STOP!

This is the back of the book!

RG Veda is published in its original Japanese right-to-left reading format, meaning that this is the last page of this book, rather than the first. If you are unfamiliar with manga, here is a diagram showing the order in which word balloons and panels should be read.

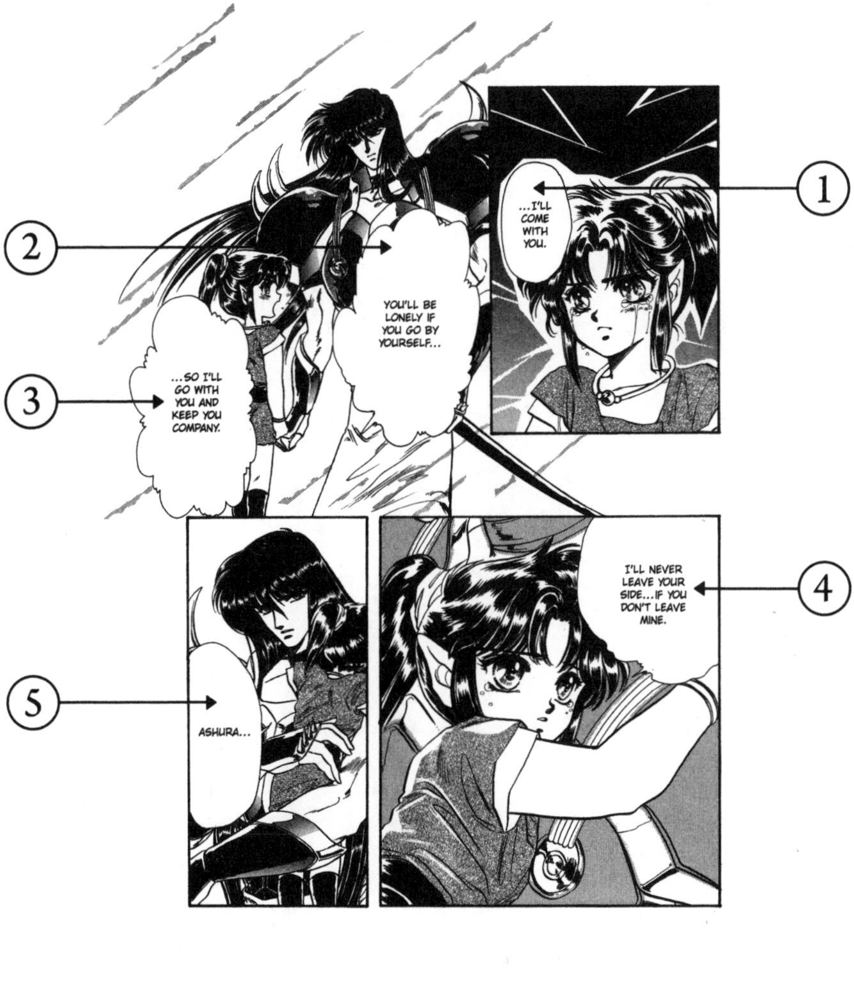
1
...I'LL COME WITH YOU.
2
YOU'LL BE LONELY IF YOU GO BY YOURSELF...
3
...SO I'LL GO WITH YOU AND KEEP YOU COMPANY.
4
I'LL NEVER LEAVE YOUR SIDE...IF YOU DON'T LEAVE MINE.
5
ASHURA...

東京 TOKYO BABYLON
CLAMP

**CLAMP's early epic of dangerous work
—and dangerous attraction!**

It's 1991, the last days of Japan's bubble economy, and money and elegance run through the streets. So do the currents of darkness beneath them, nourishing the evil spirits that only the arts of the onmyoji—Japan's legendary occultists—can combat. The two most powerful onmyoji are in the unlikely guises of a handsome young veterinarian, Seishiro, and the teenage heir to the ancient Sumeragi clan, Subaru—just a couple of guys whom Subaru's sister Hokuto has decided are destined to be together!

*"Tokyo Babylon is CLAMP's
first really great work."*
—Manga: The Complete Guide

**Each omnibus-sized
volume features over
a dozen full-color
bonus pages!**

VOLUME ONE
ISBN 978-1-61655-116-2
$19.99

VOLUME TWO
ISBN 978-1-61655-189-6
$19.99

AVAILABLE AT YOUR LOCAL COMICS SHOP OR BOOKSTORE!
To find a comics shop in your area, call 1-888-266-4226
For more information or to order direct: • On the web: DarkHorse.com
E-mail: mailorder@darkhorse.com • Phone: 1-800-862-0052 Mon.–Fri. 9 AM to 5 PM Pacific Time

RG VEDA
BOOK 3

STORY AND ART BY
CLAMP

English Translation and Adaptation by
Haruko Furukawa and
Christine Schilling

Lettering and Retouch by
IHL

Editor
Carl Gustav Horn

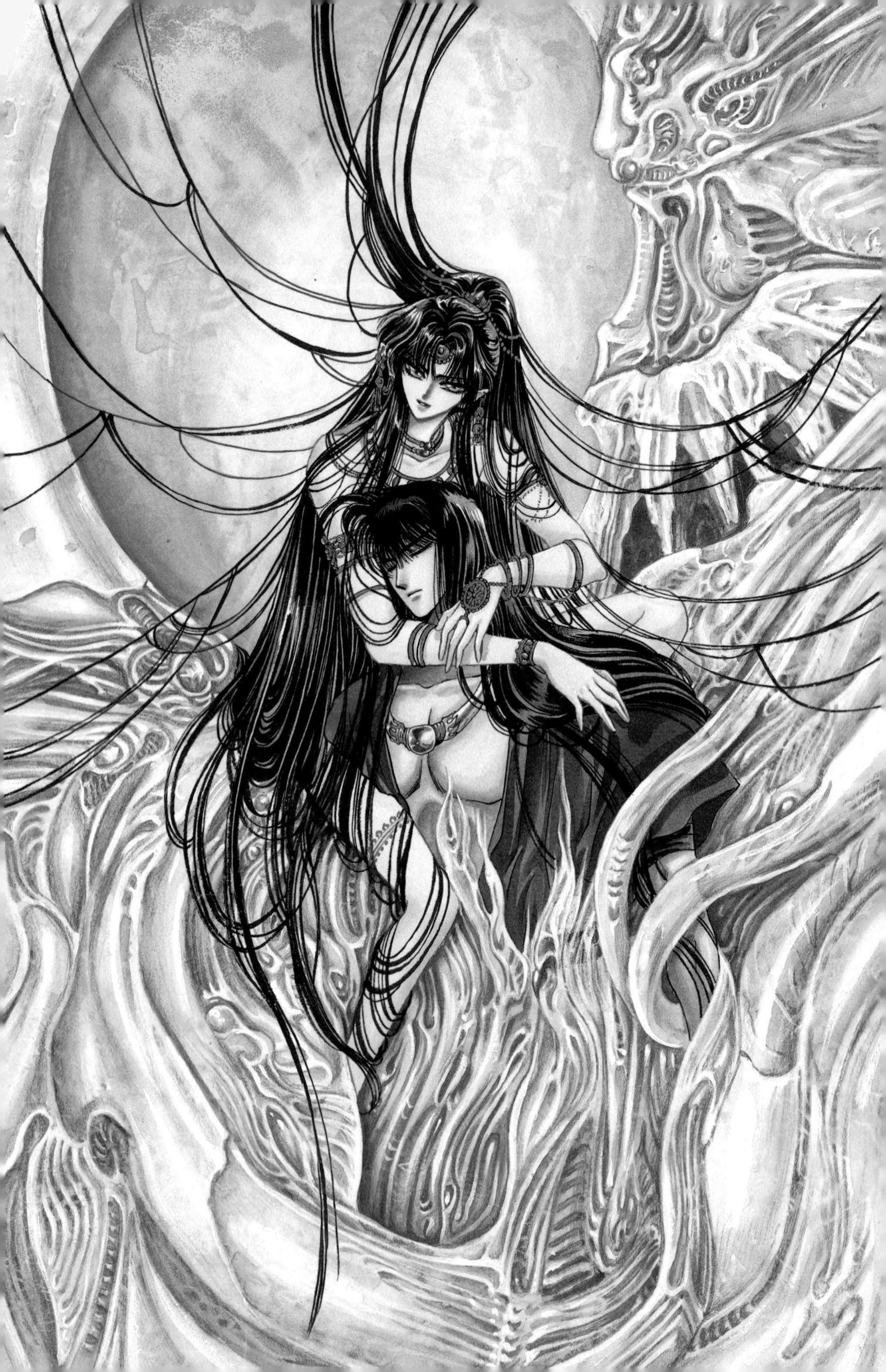

CLAMP

RG VEDA

table of contents

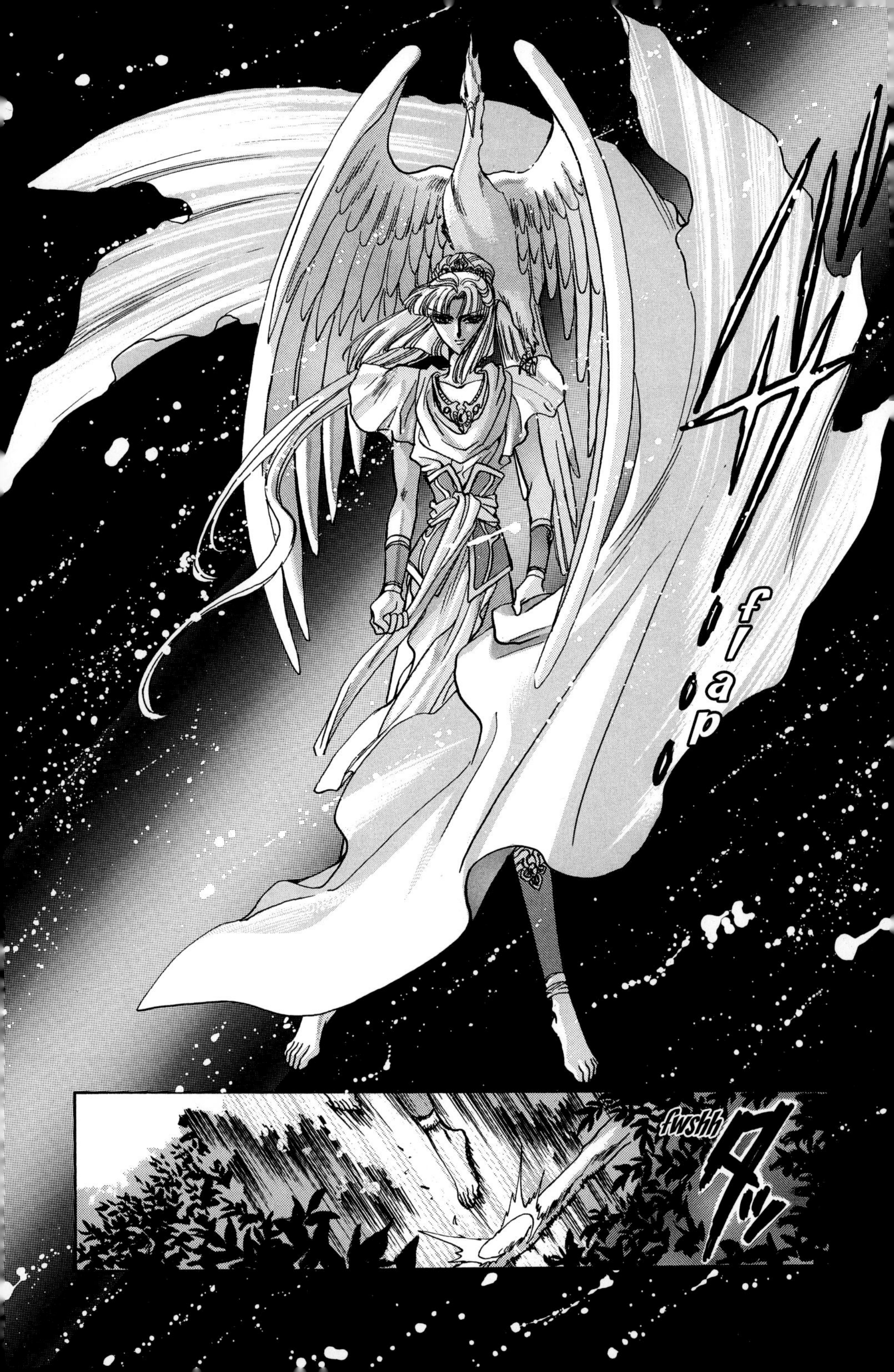
flap
fwshh
ダッ

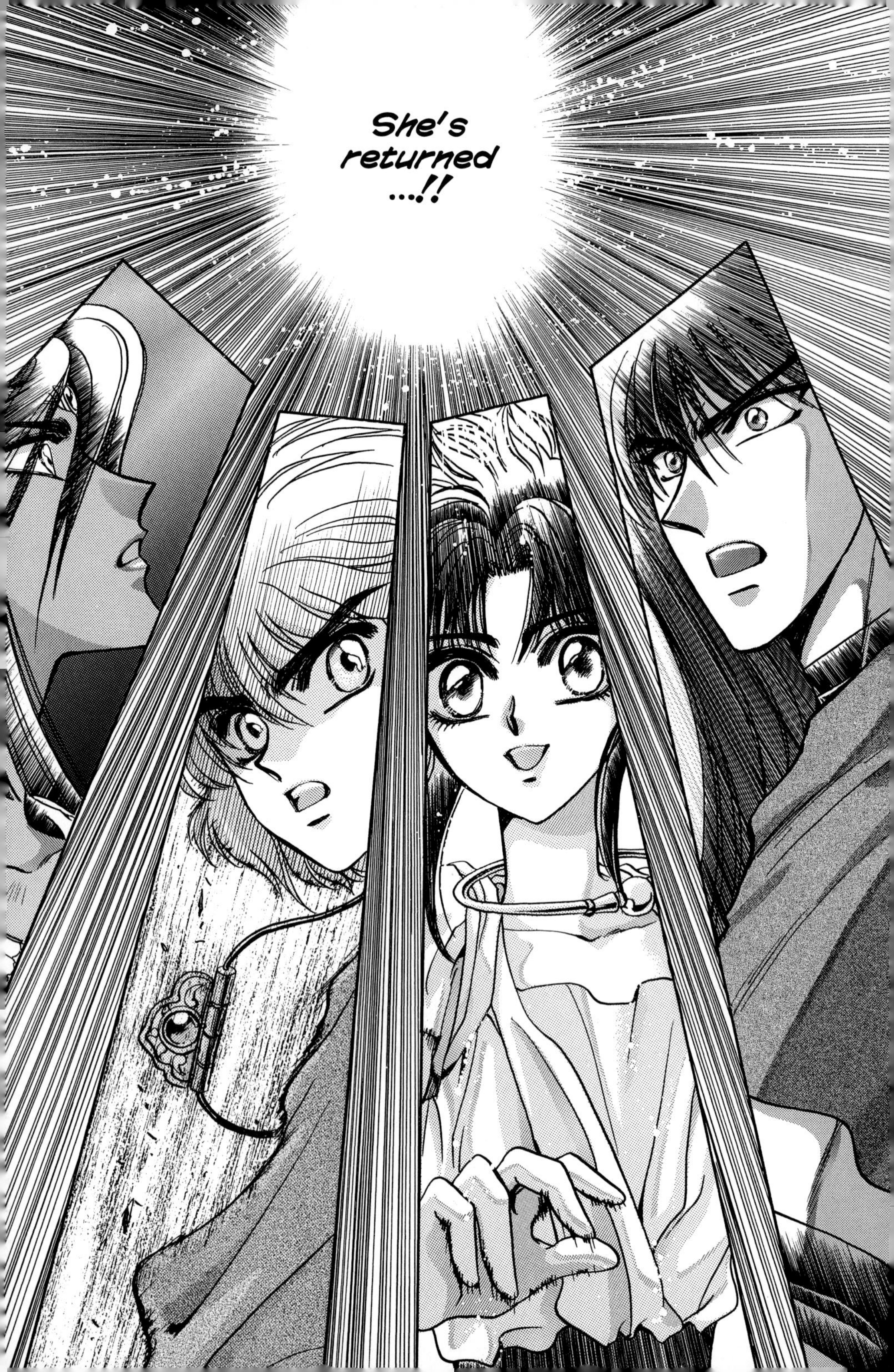
She's returned ...!!

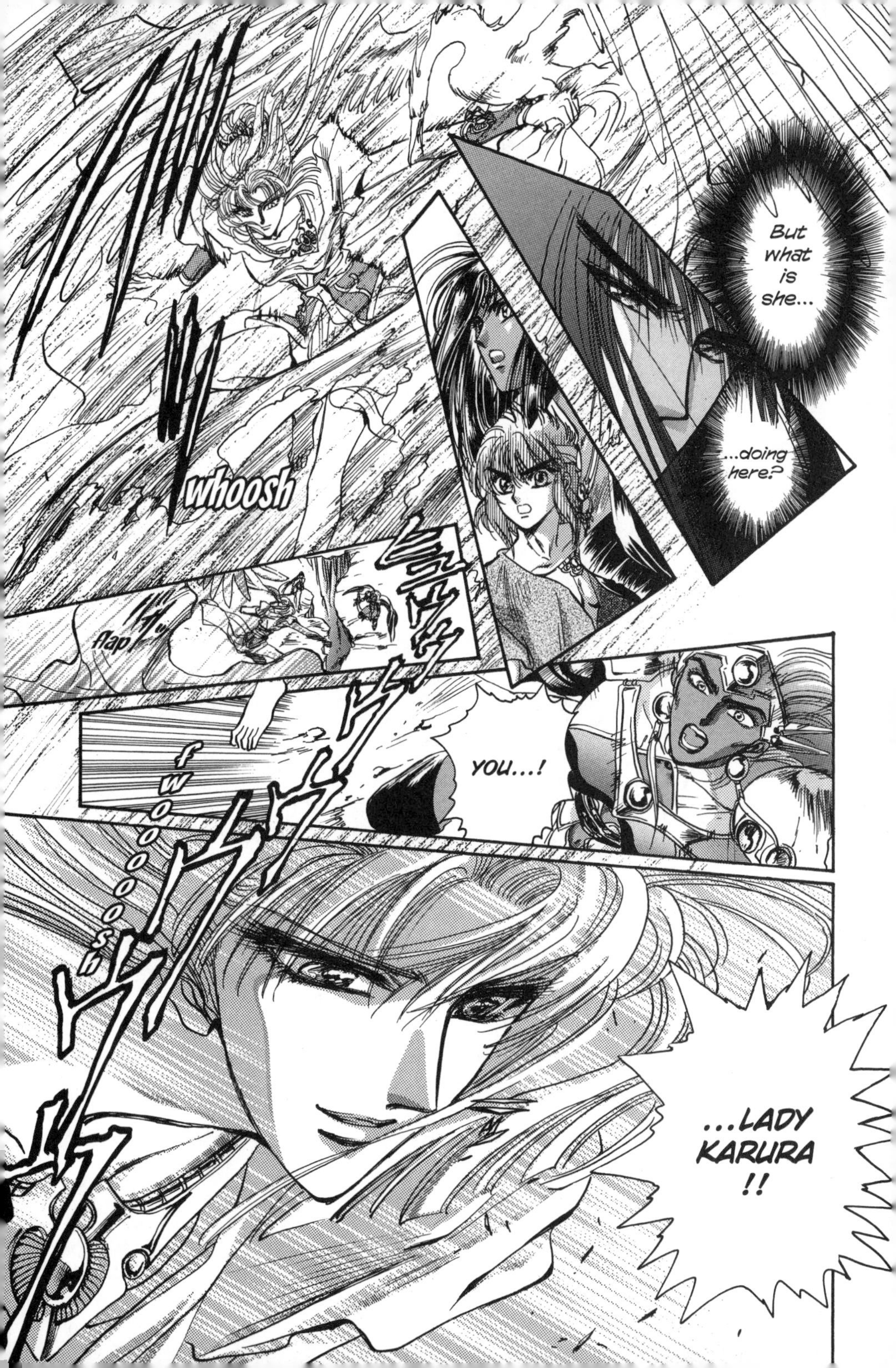

But what is she...
...doing here?
whoosh
flap
YOU...!
fwoooooosh
...LADY KARURA !!

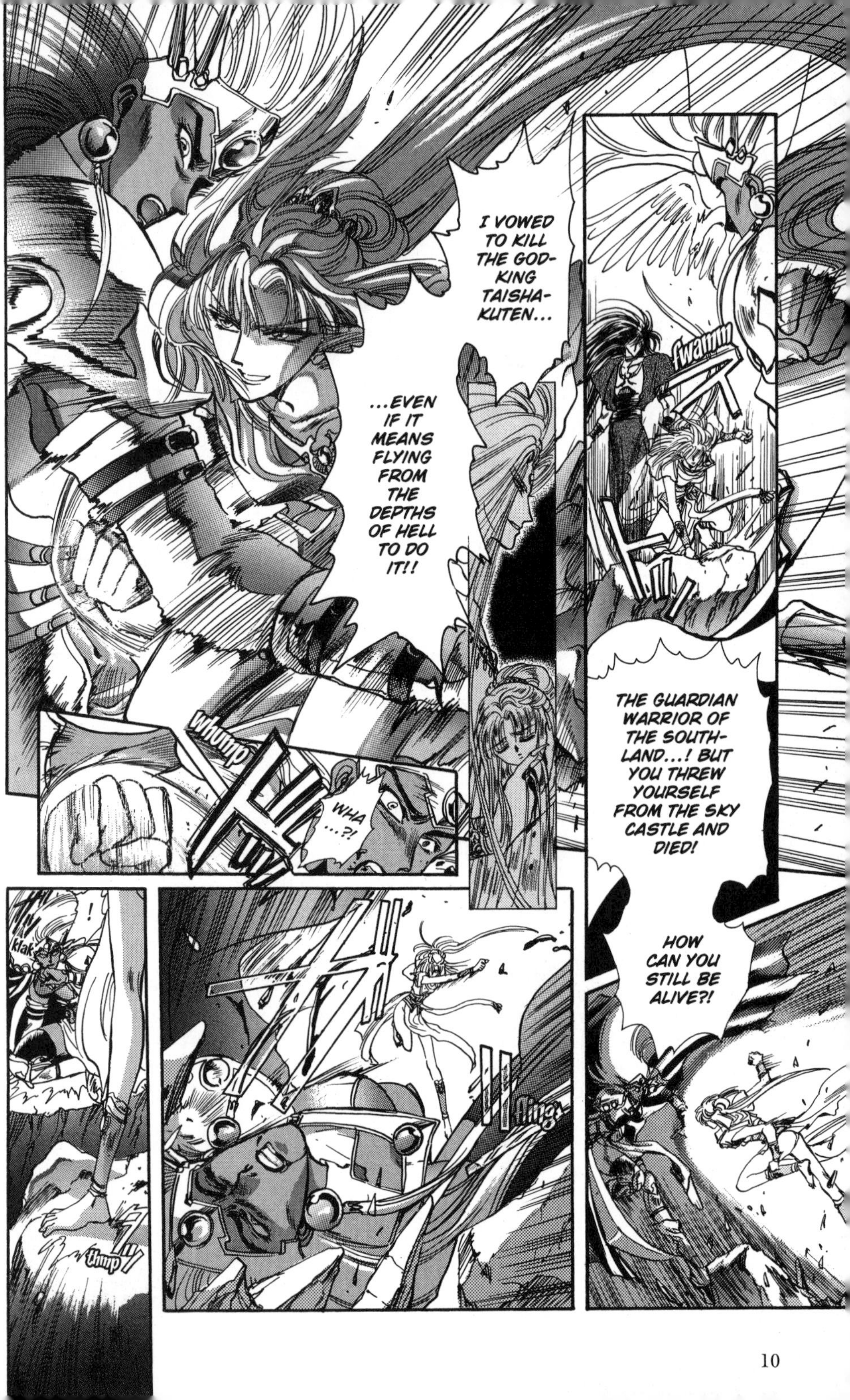
fwamm
THE GUARDIAN WARRIOR OF THE SOUTH-LAND...! BUT YOU THREW YOURSELF FROM THE SKY CASTLE AND DIED!
I VOWED TO KILL THE GOD-KING TAISHA-KUTEN...
...EVEN IF IT MEANS FLYING FROM THE DEPTHS OF HELL TO DO IT!!
whump
WHA ...?!
HOW CAN YOU STILL BE ALIVE?!
fling
!
klak
thmp

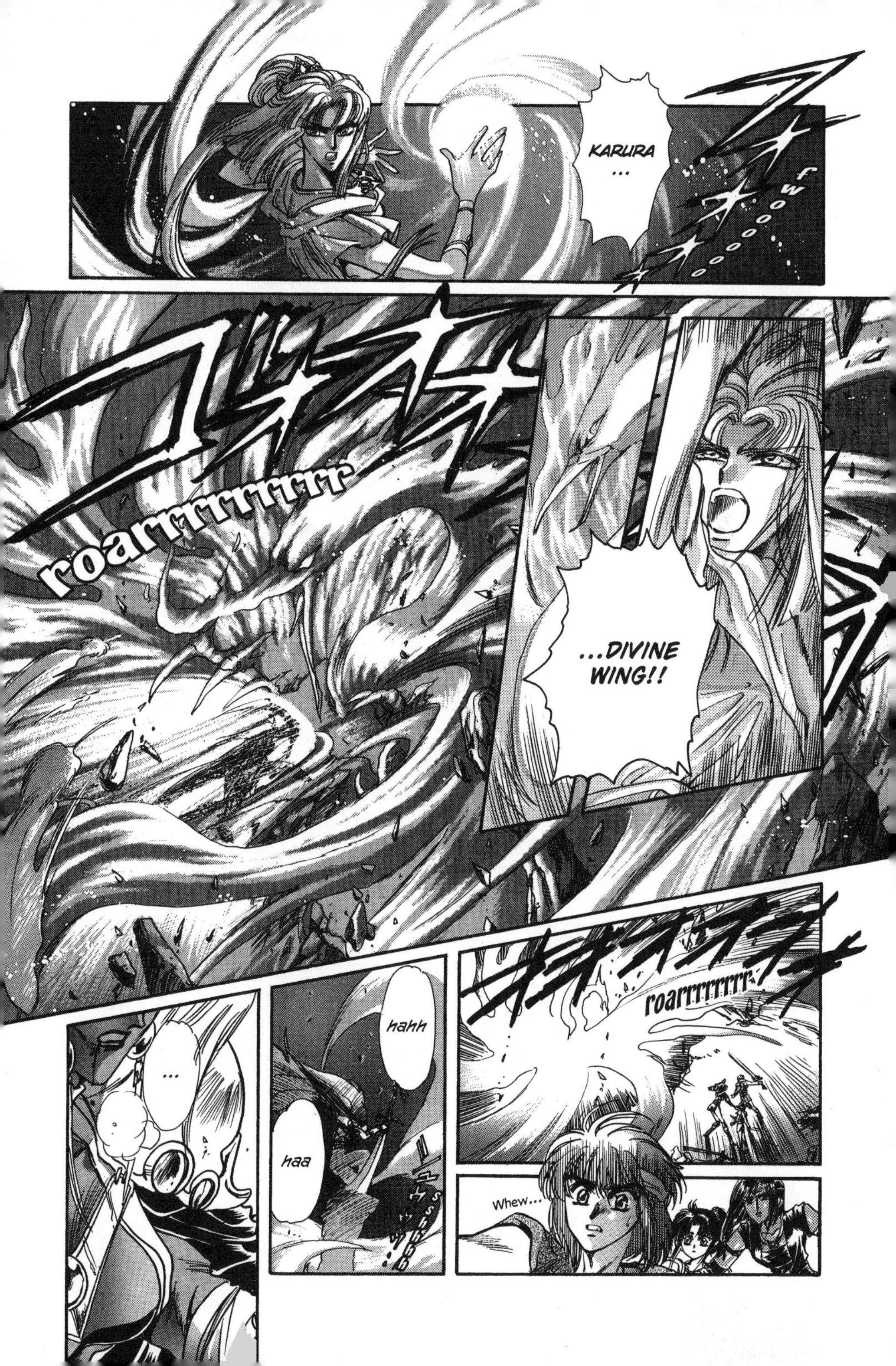

KARURA ...
fwoooooo
...DIVINE WING!!
roarrrrrrrrrrrr
roarrrrrrrr
Whew...
hahh
haa
sshhhh
...

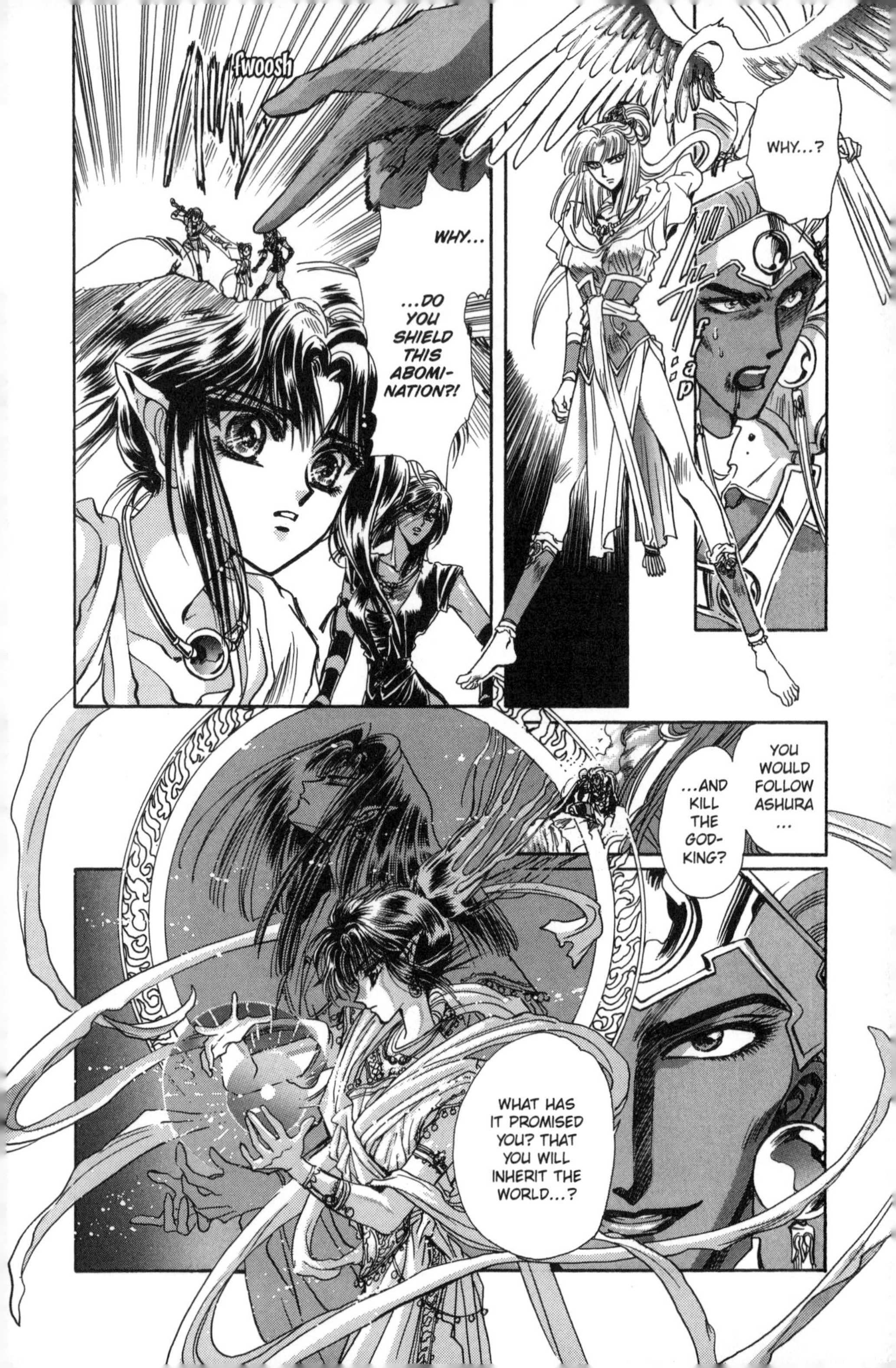
WHY...?
flap
fwoosh
WHY...
...DO YOU SHIELD THIS ABOMINATION?!
YOU WOULD FOLLOW ASHURA...
...AND KILL THE GOD-KING?
WHAT HAS IT PROMISED YOU? THAT YOU WILL INHERIT THE WORLD...?

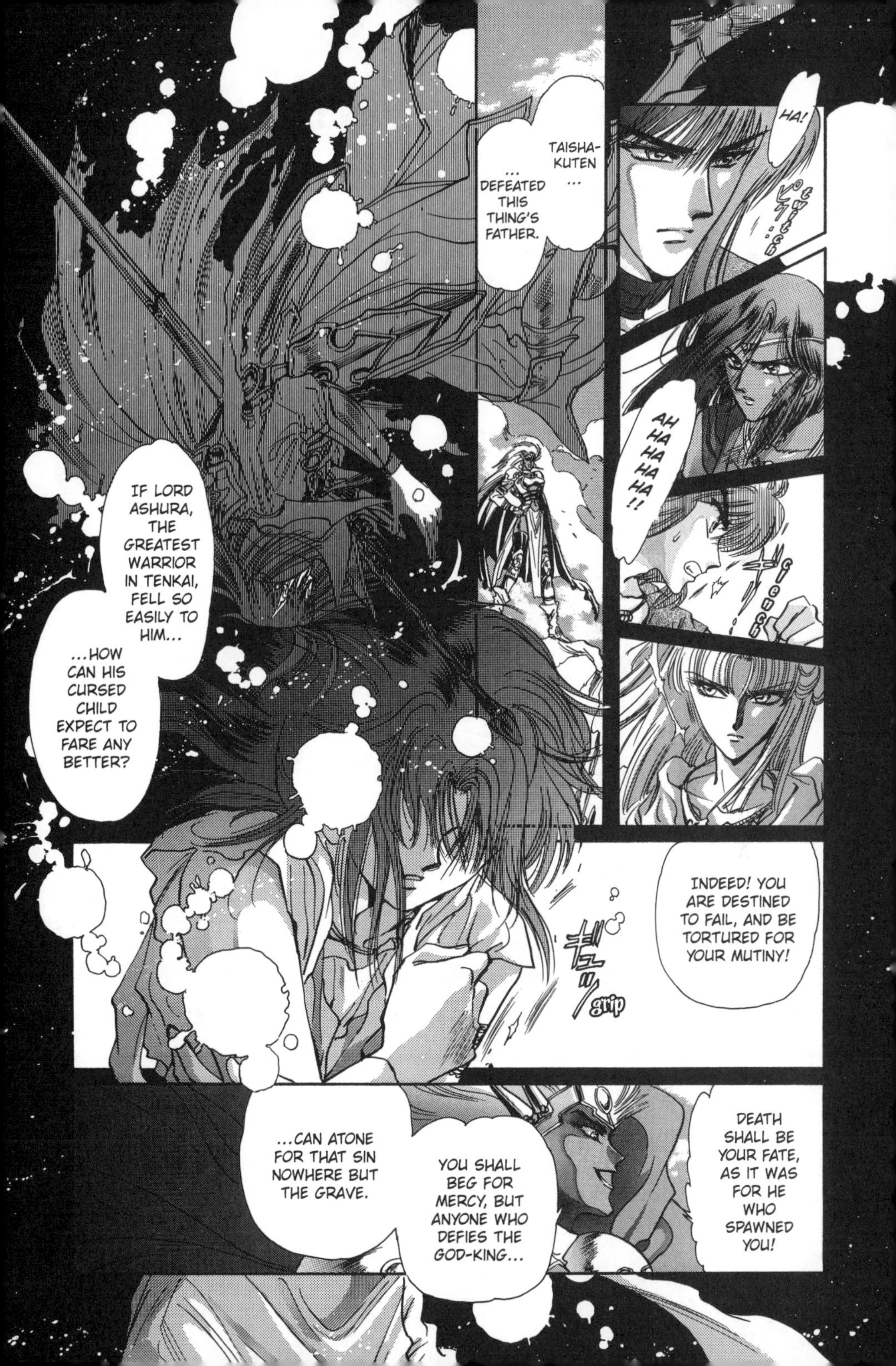
HA!
twitch
TAISHAKUTEN ...
... DEFEATED THIS THING'S FATHER.
AH HA HA HA HA!!
clench
IF LORD ASHURA, THE GREATEST WARRIOR IN TENKAI, FELL SO EASILY TO HIM...
...HOW CAN HIS CURSED CHILD EXPECT TO FARE ANY BETTER?
INDEED! YOU ARE DESTINED TO FAIL, AND BE TORTURED FOR YOUR MUTINY!
grip
DEATH SHALL BE YOUR FATE, AS IT WAS FOR HE WHO SPAWNED YOU!
YOU SHALL BEG FOR MERCY, BUT ANYONE WHO DEFIES THE GOD-KING...
...CAN ATONE FOR THAT SIN NOWHERE BUT THE GRAVE.

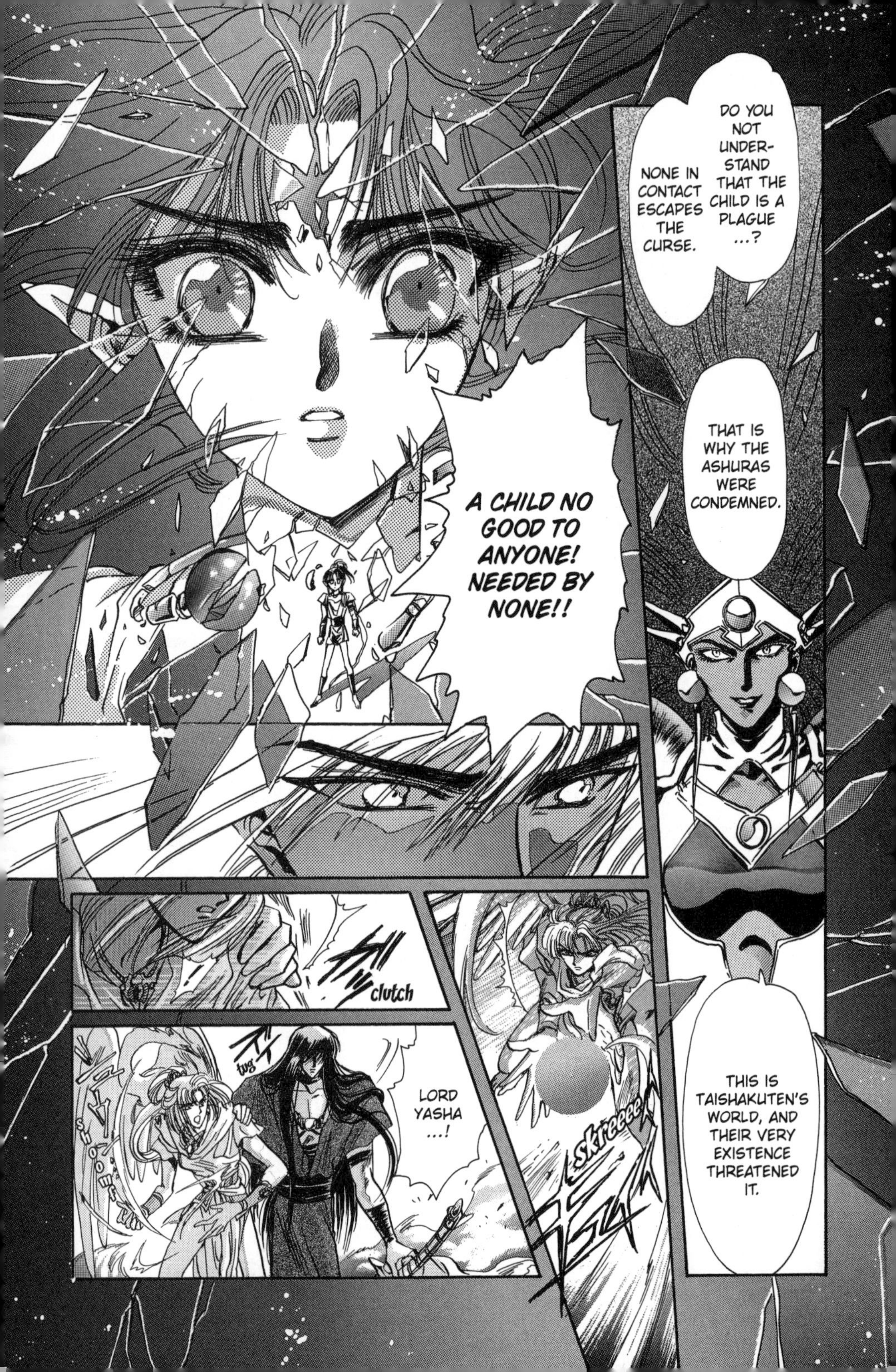
DO YOU NOT UNDER-STAND THAT THE CHILD IS A PLAGUE ...?
NONE IN CONTACT ESCAPES THE CURSE.
THAT IS WHY THE ASHURAS WERE CONDEMNED.
THIS IS TAISHAKUTEN'S WORLD, AND THEIR VERY EXISTENCE THREATENED IT.
A CHILD NO GOOD TO ANYONE! NEEDED BY NONE!!
skreeee
clutch
tug
LORD YASHA ...!
shoom

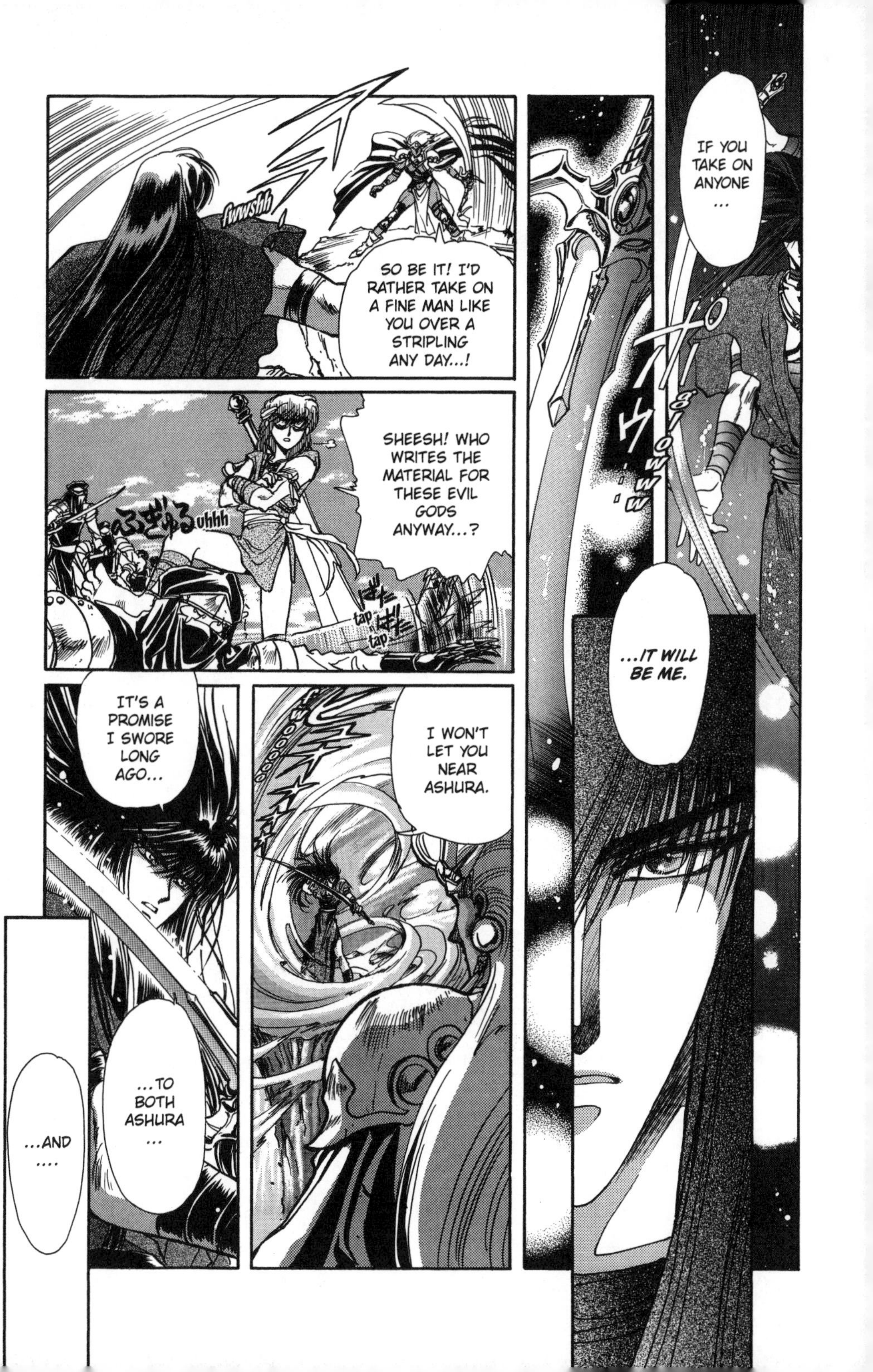
IF YOU TAKE ON ANYONE ...
...IT WILL BE ME.
fwwshh
SO BE IT! I'D RATHER TAKE ON A FINE MAN LIKE YOU OVER A STRIPLING ANY DAY...!
SHEESH! WHO WRITES THE MATERIAL FOR THESE EVIL GODS ANYWAY...?
uhhh
tap
tap
I WON'T LET YOU NEAR ASHURA.
IT'S A PROMISE I SWORE LONG AGO...
...TO BOTH ASHURA ...
...AND ....

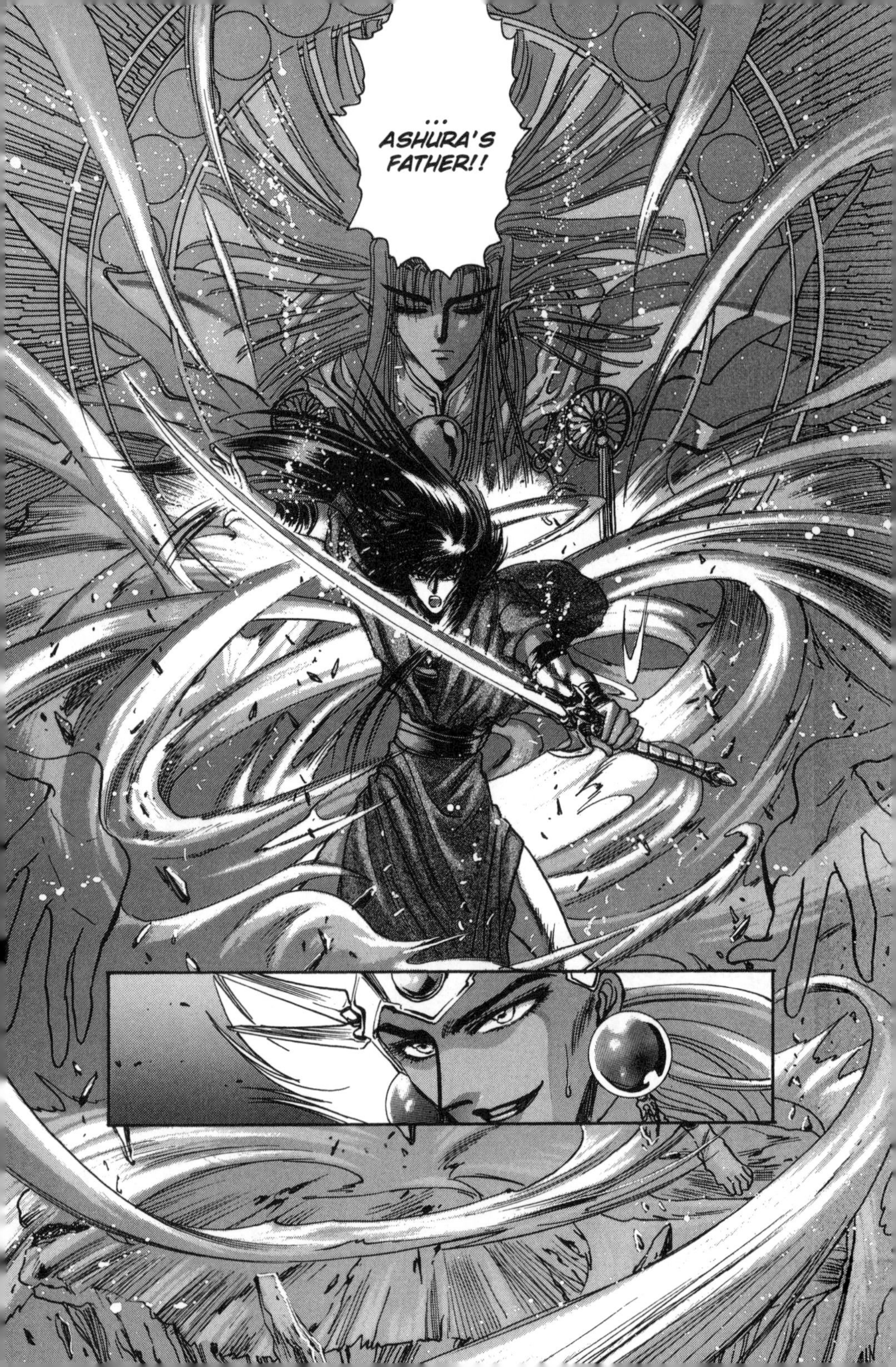
... ASHURA'S FATHER!!

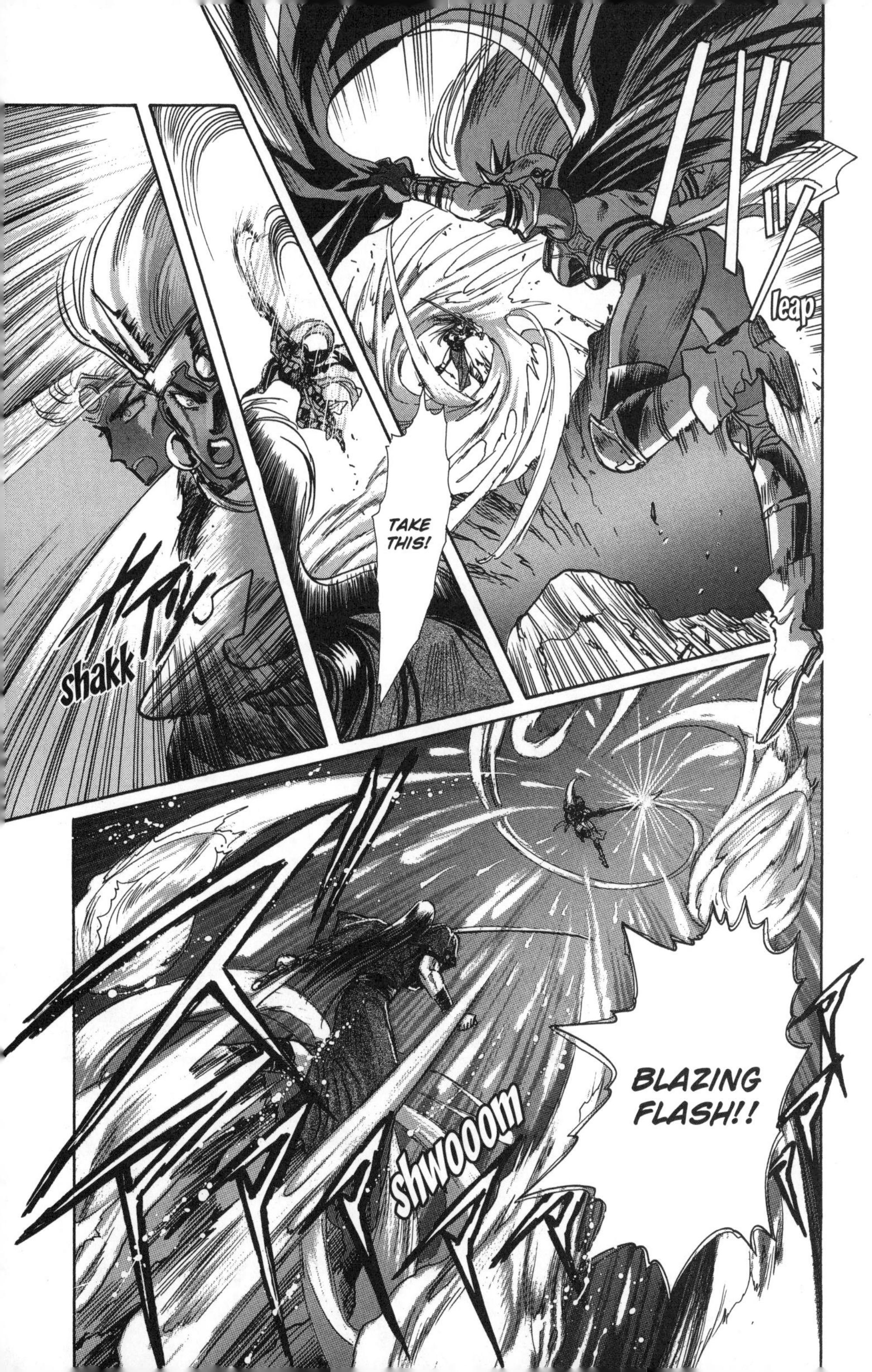
leap
TAKE THIS!
shakk
BLAZING FLASH!!
shwooom

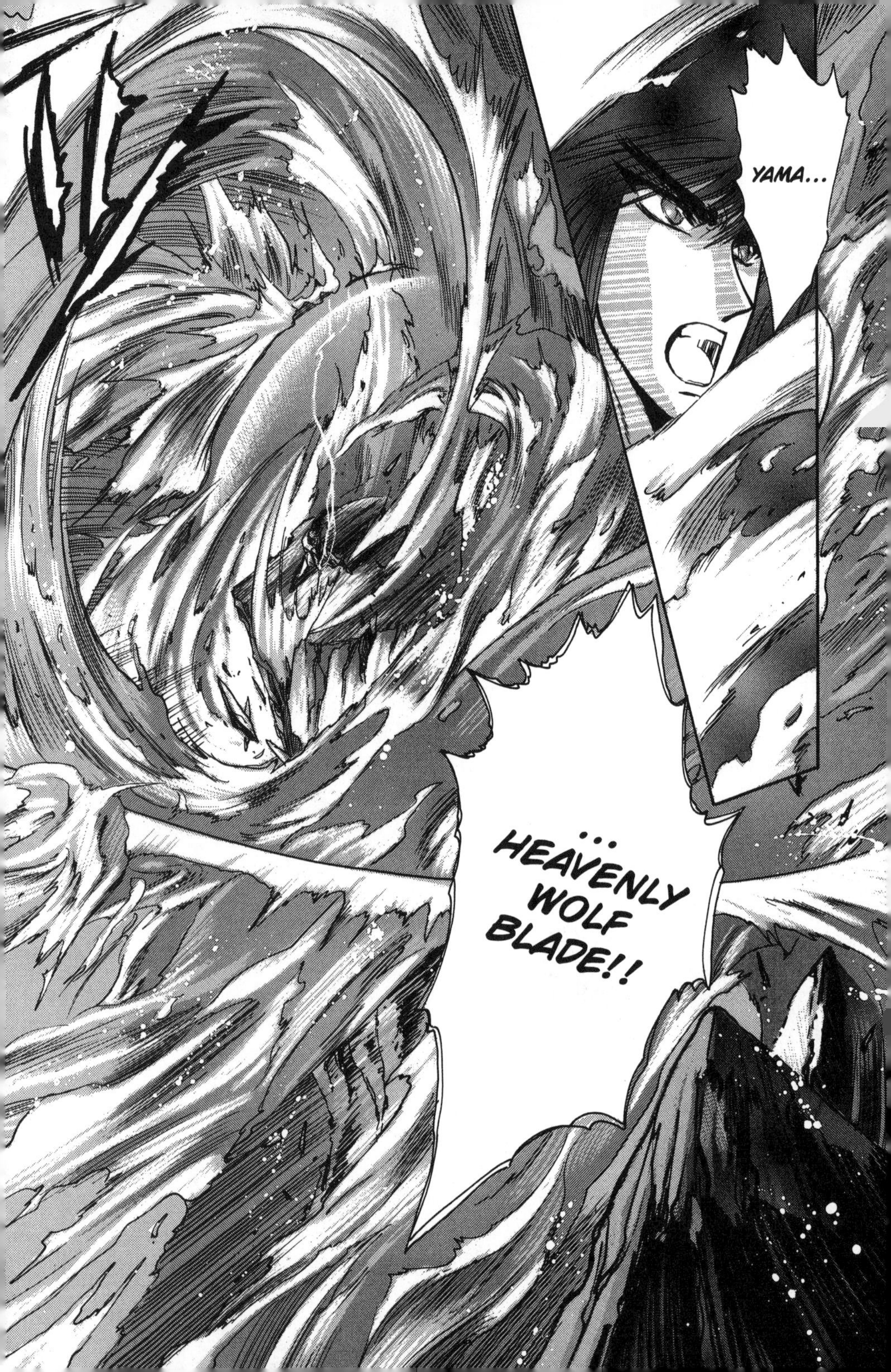
YAMA...
...HEAVENLY WOLF BLADE!!

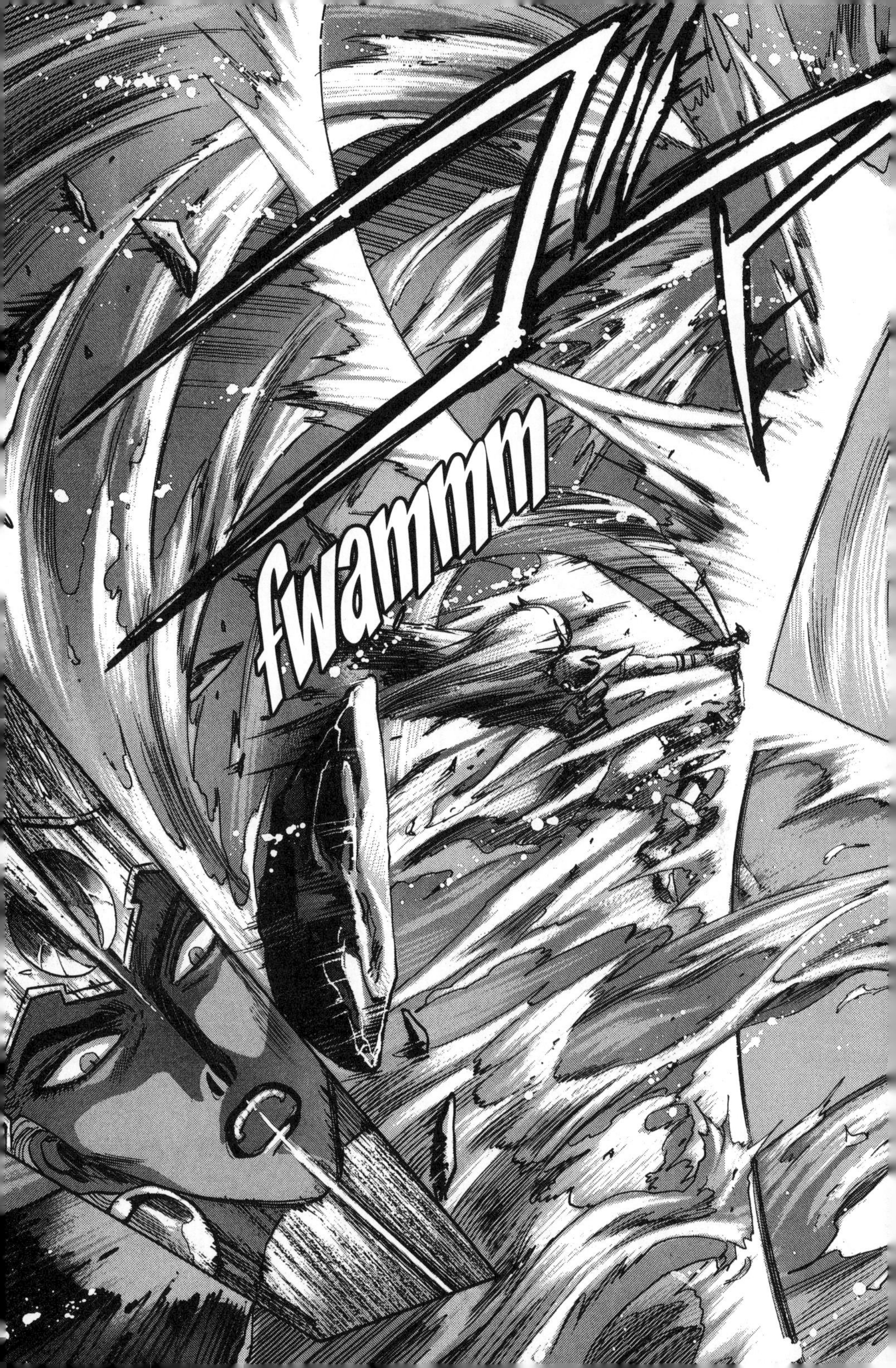
fwammm

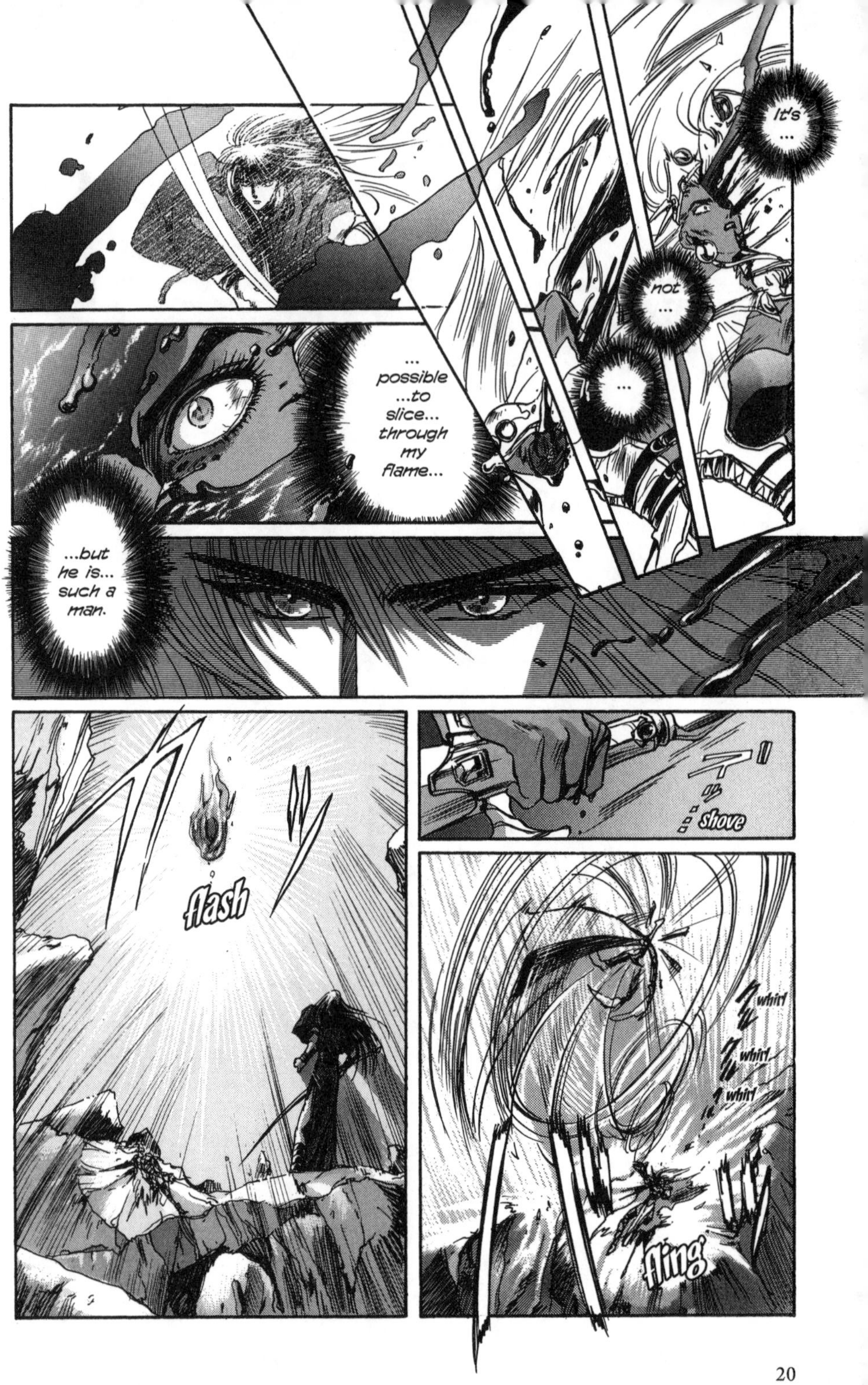
It's ...
not ...
...
... possible ...to slice... through my flame...
...but he is... such a man.
shove
whirl
whirl
whirl
fling
flash

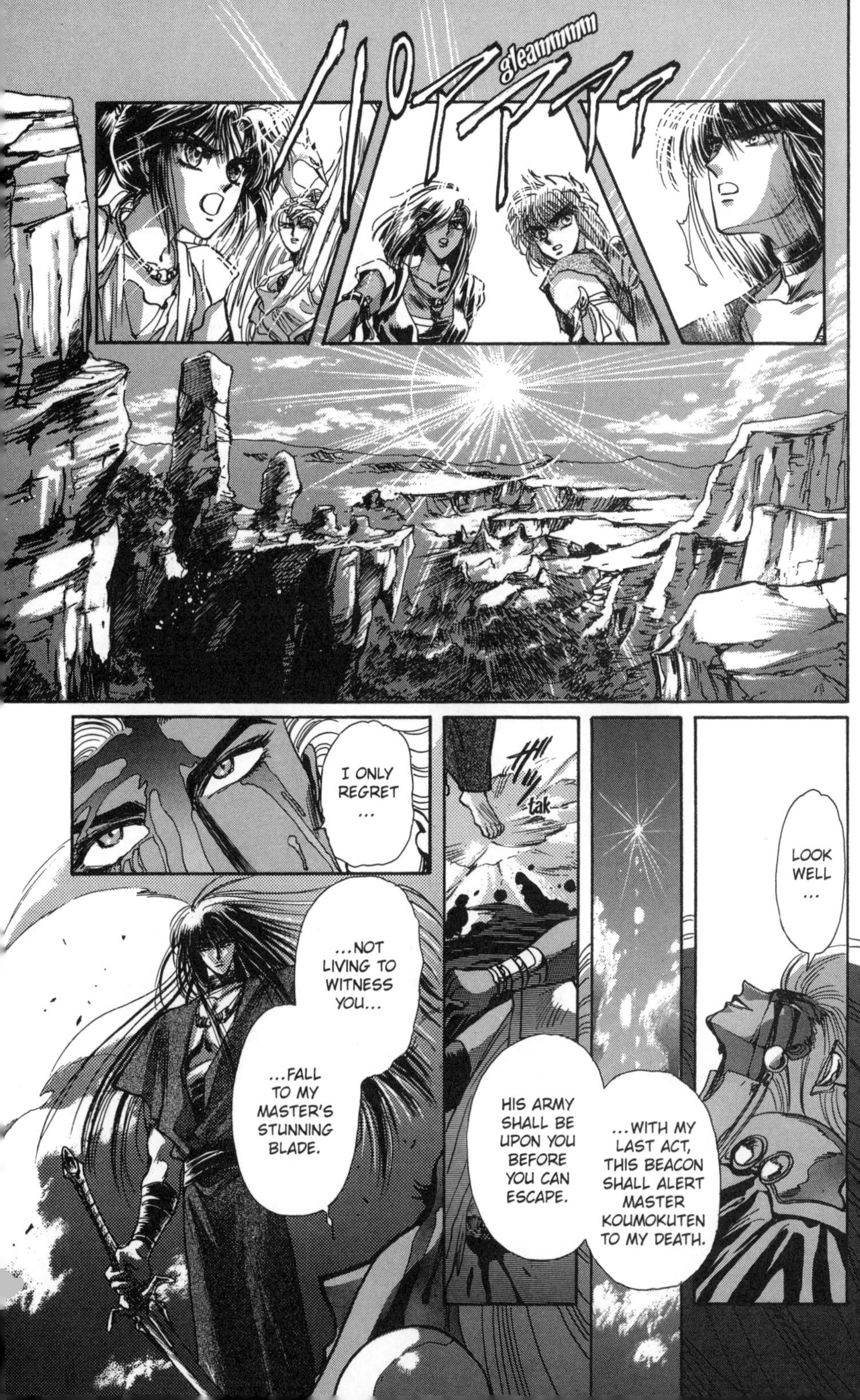
gleammmmm
LOOK WELL ...
...WITH MY LAST ACT, THIS BEACON SHALL ALERT MASTER KOUMOKUTEN TO MY DEATH.
HIS ARMY SHALL BE UPON YOU BEFORE YOU CAN ESCAPE.
tak
I ONLY REGRET ...
...NOT LIVING TO WITNESS YOU...
...FALL TO MY MASTER'S STUNNING BLADE.

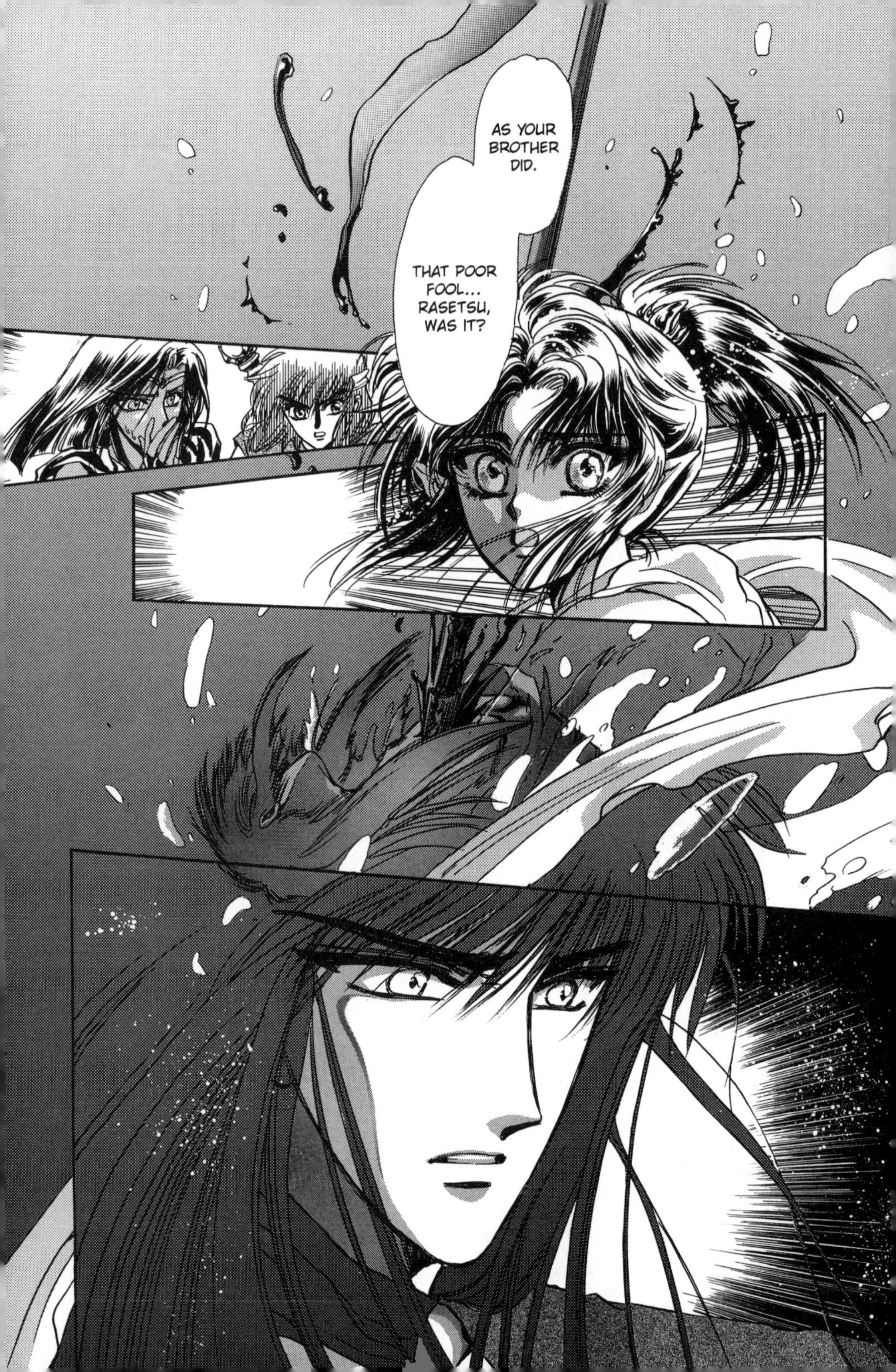

AS YOUR BROTHER DID.
THAT POOR FOOL... RASETSU, WAS IT?

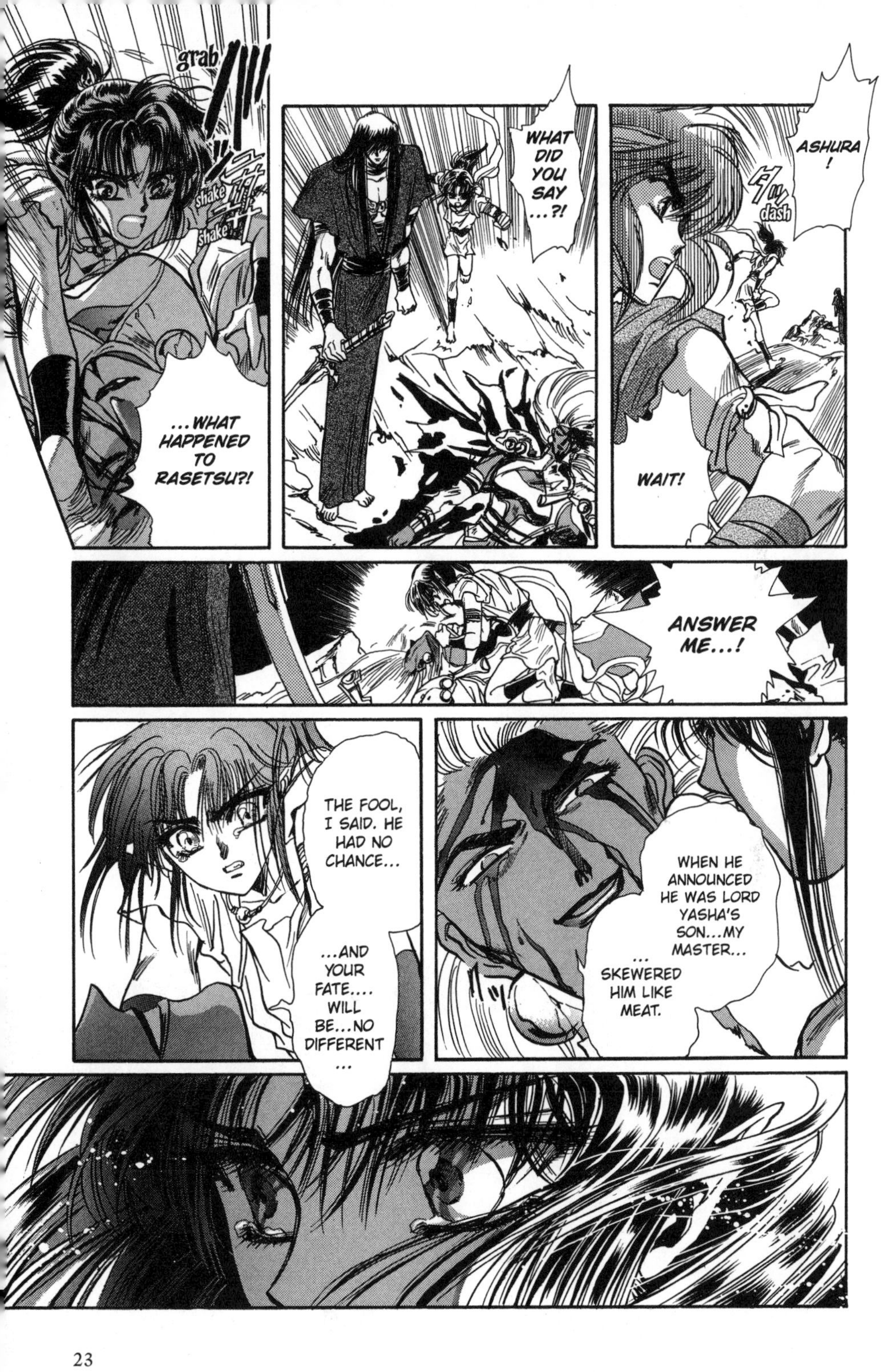
ASHURA!
dash
WAIT!
WHAT DID YOU SAY...?!
grab
shake
shake
...WHAT HAPPENED TO RASETSU?!
ANSWER ME...!
WHEN HE ANNOUNCED HE WAS LORD YASHA'S SON...MY MASTER...
... SKEWERED HIM LIKE MEAT.
THE FOOL, I SAID. HE HAD NO CHANCE...
...AND YOUR FATE.... WILL BE...NO DIFFERENT ...

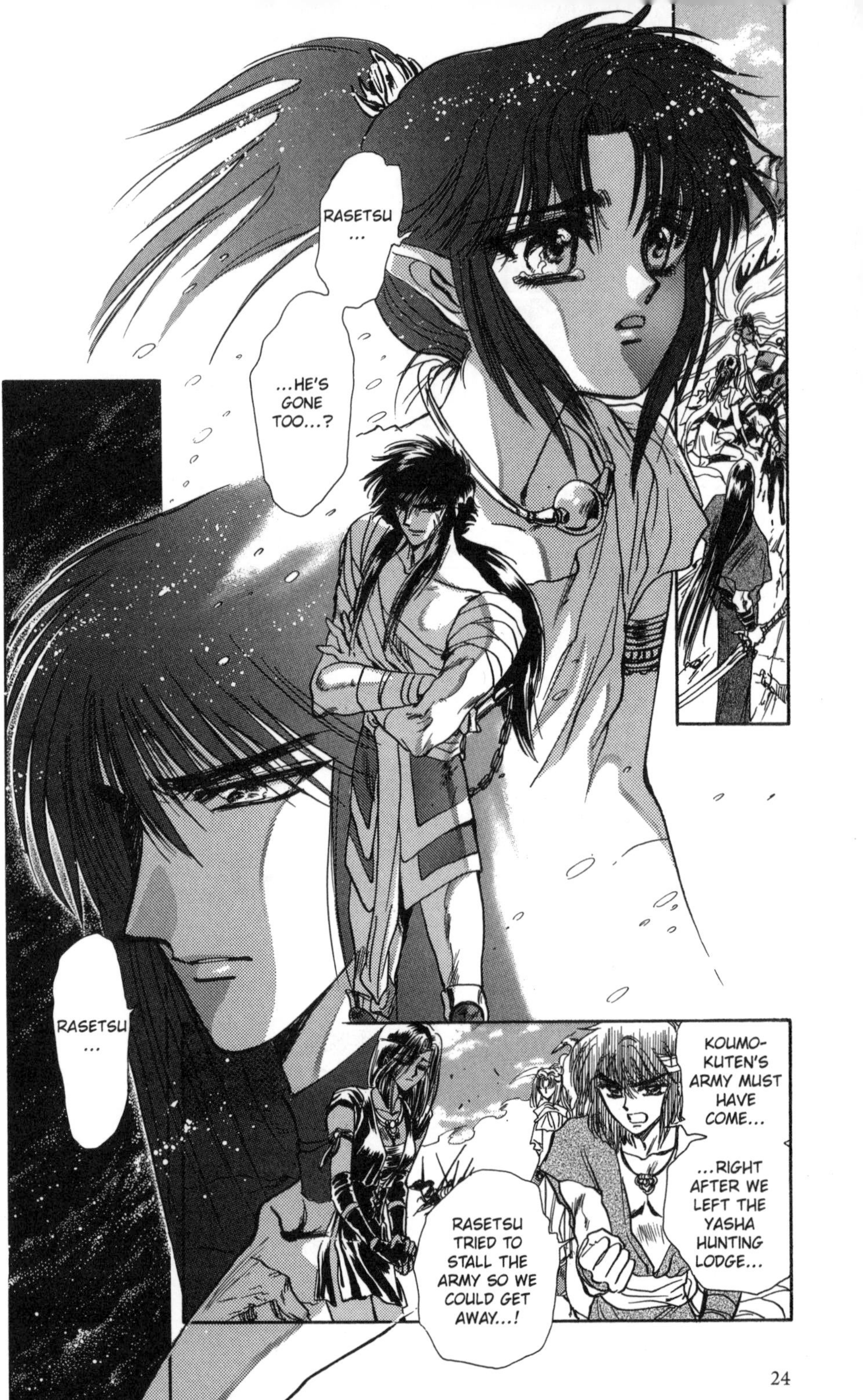
RASETSU...
...HE'S GONE TOO...?
KOUMOKUTEN'S ARMY MUST HAVE COME...
...RIGHT AFTER WE LEFT THE YASHA HUNTING LODGE...
RASETSU TRIED TO STALL THE ARMY SO WE COULD GET AWAY...!
RASETSU...

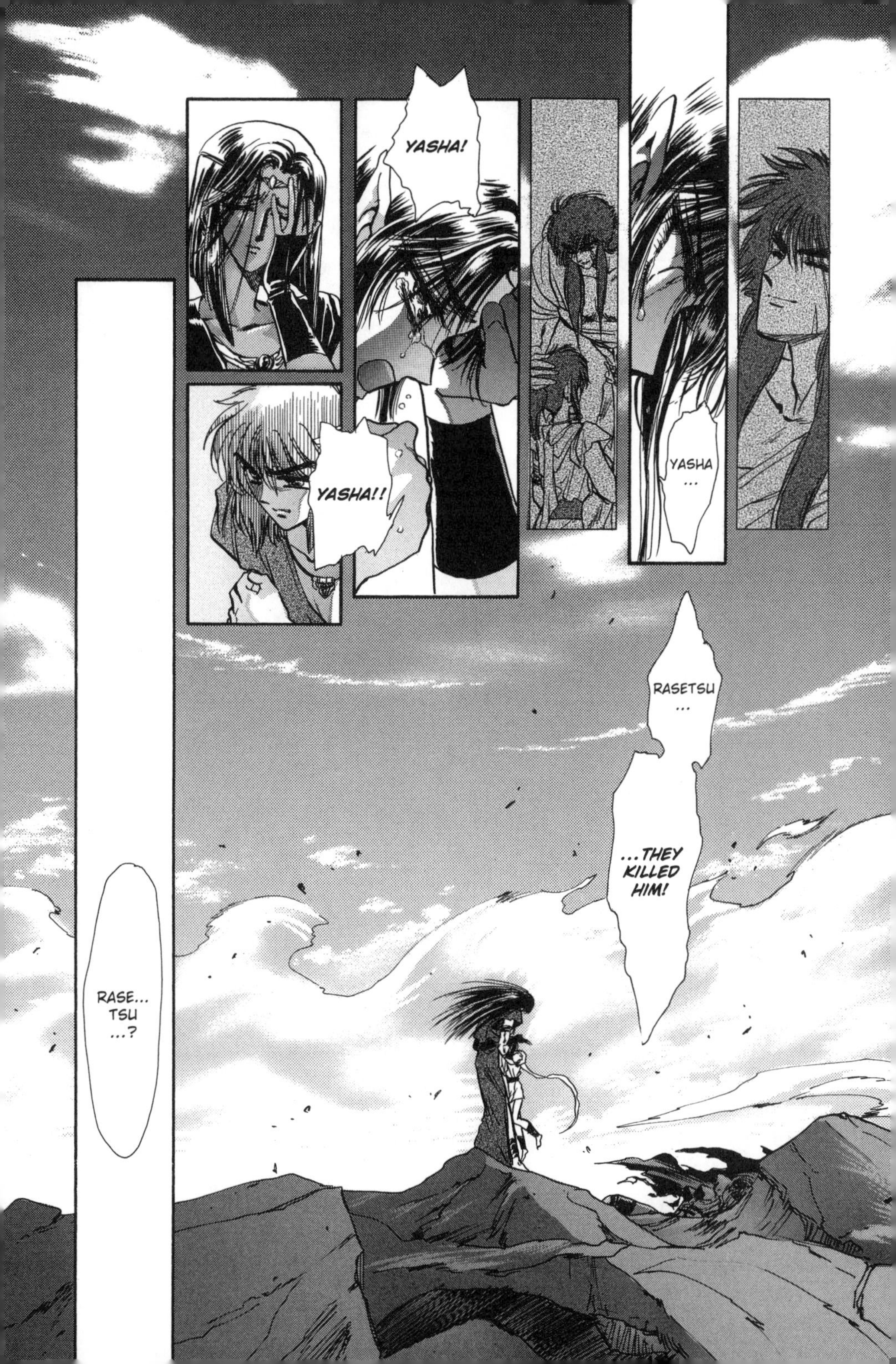
YASHA ...
YASHA!
YASHA!!
RASETSU ...
...THEY KILLED HIM!
RASE... TSU ...?

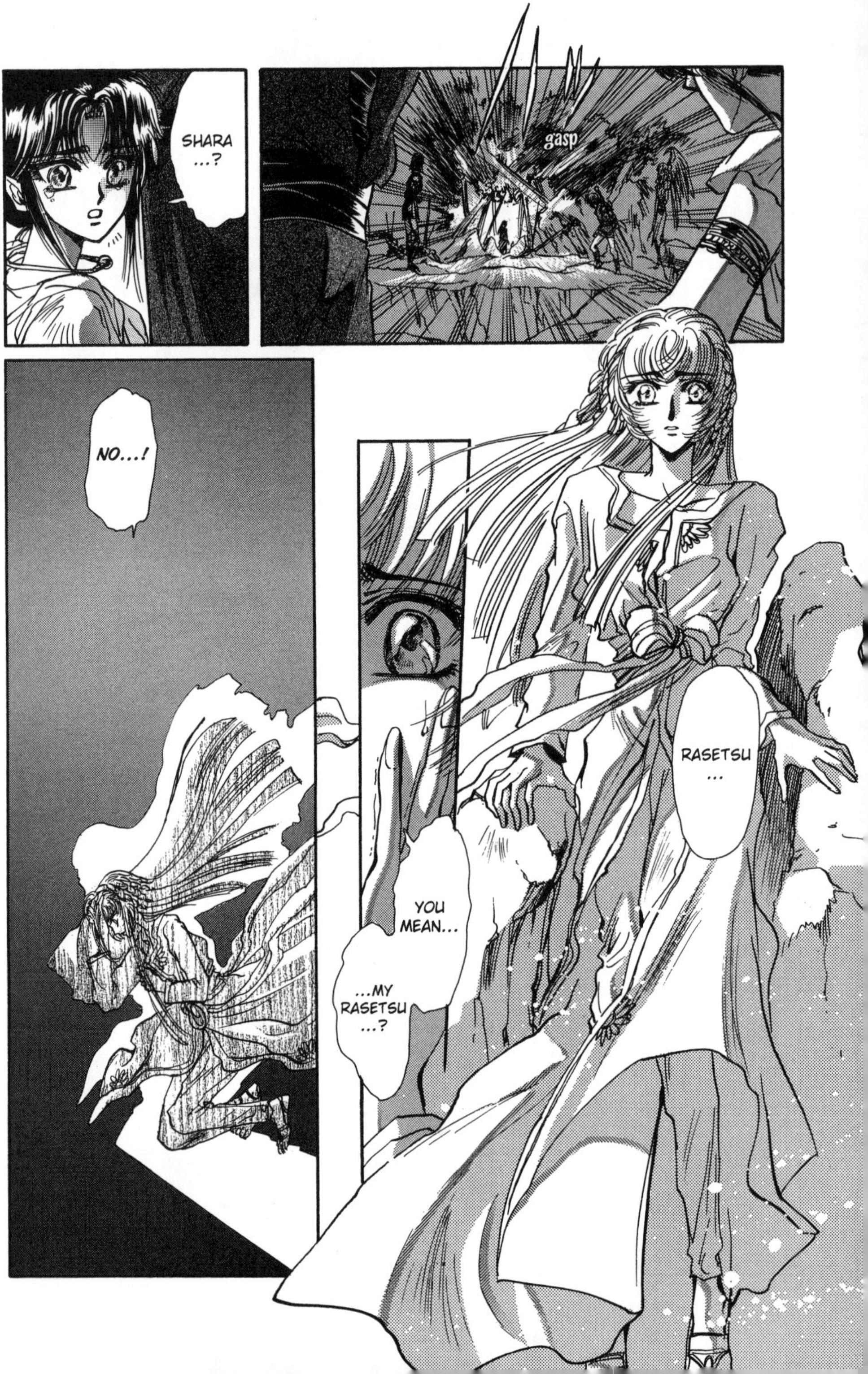
gasp
SHARA ...?
RASETSU ...
YOU MEAN...
...MY RASETSU ...?
NO...!

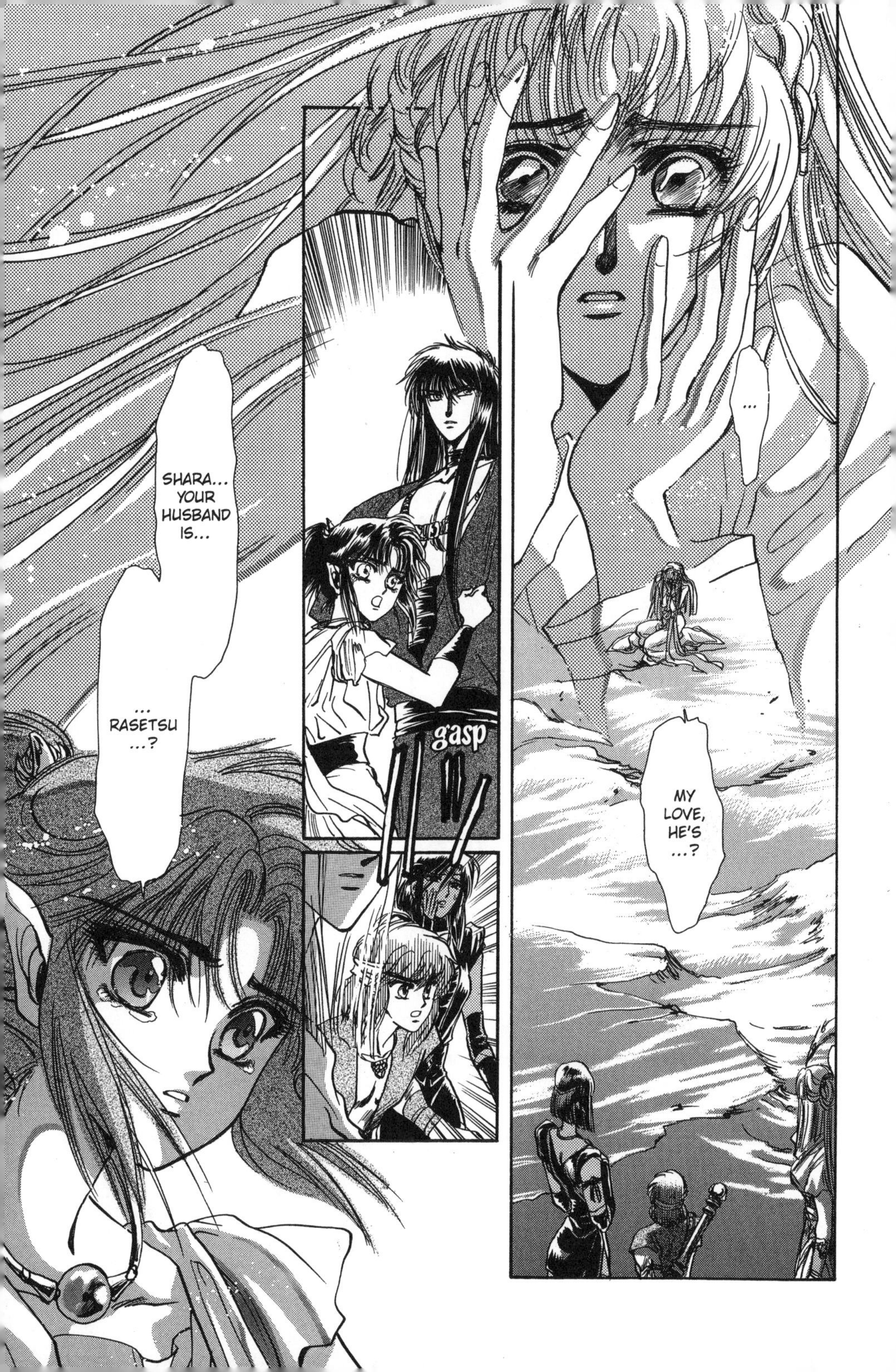
...
MY LOVE, HE'S ...?
gasp
SHARA... YOUR HUSBAND IS...
... RASETSU ...?

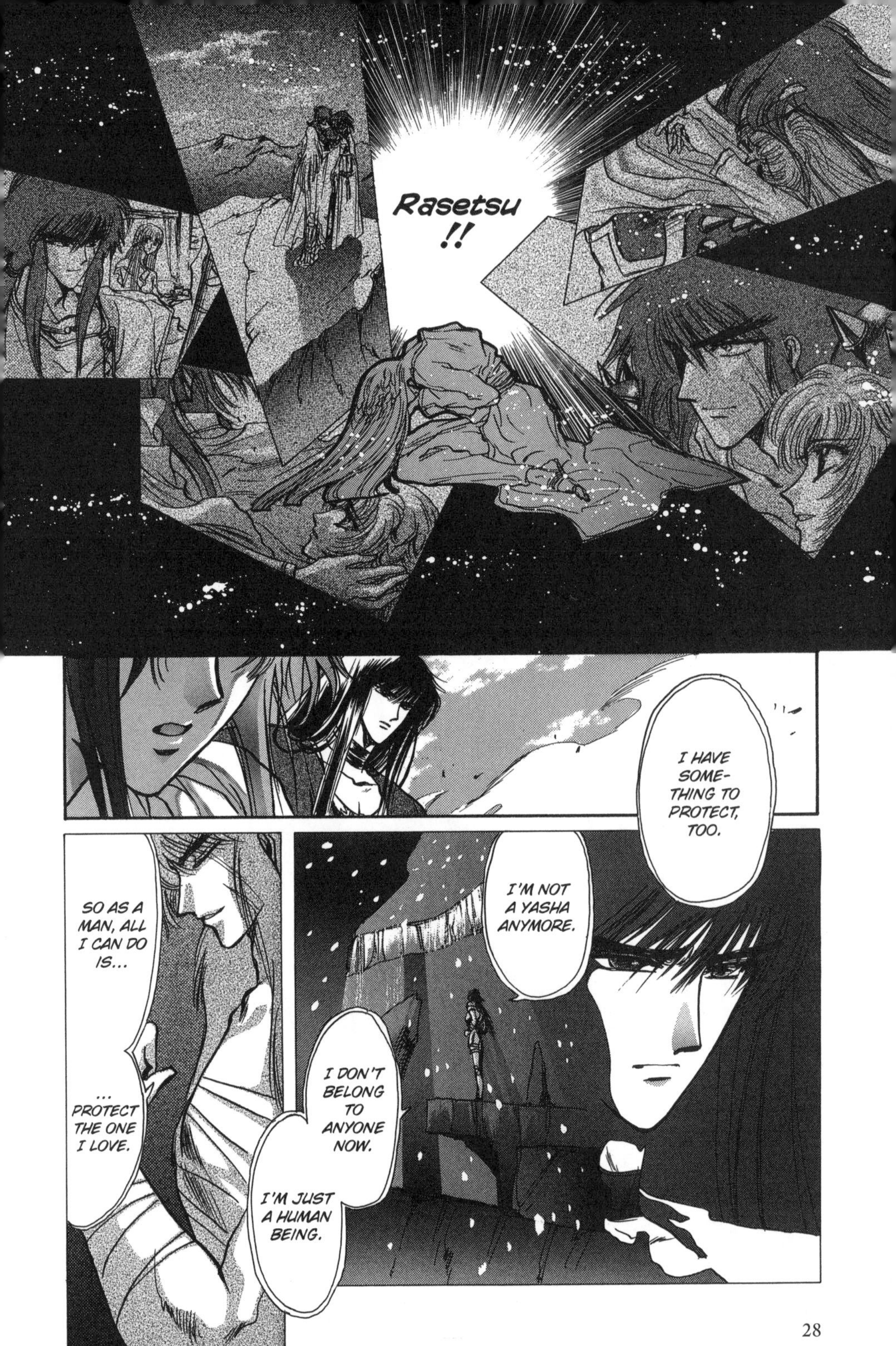
Rasetsu !!
I HAVE SOME-THING TO PROTECT, TOO.
I'M NOT A YASHA ANYMORE.
I DON'T BELONG TO ANYONE NOW.
I'M JUST A HUMAN BEING.
SO AS A MAN, ALL I CAN DO IS...
... PROTECT THE ONE I LOVE.

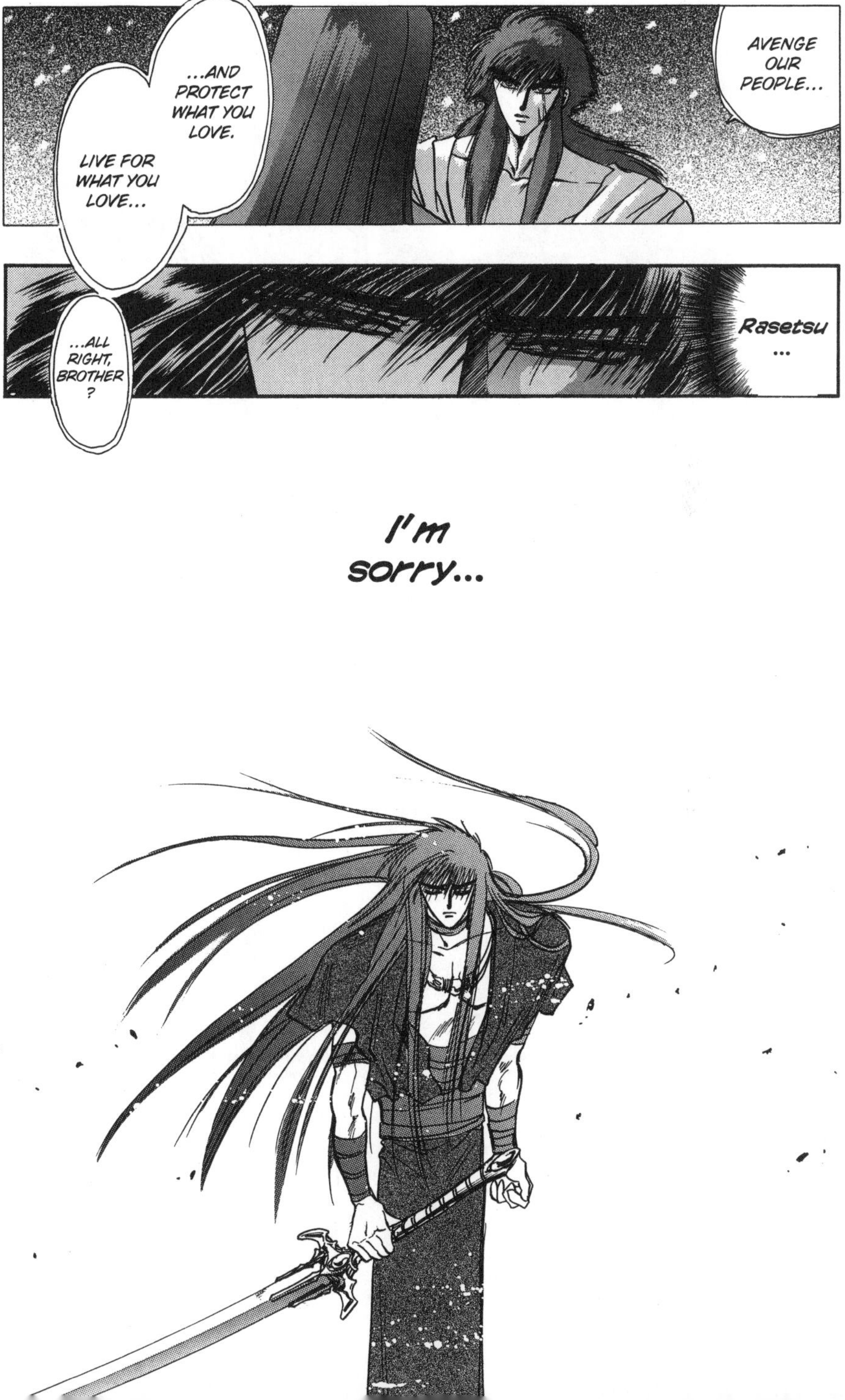
AVENGE OUR PEOPLE...
LIVE FOR WHAT YOU LOVE...
...AND PROTECT WHAT YOU LOVE.
Rasetsu ...
...ALL RIGHT, BROTHER ?
I'm sorry...

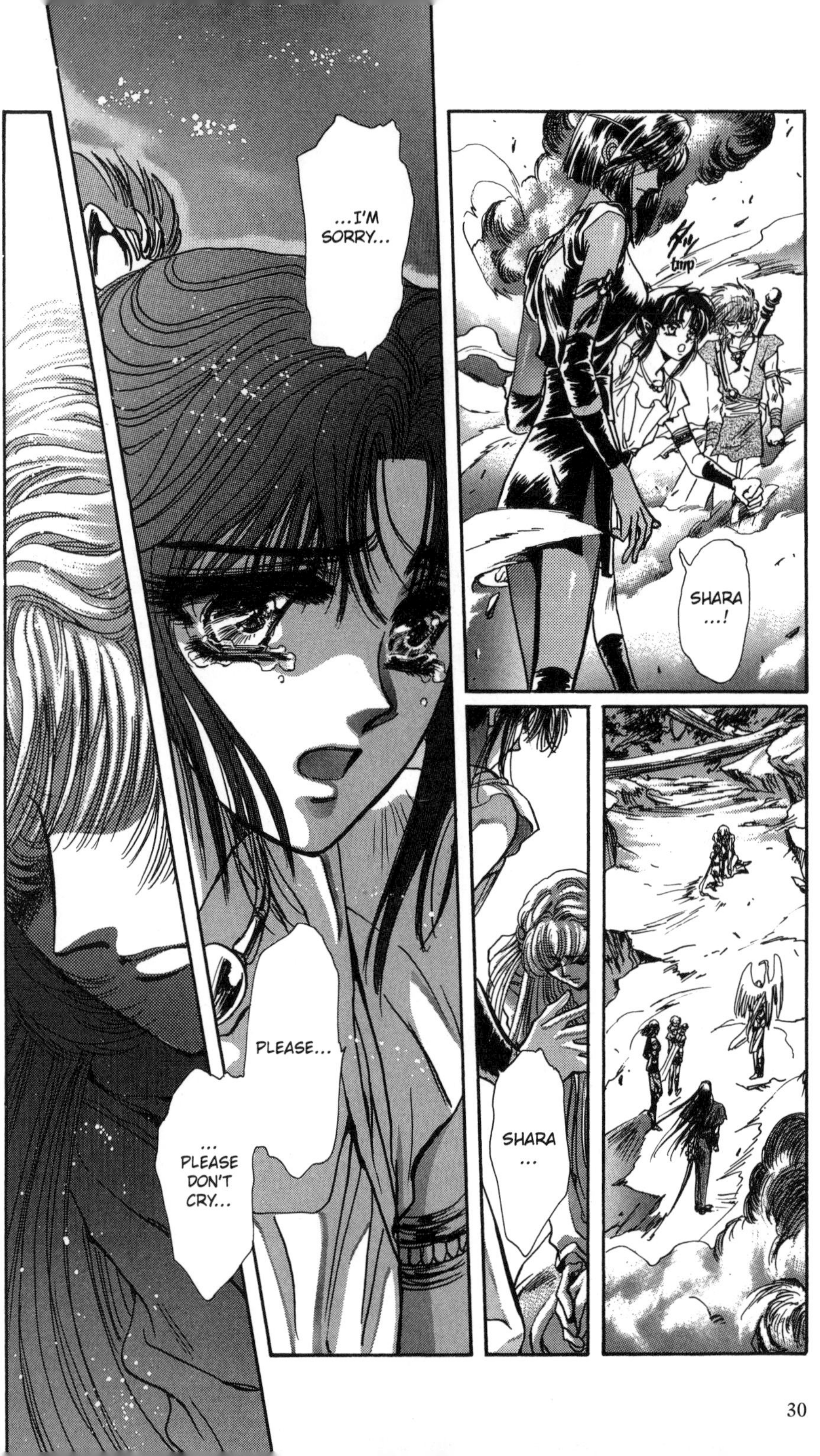
tmp
SHARA ...!
SHARA ...
...I'M SORRY...
PLEASE...
... PLEASE DON'T CRY...

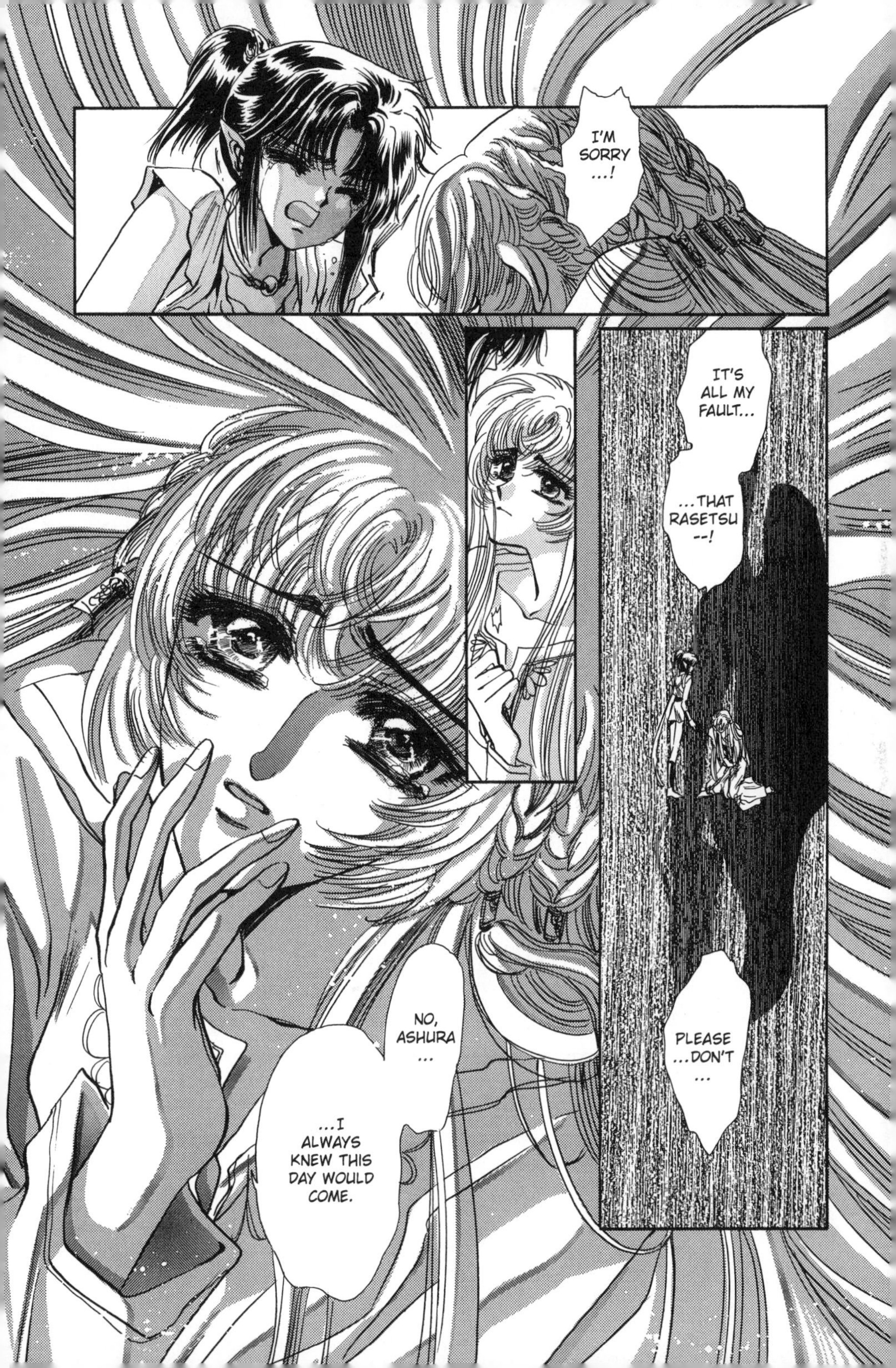
I'M SORRY ...!
IT'S ALL MY FAULT...
...THAT RASETSU --!
PLEASE ...DON'T ...
NO, ASHURA ...
...I ALWAYS KNEW THIS DAY WOULD COME.

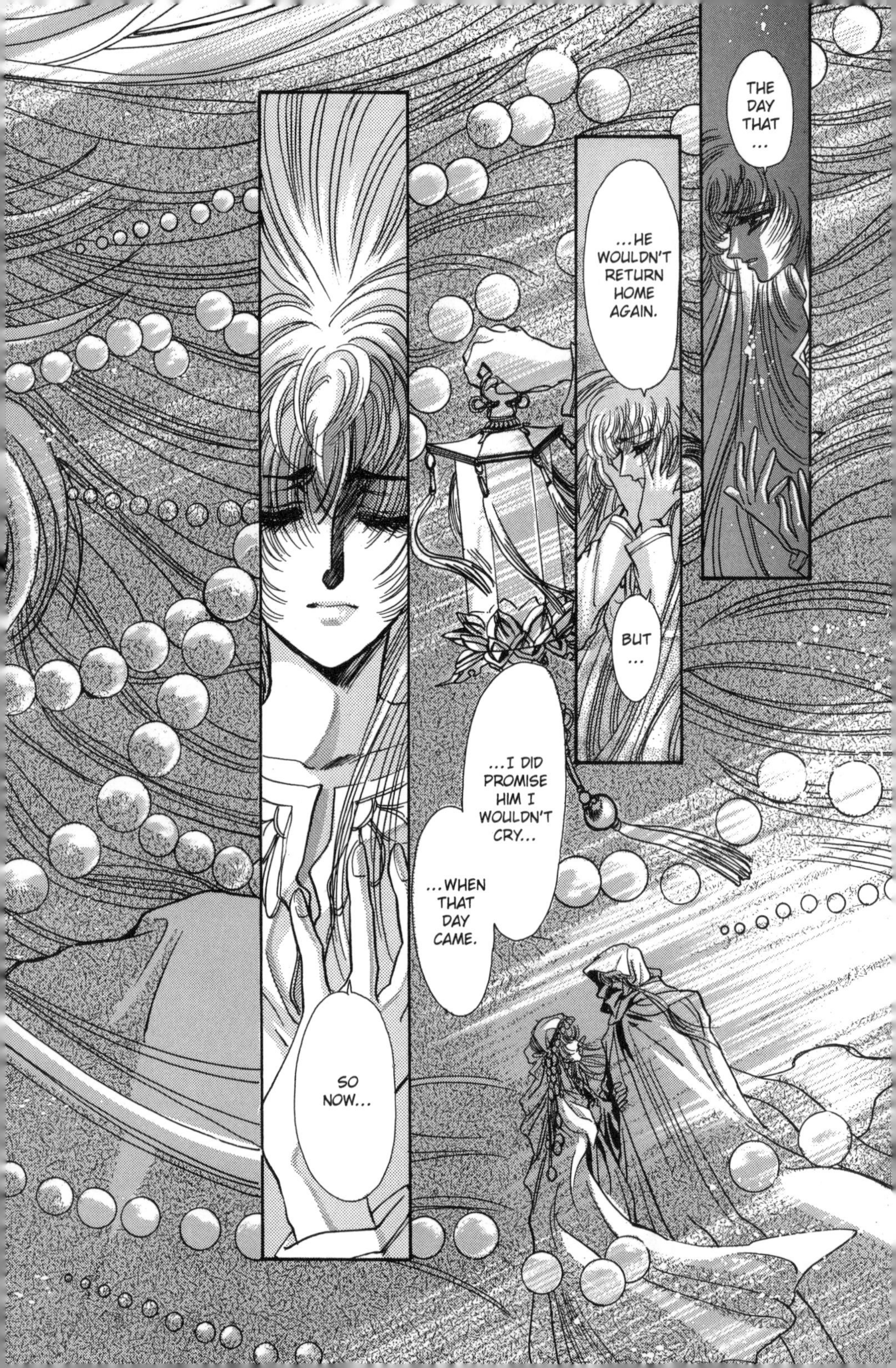
THE DAY THAT...
...HE WOULDN'T RETURN HOME AGAIN.
BUT...
...I DID PROMISE HIM I WOULDN'T CRY...
...WHEN THAT DAY CAME.
SO NOW...

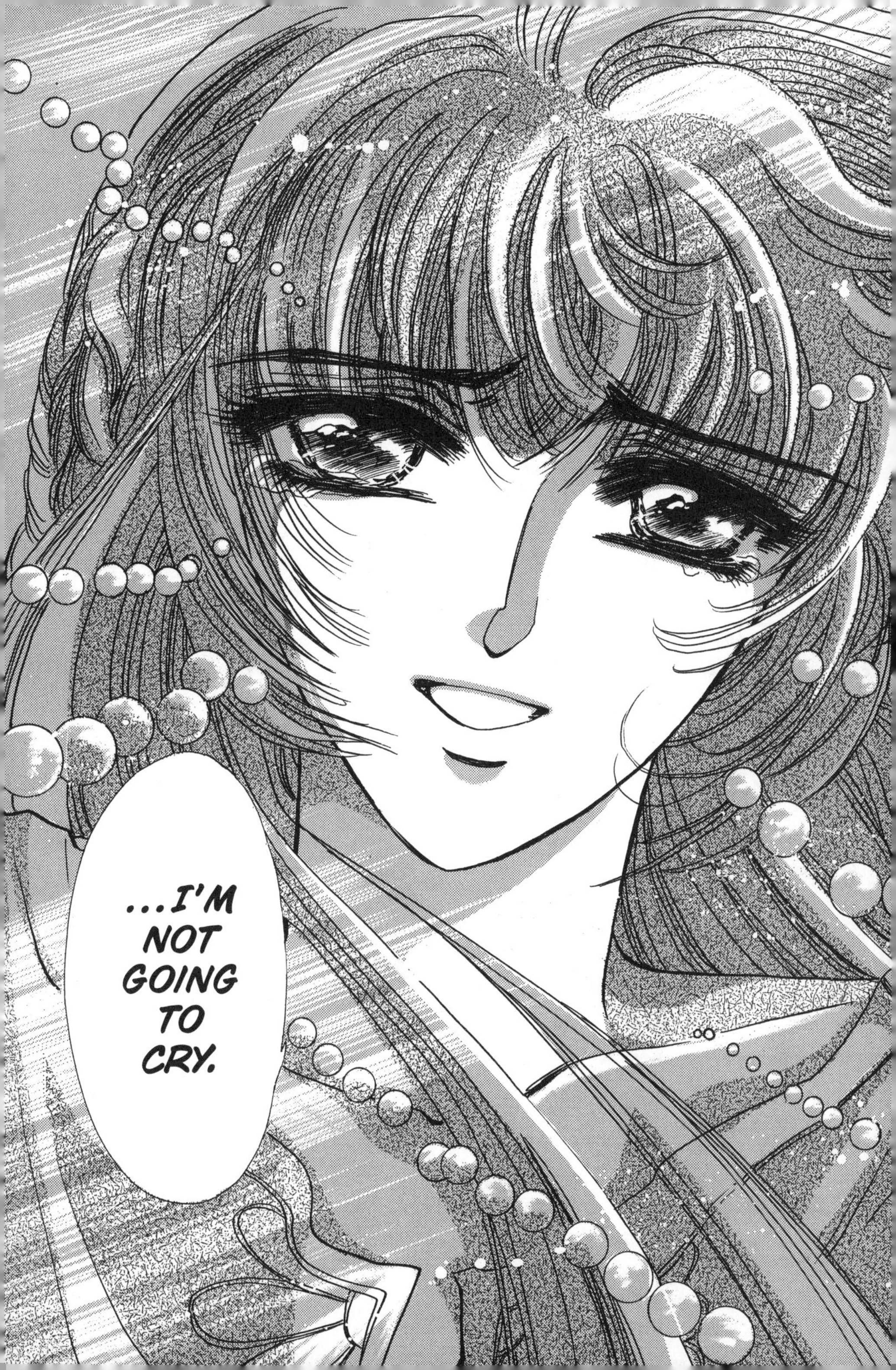
...I'M NOT GOING TO CRY.

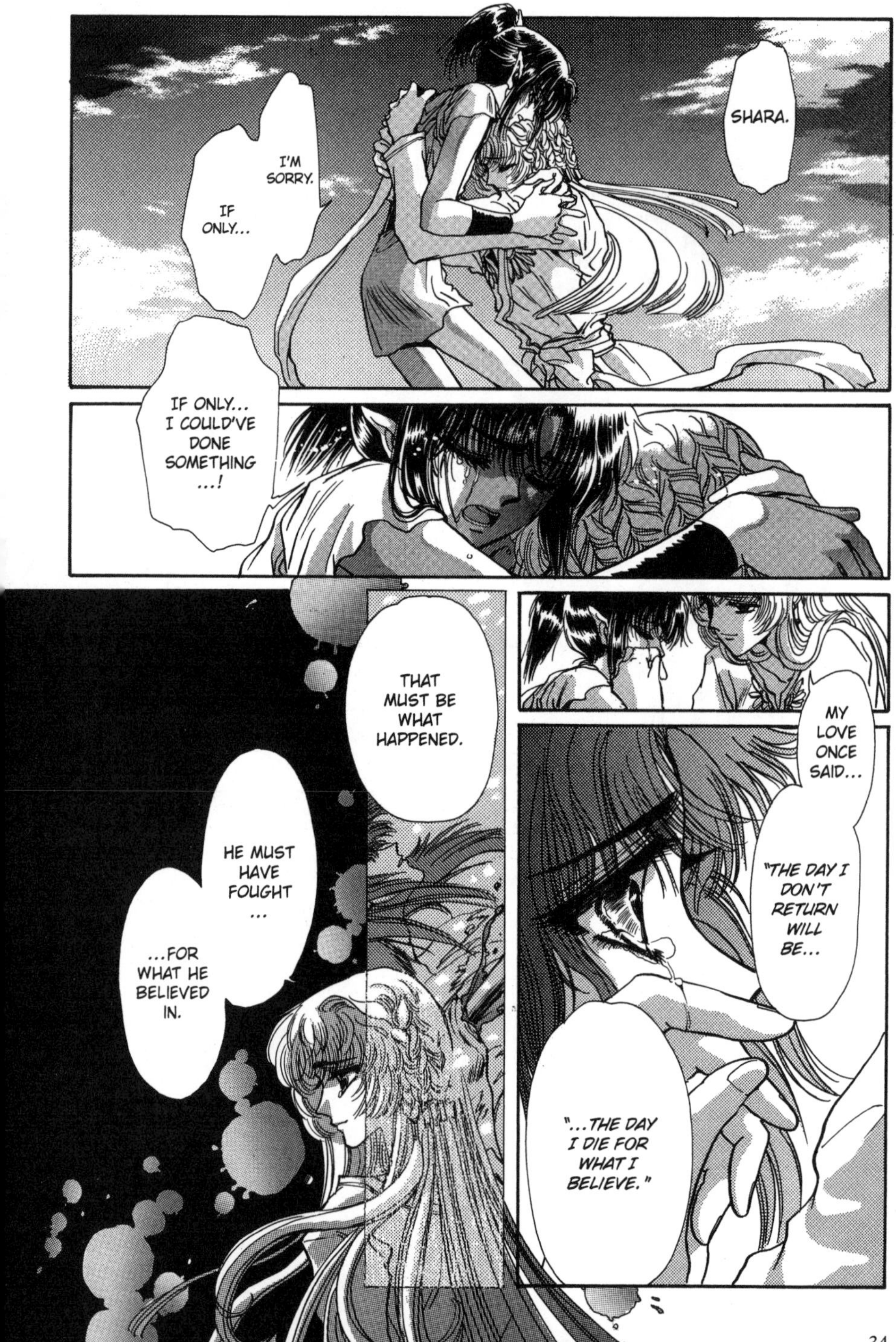
SHARA.
I'M SORRY.
IF ONLY...
IF ONLY... I COULD'VE DONE SOMETHING ...!
MY LOVE ONCE SAID...
"THE DAY I DON'T RETURN WILL BE...
"...THE DAY I DIE FOR WHAT I BELIEVE."
THAT MUST BE WHAT HAPPENED.
HE MUST HAVE FOUGHT ...
...FOR WHAT HE BELIEVED IN.

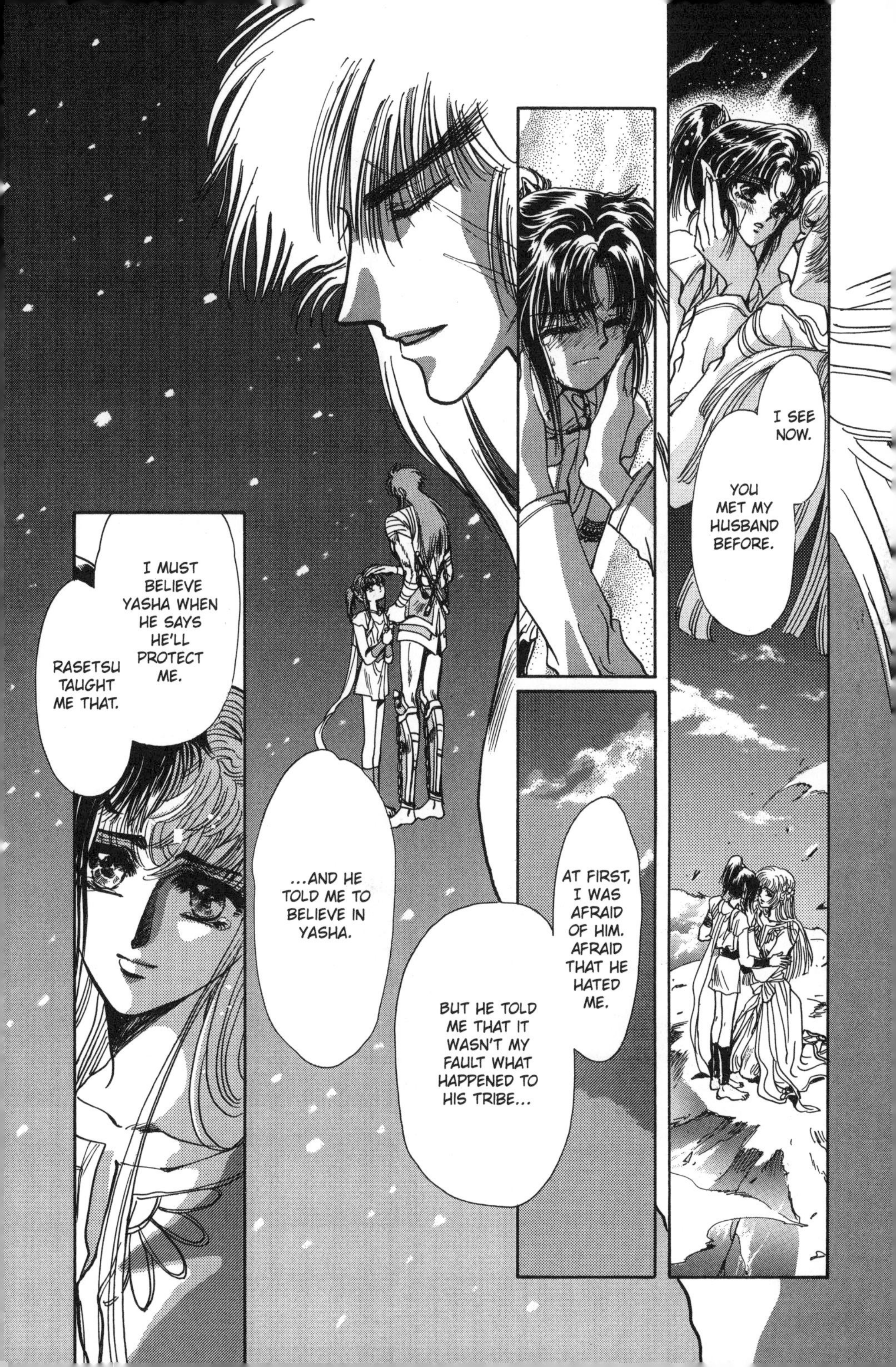
I SEE NOW.
YOU MET MY HUSBAND BEFORE.
AT FIRST, I WAS AFRAID OF HIM. AFRAID THAT HE HATED ME.
BUT HE TOLD ME THAT IT WASN'T MY FAULT WHAT HAPPENED TO HIS TRIBE...
...AND HE TOLD ME TO BELIEVE IN YASHA.
I MUST BELIEVE YASHA WHEN HE SAYS HE'LL PROTECT ME.
RASETSU TAUGHT ME THAT.

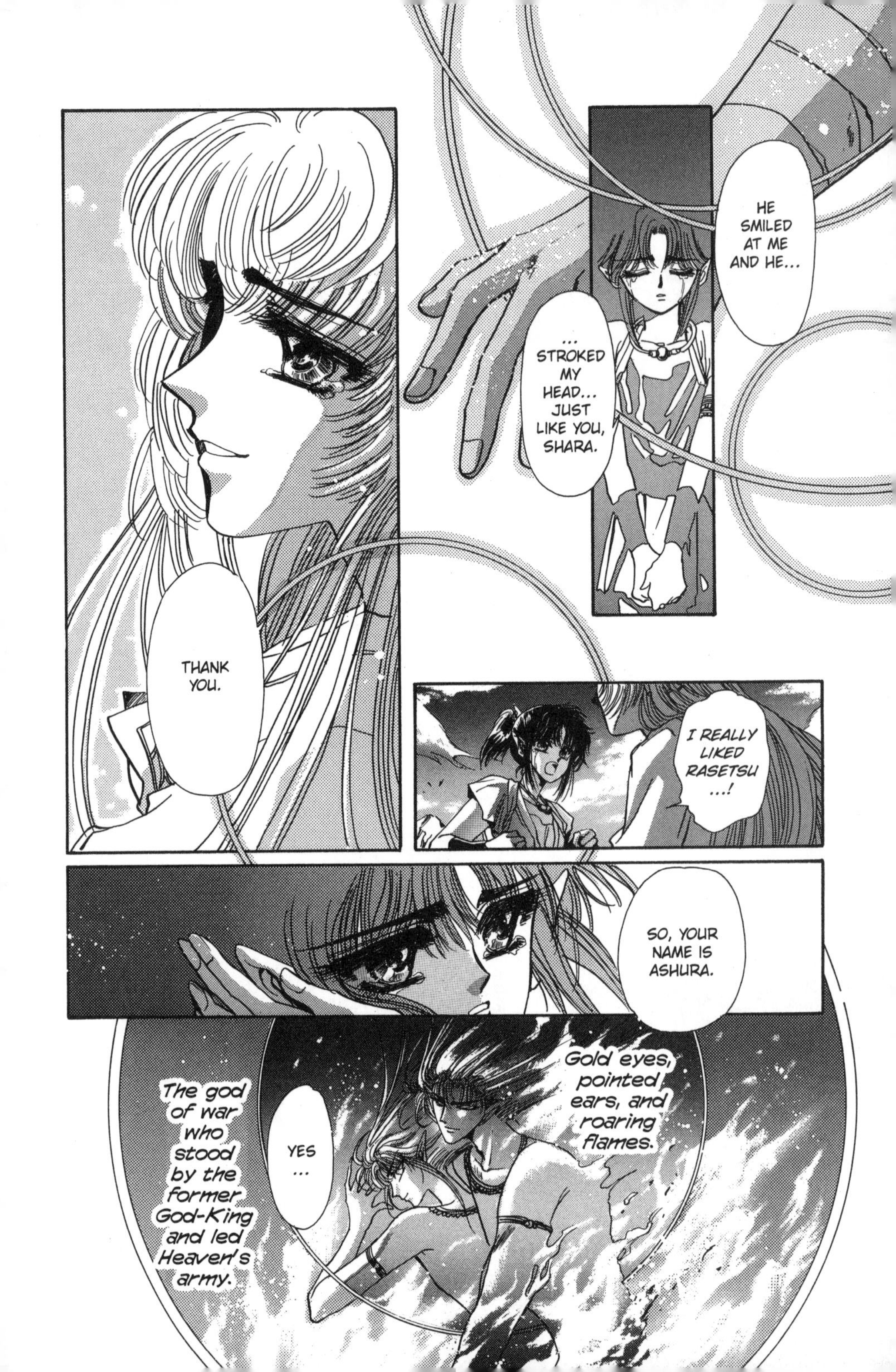
HE SMILED AT ME AND HE...
...STROKED MY HEAD... JUST LIKE YOU, SHARA.
I REALLY LIKED RASETSU ...!
THANK YOU.
SO, YOUR NAME IS ASHURA.
Gold eyes, pointed ears, and roaring flames.
YES ...
The god of war who stood by the former God-King and led Heaven's army.

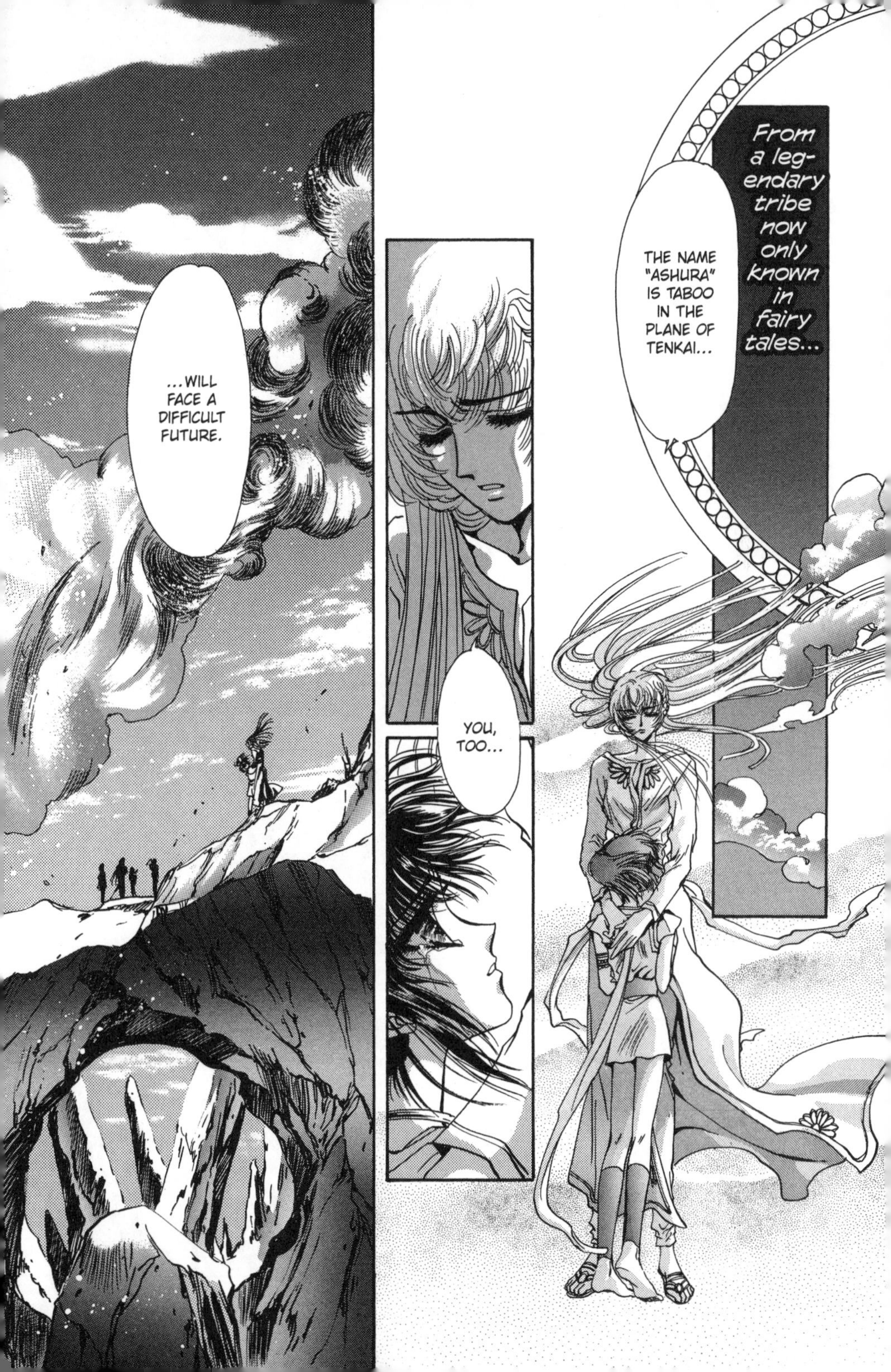
From a leg-endary tribe now only known in fairy tales...
THE NAME "ASHURA" IS TABOO IN THE PLANE OF TENKAI...
YOU, TOO...
...WILL FACE A DIFFICULT FUTURE.

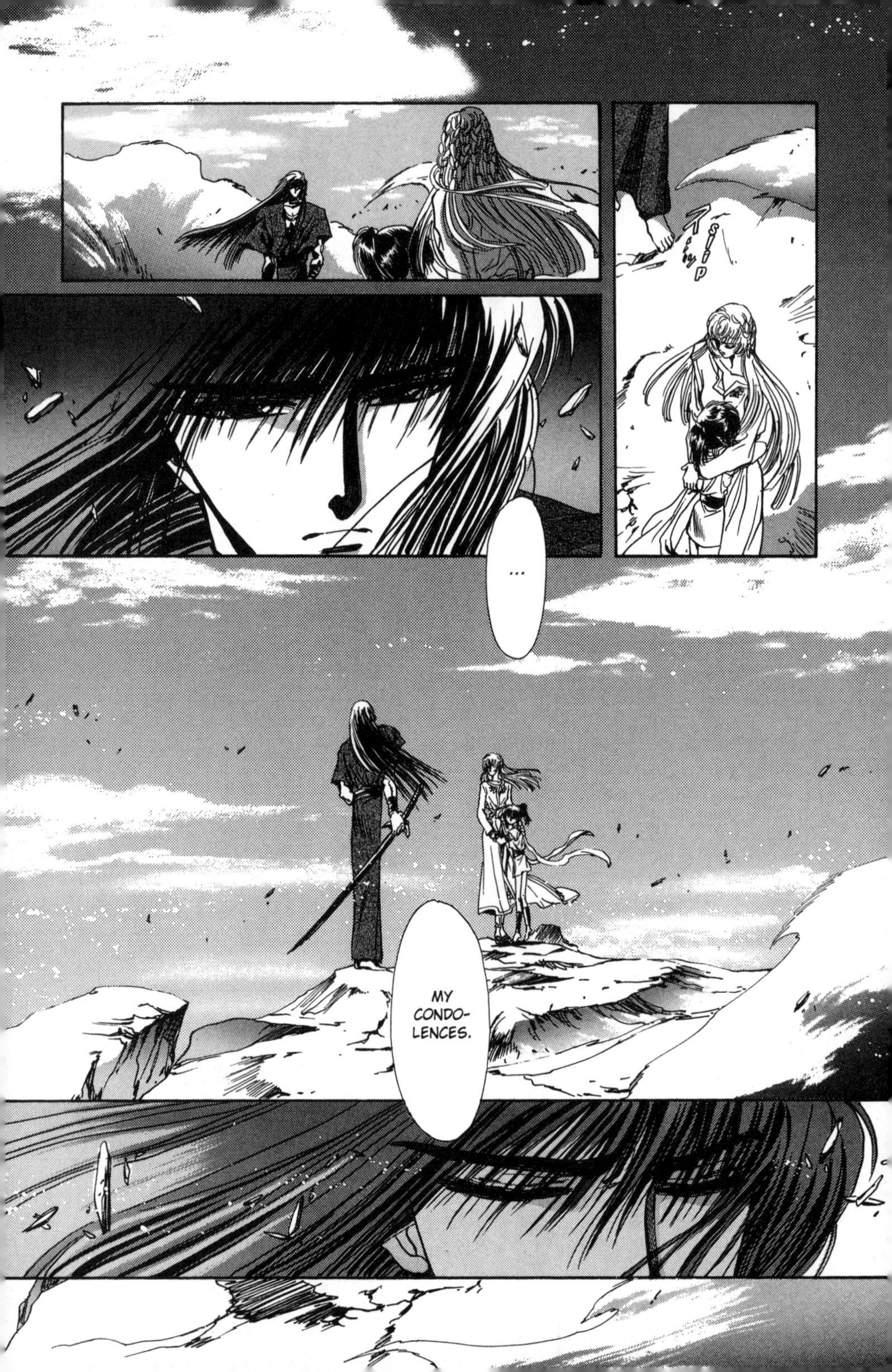
SLIP
...
MY CONDOLENCES.

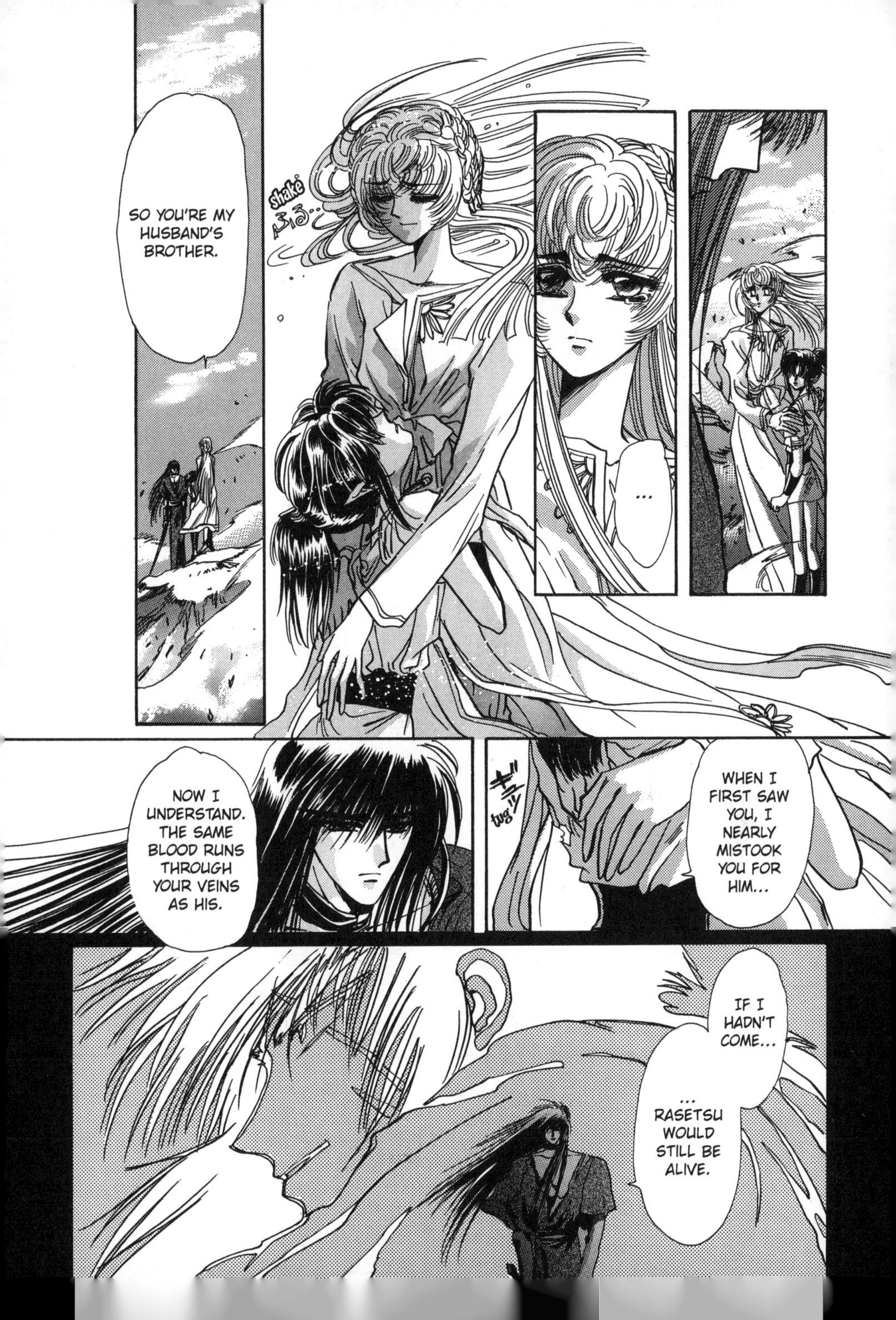
...
shake
SO YOU'RE MY HUSBAND'S BROTHER.
tug
WHEN I FIRST SAW YOU, I NEARLY MISTOOK YOU FOR HIM...
NOW I UNDERSTAND. THE SAME BLOOD RUNS THROUGH YOUR VEINS AS HIS.
IF I HADN'T COME...
...RASETSU WOULD STILL BE ALIVE.

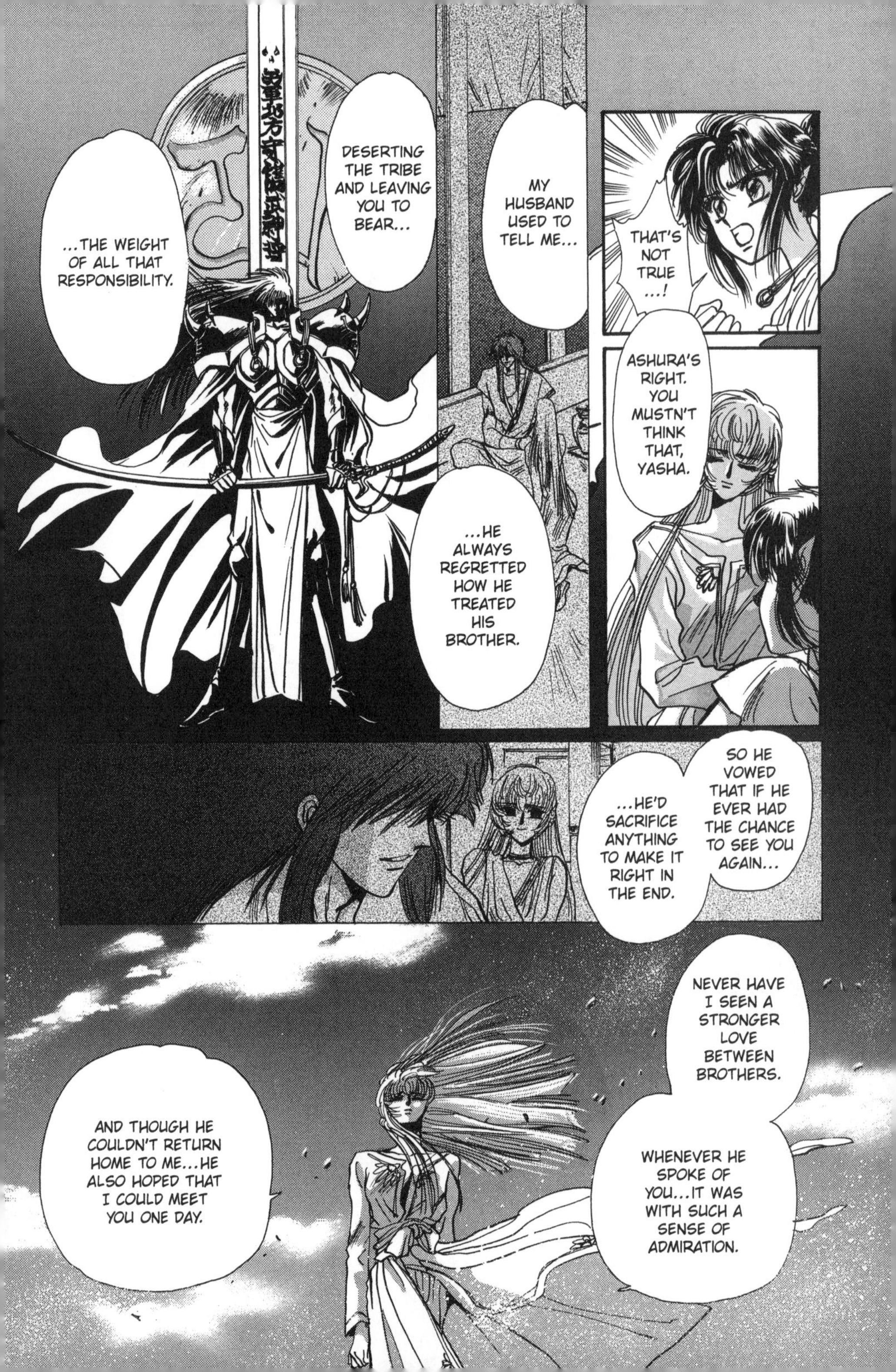
THAT'S NOT TRUE…!
ASHURA'S RIGHT. YOU MUSTN'T THINK THAT, YASHA.
MY HUSBAND USED TO TELL ME…
…HE ALWAYS REGRETTED HOW HE TREATED HIS BROTHER.
DESERTING THE TRIBE AND LEAVING YOU TO BEAR…
…THE WEIGHT OF ALL THAT RESPONSIBILITY.
SO HE VOWED THAT IF HE EVER HAD THE CHANCE TO SEE YOU AGAIN…
…HE'D SACRIFICE ANYTHING TO MAKE IT RIGHT IN THE END.
NEVER HAVE I SEEN A STRONGER LOVE BETWEEN BROTHERS.
WHENEVER HE SPOKE OF YOU…IT WAS WITH SUCH A SENSE OF ADMIRATION.
AND THOUGH HE COULDN'T RETURN HOME TO ME…HE ALSO HOPED THAT I COULD MEET YOU ONE DAY.

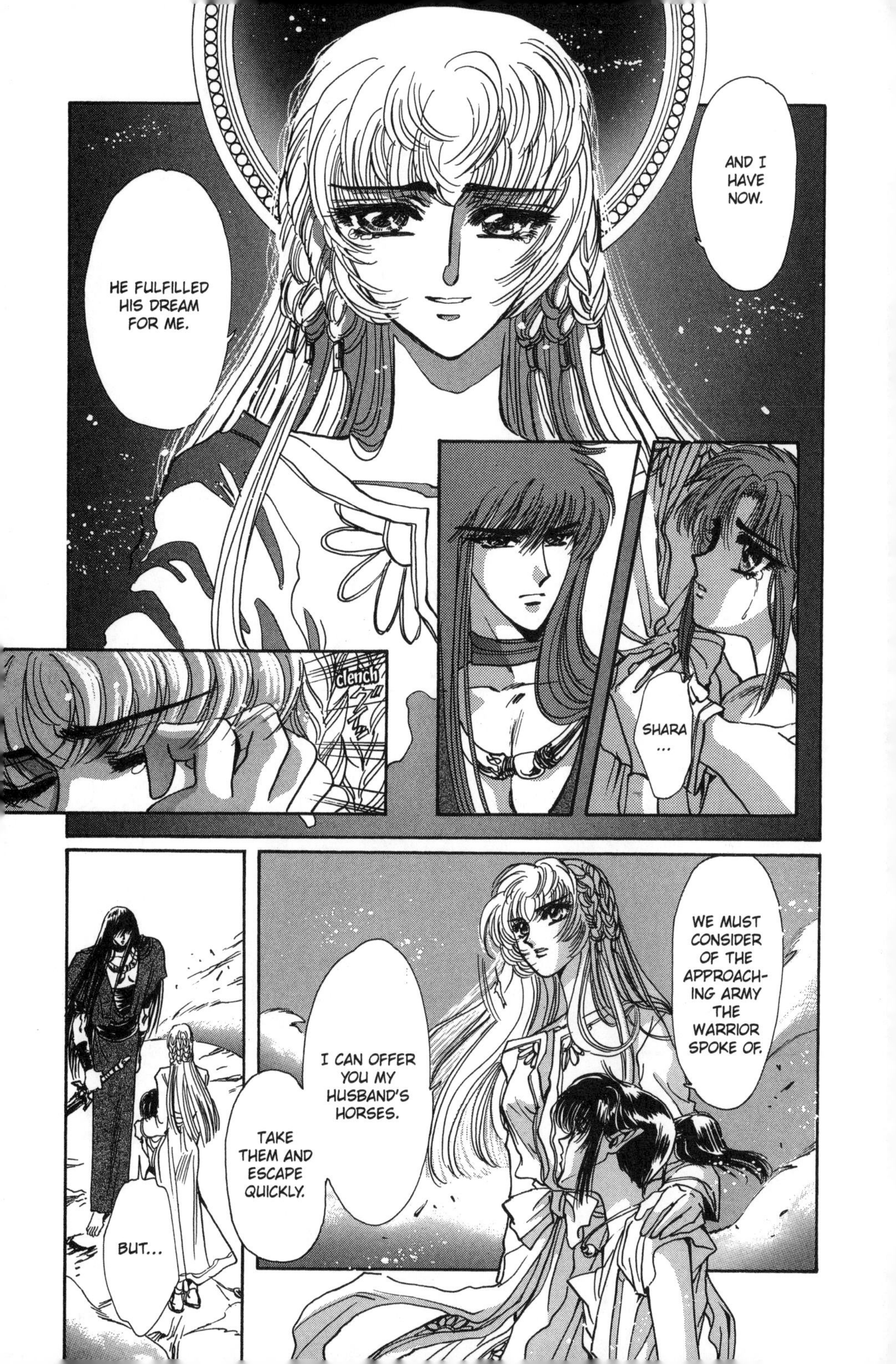
AND I HAVE NOW.
HE FULFILLED HIS DREAM FOR ME.
SHARA ...
clench
WE MUST CONSIDER OF THE APPROACHING ARMY THE WARRIOR SPOKE OF.
I CAN OFFER YOU MY HUSBAND'S HORSES.
TAKE THEM AND ESCAPE QUICKLY.
BUT...

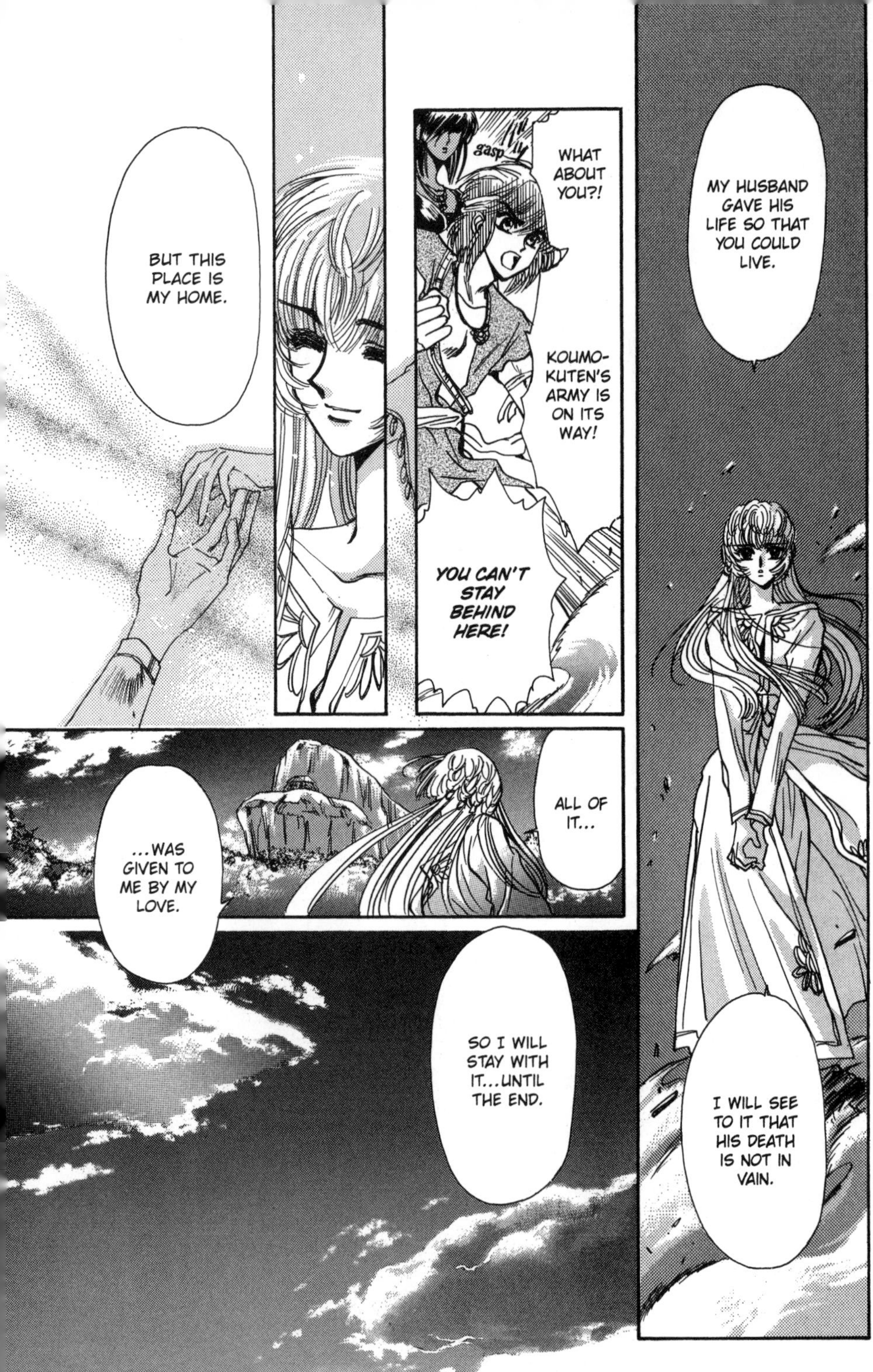
MY HUSBAND GAVE HIS LIFE SO THAT YOU COULD LIVE.
I WILL SEE TO IT THAT HIS DEATH IS NOT IN VAIN.
gasp
WHAT ABOUT YOU?!
KOUMOKUTEN'S ARMY IS ON ITS WAY!
YOU CAN'T STAY BEHIND HERE!
BUT THIS PLACE IS MY HOME.
ALL OF IT...
...WAS GIVEN TO ME BY MY LOVE.
SO I WILL STAY WITH IT...UNTIL THE END.

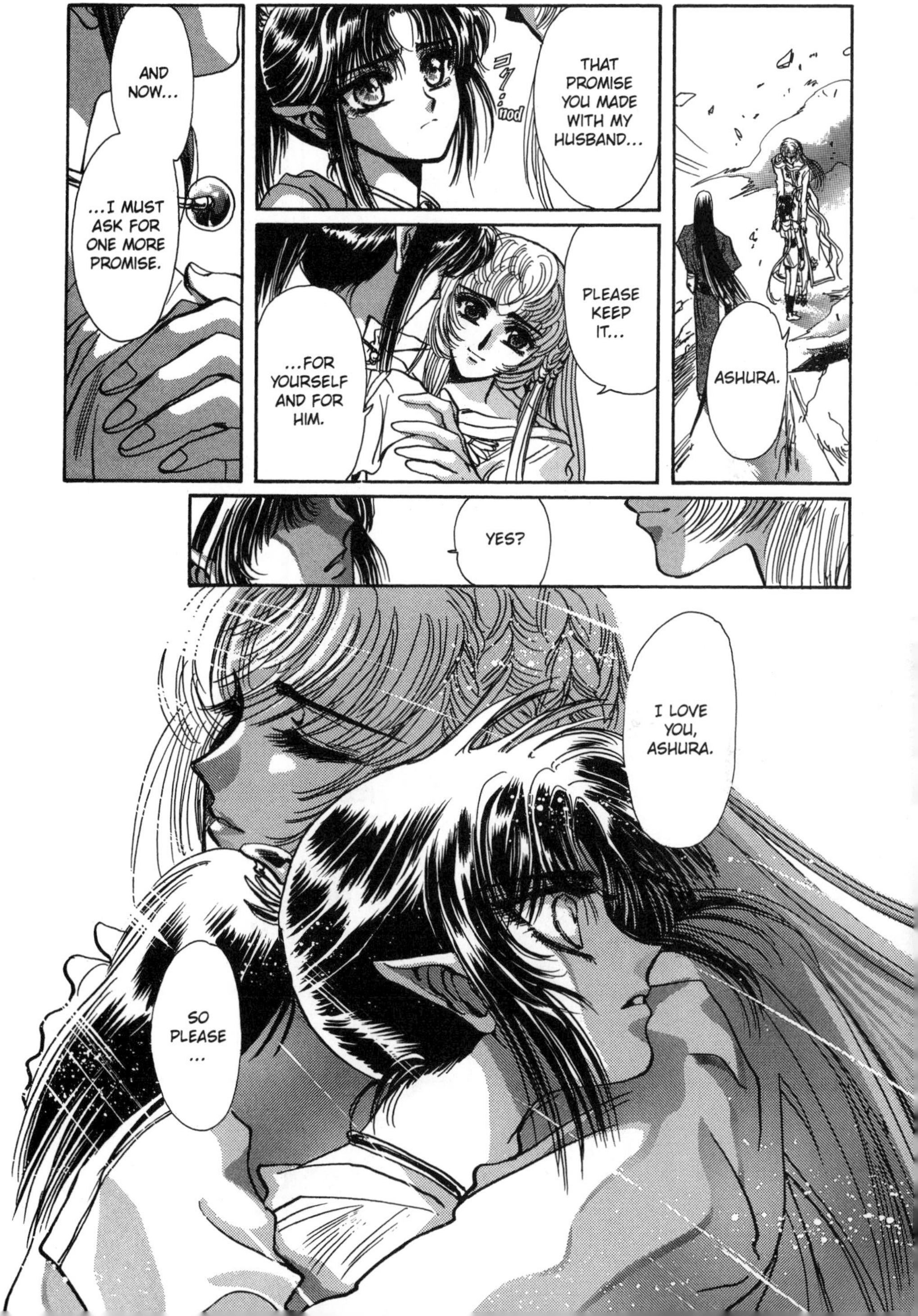
ASHURA.
THAT PROMISE YOU MADE WITH MY HUSBAND...
nod
PLEASE KEEP IT...
...FOR YOURSELF AND FOR HIM.
AND NOW...
...I MUST ASK FOR ONE MORE PROMISE.
YES?
I LOVE YOU, ASHURA.
SO PLEASE ...

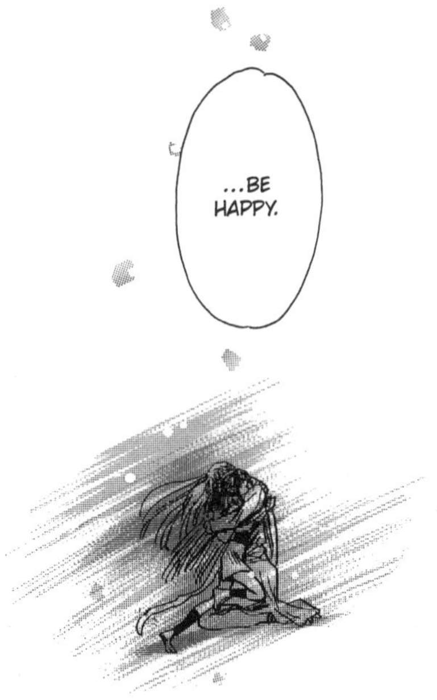
...BE HAPPY.

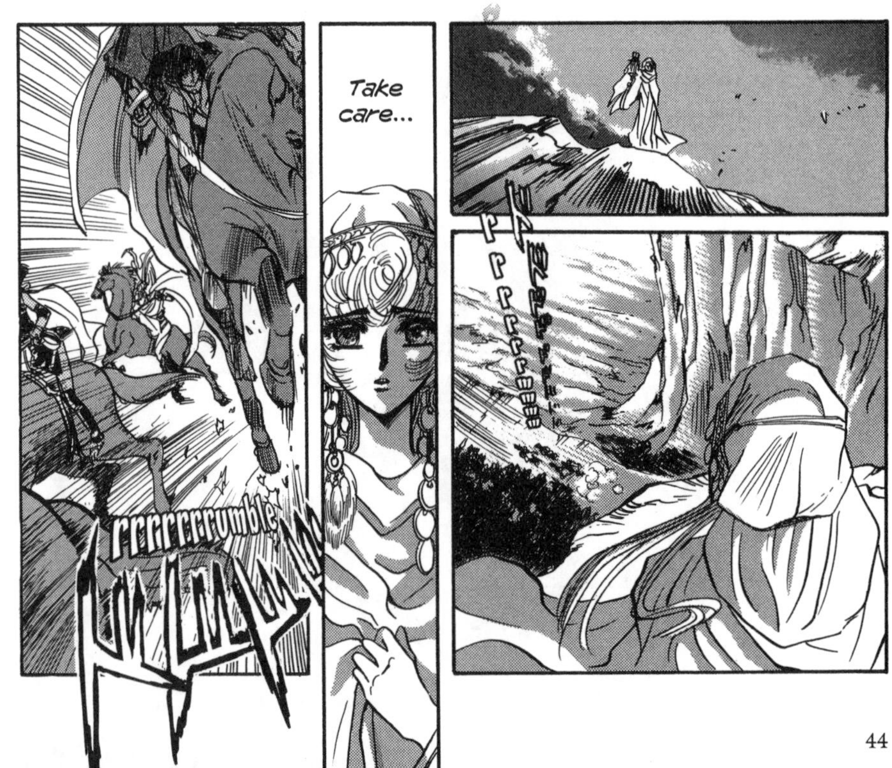
rrrrrrrmmmm
Take care...
rrrrrrrrumble

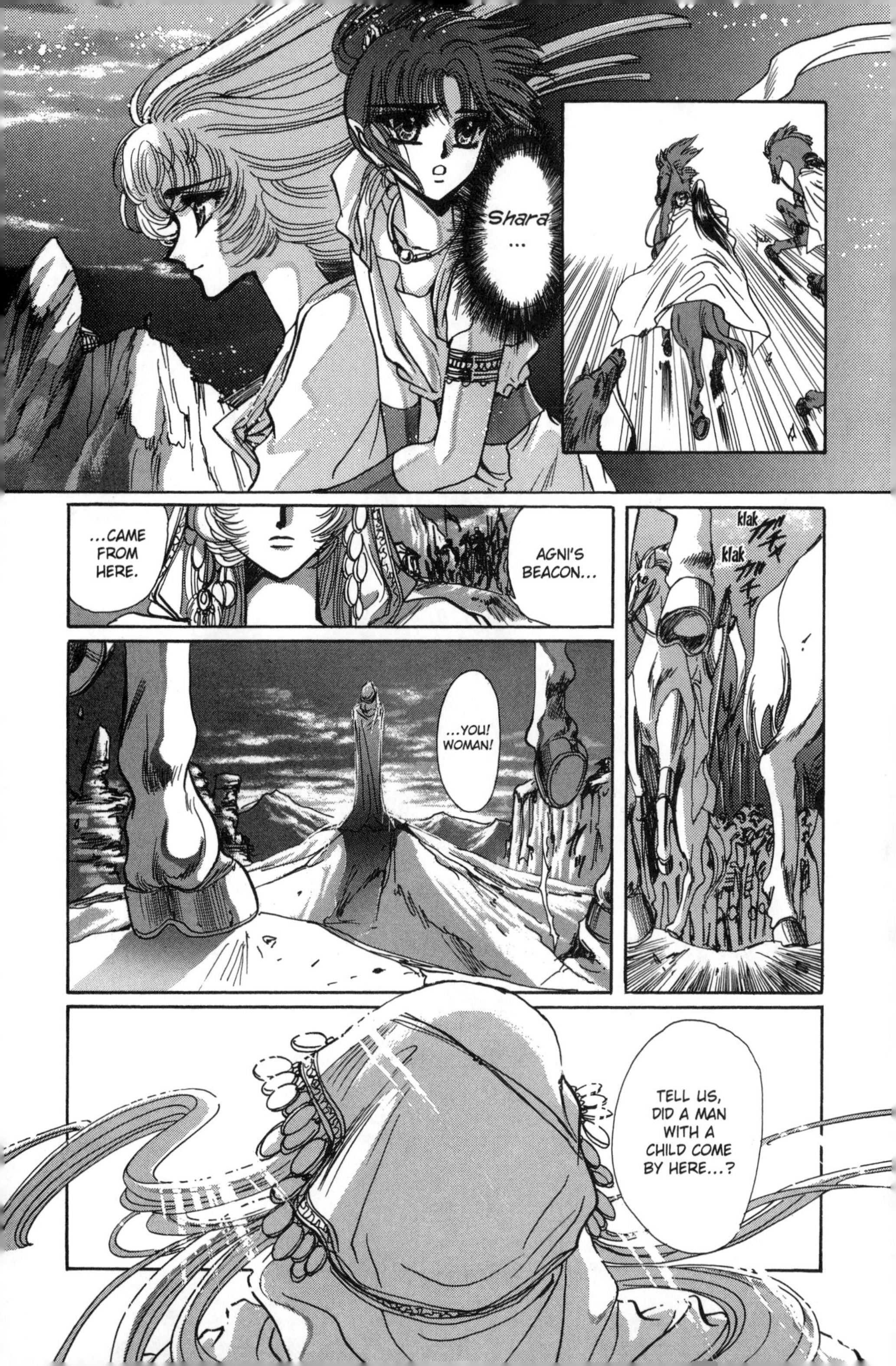
Shara
...
klak
klak
AGNI'S BEACON...
...CAME FROM HERE.
...YOU! WOMAN!
TELL US, DID A MAN WITH A CHILD COME BY HERE...?

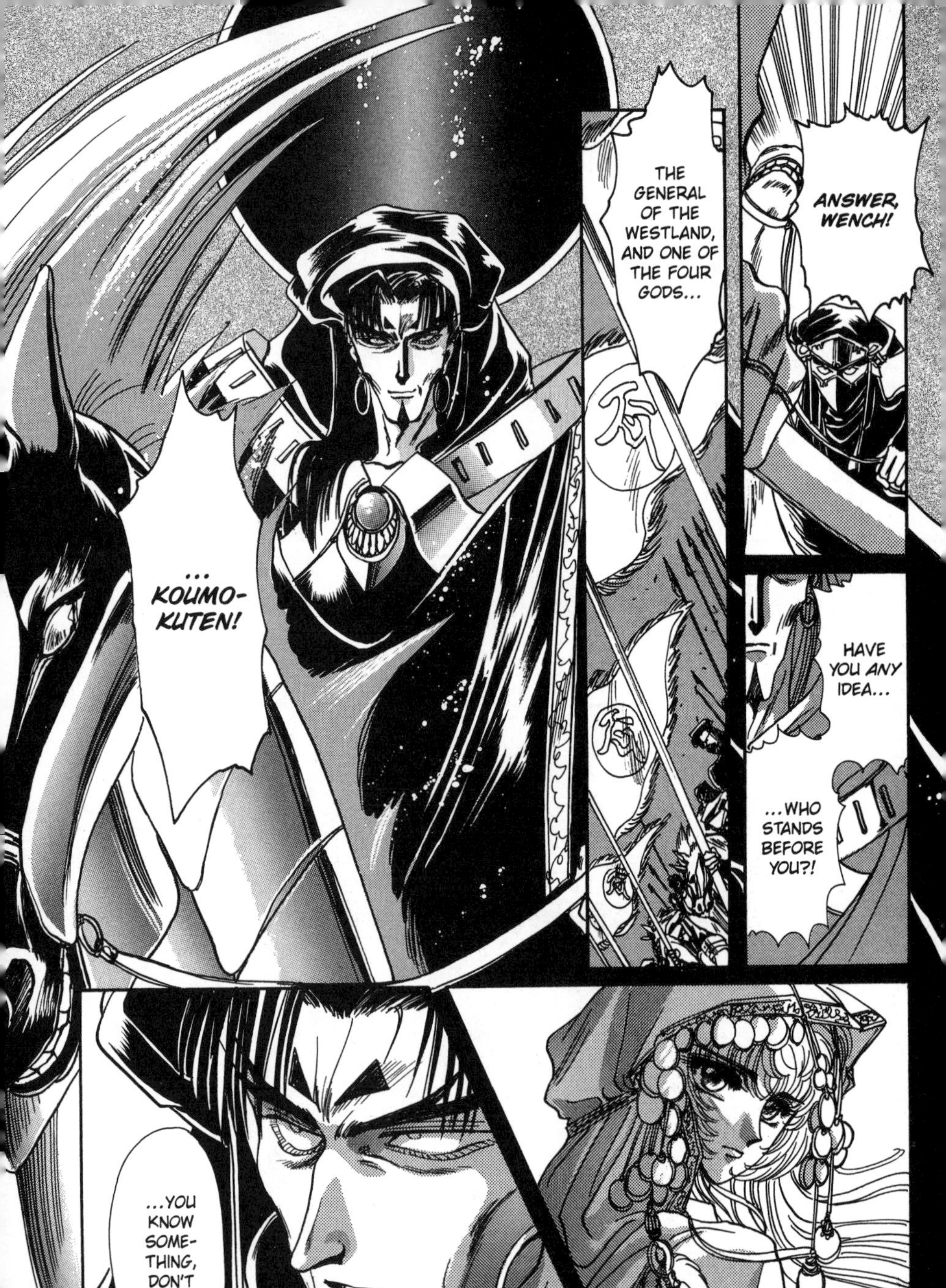

ANSWER, WENCH!
HAVE YOU ANY IDEA...
...WHO STANDS BEFORE YOU?!
THE GENERAL OF THE WESTLAND, AND ONE OF THE FOUR GODS...
...KOUMOKUTEN!
...YOU KNOW SOMETHING, DON'T YOU?

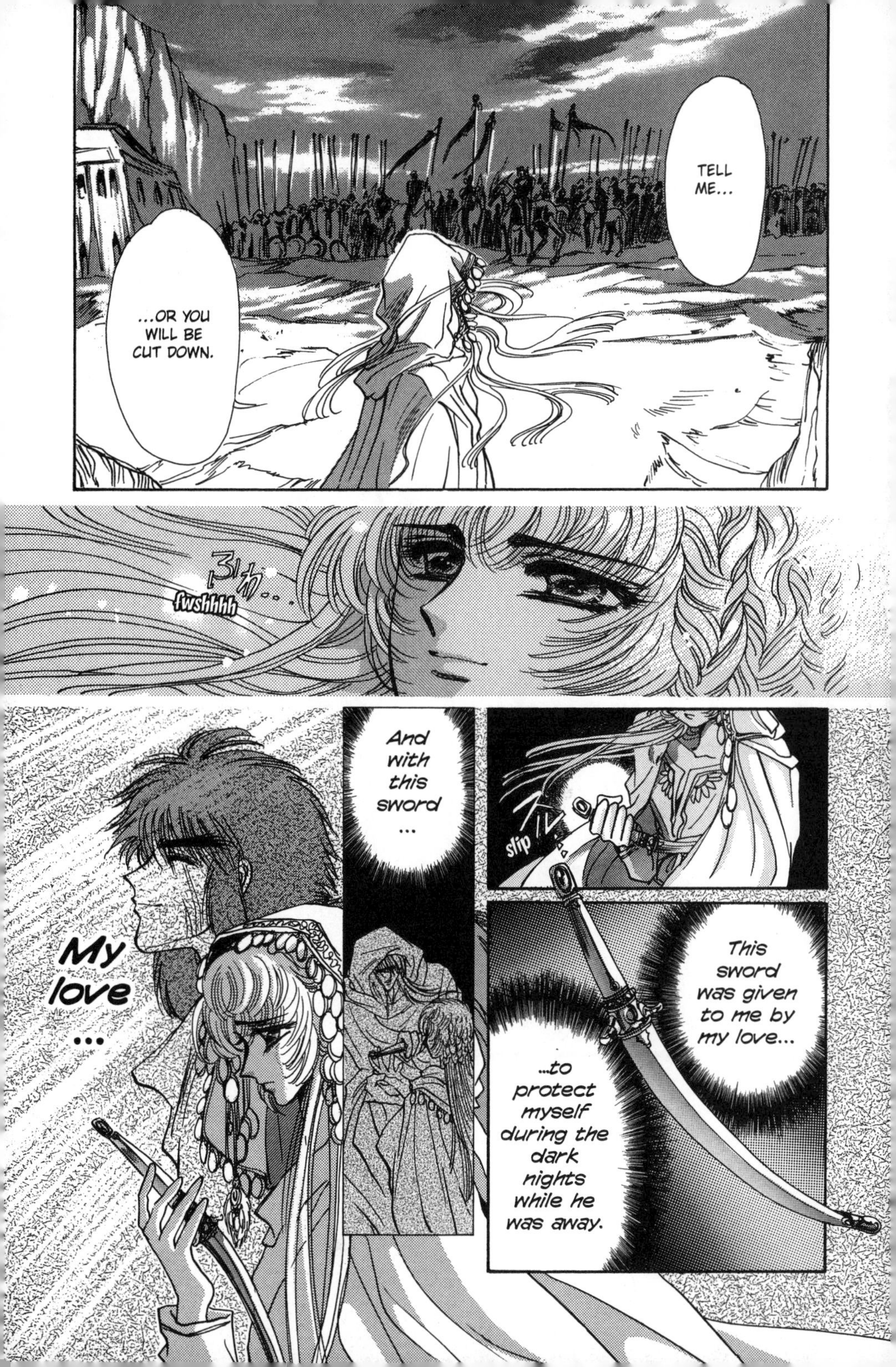
TELL ME...
...OR YOU WILL BE CUT DOWN.
fwshhhh
slip
This sword was given to me by my love...
...to protect myself during the dark nights while he was away.
And with this sword ...
My love ...

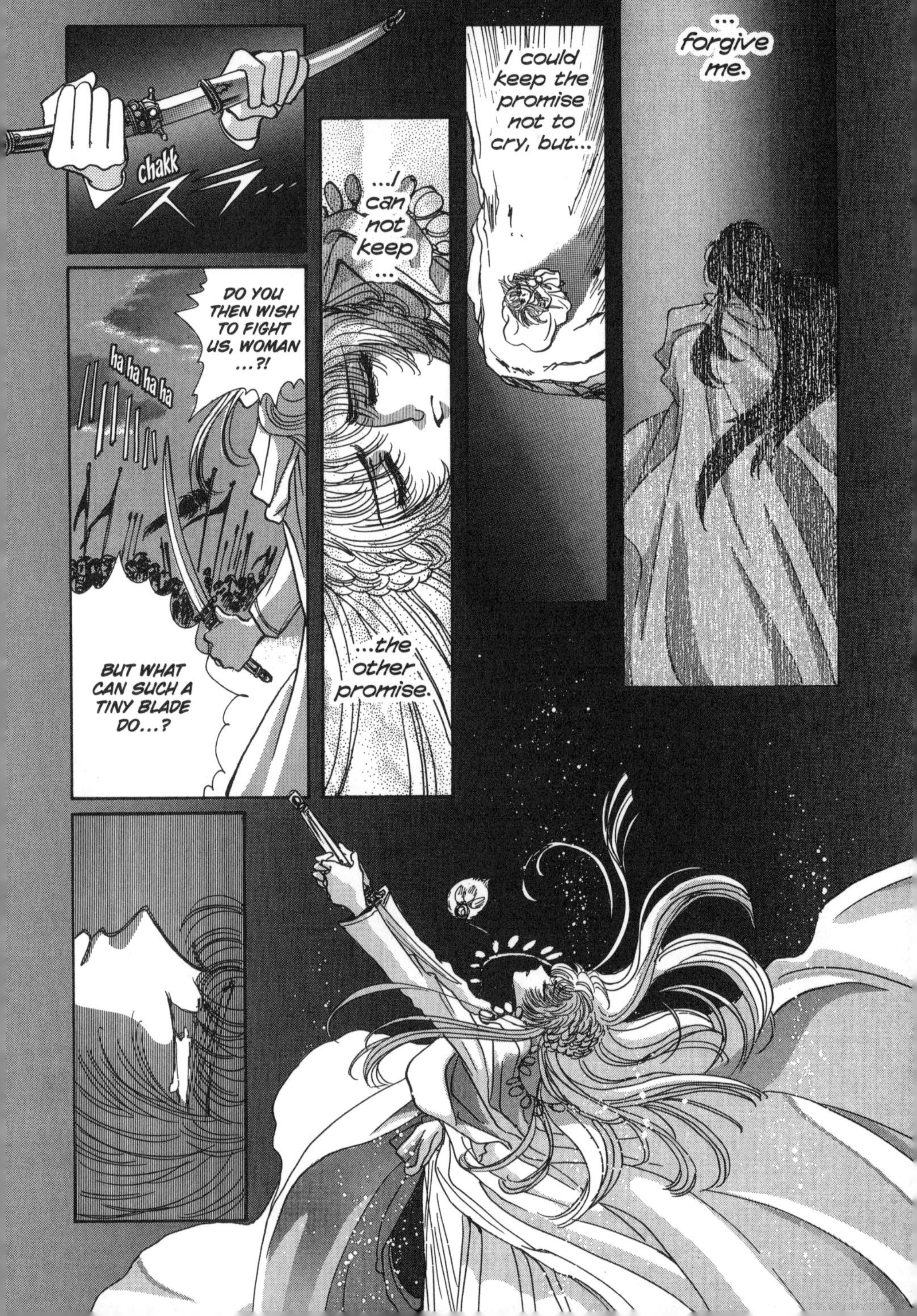
...forgive me.
I could keep the promise not to cry, but...
...I can not keep ...
...the other promise.
chakk
スラ...
DO YOU THEN WISH TO FIGHT US, WOMAN ...?!
ha ha ha ha
BUT WHAT CAN SUCH A TINY BLADE DO...?

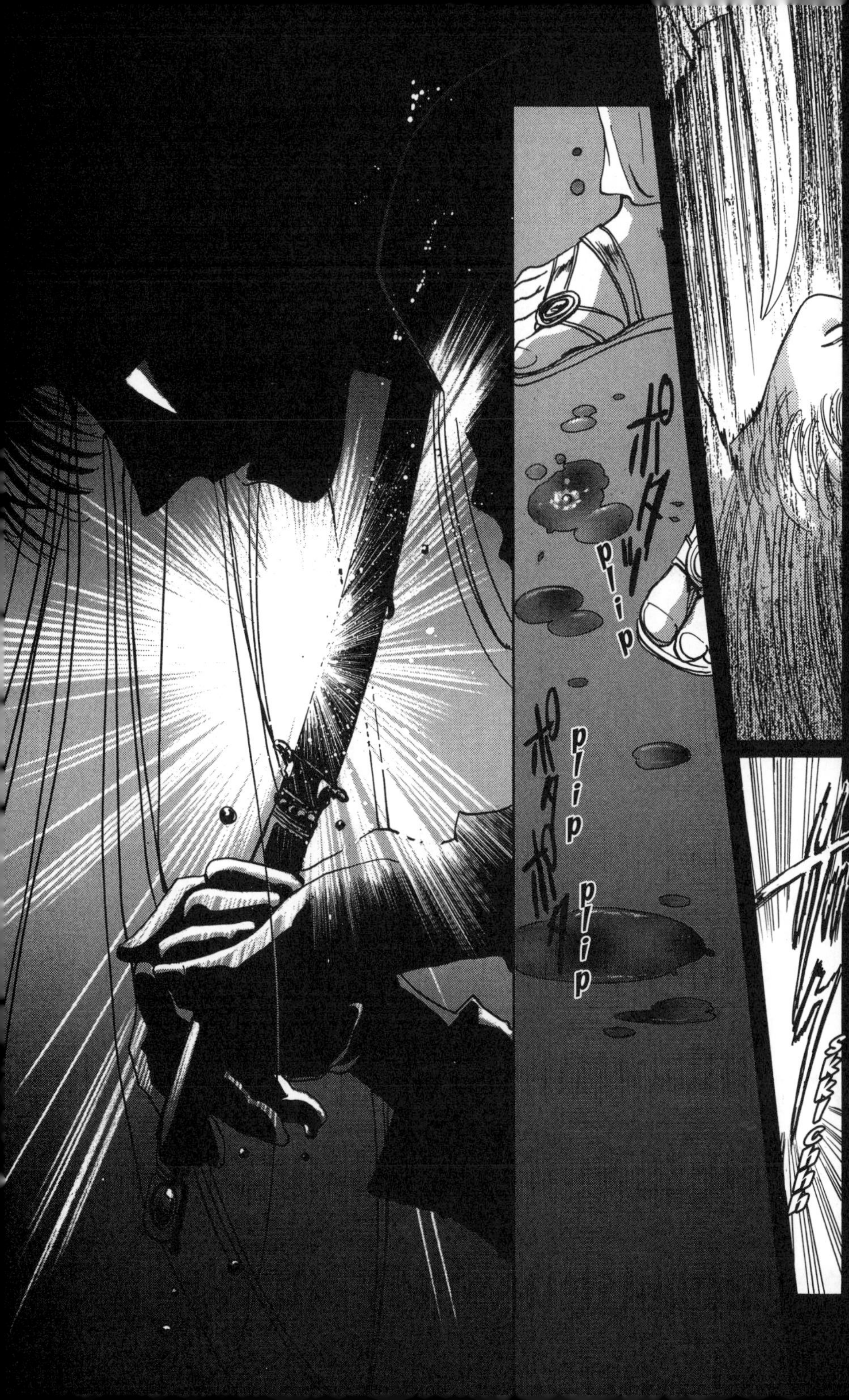
skkichhh
plip
plip
plip
plip

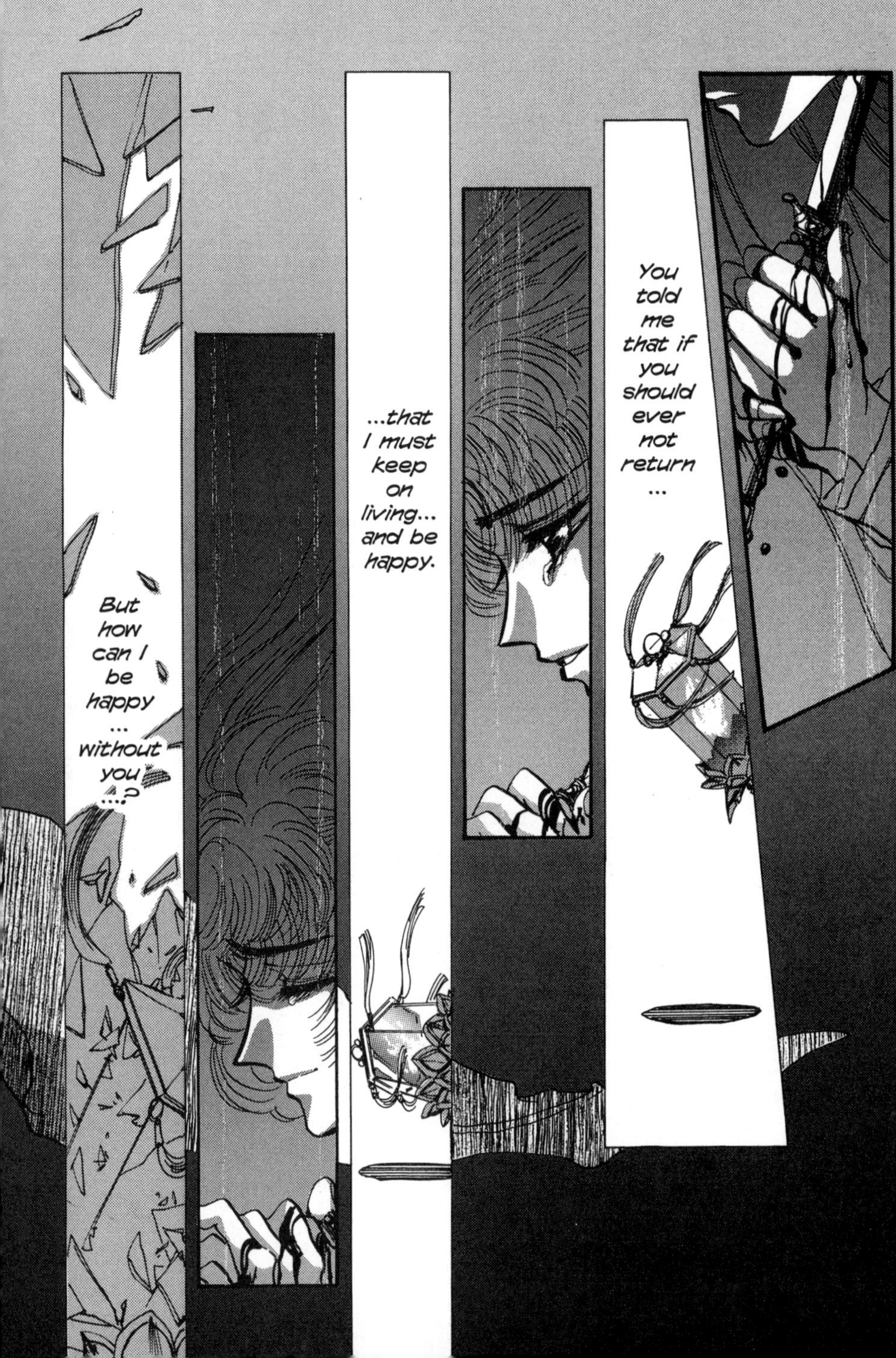
You told me that if you should ever not return ...
...that I must keep on living... and be happy.
But how can I be happy ... without you ...?

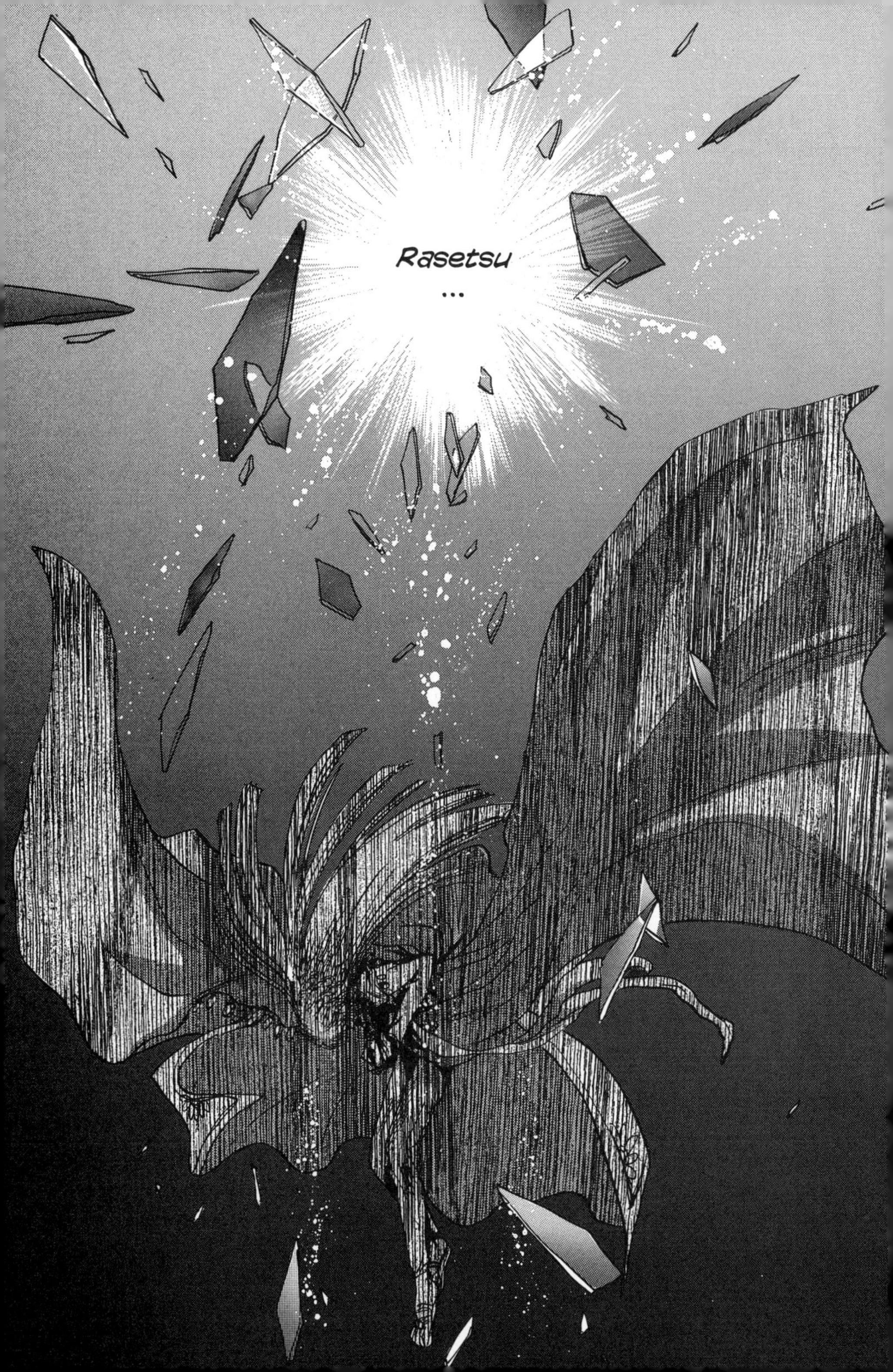
Rasetsu
...

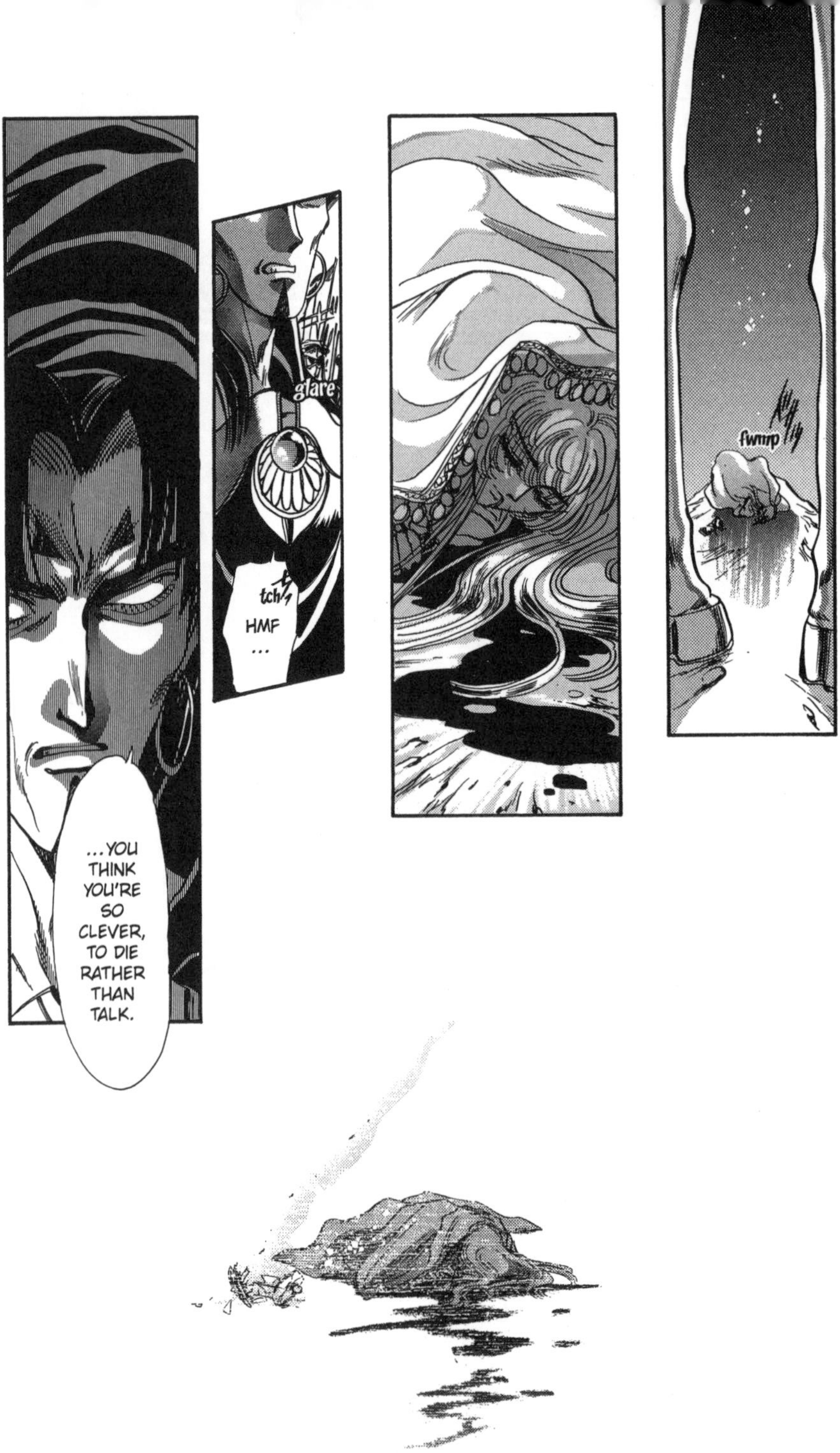
fwmp
glare
tch
HMF …
…YOU THINK YOU'RE SO CLEVER, TO DIE RATHER THAN TALK.

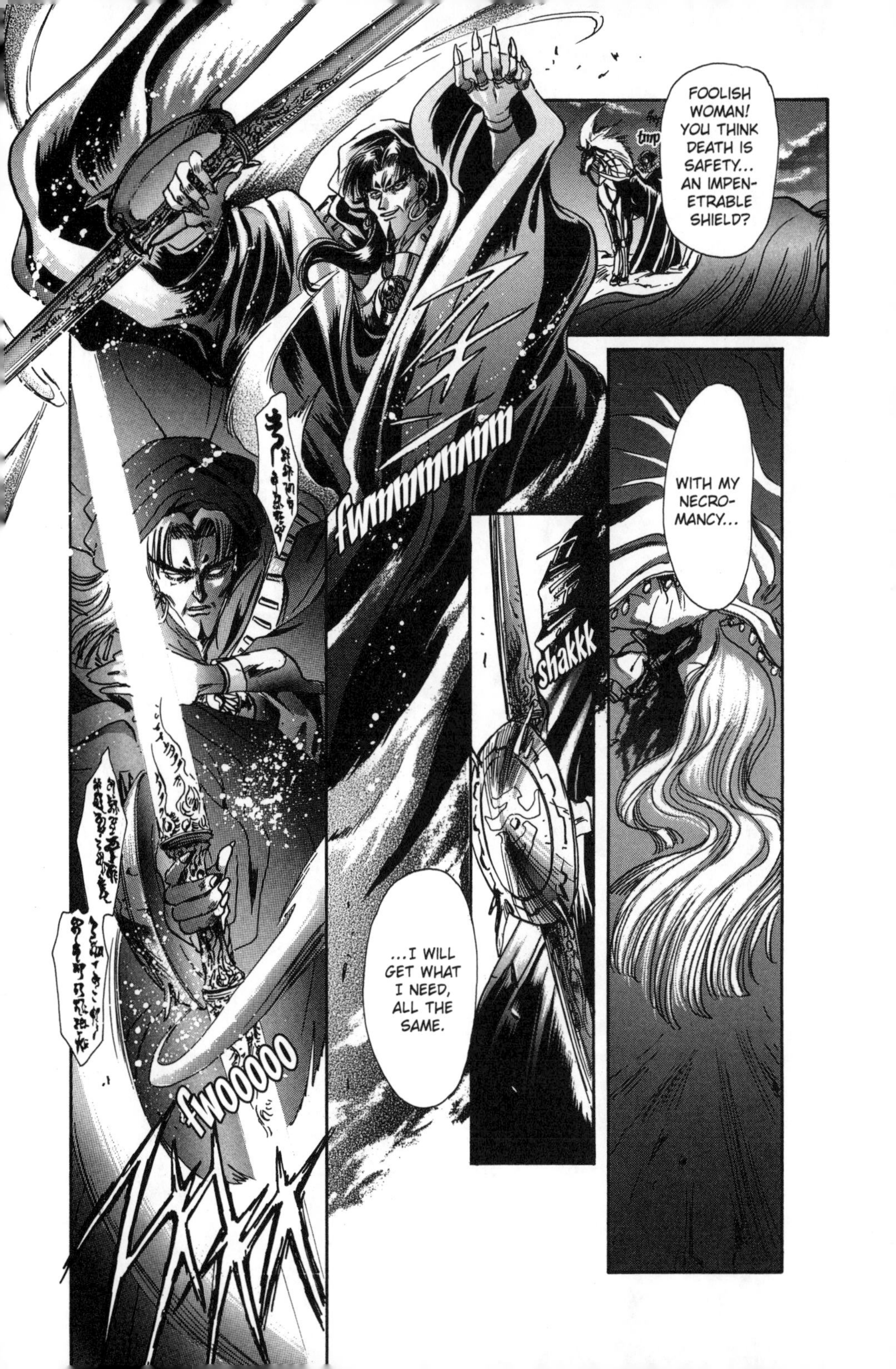
FOOLISH WOMAN! YOU THINK DEATH IS SAFETY... AN IMPENETRABLE SHIELD?
tmp
fwmmmmmmm
WITH MY NECROMANCY...
shakkk
...I WILL GET WHAT I NEED, ALL THE SAME.
fwooooo

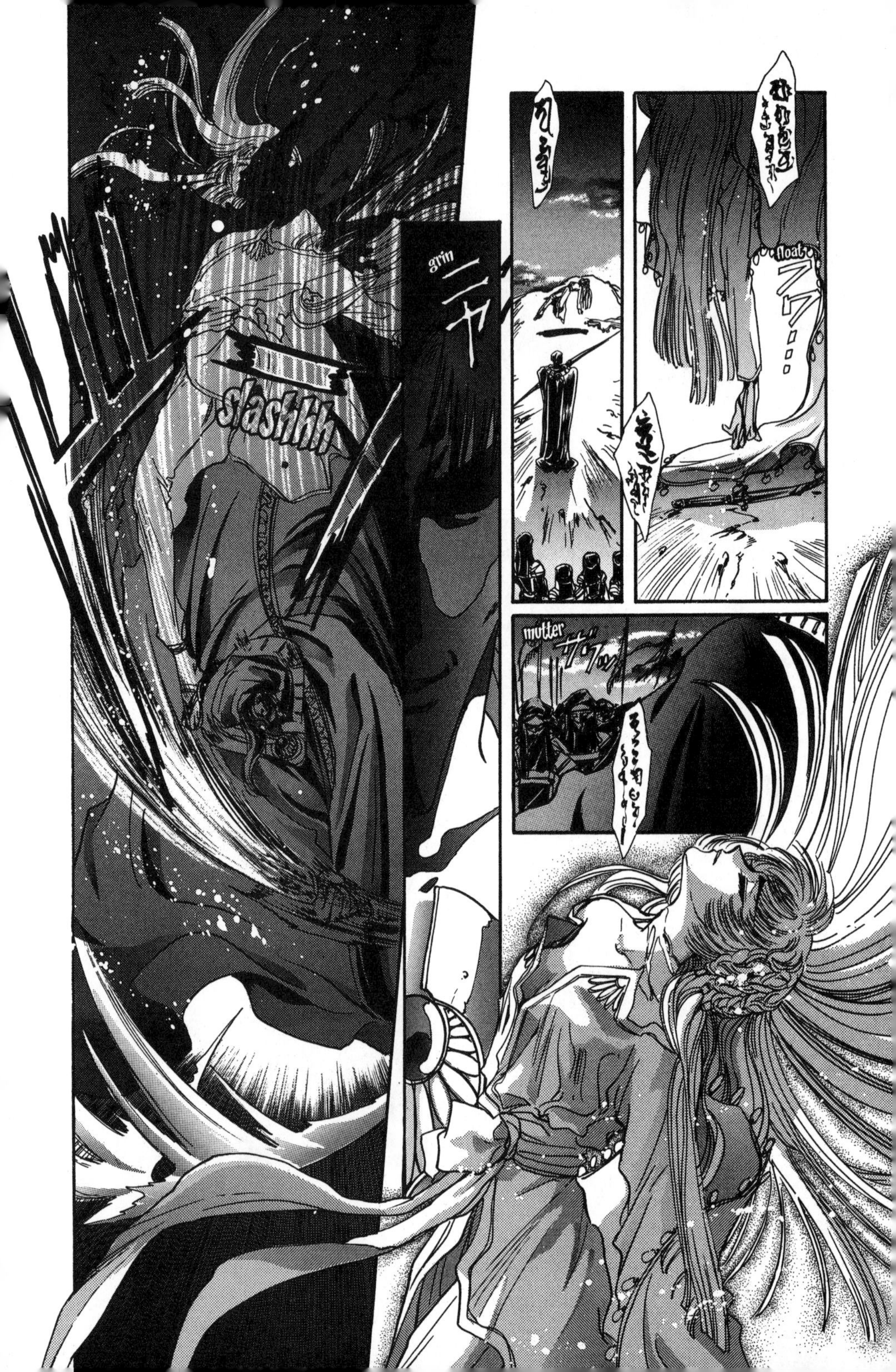
float
フワ
mutter
grin
ニヤ
slashhh

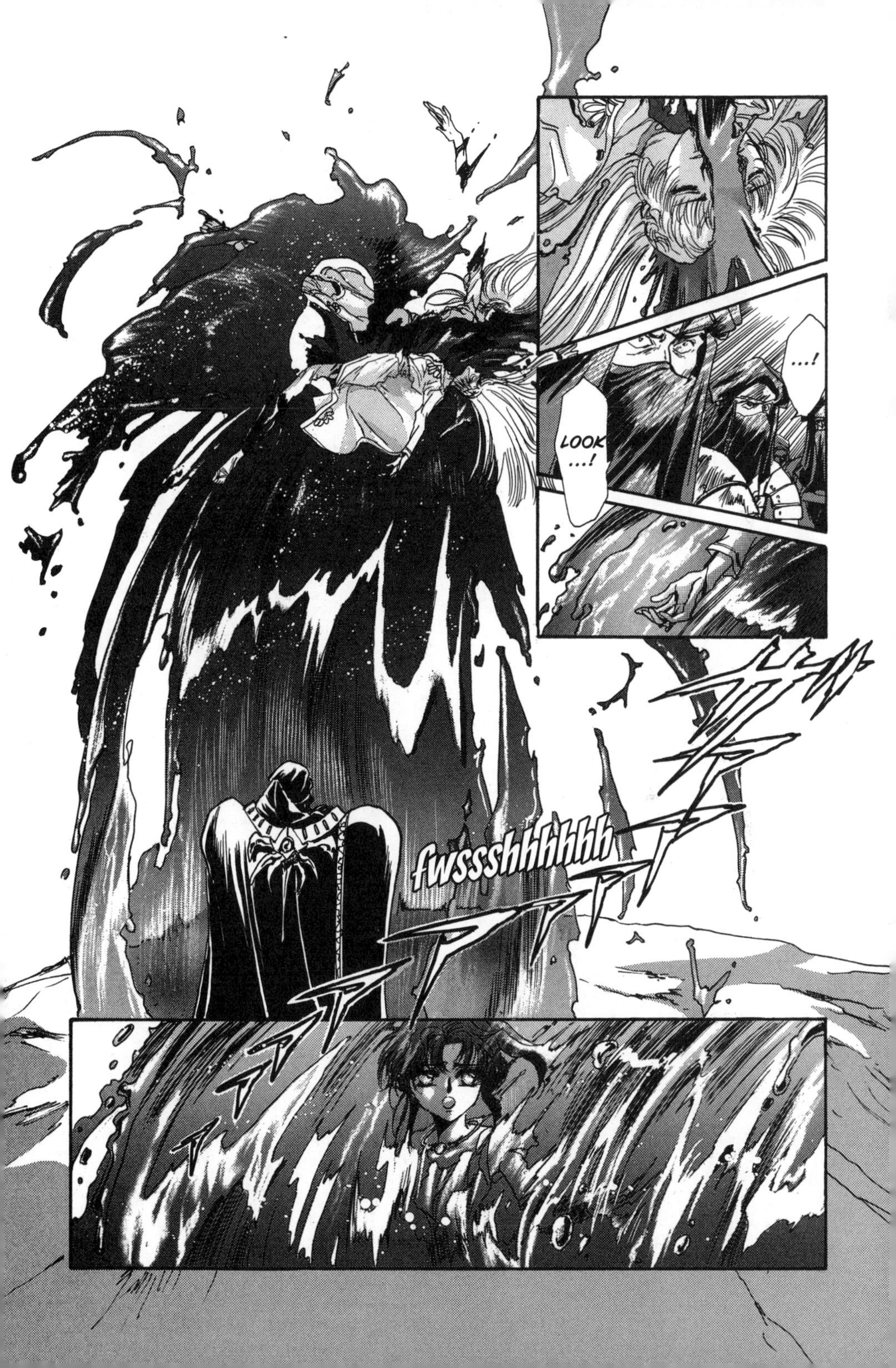

...!
LOOK ...!
fwssshhhhhh

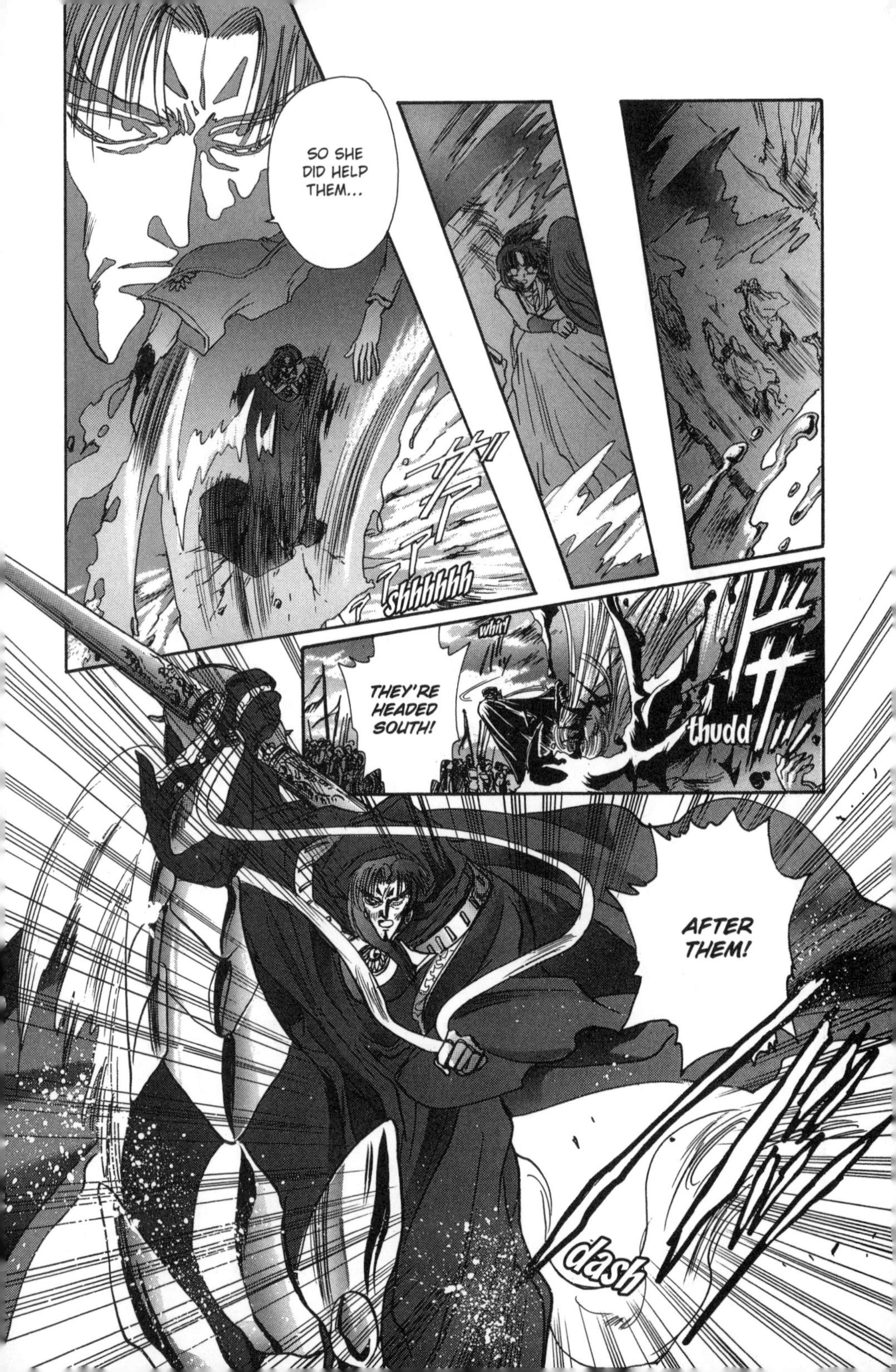
SO SHE DID HELP THEM...
shhhhhh
thudd
whirl
THEY'RE HEADED SOUTH!
AFTER THEM!
dash

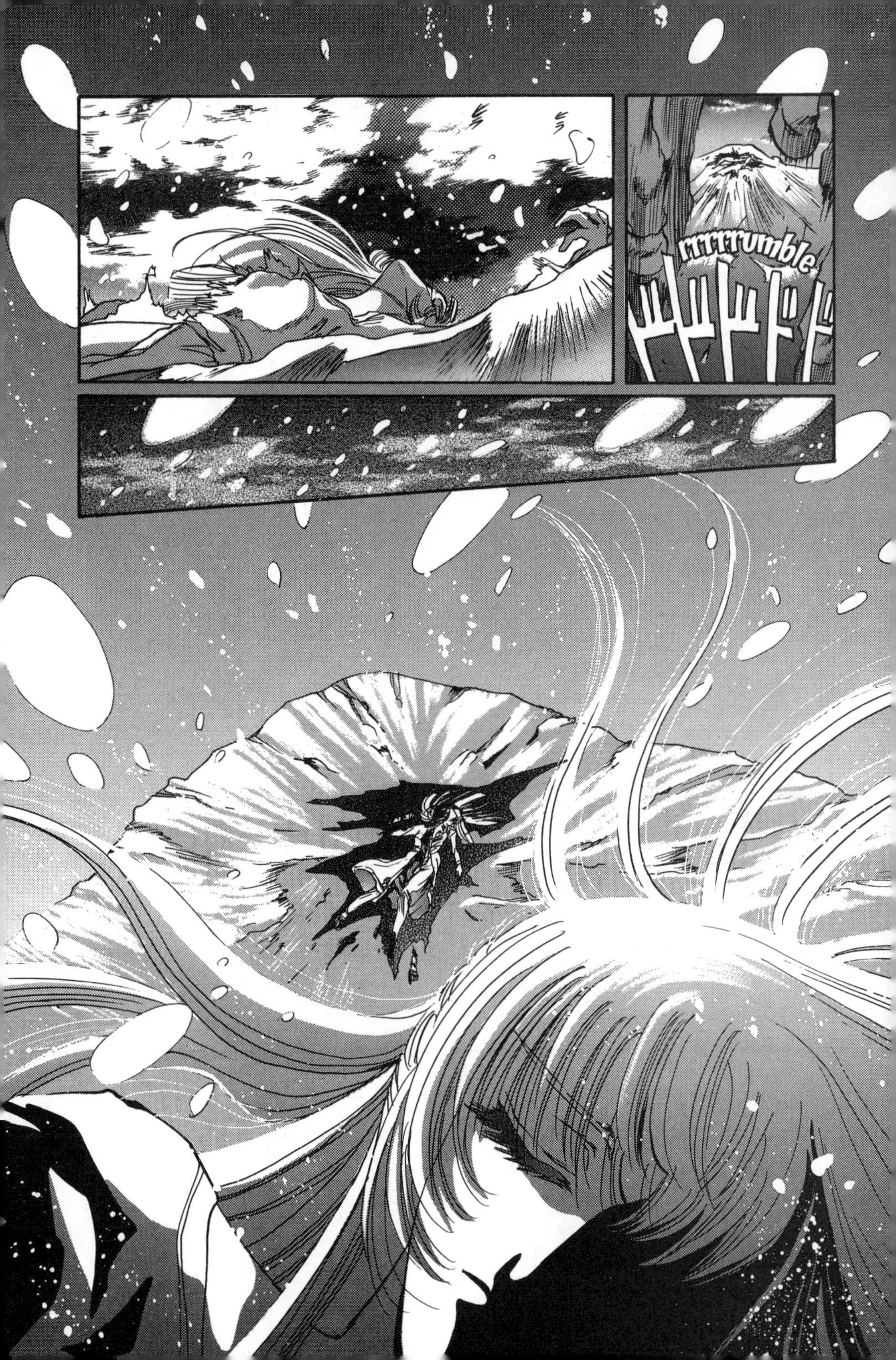
rrrrrrumble
ドドドドド

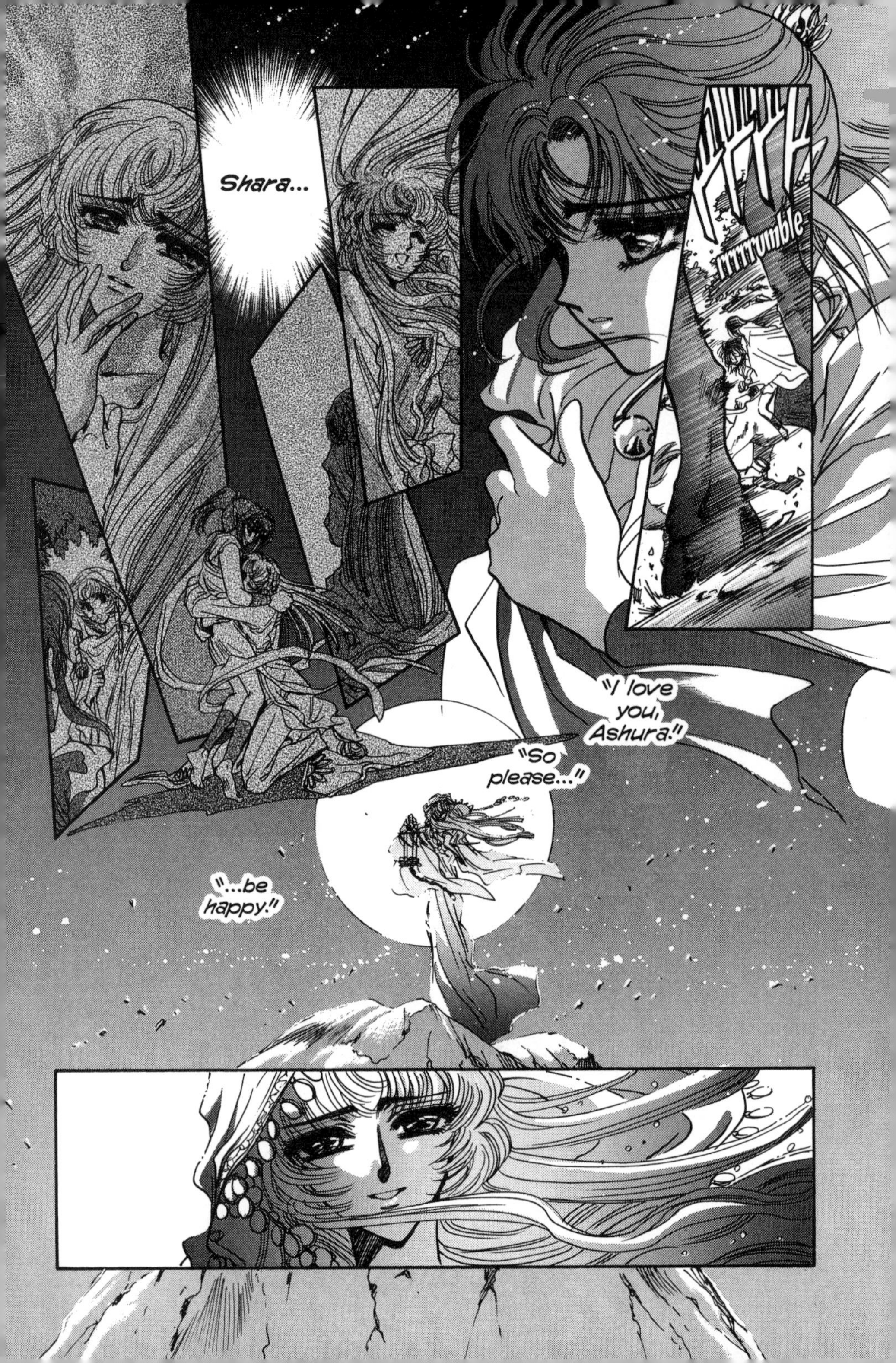
rrrrrumble
Shara...
"I love you, Ashura."
"So please..."
"...be happy."

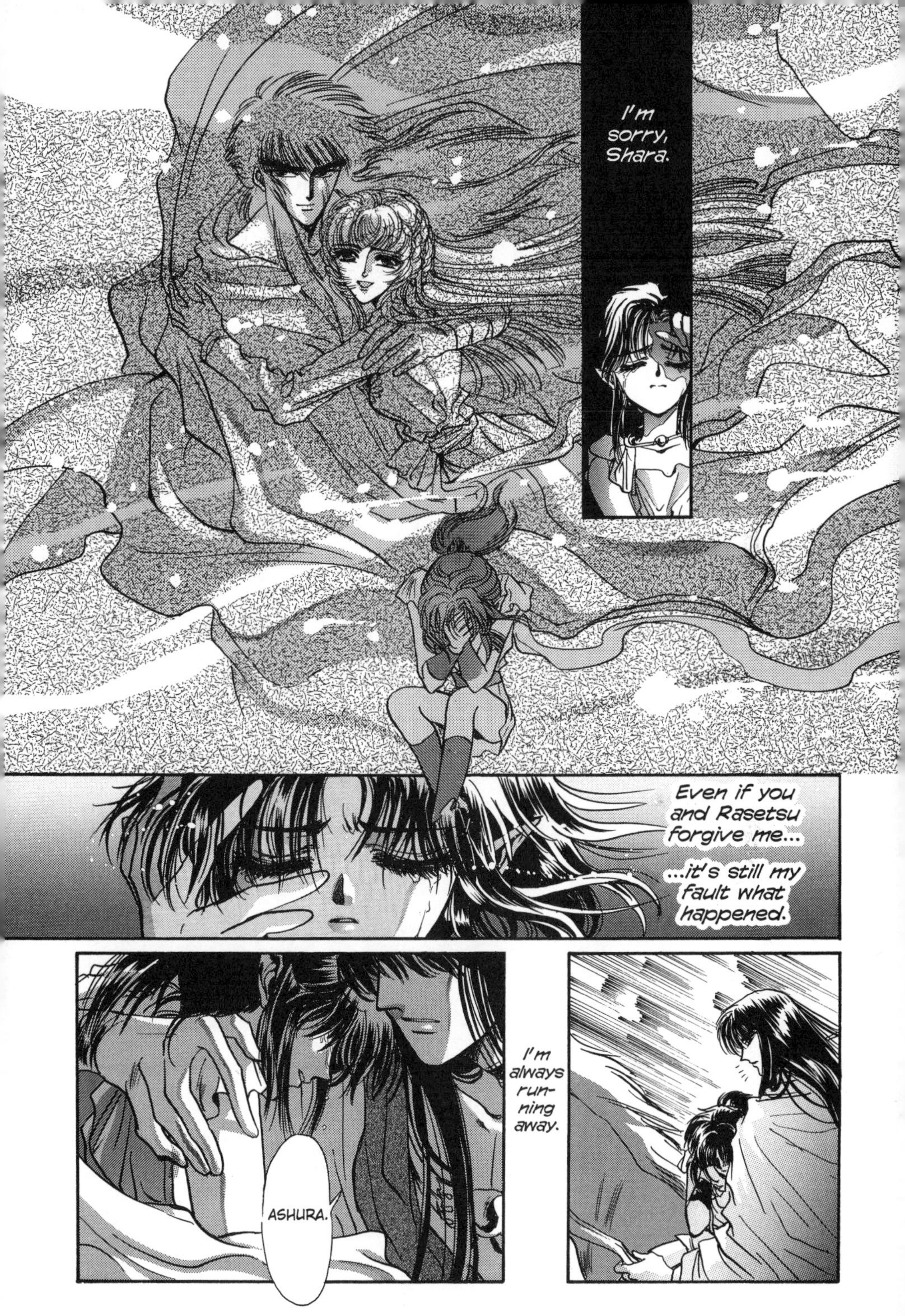
I'm sorry, Shara.
Even if you and Rasetsu forgive me...
...it's still my fault what happened.
I'm always run-ning away.
ASHURA.

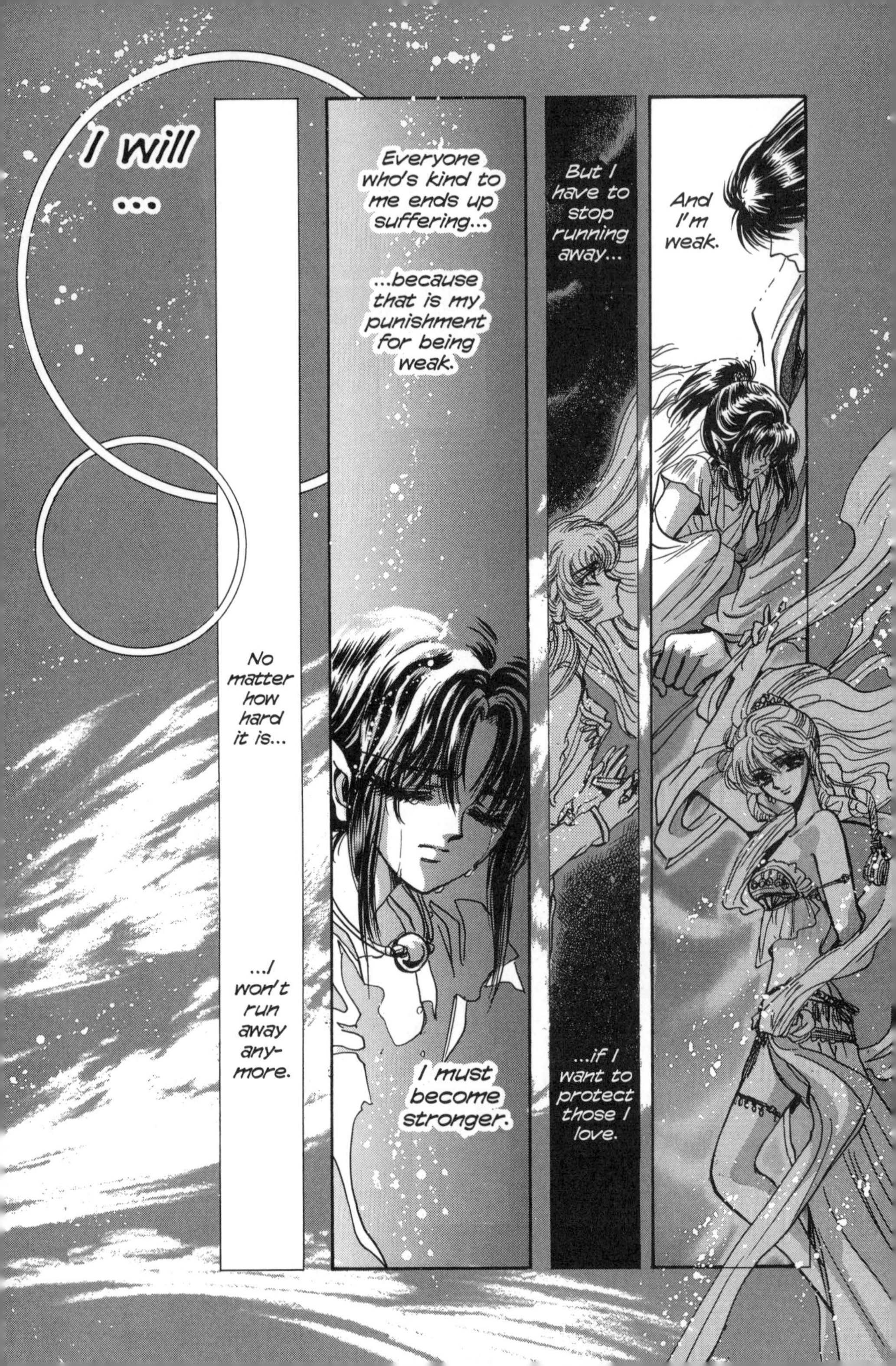
And I'm weak.
But I have to stop running away...
...if I want to protect those I love.
Everyone who's kind to me ends up suffering...
...because that is my punishment for being weak.
I must become stronger.
No matter how hard it is...
...I won't run away anymore.
I will ...

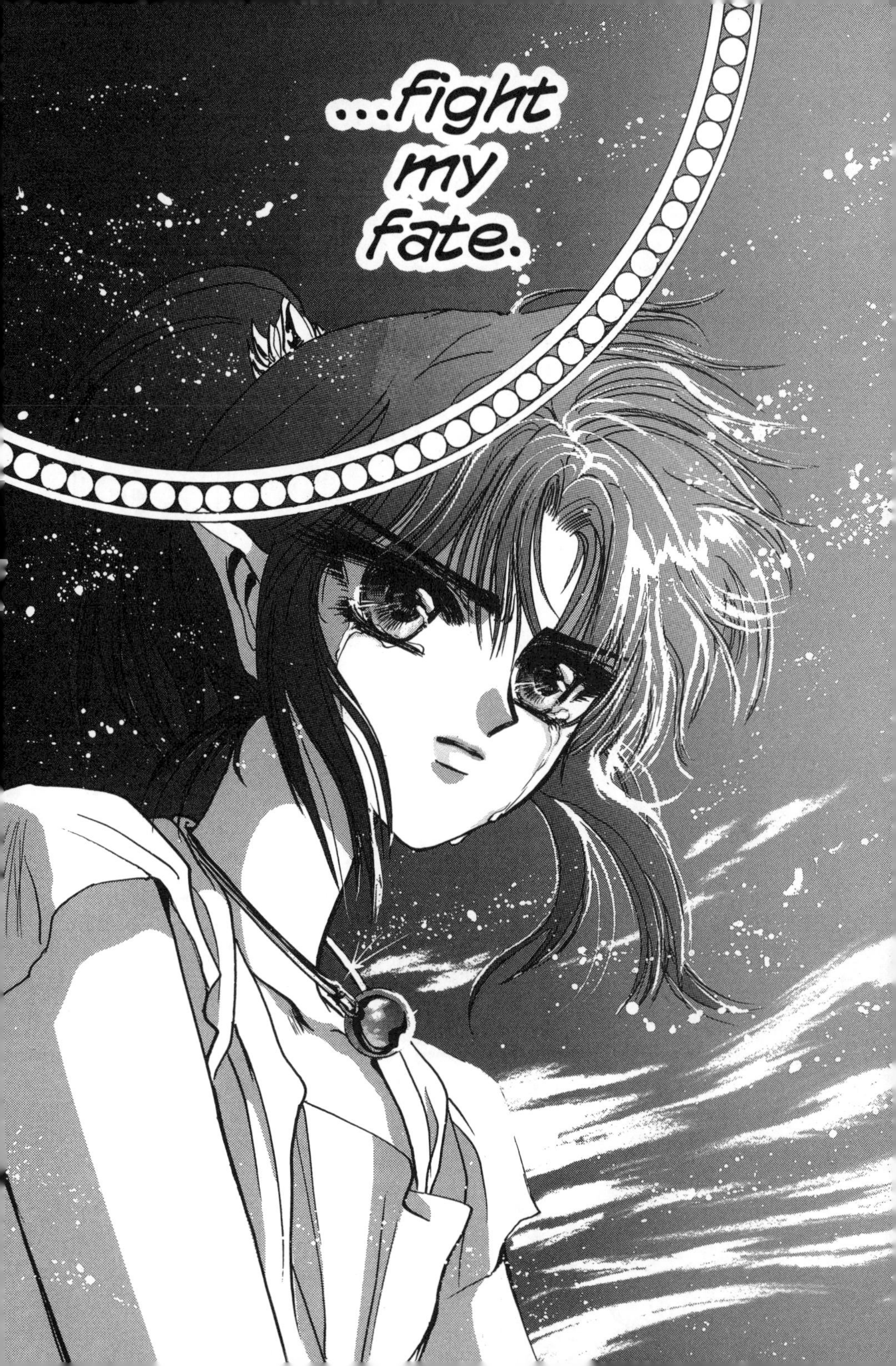
...fight my fate.

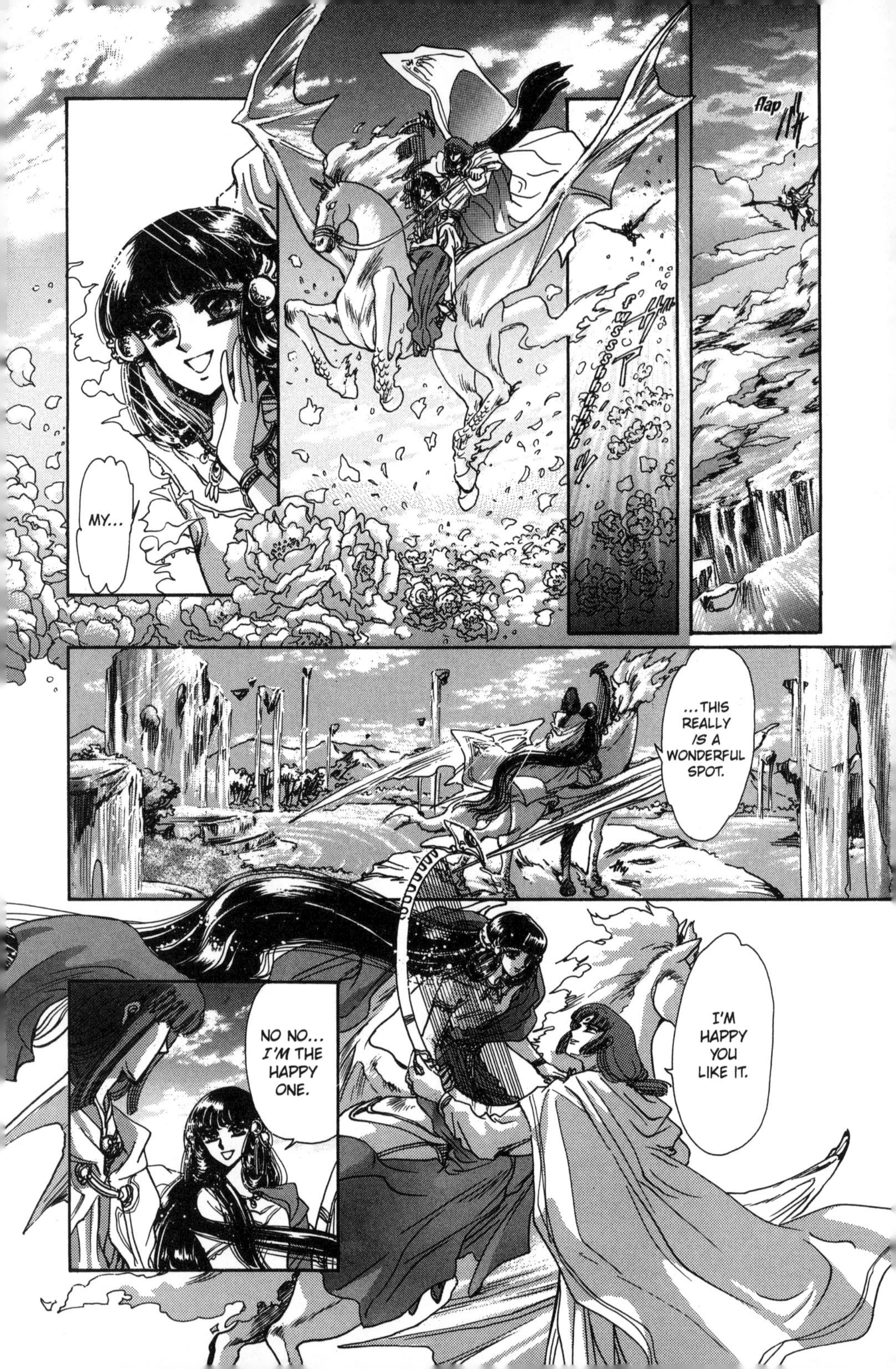
flap
FWSSSHHHHH
MY...
...THIS REALLY IS A WONDERFUL SPOT.
I'M HAPPY YOU LIKE IT.
NO NO... *I'M* THE HAPPY ONE.

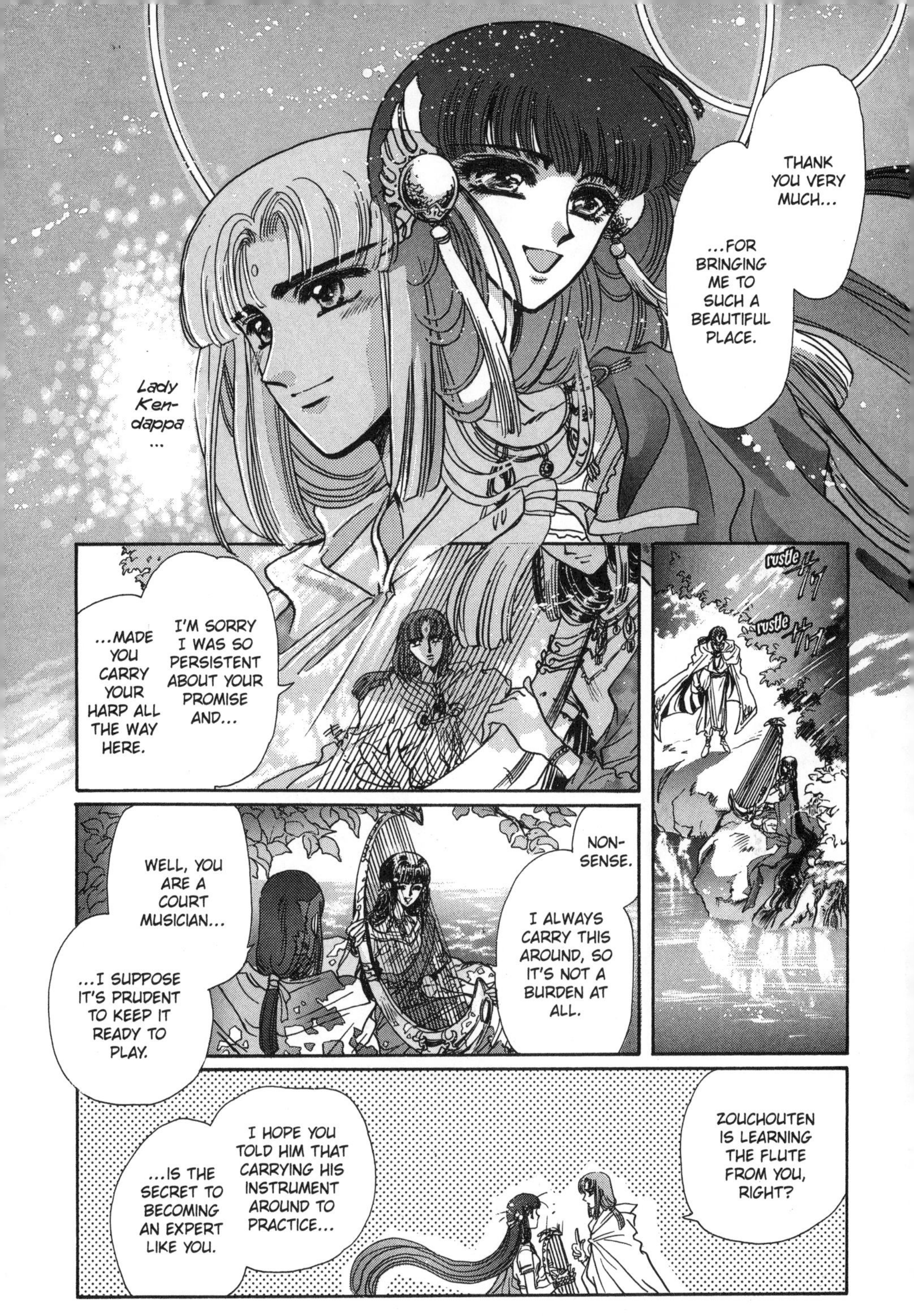
THANK YOU VERY MUCH...
...FOR BRINGING ME TO SUCH A BEAUTIFUL PLACE.
Lady Ken-dappa ...
rustle
rustle
I'M SORRY I WAS SO PERSISTENT ABOUT YOUR PROMISE AND...
...MADE YOU CARRY YOUR HARP ALL THE WAY HERE.
NON-SENSE.
I ALWAYS CARRY THIS AROUND, SO IT'S NOT A BURDEN AT ALL.
WELL, YOU ARE A COURT MUSICIAN...
...I SUPPOSE IT'S PRUDENT TO KEEP IT READY TO PLAY.
ZOUCHOUTEN IS LEARNING THE FLUTE FROM YOU, RIGHT?
I HOPE YOU TOLD HIM THAT CARRYING HIS INSTRUMENT AROUND TO PRACTICE...
...IS THE SECRET TO BECOMING AN EXPERT LIKE YOU.

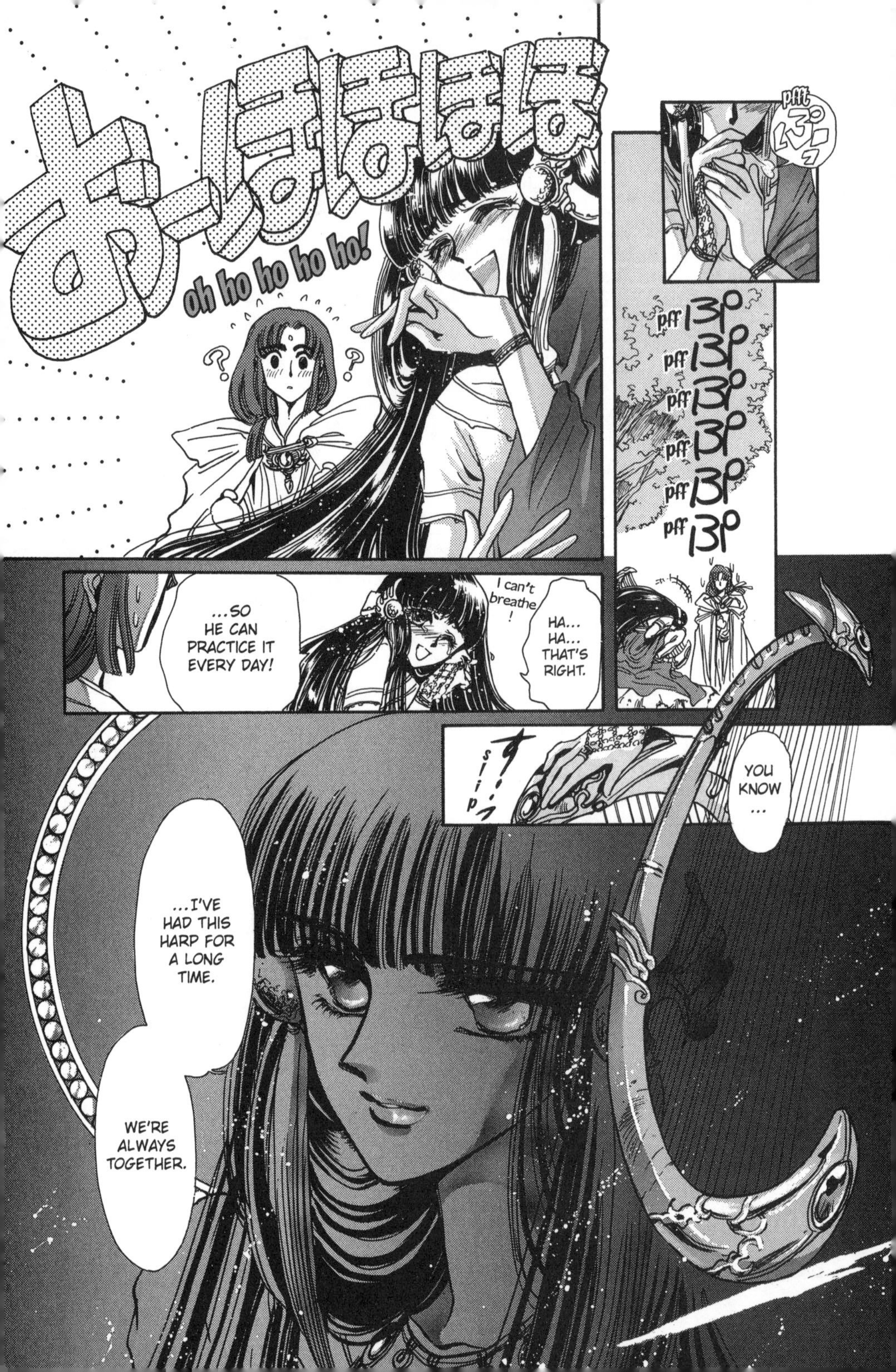
pfft
pfft
pfft
pfft
pfft
pfft
pfft
おーほほほほ
oh ho ho ho ho!
HA... HA... THAT'S RIGHT.
I can't breathe!
...SO HE CAN PRACTICE IT EVERY DAY!
slip
YOU KNOW...
...I'VE HAD THIS HARP FOR A LONG TIME.
WE'RE ALWAYS TOGETHER.

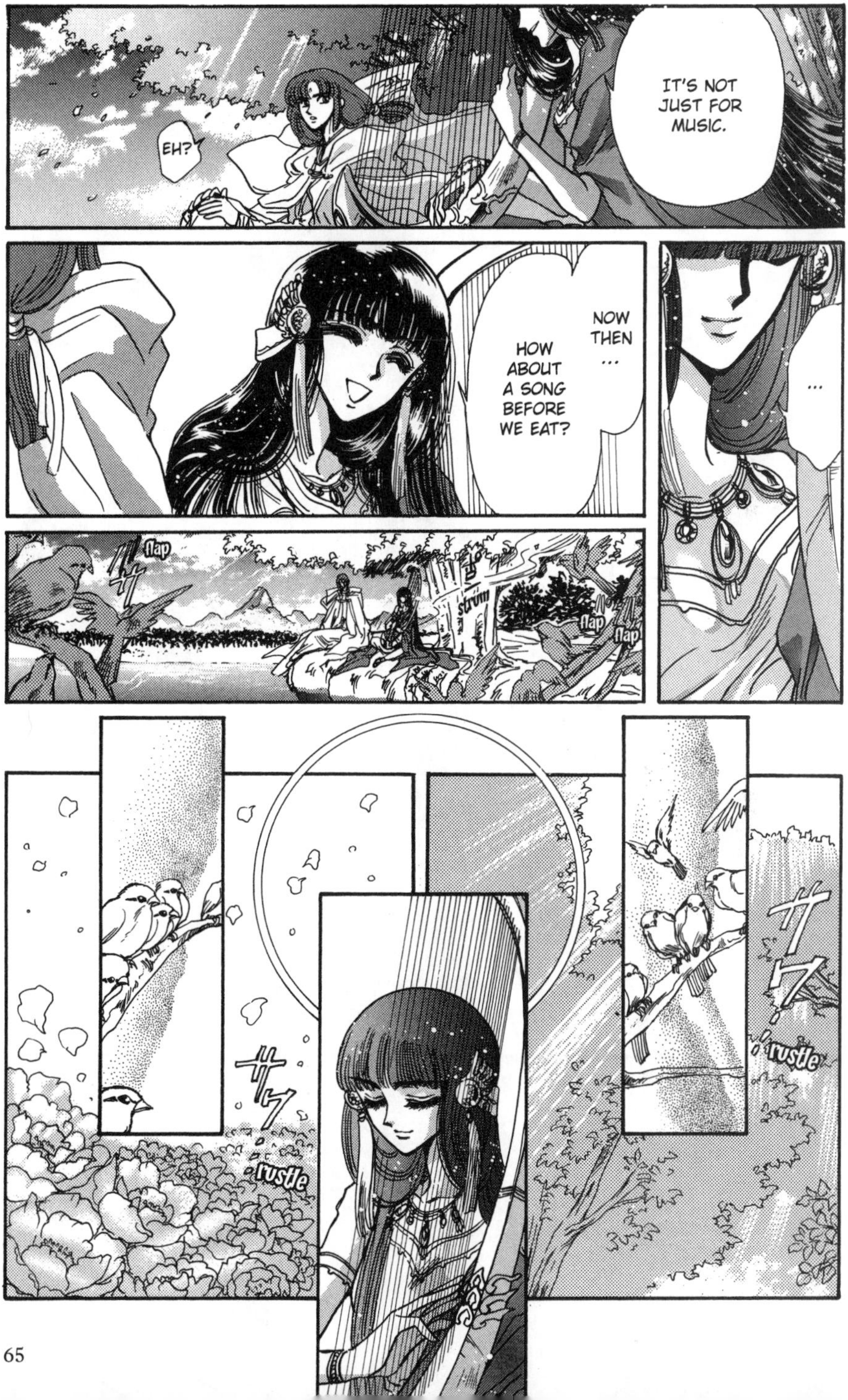

IT'S NOT JUST FOR MUSIC.
EH?
...
NOW THEN ...
HOW ABOUT A SONG BEFORE WE EAT?
flap flap
strum
flap
サワ
rustle
サワ
rustle

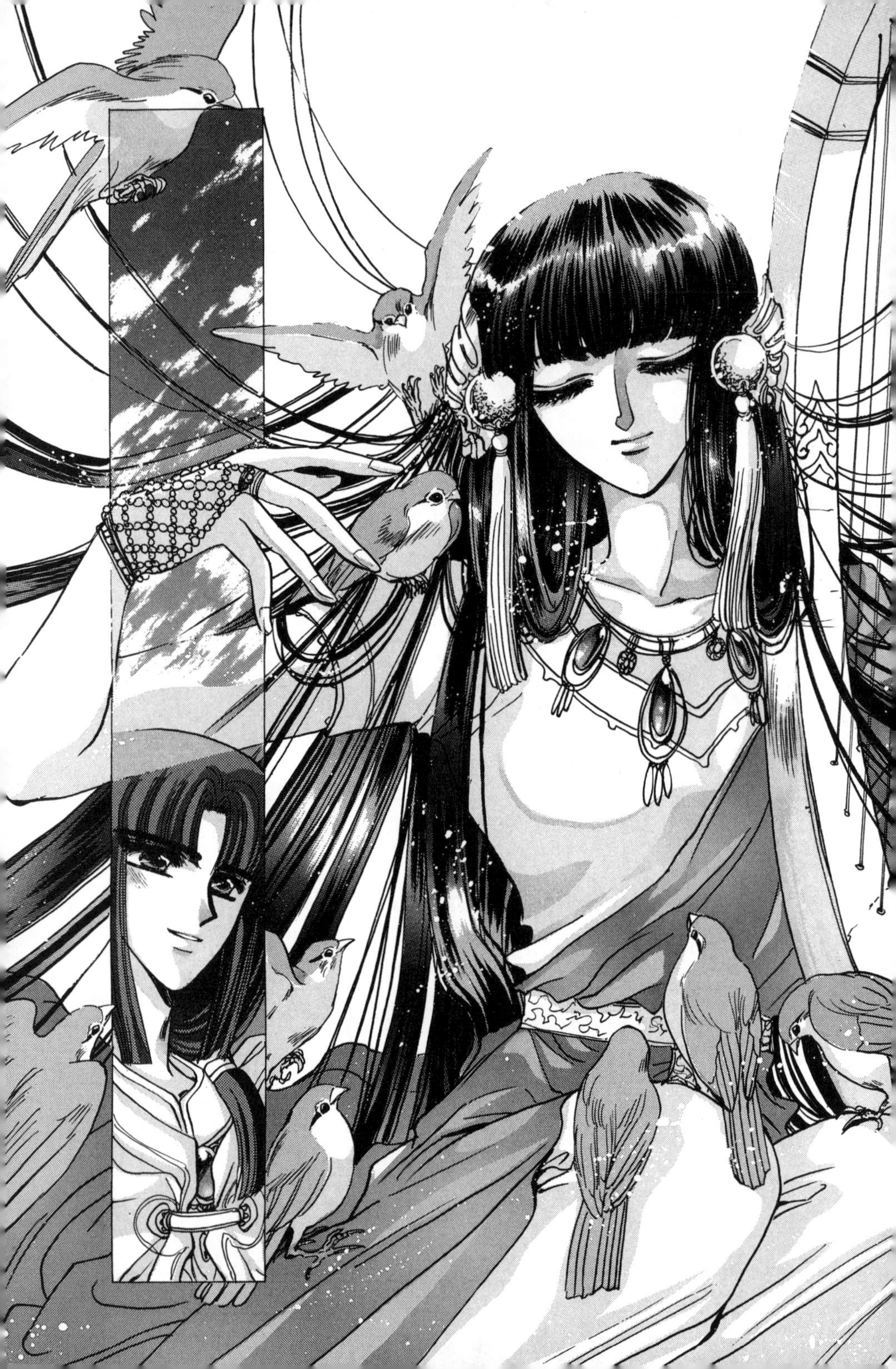

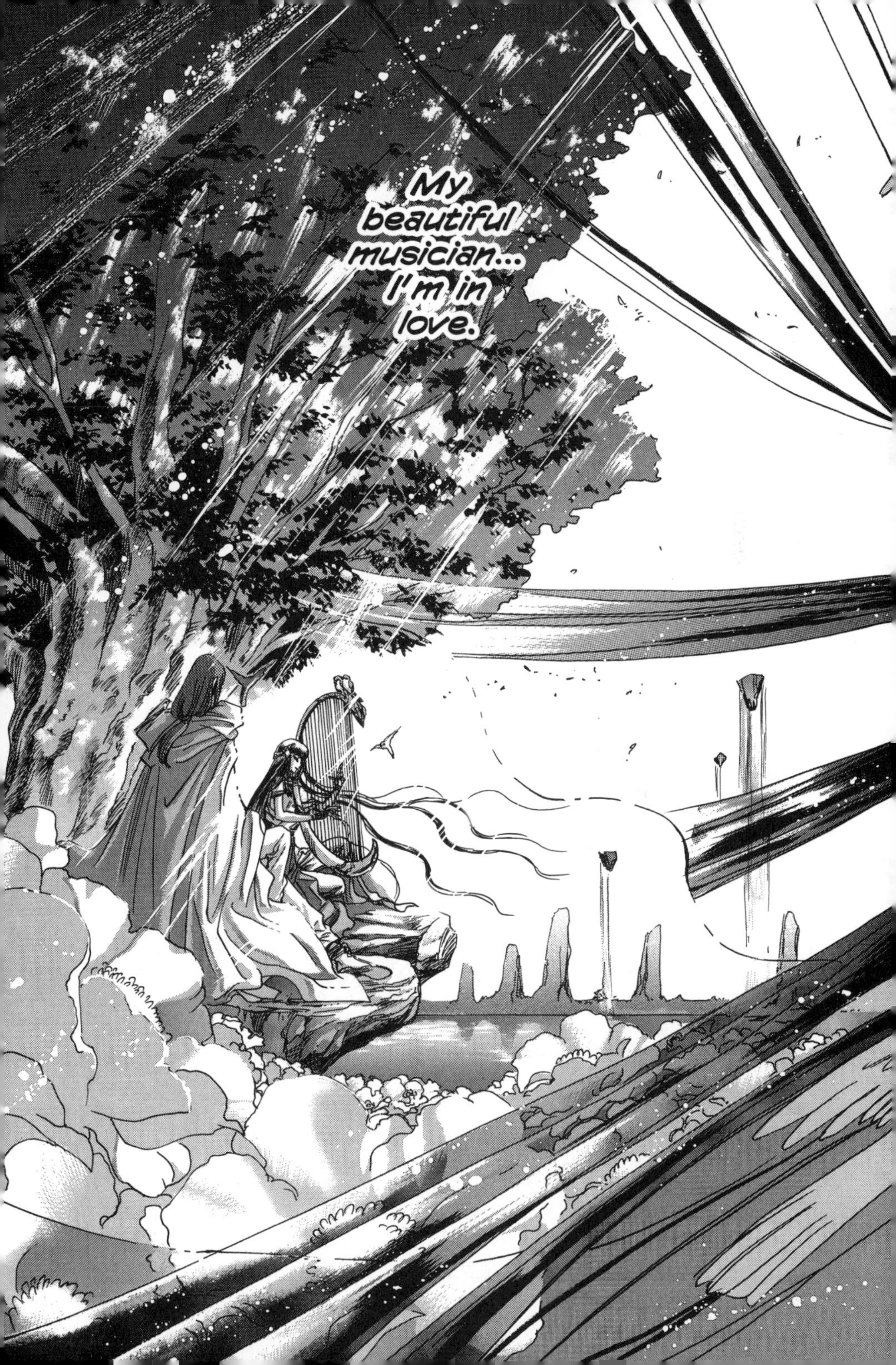
My beautiful musician... I'm in love.

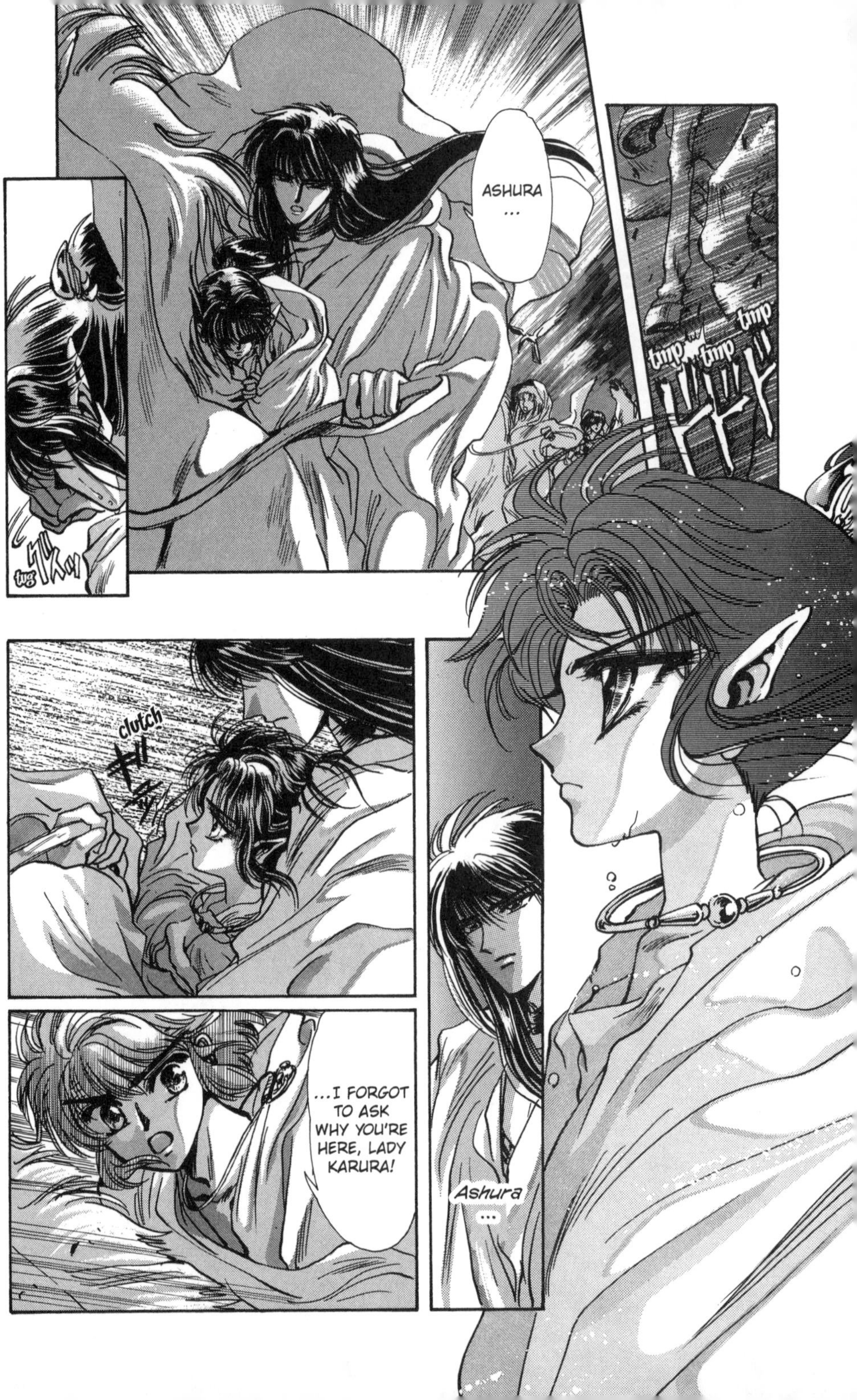

tmp tmp tmp
ASHURA ...
tug
Ashura ...
clutch
...I FORGOT TO ASK WHY YOU'RE HERE, LADY KARURA!

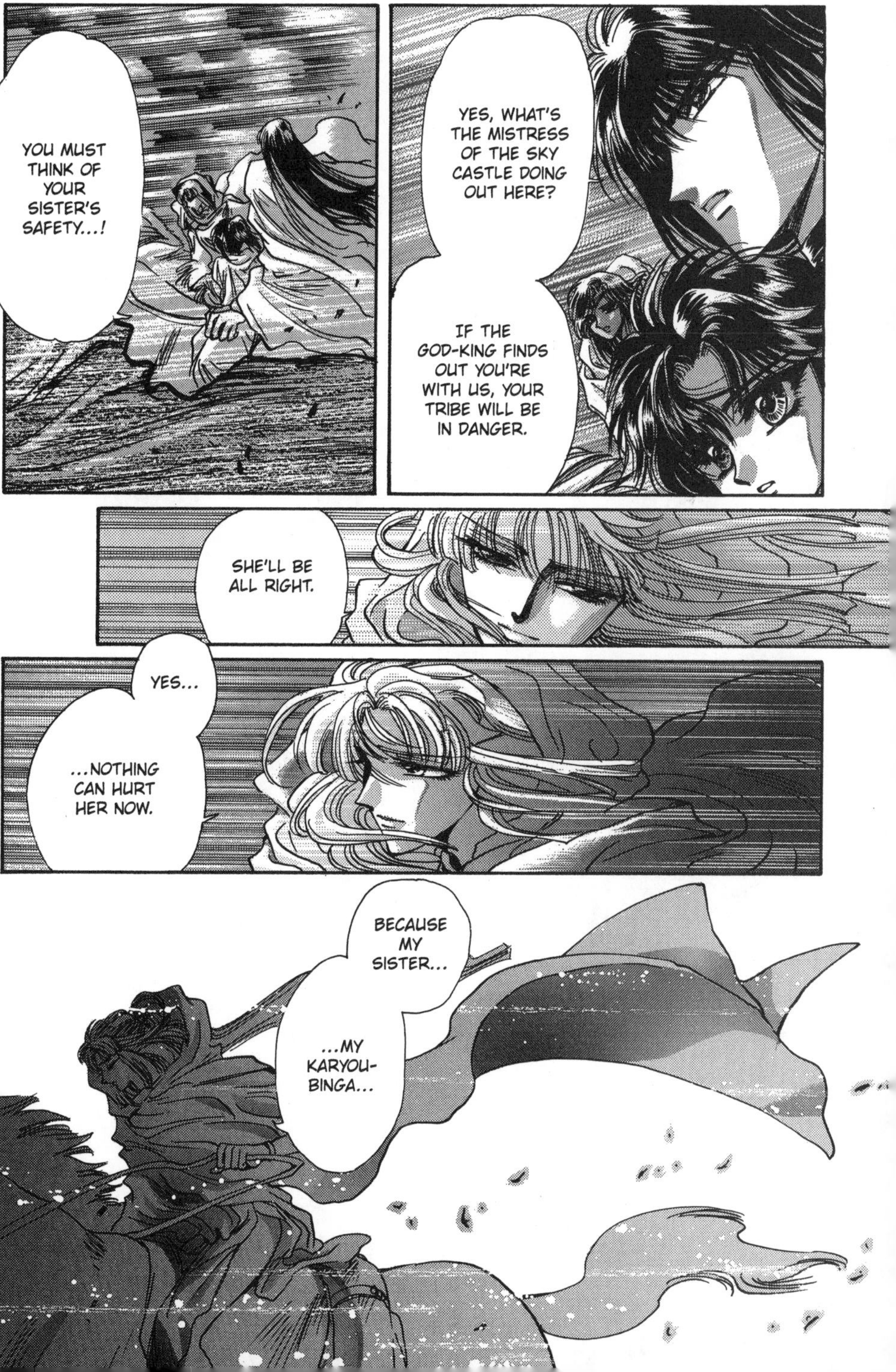
YES, WHAT'S THE MISTRESS OF THE SKY CASTLE DOING OUT HERE?
IF THE GOD-KING FINDS OUT YOU'RE WITH US, YOUR TRIBE WILL BE IN DANGER.
YOU MUST THINK OF YOUR SISTER'S SAFETY...!
SHE'LL BE ALL RIGHT.
YES...
...NOTHING CAN HURT HER NOW.
BECAUSE MY SISTER...
...MY KARYOU-BINGA...

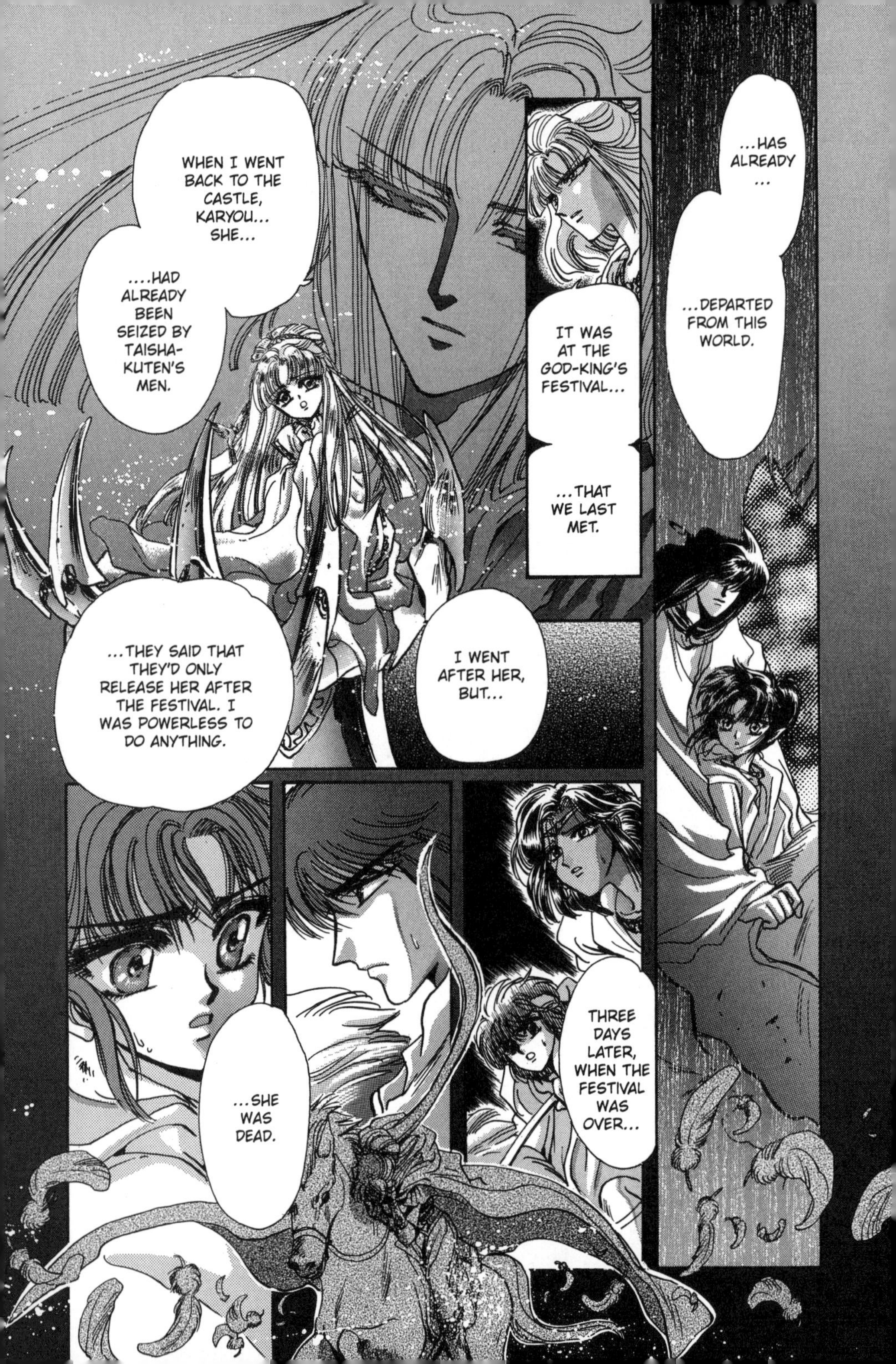
...HAS ALREADY ...
...DEPARTED FROM THIS WORLD.
IT WAS AT THE GOD-KING'S FESTIVAL...
...THAT WE LAST MET.
WHEN I WENT BACK TO THE CASTLE, KARYOU... SHE...
....HAD ALREADY BEEN SEIZED BY TAISHA-KUTEN'S MEN.
I WENT AFTER HER, BUT...
...THEY SAID THAT THEY'D ONLY RELEASE HER AFTER THE FESTIVAL. I WAS POWERLESS TO DO ANYTHING.
THREE DAYS LATER, WHEN THE FESTIVAL WAS OVER...
...SHE WAS DEAD.

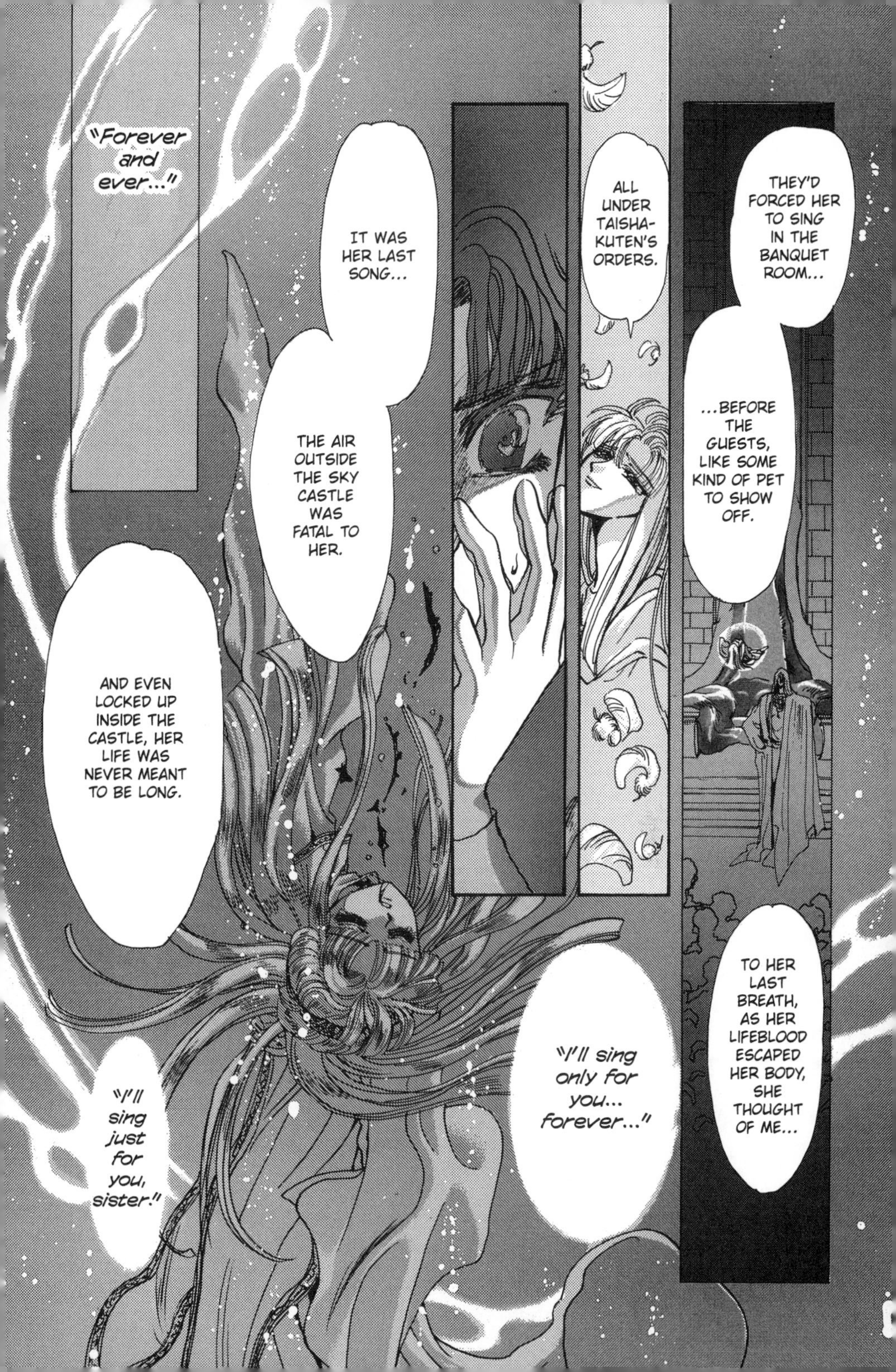
THEY'D FORCED HER TO SING IN THE BANQUET ROOM...
...BEFORE THE GUESTS, LIKE SOME KIND OF PET TO SHOW OFF.
ALL UNDER TAISHAKUTEN'S ORDERS.
IT WAS HER LAST SONG...
"Forever and ever..."
THE AIR OUTSIDE THE SKY CASTLE WAS FATAL TO HER.
AND EVEN LOCKED UP INSIDE THE CASTLE, HER LIFE WAS NEVER MEANT TO BE LONG.
TO HER LAST BREATH, AS HER LIFEBLOOD ESCAPED HER BODY, SHE THOUGHT OF ME...
"I'll sing only for you... forever..."
"I'll sing just for you, sister."

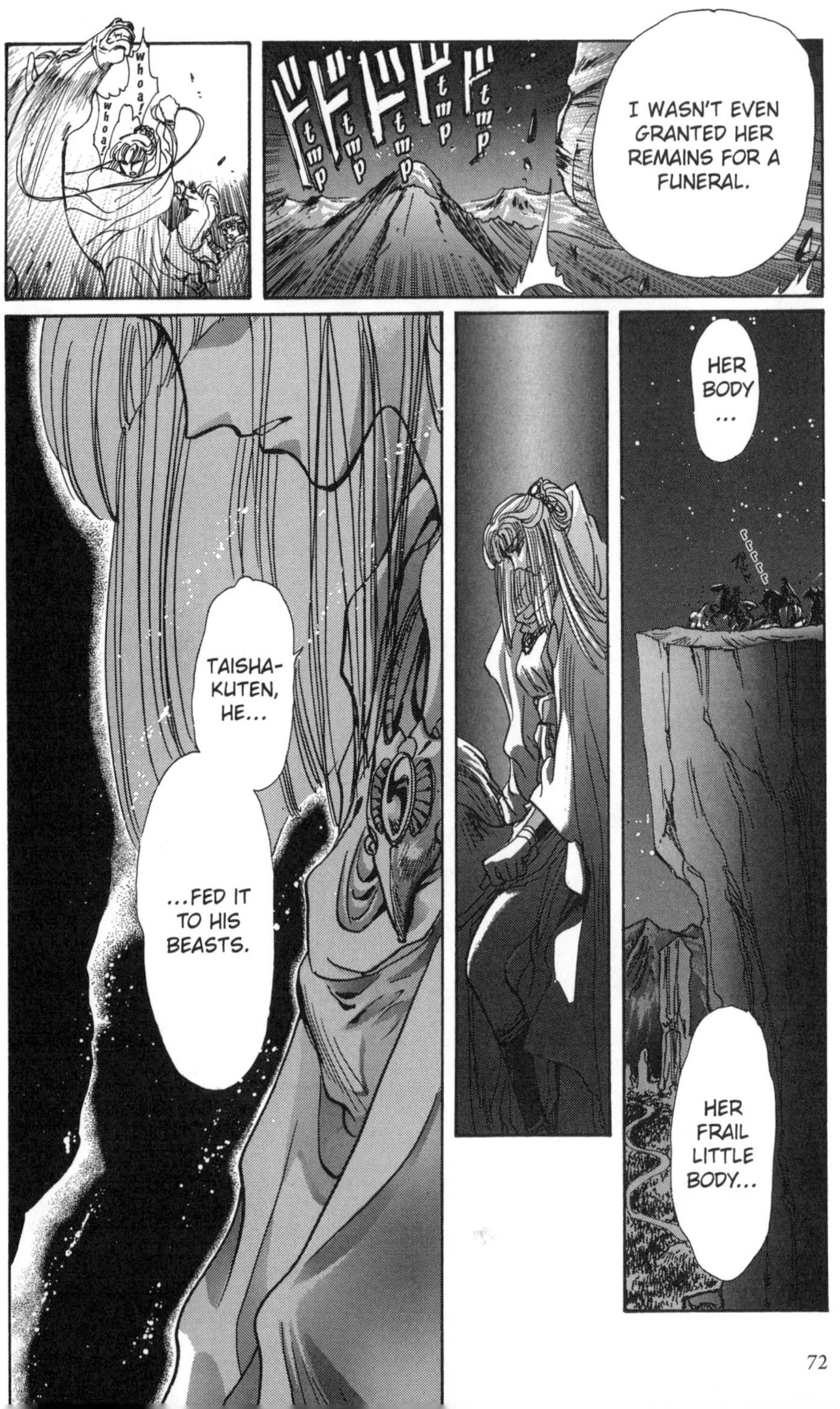
I WASN'T EVEN GRANTED HER REMAINS FOR A FUNERAL.
ドドドドド
tmp tmp tmp tmp tmp
whoa! whoa! whoa!
HER BODY...
HER FRAIL LITTLE BODY...
TAISHA-KUTEN, HE...
...FED IT TO HIS BEASTS.

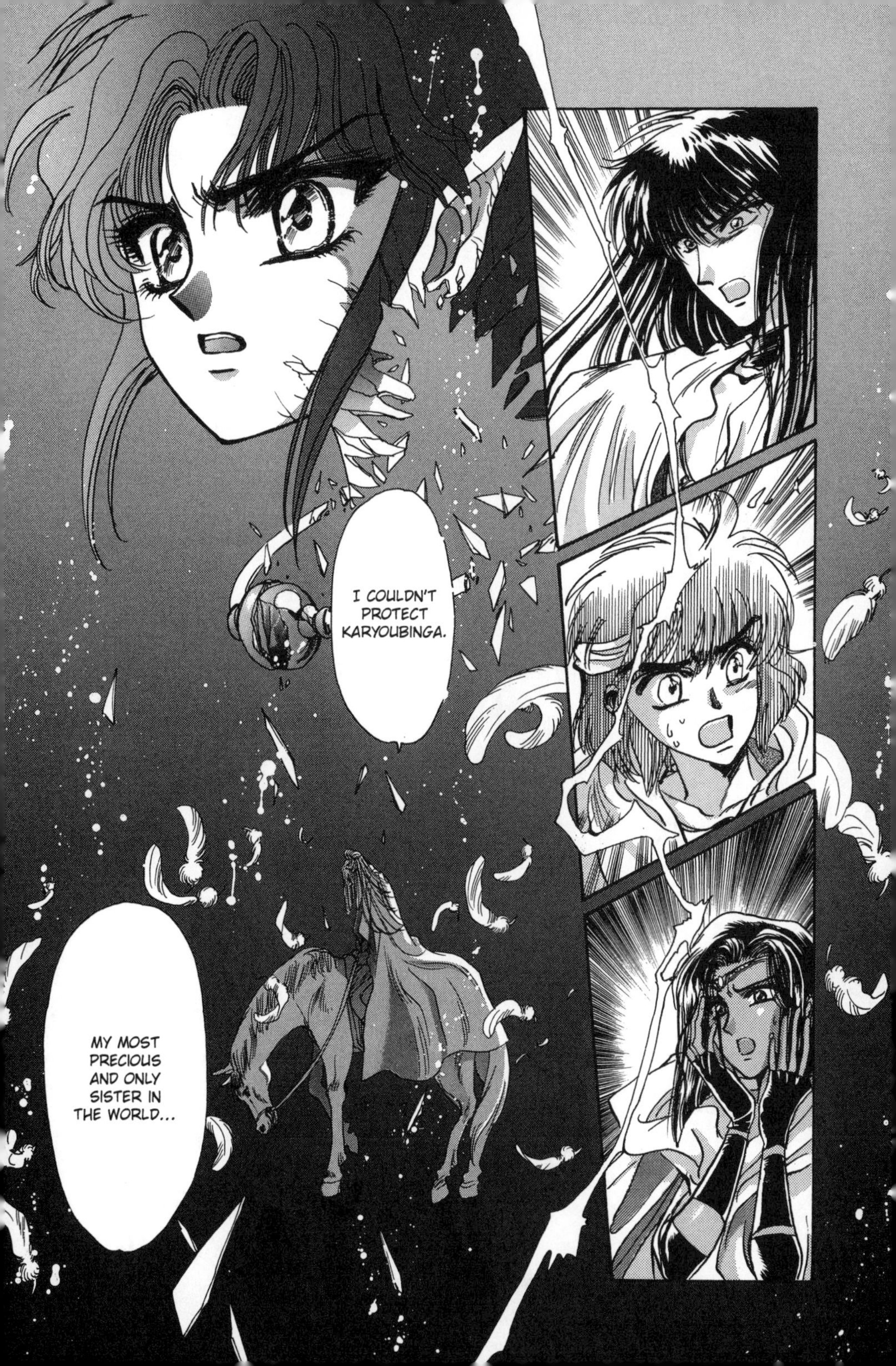
I COULDN'T PROTECT KARYOUBINGA.
MY MOST PRECIOUS AND ONLY SISTER IN THE WORLD...

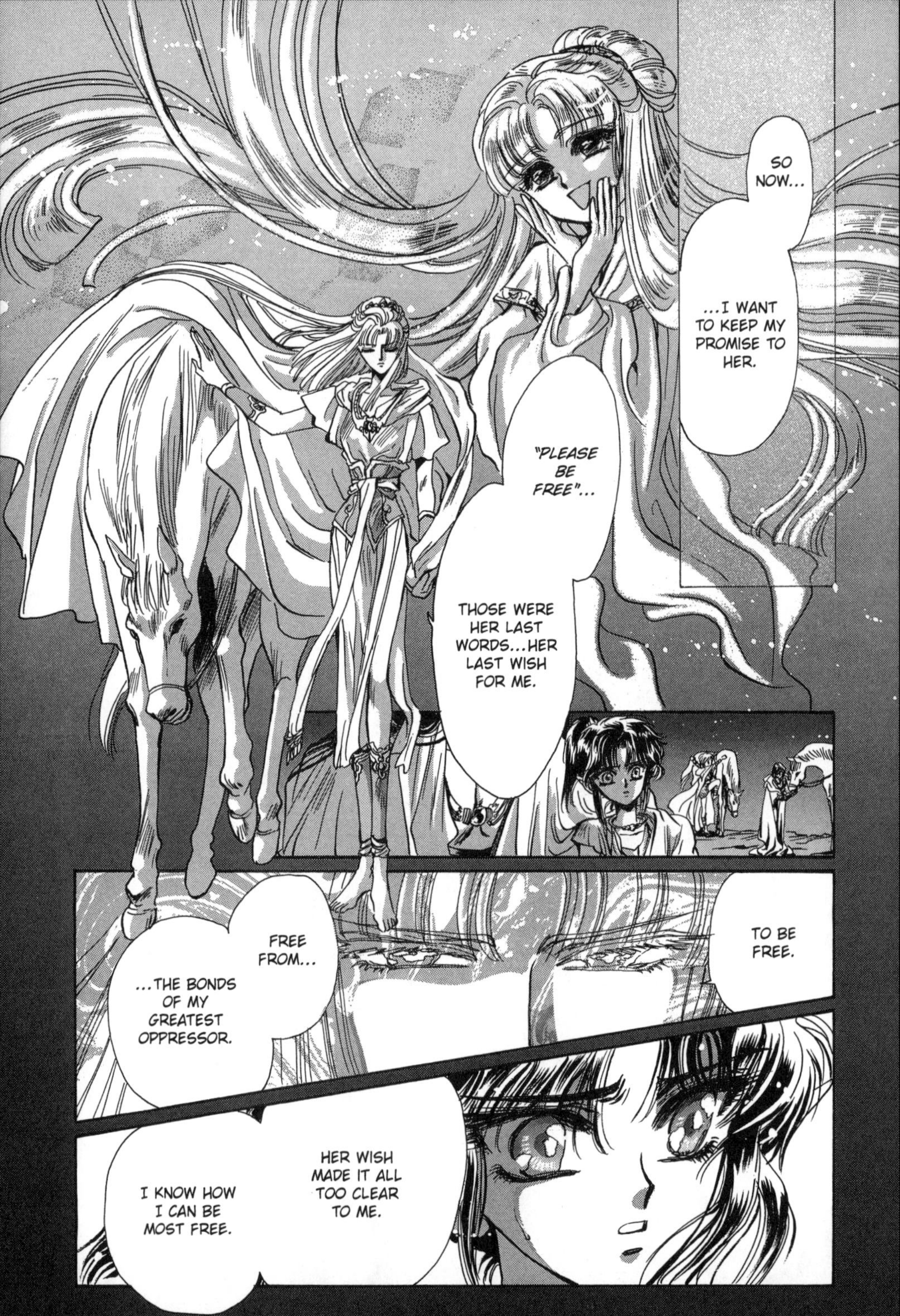
SO NOW...
...I WANT TO KEEP MY PROMISE TO HER.
"PLEASE BE FREE"...
THOSE WERE HER LAST WORDS...HER LAST WISH FOR ME.
TO BE FREE.
FREE FROM...
...THE BONDS OF MY GREATEST OPPRESSOR.
HER WISH MADE IT ALL TOO CLEAR TO ME.
I KNOW HOW I CAN BE MOST FREE.

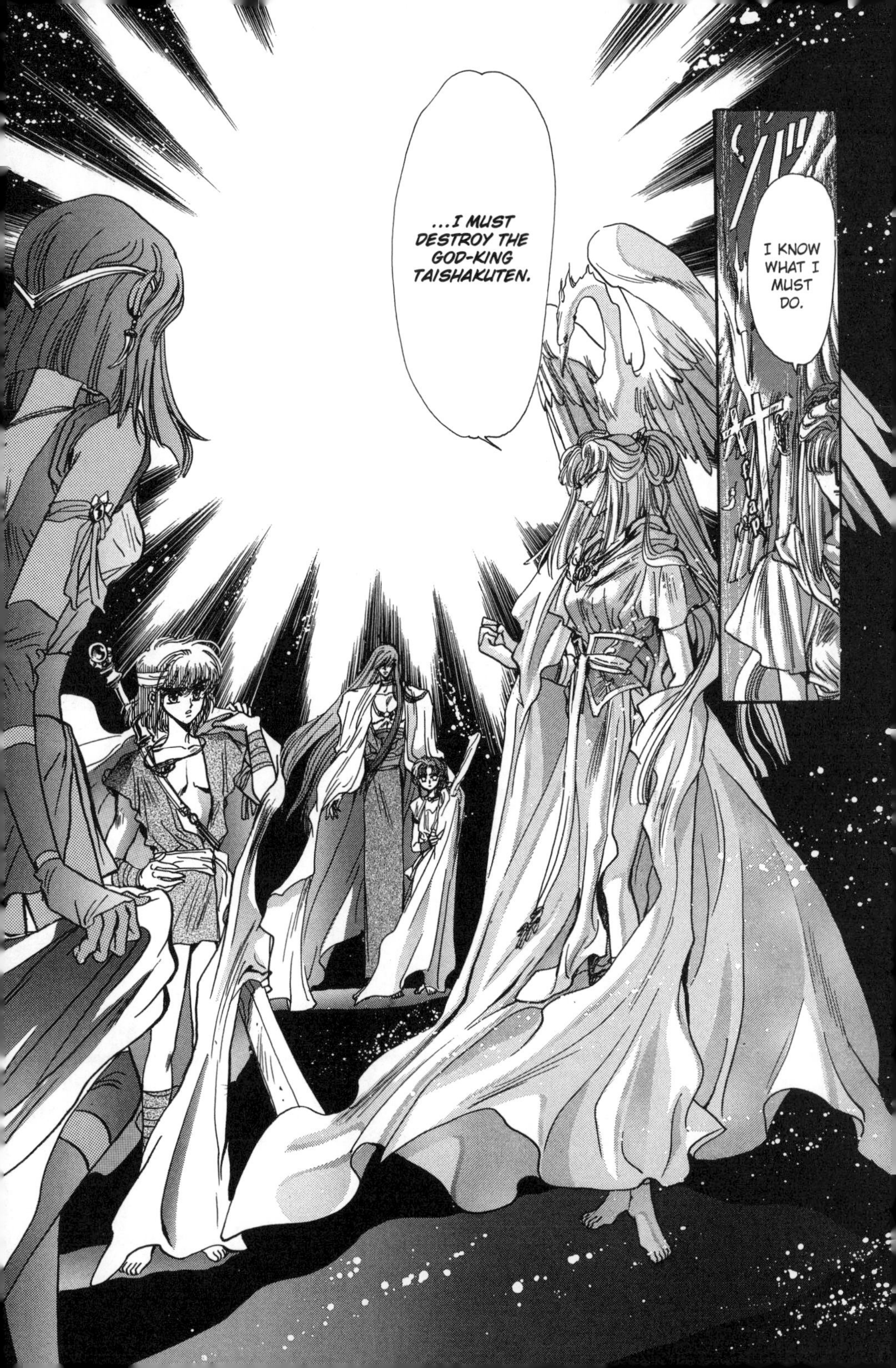
I KNOW WHAT I MUST DO.
flap
...I MUST DESTROY THE GOD-KING TAISHAKUTEN.

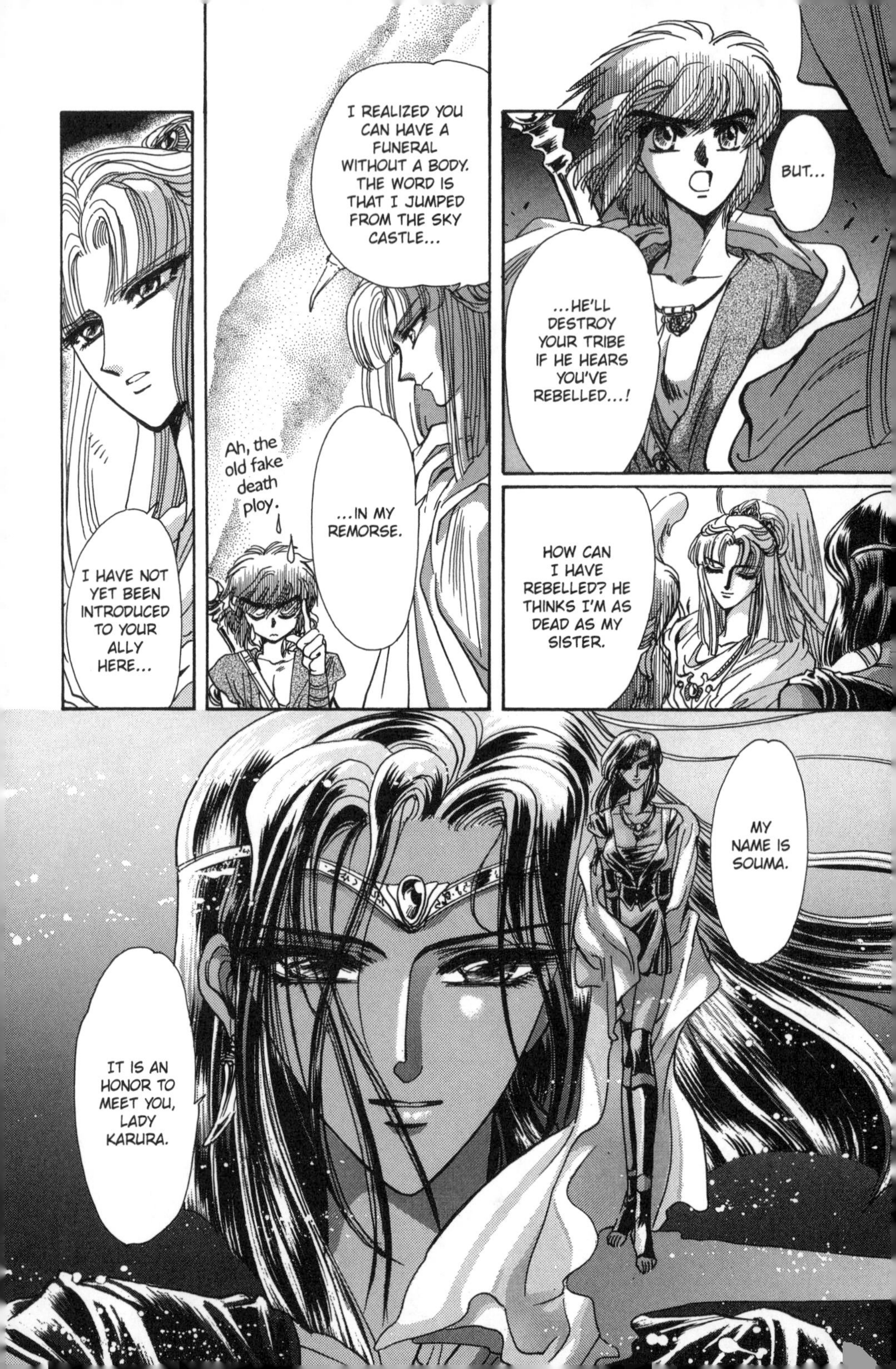
BUT...
...HE'LL DESTROY YOUR TRIBE IF HE HEARS YOU'VE REBELLED...!
HOW CAN I HAVE REBELLED? HE THINKS I'M AS DEAD AS MY SISTER.
I REALIZED YOU CAN HAVE A FUNERAL WITHOUT A BODY. THE WORD IS THAT I JUMPED FROM THE SKY CASTLE...
...IN MY REMORSE.
Ah, the old fake death ploy.
I HAVE NOT YET BEEN INTRODUCED TO YOUR ALLY HERE...
MY NAME IS SOUMA.
IT IS AN HONOR TO MEET YOU, LADY KARURA.

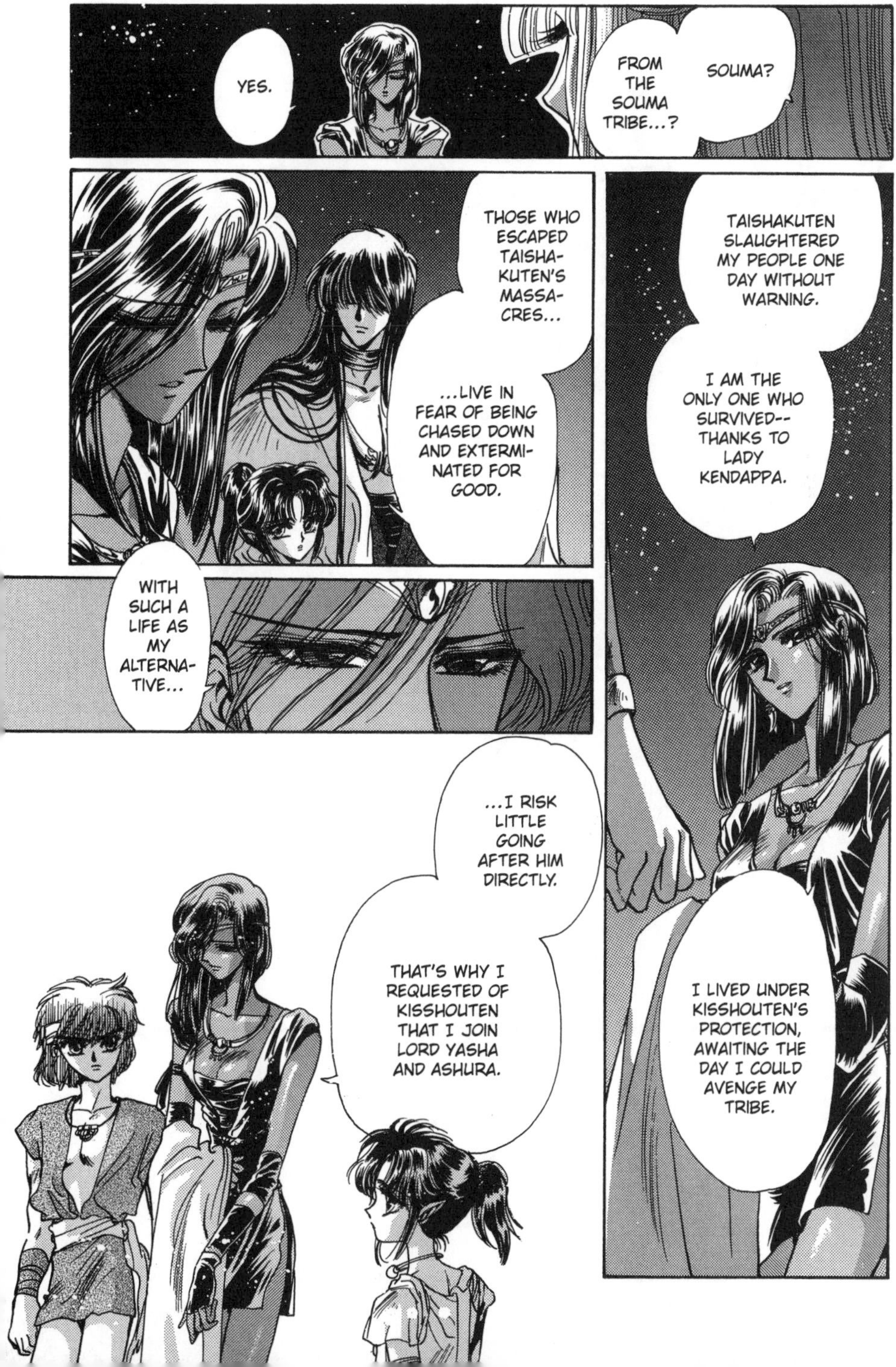
SOUMA?
FROM THE SOUMA TRIBE...?
YES.
TAISHAKUTEN SLAUGHTERED MY PEOPLE ONE DAY WITHOUT WARNING.
I AM THE ONLY ONE WHO SURVIVED--THANKS TO LADY KENDAPPA.
I LIVED UNDER KISSHOUTEN'S PROTECTION, AWAITING THE DAY I COULD AVENGE MY TRIBE.
THOSE WHO ESCAPED TAISHA-KUTEN'S MASSA-CRES...
...LIVE IN FEAR OF BEING CHASED DOWN AND EXTERMI-NATED FOR GOOD.
WITH SUCH A LIFE AS MY ALTERNA-TIVE...
...I RISK LITTLE GOING AFTER HIM DIRECTLY.
THAT'S WHY I REQUESTED OF KISSHOUTEN THAT I JOIN LORD YASHA AND ASHURA.

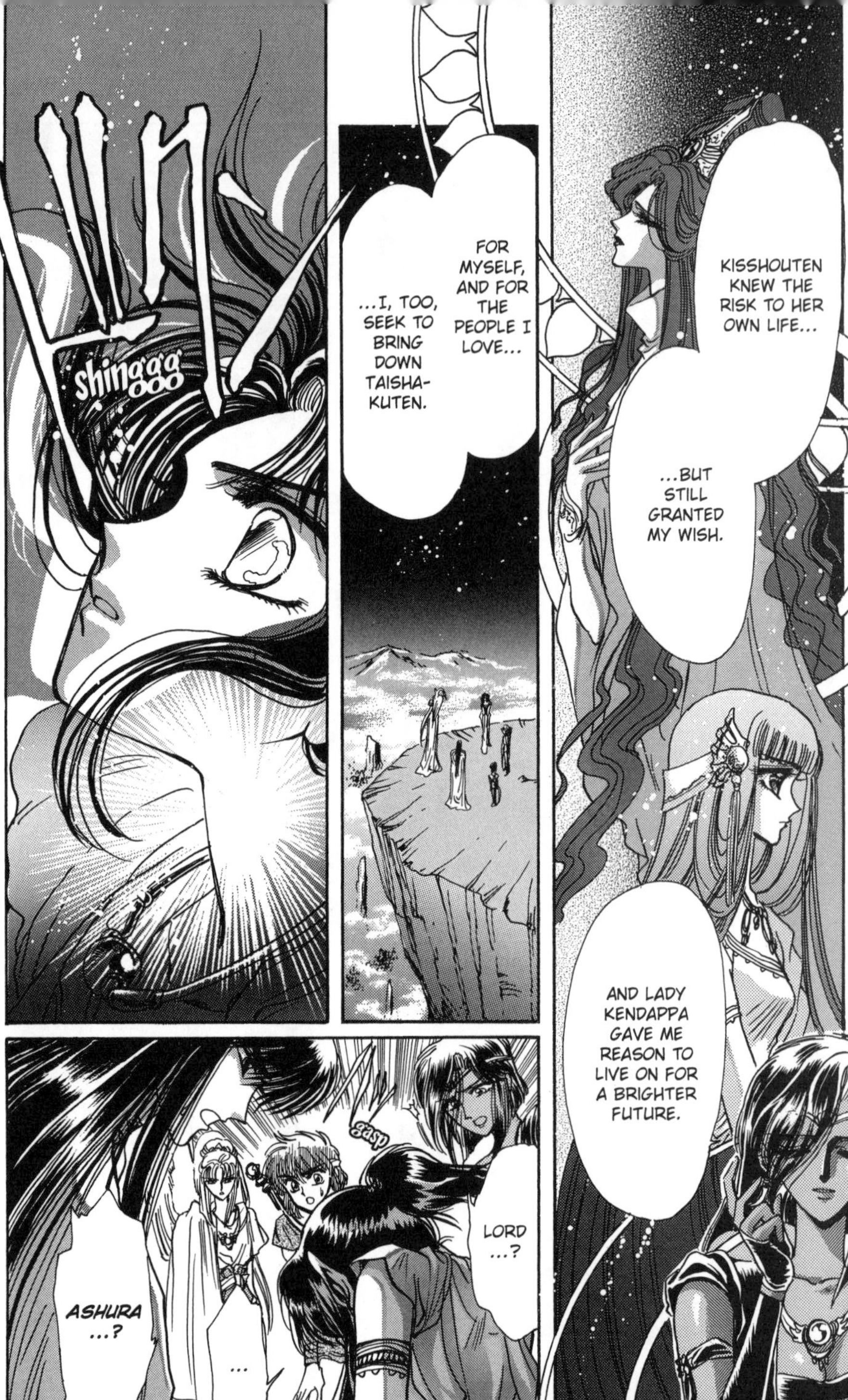
KISSHOUTEN KNEW THE RISK TO HER OWN LIFE...
...BUT STILL GRANTED MY WISH.
AND LADY KENDAPPA GAVE ME REASON TO LIVE ON FOR A BRIGHTER FUTURE.
FOR MYSELF, AND FOR THE PEOPLE I LOVE...
...I, TOO, SEEK TO BRING DOWN TAISHA-KUTEN.
shinggg
gasp
LORD ...?
ASHURA ...?
...

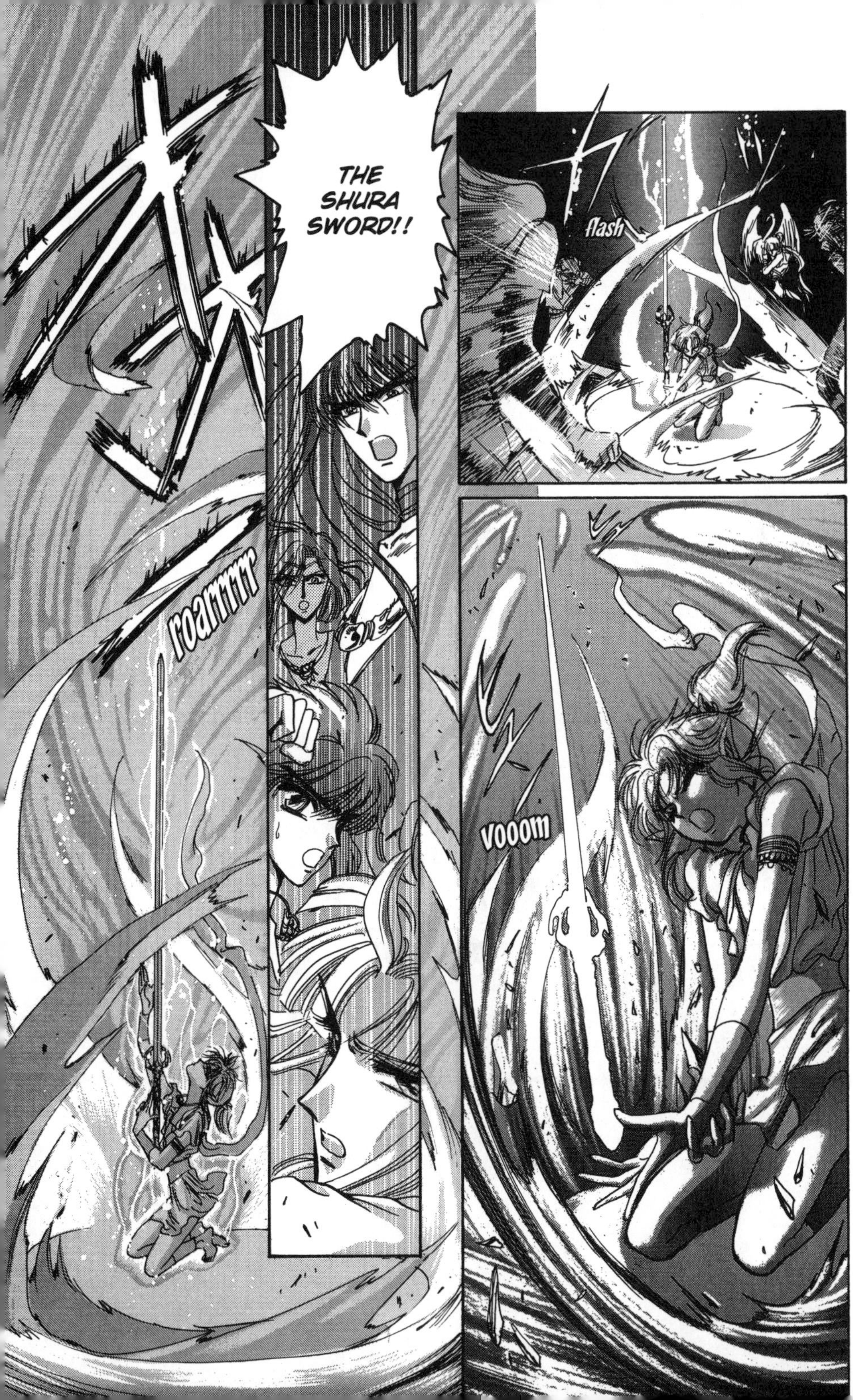
flash
vooom
THE SHURA SWORD!!
roarrrr

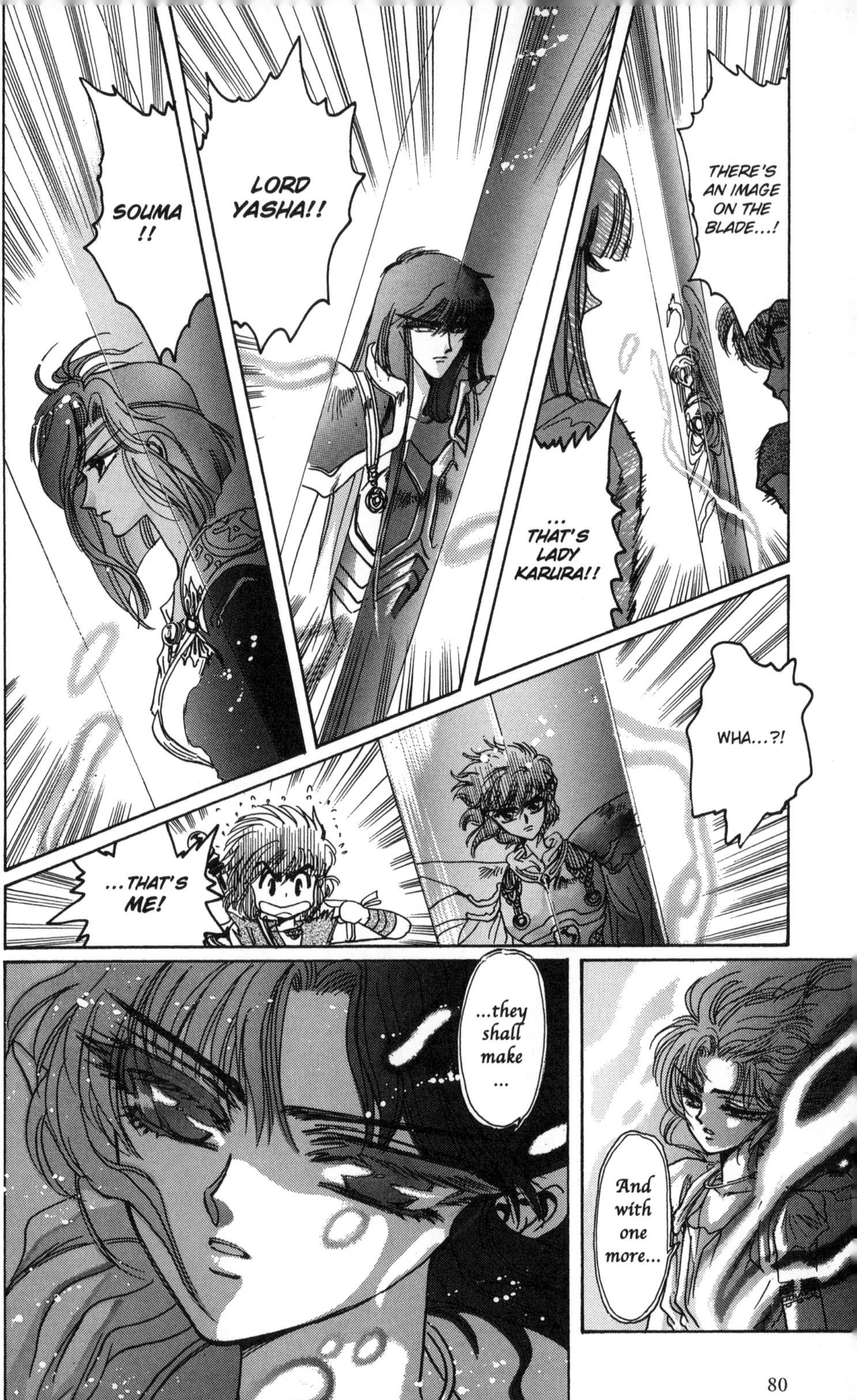
THERE'S AN IMAGE ON THE BLADE...!
...THAT'S LADY KARURA!!
LORD YASHA!!
SOUMA!!
WHA...?!
...THAT'S ME!
And with one more...
...they shall make ...

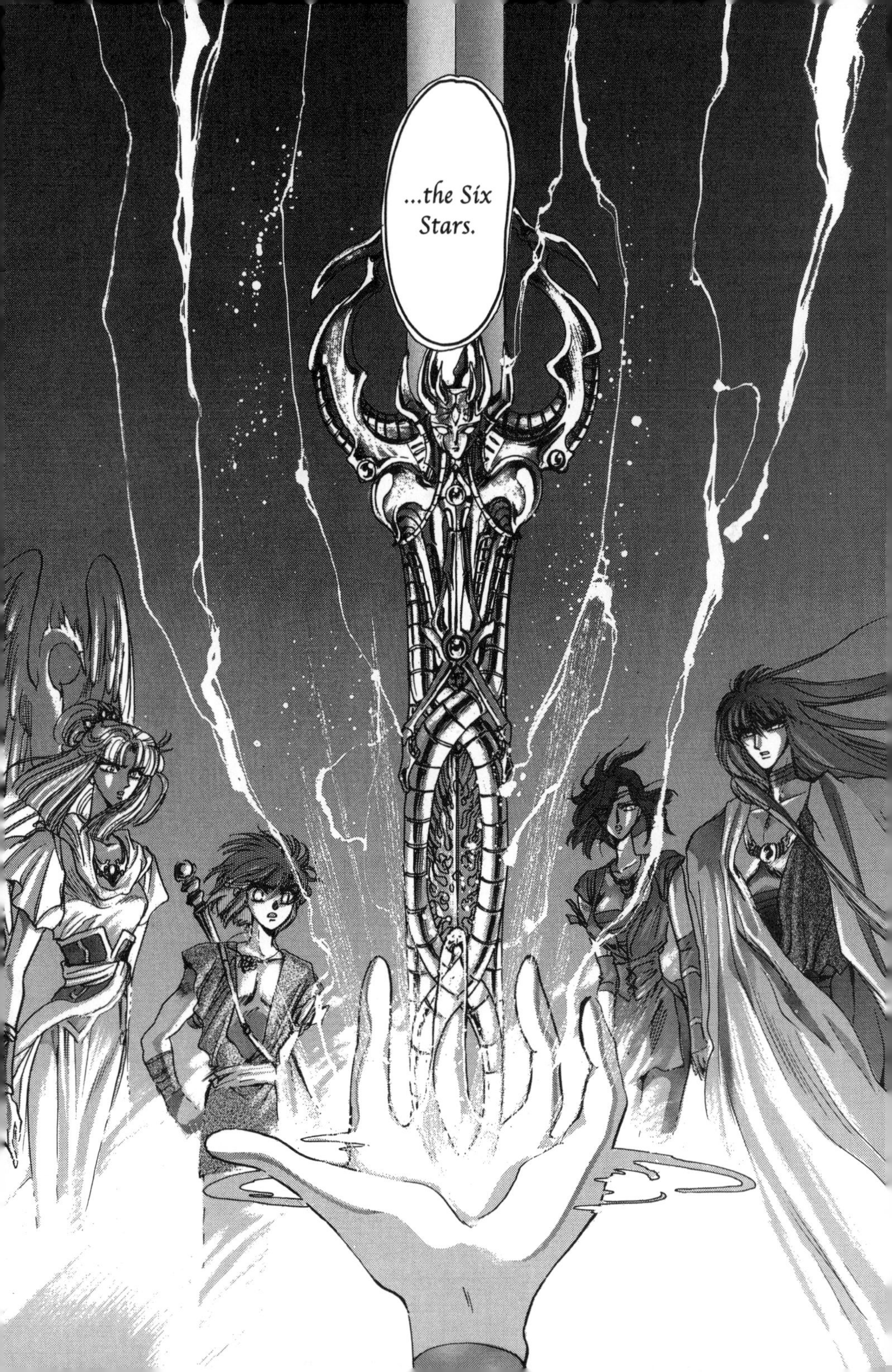
...the Six Stars.

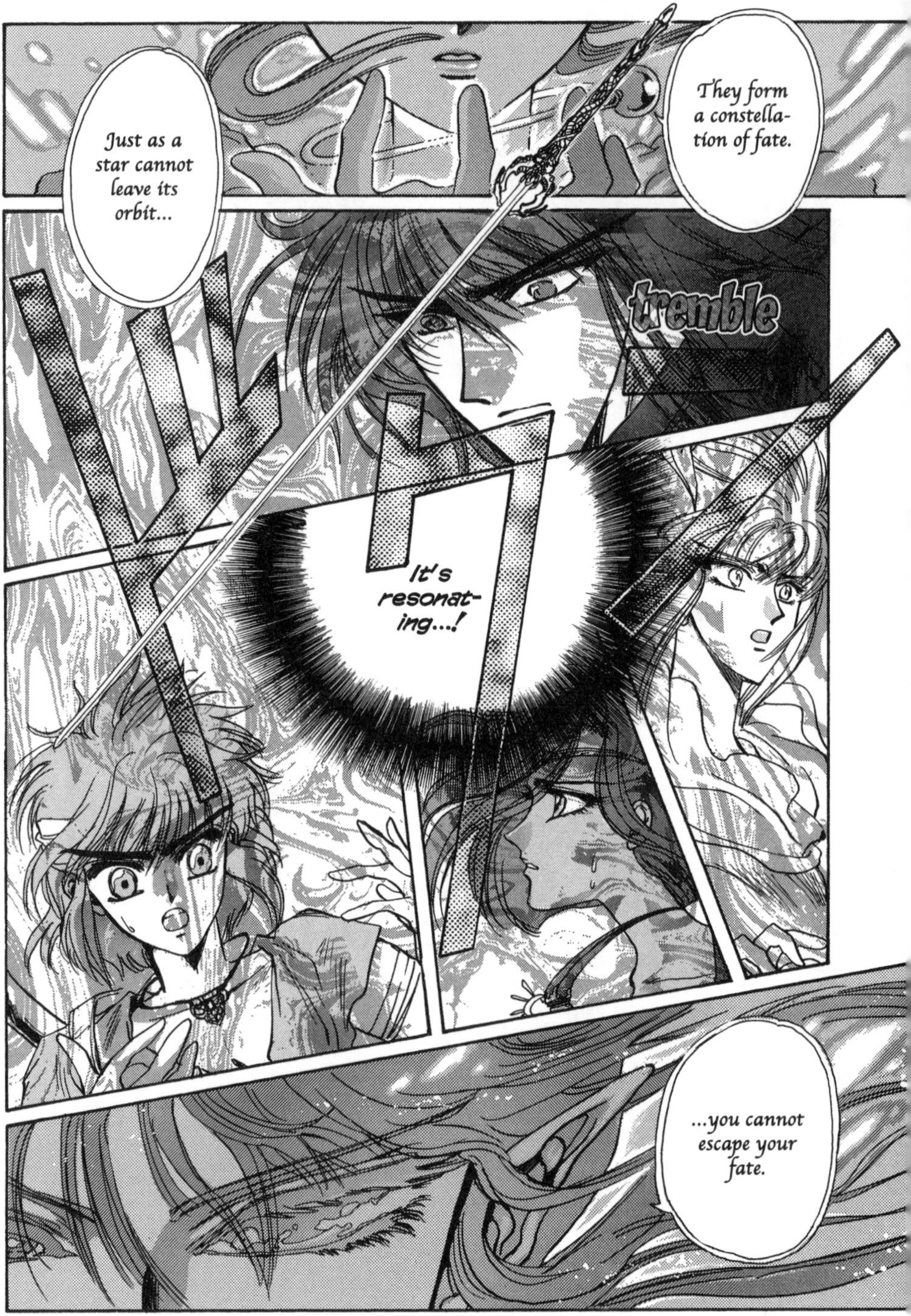
They form a constellation of fate.
Just as a star cannot leave its orbit...
tremble
It's resonating...!
...you cannot escape your fate.

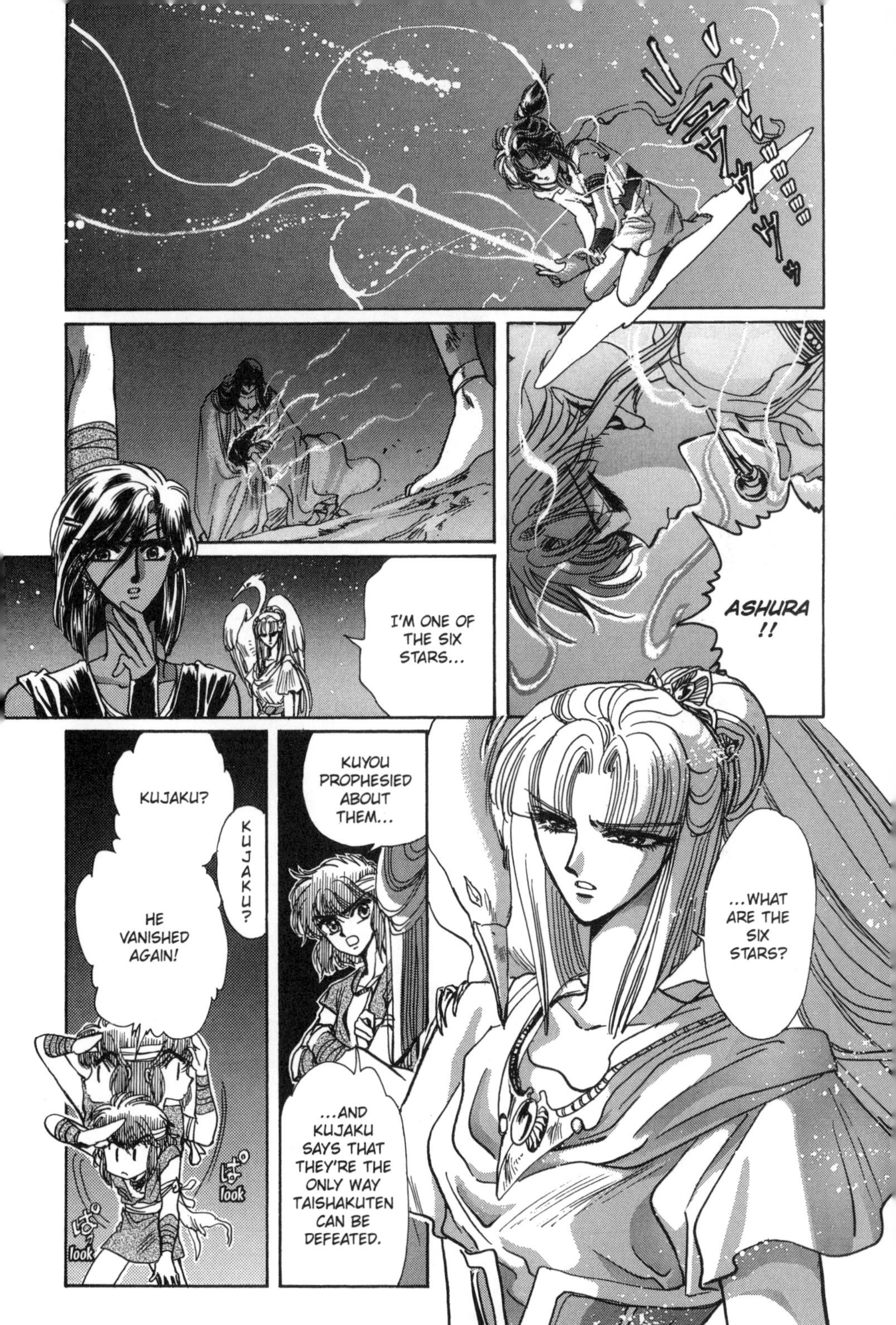

ASHURA !!
I'M ONE OF THE SIX STARS...
...WHAT ARE THE SIX STARS?
KUYOU PROPHESIED ABOUT THEM...
...AND KUJAKU SAYS THAT THEY'RE THE ONLY WAY TAISHAKUTEN CAN BE DEFEATED.
KUJAKU?
KUJAKU?
HE VANISHED AGAIN!
ぱ look
ぱ look

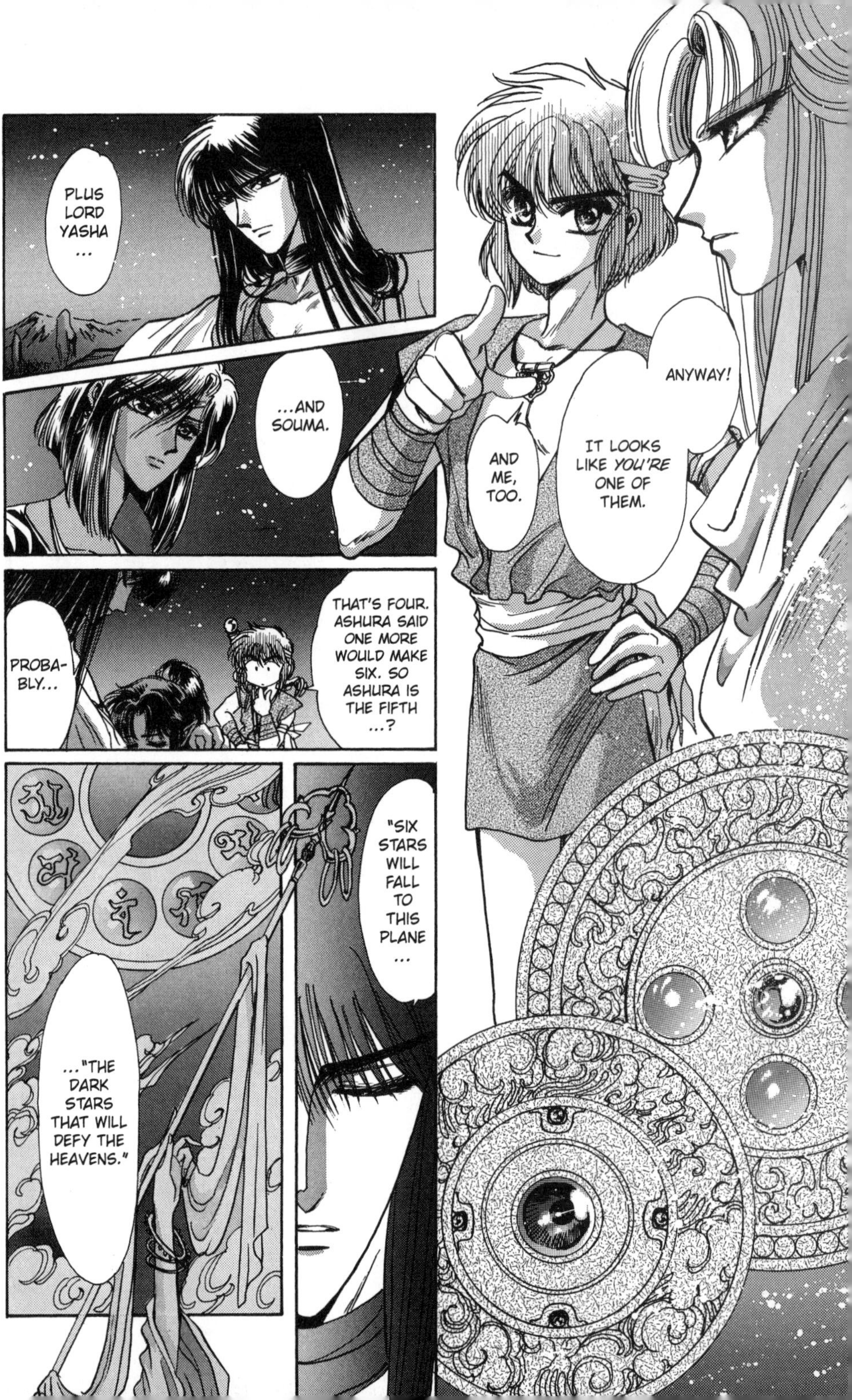
ANYWAY!
IT LOOKS LIKE *YOU'RE* ONE OF THEM.
AND ME, TOO.
PLUS LORD YASHA ...
...AND SOUMA.
THAT'S FOUR. ASHURA SAID ONE MORE WOULD MAKE SIX. SO ASHURA IS THE FIFTH ...?
PROBA-BLY...
"SIX STARS WILL FALL TO THIS PLANE ...
..."THE DARK STARS THAT WILL DEFY THE HEAVENS."

...And you shall undertake a journey that begins when you find the child of a vanished race. I cannot discern the child's true alignment, but I know that the child alone can turn the wheel of Tenkai's destiny. For it is by heavenly mandate that through this child, the Six Stars shall begin to gather. And then a figure shall appear from the shadows. Even my powers cannot clearly discern him...but he knows the future...and can turn the path of those stars, whether evil or heavenly. A roaring flame will raze the wicked. Six Stars will overpower all others...and inevitably...they will form the schism that splits the heavens.

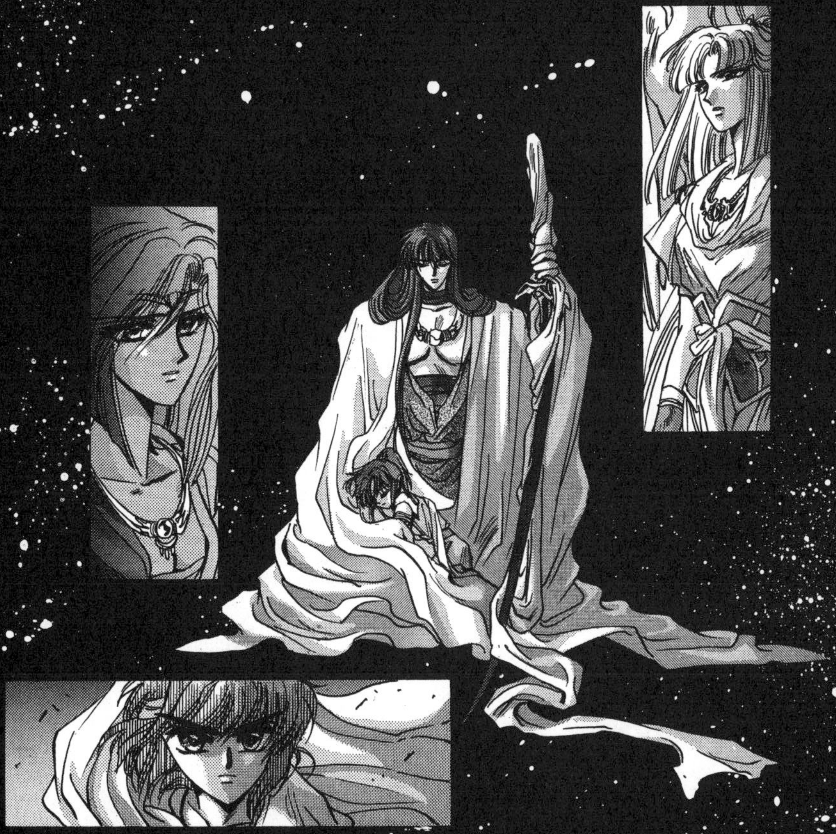

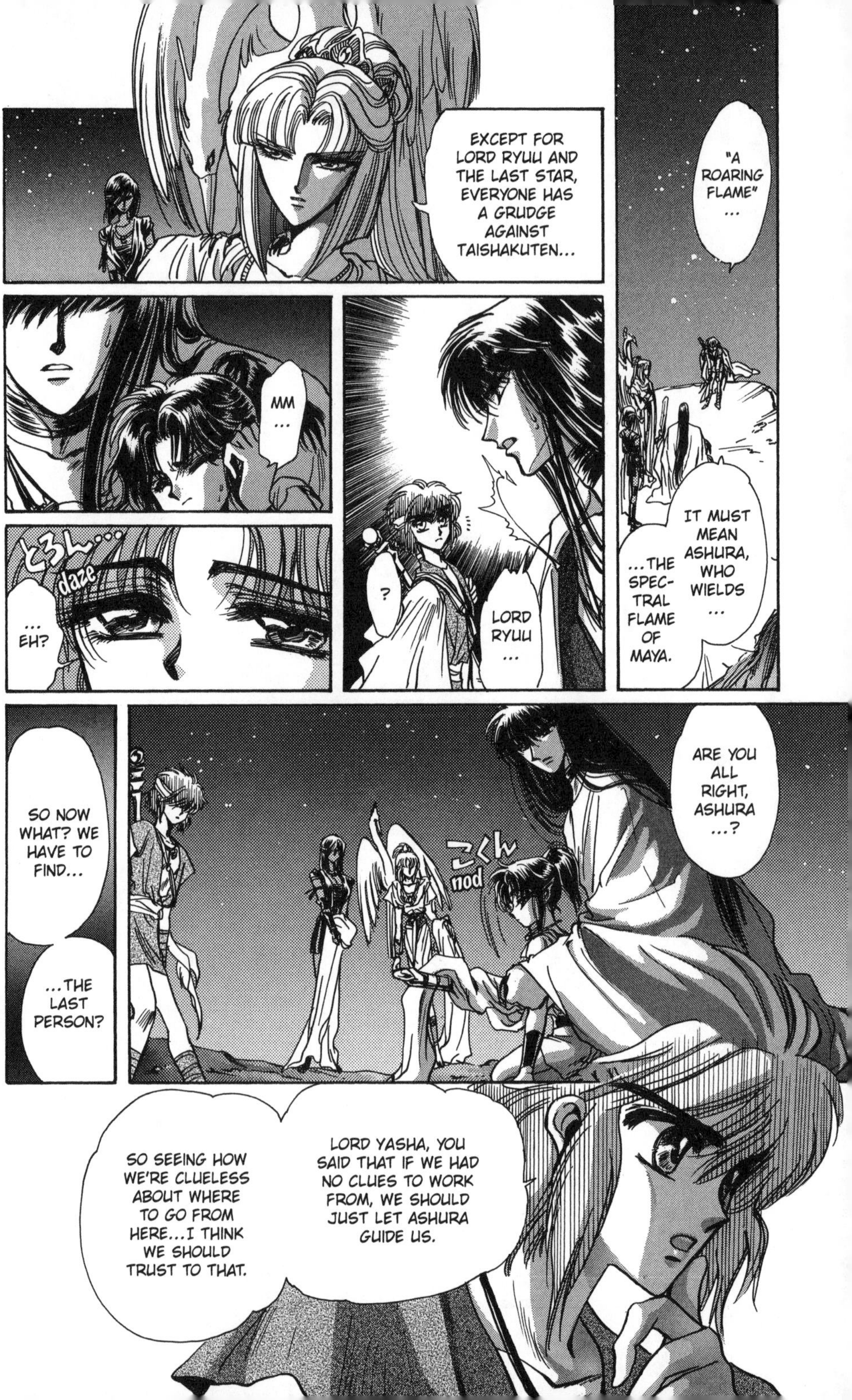

"A ROARING FLAME" ...
EXCEPT FOR LORD RYUU AND THE LAST STAR, EVERYONE HAS A GRUDGE AGAINST TAISHAKUTEN...
IT MUST MEAN ASHURA, WHO WIELDS ...
...THE SPECTRAL FLAME OF MAYA.
LORD RYUU ...
?
MM ...
とろん...
daze
... EH?
ARE YOU ALL RIGHT, ASHURA ...?
こくん
nod
SO NOW WHAT? WE HAVE TO FIND...
...THE LAST PERSON?
LORD YASHA, YOU SAID THAT IF WE HAD NO CLUES TO WORK FROM, WE SHOULD JUST LET ASHURA GUIDE US.
SO SEEING HOW WE'RE CLUELESS ABOUT WHERE TO GO FROM HERE...I THINK WE SHOULD TRUST TO THAT.

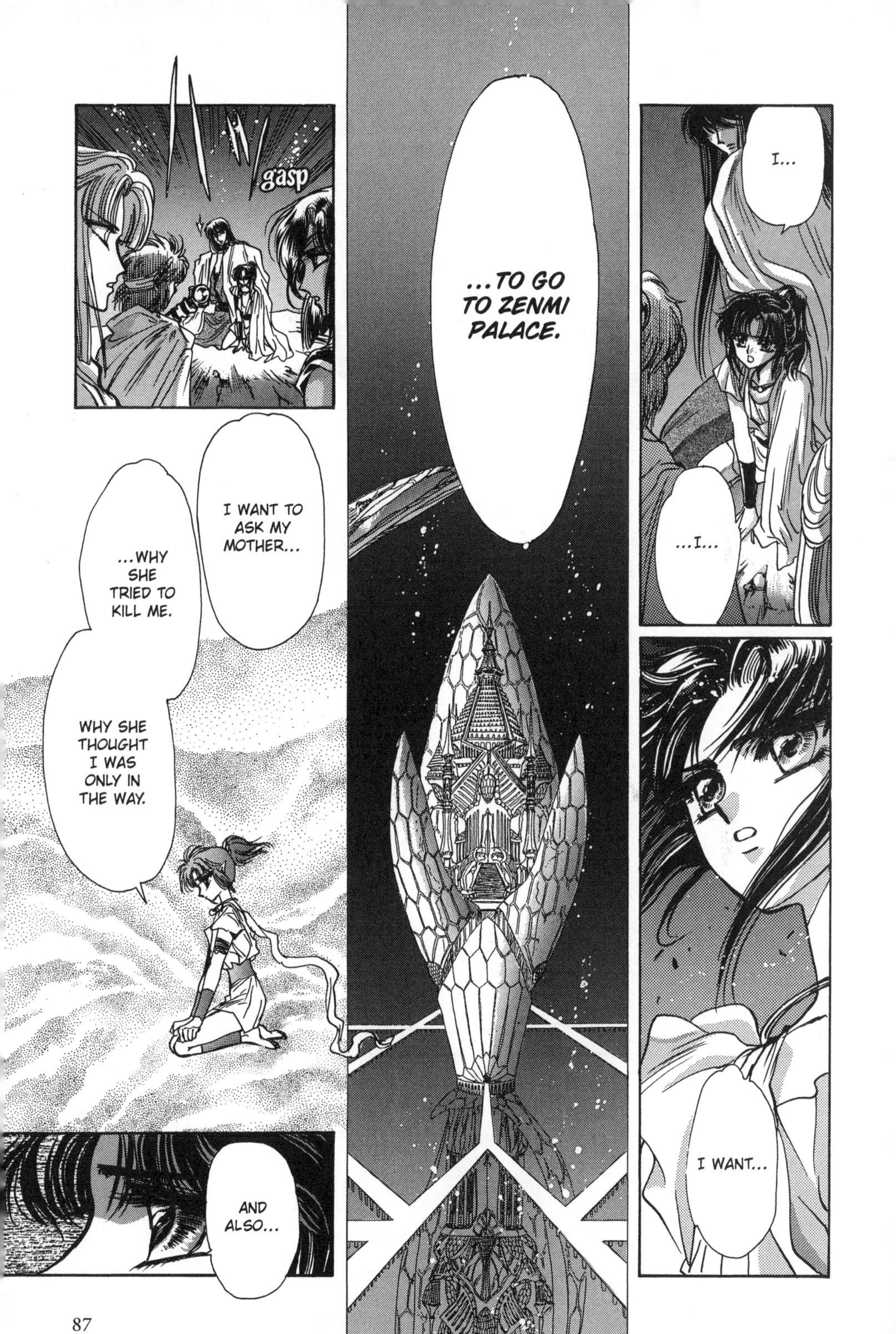
I...
...I...
I WANT...
...TO GO TO ZENMI PALACE.
gasp
I WANT TO ASK MY MOTHER...
...WHY SHE TRIED TO KILL ME.
WHY SHE THOUGHT I WAS ONLY IN THE WAY.
AND ALSO...

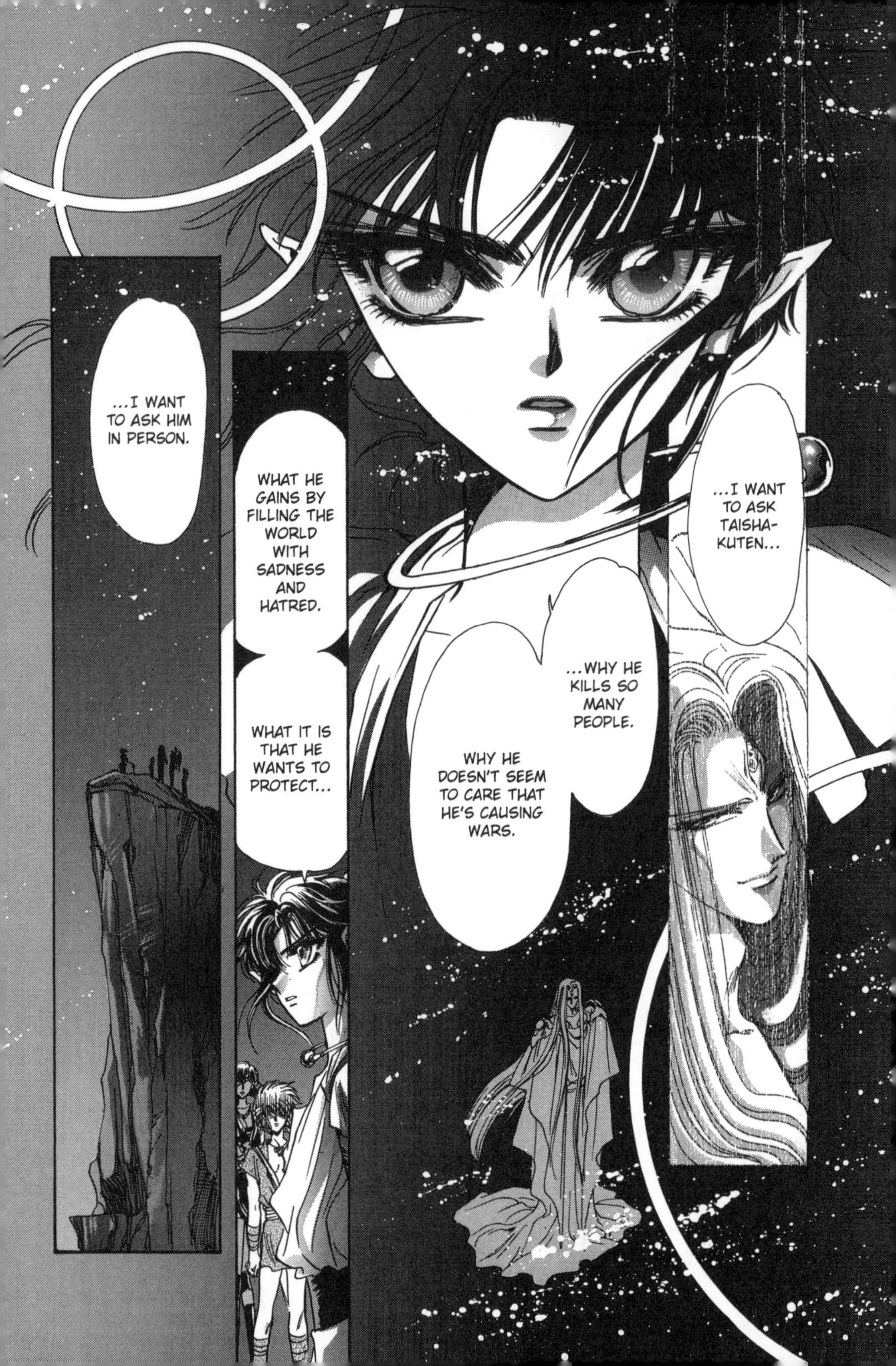
...I WANT TO ASK TAISHA-KUTEN...
...WHY HE KILLS SO MANY PEOPLE.
WHY HE DOESN'T SEEM TO CARE THAT HE'S CAUSING WARS.
WHAT HE GAINS BY FILLING THE WORLD WITH SADNESS AND HATRED.
WHAT IT IS THAT HE WANTS TO PROTECT...
...I WANT TO ASK HIM IN PERSON.

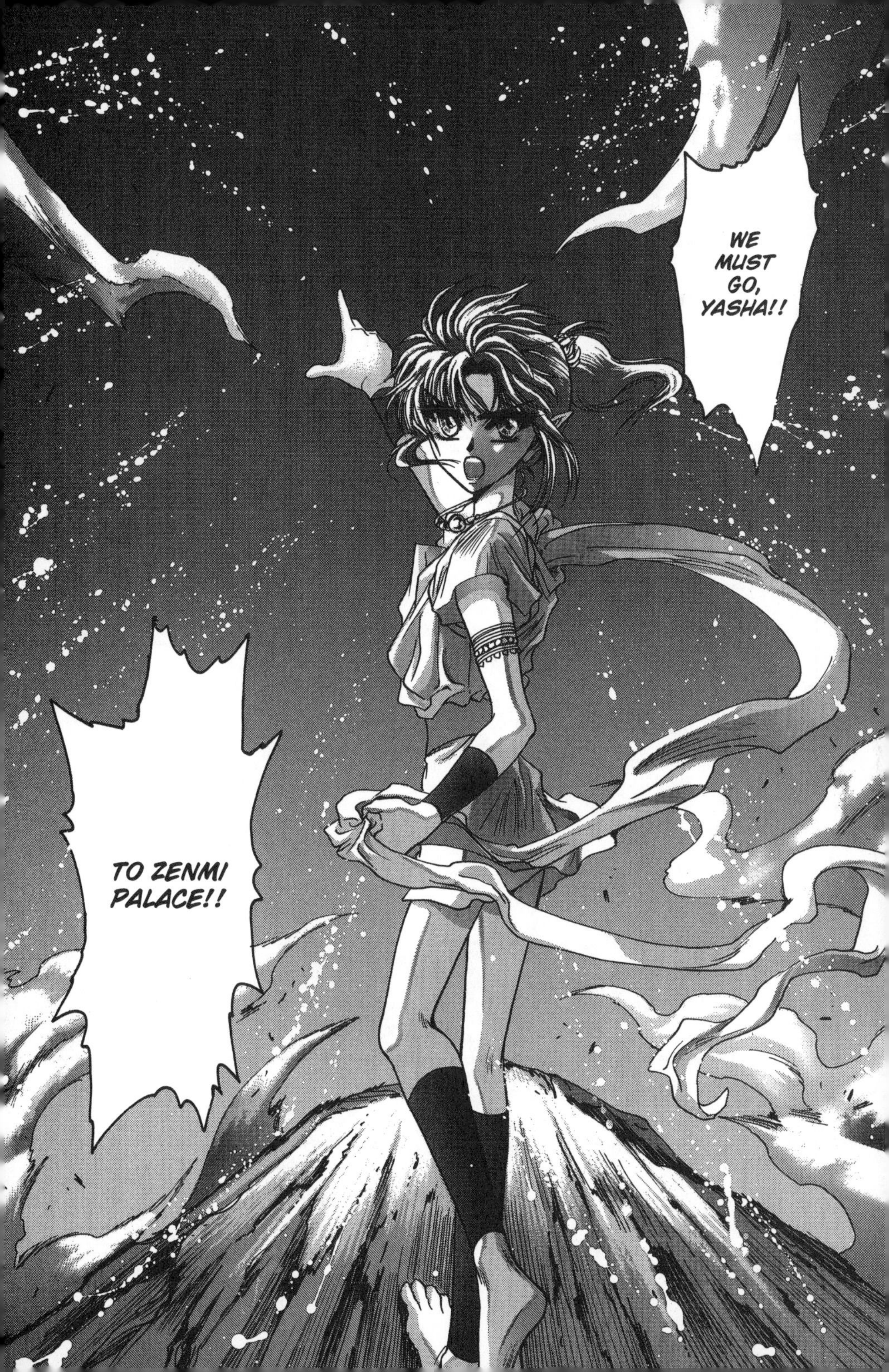
WE MUST GO, YASHA!!
TO ZENMI PALACE!!

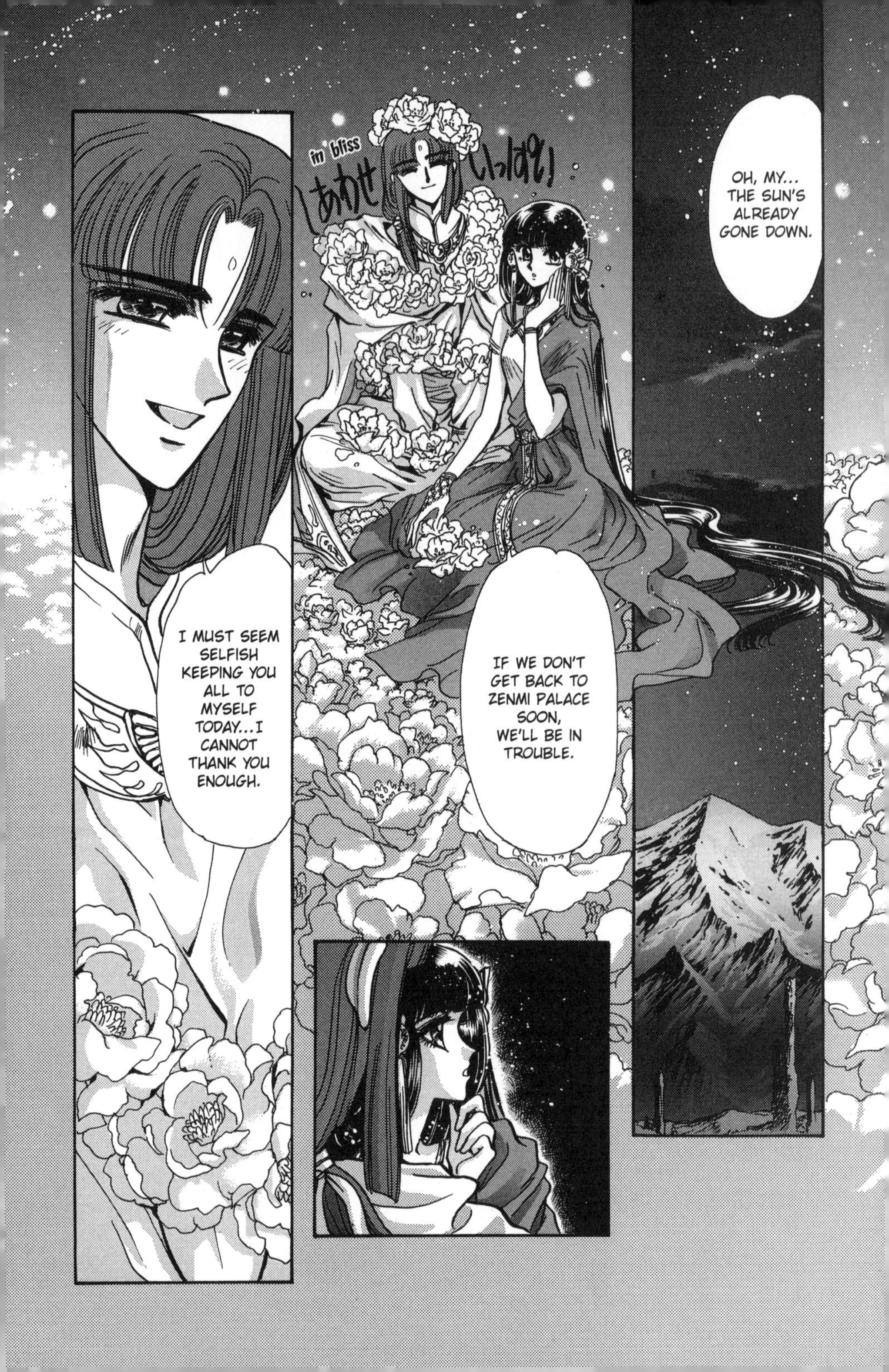

OH, MY... THE SUN'S ALREADY GONE DOWN.
in bliss
IF WE DON'T GET BACK TO ZENMI PALACE SOON, WE'LL BE IN TROUBLE.
I MUST SEEM SELFISH KEEPING YOU ALL TO MYSELF TODAY...I CANNOT THANK YOU ENOUGH.

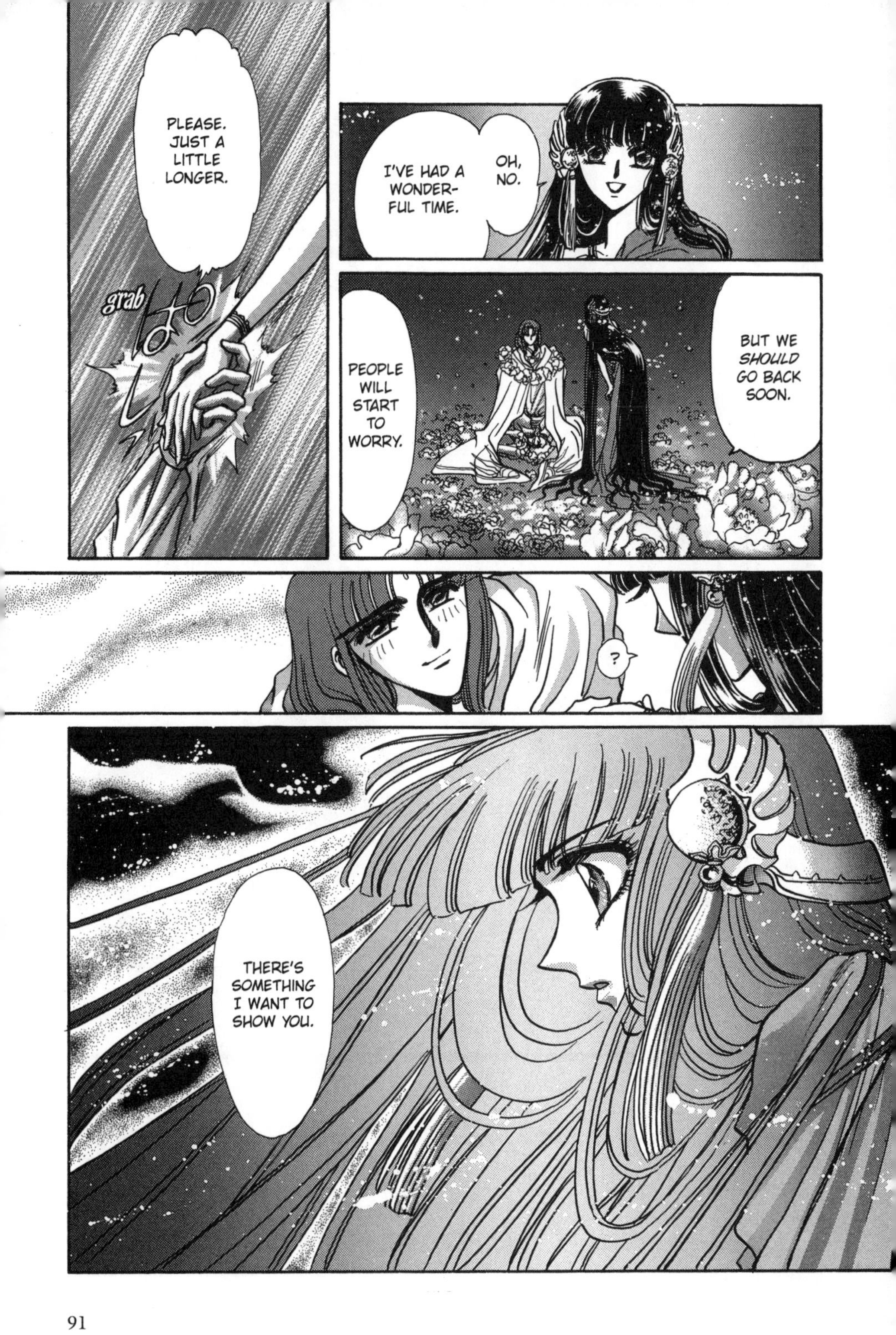
OH, NO.
I'VE HAD A WONDERFUL TIME.
BUT WE SHOULD GO BACK SOON.
PEOPLE WILL START TO WORRY.
PLEASE. JUST A LITTLE LONGER.
grab
?
THERE'S SOMETHING I WANT TO SHOW YOU.

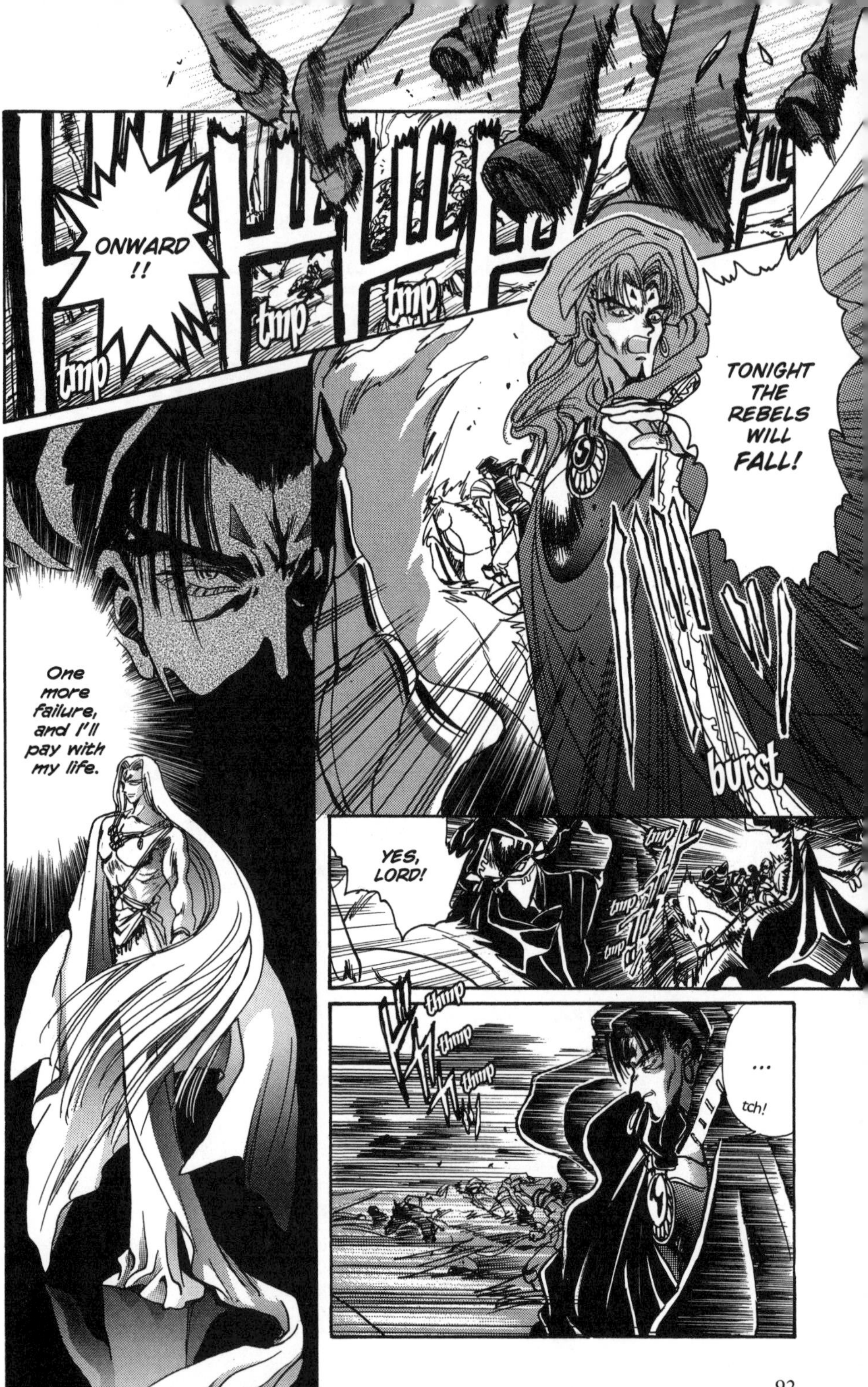
ONWARD !!
tmp
tmp
tmp
TONIGHT THE REBELS WILL FALL!
burst
YES, LORD!
tmp
tmp
tmp
thmp
thmp
thmp
...
tch!
One more failure, and I'll pay with my life.

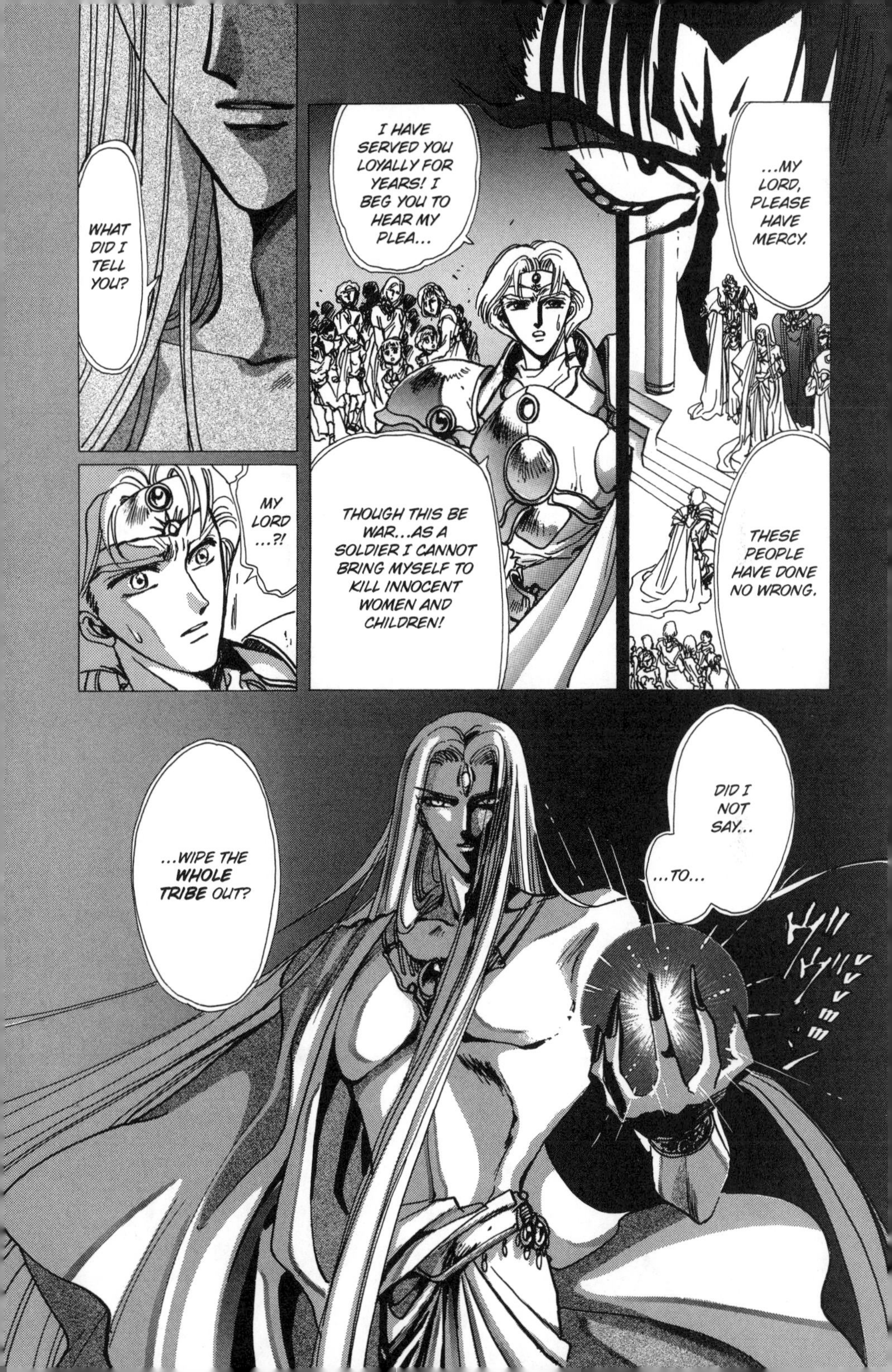
...MY LORD, PLEASE HAVE MERCY.
THESE PEOPLE HAVE DONE NO WRONG.
I HAVE SERVED YOU LOYALLY FOR YEARS! I BEG YOU TO HEAR MY PLEA...
THOUGH THIS BE WAR...AS A SOLDIER I CANNOT BRING MYSELF TO KILL INNOCENT WOMEN AND CHILDREN!
WHAT DID I TELL YOU?
MY LORD ...?!
DID I NOT SAY...
...TO...
...WIPE THE WHOLE TRIBE OUT?

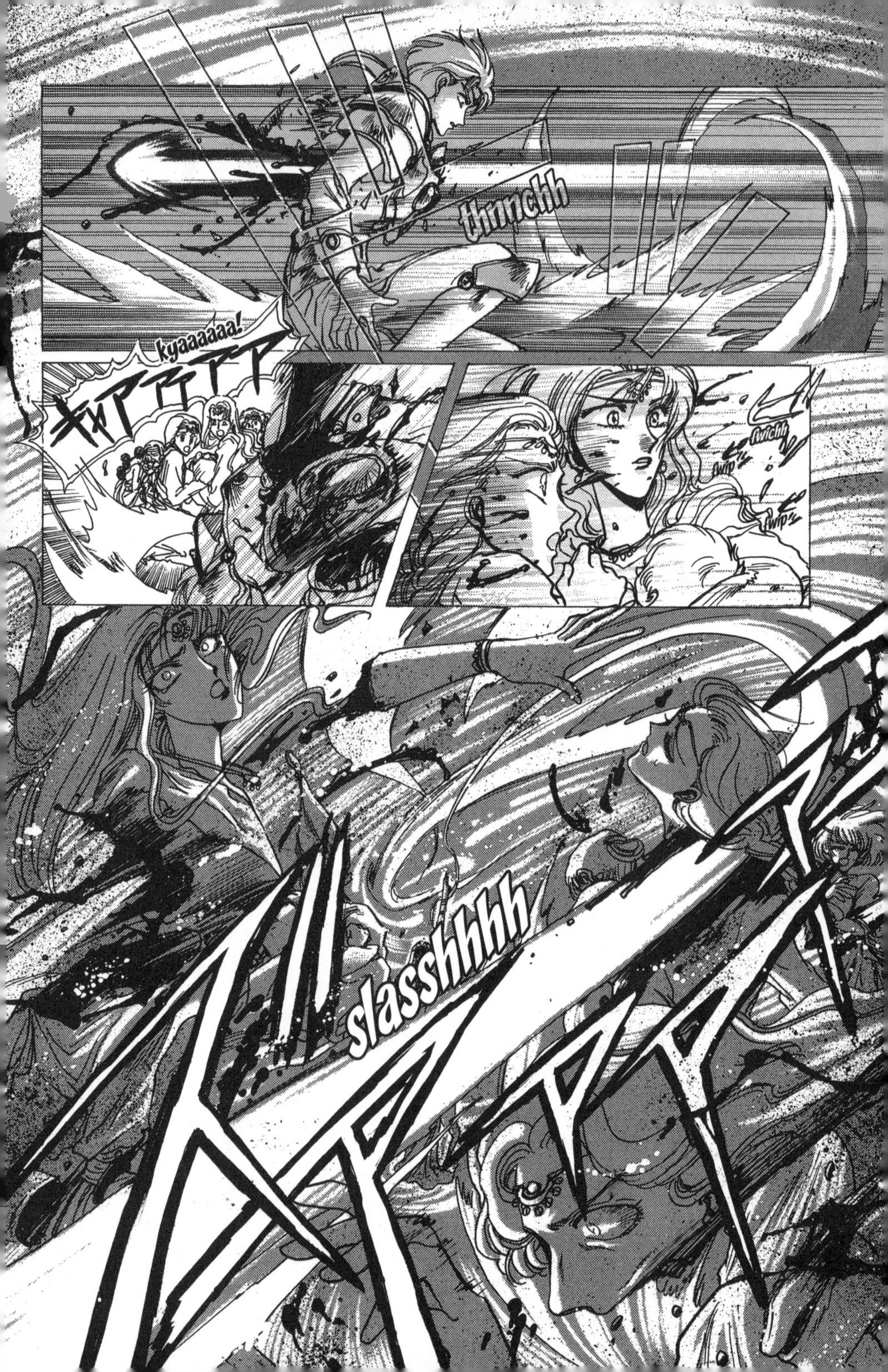
thnnchh
fwichh
fwip
fwip
kyaaaaaa!
キャアアアア
slasshhhh

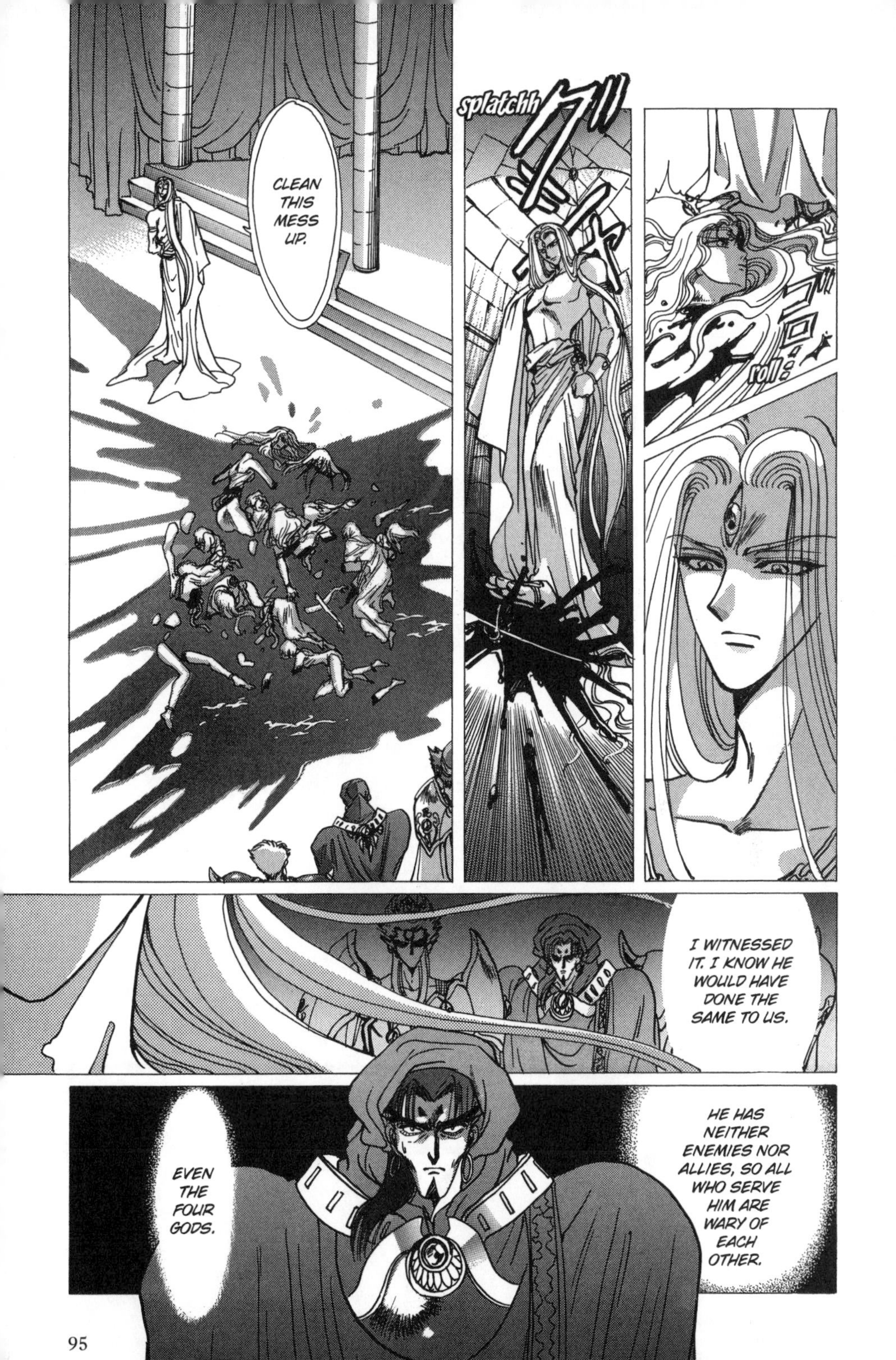
roll
splatchh
CLEAN THIS MESS UP.
I WITNESSED IT. I KNOW HE WOULD HAVE DONE THE SAME TO US.
HE HAS NEITHER ENEMIES NOR ALLIES, SO ALL WHO SERVE HIM ARE WARY OF EACH OTHER.
EVEN THE FOUR GODS.

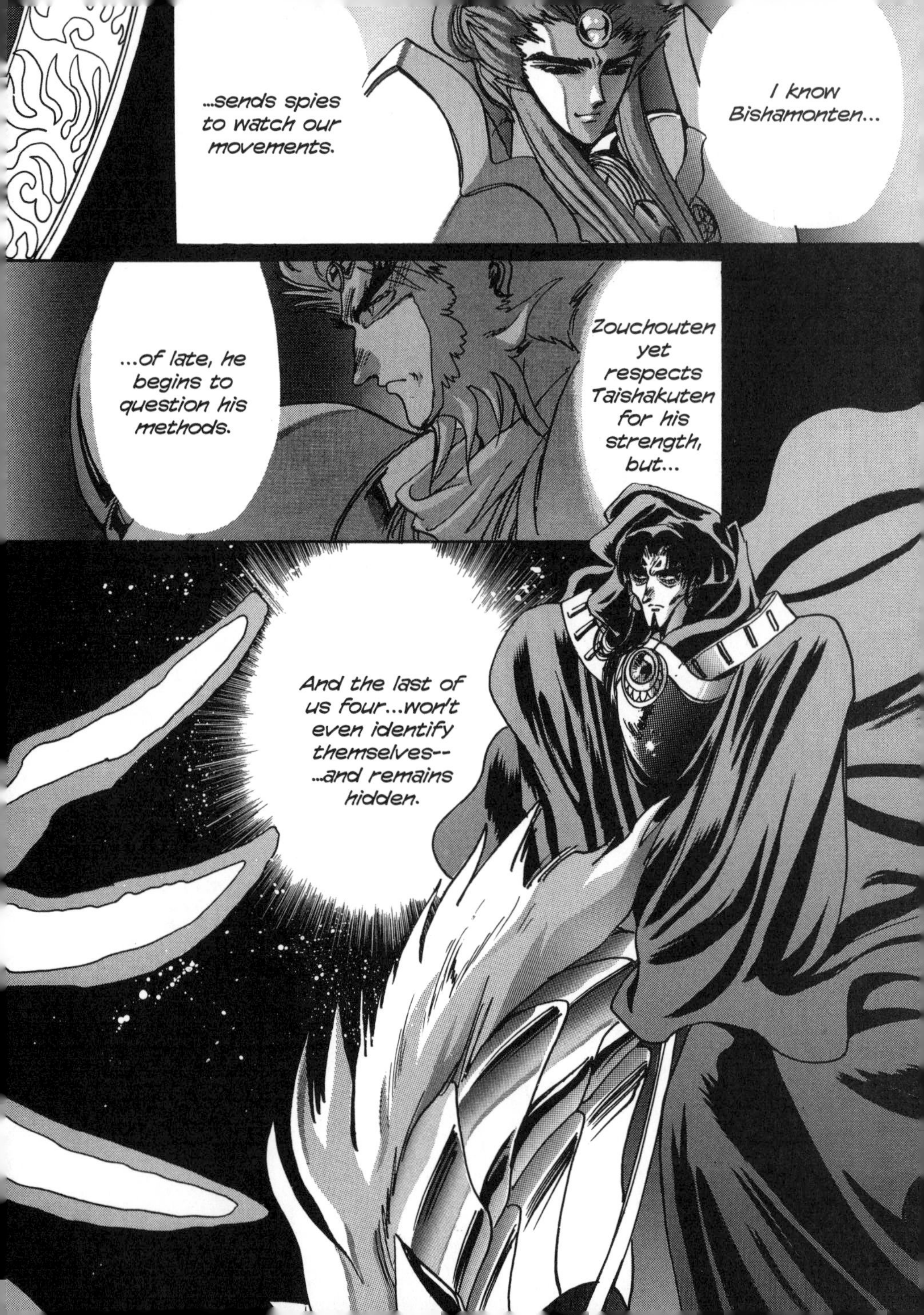
I know Bishamonten...
...sends spies to watch our movements.
Zouchouten yet respects Taishakuten for his strength, but...
...of late, he begins to question his methods.
And the last of us four...won't even identify themselves--
...and remains hidden.

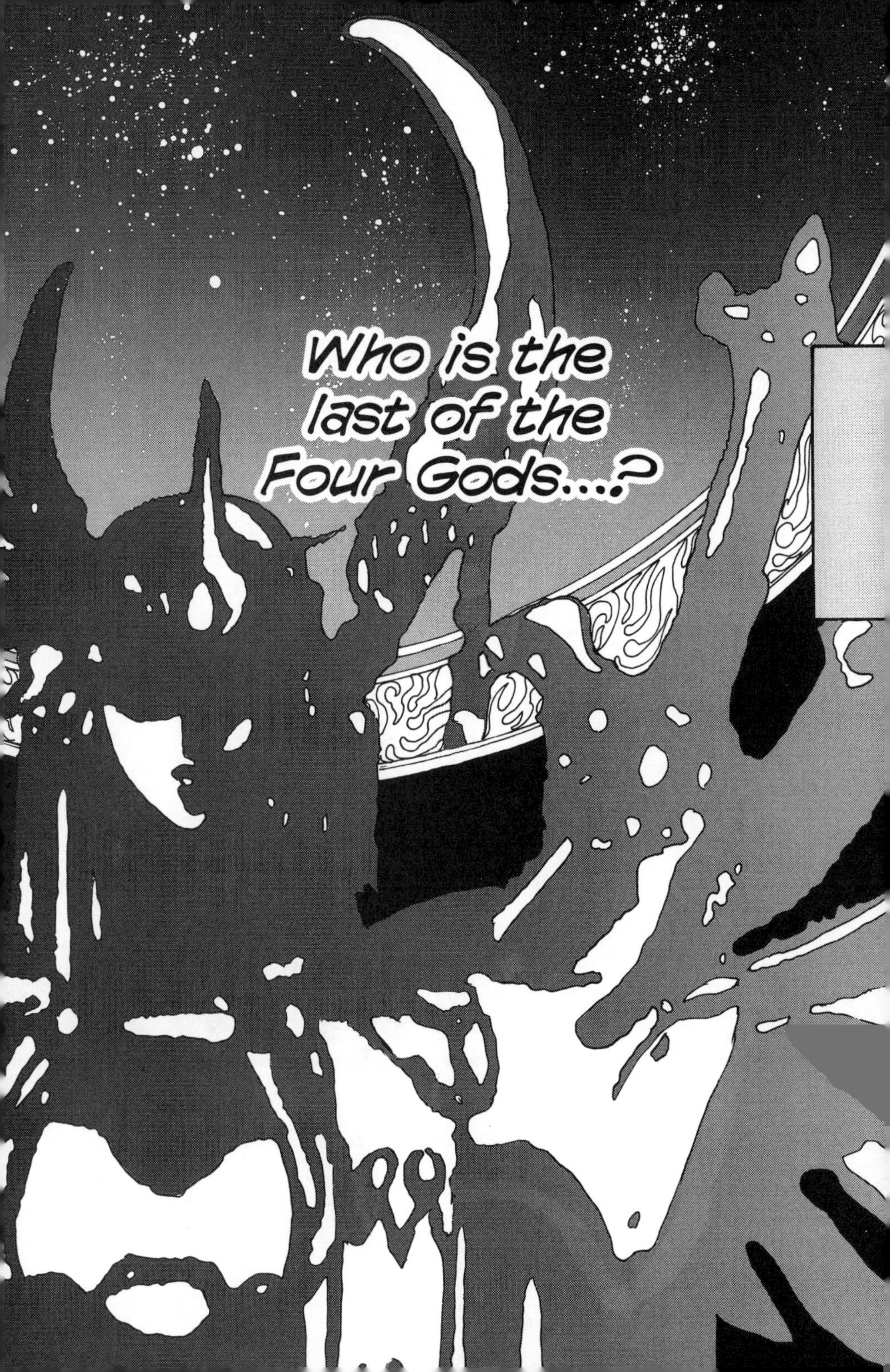
Who is the last of the Four Gods...?

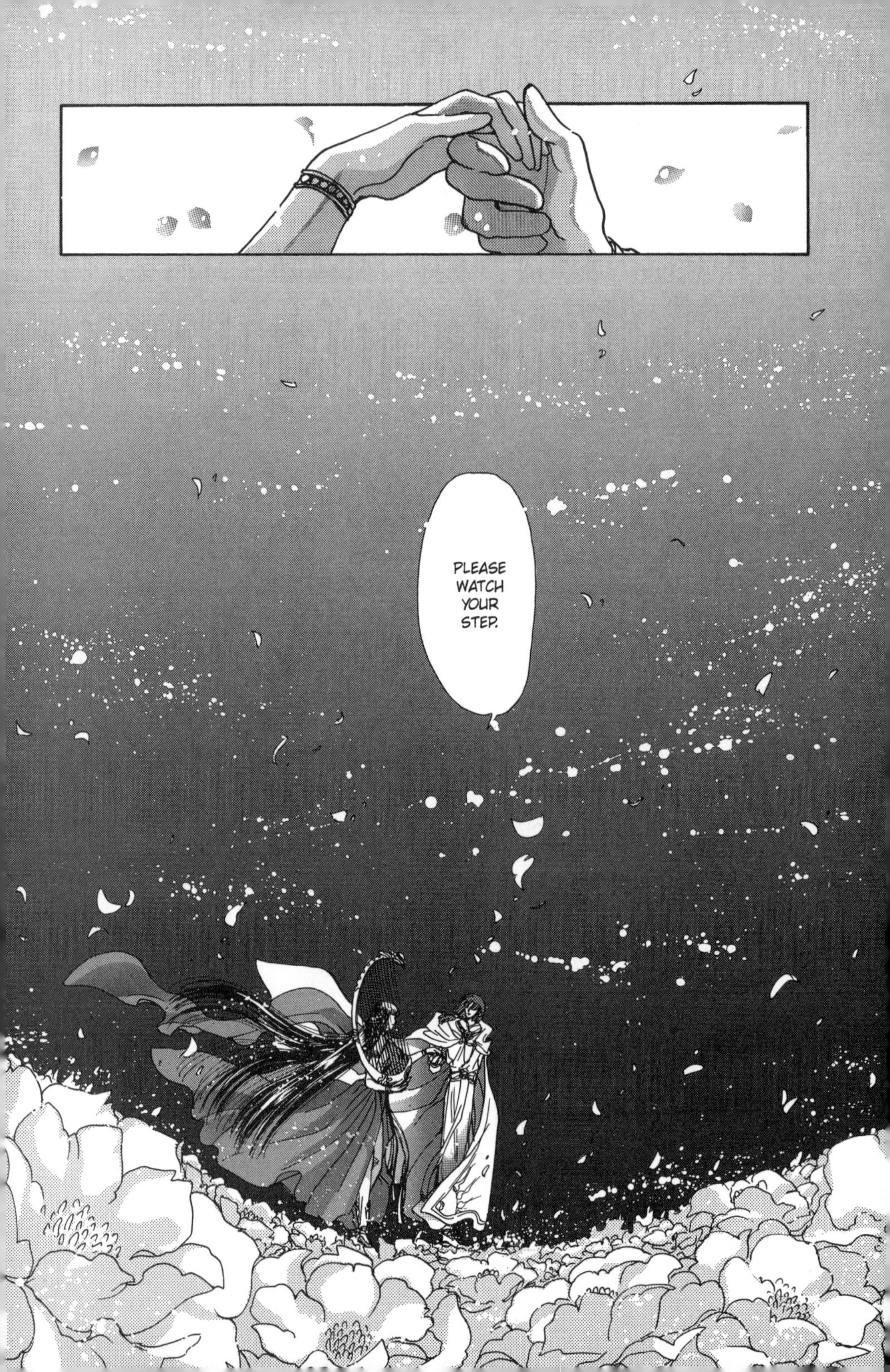
PLEASE WATCH YOUR STEP.

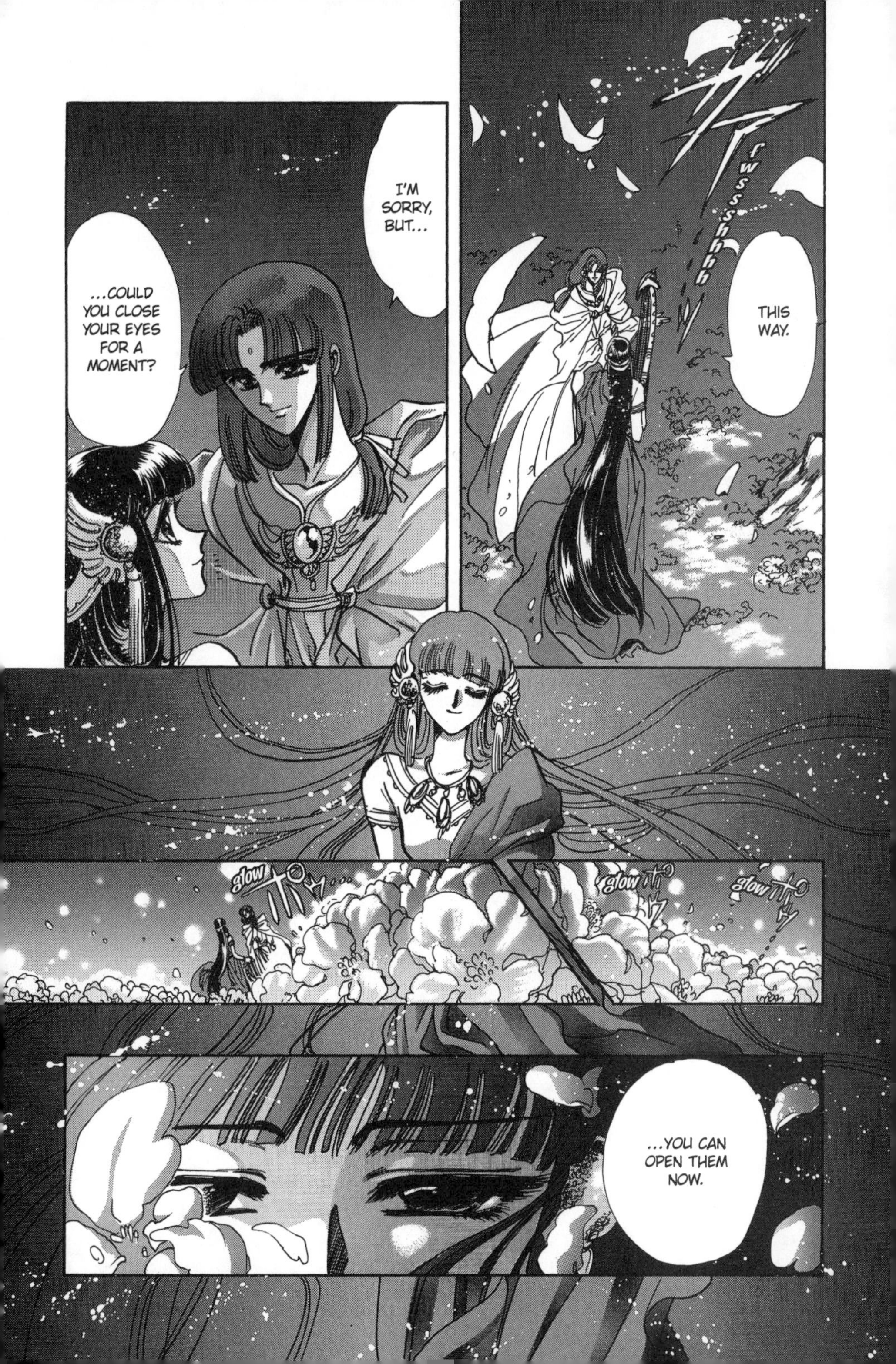

fwssshhhh
THIS WAY.
I'M SORRY, BUT...
...COULD YOU CLOSE YOUR EYES FOR A MOMENT?
glow
glow
glow
...YOU CAN OPEN THEM NOW.

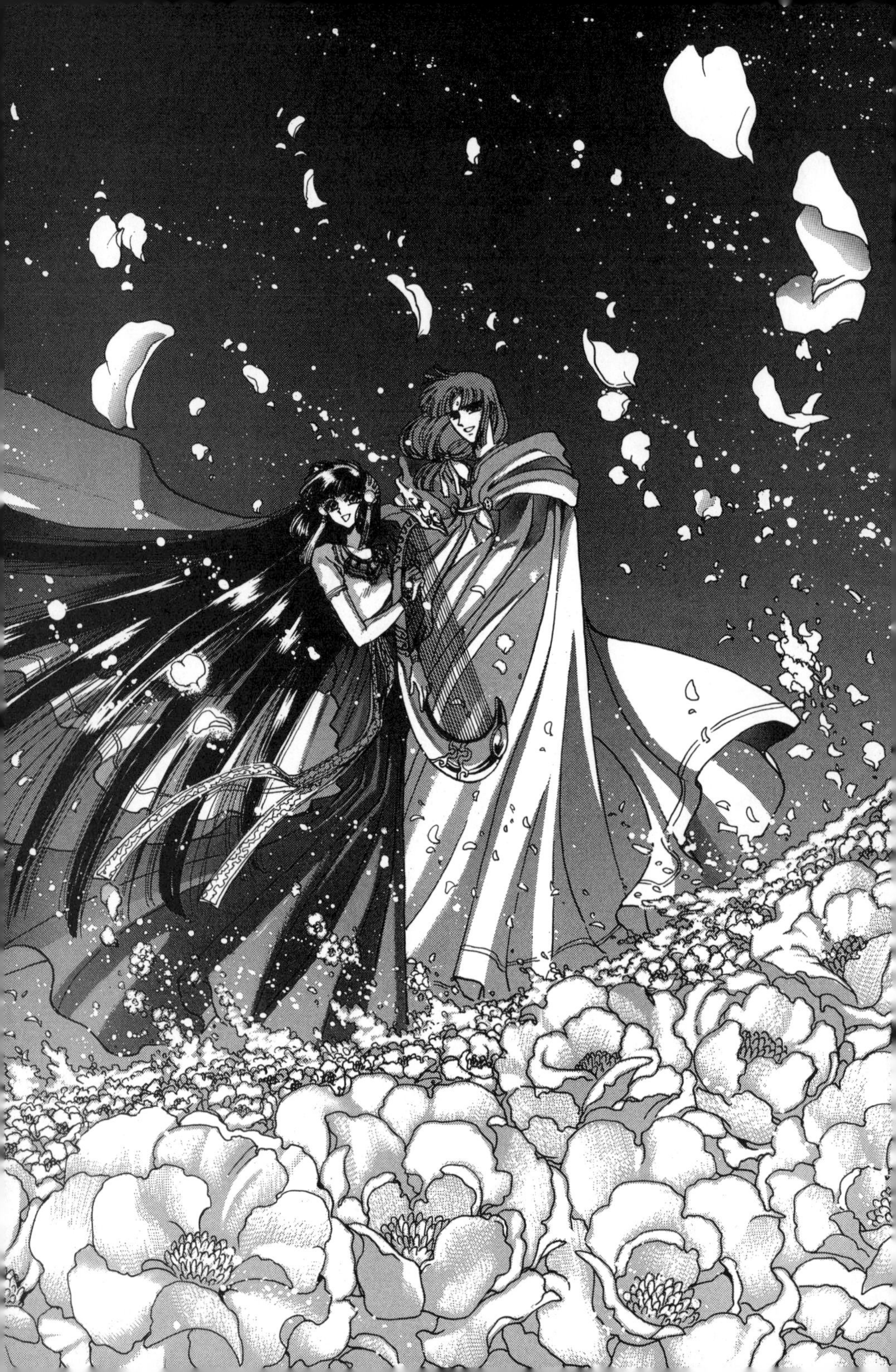

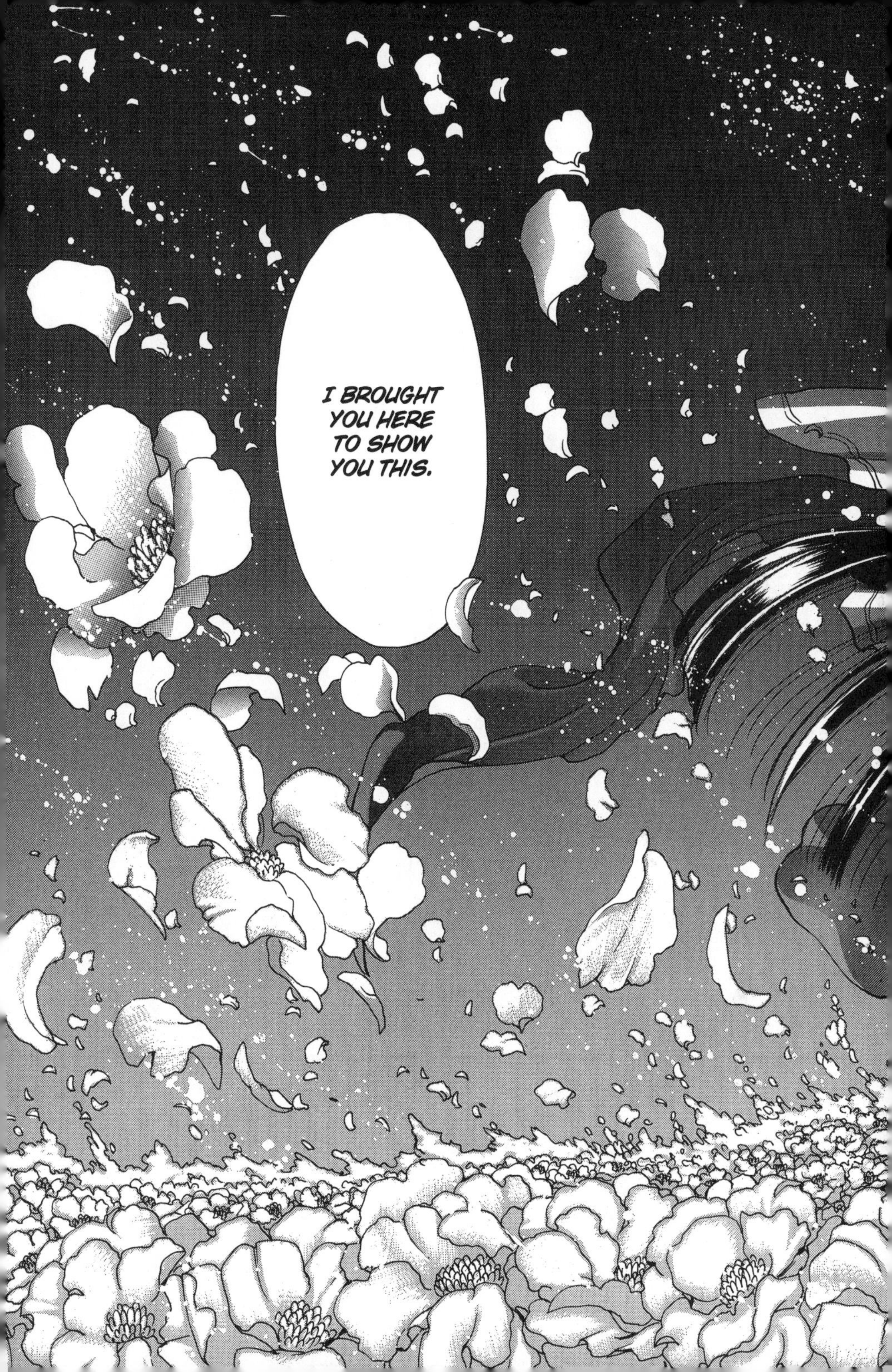
I BROUGHT YOU HERE TO SHOW YOU THIS.

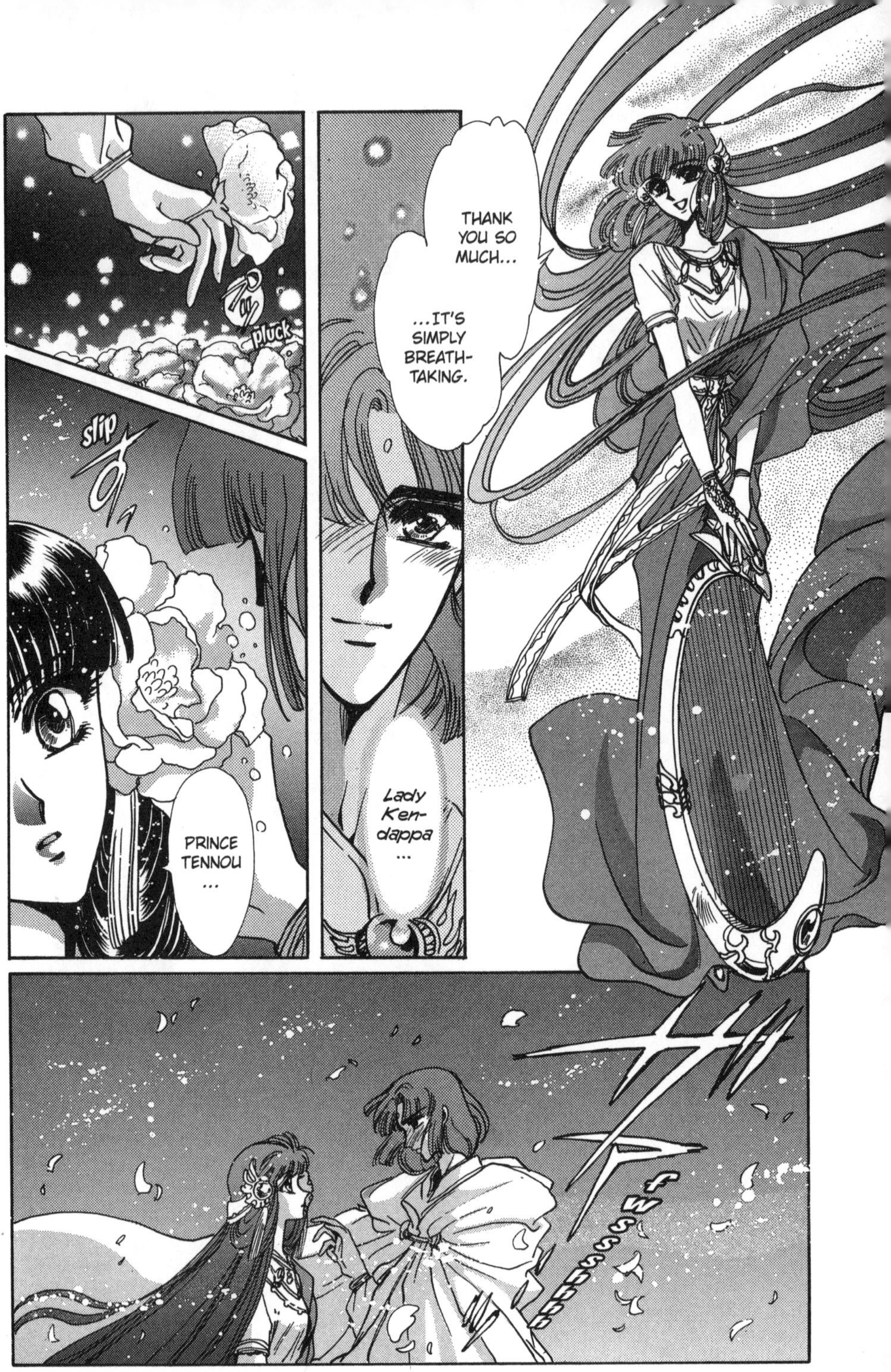
THANK YOU SO MUCH…
…IT'S SIMPLY BREATH-TAKING.
Lady Ken-dappa …
pluck
slip
PRINCE TENNOU …
fwsssssh

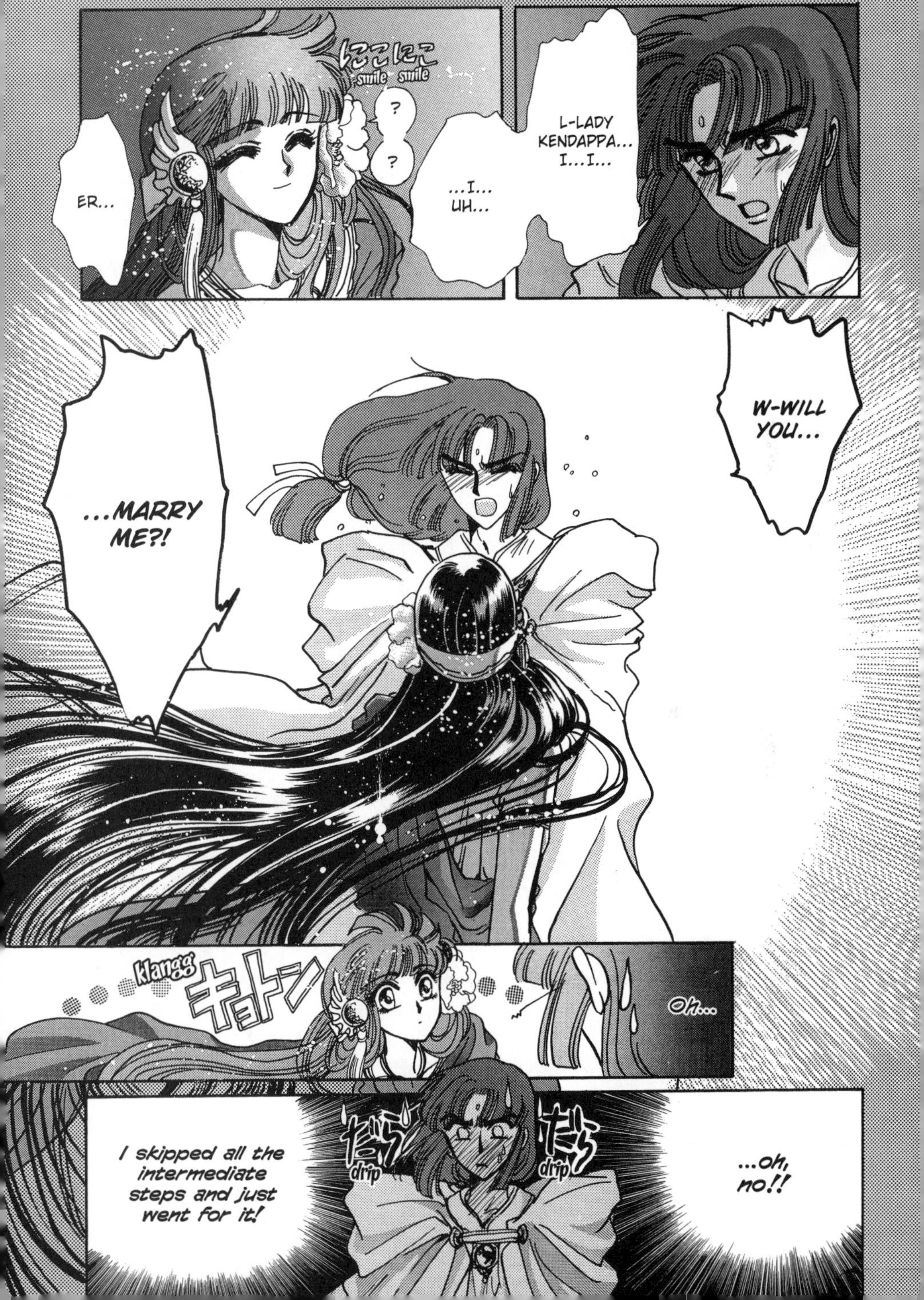
L-LADY KENDAPPA... I...I...
...I... UH...
?
?
にこにこ
smile smile
ER...
W-WILL YOU...
...MARRY ME?!
Oh...
キョトーン
klangg
...oh, no!!
だらだら
drip drip
I skipped all the intermediate steps and just went for it!

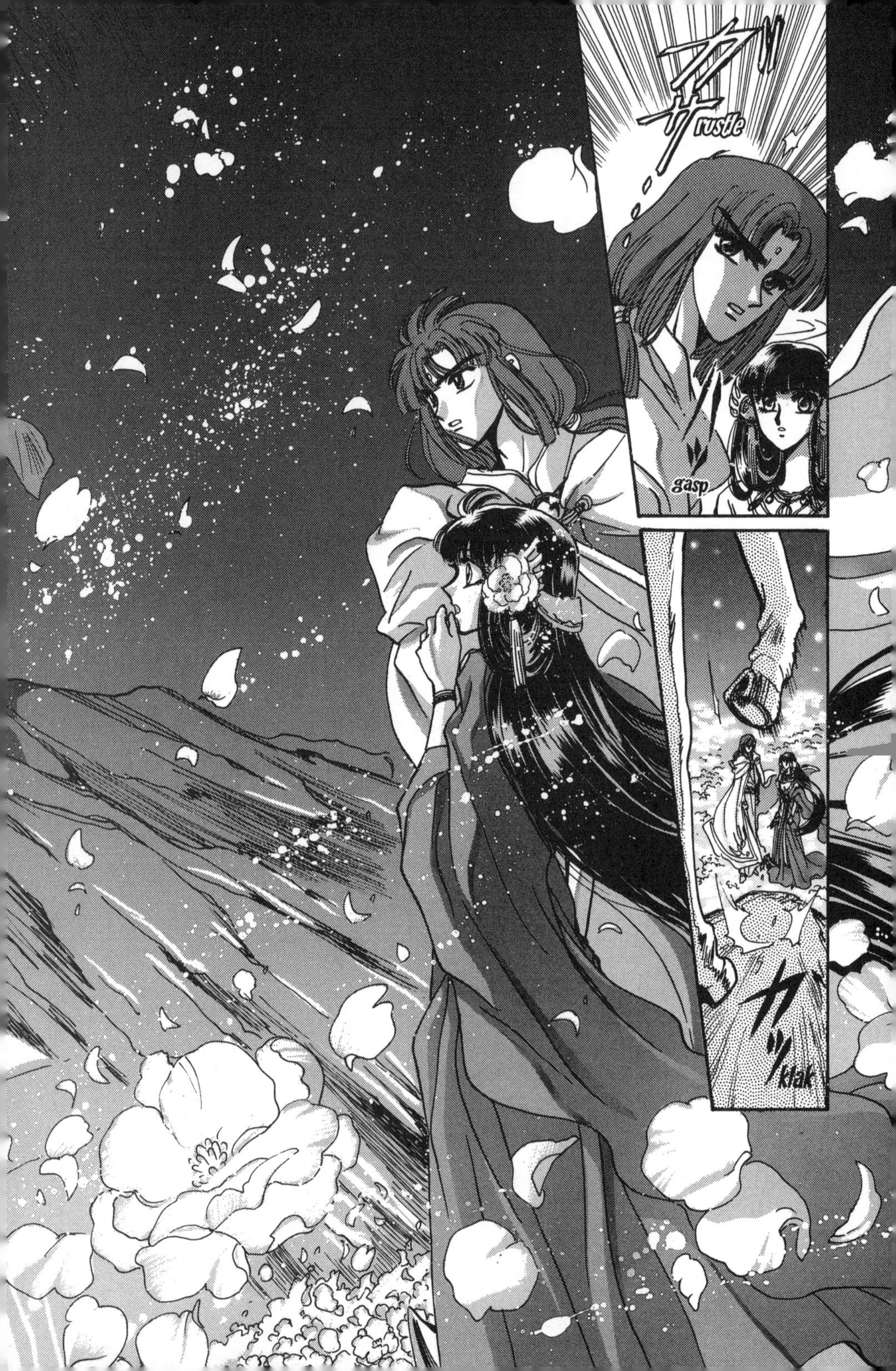
rustle
gasp
klak

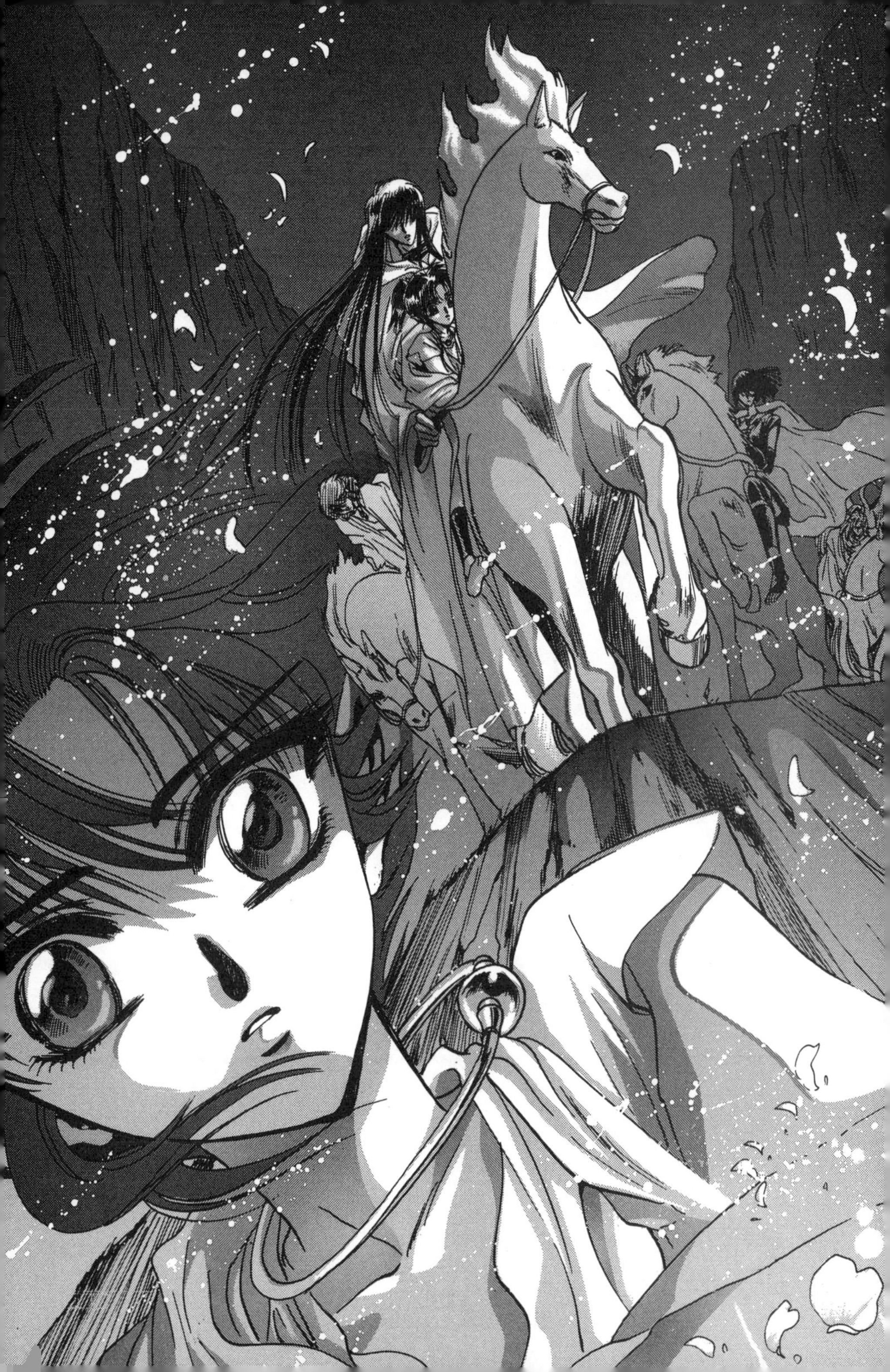

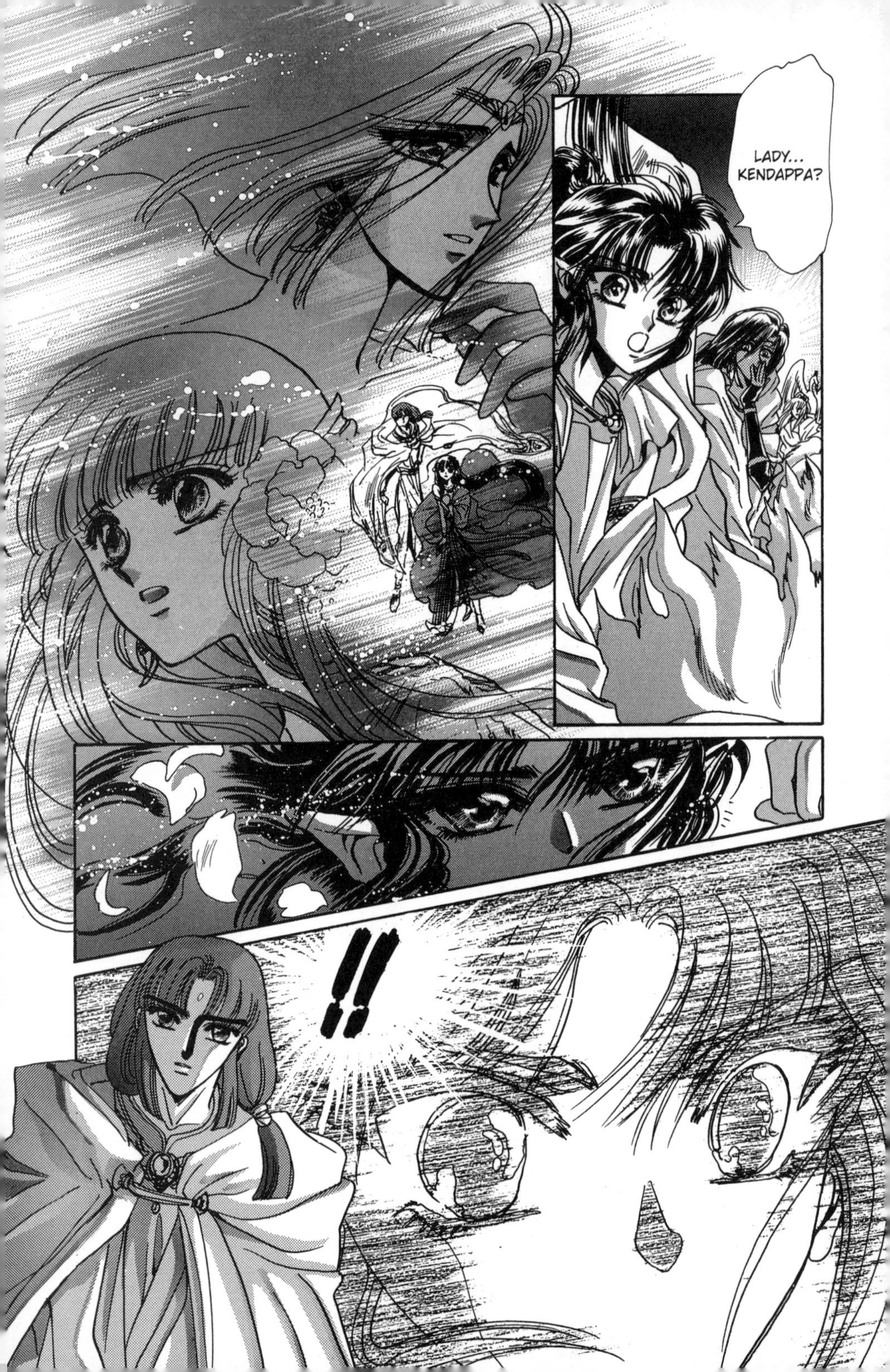
LADY... KENDAPPA?

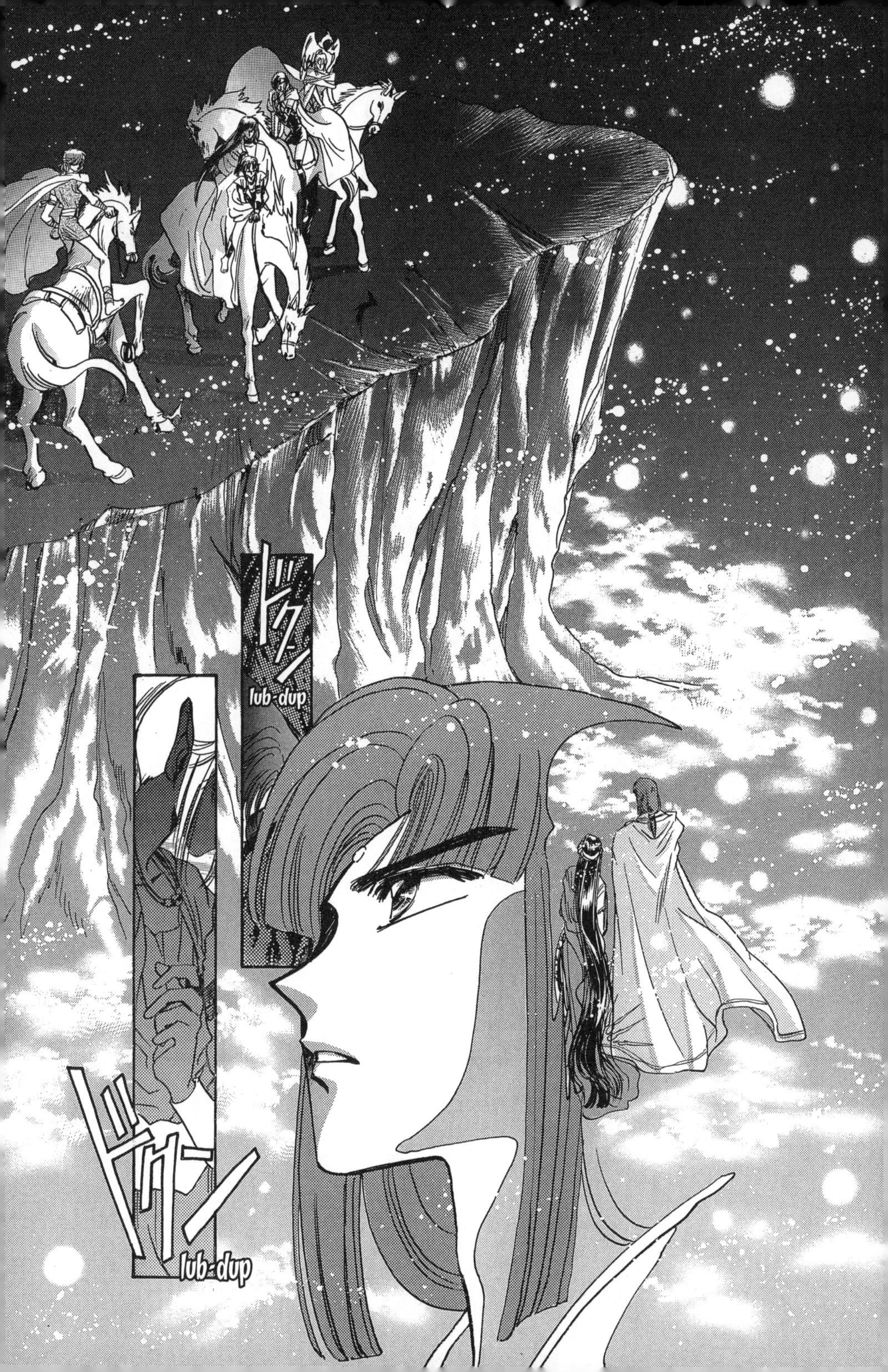
ドクン
lub-dup
ドクン
lub-dup

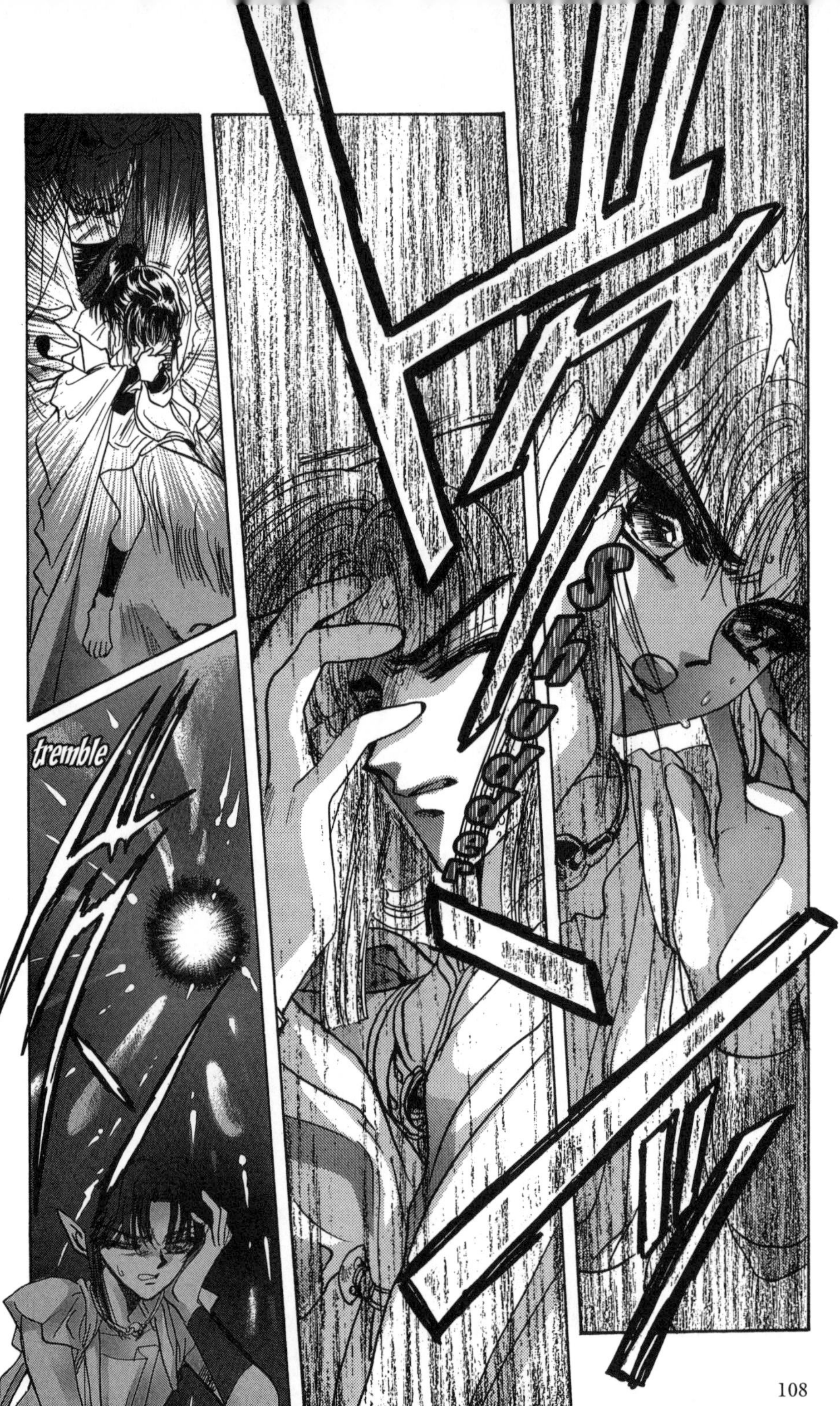
shudder
tremble

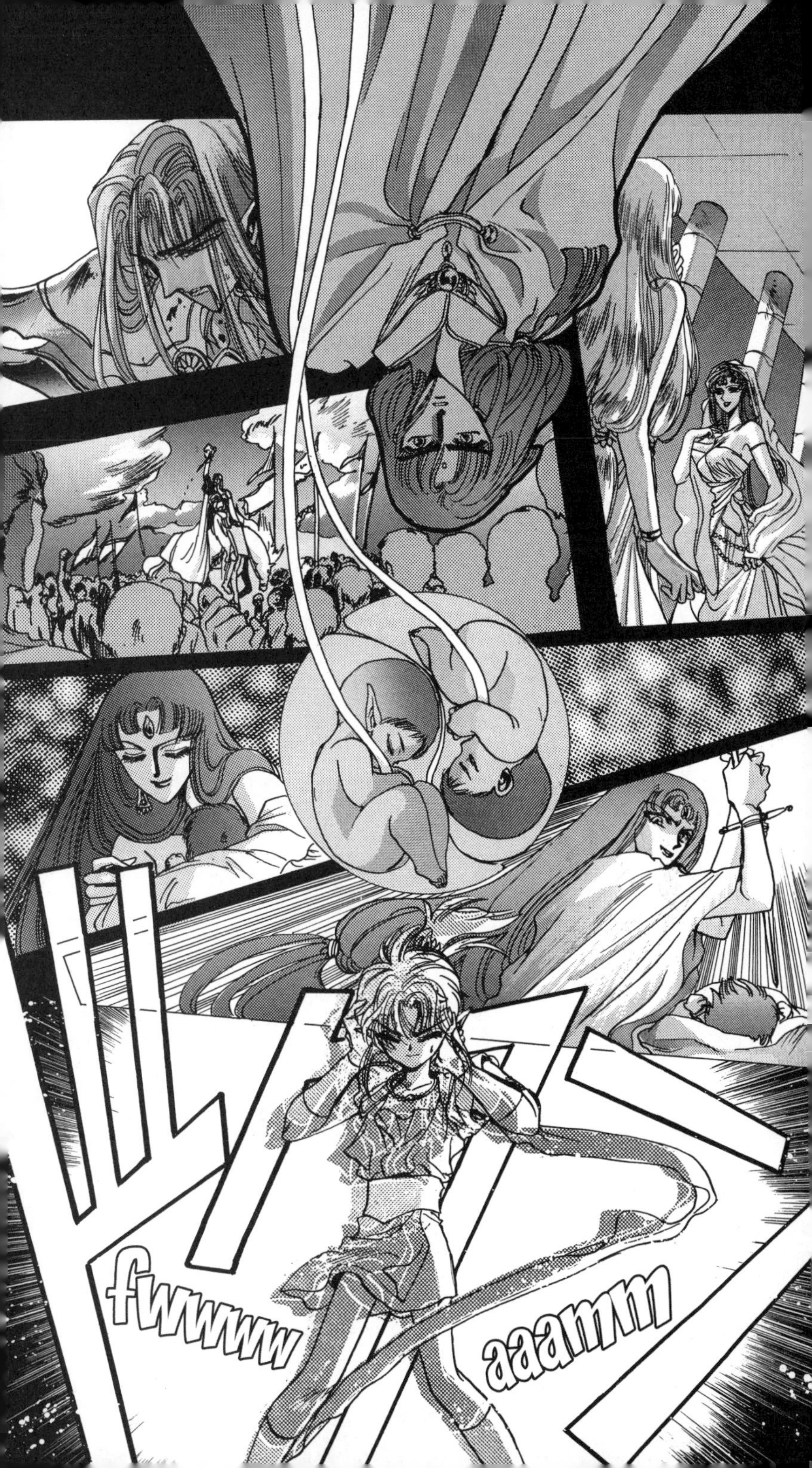
fwwwww
aaamm

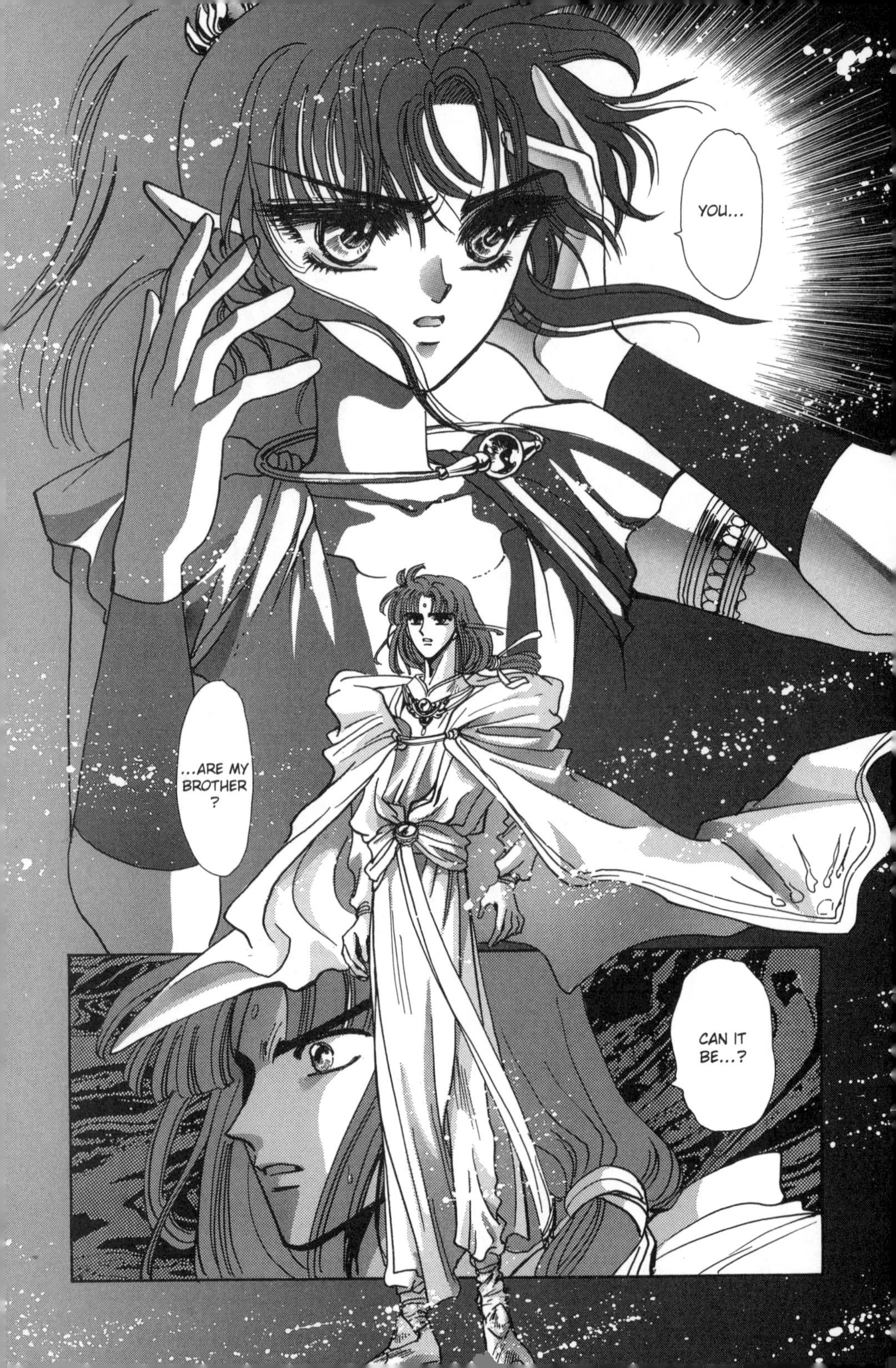
YOU...
...ARE MY BROTHER?
CAN IT BE...?

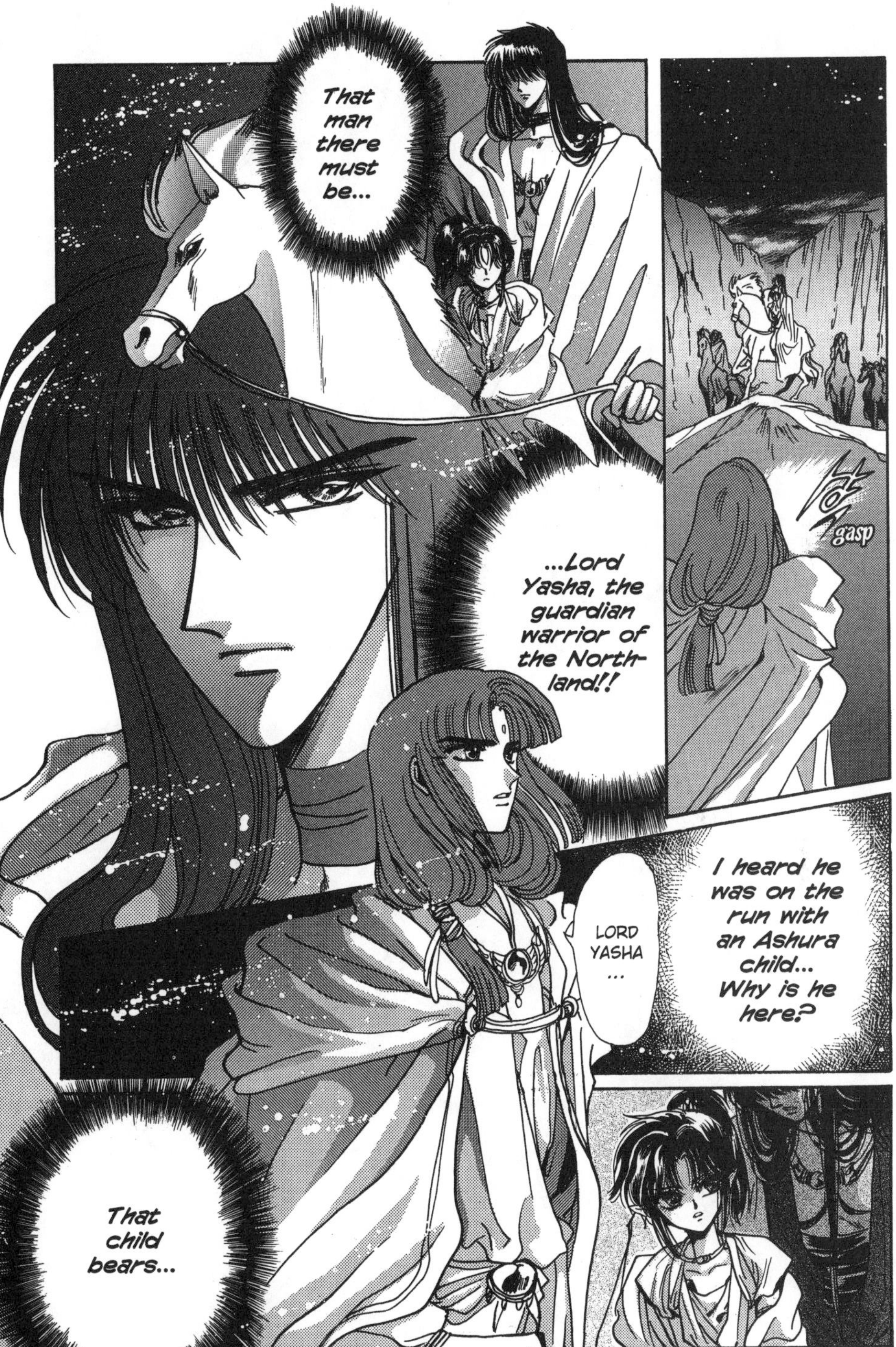
gasp
I heard he was on the run with an Ashura child... Why is he here?
LORD YASHA ...
That man there must be...
...Lord Yasha, the guardian warrior of the North-land!!
That child bears...

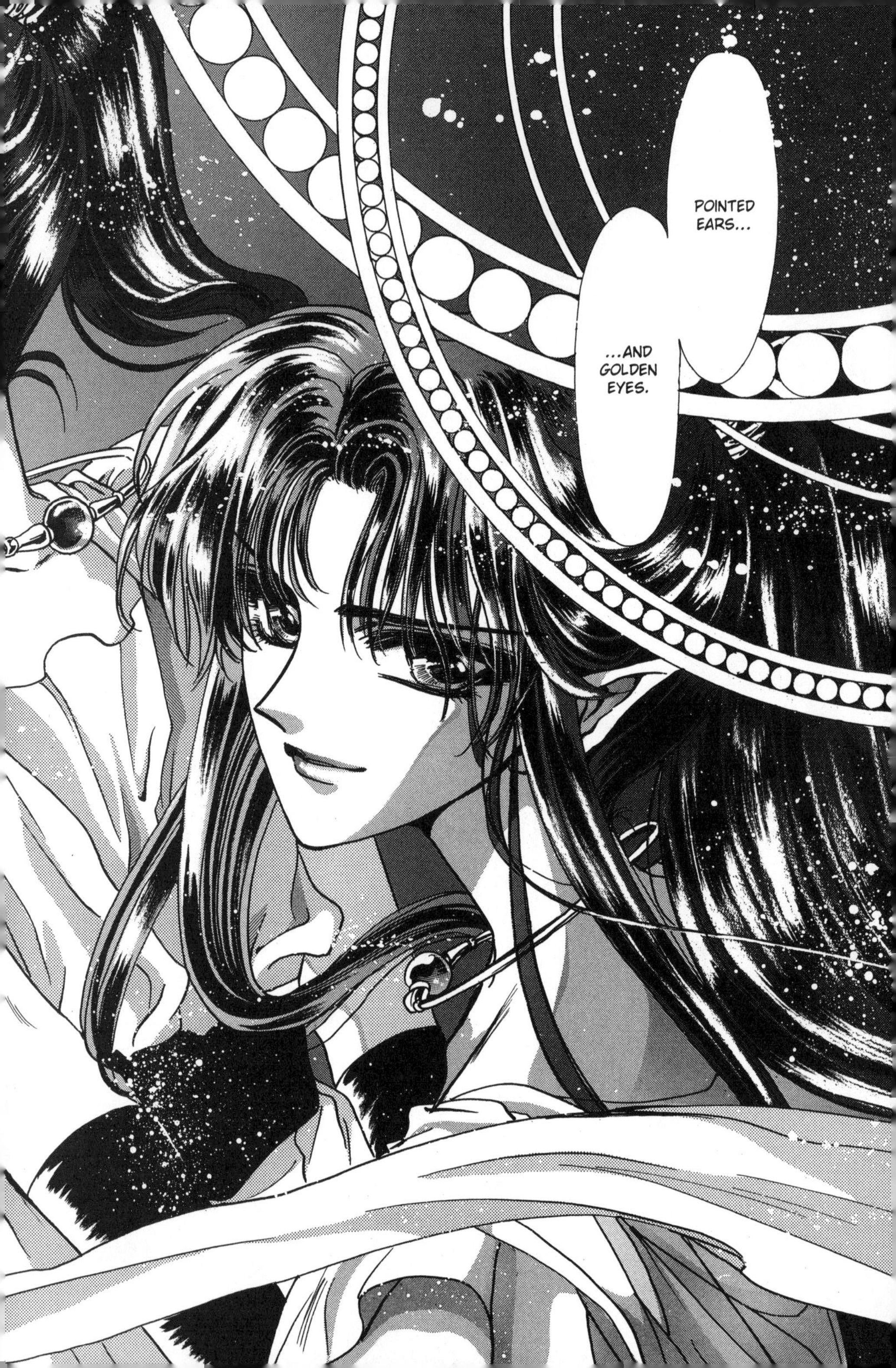
POINTED EARS...
...AND GOLDEN EYES.

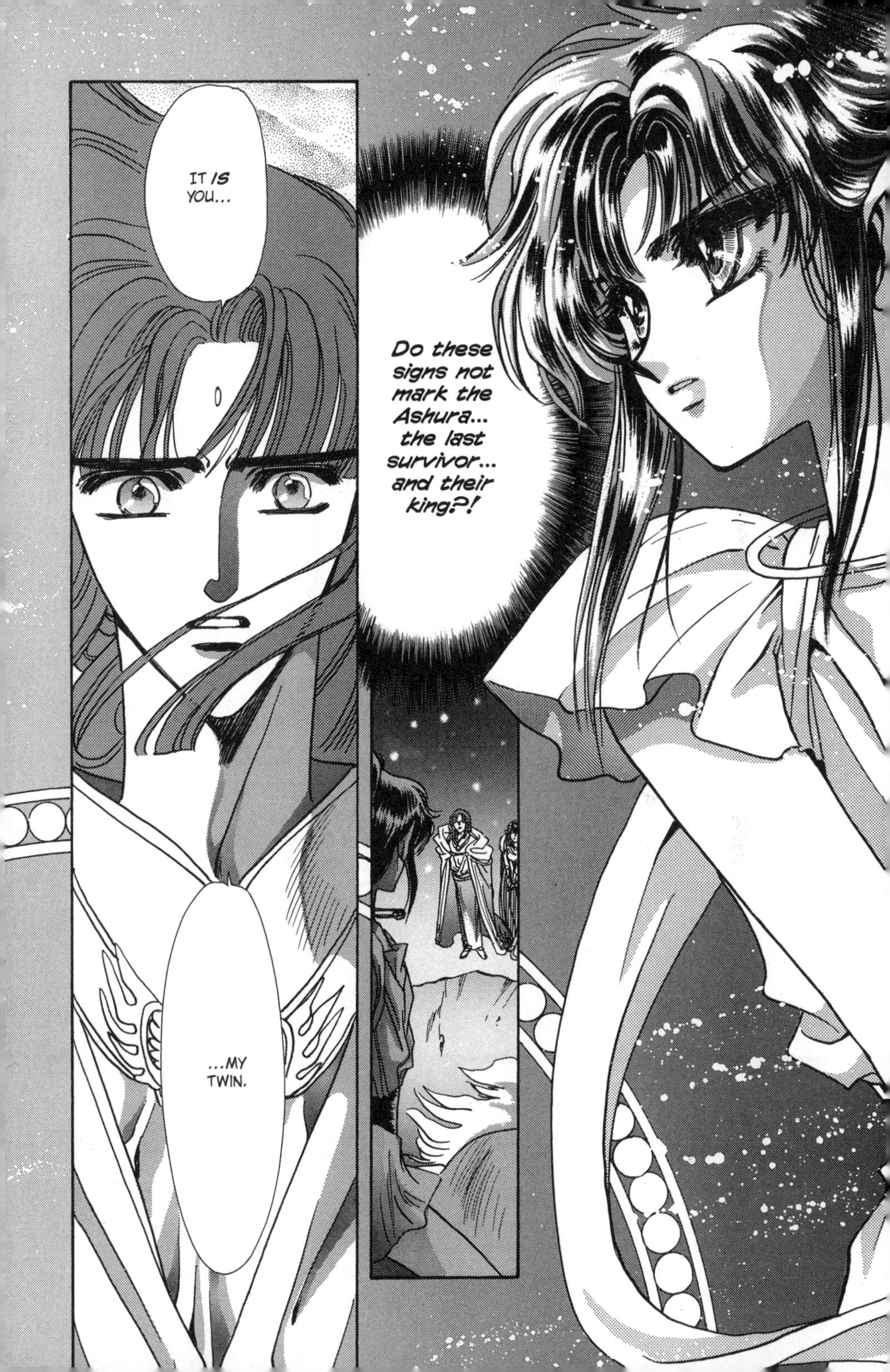
Do these signs not mark the Ashura... the last survivor... and their king?!
IT IS YOU...
...MY TWIN.

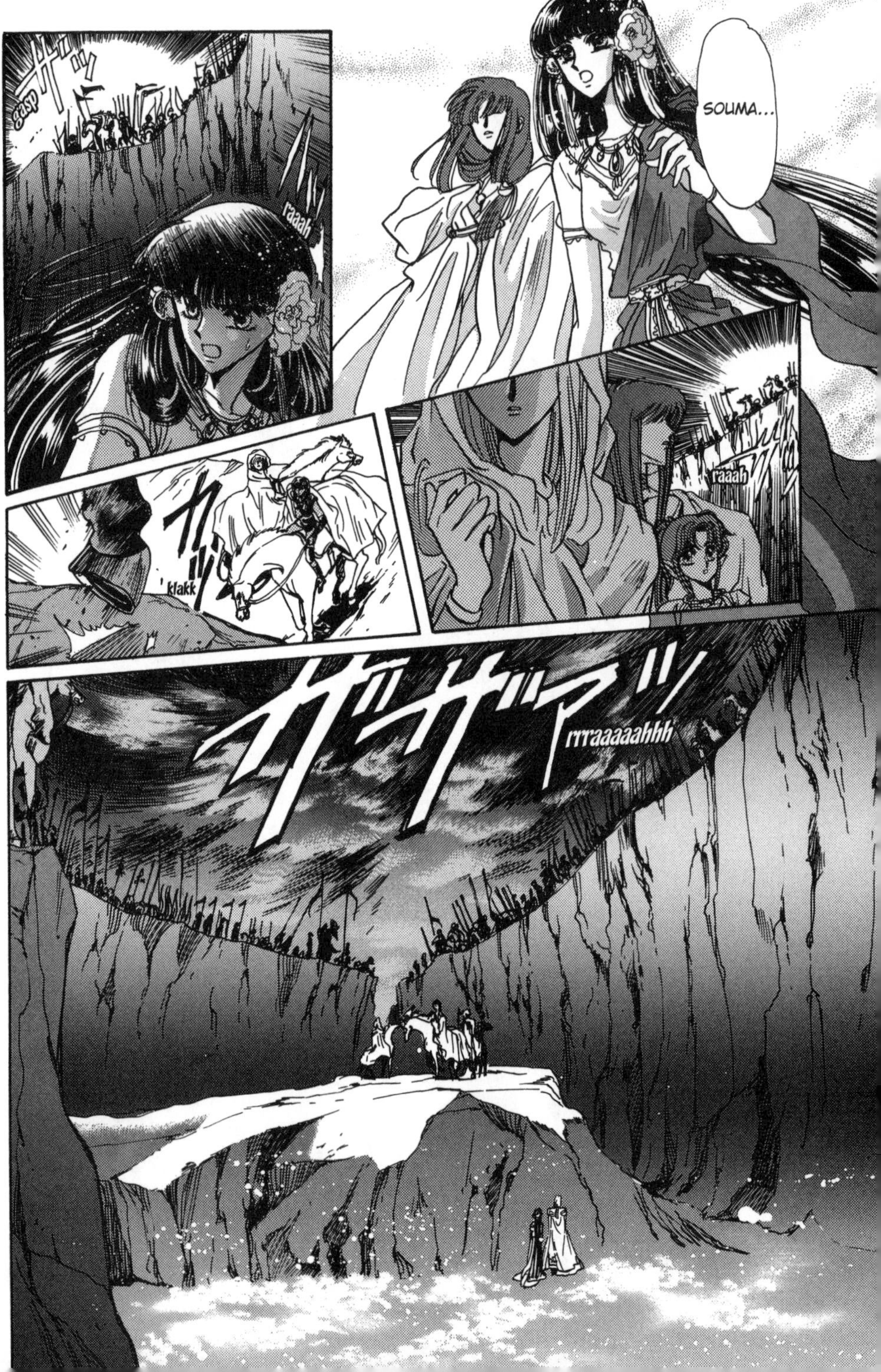
SOUMA...
gasp
raaah
raaah
klakk
rrraaaaahhh

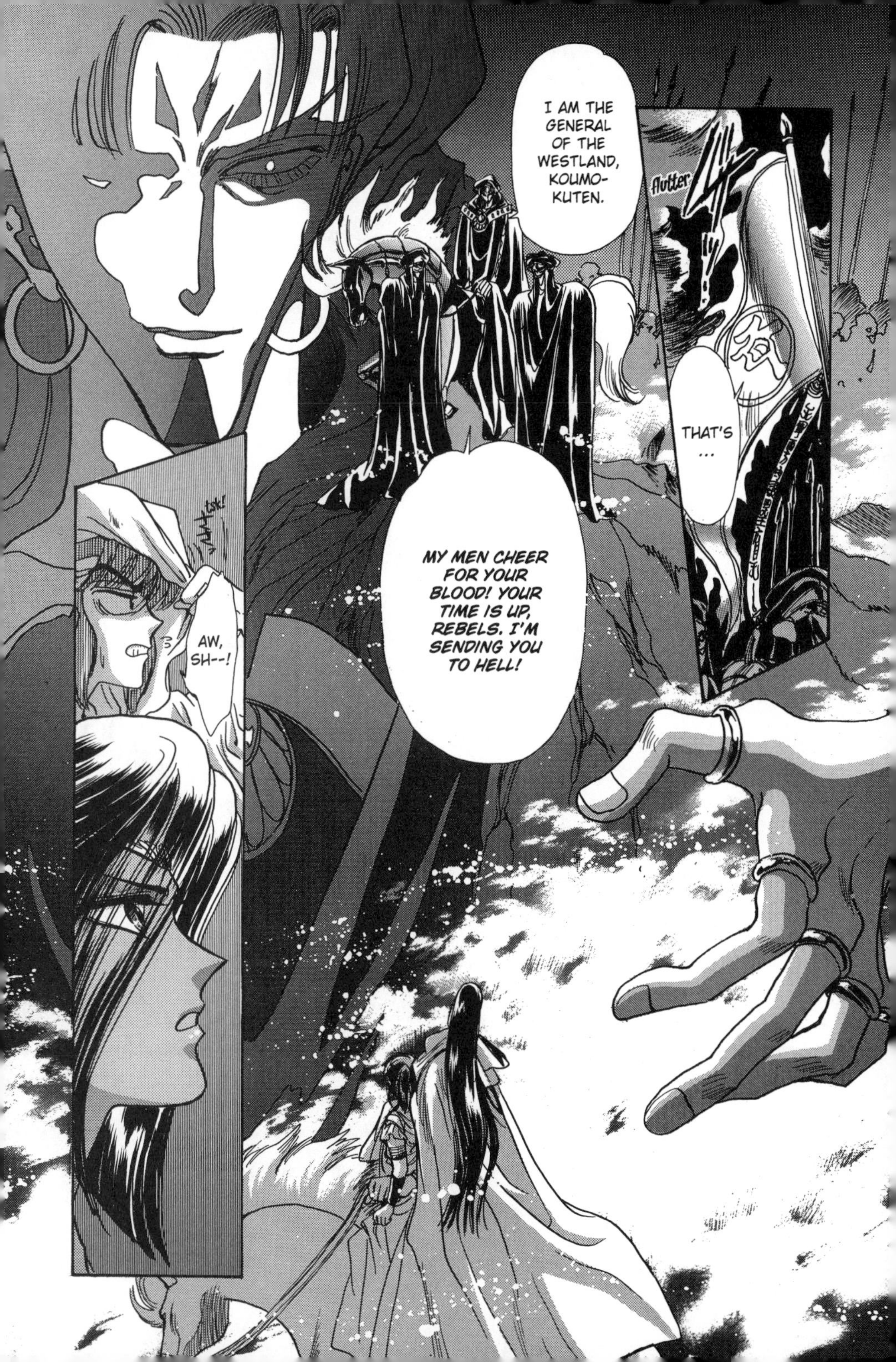
I AM THE GENERAL OF THE WESTLAND, KOUMOKUTEN.
flutter
THAT'S ...
MY MEN CHEER FOR YOUR BLOOD! YOUR TIME IS UP, REBELS. I'M SENDING YOU TO HELL!
tsk!
AW, SH--!

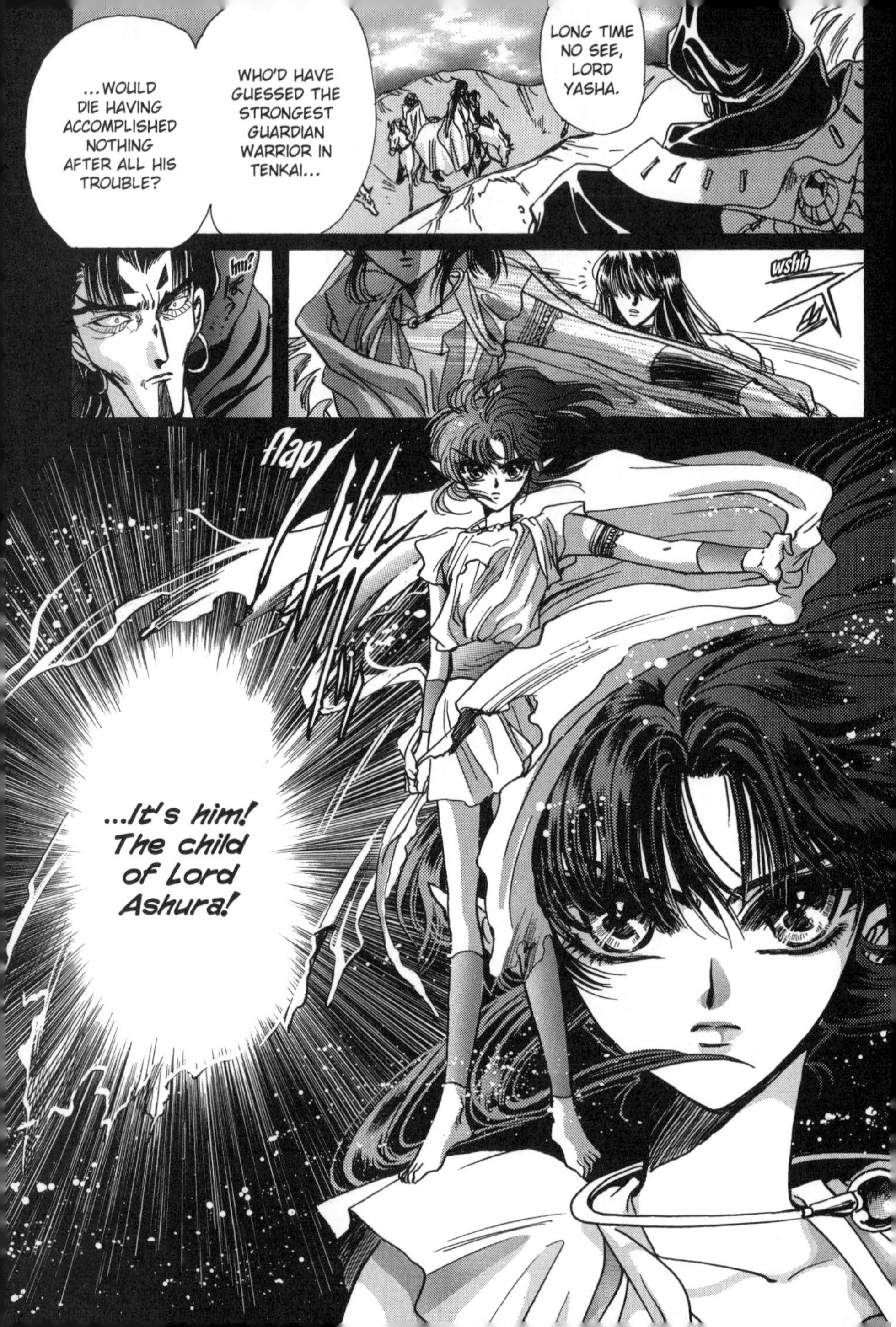
LONG TIME NO SEE, LORD YASHA.
WHO'D HAVE GUESSED THE STRONGEST GUARDIAN WARRIOR IN TENKAI...
...WOULD DIE HAVING ACCOMPLISHED NOTHING AFTER ALL HIS TROUBLE?
wshh
hm?
flap
...It's him! The child of Lord Ashura!

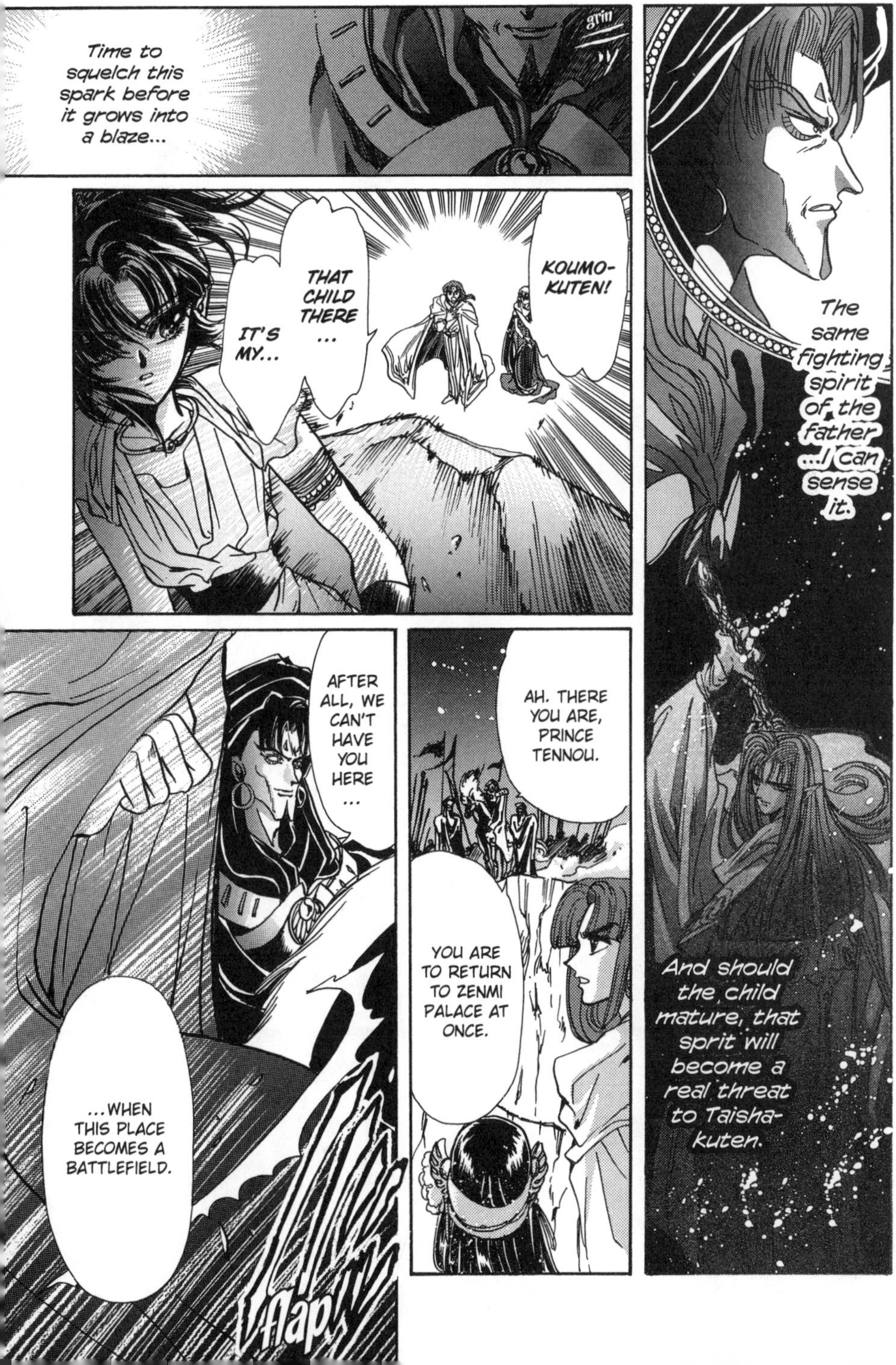
The same fighting spirit of the father ...I can sense it.
And should the child mature, that sprit will become a real threat to Taisha-kuten.
grin
Time to squelch this spark before it grows into a blaze...
KOUMO-KUTEN!
THAT CHILD THERE ...
IT'S MY...
AH. THERE YOU ARE, PRINCE TENNOU.
YOU ARE TO RETURN TO ZENMI PALACE AT ONCE.
AFTER ALL, WE CAN'T HAVE YOU HERE ...
...WHEN THIS PLACE BECOMES A BATTLEFIELD.
flap!

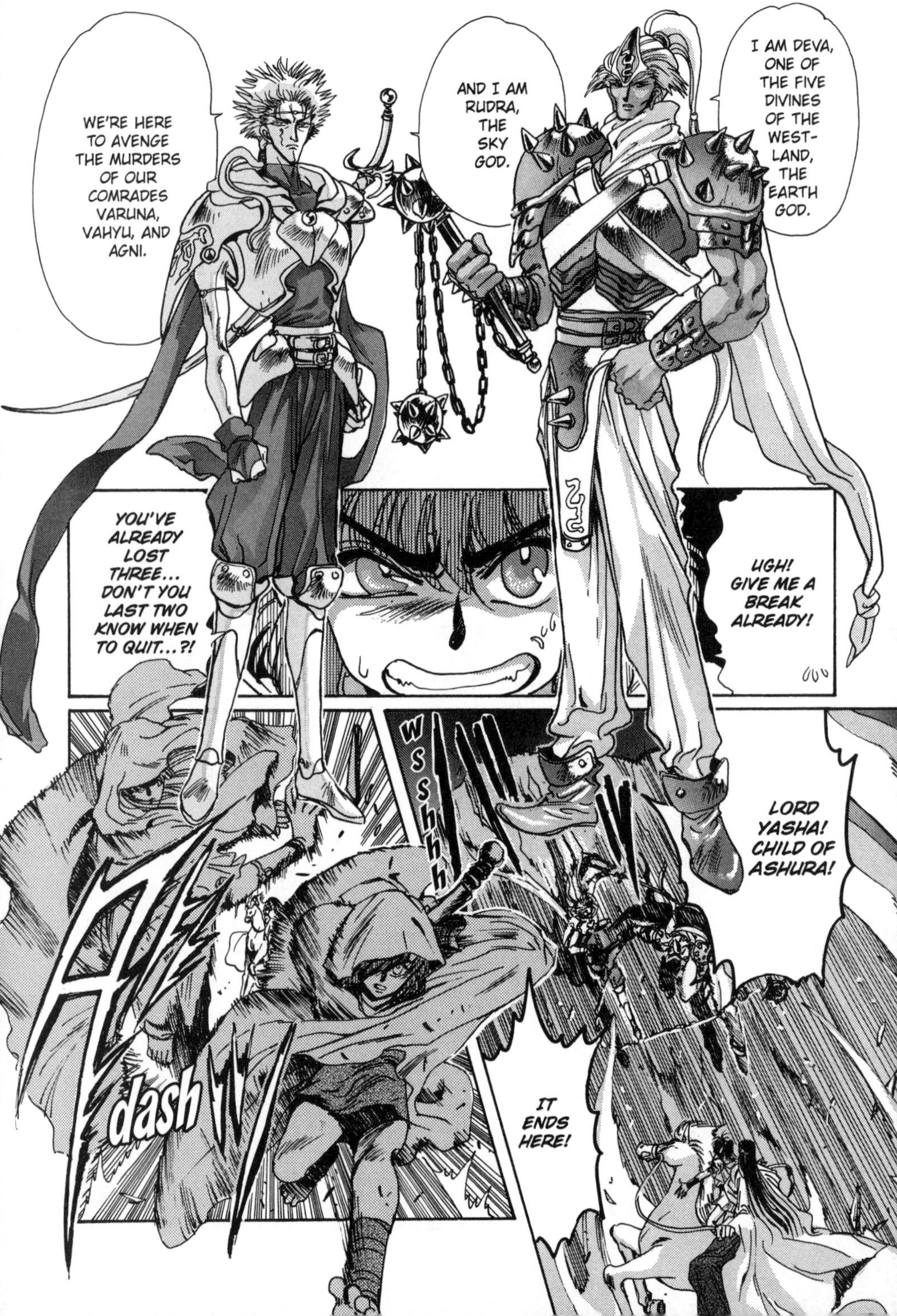
I AM DEVA, ONE OF THE FIVE DIVINES OF THE WEST-LAND, THE EARTH GOD.
AND I AM RUDRA, THE SKY GOD.
WE'RE HERE TO AVENGE THE MURDERS OF OUR COMRADES VARUNA, VAHYU, AND AGNI.
YOU'VE ALREADY LOST THREE... DON'T YOU LAST TWO KNOW WHEN TO QUIT...?!
UGH! GIVE ME A BREAK ALREADY!
LORD YASHA! CHILD OF ASHURA!
IT ENDS HERE!
WSShhh
dash

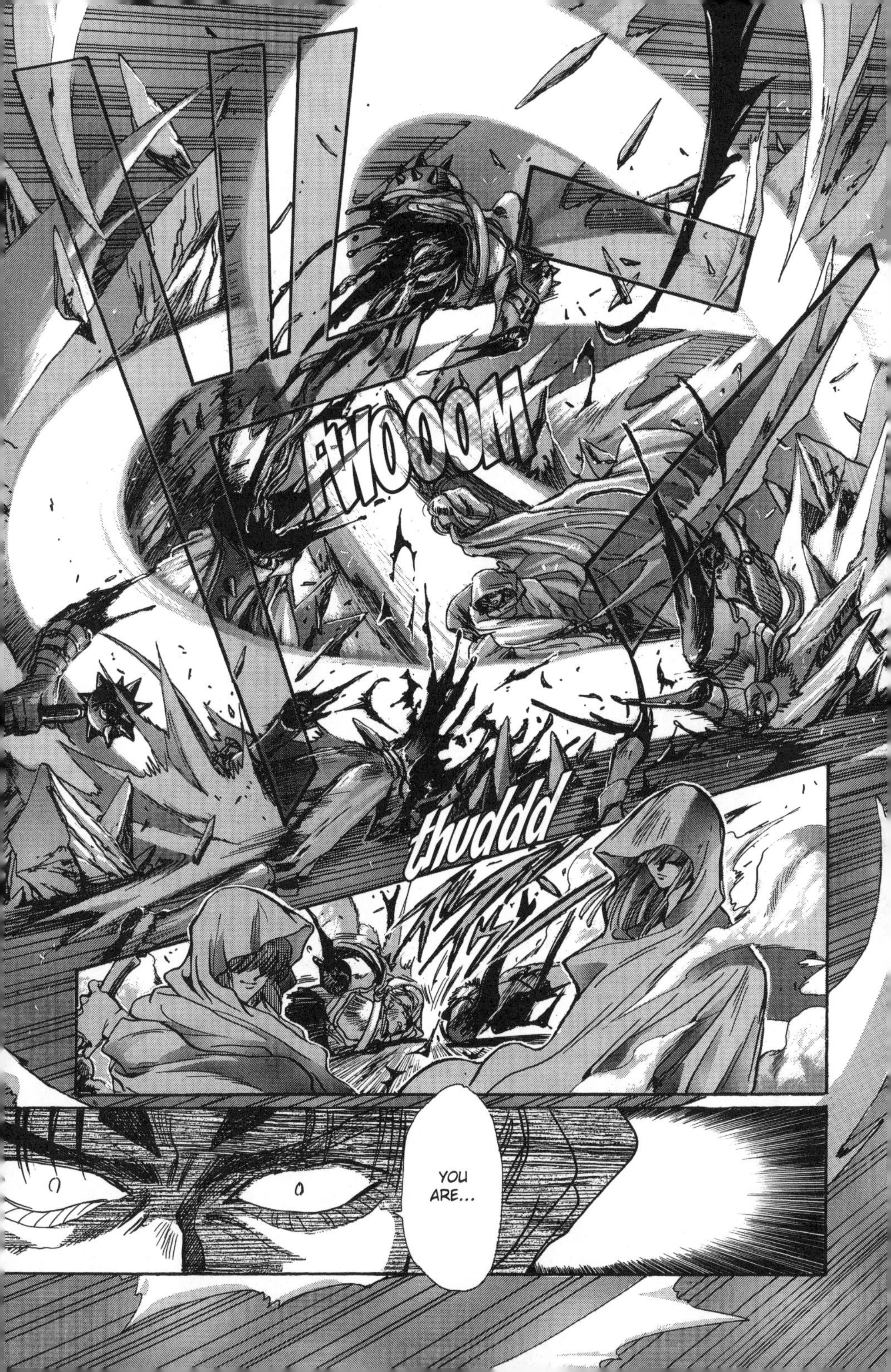
FWOOOM
thuddd
YOU ARE...

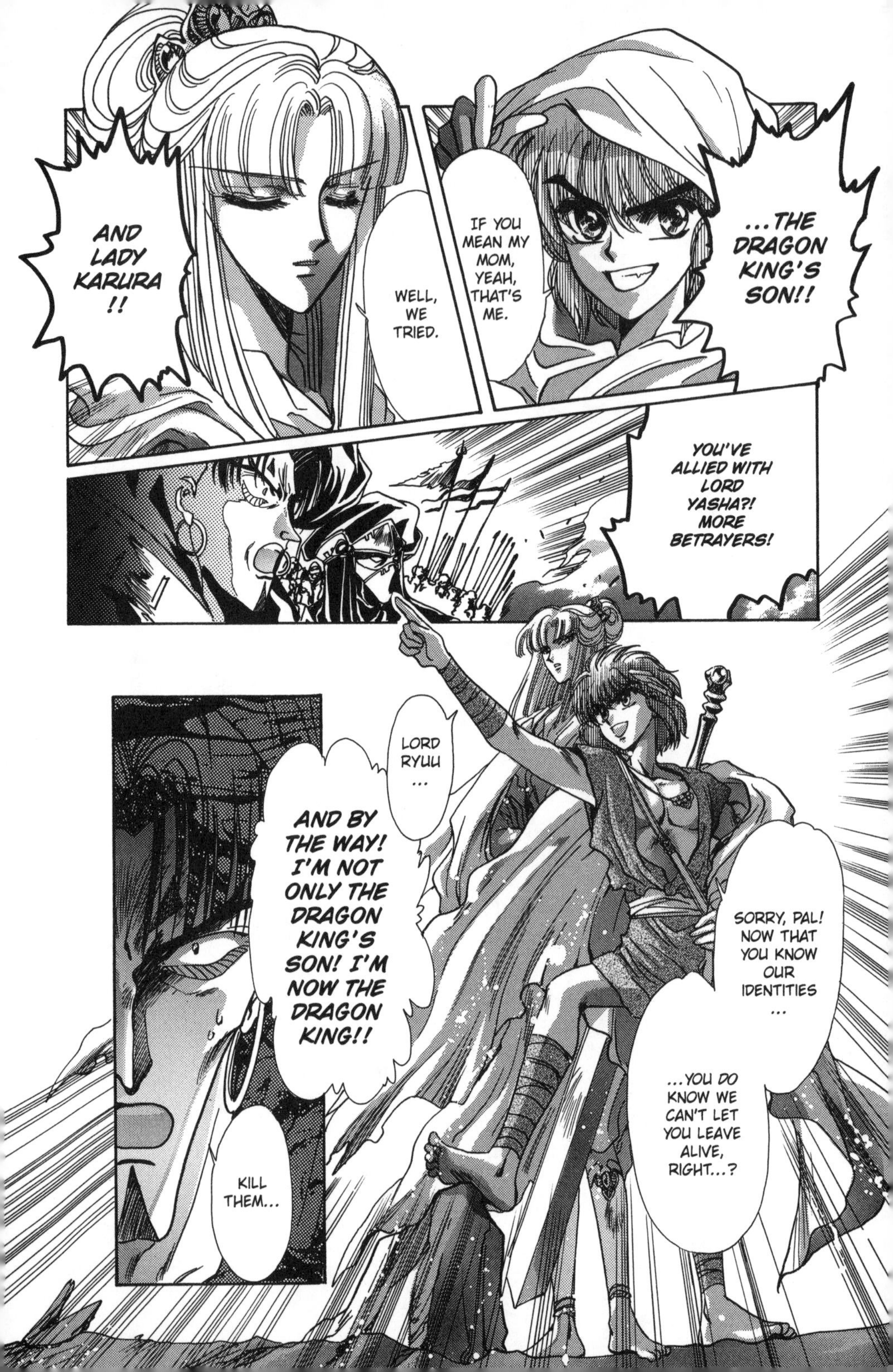
...THE DRAGON KING'S SON!!
IF YOU MEAN MY MOM, YEAH, THAT'S ME.
WELL, WE TRIED.
AND LADY KARURA!!
YOU'VE ALLIED WITH LORD YASHA?! MORE BETRAYERS!
LORD RYUU...
AND BY THE WAY! I'M NOT ONLY THE DRAGON KING'S SON! I'M NOW THE DRAGON KING!!
SORRY, PAL! NOW THAT YOU KNOW OUR IDENTITIES...
...YOU DO KNOW WE CAN'T LET YOU LEAVE ALIVE, RIGHT...?
KILL THEM...

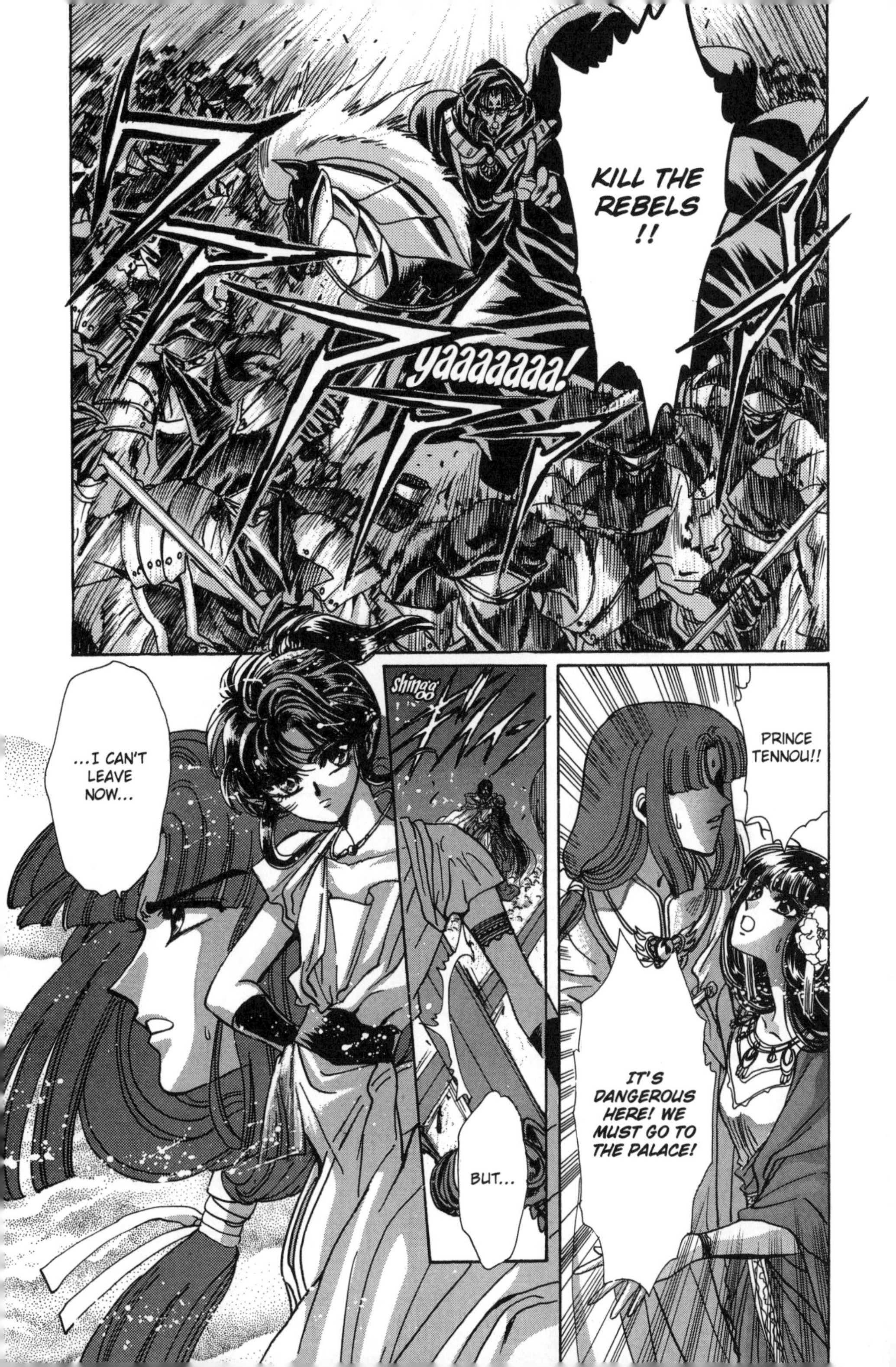
KILL THE REBELS !!
yaaaaaaa!
PRINCE TENNOU!!
IT'S DANGEROUS HERE! WE MUST GO TO THE PALACE!
BUT...
...I CAN'T LEAVE NOW...

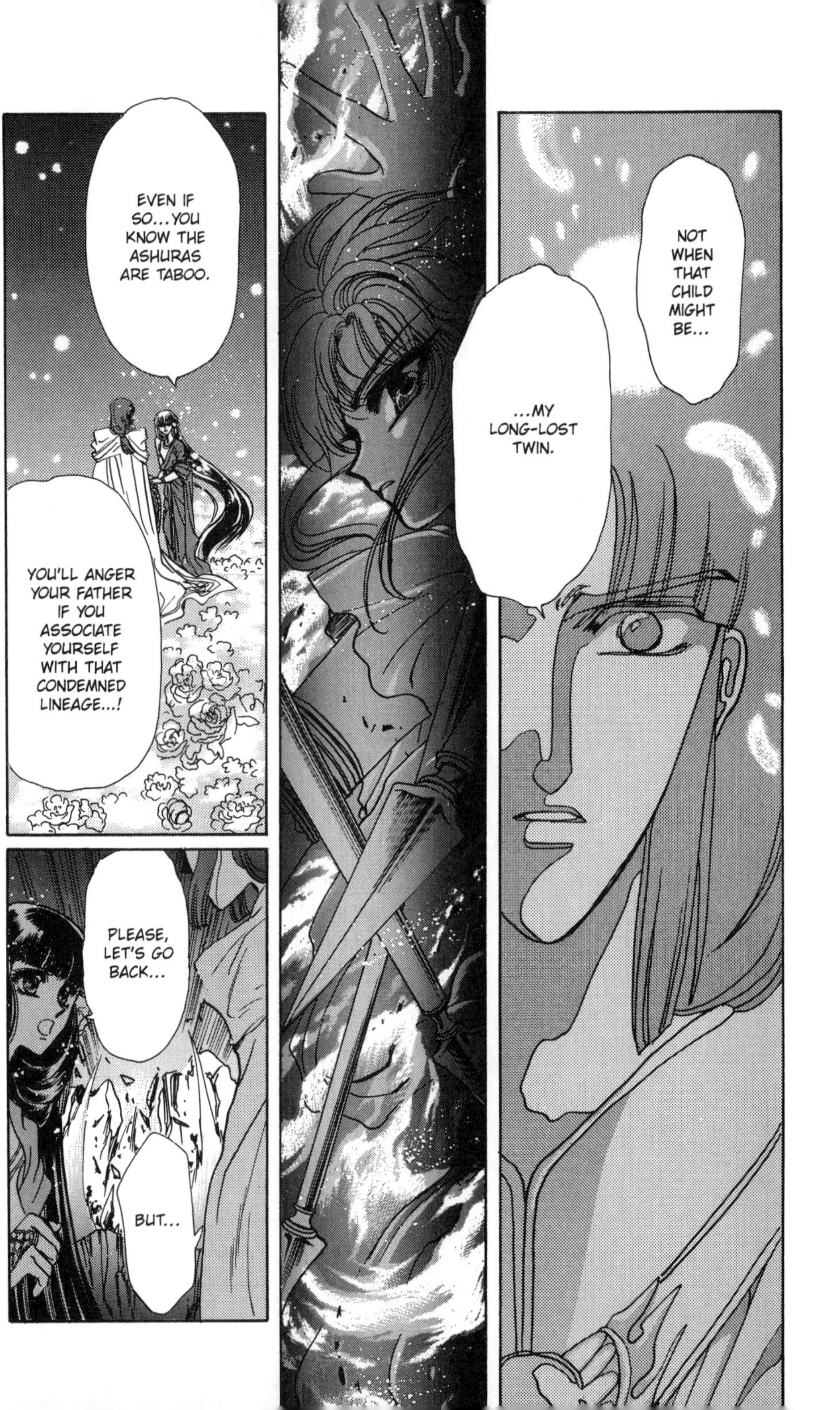
NOT WHEN THAT CHILD MIGHT BE...
...MY LONG-LOST TWIN.
EVEN IF SO...YOU KNOW THE ASHURAS ARE TABOO.
YOU'LL ANGER YOUR FATHER IF YOU ASSOCIATE YOURSELF WITH THAT CONDEMNED LINEAGE...!
PLEASE, LET'S GO BACK...
BUT...

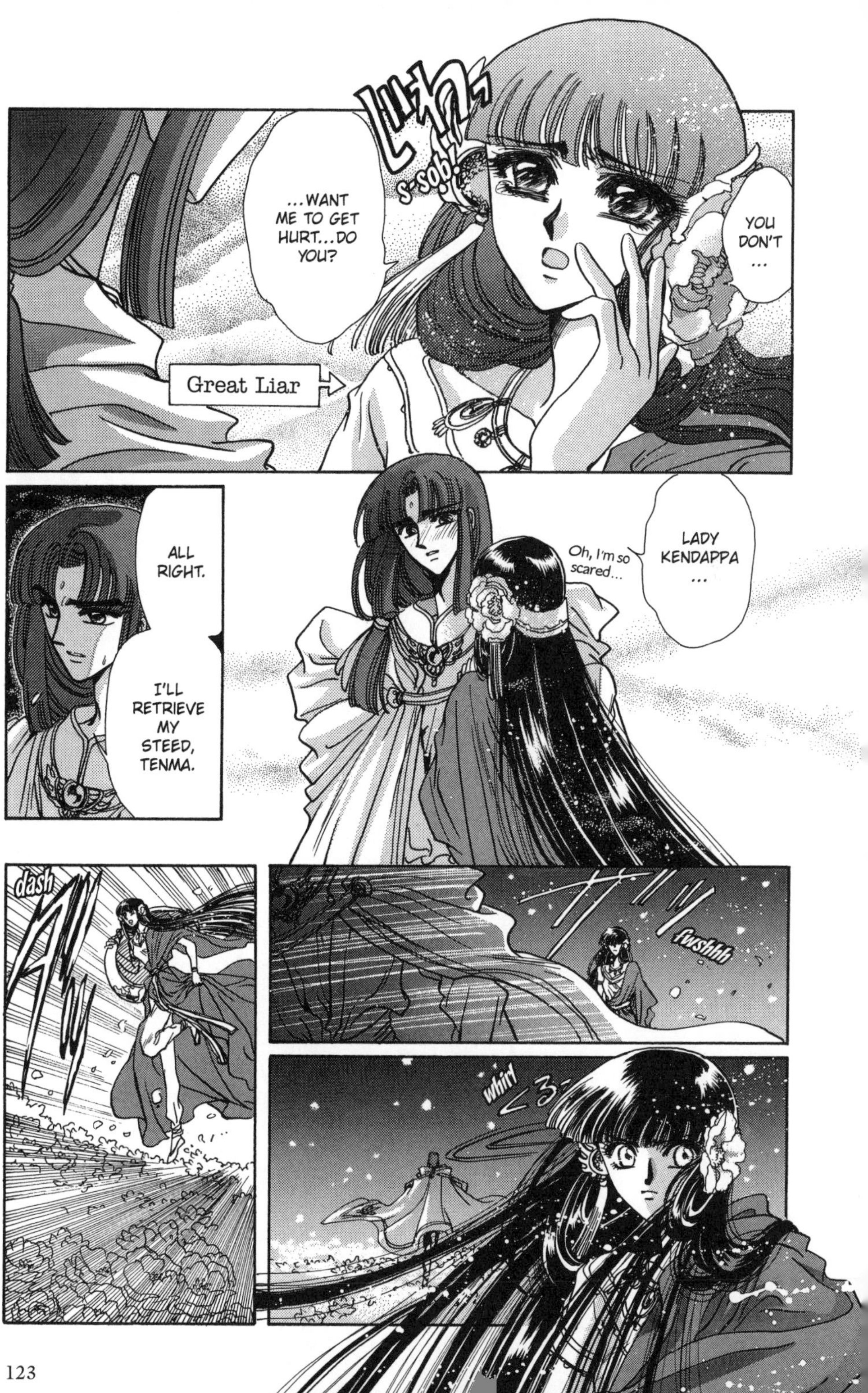
YOU DON'T ...
S-SOB!
...WANT ME TO GET HURT...DO YOU?
Great Liar
LADY KENDAPPA ...
Oh, I'm so scared...
ALL RIGHT.
I'LL RETRIEVE MY STEED, TENMA.
fwshhh
whirl
dash

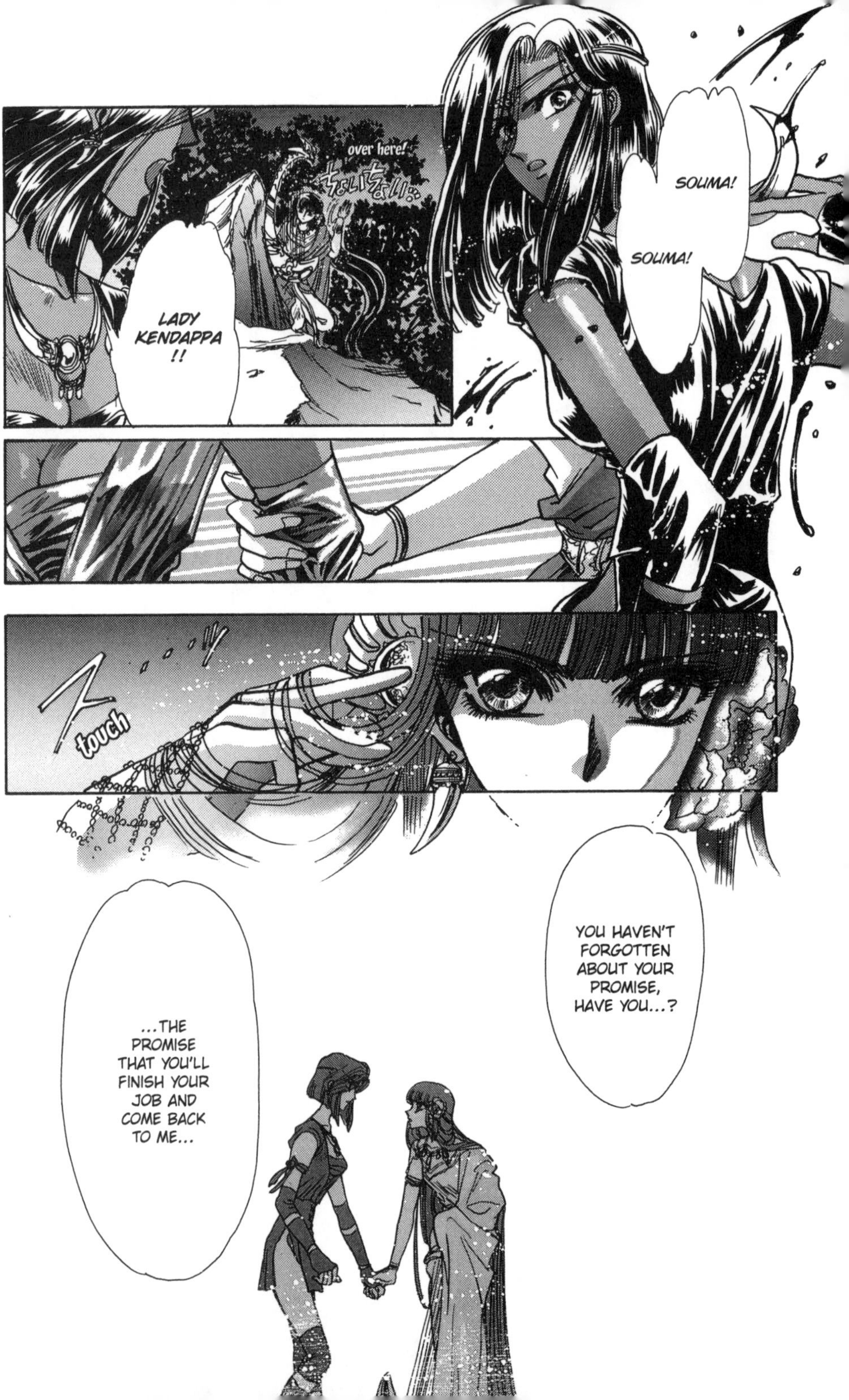
SOUMA!
SOUMA!
over here!
ちょいちょい
LADY KENDAPPA !!
touch
YOU HAVEN'T FORGOTTEN ABOUT YOUR PROMISE, HAVE YOU...?
...THE PROMISE THAT YOU'LL FINISH YOUR JOB AND COME BACK TO ME...

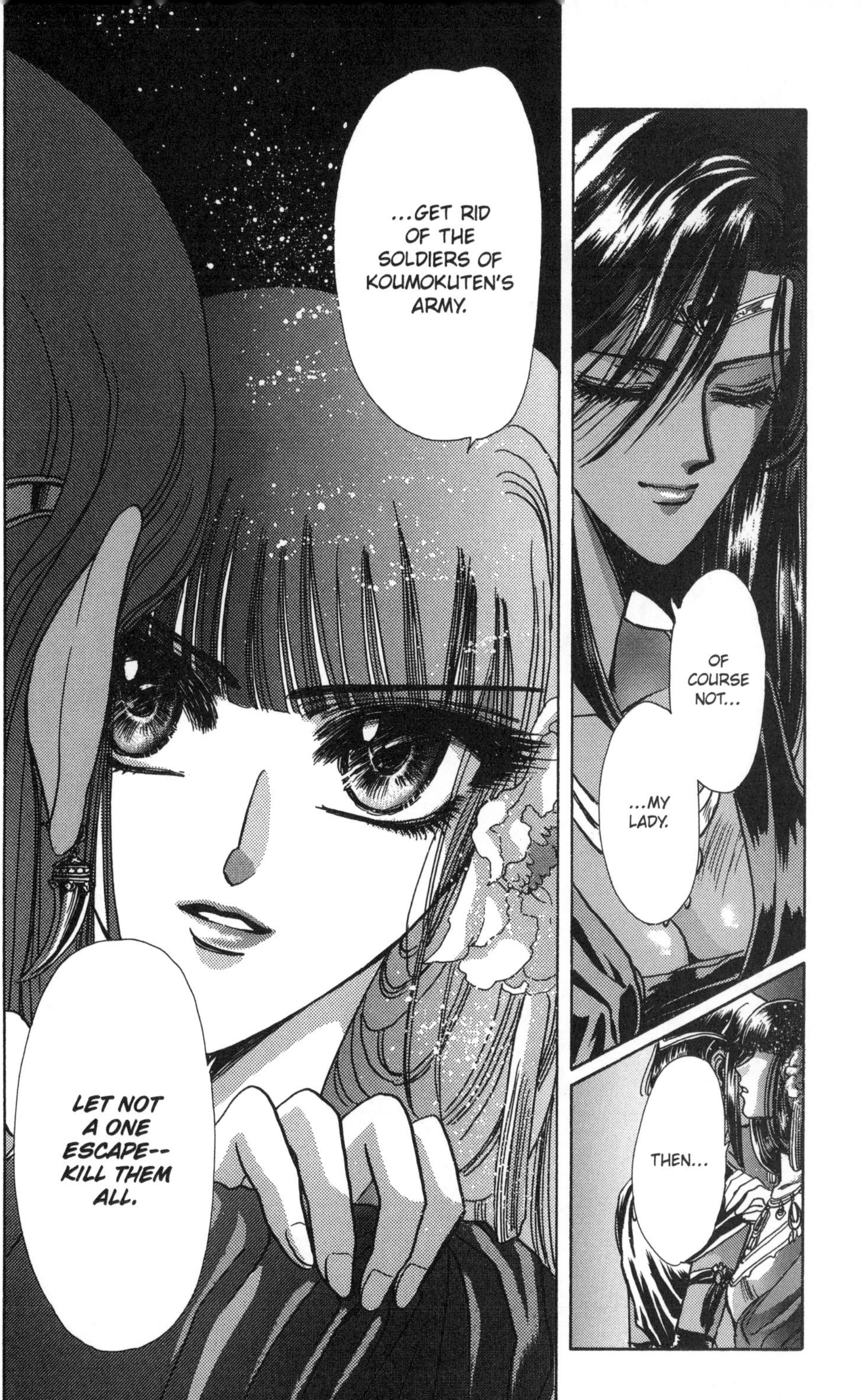
OF COURSE NOT...
...MY LADY.
THEN...
...GET RID OF THE SOLDIERS OF KOUMOKUTEN'S ARMY.
LET NOT A ONE ESCAPE-- KILL THEM ALL.

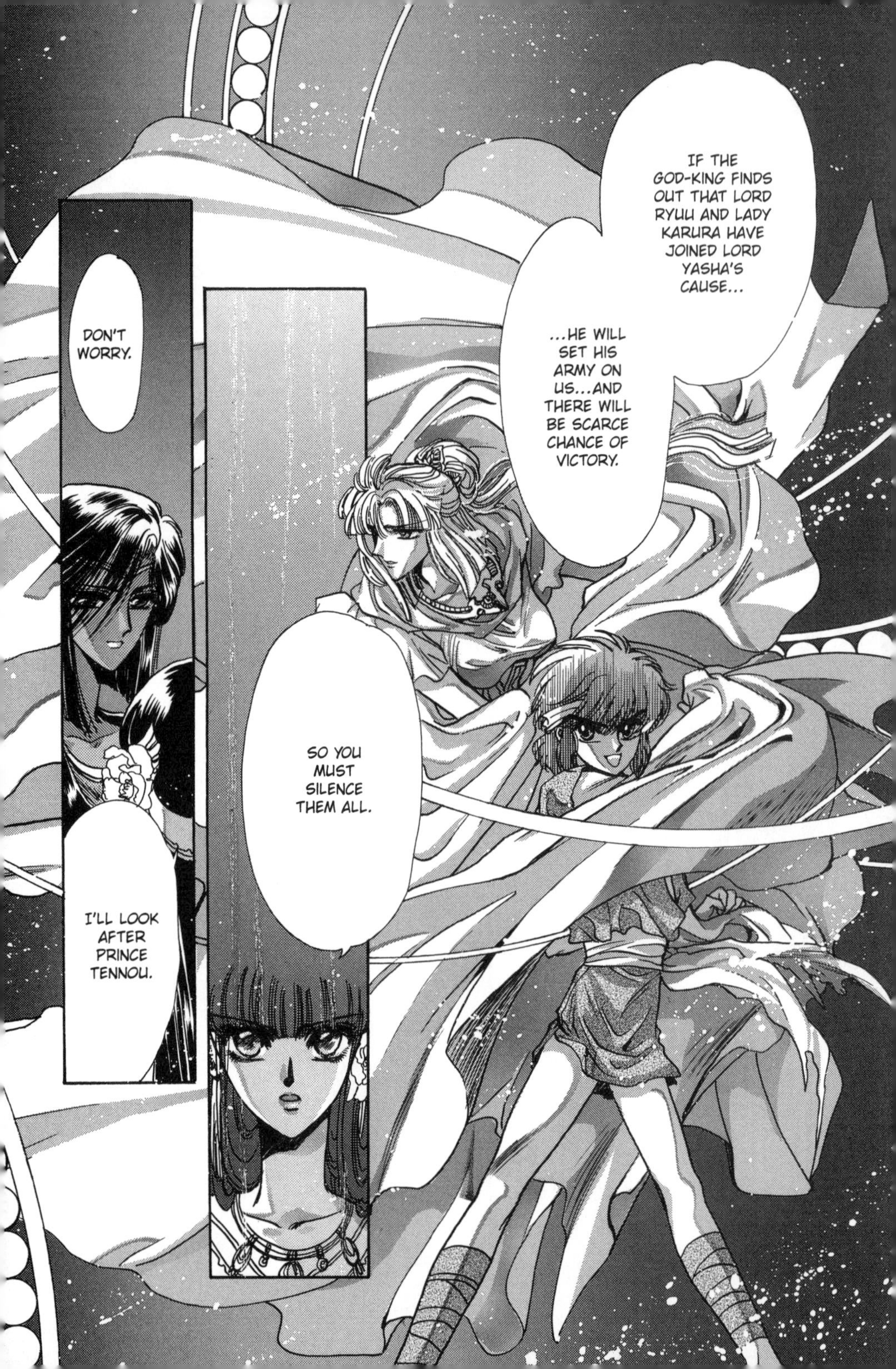
IF THE GOD-KING FINDS OUT THAT LORD RYUU AND LADY KARURA HAVE JOINED LORD YASHA'S CAUSE...
...HE WILL SET HIS ARMY ON US...AND THERE WILL BE SCARCE CHANCE OF VICTORY.
SO YOU MUST SILENCE THEM ALL.
DON'T WORRY.
I'LL LOOK AFTER PRINCE TENNOU.

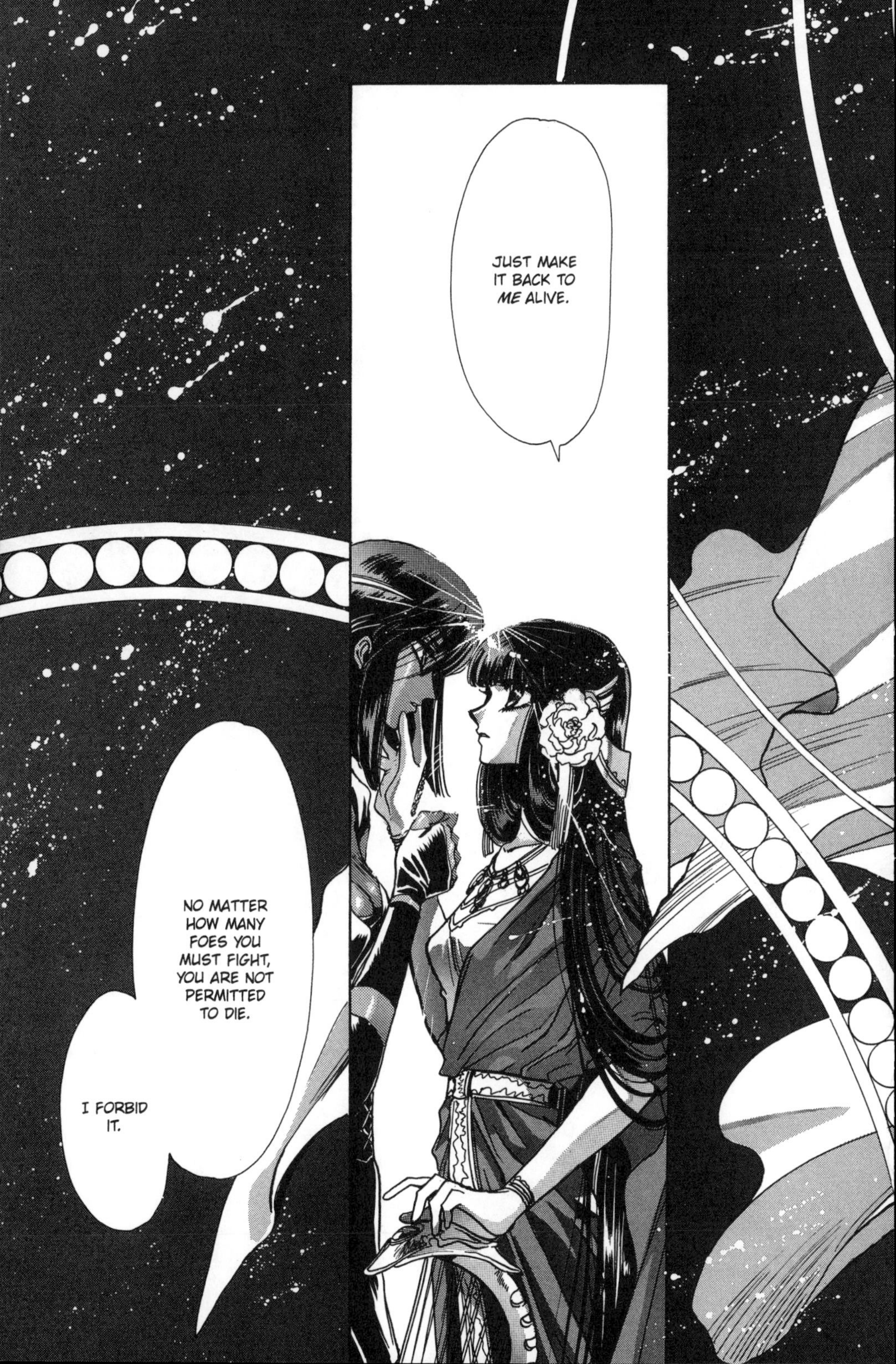

JUST MAKE IT BACK TO *ME* ALIVE.
NO MATTER HOW MANY FOES YOU MUST FIGHT, YOU ARE NOT PERMITTED TO DIE.
I FORBID IT.

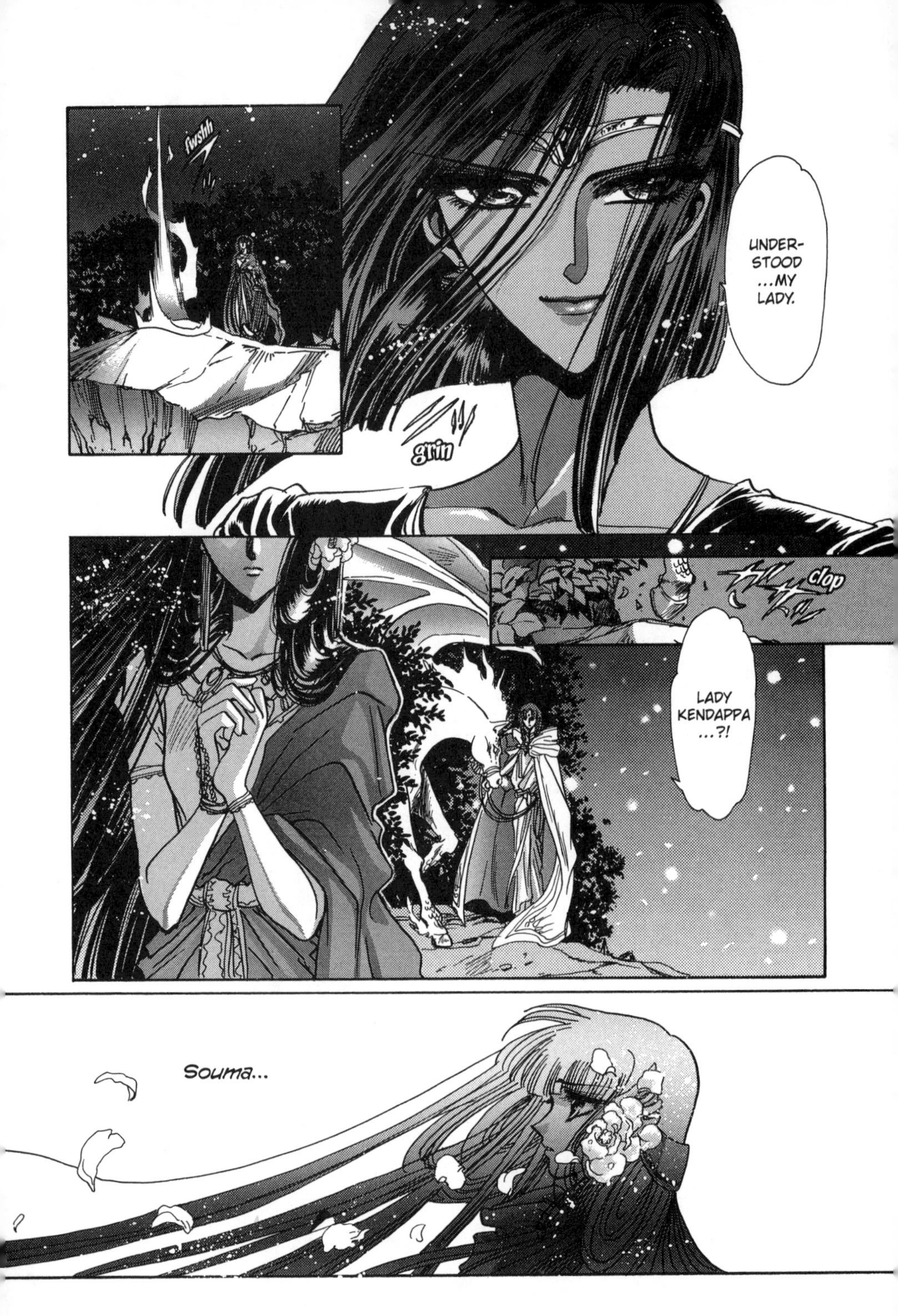
UNDER-STOOD ...MY LADY.
grin
fwshh
clop
LADY KENDAPPA ...?!
Souma...

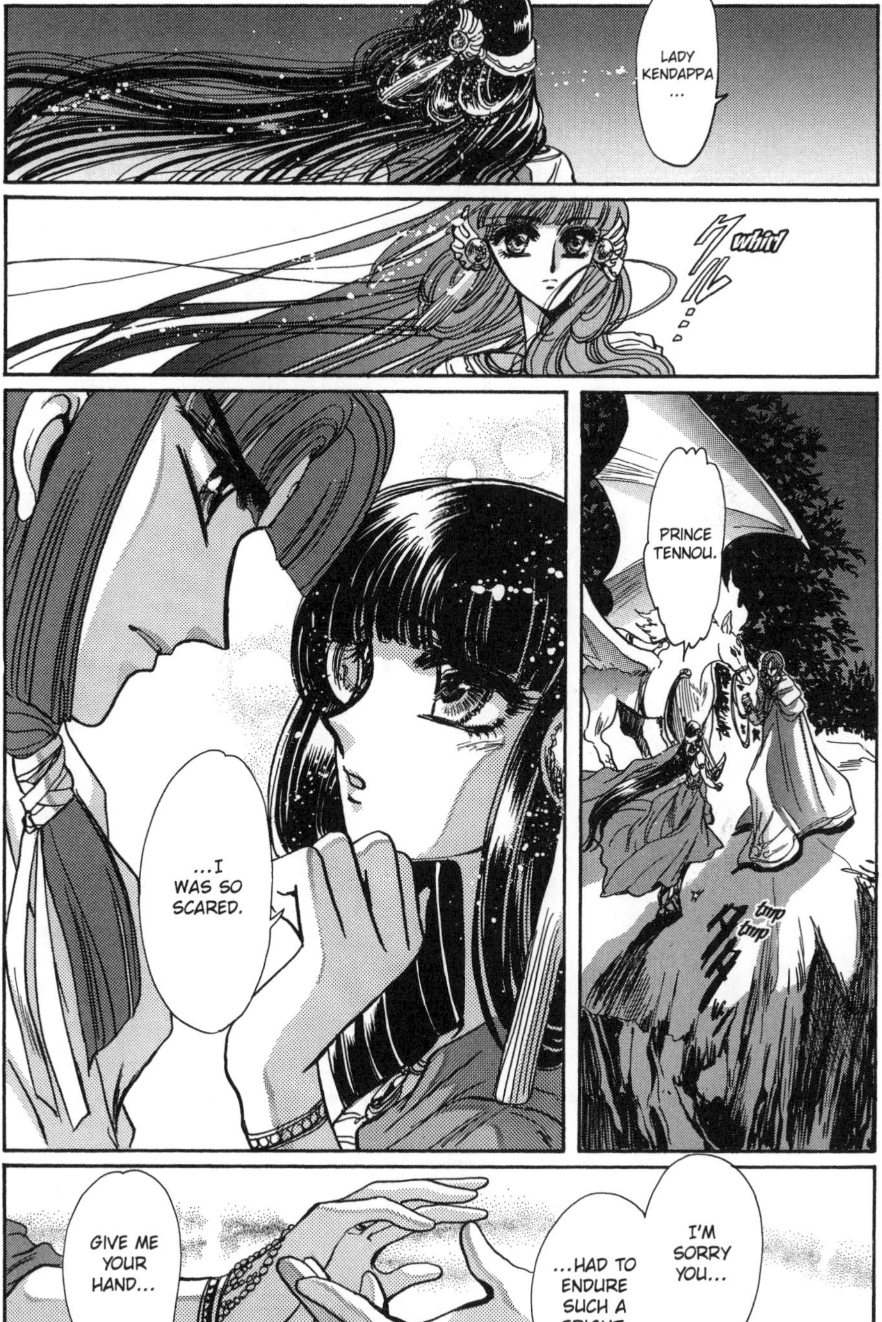
LADY KENDAPPA ...
whirl
PRINCE TENNOU.
tmp tmp
...I WAS SO SCARED.
I'M SORRY YOU...
...HAD TO ENDURE SUCH A FRIGHT.
GIVE ME YOUR HAND...

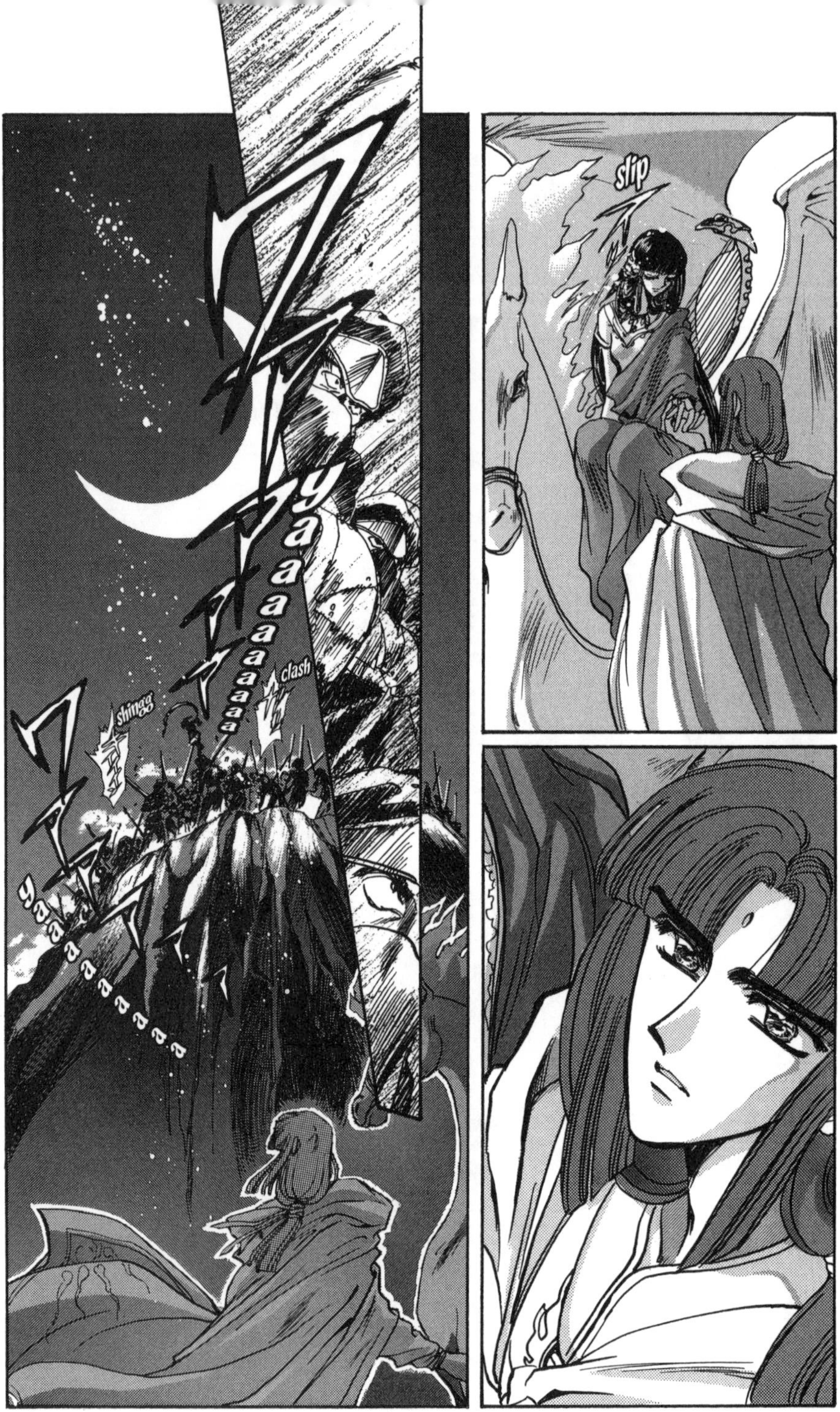
slip
yaaaaaaaaaa
clash
shinggg
yaaaaaaaaaaa

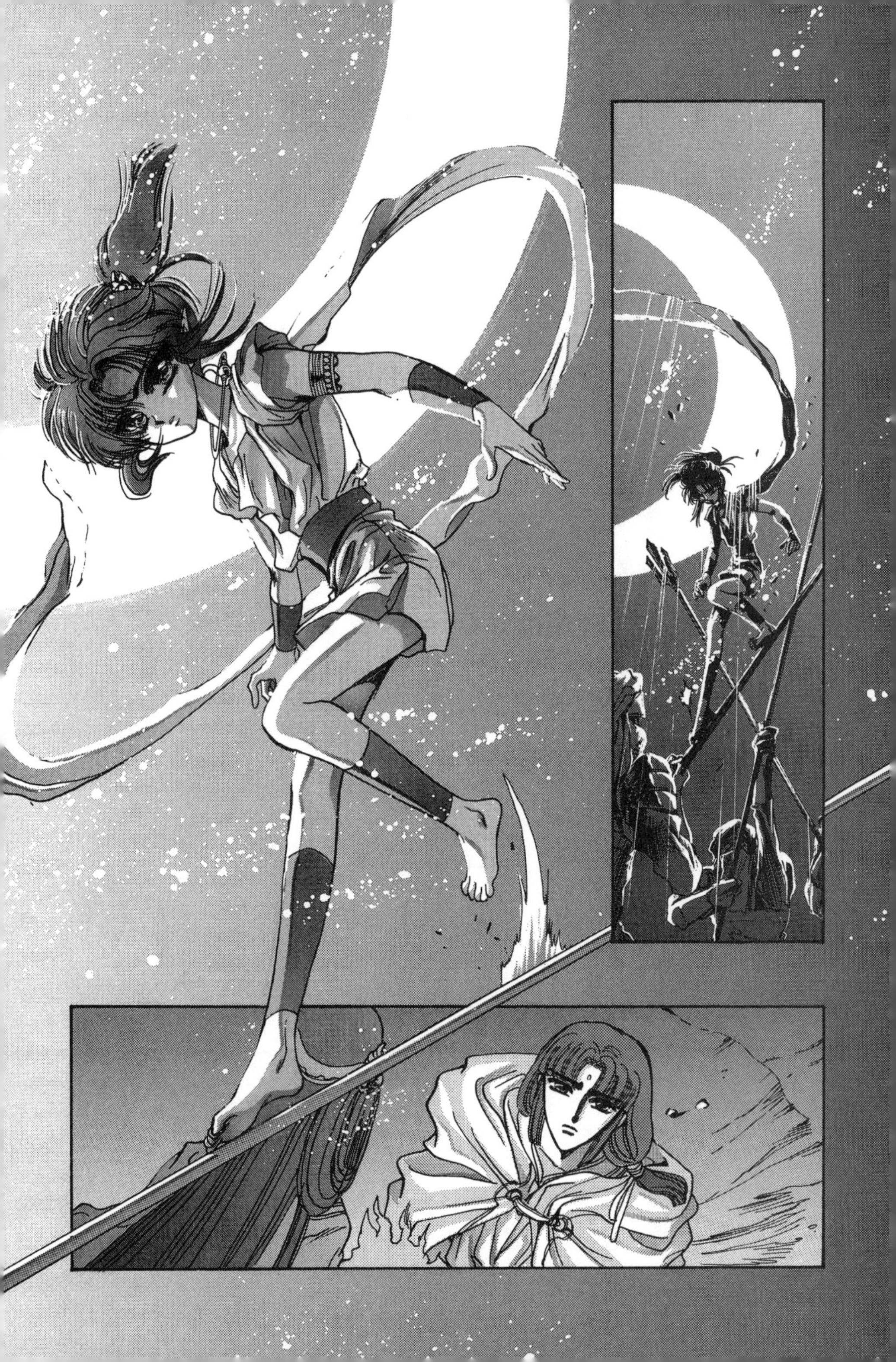

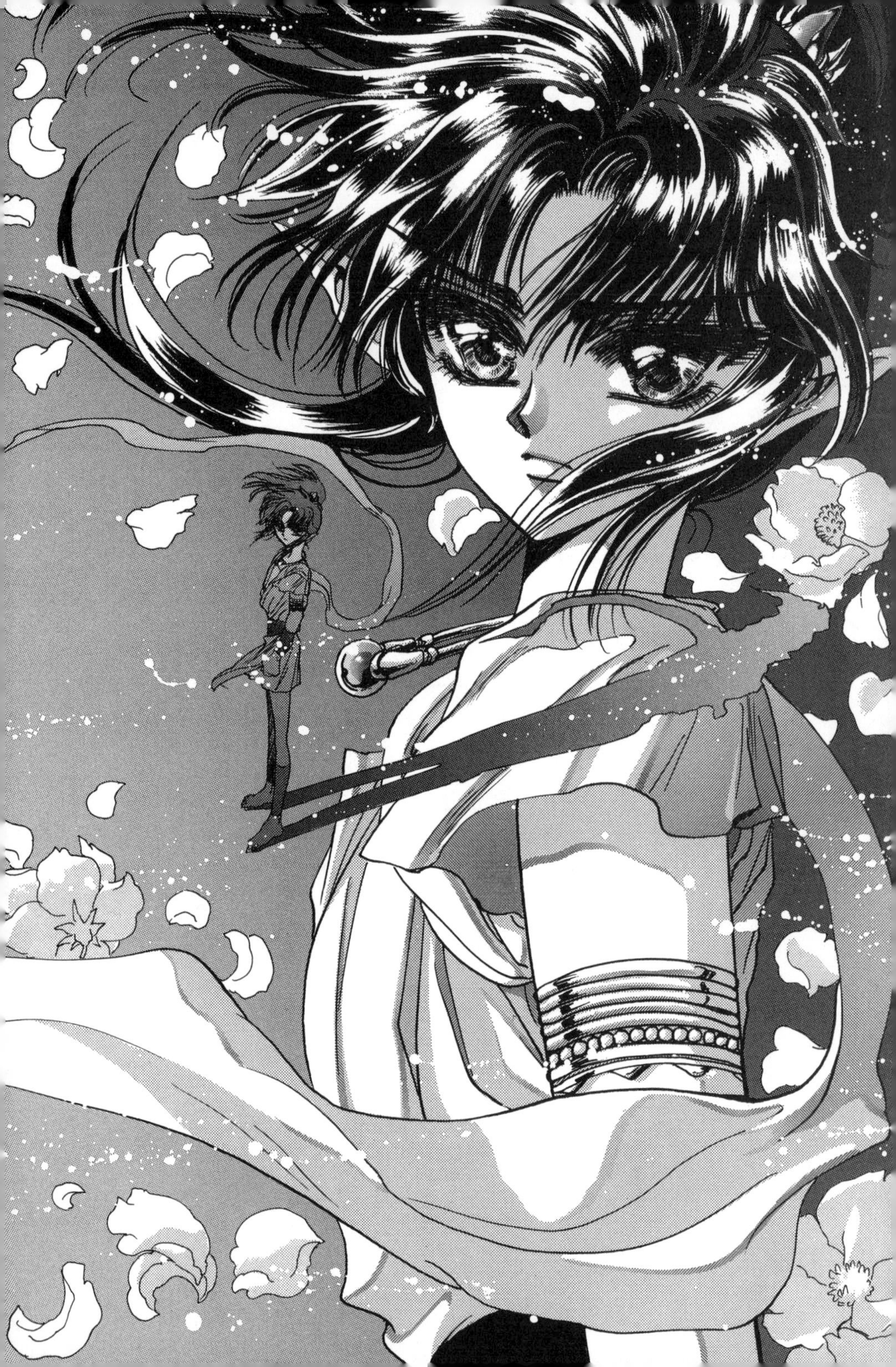

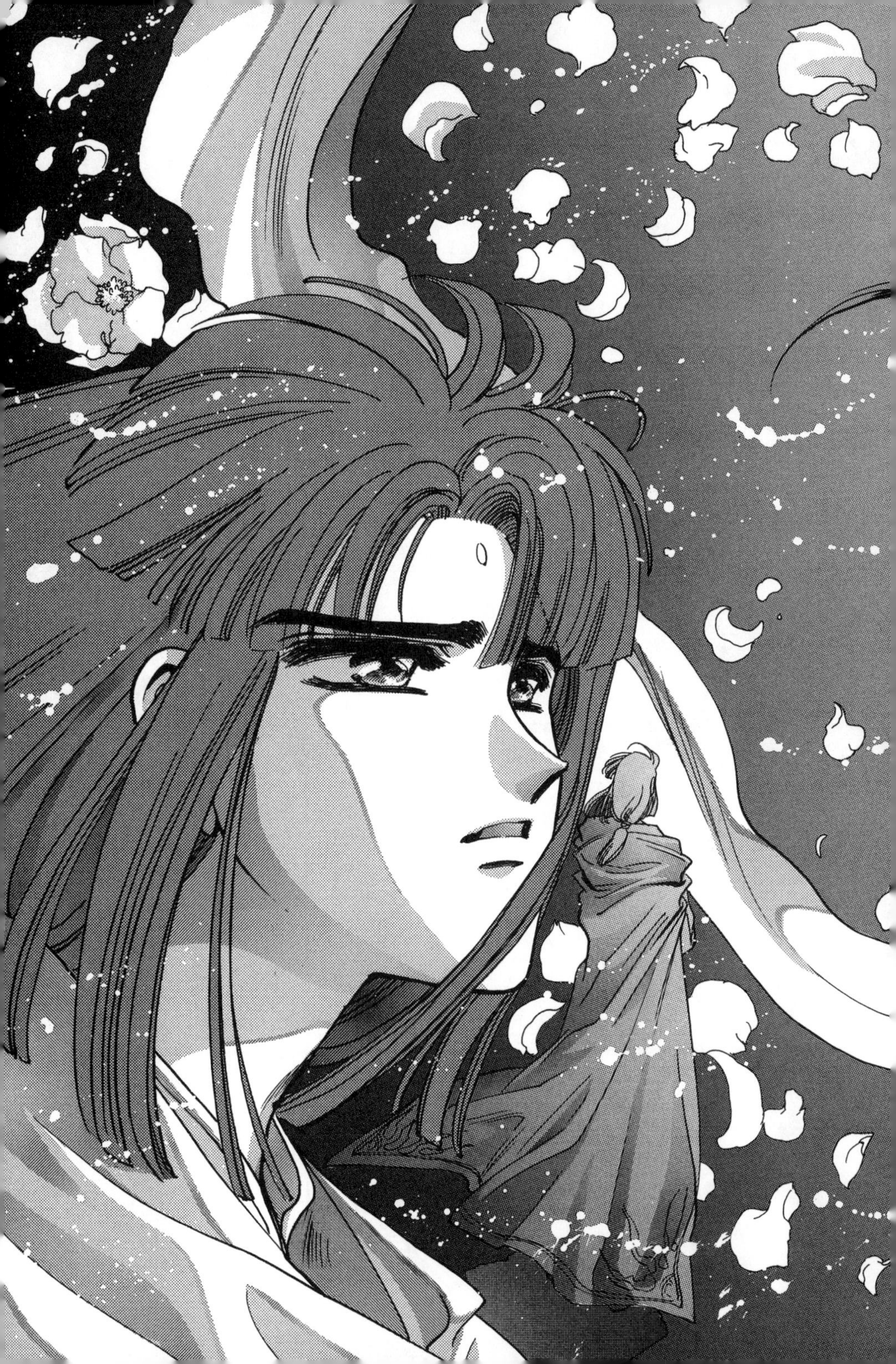

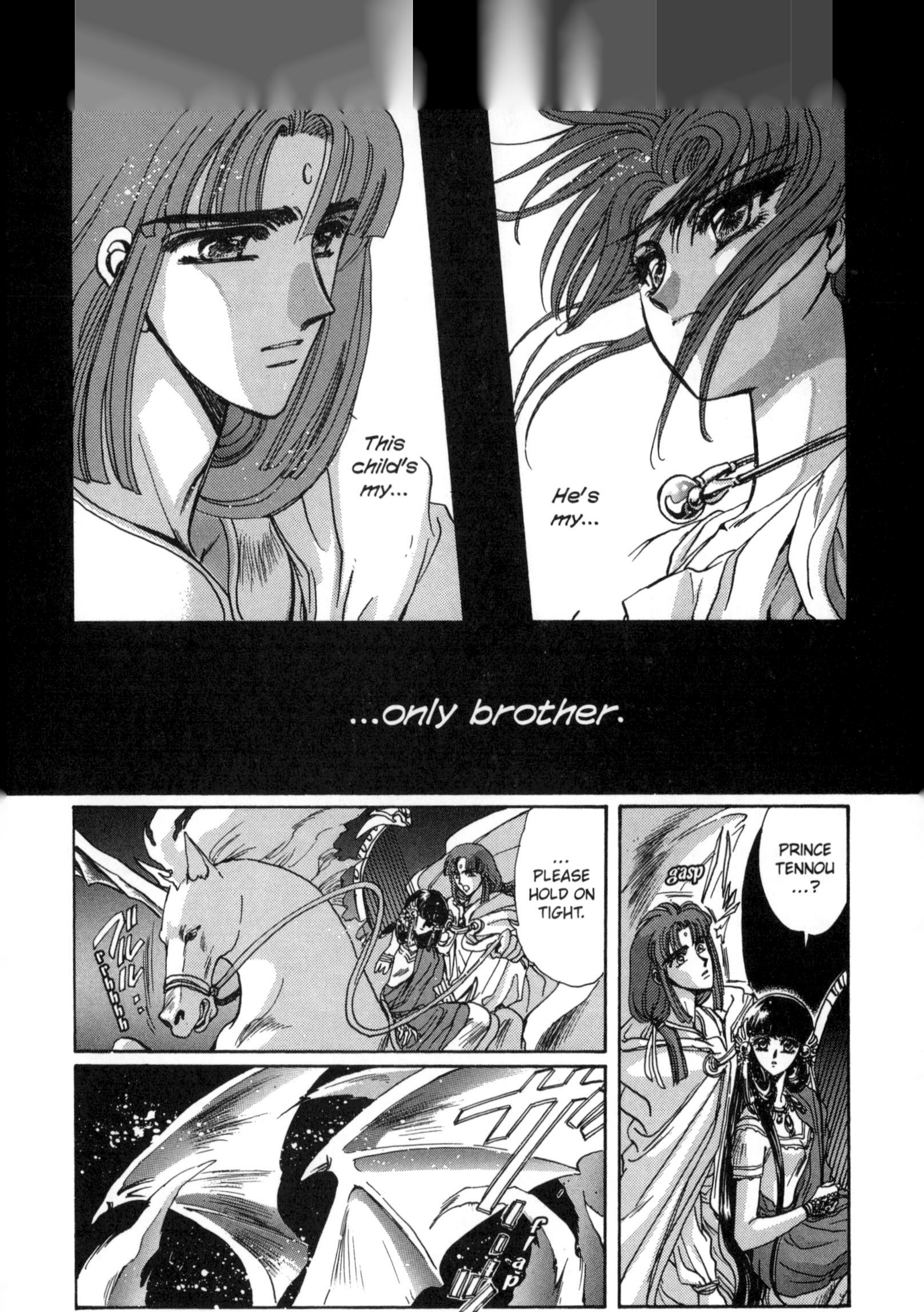
He's my...
This child's my...
...only brother.
gasp
PRINCE TENNOU ...?
... PLEASE HOLD ON TIGHT.
rrhhhh
flap

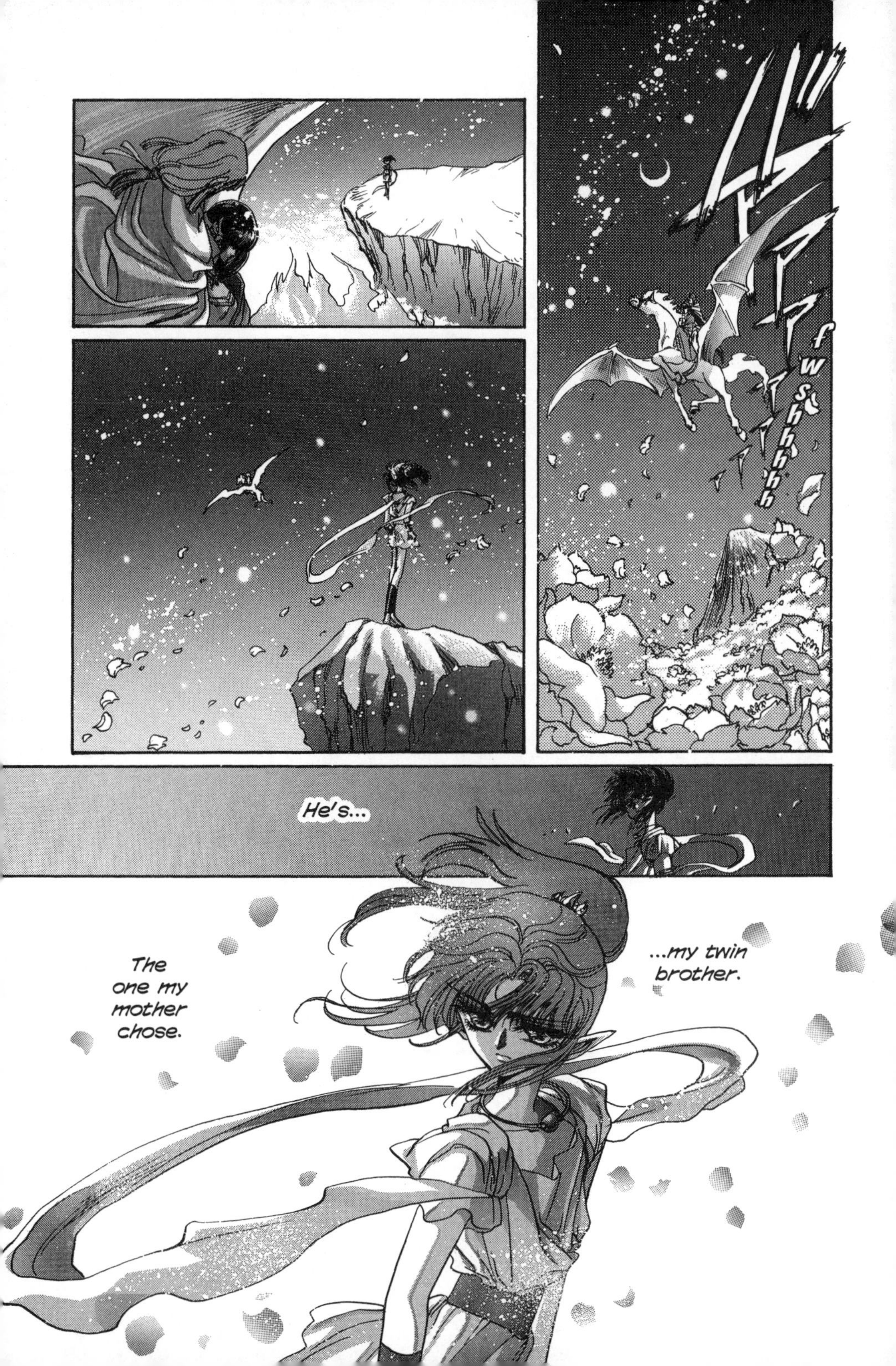
fwshhhhhh
He's...
...my twin brother.
The one my mother chose.

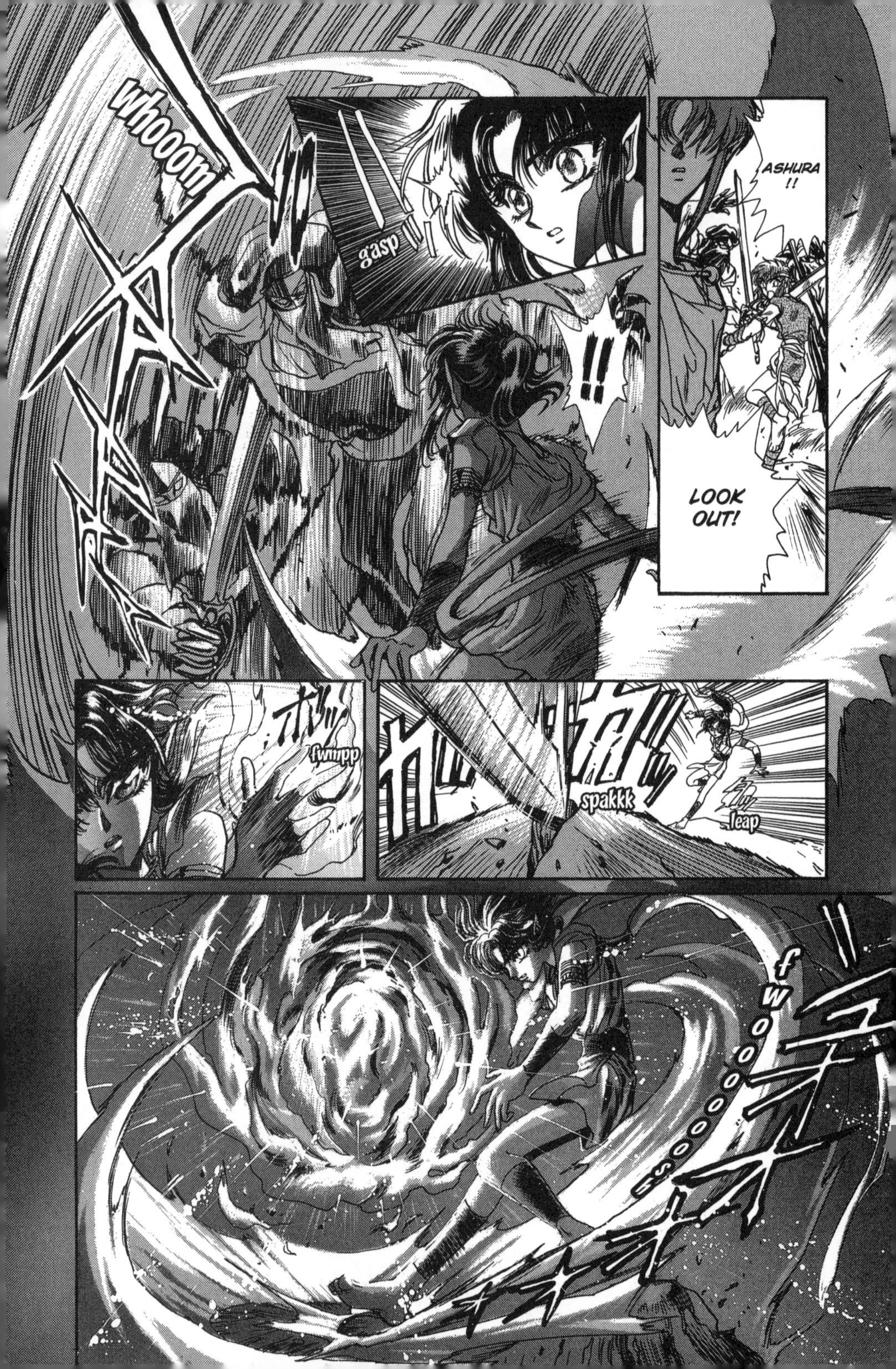
ASHURA !!
LOOK OUT!
gasp
whoooom
!!
spakkk
leap
fwmpp
fwooooooosh

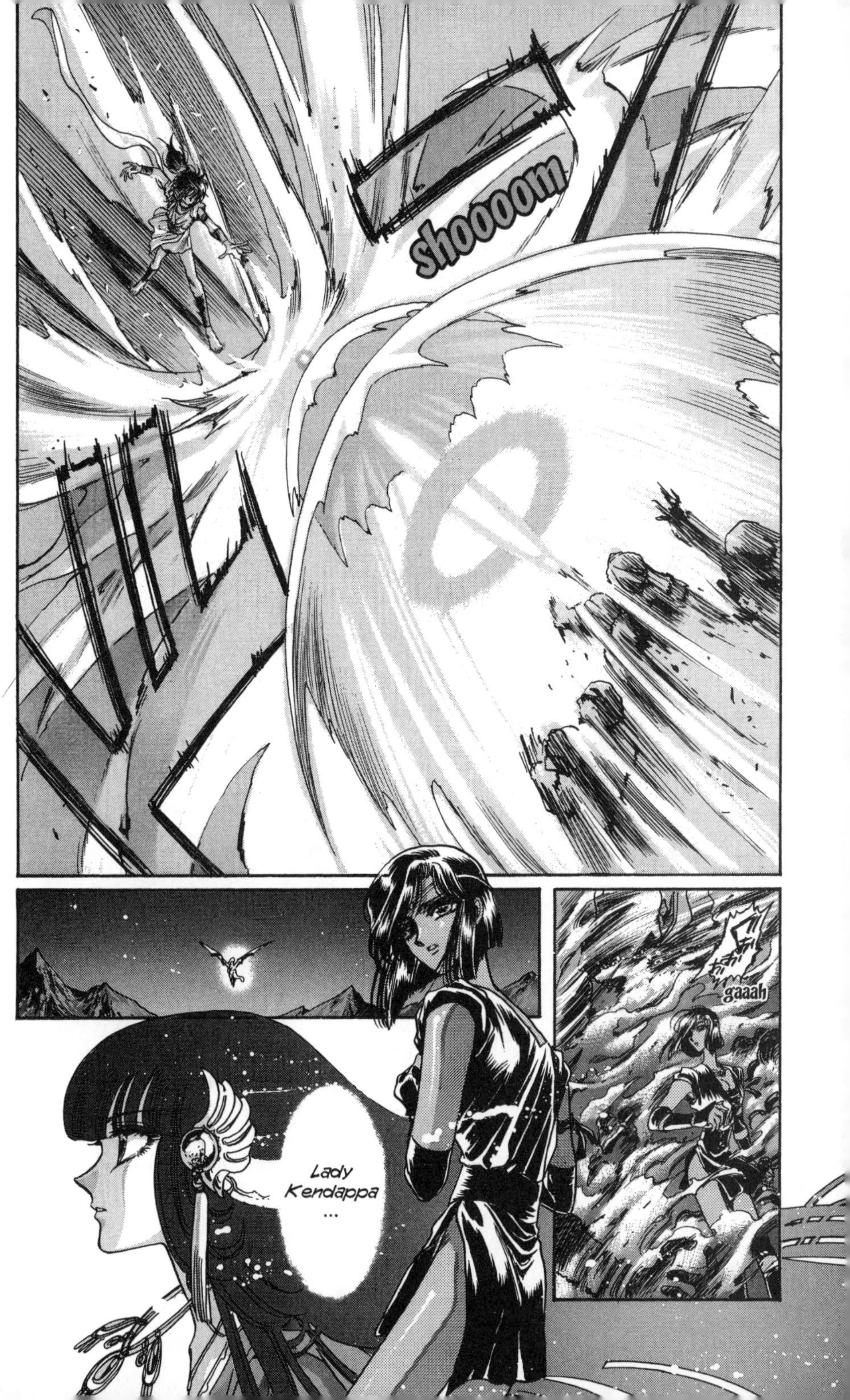
shoooom
gaaah
Lady Kendappa ...

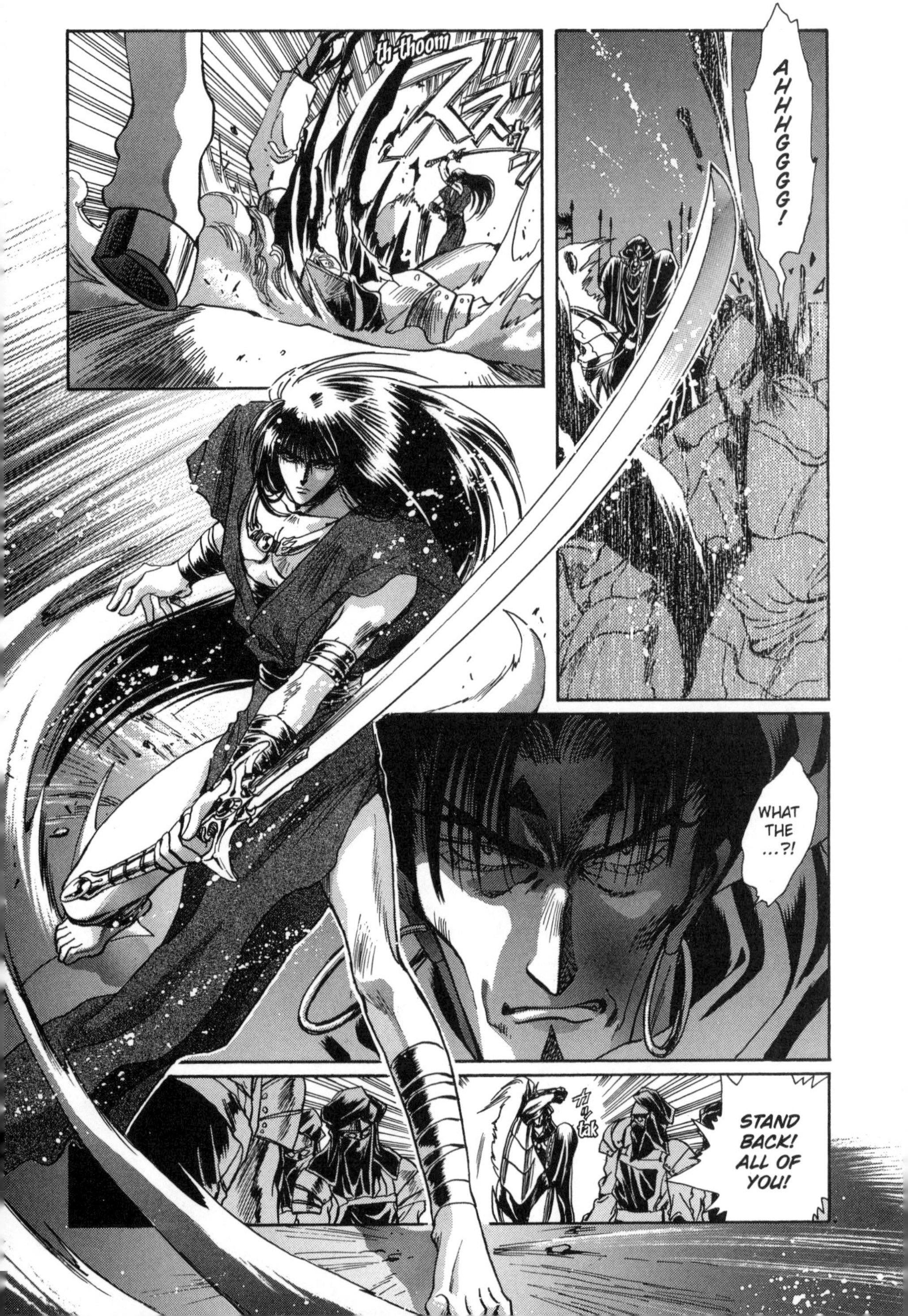
AHHHGGGG!
th-thoom
WHAT THE ...?!
STAND BACK! ALL OF YOU!
tak

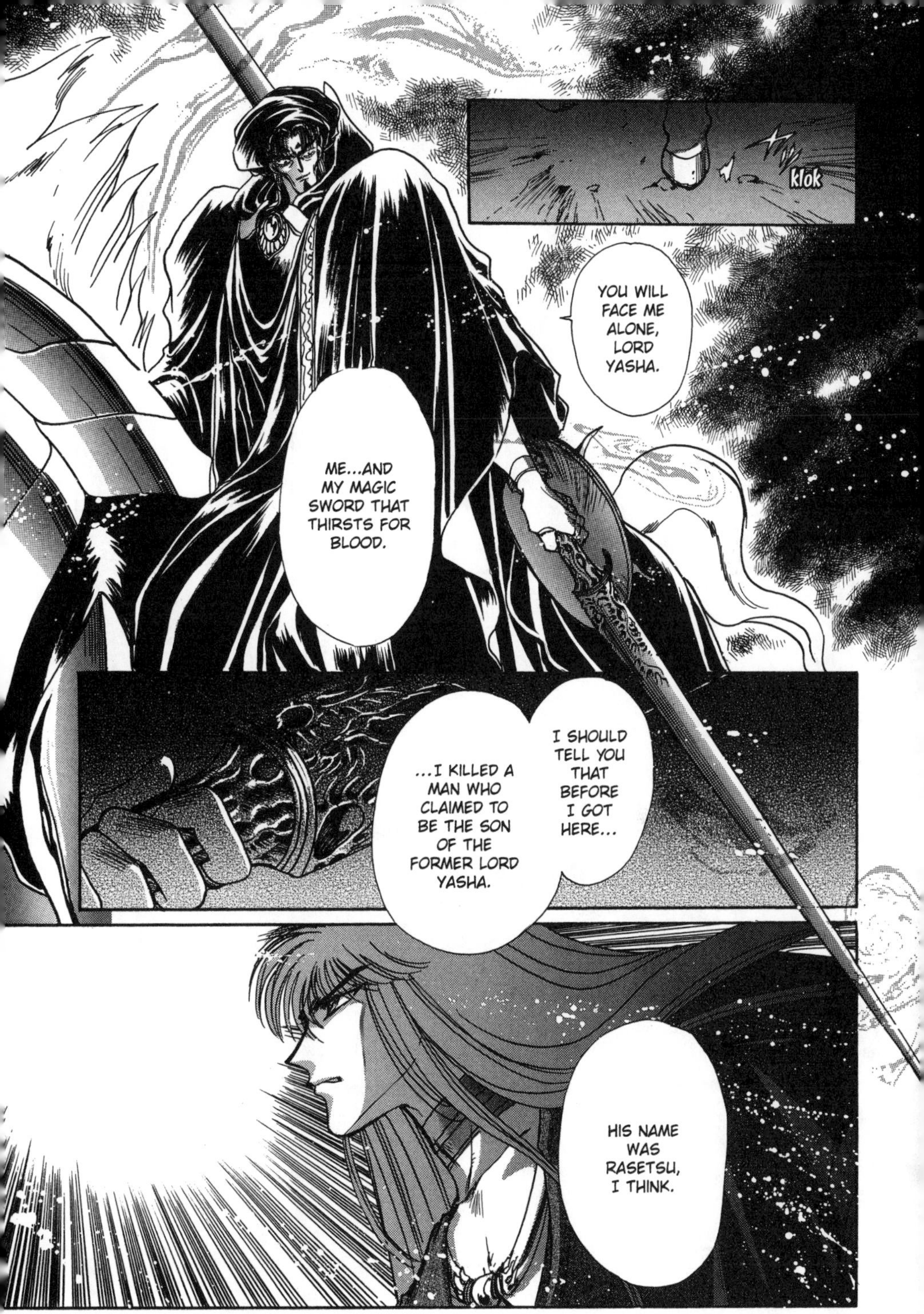

klok
YOU WILL FACE ME ALONE, LORD YASHA.
ME...AND MY MAGIC SWORD THAT THIRSTS FOR BLOOD.
I SHOULD TELL YOU THAT BEFORE I GOT HERE...
...I KILLED A MAN WHO CLAIMED TO BE THE SON OF THE FORMER LORD YASHA.
HIS NAME WAS RASETSU, I THINK.

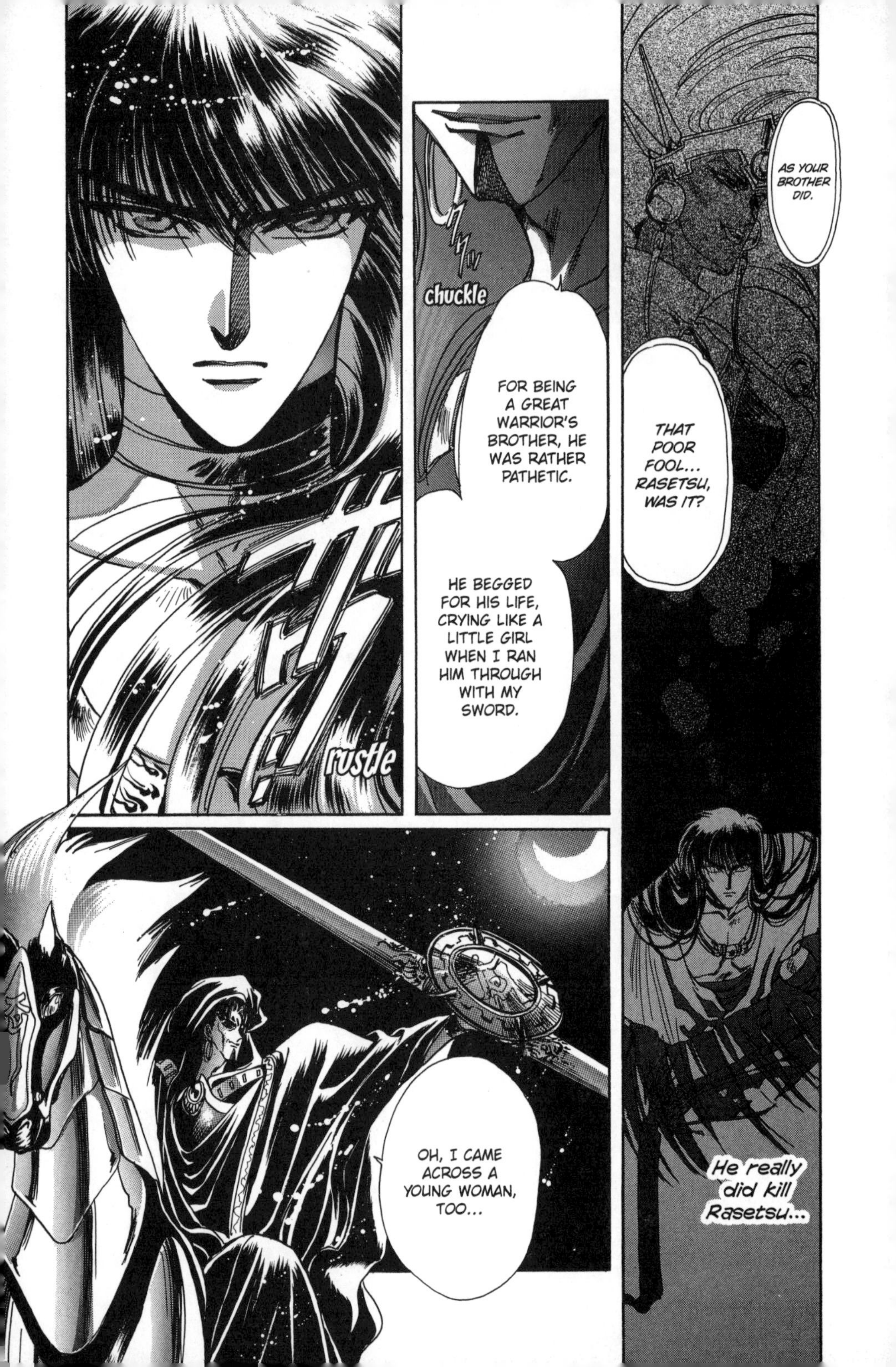
AS YOUR BROTHER DID.
THAT POOR FOOL... RASETSU, WAS IT?
chuckle
FOR BEING A GREAT WARRIOR'S BROTHER, HE WAS RATHER PATHETIC.
HE BEGGED FOR HIS LIFE, CRYING LIKE A LITTLE GIRL WHEN I RAN HIM THROUGH WITH MY SWORD.
rustle
He really did kill Rasetsu...
OH, I CAME ACROSS A YOUNG WOMAN, TOO...

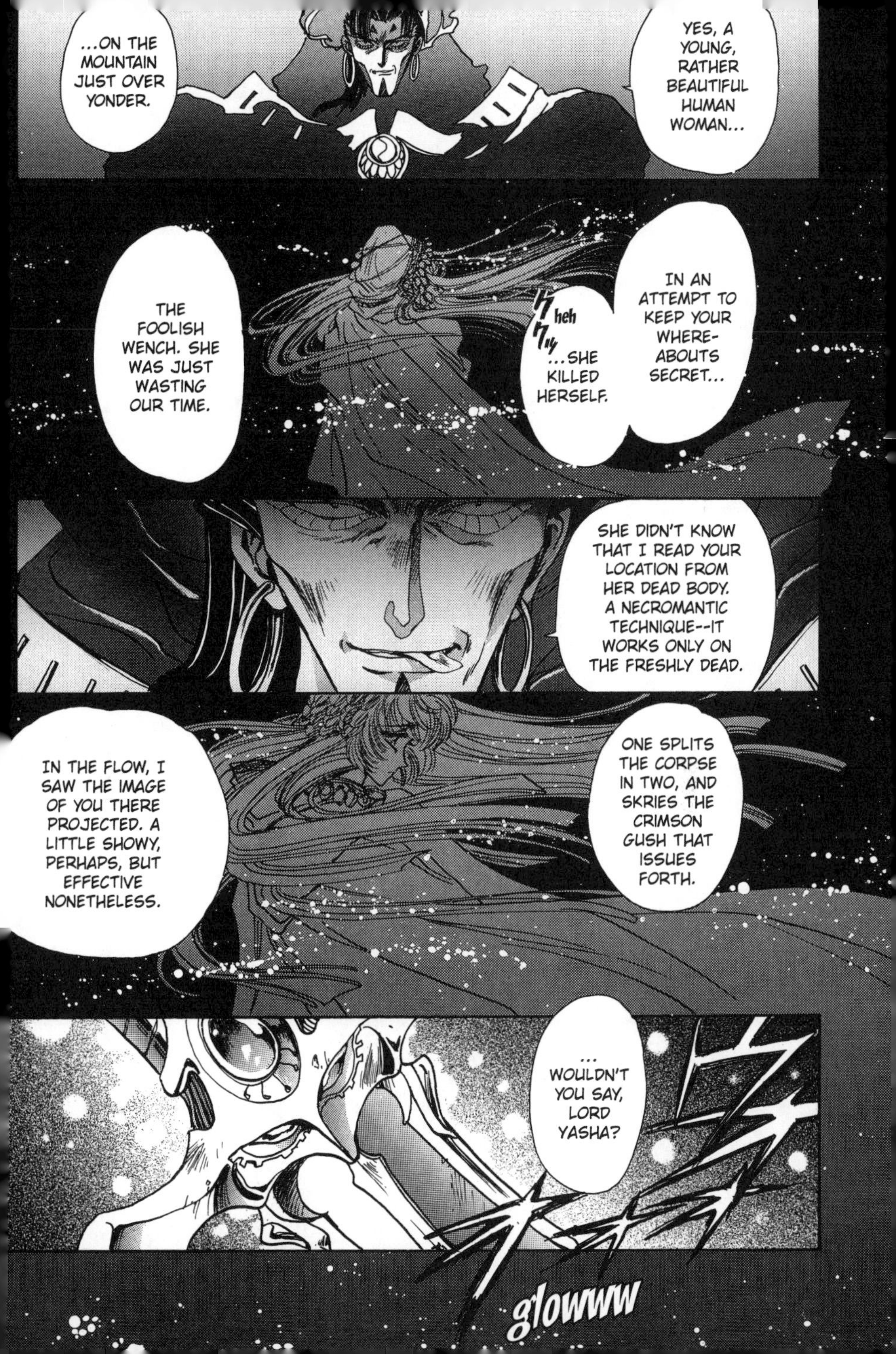
YES, A YOUNG, RATHER BEAUTIFUL HUMAN WOMAN...
...ON THE MOUNTAIN JUST OVER YONDER.
IN AN ATTEMPT TO KEEP YOUR WHERE-ABOUTS SECRET...
heh
...SHE KILLED HERSELF.
THE FOOLISH WENCH. SHE WAS JUST WASTING OUR TIME.
SHE DIDN'T KNOW THAT I READ YOUR LOCATION FROM HER DEAD BODY. A NECROMANTIC TECHNIQUE--IT WORKS ONLY ON THE FRESHLY DEAD.
ONE SPLITS THE CORPSE IN TWO, AND SKRIES THE CRIMSON GUSH THAT ISSUES FORTH.
IN THE FLOW, I SAW THE IMAGE OF YOU THERE PROJECTED. A LITTLE SHOWY, PERHAPS, BUT EFFECTIVE NONETHELESS.
...WOULDN'T YOU SAY, LORD YASHA?
glowww

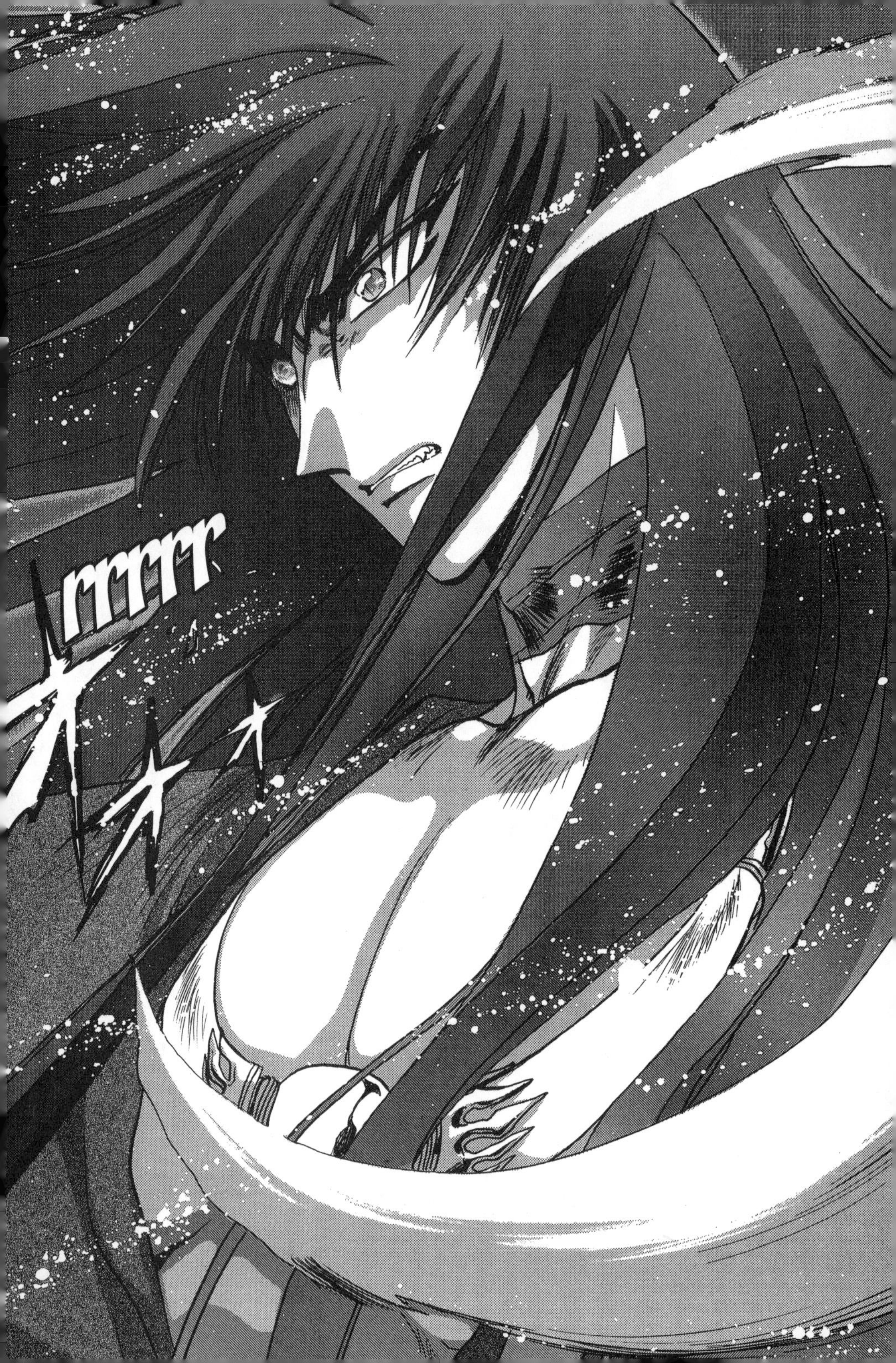
rrrrrr

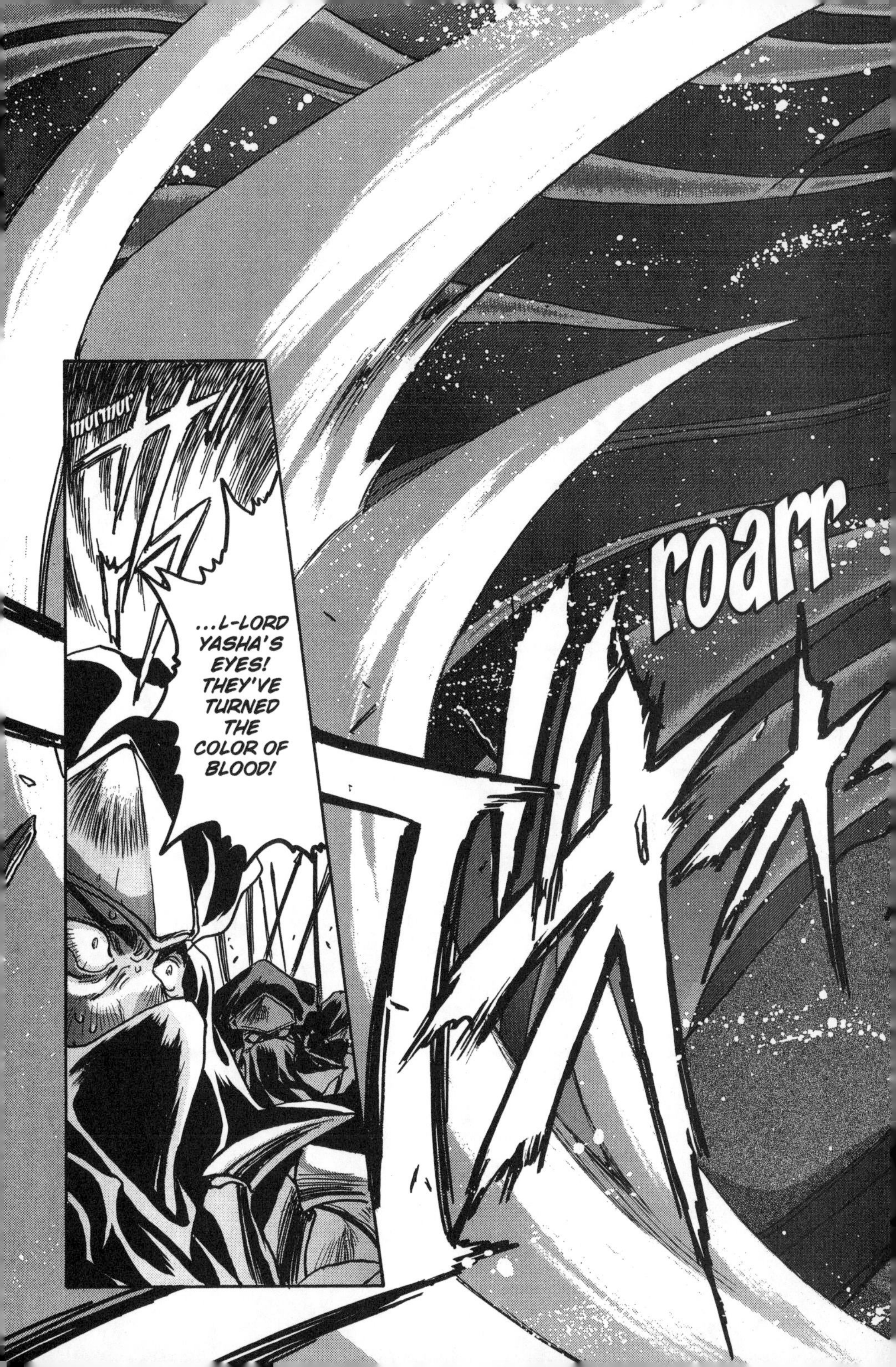
roarr
murmur
...L-LORD YASHA'S EYES! THEY'VE TURNED THE COLOR OF BLOOD!

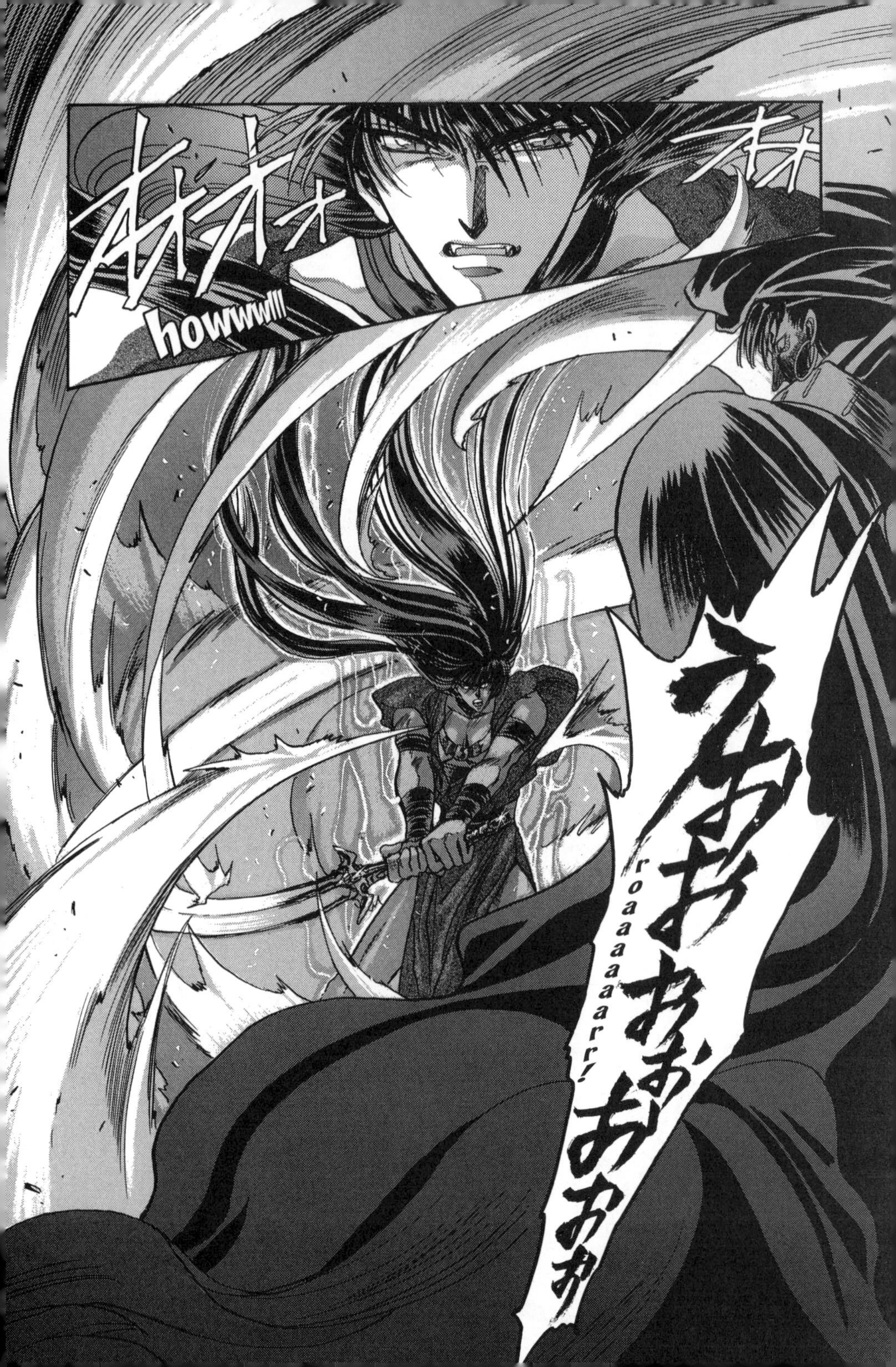

オオオオ
オオ
howwwlll
うおおおおおお
roaaaaaaarr!

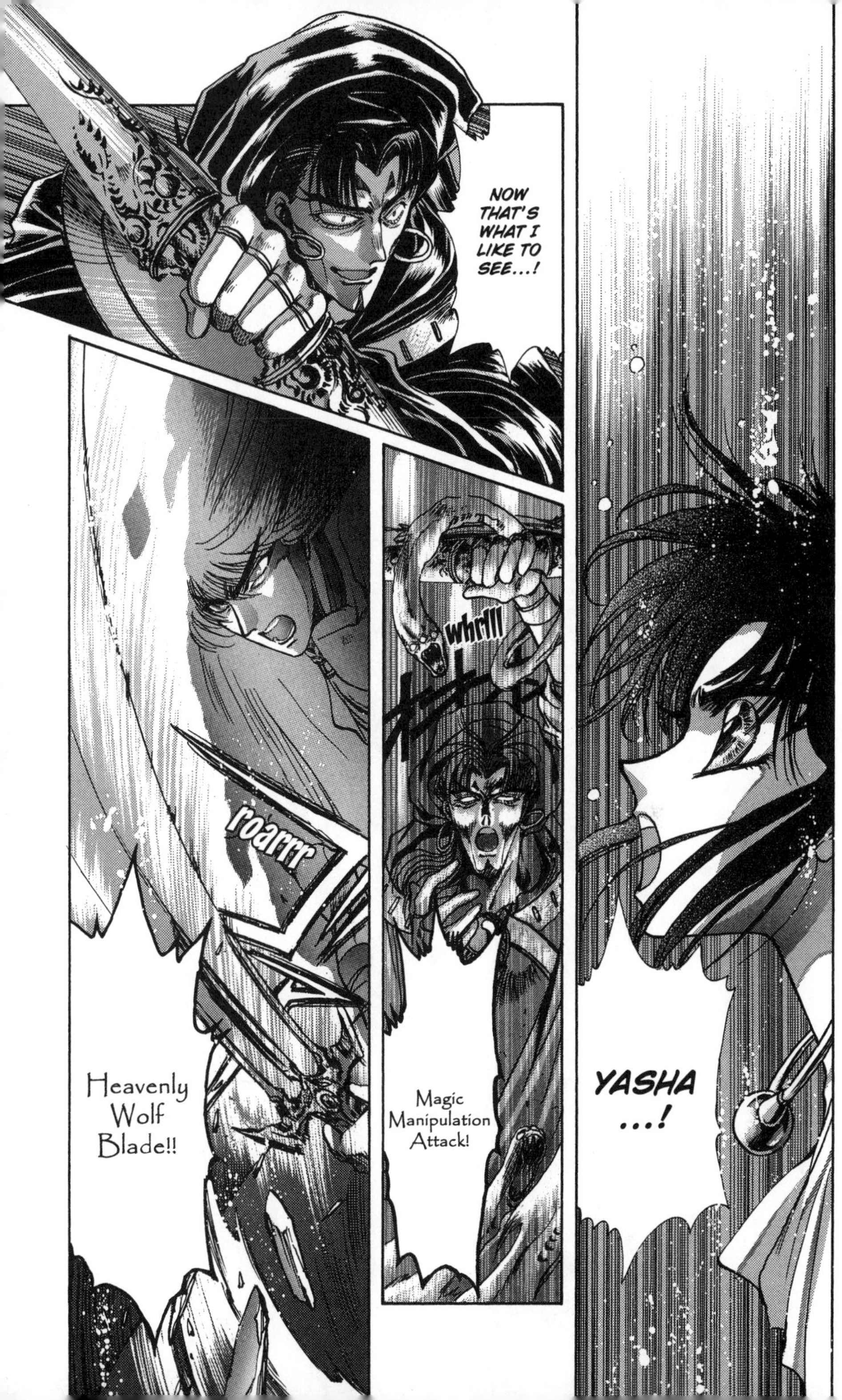
YASHA
...!
NOW THAT'S WHAT I LIKE TO SEE...!
whrlll
Magic Manipulation Attack!
roarrrr
Heavenly Wolf Blade!!

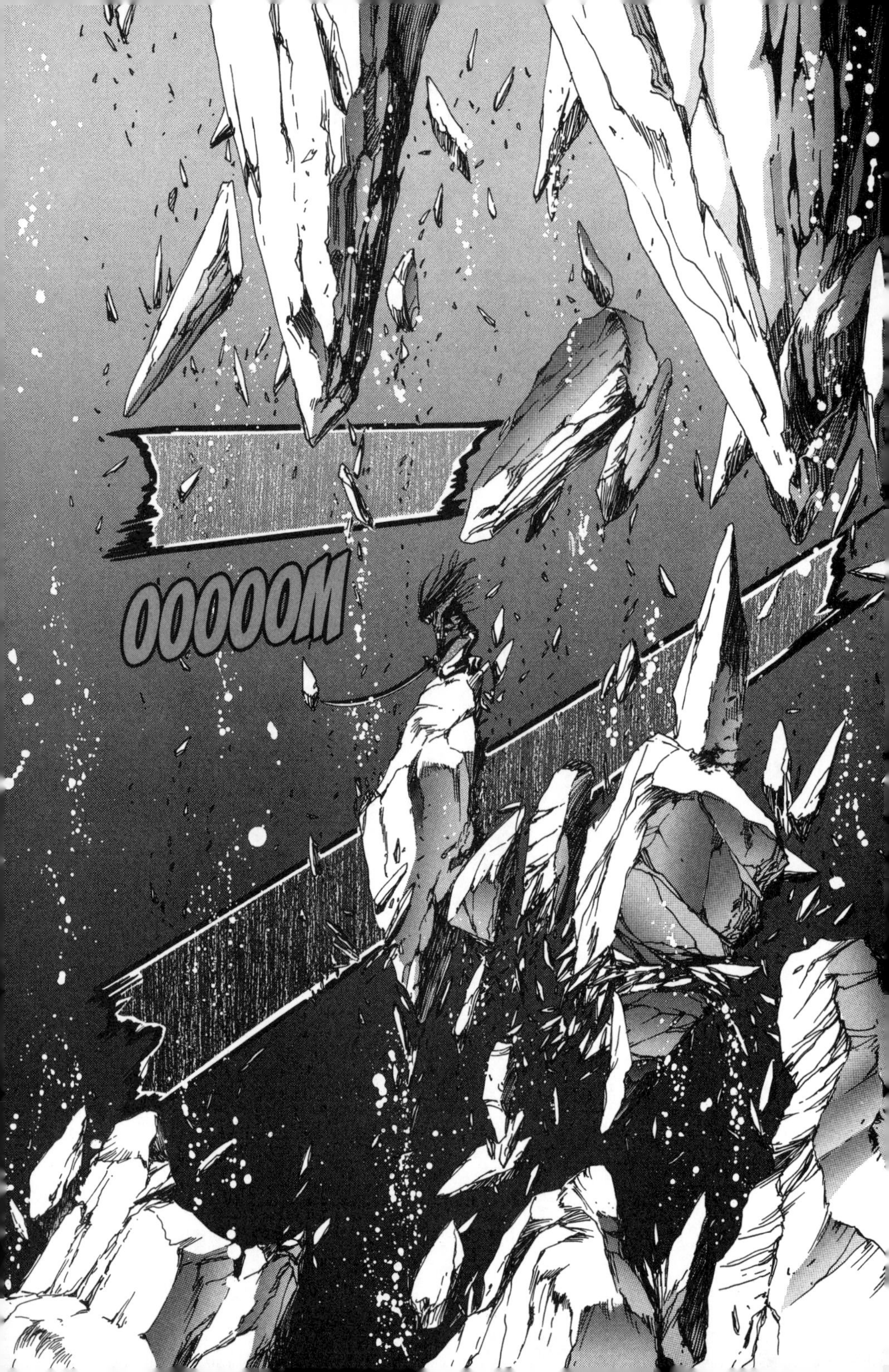
OOOOOM

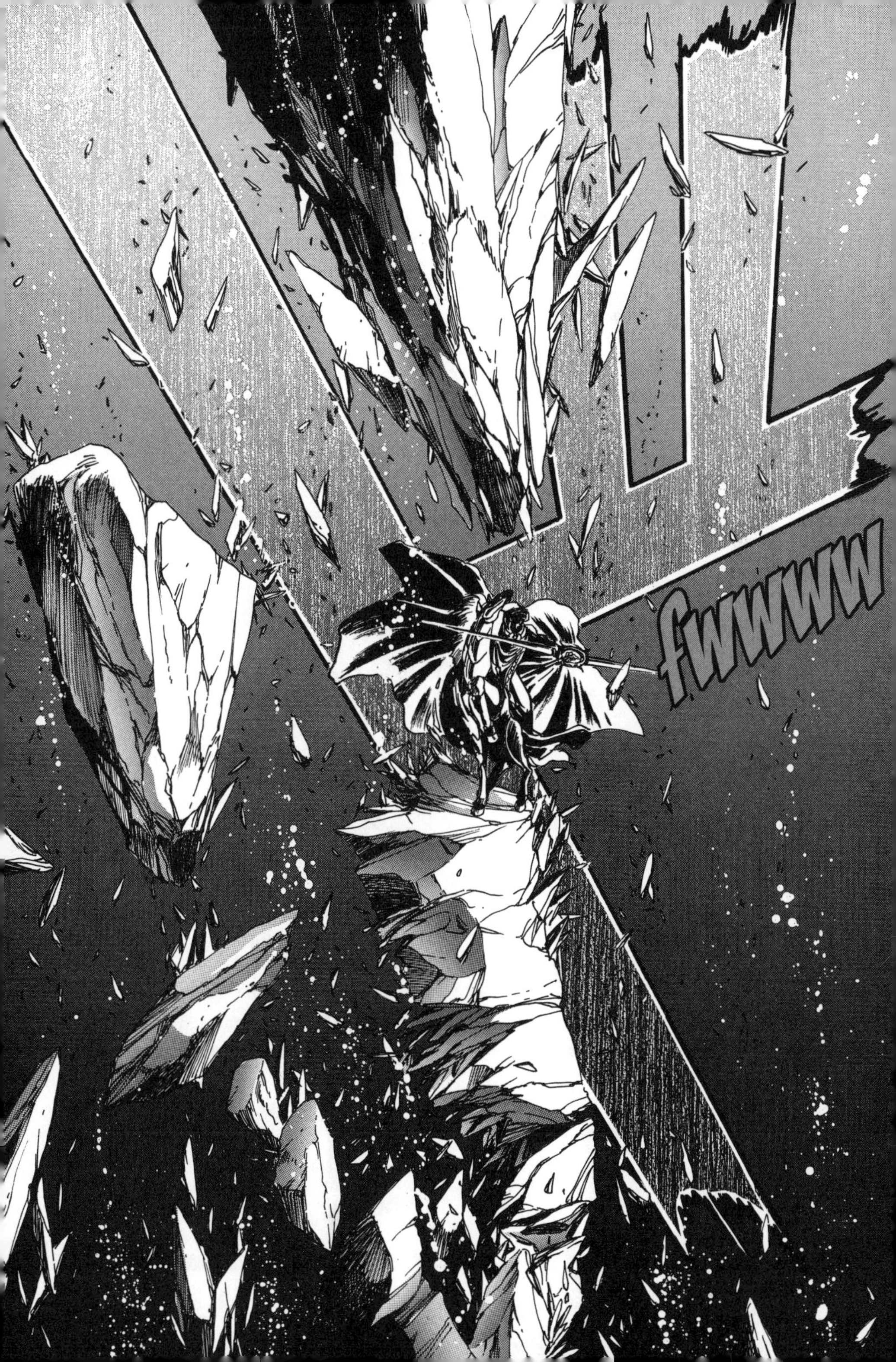
fwwww

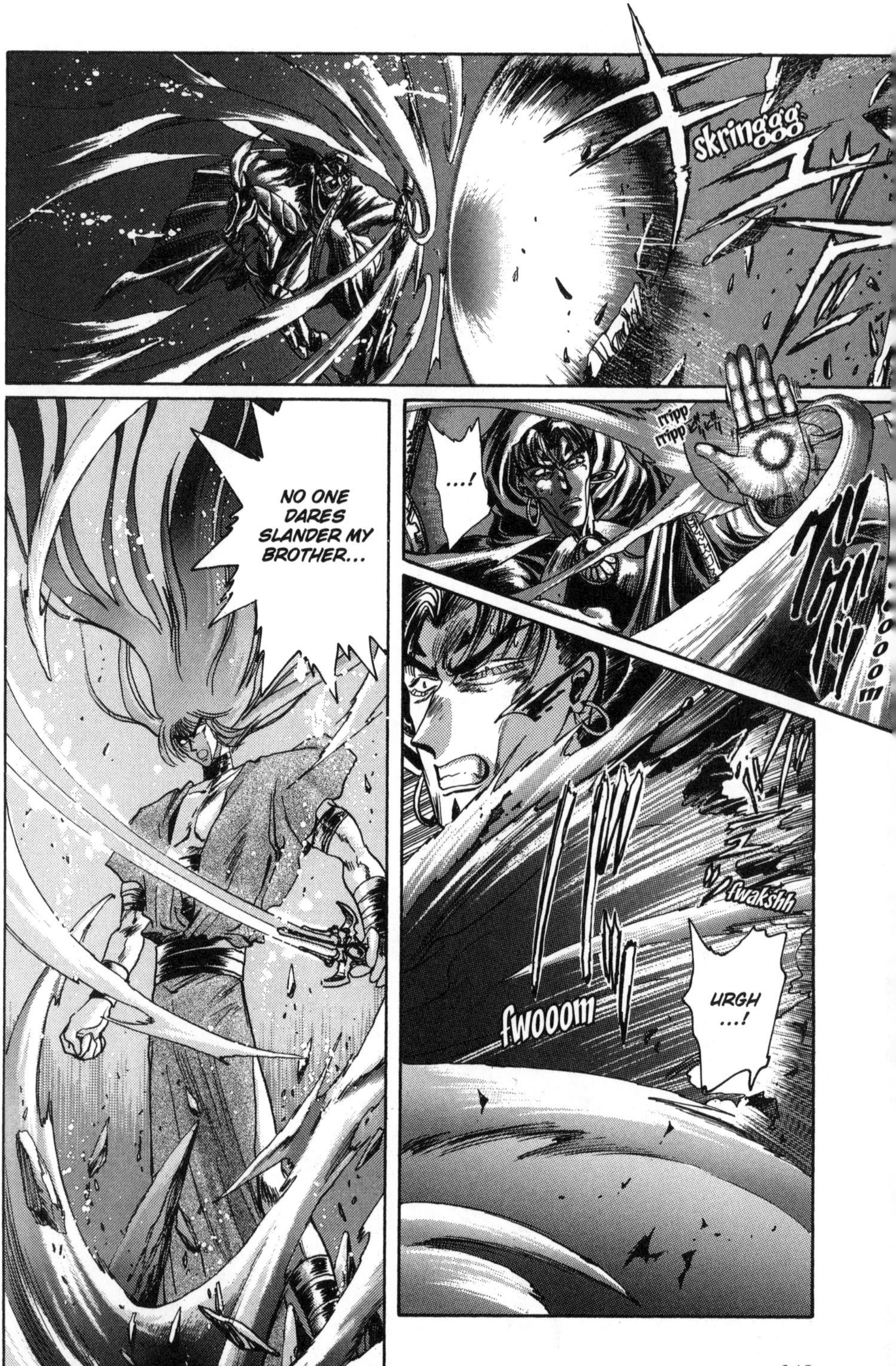
skringgg ooo
rripp rripp
...!
oooo!!
fwakshh
fwooom
URGH ...!
NO ONE DARES SLANDER MY BROTHER...

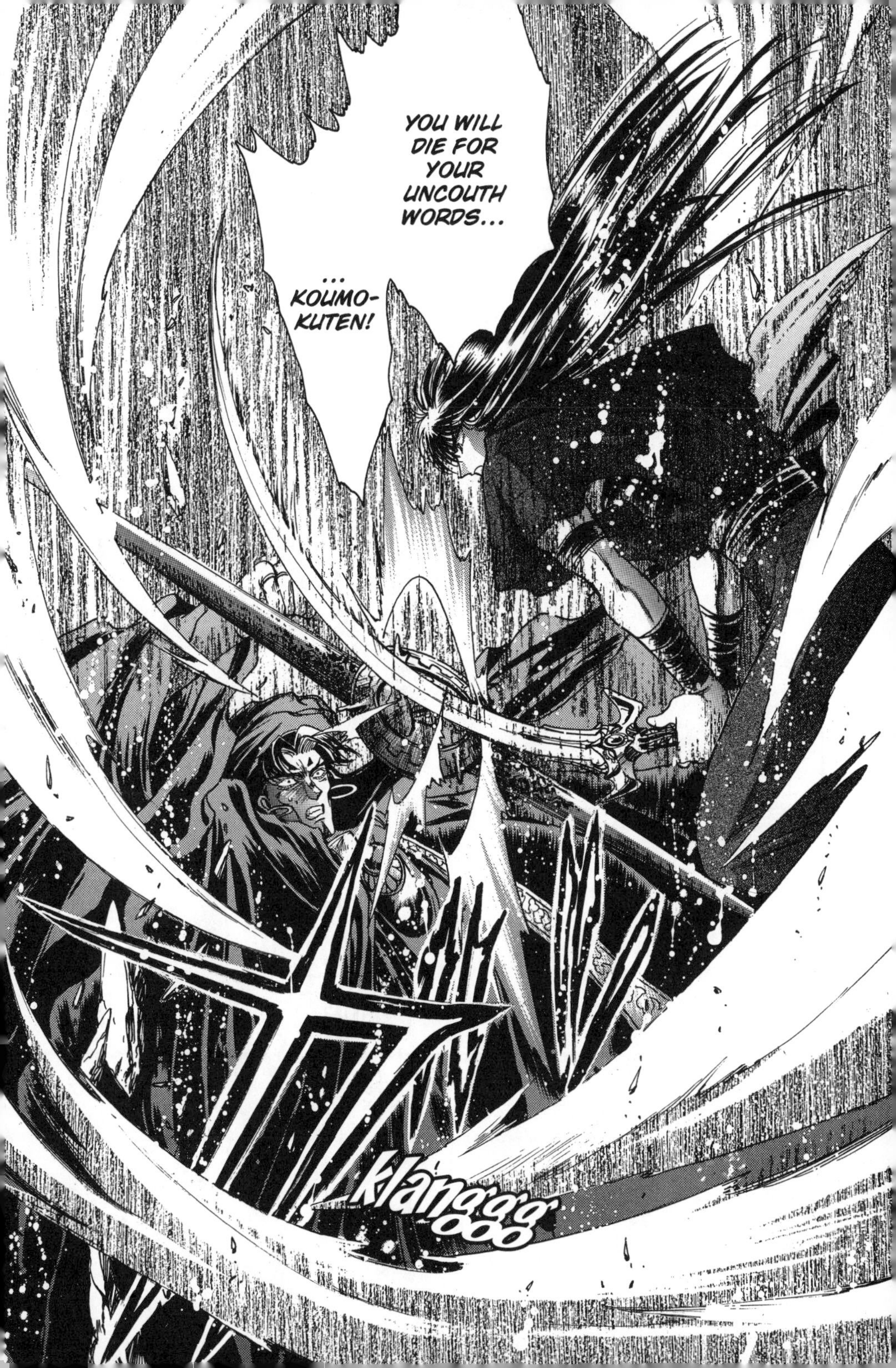
YOU WILL DIE FOR YOUR UNCOUTH WORDS...
...KOUMOKUTEN!
klanggg

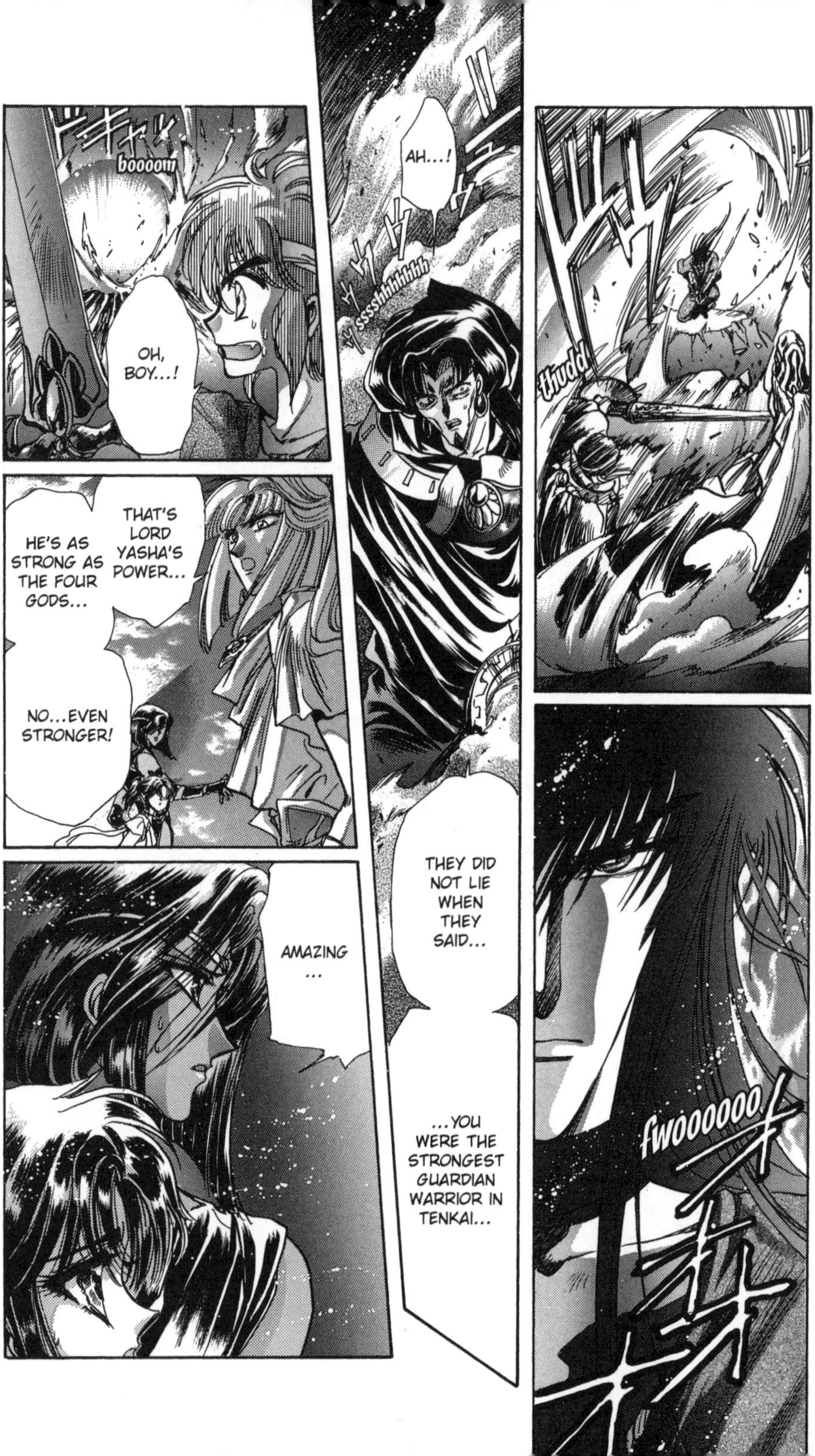
thudd
fwoooooo
AH...!
sssshhhhhhh
THEY DID NOT LIE WHEN THEY SAID...
...YOU WERE THE STRONGEST GUARDIAN WARRIOR IN TENKAI...
booooom
OH, BOY...!
THAT'S LORD YASHA'S POWER...
HE'S AS STRONG AS THE FOUR GODS...
NO...EVEN STRONGER!
AMAZING ...

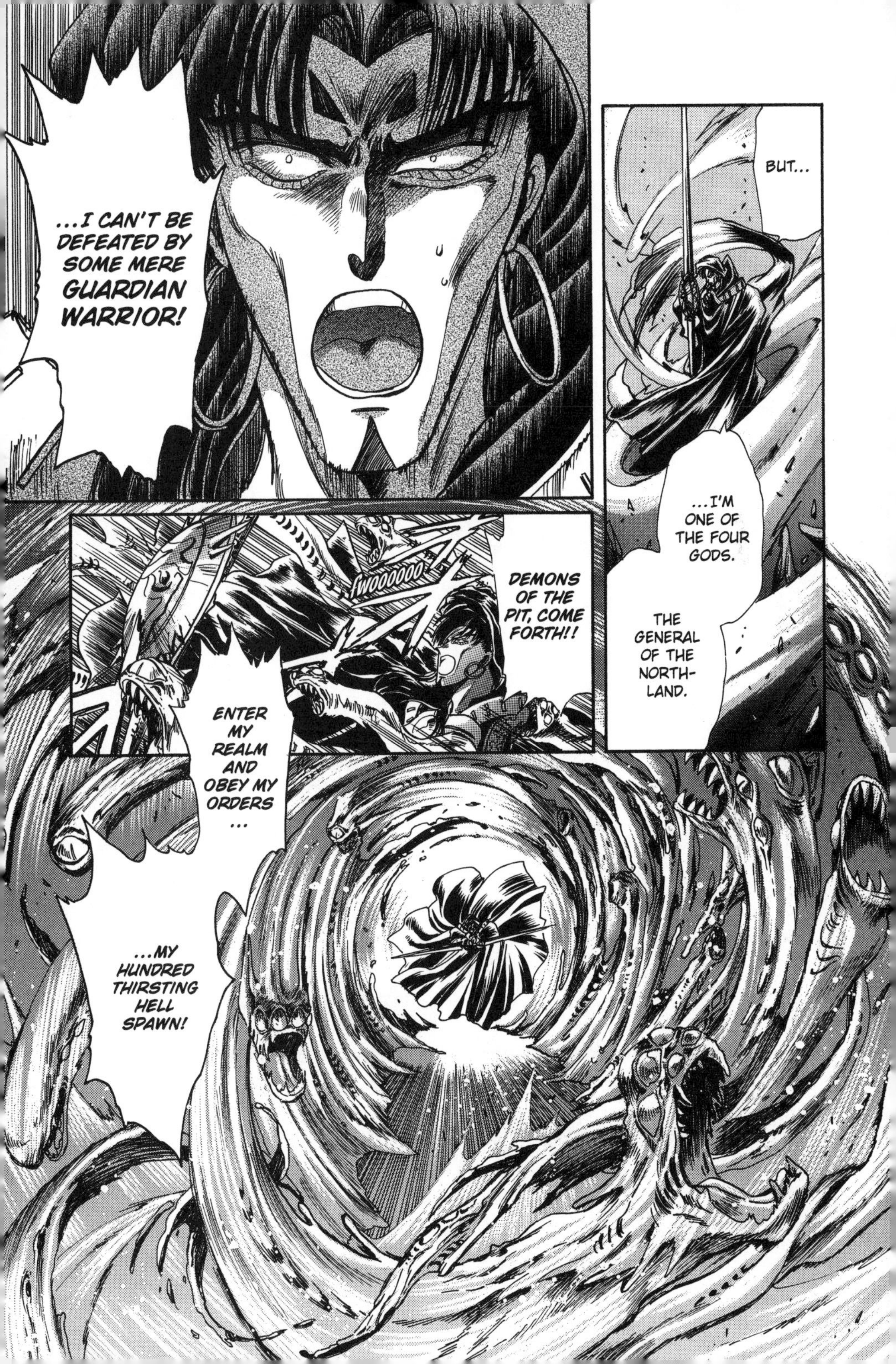
BUT...
...I'M ONE OF THE FOUR GODS.
THE GENERAL OF THE NORTH-LAND.
...I CAN'T BE DEFEATED BY SOME MERE GUARDIAN WARRIOR!
DEMONS OF THE PIT, COME FORTH!!
fwoooooo
ENTER MY REALM AND OBEY MY ORDERS ...
...MY HUNDRED THIRSTING HELL SPAWN!

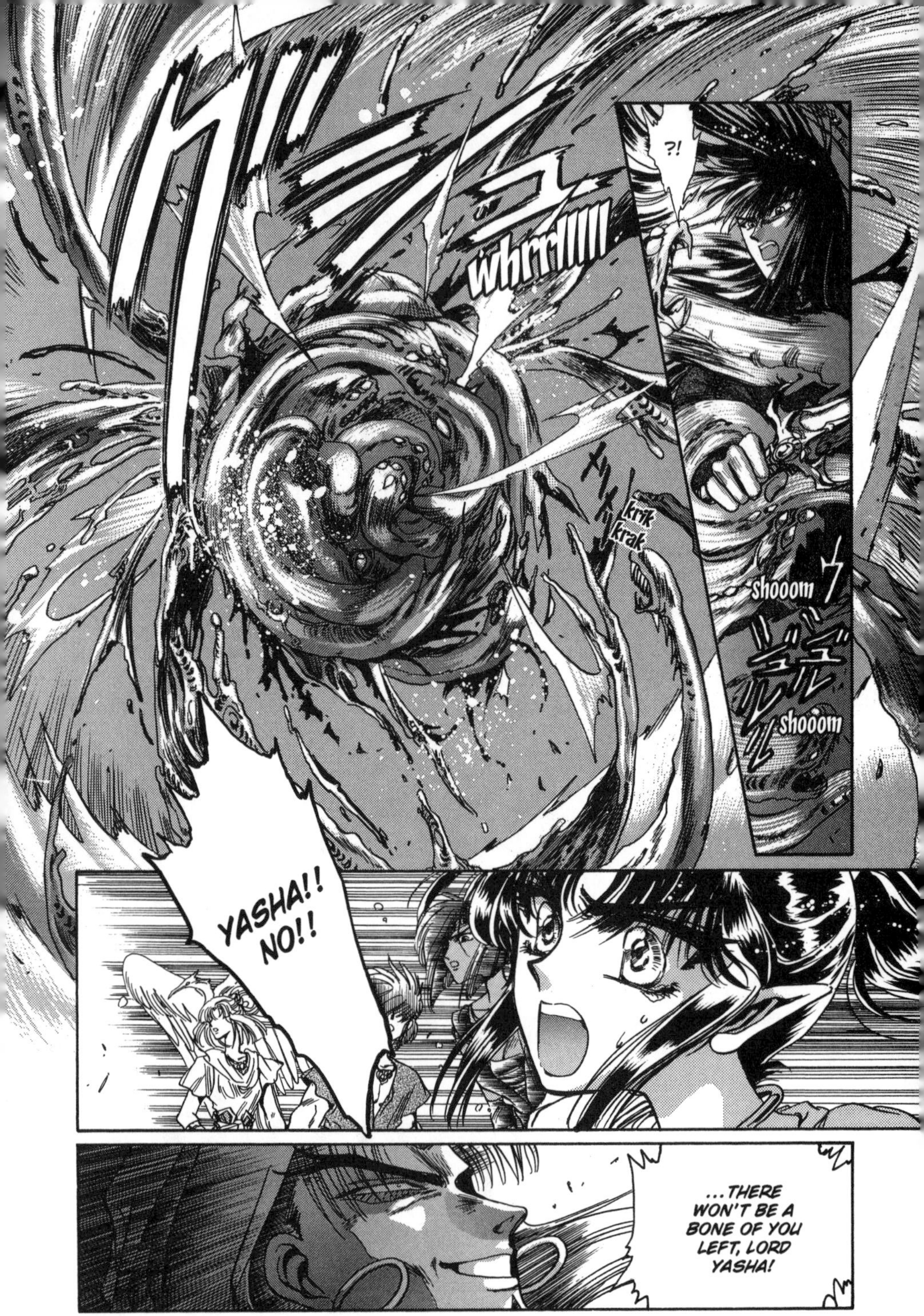
?!
shooom
shooom
whrrllllll
krik krak
YASHA!! NO!!
...THERE WON'T BE A BONE OF YOU LEFT, LORD YASHA!

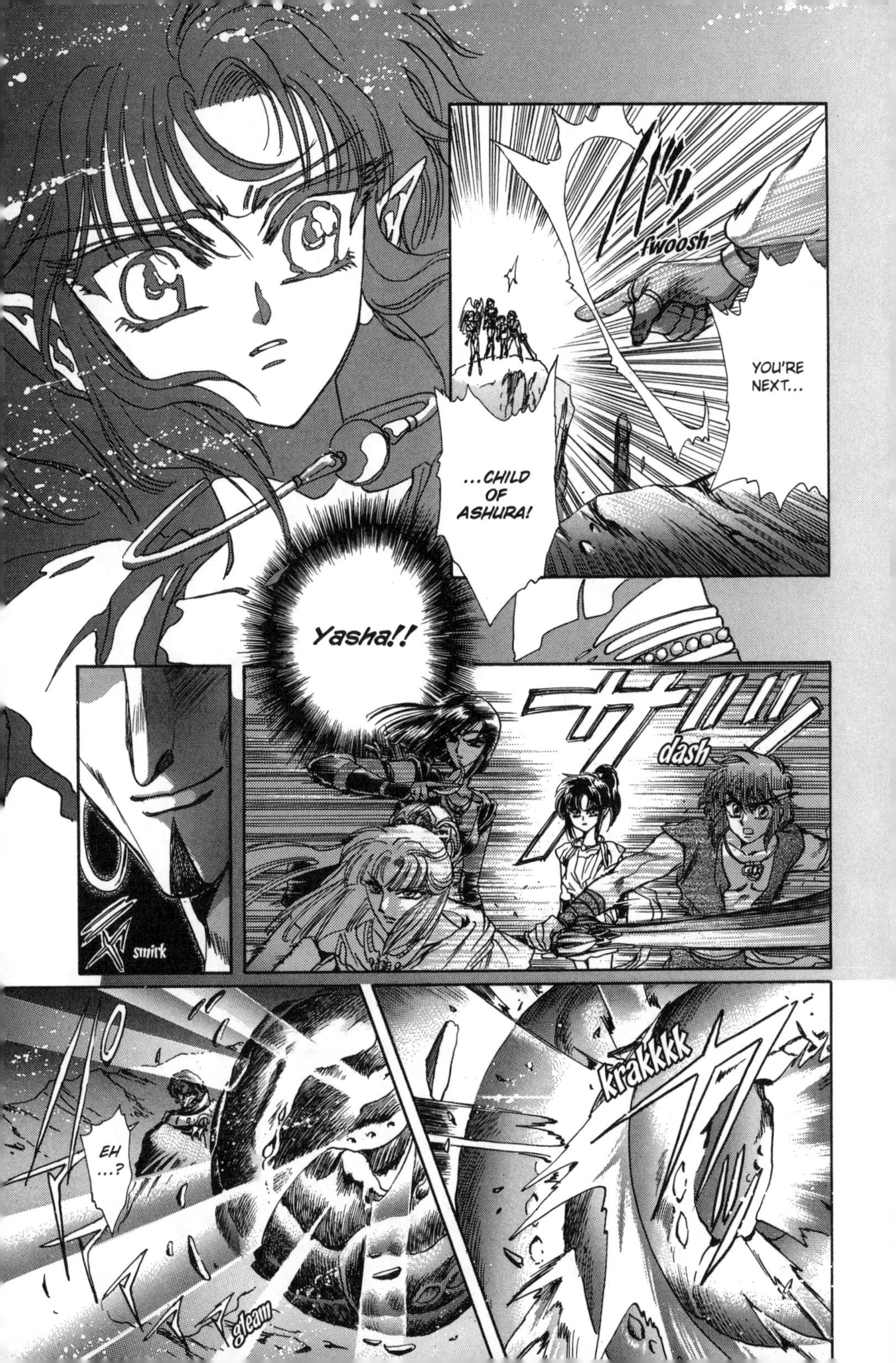
fwoosh
YOU'RE NEXT...
...CHILD OF ASHURA!
Yasha!!
dash
smirk
krakkkk
EH ...?
gleam

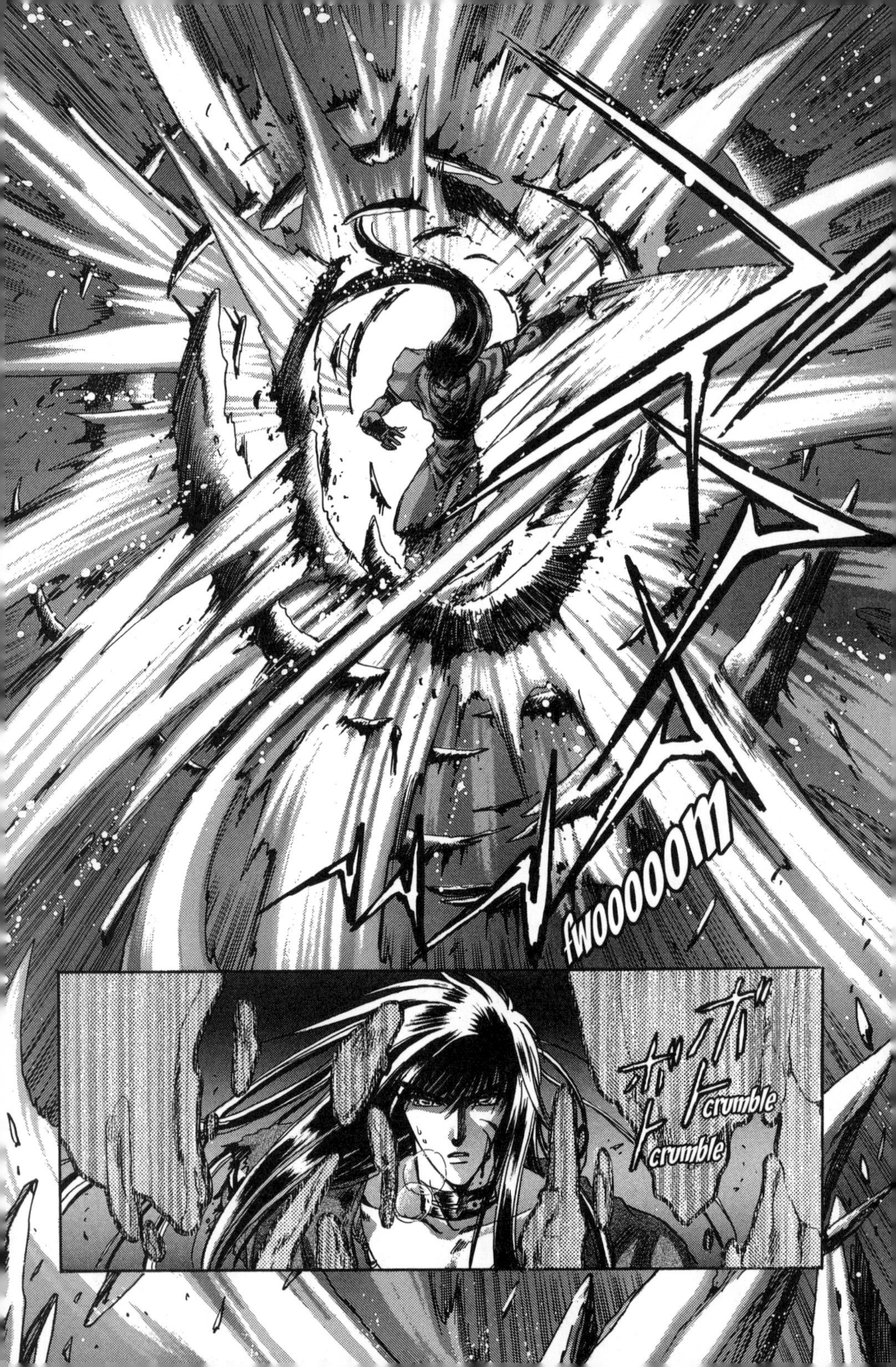
fwooooom
crumble
crumble

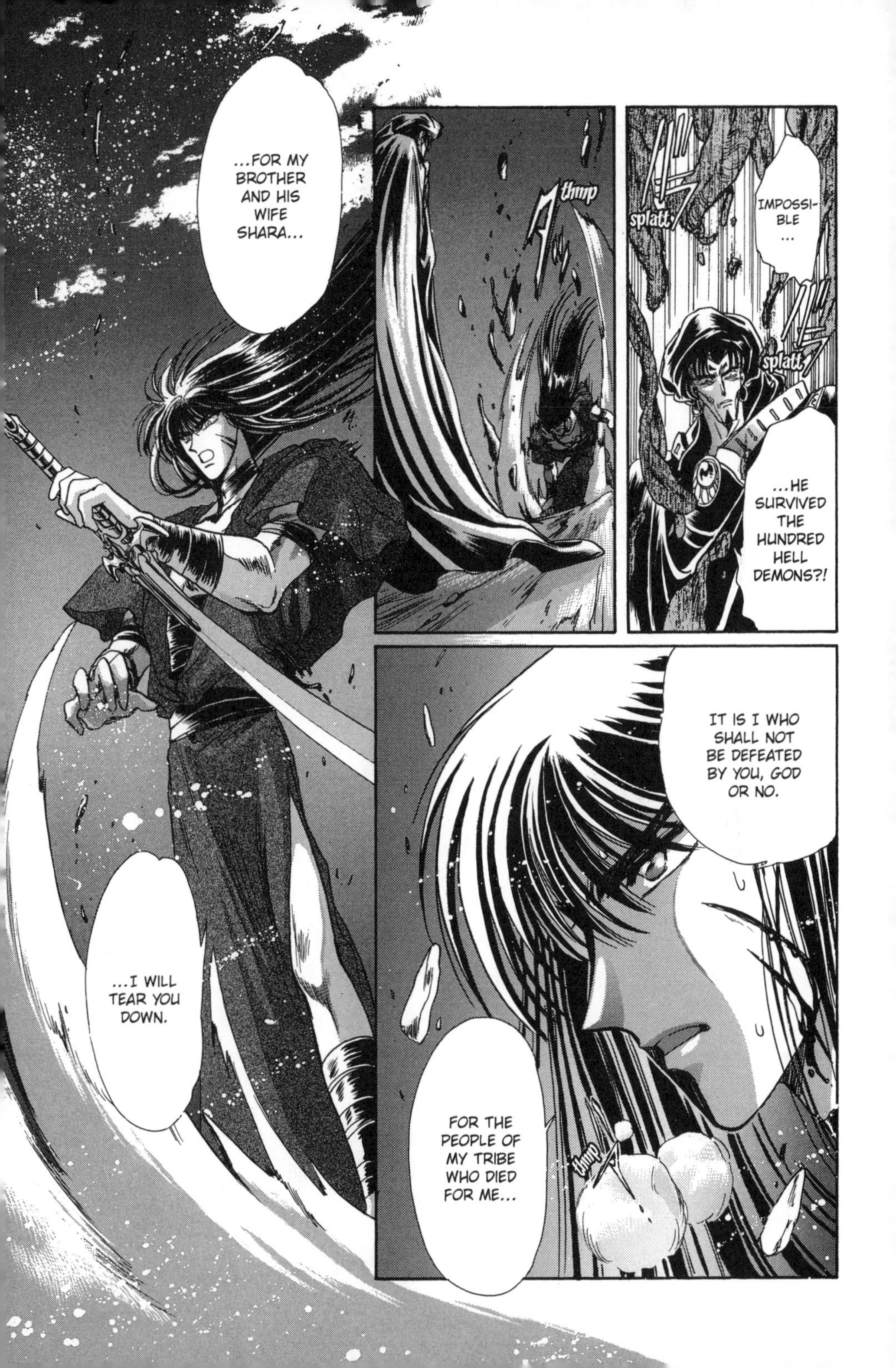
splatt
IMPOSSIBLE...
splatt
...HE SURVIVED THE HUNDRED HELL DEMONS?!
thmp
IT IS I WHO SHALL NOT BE DEFEATED BY YOU, GOD OR NO.
FOR THE PEOPLE OF MY TRIBE WHO DIED FOR ME...
thmp
...FOR MY BROTHER AND HIS WIFE SHARA...
...I WILL TEAR YOU DOWN.

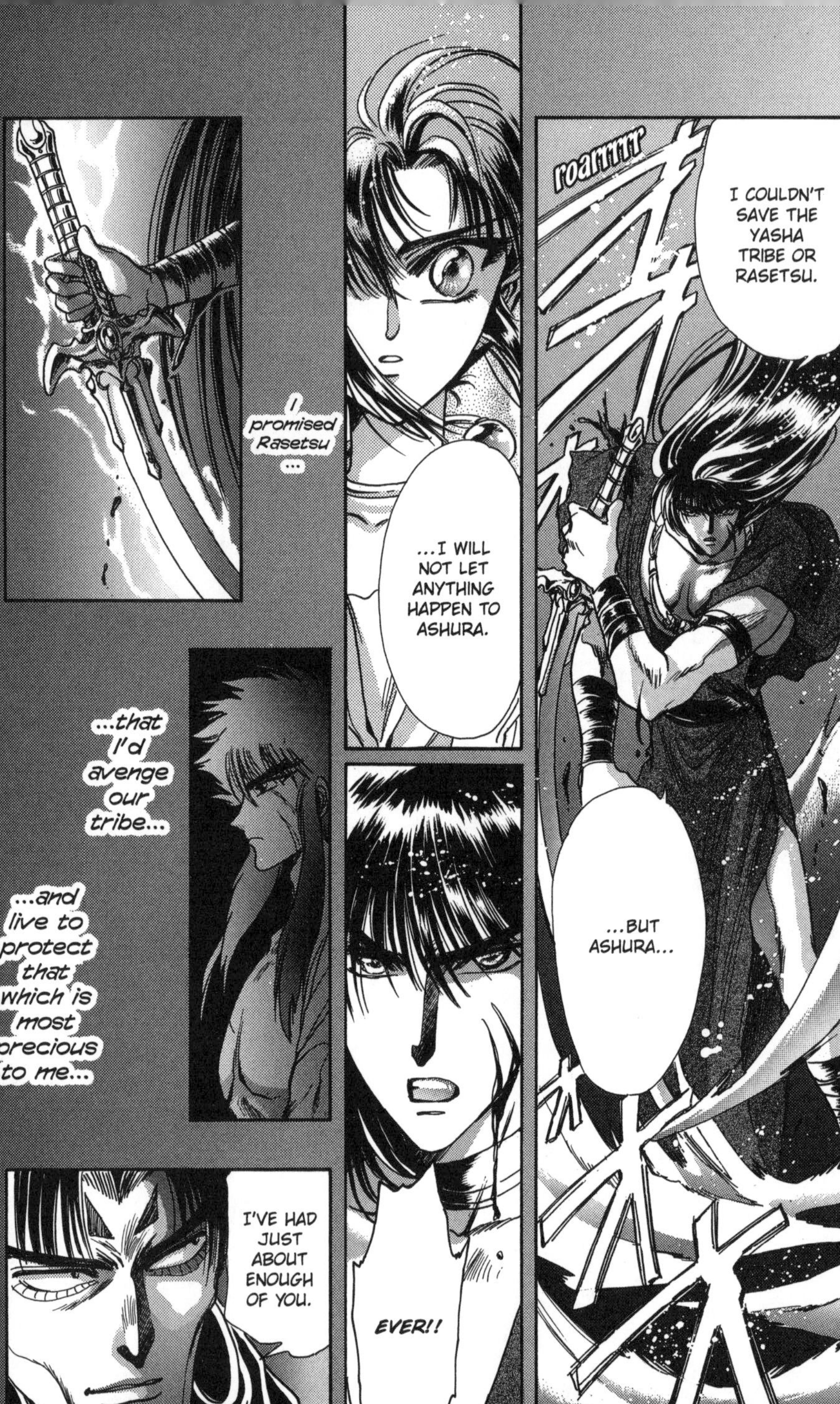
roarrrrr
I COULDN'T SAVE THE YASHA TRIBE OR RASETSU.
...BUT ASHURA...
...I WILL NOT LET ANYTHING HAPPEN TO ASHURA.
EVER!!
I promised Rasetsu ...
...that I'd avenge our tribe...
...and live to protect that which is most precious to me...
I'VE HAD JUST ABOUT ENOUGH OF YOU.

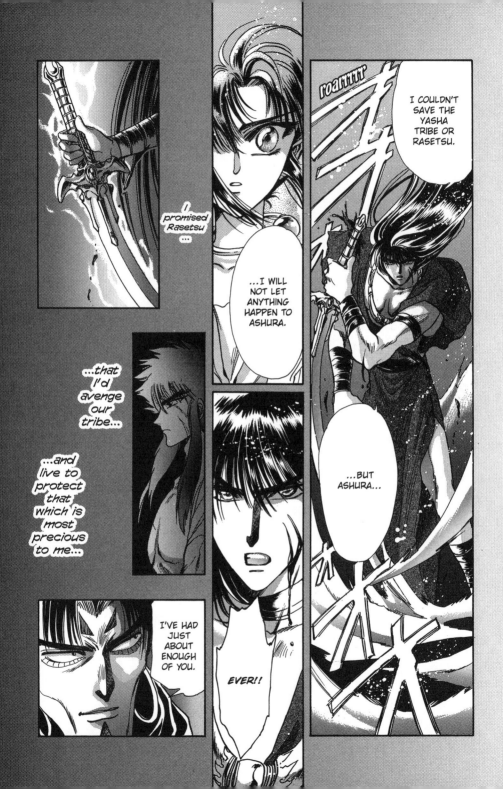

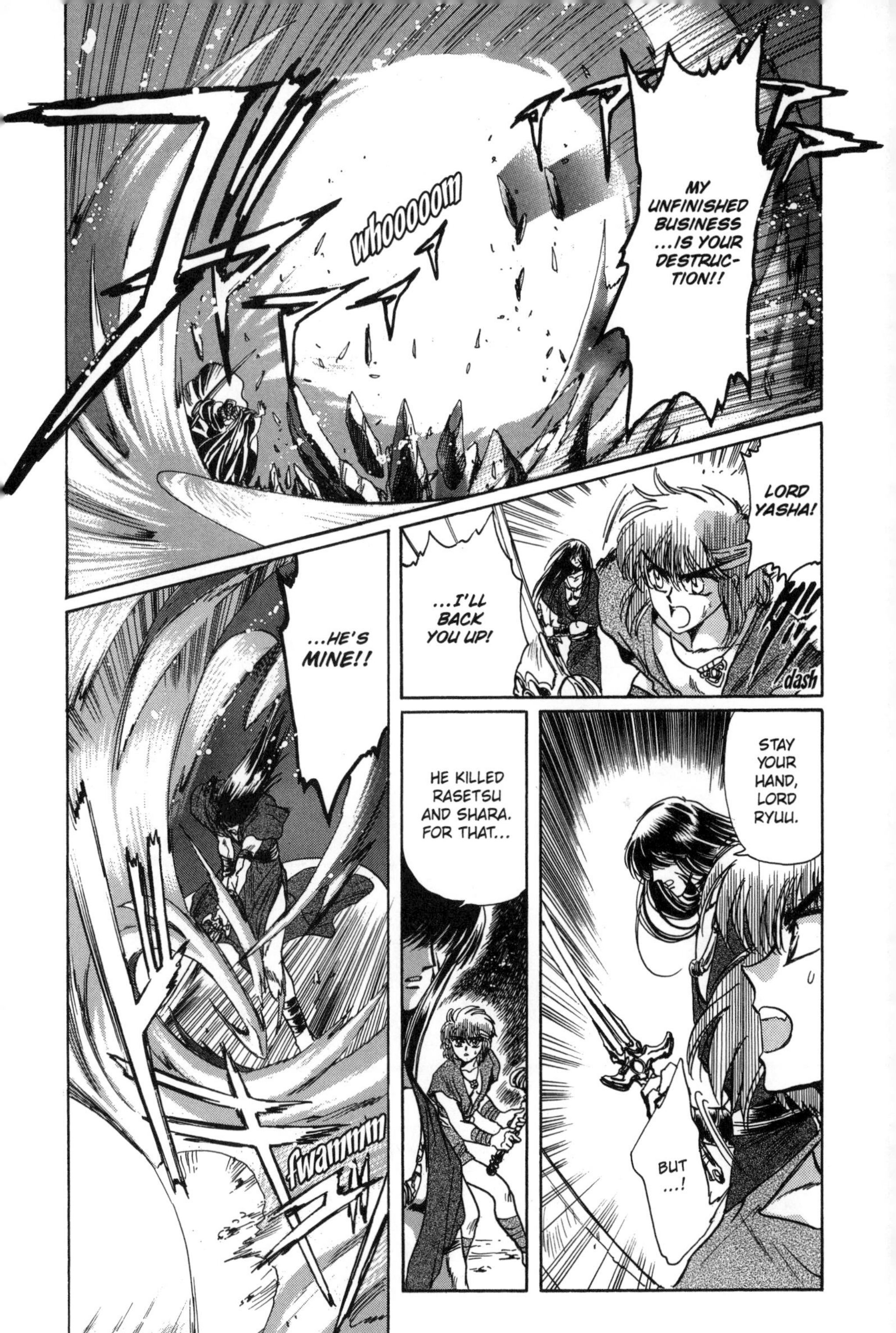
MY UNFINISHED BUSINESS ...IS YOUR DESTRUC-TION!!
whoooooom
LORD YASHA!
...I'LL BACK YOU UP!
dash
STAY YOUR HAND, LORD RYUU.
BUT ...!
HE KILLED RASETSU AND SHARA. FOR THAT...
...HE'S MINE!!
fwammm

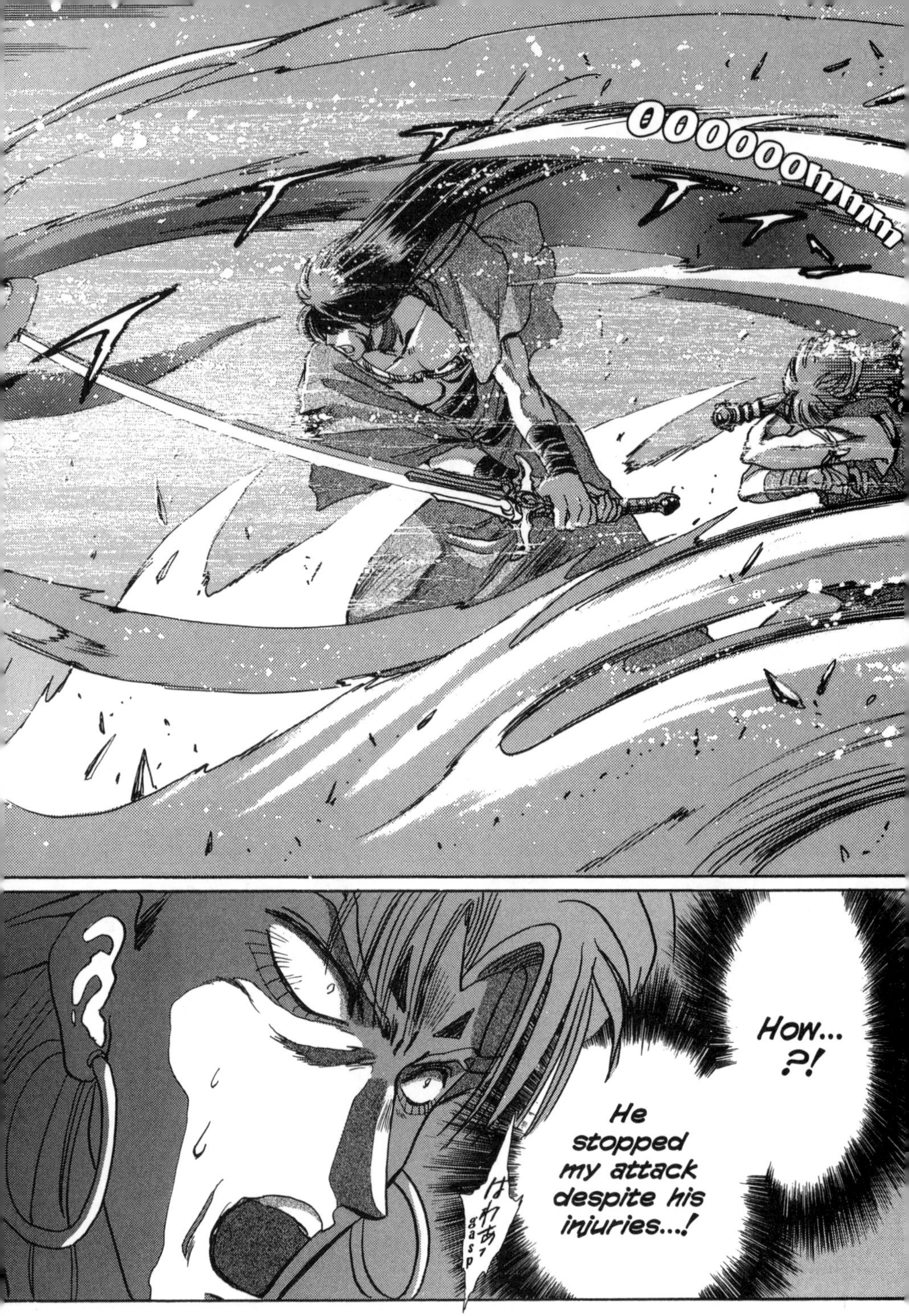
Ooooooommmm
How...?!
He stopped my attack despite his injuries...!
はわあっ
gasp

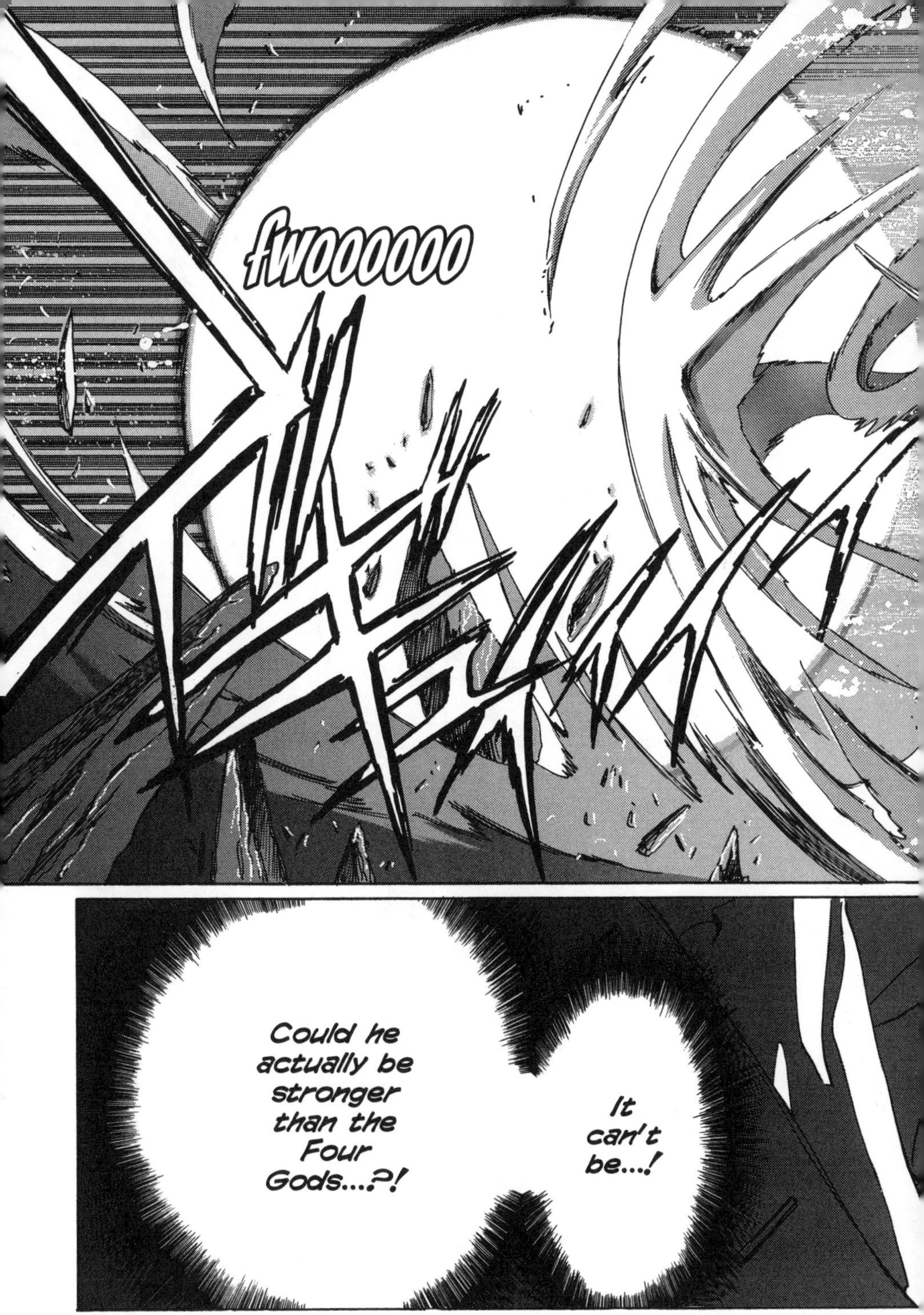
fwoooooo
It can't be...!
Could he actually be stronger than the Four Gods...?!

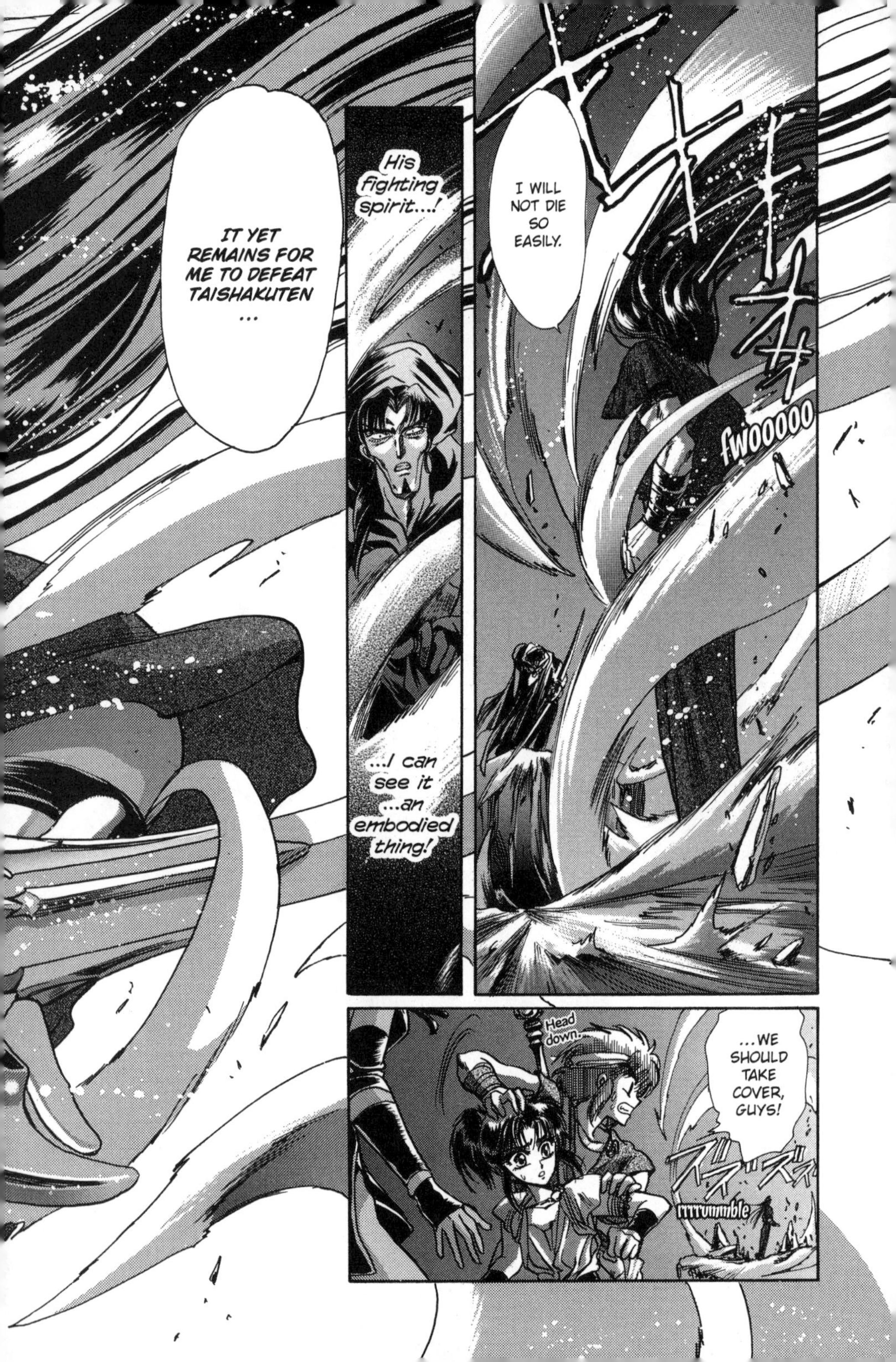
I WILL NOT DIE SO EASILY.
fwoooooo
His fighting spirit....!
...I can see it ...an embodied thing!
...WE SHOULD TAKE COVER, GUYS!
Head down...
rrrrummble
IT YET REMAINS FOR ME TO DEFEAT TAISHAKUTEN ...

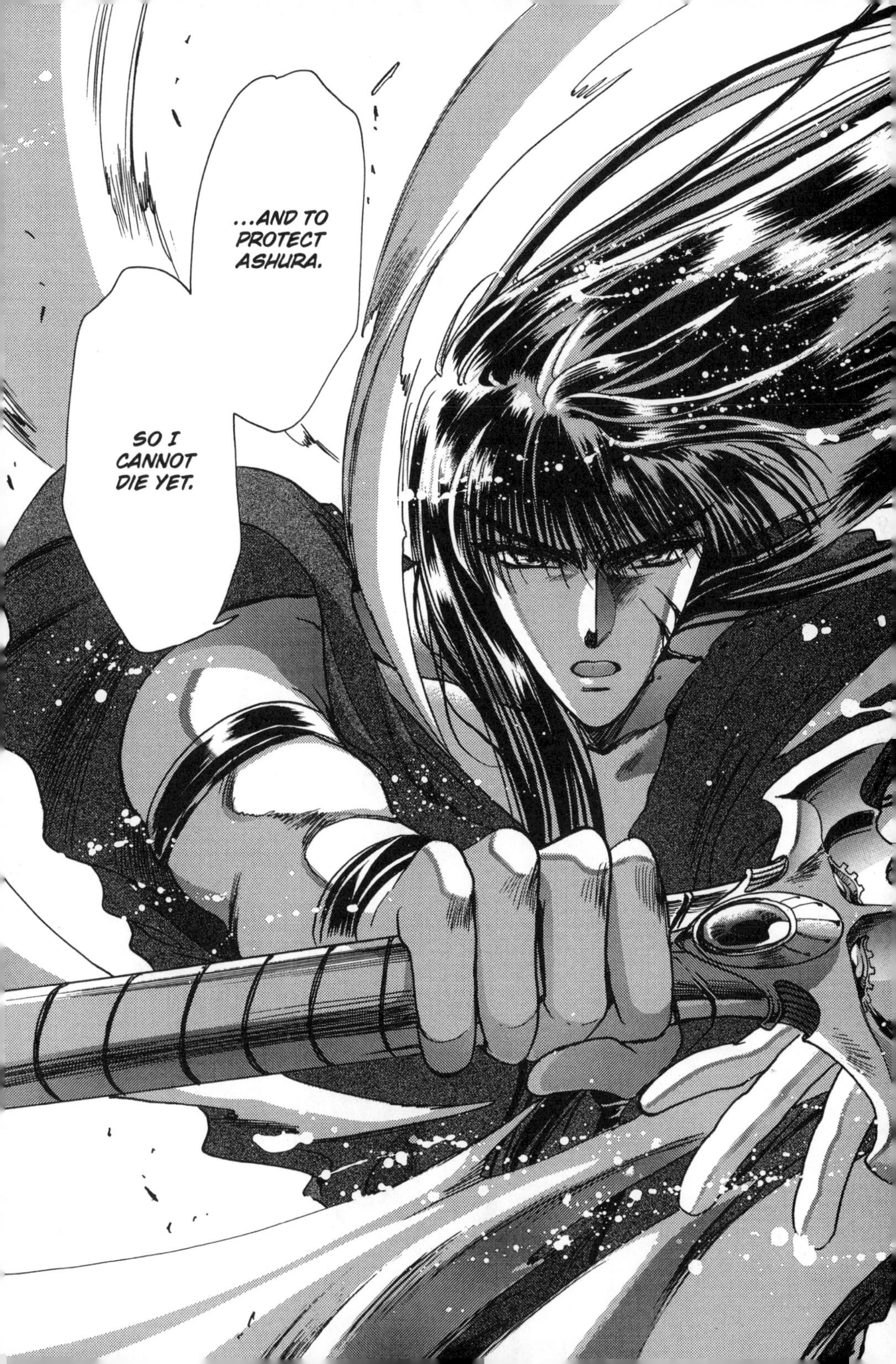
...AND TO PROTECT ASHURA.
SO I CANNOT DIE YET.

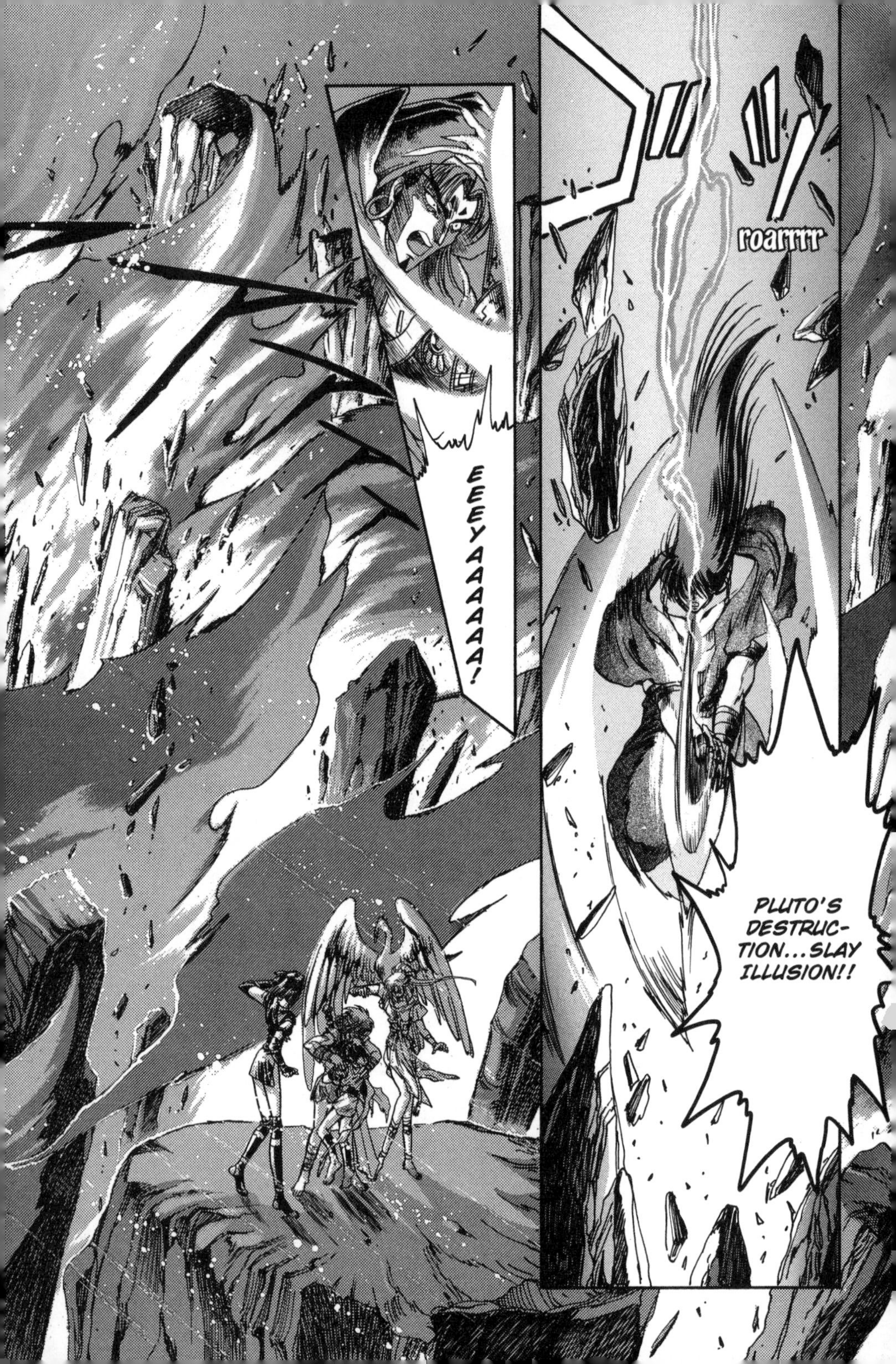
roarrrr
PLUTO'S DESTRUCTION...SLAY ILLUSION!!
EEEYAAAAAAA!

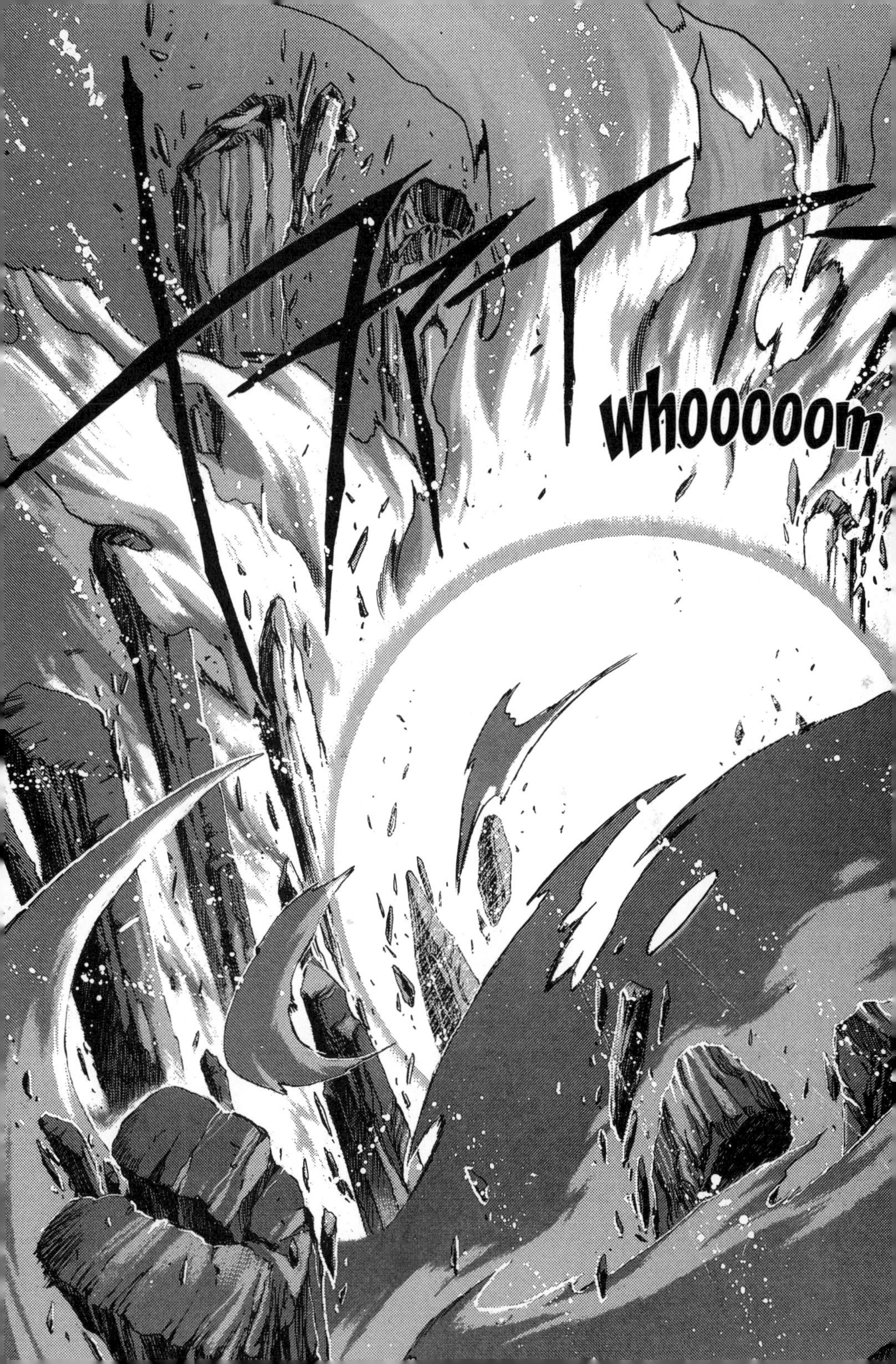
whoooooom

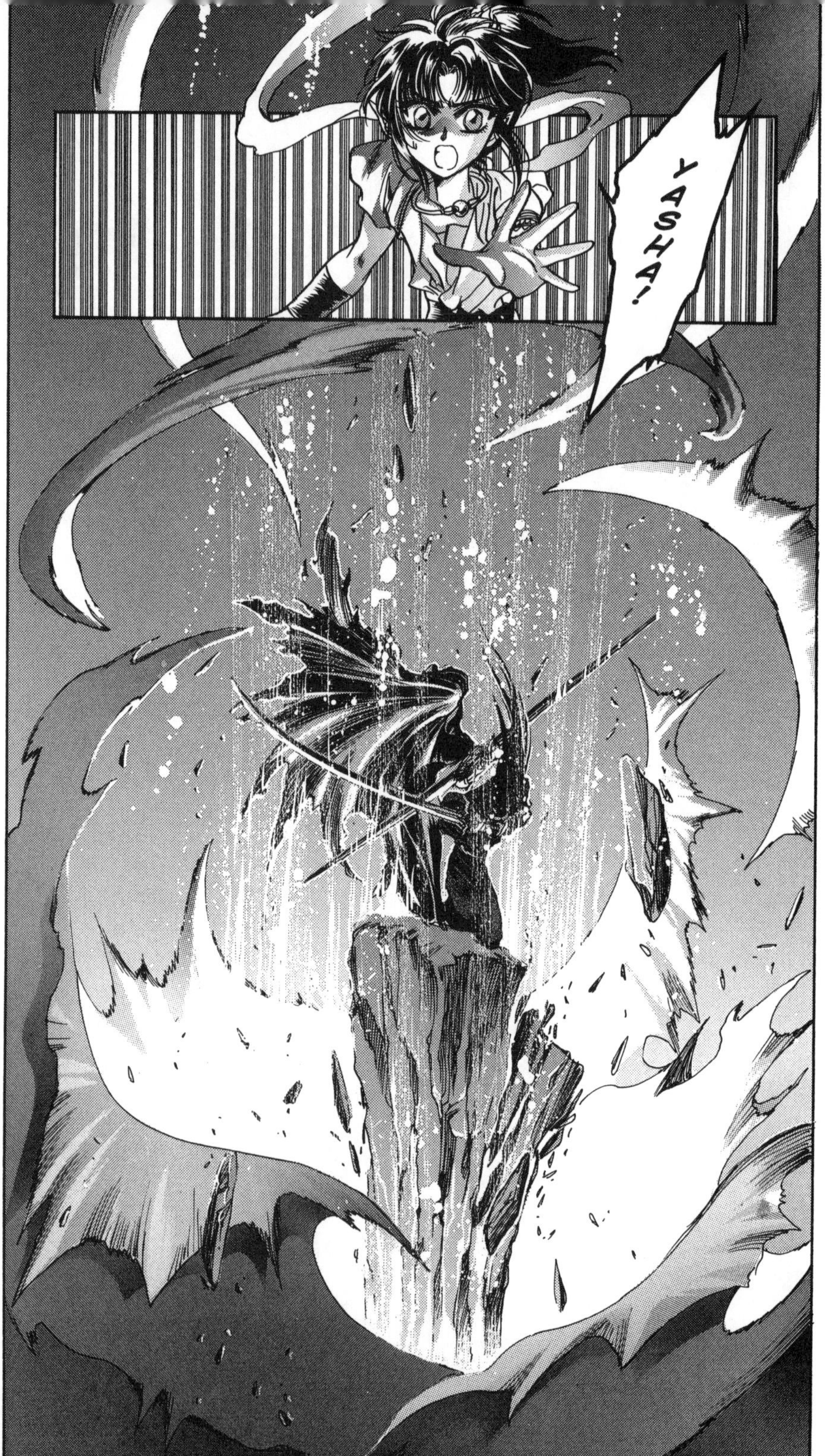
YASHA!

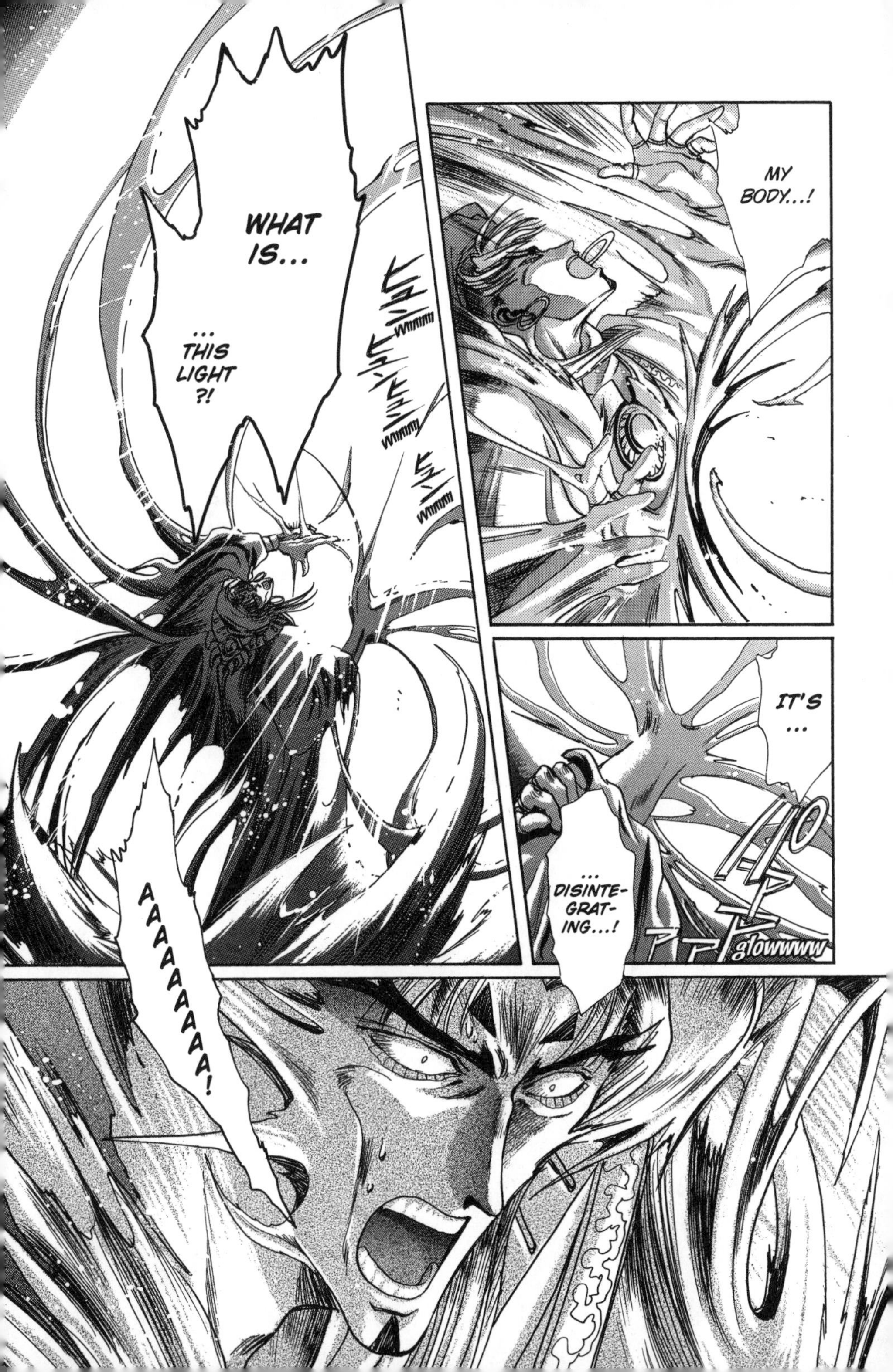
MY BODY...!
IT'S ...
...DISINTEGRATING...!
glowwww
WHAT IS...
...THIS LIGHT ?!
wiiiiin
wiiiiin
wiiiiin
AAAAAAAAAA!

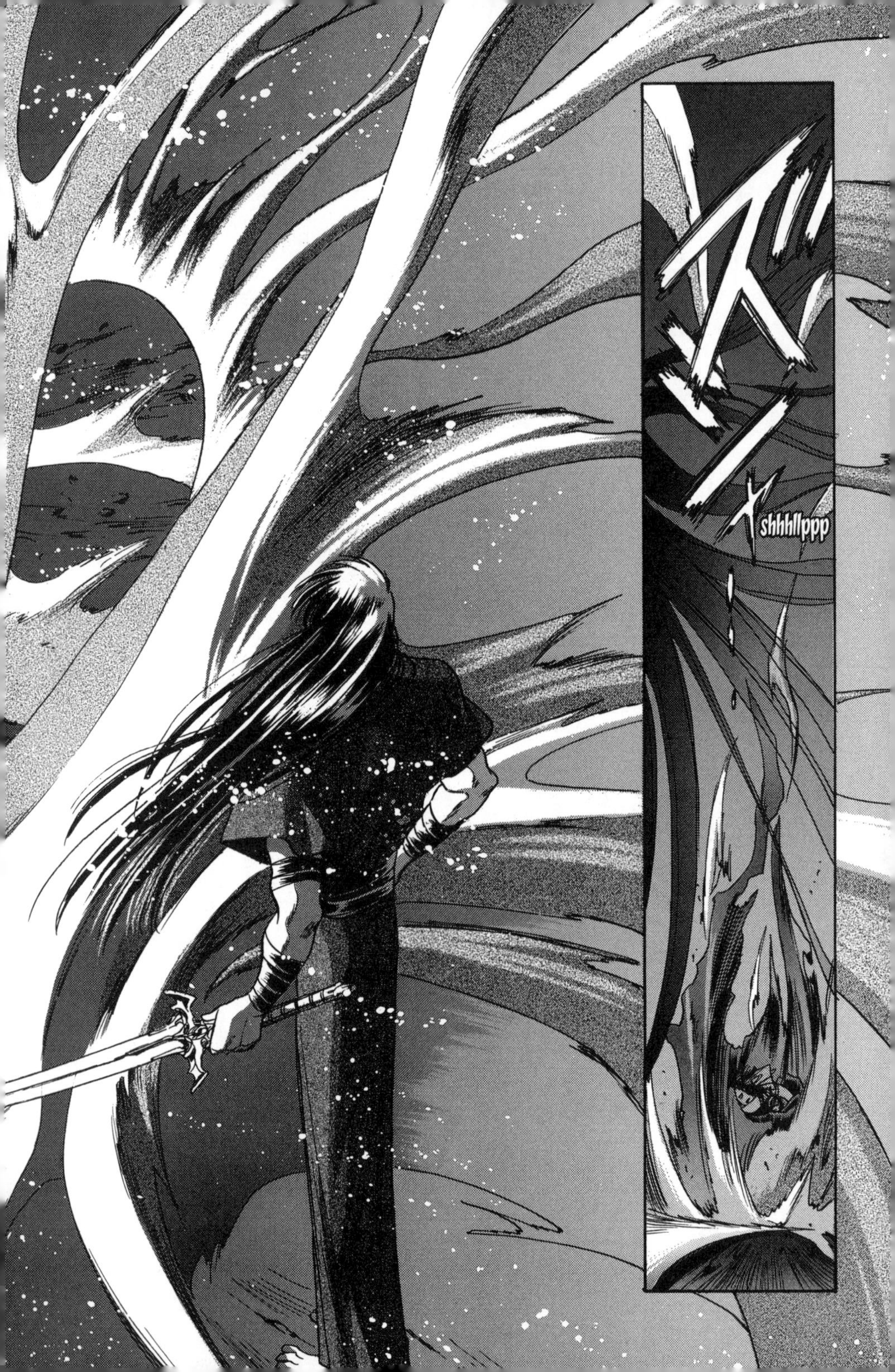
shhhllppp

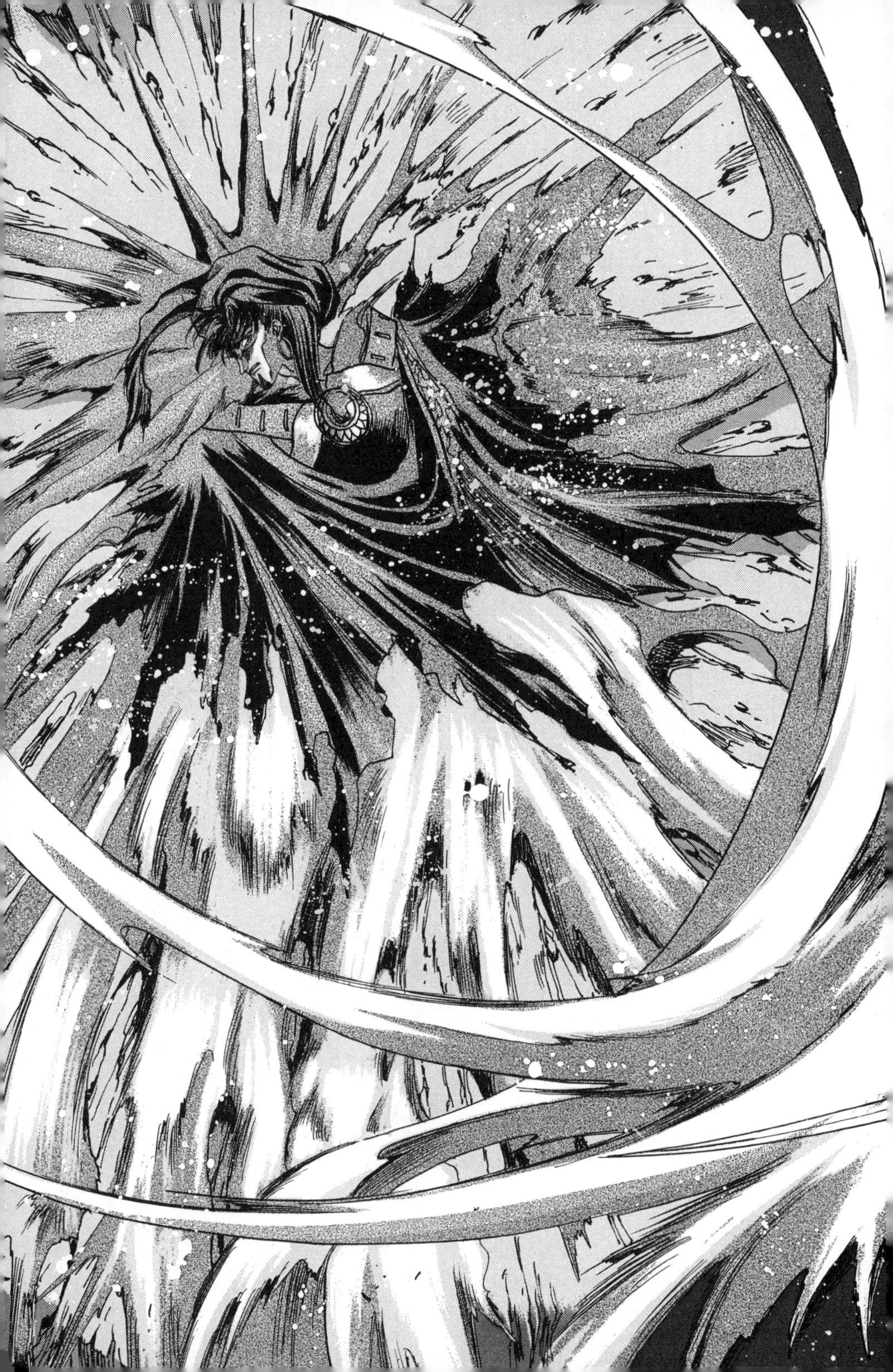

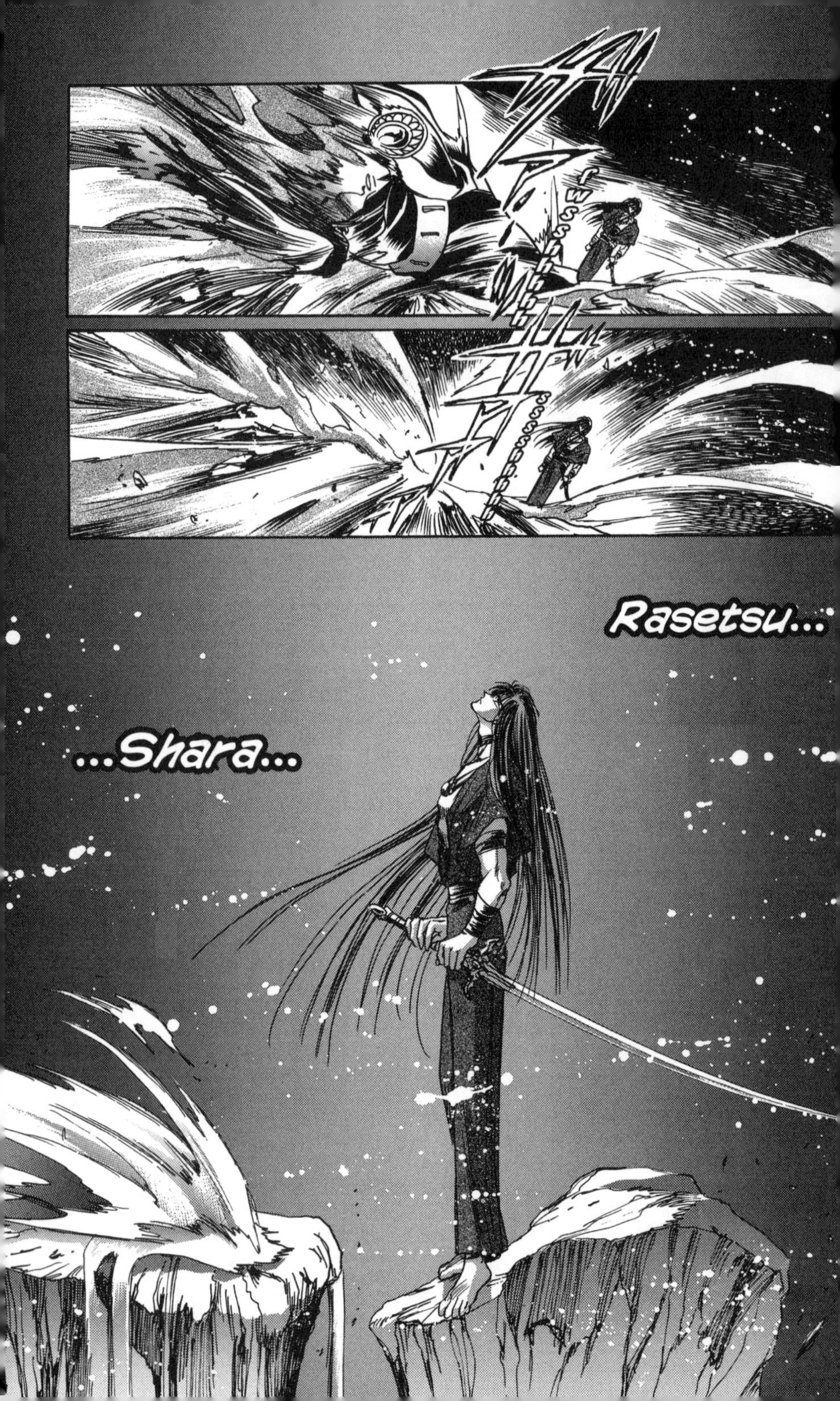
fwsshhhhhh
ssssshhhhh
Rasetsu...
...Shara...

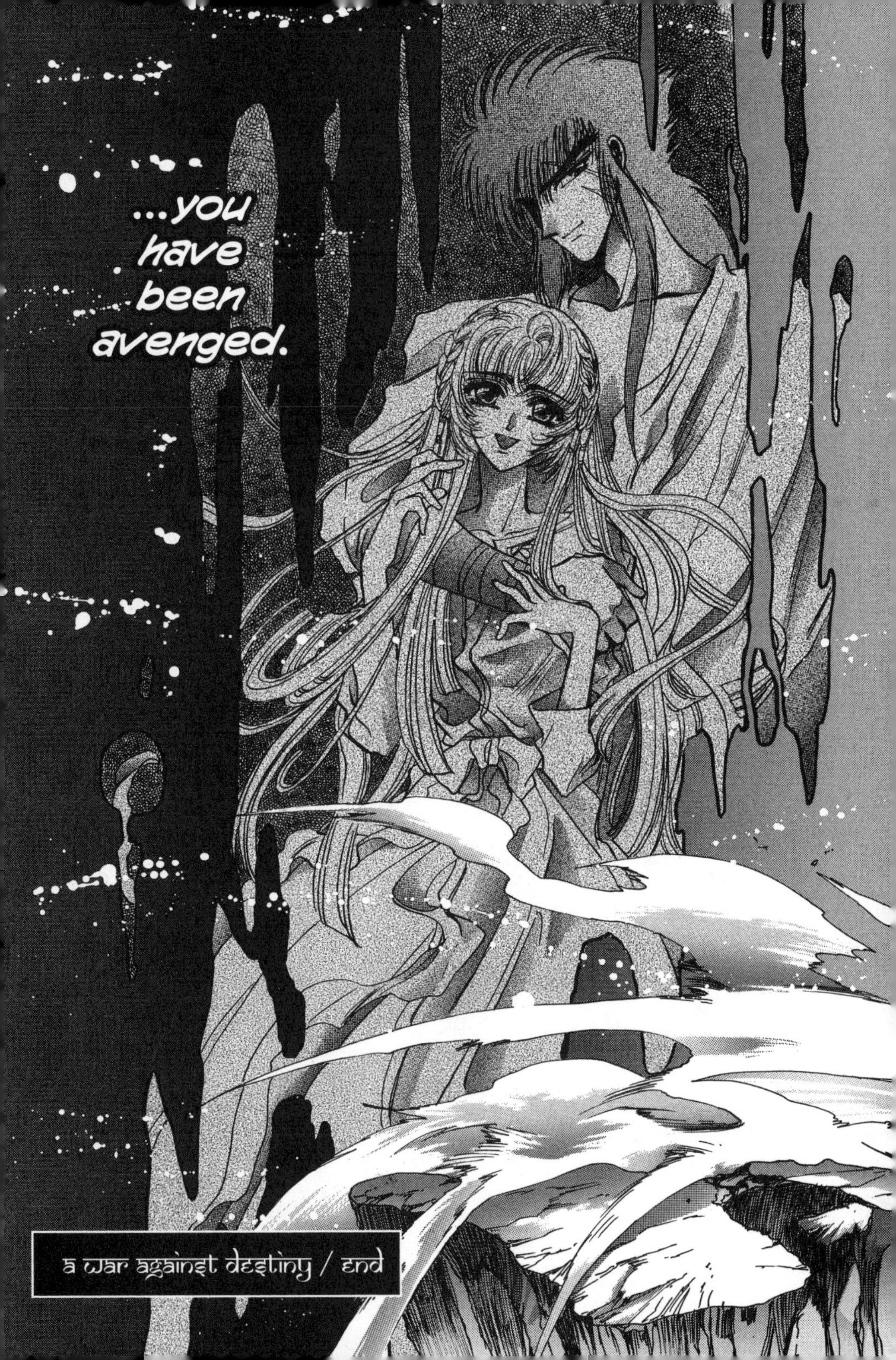
...you have been avenged.
a war against destiny / end

CLAMP

RG VEDA

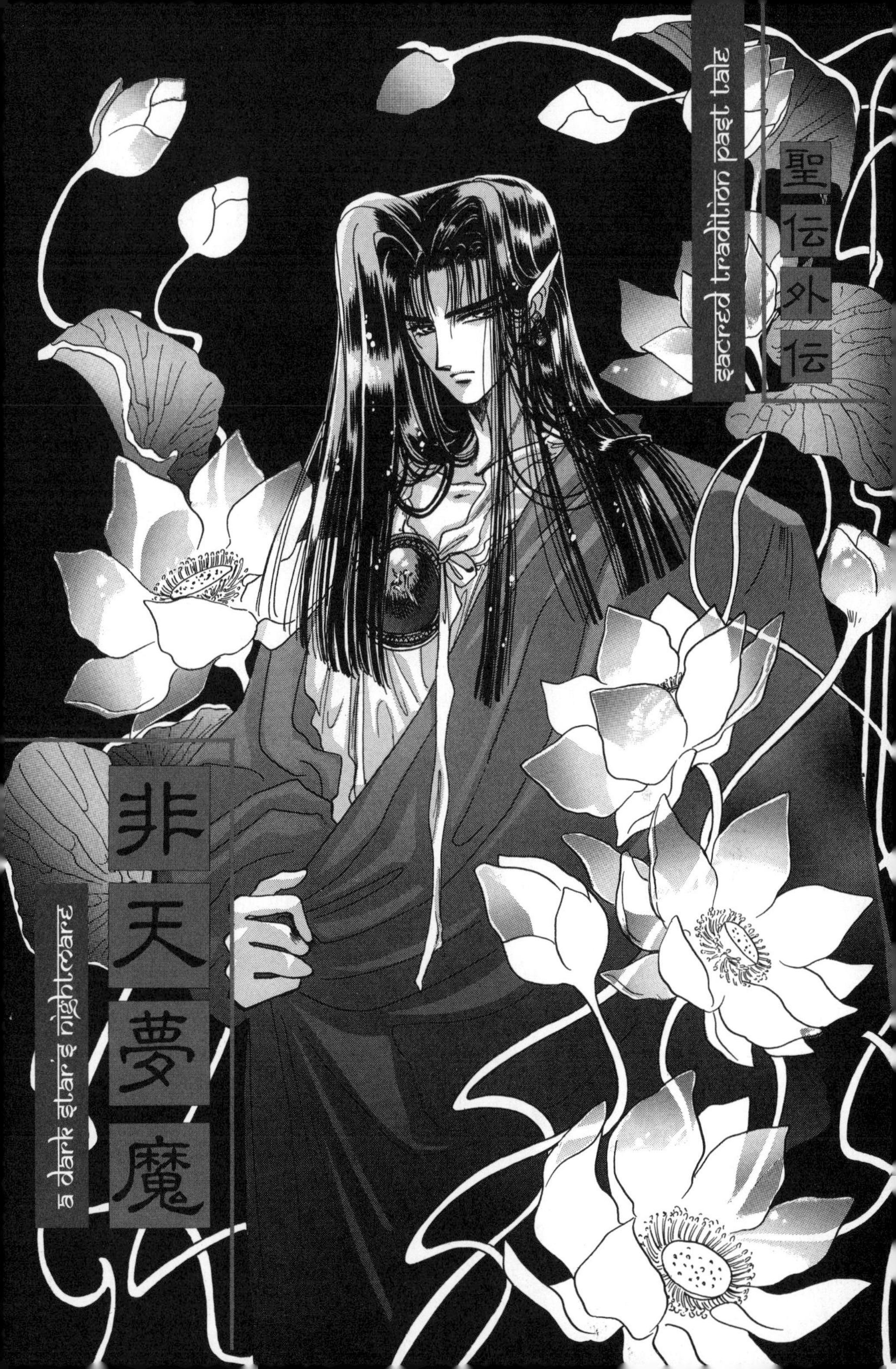
聖伝外伝
sacred tradition past tale
非天夢魔
a dark star's nightmare

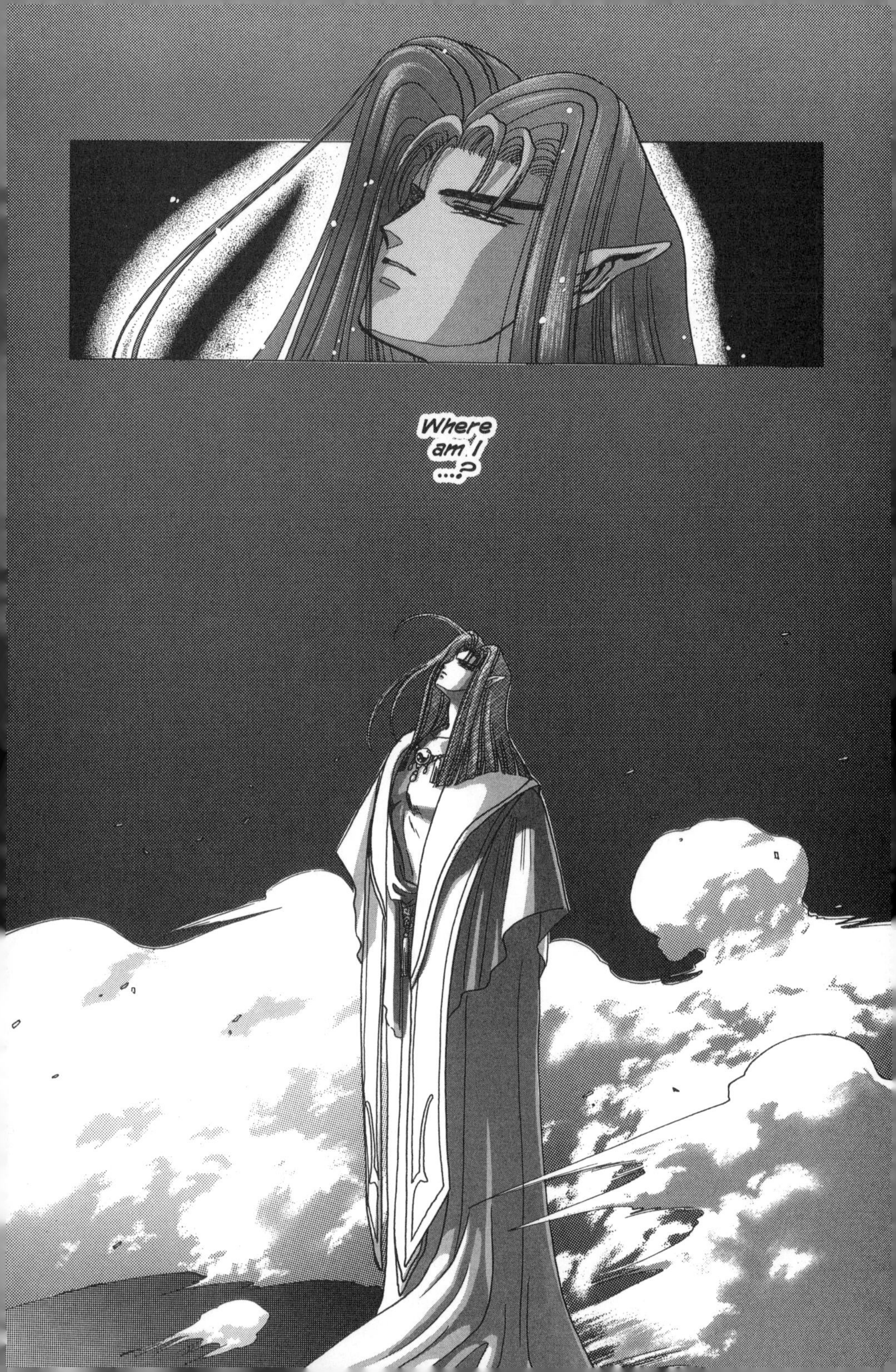
Where am I ...?

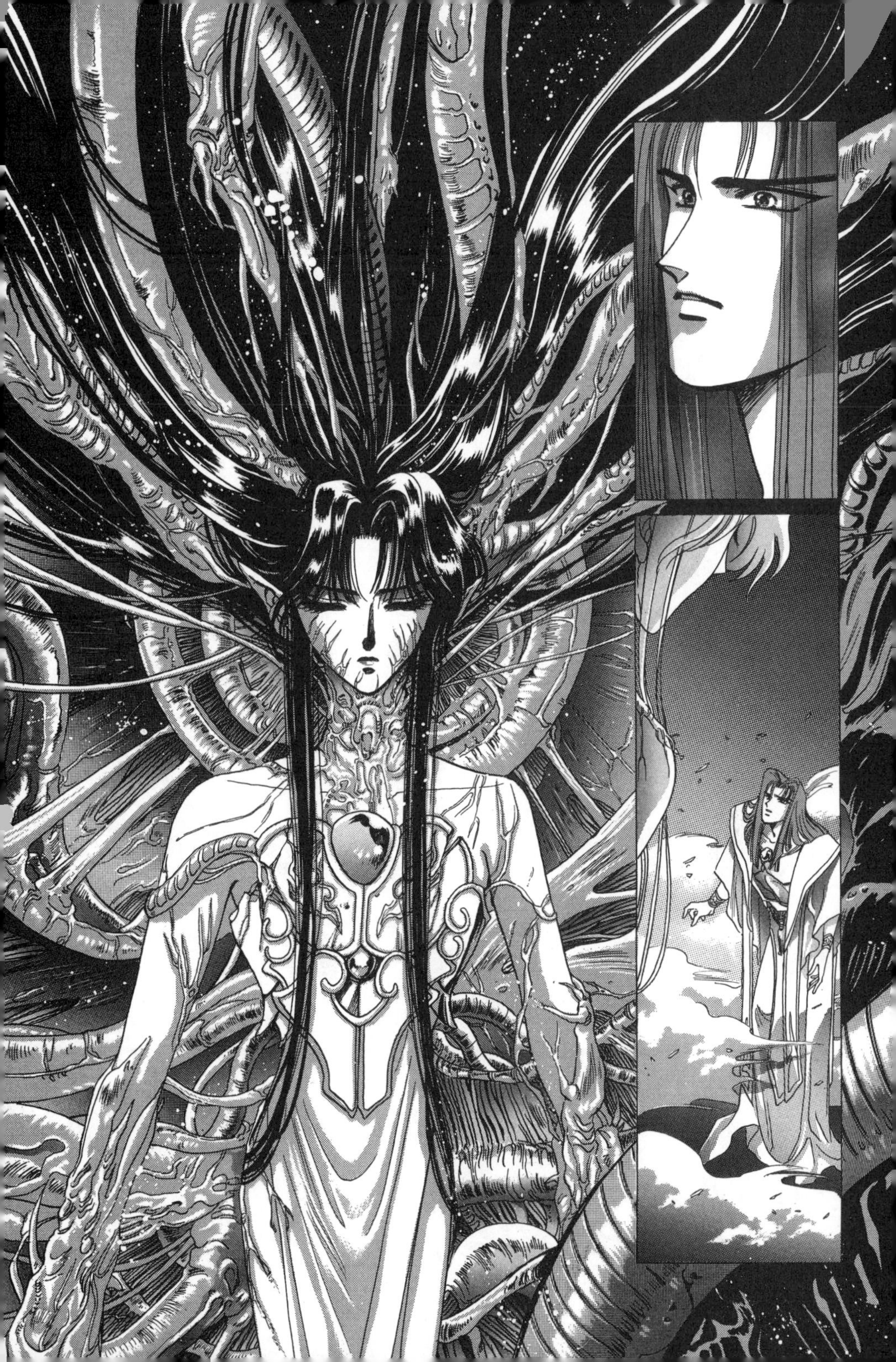

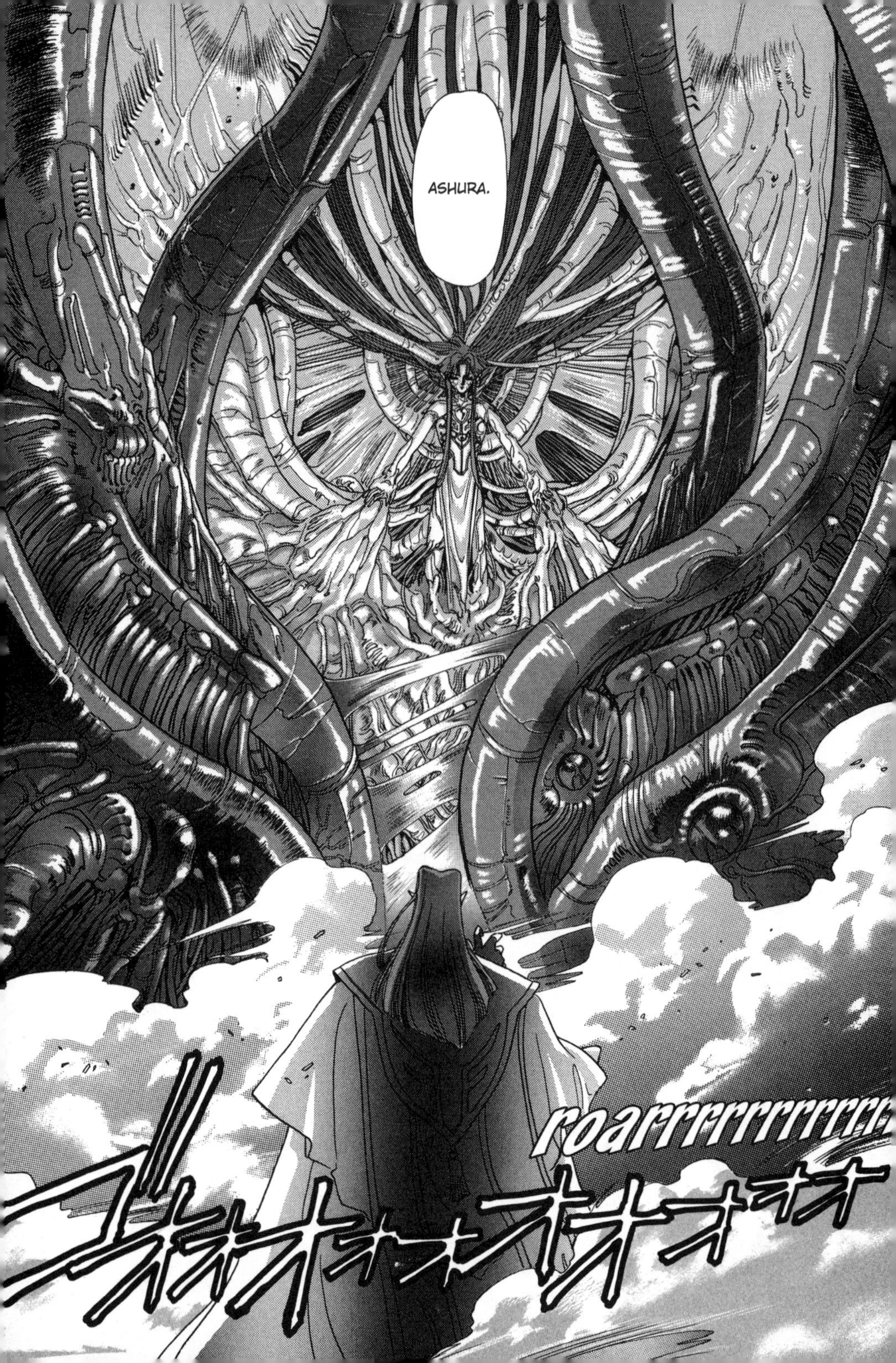
ASHURA.
roarrrrrrrrrrr

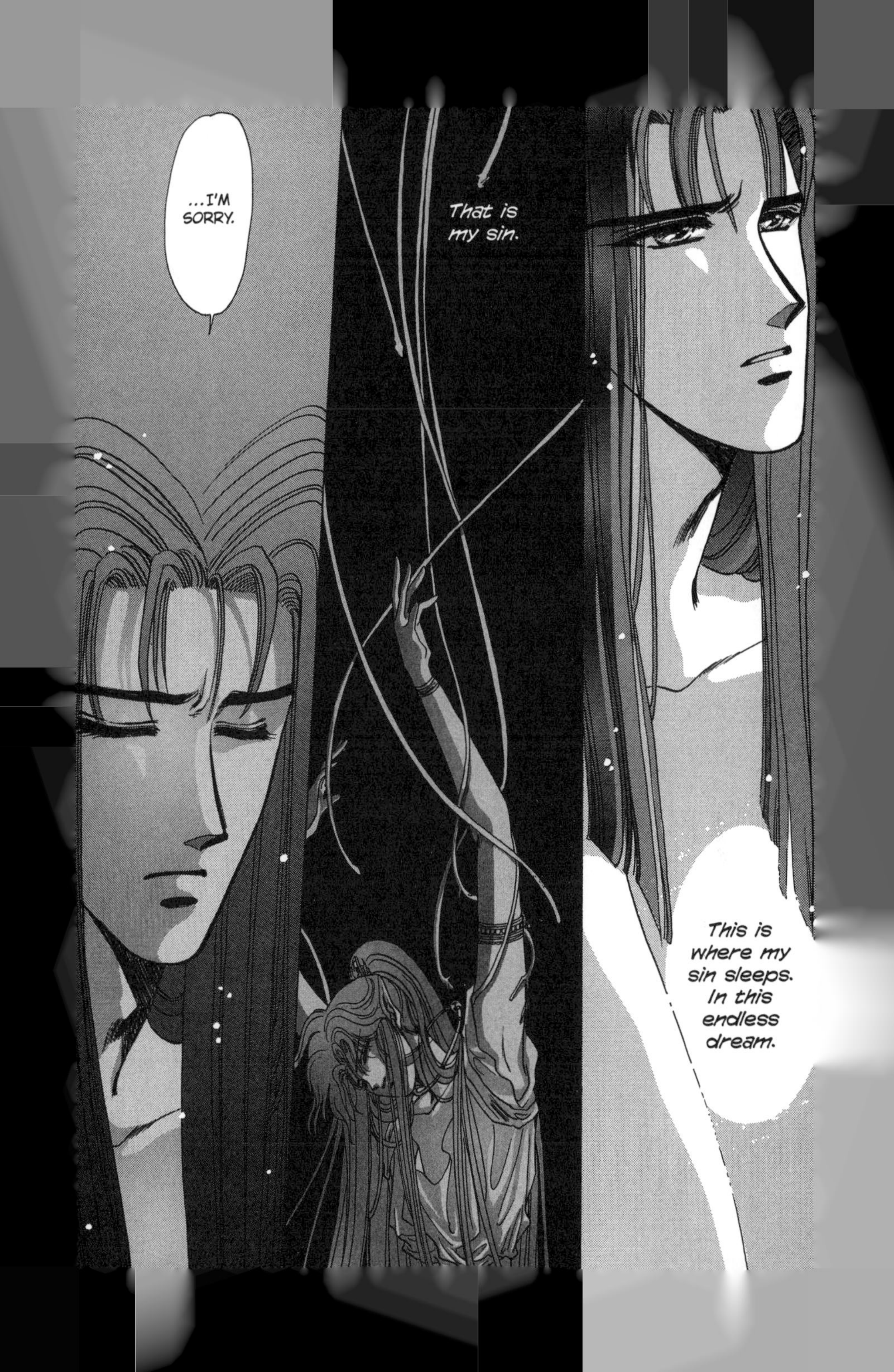
This is where my sin sleeps. In this endless dream.
That is my sin.
...I'M SORRY.

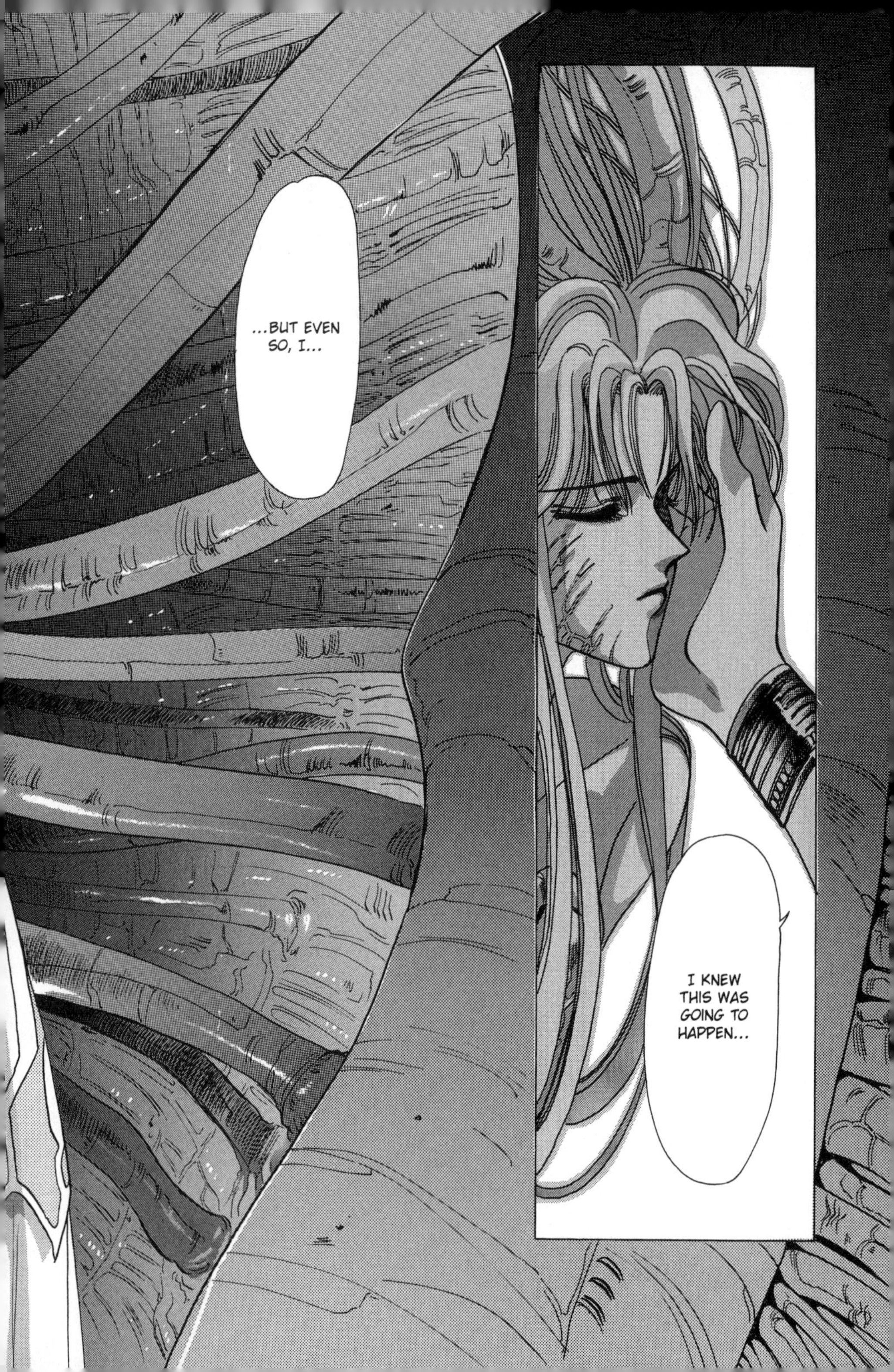
I KNEW THIS WAS GOING TO HAPPEN...
...BUT EVEN SO, I...

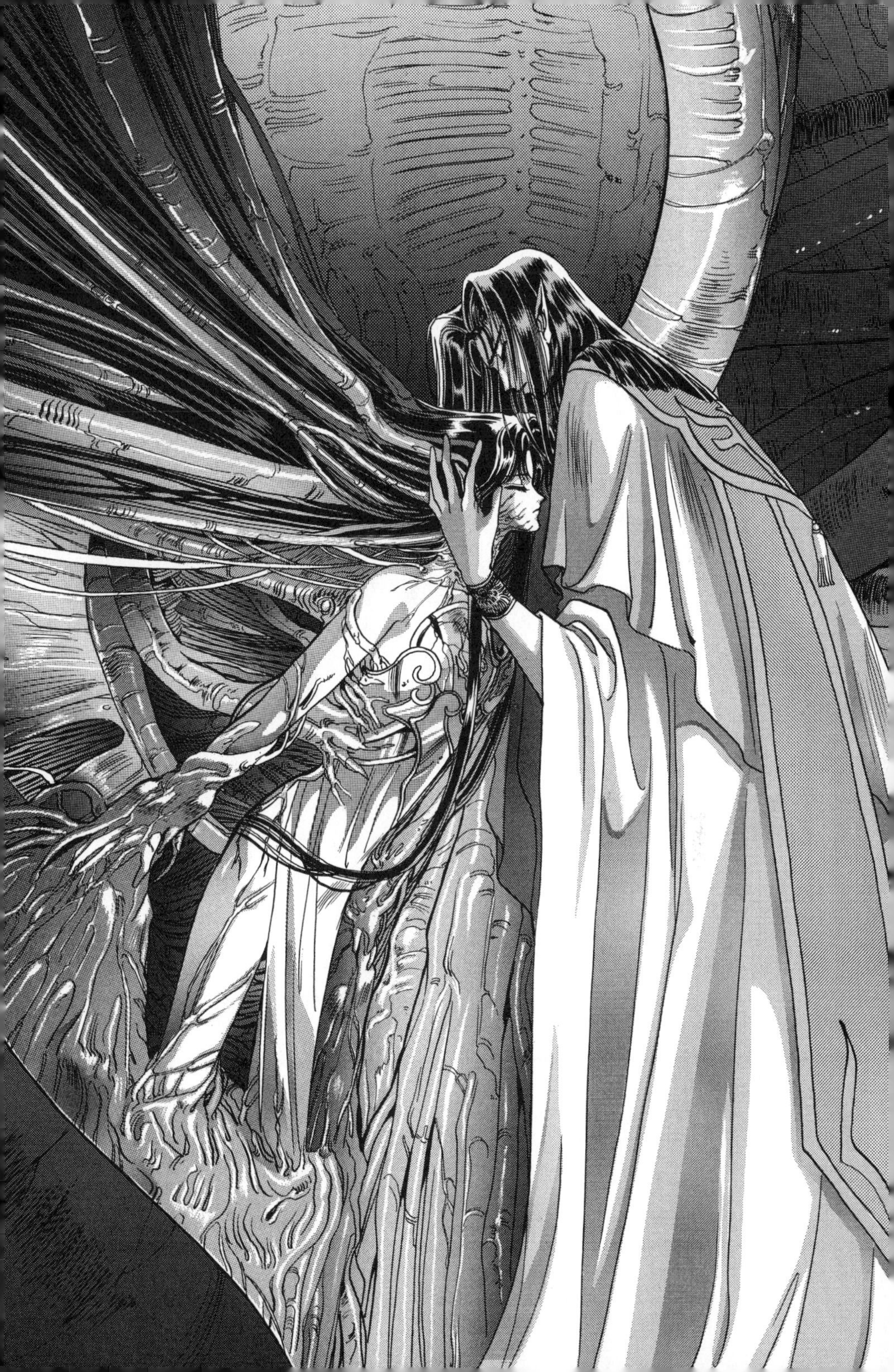

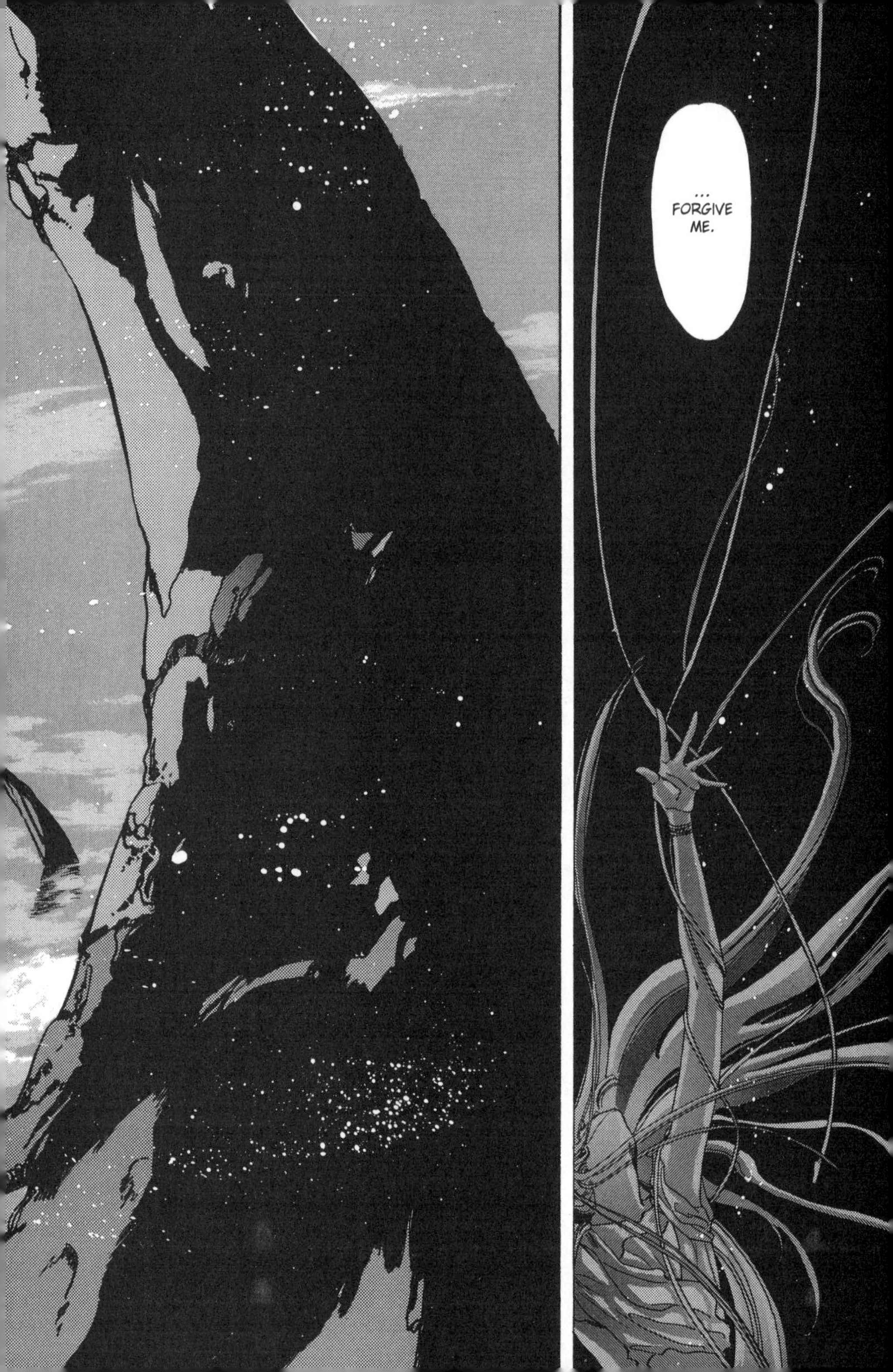
...
FORGIVE
ME.

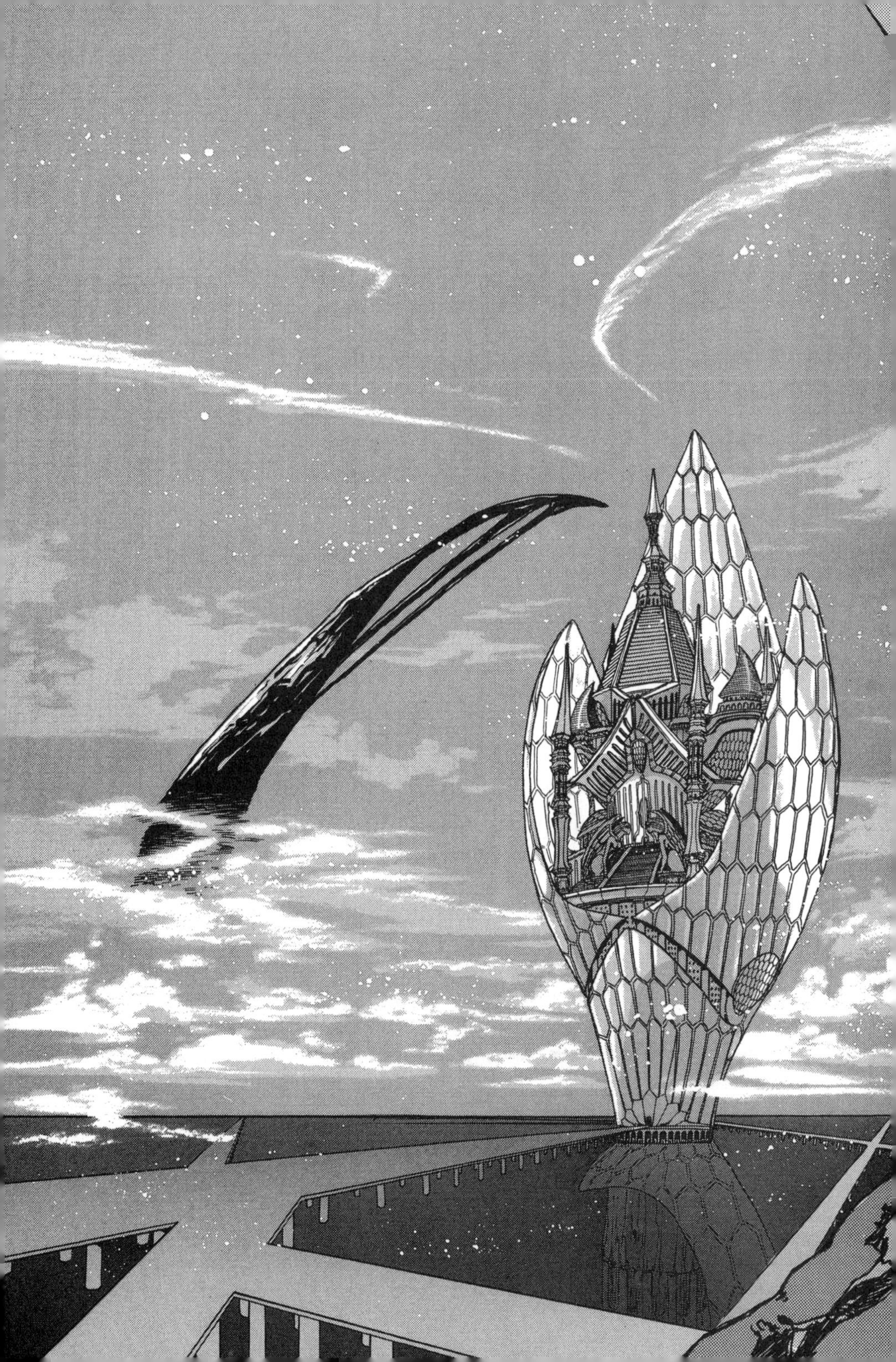

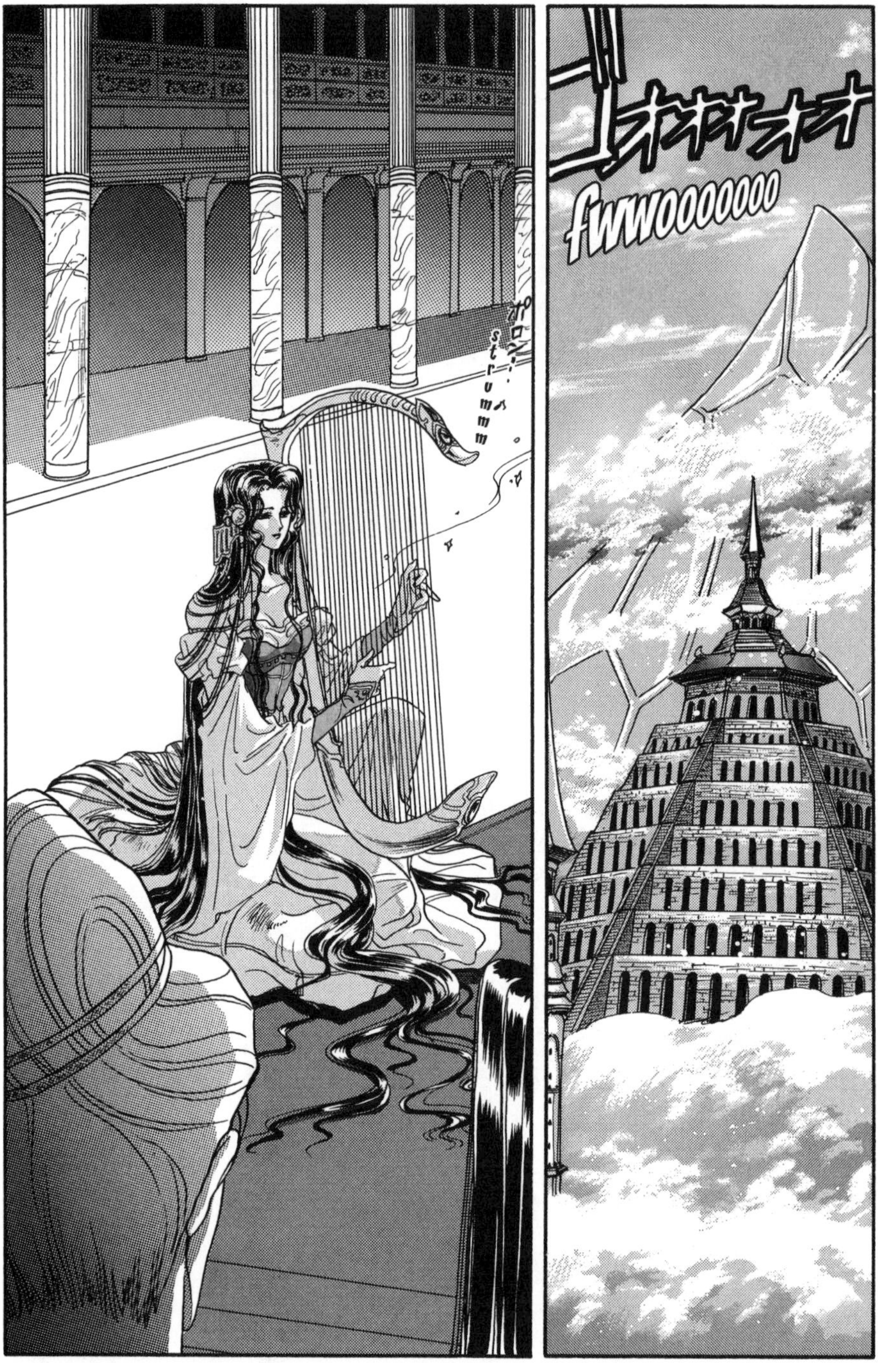
ゴオオオオオオ
fwwooooooo
ポロン…♪
strummm

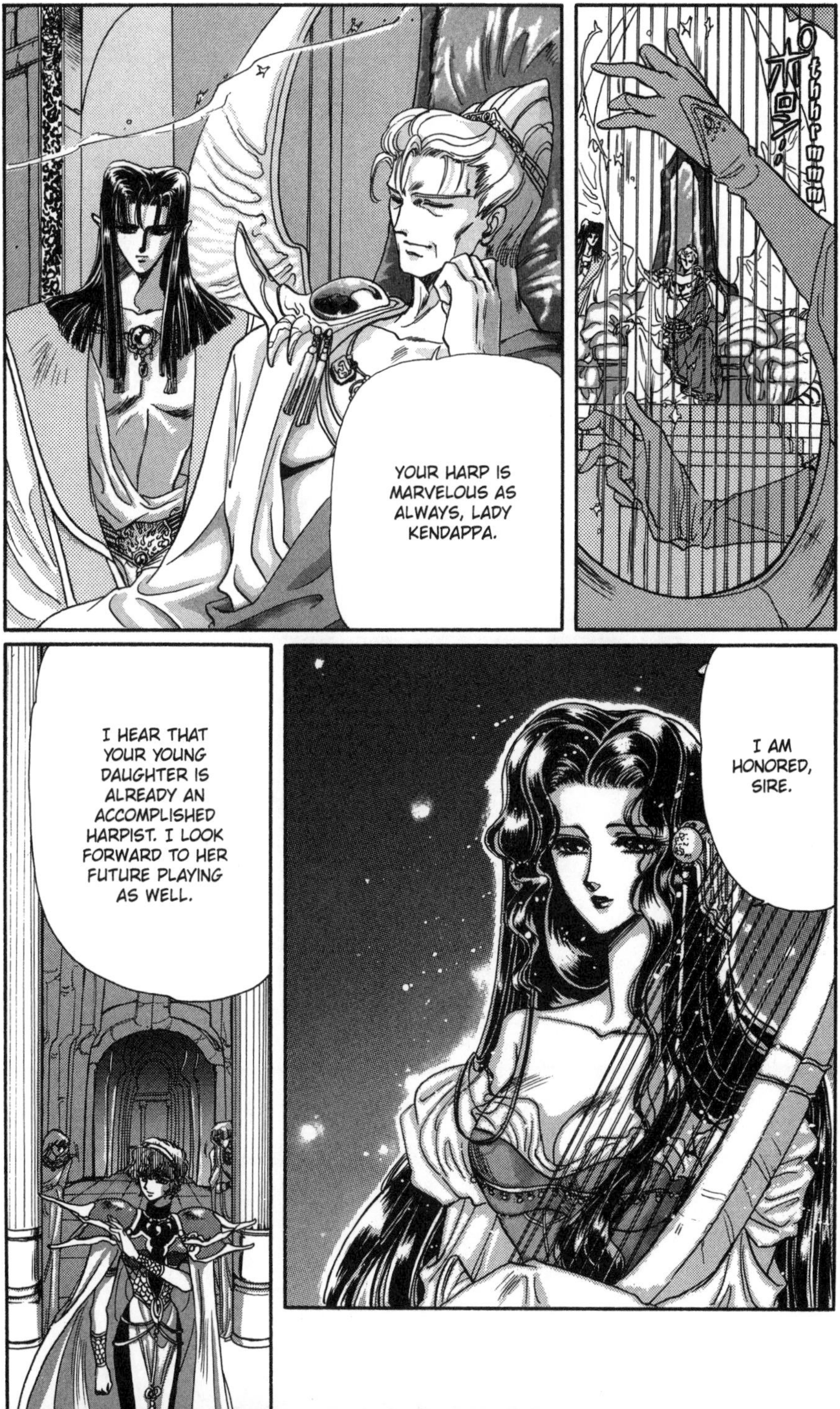
ポロン…
thhrmmm
YOUR HARP IS MARVELOUS AS ALWAYS, LADY KENDAPPA.
I AM HONORED, SIRE.
I HEAR THAT YOUR YOUNG DAUGHTER IS ALREADY AN ACCOMPLISHED HARPIST. I LOOK FORWARD TO HER FUTURE PLAYING AS WELL.

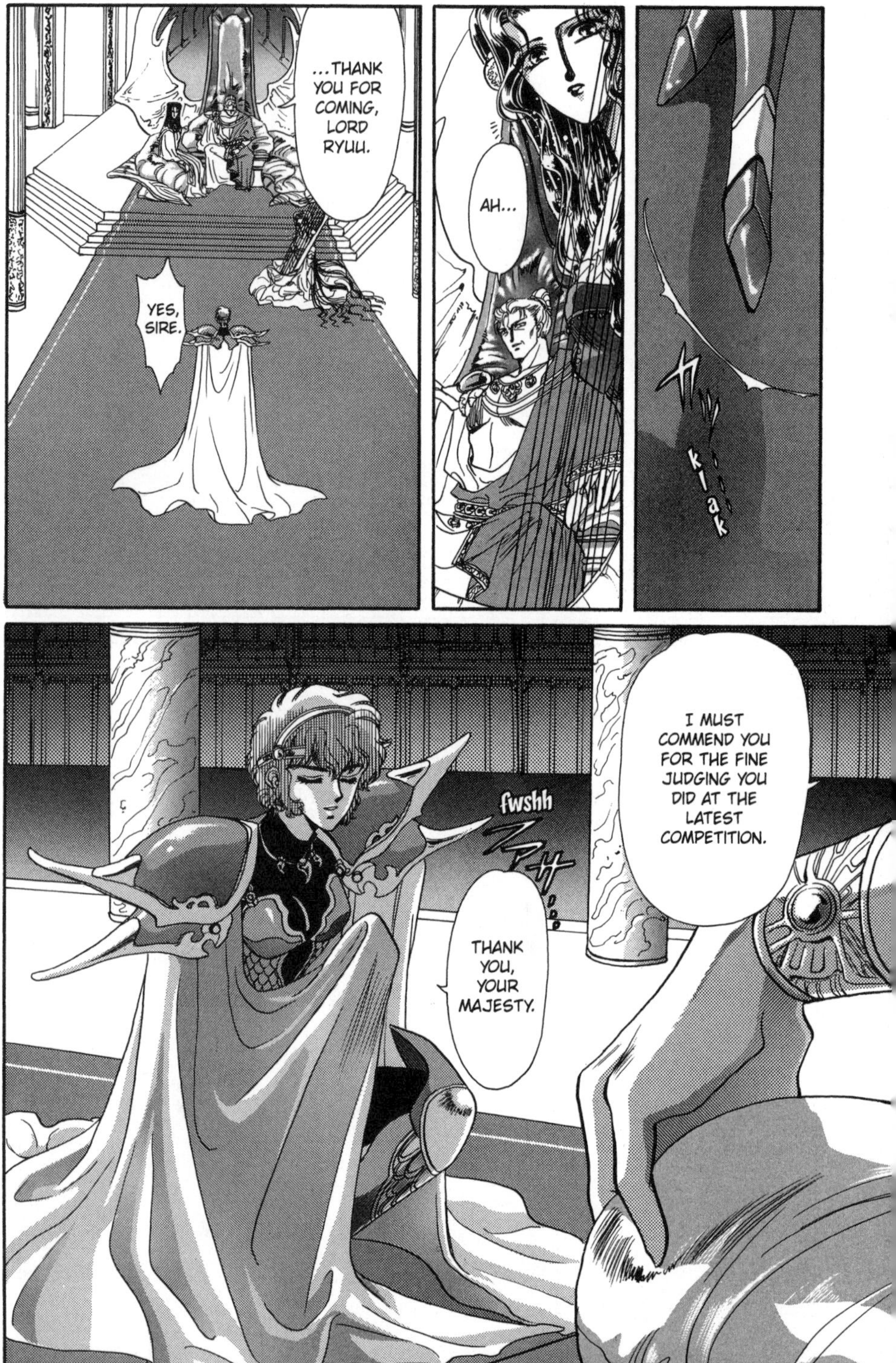
klak
AH...
...THANK YOU FOR COMING, LORD RYUU.
YES, SIRE.
I MUST COMMEND YOU FOR THE FINE JUDGING YOU DID AT THE LATEST COMPETITION.
fwshh
THANK YOU, YOUR MAJESTY.

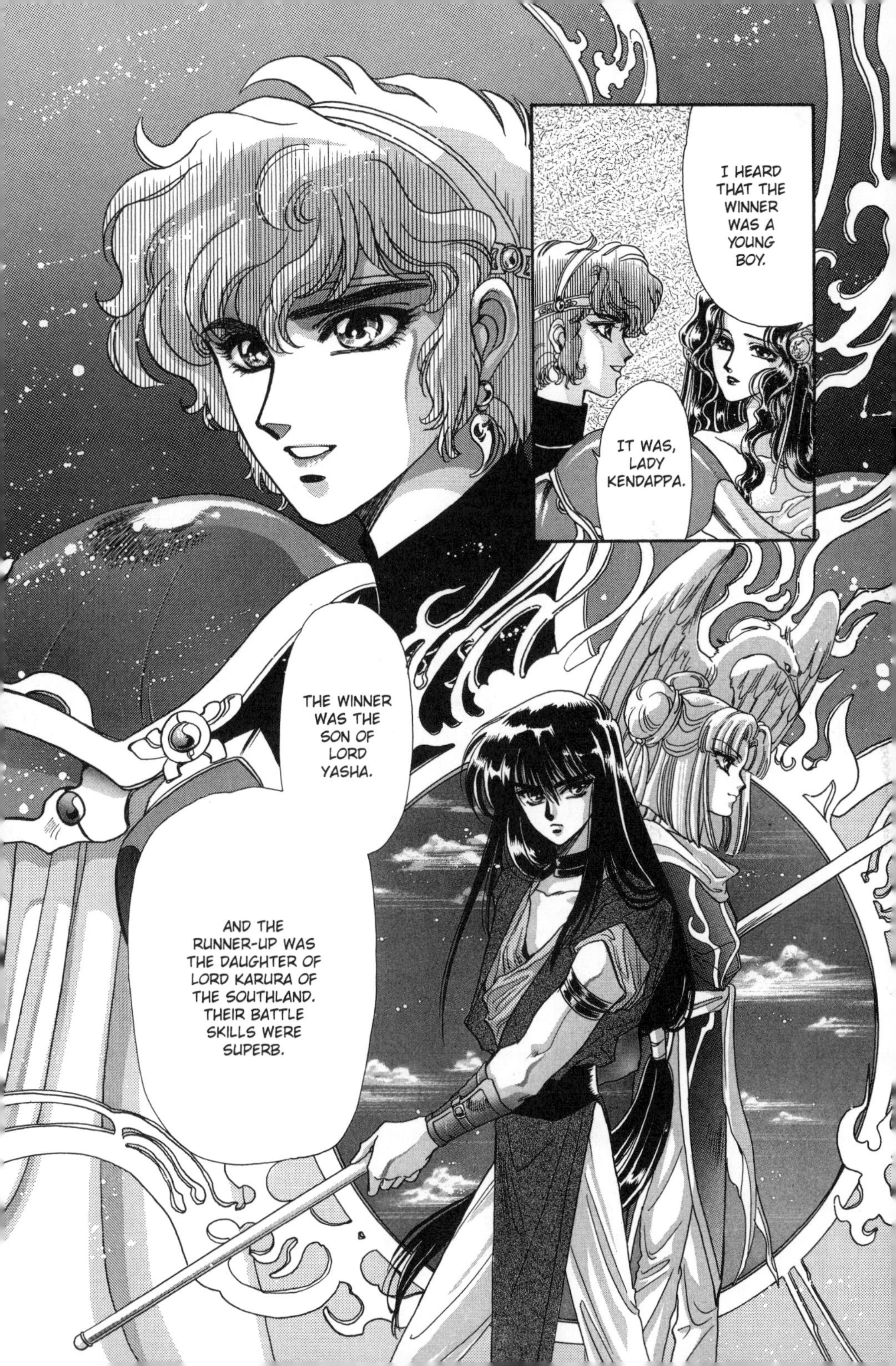
I HEARD THAT THE WINNER WAS A YOUNG BOY.
IT WAS, LADY KENDAPPA.
THE WINNER WAS THE SON OF LORD YASHA.
AND THE RUNNER-UP WAS THE DAUGHTER OF LORD KARURA OF THE SOUTHLAND. THEIR BATTLE SKILLS WERE SUPERB.

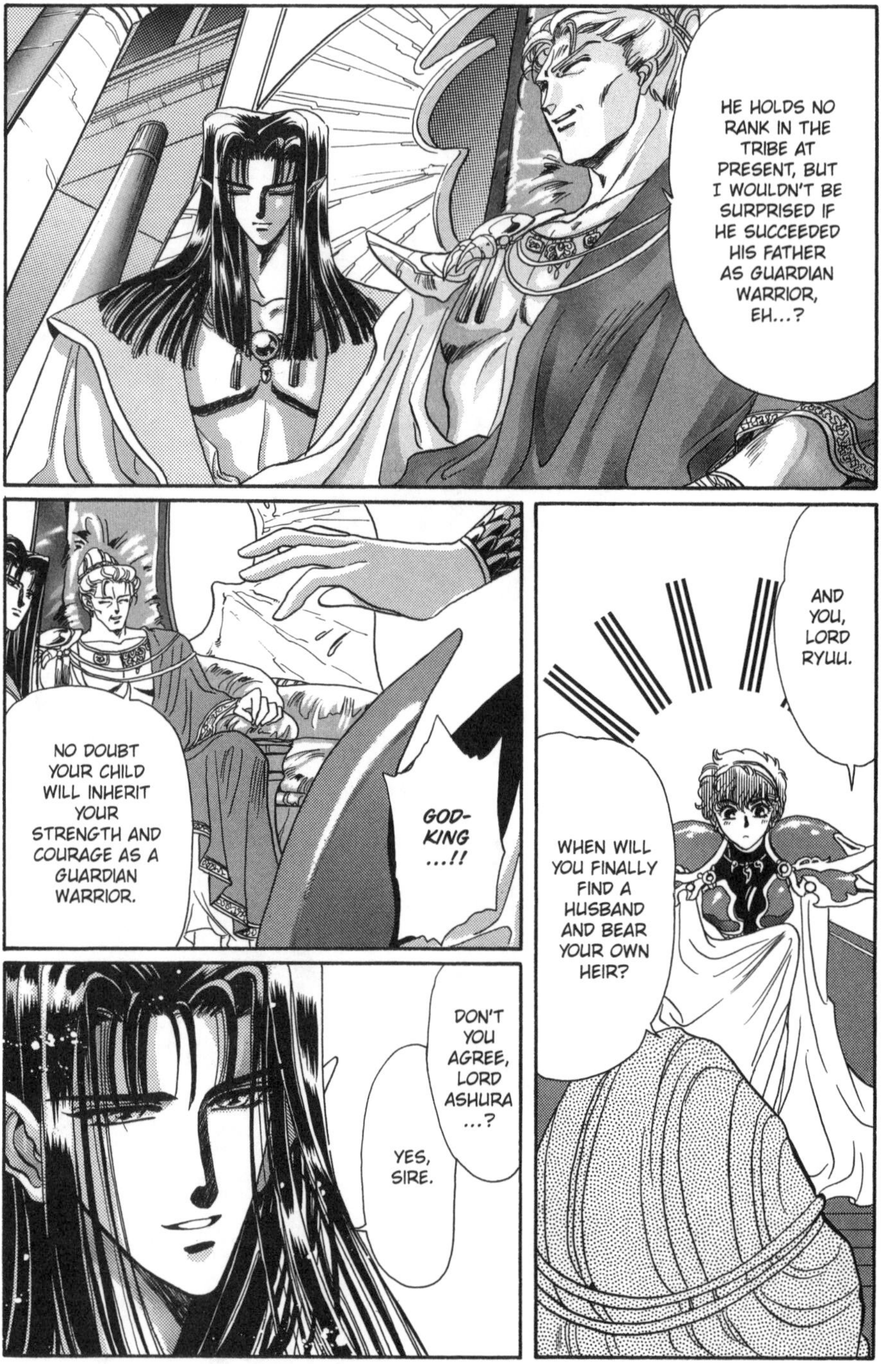
HE HOLDS NO RANK IN THE TRIBE AT PRESENT, BUT I WOULDN'T BE SURPRISED IF HE SUCCEEDED HIS FATHER AS GUARDIAN WARRIOR, EH...?
AND YOU, LORD RYUU.
WHEN WILL YOU FINALLY FIND A HUSBAND AND BEAR YOUR OWN HEIR?
GOD-KING ...!!
NO DOUBT YOUR CHILD WILL INHERIT YOUR STRENGTH AND COURAGE AS A GUARDIAN WARRIOR.
DON'T YOU AGREE, LORD ASHURA ...?
YES, SIRE.

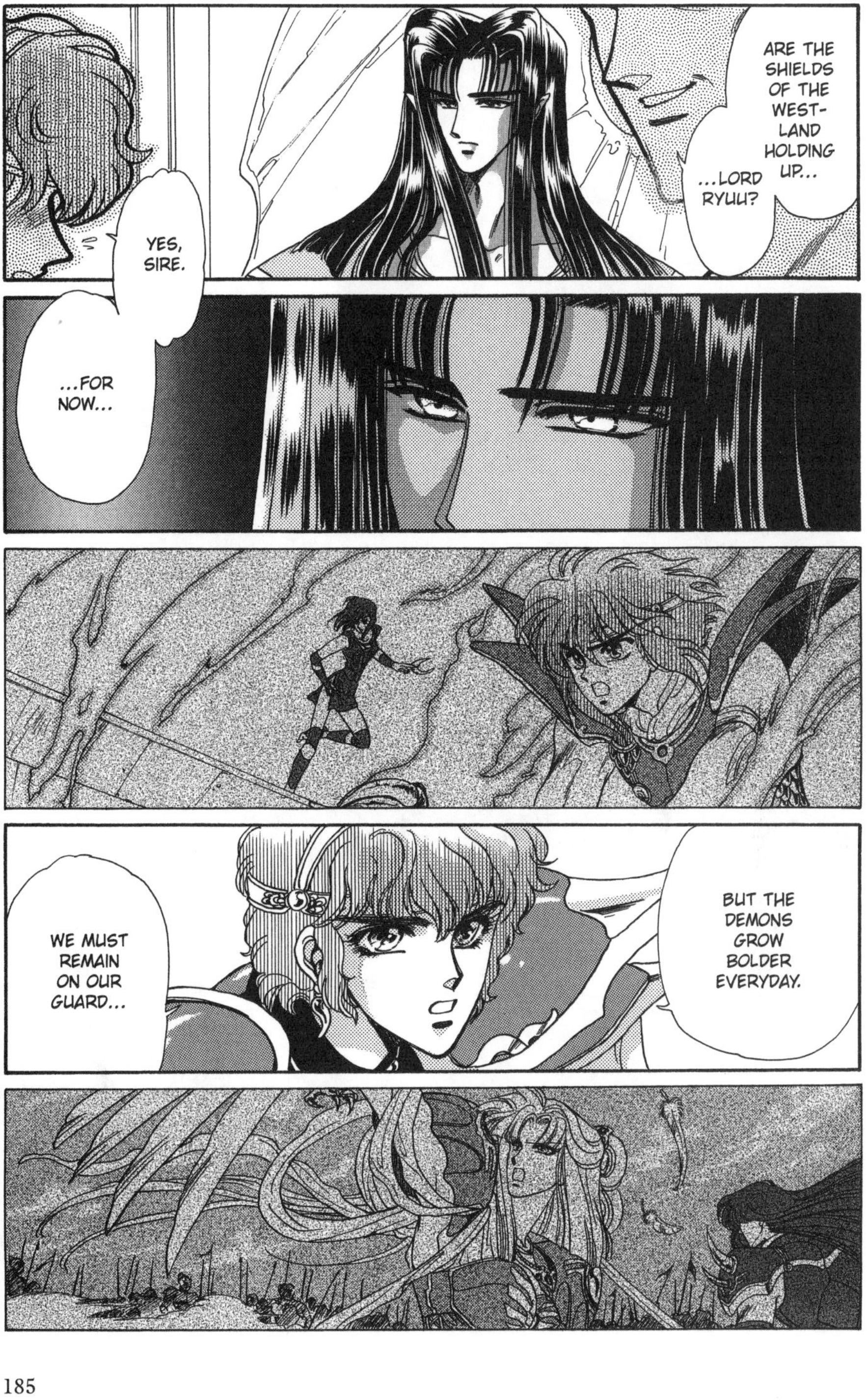
ARE THE SHIELDS OF THE WEST-LAND HOLDING UP...
...LORD RYUU?
YES, SIRE.
...FOR NOW...
BUT THE DEMONS GROW BOLDER EVERYDAY.
WE MUST REMAIN ON OUR GUARD...

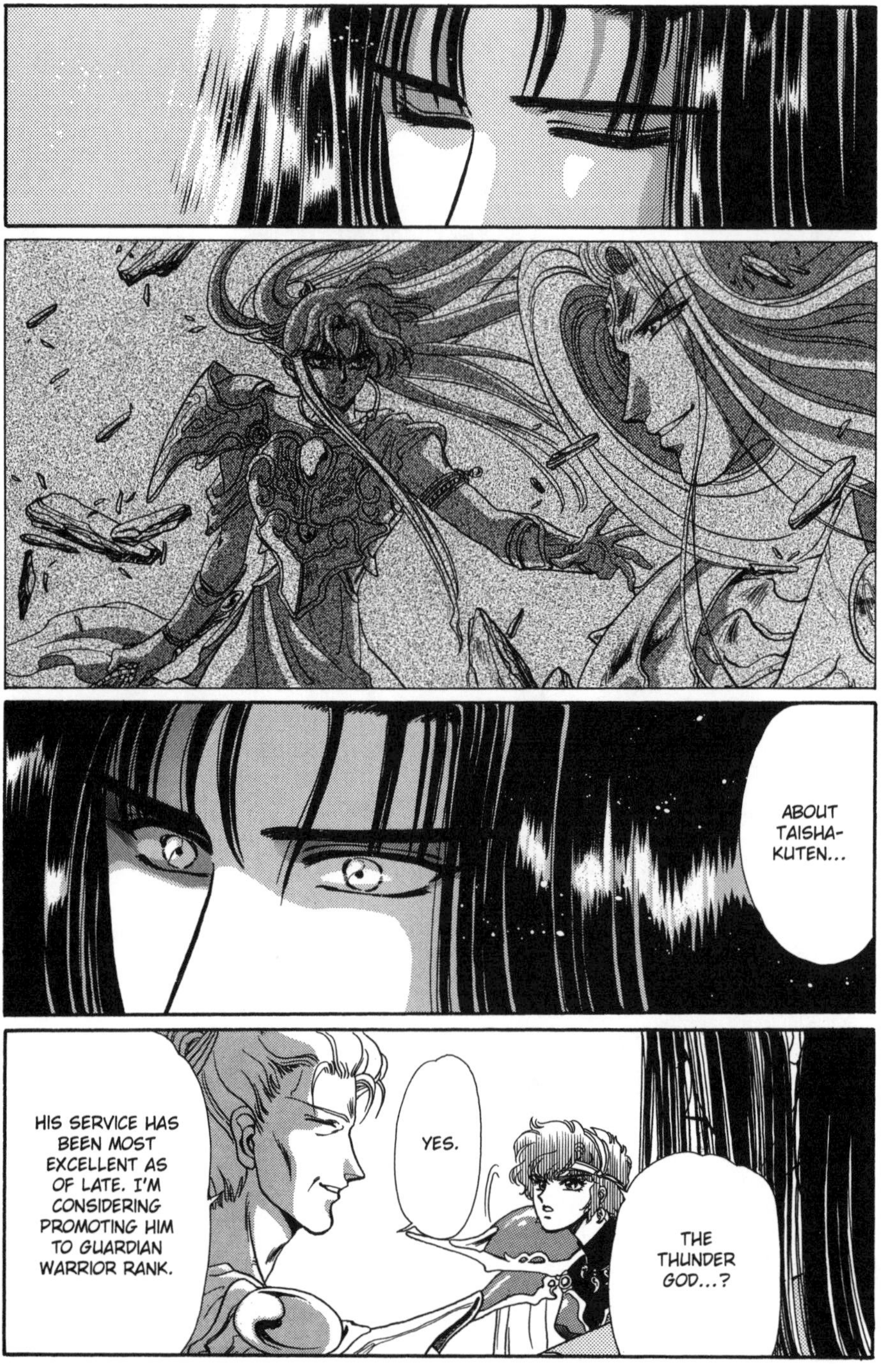
ABOUT TAISHA-KUTEN...
THE THUNDER GOD...?
YES.
HIS SERVICE HAS BEEN MOST EXCELLENT AS OF LATE. I'M CONSIDERING PROMOTING HIM TO GUARDIAN WARRIOR RANK.

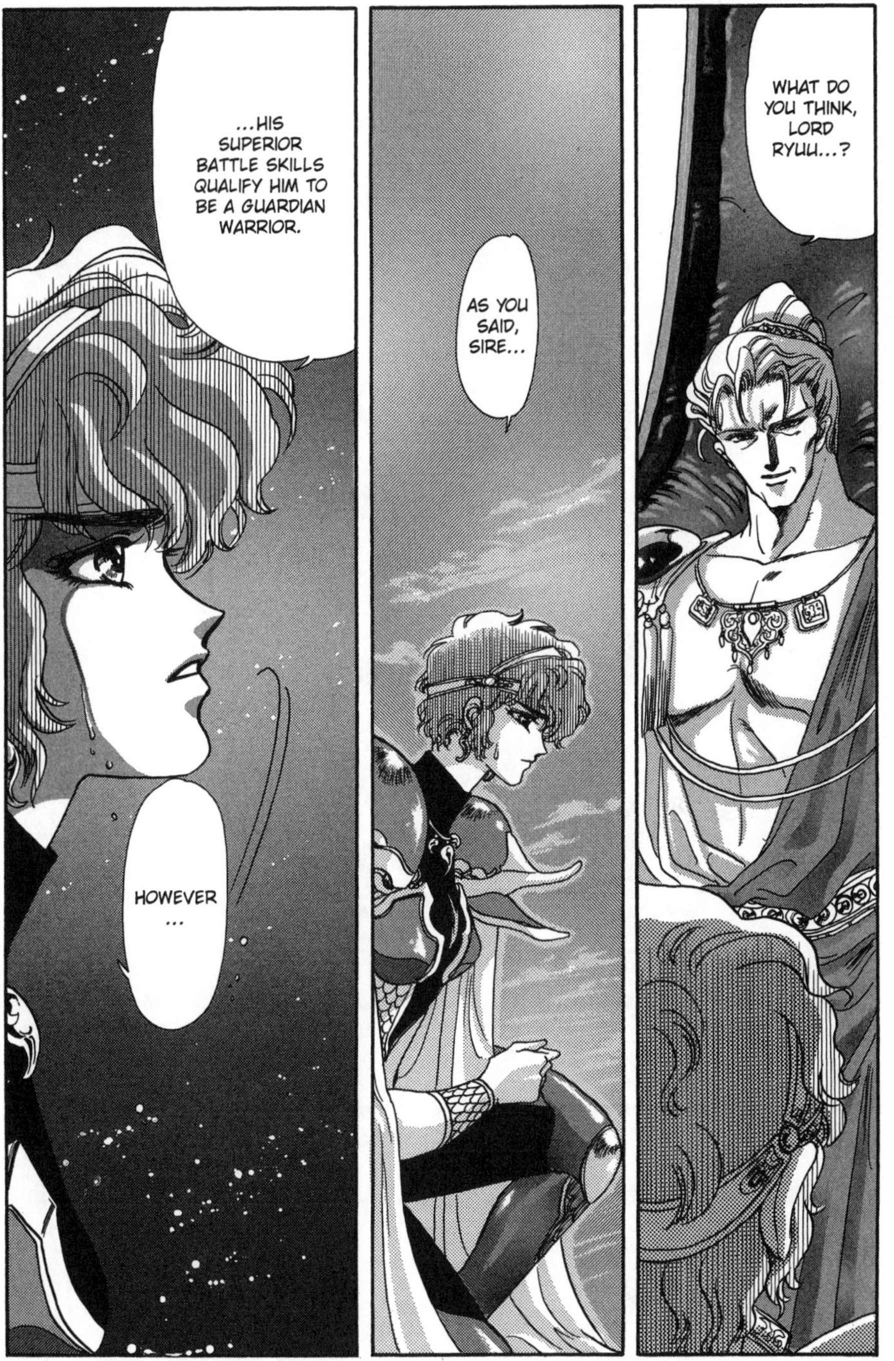
WHAT DO YOU THINK, LORD RYUU...?
AS YOU SAID, SIRE...
...HIS SUPERIOR BATTLE SKILLS QUALIFY HIM TO BE A GUARDIAN WARRIOR.
HOWEVER ...

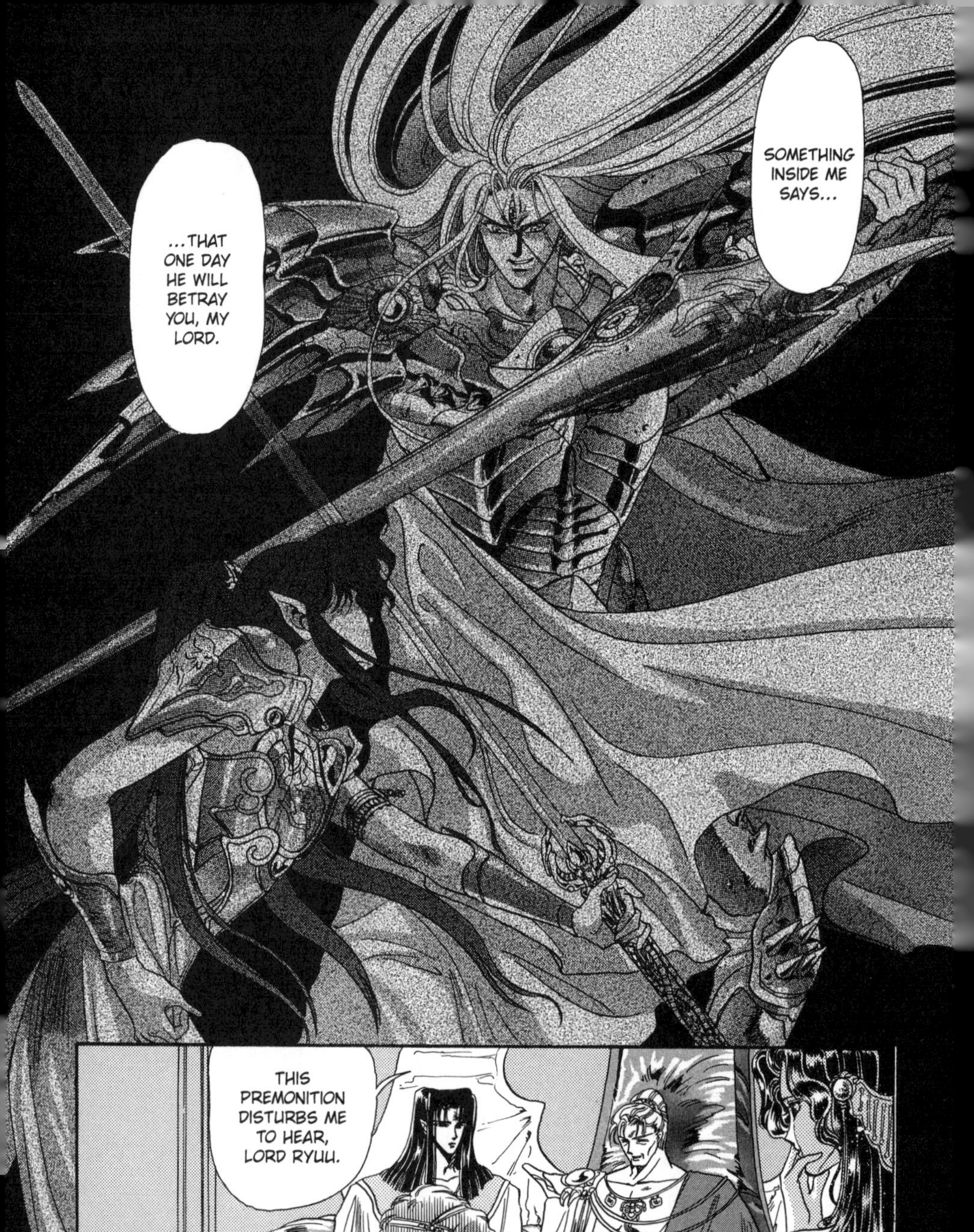
SOMETHING INSIDE ME SAYS...
...THAT ONE DAY HE WILL BETRAY YOU, MY LORD.
THIS PREMONITION DISTURBS ME TO HEAR, LORD RYUU.

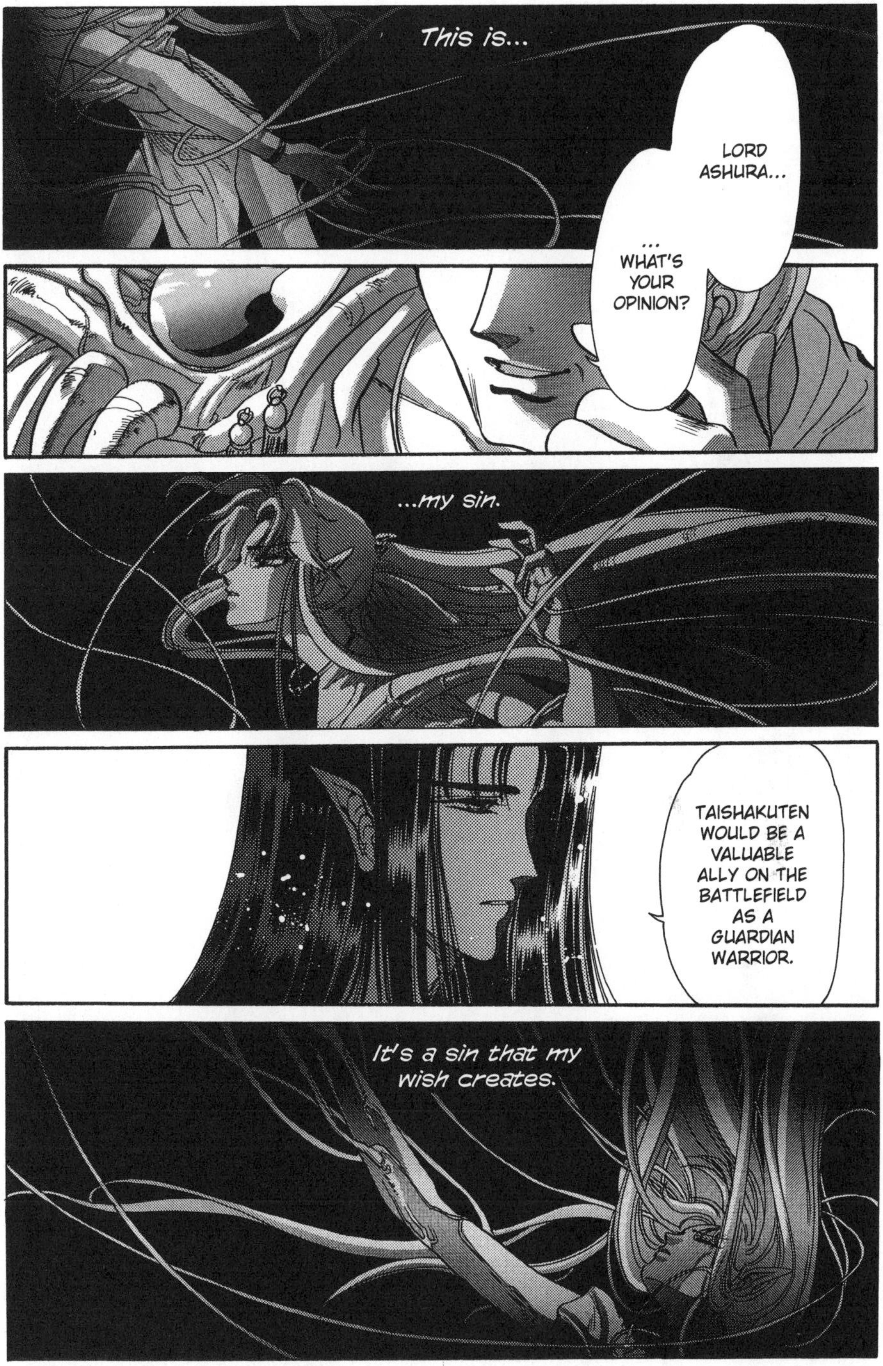

This is...
LORD ASHURA...
... WHAT'S YOUR OPINION?
...my sin.
TAISHAKUTEN WOULD BE A VALUABLE ALLY ON THE BATTLEFIELD AS A GUARDIAN WARRIOR.
It's a sin that my wish creates.

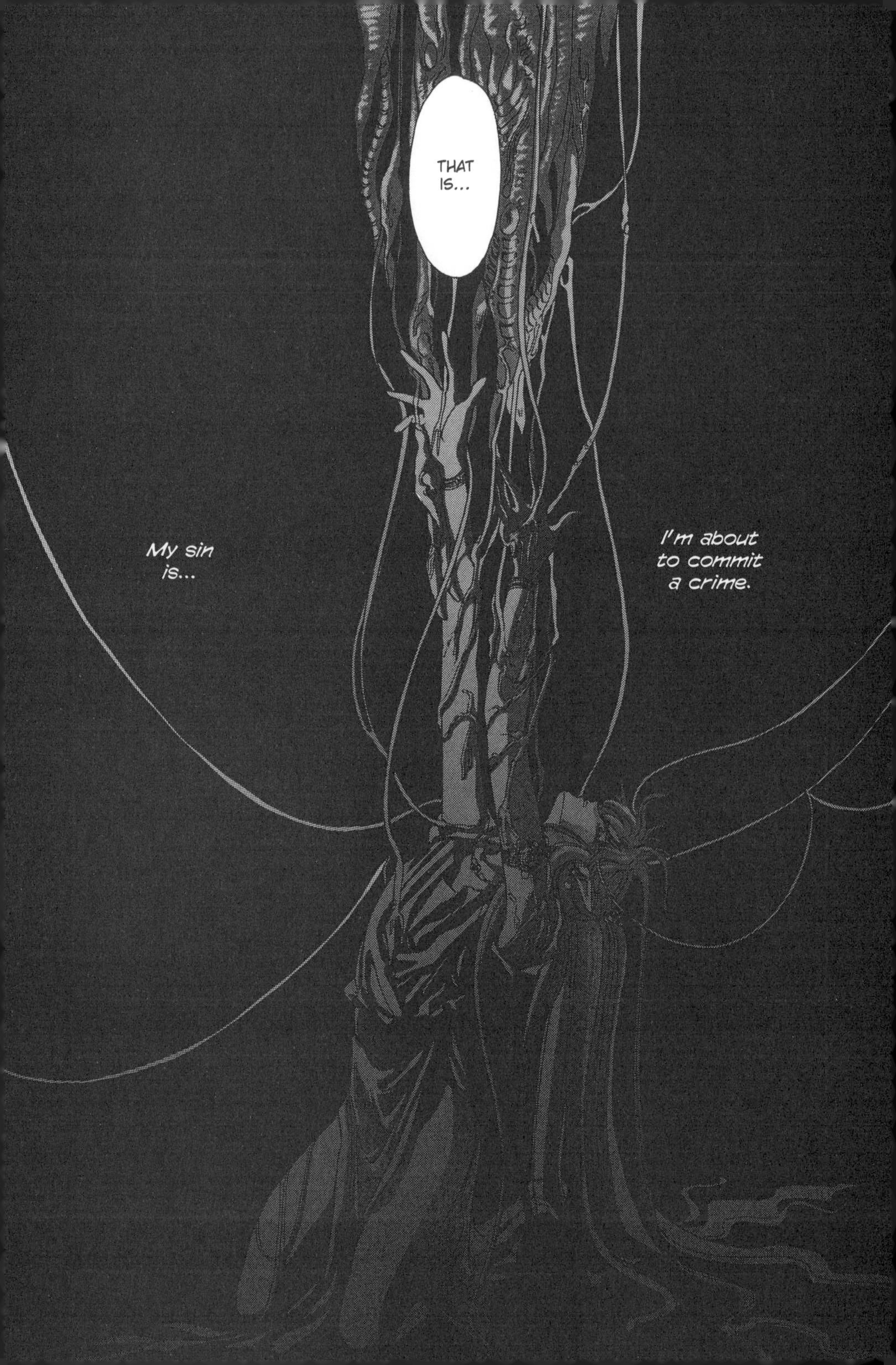
THAT IS...
I'm about to commit a crime.
My sin is...

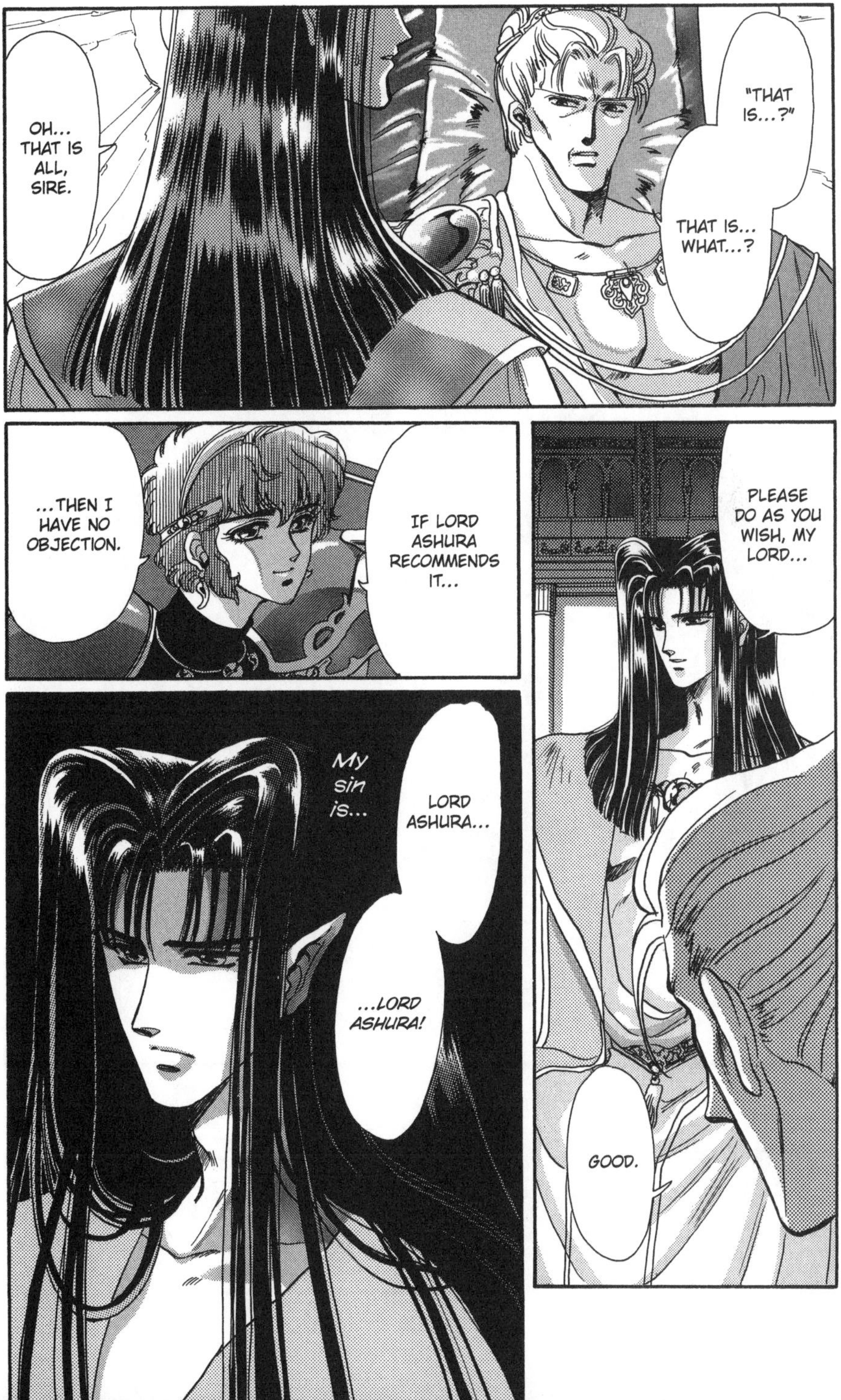
"THAT IS...?"
THAT IS... WHAT...?
OH... THAT IS ALL, SIRE.
PLEASE DO AS YOU WISH, MY LORD...
GOOD.
IF LORD ASHURA RECOMMENDS IT...
...THEN I HAVE NO OBJECTION.
LORD ASHURA...
My sin is...
...LORD ASHURA!

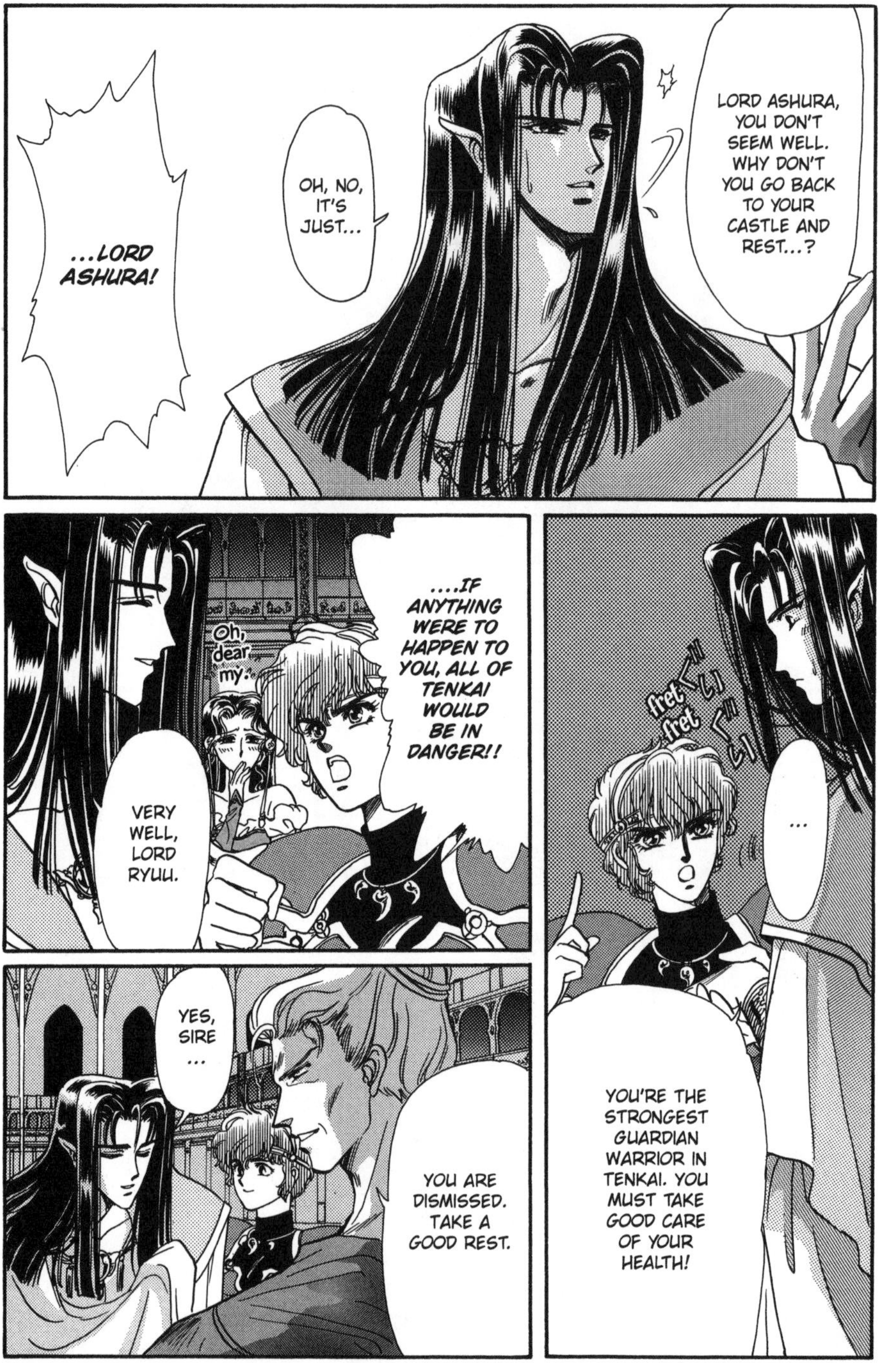

LORD ASHURA, YOU DON'T SEEM WELL. WHY DON'T YOU GO BACK TO YOUR CASTLE AND REST...?
OH, NO, IT'S JUST...
...LORD ASHURA!
fret fret
...
YOU'RE THE STRONGEST GUARDIAN WARRIOR IN TENKAI. YOU MUST TAKE GOOD CARE OF YOUR HEALTH!
....IF ANYTHING WERE TO HAPPEN TO YOU, ALL OF TENKAI WOULD BE IN DANGER!!
Oh, dear my.
VERY WELL, LORD RYUU.
YOU ARE DISMISSED. TAKE A GOOD REST.
YES, SIRE ...

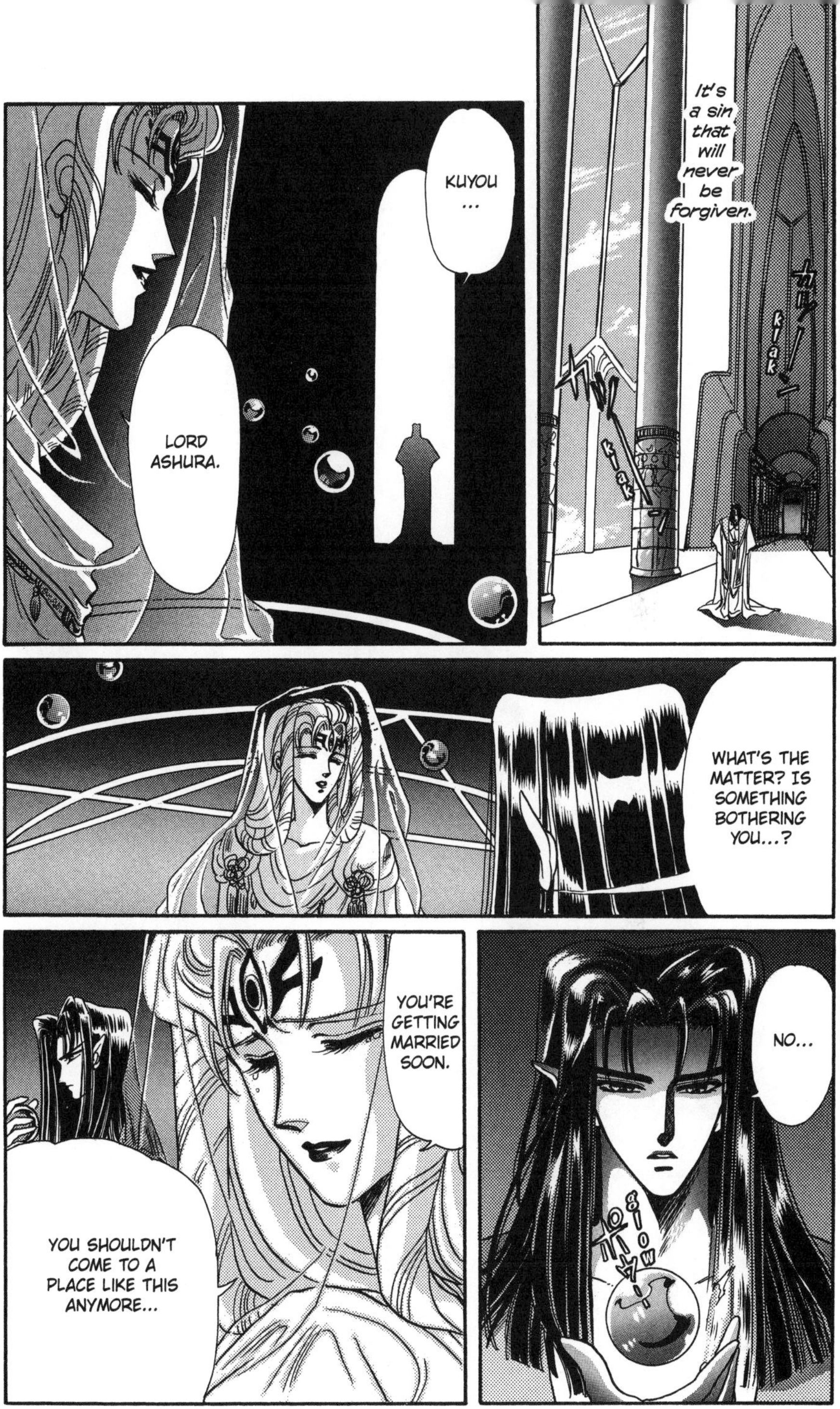
It's a sin that will never be forgiven.
klak
klak
KUYOU ...
LORD ASHURA.
WHAT'S THE MATTER? IS SOMETHING BOTHERING YOU...?
NO...
glow
YOU'RE GETTING MARRIED SOON.
YOU SHOULDN'T COME TO A PLACE LIKE THIS ANYMORE...

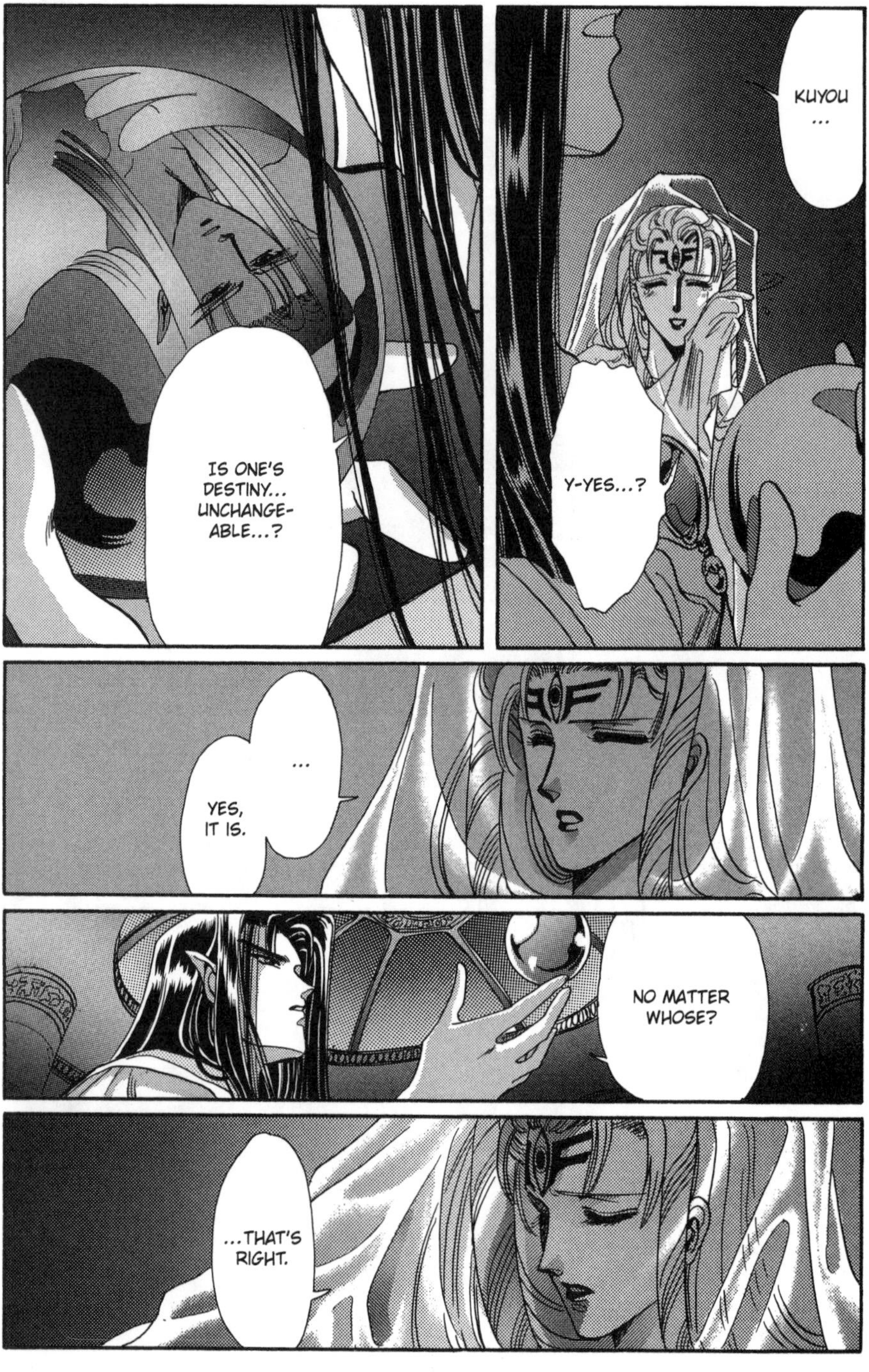
KUYOU ...
Y-YES...?
IS ONE'S DESTINY... UNCHANGE-ABLE...?
...
YES, IT IS.
NO MATTER WHOSE?
...THAT'S RIGHT.

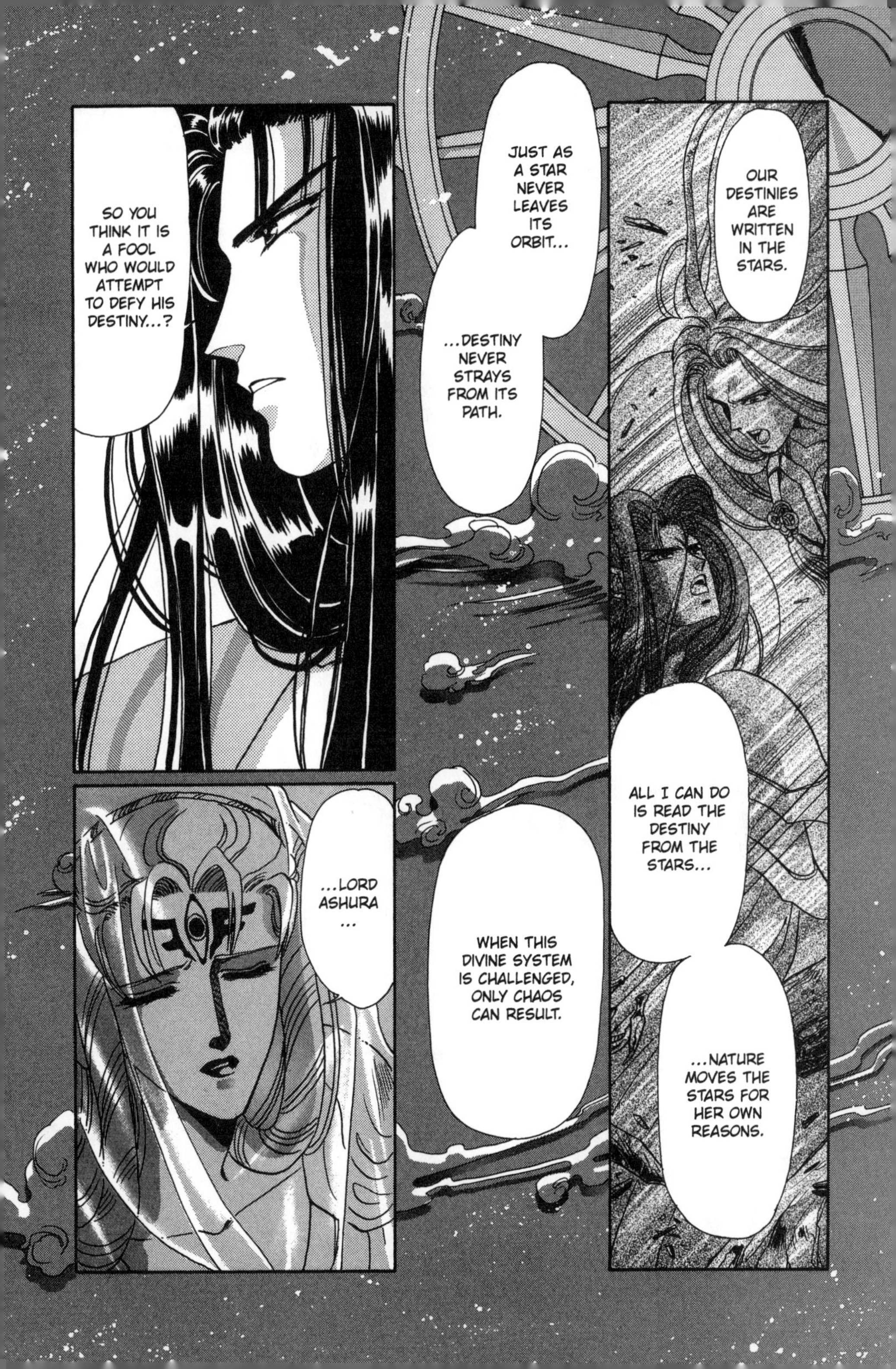
OUR DESTINIES ARE WRITTEN IN THE STARS.
JUST AS A STAR NEVER LEAVES ITS ORBIT...
...DESTINY NEVER STRAYS FROM ITS PATH.
SO YOU THINK IT IS A FOOL WHO WOULD ATTEMPT TO DEFY HIS DESTINY...?
ALL I CAN DO IS READ THE DESTINY FROM THE STARS...
...NATURE MOVES THE STARS FOR HER OWN REASONS.
WHEN THIS DIVINE SYSTEM IS CHALLENGED, ONLY CHAOS CAN RESULT.
...LORD ASHURA ...

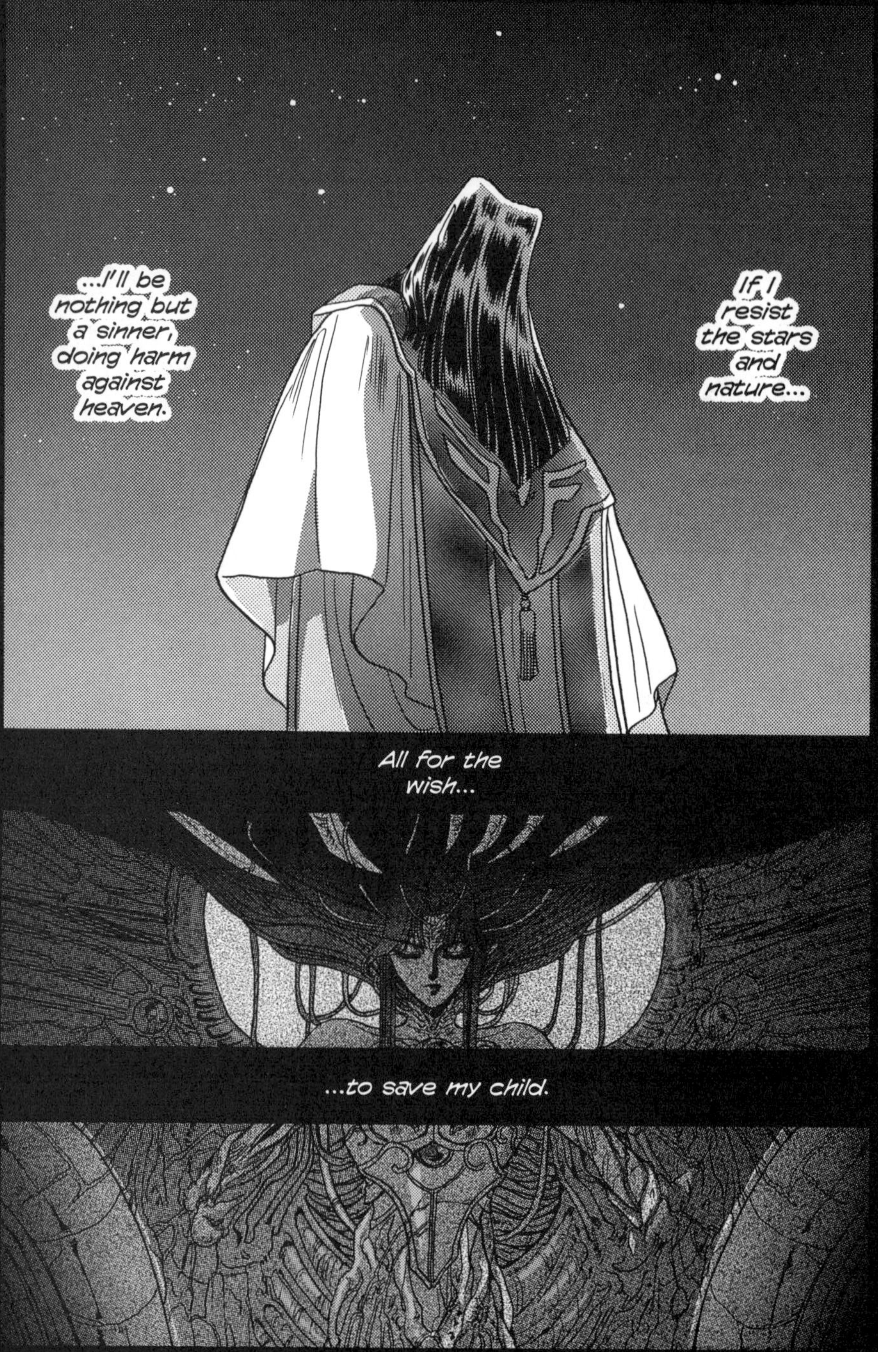
If I resist the stars and nature...
...I'll be nothing but a sinner, doing harm against heaven.
All for the wish...
...to save my child.

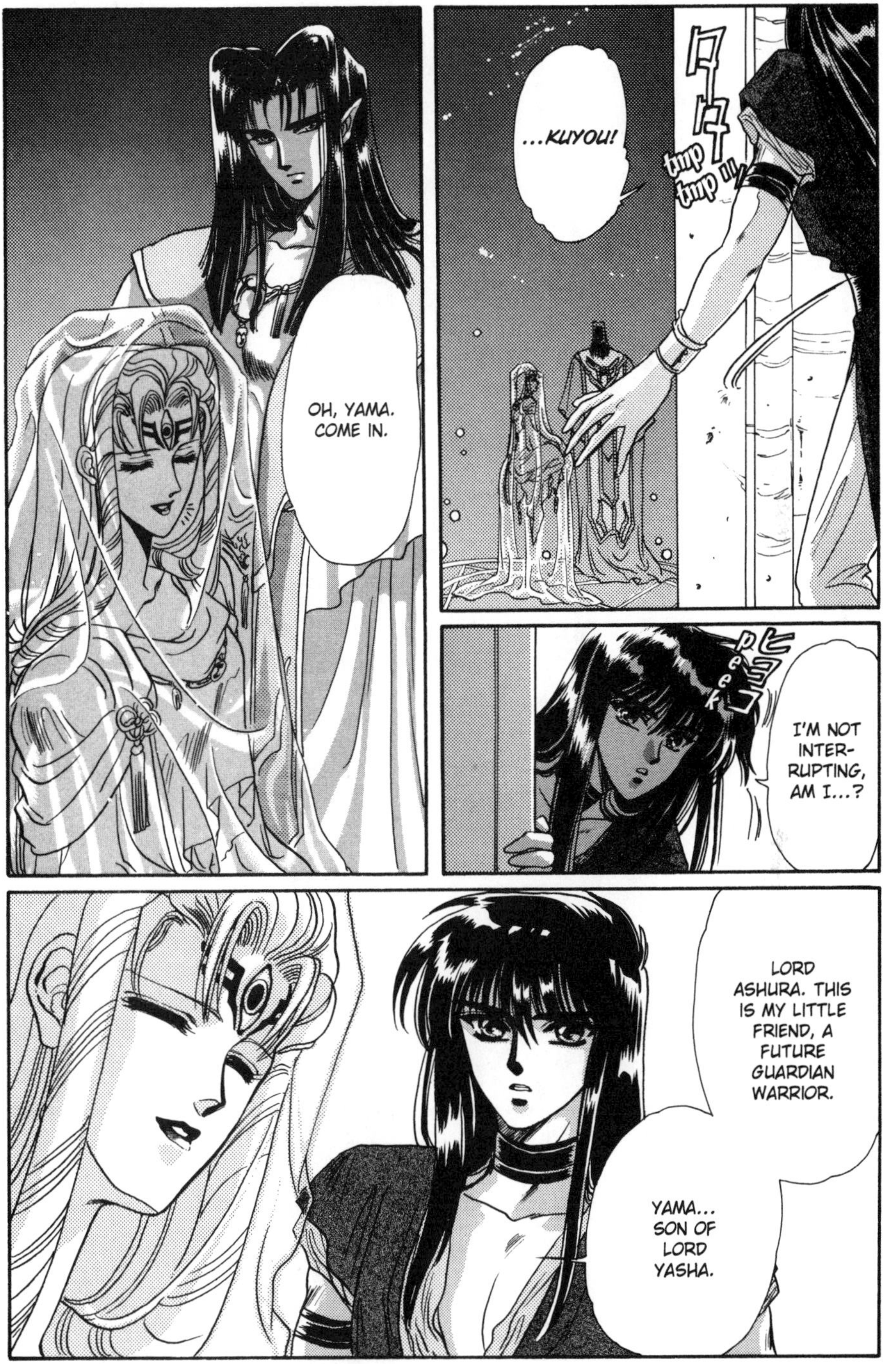
...KUYOU!
tmp tmp
ヒョコ
peek
I'M NOT INTER-RUPTING, AM I...?
OH, YAMA. COME IN.
LORD ASHURA. THIS IS MY LITTLE FRIEND, A FUTURE GUARDIAN WARRIOR.
YAMA... SON OF LORD YASHA.

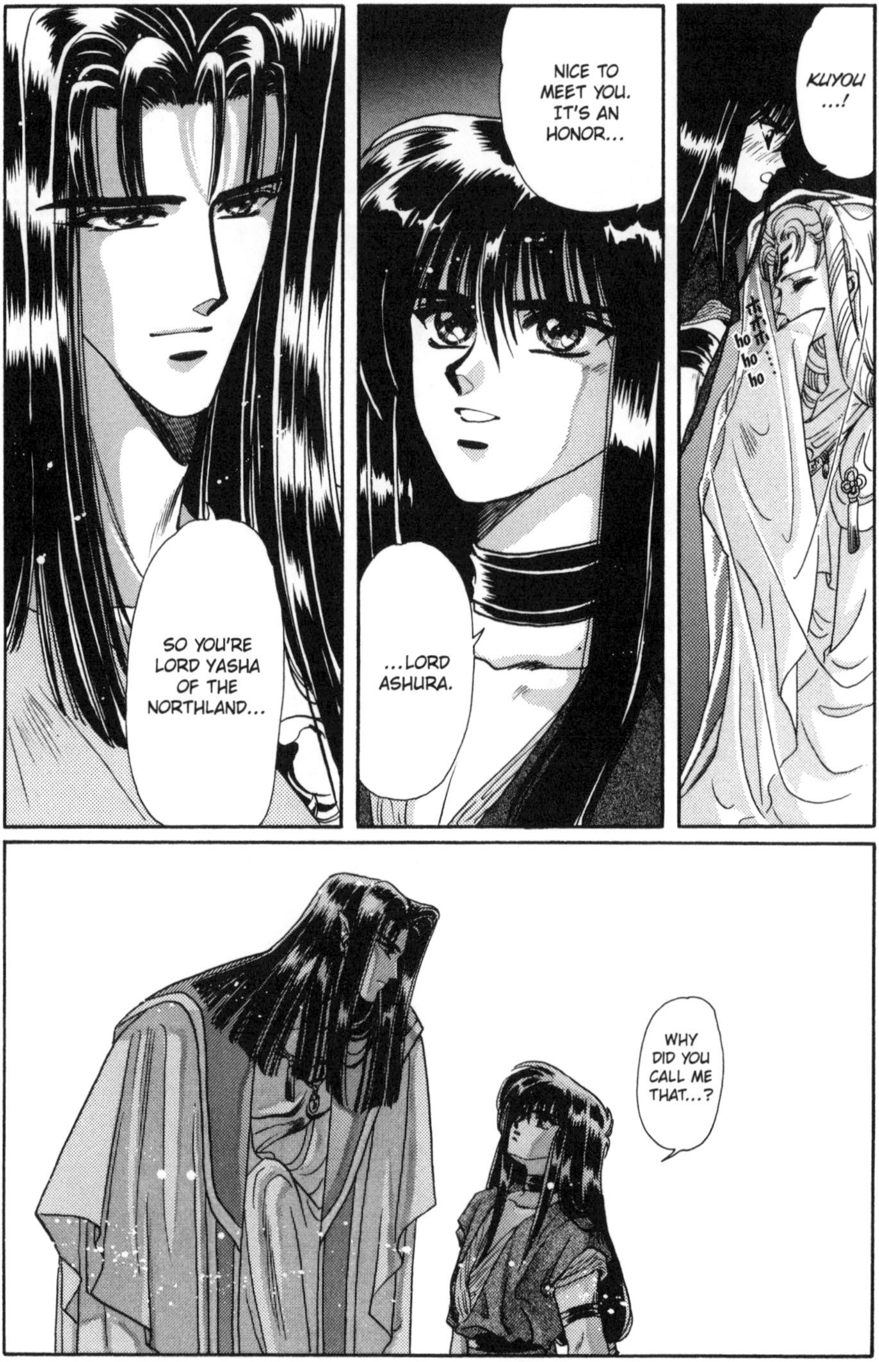
KUYOU ...!
ho ho ho
NICE TO MEET YOU. IT'S AN HONOR...
...LORD ASHURA.
SO YOU'RE LORD YASHA OF THE NORTHLAND...
WHY DID YOU CALL ME THAT...?

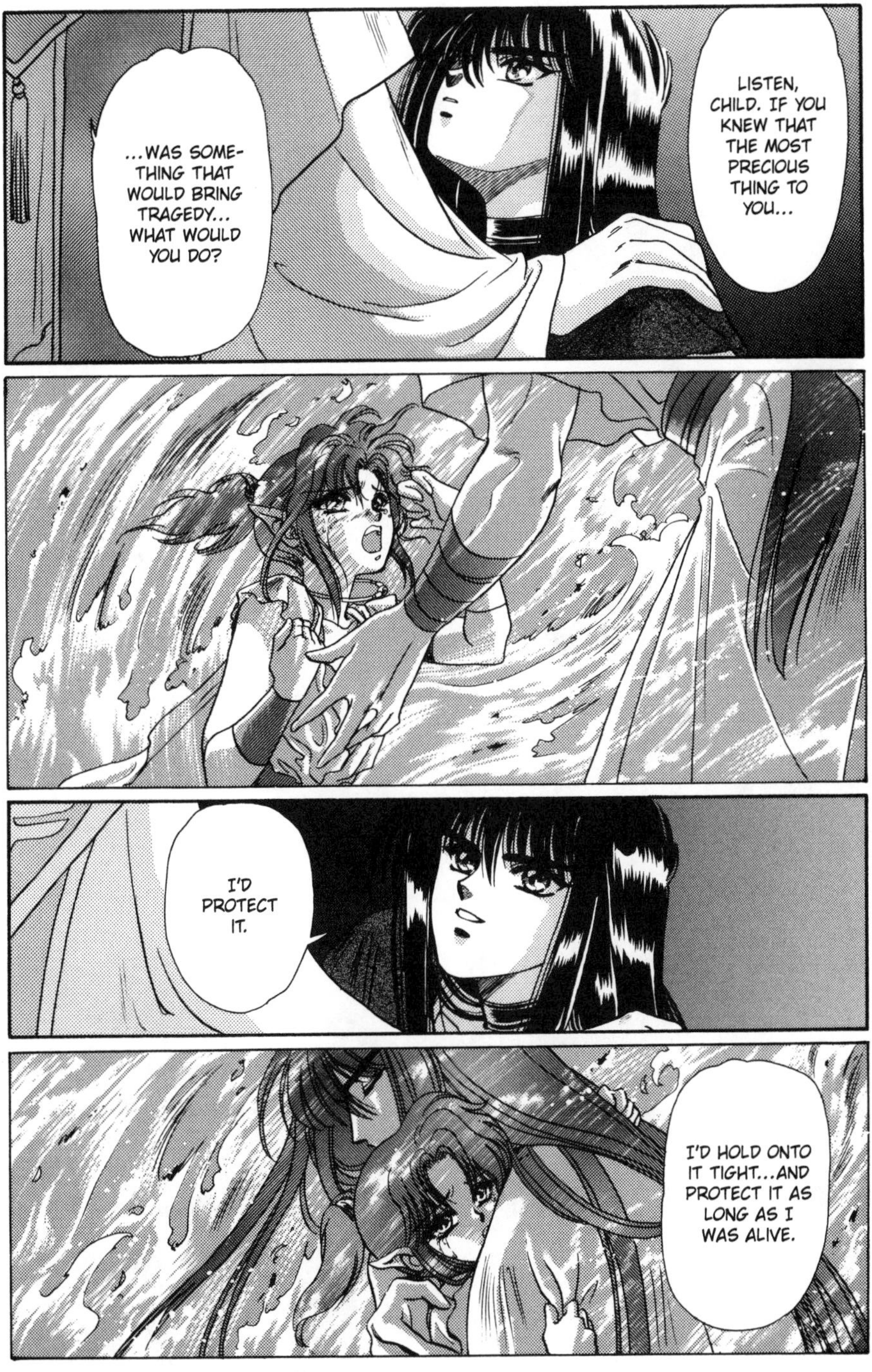
LISTEN, CHILD. IF YOU KNEW THAT THE MOST PRECIOUS THING TO YOU...
...WAS SOME-THING THAT WOULD BRING TRAGEDY... WHAT WOULD YOU DO?
I'D PROTECT IT.
I'D HOLD ONTO IT TIGHT...AND PROTECT IT AS LONG AS I WAS ALIVE.

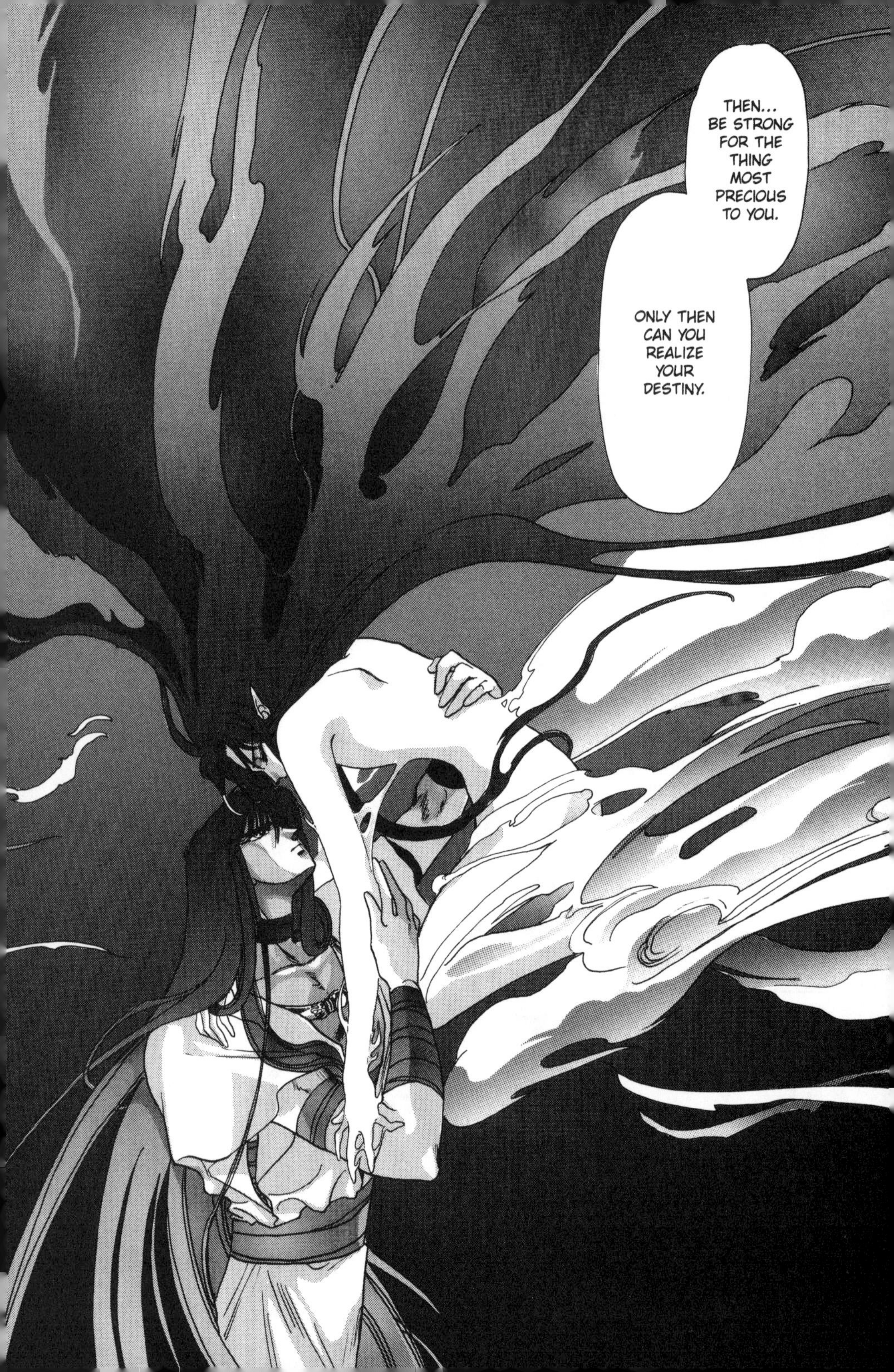
THEN... BE STRONG FOR THE THING MOST PRECIOUS TO YOU.
ONLY THEN CAN YOU REALIZE YOUR DESTINY.

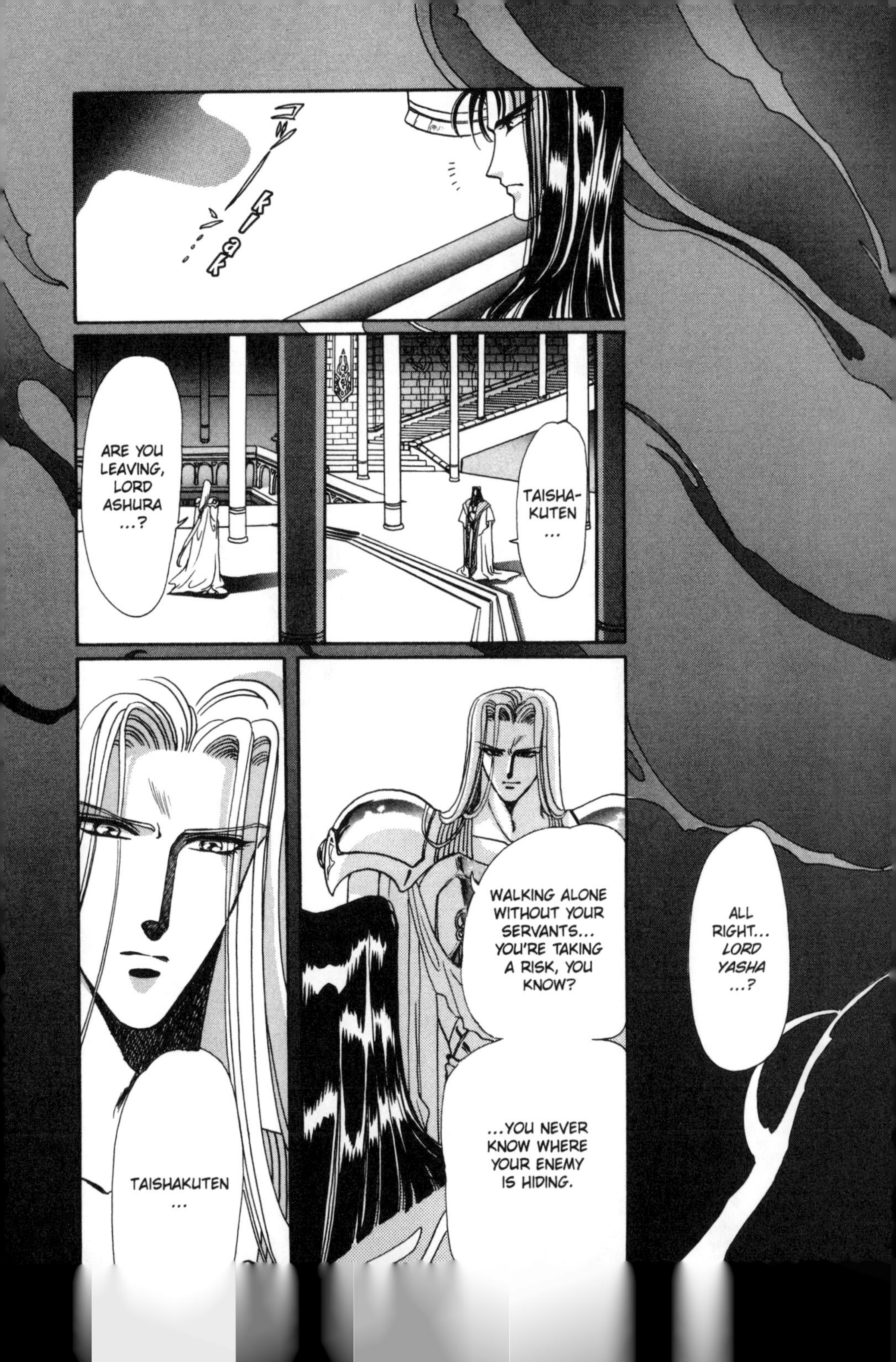
TAISHA-KUTEN...
ARE YOU LEAVING, LORD ASHURA...?
ALL RIGHT... LORD YASHA...?
WALKING ALONE WITHOUT YOUR SERVANTS... YOU'RE TAKING A RISK, YOU KNOW?
...YOU NEVER KNOW WHERE YOUR ENEMY IS HIDING.
TAISHAKUTEN...

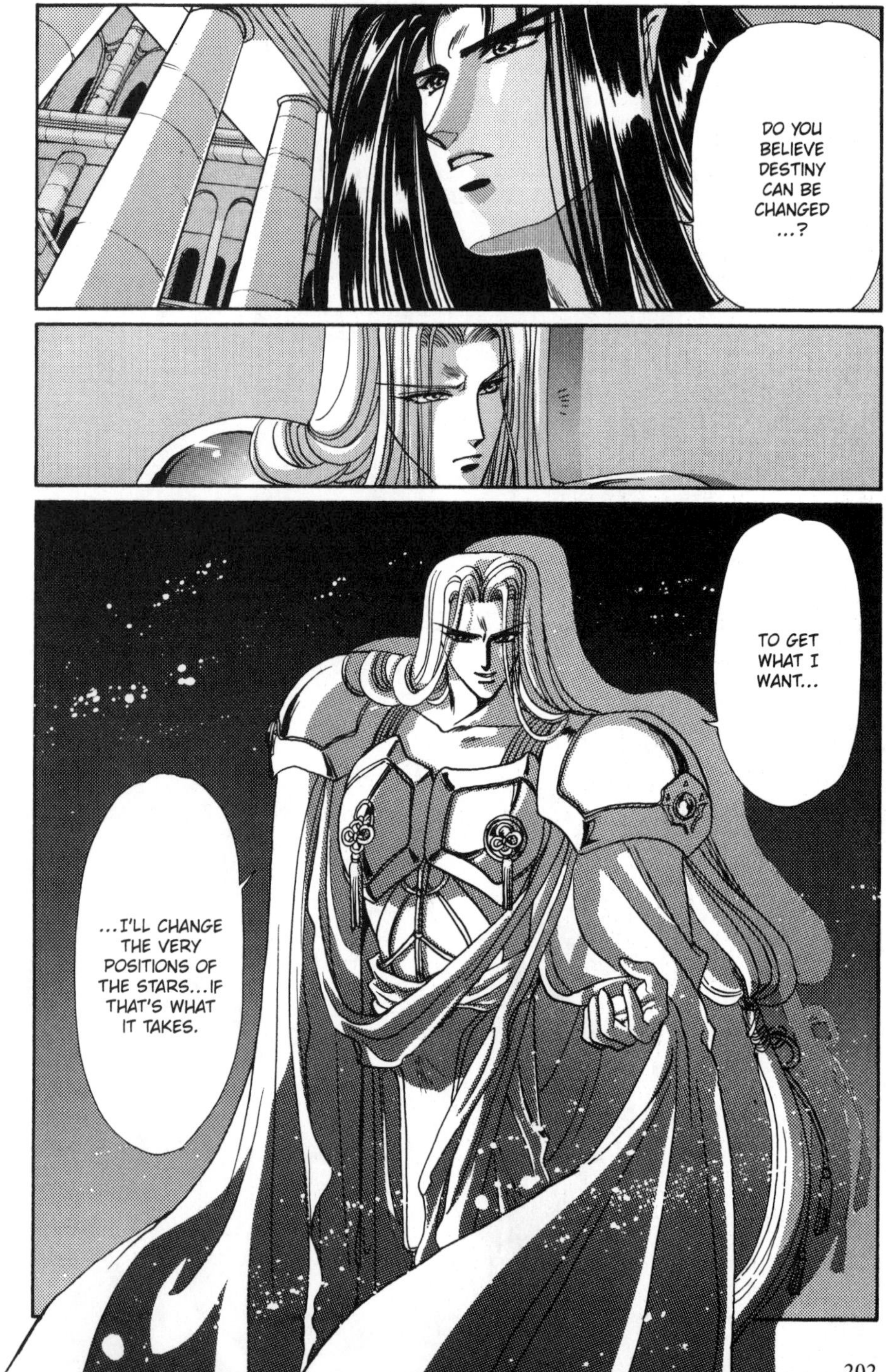
DO YOU BELIEVE DESTINY CAN BE CHANGED ...?
TO GET WHAT I WANT...
...I'LL CHANGE THE VERY POSITIONS OF THE STARS...IF THAT'S WHAT IT TAKES.

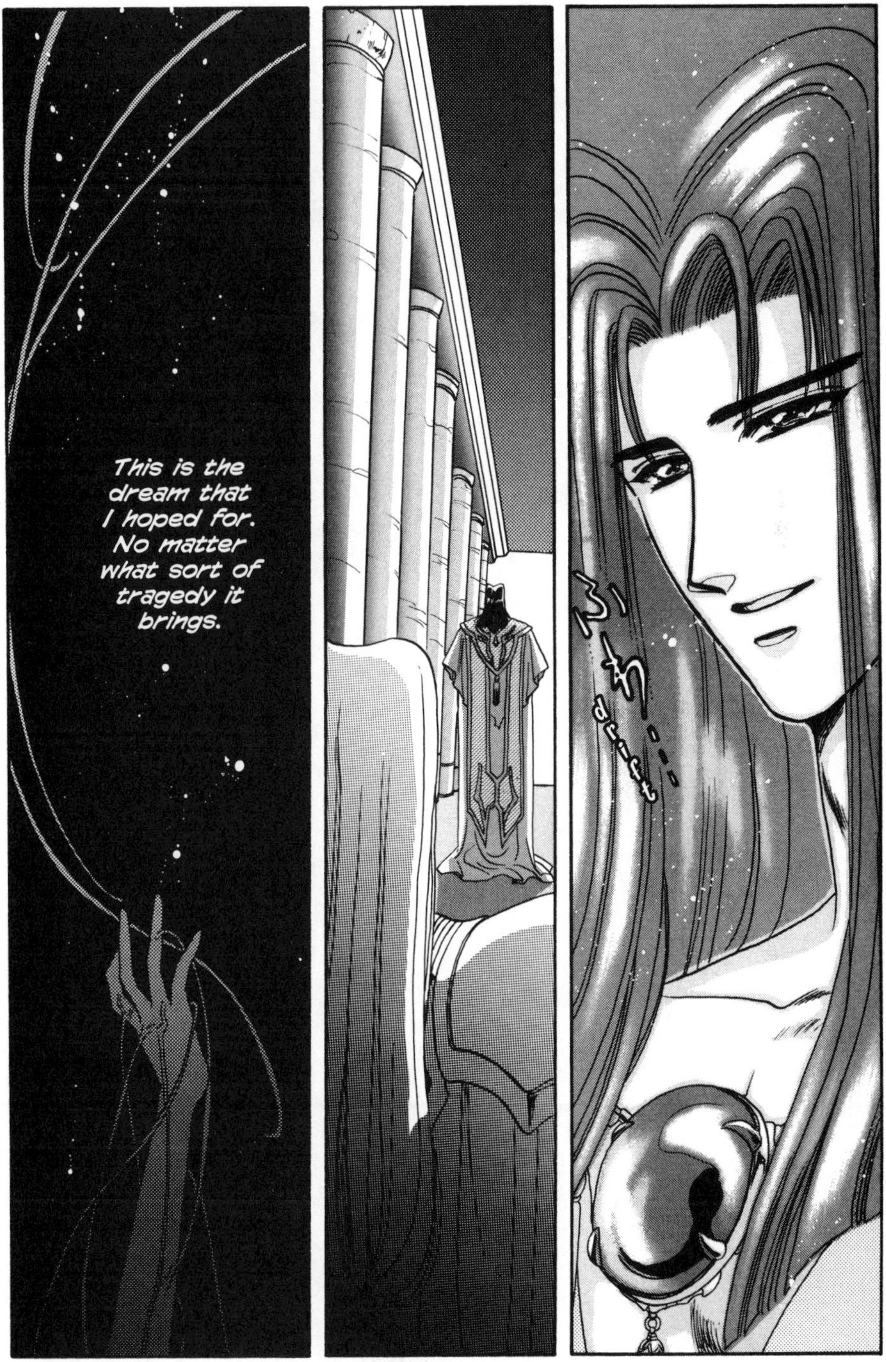
drift
This is the dream that I hoped for. No matter what sort of tragedy it brings.

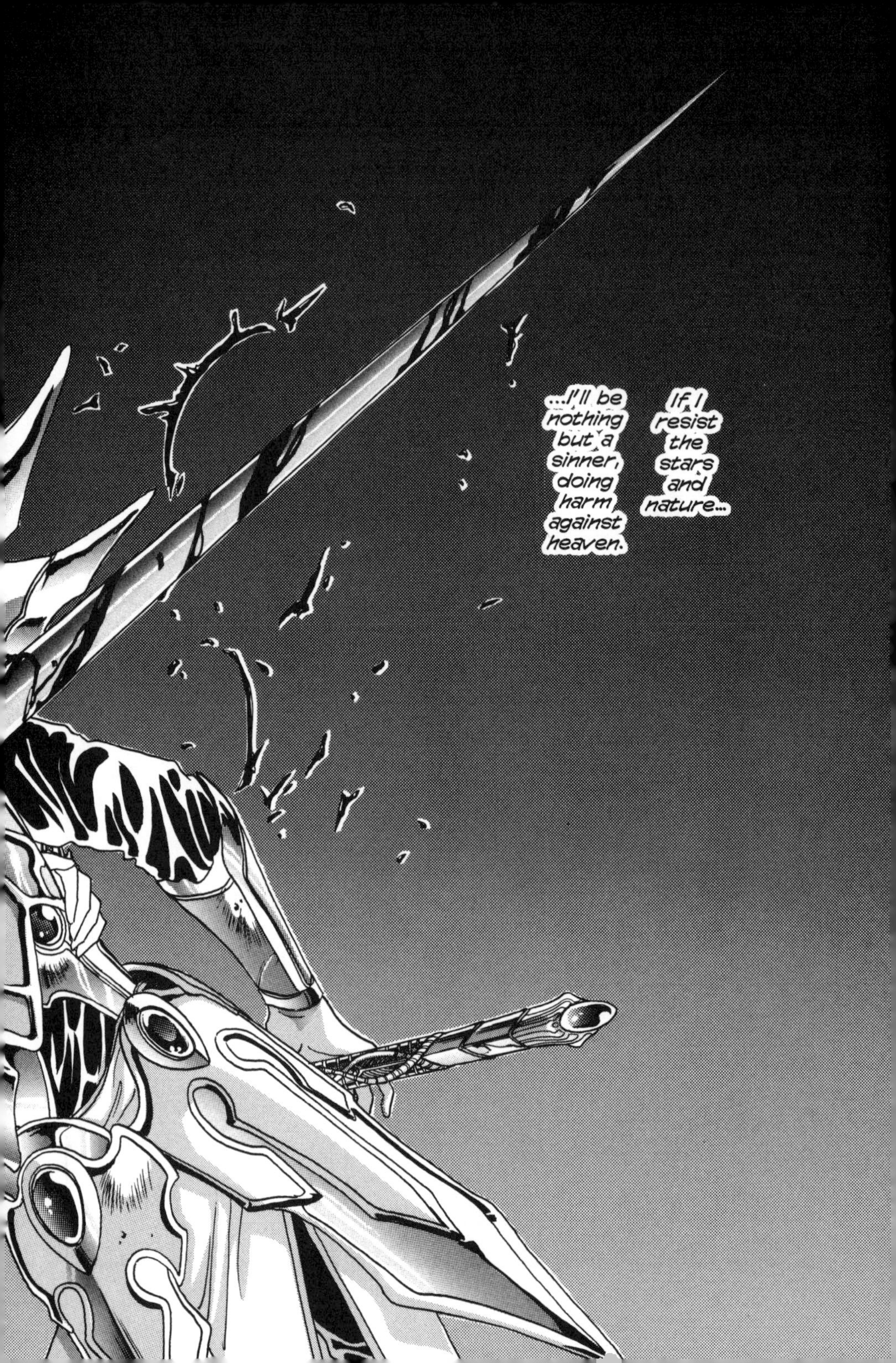
If I resist the stars and nature...
...I'll be nothing but a sinner, doing harm against heaven.

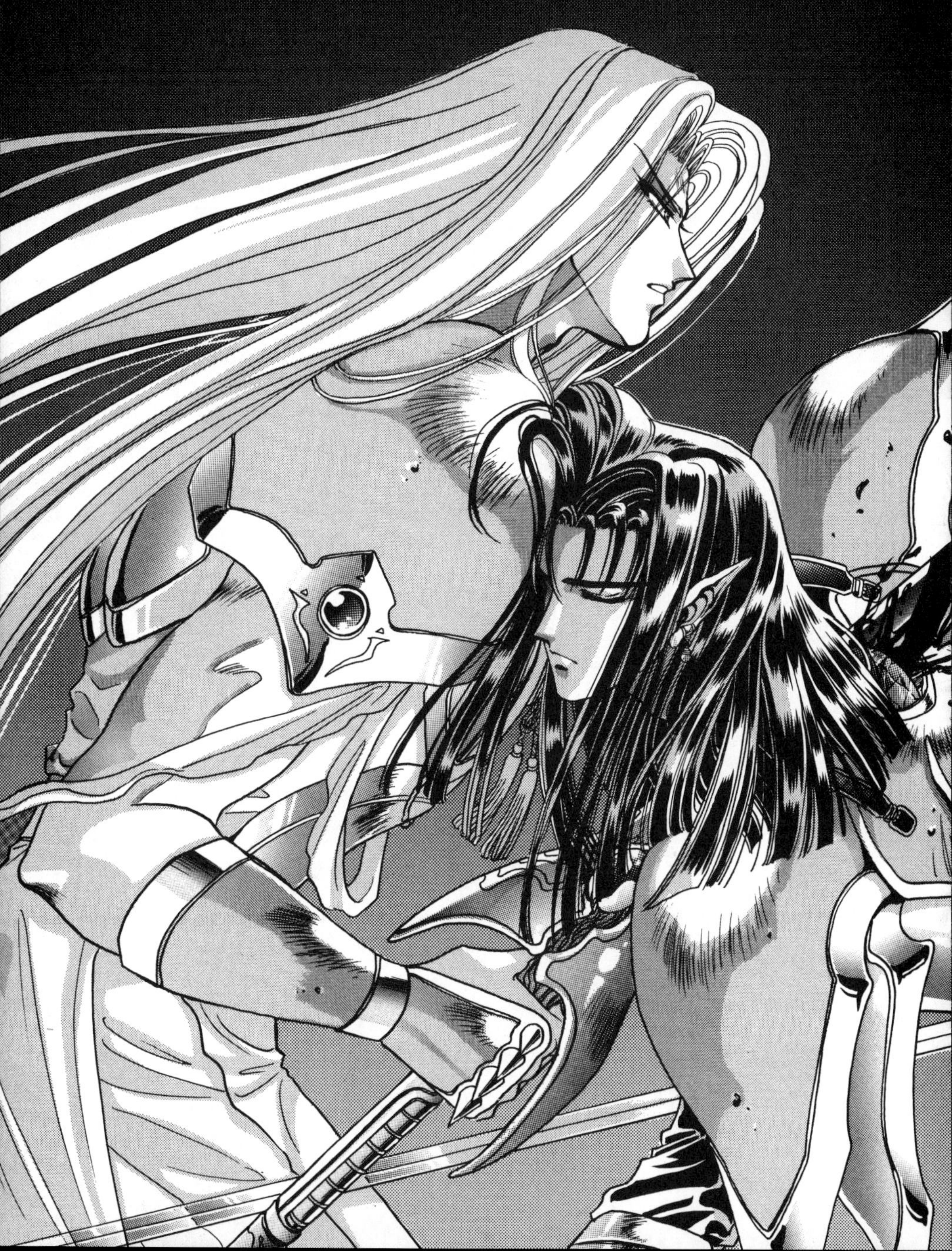

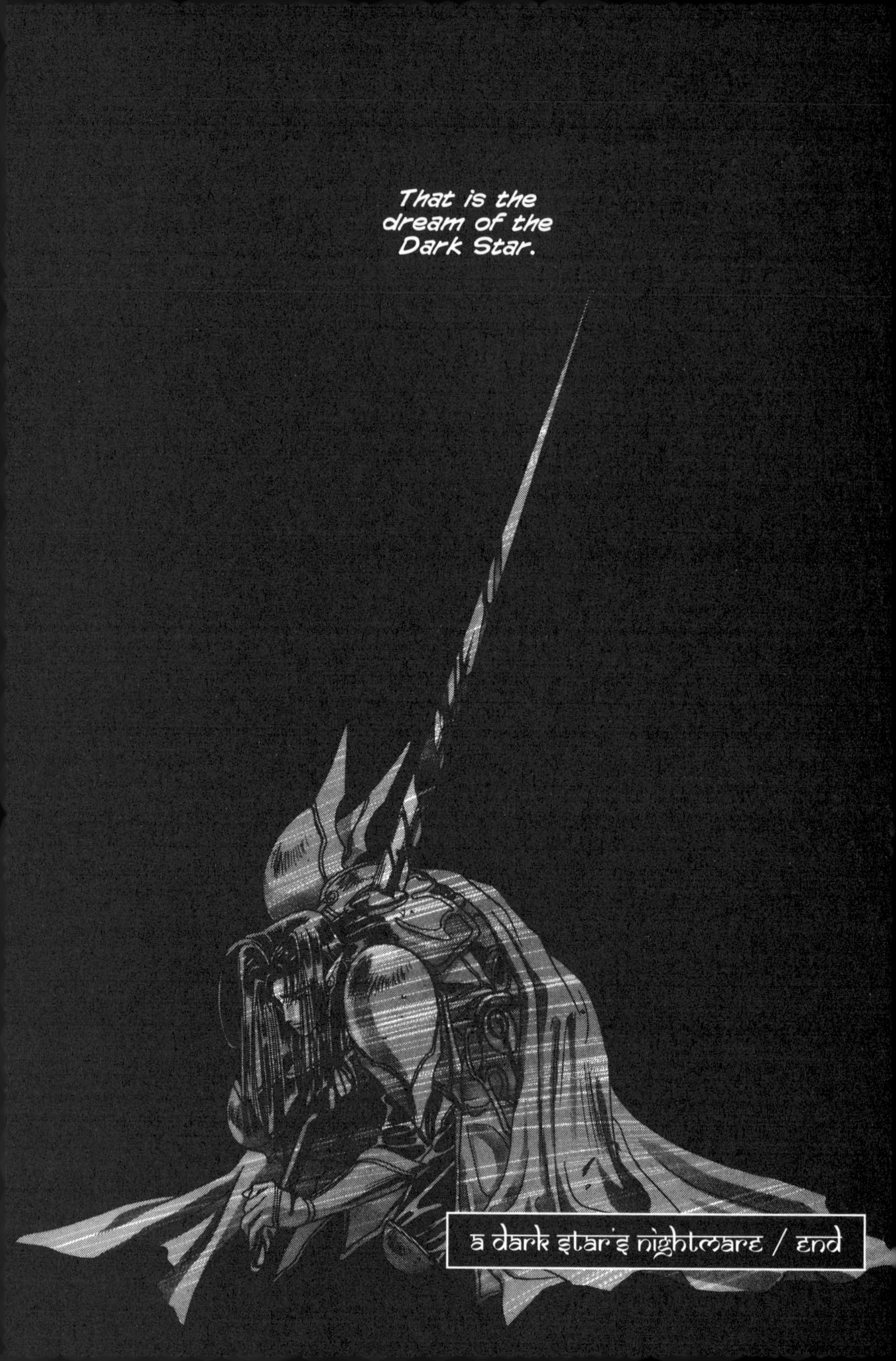
That is the dream of the Dark Star.
a dark star's nightmare / end

CLAMP
RG VEDA

CLAMP
RG VEDA

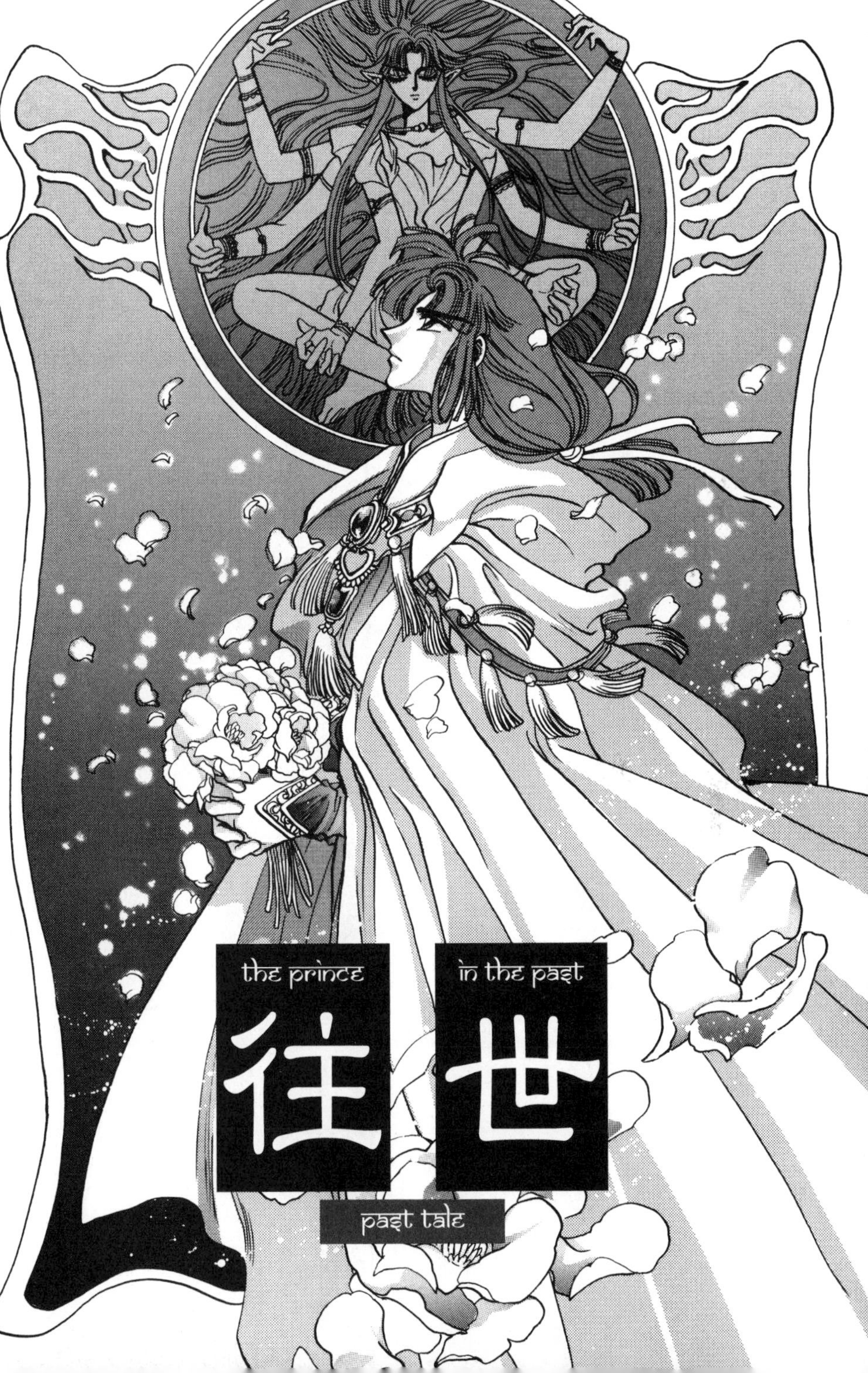
the prince
in the past
往世
past tale

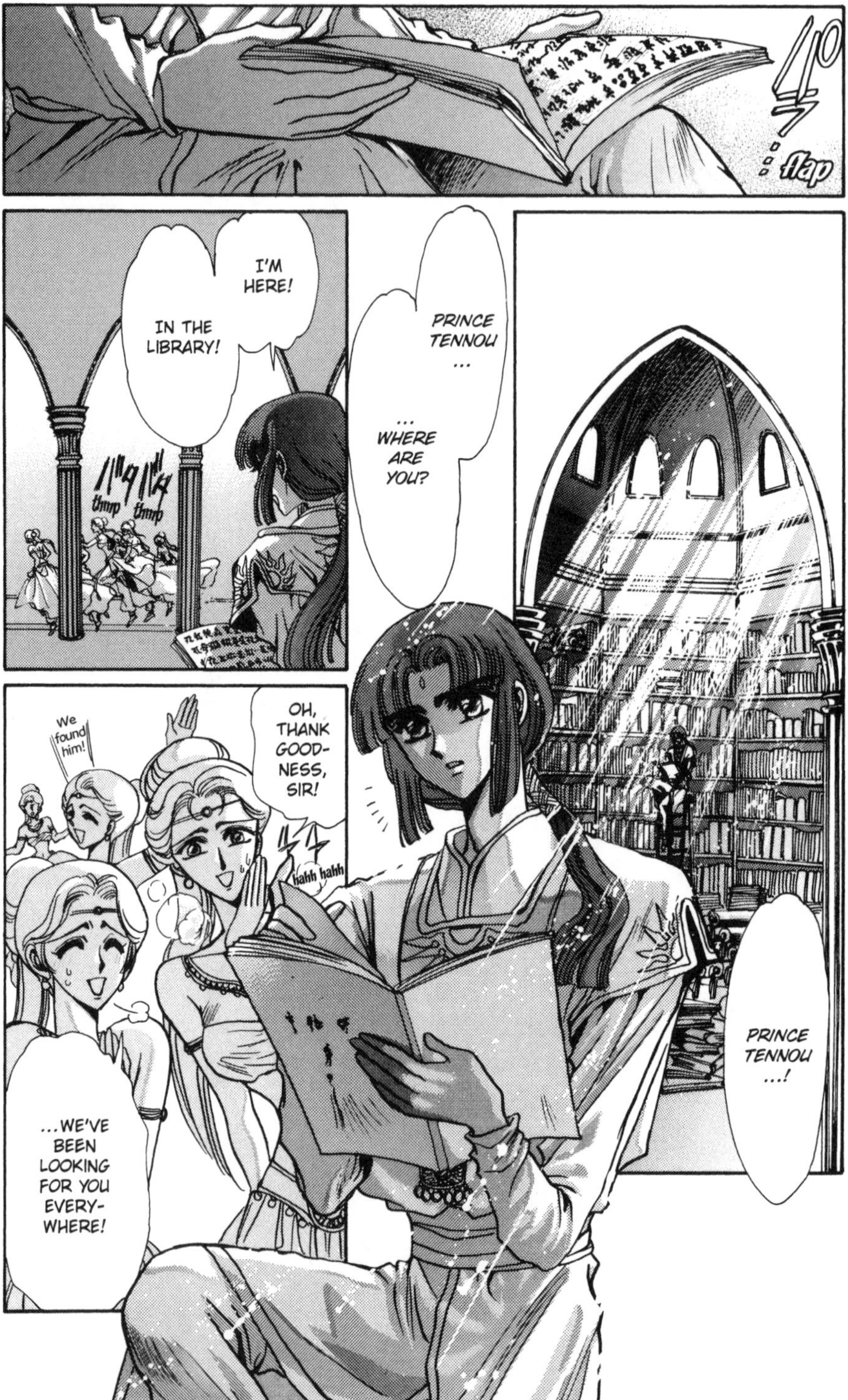
flap
PRINCE TENNOU ...
... WHERE ARE YOU?
I'M HERE!
IN THE LIBRARY!
thmp thmp
PRINCE TENNOU ...!
OH, THANK GOODNESS, SIR!
We found him!
hahh hahh
...WE'VE BEEN LOOKING FOR YOU EVERY-WHERE!

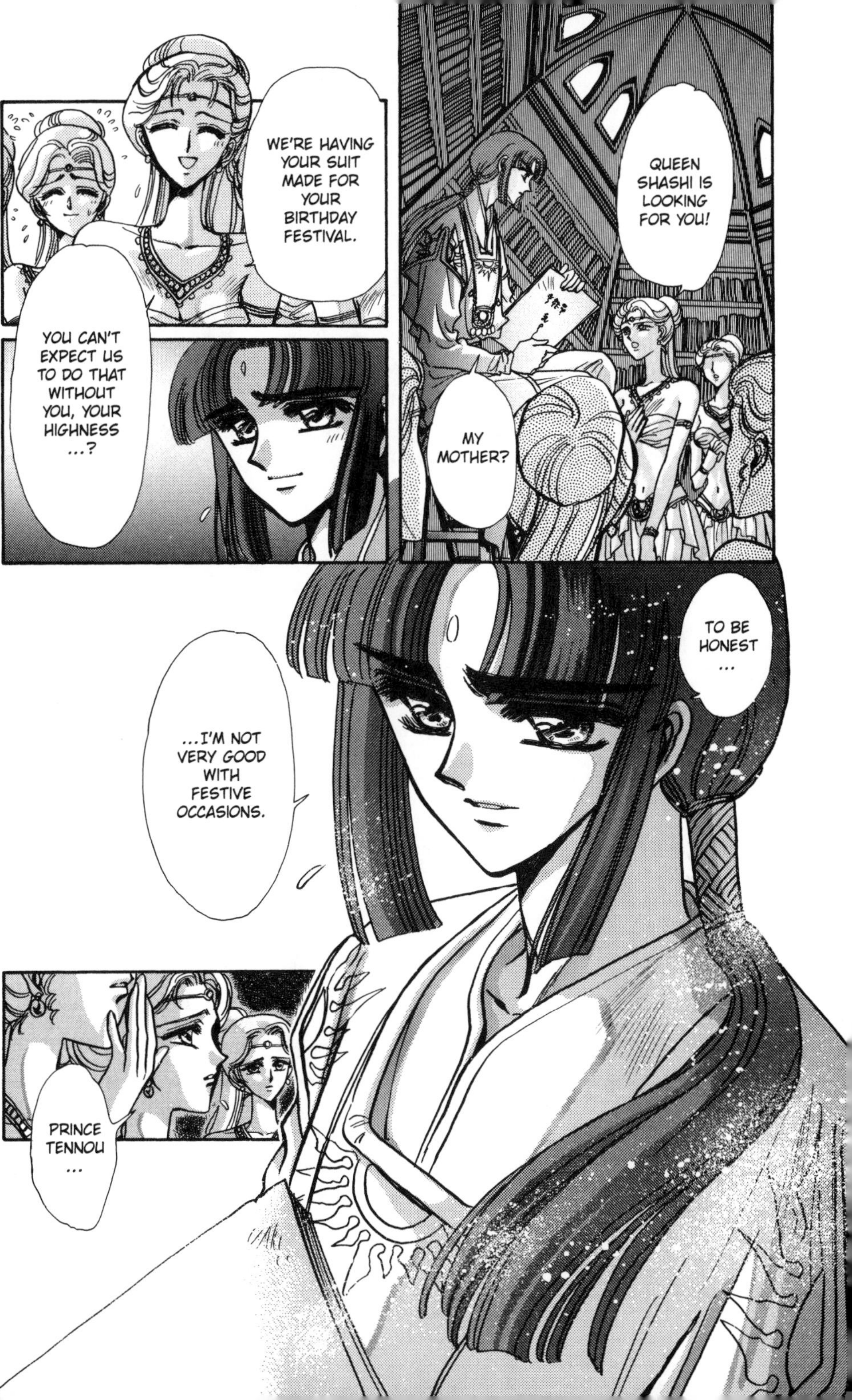
QUEEN SHASHI IS LOOKING FOR YOU!
MY MOTHER?
WE'RE HAVING YOUR SUIT MADE FOR YOUR BIRTHDAY FESTIVAL.
YOU CAN'T EXPECT US TO DO THAT WITHOUT YOU, YOUR HIGHNESS ...?
TO BE HONEST ...
...I'M NOT VERY GOOD WITH FESTIVE OCCASIONS.
PRINCE TENNOU ...

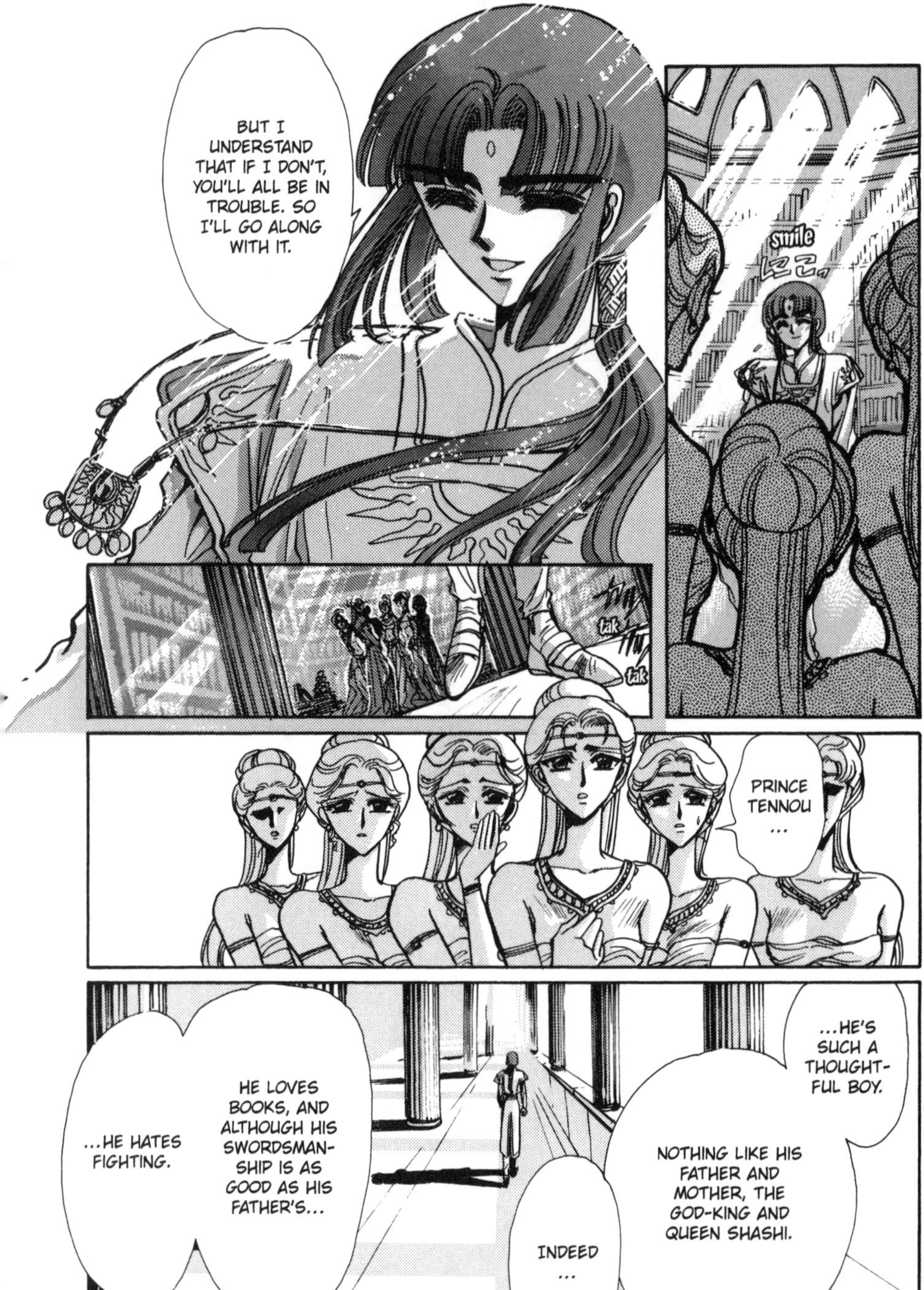
smile
BUT I UNDERSTAND THAT IF I DON'T, YOU'LL ALL BE IN TROUBLE. SO I'LL GO ALONG WITH IT.
tak
tak
PRINCE TENNOU ...
...HE'S SUCH A THOUGHT-FUL BOY.
NOTHING LIKE HIS FATHER AND MOTHER, THE GOD-KING AND QUEEN SHASHI.
INDEED ...
HE LOVES BOOKS, AND ALTHOUGH HIS SWORDSMAN-SHIP IS AS GOOD AS HIS FATHER'S...
...HE HATES FIGHTING.

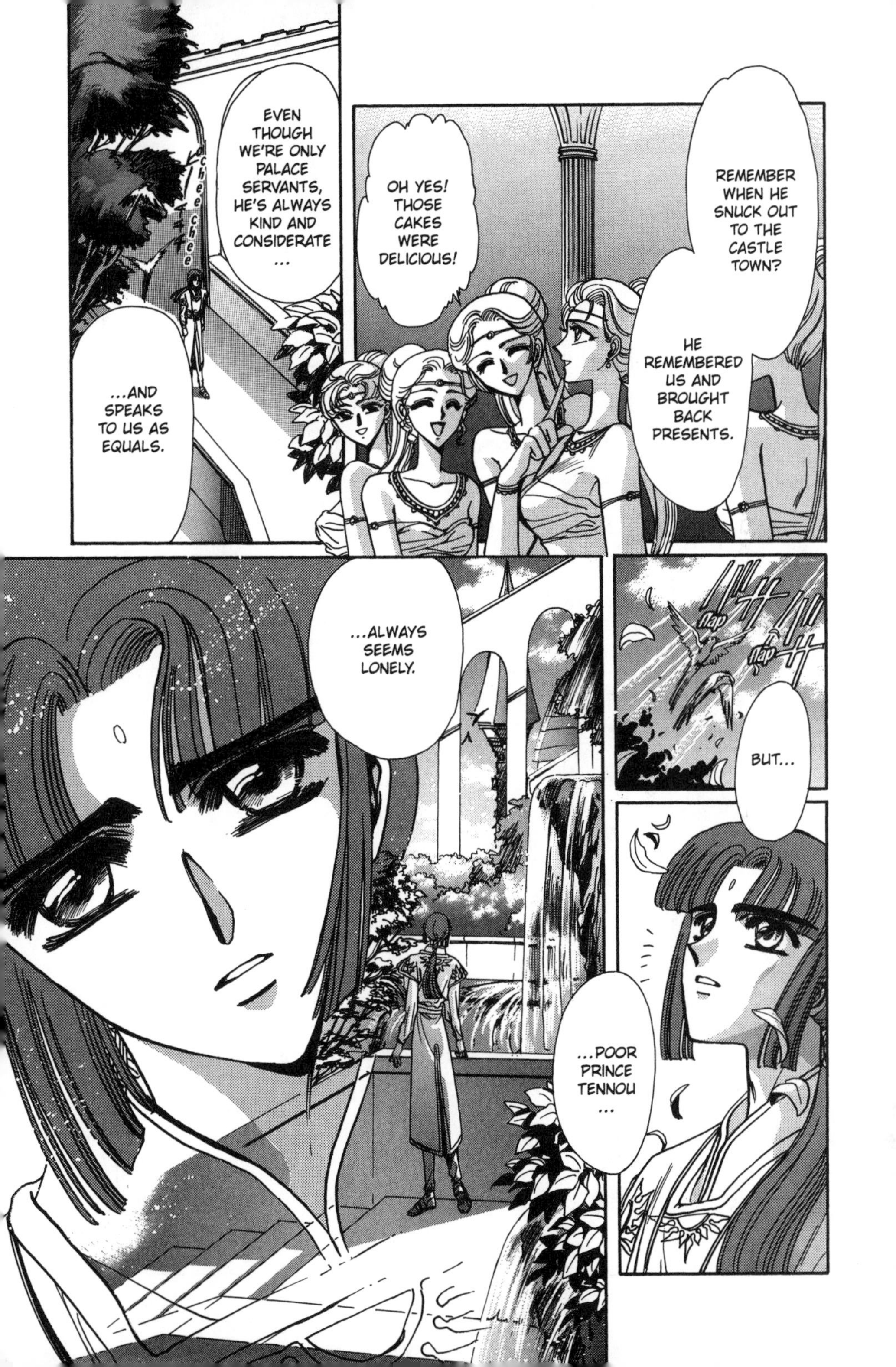
REMEMBER WHEN HE SNUCK OUT TO THE CASTLE TOWN?
HE REMEMBERED US AND BROUGHT BACK PRESENTS.
OH YES! THOSE CAKES WERE DELICIOUS!
EVEN THOUGH WE'RE ONLY PALACE SERVANTS, HE'S ALWAYS KIND AND CONSIDERATE ...
chee chee
...AND SPEAKS TO US AS EQUALS.
flap
flap
BUT...
...POOR PRINCE TENNOU ...
...ALWAYS SEEMS LONELY.

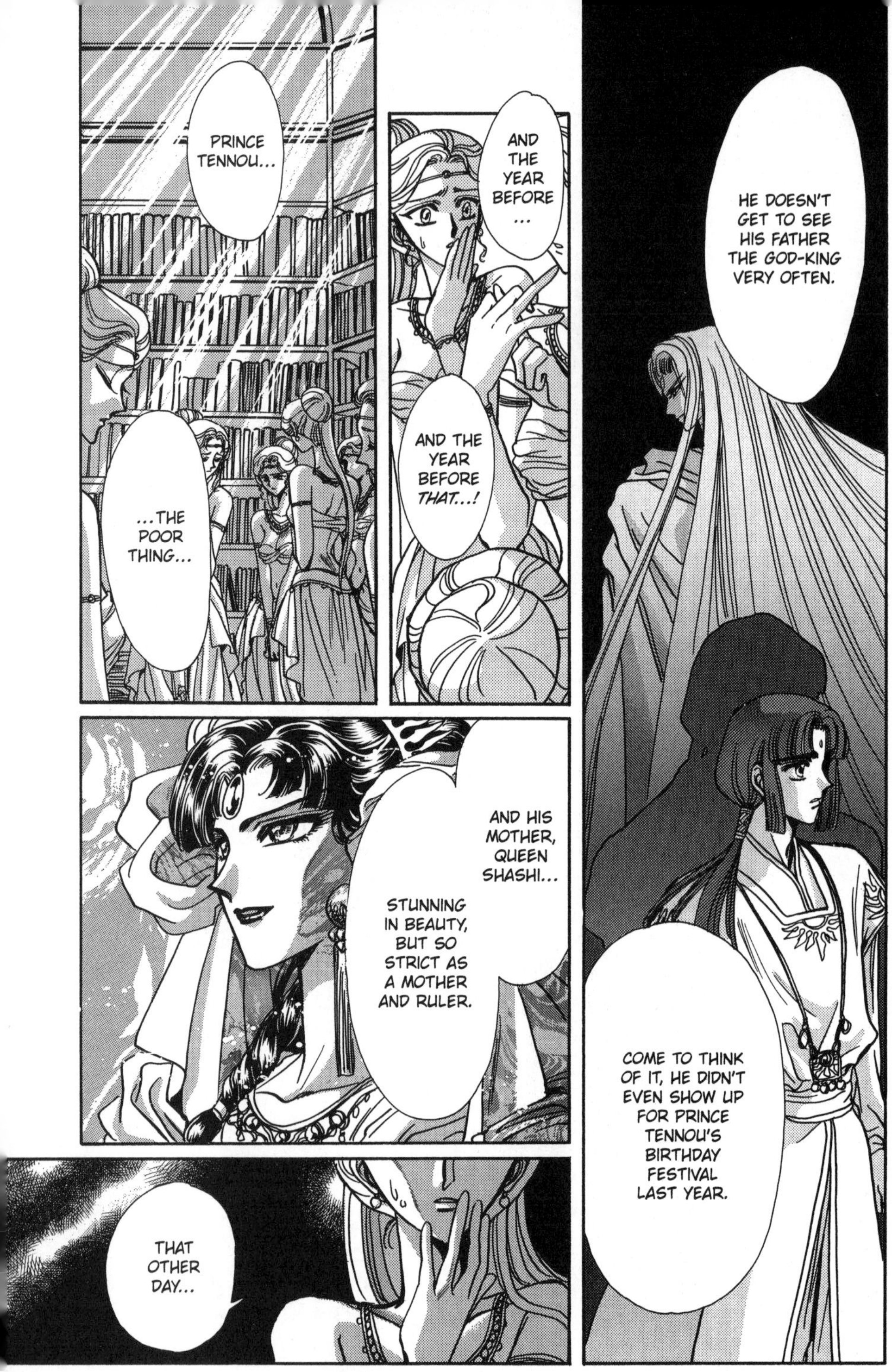

HE DOESN'T GET TO SEE HIS FATHER THE GOD-KING VERY OFTEN.
COME TO THINK OF IT, HE DIDN'T EVEN SHOW UP FOR PRINCE TENNOU'S BIRTHDAY FESTIVAL LAST YEAR.
AND THE YEAR BEFORE ...
AND THE YEAR BEFORE *THAT*...!
PRINCE TENNOU...
...THE POOR THING...
AND HIS MOTHER, QUEEN SHASHI...
STUNNING IN BEAUTY, BUT SO STRICT AS A MOTHER AND RULER.
THAT OTHER DAY...

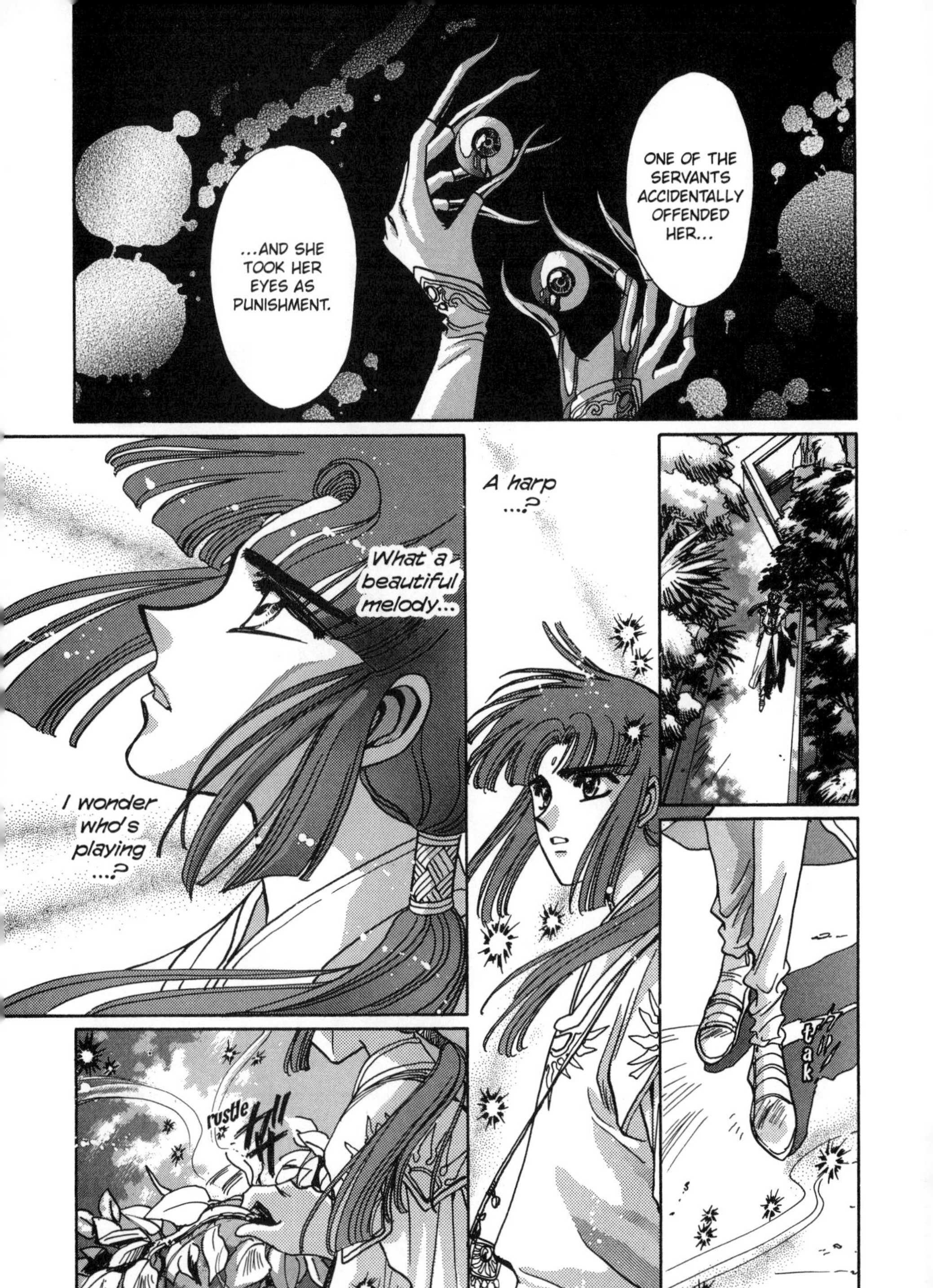
ONE OF THE SERVANTS ACCIDENTALLY OFFENDED HER...
...AND SHE TOOK HER EYES AS PUNISHMENT.
tak
A harp ...?
What a beautiful melody...
I wonder who's playing ...?
rustle

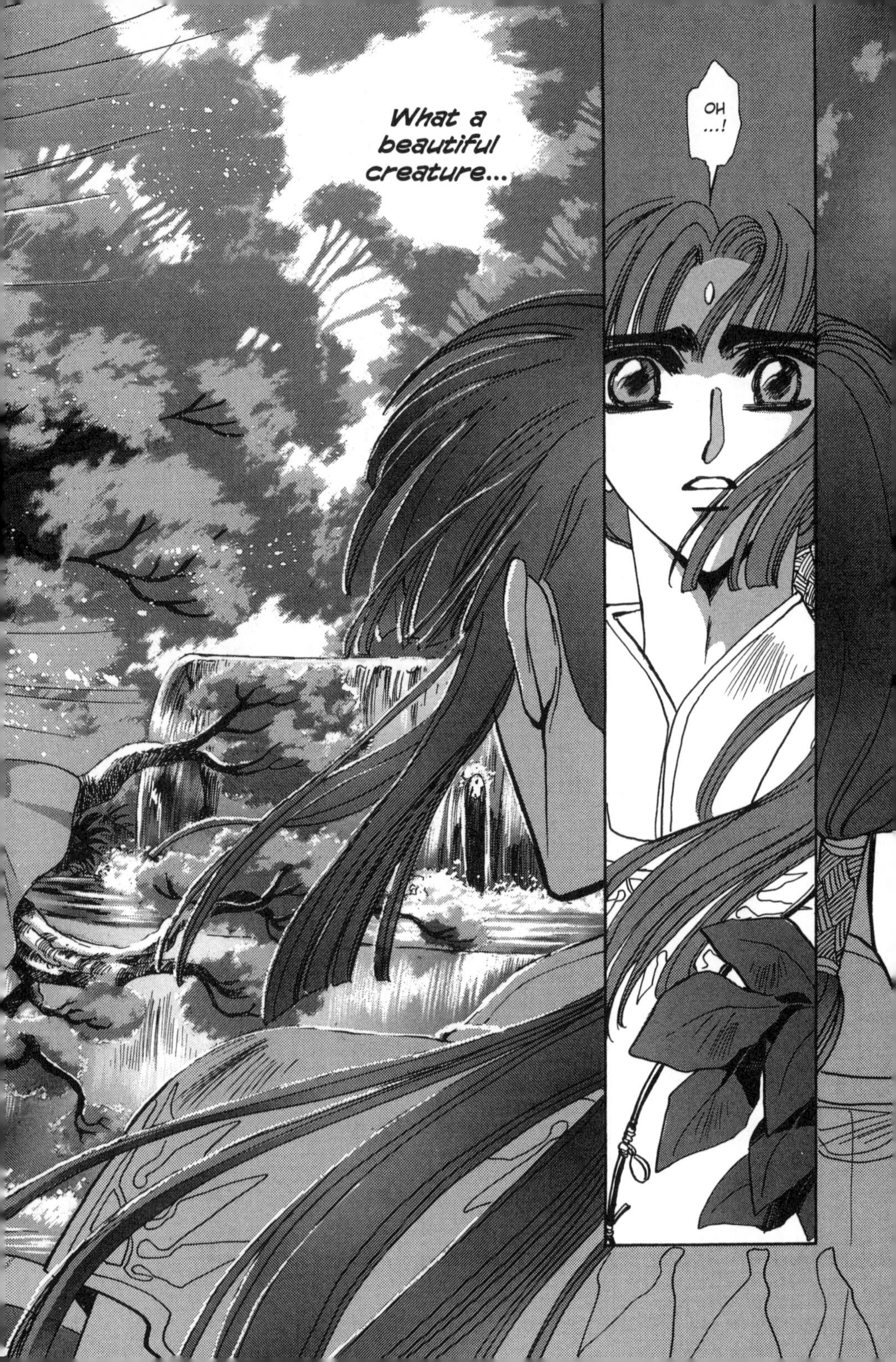
OH ...!
What a beautiful creature...

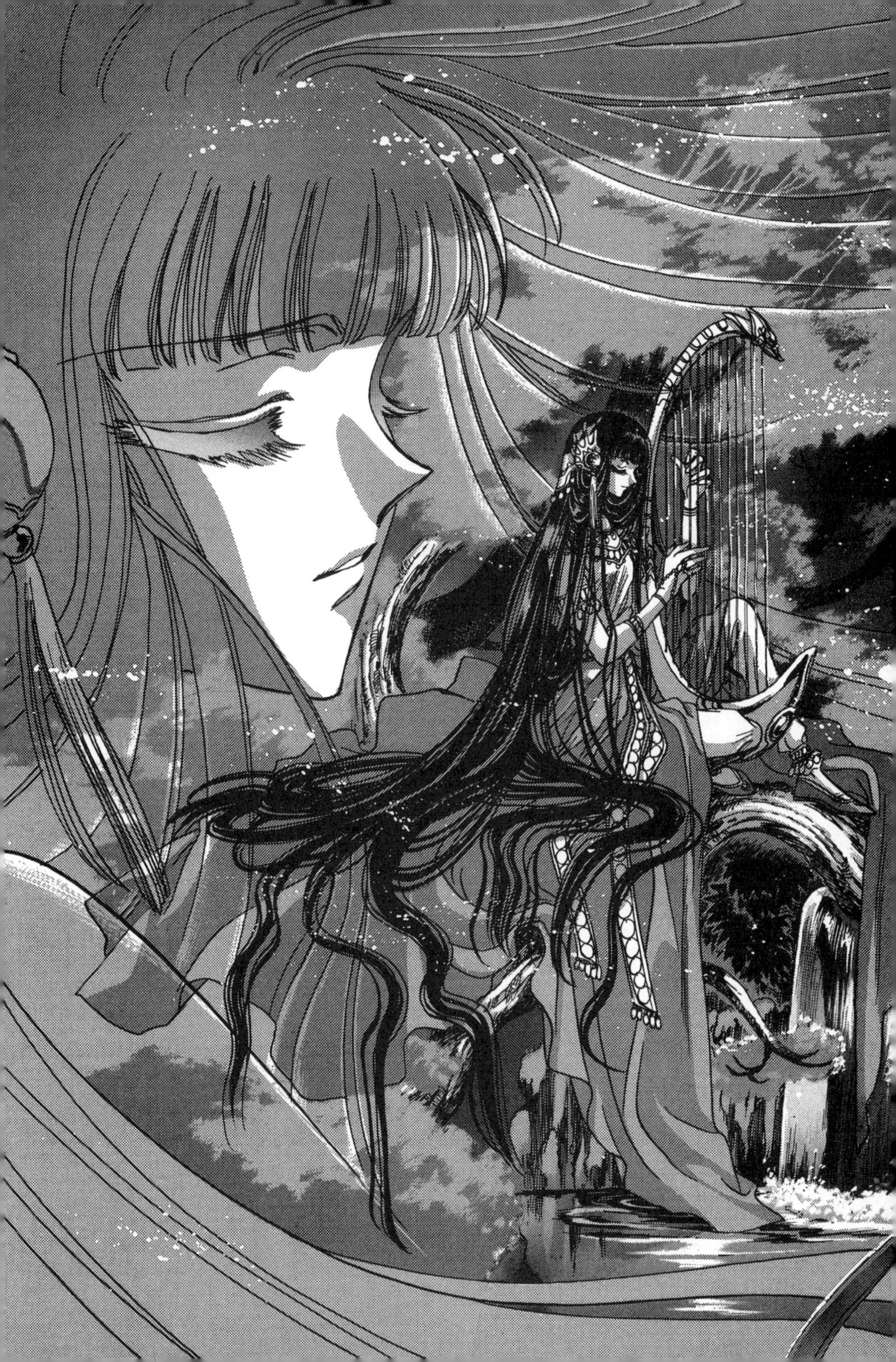

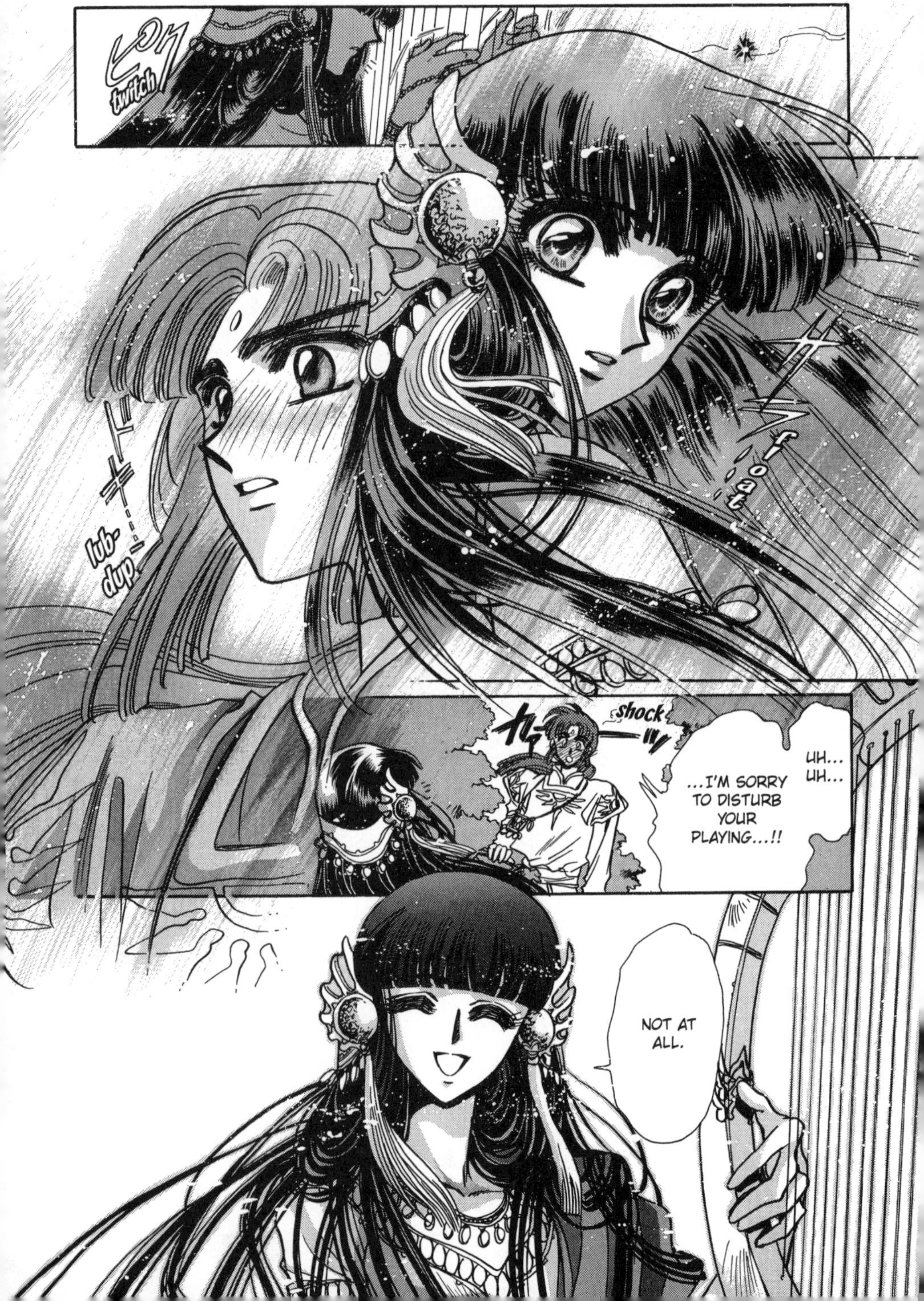
twitch
float
lub-dup
UH... UH...
shock
...I'M SORRY TO DISTURB YOUR PLAYING...!!
NOT AT ALL.

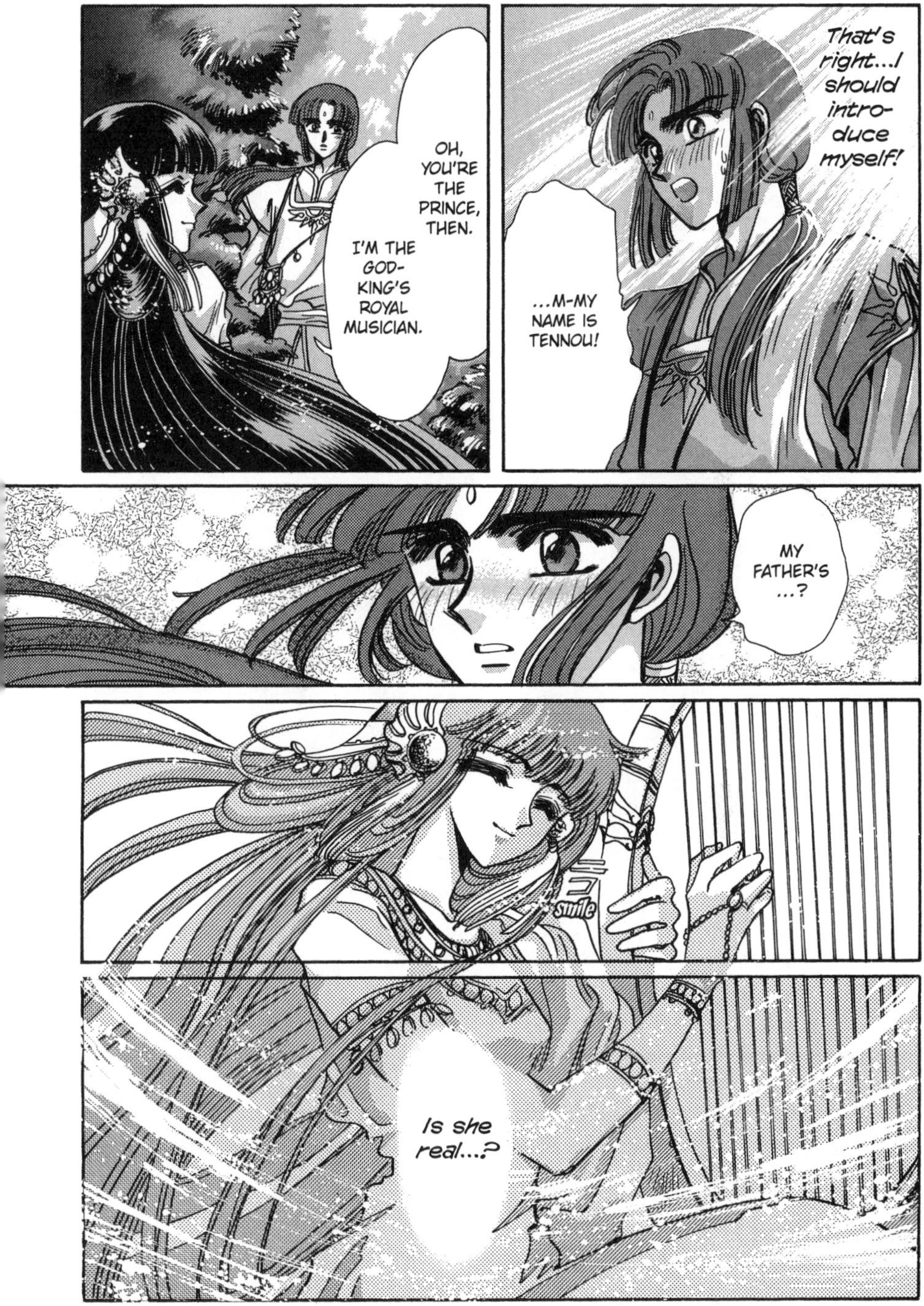
That's right...I should intro-duce myself!
...M-MY NAME IS TENNOU!
OH, YOU'RE THE PRINCE, THEN.
I'M THE GOD-KING'S ROYAL MUSICIAN.
MY FATHER'S ...?
smile
Is she real...?

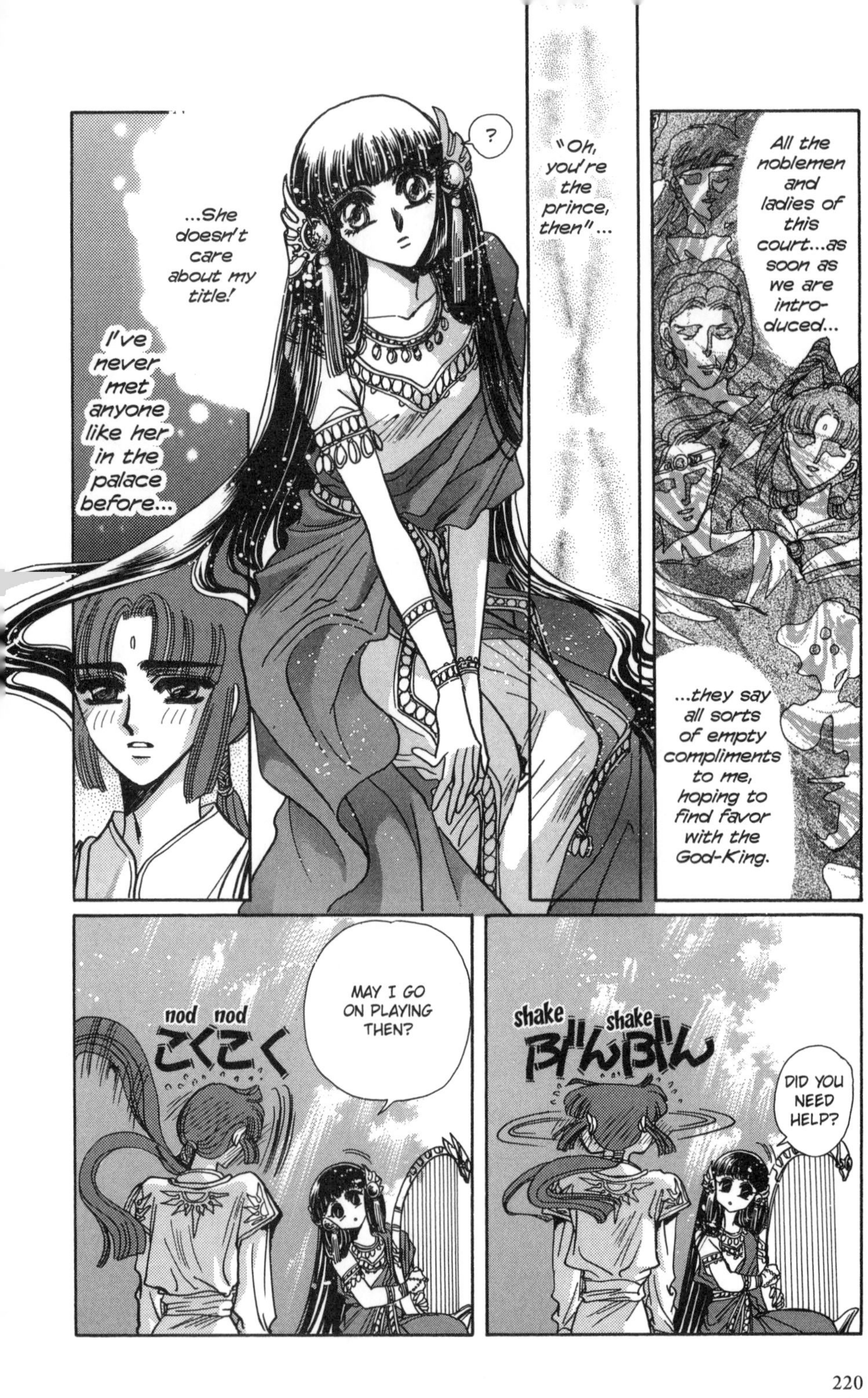

All the noblemen and ladies of this court...as soon as we are introduced...
...they say all sorts of empty compliments to me, hoping to find favor with the God-King.
"Oh, you're the prince, then"...
?
...She doesn't care about my title!
I've never met anyone like her in the palace before...
shake shake
ぶんぶん
DID YOU NEED HELP?
MAY I GO ON PLAYING THEN?
nod nod
こくこく

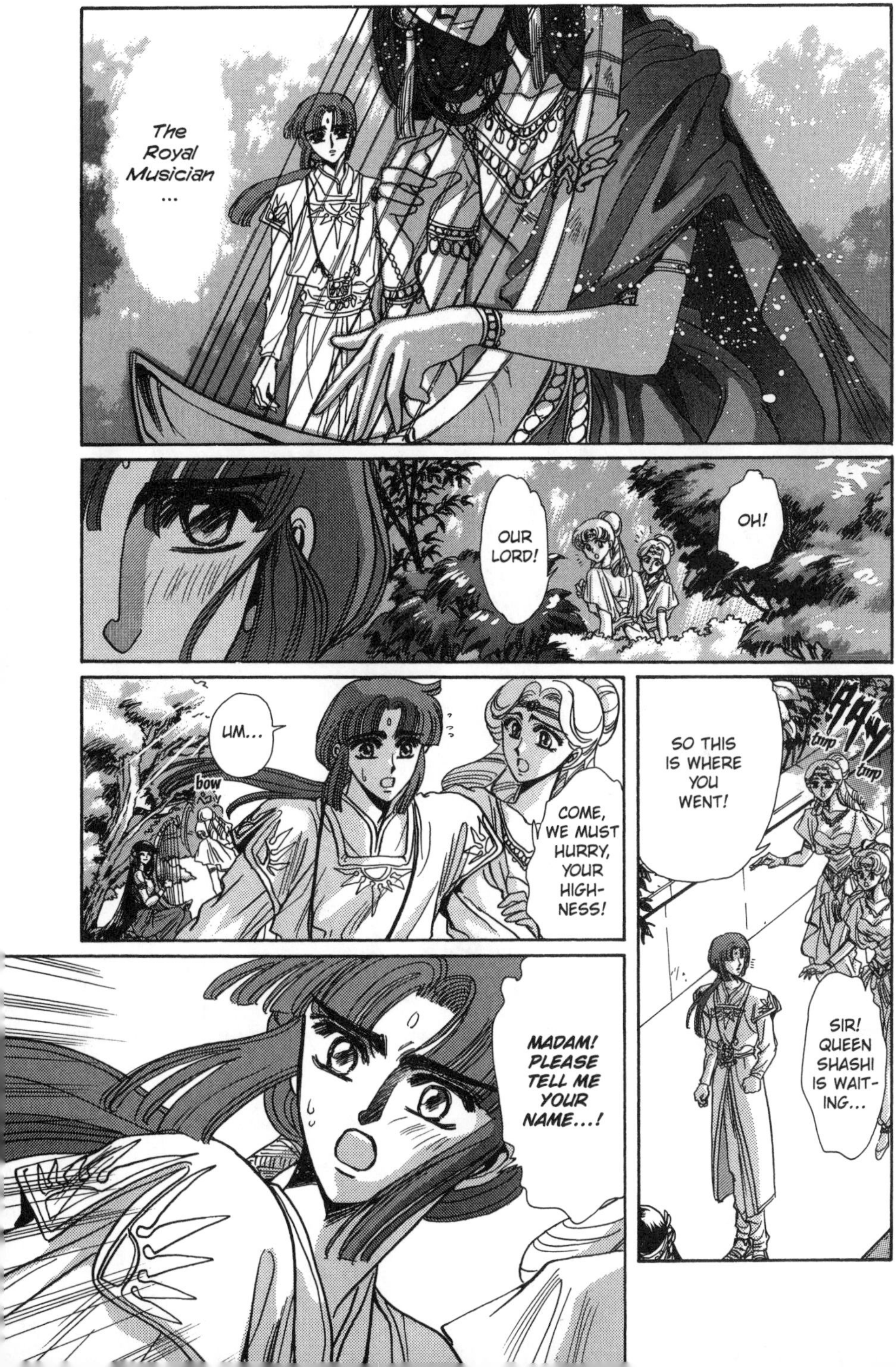
The Royal Musician ...
OH!
OUR LORD!
SO THIS IS WHERE YOU WENT!
tmp tmp
SIR! QUEEN SHASHI IS WAIT-ING...
COME, WE MUST HURRY, YOUR HIGH-NESS!
UM...
bow
MADAM! PLEASE TELL ME YOUR NAME...!

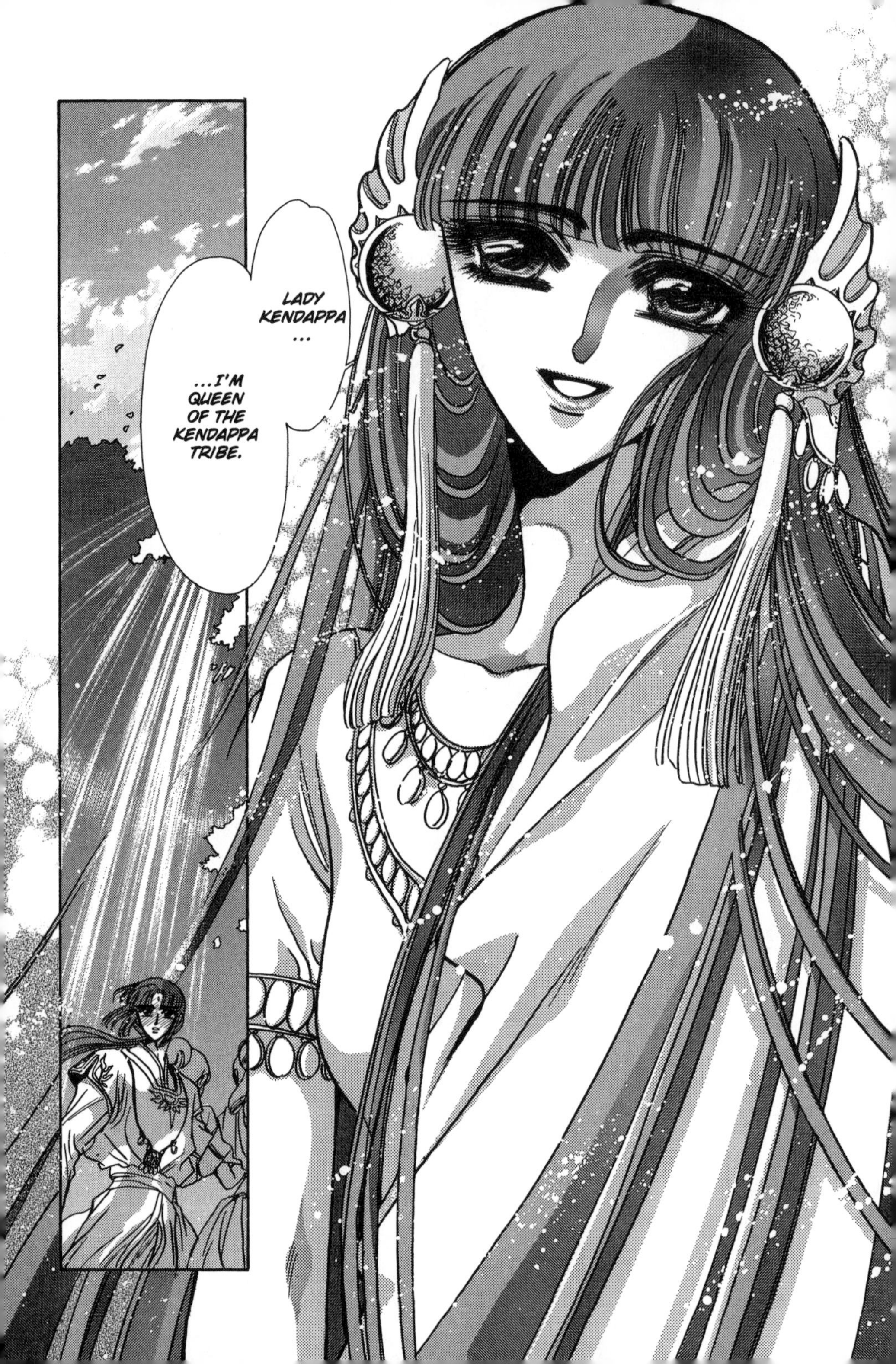
LADY KENDAPPA ...
...I'M QUEEN OF THE KENDAPPA TRIBE.

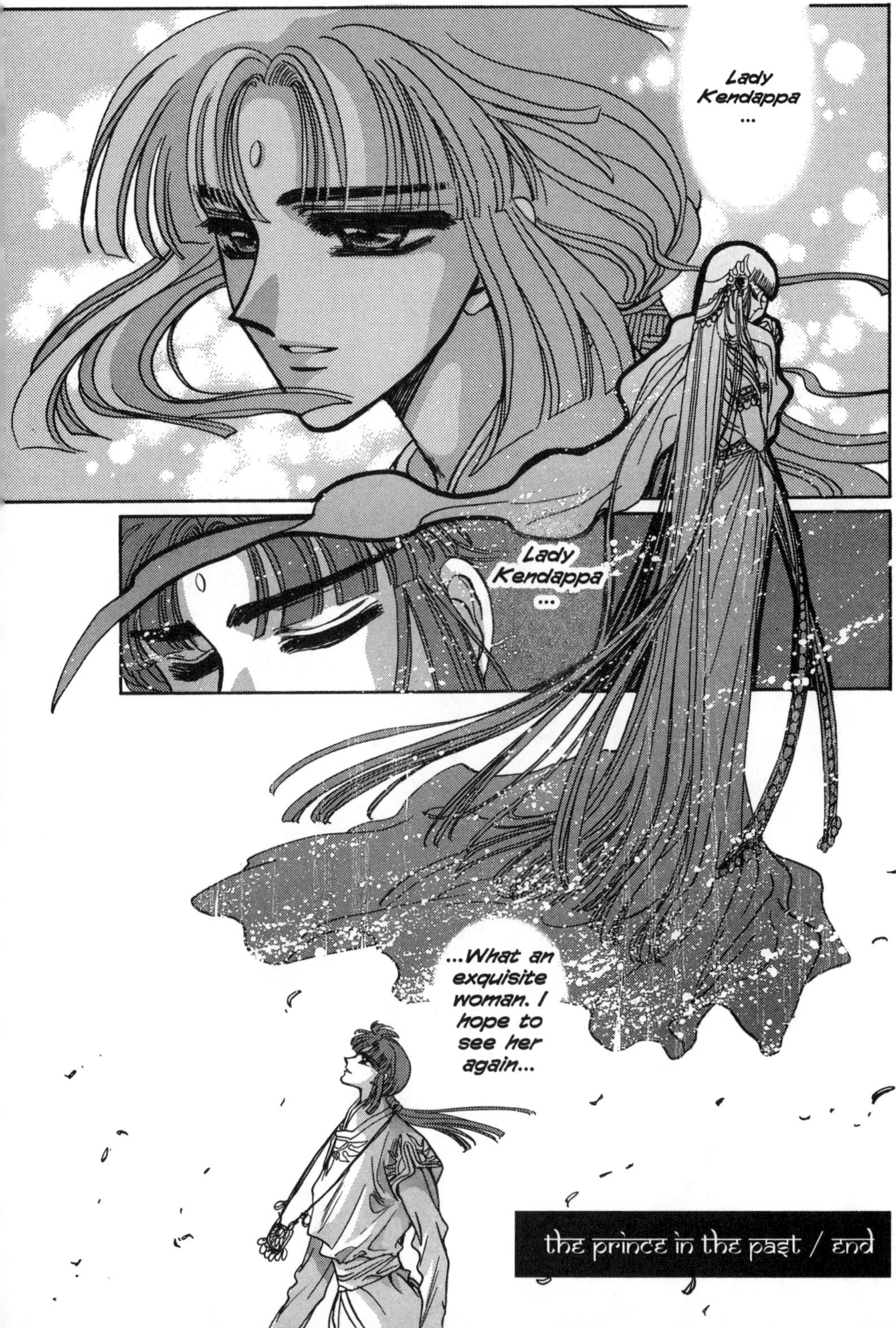
Lady Kendappa ...
Lady Kendappa ...
...What an exquisite woman. I hope to see her again...
the prince in the past / end

CLAMP
RG VEDA

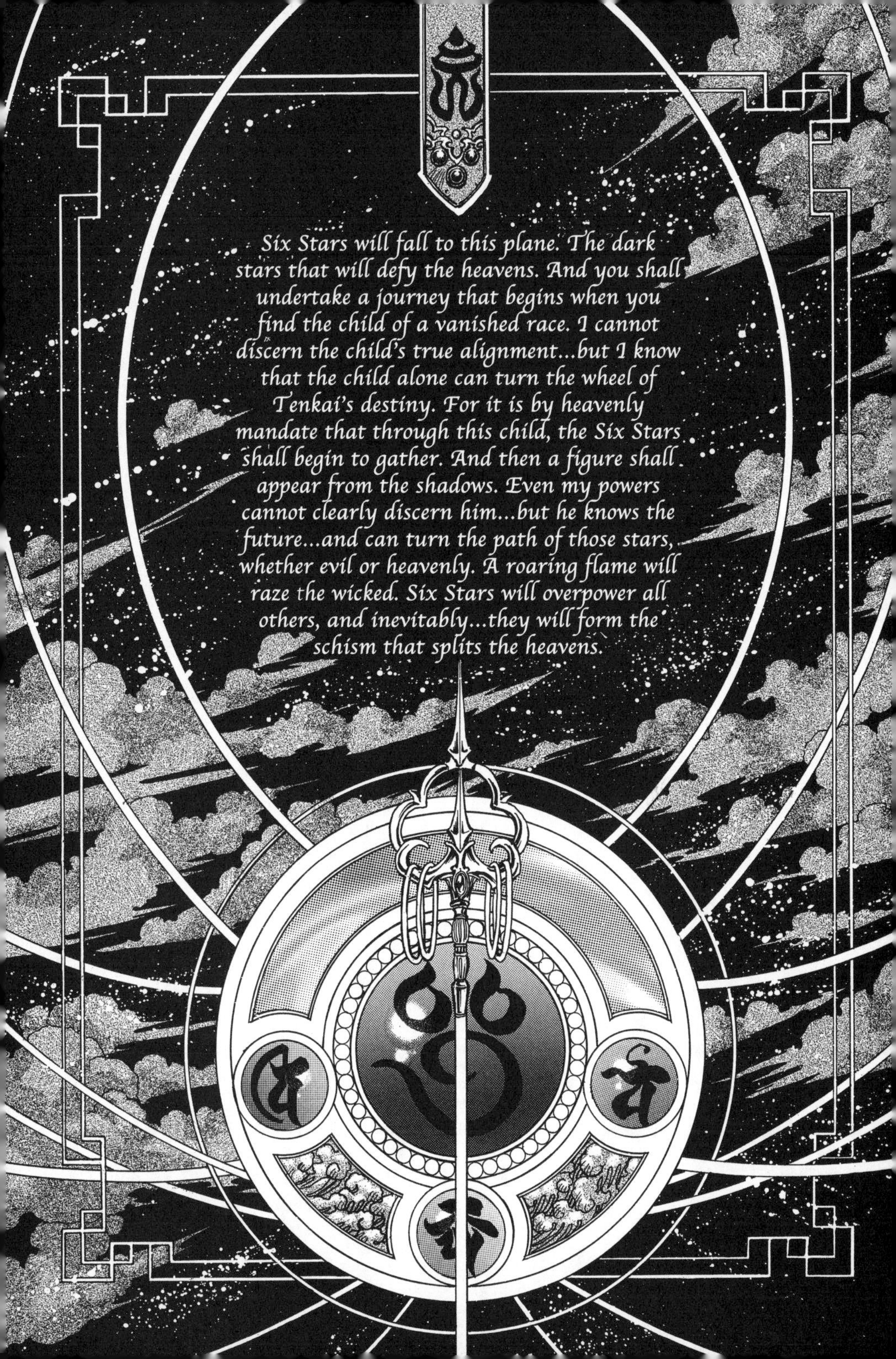
Six Stars will fall to this plane. The dark stars that will defy the heavens. And you shall undertake a journey that begins when you find the child of a vanished race. I cannot discern the child's true alignment...but I know that the child alone can turn the wheel of Tenkai's destiny. For it is by heavenly mandate that through this child, the Six Stars shall begin to gather. And then a figure shall appear from the shadows. Even my powers cannot clearly discern him...but he knows the future...and can turn the path of those stars, whether evil or heavenly. A roaring flame will raze the wicked. Six Stars will overpower all others, and inevitably...they will form the schism that splits the heavens.

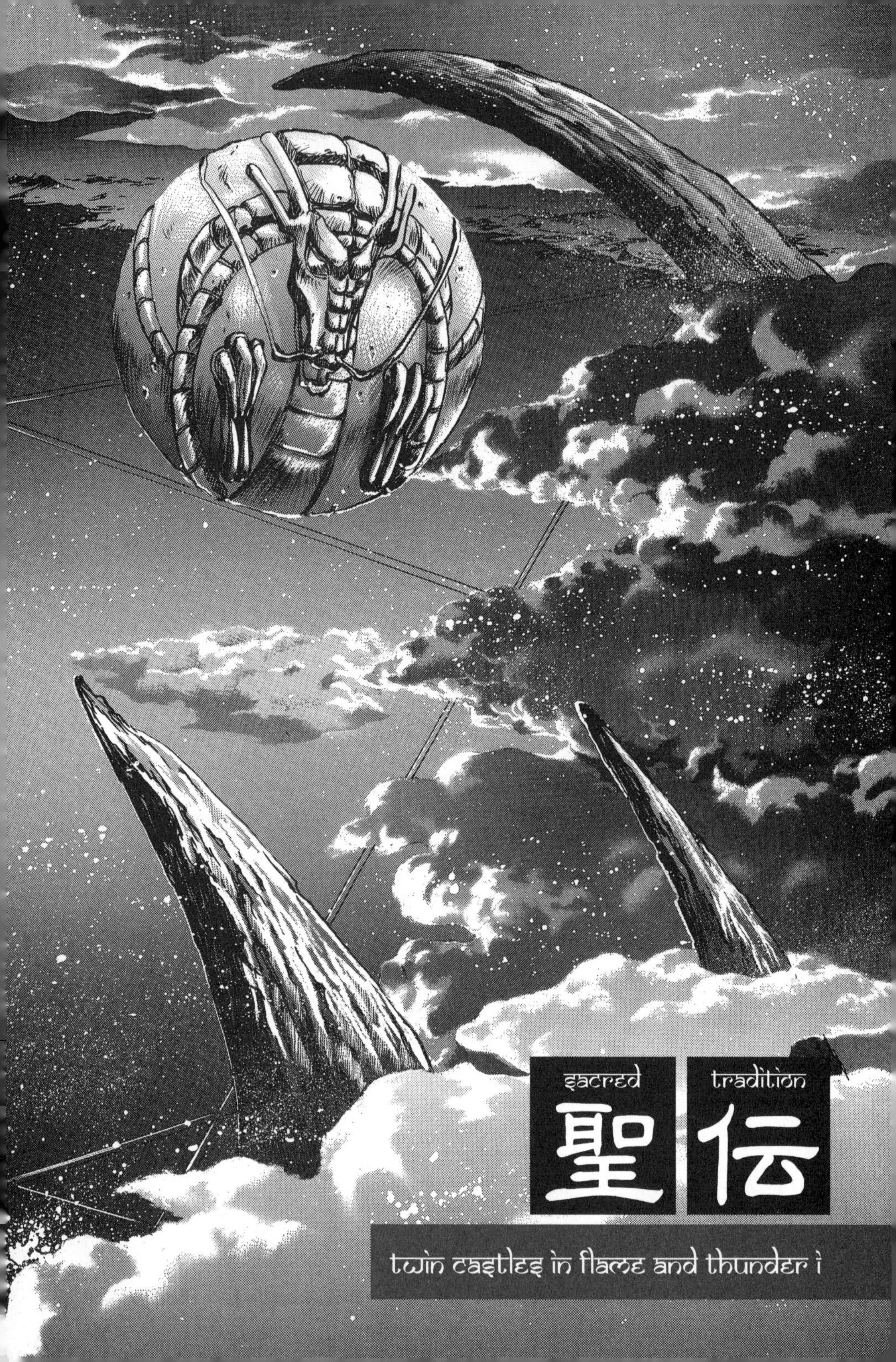
sacred
tradition
聖伝
twin castles in flame and thunder i

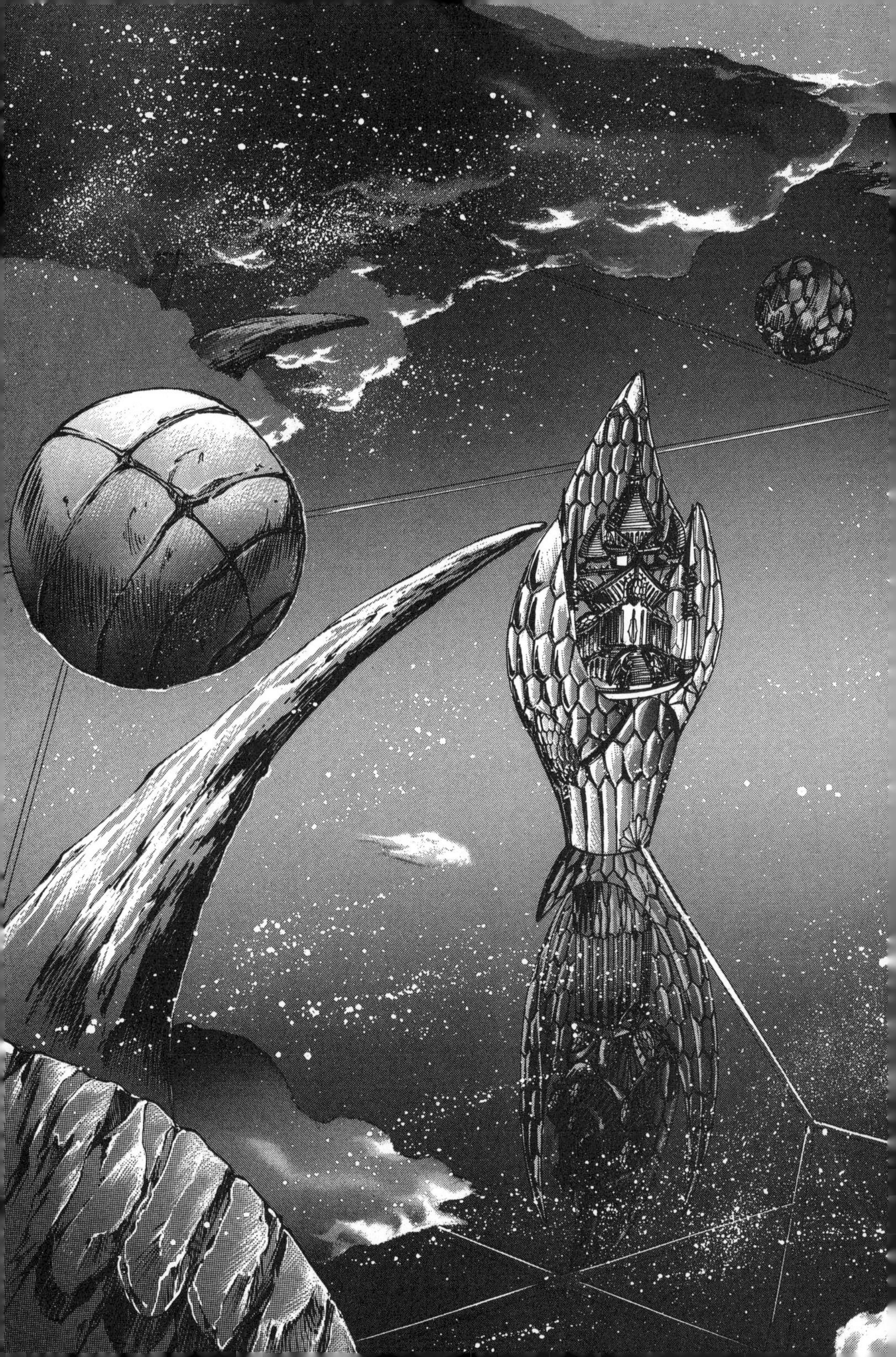

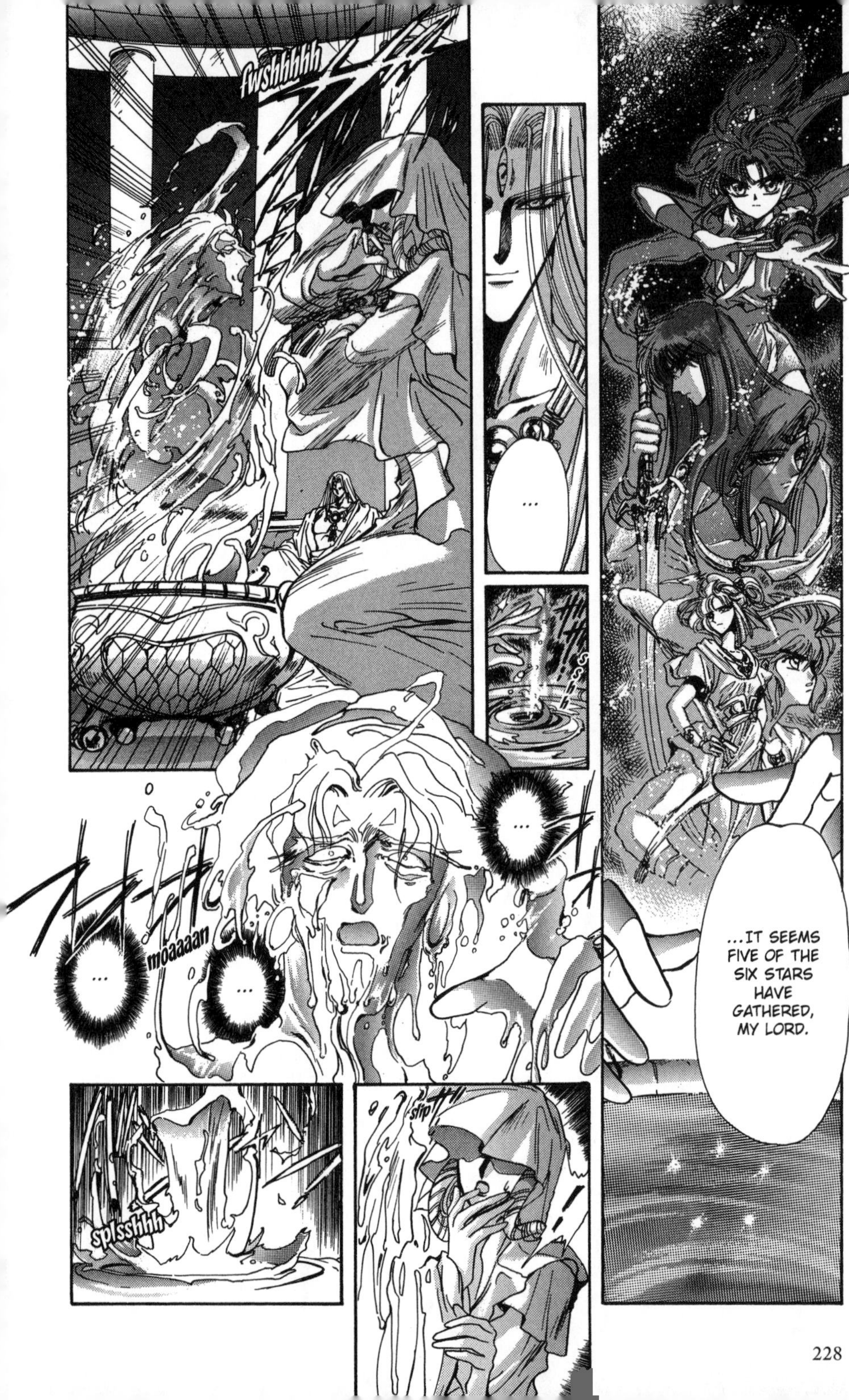
...IT SEEMS FIVE OF THE SIX STARS HAVE GATHERED, MY LORD.
...
sshhh
fwshhhhh
...
moaaaan
...
...
...
slip
splsshhh

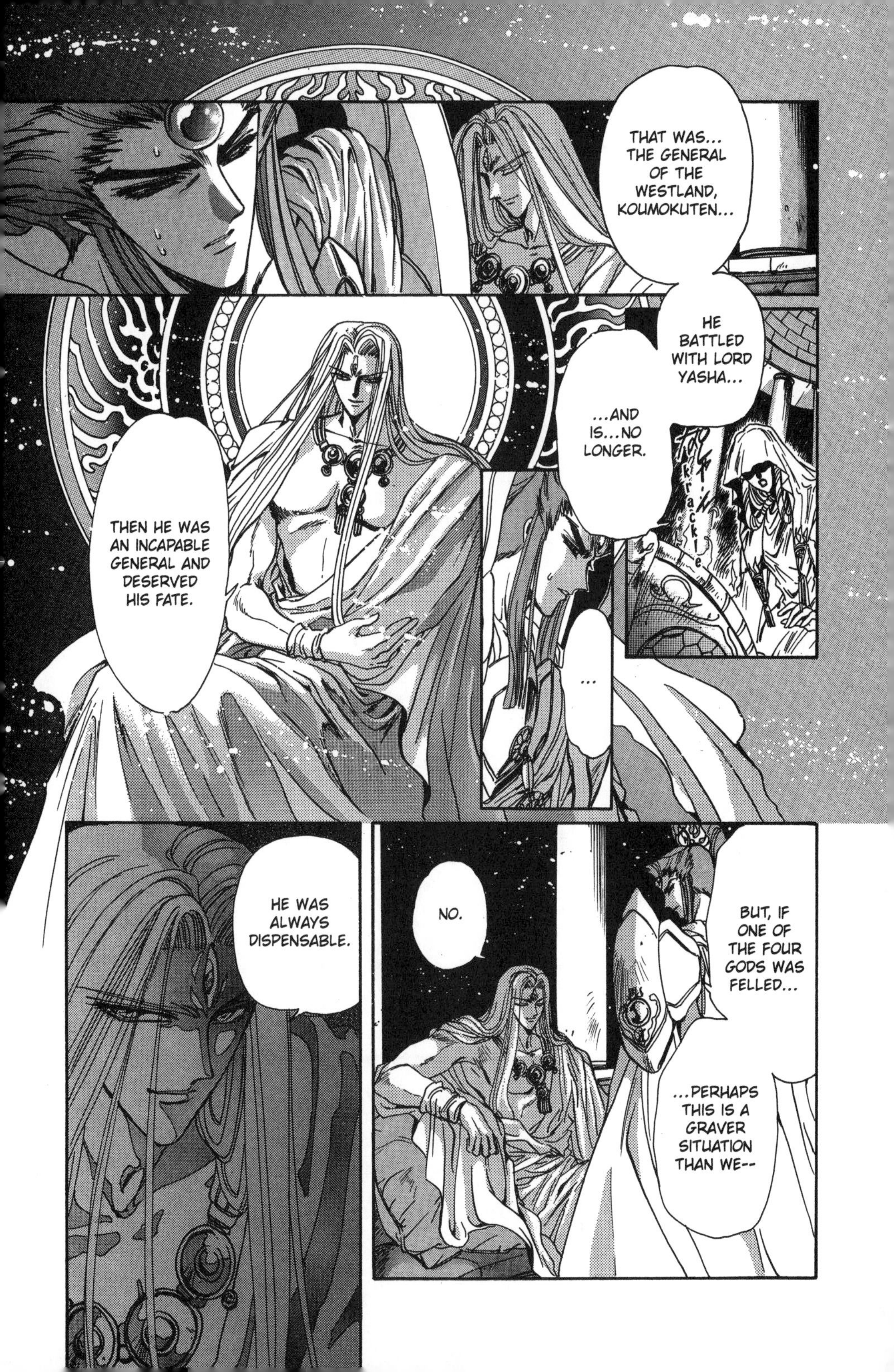
THAT WAS... THE GENERAL OF THE WESTLAND, KOUMOKUTEN...
HE BATTLED WITH LORD YASHA...
...AND IS...NO LONGER.
krackle
...
THEN HE WAS AN INCAPABLE GENERAL AND DESERVED HIS FATE.
BUT, IF ONE OF THE FOUR GODS WAS FELLED...
...PERHAPS THIS IS A GRAVER SITUATION THAN WE--
NO.
HE WAS ALWAYS DISPENSABLE.

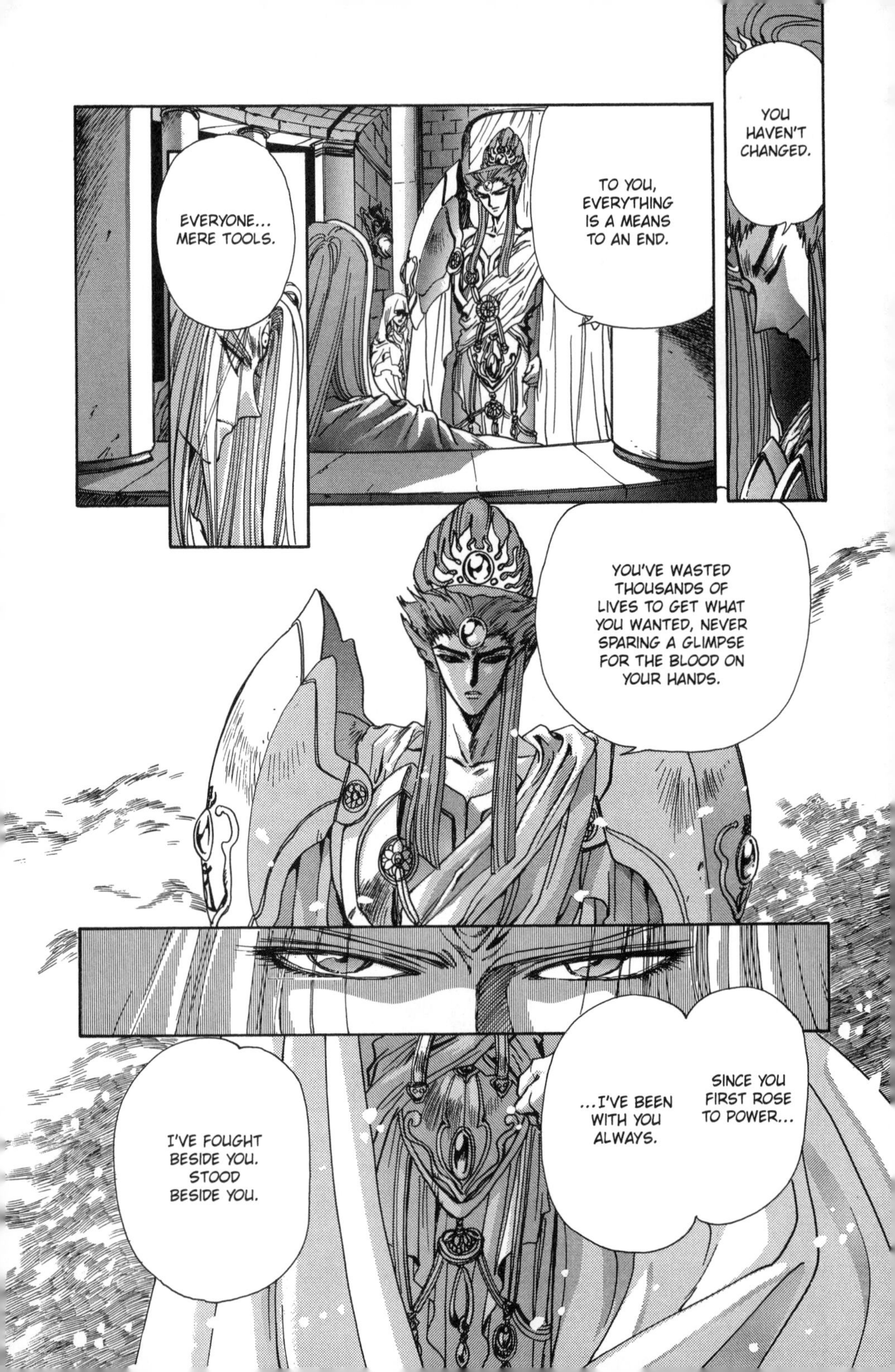
YOU HAVEN'T CHANGED.
TO YOU, EVERYTHING IS A MEANS TO AN END.
EVERYONE... MERE TOOLS.
YOU'VE WASTED THOUSANDS OF LIVES TO GET WHAT YOU WANTED, NEVER SPARING A GLIMPSE FOR THE BLOOD ON YOUR HANDS.
SINCE YOU FIRST ROSE TO POWER...
...I'VE BEEN WITH YOU ALWAYS.
I'VE FOUGHT BESIDE YOU. STOOD BESIDE YOU.

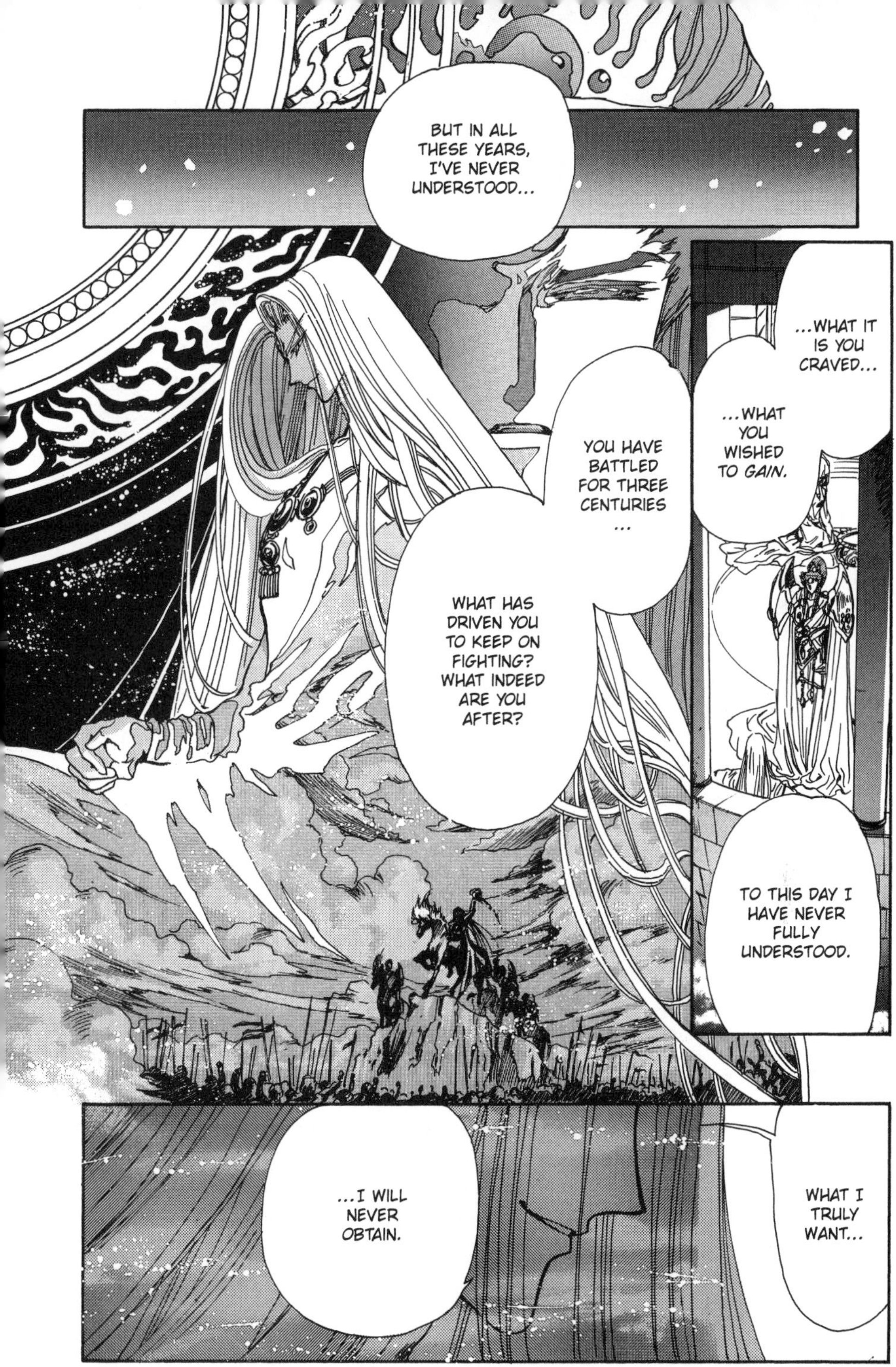
BUT IN ALL THESE YEARS, I'VE NEVER UNDERSTOOD...
...WHAT IT IS YOU CRAVED...
...WHAT YOU WISHED TO GAIN.
TO THIS DAY I HAVE NEVER FULLY UNDERSTOOD.
YOU HAVE BATTLED FOR THREE CENTURIES ...
WHAT HAS DRIVEN YOU TO KEEP ON FIGHTING? WHAT INDEED ARE YOU AFTER?
WHAT I TRULY WANT...
...I WILL NEVER OBTAIN.

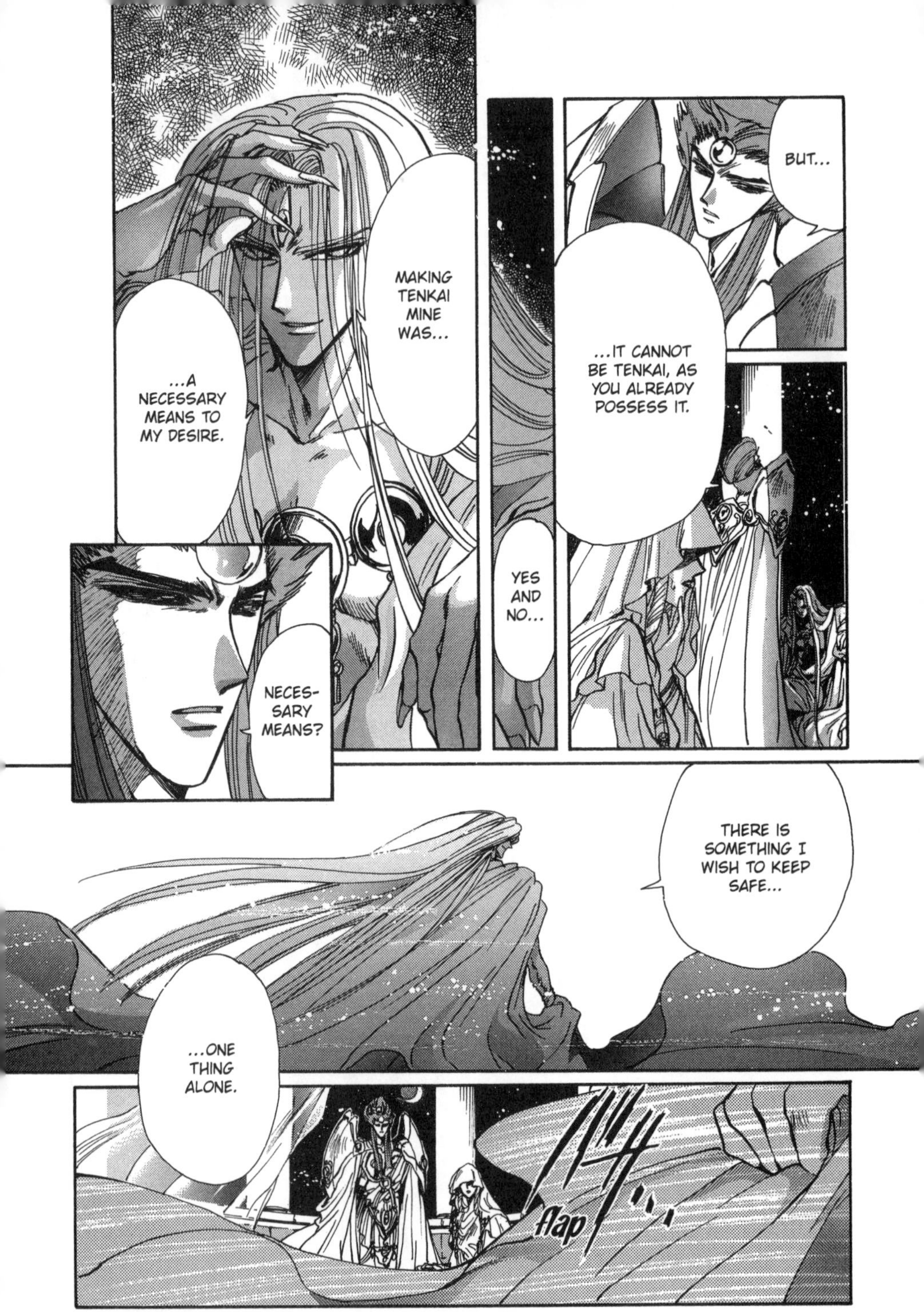
BUT...
...IT CANNOT BE TENKAI, AS YOU ALREADY POSSESS IT.
YES AND NO...
MAKING TENKAI MINE WAS...
...A NECESSARY MEANS TO MY DESIRE.
NECES-SARY MEANS?
THERE IS SOMETHING I WISH TO KEEP SAFE...
...ONE THING ALONE.
flap

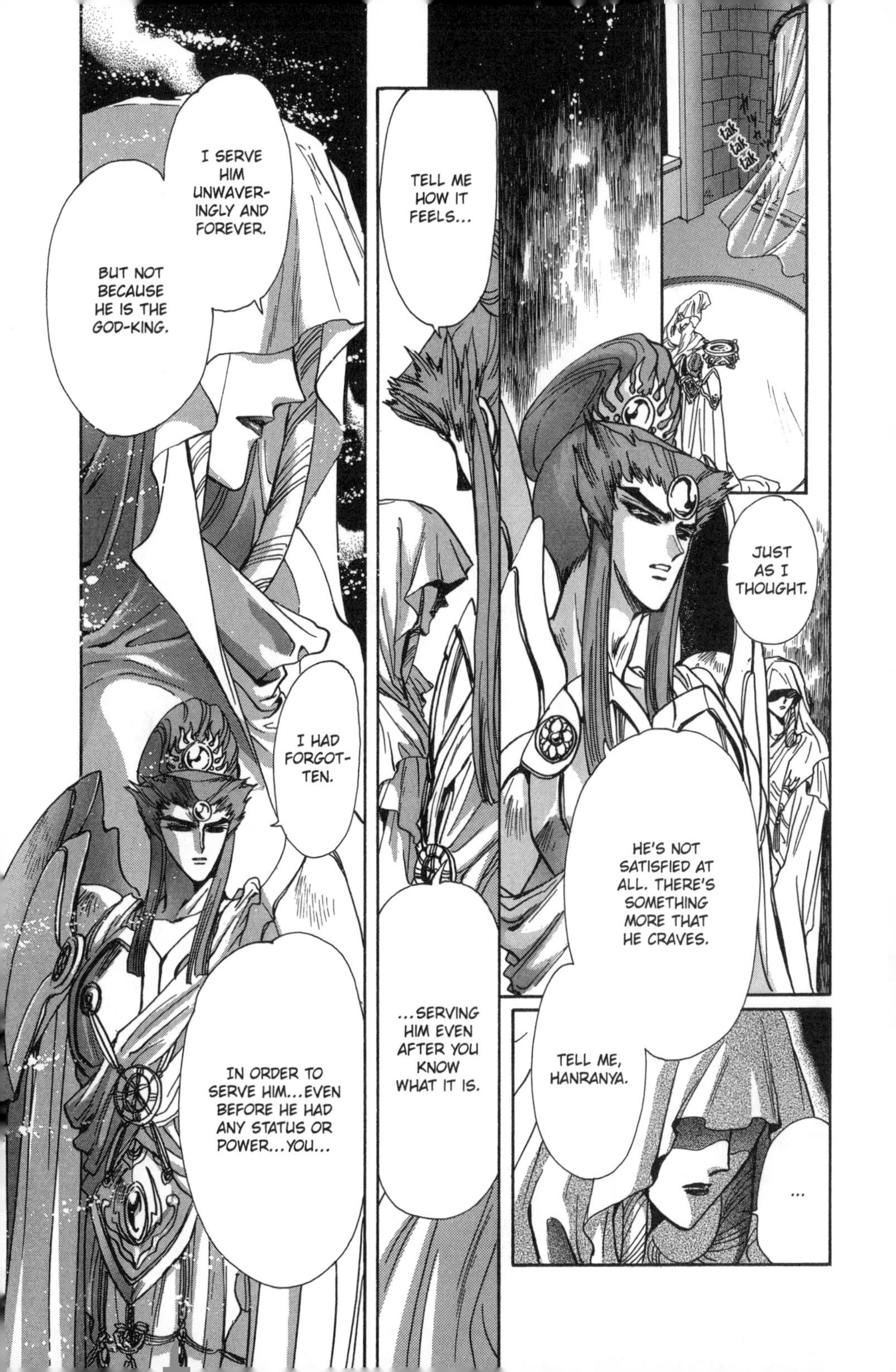
tak tak tak
JUST AS I THOUGHT.
HE'S NOT SATISFIED AT ALL. THERE'S SOMETHING MORE THAT HE CRAVES.
TELL ME, HANRANYA.
...
TELL ME HOW IT FEELS...
...SERVING HIM EVEN AFTER YOU KNOW WHAT IT IS.
I SERVE HIM UNWAVER-INGLY AND FOREVER.
BUT NOT BECAUSE HE IS THE GOD-KING.
I HAD FORGOT-TEN.
IN ORDER TO SERVE HIM...EVEN BEFORE HE HAD ANY STATUS OR POWER...YOU...

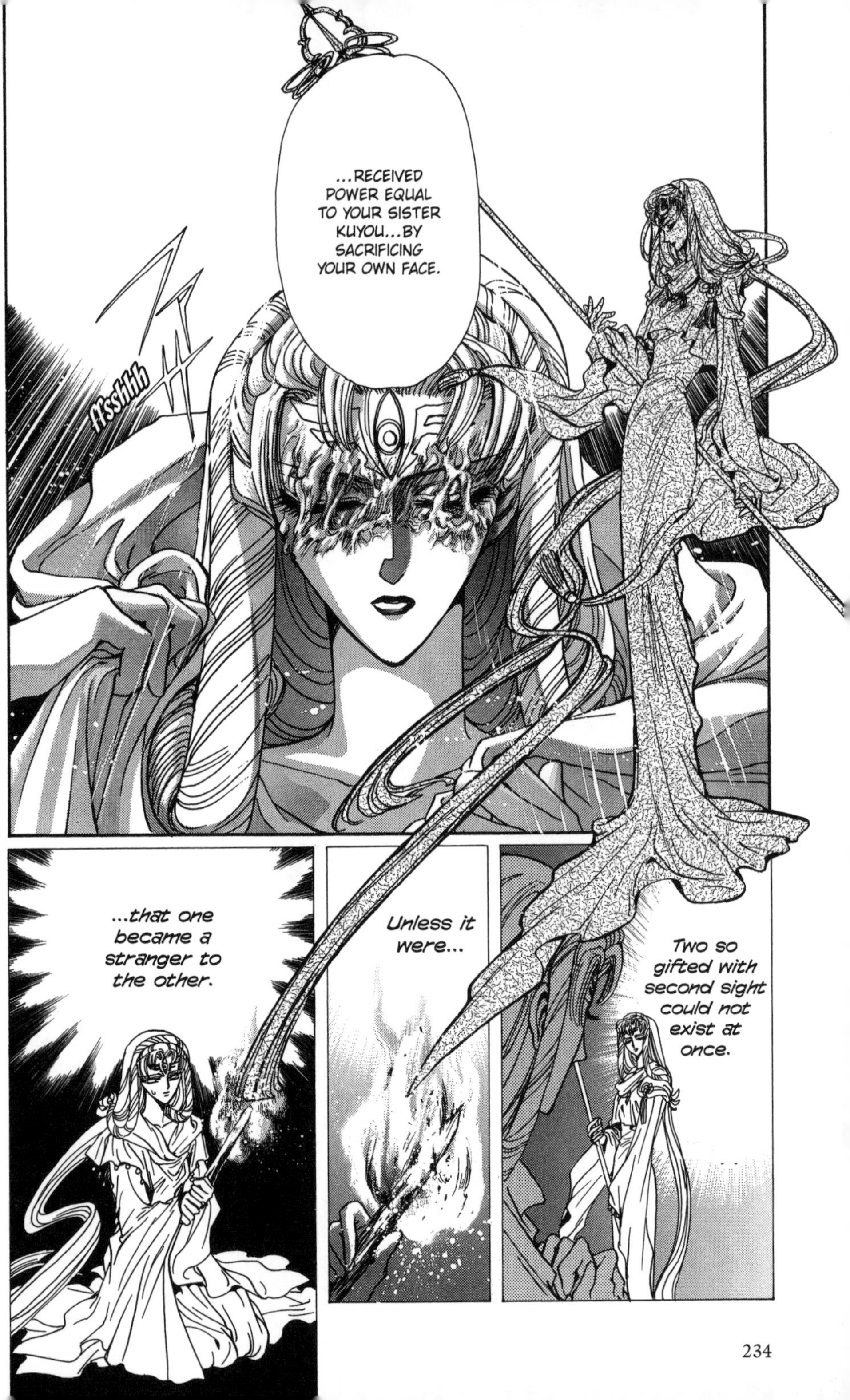
...RECEIVED POWER EQUAL TO YOUR SISTER KUYOU...BY SACRIFICING YOUR OWN FACE.
Ffsshhh
Two so gifted with second sight could not exist at once.
Unless it were...
...that one became a stranger to the other.

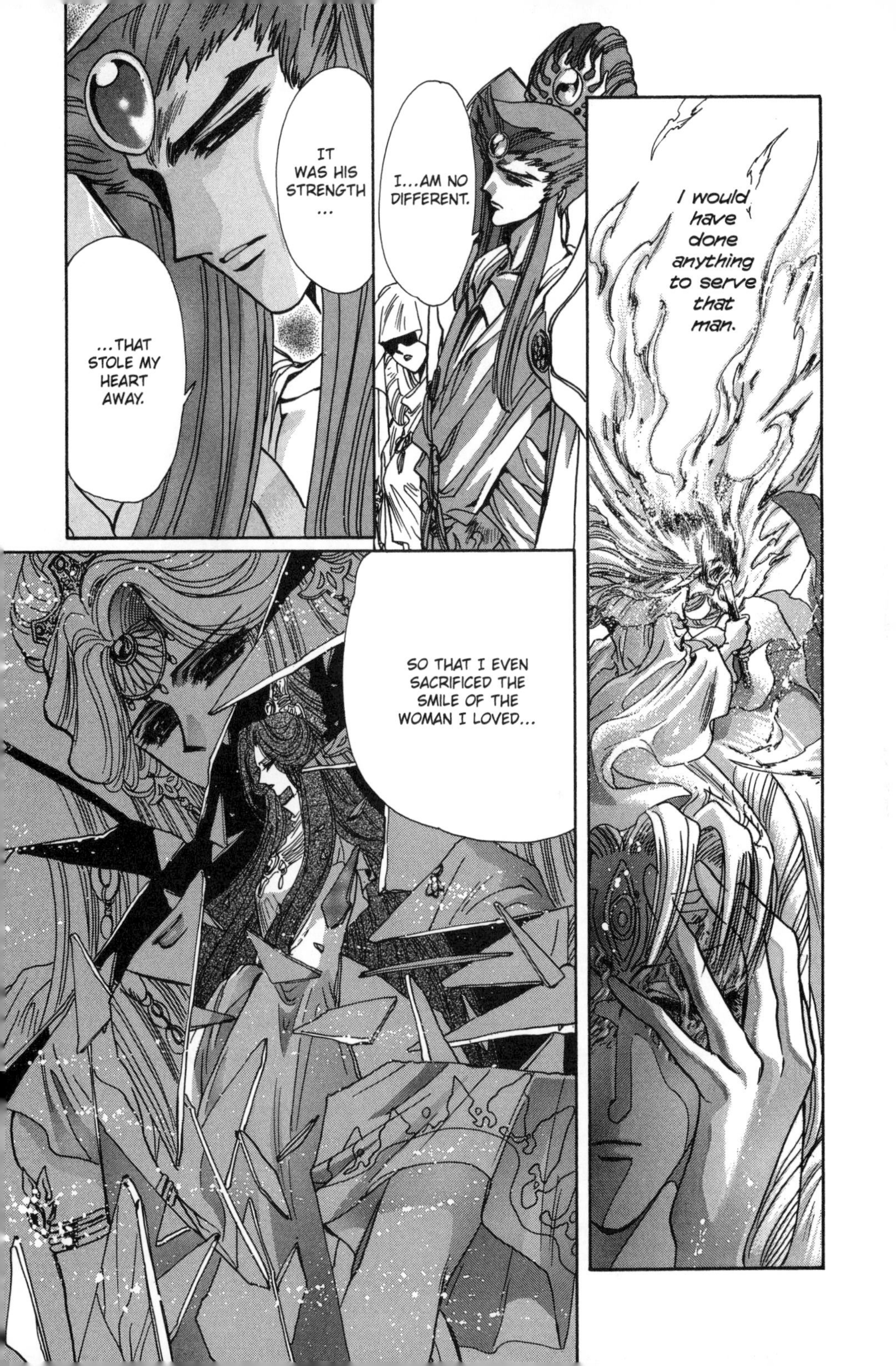
I would have done anything to serve that man.
I...AM NO DIFFERENT.
IT WAS HIS STRENGTH...
...THAT STOLE MY HEART AWAY.
SO THAT I EVEN SACRIFICED THE SMILE OF THE WOMAN I LOVED...

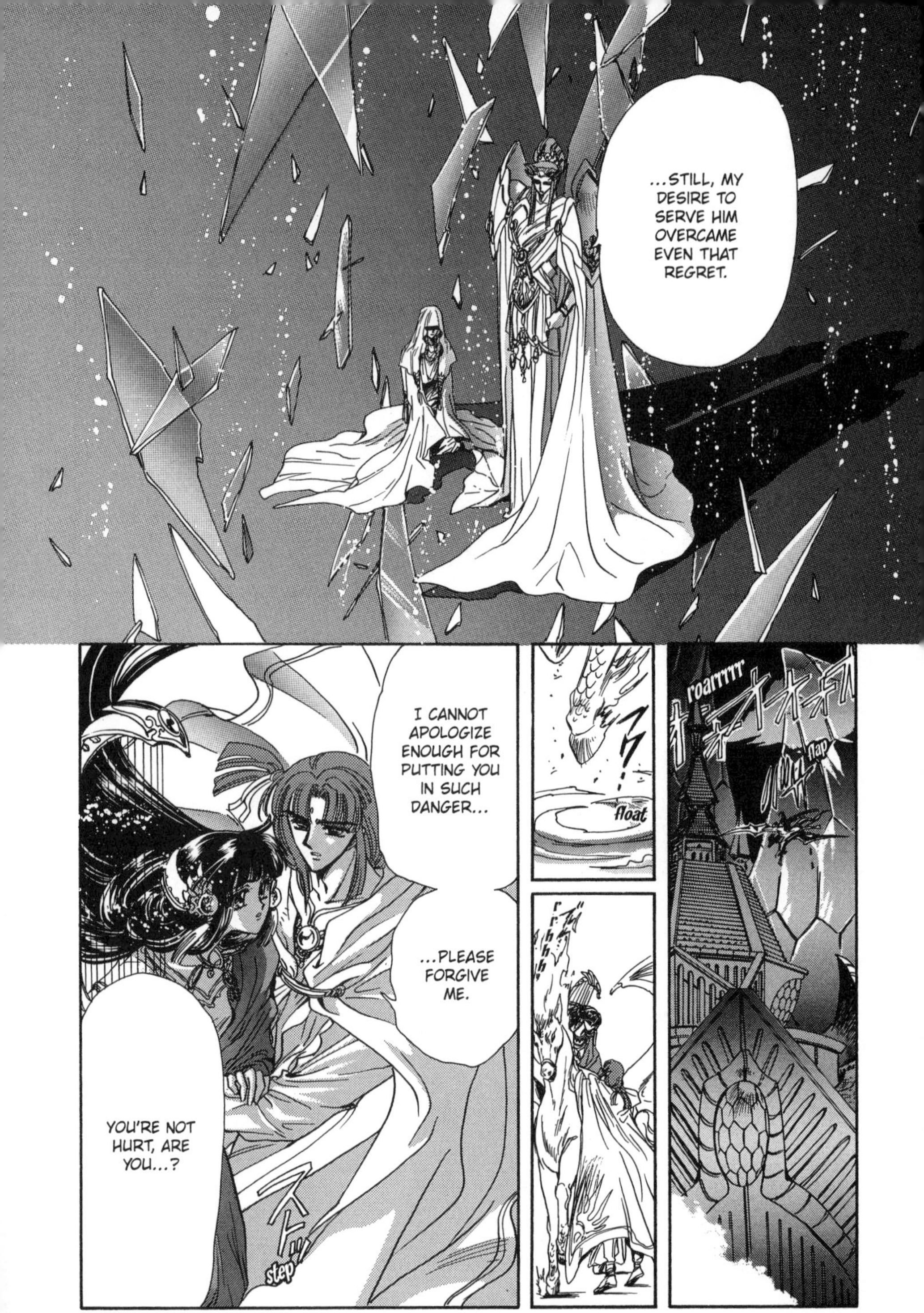
...STILL, MY DESIRE TO SERVE HIM OVERCAME EVEN THAT REGRET.
roarrrrr
flap
float
rrhhh!
I CANNOT APOLOGIZE ENOUGH FOR PUTTING YOU IN SUCH DANGER...
...PLEASE FORGIVE ME.
YOU'RE NOT HURT, ARE YOU...?
step

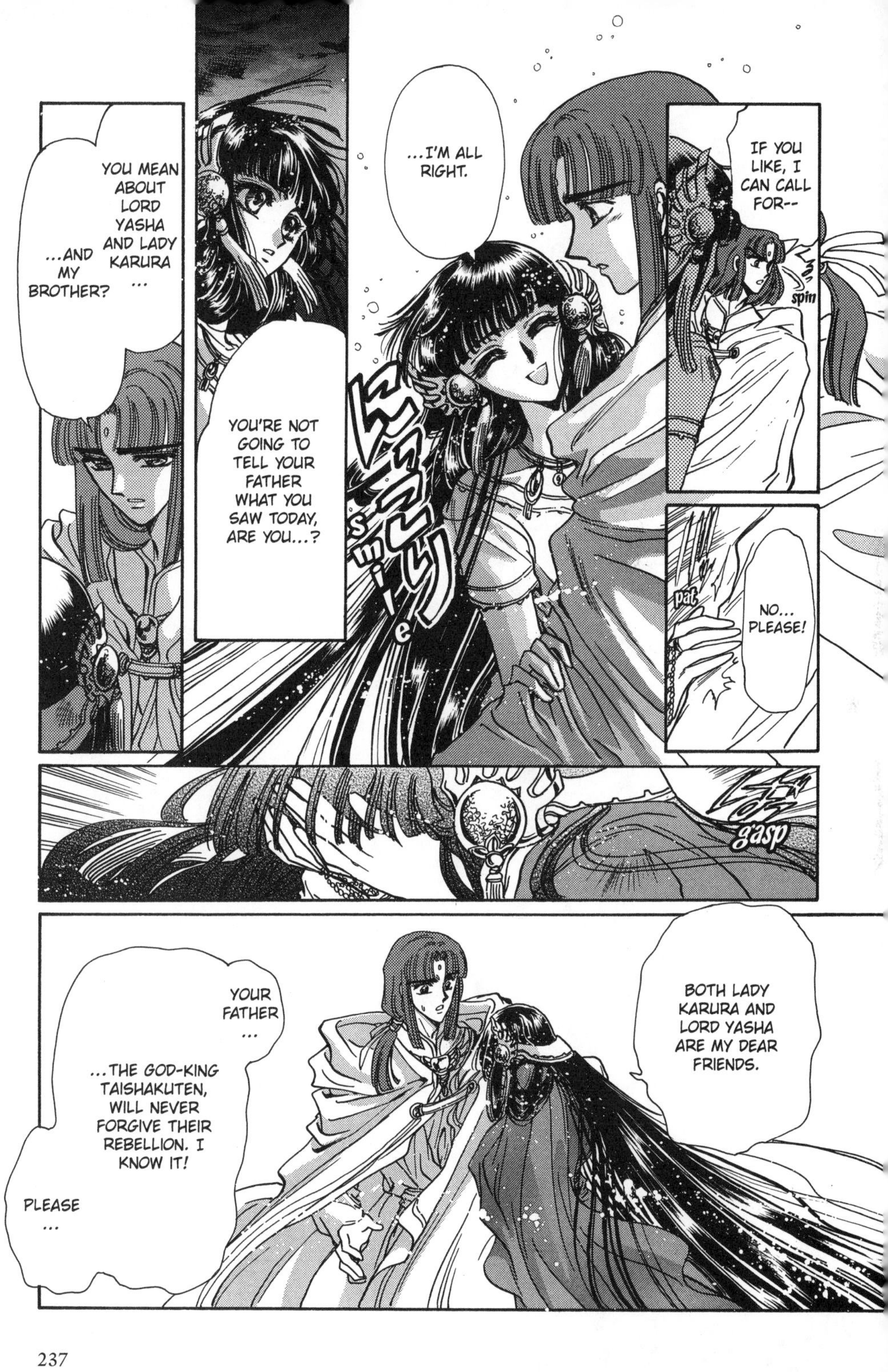
IF YOU LIKE, I CAN CALL FOR--
spin
pat
NO... PLEASE!
...I'M ALL RIGHT.
smile
YOU'RE NOT GOING TO TELL YOUR FATHER WHAT YOU SAW TODAY, ARE YOU...?
YOU MEAN ABOUT LORD YASHA AND LADY KARURA ...
...AND MY BROTHER?
gasp
BOTH LADY KARURA AND LORD YASHA ARE MY DEAR FRIENDS.
YOUR FATHER ...
...THE GOD-KING TAISHAKUTEN, WILL NEVER FORGIVE THEIR REBELLION. I KNOW IT!
PLEASE ...

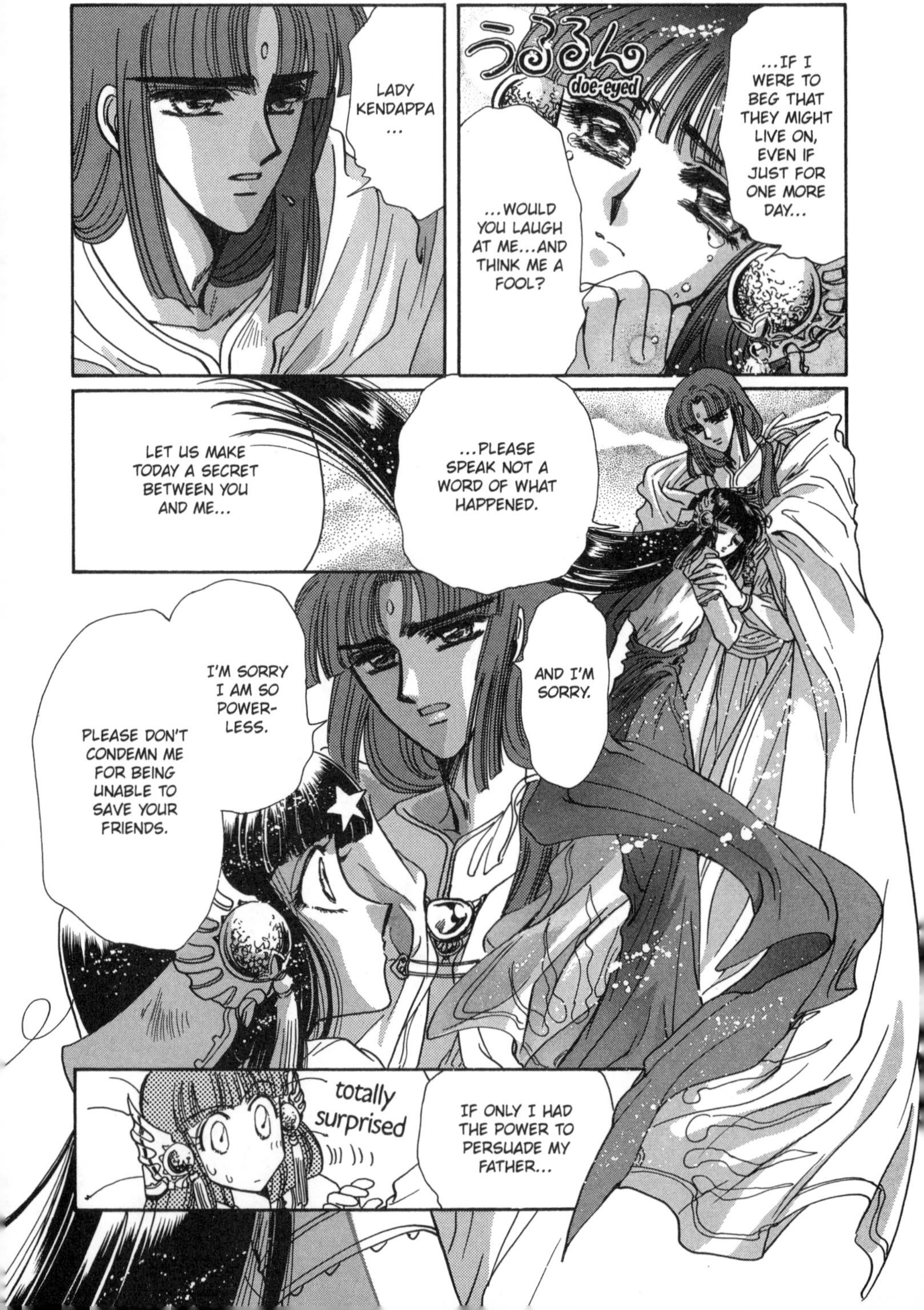
...IF I WERE TO BEG THAT THEY MIGHT LIVE ON, EVEN IF JUST FOR ONE MORE DAY...
うるるん
doe-eyed
...WOULD YOU LAUGH AT ME...AND THINK ME A FOOL?
LADY KENDAPPA ...
...PLEASE SPEAK NOT A WORD OF WHAT HAPPENED.
LET US MAKE TODAY A SECRET BETWEEN YOU AND ME...
AND I'M SORRY.
I'M SORRY I AM SO POWER-LESS.
PLEASE DON'T CONDEMN ME FOR BEING UNABLE TO SAVE YOUR FRIENDS.
IF ONLY I HAD THE POWER TO PERSUADE MY FATHER...
totally surprised

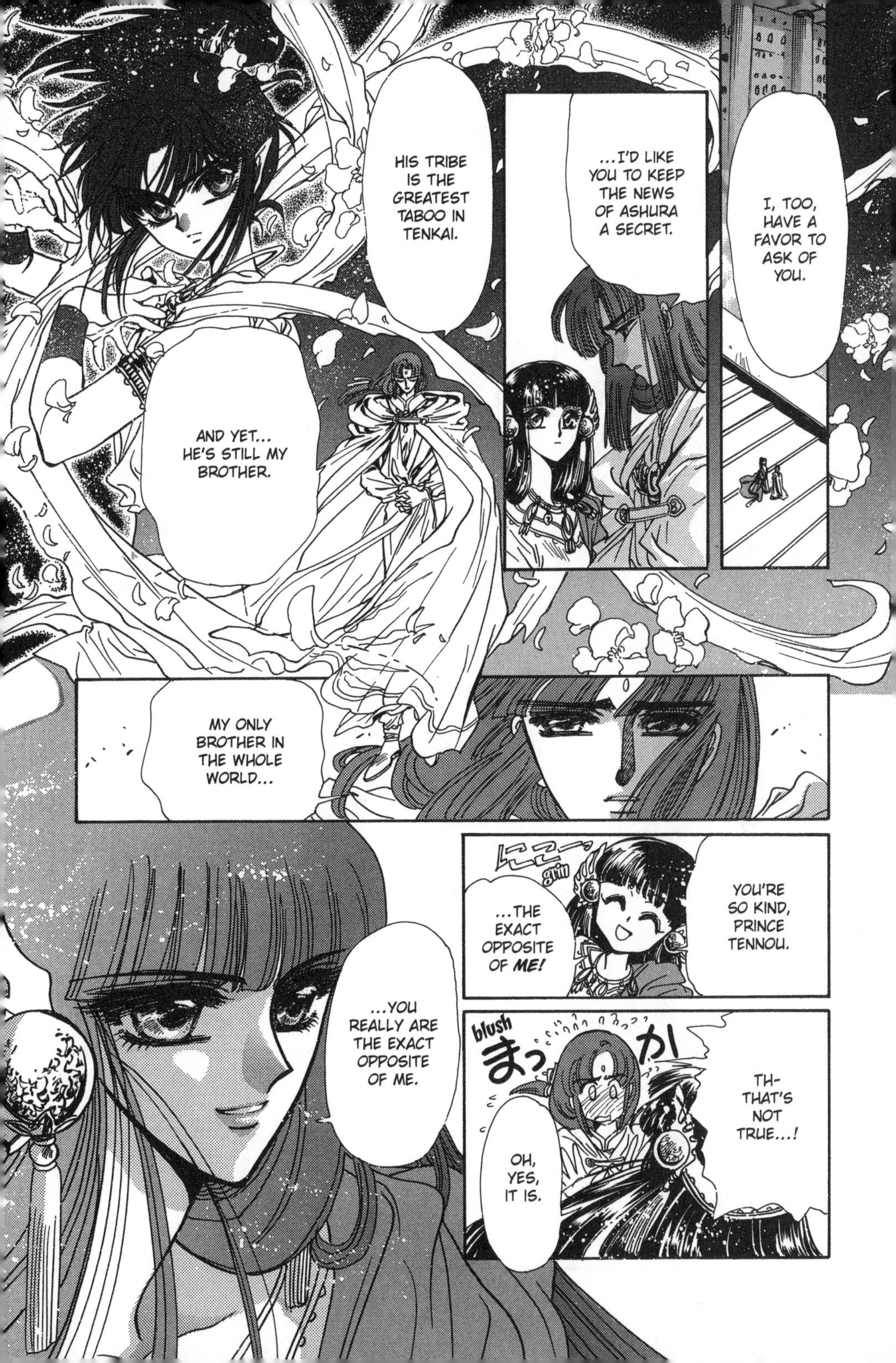
I, TOO, HAVE A FAVOR TO ASK OF YOU.
...I'D LIKE YOU TO KEEP THE NEWS OF ASHURA A SECRET.
HIS TRIBE IS THE GREATEST TABOO IN TENKAI.
AND YET... HE'S STILL MY BROTHER.
MY ONLY BROTHER IN THE WHOLE WORLD...
grin
YOU'RE SO KIND, PRINCE TENNOU.
...THE EXACT OPPOSITE OF ***ME!***
blush
TH-THAT'S NOT TRUE...!
OH, YES, IT IS.
...YOU REALLY ARE THE EXACT OPPOSITE OF ME.

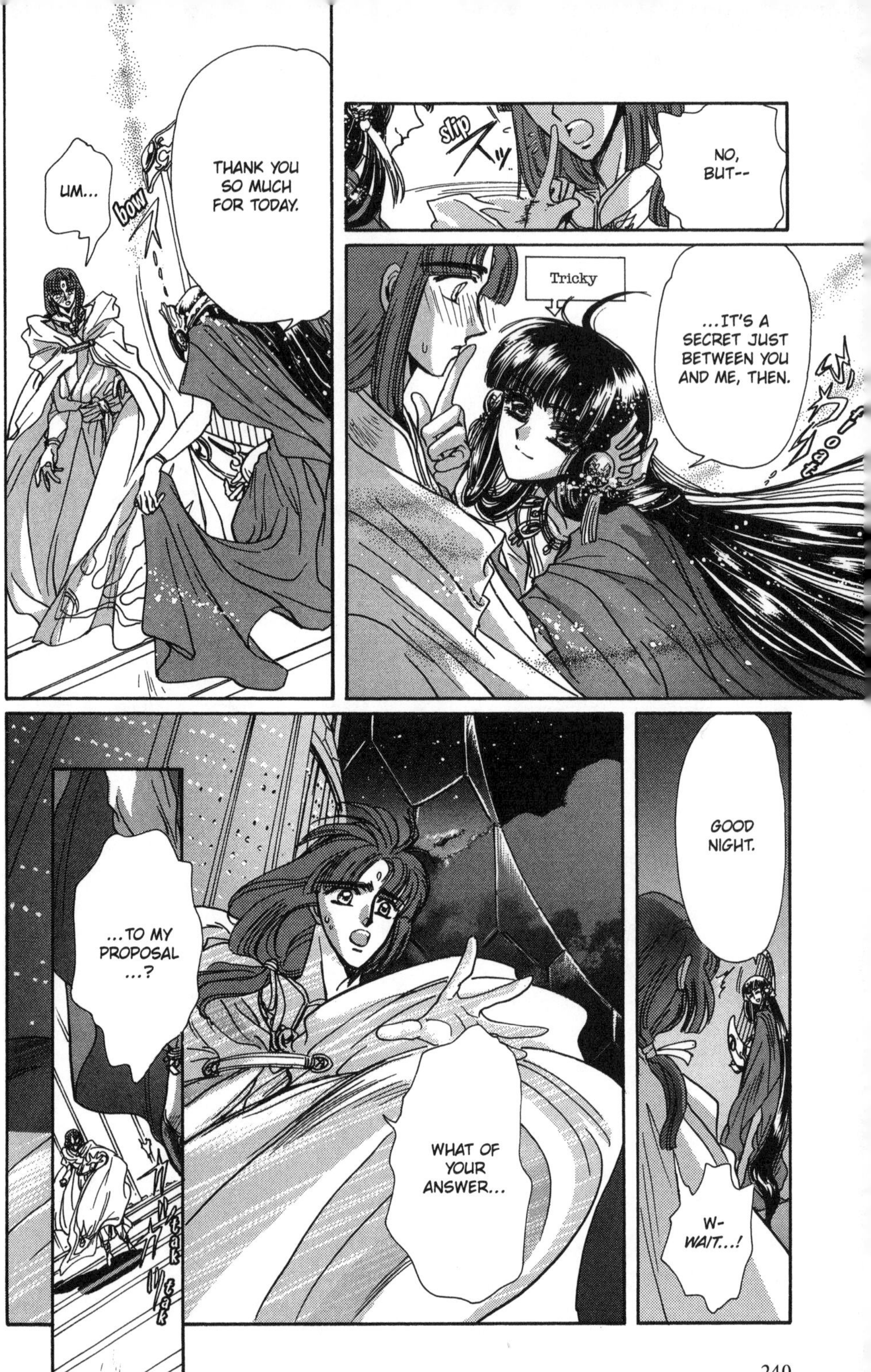
slip
NO, BUT--
Tricky
...IT'S A SECRET JUST BETWEEN YOU AND ME, THEN.
float
THANK YOU SO MUCH FOR TODAY.
bow
UM...
GOOD NIGHT.
W-WAIT...!
WHAT OF YOUR ANSWER...
...TO MY PROPOSAL ...?
tak tak

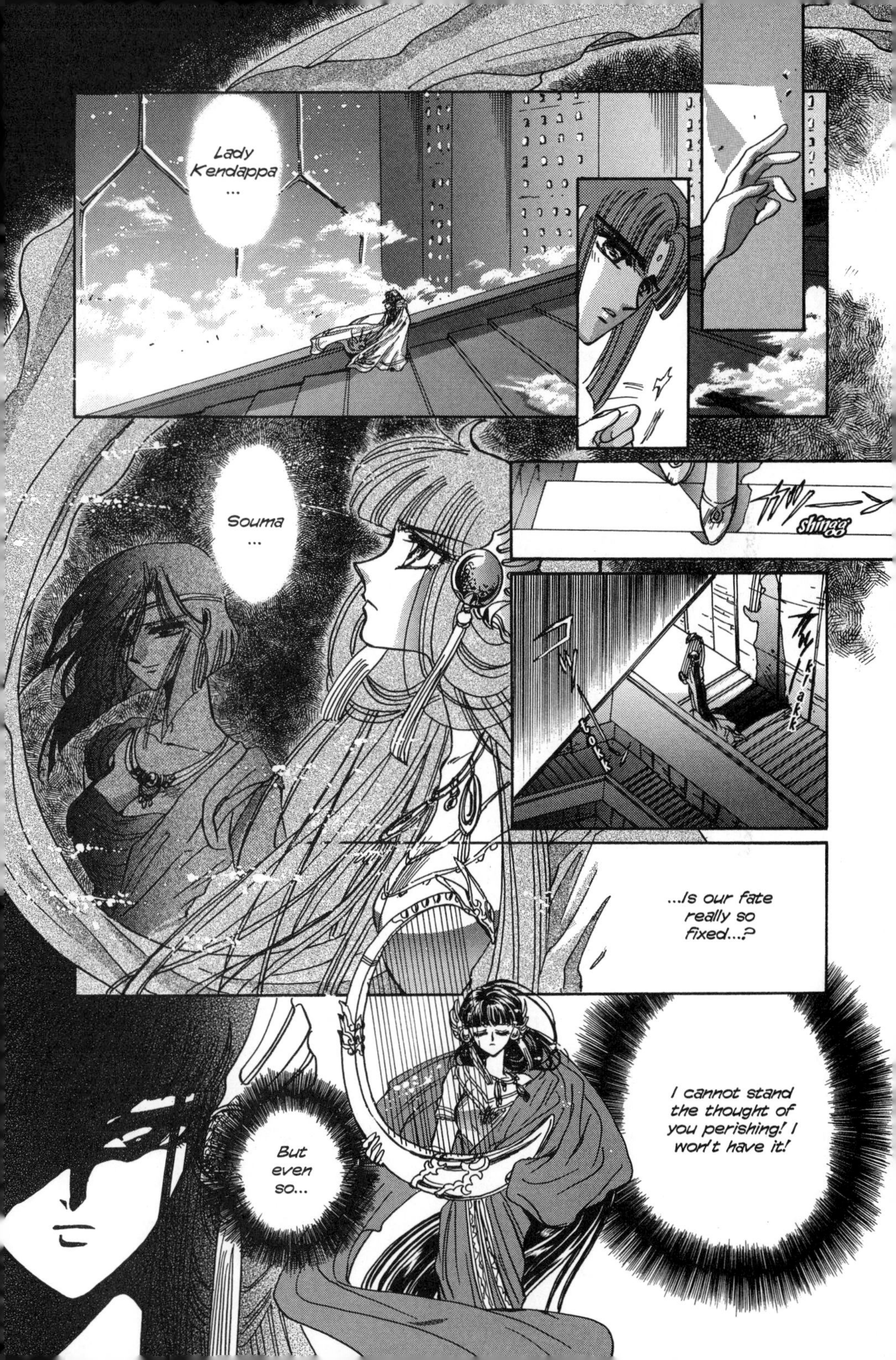
Lady Kendappa ...
shingg
klakk
tokk
Souma ...
...Is our fate really so fixed...?
I cannot stand the thought of you perishing! I won't have it!
But even so...

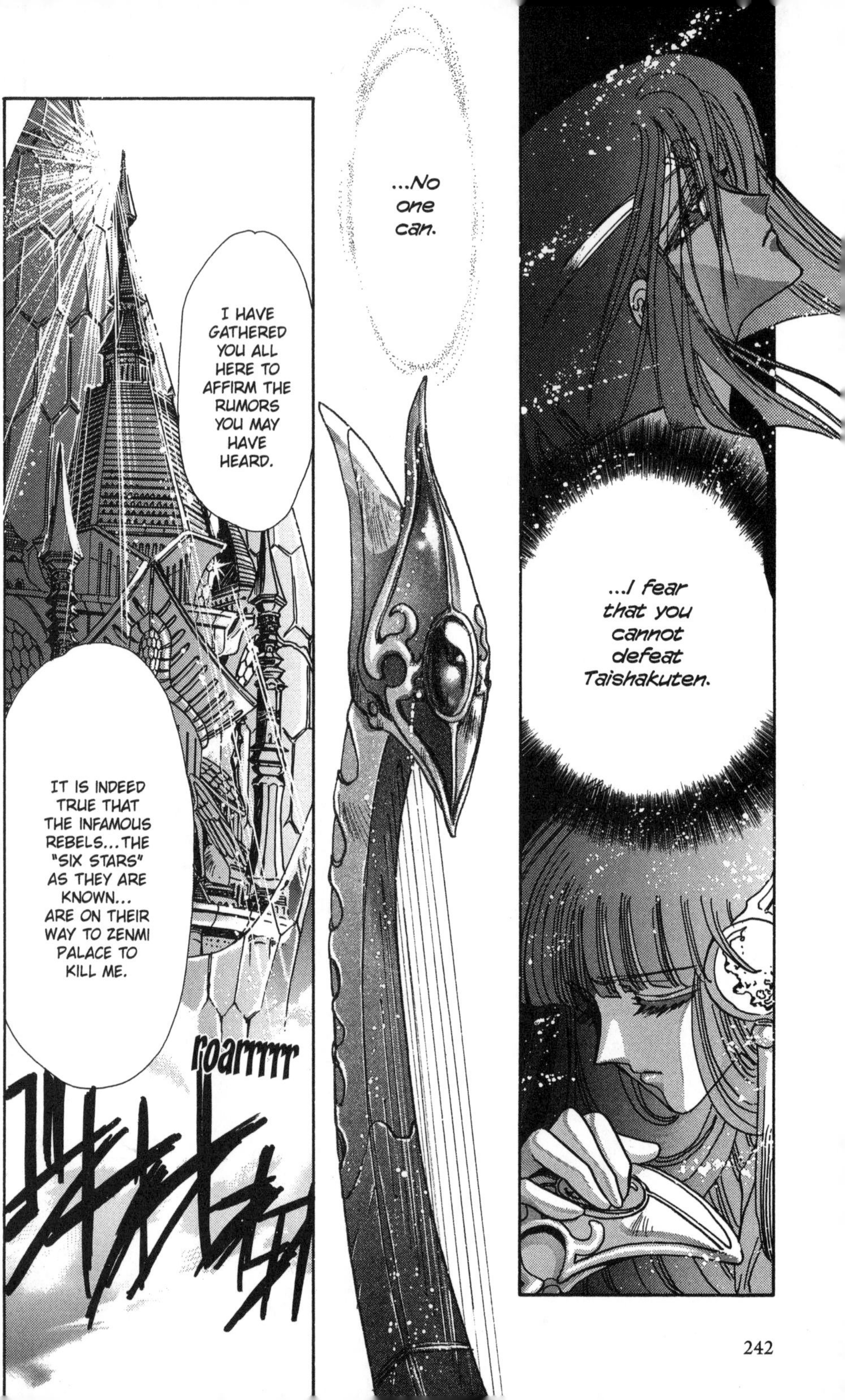
...I fear that you cannot defeat Taishakuten.
...No one can.
I HAVE GATHERED YOU ALL HERE TO AFFIRM THE RUMORS YOU MAY HAVE HEARD.
IT IS INDEED TRUE THAT THE INFAMOUS REBELS...THE "SIX STARS" AS THEY ARE KNOWN... ARE ON THEIR WAY TO ZENMI PALACE TO KILL ME.
roarrrrr

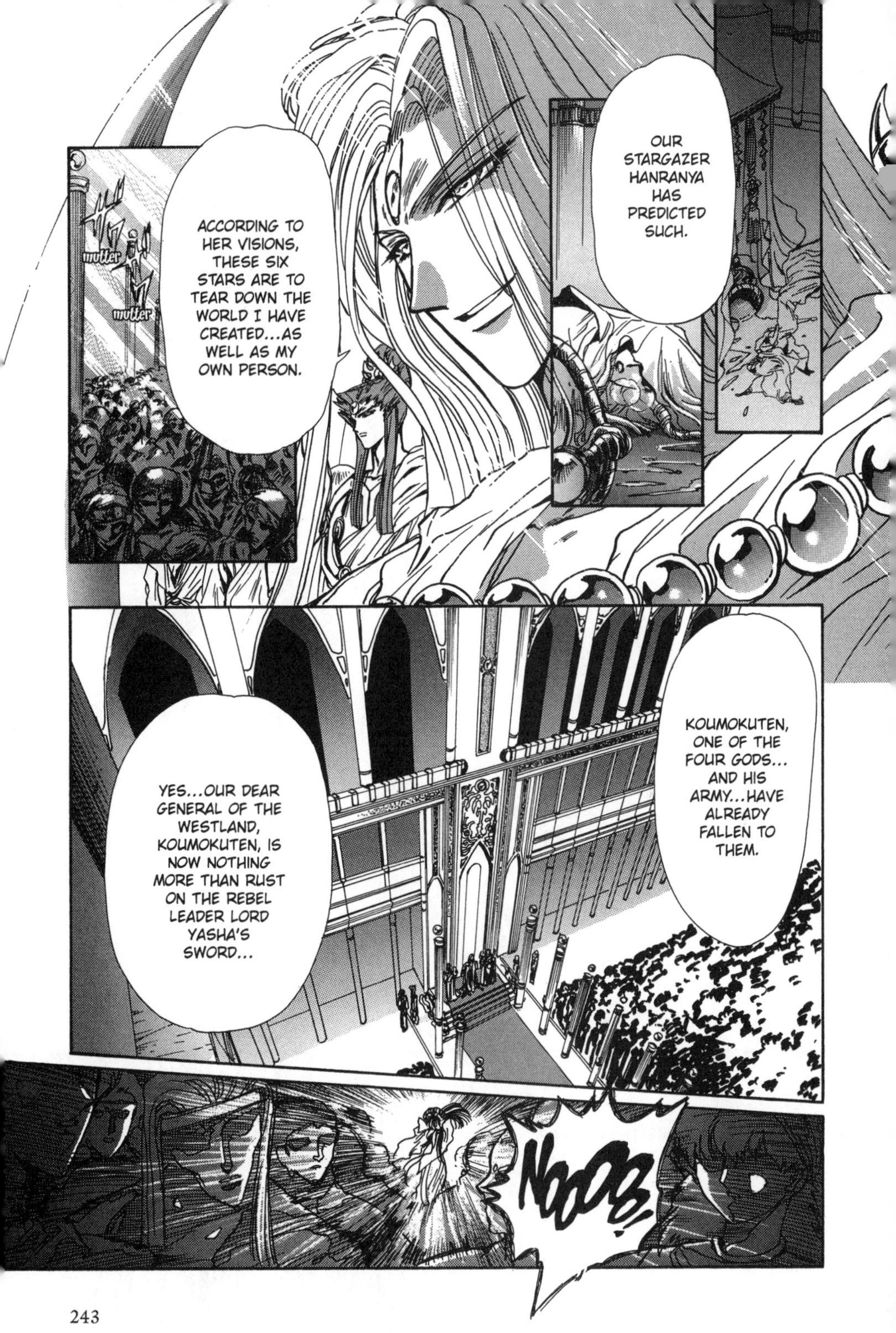
OUR STARGAZER HANRANYA HAS PREDICTED SUCH.
ACCORDING TO HER VISIONS, THESE SIX STARS ARE TO TEAR DOWN THE WORLD I HAVE CREATED...AS WELL AS MY OWN PERSON.
mutter
mutter
KOUMOKUTEN, ONE OF THE FOUR GODS... AND HIS ARMY...HAVE ALREADY FALLEN TO THEM.
YES...OUR DEAR GENERAL OF THE WESTLAND, KOUMOKUTEN, IS NOW NOTHING MORE THAN RUST ON THE REBEL LEADER LORD YASHA'S SWORD...
NOOO!

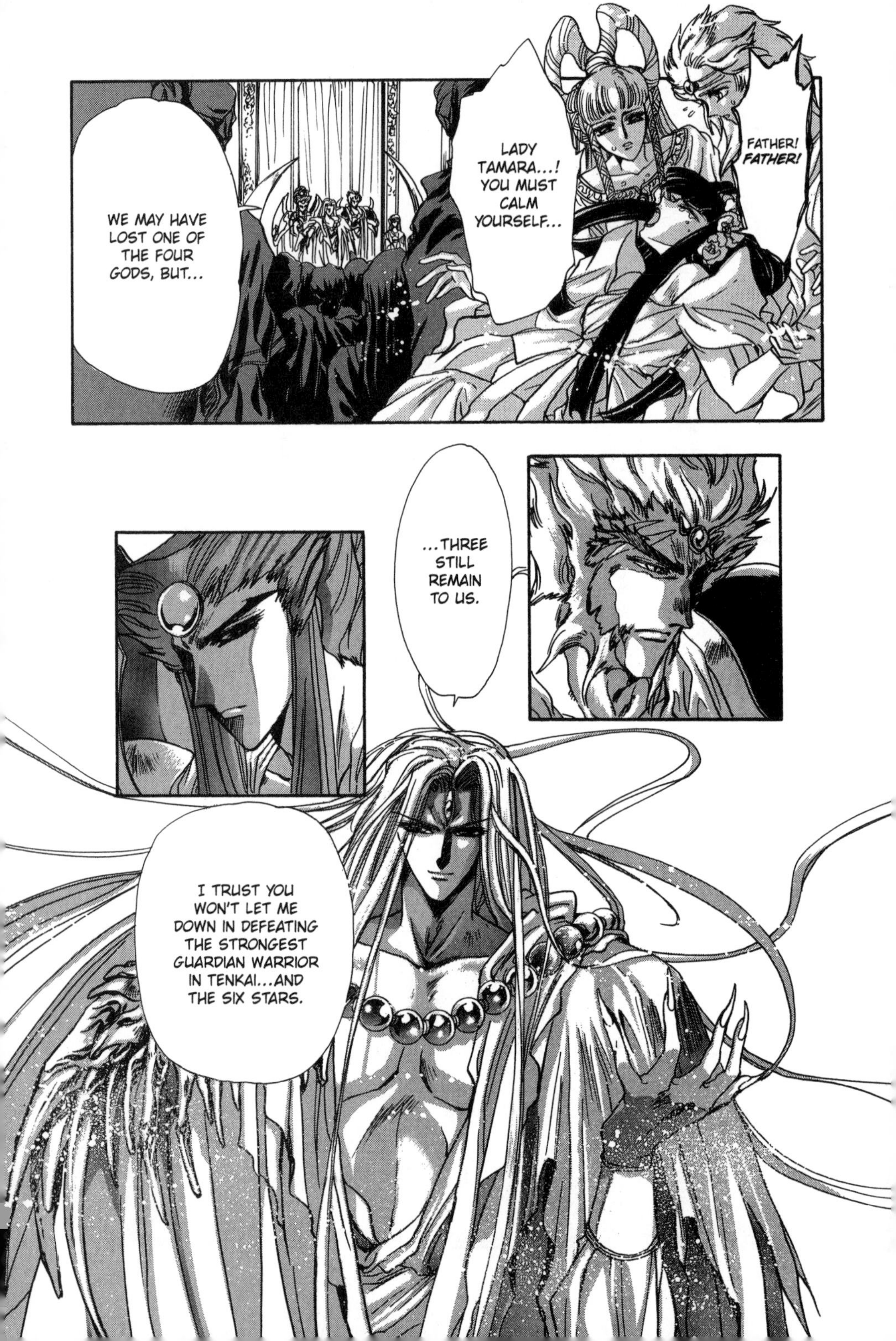
FATHER! FATHER!
LADY TAMARA...! YOU MUST CALM YOURSELF...
WE MAY HAVE LOST ONE OF THE FOUR GODS, BUT...
...THREE STILL REMAIN TO US.
I TRUST YOU WON'T LET ME DOWN IN DEFEATING THE STRONGEST GUARDIAN WARRIOR IN TENKAI...AND THE SIX STARS.

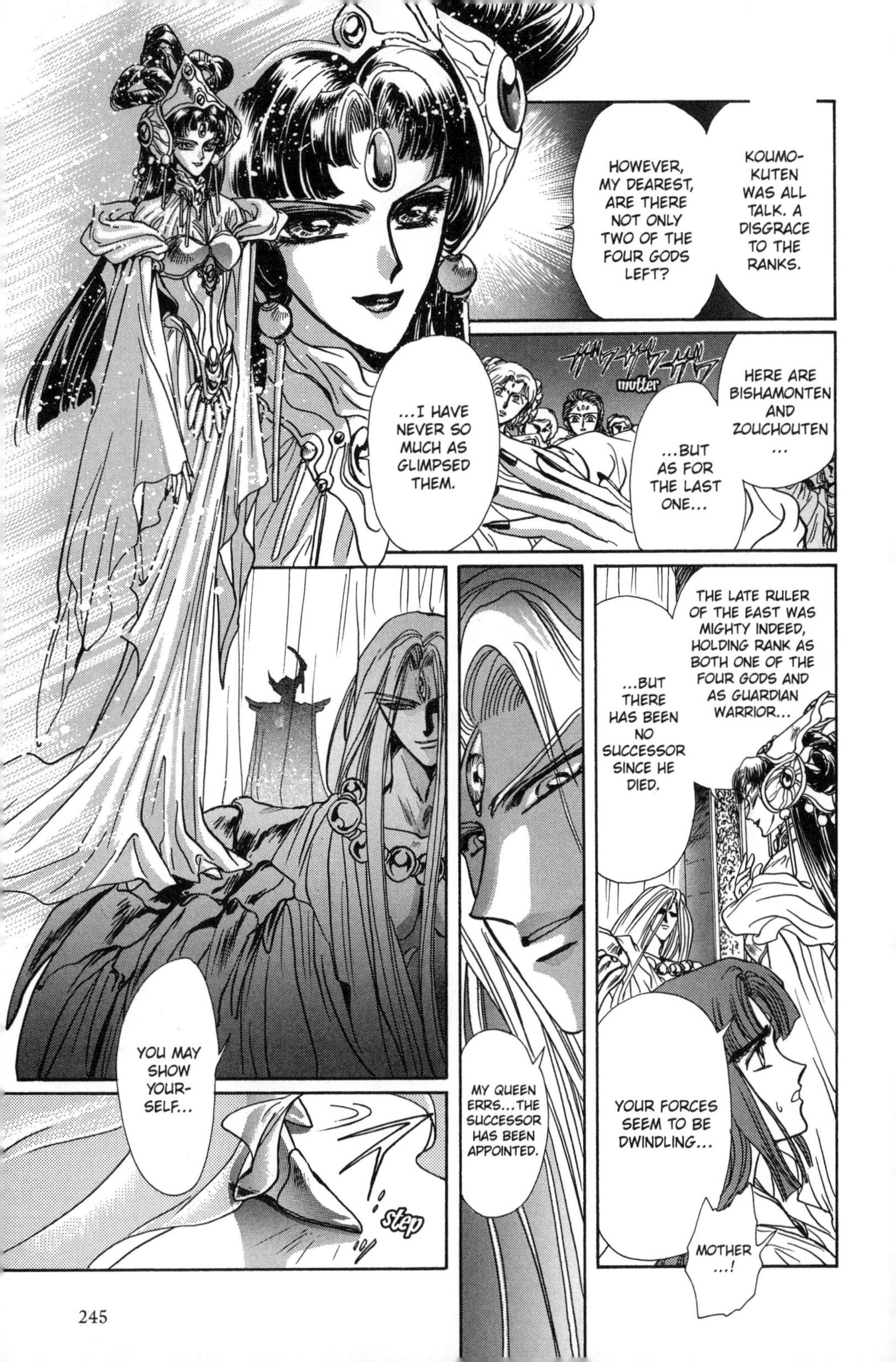

KOUMOKUTEN WAS ALL TALK. A DISGRACE TO THE RANKS.
HOWEVER, MY DEAREST, ARE THERE NOT ONLY TWO OF THE FOUR GODS LEFT?
HERE ARE BISHAMONTEN AND ZOUCHOUTEN...
mutter
...BUT AS FOR THE LAST ONE...
...I HAVE NEVER SO MUCH AS GLIMPSED THEM.
THE LATE RULER OF THE EAST WAS MIGHTY INDEED, HOLDING RANK AS BOTH ONE OF THE FOUR GODS AND AS GUARDIAN WARRIOR...
...BUT THERE HAS BEEN NO SUCCESSOR SINCE HE DIED.
YOUR FORCES SEEM TO BE DWINDLING...
MOTHER ...!
MY QUEEN ERRS...THE SUCCESSOR HAS BEEN APPOINTED.
YOU MAY SHOW YOURSELF...
step

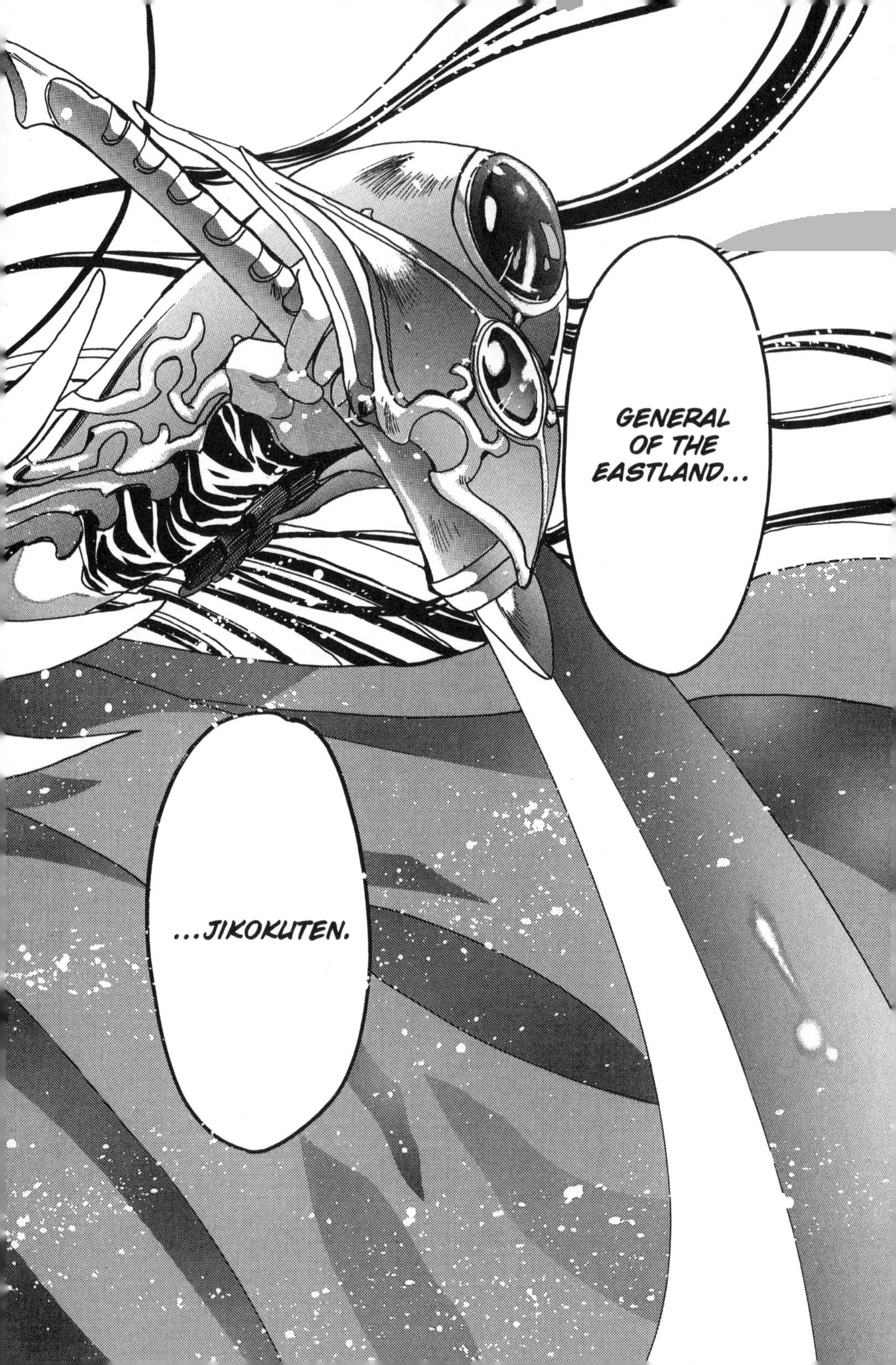
GENERAL OF THE EASTLAND...
...JIKOKUTEN.

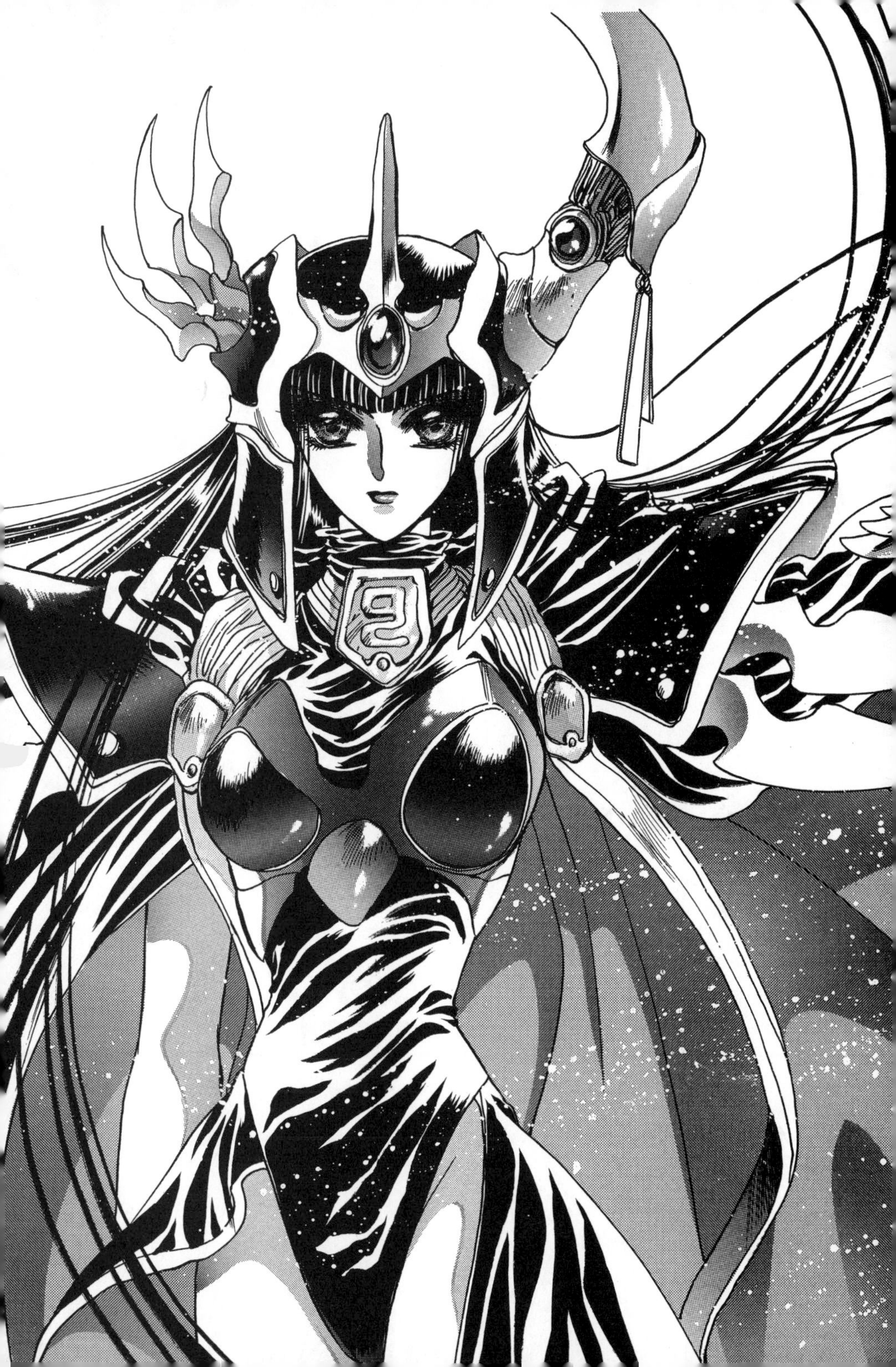

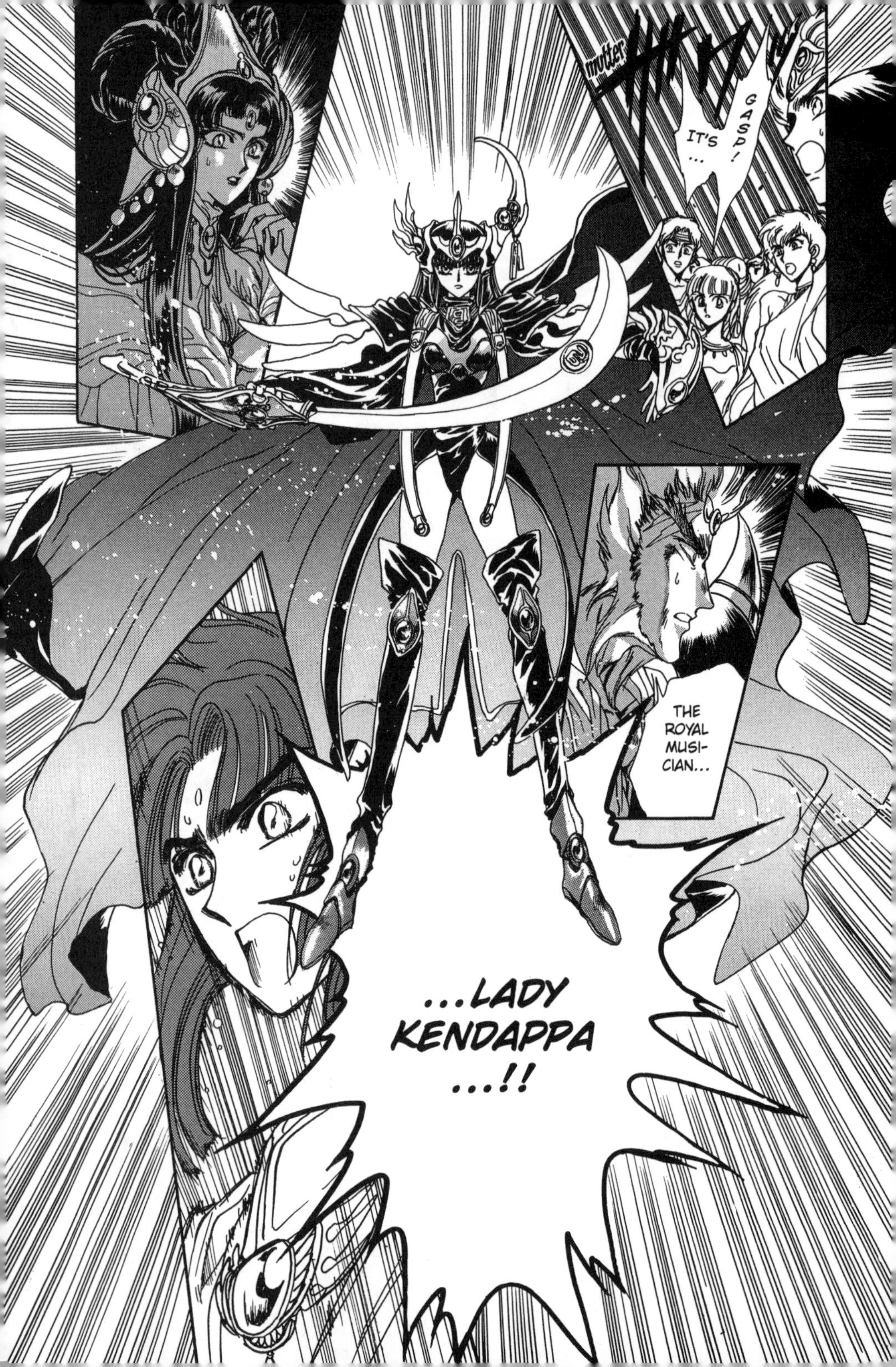
mutter
GASP!
IT'S ...
THE ROYAL MUSICIAN...
...LADY KENDAPPA ...!!

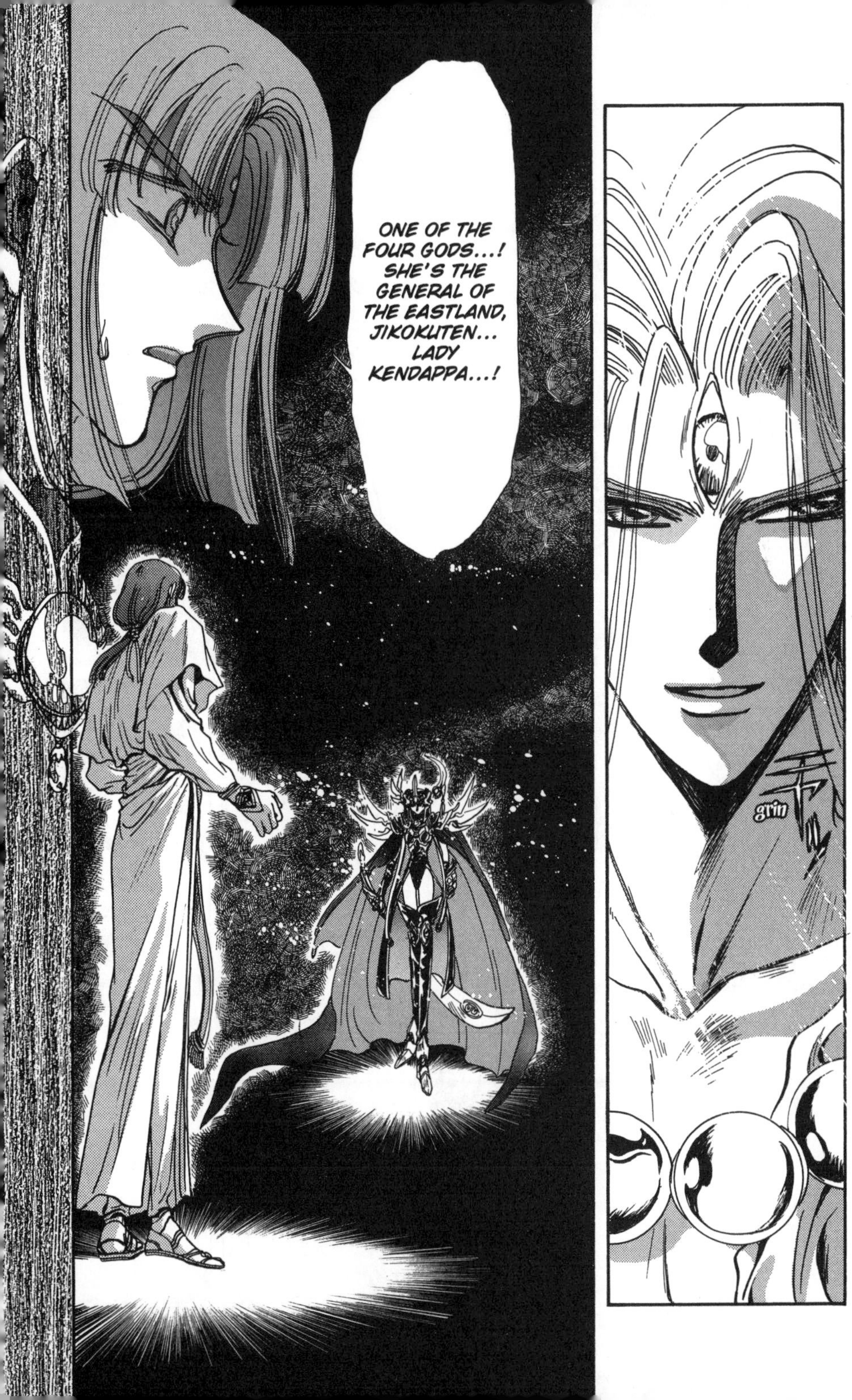
grin
ONE OF THE FOUR GODS...! SHE'S THE GENERAL OF THE EASTLAND, JIKOKUTEN... LADY KENDAPPA...!

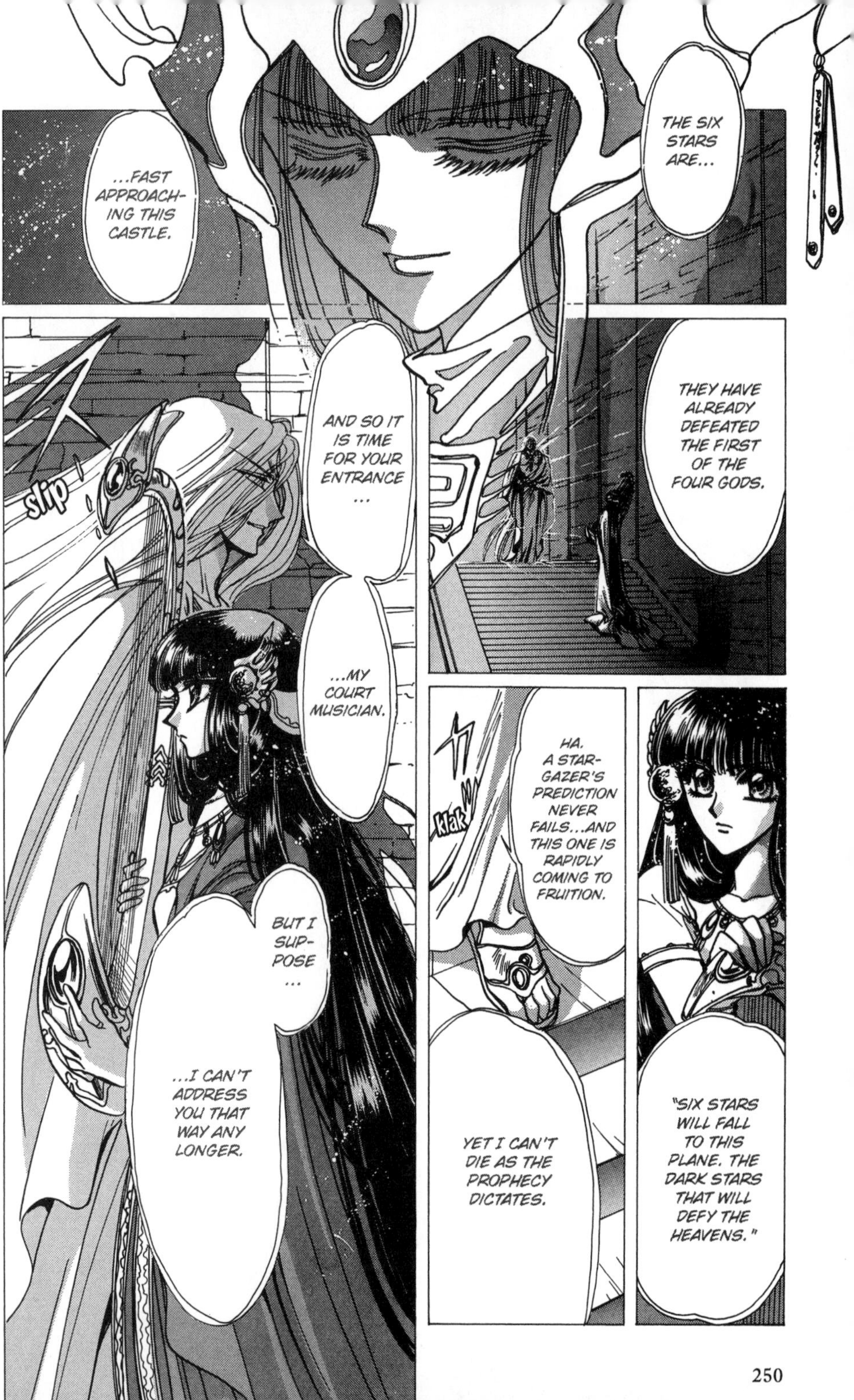
THE SIX STARS ARE...
...FAST APPROACHING THIS CASTLE.
THEY HAVE ALREADY DEFEATED THE FIRST OF THE FOUR GODS.
"SIX STARS WILL FALL TO THIS PLANE. THE DARK STARS THAT WILL DEFY THE HEAVENS."
HA. A STARGAZER'S PREDICTION NEVER FAILS...AND THIS ONE IS RAPIDLY COMING TO FRUITION.
klak
YET I CAN'T DIE AS THE PROPHECY DICTATES.
AND SO IT IS TIME FOR YOUR ENTRANCE...
...MY COURT MUSICIAN.
slip
BUT I SUPPOSE...
...I CAN'T ADDRESS YOU THAT WAY ANY LONGER.

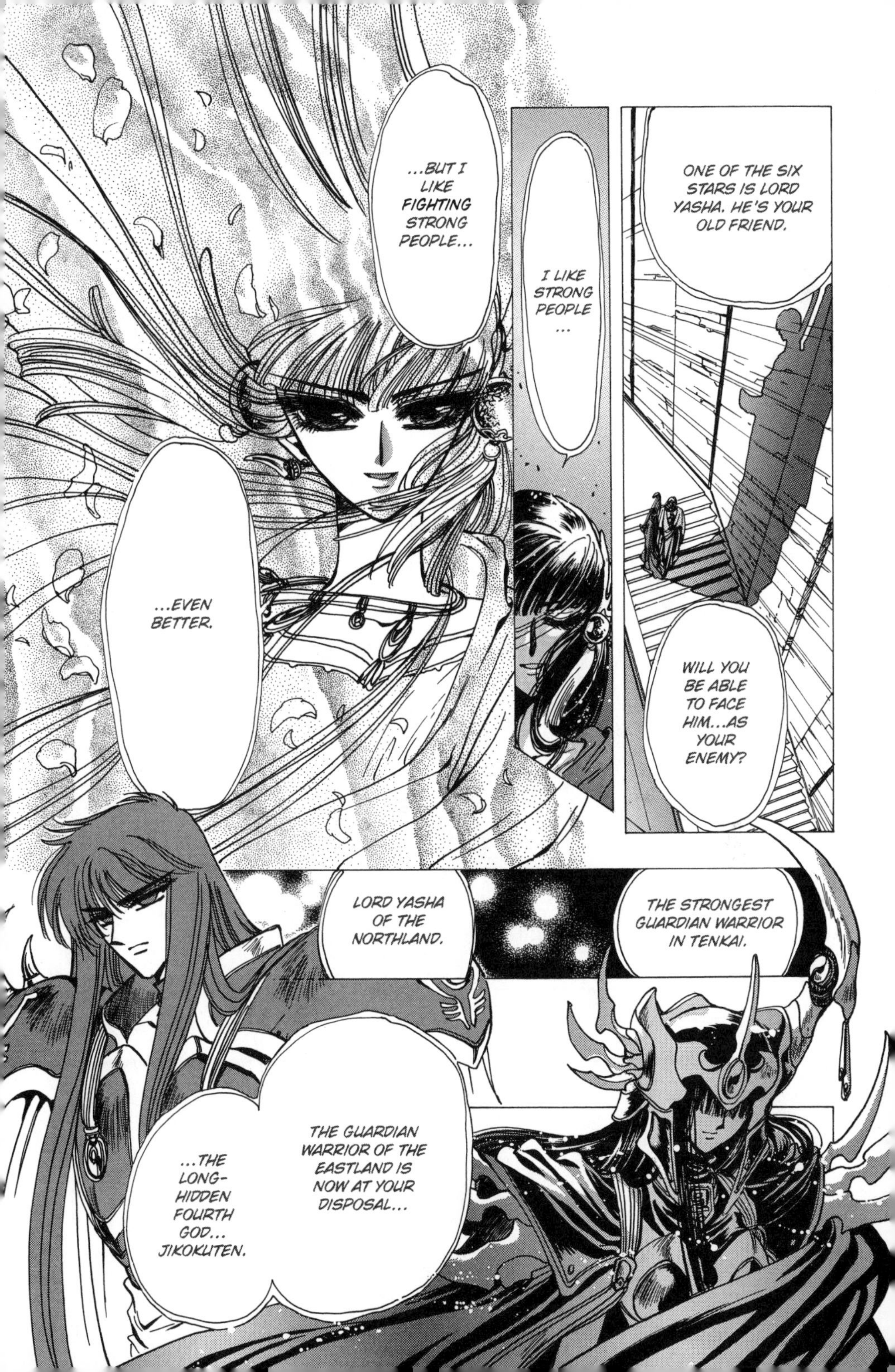
ONE OF THE SIX STARS IS LORD YASHA. HE'S YOUR OLD FRIEND.
WILL YOU BE ABLE TO FACE HIM...AS YOUR ENEMY?
I LIKE STRONG PEOPLE...
...BUT I LIKE FIGHTING STRONG PEOPLE...
...EVEN BETTER.
THE STRONGEST GUARDIAN WARRIOR IN TENKAI.
LORD YASHA OF THE NORTHLAND.
THE GUARDIAN WARRIOR OF THE EASTLAND IS NOW AT YOUR DISPOSAL...
...THE LONG-HIDDEN FOURTH GOD... JIKOKUTEN.

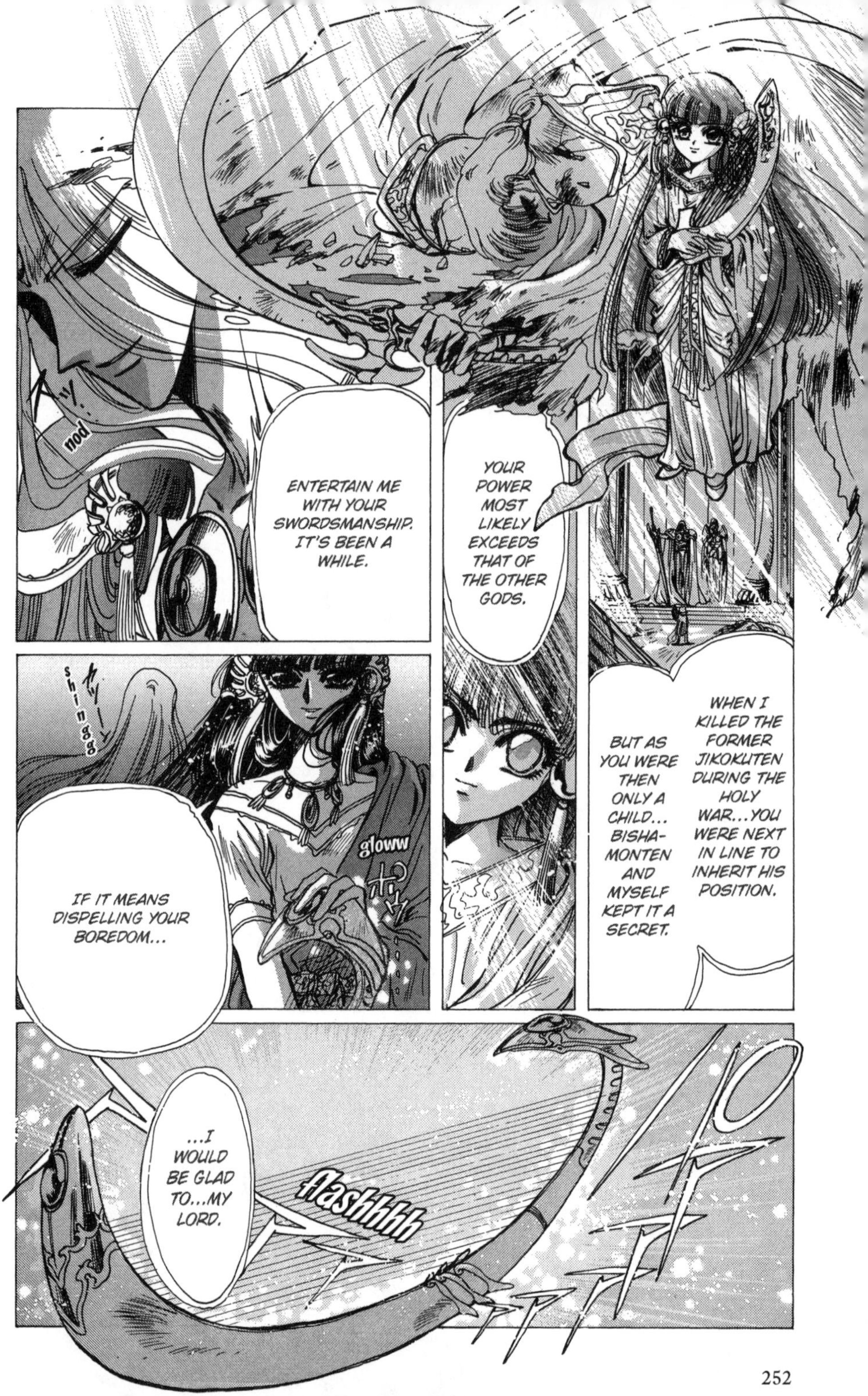

WHEN I KILLED THE FORMER JIKOKUTEN DURING THE HOLY WAR...YOU WERE NEXT IN LINE TO INHERIT HIS POSITION.
BUT AS YOU WERE THEN ONLY A CHILD... BISHA-MONTEN AND MYSELF KEPT IT A SECRET.
YOUR POWER MOST LIKELY EXCEEDS THAT OF THE OTHER GODS.
ENTERTAIN ME WITH YOUR SWORDSMANSHIP. IT'S BEEN A WHILE.
nod
shingg
gloww
IF IT MEANS DISPELLING YOUR BOREDOM...
...I WOULD BE GLAD TO...MY LORD.
flashhhh

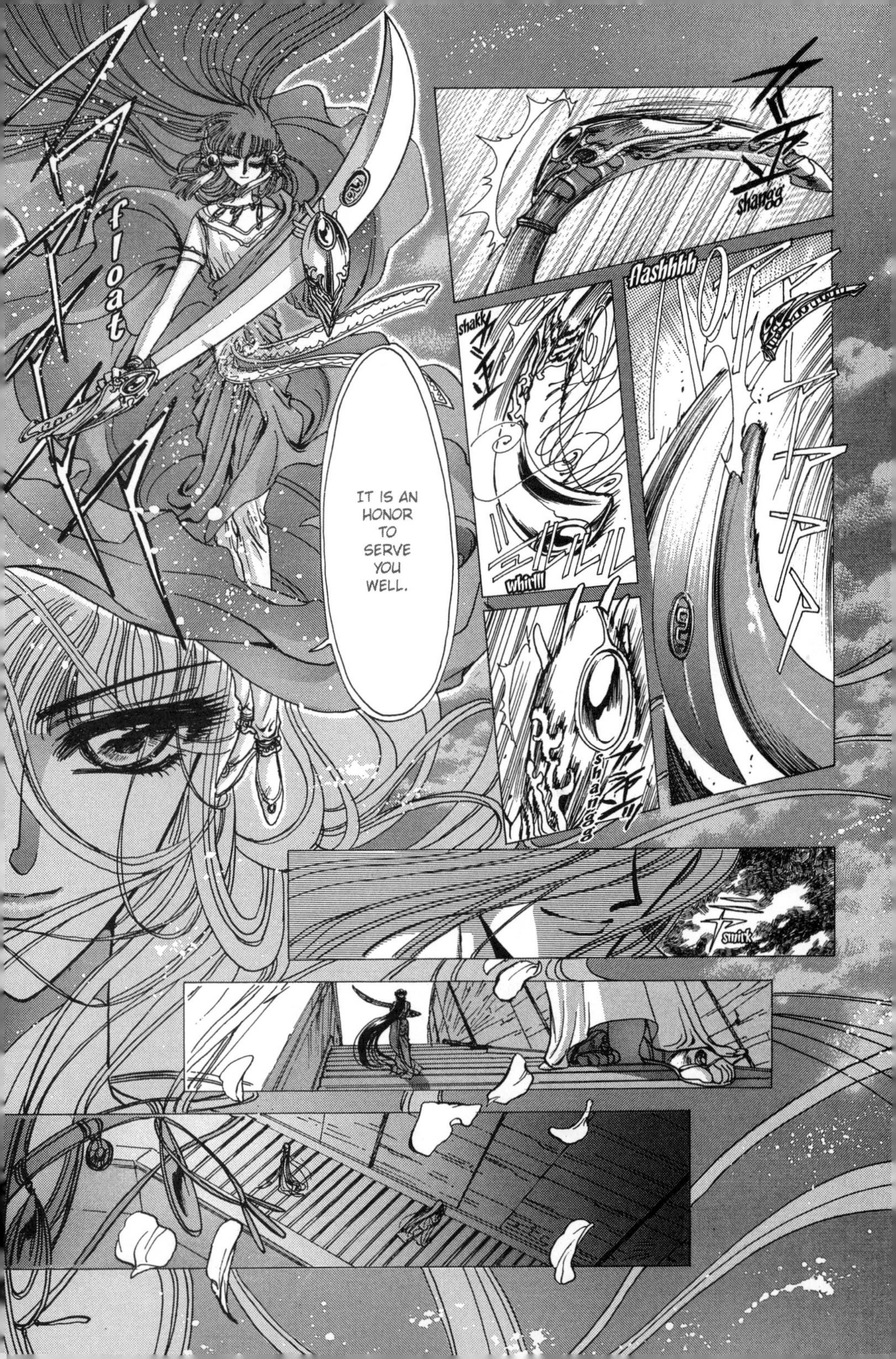
shanggg
flashhhh
shakk
whirlll
shanggg
float
IT IS AN HONOR TO SERVE YOU WELL.
snick

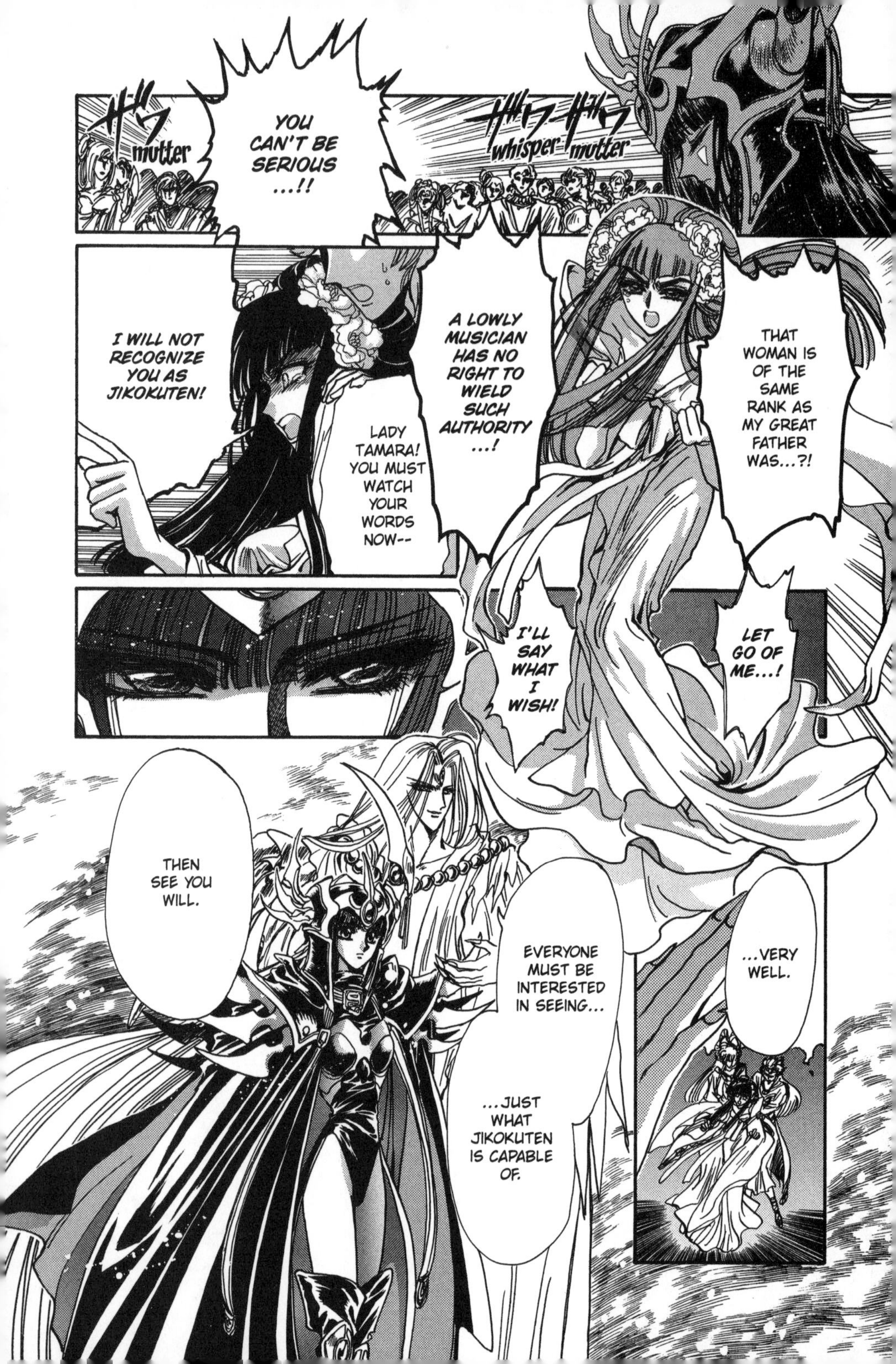
ザワザワ whisper mutter
YOU CAN'T BE SERIOUS ...!!
ザワ mutter
THAT WOMAN IS OF THE SAME RANK AS MY GREAT FATHER WAS...?!
A LOWLY MUSICIAN HAS NO RIGHT TO WIELD SUCH AUTHORITY ...!
LADY TAMARA! YOU MUST WATCH YOUR WORDS NOW--
I WILL NOT RECOGNIZE YOU AS JIKOKUTEN!
LET GO OF ME...!
I'LL SAY WHAT I WISH!
...VERY WELL.
EVERYONE MUST BE INTERESTED IN SEEING...
...JUST WHAT JIKOKUTEN IS CAPABLE OF.
THEN SEE YOU WILL.

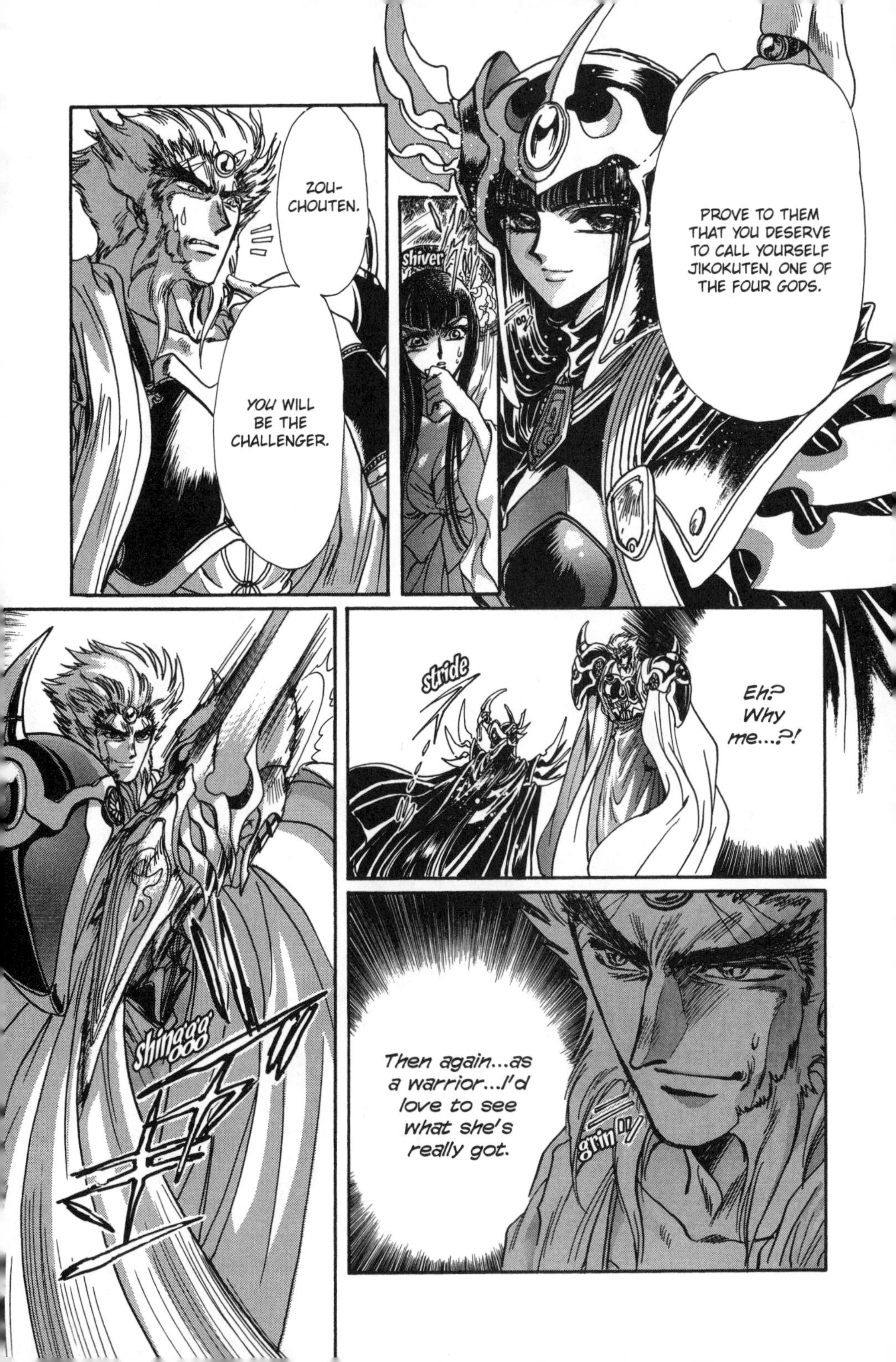
PROVE TO THEM THAT YOU DESERVE TO CALL YOURSELF JIKOKUTEN, ONE OF THE FOUR GODS.
shiver
ZOU-CHOUTEN.
YOU WILL BE THE CHALLENGER.
stride
Eh? Why me...?!
Then again...as a warrior...I'd love to see what she's really got.
grin
shinaaaooo

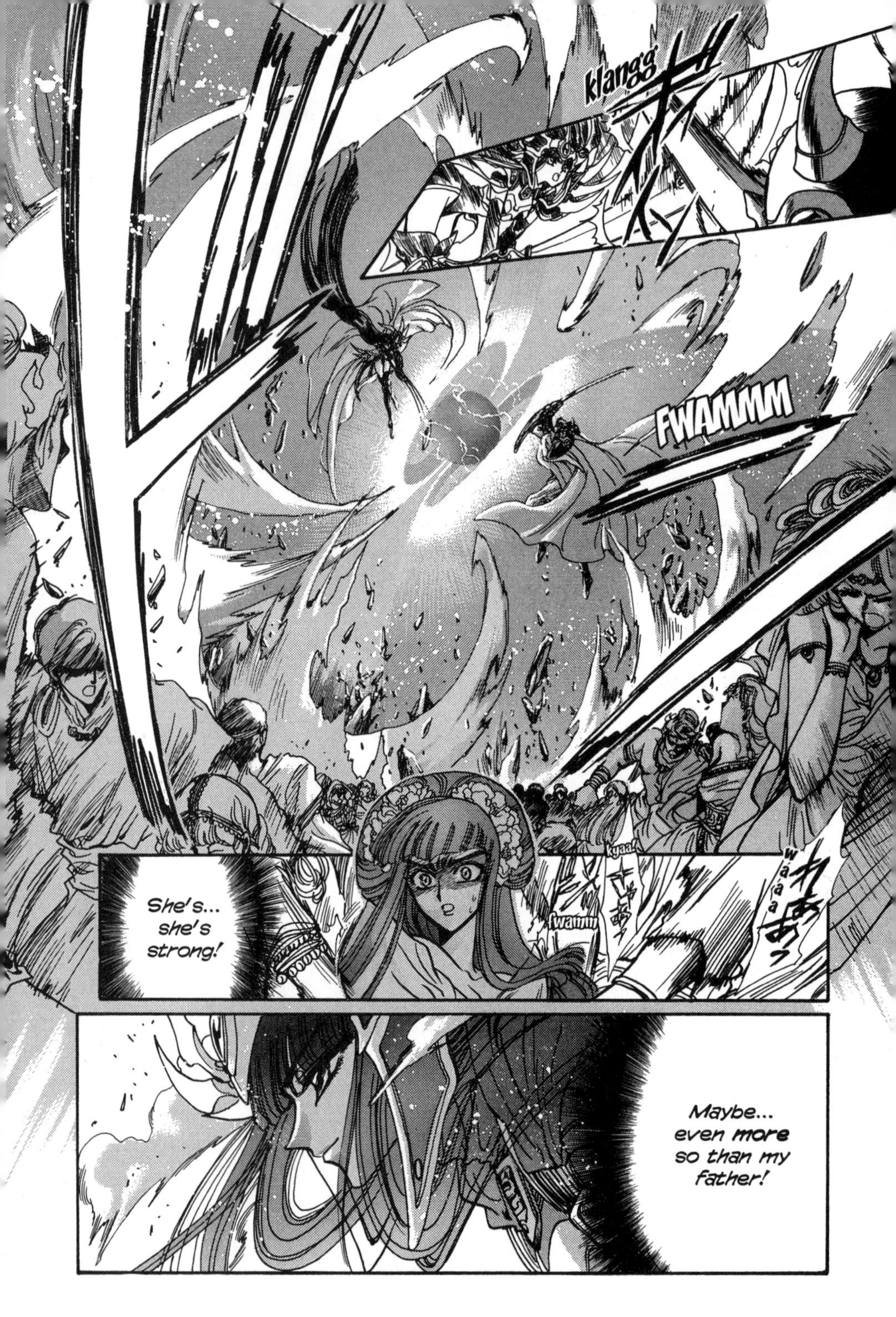
klangg
FWAMMM
waaaa
kyaa!
fwamm
She's... she's strong!
Maybe... even more so than my father!

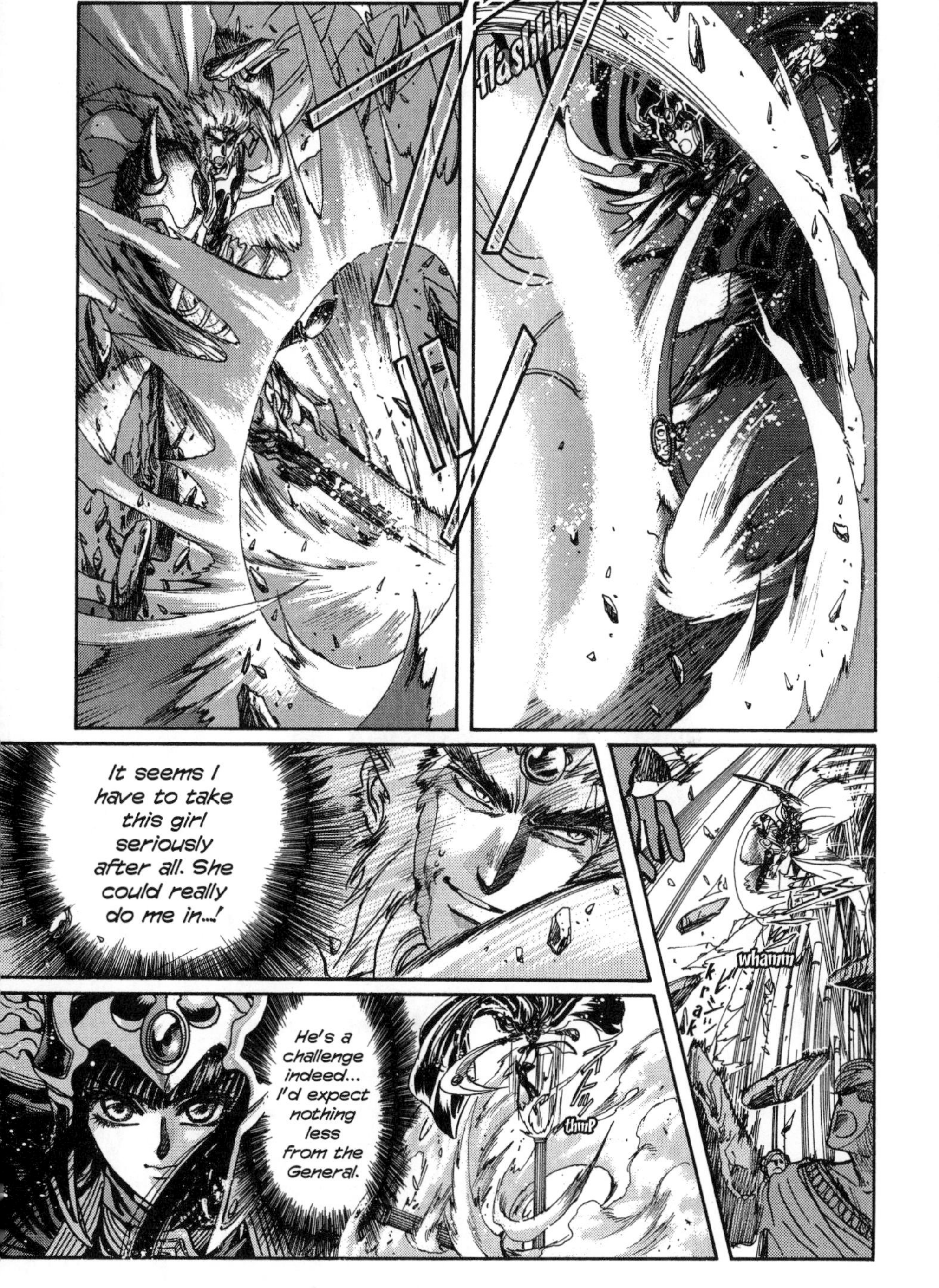
flashhh
whamm
It seems I have to take this girl seriously after all. She could really do me in...!
He's a challenge indeed... I'd expect nothing less from the General.
thmp

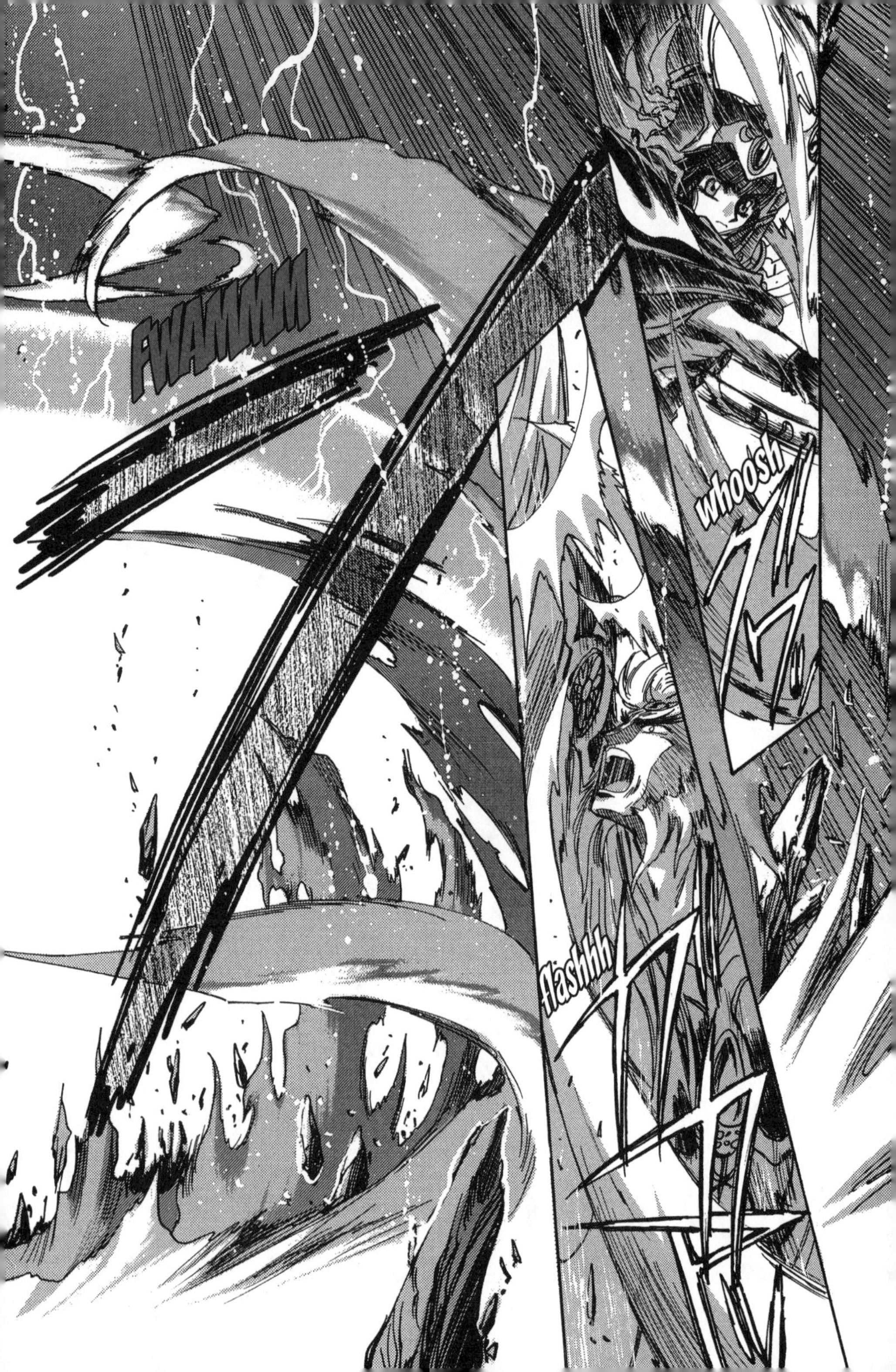
whoosh
flashhh
FWAMMM

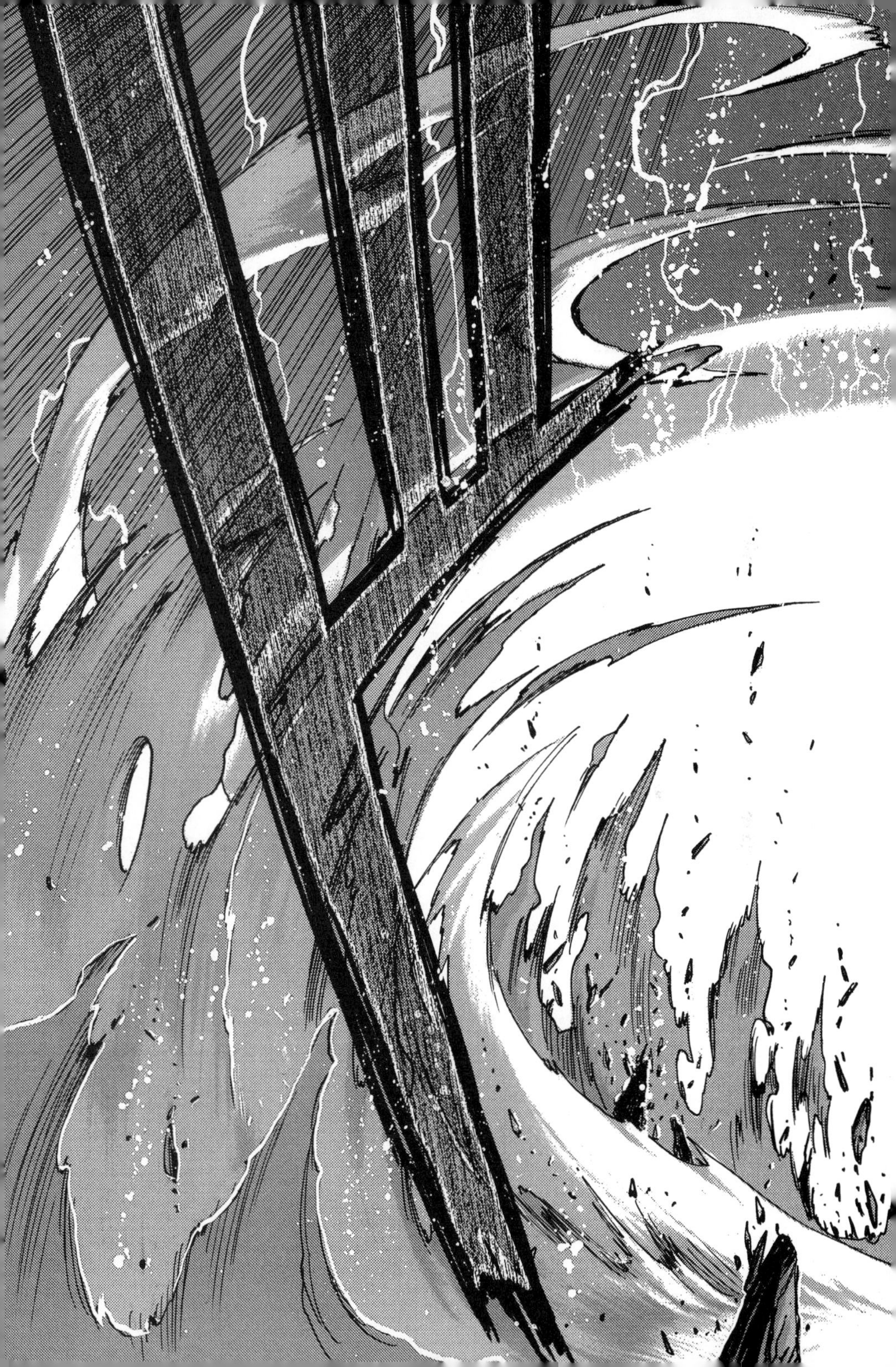

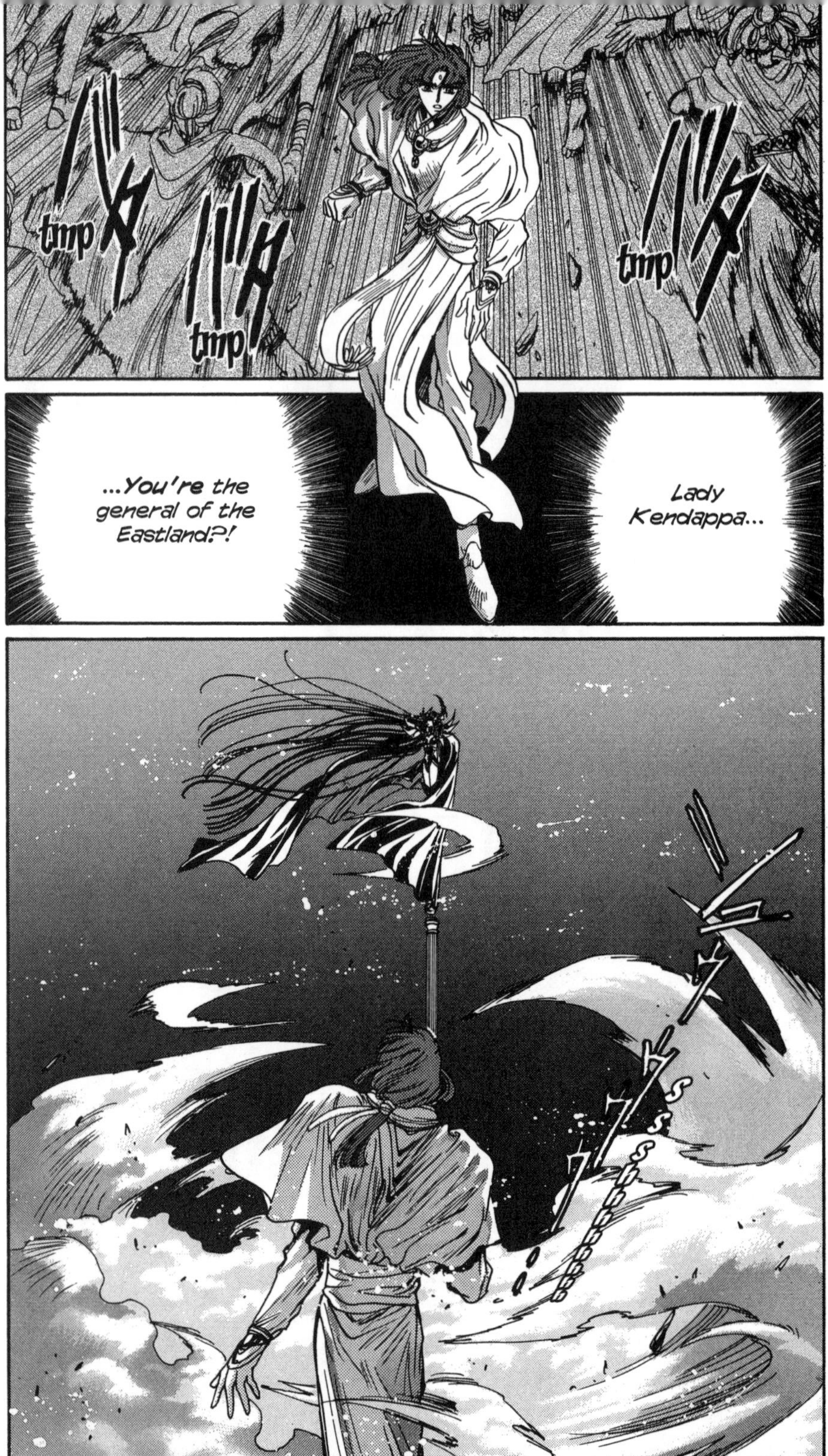
tmp
tmp
tmp
Lady Kendappa...
...You're the general of the Eastland?!

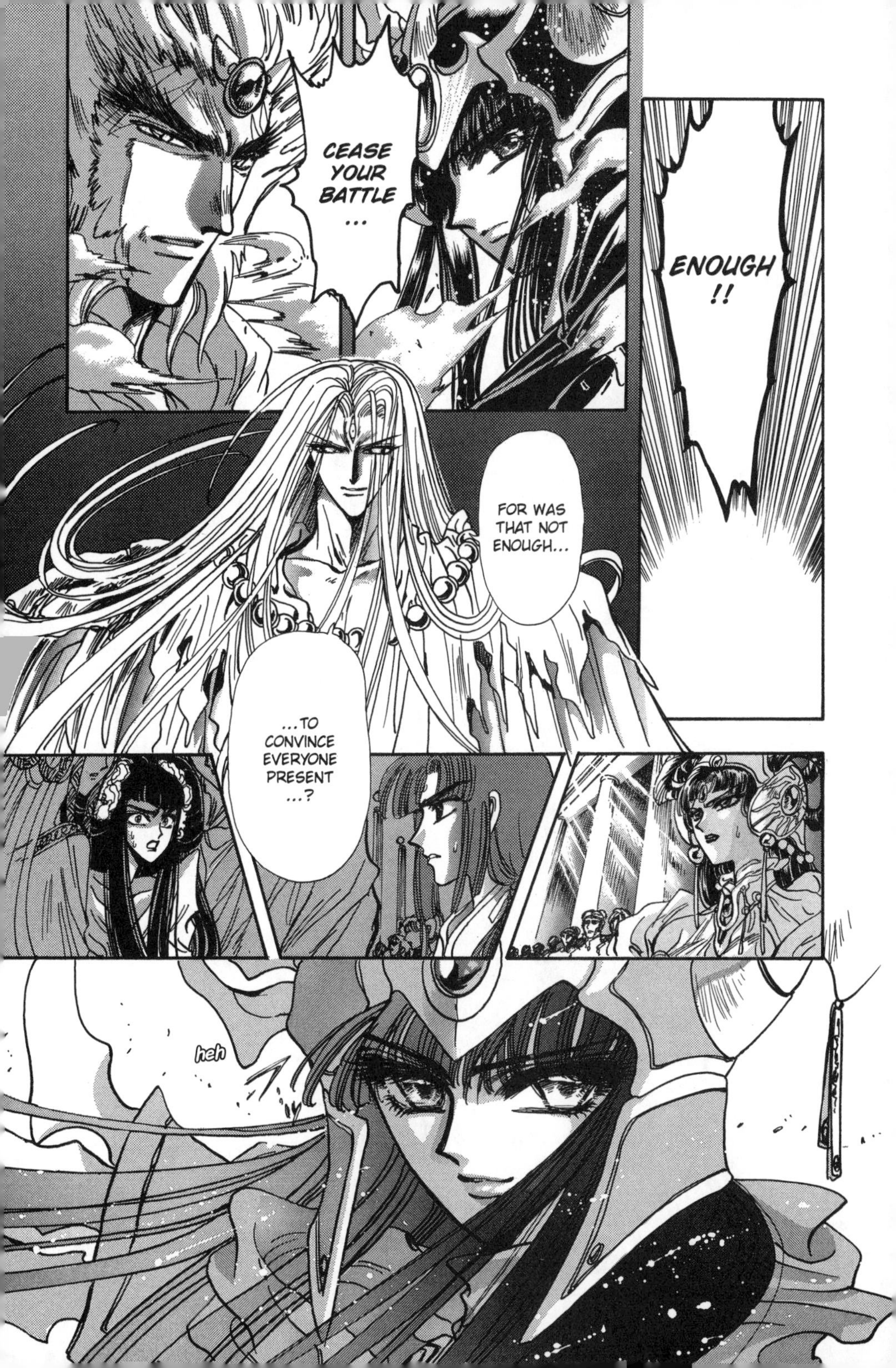
ENOUGH !!
CEASE YOUR BATTLE ...
FOR WAS THAT NOT ENOUGH...
...TO CONVINCE EVERYONE PRESENT ...?
heh

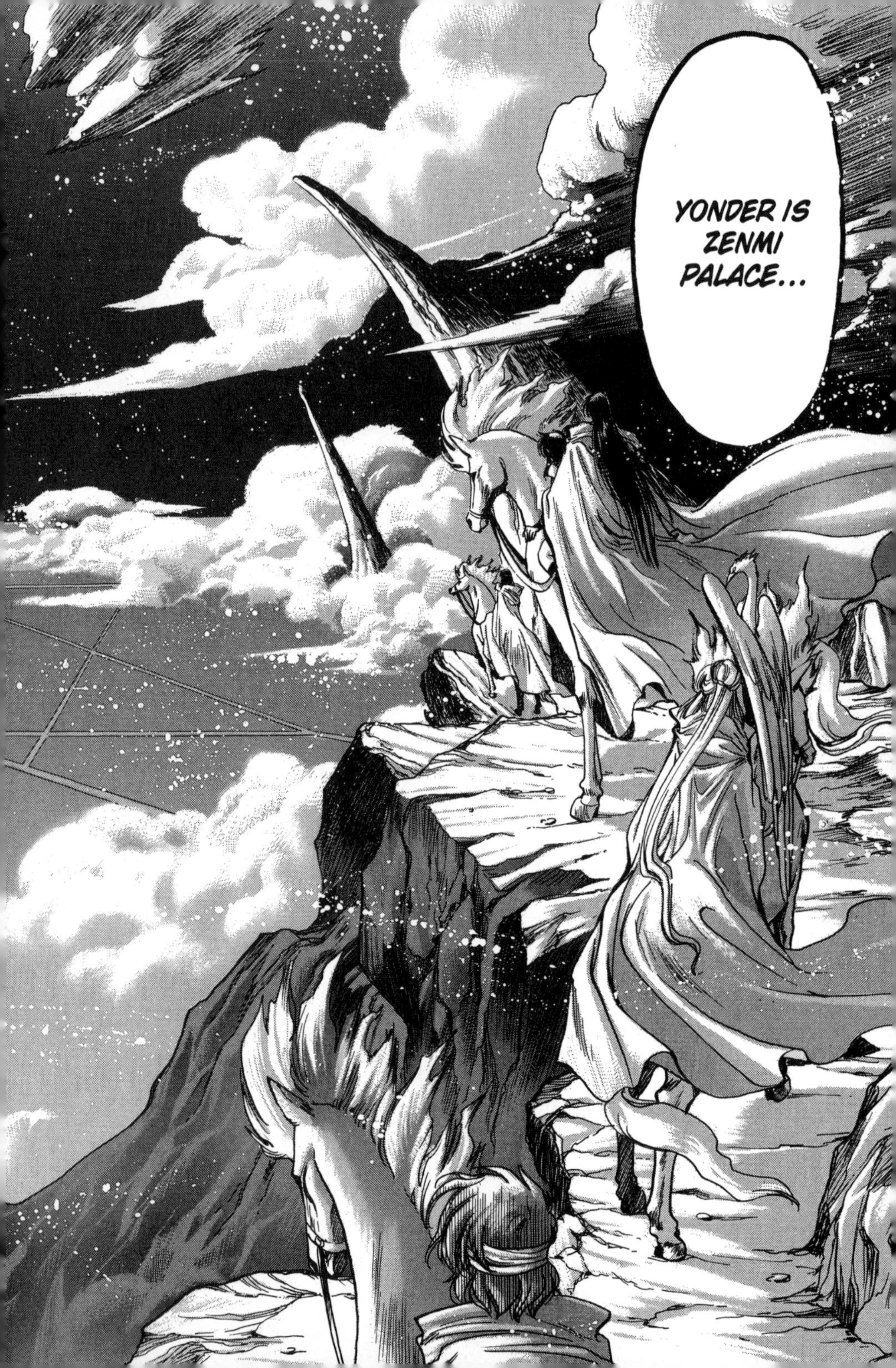
YONDER IS ZENMI PALACE...

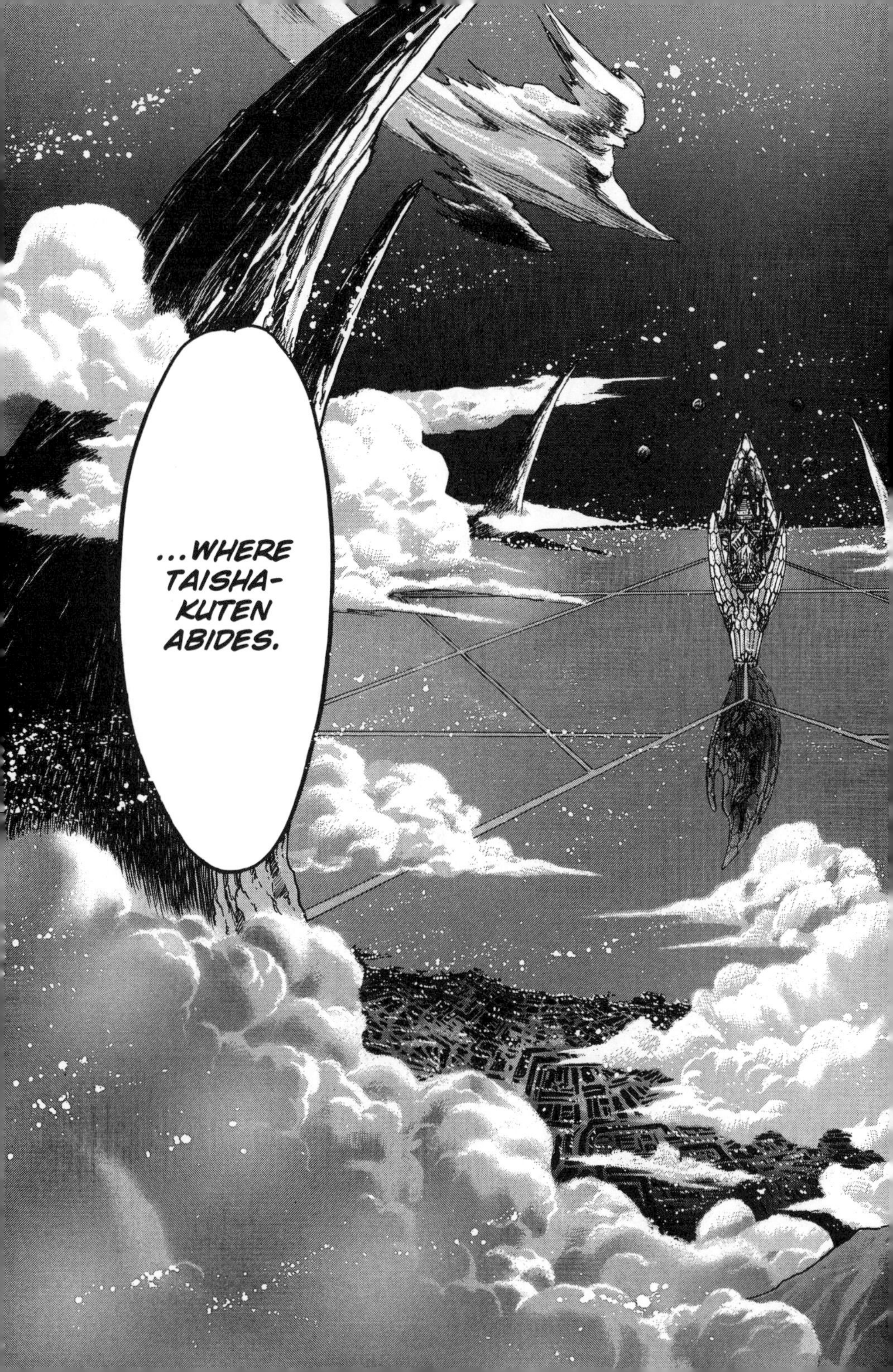
...WHERE TAISHA-KUTEN ABIDES.

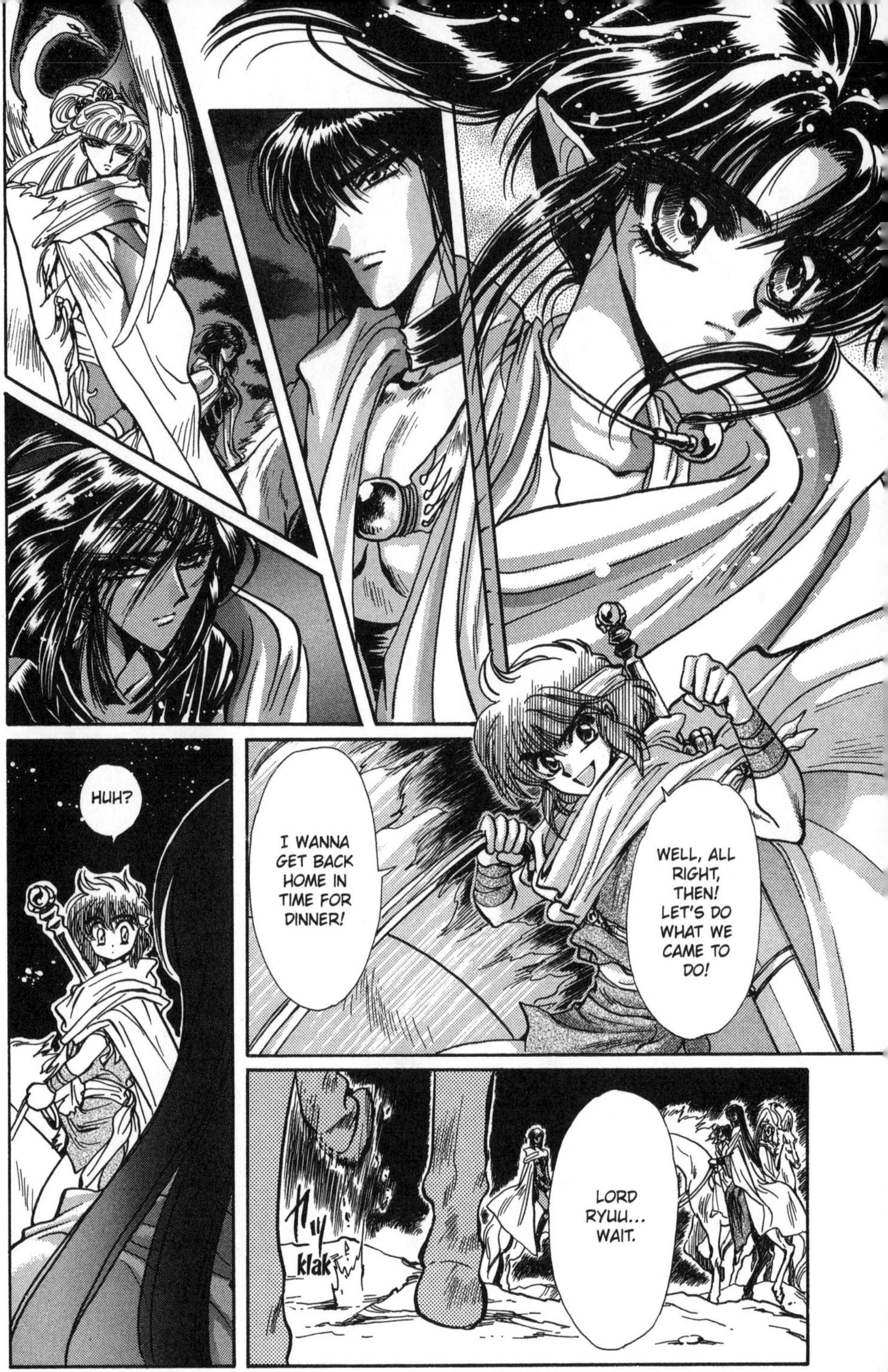

WELL, ALL RIGHT, THEN! LET'S DO WHAT WE CAME TO DO!
I WANNA GET BACK HOME IN TIME FOR DINNER!
LORD RYUU... WAIT.
klak
HUH?

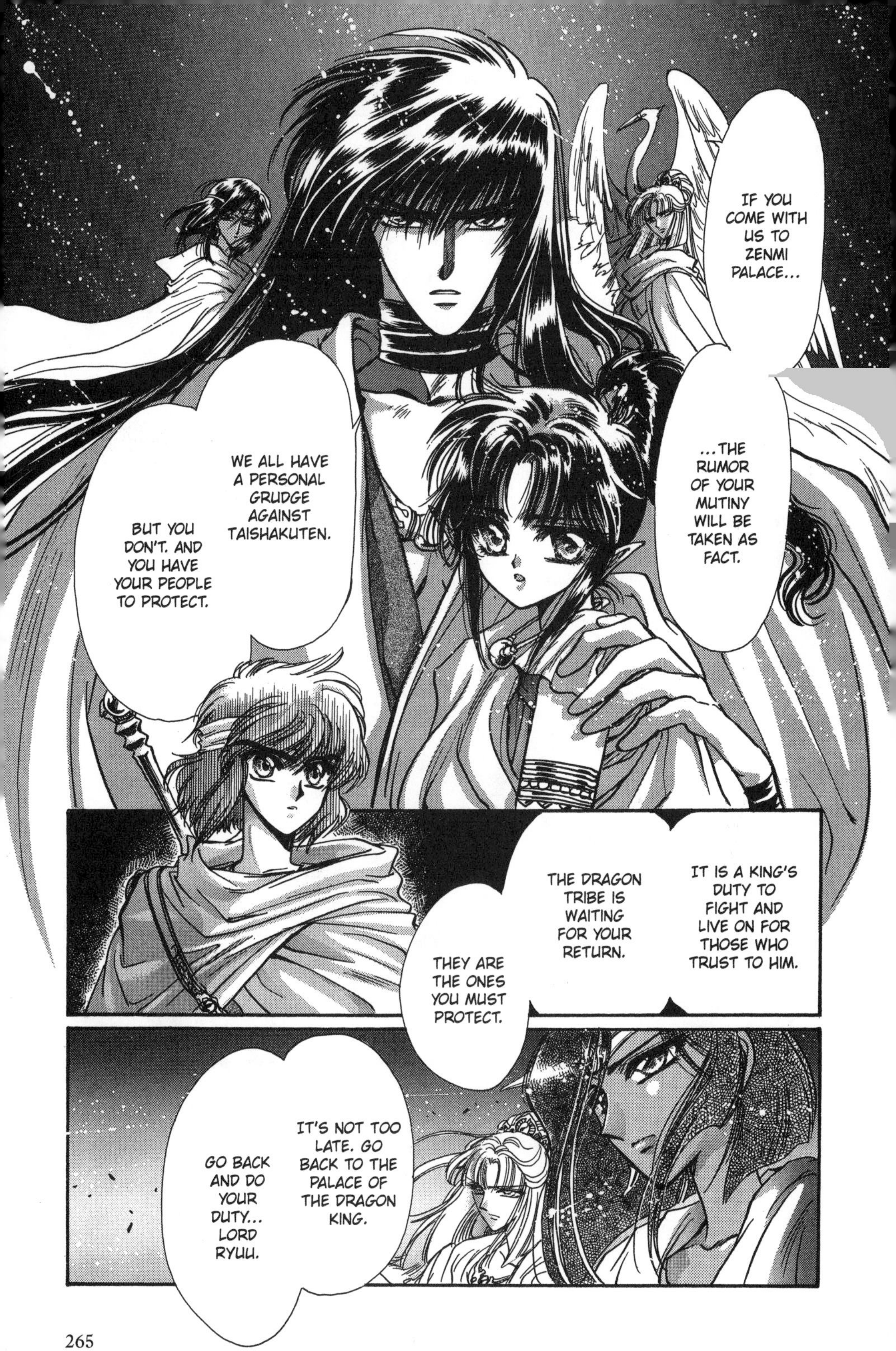
IF YOU COME WITH US TO ZENMI PALACE...
...THE RUMOR OF YOUR MUTINY WILL BE TAKEN AS FACT.
WE ALL HAVE A PERSONAL GRUDGE AGAINST TAISHAKUTEN.
BUT YOU DON'T. AND YOU HAVE YOUR PEOPLE TO PROTECT.
IT IS A KING'S DUTY TO FIGHT AND LIVE ON FOR THOSE WHO TRUST TO HIM.
THE DRAGON TRIBE IS WAITING FOR YOUR RETURN.
THEY ARE THE ONES YOU MUST PROTECT.
IT'S NOT TOO LATE. GO BACK TO THE PALACE OF THE DRAGON KING.
GO BACK AND DO YOUR DUTY... LORD RYUU.

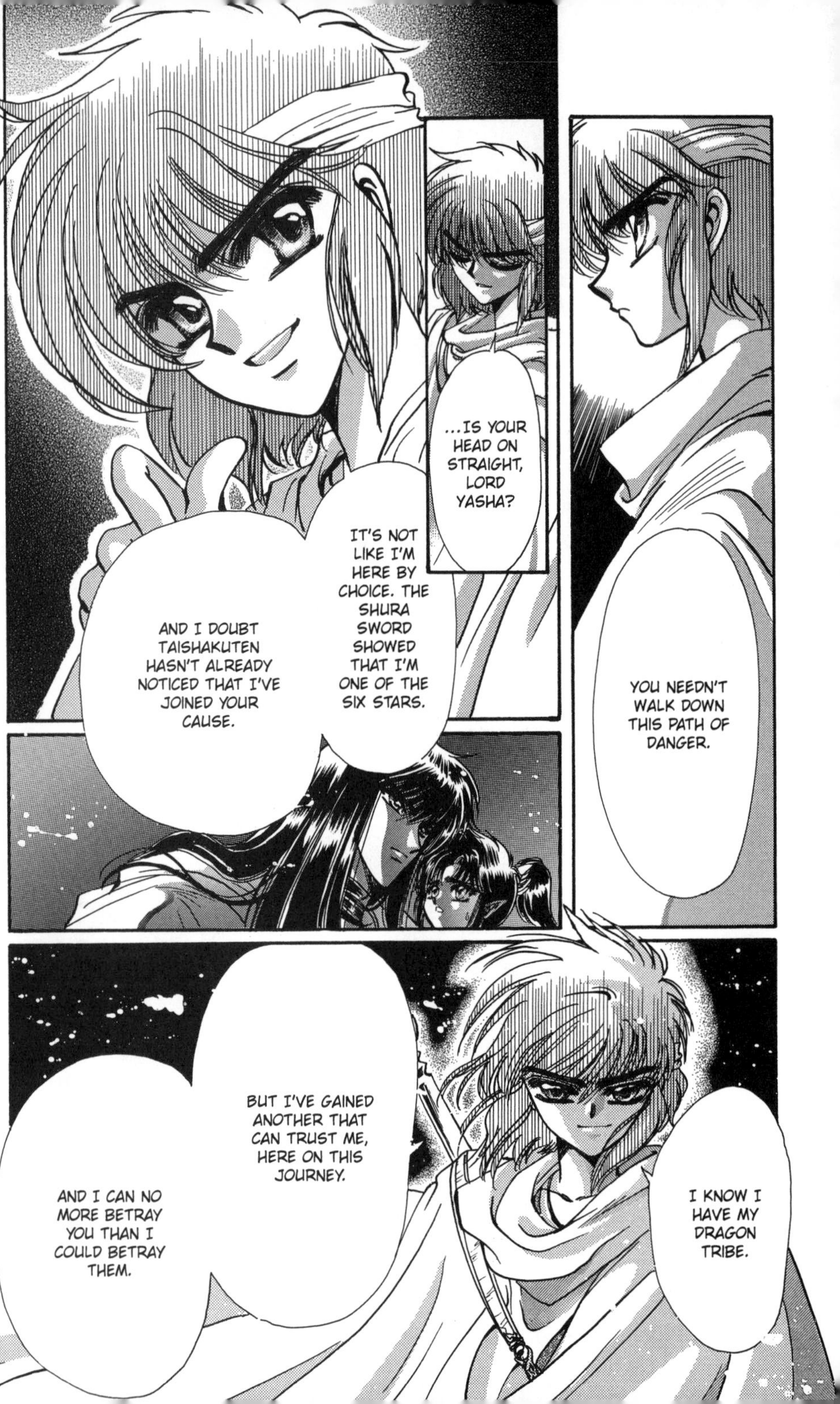
YOU NEEDN'T WALK DOWN THIS PATH OF DANGER.
...IS YOUR HEAD ON STRAIGHT, LORD YASHA?
IT'S NOT LIKE I'M HERE BY CHOICE. THE SHURA SWORD SHOWED THAT I'M ONE OF THE SIX STARS.
AND I DOUBT TAISHAKUTEN HASN'T ALREADY NOTICED THAT I'VE JOINED YOUR CAUSE.
I KNOW I HAVE MY DRAGON TRIBE.
BUT I'VE GAINED ANOTHER THAT CAN TRUST ME, HERE ON THIS JOURNEY.
AND I CAN NO MORE BETRAY YOU THAN I COULD BETRAY THEM.

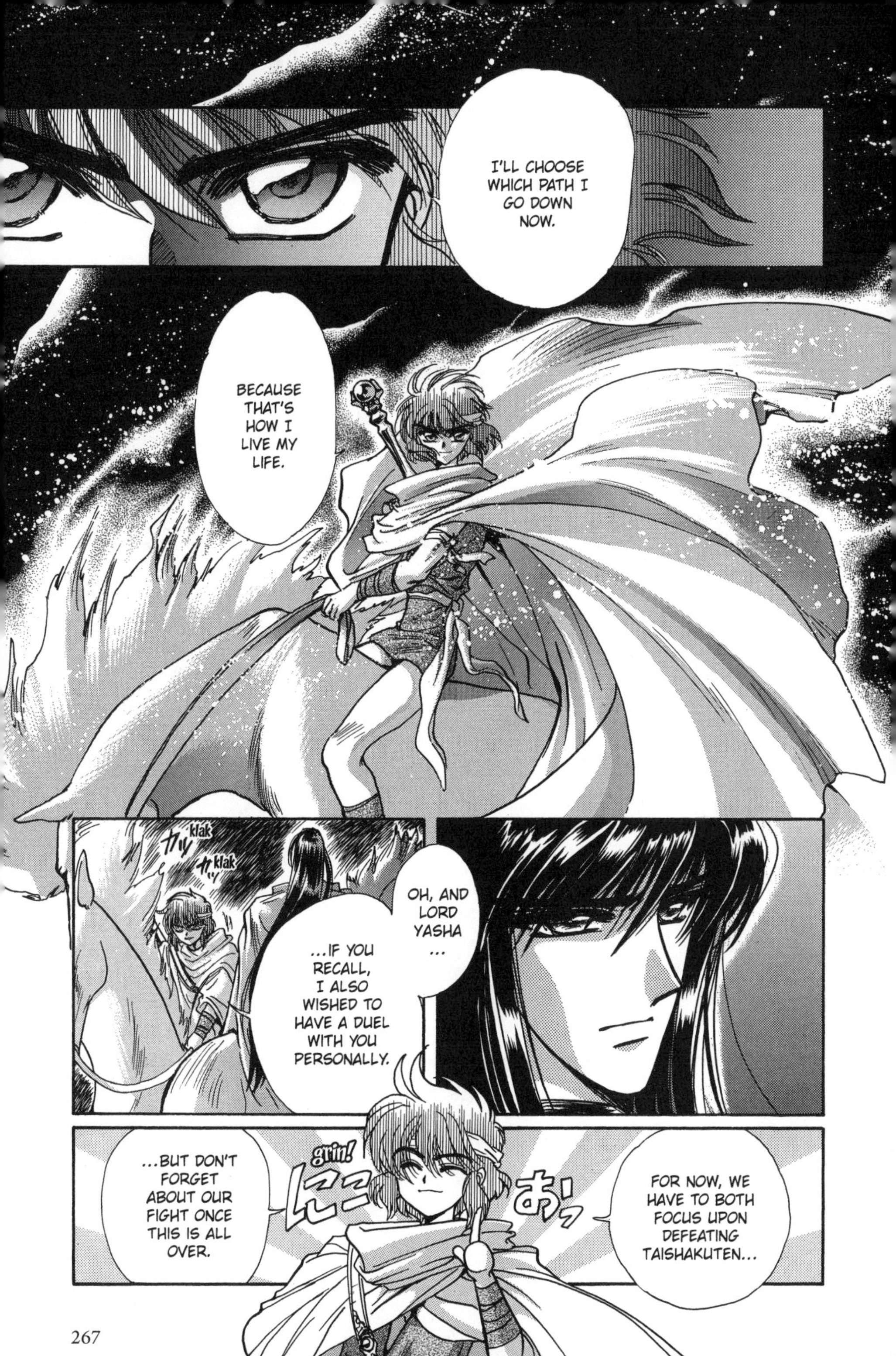
I'LL CHOOSE WHICH PATH I GO DOWN NOW.
BECAUSE THAT'S HOW I LIVE MY LIFE.
OH, AND LORD YASHA ...
...IF YOU RECALL, I ALSO WISHED TO HAVE A DUEL WITH YOU PERSONALLY.
カッ klak
カッ klak
FOR NOW, WE HAVE TO BOTH FOCUS UPON DEFEATING TAISHAKUTEN...
おっ
にこ grin!
...BUT DON'T FORGET ABOUT OUR FIGHT ONCE THIS IS ALL OVER.

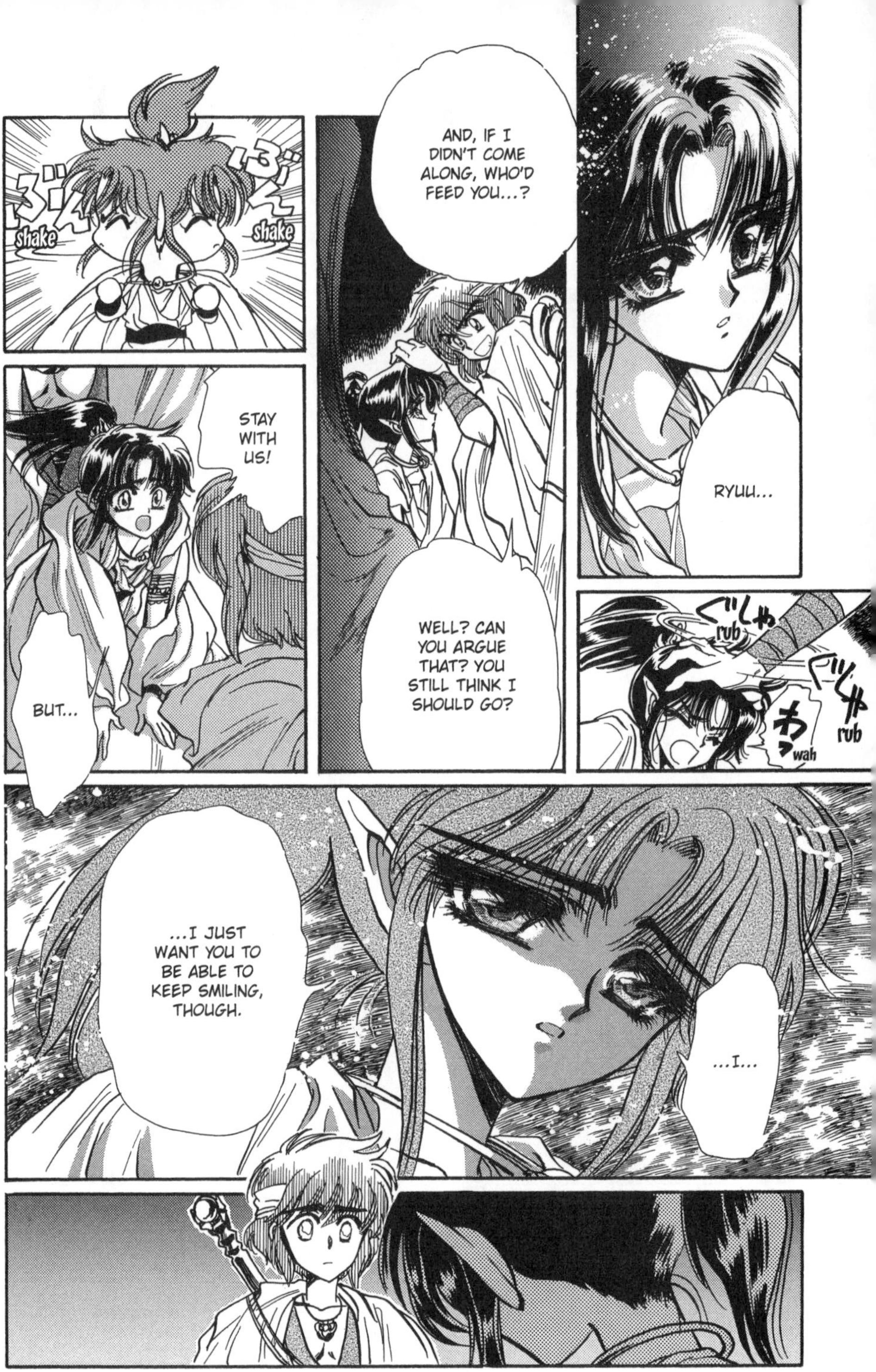
RYUU...
rub
rub
wah
AND, IF I DIDN'T COME ALONG, WHO'D FEED YOU...?
WELL? CAN YOU ARGUE THAT? YOU STILL THINK I SHOULD GO?
shake
shake
STAY WITH US!
BUT...
...I...
...I JUST WANT YOU TO BE ABLE TO KEEP SMILING, THOUGH.

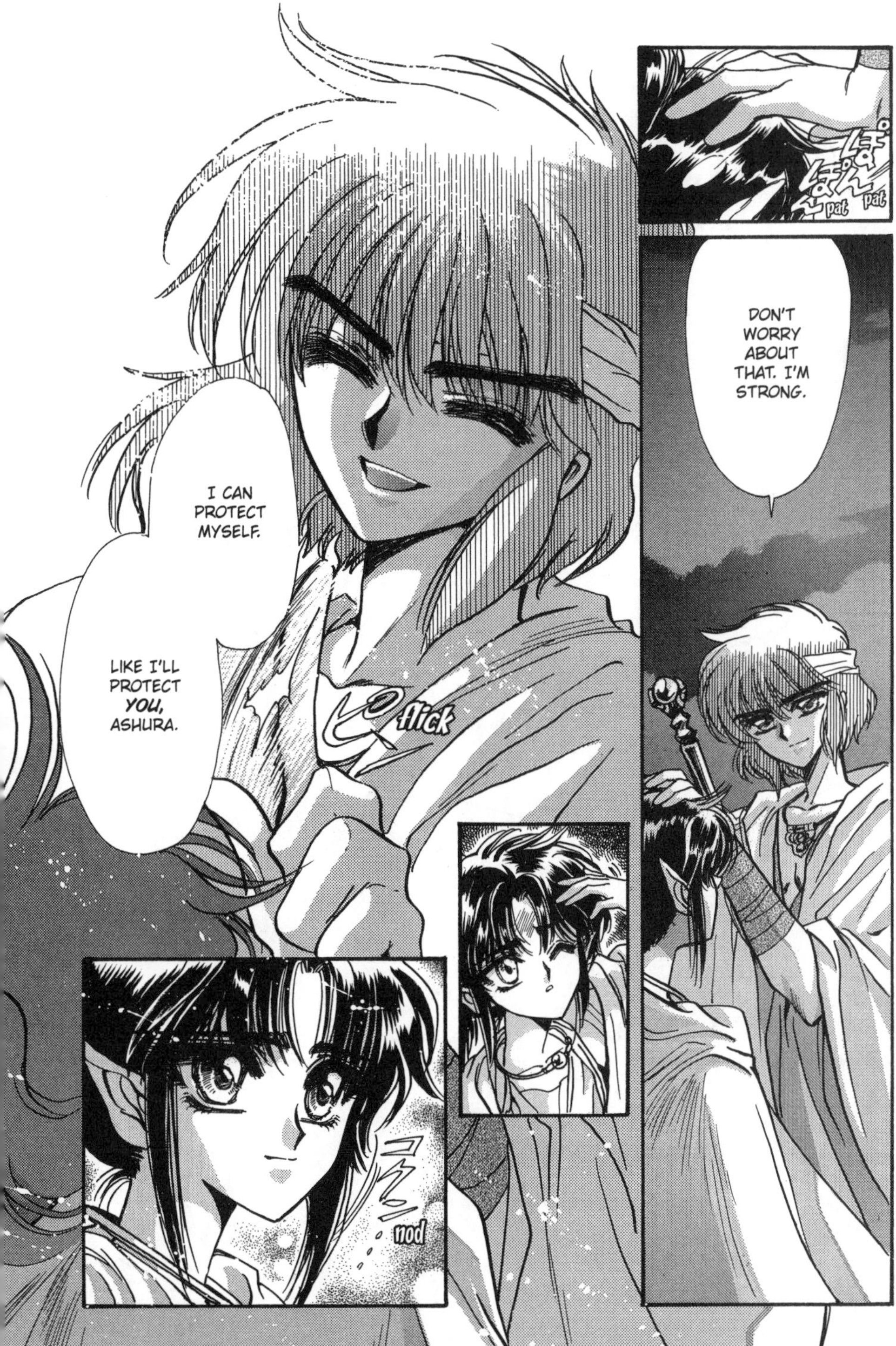
pat pat
DON'T WORRY ABOUT THAT. I'M STRONG.
I CAN PROTECT MYSELF.
LIKE I'LL PROTECT *YOU*, ASHURA.
flick
nod

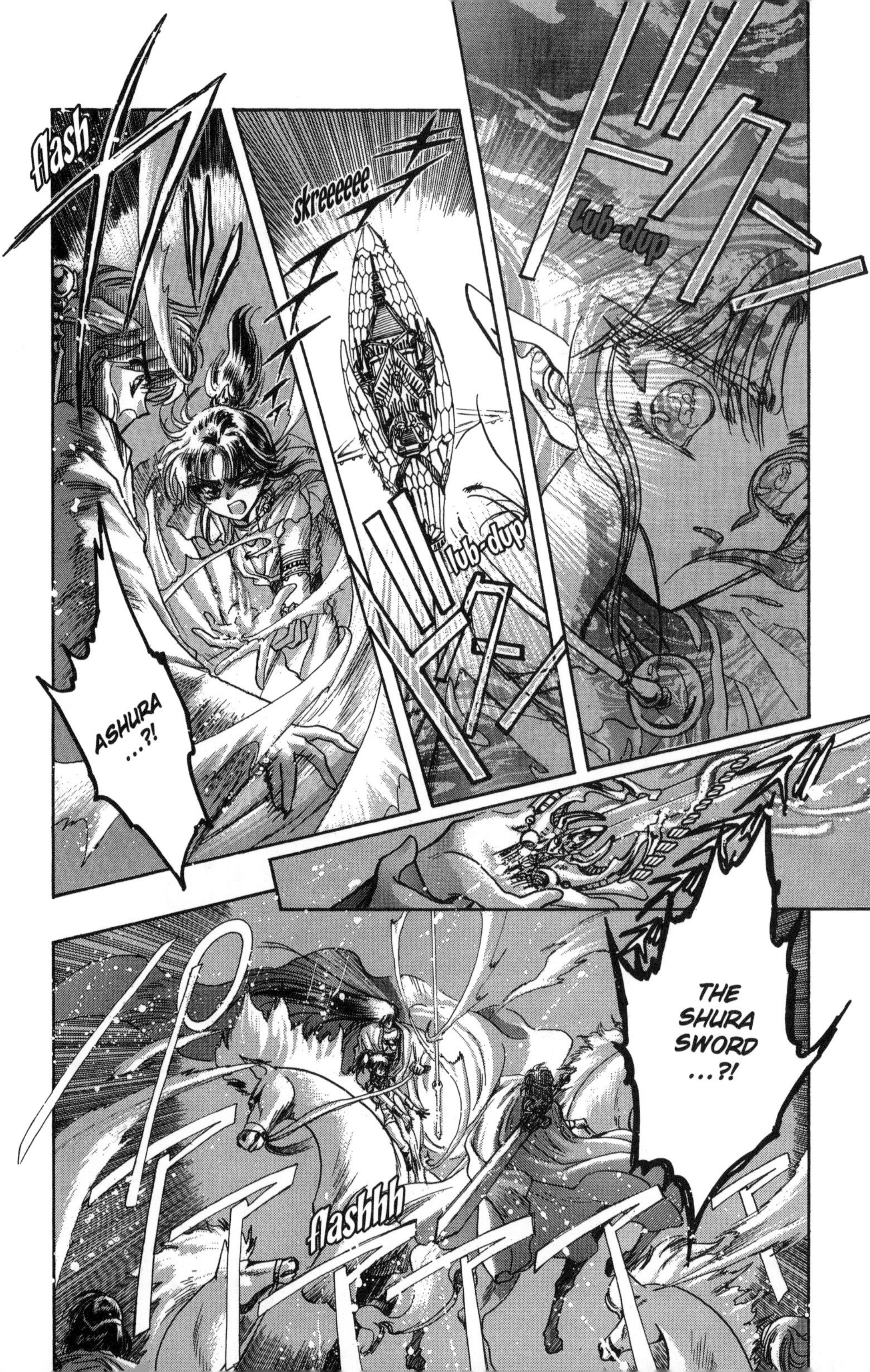

lub-dup
skreeeeee
lub-dup
flash
ASHURA ...?!
THE SHURA SWORD ...?!
flashhh

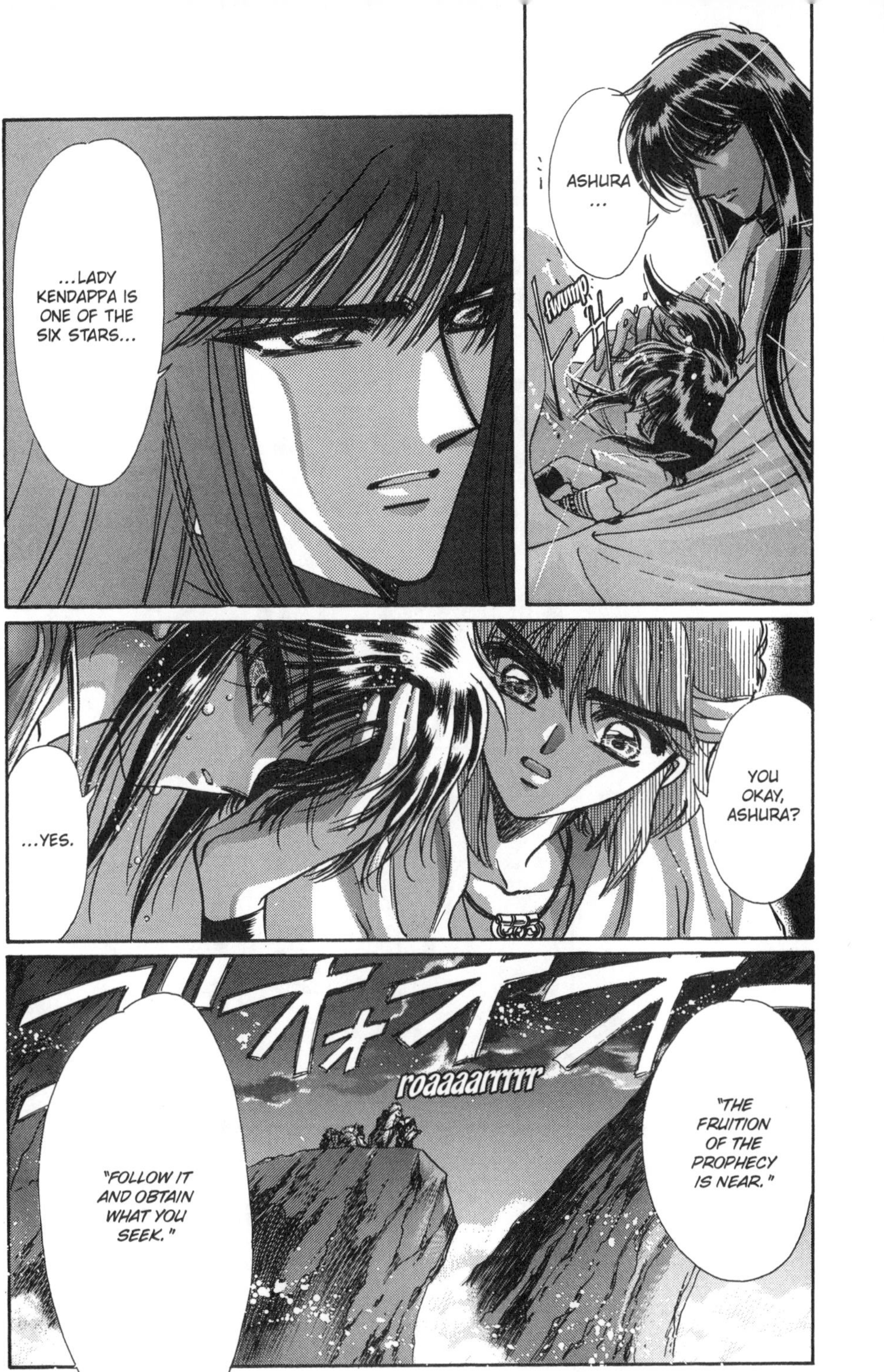

ASHURA ...
fwump
...LADY KENDAPPA IS ONE OF THE SIX STARS...
YOU OKAY, ASHURA?
...YES.
roaaaarrrrr
"THE FRUITION OF THE PROPHECY IS NEAR."
"FOLLOW IT AND OBTAIN WHAT YOU SEEK."

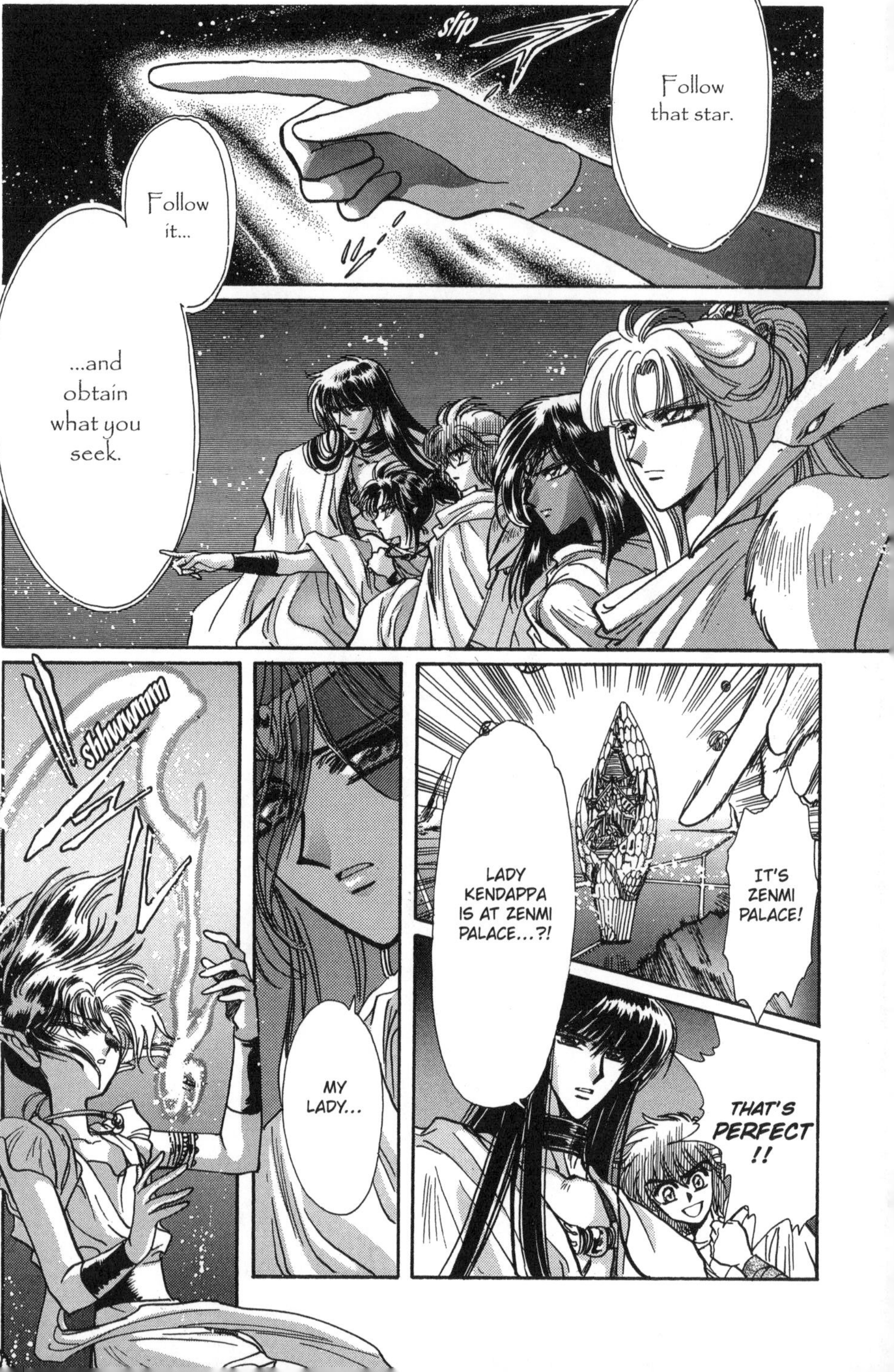
slip
Follow that star.
Follow it...
...and obtain what you seek.
IT'S ZENMI PALACE!
LADY KENDAPPA IS AT ZENMI PALACE...?!
THAT'S PERFECT!!
MY LADY...
shhwwmm

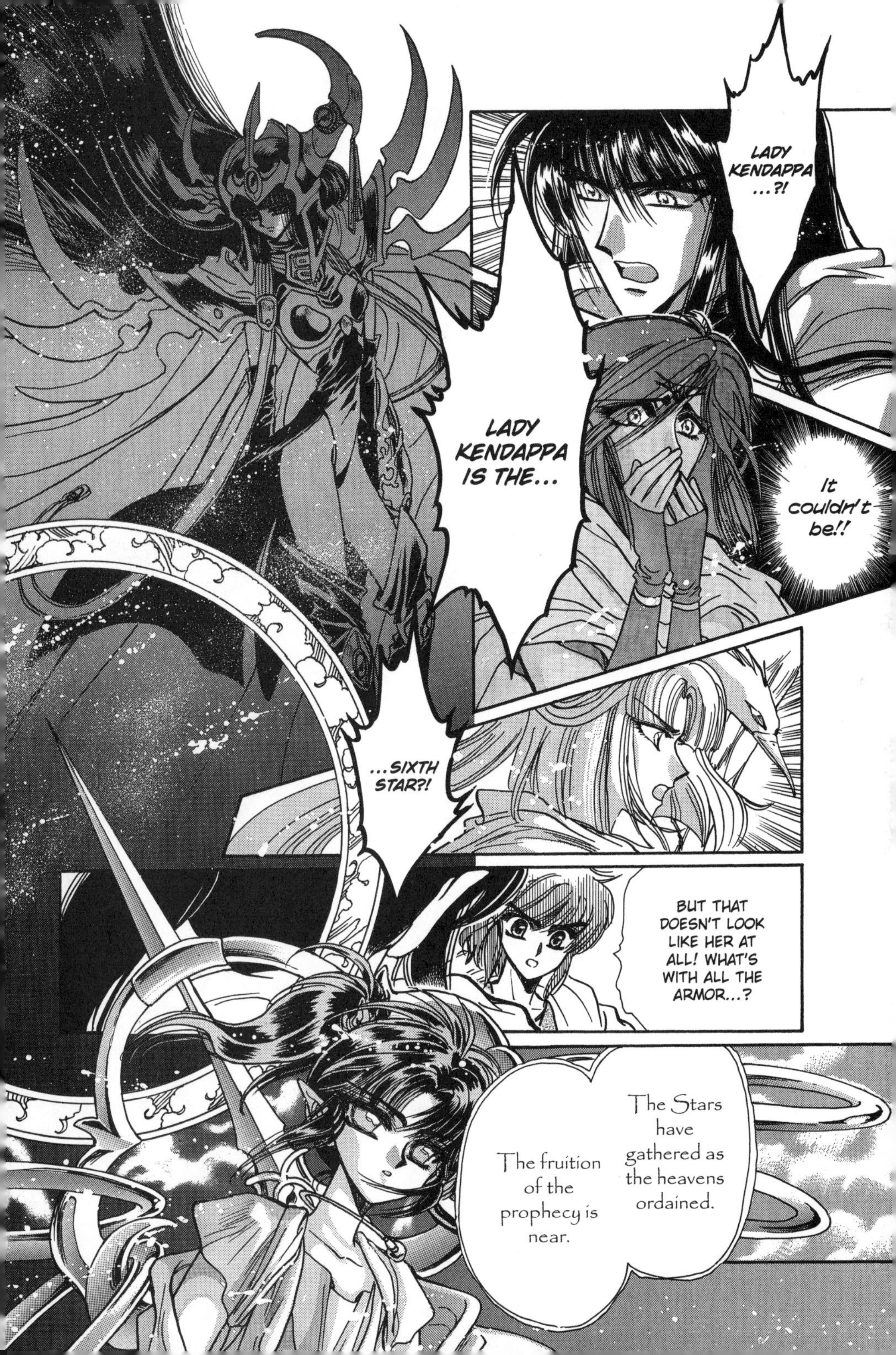
LADY KENDAPPA ...?!
It couldn't be!!
LADY KENDAPPA IS THE...
...SIXTH STAR?!
BUT THAT DOESN'T LOOK LIKE HER AT ALL! WHAT'S WITH ALL THE ARMOR...?
The Stars have gathered as the heavens ordained.
The fruition of the prophecy is near.

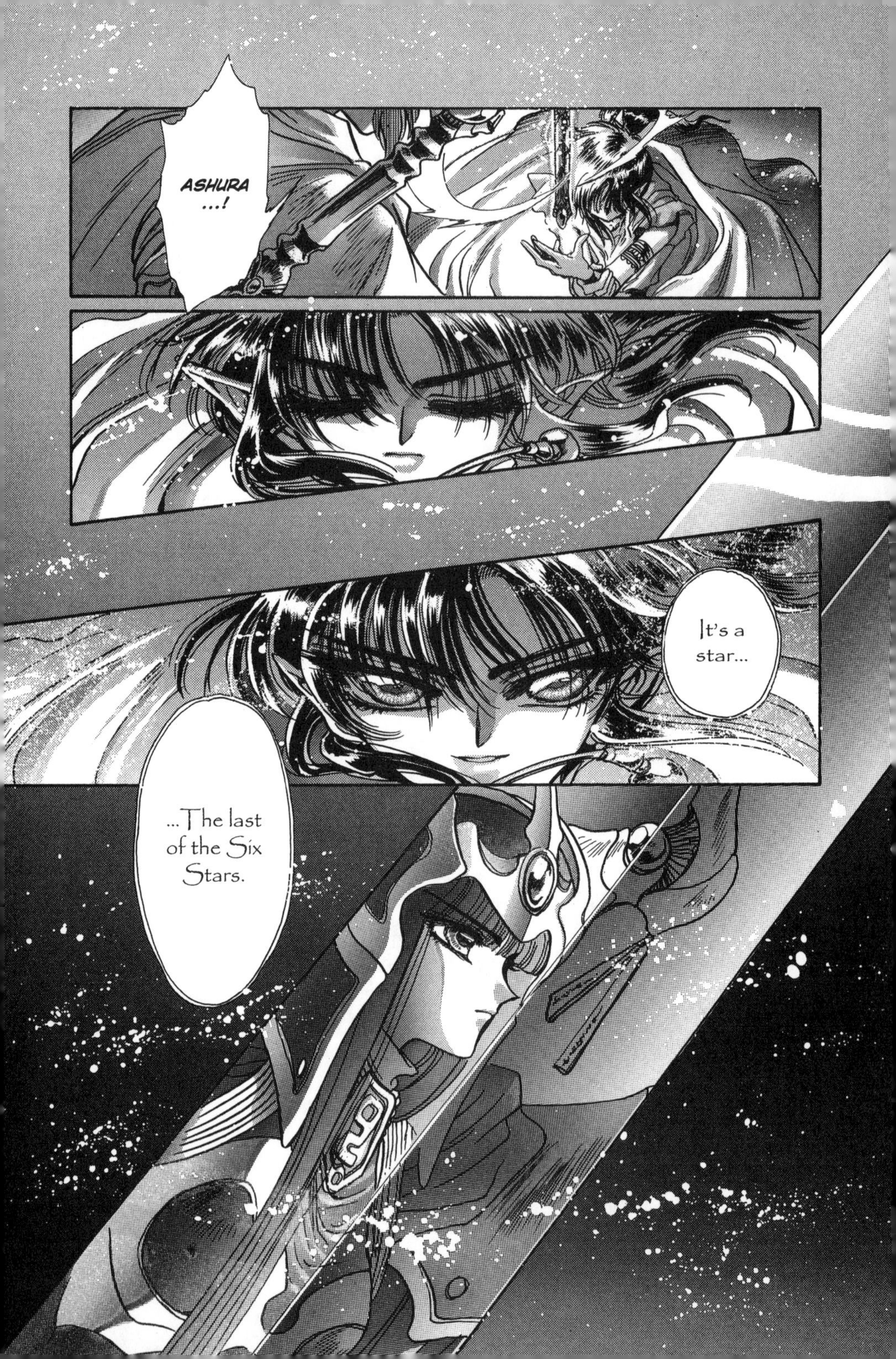

ASHURA ...!
It's a star...
...The last of the Six Stars.

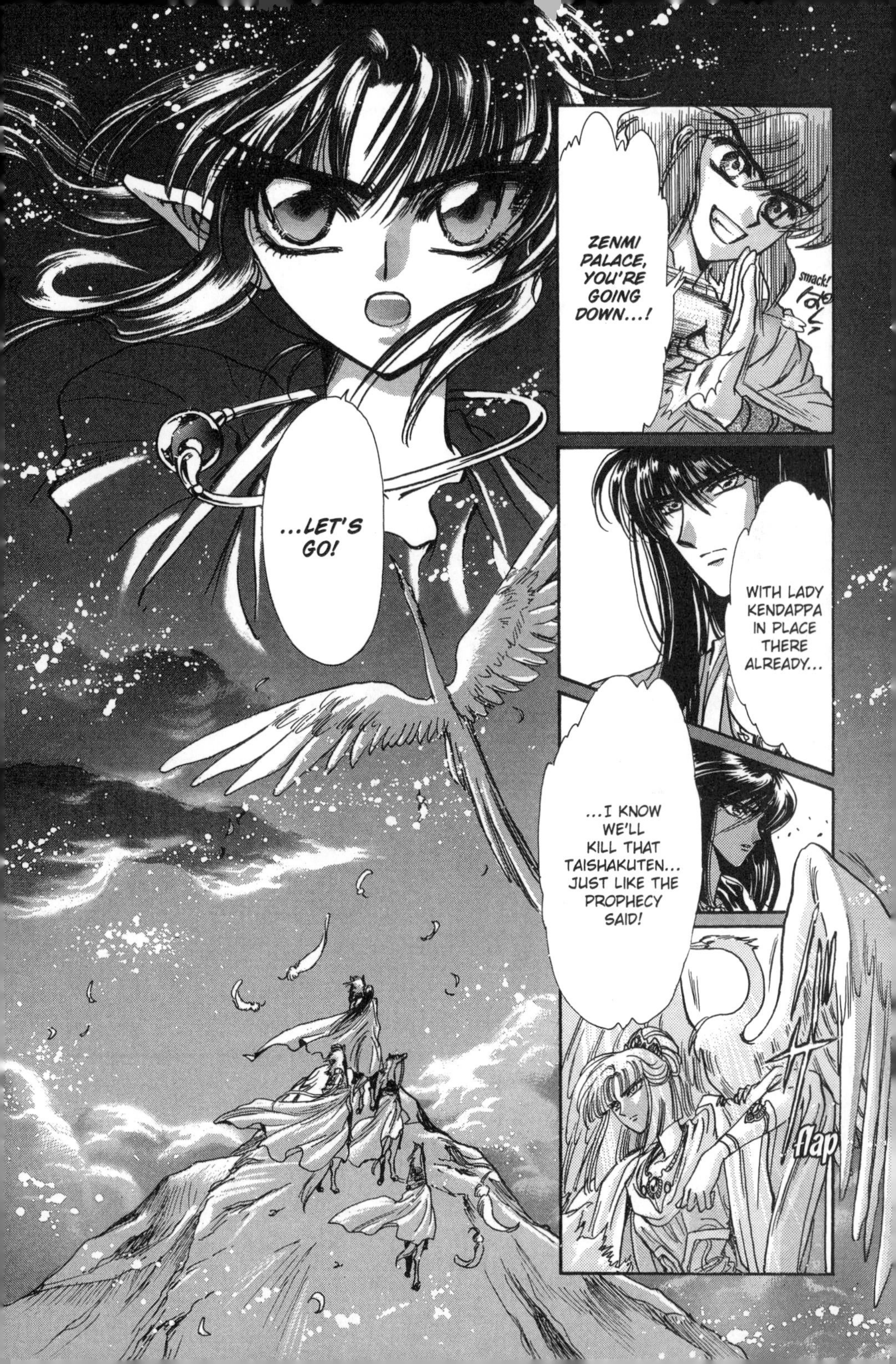
ZENMI PALACE, YOU'RE GOING DOWN...!
smack!
WITH LADY KENDAPPA IN PLACE THERE ALREADY...
...I KNOW WE'LL KILL THAT TAISHAKUTEN... JUST LIKE THE PROPHECY SAID!
flap
...LET'S GO!

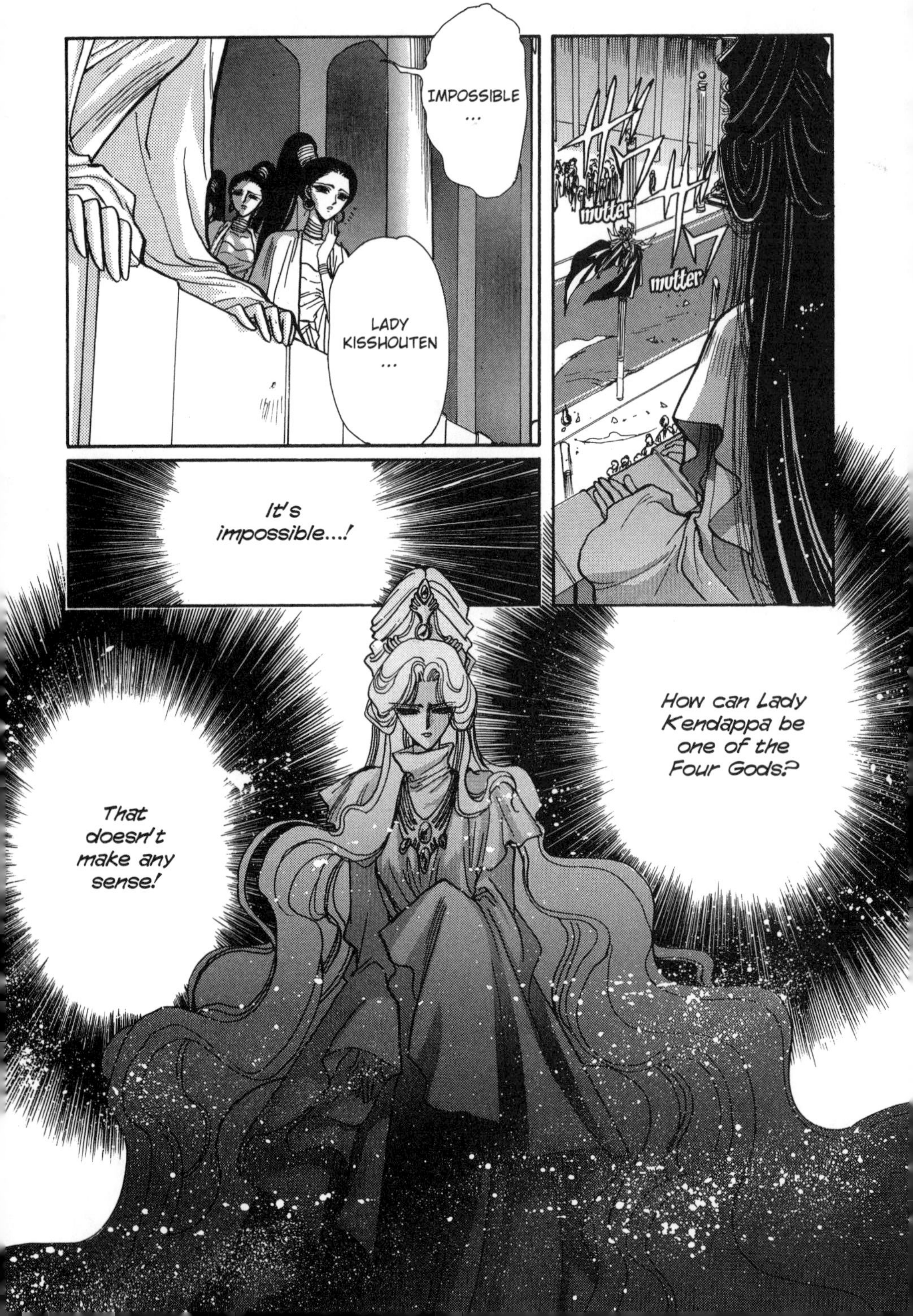
mutter
mutter
IMPOSSIBLE ...
LADY KISSHOUTEN ...
It's impossible...!
How can Lady Kendappa be one of the Four Gods?
That doesn't make any sense!

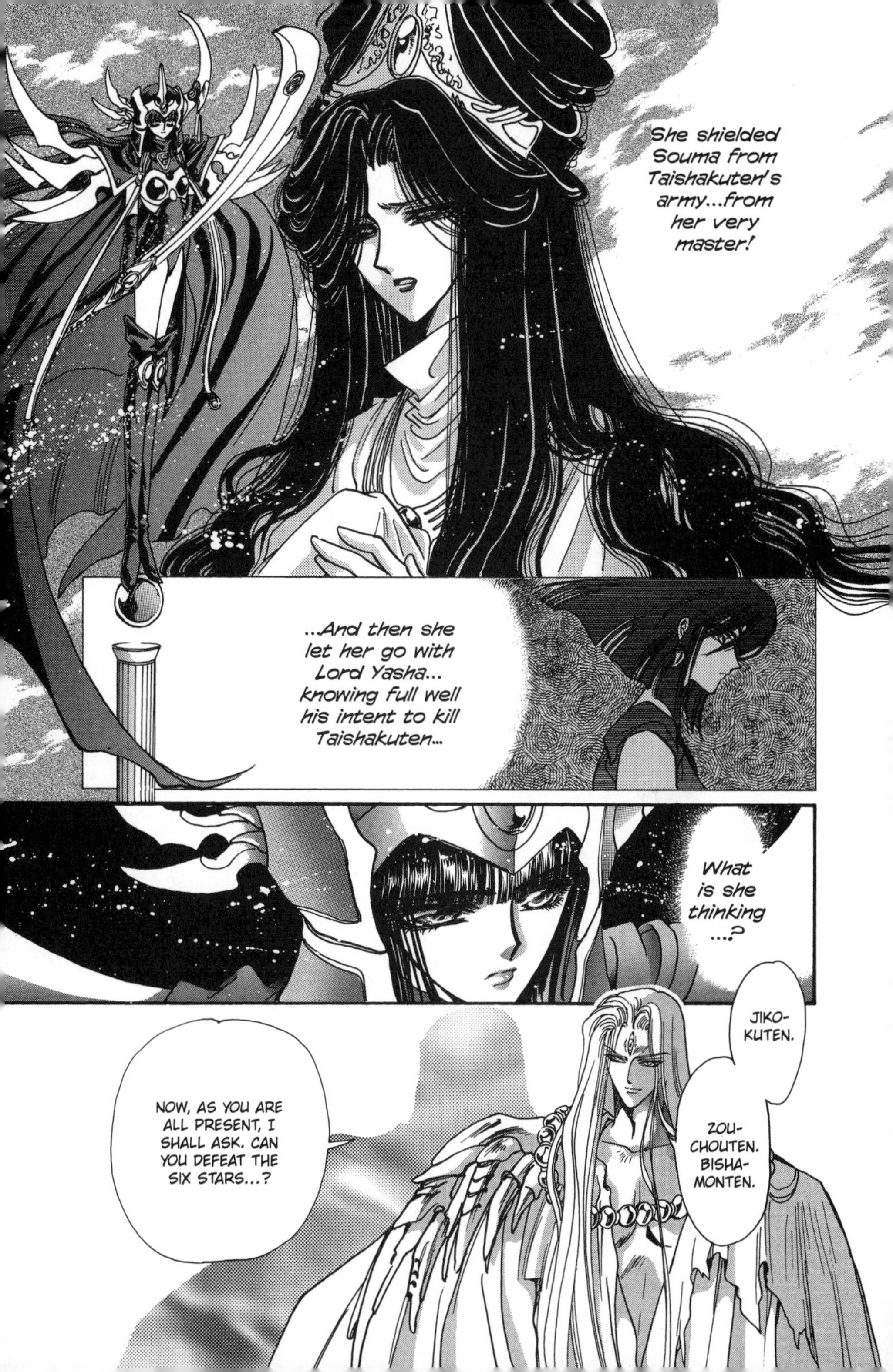
She shielded Souma from Taishakuten's army...from her very master!
...And then she let her go with Lord Yasha... knowing full well his intent to kill Taishakuten...
What is she thinking ...?
JIKO-KUTEN.
ZOU-CHOUTEN. BISHA-MONTEN.
NOW, AS YOU ARE ALL PRESENT, I SHALL ASK. CAN YOU DEFEAT THE SIX STARS...?

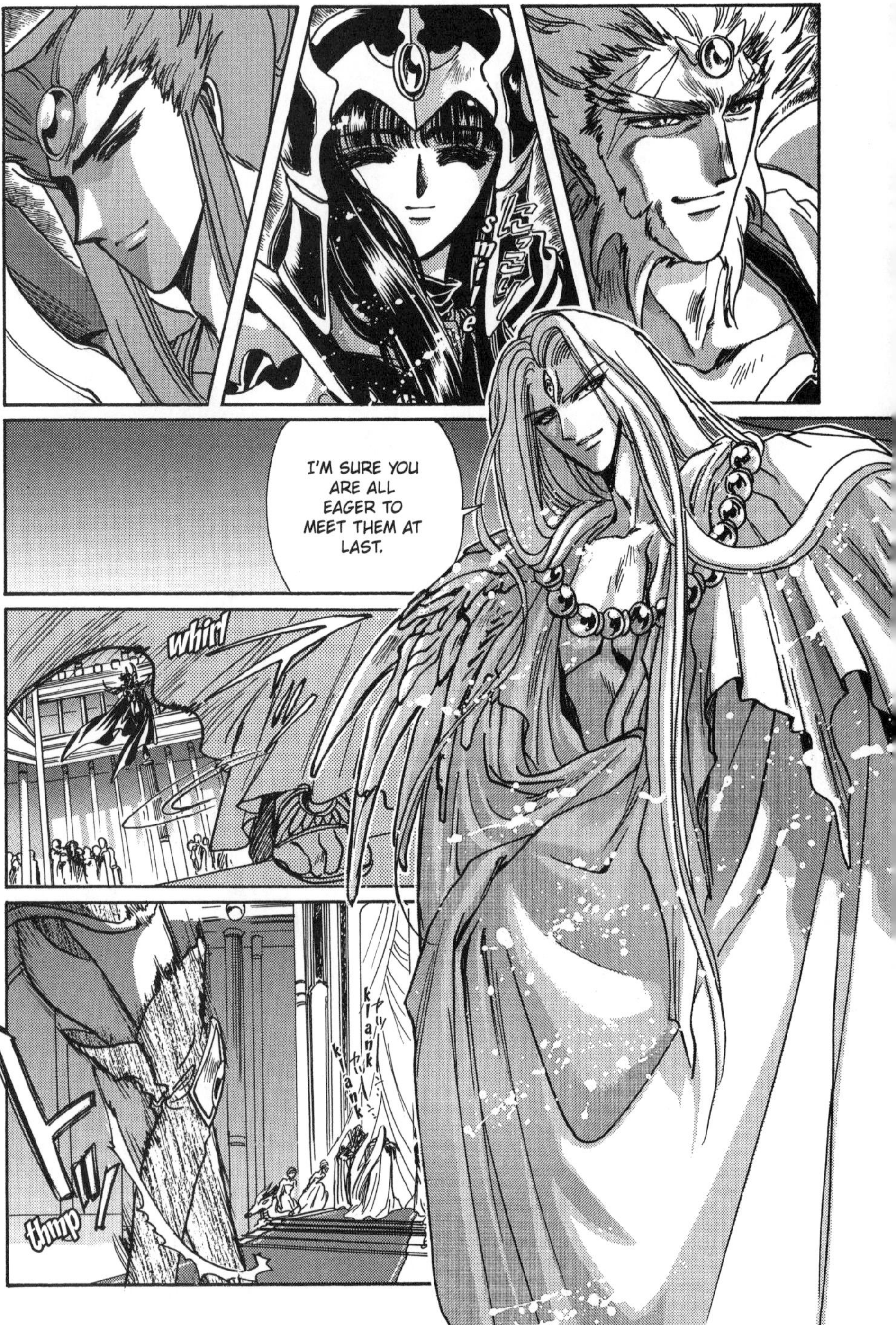
smile
I'M SURE YOU ARE ALL EAGER TO MEET THEM AT LAST.
whirl
klank
klank
thmp

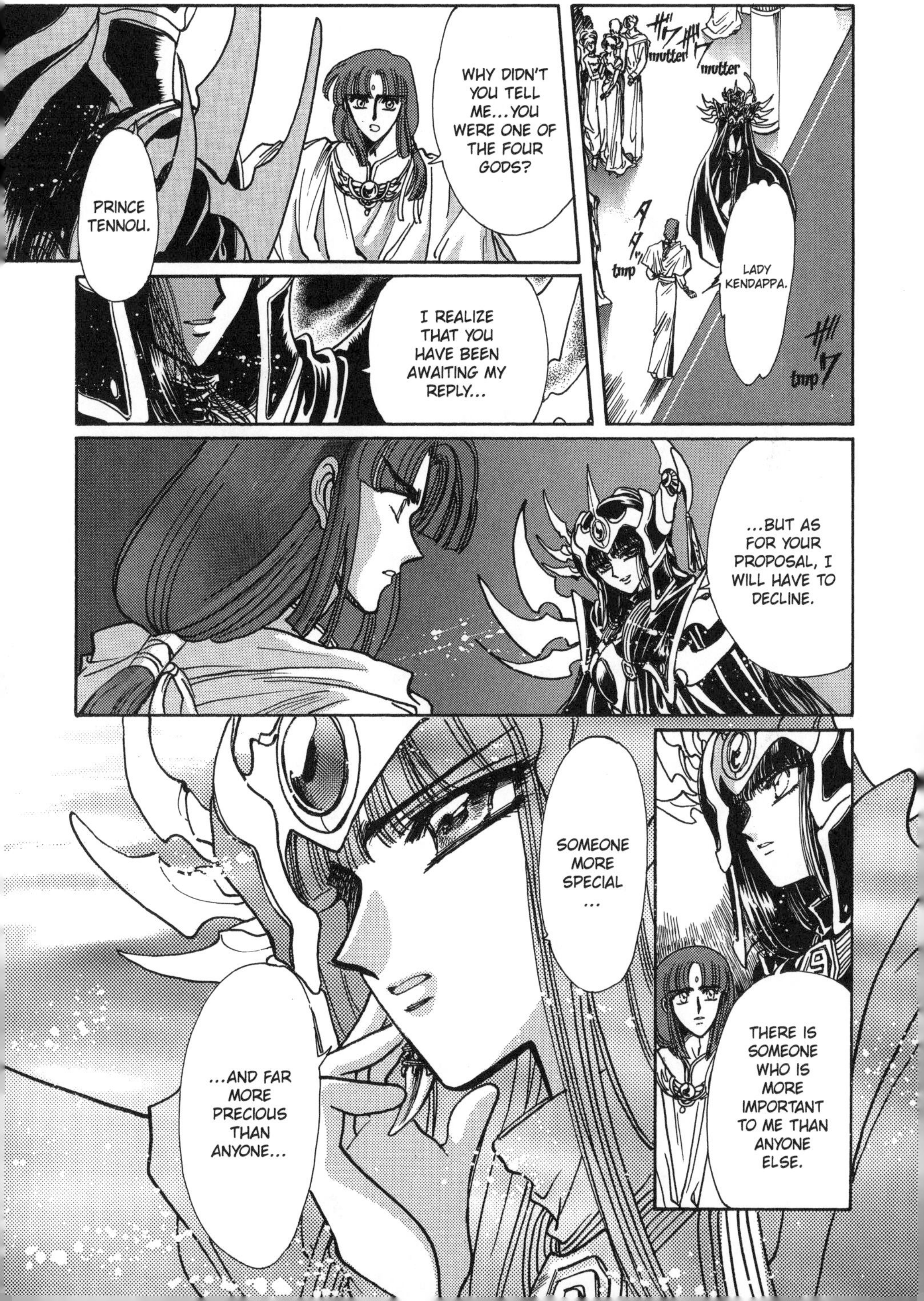
mutter
mutter
tmp
LADY KENDAPPA.
tmp
WHY DIDN'T YOU TELL ME...YOU WERE ONE OF THE FOUR GODS?
PRINCE TENNOU.
I REALIZE THAT YOU HAVE BEEN AWAITING MY REPLY...
...BUT AS FOR YOUR PROPOSAL, I WILL HAVE TO DECLINE.
THERE IS SOMEONE WHO IS MORE IMPORTANT TO ME THAN ANYONE ELSE.
SOMEONE MORE SPECIAL ...
...AND FAR MORE PRECIOUS THAN ANYONE...

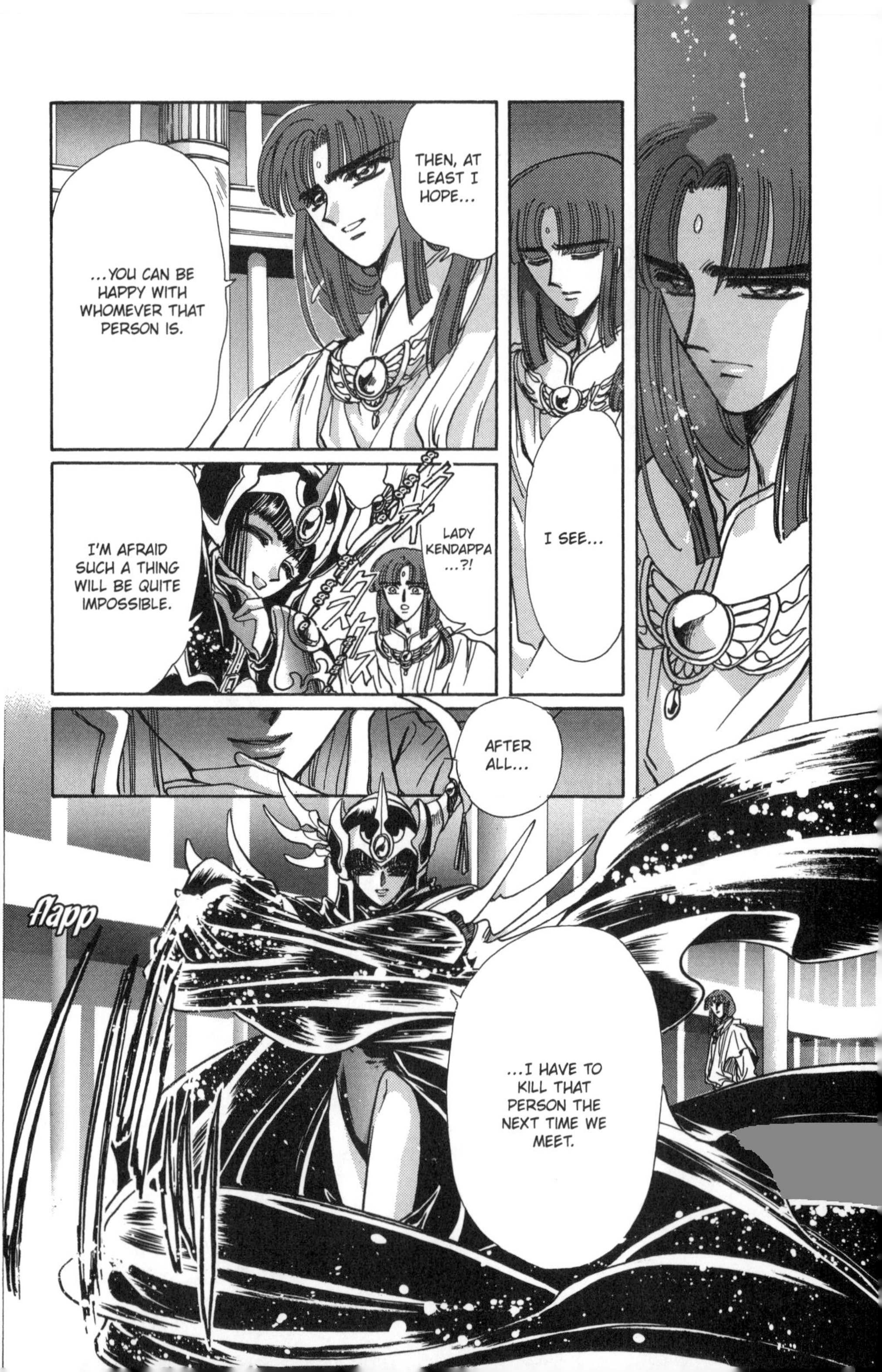
I SEE...
THEN, AT LEAST I HOPE...
...YOU CAN BE HAPPY WITH WHOMEVER THAT PERSON IS.
LADY KENDAPPA ...?!
I'M AFRAID SUCH A THING WILL BE QUITE IMPOSSIBLE.
AFTER ALL...
flapp
...I HAVE TO KILL THAT PERSON THE NEXT TIME WE MEET.

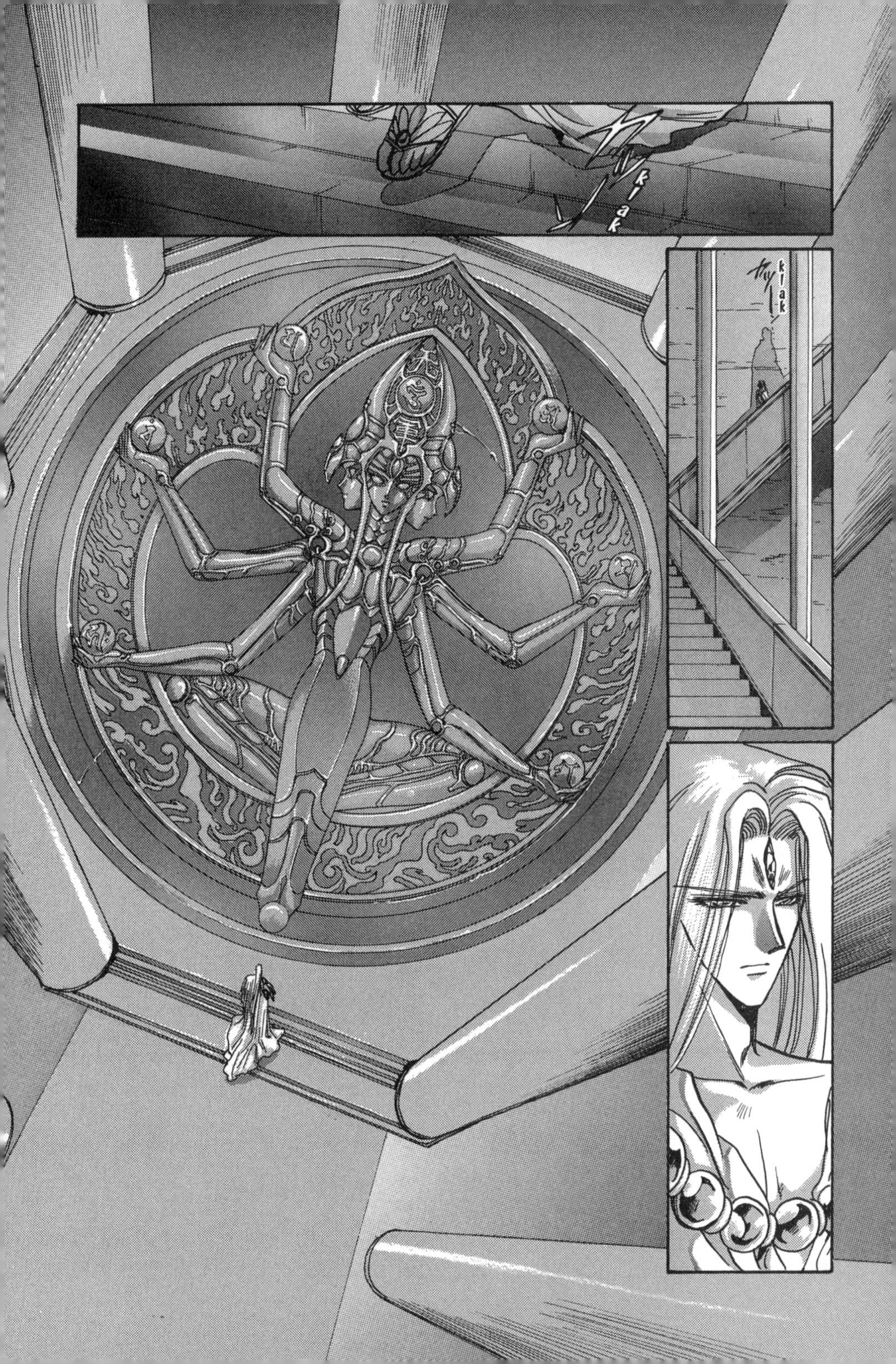
klak
klak

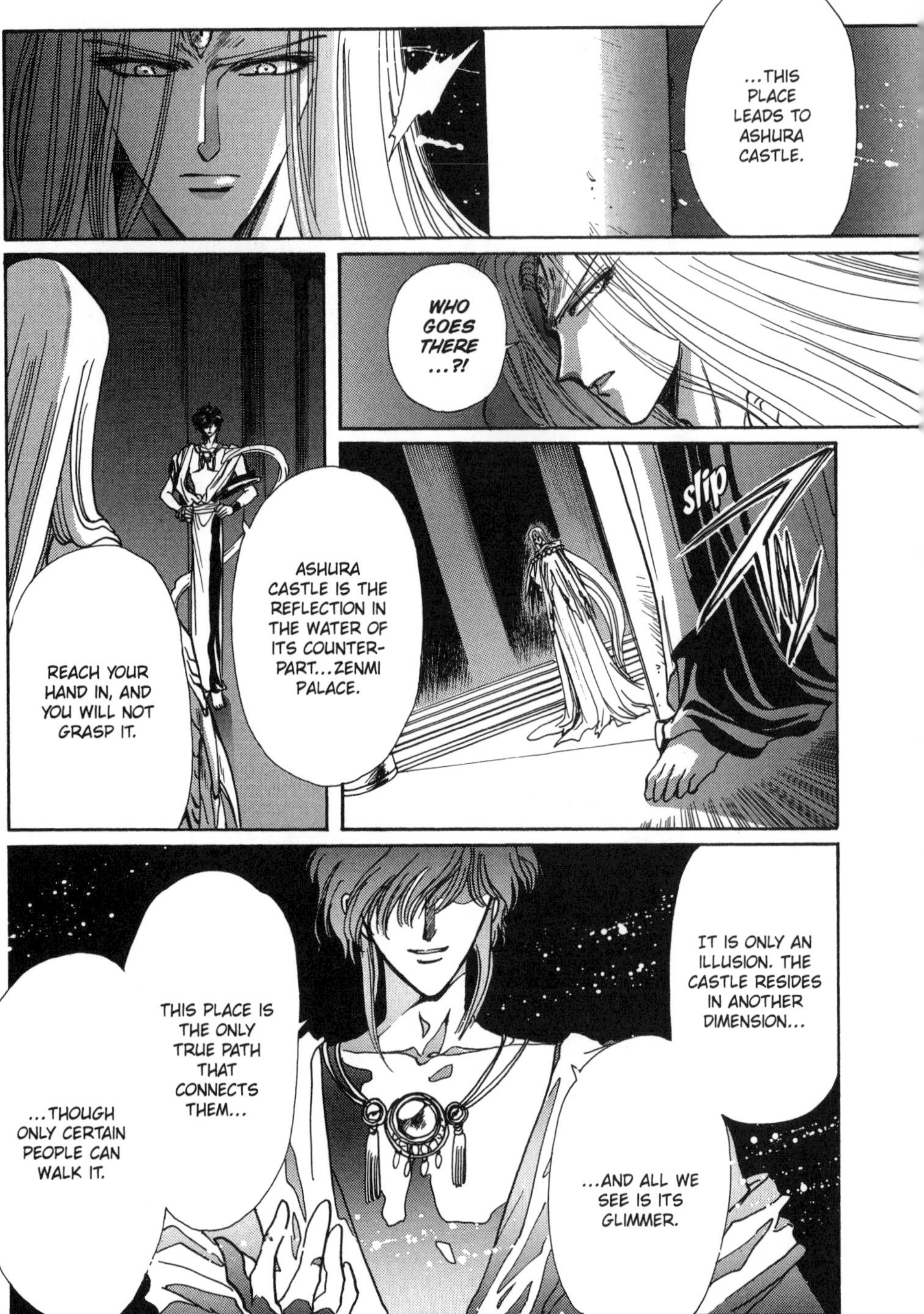
...THIS PLACE LEADS TO ASHURA CASTLE.
WHO GOES THERE ...?!
slip
ASHURA CASTLE IS THE REFLECTION IN THE WATER OF ITS COUNTER-PART...ZENMI PALACE.
REACH YOUR HAND IN, AND YOU WILL NOT GRASP IT.
IT IS ONLY AN ILLUSION. THE CASTLE RESIDES IN ANOTHER DIMENSION...
...AND ALL WE SEE IS ITS GLIMMER.
THIS PLACE IS THE ONLY TRUE PATH THAT CONNECTS THEM...
...THOUGH ONLY CERTAIN PEOPLE CAN WALK IT.

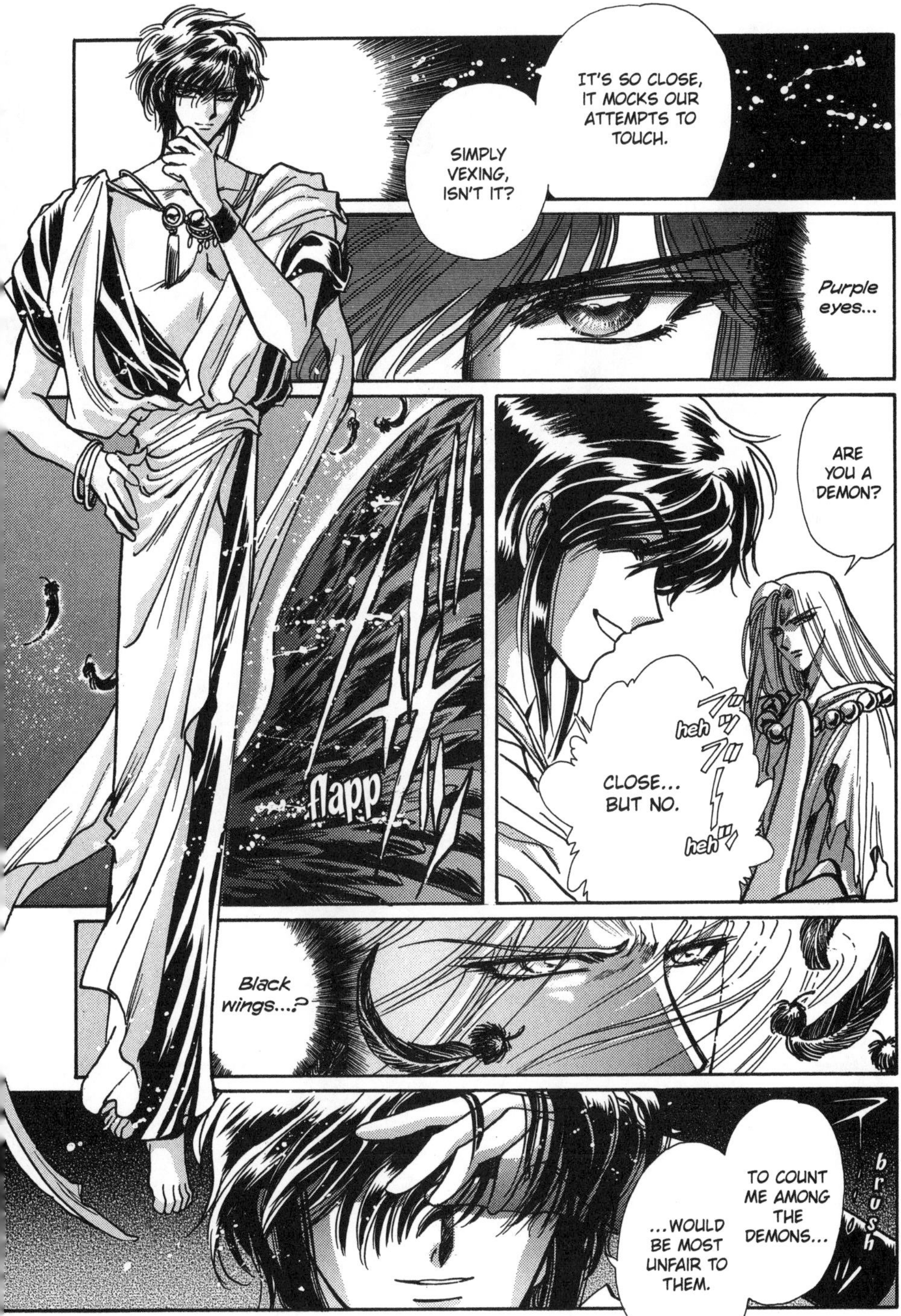
IT'S SO CLOSE, IT MOCKS OUR ATTEMPTS TO TOUCH.
SIMPLY VEXING, ISN'T IT?
Purple eyes...
ARE YOU A DEMON?
heh
CLOSE... BUT NO.
heh
flapp
Black wings...?
brush
TO COUNT ME AMONG THE DEMONS...
...WOULD BE MOST UNFAIR TO THEM.

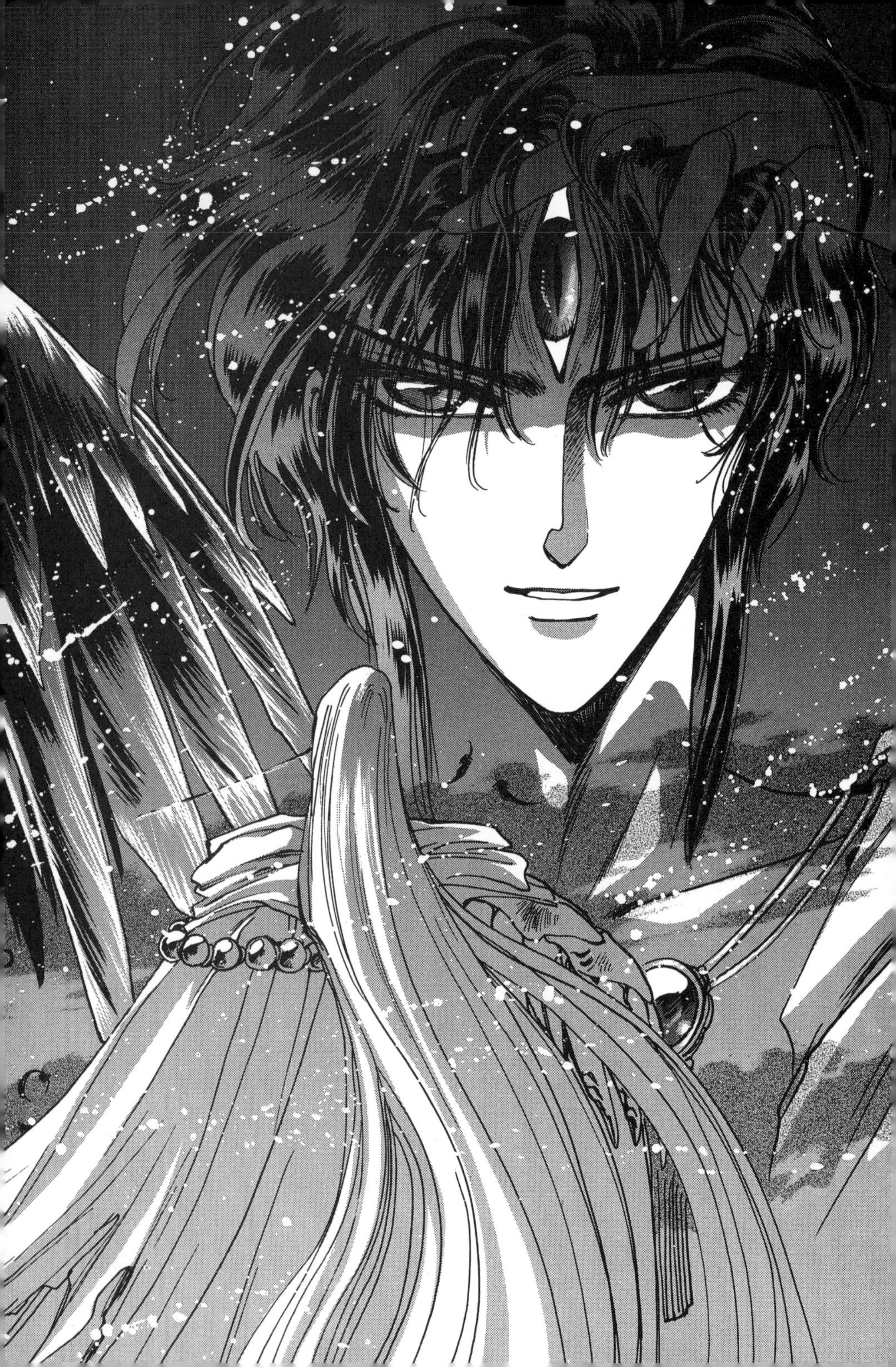

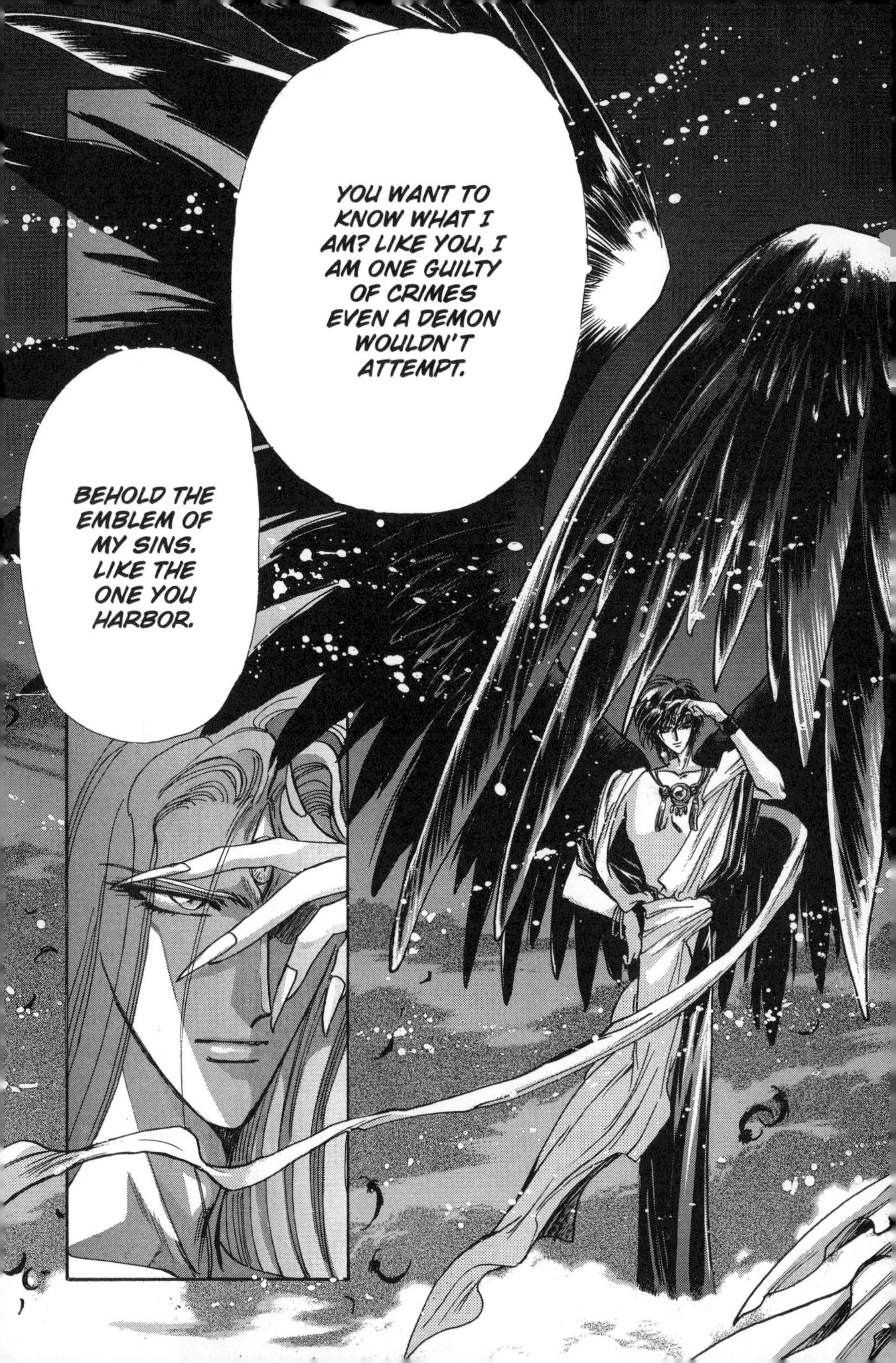
YOU WANT TO KNOW WHAT I AM? LIKE YOU, I AM ONE GUILTY OF CRIMES EVEN A DEMON WOULDN'T ATTEMPT.
BEHOLD THE EMBLEM OF MY SINS. LIKE THE ONE YOU HARBOR.

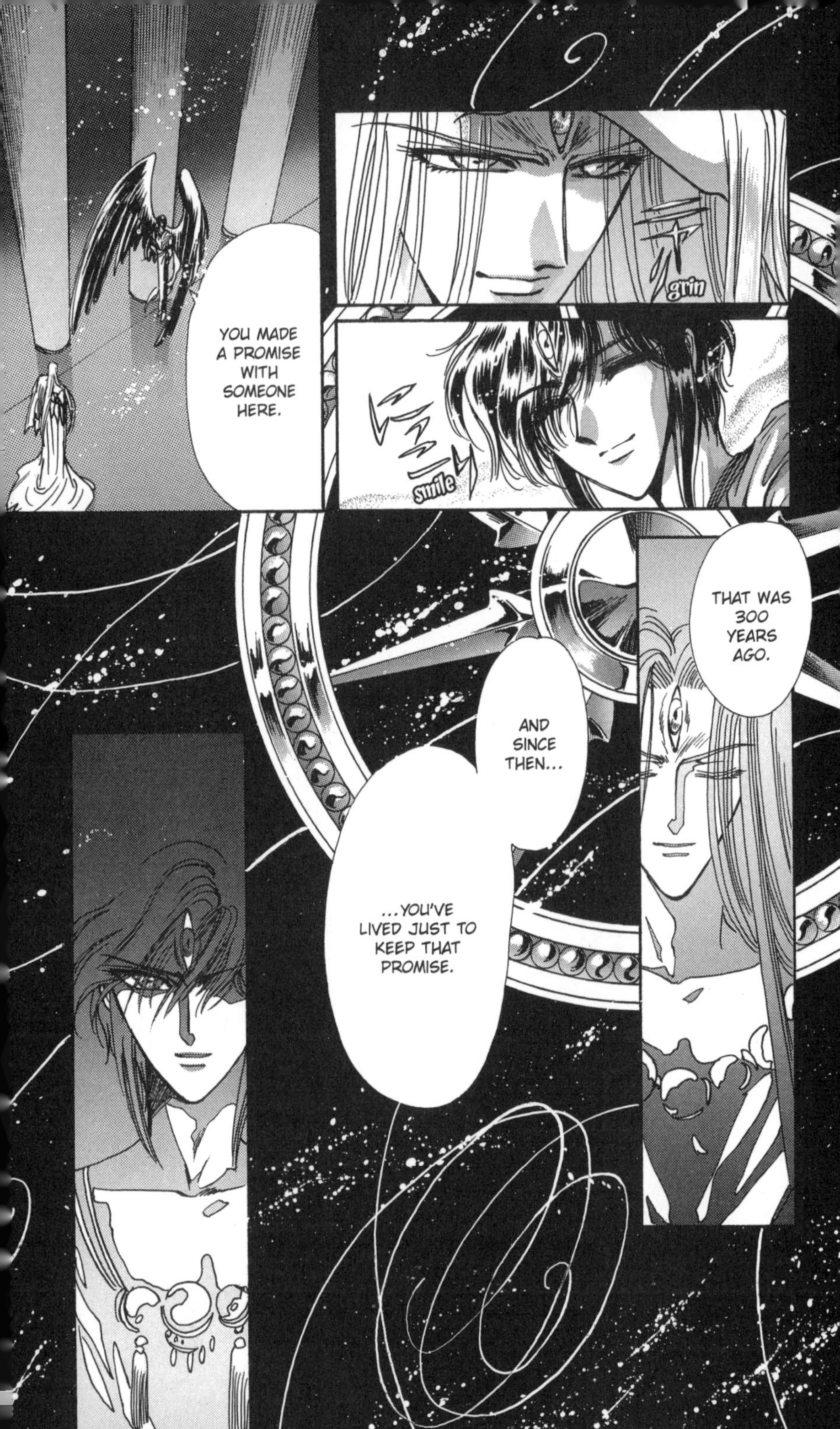
grin
smile
YOU MADE A PROMISE WITH SOMEONE HERE.
THAT WAS 300 YEARS AGO.
AND SINCE THEN...
...YOU'VE LIVED JUST TO KEEP THAT PROMISE.

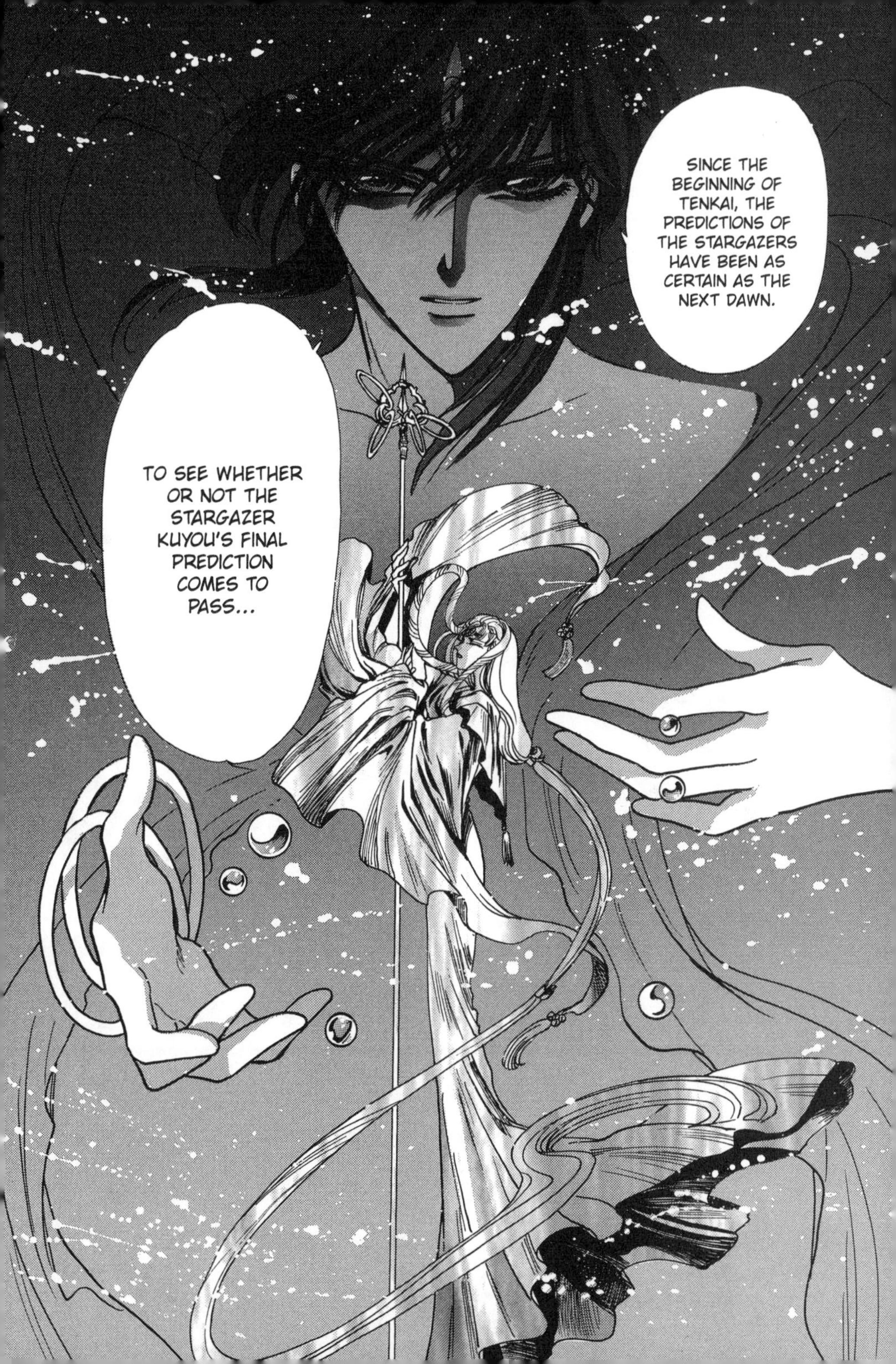
SINCE THE BEGINNING OF TENKAI, THE PREDICTIONS OF THE STARGAZERS HAVE BEEN AS CERTAIN AS THE NEXT DAWN.
TO SEE WHETHER OR NOT THE STARGAZER KUYOU'S FINAL PREDICTION COMES TO PASS...

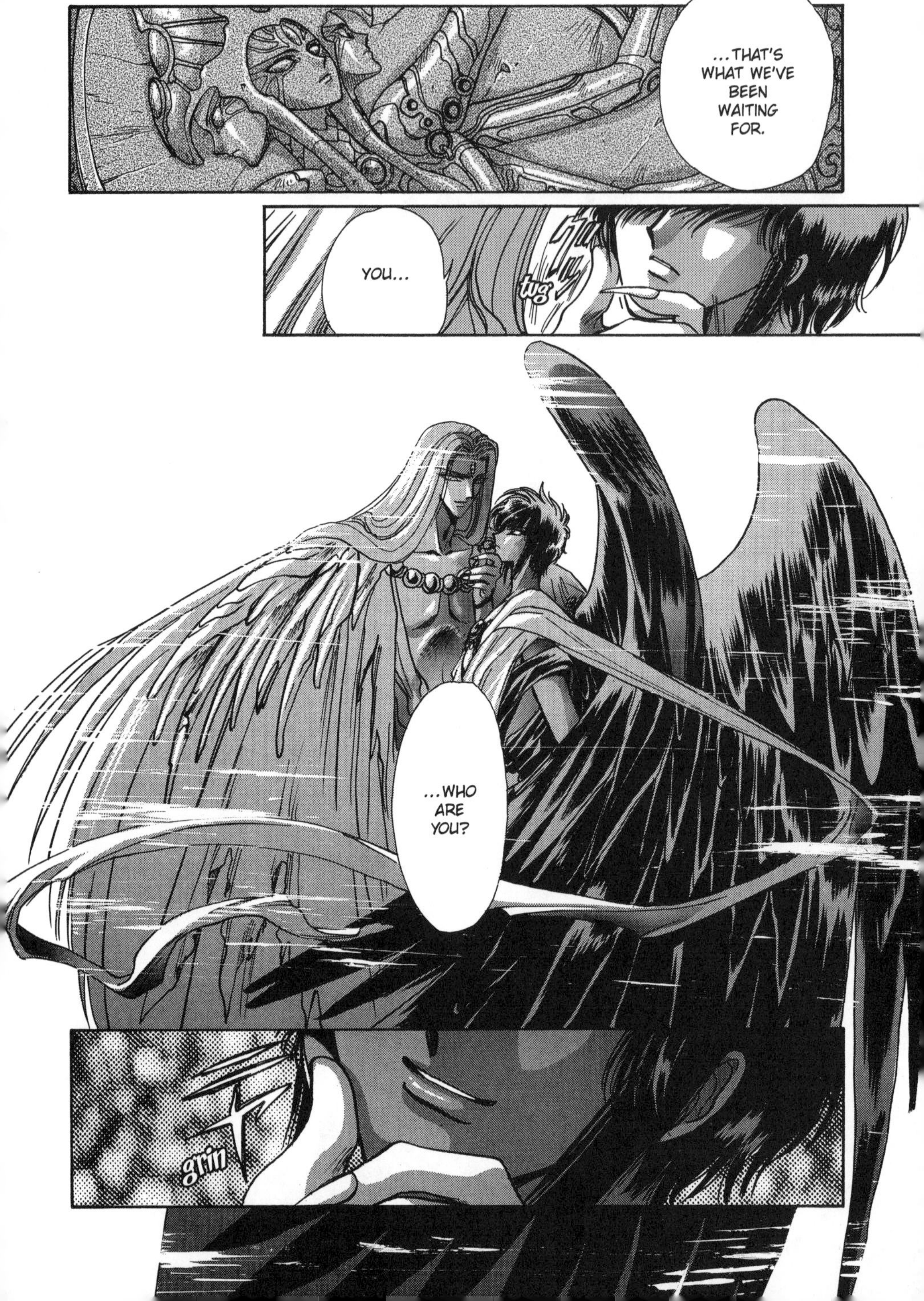
...THAT'S WHAT WE'VE BEEN WAITING FOR.
tug
YOU...
...WHO ARE YOU?
grin

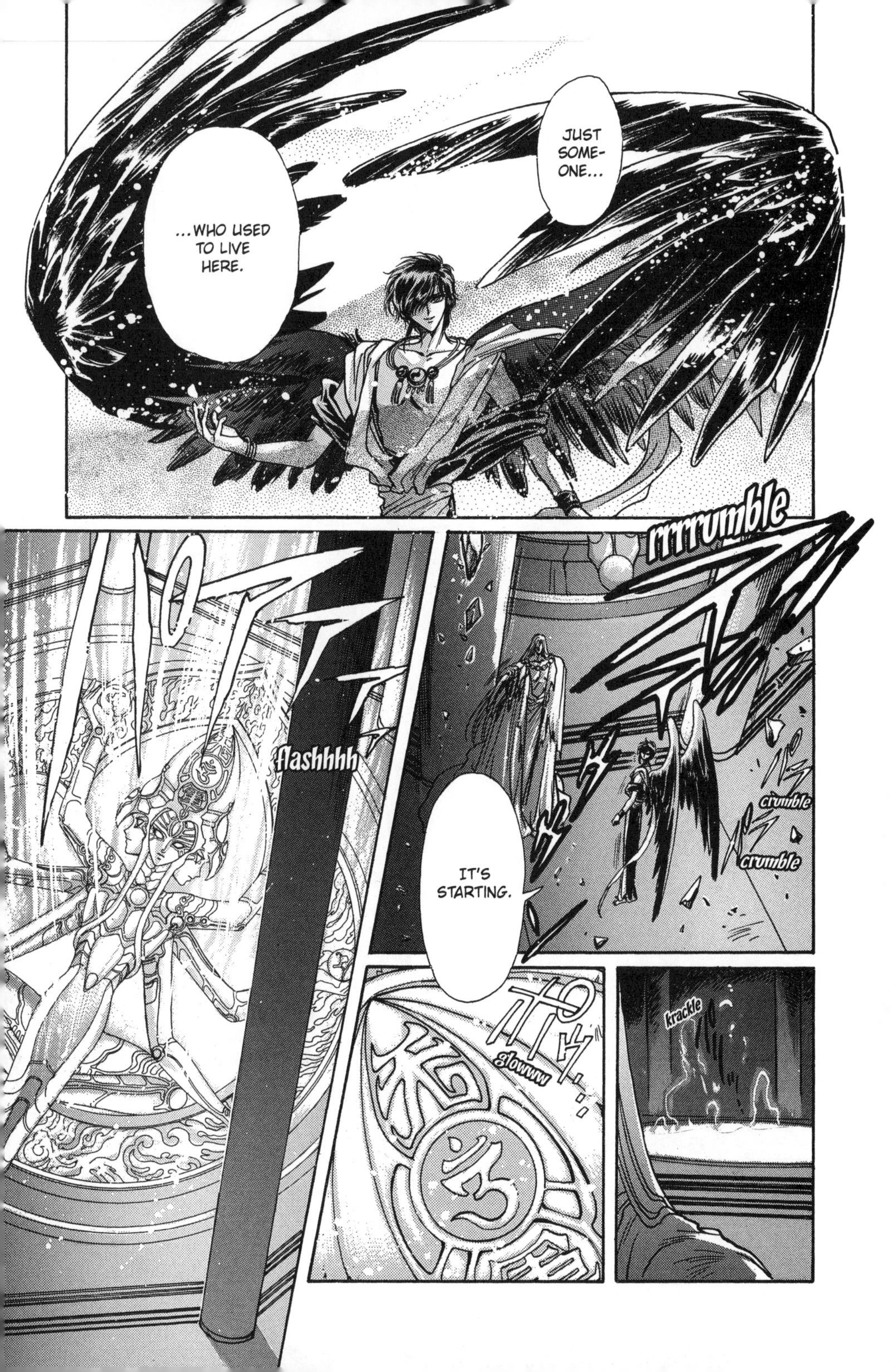
JUST SOME-ONE...
...WHO USED TO LIVE HERE.
rrrrumble
IT'S STARTING.
crumble
crumble
krackle
glowww
flashhhh

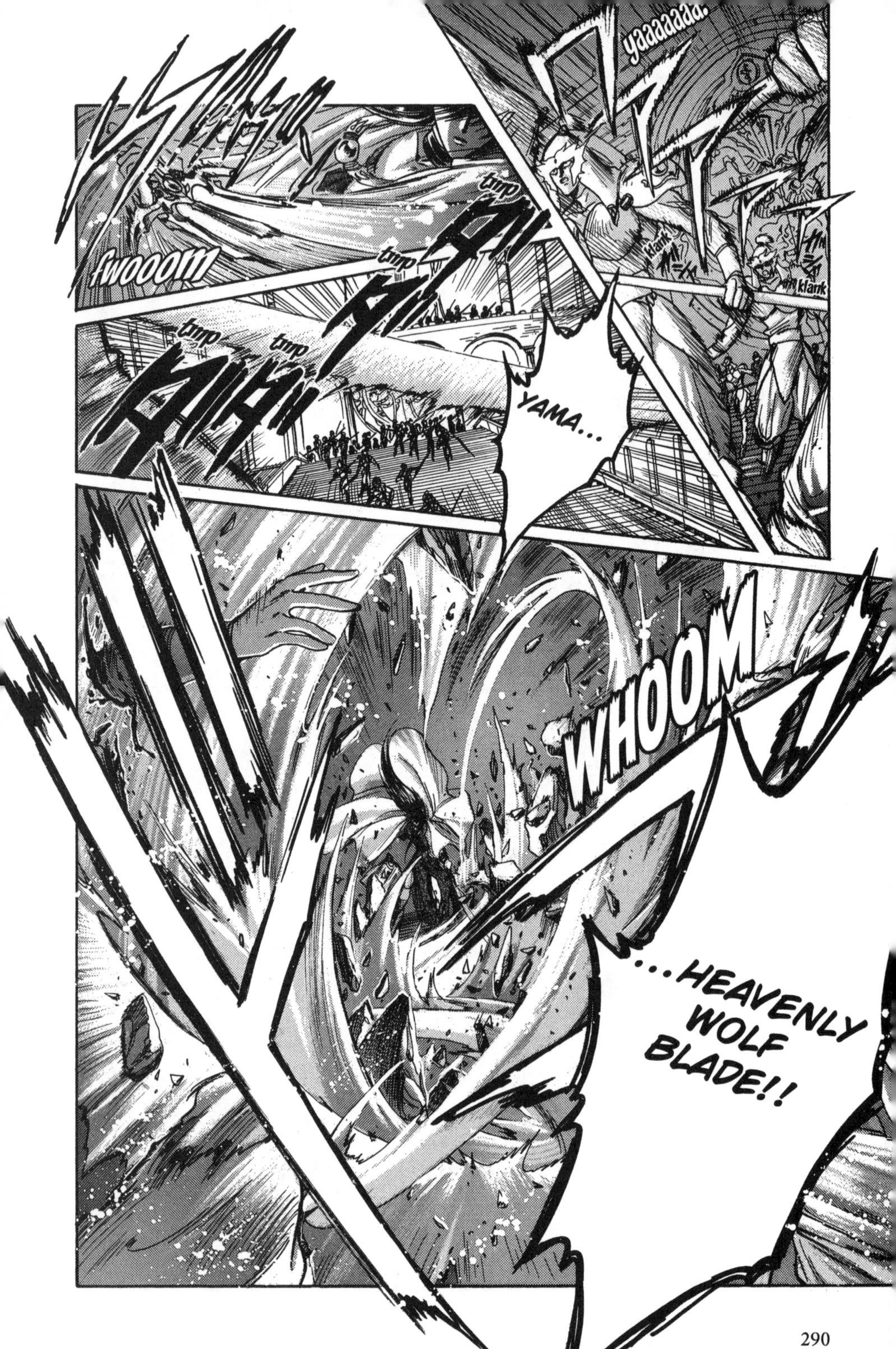
yaaaaaaa.
klank
klank
tmp
tmp
fwooom
tmp
tmp
YAMA...
WHOOM
...HEAVENLY WOLF BLADE!!

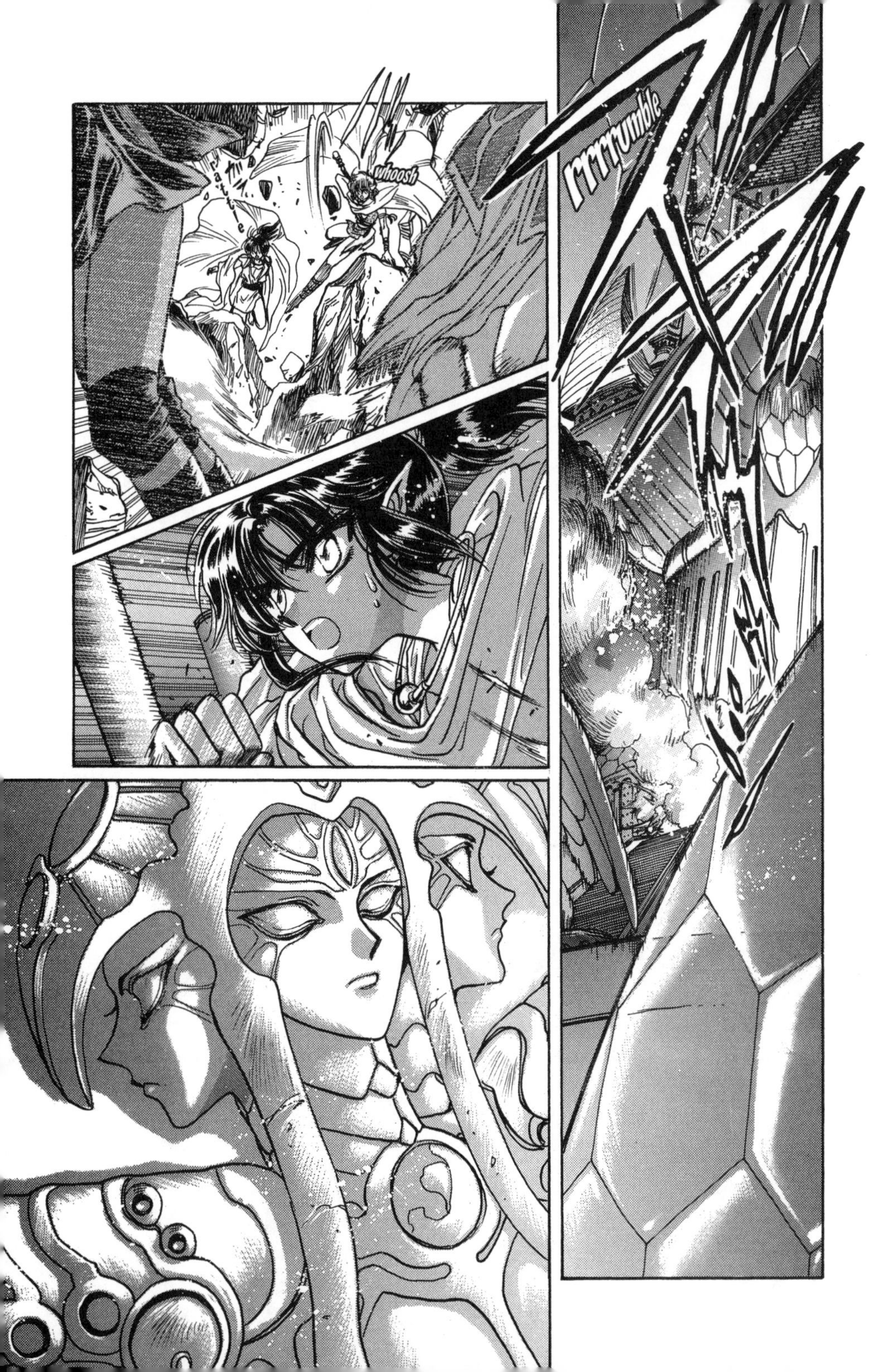
rrrrrumble
whoosh
rattle

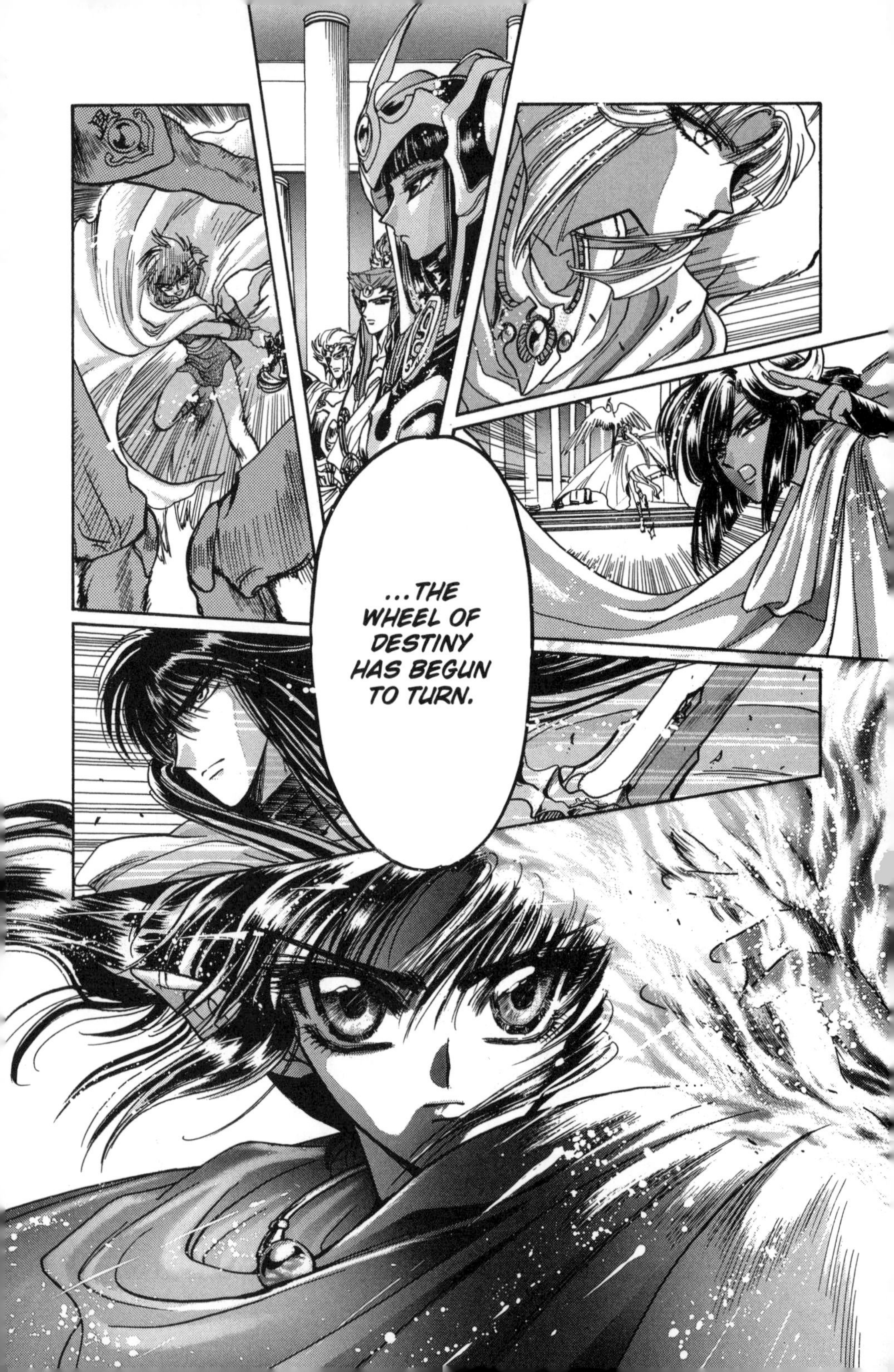
...THE WHEEL OF DESTINY HAS BEGUN TO TURN.

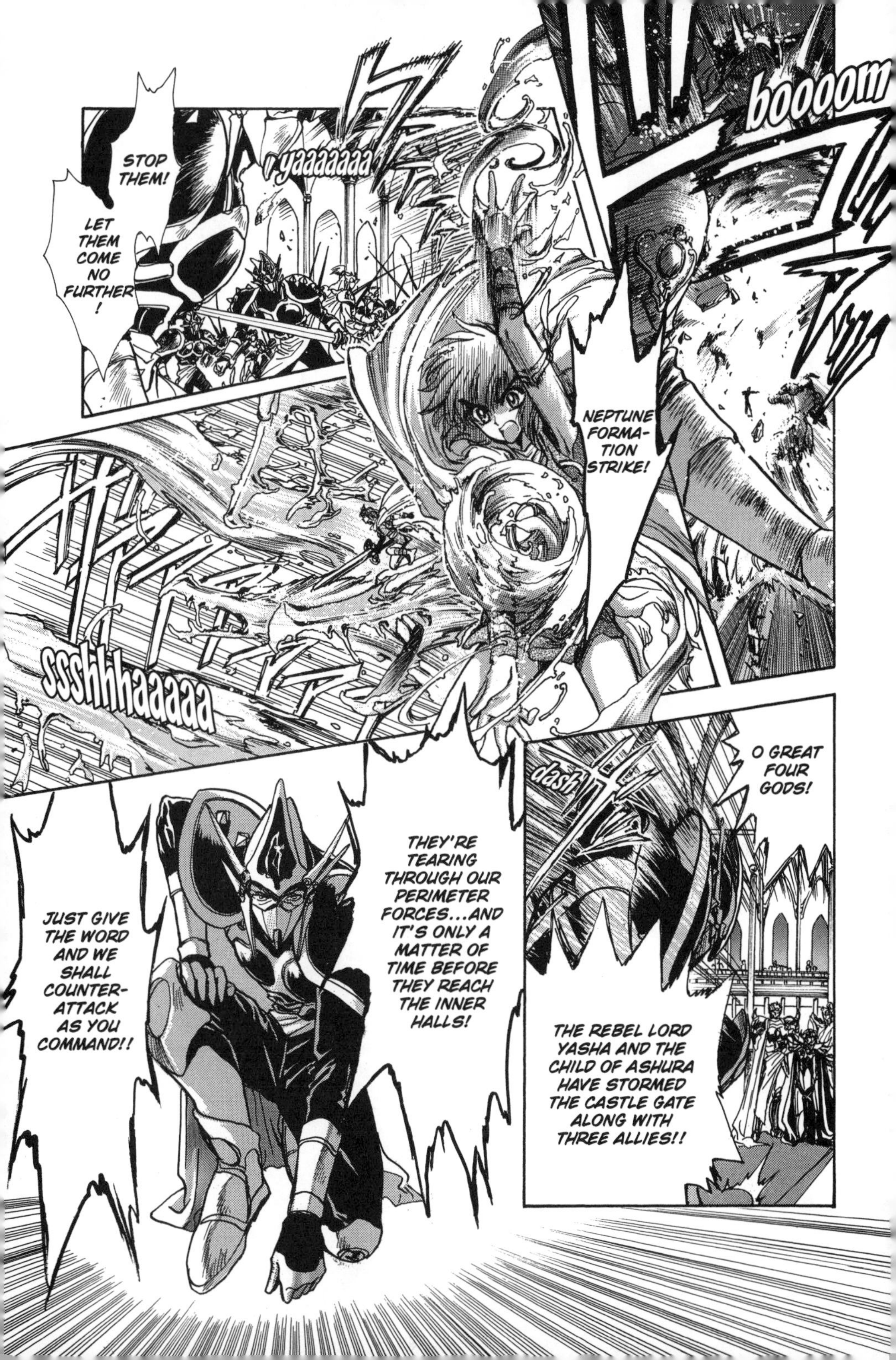
boooom
STOP THEM!
LET THEM COME NO FURTHER!
yaaaaaaa
NEPTUNE FORMATION STRIKE!
ssshhhaaaaa
dash
O GREAT FOUR GODS!
THE REBEL LORD YASHA AND THE CHILD OF ASHURA HAVE STORMED THE CASTLE GATE ALONG WITH THREE ALLIES!!
THEY'RE TEARING THROUGH OUR PERIMETER FORCES...AND IT'S ONLY A MATTER OF TIME BEFORE THEY REACH THE INNER HALLS!
JUST GIVE THE WORD AND WE SHALL COUNTER-ATTACK AS YOU COMMAND!!

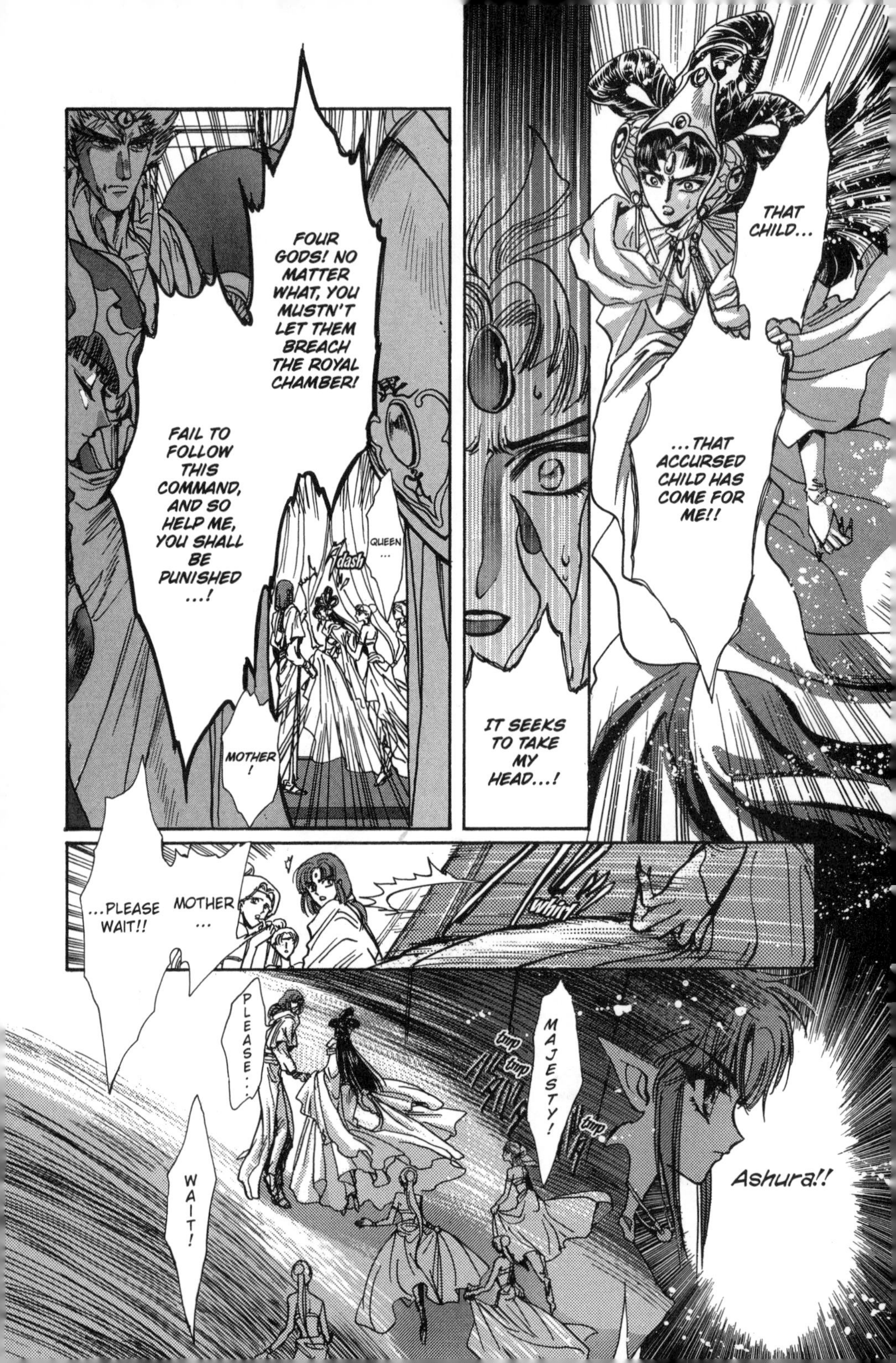
THAT CHILD...
...THAT ACCURSED CHILD HAS COME FOR ME!!
IT SEEKS TO TAKE MY HEAD...!
FOUR GODS! NO MATTER WHAT, YOU MUSTN'T LET THEM BREACH THE ROYAL CHAMBER!
QUEEN ...
dash
FAIL TO FOLLOW THIS COMMAND, AND SO HELP ME, YOU SHALL BE PUNISHED ...!
MOTHER !
whirl
MOTHER ...
...PLEASE WAIT!!
Ashura!!
MAJESTY!
tmp tmp tmp
PLEASE...
WAIT!

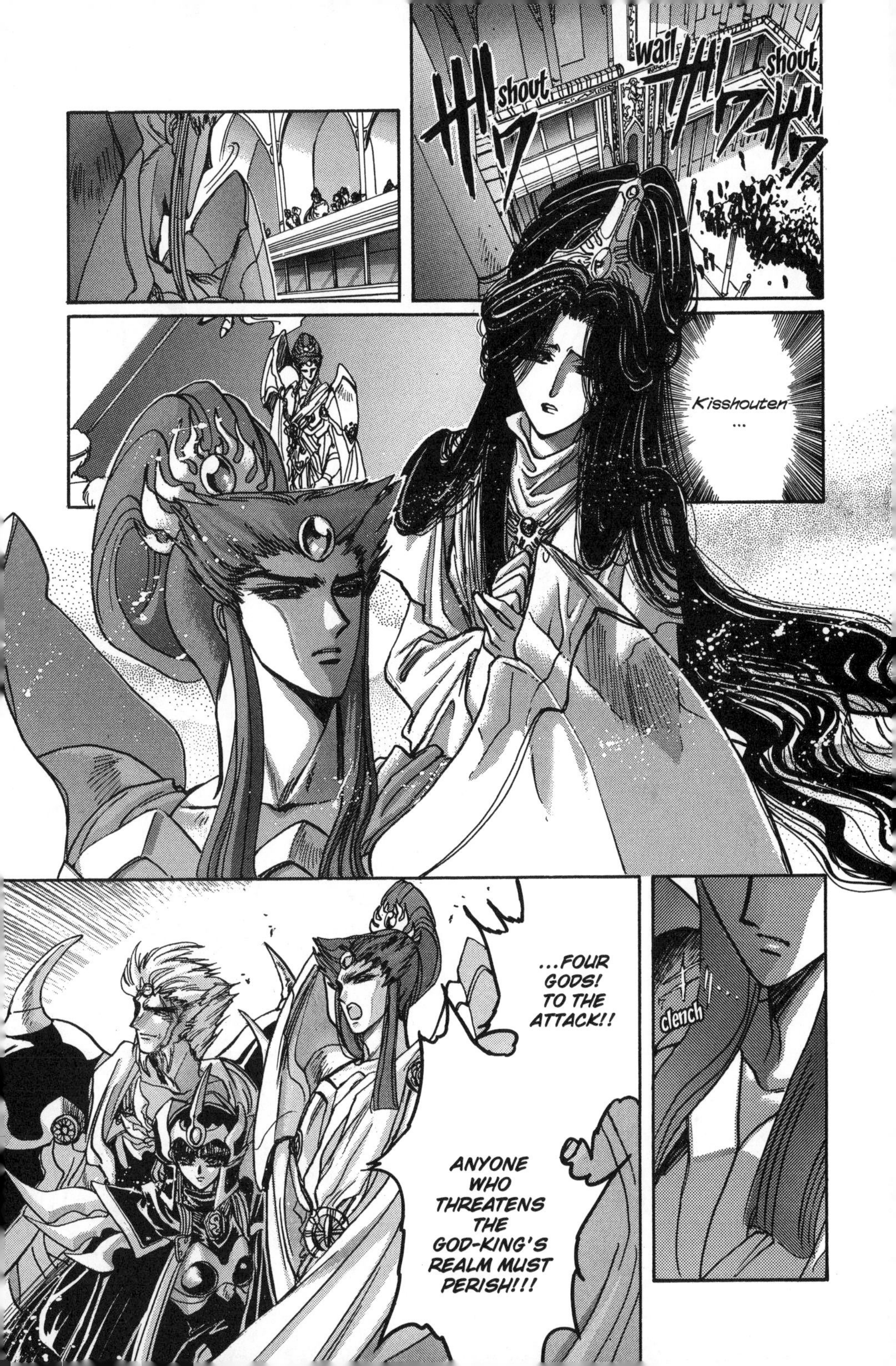
shout
wail
shout
Kisshouten
...
clench
...FOUR GODS! TO THE ATTACK!!
ANYONE WHO THREATENS THE GOD-KING'S REALM MUST PERISH!!!

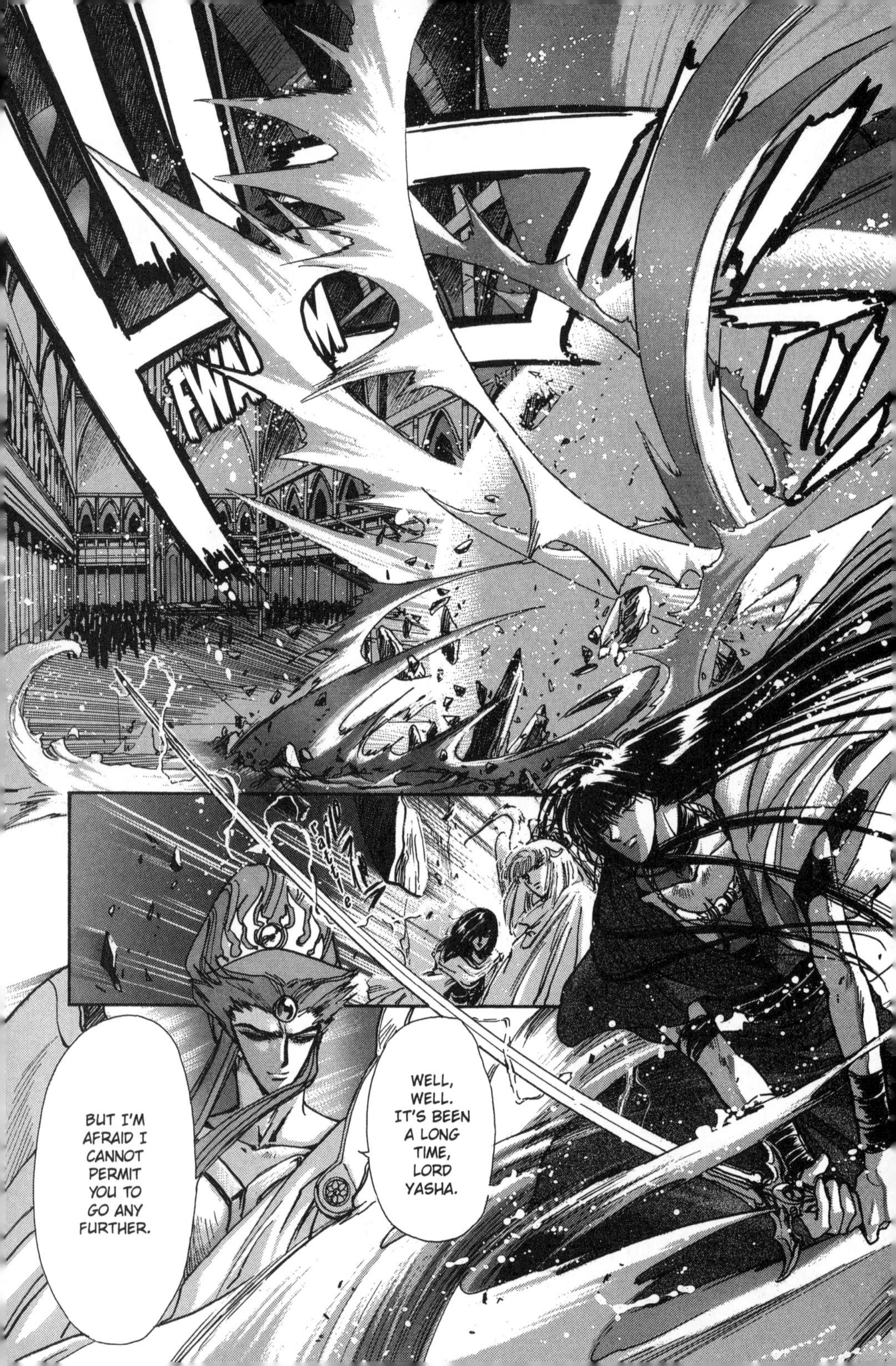
FWAM
rattle
WELL, WELL. IT'S BEEN A LONG TIME, LORD YASHA.
BUT I'M AFRAID I CANNOT PERMIT YOU TO GO ANY FURTHER.

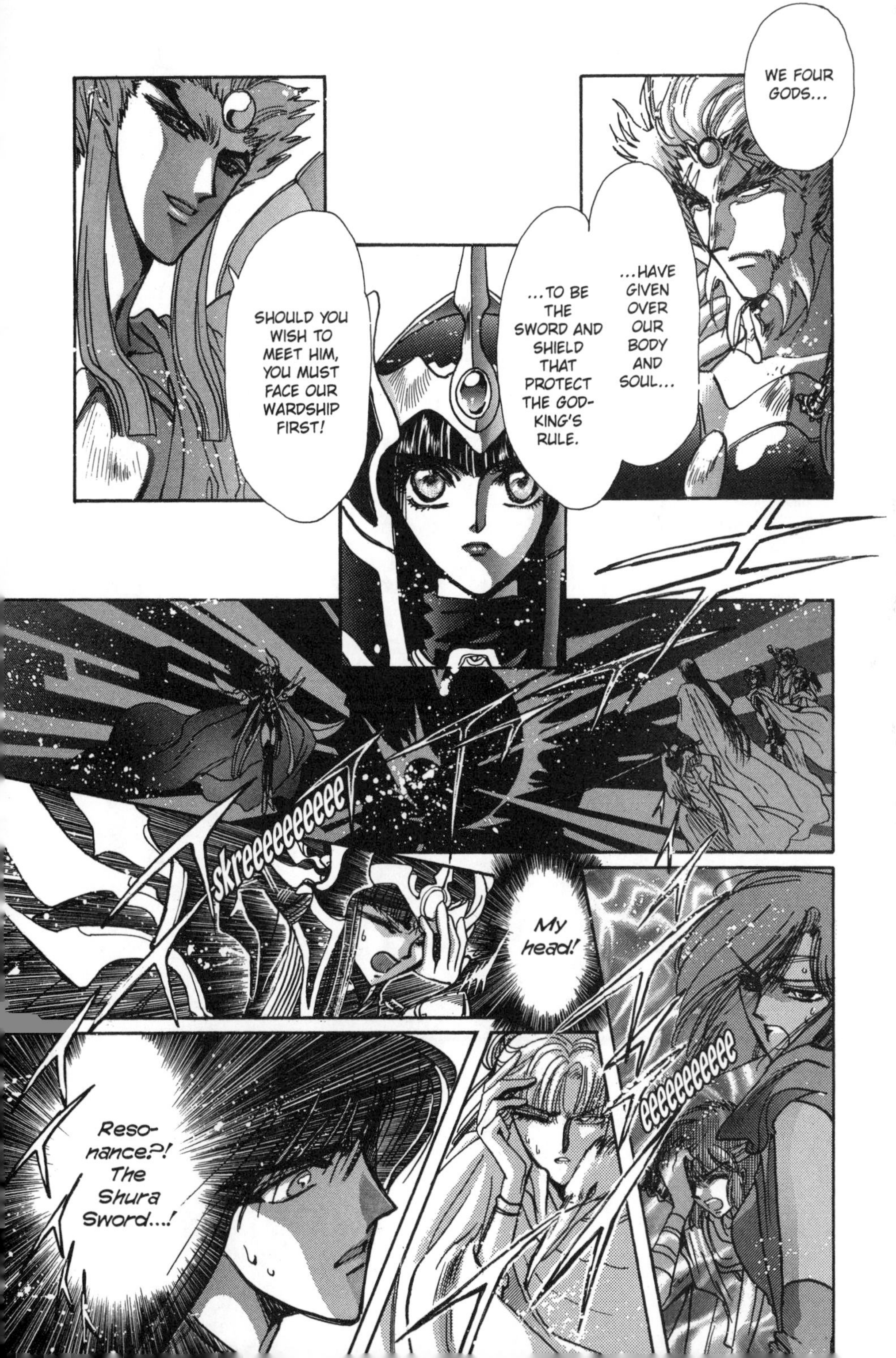
WE FOUR GODS...
...HAVE GIVEN OVER OUR BODY AND SOUL...
...TO BE THE SWORD AND SHIELD THAT PROTECT THE GOD-KING'S RULE.
SHOULD YOU WISH TO MEET HIM, YOU MUST FACE OUR WARDSHIP FIRST!
skreeeeeeeeeeeee
My head!
eeeeeeeeeeee
Reso-nance?! The Shura Sword...!

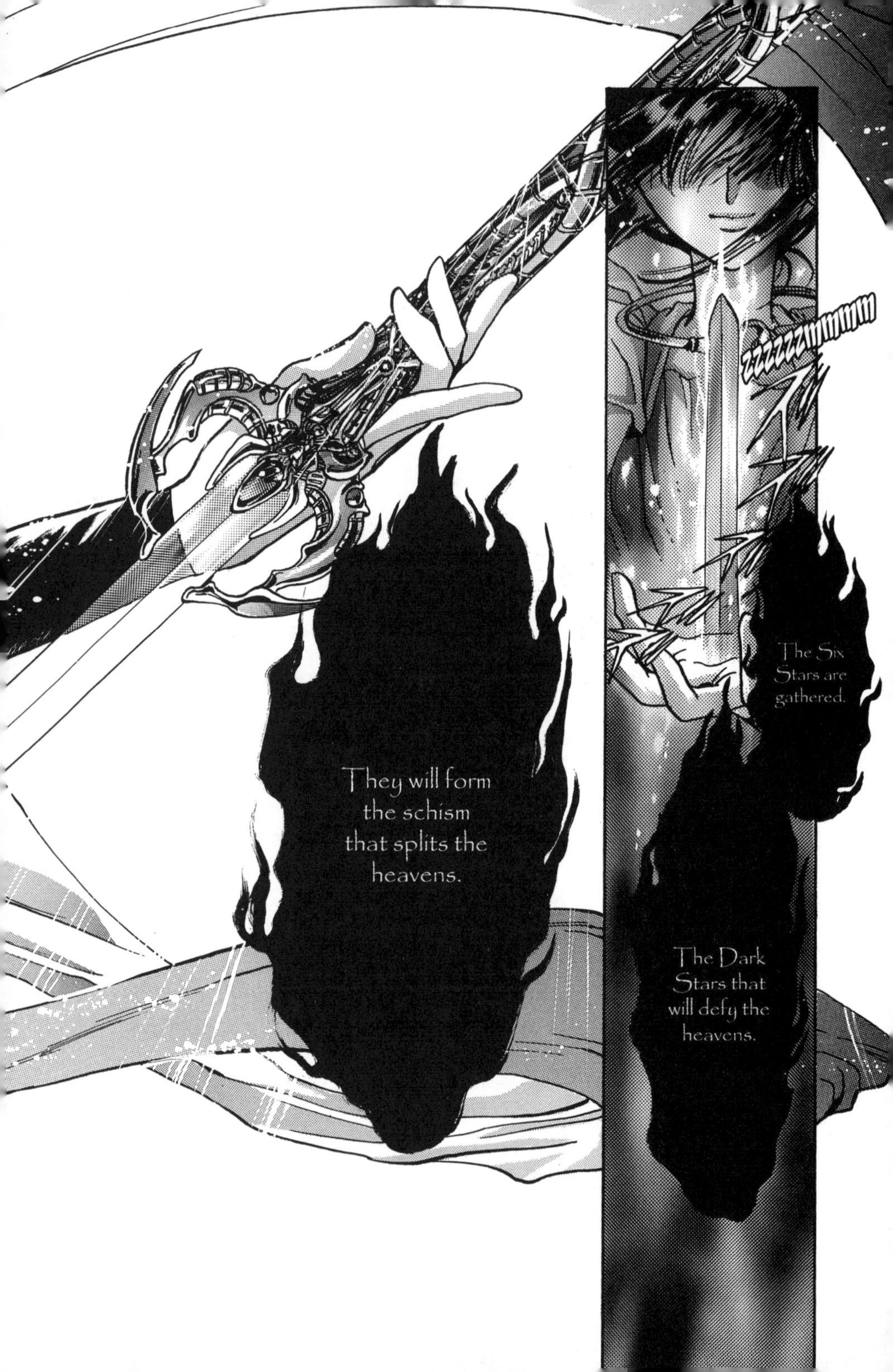
zzzzzzmmmmm
The Six Stars are gathered.
The Dark Stars that will defy the heavens.
They will form the schism that splits the heavens.

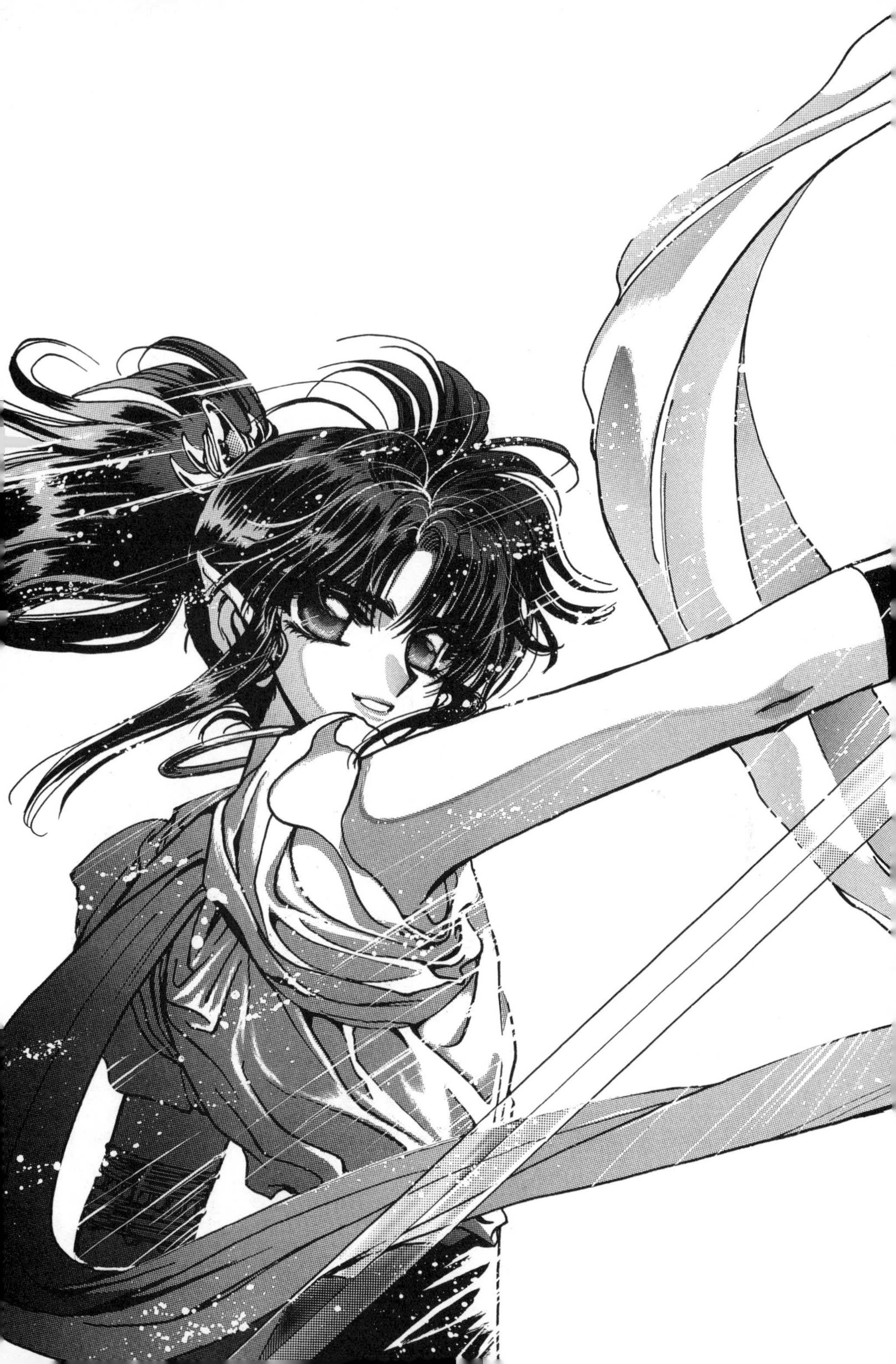

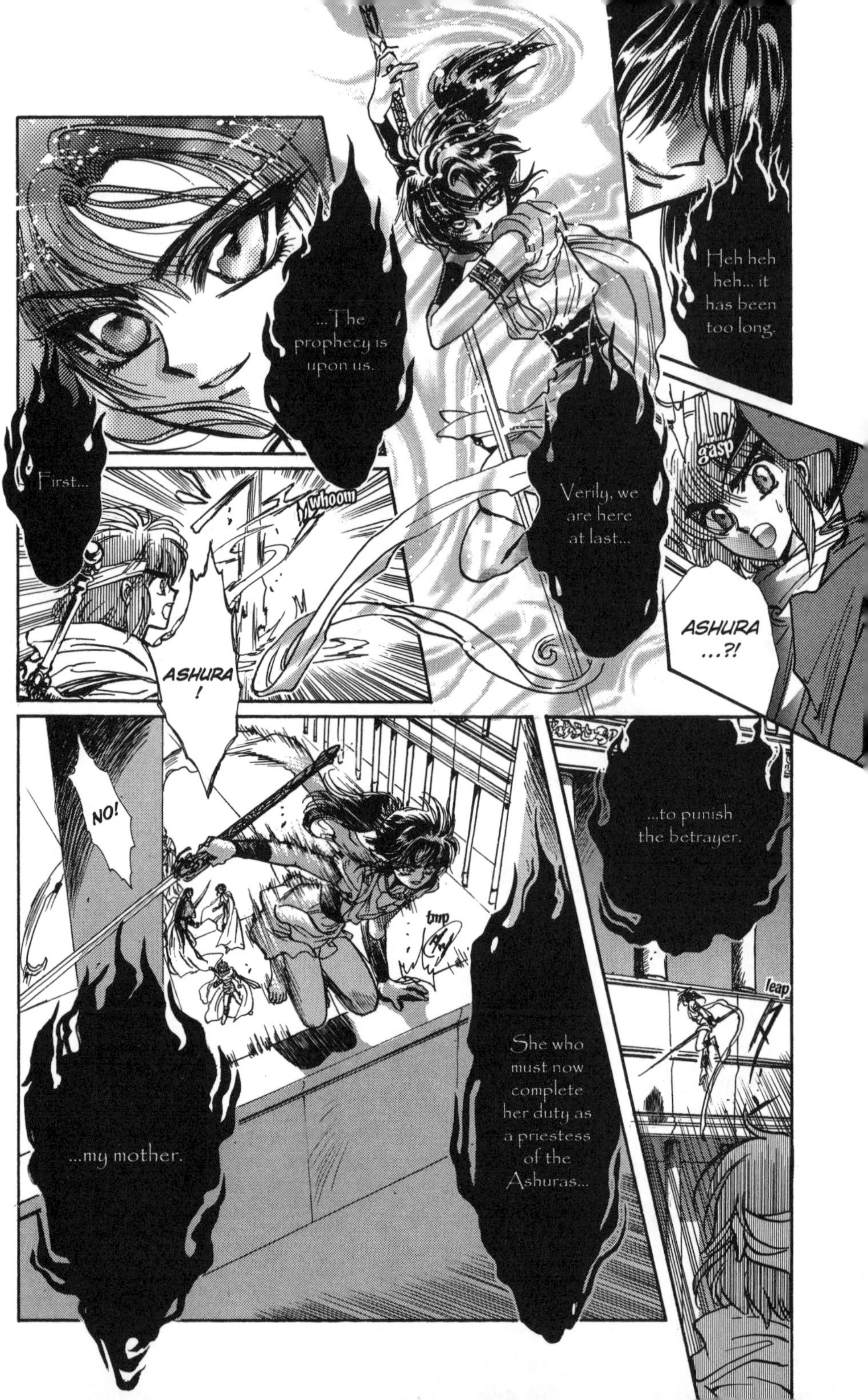

Heh heh heh... it has been too long.
Verily, we are here at last...
...The prophecy is upon us.
gasp
ASHURA ...?!
First...
whoom
ASHURA!
...to punish the betrayer.
leap
She who must now complete her duty as a priestess of the Ashuras...
tmp
NO!
...my mother.

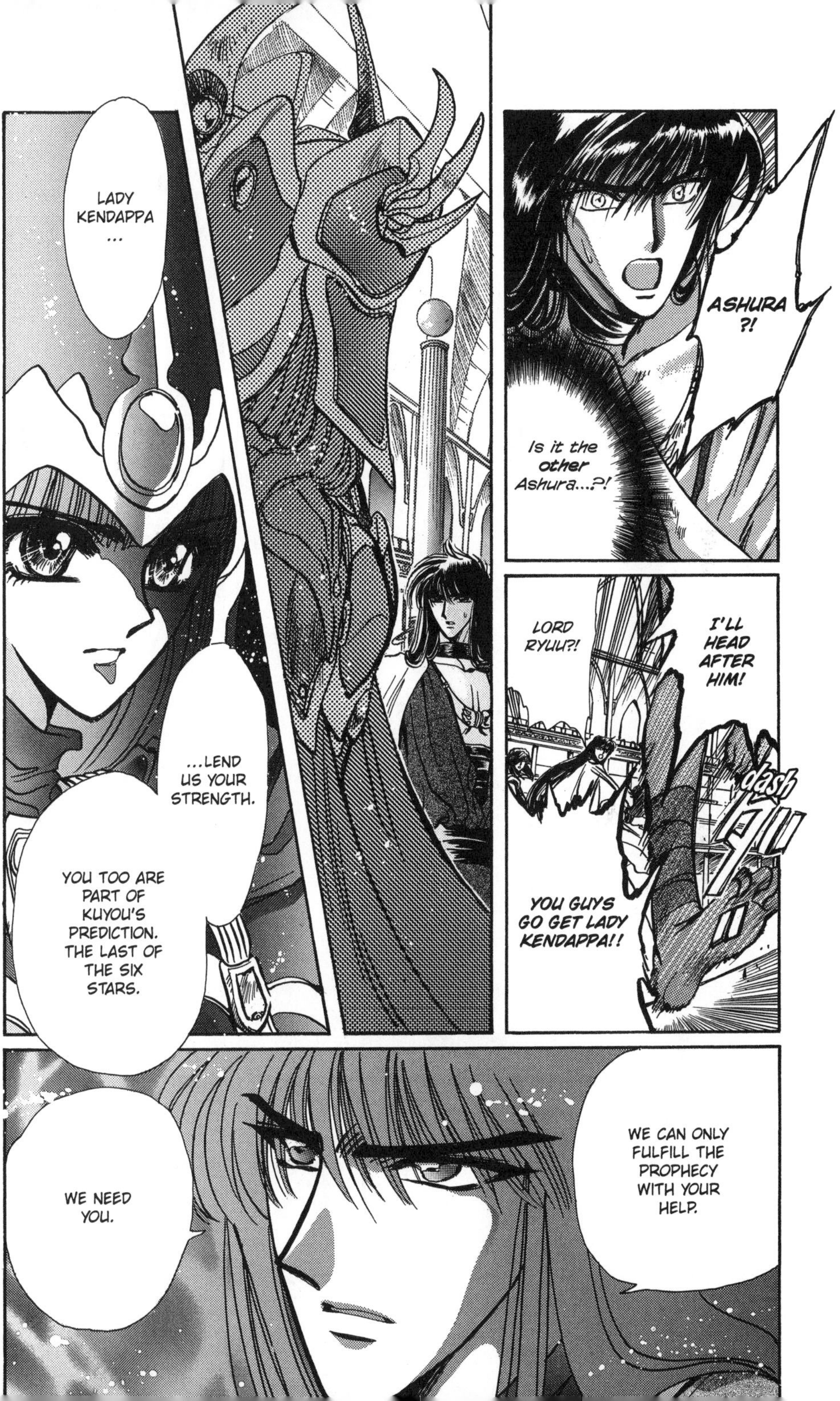
ASHURA ?!
Is it the other Ashura...?!
I'LL HEAD AFTER HIM!
LORD RYUU?!
dash
YOU GUYS GO GET LADY KENDAPPA!!
LADY KENDAPPA ...
...LEND US YOUR STRENGTH.
YOU TOO ARE PART OF KUYOU'S PREDICTION. THE LAST OF THE SIX STARS.
WE CAN ONLY FULFILL THE PROPHECY WITH YOUR HELP.
WE NEED YOU.

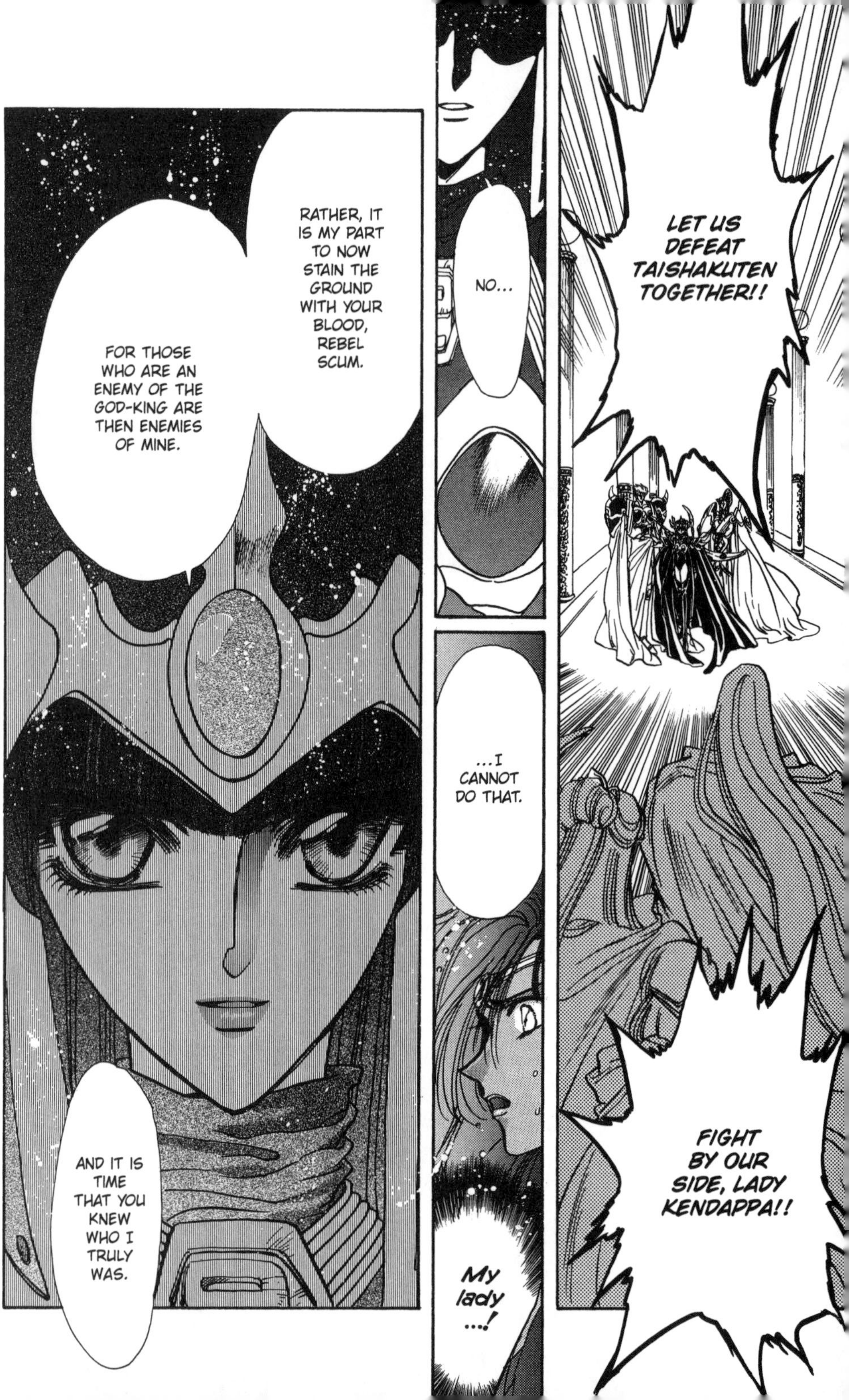
LET US DEFEAT TAISHAKUTEN TOGETHER!!
FIGHT BY OUR SIDE, LADY KENDAPPA!!
NO...
...I CANNOT DO THAT.
My lady...!
RATHER, IT IS MY PART TO NOW STAIN THE GROUND WITH YOUR BLOOD, REBEL SCUM.
FOR THOSE WHO ARE AN ENEMY OF THE GOD-KING ARE THEN ENEMIES OF MINE.
AND IT IS TIME THAT YOU KNEW WHO I TRULY WAS.

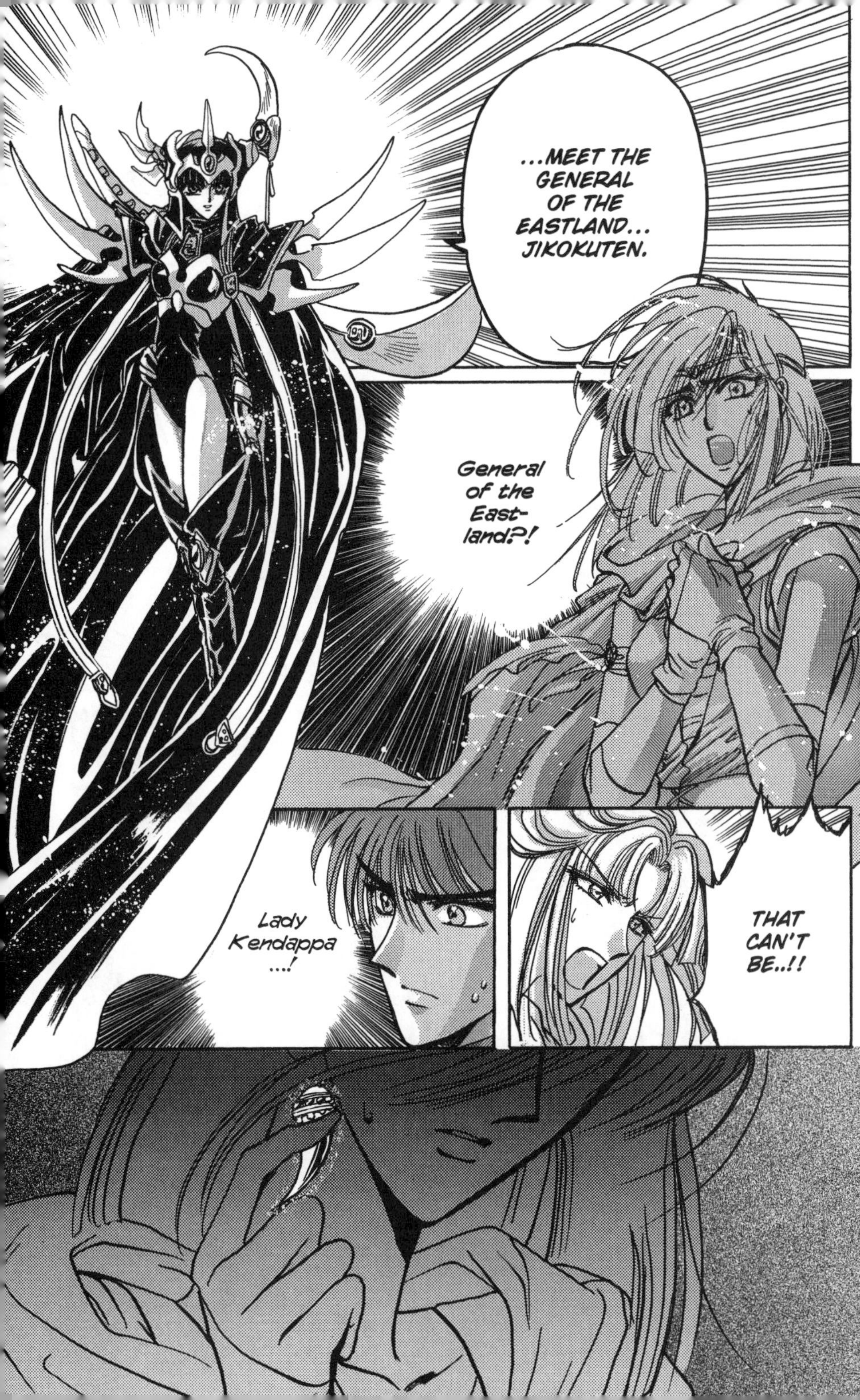
...MEET THE GENERAL OF THE EASTLAND... JIKOKUTEN.
General of the East-land?!
THAT CAN'T BE..!!
Lady Kendappa ...!

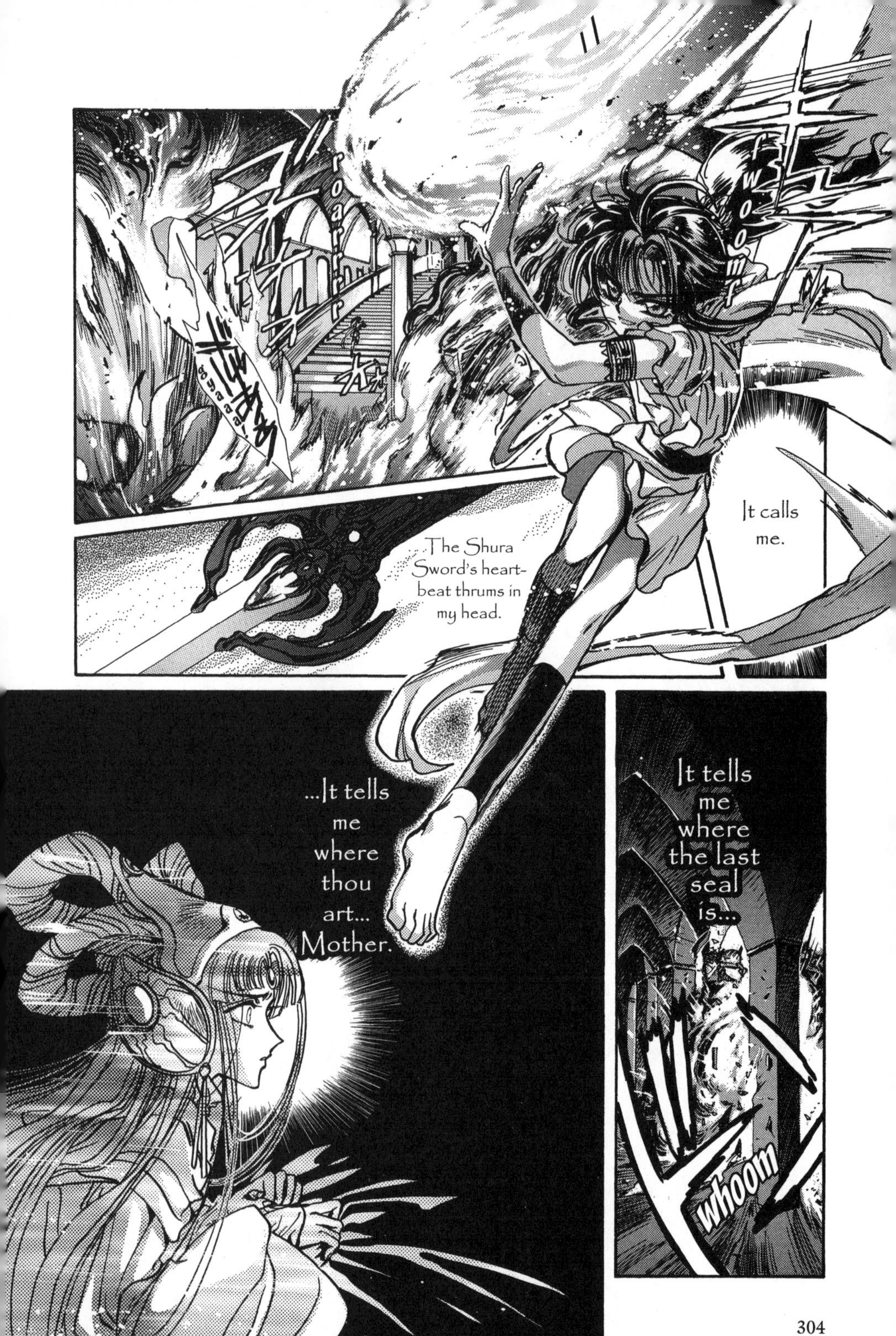
fwoomf
roarrrrr
ギャああ
gyaaa!
It calls me.
The Shura Sword's heartbeat thrums in my head.
It tells me where the last seal is...
whoom
...It tells me where thou art... Mother.

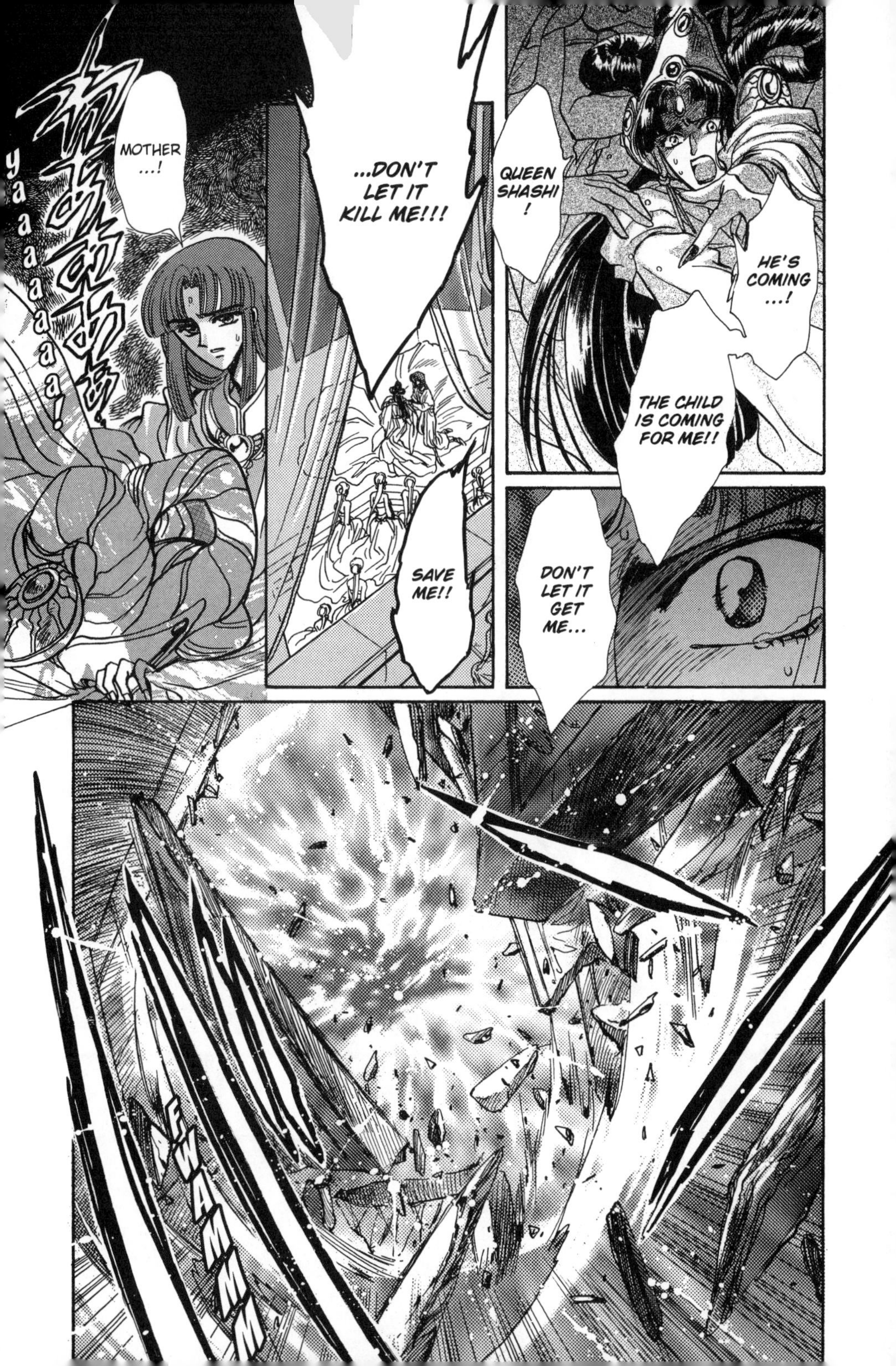
QUEEN SHASHI!
HE'S COMING...!
THE CHILD IS COMING FOR ME!!
DON'T LET IT GET ME...
...DON'T LET IT KILL ME!!!
SAVE ME!!
MOTHER...!
yaaaaaaaaa!
FWAMMM

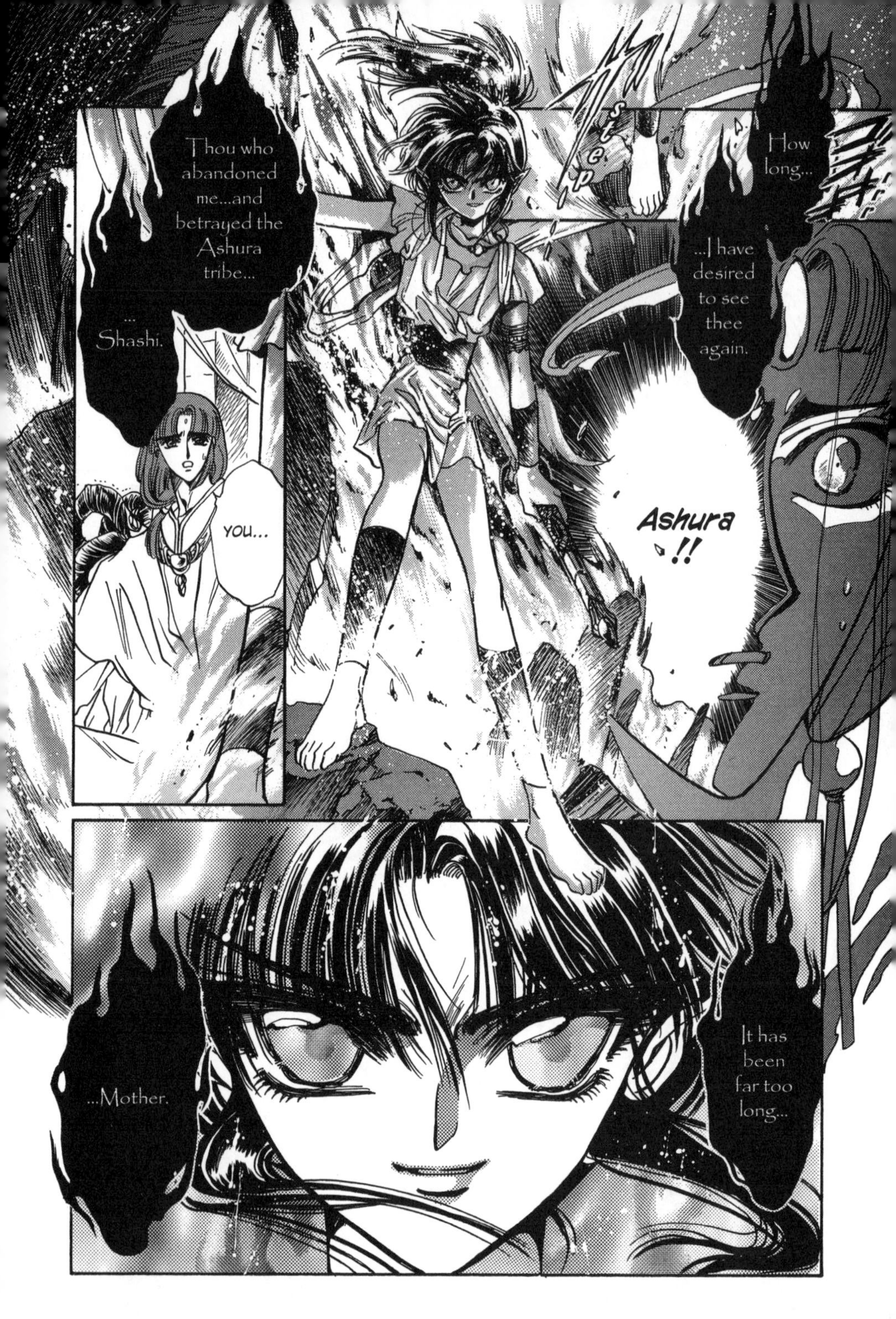
How long...
...I have desired to see thee again.
Ashura!!
step
Thou who abandoned me...and betrayed the Ashura tribe...
...Shashi.
You...
It has been far too long...
...Mother.

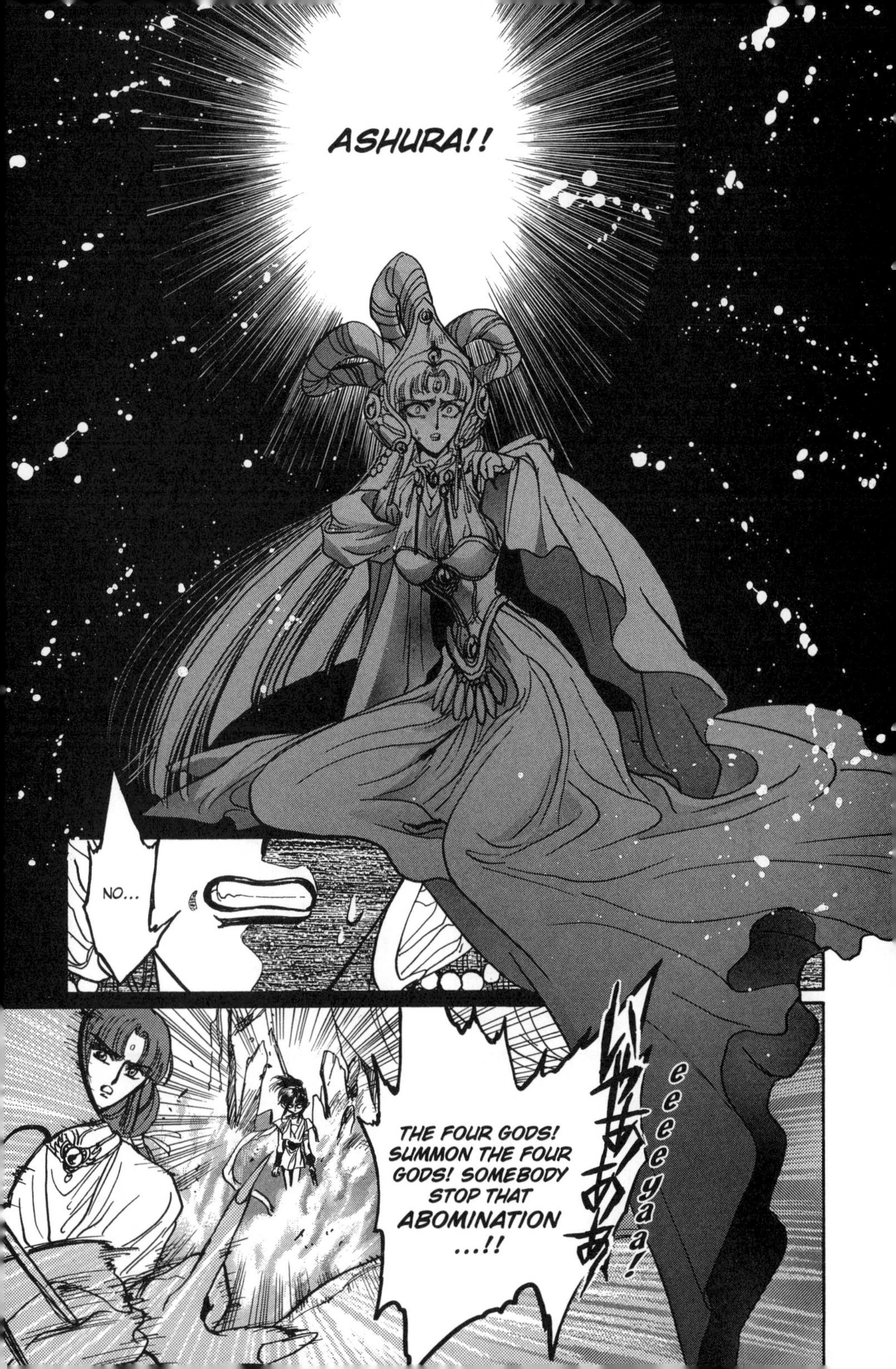
ASHURA!!
NO...
eeeeyaaa!
THE FOUR GODS! SUMMON THE FOUR GODS! SOMEBODY STOP THAT ABOMINATION ...!!

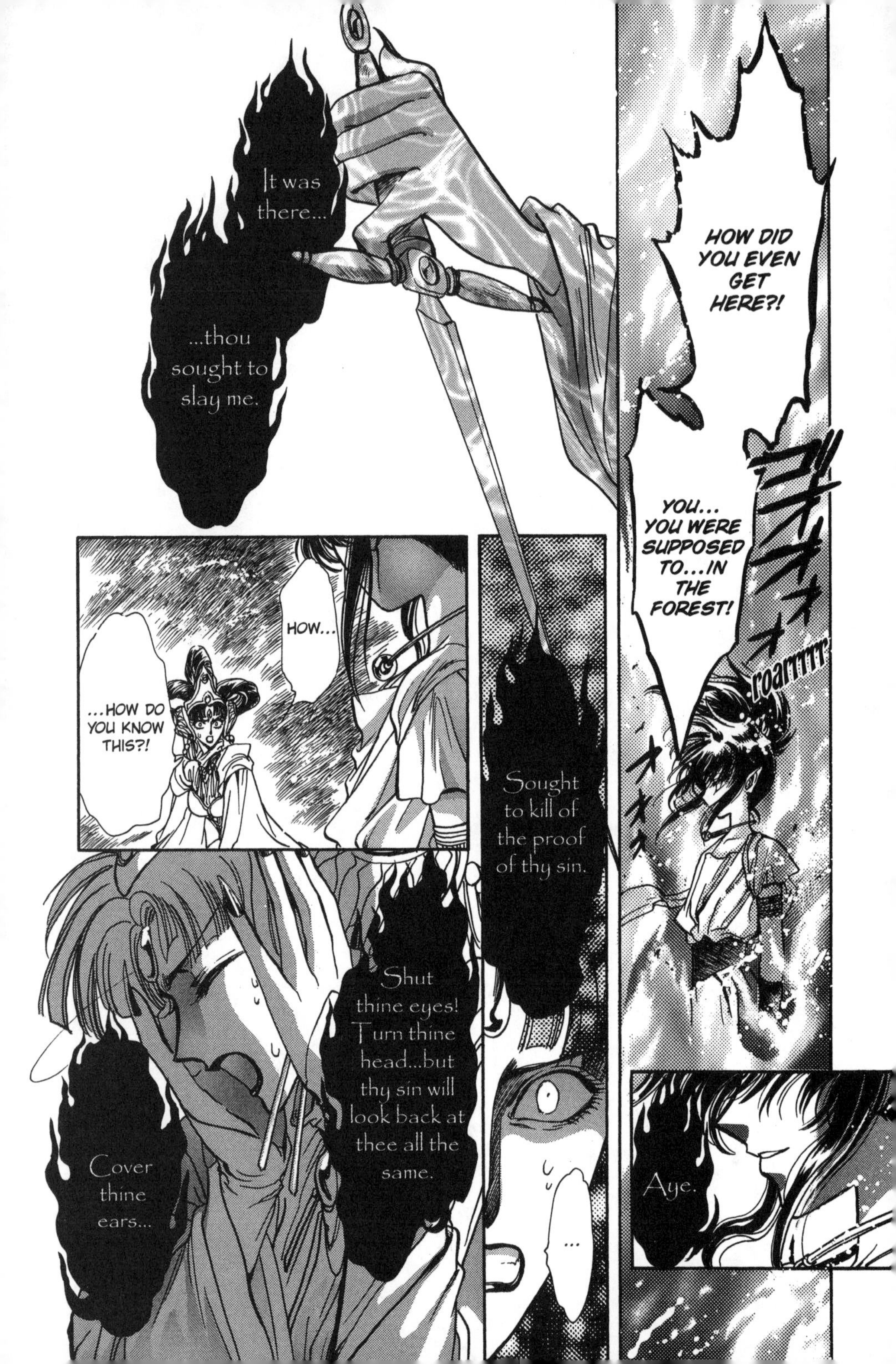
HOW DID YOU EVEN GET HERE?!
YOU... YOU WERE SUPPOSED TO...IN THE FOREST!
roarrrr
It was there...
...thou sought to slay me.
Sought to kill of the proof of thy sin.
HOW...
...HOW DO YOU KNOW THIS?!
Aye.
...
Shut thine eyes! Turn thine head...but thy sin will look back at thee all the same.
Cover thine ears...

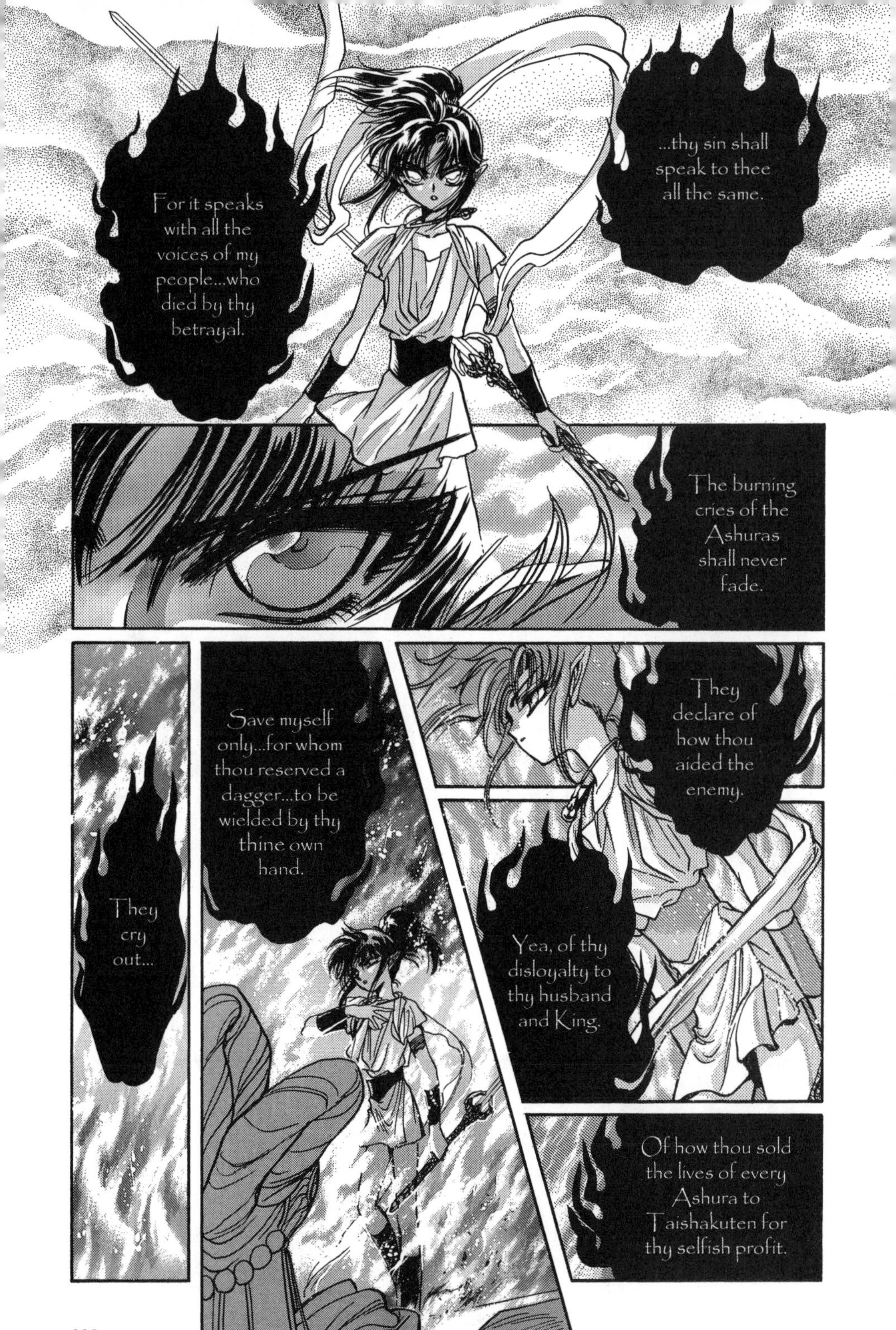
...thy sin shall speak to thee all the same.
For it speaks with all the voices of my people...who died by thy betrayal.
The burning cries of the Ashuras shall never fade.
They declare of how thou aided the enemy.
Yea, of thy disloyalty to thy husband and King.
Of how thou sold the lives of every Ashura to Taishakuten for thy selfish profit.
Save myself only...for whom thou reserved a dagger...to be wielded by thy thine own hand.
They cry out...

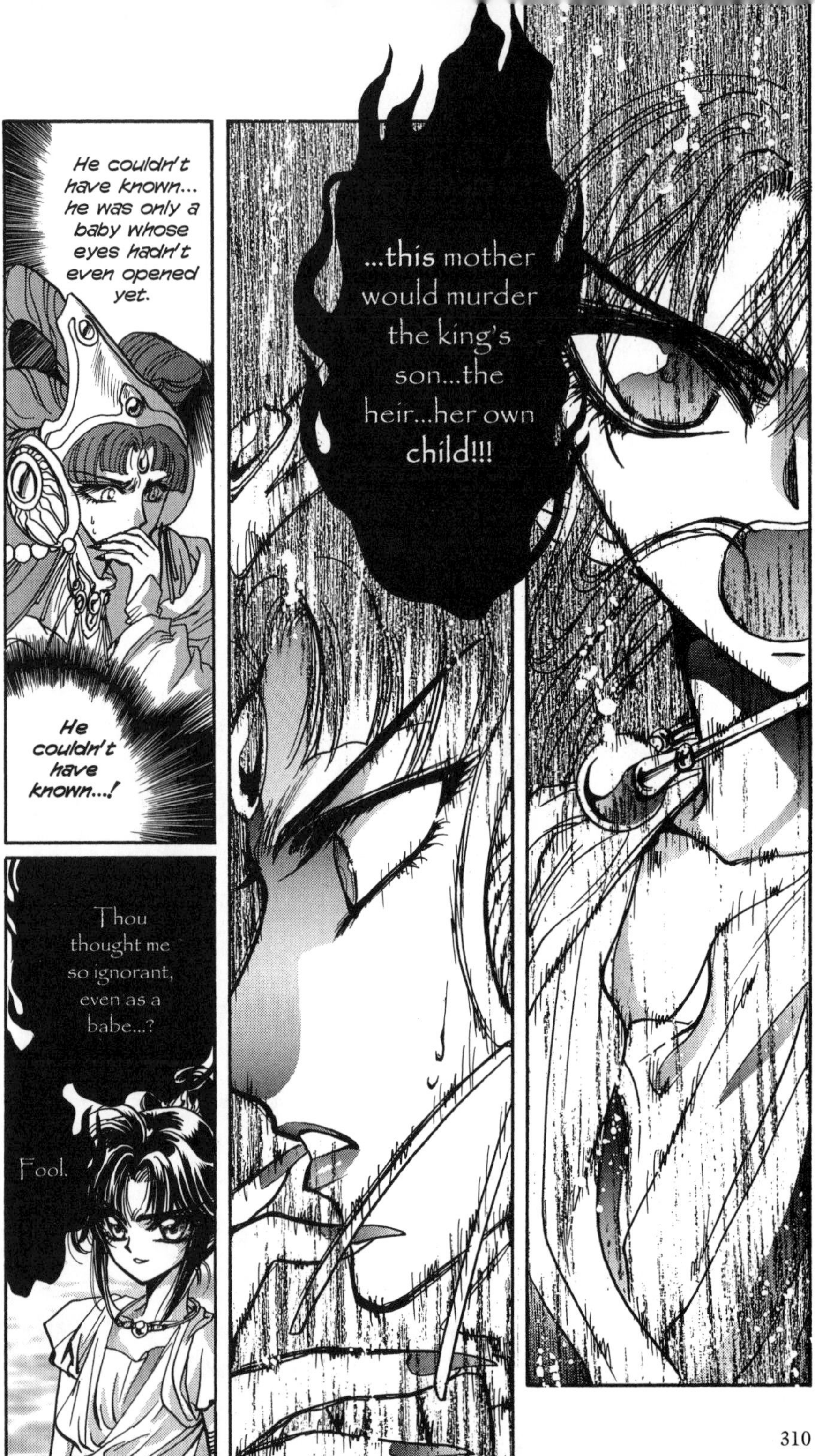
...this mother would murder the king's son...the heir...her own child!!!
He couldn't have known... he was only a baby whose eyes hadn't even opened yet.
He couldn't have known...!
Thou thought me so ignorant, even as a babe...?
Fool.

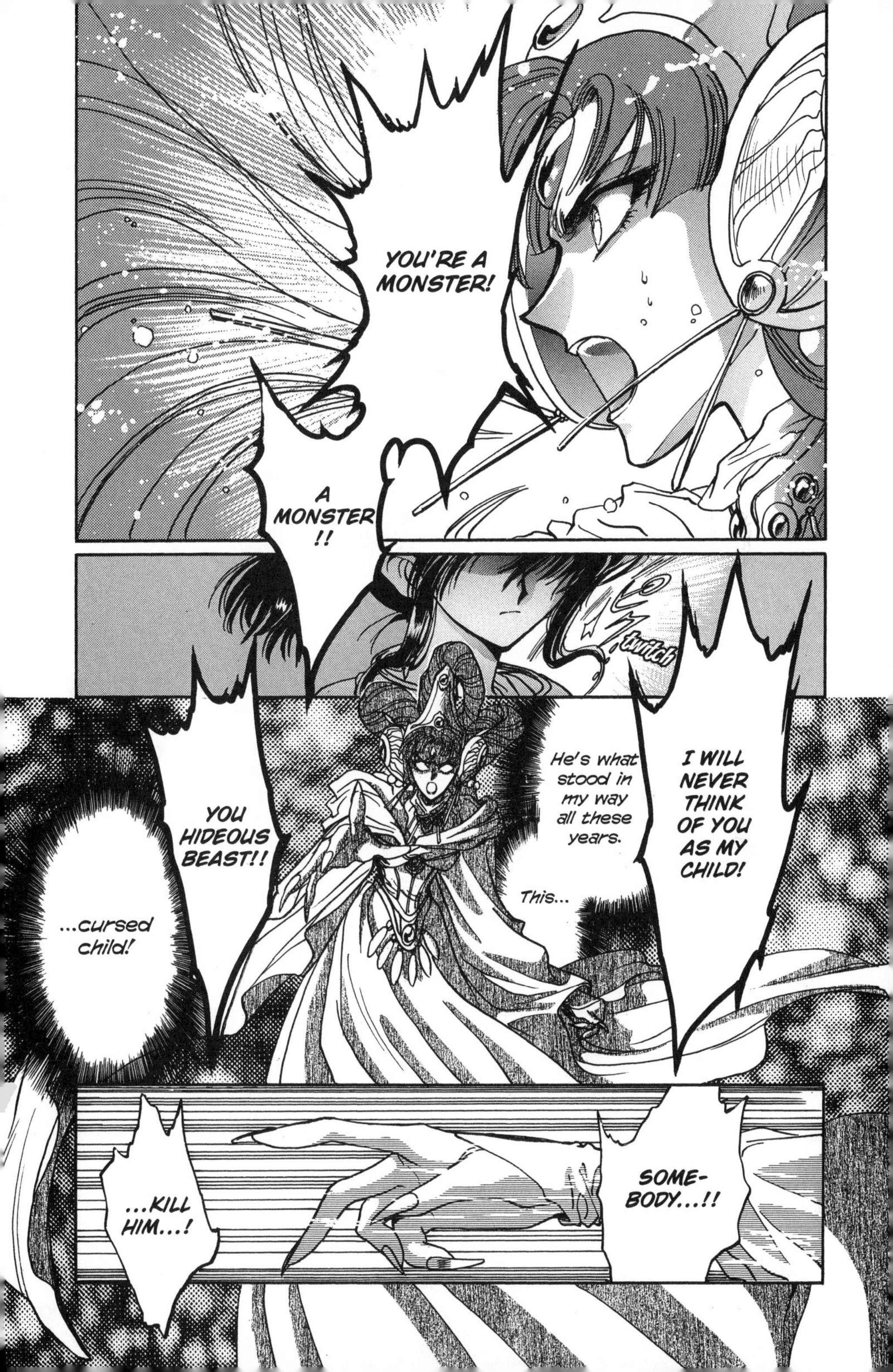
YOU'RE A MONSTER!
A MONSTER !!
twitch
I WILL NEVER THINK OF YOU AS MY CHILD!
He's what stood in my way all these years.
This...
YOU HIDEOUS BEAST!!
...cursed child!
SOME-BODY...!!
...KILL HIM...!

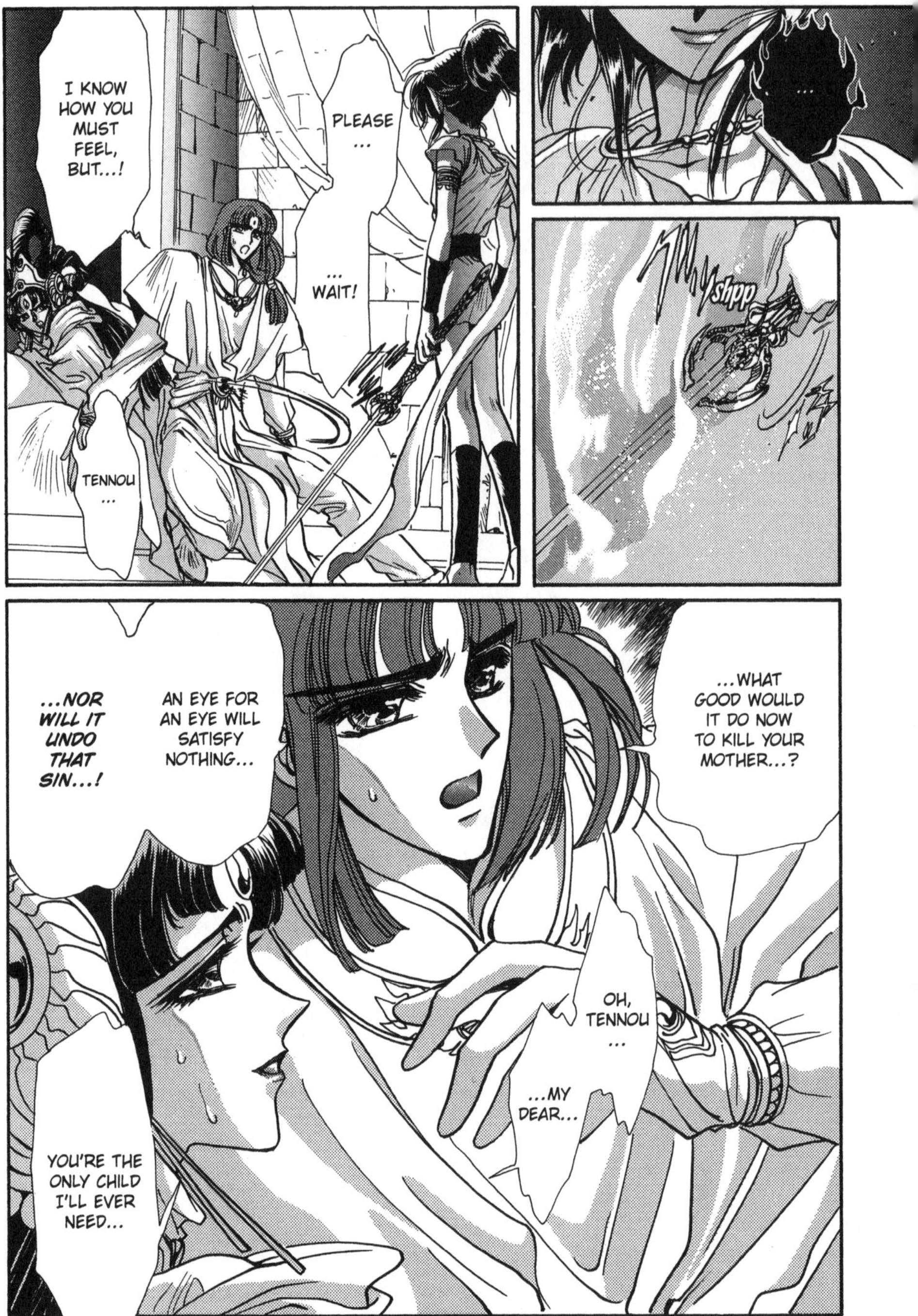
...
SHPP
PLEASE ...
... WAIT!
I KNOW HOW YOU MUST FEEL, BUT...!
TENNOU ...
...WHAT GOOD WOULD IT DO NOW TO KILL YOUR MOTHER...?
AN EYE FOR AN EYE WILL SATISFY NOTHING...
...NOR WILL IT UNDO THAT SIN...!
OH, TENNOU ...
...MY DEAR...
YOU'RE THE ONLY CHILD I'LL EVER NEED...

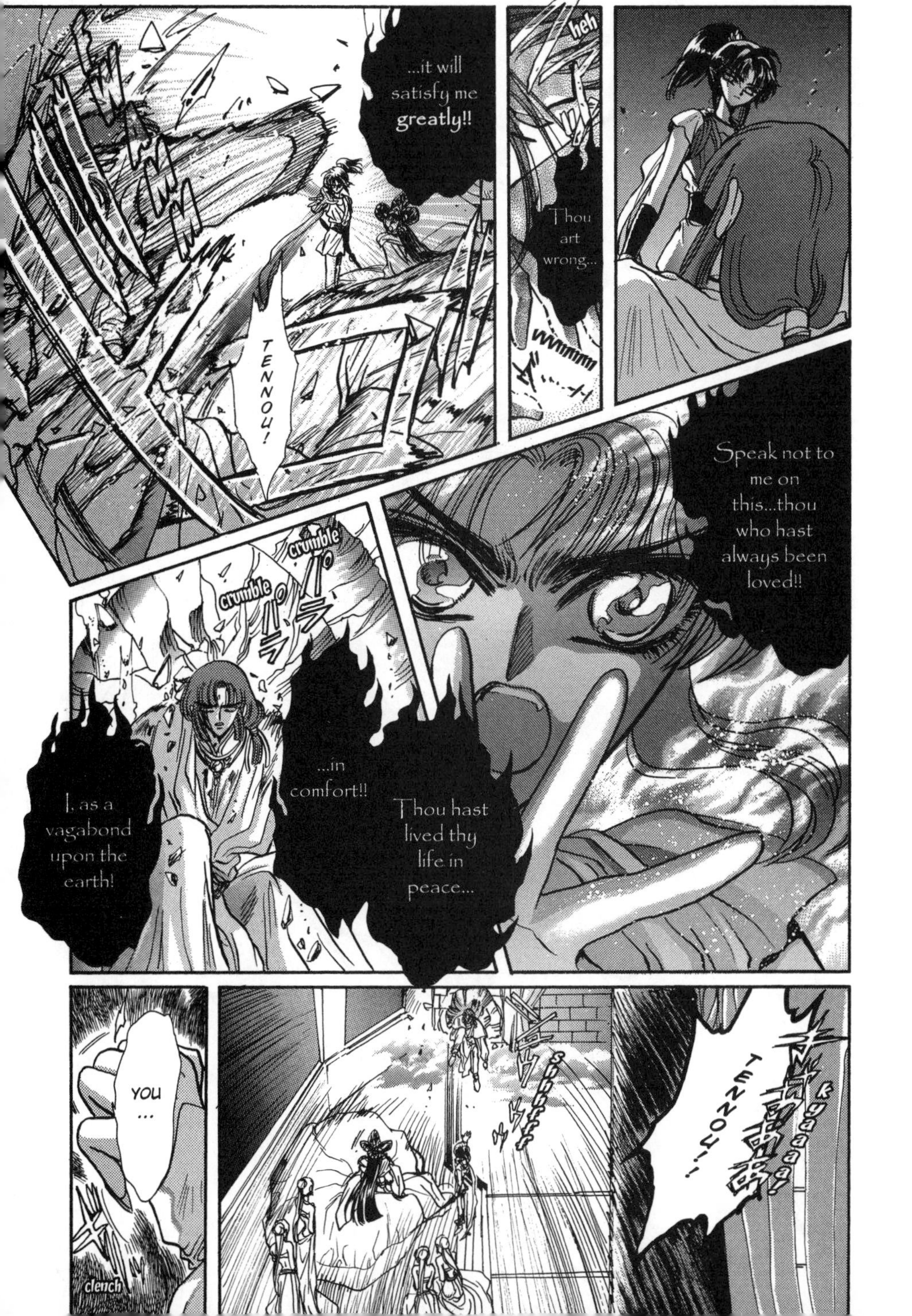
heh
Thou art wrong...
...it will satisfy me greatly!!
TENNOU!
Speak not to me on this...thou who hast always been loved!!
Thou hast lived thy life in peace...
...in comfort!!
crumble
crumble
I, as a vagabond upon the earth!
kyaaaa!
TENNOU--!!
YOU ...
clench

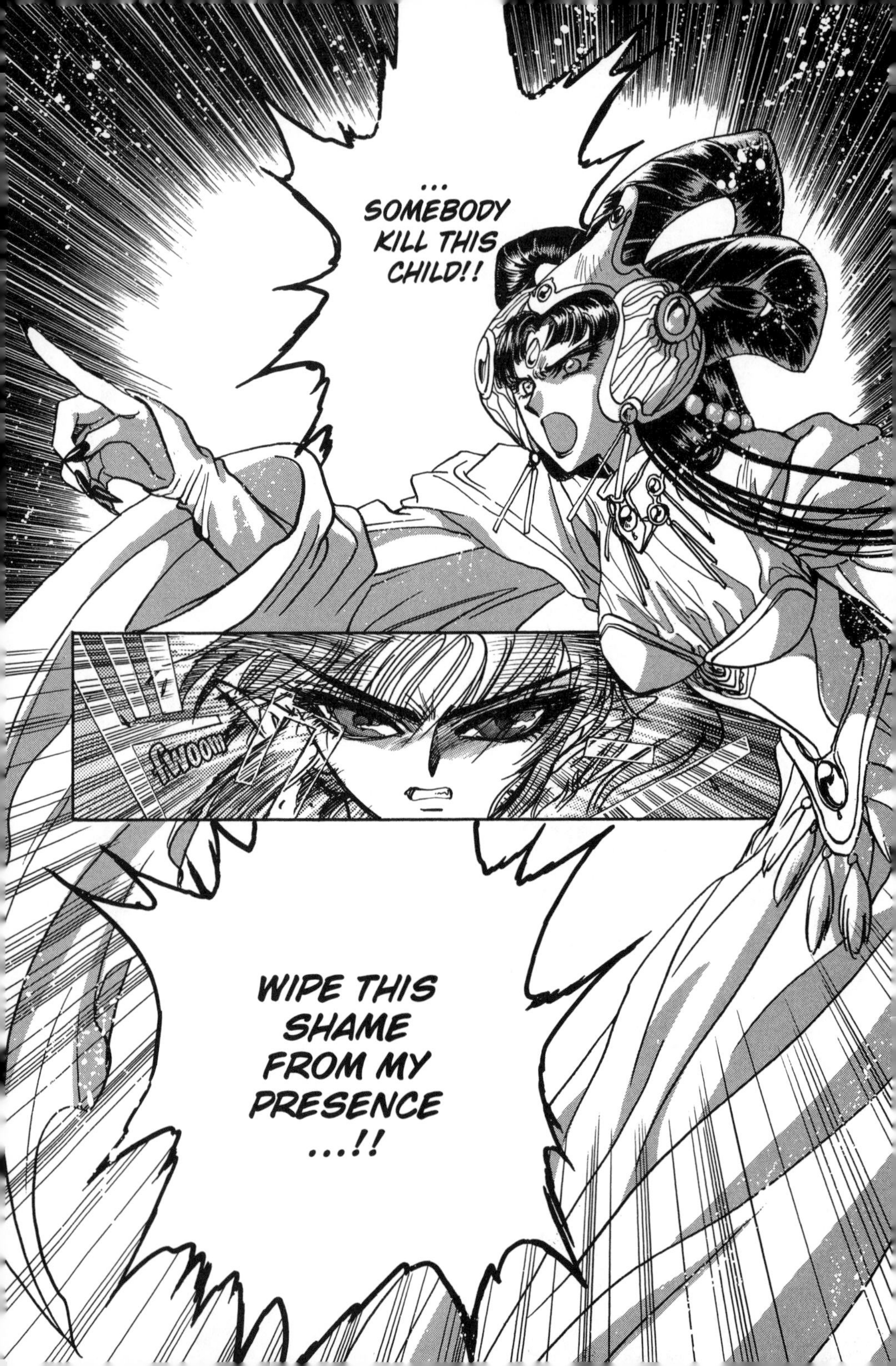

... SOMEBODY KILL THIS CHILD!!
FWOOM
WIPE THIS SHAME FROM MY PRESENCE ...!!

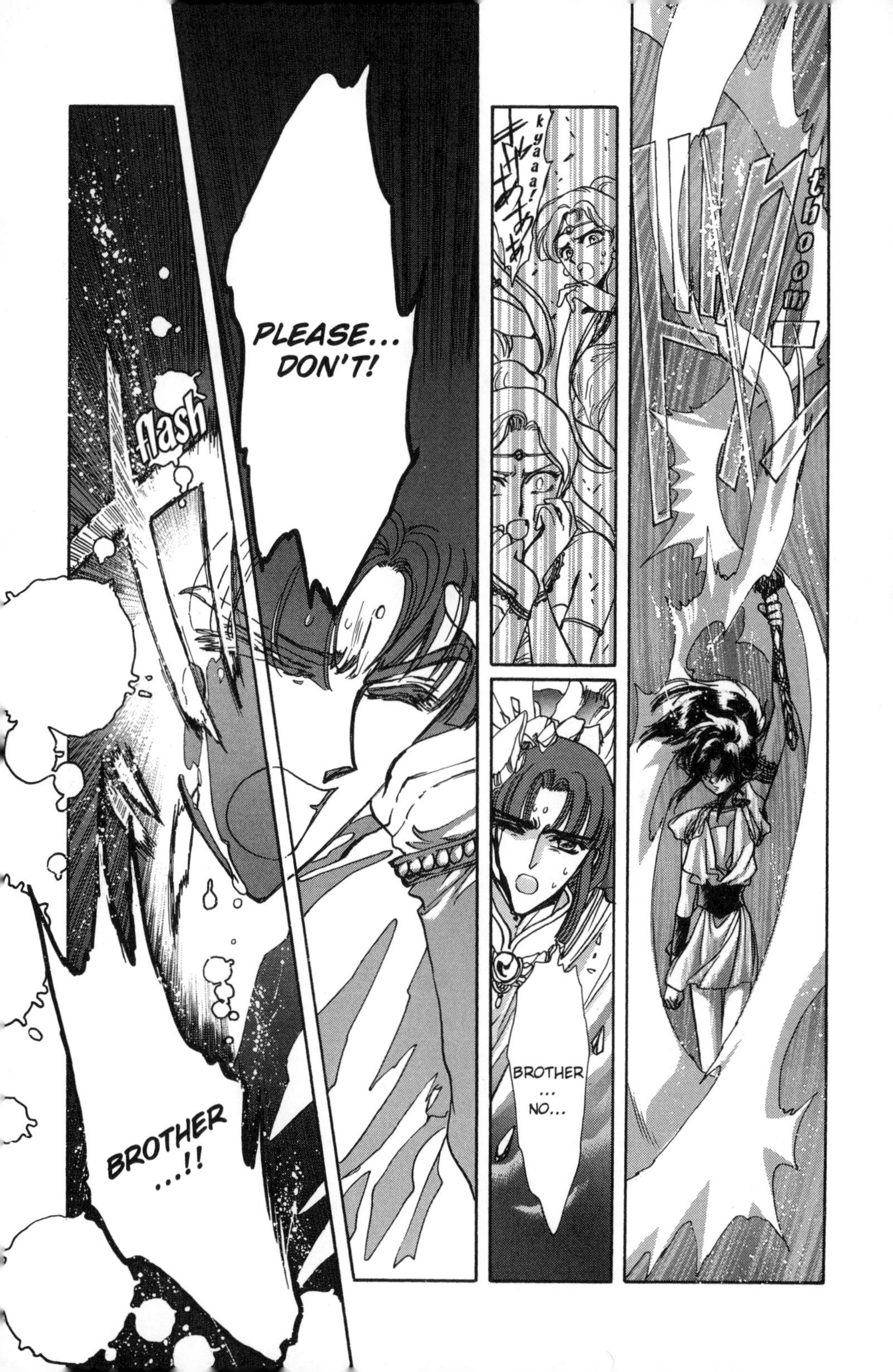
thooom
kyaaa!
BROTHER
...
NO...
PLEASE...
DON'T!
flash
BROTHER
...!!

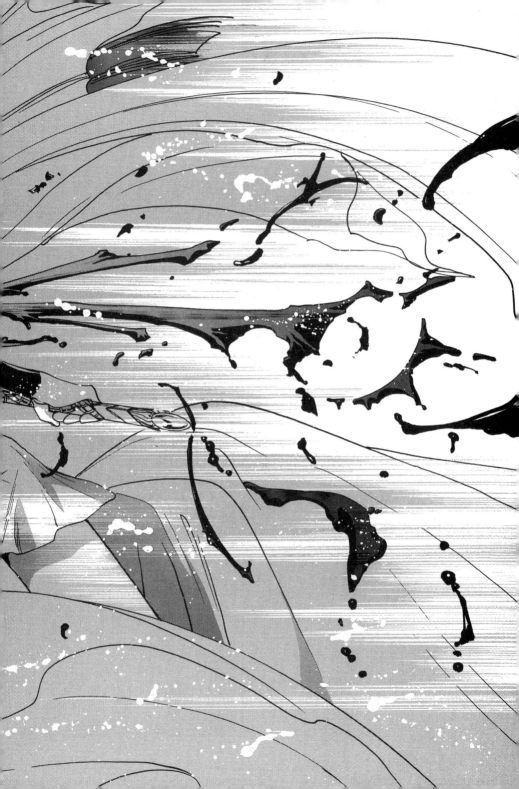

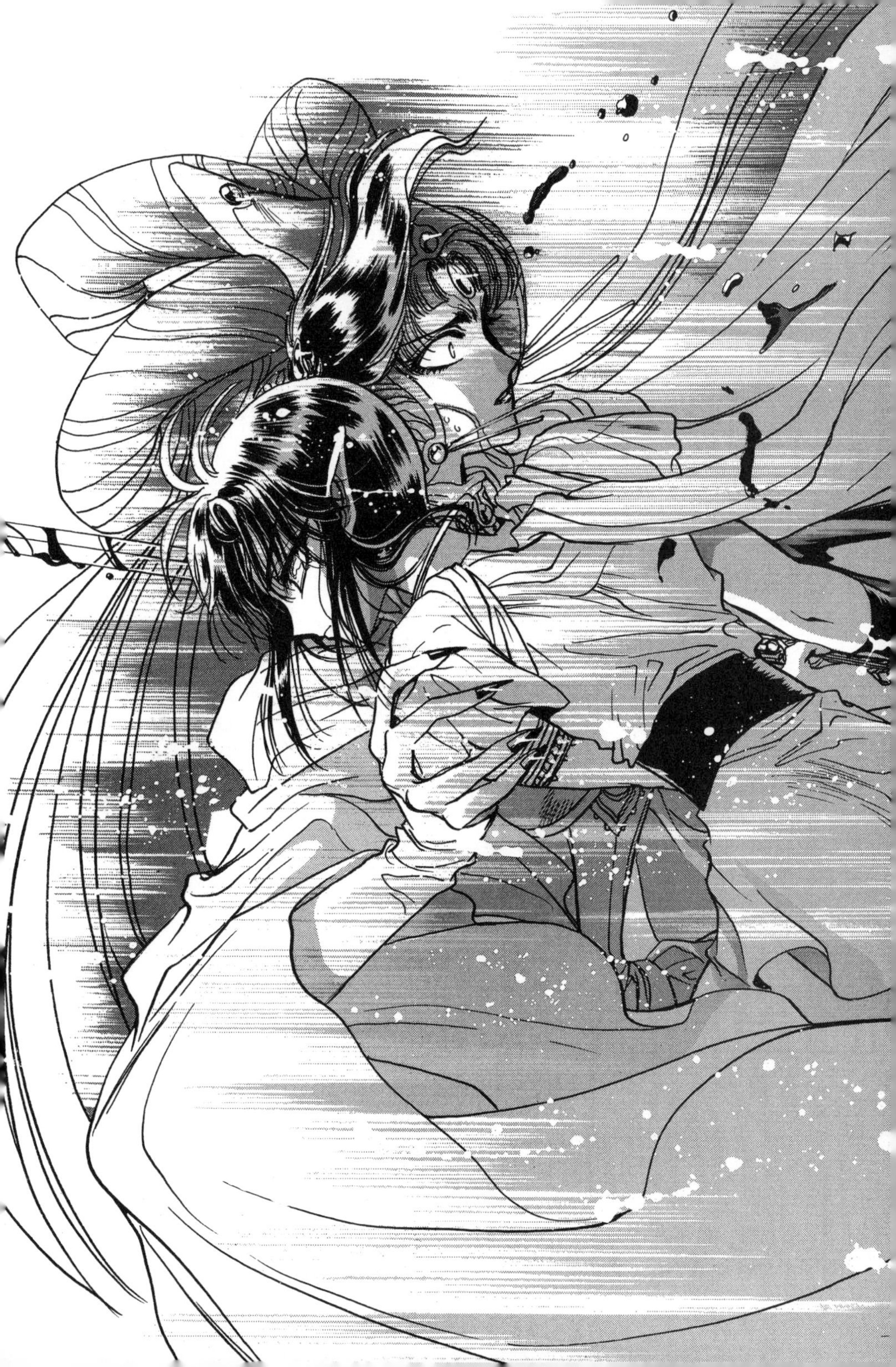

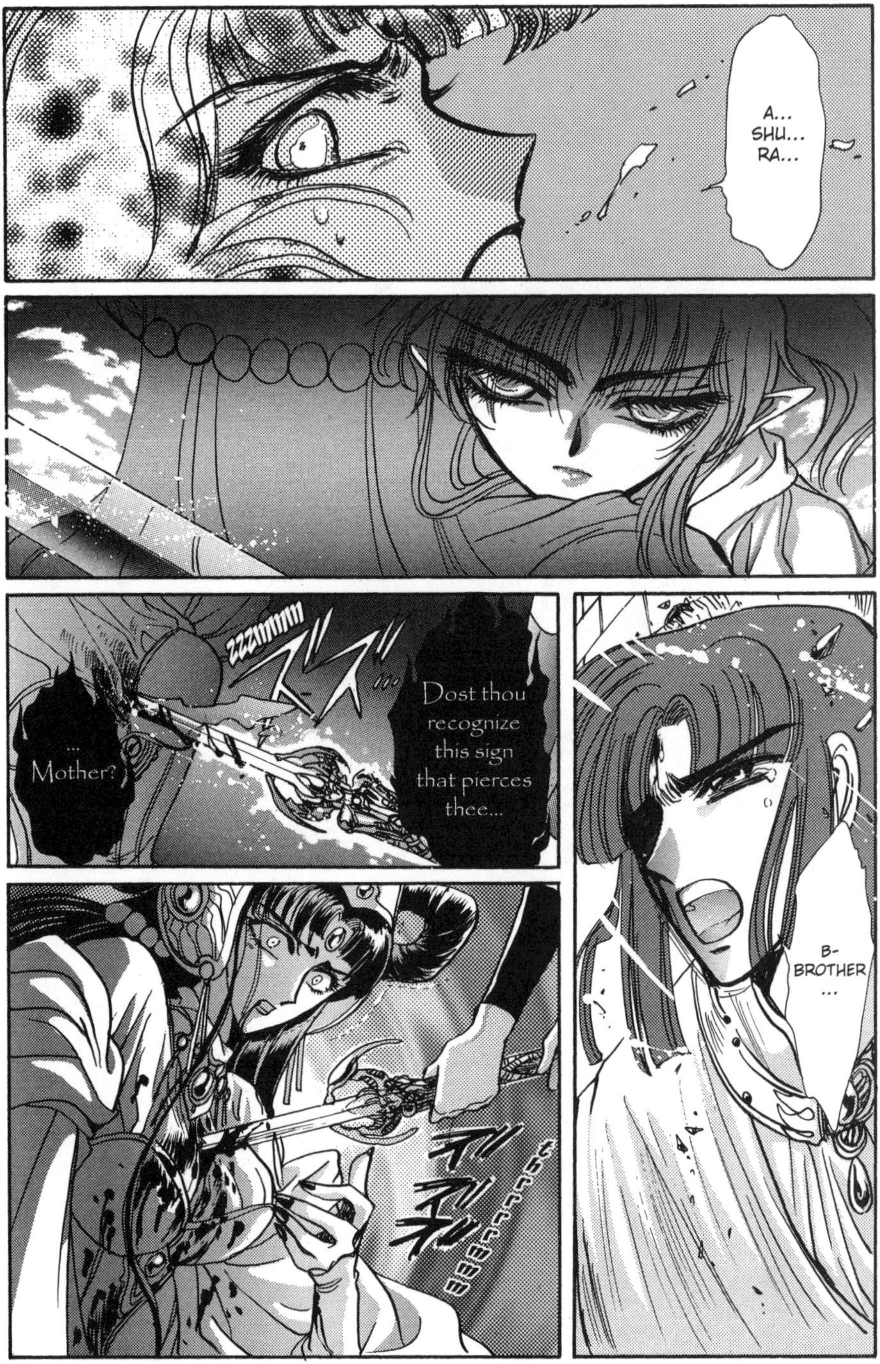
A... SHU... RA...
B-BROTHER ...
zzzmmmm
Dost thou recognize this sign that pierces thee...
... Mother?
thrrrrrmmm

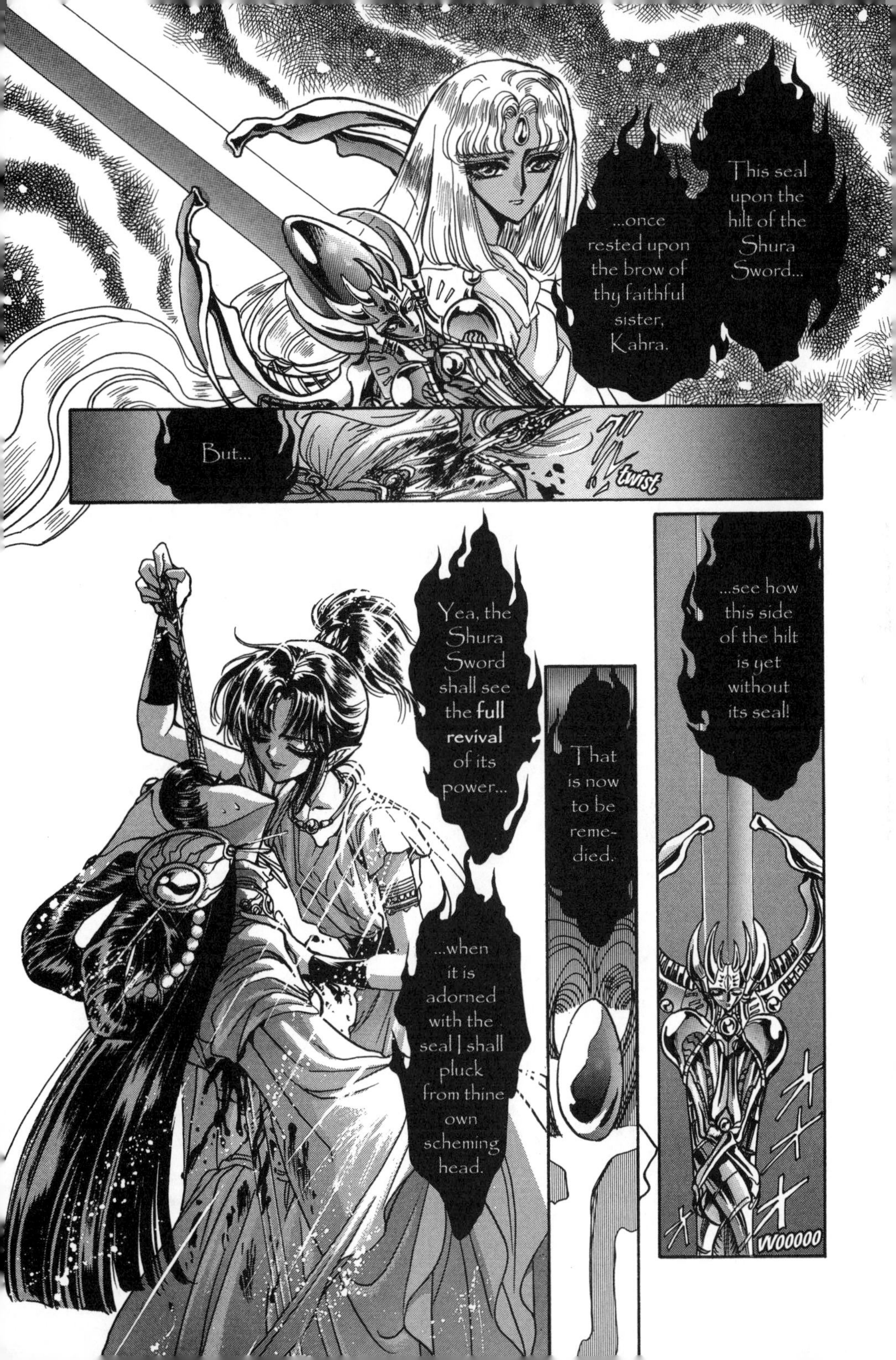
This seal upon the hilt of the Shura Sword...
...once rested upon the brow of thy faithful sister, Kahra.
twist
But...
...see how this side of the hilt is yet without its seal!
WOOOOO
That is now to be reme-died.
Yea, the Shura Sword shall see the **full revival** of its power...
...when it is adorned with the seal I shall pluck from thine own scheming head.

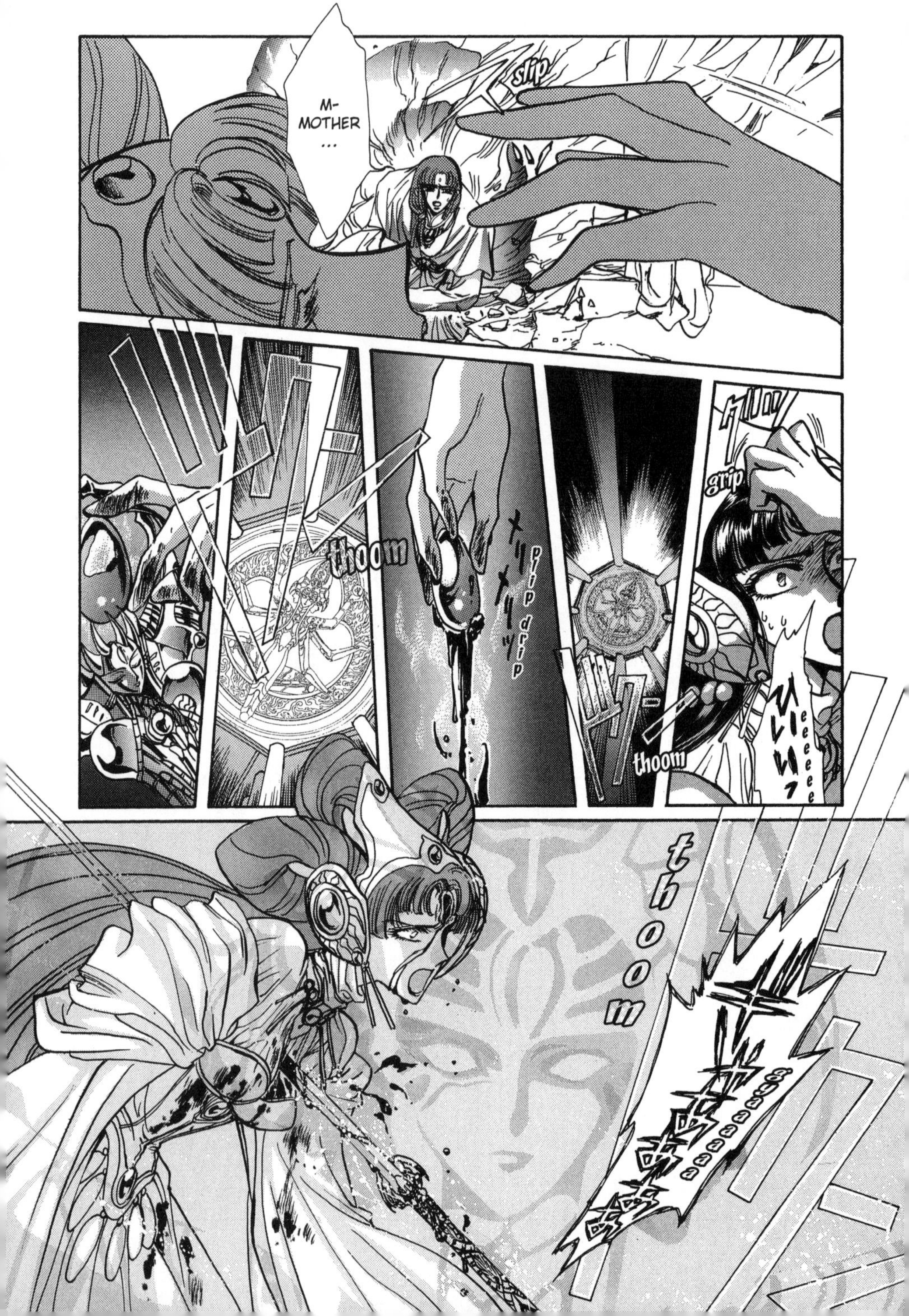
slip
M-MOTHER ...
grip
eeeeeee
thoom
plip drip
thoom
thooom
aaaaaaa

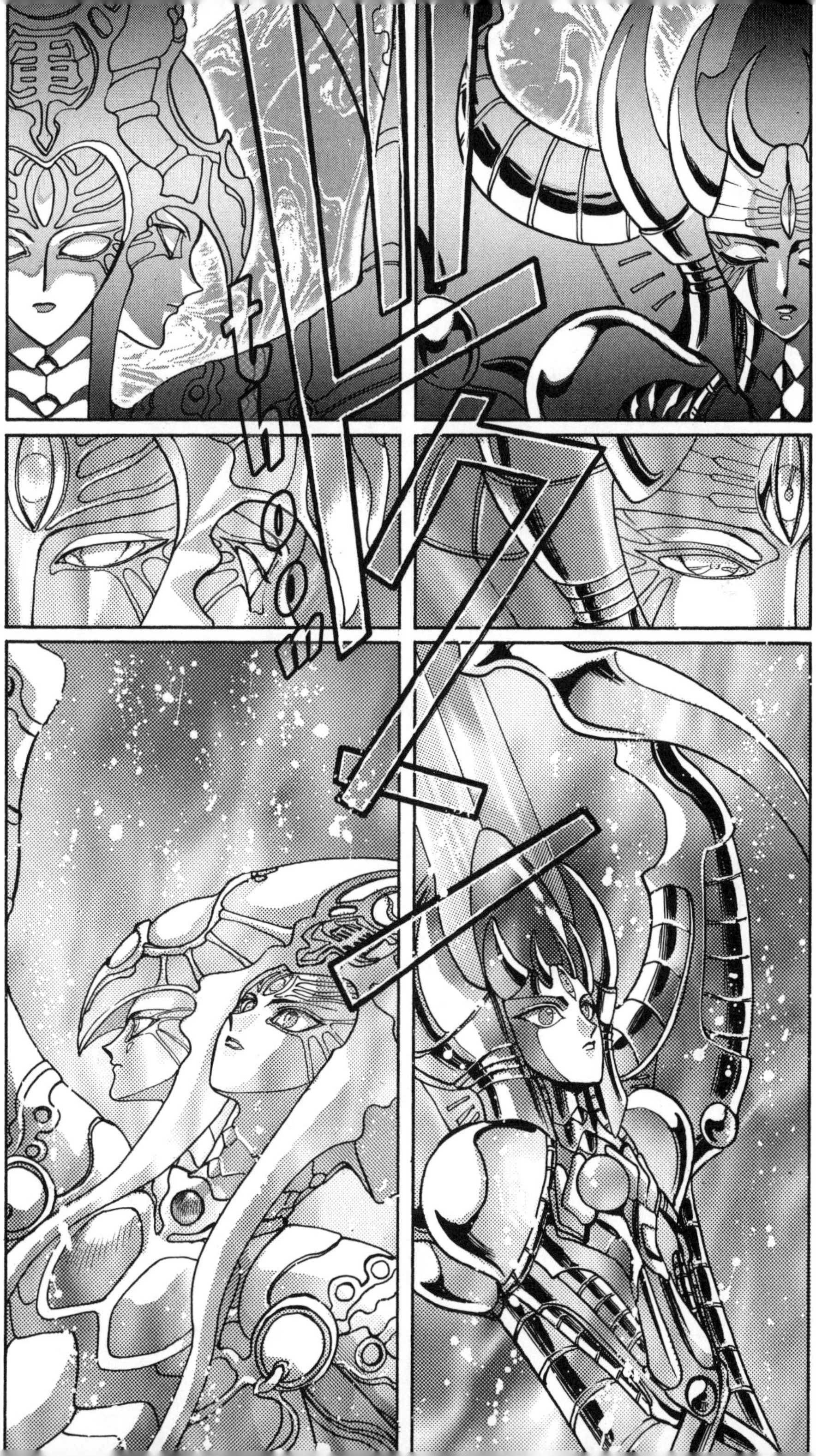

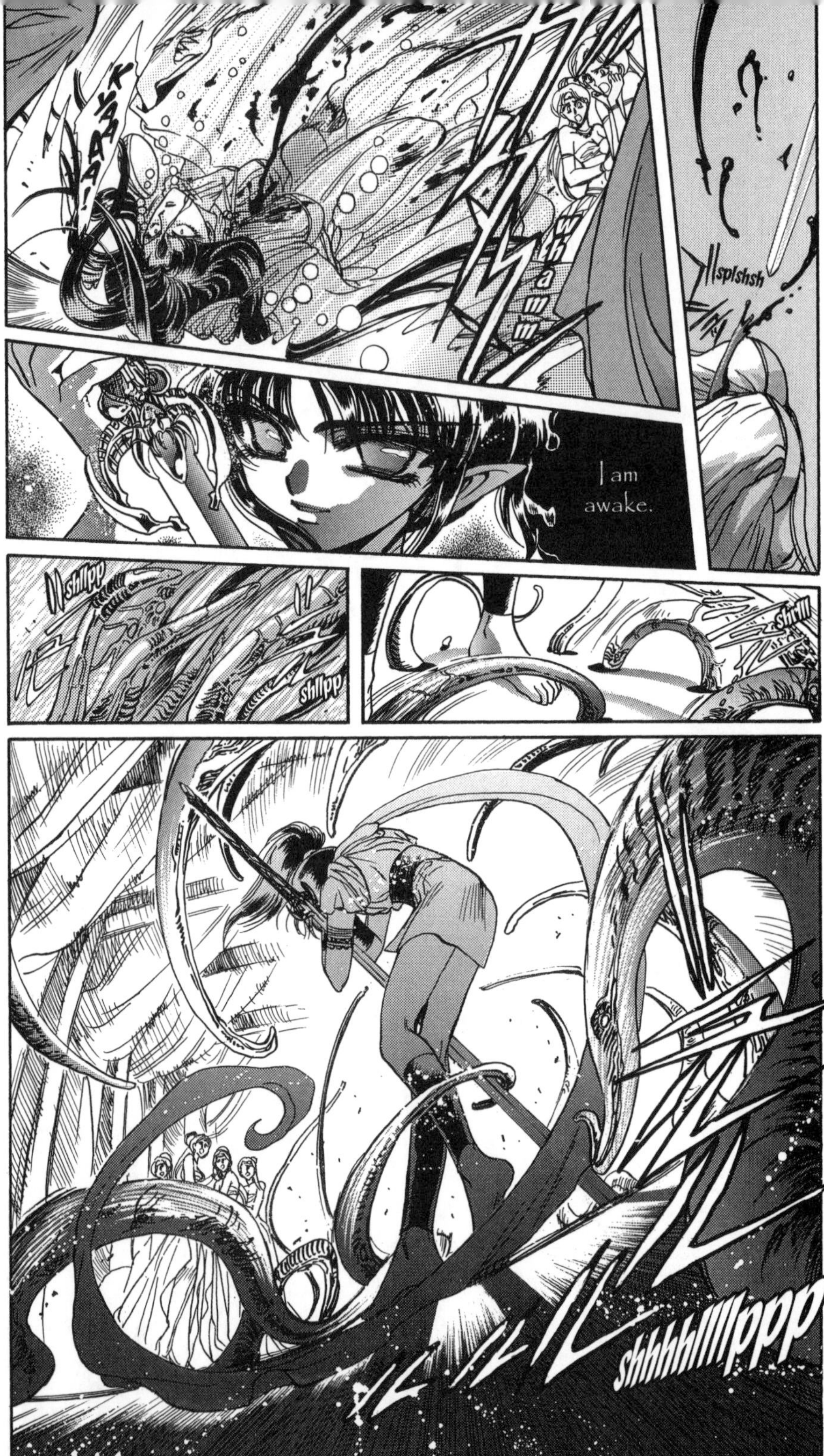

splshsh
whamm
KYAAA!
I am awake.
shrlll
shllpp
shllpp
shhhlllllppp

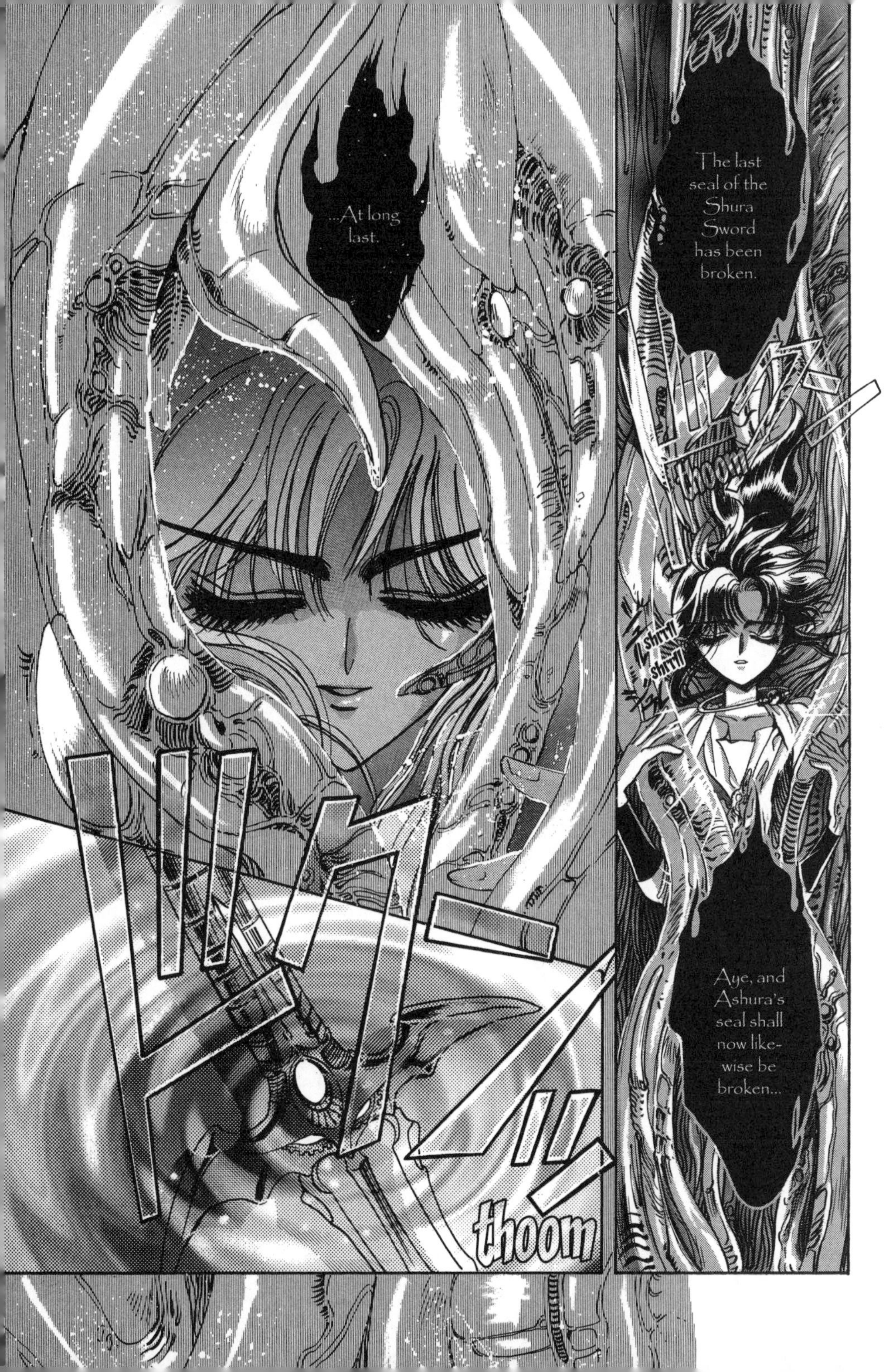
The last seal of the Shura Sword has been broken.
thoom
shrrl shrrl
Aye, and Ashura's seal shall now like-wise be broken...
...At long last.
thoom

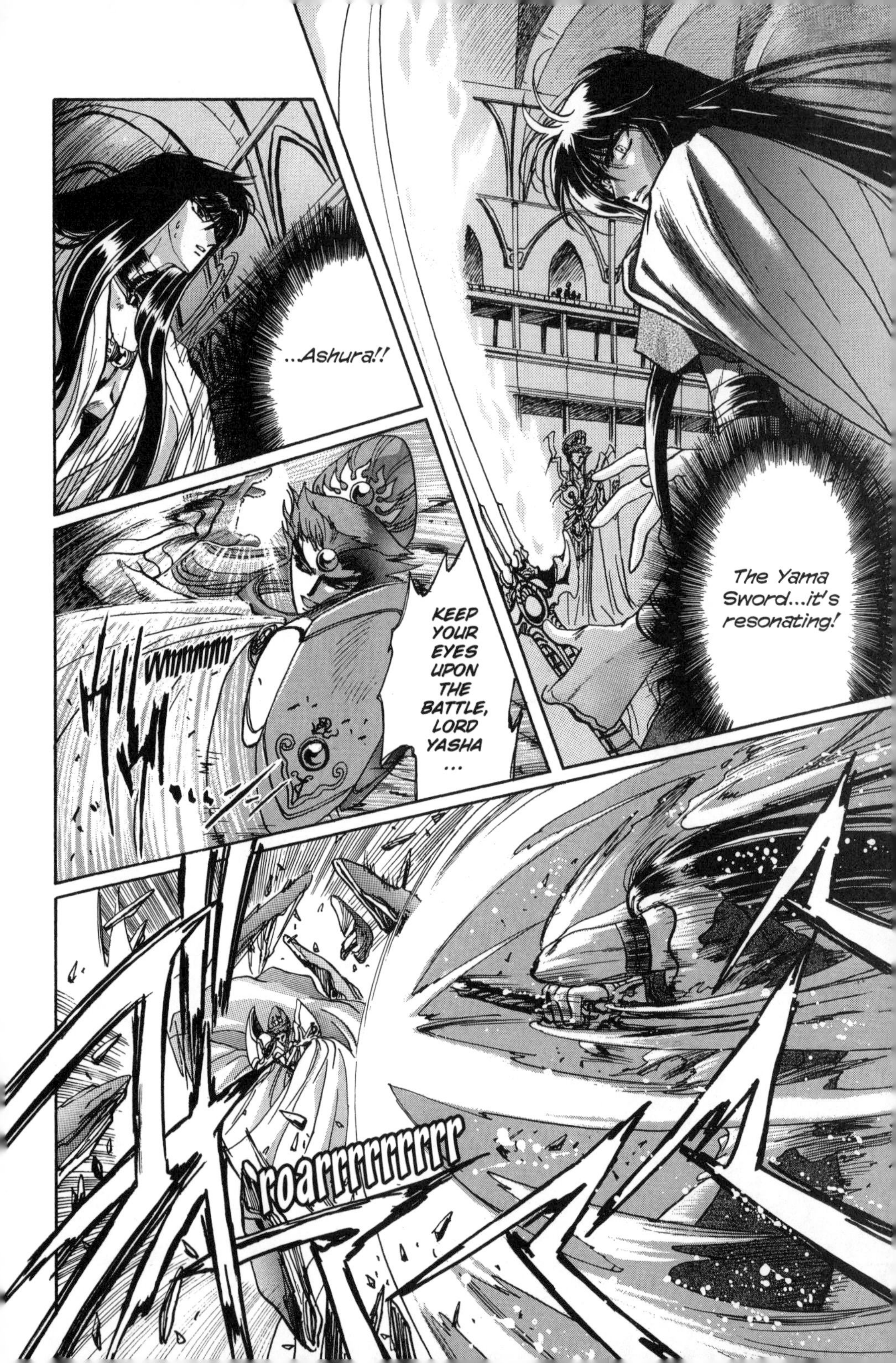
The Yama Sword...it's resonating!
...Ashura!!
KEEP YOUR EYES UPON THE BATTLE, LORD YASHA ...
roarrrrrrrrrr

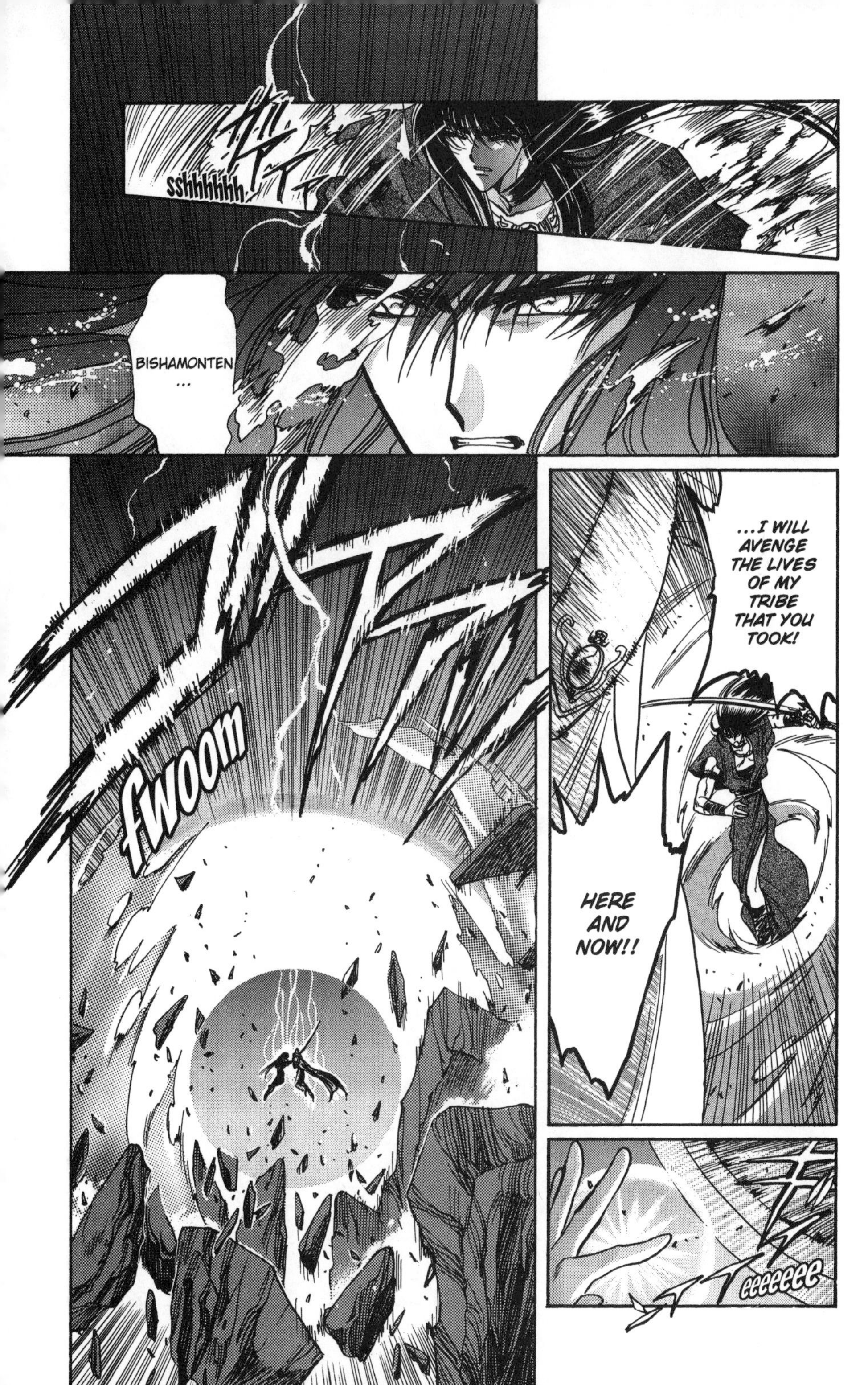
sshhhhhh
BISHAMONTEN ...
...I WILL AVENGE THE LIVES OF MY TRIBE THAT YOU TOOK!
HERE AND NOW!!
eeeeeee
fwoom

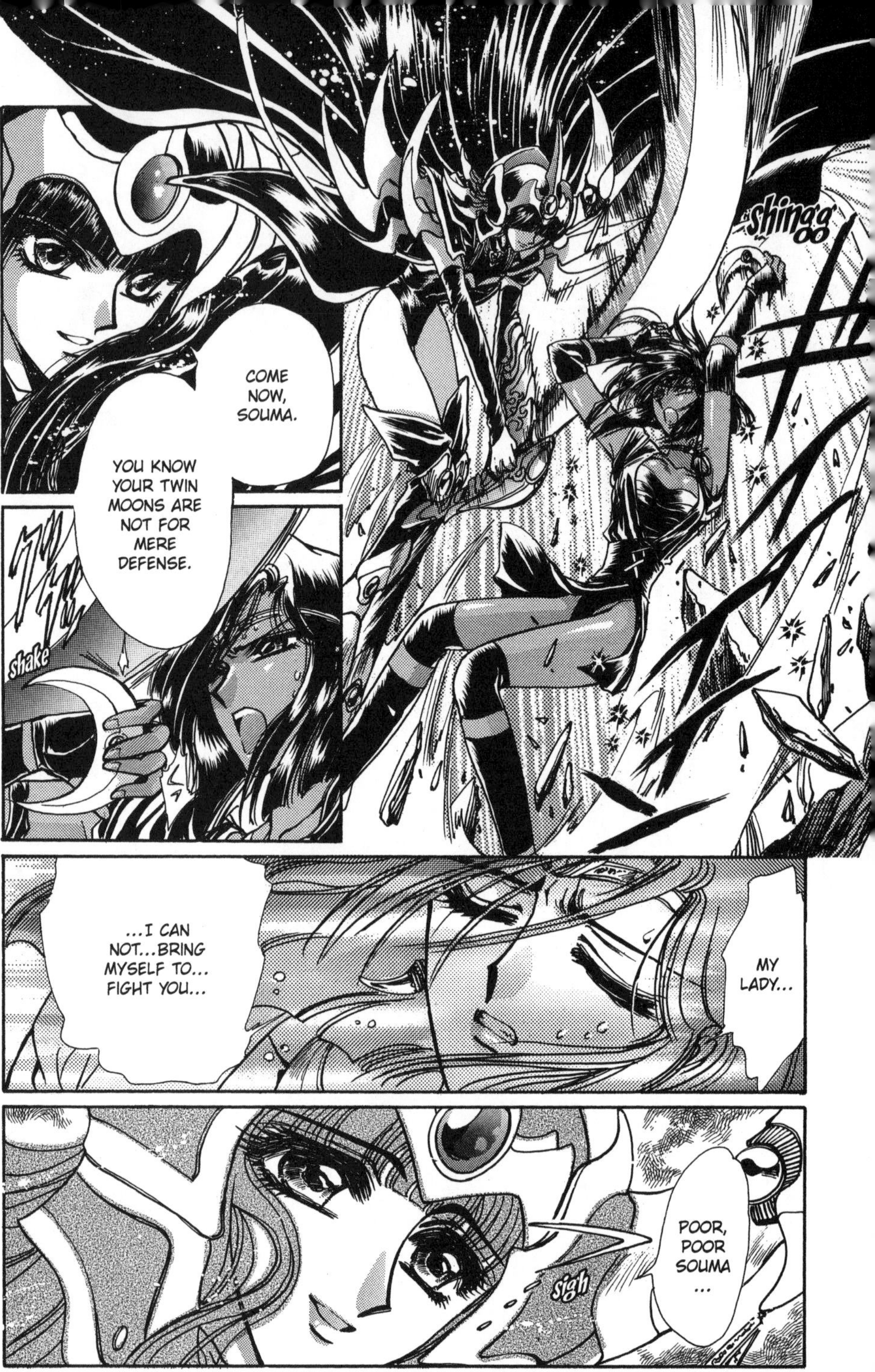
shingg
COME NOW, SOUMA.
YOU KNOW YOUR TWIN MOONS ARE NOT FOR MERE DEFENSE.
shake
MY LADY...
...I CAN NOT...BRING MYSELF TO... FIGHT YOU...
sigh
POOR, POOR SOUMA ...

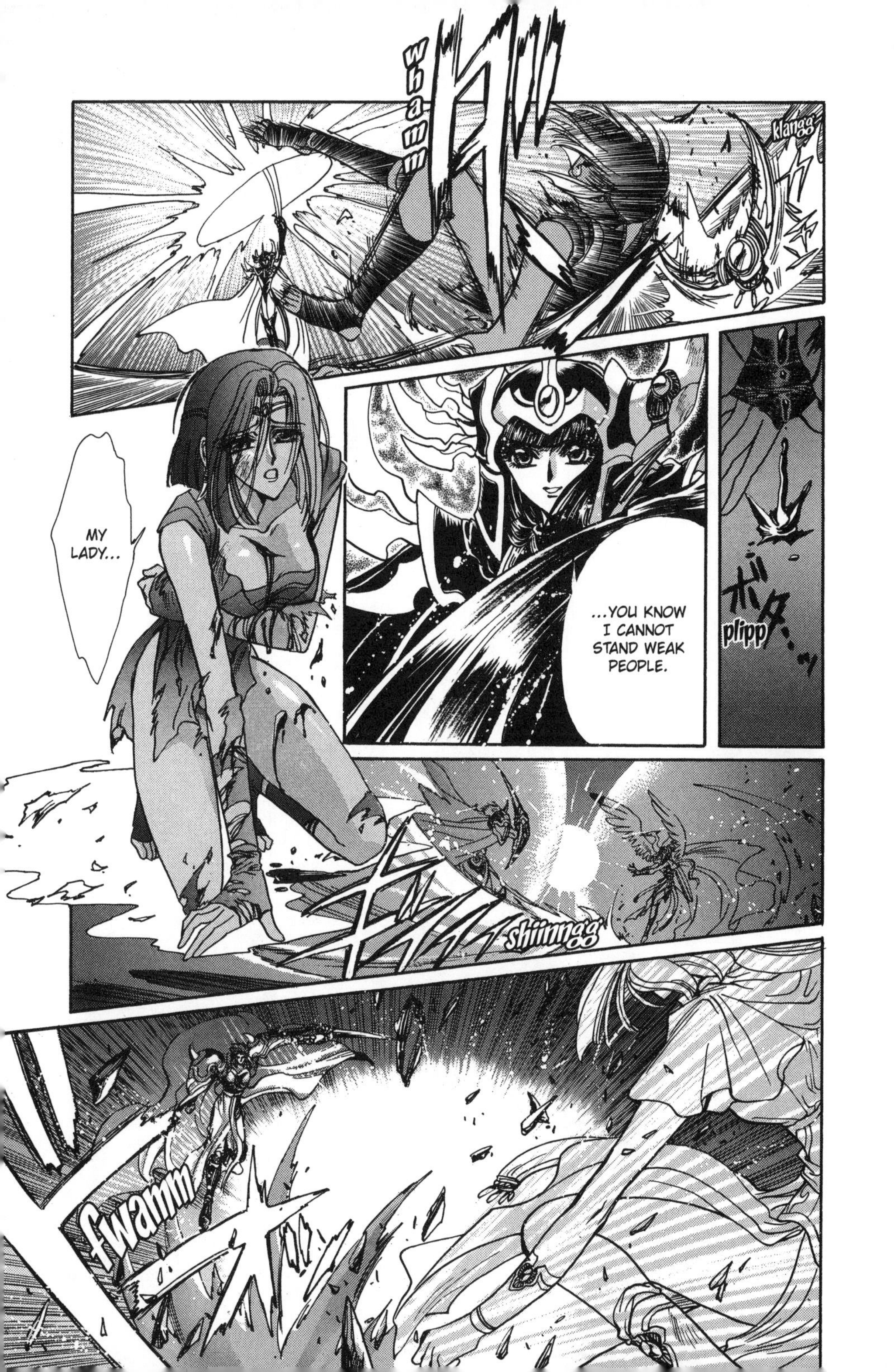
klangg
whamm
ボタ
plipp
...YOU KNOW I CANNOT STAND WEAK PEOPLE.
MY LADY...
shiinngg
fwamm

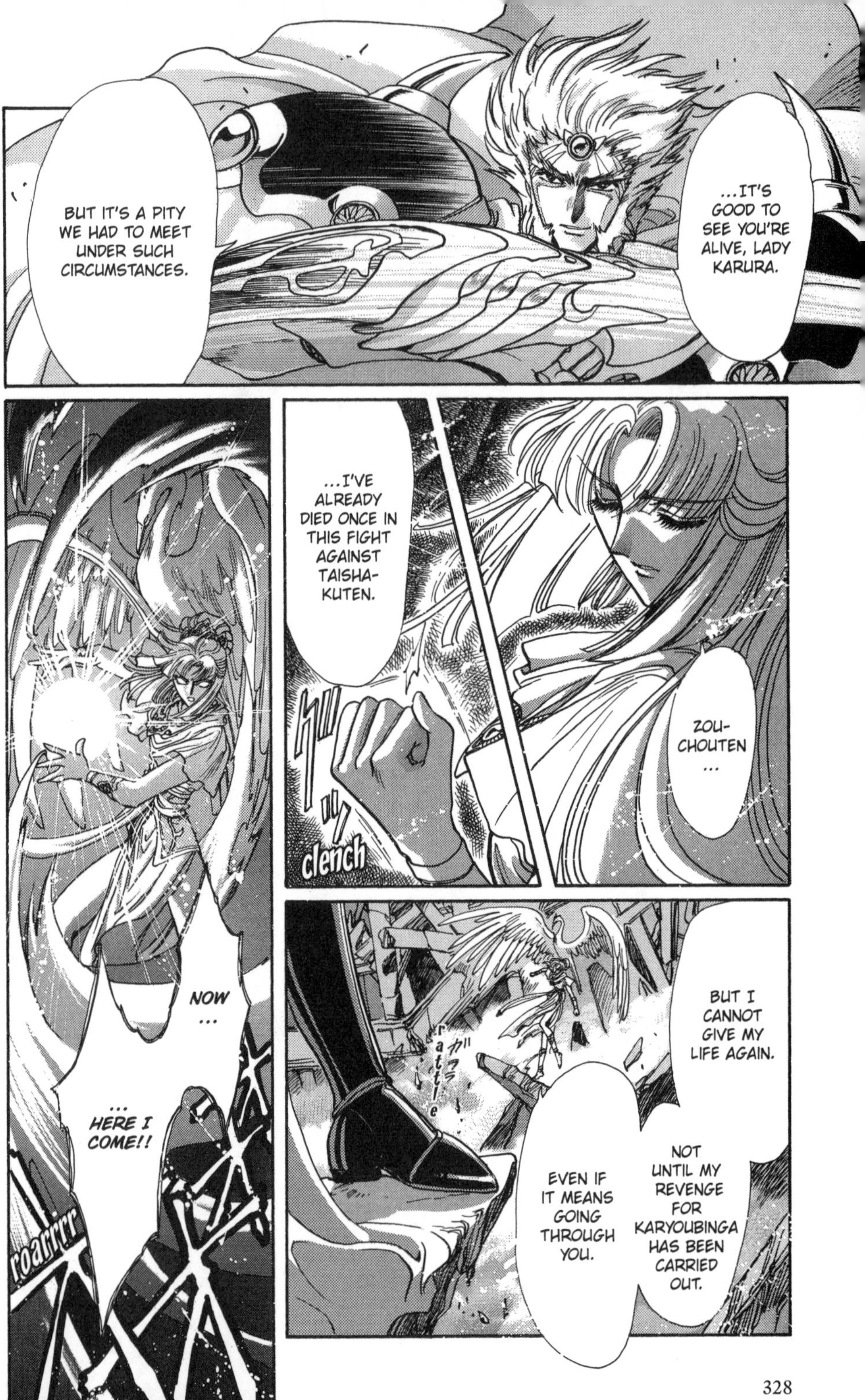
...IT'S GOOD TO SEE YOU'RE ALIVE, LADY KARURA.
BUT IT'S A PITY WE HAD TO MEET UNDER SUCH CIRCUMSTANCES.
ZOU-CHOUTEN ...
...I'VE ALREADY DIED ONCE IN THIS FIGHT AGAINST TAISHA-KUTEN.
clench
BUT I CANNOT GIVE MY LIFE AGAIN.
NOT UNTIL MY REVENGE FOR KARYOUBINGA HAS BEEN CARRIED OUT.
EVEN IF IT MEANS GOING THROUGH YOU.
rattle
NOW ...
... HERE I COME!!
roarrrr

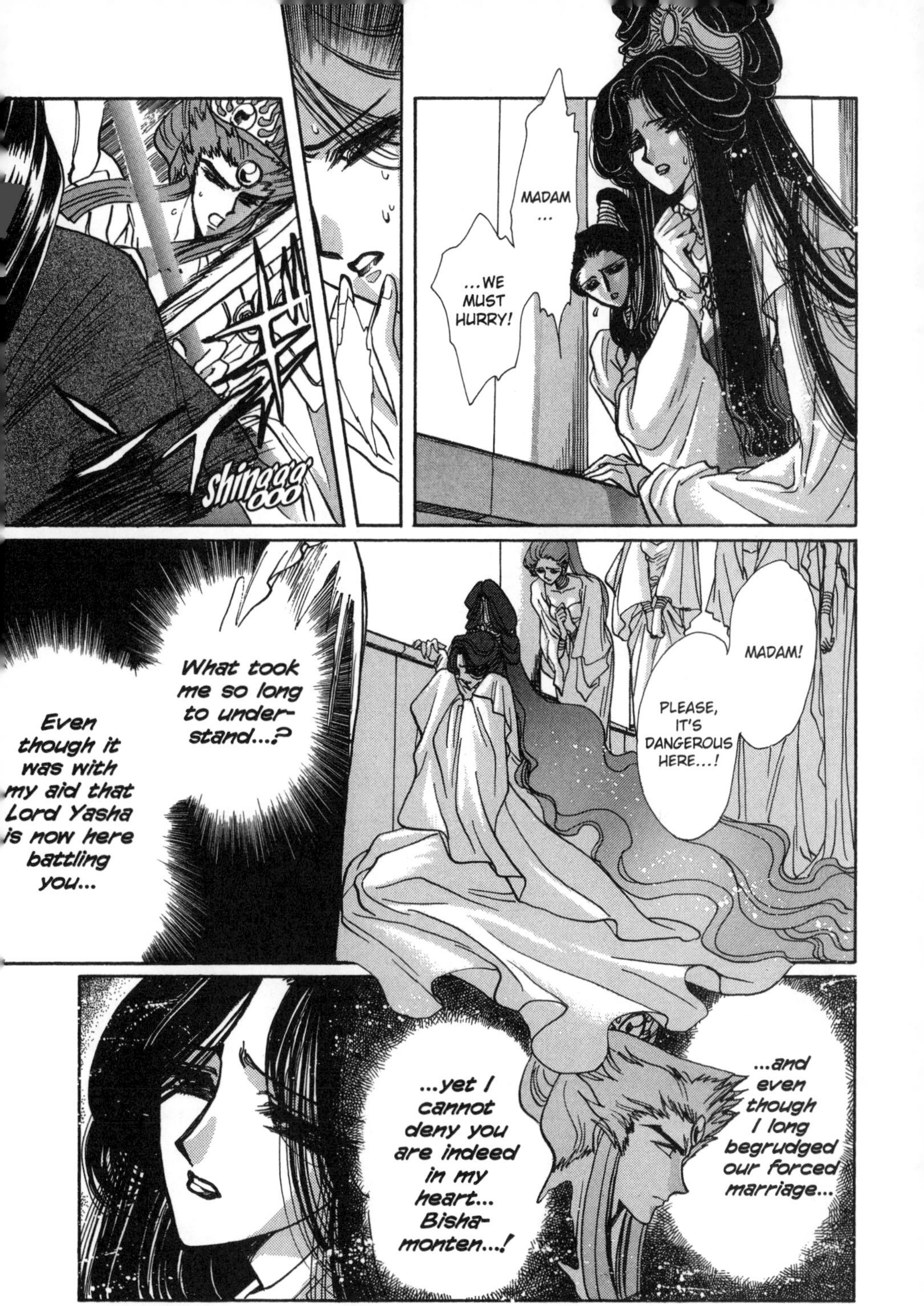
MADAM ...
...WE MUST HURRY!
shinggg ooo
MADAM!
PLEASE, IT'S DANGEROUS HERE...!
What took me so long to understand...?
Even though it was with my aid that Lord Yasha is now here battling you...
...and even though I long begrudged our forced marriage...
...yet I cannot deny you are indeed in my heart... Bisha-monten...!

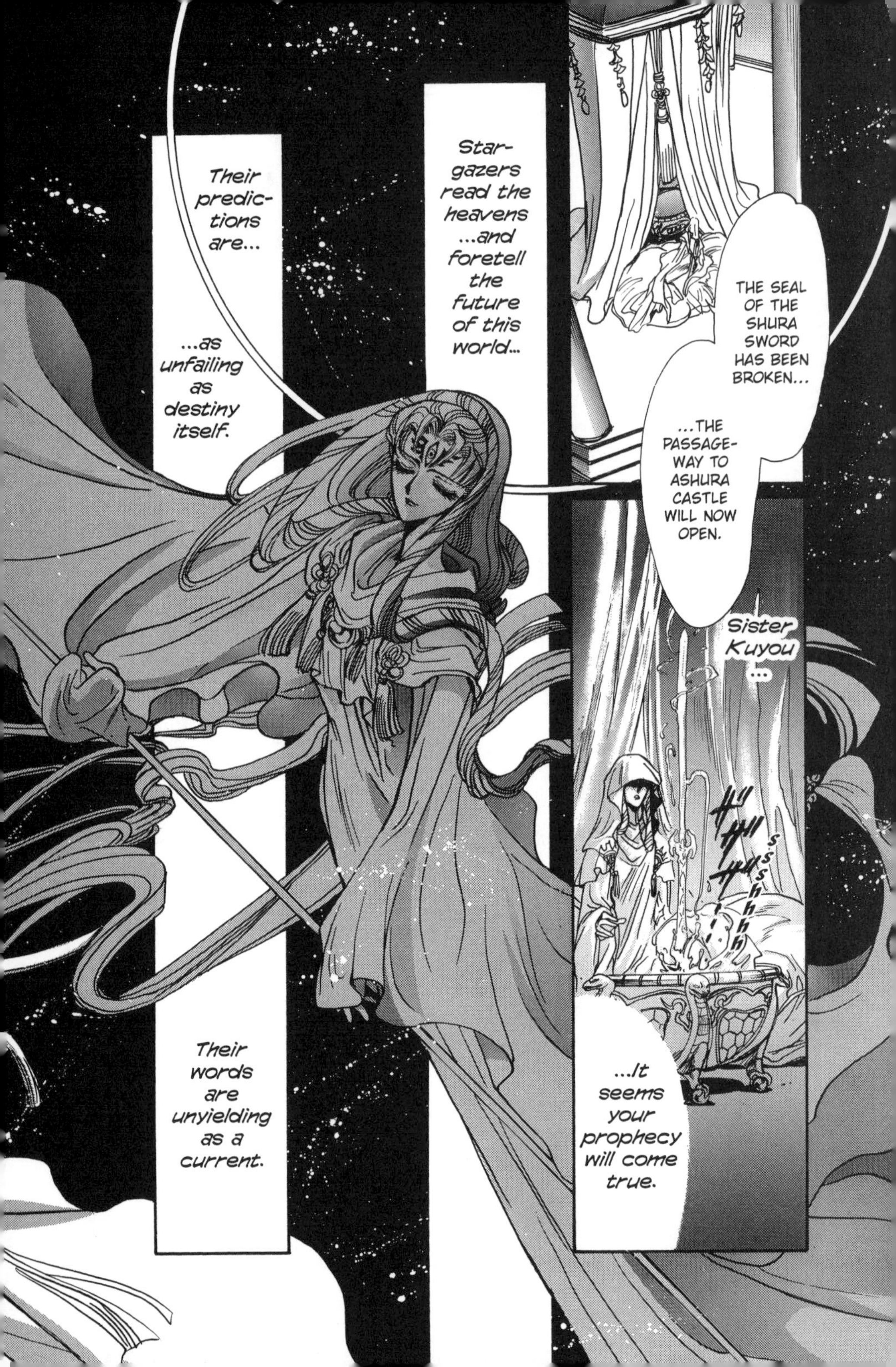

THE SEAL OF THE SHURA SWORD HAS BEEN BROKEN...
...THE PASSAGE-WAY TO ASHURA CASTLE WILL NOW OPEN.
Sister Kuyou ...
ssshhhh!!!
...It seems your prophecy will come true.
Star-gazers read the heavens ...and foretell the future of this world...
Their predic-tions are...
...as unfailing as destiny itself.
Their words are unyielding as a current.

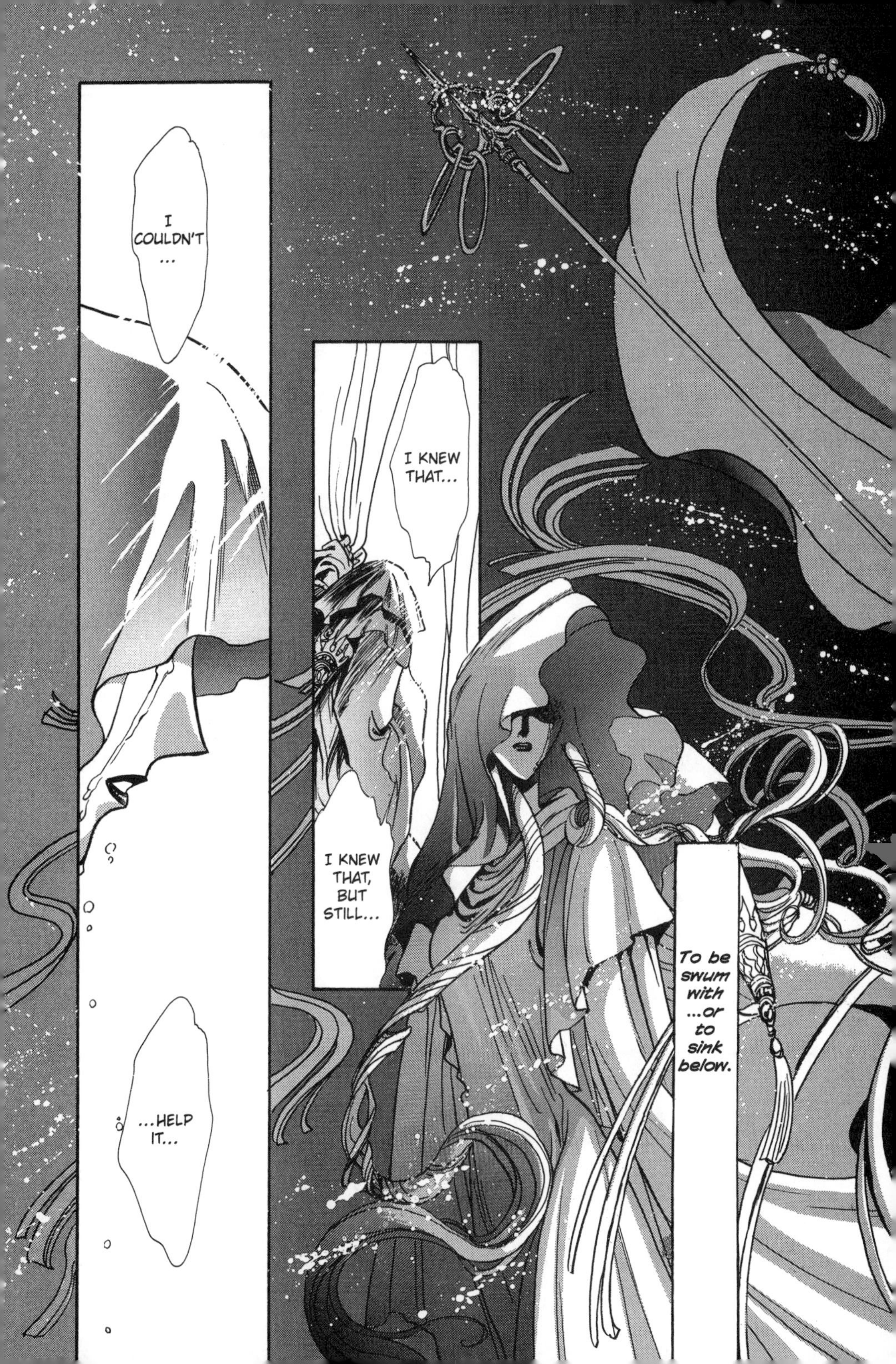
To be swum with ...or to sink below.
I KNEW THAT...
I KNEW THAT, BUT STILL...
I COULDN'T ...
...HELP IT...

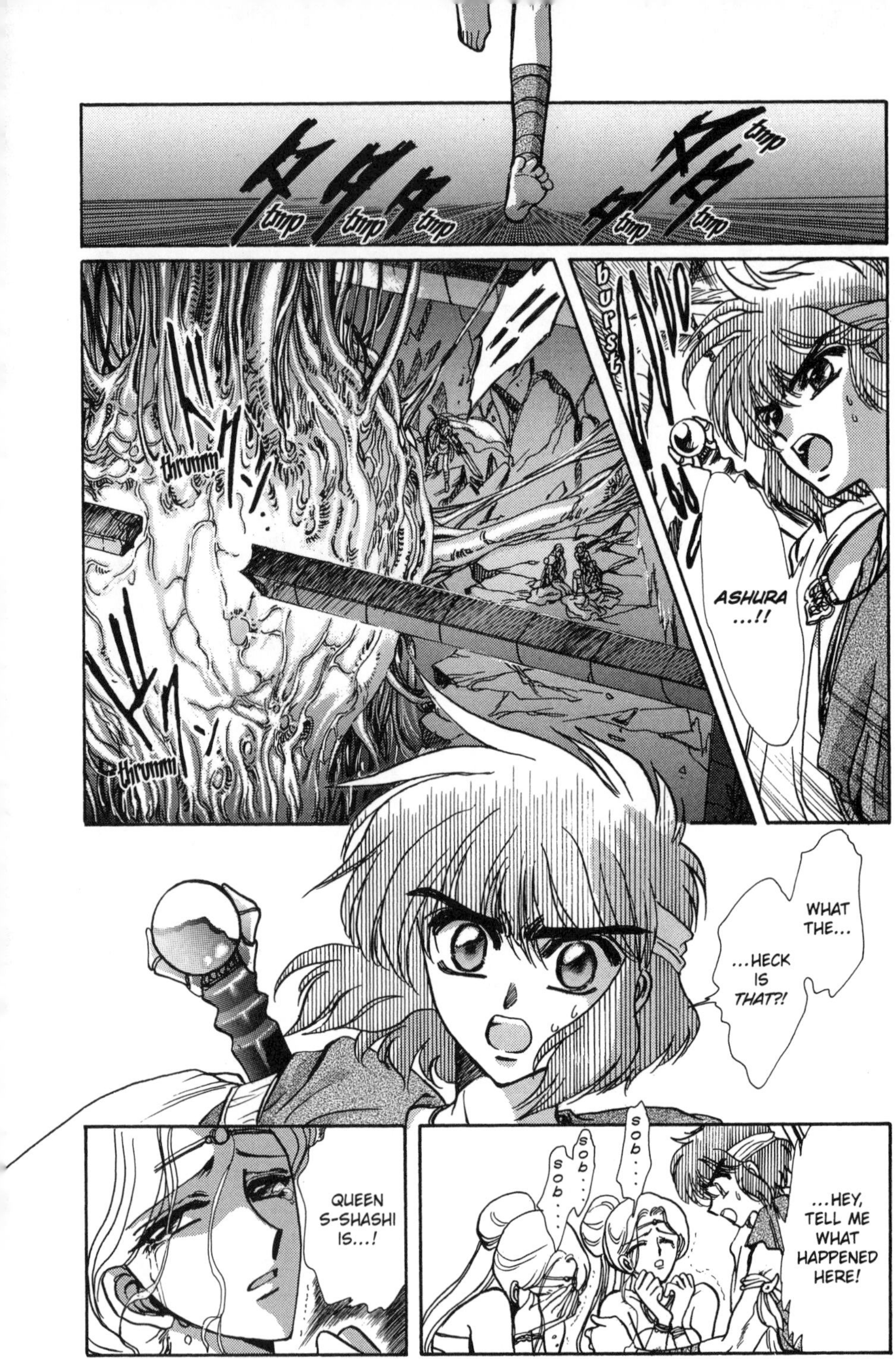
tmp
tmp
tmp
tmp
tmp
tmp
burst
ASHURA ...!!
thrummm
thrummm
WHAT THE...
...HECK IS THAT?!
sob...
sob...
sob...
...HEY, TELL ME WHAT HAPPENED HERE!
QUEEN S-SHASHI IS...!

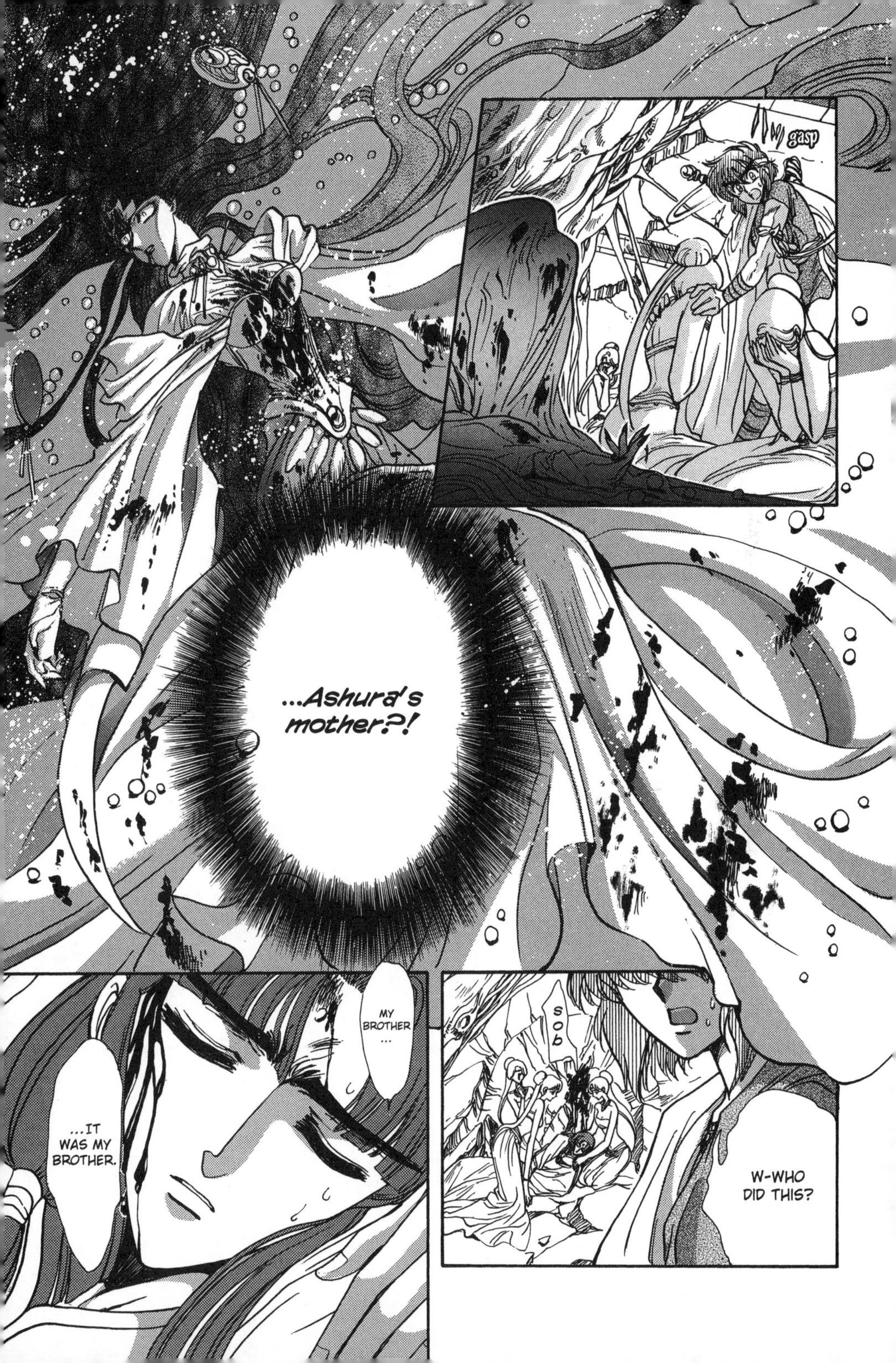
gasp
...Ashura's mother?!
sob
W-WHO DID THIS?
MY BROTHER ...
...IT WAS MY BROTHER.

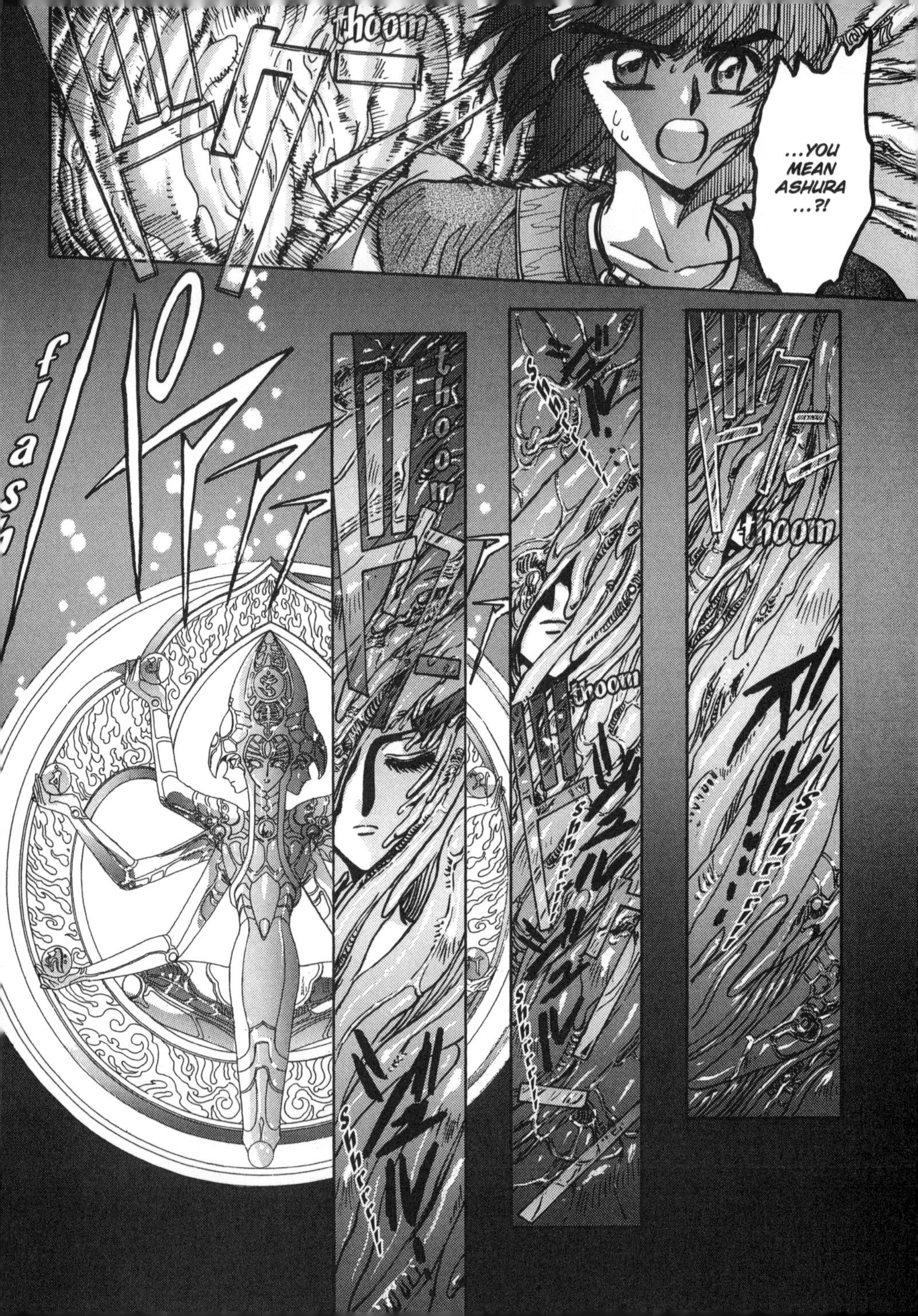
...YOU MEAN ASHURA ...?!
thoom
thoom
shhhrrr...
thoom
shhhrrr
thoom
shhhrrr
flash

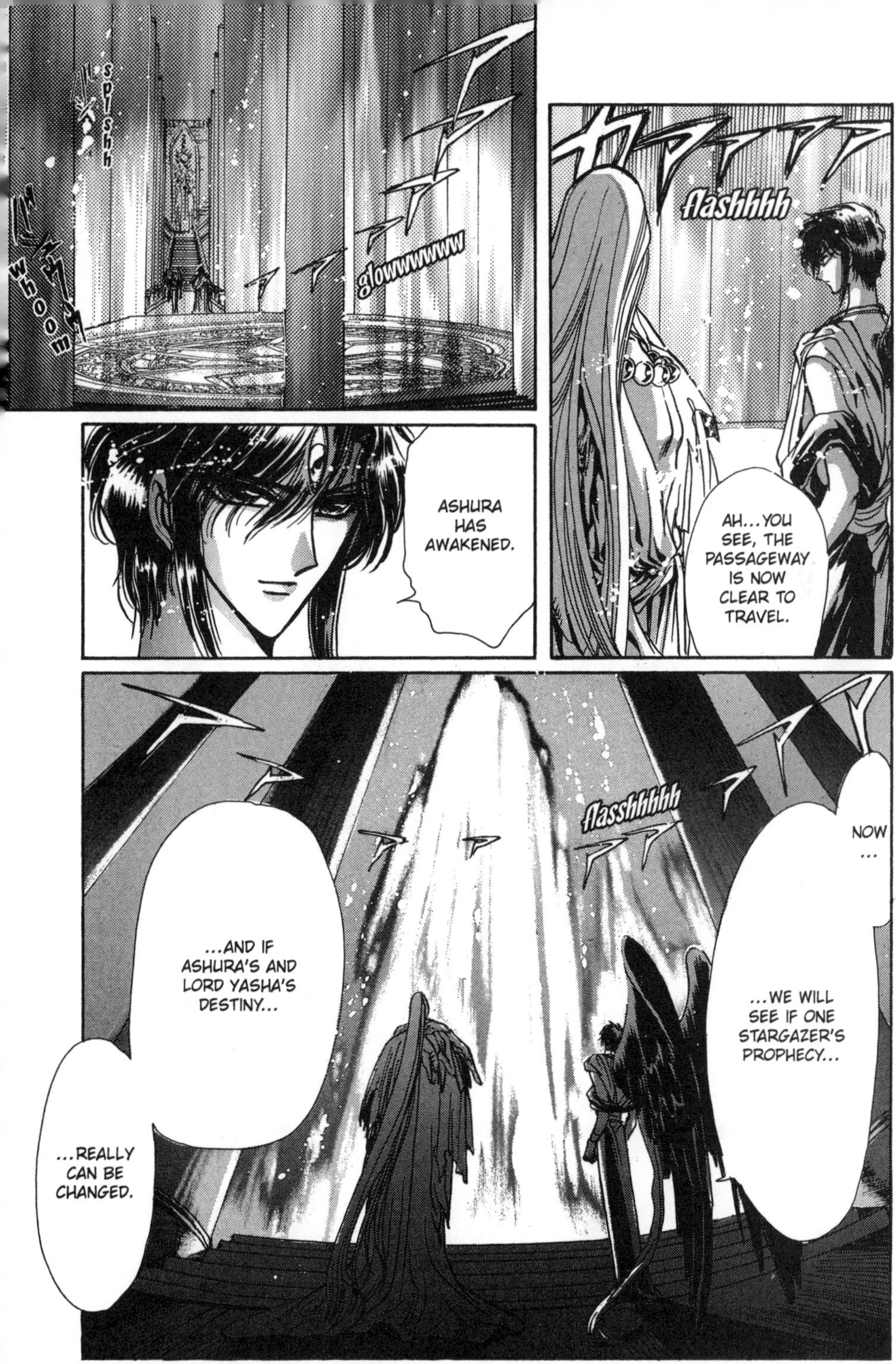
flashhhh
AH...YOU SEE, THE PASSAGEWAY IS NOW CLEAR TO TRAVEL.
splshh
whoom
glowwwwww
ASHURA HAS AWAKENED.
flasshhhhh
NOW...
...WE WILL SEE IF ONE STARGAZER'S PROPHECY...
...AND IF ASHURA'S AND LORD YASHA'S DESTINY...
...REALLY CAN BE CHANGED.

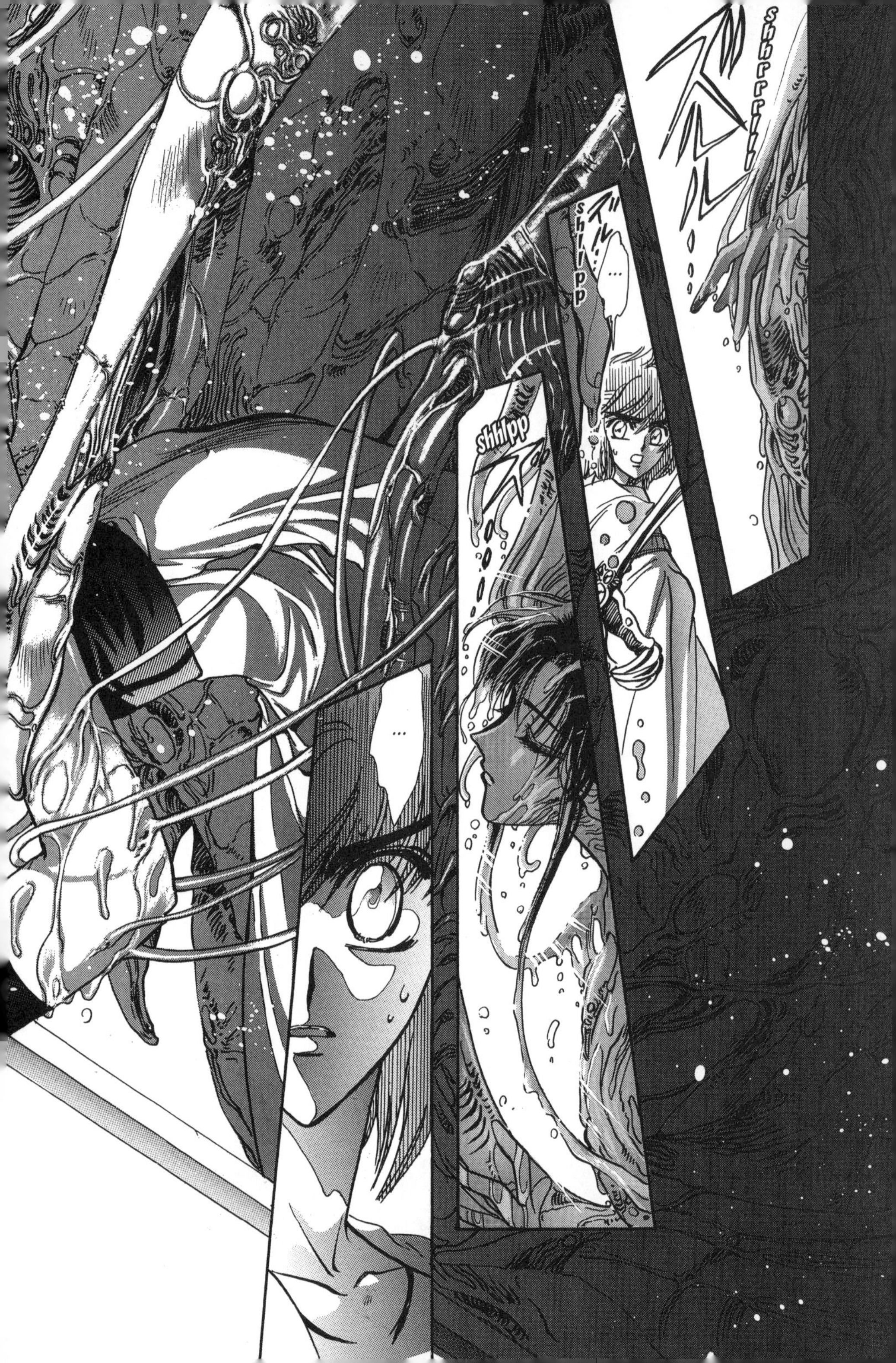
ズルル
shhrrrrlll
ズル…
shllpp
…
ズ…
shllpp
…

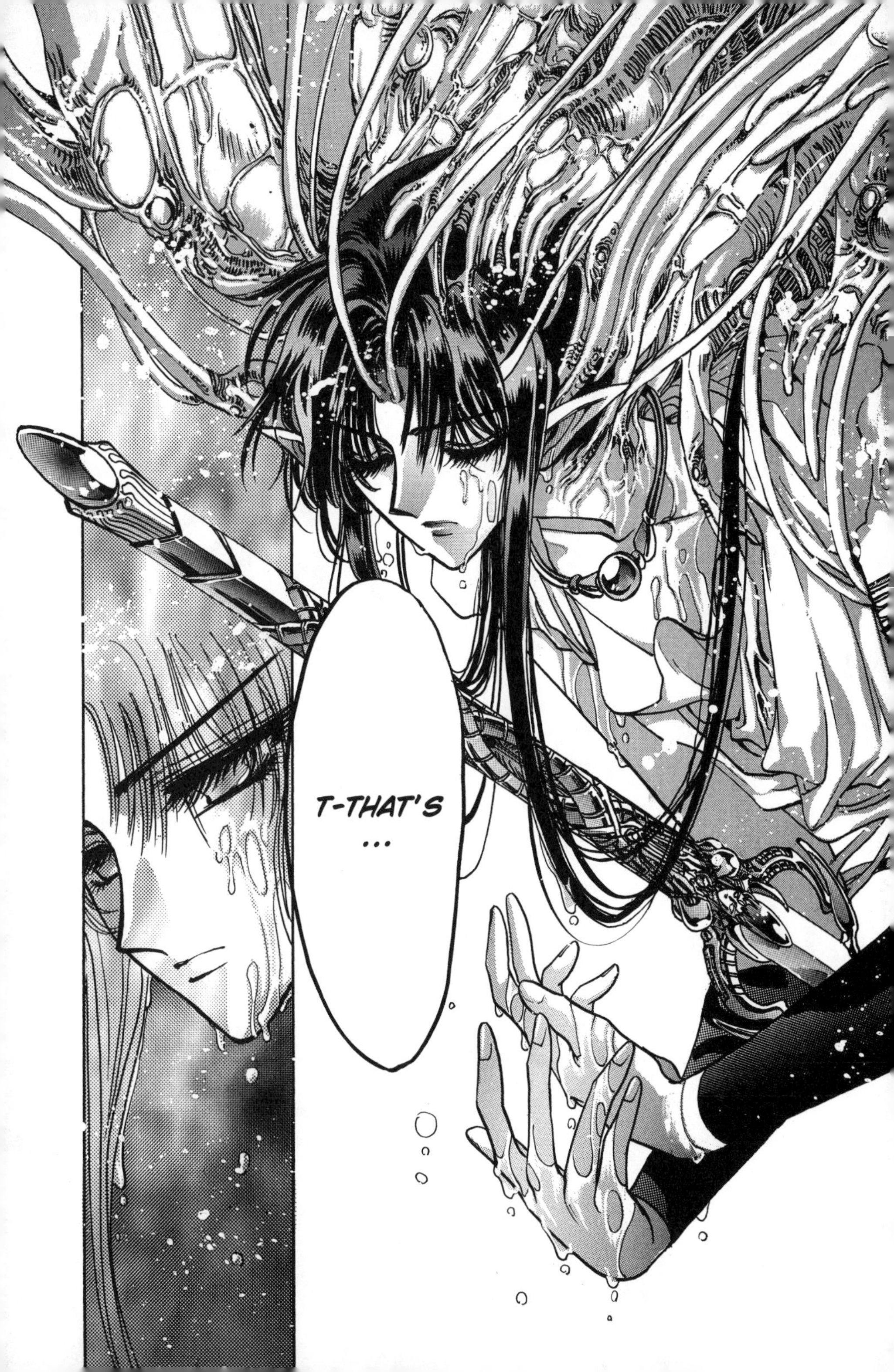
T-THAT'S
...

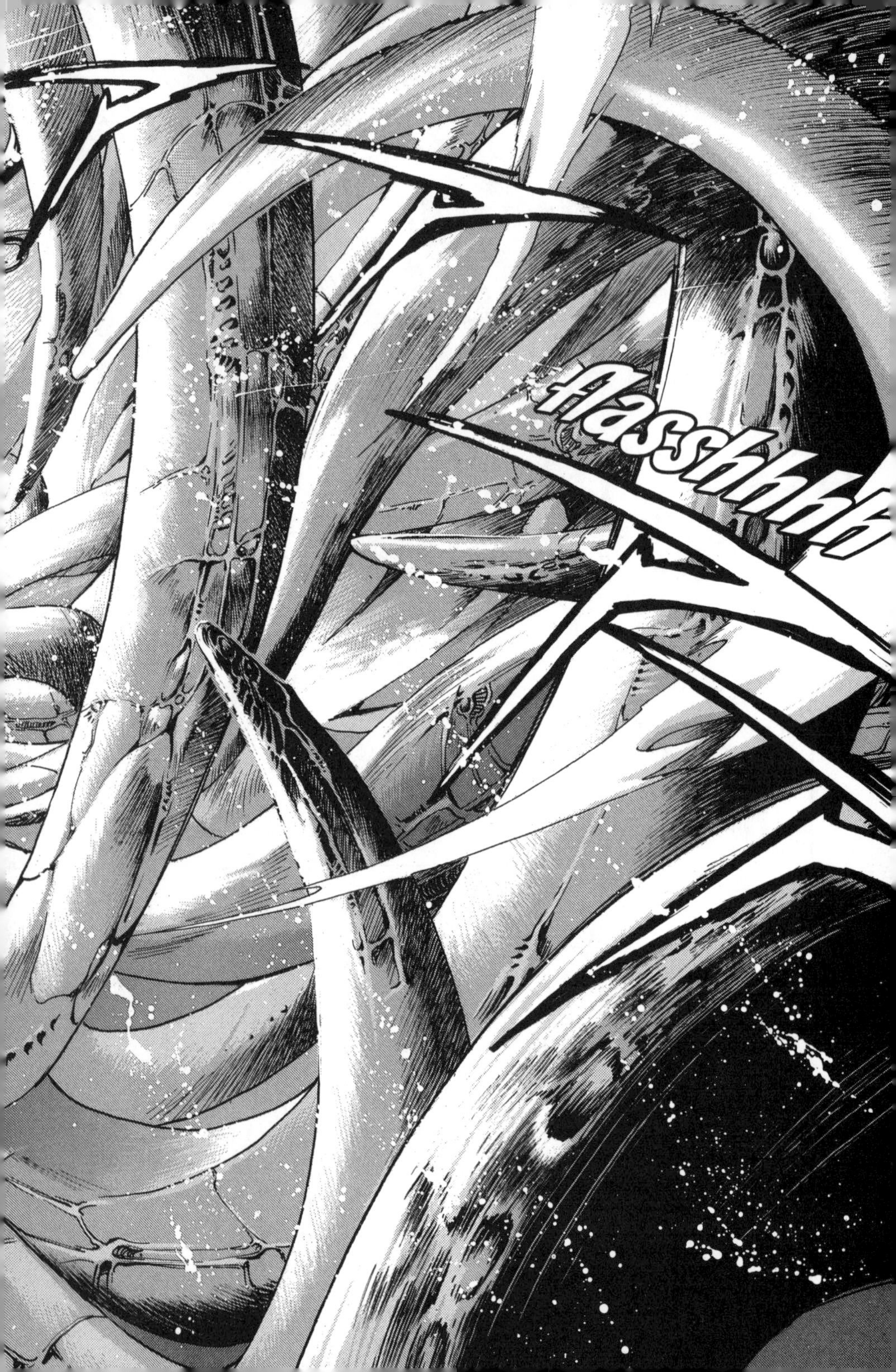
flasshhh

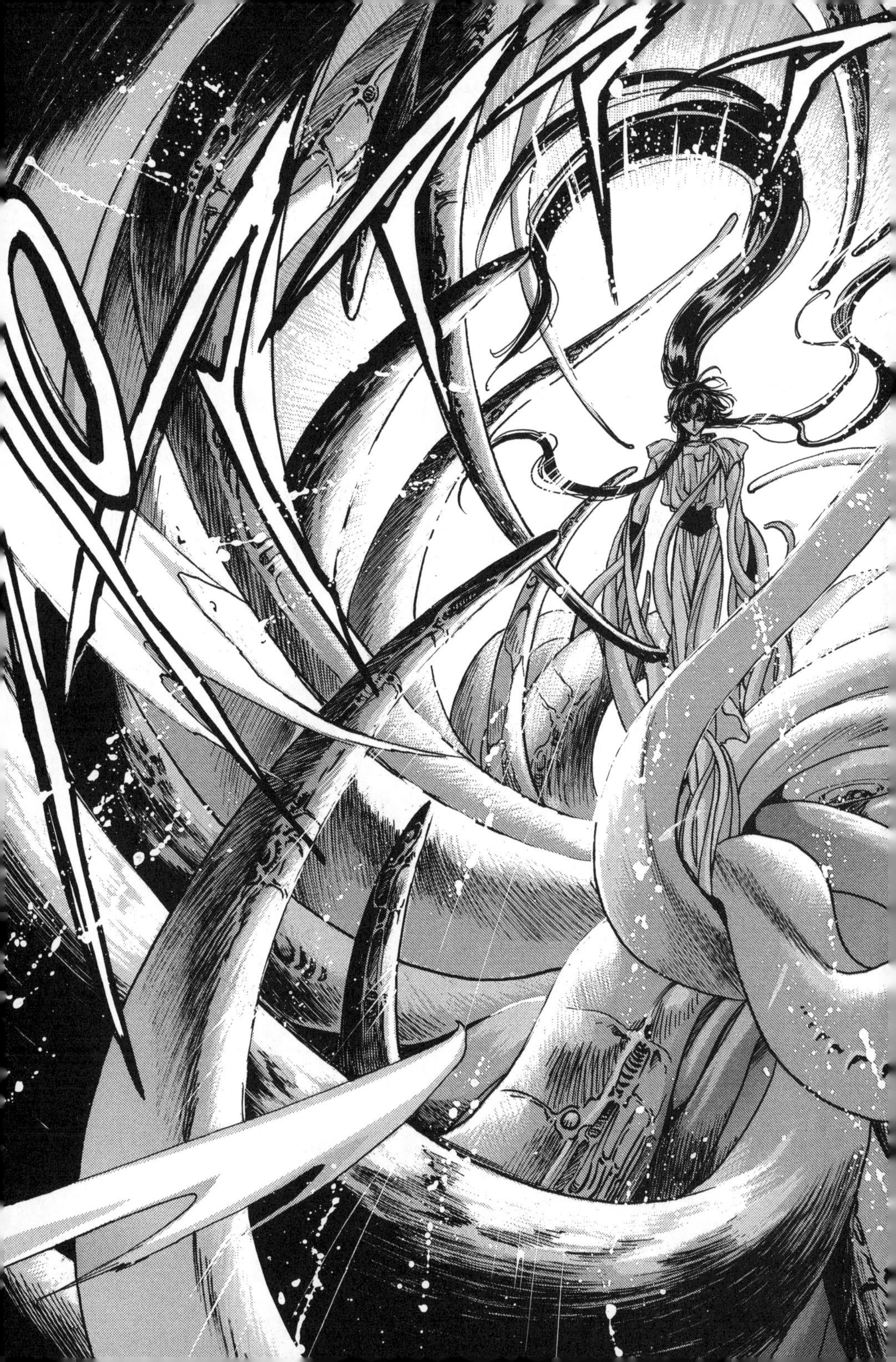

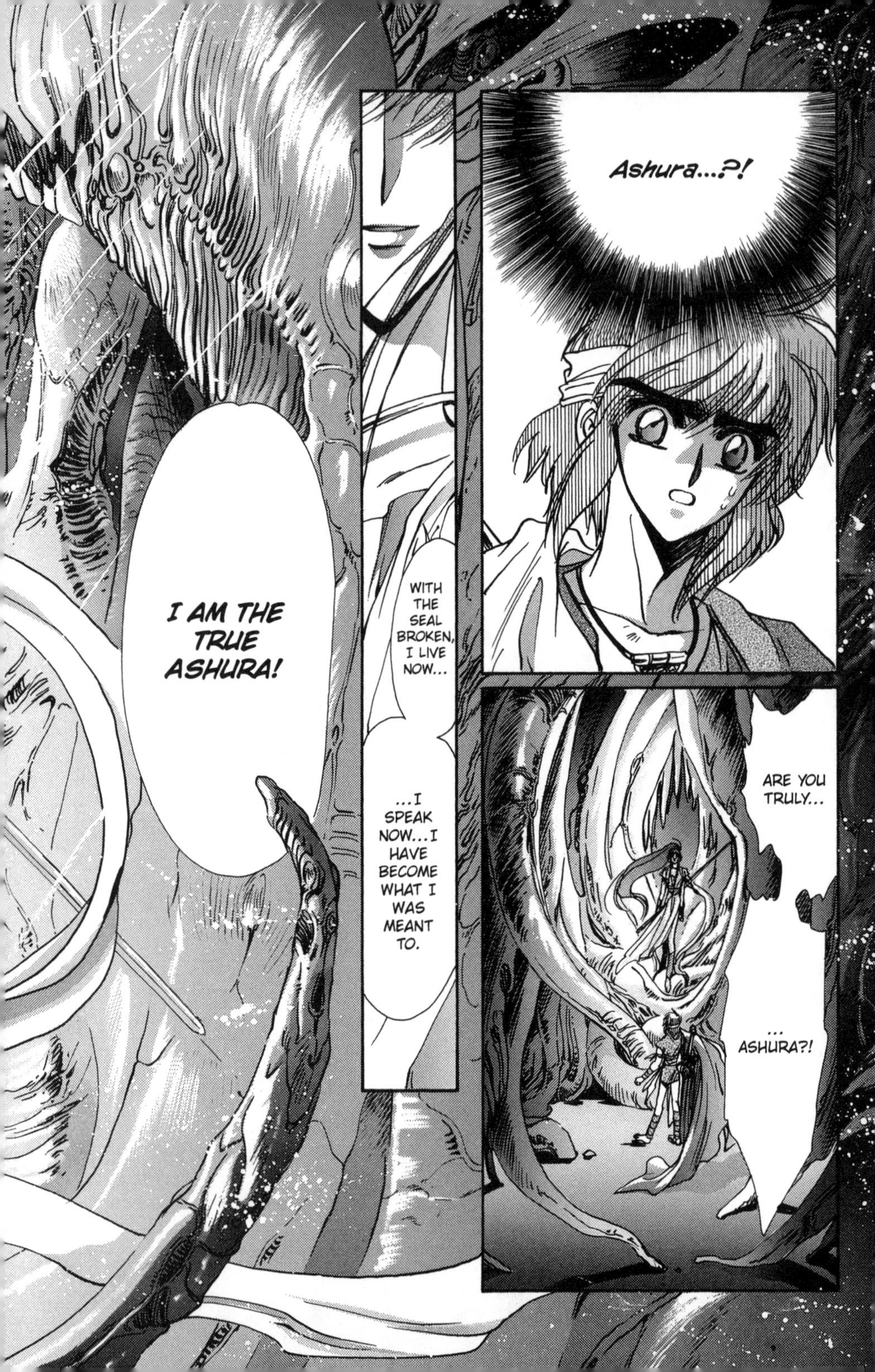
Ashura...?!
ARE YOU TRULY...
...ASHURA?!
WITH THE SEAL BROKEN, I LIVE NOW...
...I SPEAK NOW...I HAVE BECOME WHAT I WAS MEANT TO.
I AM THE TRUE ASHURA!

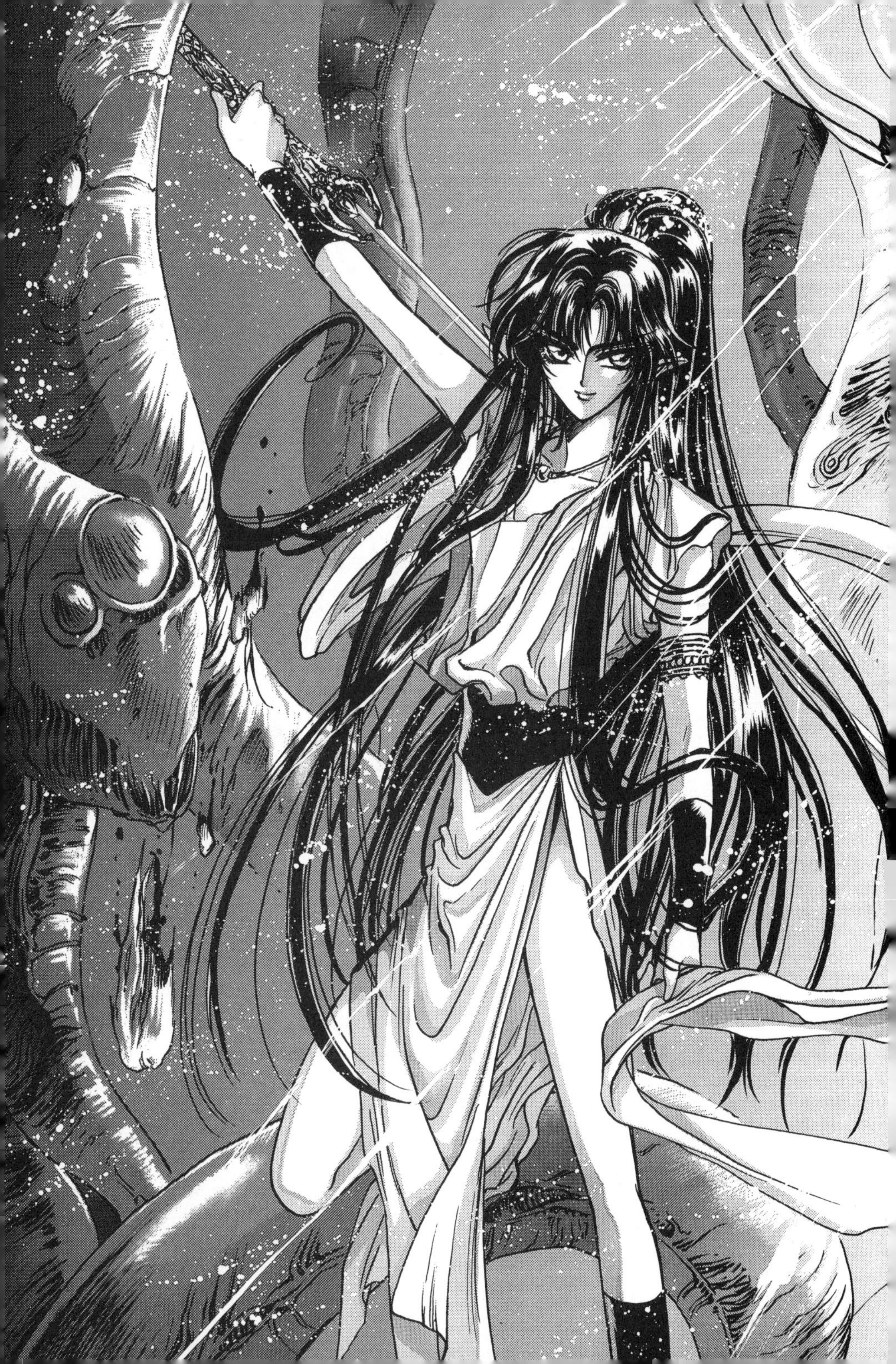

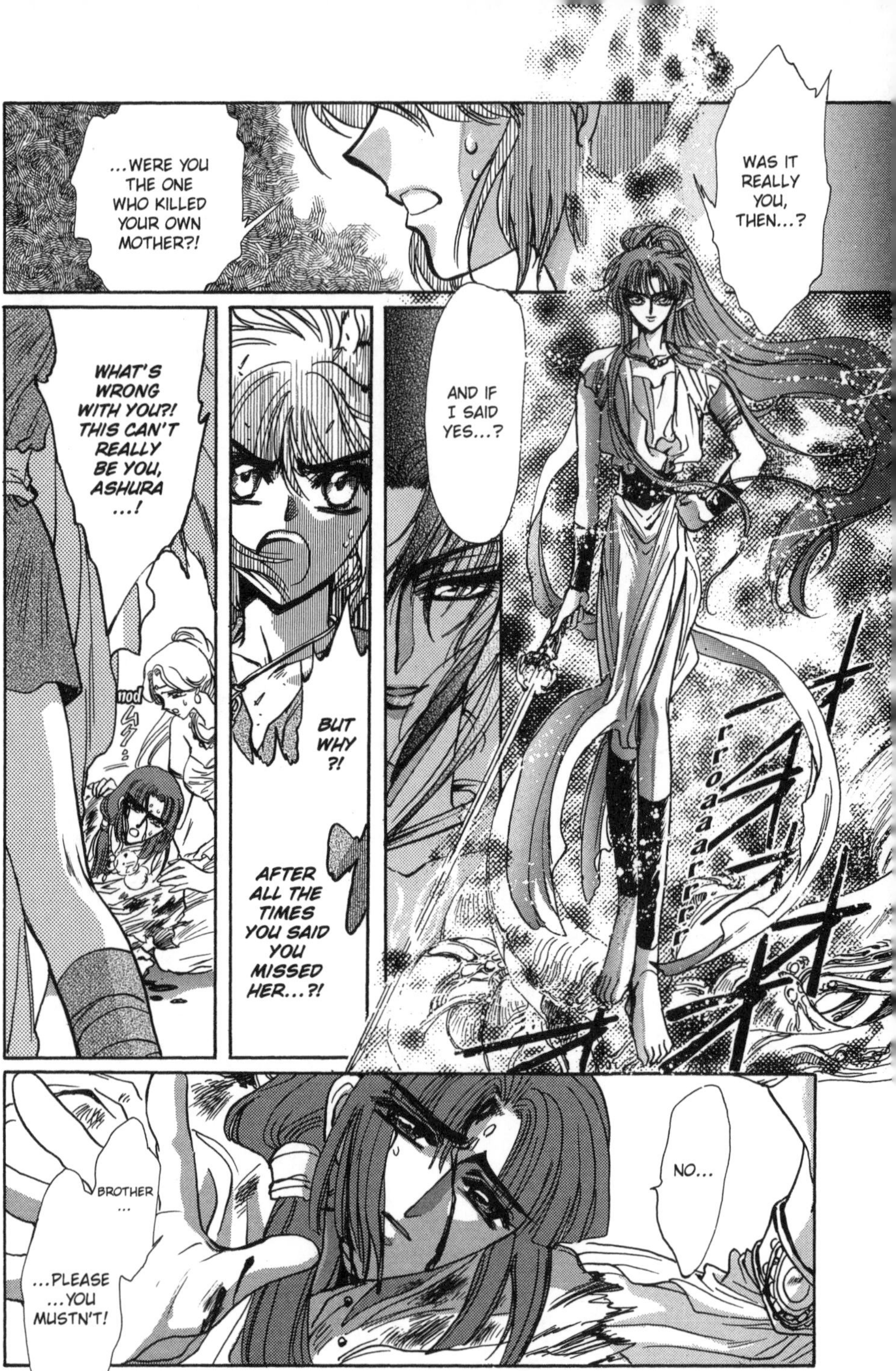
WAS IT REALLY YOU, THEN...?
...WERE YOU THE ONE WHO KILLED YOUR OWN MOTHER?!
AND IF I SAID YES...?
rroaaarrrr
!
BUT WHY?!
AFTER ALL THE TIMES YOU SAID YOU MISSED HER...?!
WHAT'S WRONG WITH YOU?! THIS CAN'T REALLY BE YOU, ASHURA...!
nod
NO...
BROTHER...
...PLEASE ...YOU MUSTN'T!

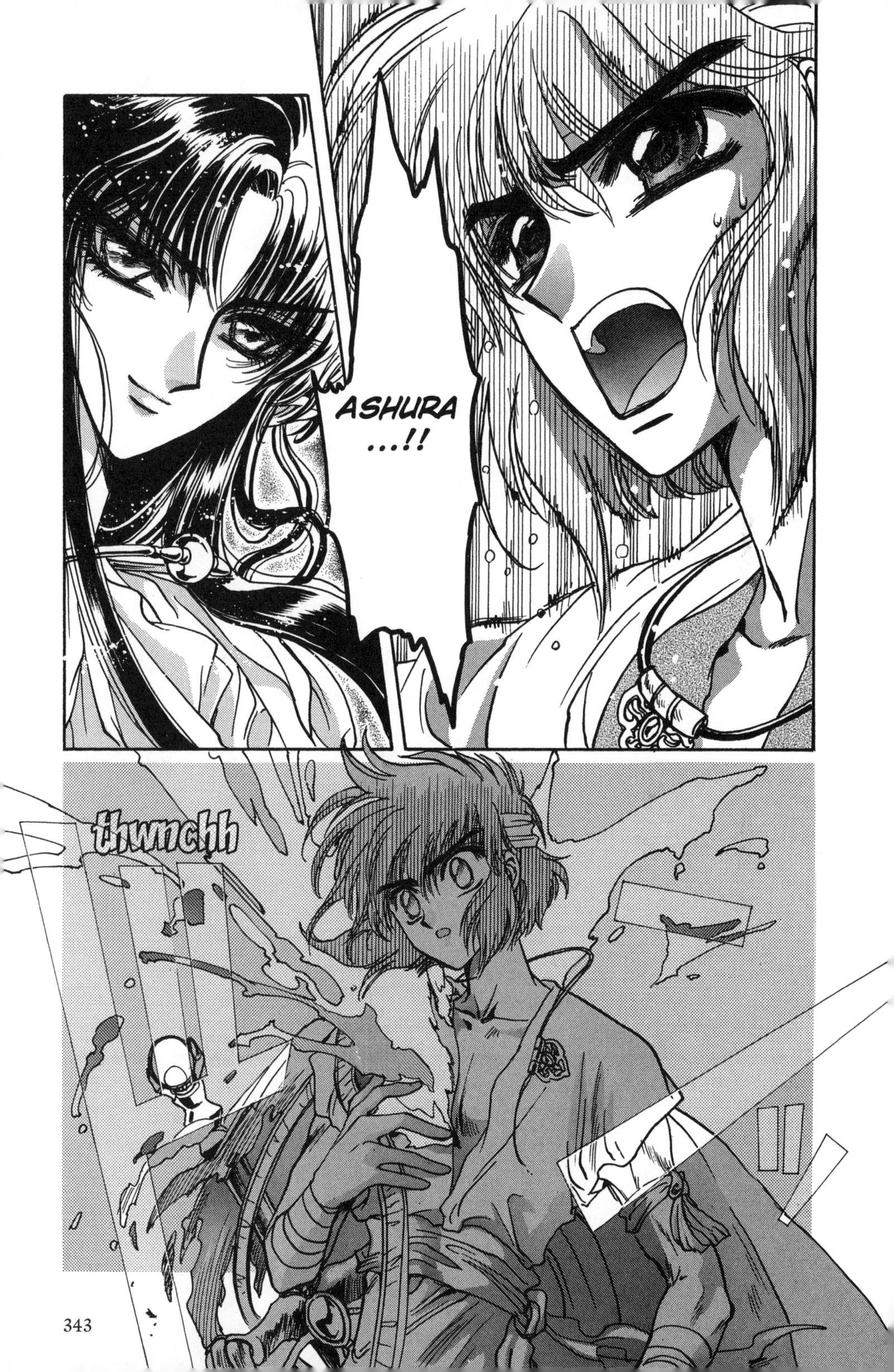
ASHURA ...!!
thwnchh

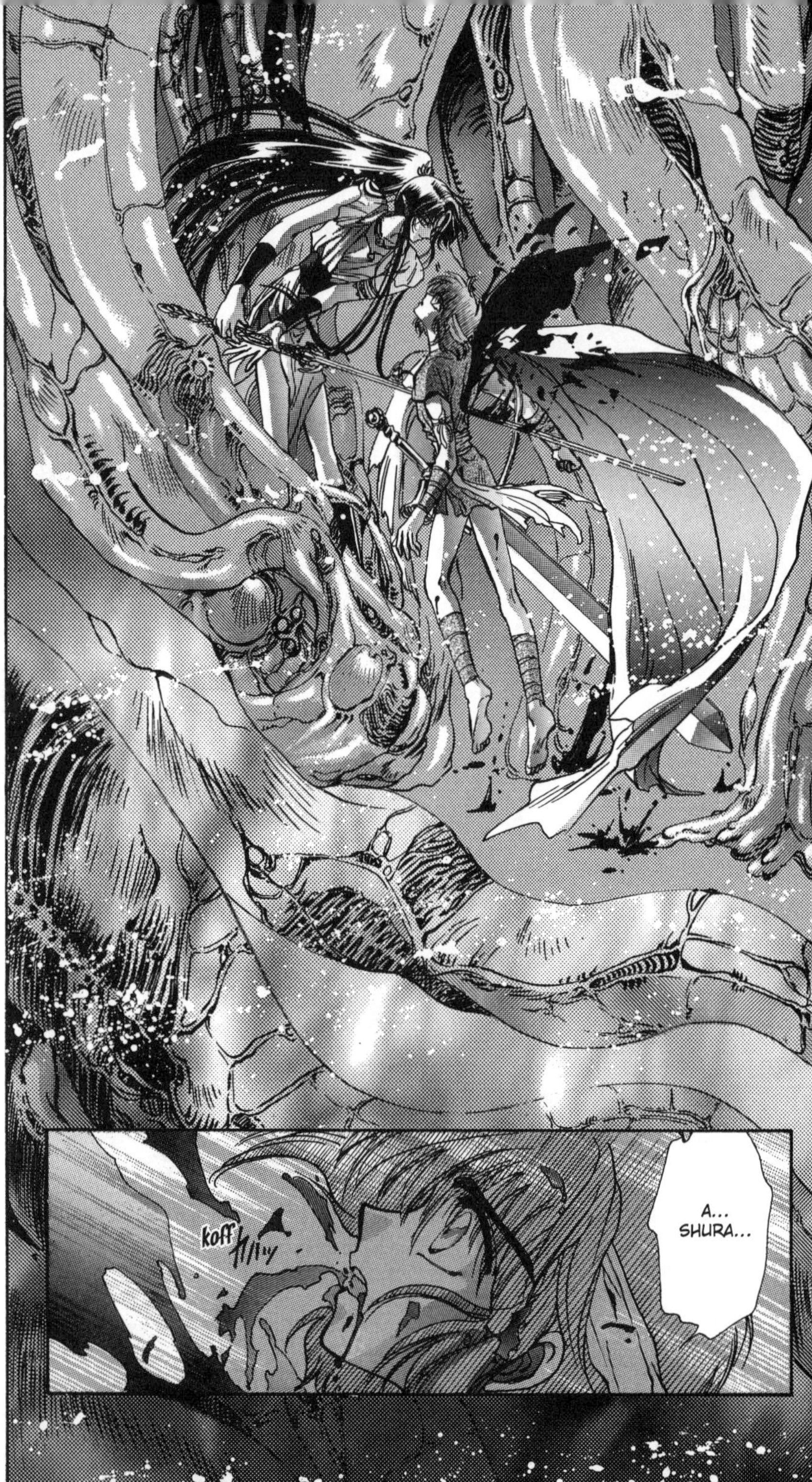
A... SHURA...
koff

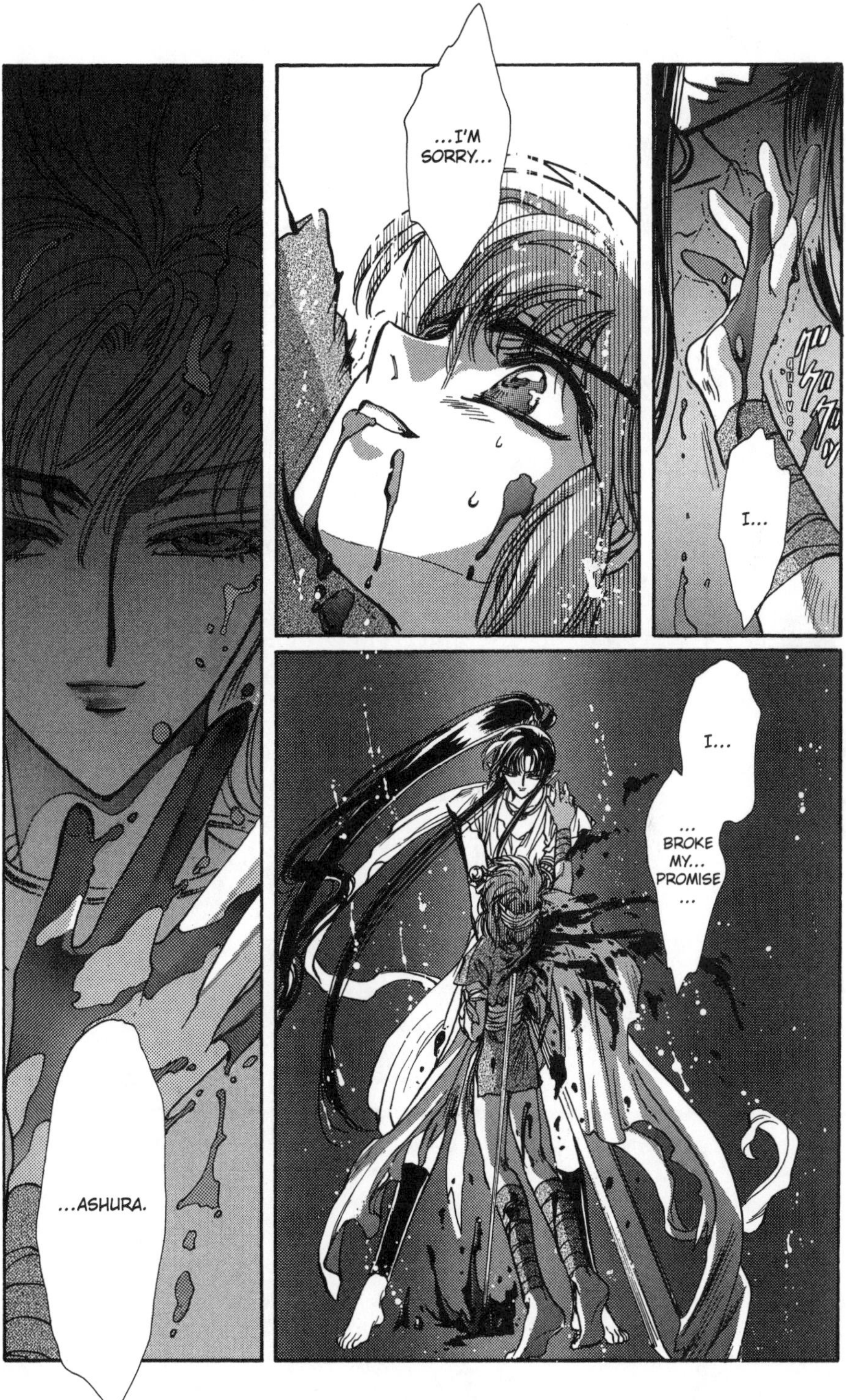

quiver
I...
...I'M SORRY...
I...
...BROKE MY... PROMISE...
...ASHURA.

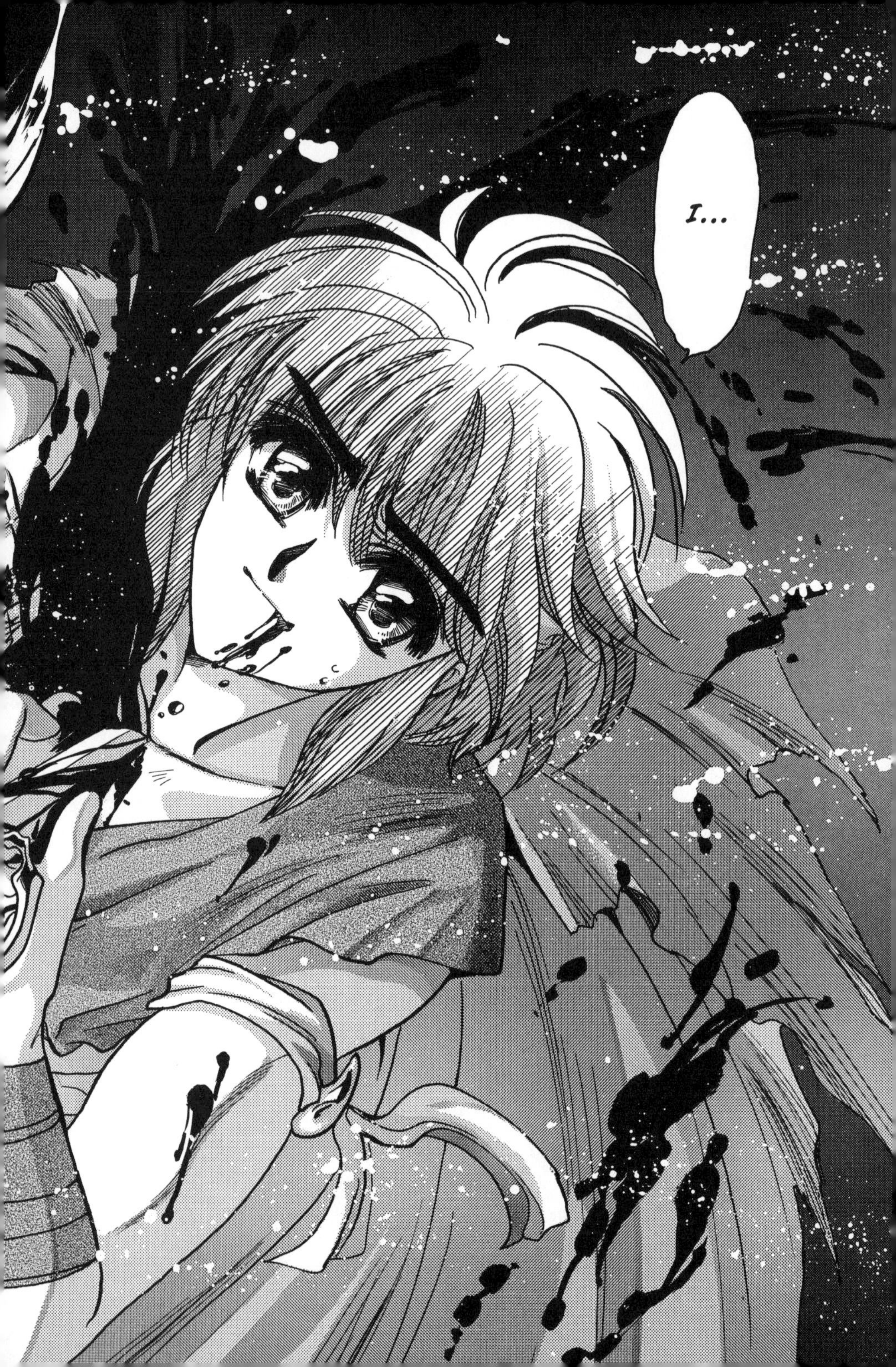
I...

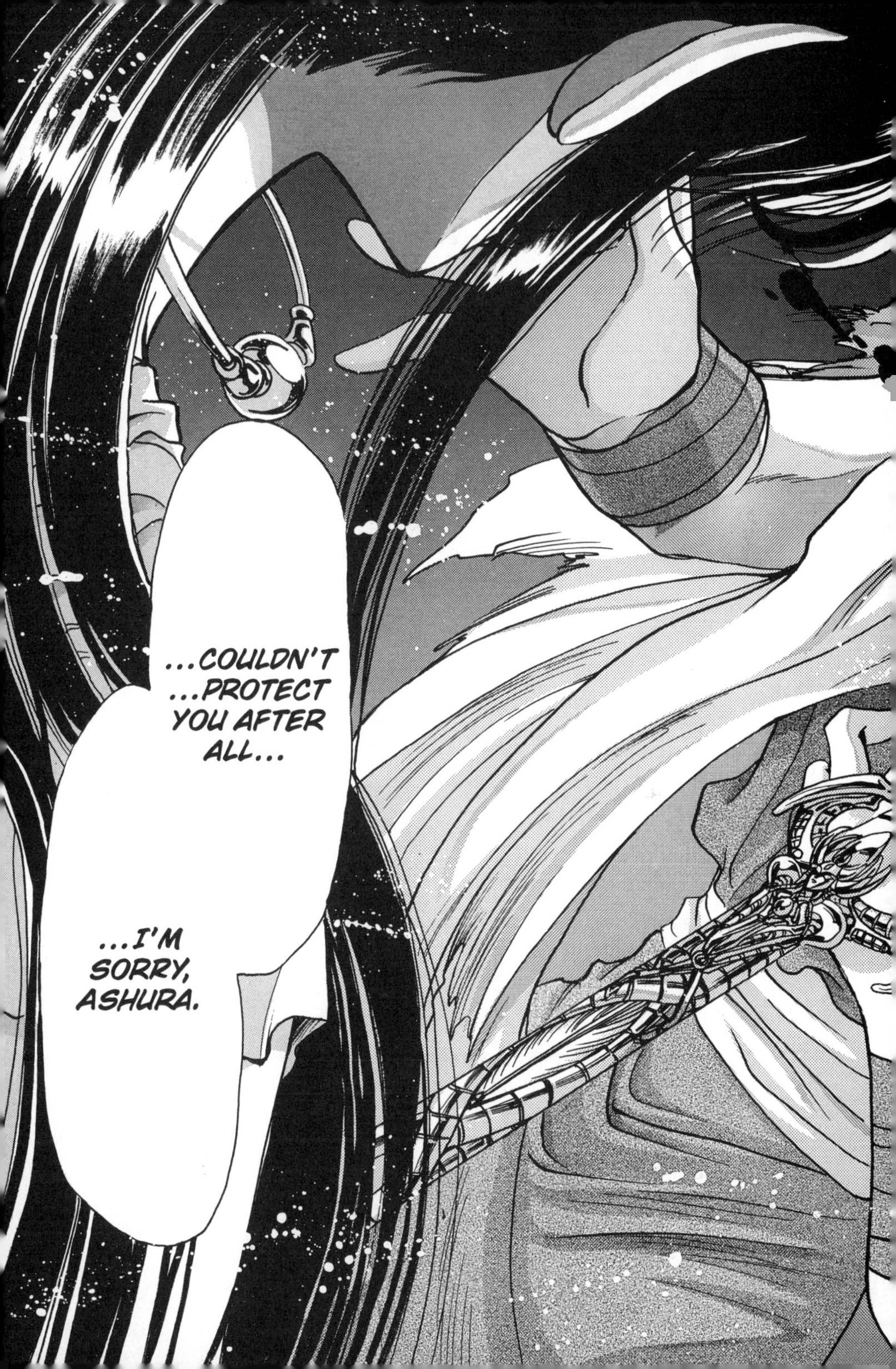
...COULDN'T ...PROTECT YOU AFTER ALL...
...I'M SORRY, ASHURA.

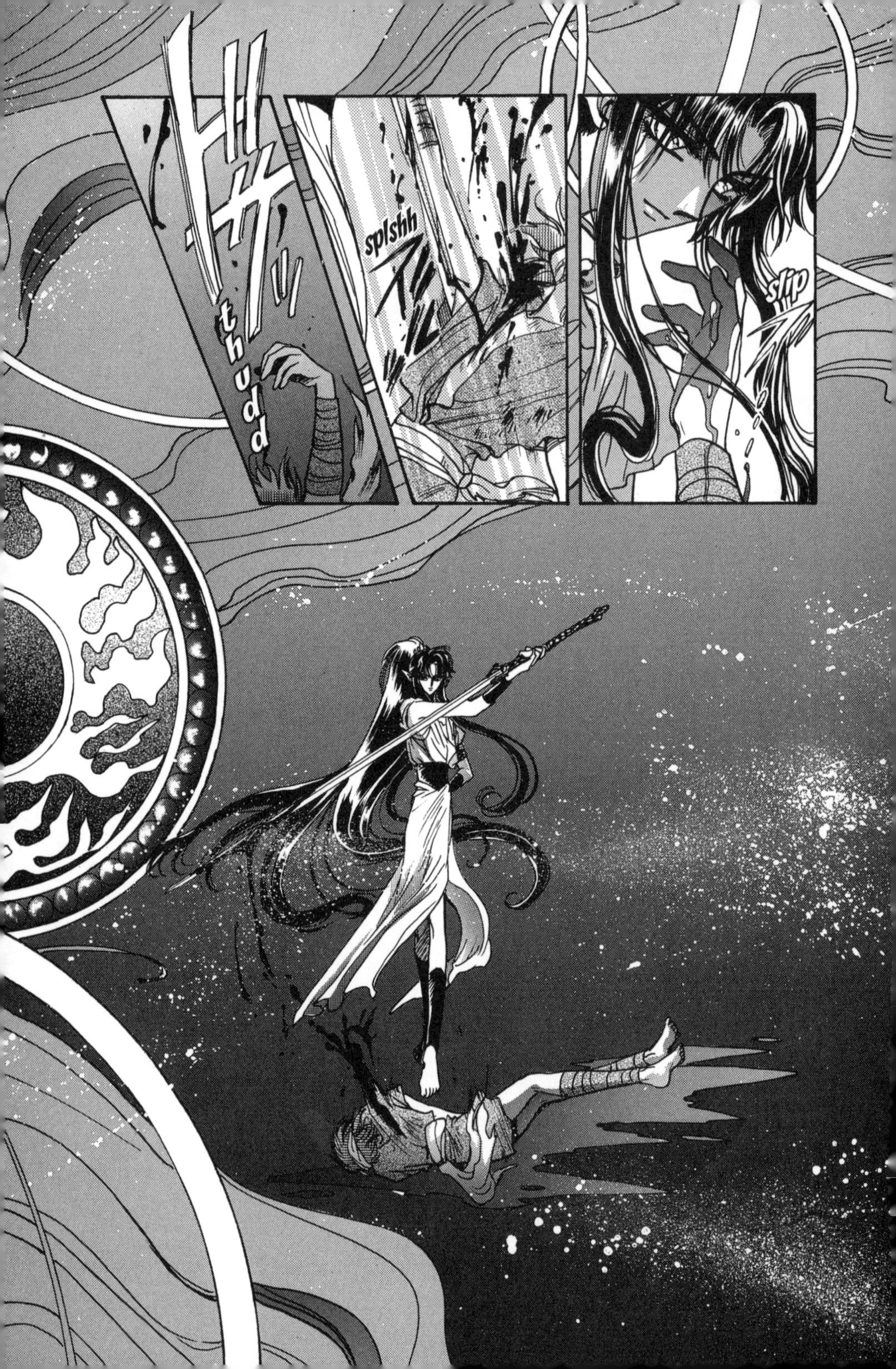

slip
splshh
thudd

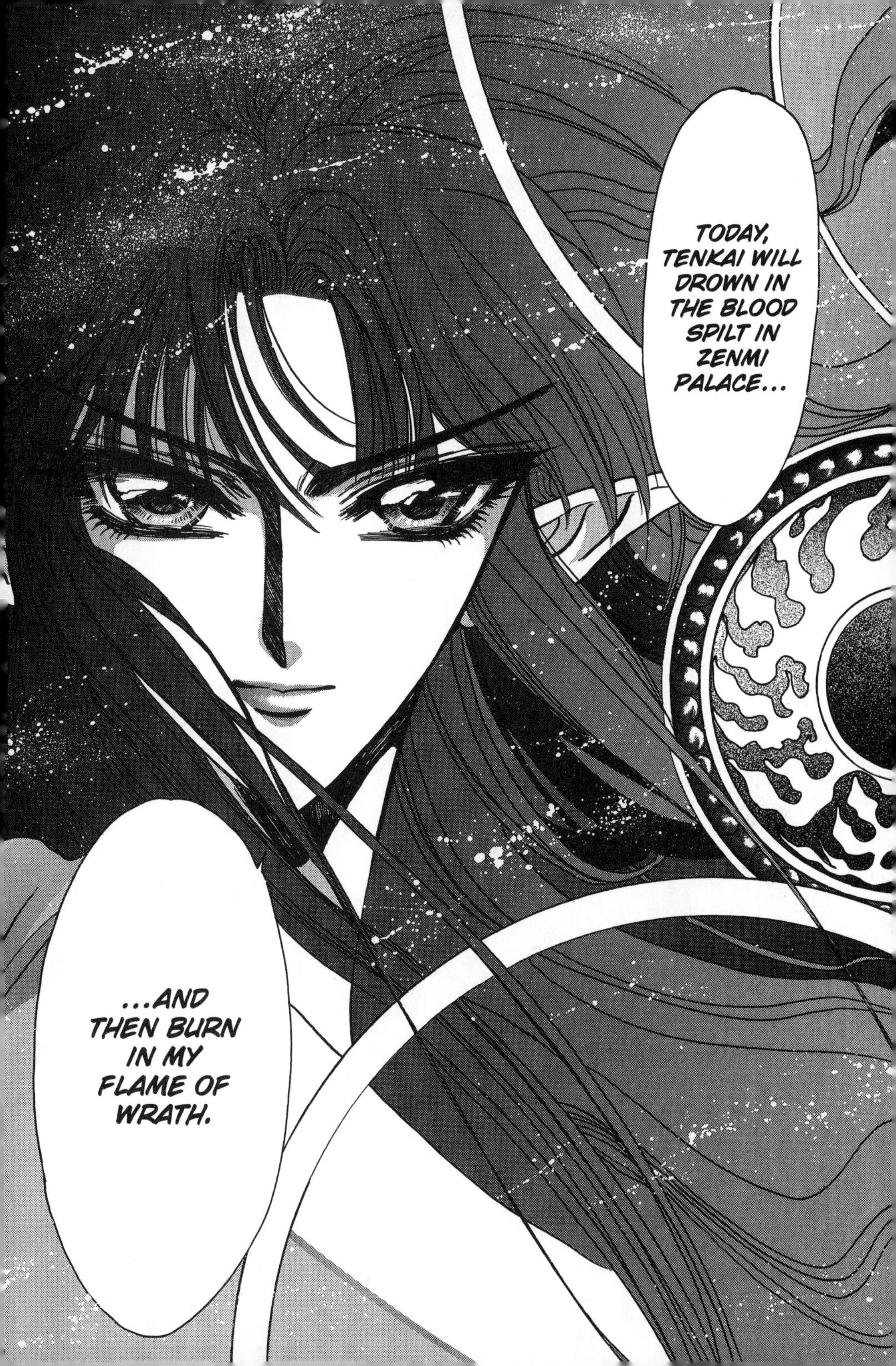
TODAY, TENKAI WILL DROWN IN THE BLOOD SPILT IN ZENMI PALACE...
...AND THEN BURN IN MY FLAME OF WRATH.

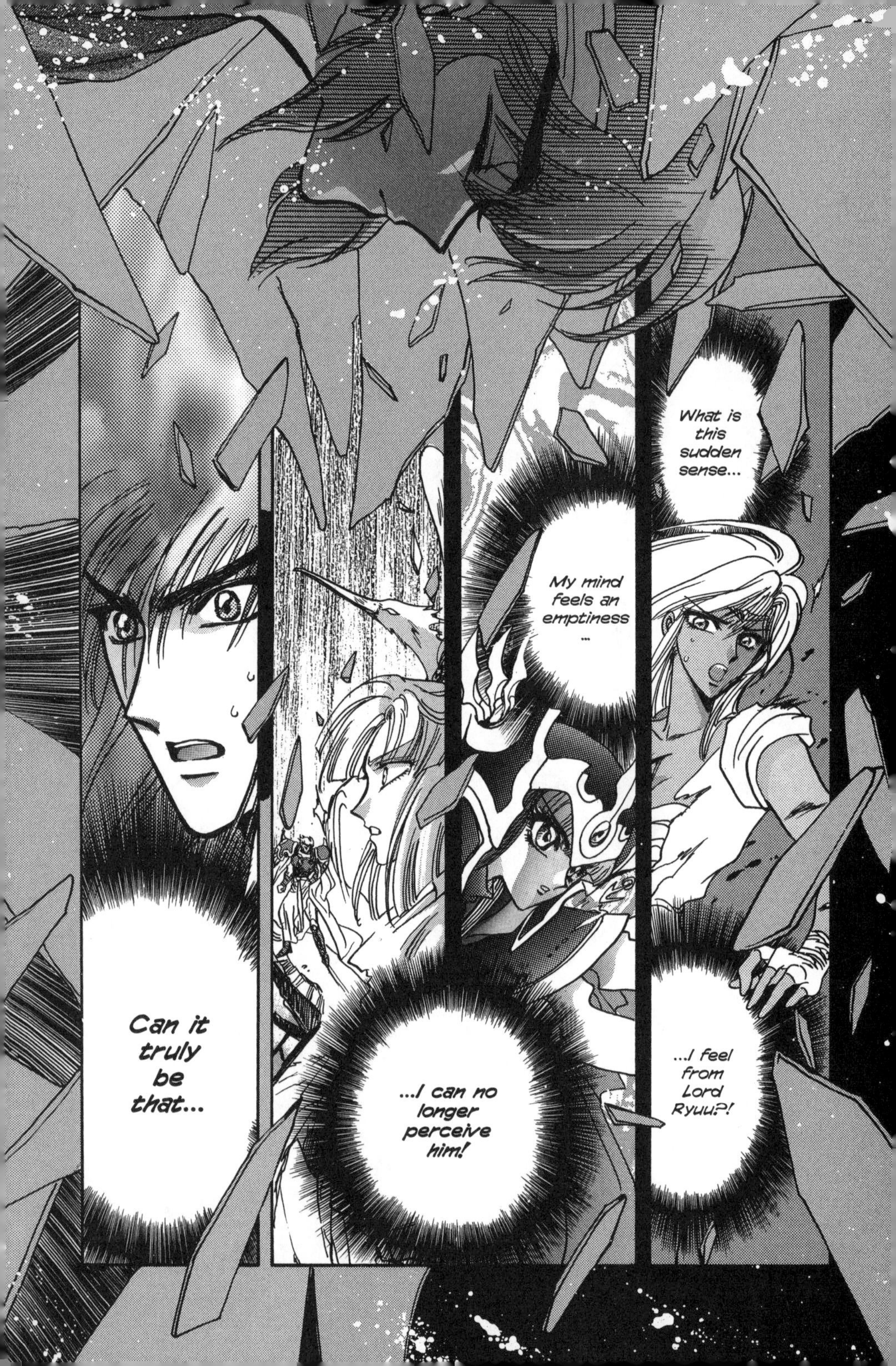
What is this sudden sense...
...I feel from Lord Ryuu?!
My mind feels an emptiness ...
...I can no longer perceive him!
Can it truly be that...

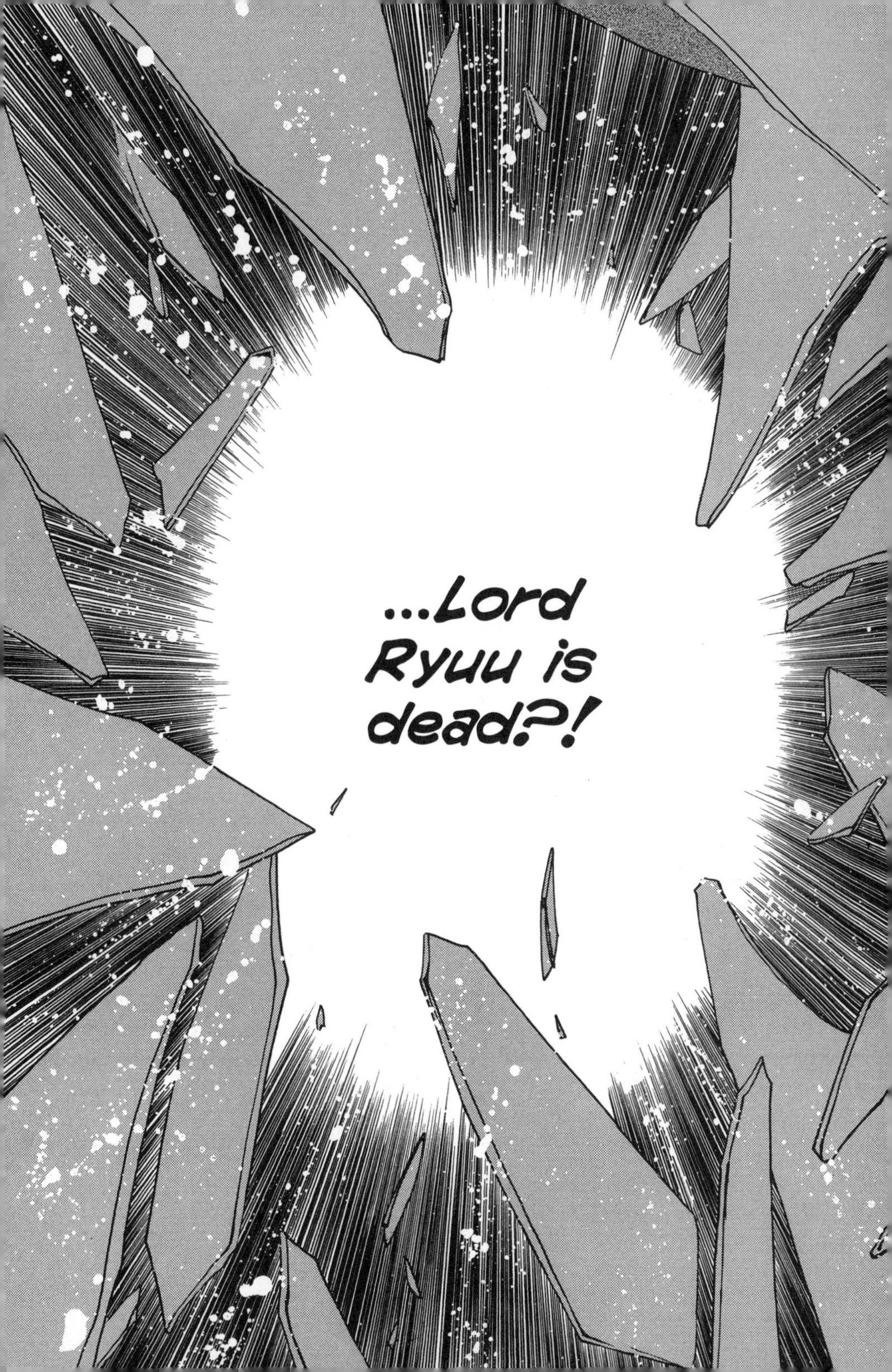
...Lord Ryuu is dead?!

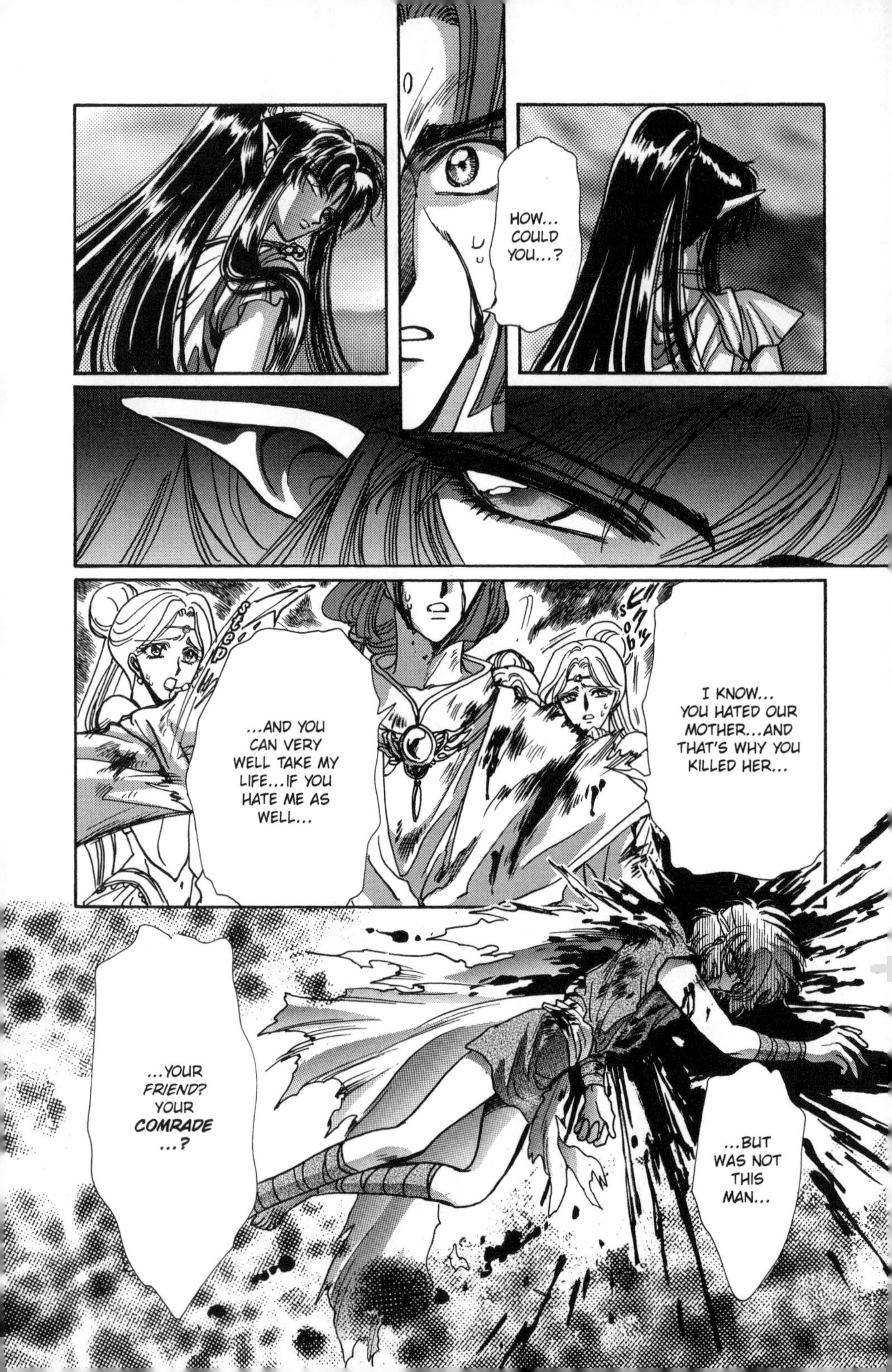
HOW... COULD YOU...?
I KNOW... YOU HATED OUR MOTHER...AND THAT'S WHY YOU KILLED HER...
...AND YOU CAN VERY WELL TAKE MY LIFE...IF YOU HATE ME AS WELL...
...BUT WAS NOT THIS MAN...
...YOUR FRIEND? YOUR **COMRADE** ...?

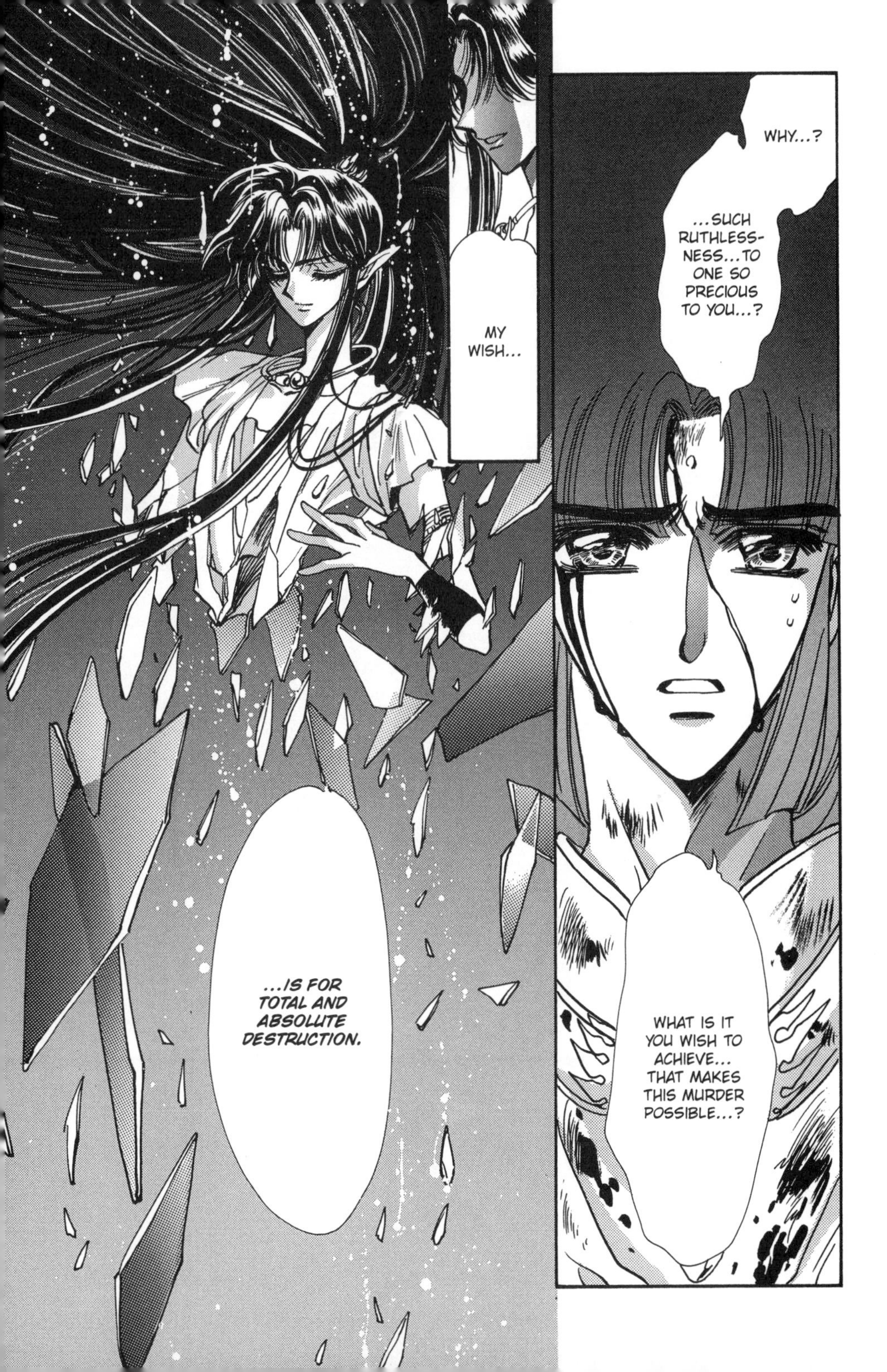
WHY...?
...SUCH RUTHLESS-NESS...TO ONE SO PRECIOUS TO YOU...?
WHAT IS IT YOU WISH TO ACHIEVE... THAT MAKES THIS MURDER POSSIBLE...?
MY WISH...
...IS FOR TOTAL AND ABSOLUTE DESTRUCTION.

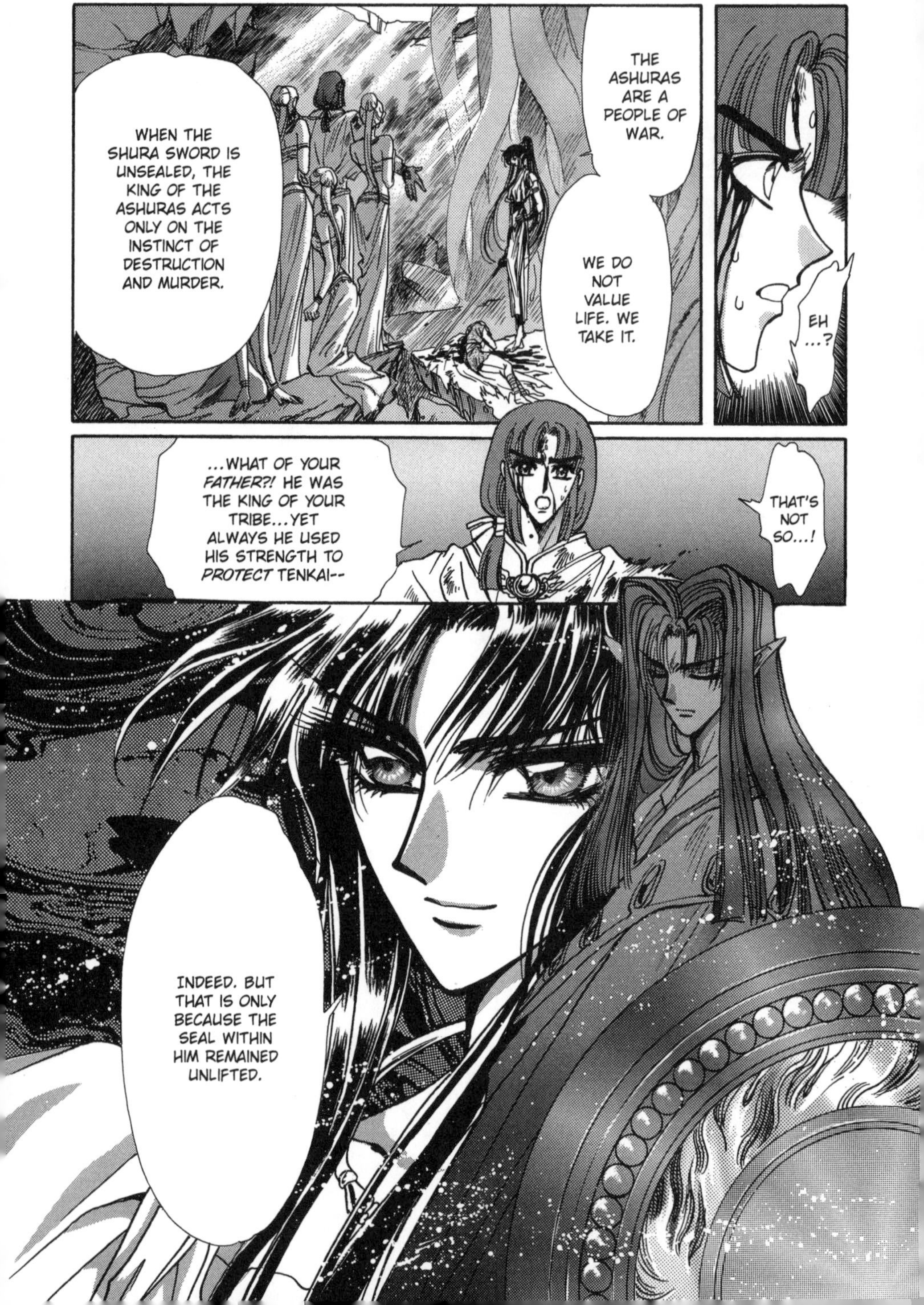
EH ...?
THE ASHURAS ARE A PEOPLE OF WAR.
WE DO NOT VALUE LIFE. WE TAKE IT.
WHEN THE SHURA SWORD IS UNSEALED, THE KING OF THE ASHURAS ACTS ONLY ON THE INSTINCT OF DESTRUCTION AND MURDER.
THAT'S NOT SO...!
...WHAT OF YOUR *FATHER?!* HE WAS THE KING OF YOUR TRIBE...YET ALWAYS HE USED HIS STRENGTH TO *PROTECT* TENKAI--
INDEED. BUT THAT IS ONLY BECAUSE THE SEAL WITHIN HIM REMAINED UNLIFTED.

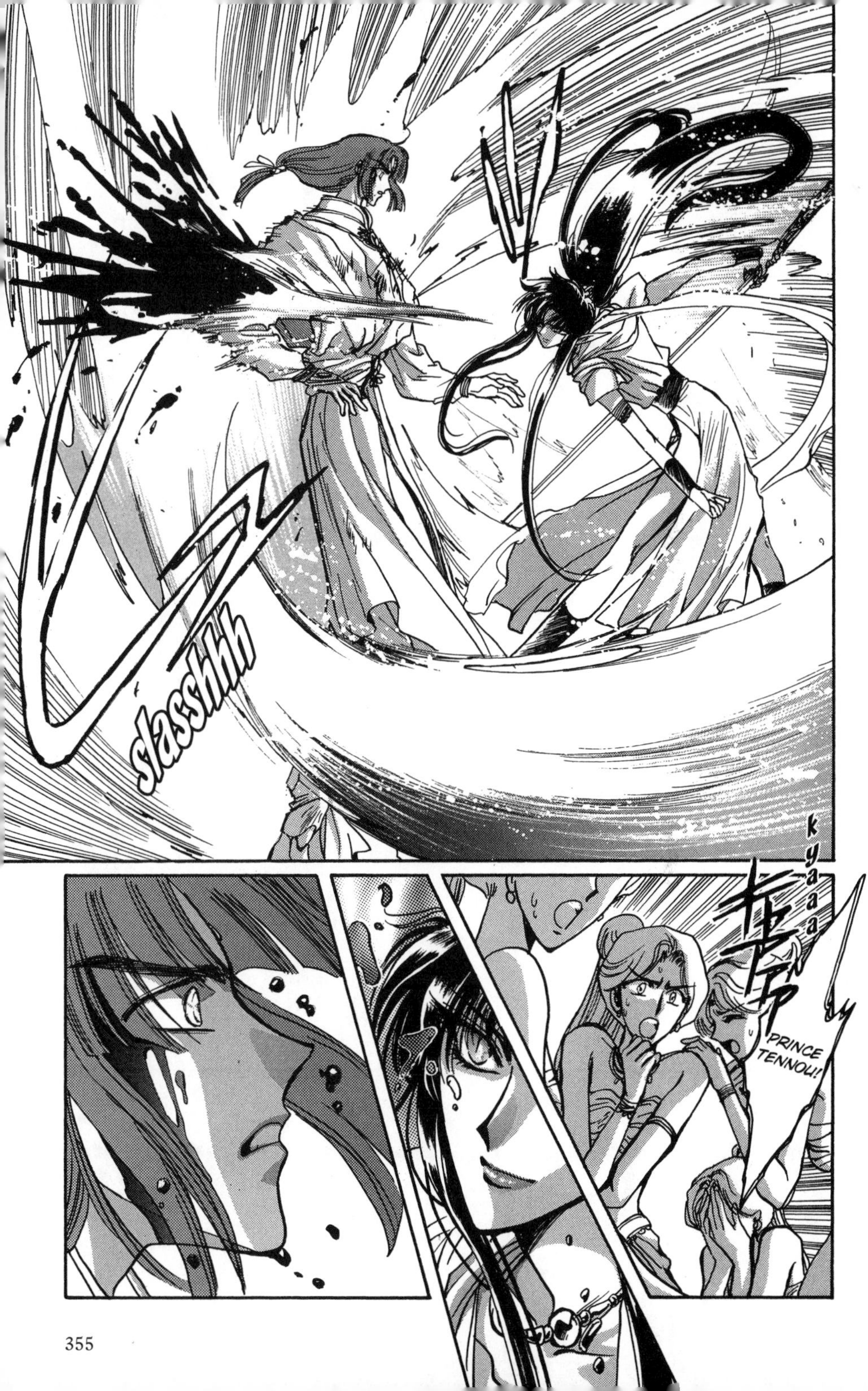
slasshhh
kyaaaa
PRINCE TENNOU!

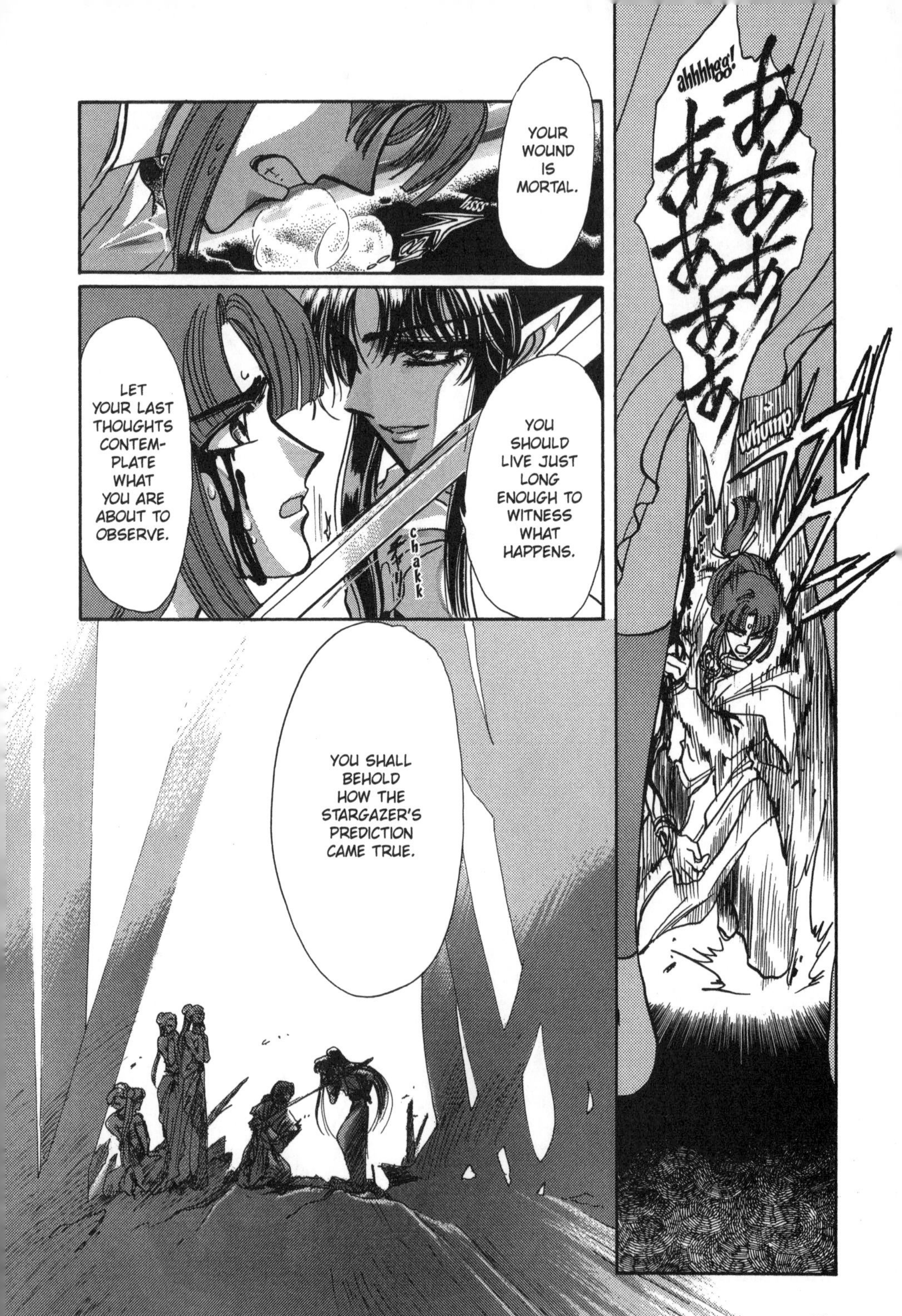

ahhhhgg!
ああぁ
あああぁ
whump
hisss
YOUR WOUND IS MORTAL.
YOU SHOULD LIVE JUST LONG ENOUGH TO WITNESS WHAT HAPPENS.
chakk
LET YOUR LAST THOUGHTS CONTEM-PLATE WHAT YOU ARE ABOUT TO OBSERVE.
YOU SHALL BEHOLD HOW THE STARGAZER'S PREDICTION CAME TRUE.

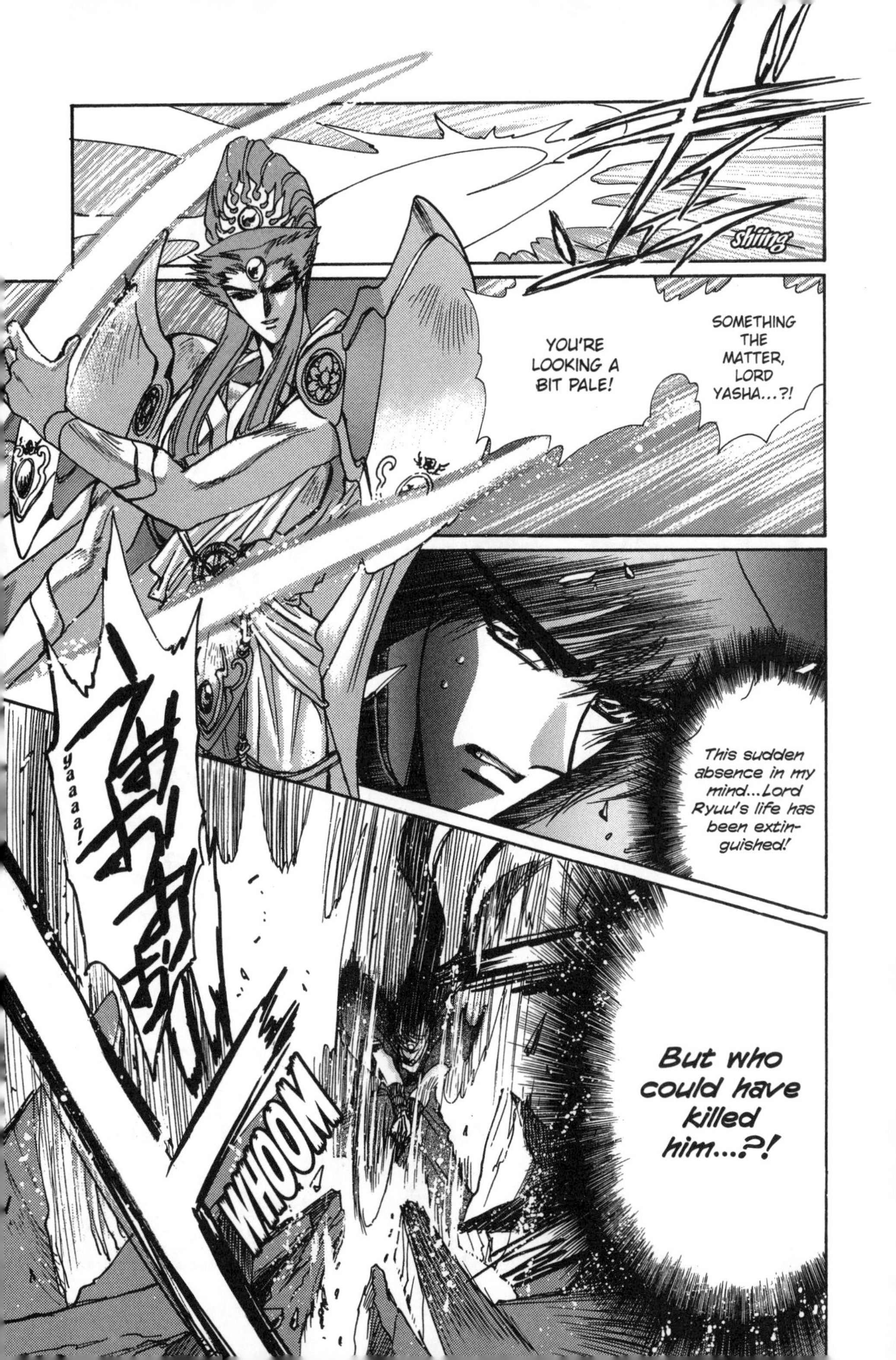
shiing
SOMETHING THE MATTER, LORD YASHA...?!
YOU'RE LOOKING A BIT PALE!
This sudden absence in my mind...Lord Ryuu's life has been extinguished!
yaaaaa!
But who could have killed him...?!
WHOOM

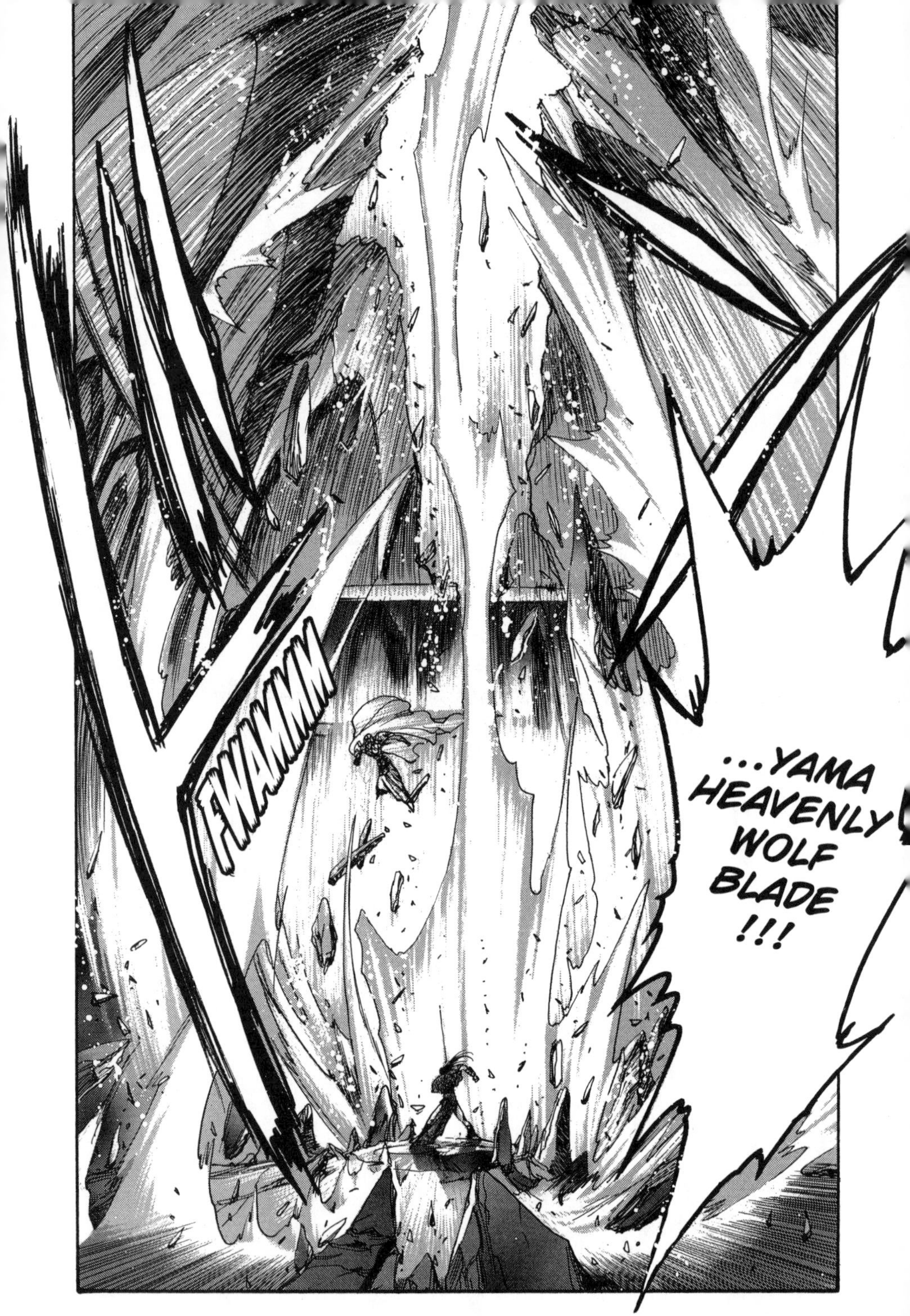
...YAMA HEAVENLY WOLF BLADE!!!
FWAMMM

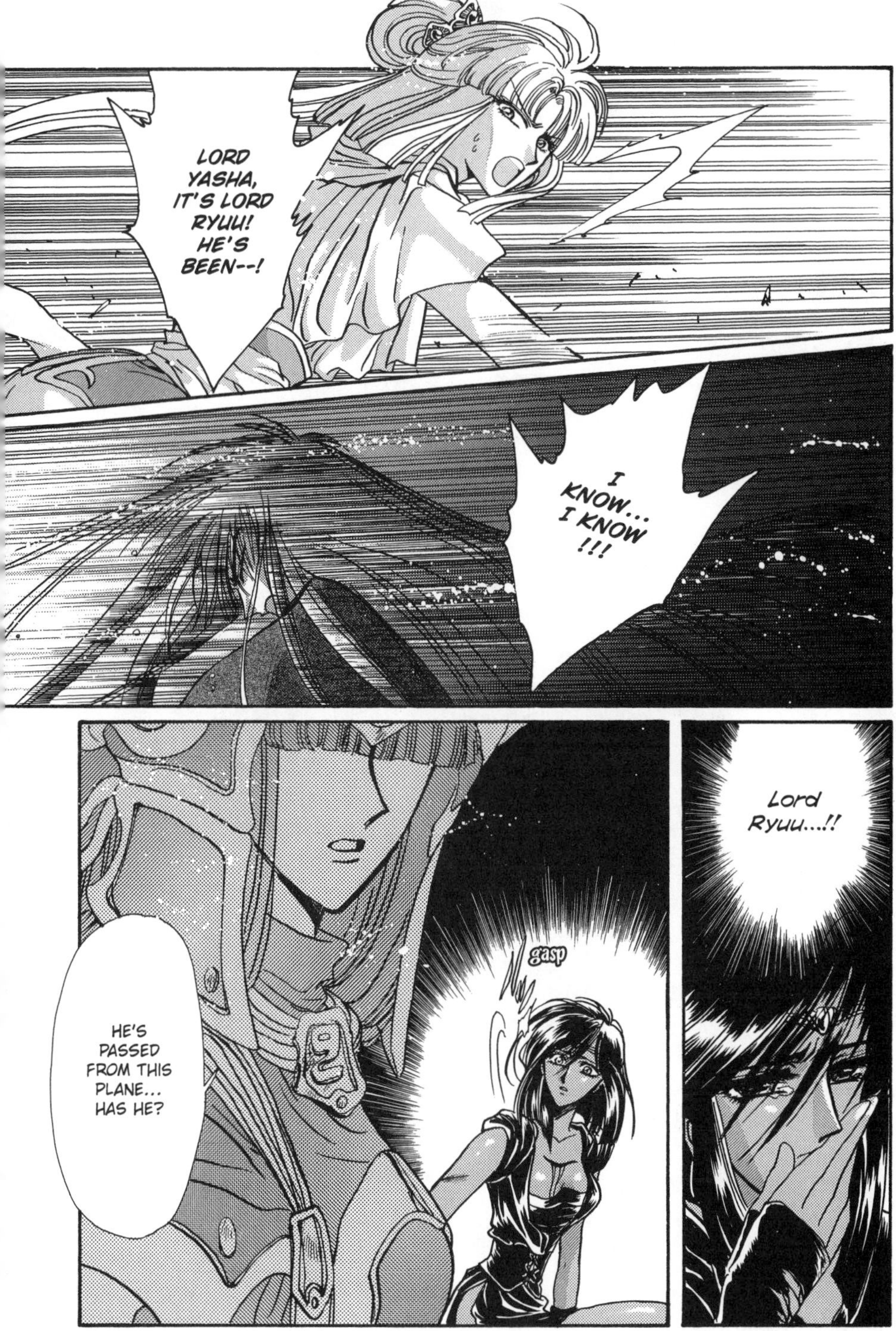
LORD YASHA, IT'S LORD RYUU! HE'S BEEN--!
I KNOW... I KNOW !!!
Lord Ryuu...!!
gasp
HE'S PASSED FROM THIS PLANE... HAS HE?

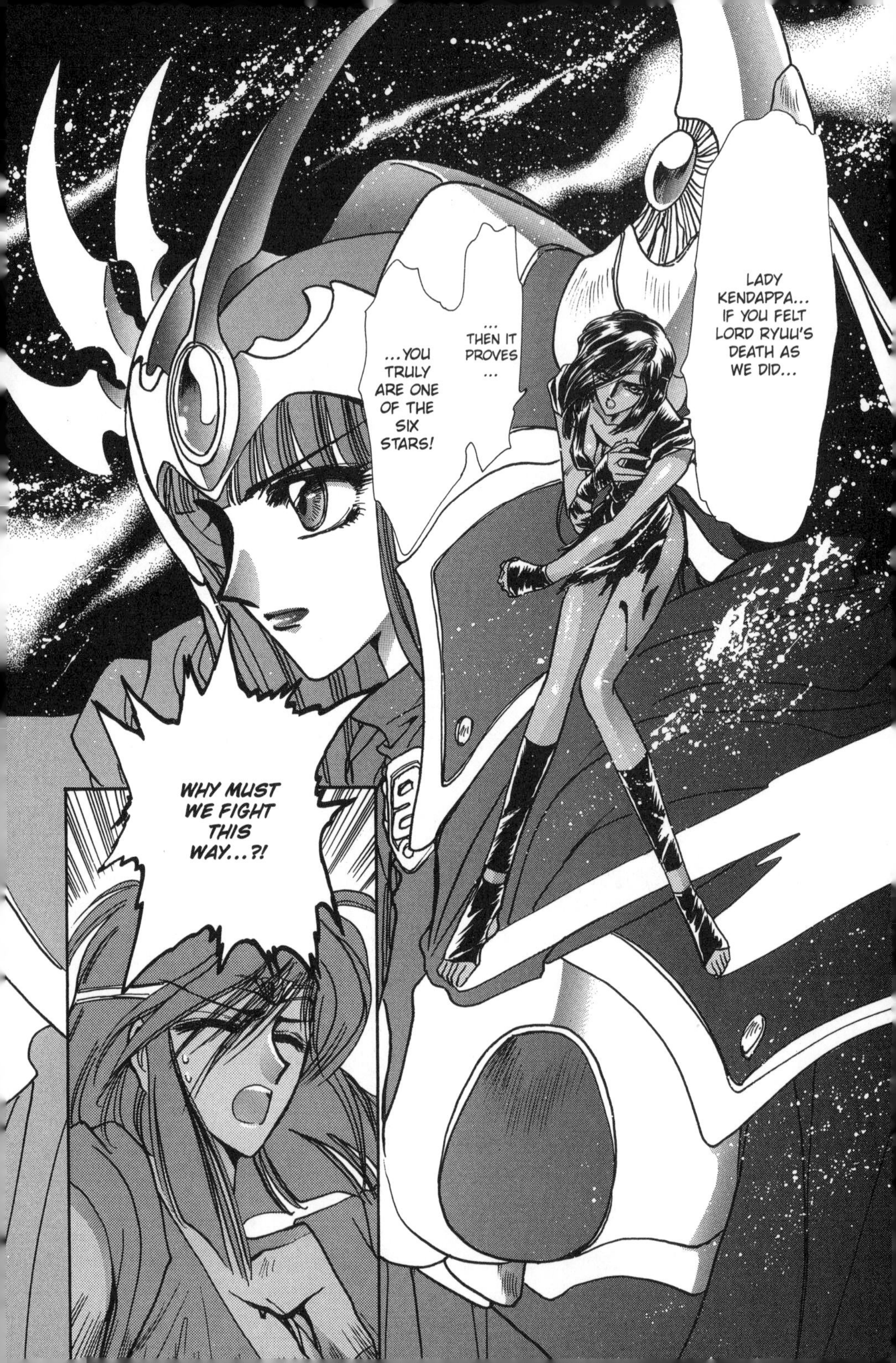

LADY KENDAPPA... IF YOU FELT LORD RYUU'S DEATH AS WE DID...
...THEN IT PROVES...
...YOU TRULY ARE ONE OF THE SIX STARS!
WHY MUST WE FIGHT THIS WAY...?!

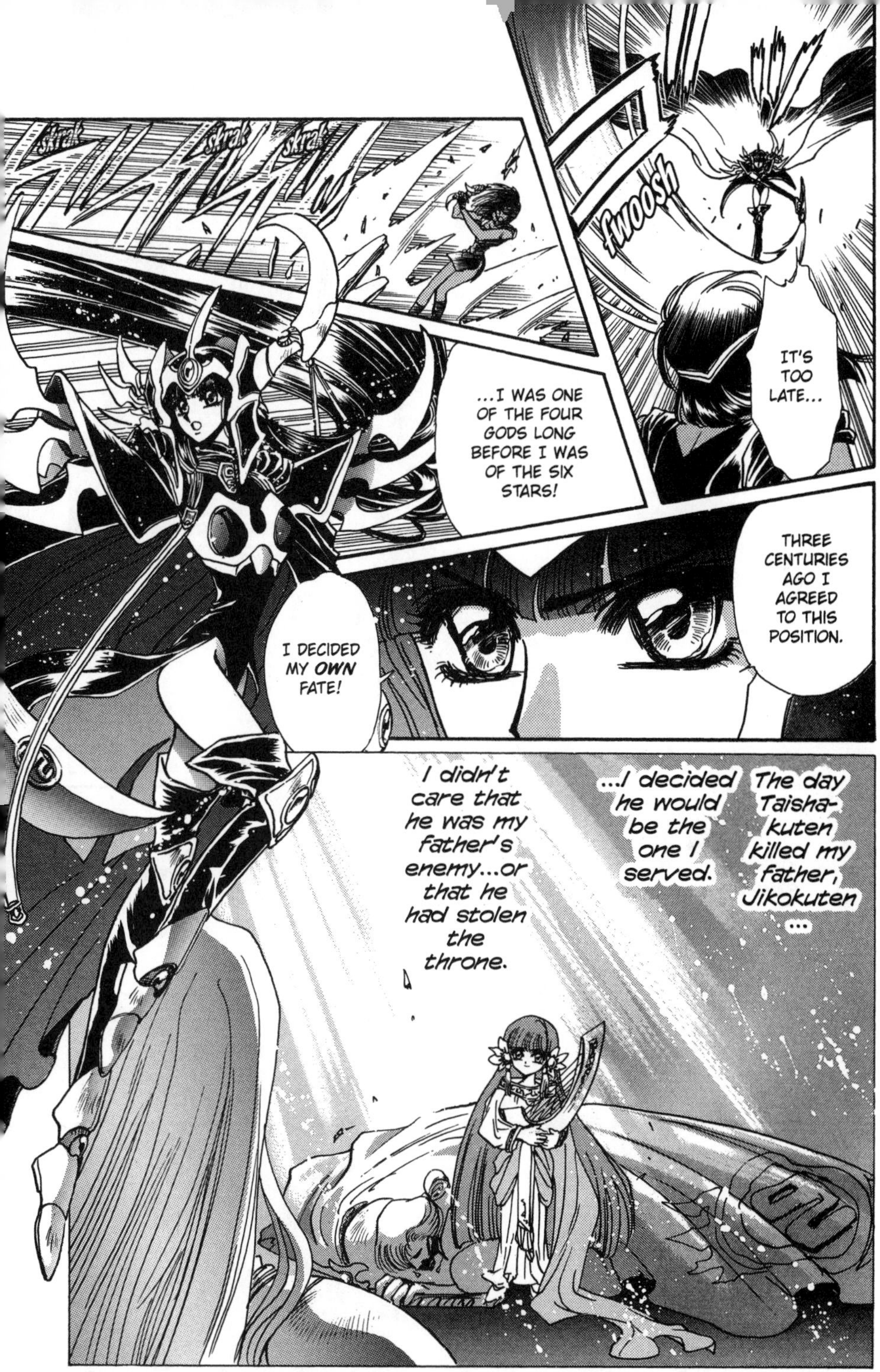
fwoosh
IT'S TOO LATE...
skrak
skrak
skrak
...I WAS ONE OF THE FOUR GODS LONG BEFORE I WAS OF THE SIX STARS!
THREE CENTURIES AGO I AGREED TO THIS POSITION.
I DECIDED MY *OWN* FATE!
The day Taishakuten killed my father, Jikokuten ...
...I decided he would be the one I served.
I didn't care that he was my father's enemy...or that he had stolen the throne.

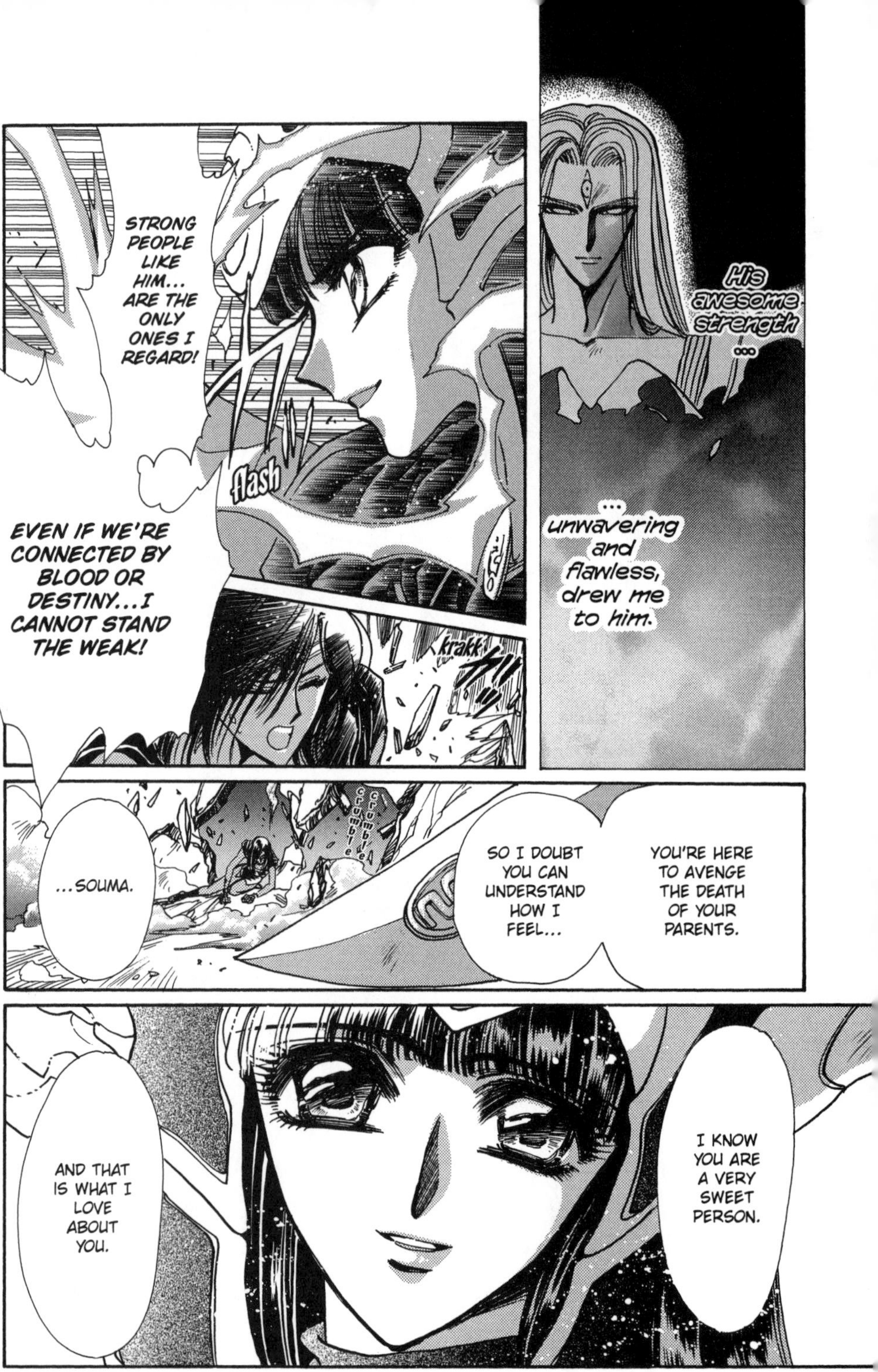

His awesome strength...
...unwavering and flawless, drew me to him.
STRONG PEOPLE LIKE HIM... ARE THE ONLY ONES I REGARD!
flash
krakk
EVEN IF WE'RE CONNECTED BY BLOOD OR DESTINY... I CANNOT STAND THE WEAK!
YOU'RE HERE TO AVENGE THE DEATH OF YOUR PARENTS.
SO I DOUBT YOU CAN UNDERSTAND HOW I FEEL...
crumble
crumble
...SOUMA.
I KNOW YOU ARE A VERY SWEET PERSON.
AND THAT IS WHAT I LOVE ABOUT YOU.

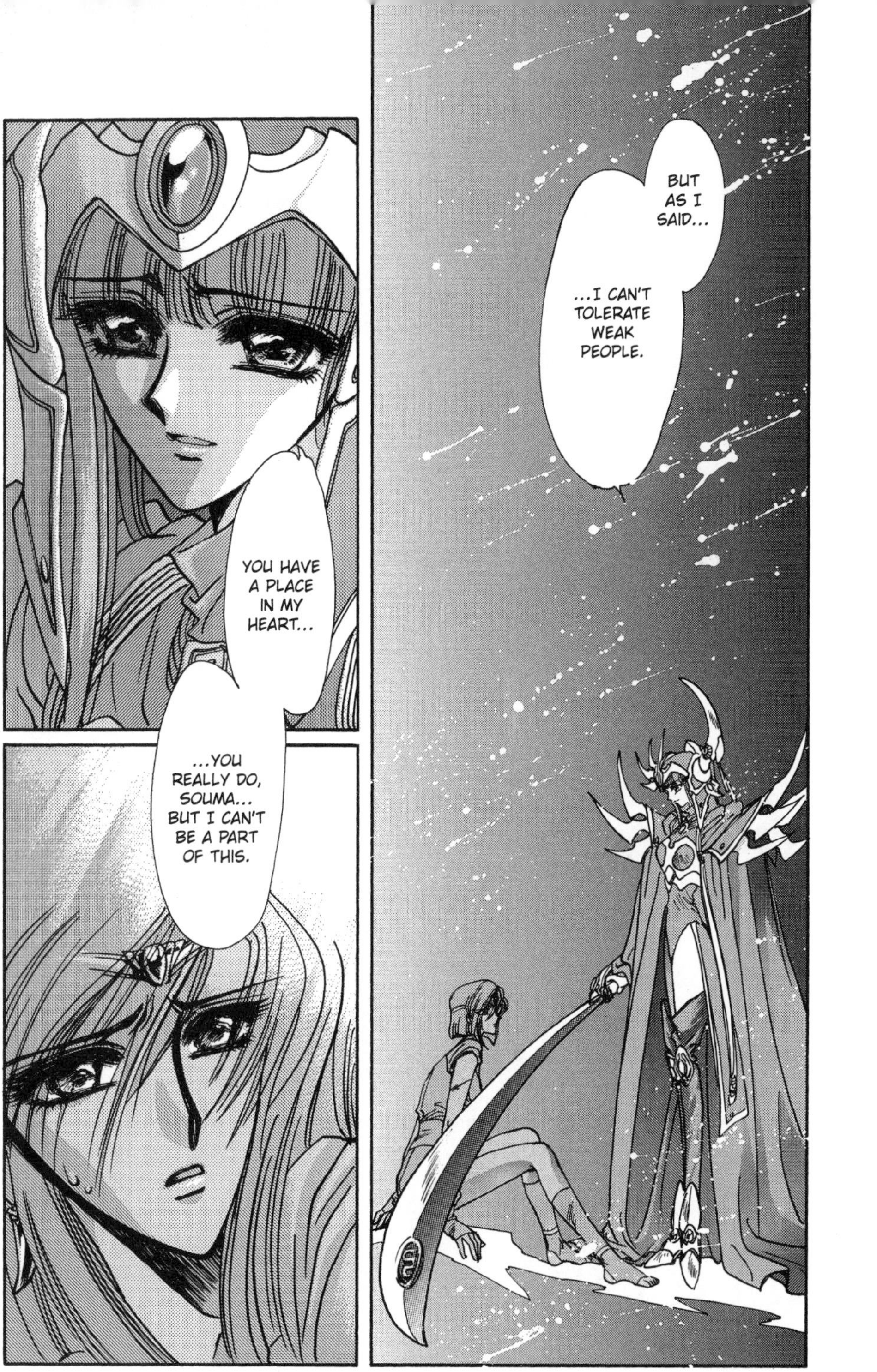
BUT AS I SAID...
...I CAN'T TOLERATE WEAK PEOPLE.
YOU HAVE A PLACE IN MY HEART...
...YOU REALLY DO, SOUMA... BUT I CAN'T BE A PART OF THIS.

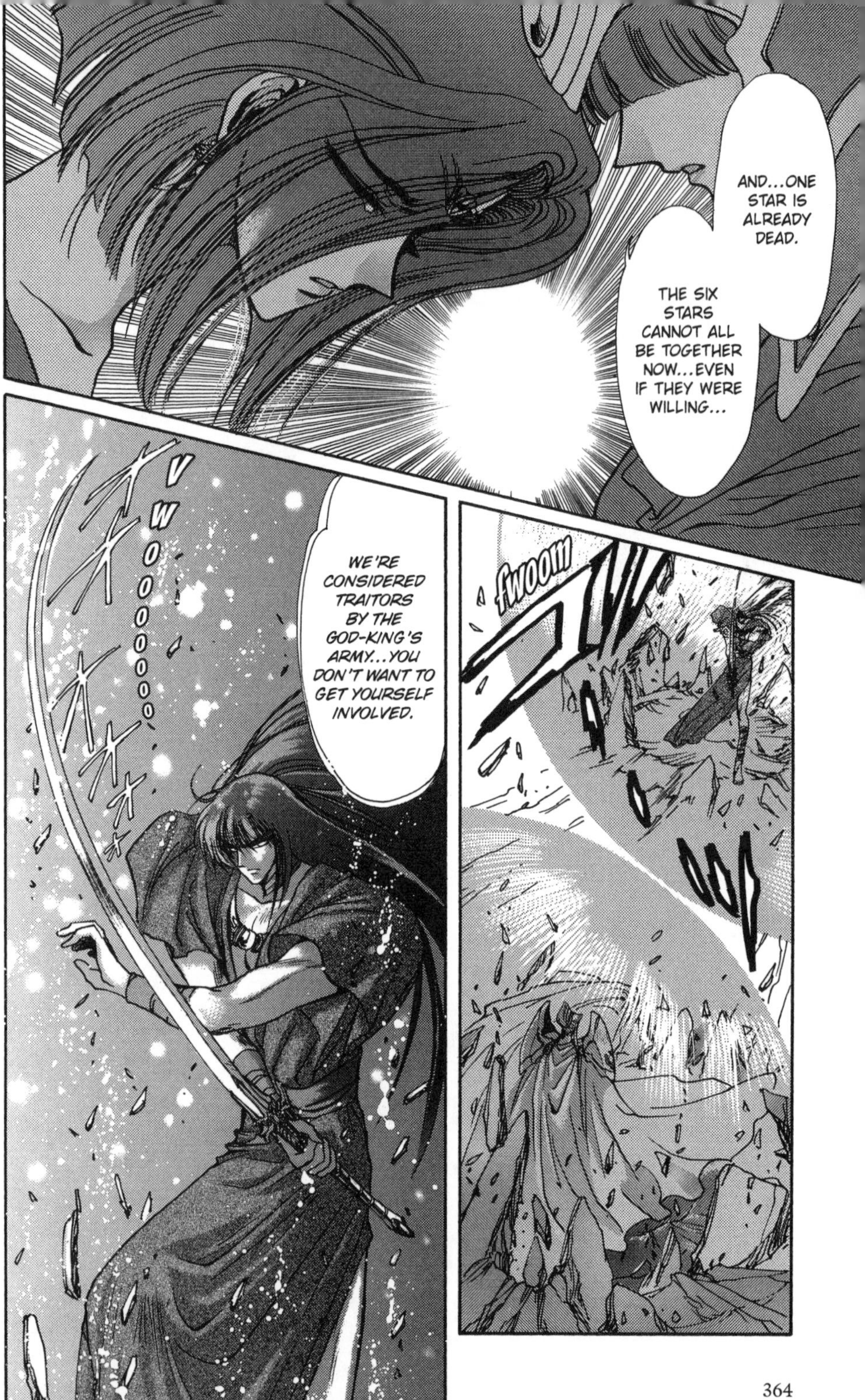
AND...ONE STAR IS ALREADY DEAD.
THE SIX STARS CANNOT ALL BE TOGETHER NOW...EVEN IF THEY WERE WILLING...
fwoom
WE'RE CONSIDERED TRAITORS BY THE GOD-KING'S ARMY...YOU DON'T WANT TO GET YOURSELF INVOLVED.
VWOOOOOOOOOOO

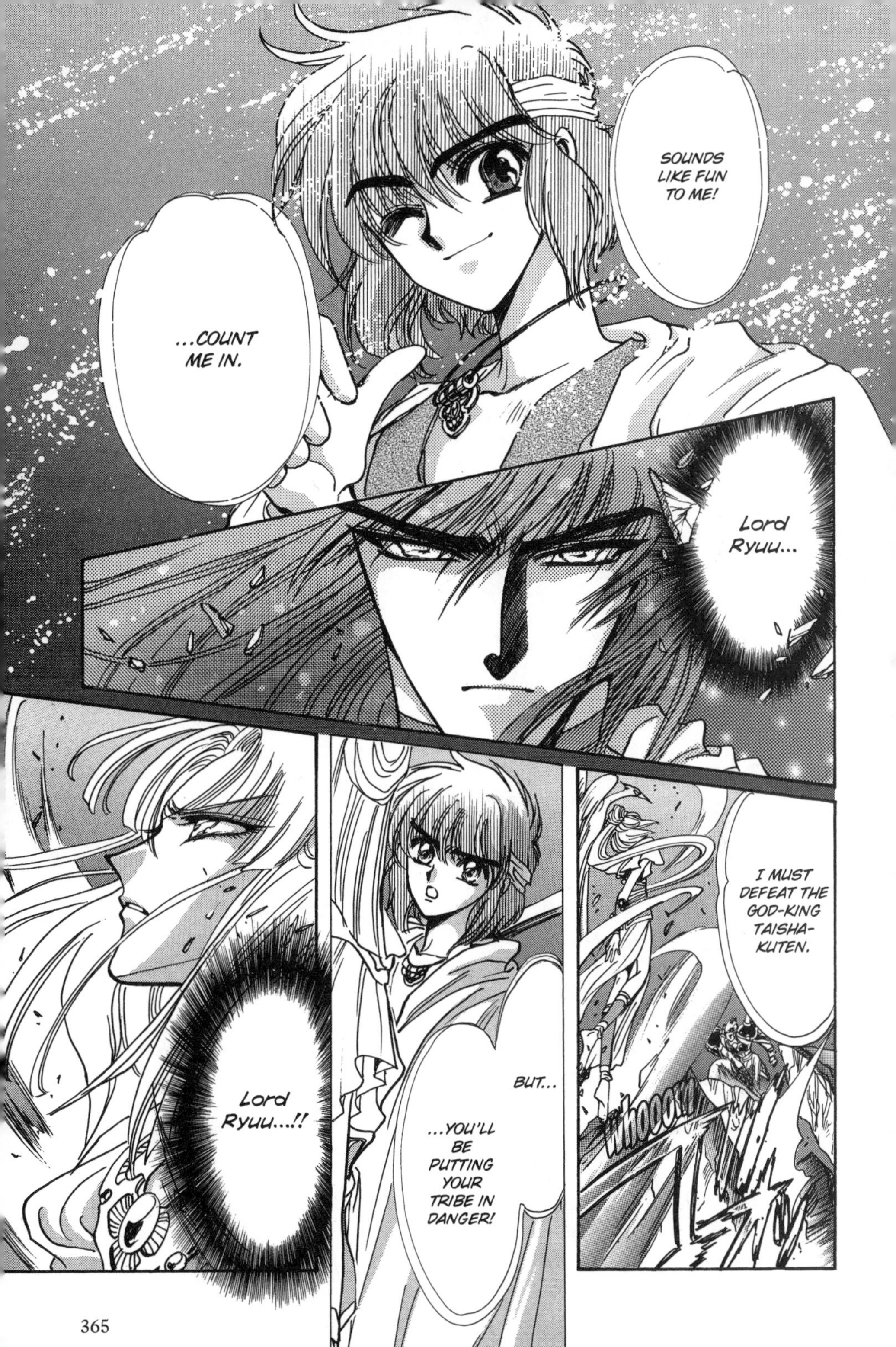
SOUNDS LIKE FUN TO ME!
...COUNT ME IN.
Lord Ryuu...
I MUST DEFEAT THE GOD-KING TAISHA-KUTEN.
BUT...
...YOU'LL BE PUTTING YOUR TRIBE IN DANGER!
Lord Ryuu...!!

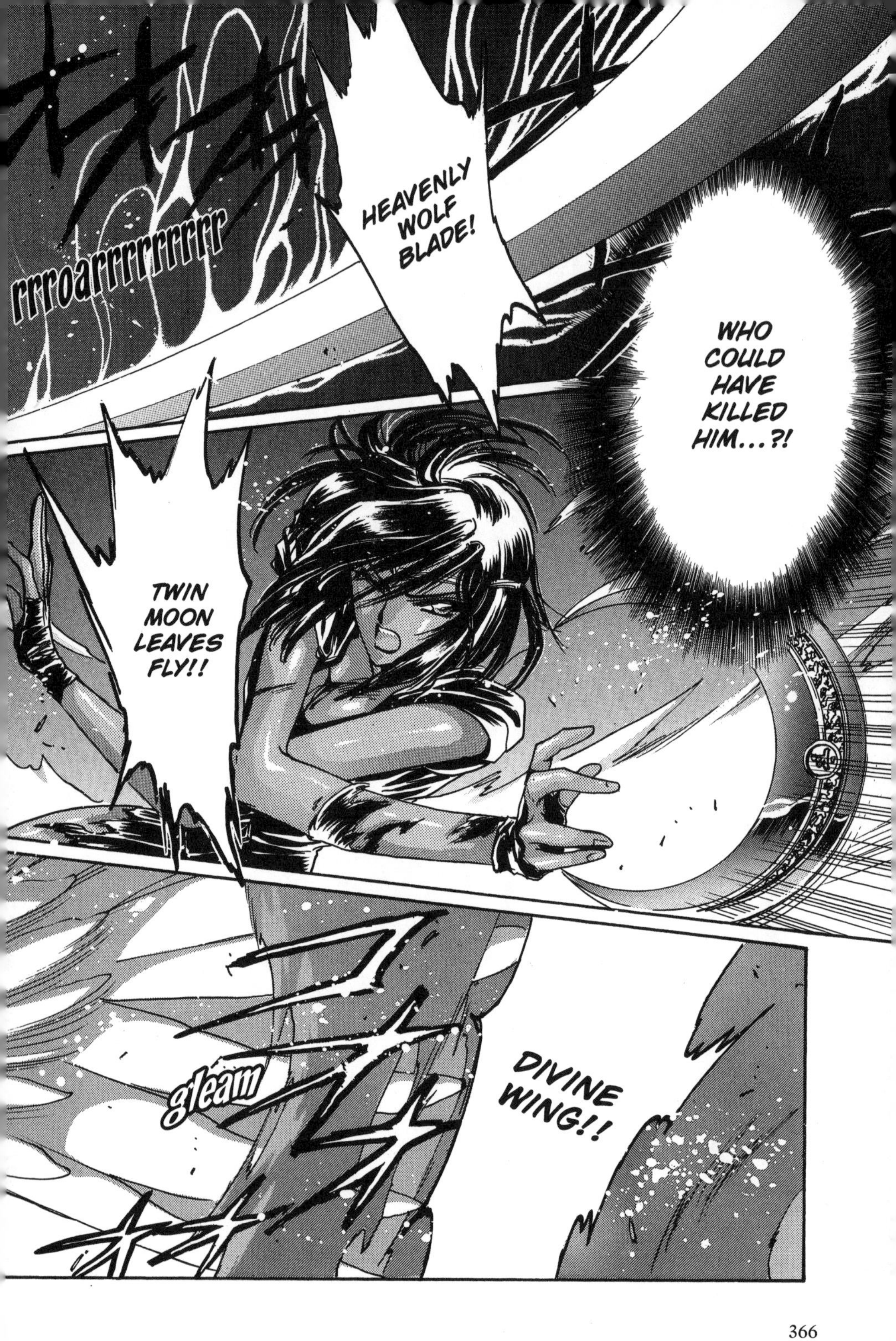
HEAVENLY WOLF BLADE!
rrroarrrrrrrrr
WHO COULD HAVE KILLED HIM...?!
TWIN MOON LEAVES FLY!!
DIVINE WING!!
gleam

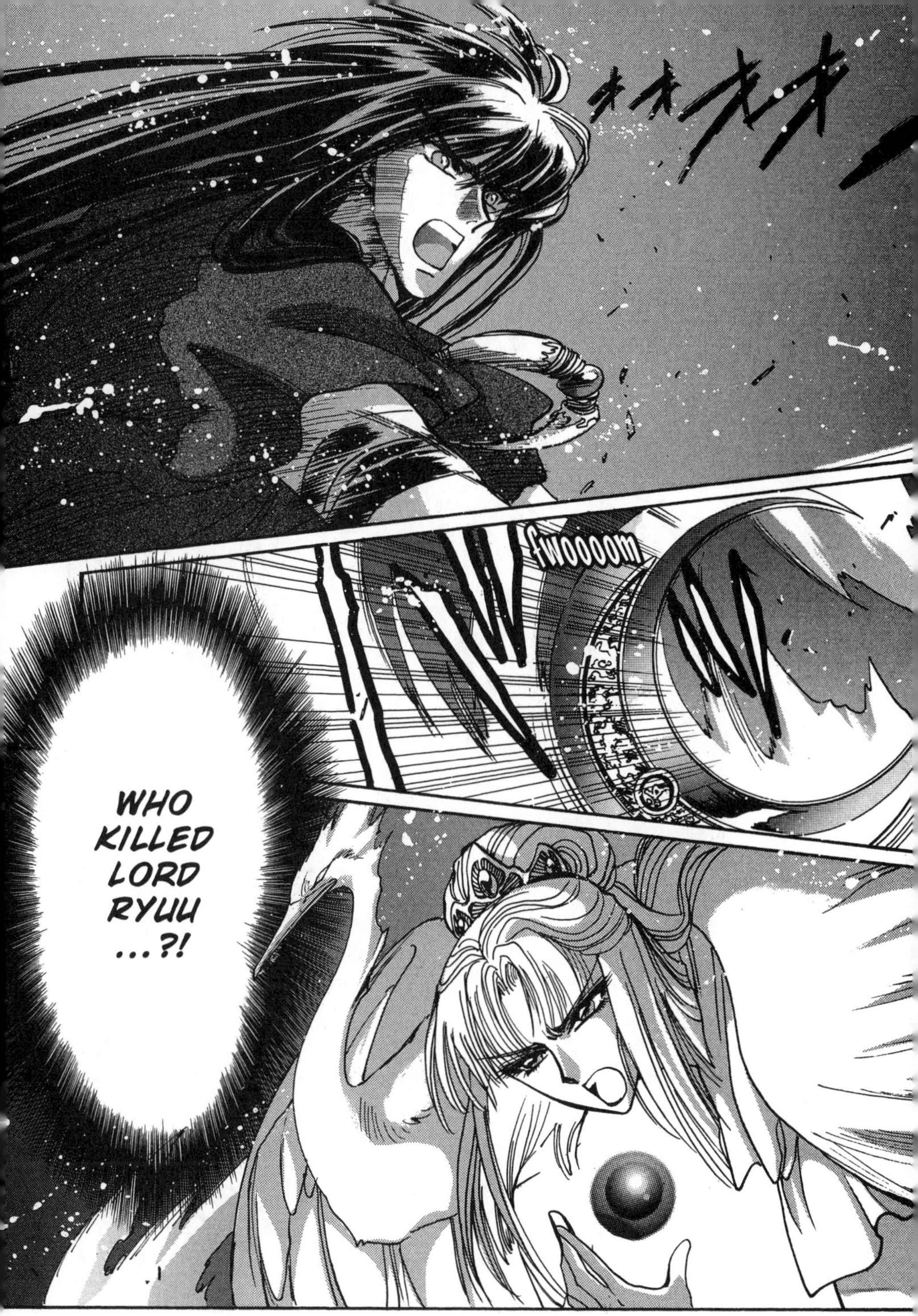

オオオオ
fwoooom
WHO KILLED LORD RYUU ...?!

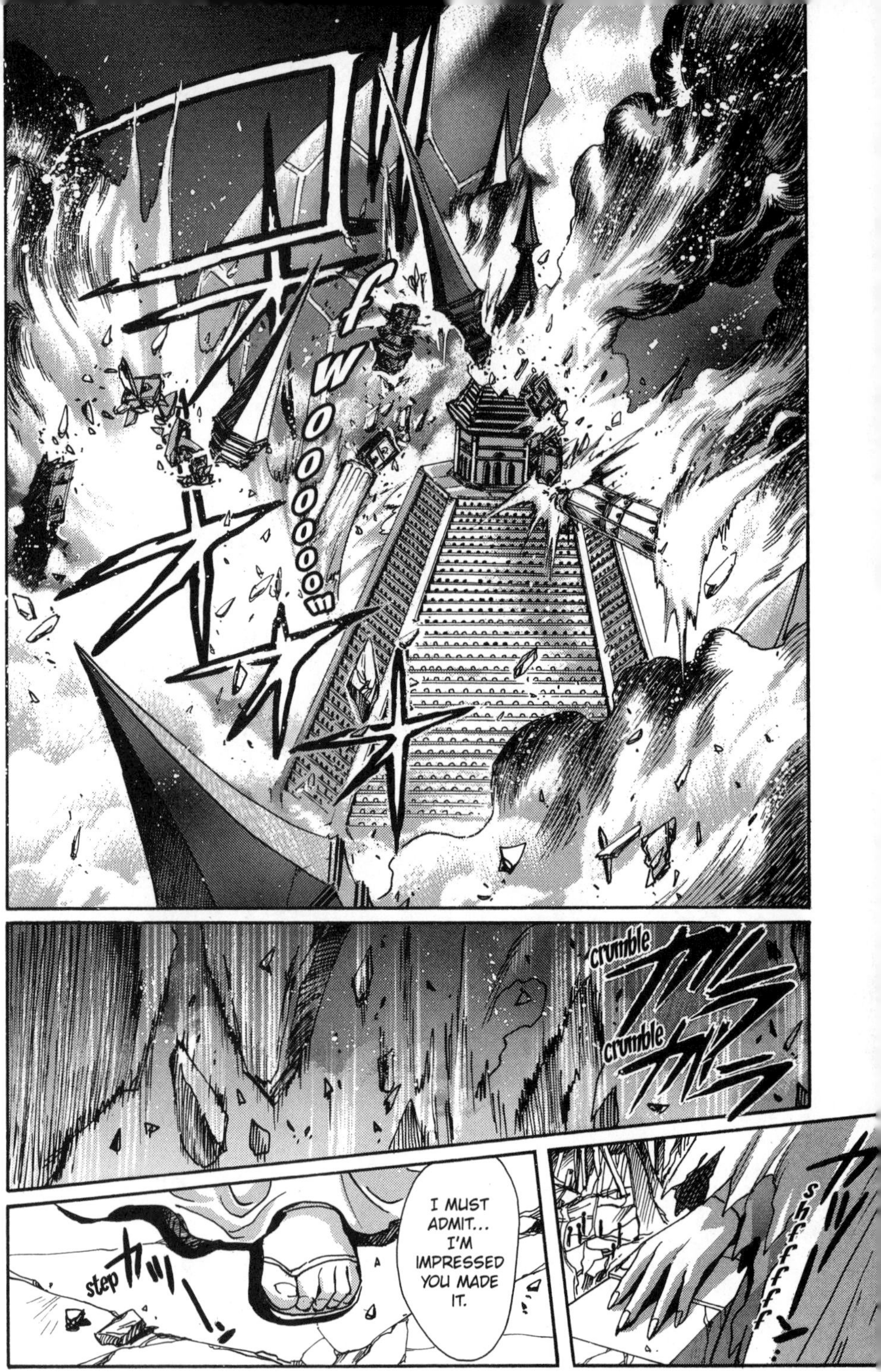
fwoooooooom
crumble
crumble
shffffff
I MUST ADMIT... I'M IMPRESSED YOU MADE IT.
step

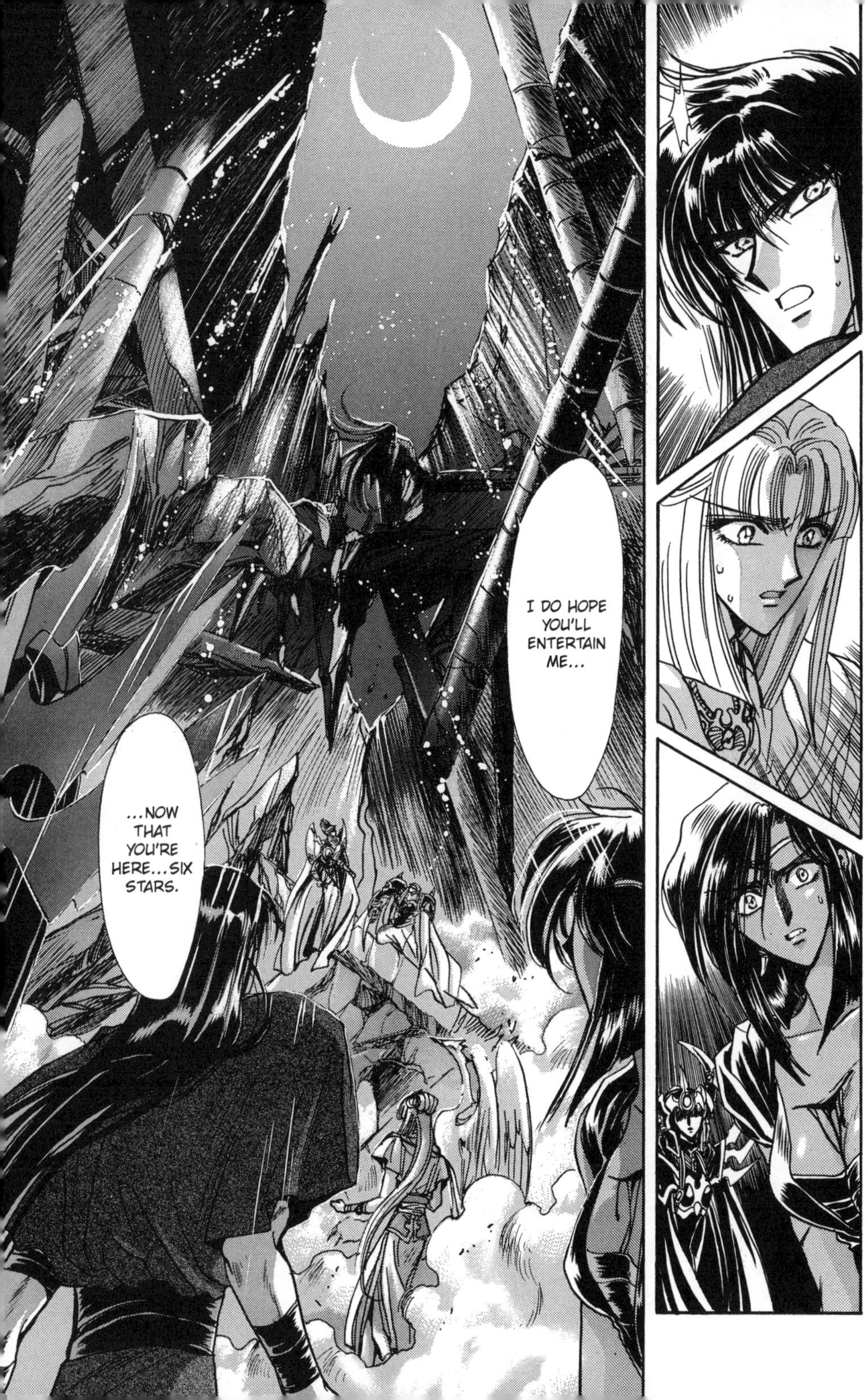
I DO HOPE YOU'LL ENTERTAIN ME...
...NOW THAT YOU'RE HERE...SIX STARS.

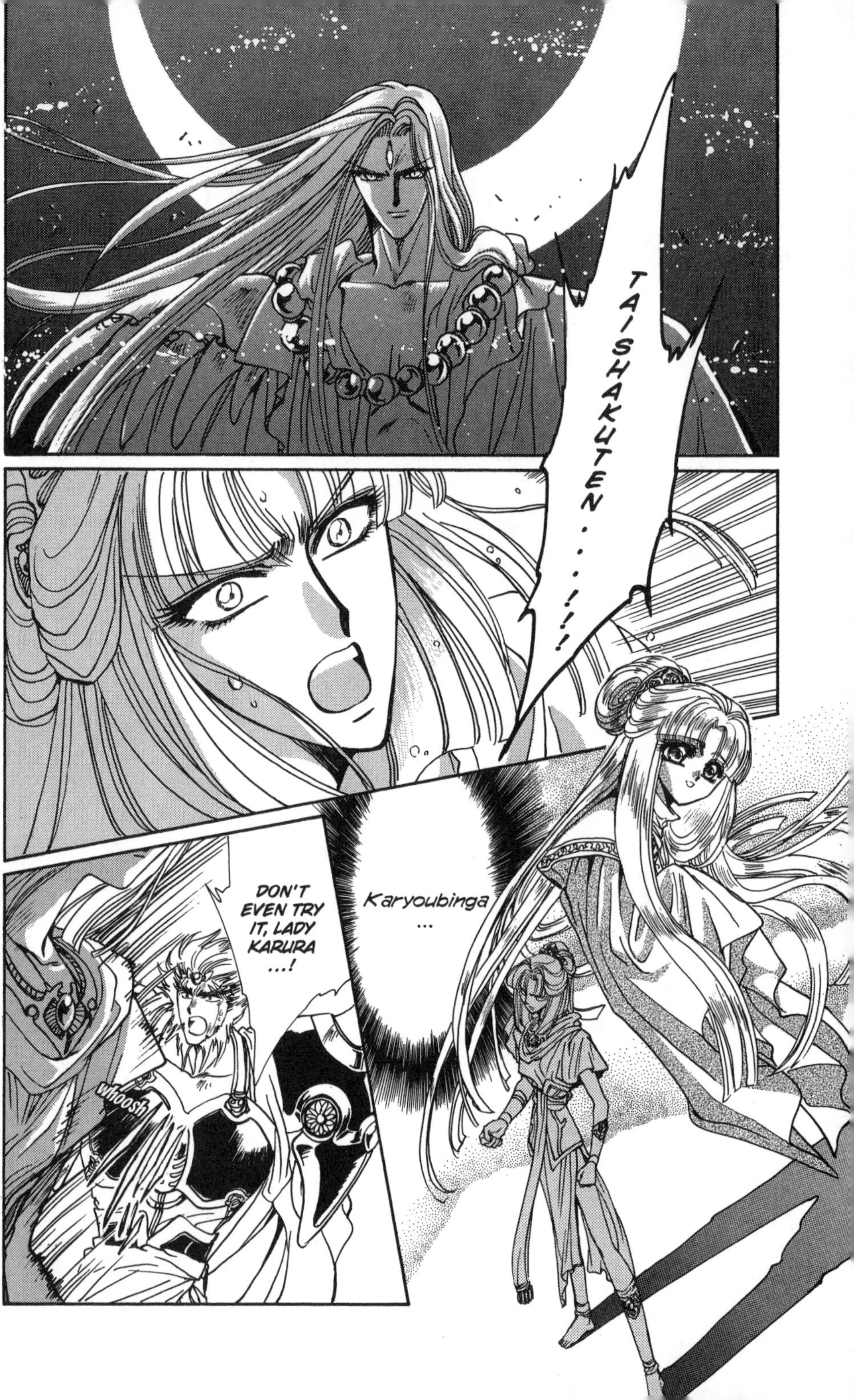

TAISHAKUTEN.....!!!
Karyoubinga ...
DON'T EVEN TRY IT, LADY KARURA ...!
whoosh

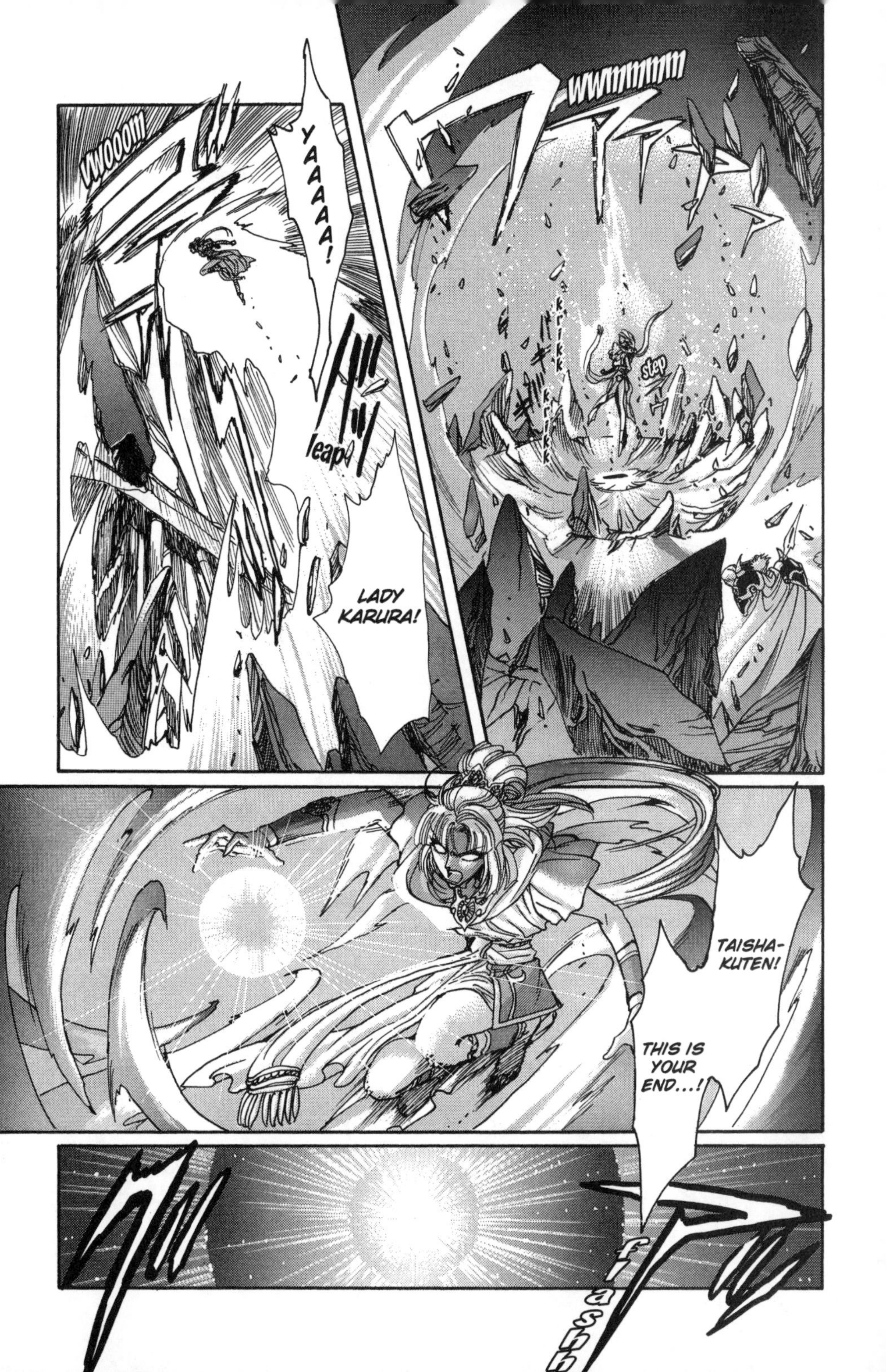
wwmmmm
krikk
krikk
step
vwooom
YAAAAAA!
leap
LADY KARURA!
TAISHA-KUTEN!
THIS IS YOUR END...!
flash

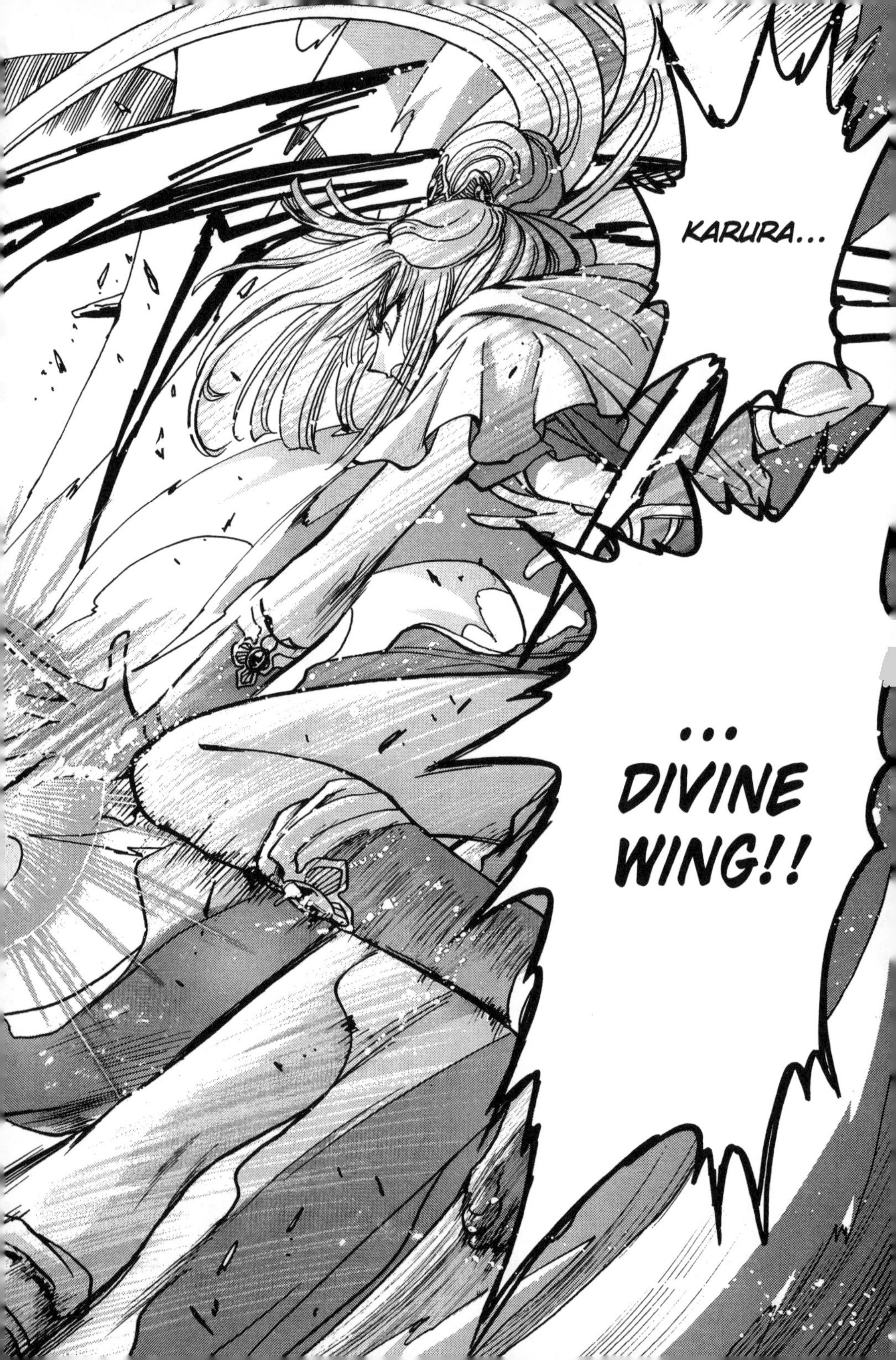
KARURA...
... DIVINE WING!!

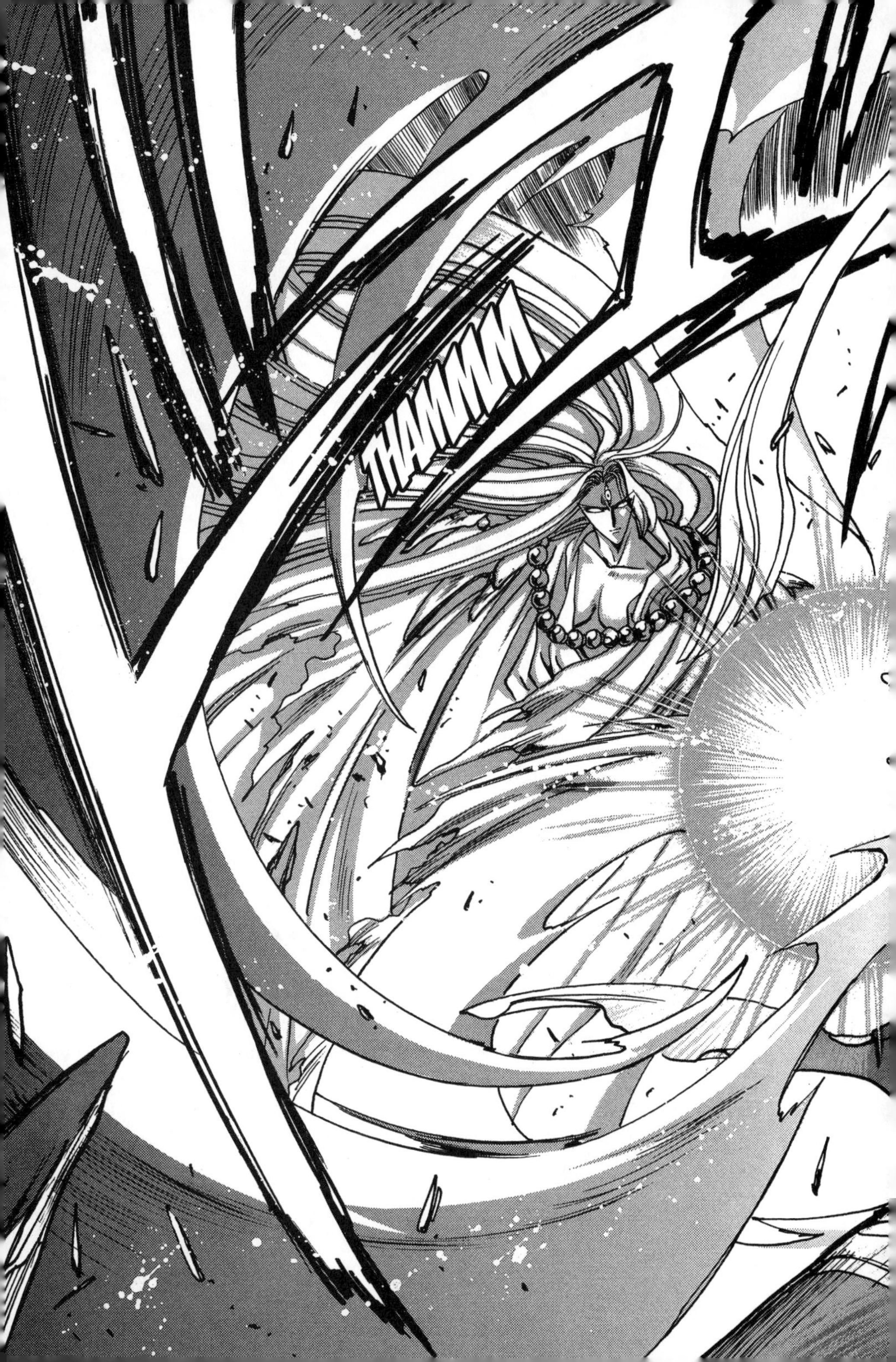
THAMMM

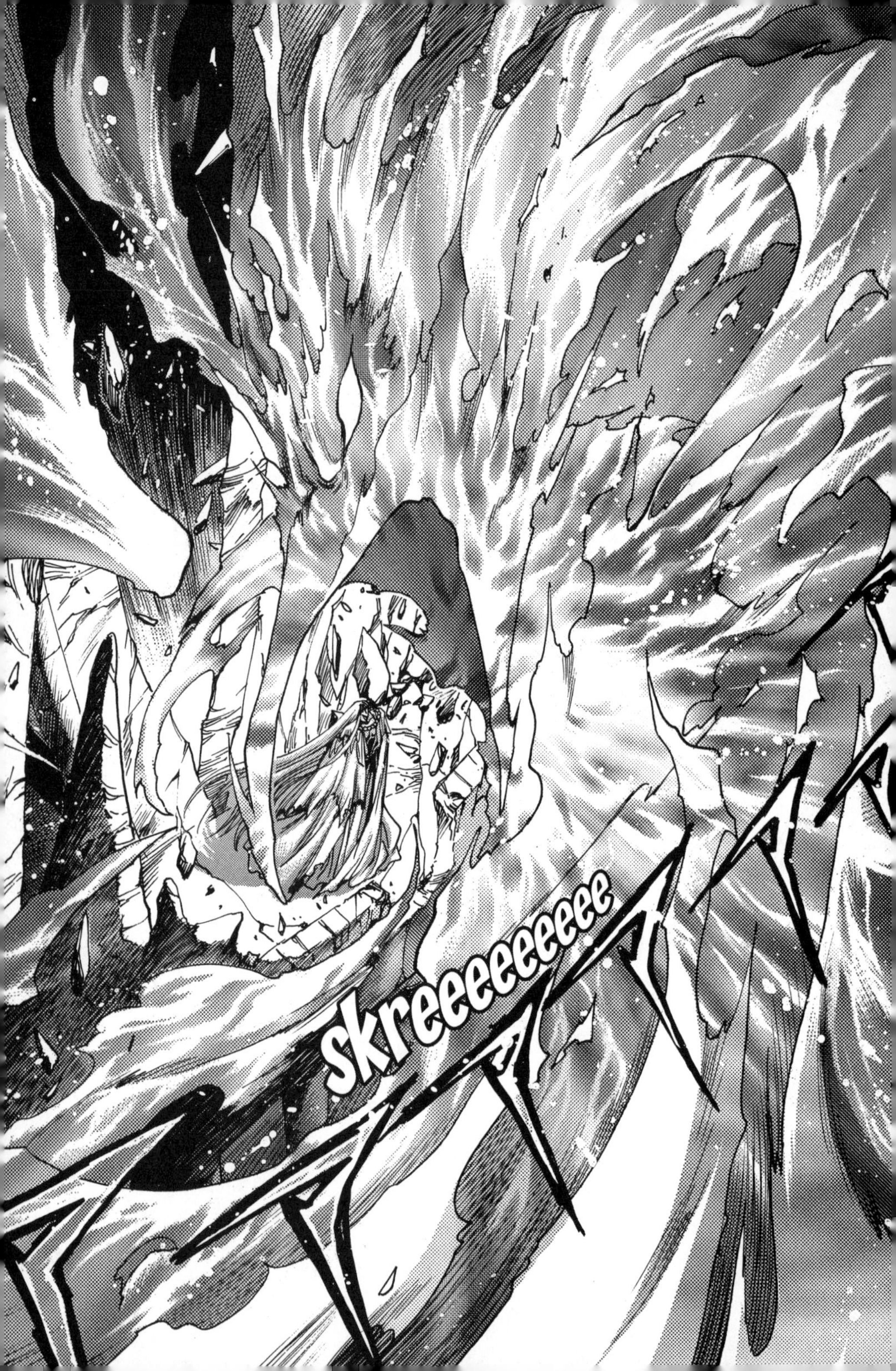
skreeeeeeeeee

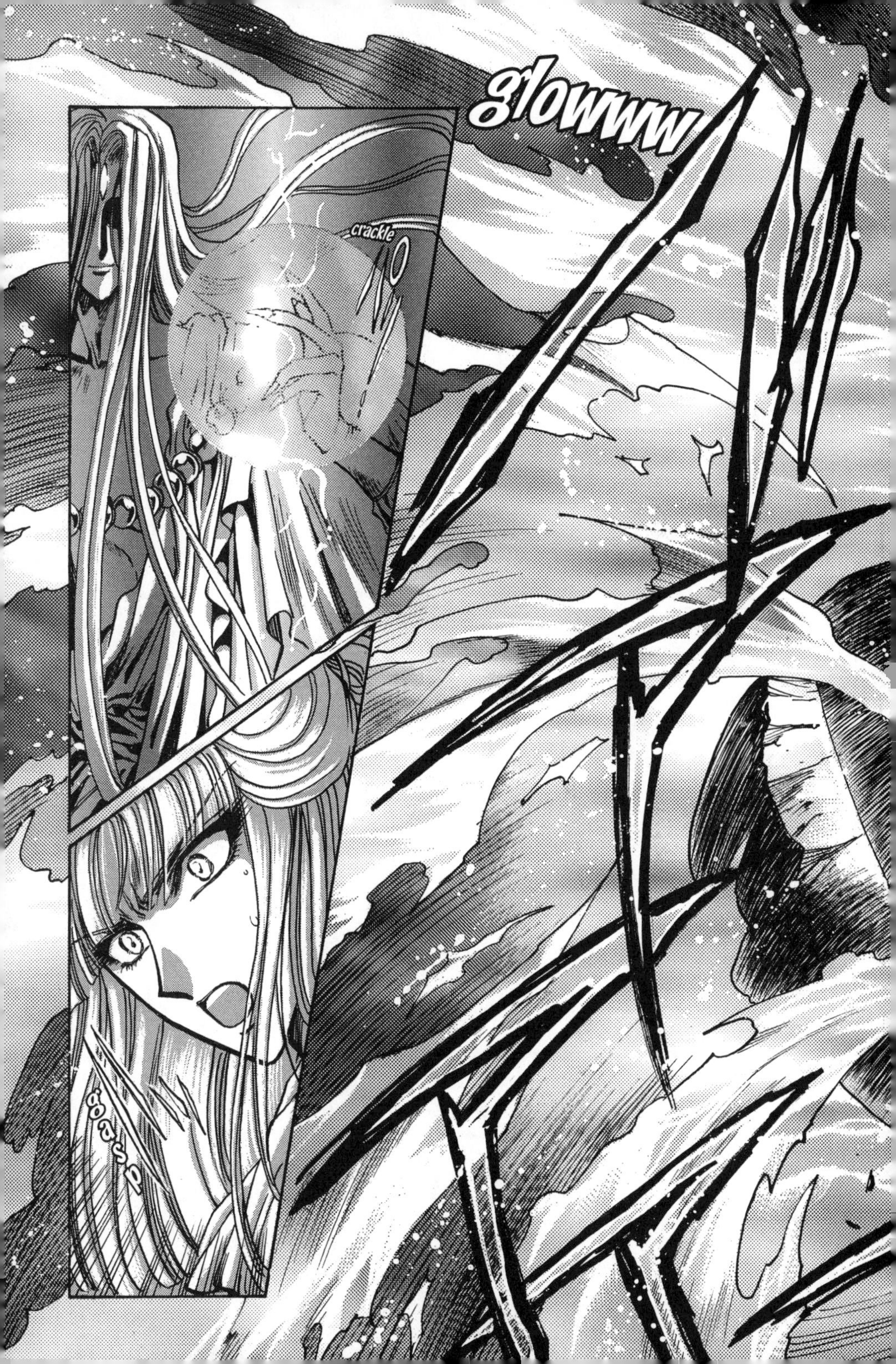
glowww
crackle
gasp

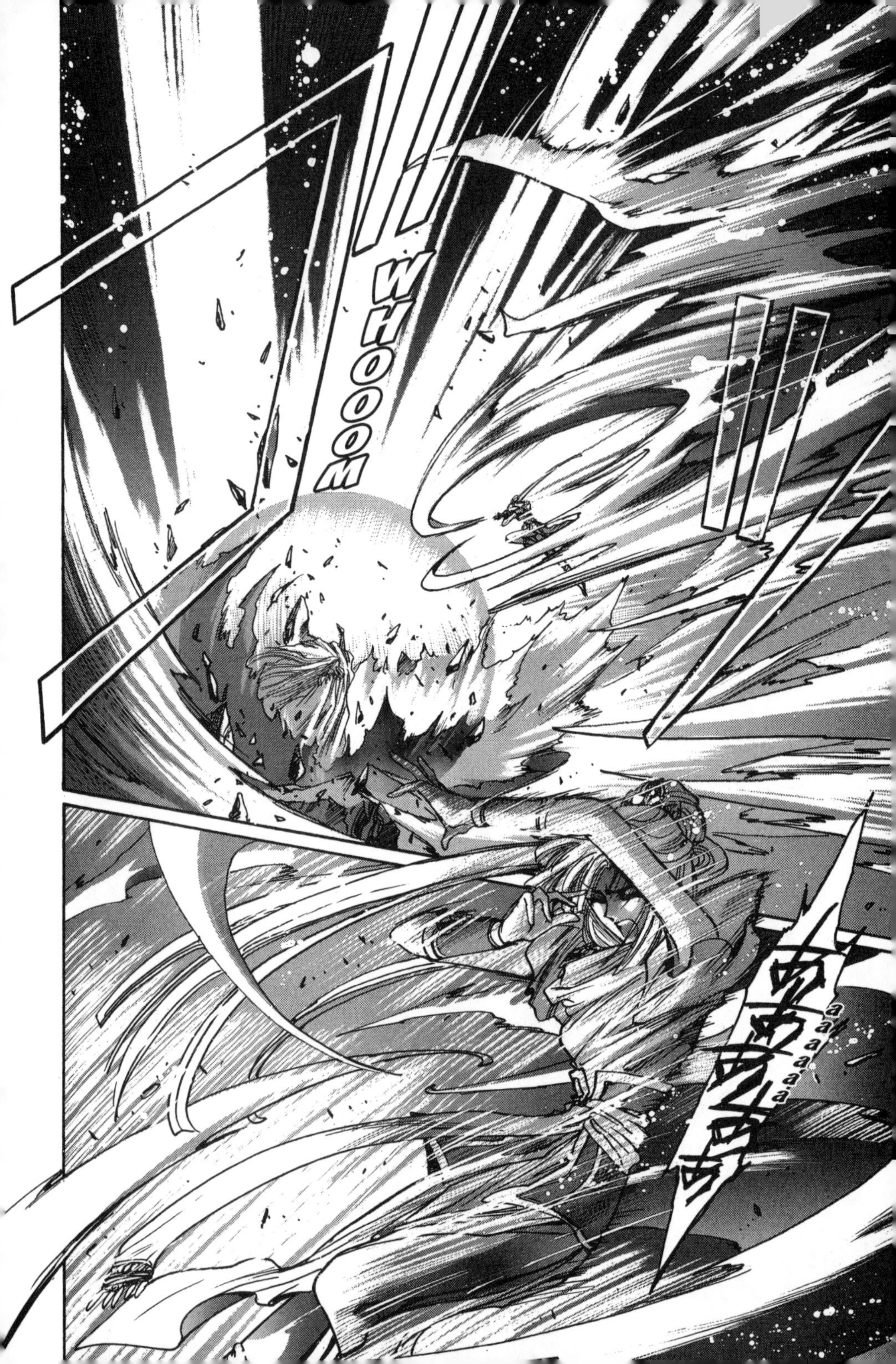
WHOOOOOM
あああああ
aaaaaa

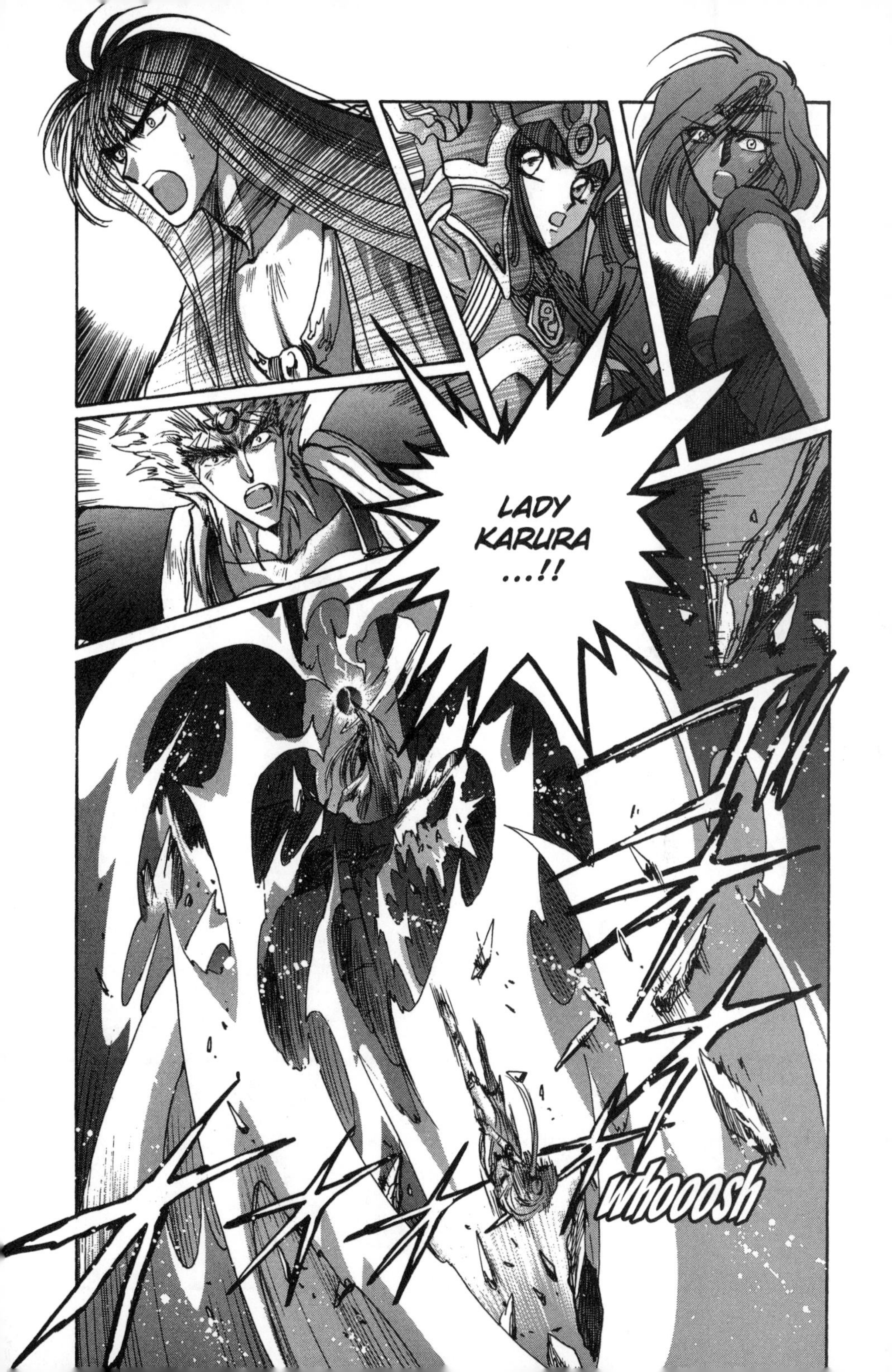
LADY KARURA ...!!
whooosh

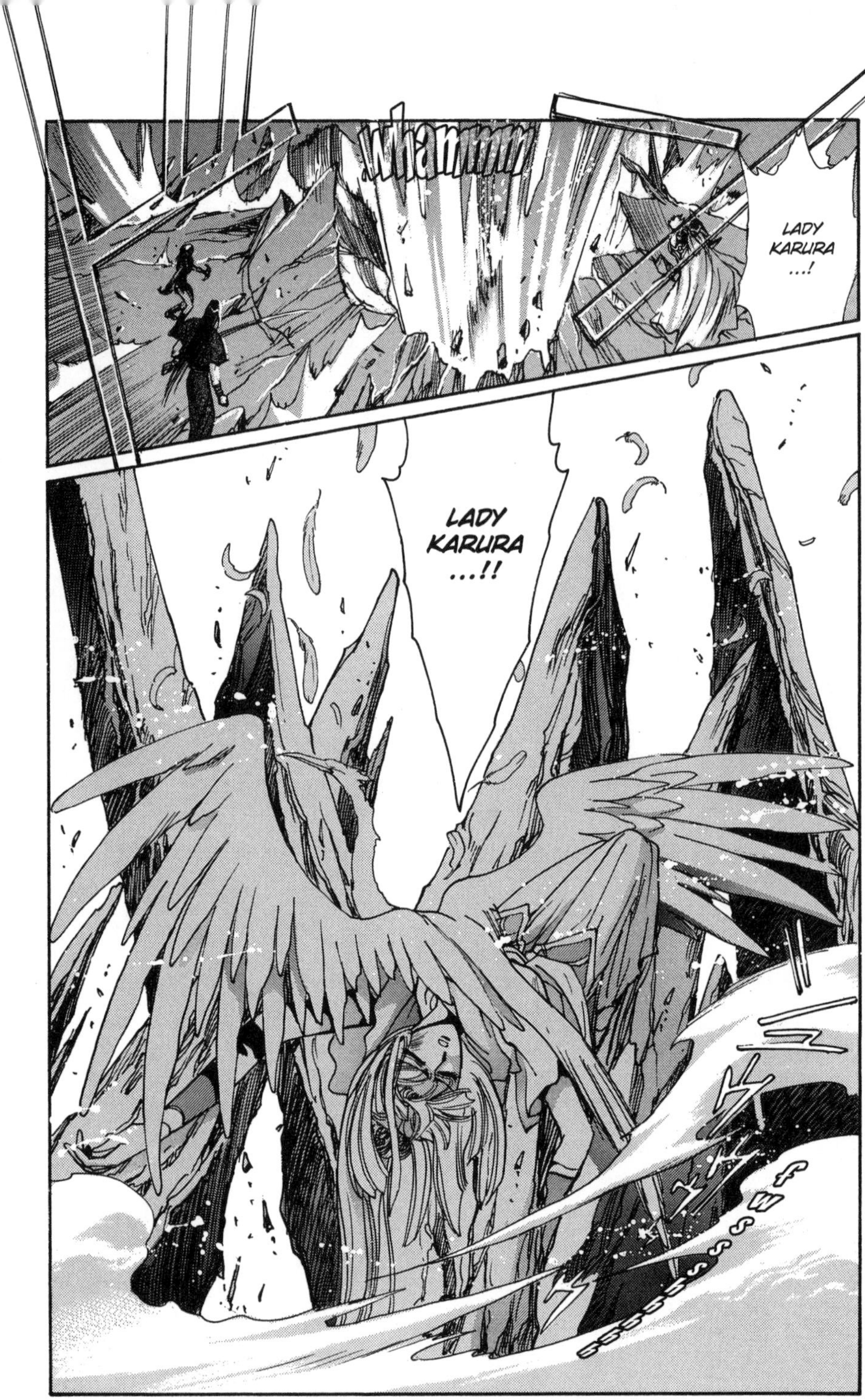
LADY KARURA ...!
whammm
LADY KARURA ...!!
fwssssssss

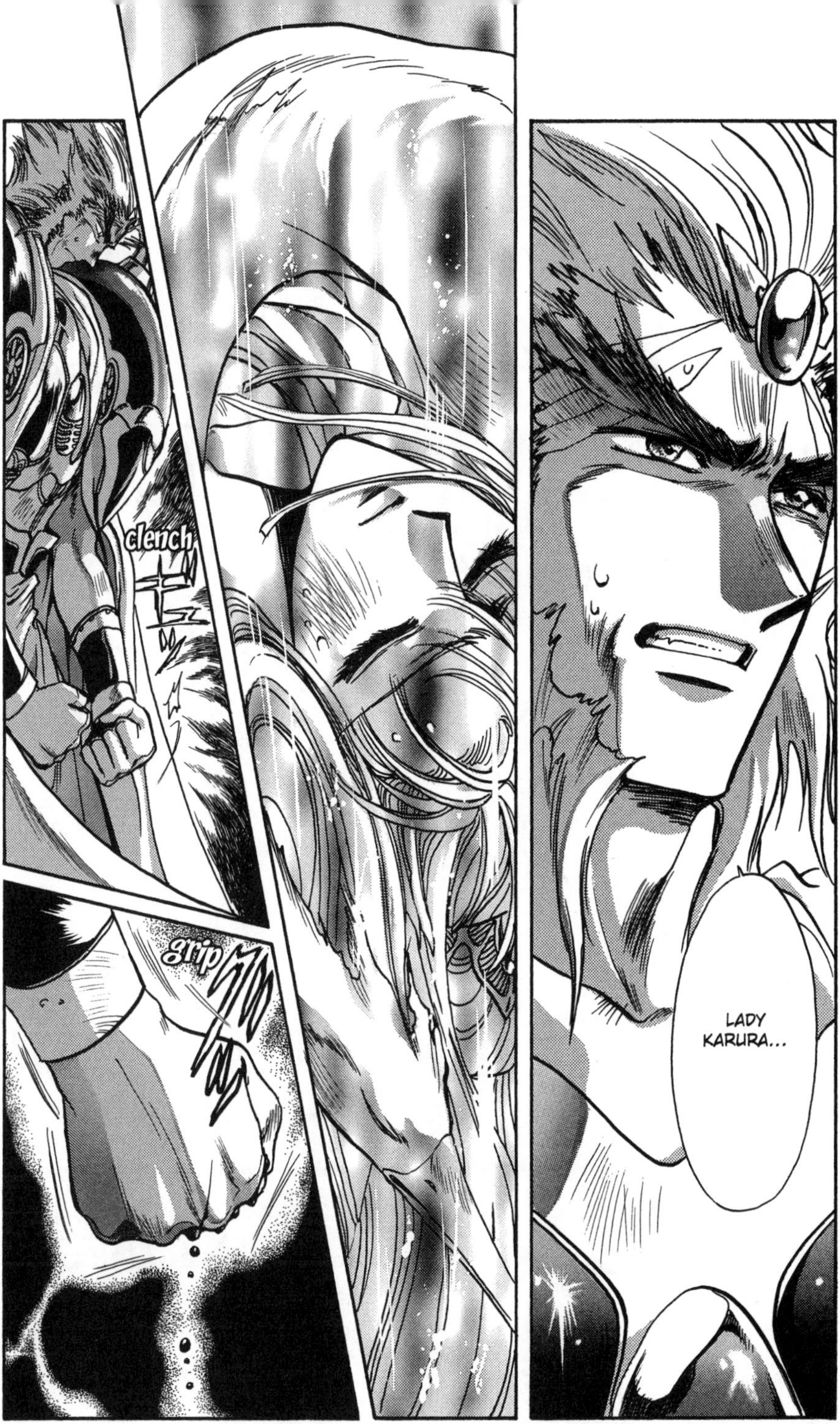
LADY KARURA...
clench
grip

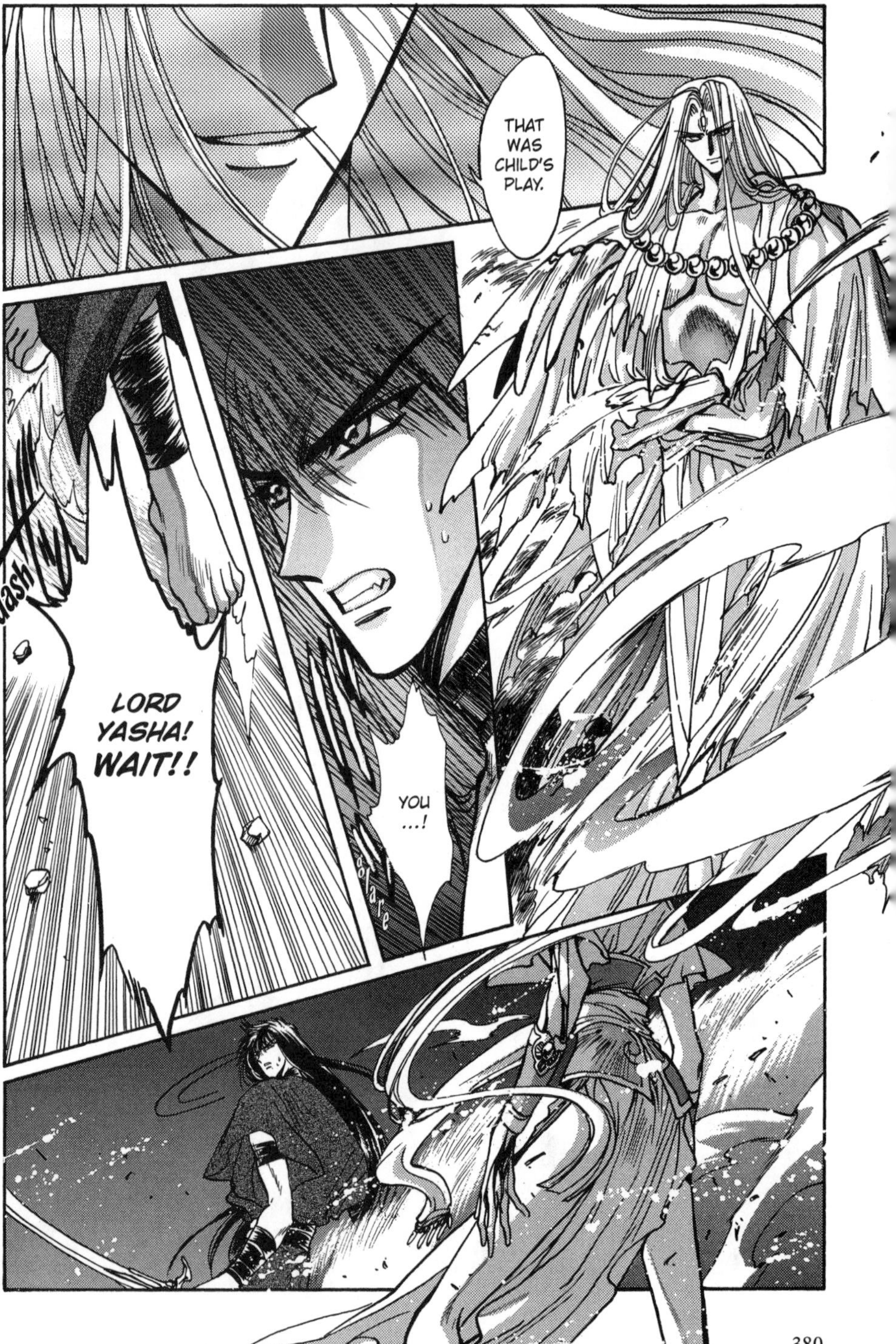
THAT WAS CHILD'S PLAY.
YOU ...!
glare
dash
LORD YASHA! WAIT!!

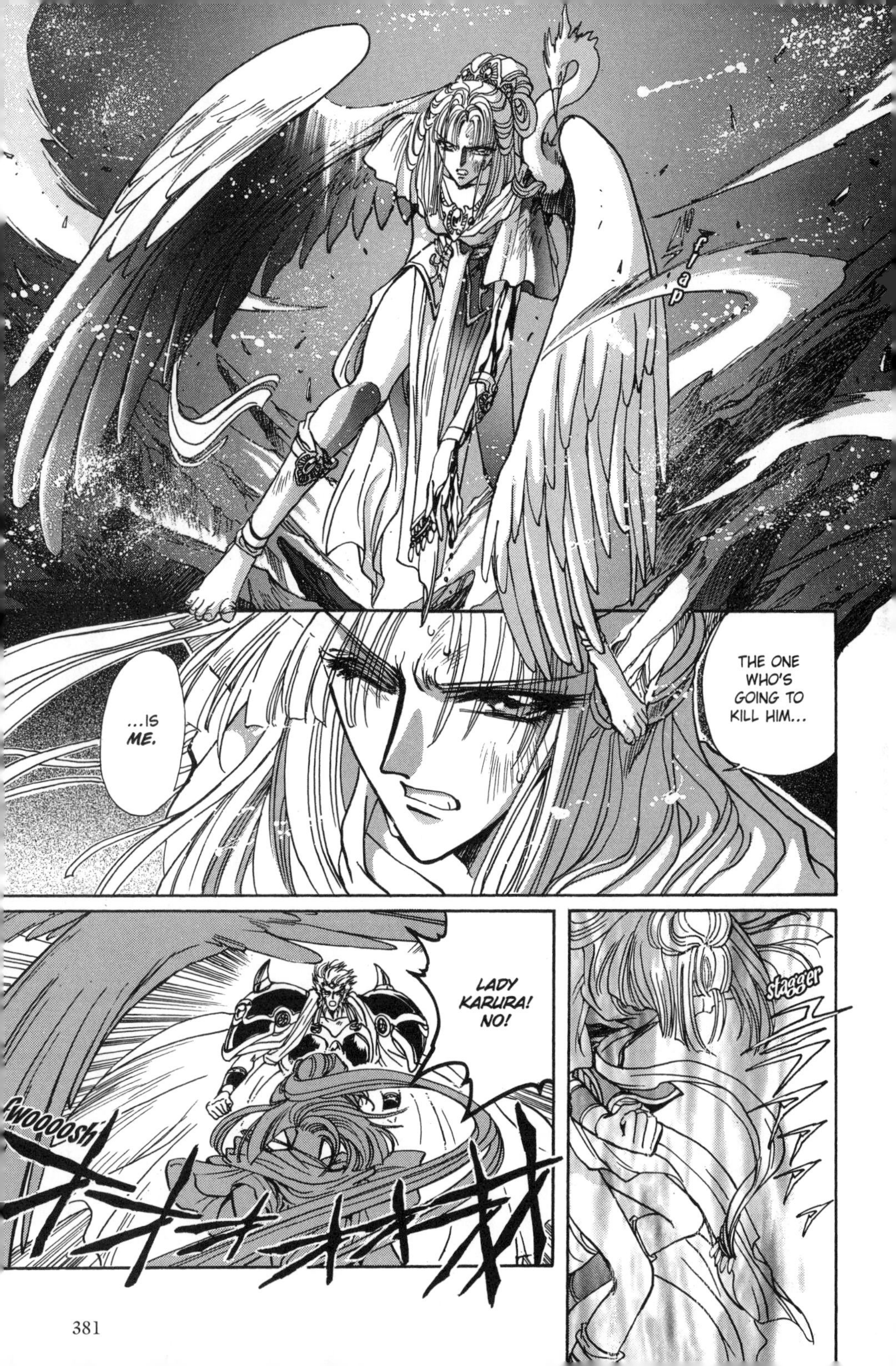
flap
THE ONE WHO'S GOING TO KILL HIM...
...IS ME.
stagger
LADY KARURA! NO!
Gwoooosh

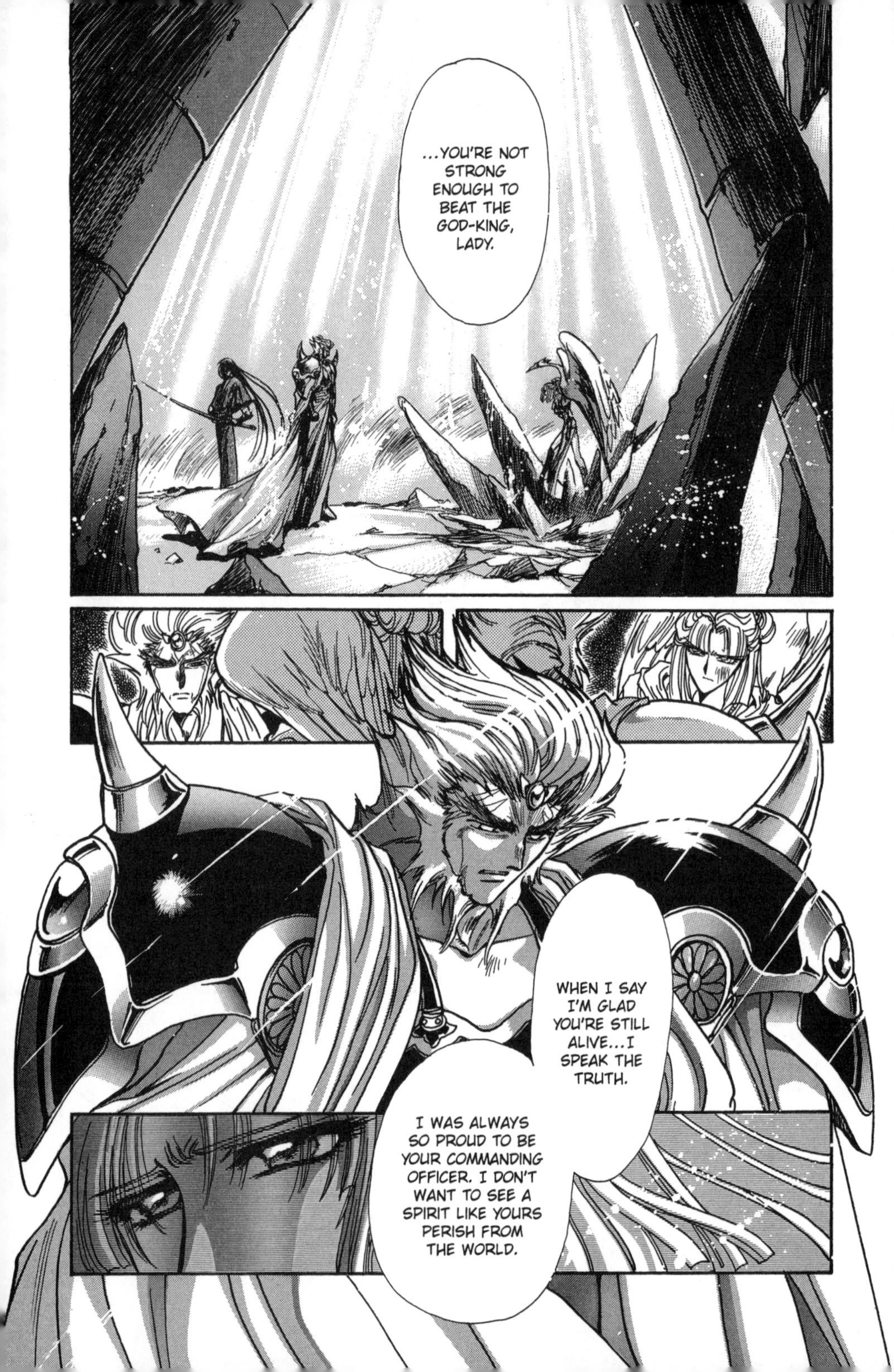
...YOU'RE NOT STRONG ENOUGH TO BEAT THE GOD-KING, LADY.
WHEN I SAY I'M GLAD YOU'RE STILL ALIVE...I SPEAK THE TRUTH.
I WAS ALWAYS SO PROUD TO BE YOUR COMMANDING OFFICER. I DON'T WANT TO SEE A SPIRIT LIKE YOURS PERISH FROM THE WORLD.

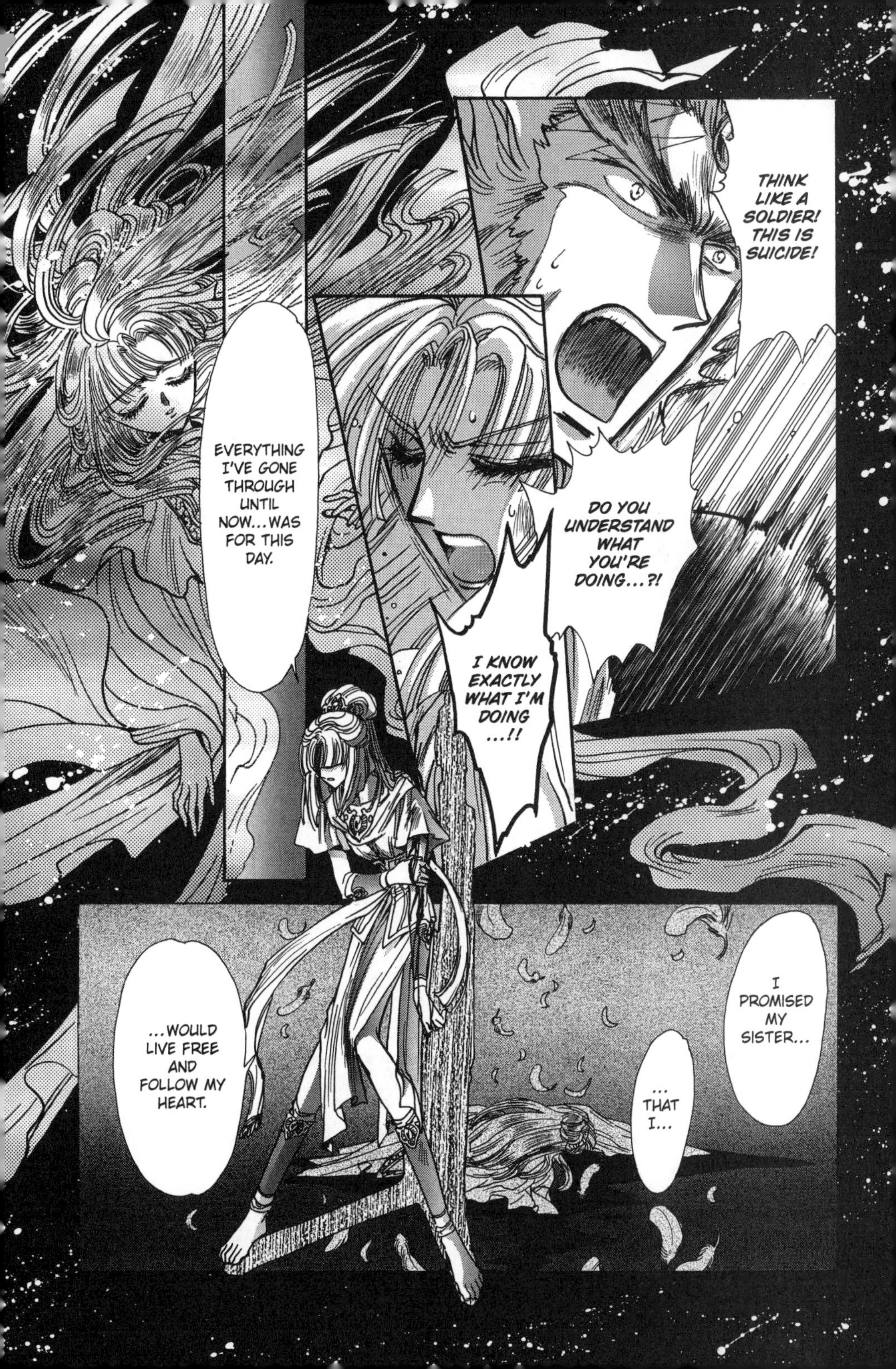
THINK LIKE A SOLDIER! THIS IS SUICIDE!
DO YOU UNDERSTAND WHAT YOU'RE DOING...?!
I KNOW EXACTLY WHAT I'M DOING ...!!
EVERYTHING I'VE GONE THROUGH UNTIL NOW...WAS FOR THIS DAY.
I PROMISED MY SISTER...
...THAT I...
...WOULD LIVE FREE AND FOLLOW MY HEART.

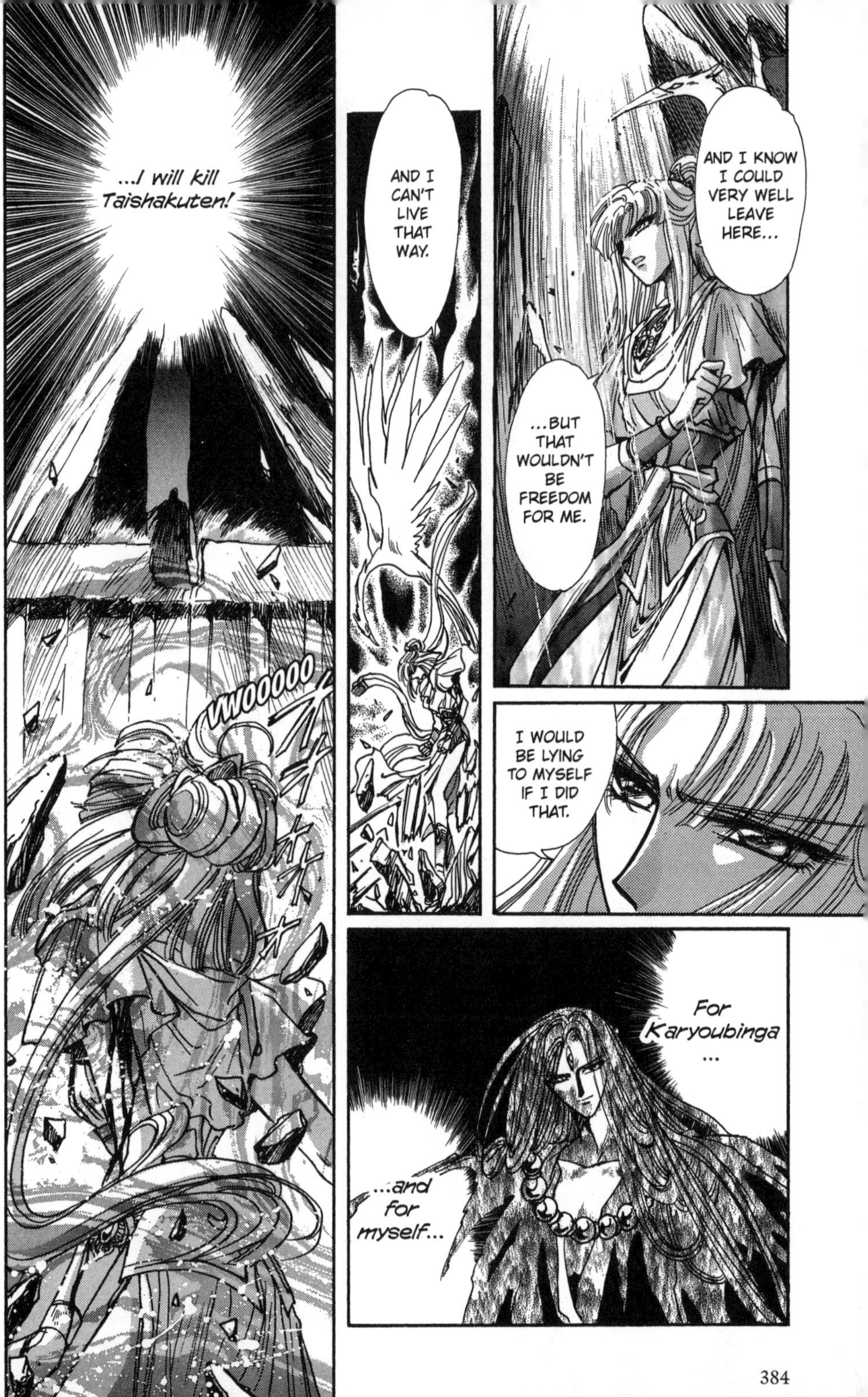
AND I KNOW I COULD VERY WELL LEAVE HERE...
...BUT THAT WOULDN'T BE FREEDOM FOR ME.
I WOULD BE LYING TO MYSELF IF I DID THAT.
AND I CAN'T LIVE THAT WAY.
For Karyoubinga ...
...and for myself...
...I will kill Taishakuten!
VWOOOOO

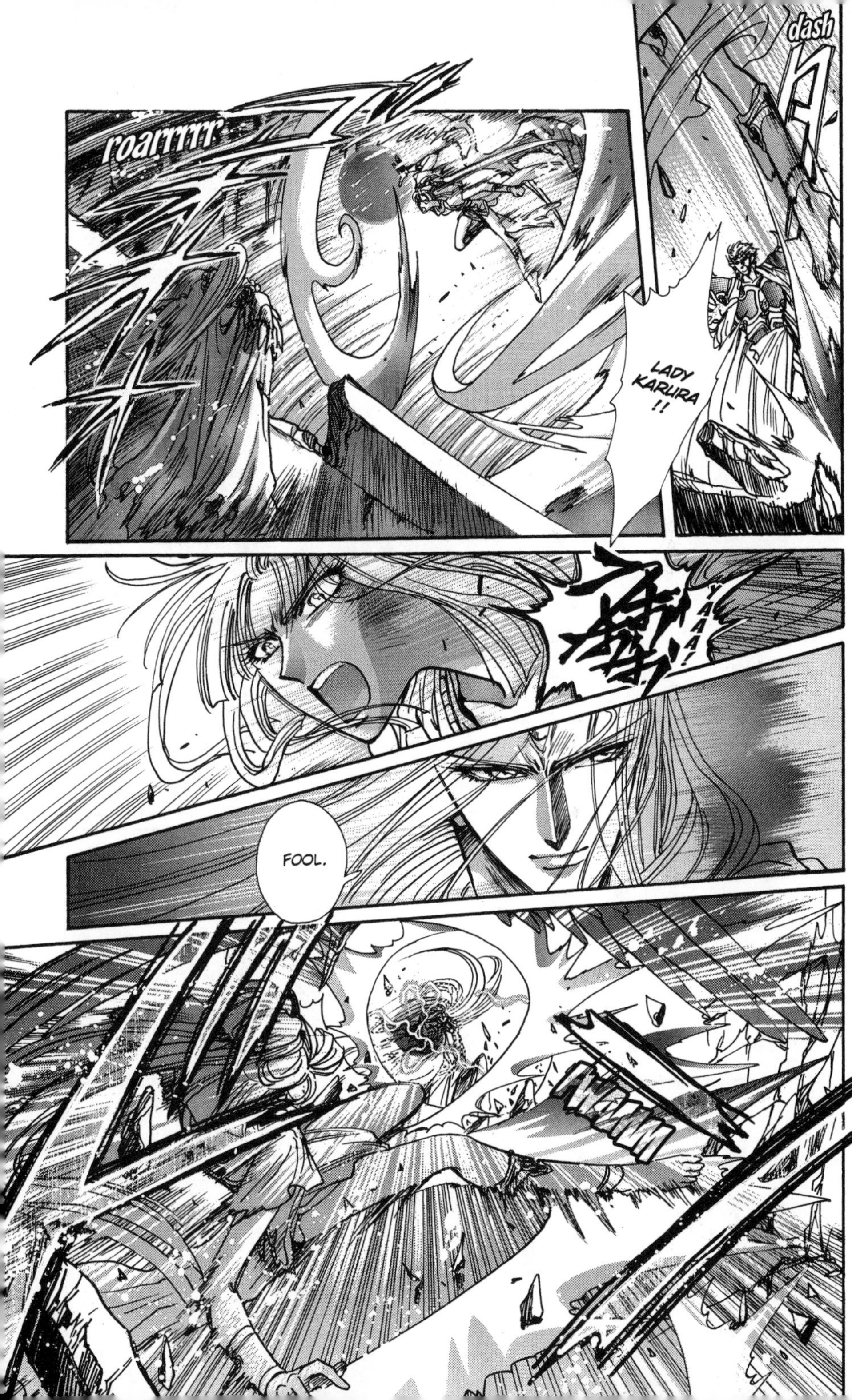
dash
LADY KARURA !!
roarrrrr
YAAAA!!
FOOL.

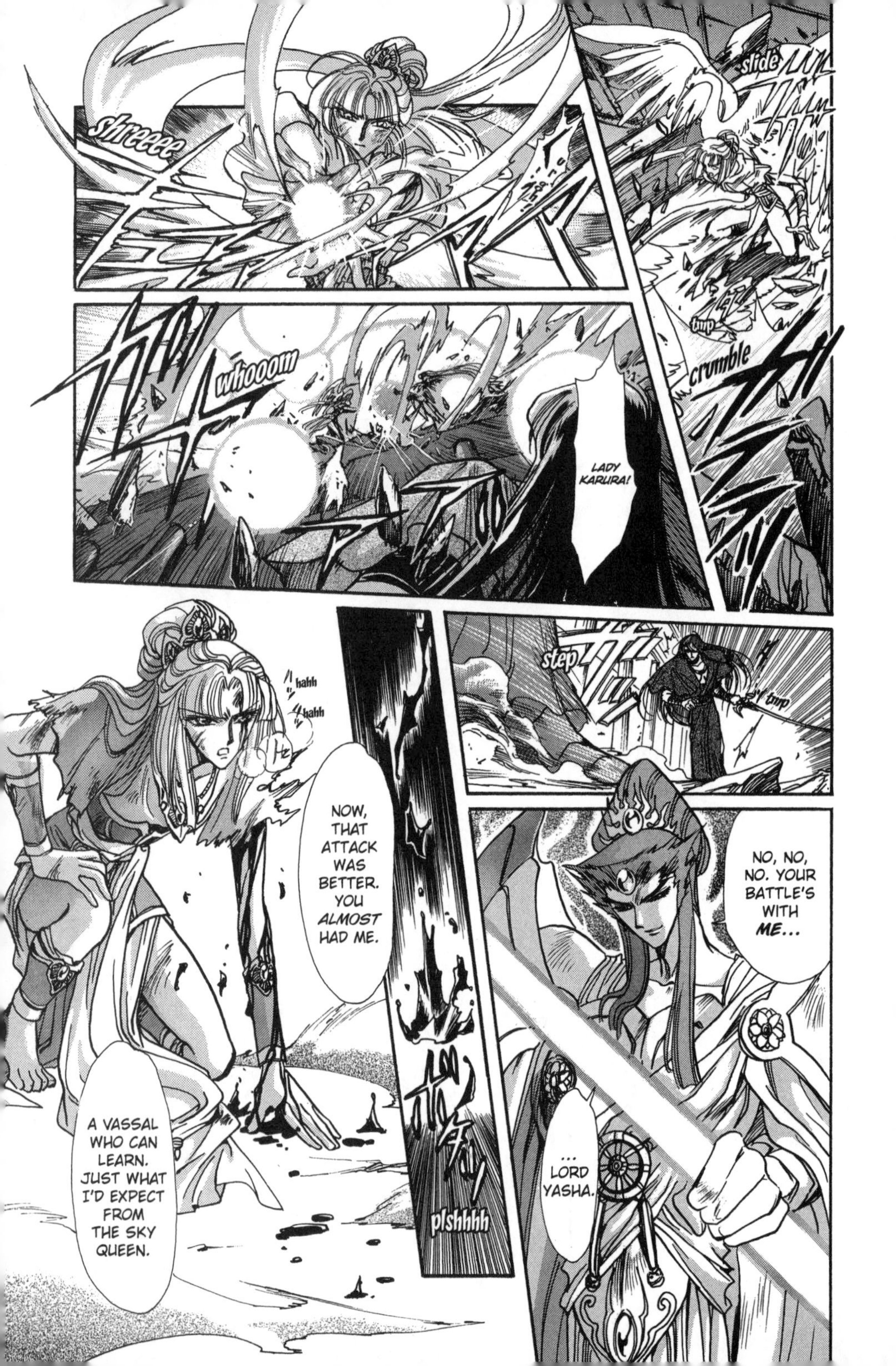
slide
tmp
crumble
shreeee
whooom
LADY KARURA!
step
tmp
NO, NO, NO. YOUR BATTLE'S WITH ME...
... LORD YASHA.
plshhhh
hahh
hahh
NOW, THAT ATTACK WAS BETTER. YOU ALMOST HAD ME.
A VASSAL WHO CAN LEARN. JUST WHAT I'D EXPECT FROM THE SKY QUEEN.

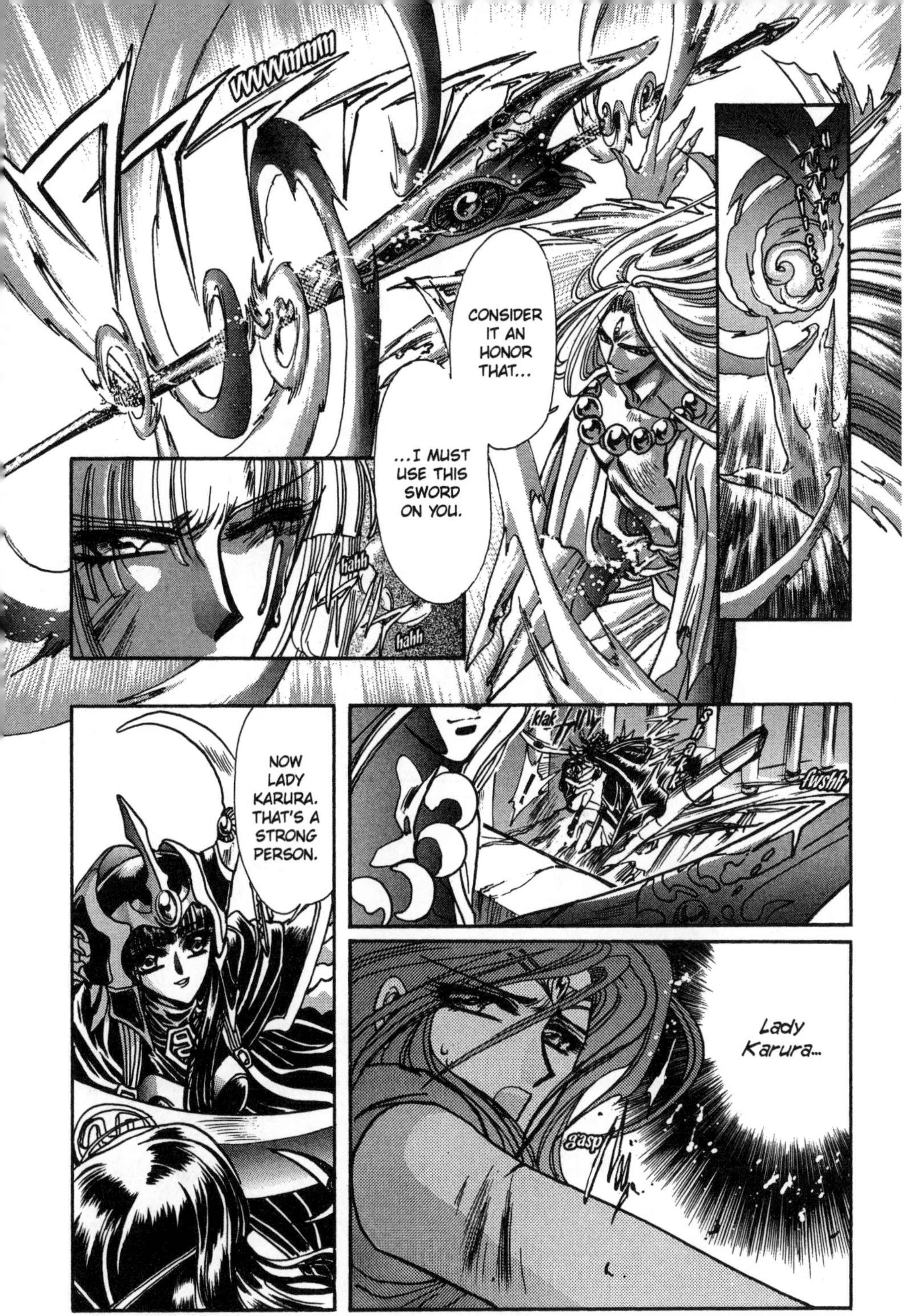
flicker
wwwmmm
CONSIDER IT AN HONOR THAT...
...I MUST USE THIS SWORD ON YOU.
hahh
hahh
klak
shakk
fwshh
gasp
Lady Karura...
NOW LADY KARURA. THAT'S A STRONG PERSON.

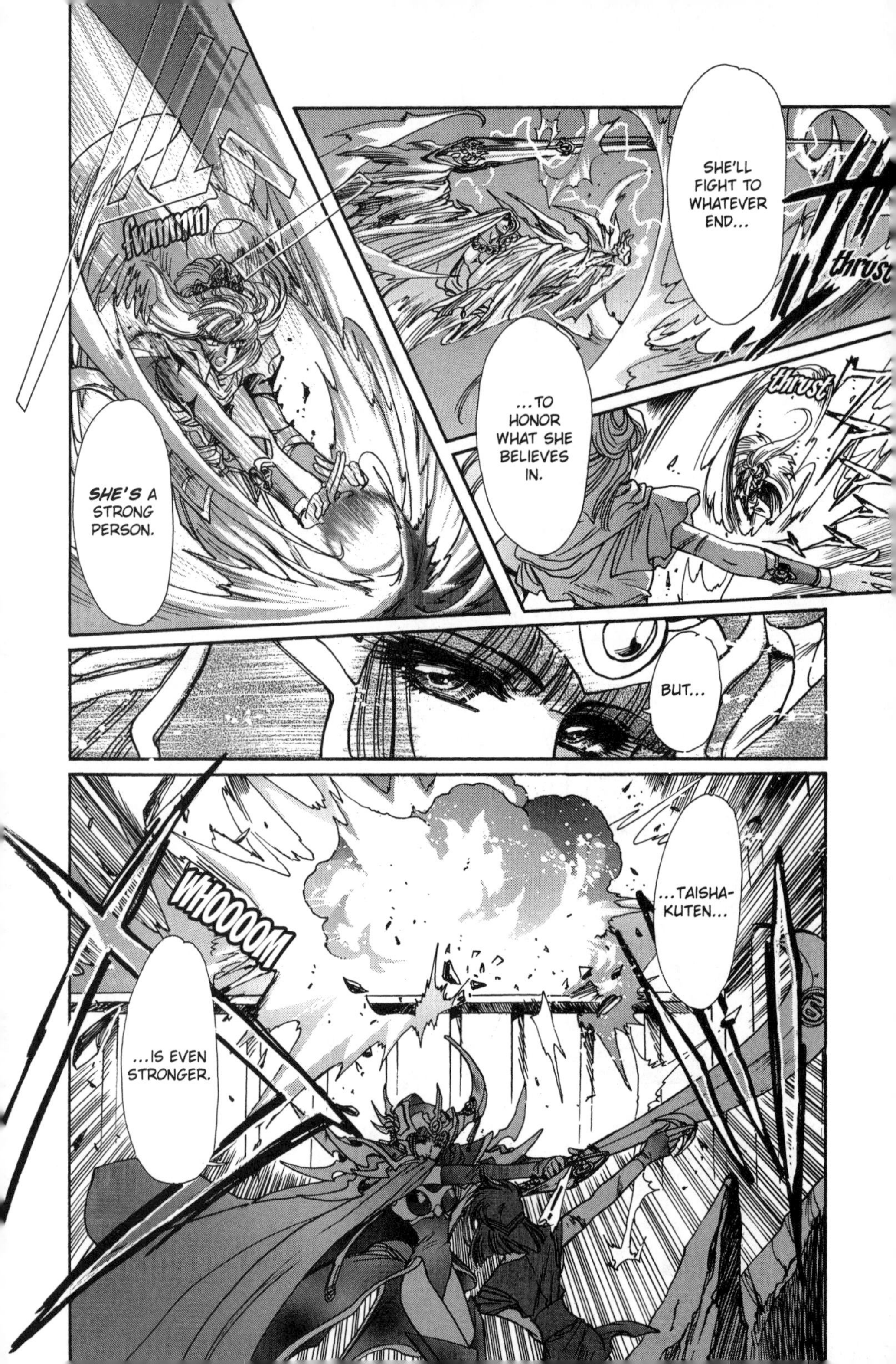
SHE'LL FIGHT TO WHATEVER END...
thrust
thrust
...TO HONOR WHAT SHE BELIEVES IN.
fwmmm
SHE'S A STRONG PERSON.
BUT...
...TAISHAKUTEN...
WHOOOOM
...IS EVEN STRONGER.

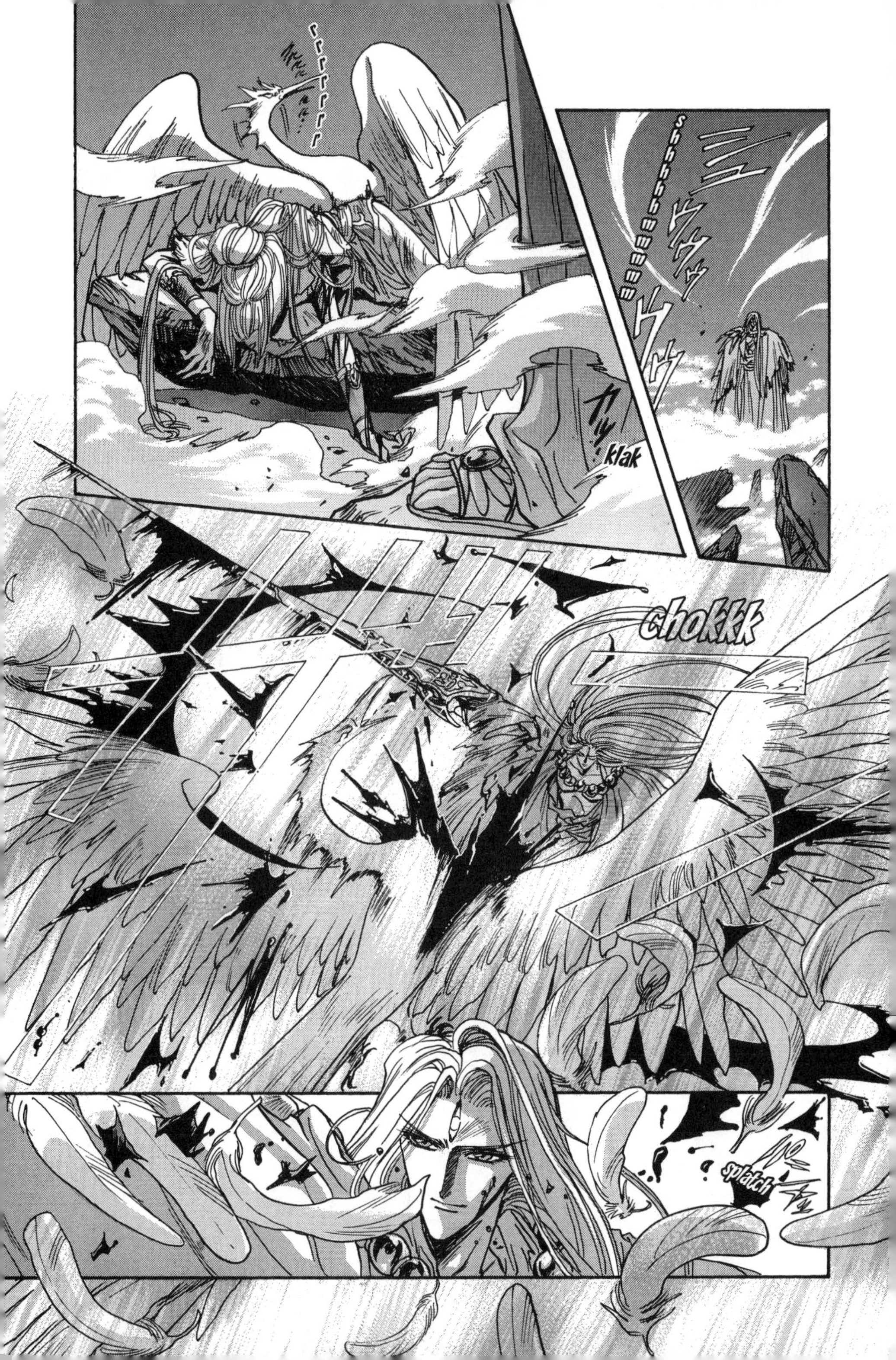
shhhhhhhhmmmmmmmm
rrrrrrrrrrr
klak
chokkk
splatch

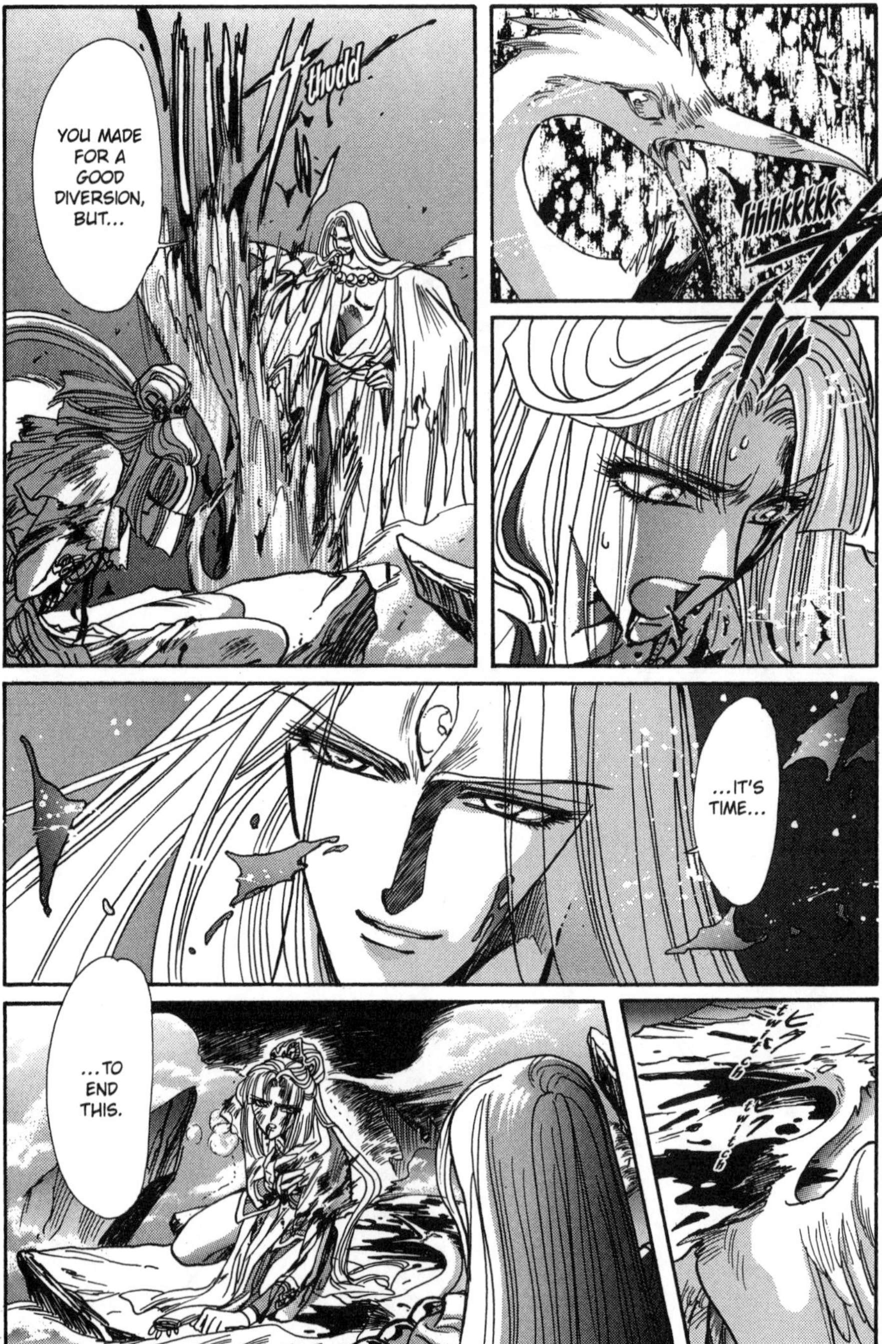
YOU MADE FOR A GOOD DIVERSION, BUT...
thudd
...IT'S TIME...
twitch
twitch
...TO END THIS.

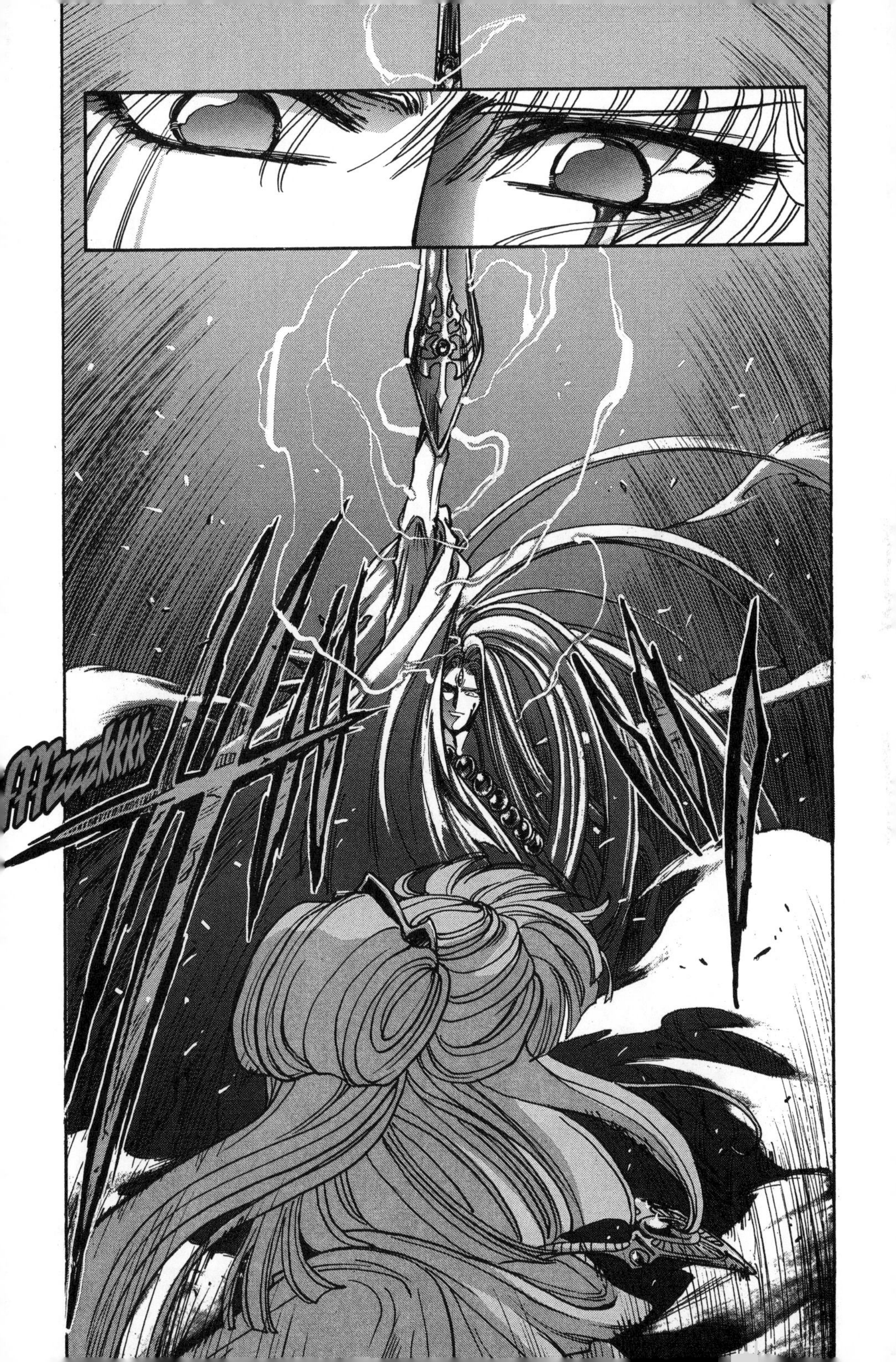
ffzzzkkkk

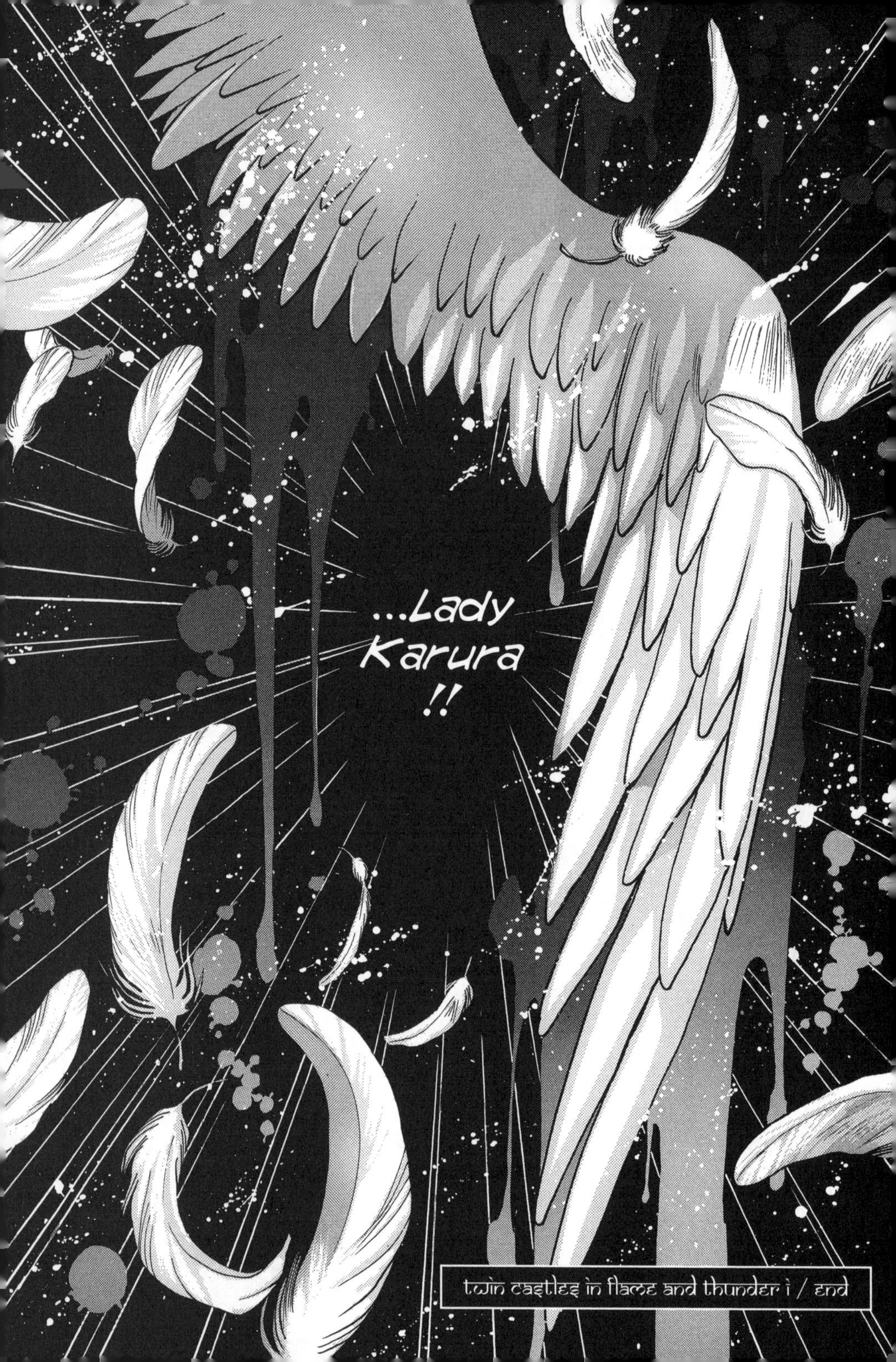
...Lady Karura !!
twin castles in flame and thunder i / end

CLAMP
RG VEDA

CLAMP
RG VEDA

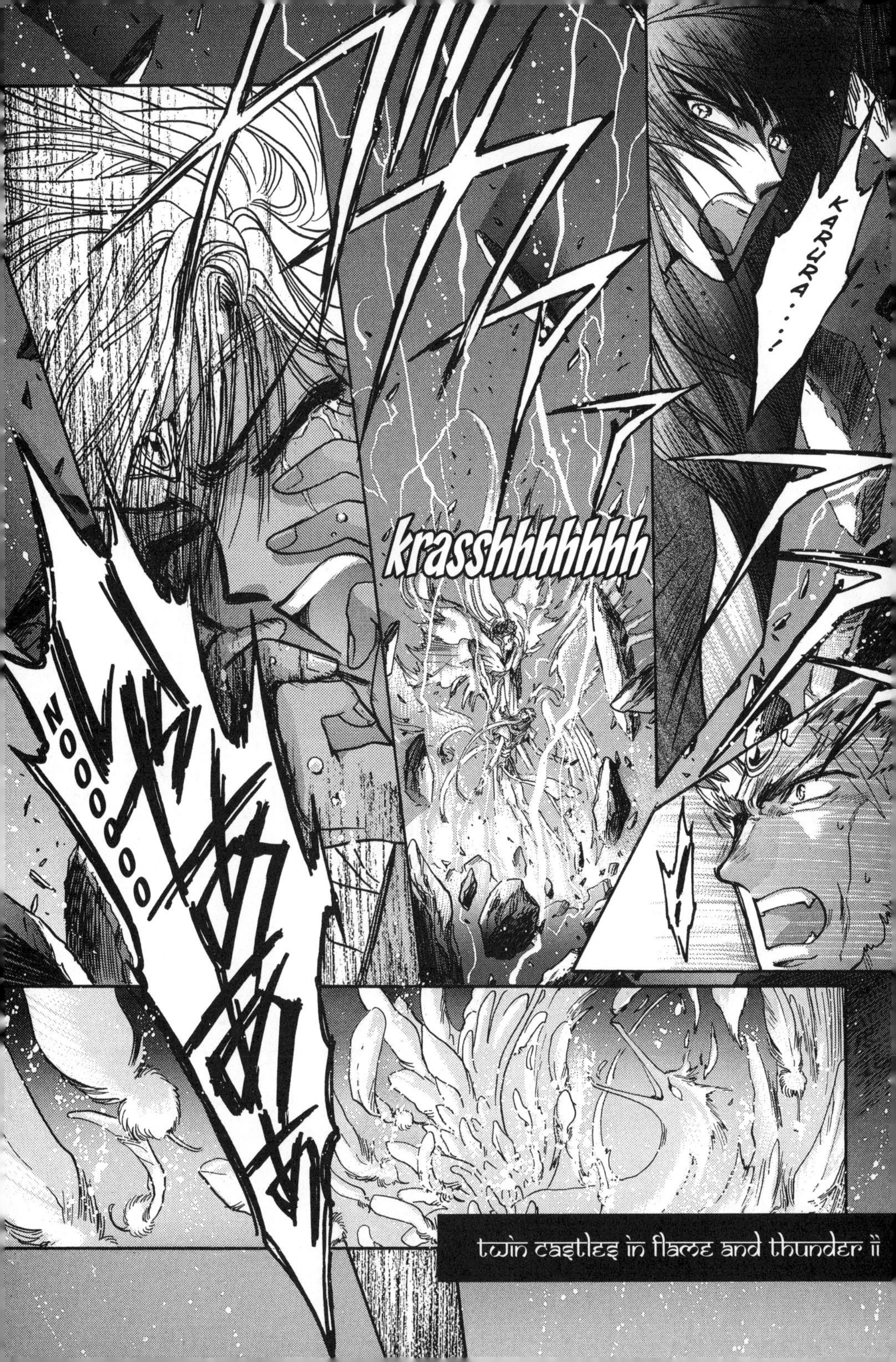
KARURA...!
krasshhhhhhh
NOOOOoooo

twin castles in flame and thunder ii

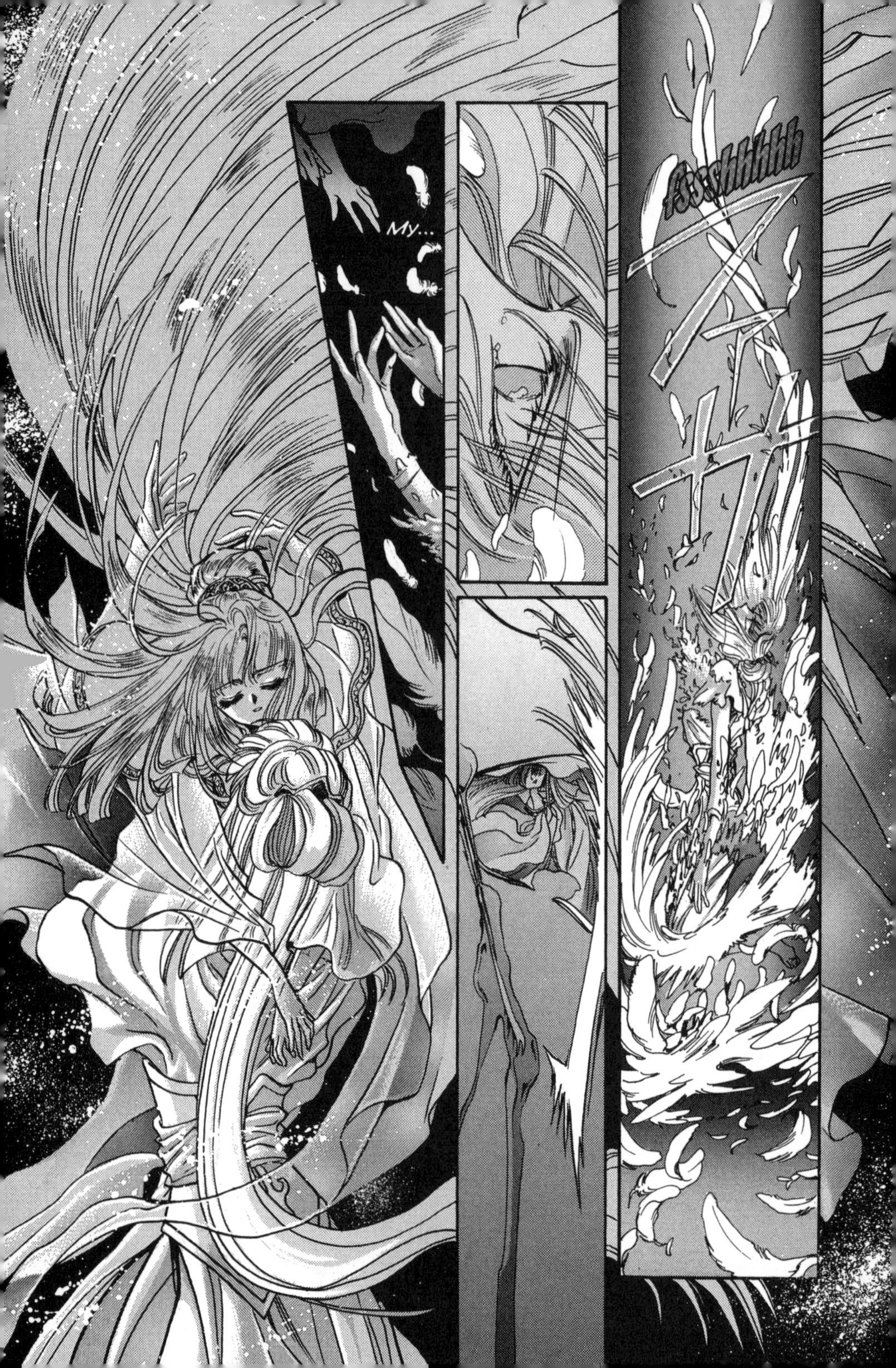
Fssshhhhhhh
My...

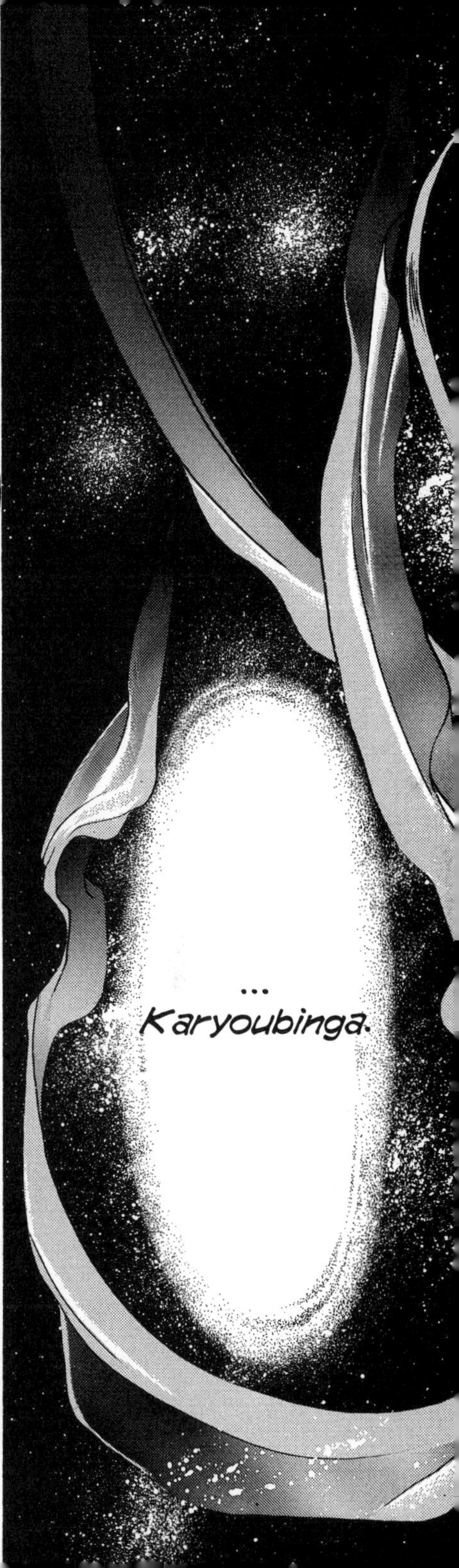

...
Karyoubinga.

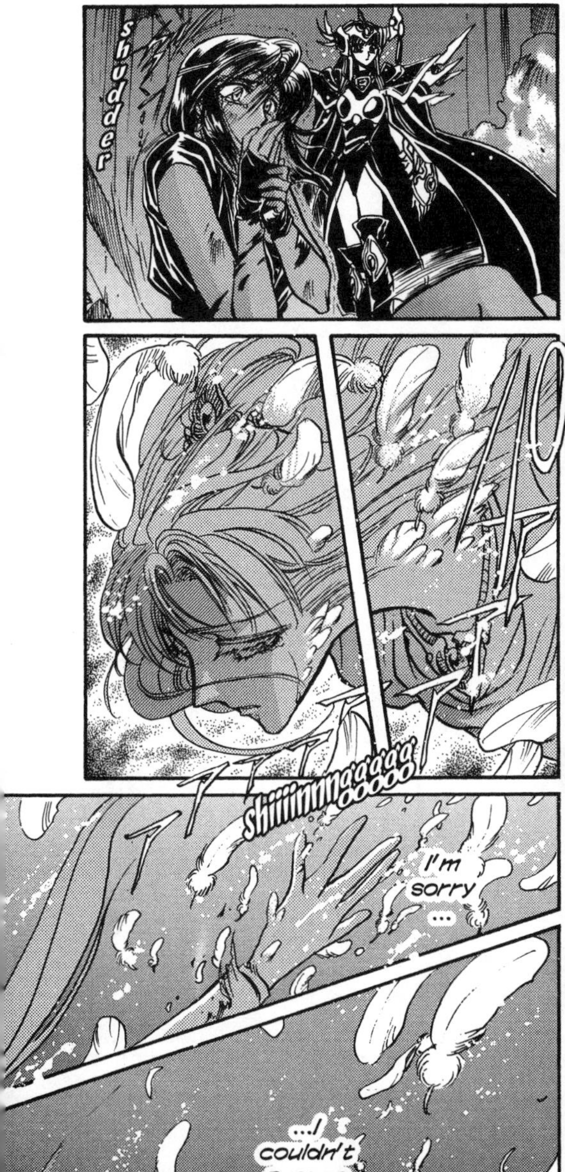

shudder
Shiiiiinnnaaaaa
ooooo
I'm sorry ...
...I couldn't avenge your death.

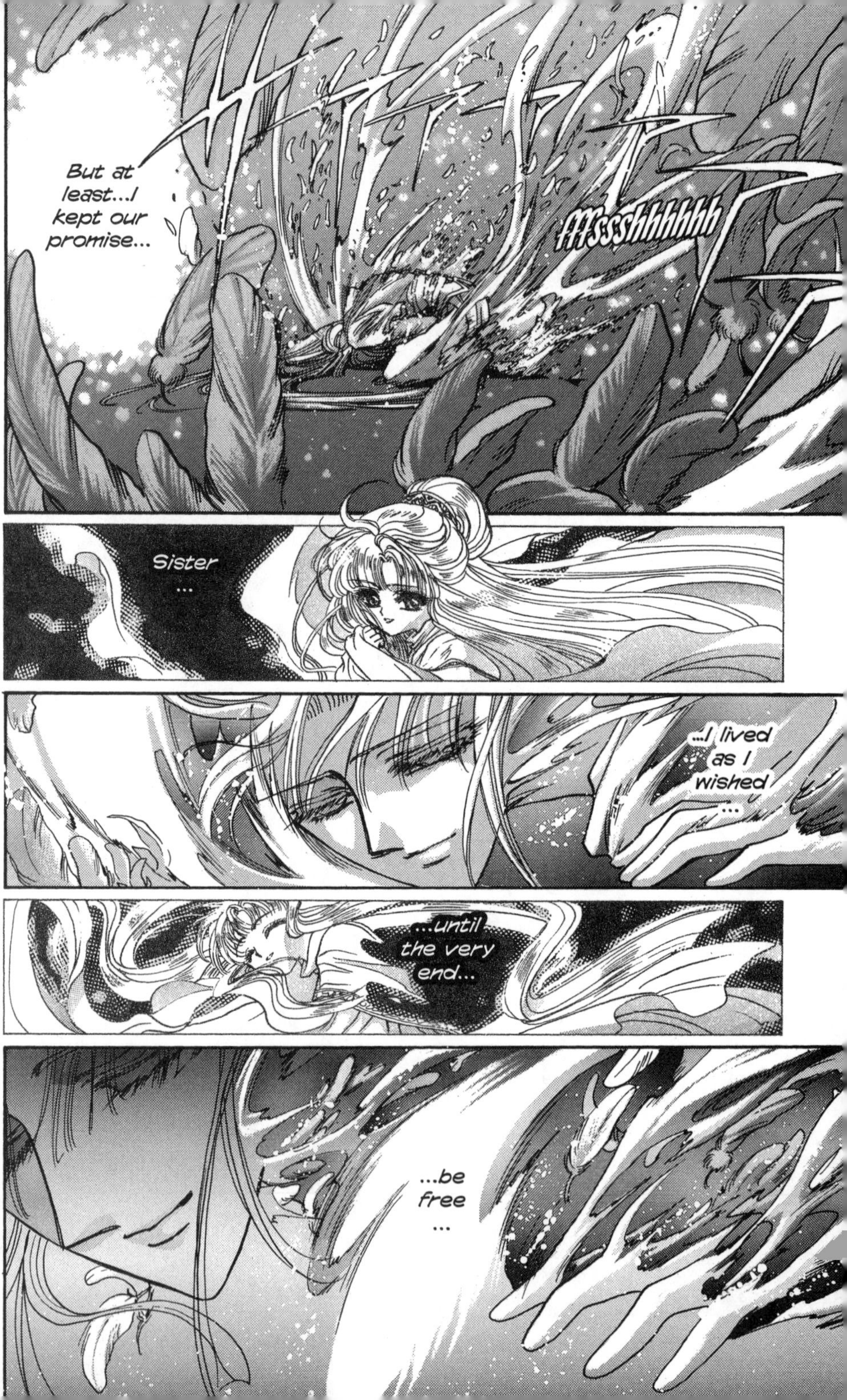
But at least...I kept our promise...
fffssshhhhhh
Sister ...
...I lived as I wished ...
...until the very end...
...be free ...

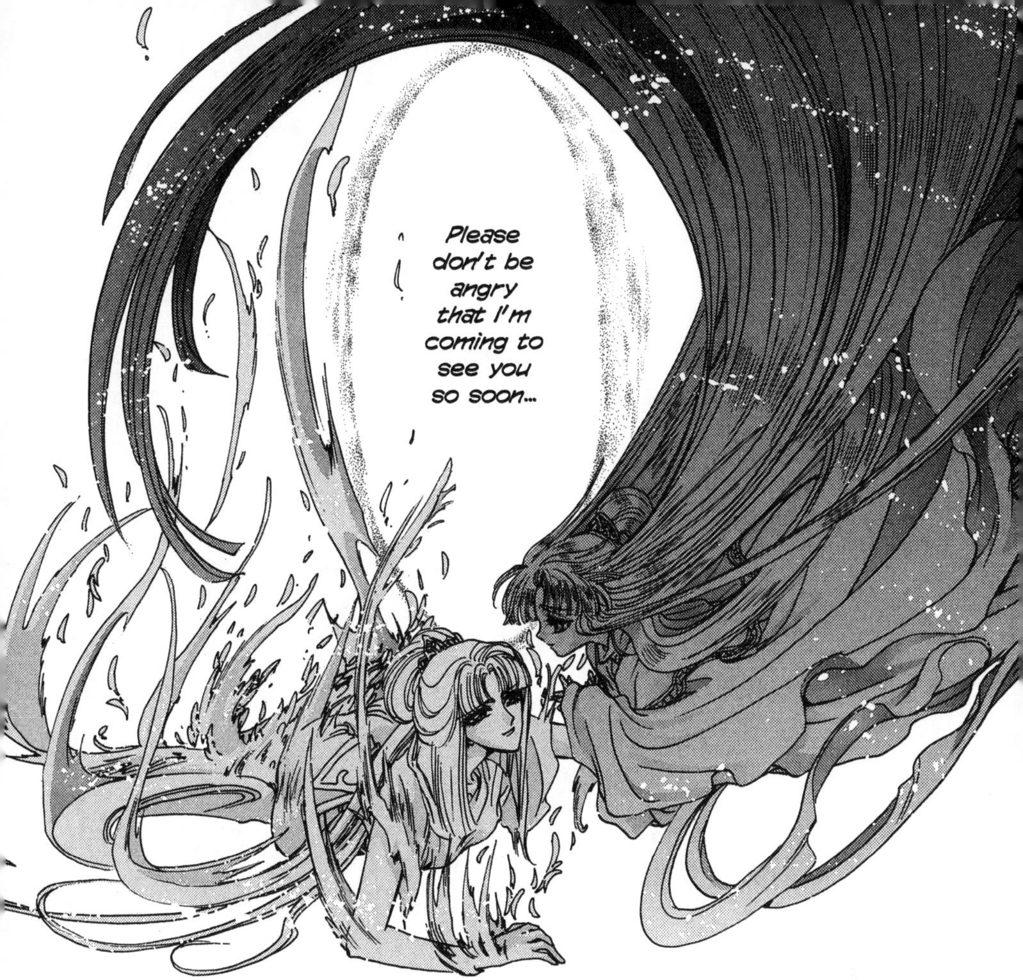
Please don't be angry that I'm coming to see you so soon...

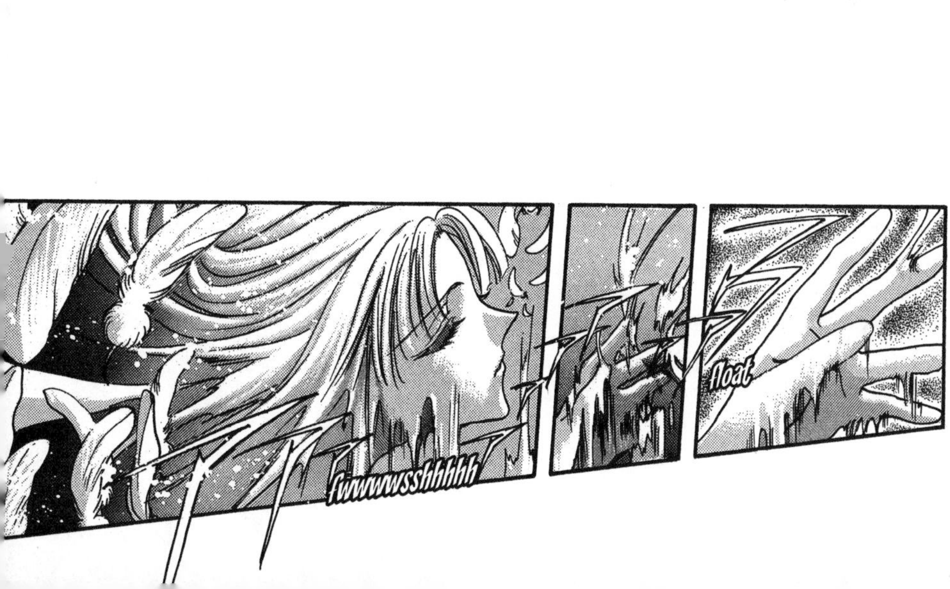
float
fwwwwwsshhhhhh

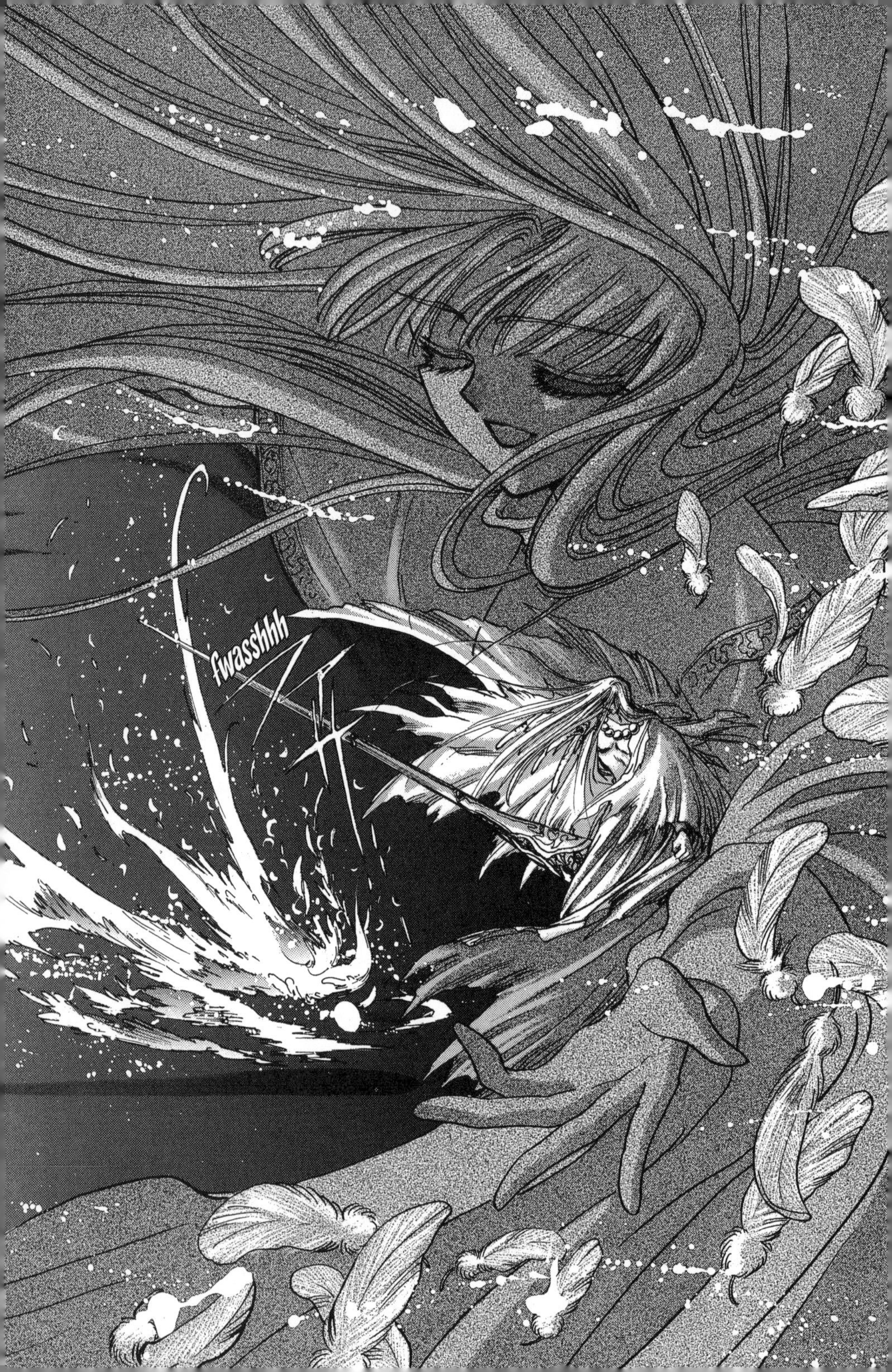
fwasshhh

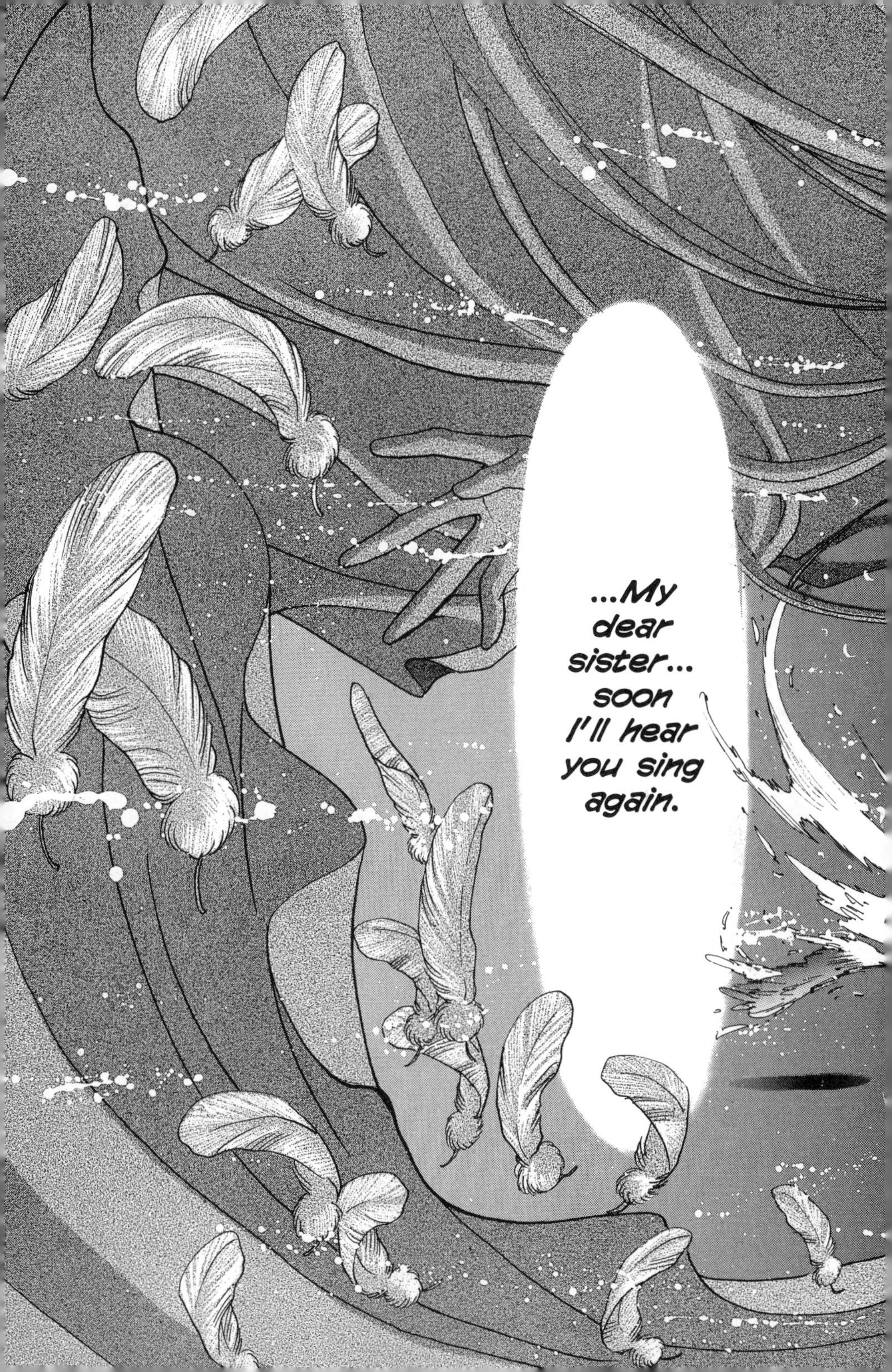
...My dear sister... soon I'll hear you sing again.

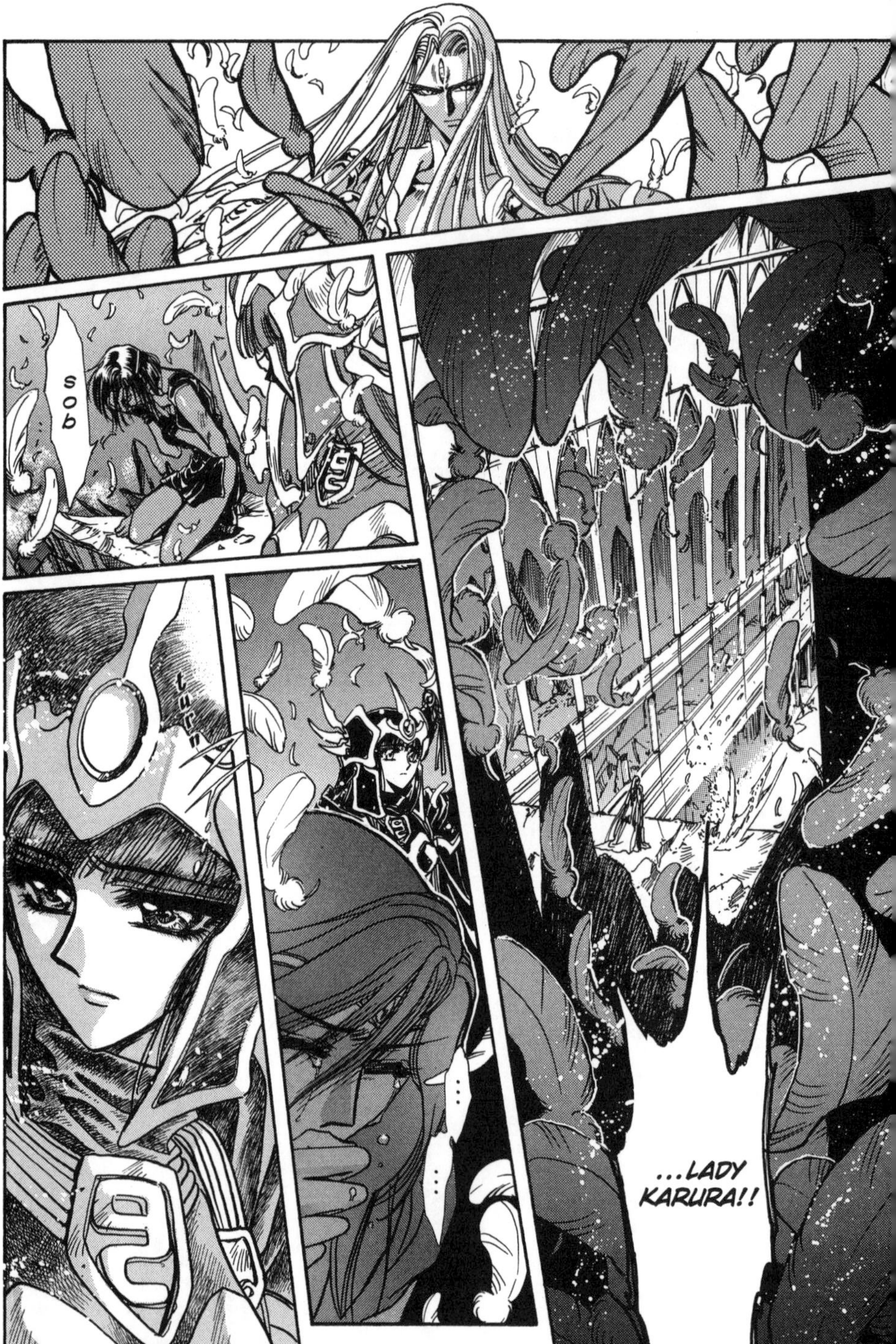
sob
turn
...
...
...LADY KARURA!!

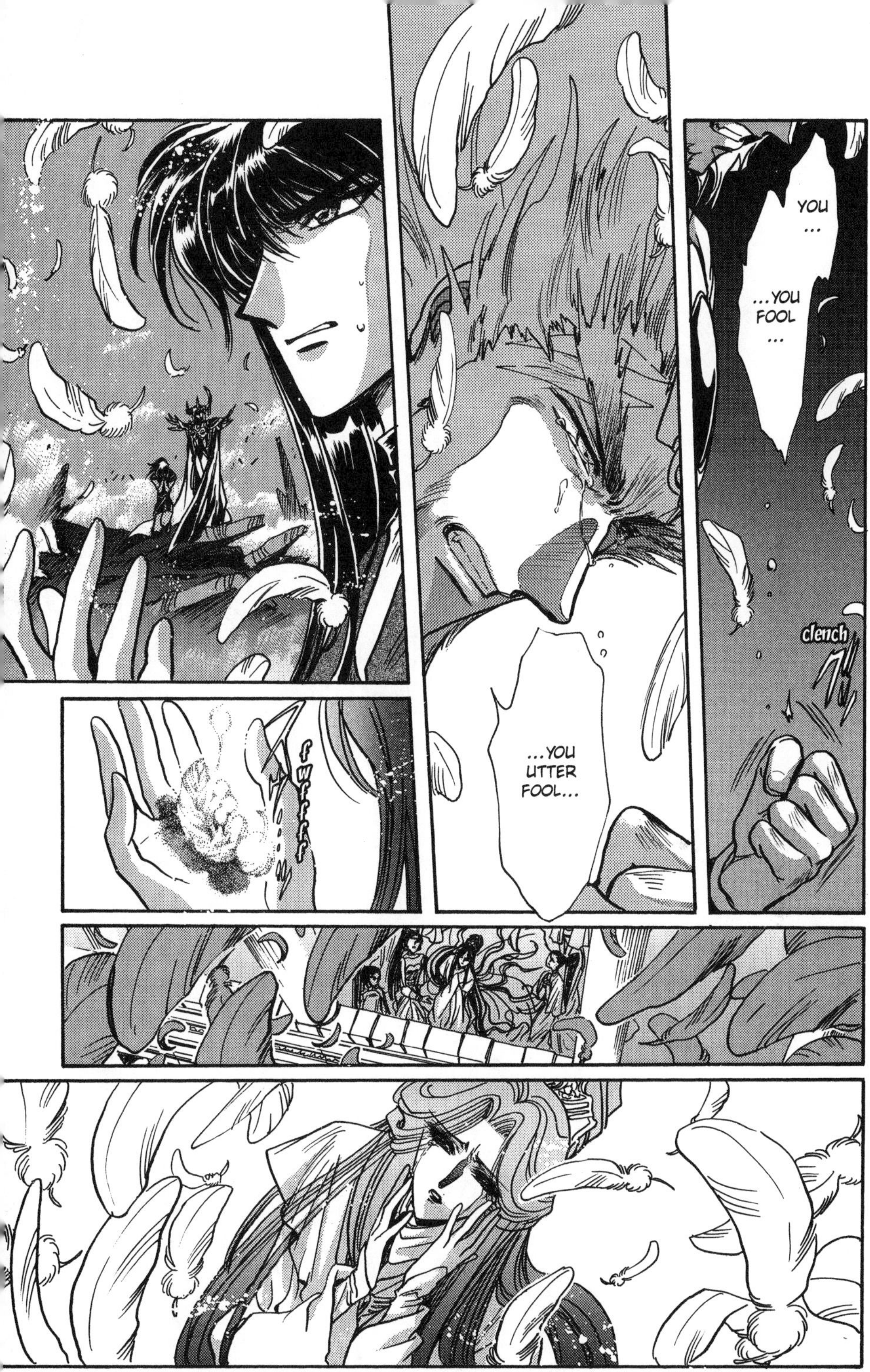
YOU ...
...YOU FOOL ...
clench
...YOU UTTER FOOL...
fwfffff

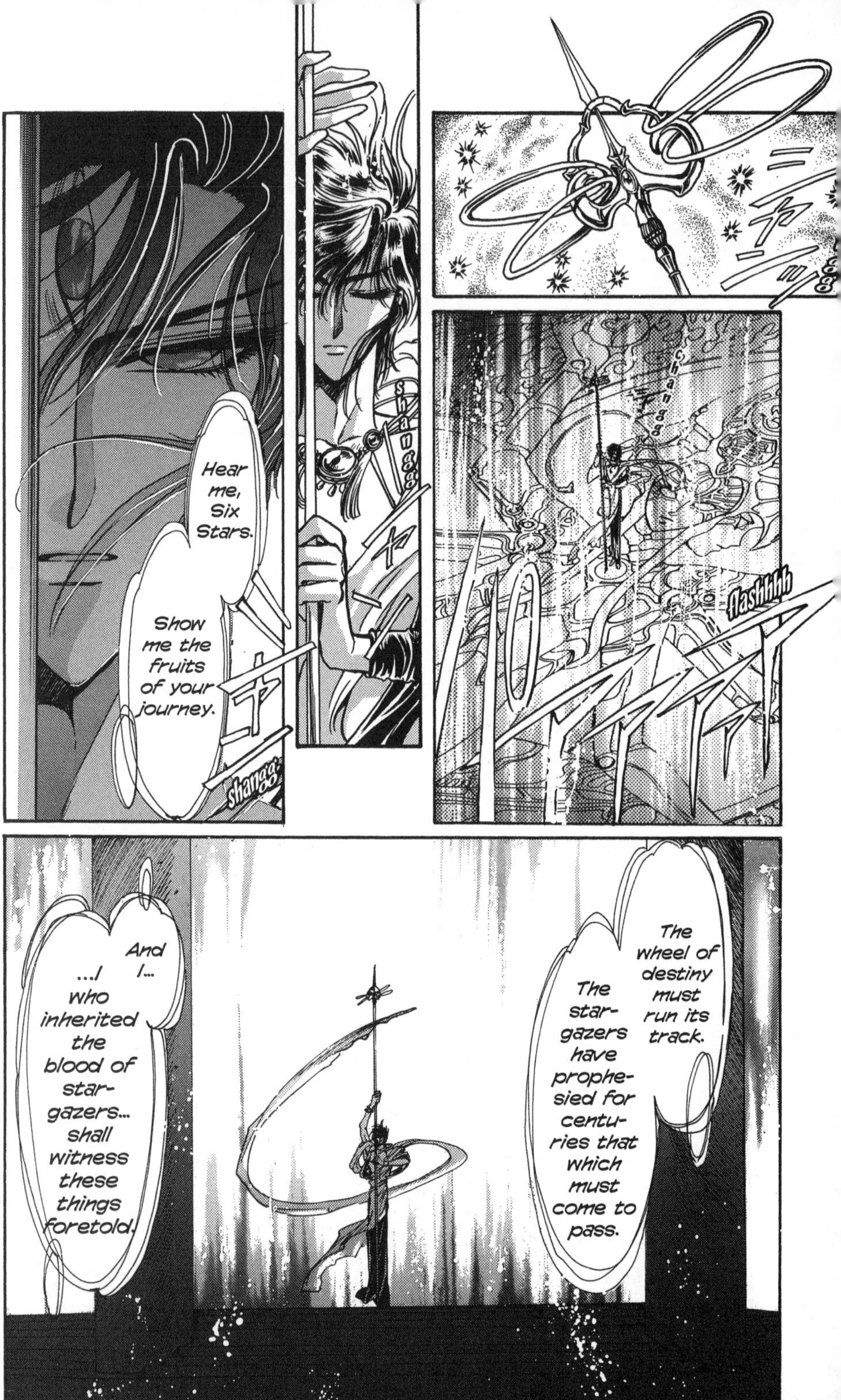
flashhhh
Hear me, Six Stars.
Show me the fruits of your journey.
shangg
The wheel of destiny must run its track.
The star-gazers have prophesied for centuries that which must come to pass.
And I... ...I who inherited the blood of star-gazers... shall witness these things foretold.

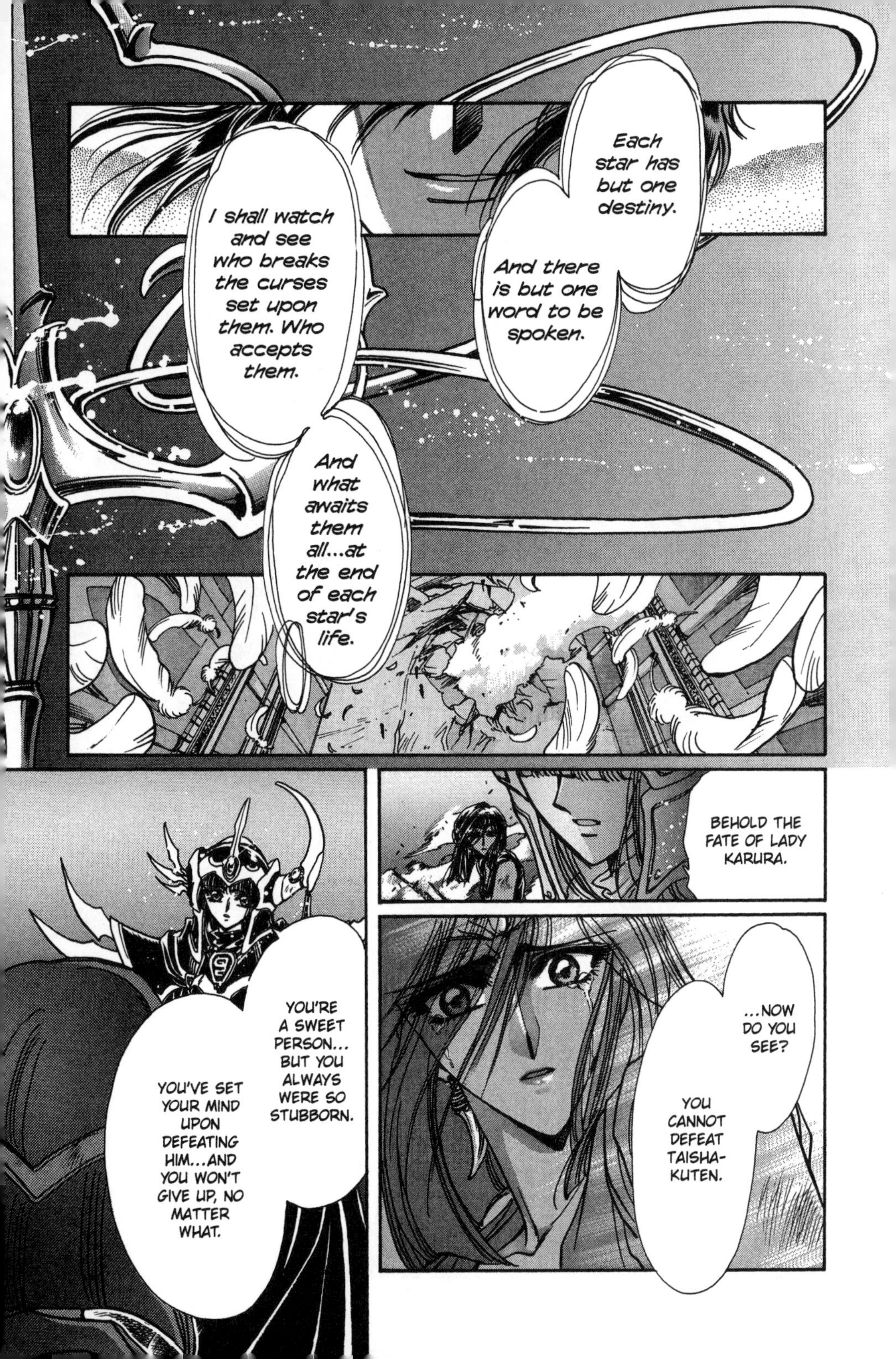
Each star has but one destiny.
And there is but one word to be spoken.
I shall watch and see who breaks the curses set upon them. Who accepts them.
And what awaits them all...at the end of each star's life.
BEHOLD THE FATE OF LADY KARURA.
...NOW DO YOU SEE?
YOU CANNOT DEFEAT TAISHA-KUTEN.
YOU'RE A SWEET PERSON... BUT YOU ALWAYS WERE SO STUBBORN.
YOU'VE SET YOUR MIND UPON DEFEATING HIM...AND YOU WON'T GIVE UP, NO MATTER WHAT.

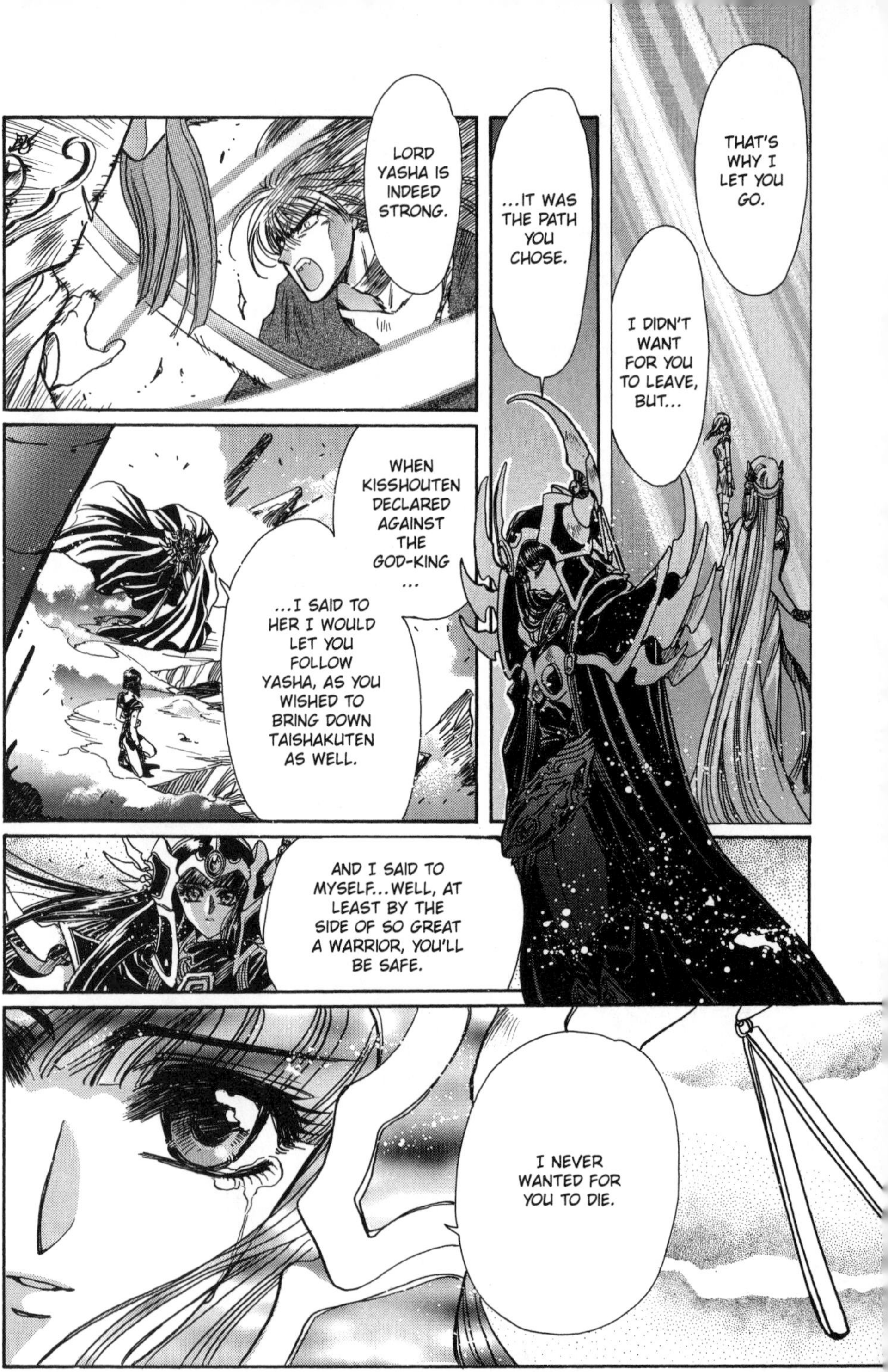
THAT'S WHY I LET YOU GO.
I DIDN'T WANT FOR YOU TO LEAVE, BUT...
...IT WAS THE PATH YOU CHOSE.
LORD YASHA IS INDEED STRONG.
WHEN KISSHOUTEN DECLARED AGAINST THE GOD-KING...
...I SAID TO HER I WOULD LET YOU FOLLOW YASHA, AS YOU WISHED TO BRING DOWN TAISHAKUTEN AS WELL.
AND I SAID TO MYSELF...WELL, AT LEAST BY THE SIDE OF SO GREAT A WARRIOR, YOU'LL BE SAFE.
I NEVER WANTED FOR YOU TO DIE.

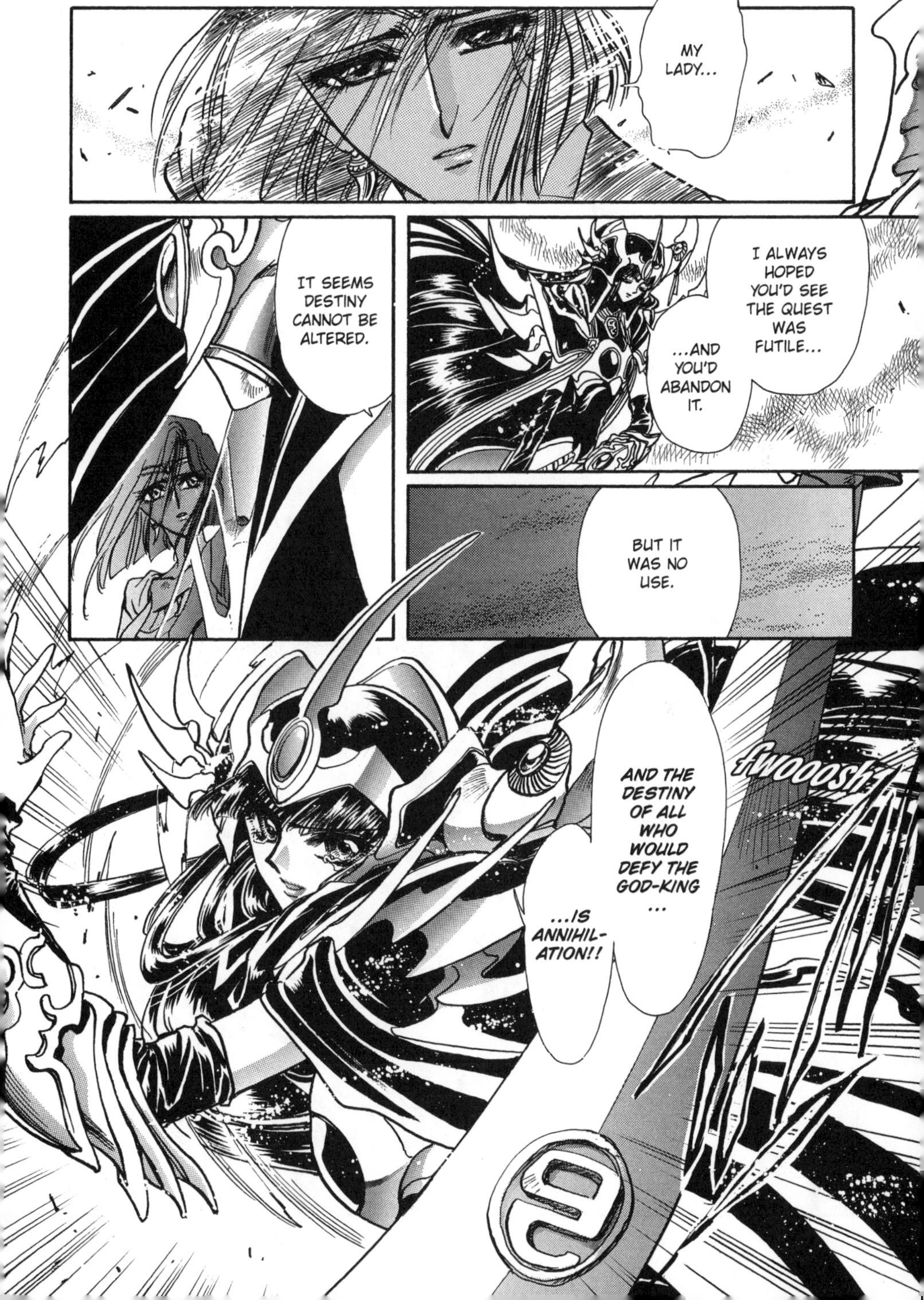
MY LADY...
I ALWAYS HOPED YOU'D SEE THE QUEST WAS FUTILE...
...AND YOU'D ABANDON IT.
IT SEEMS DESTINY CANNOT BE ALTERED.
BUT IT WAS NO USE.
fwooosh
AND THE DESTINY OF ALL WHO WOULD DEFY THE GOD-KING ...
...IS ANNIHIL-ATION!!

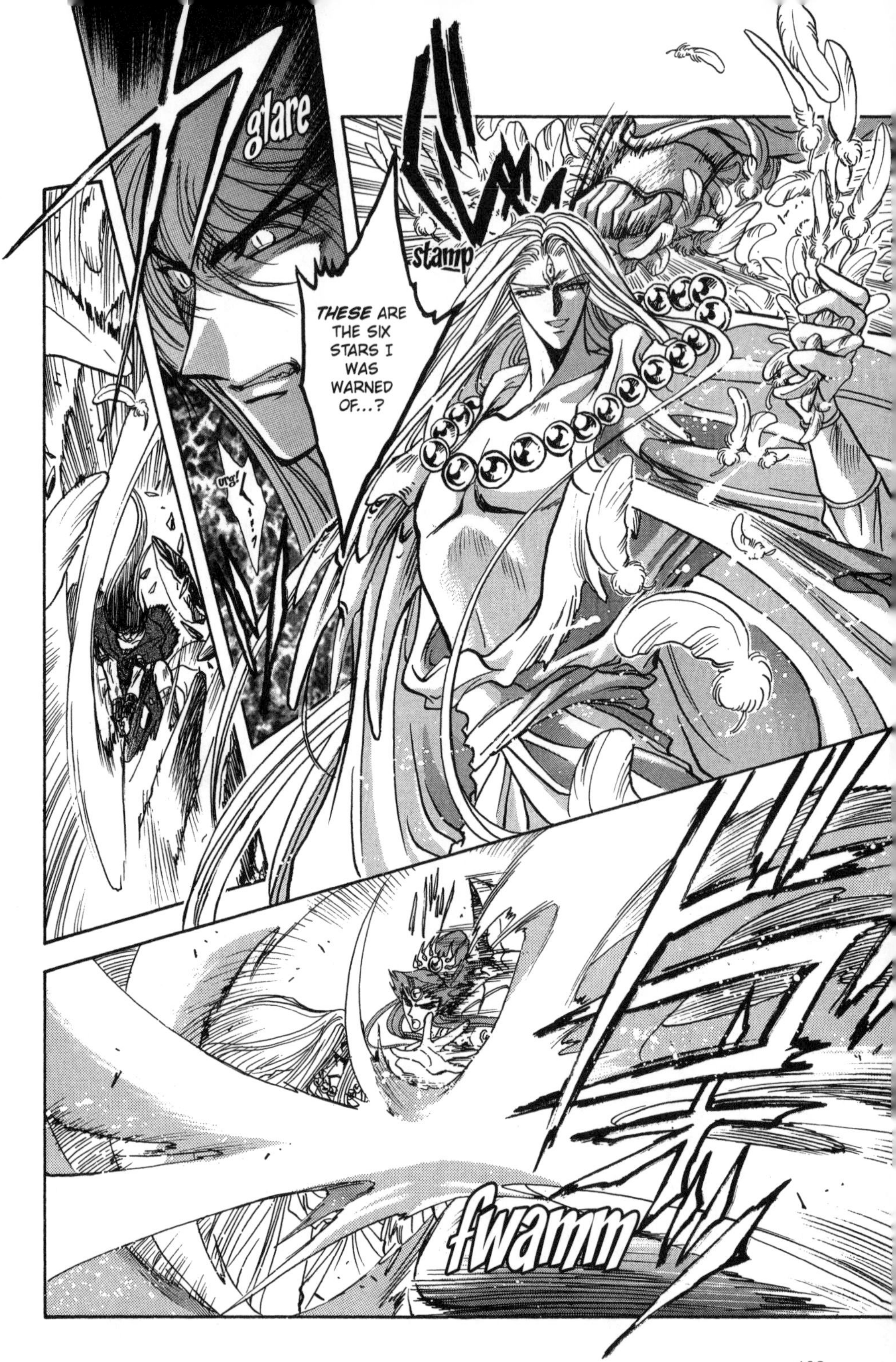
stamp
THESE ARE THE SIX STARS I WAS WARNED OF...?
glare
urg!
fwamm

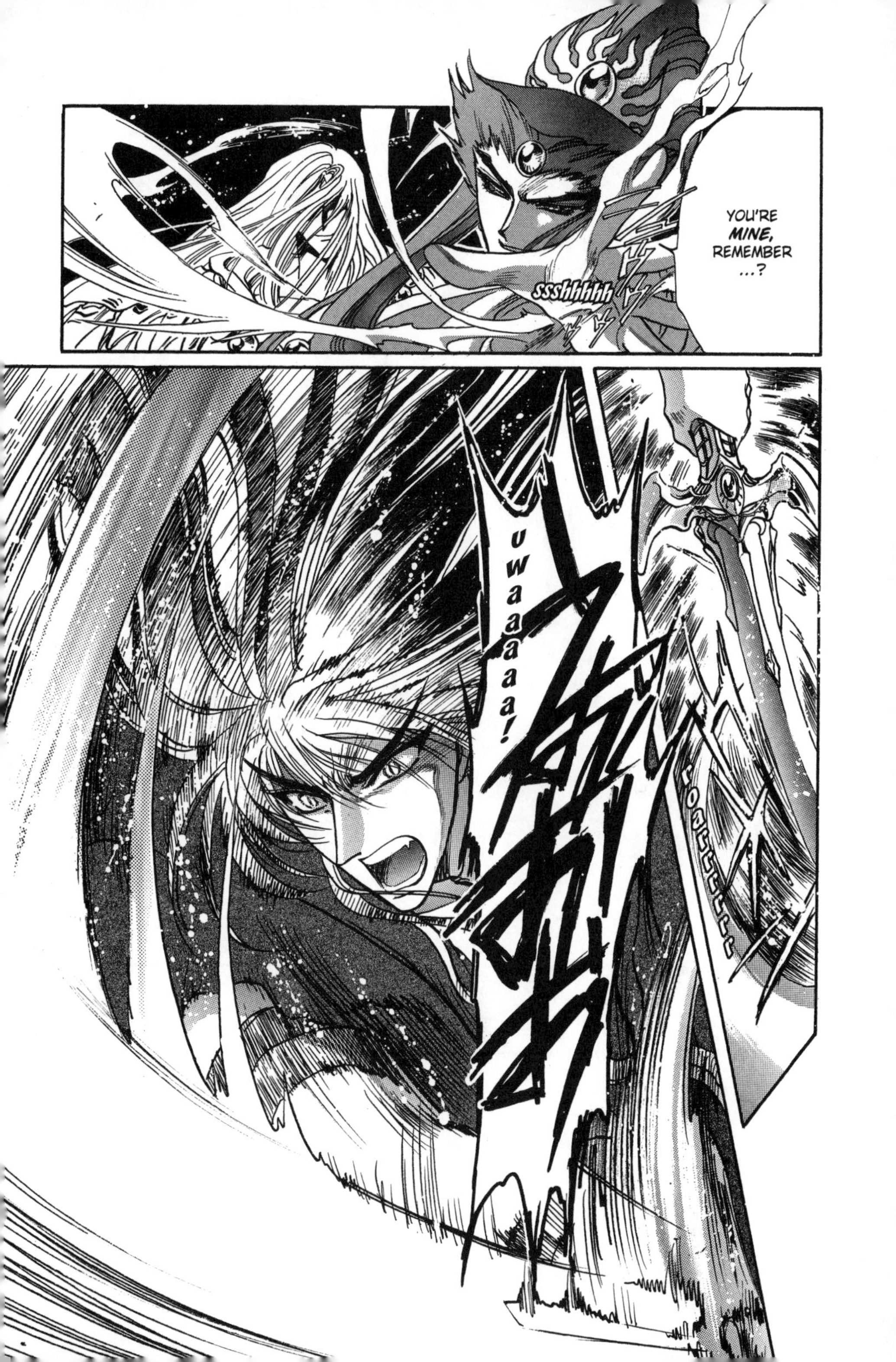
YOU'RE *MINE,* REMEMBER ...?
ssshhhhh
uwaaaaaa!
roarrrrrr

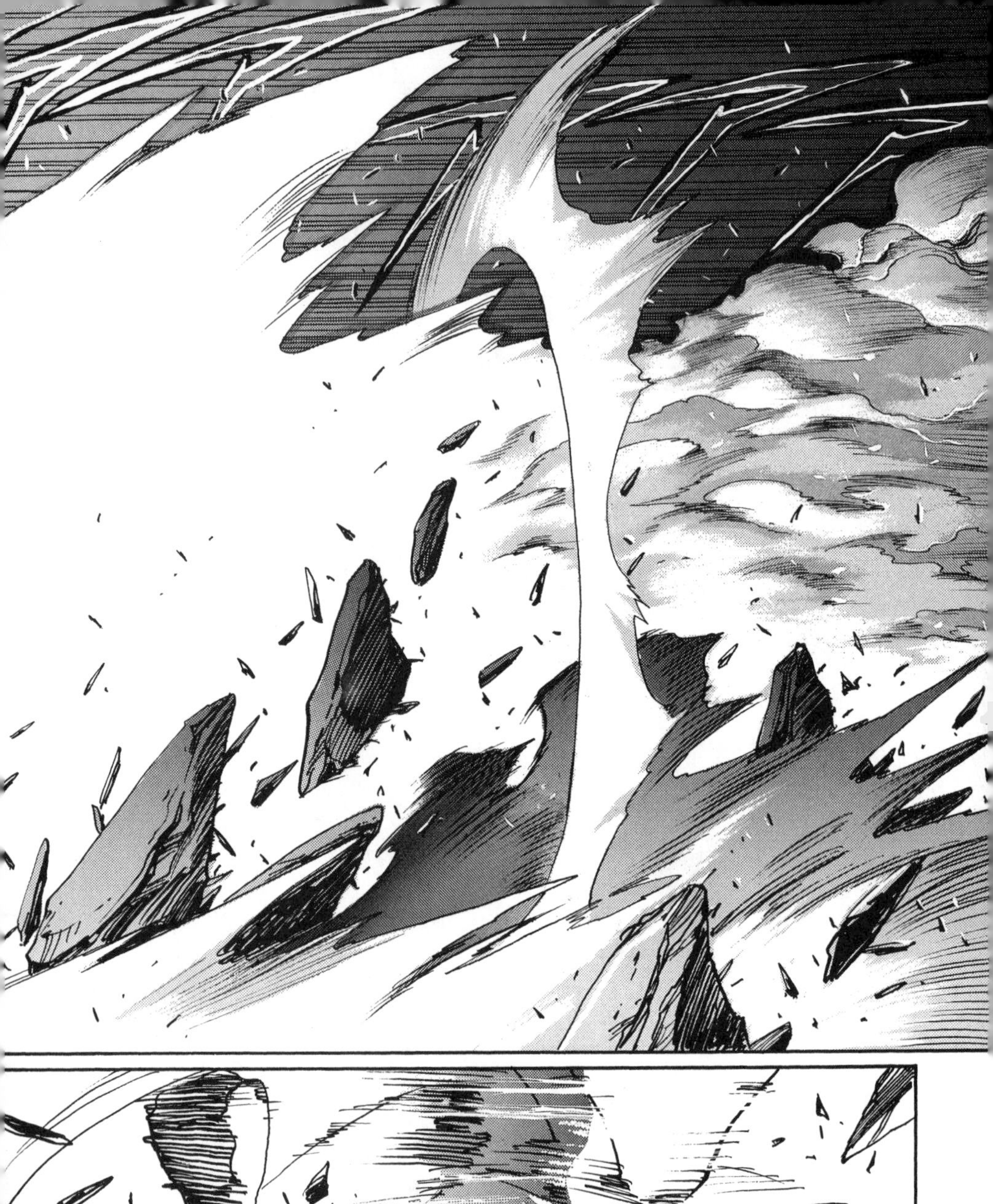

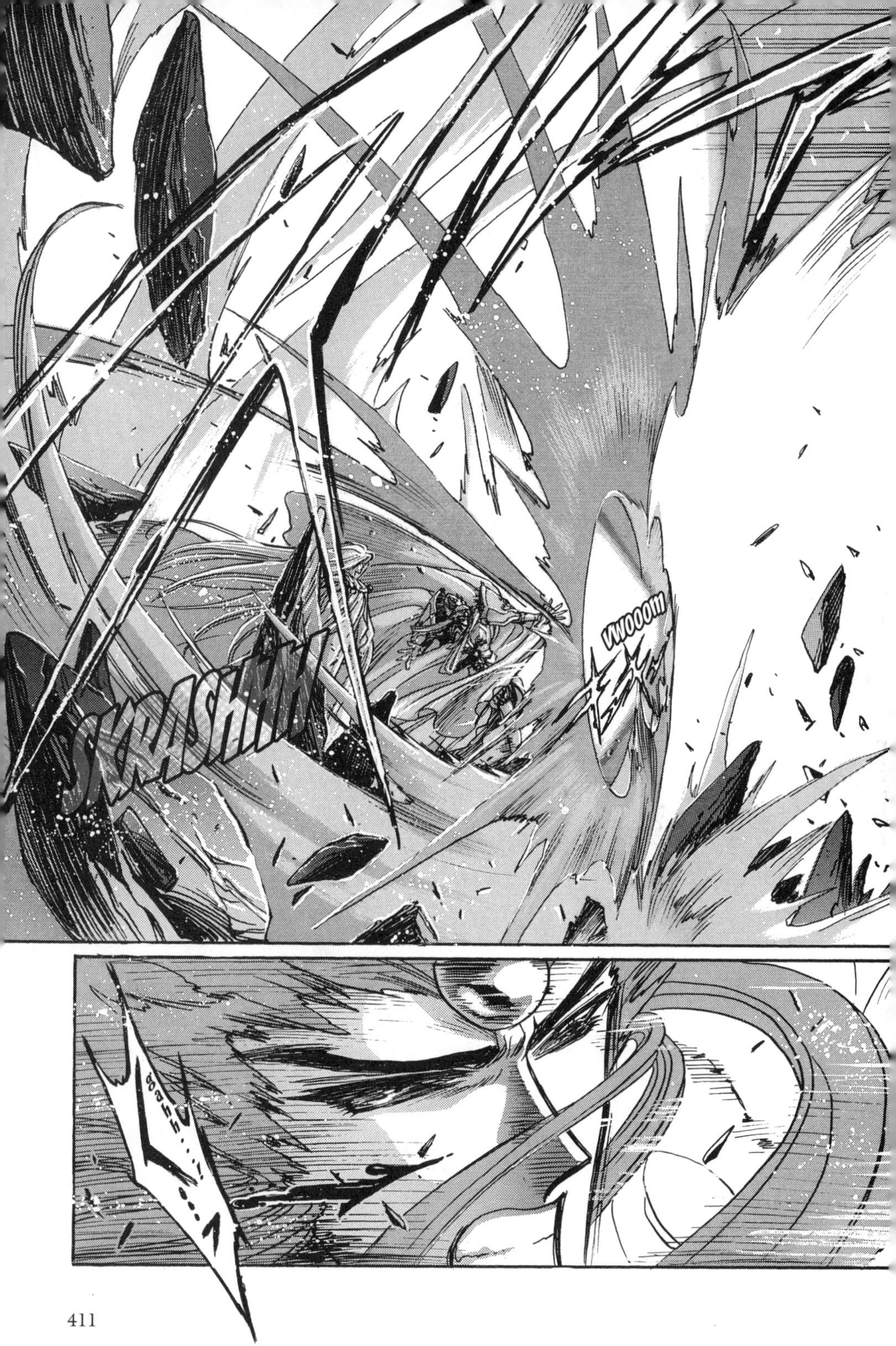
vwooom
gahh...!

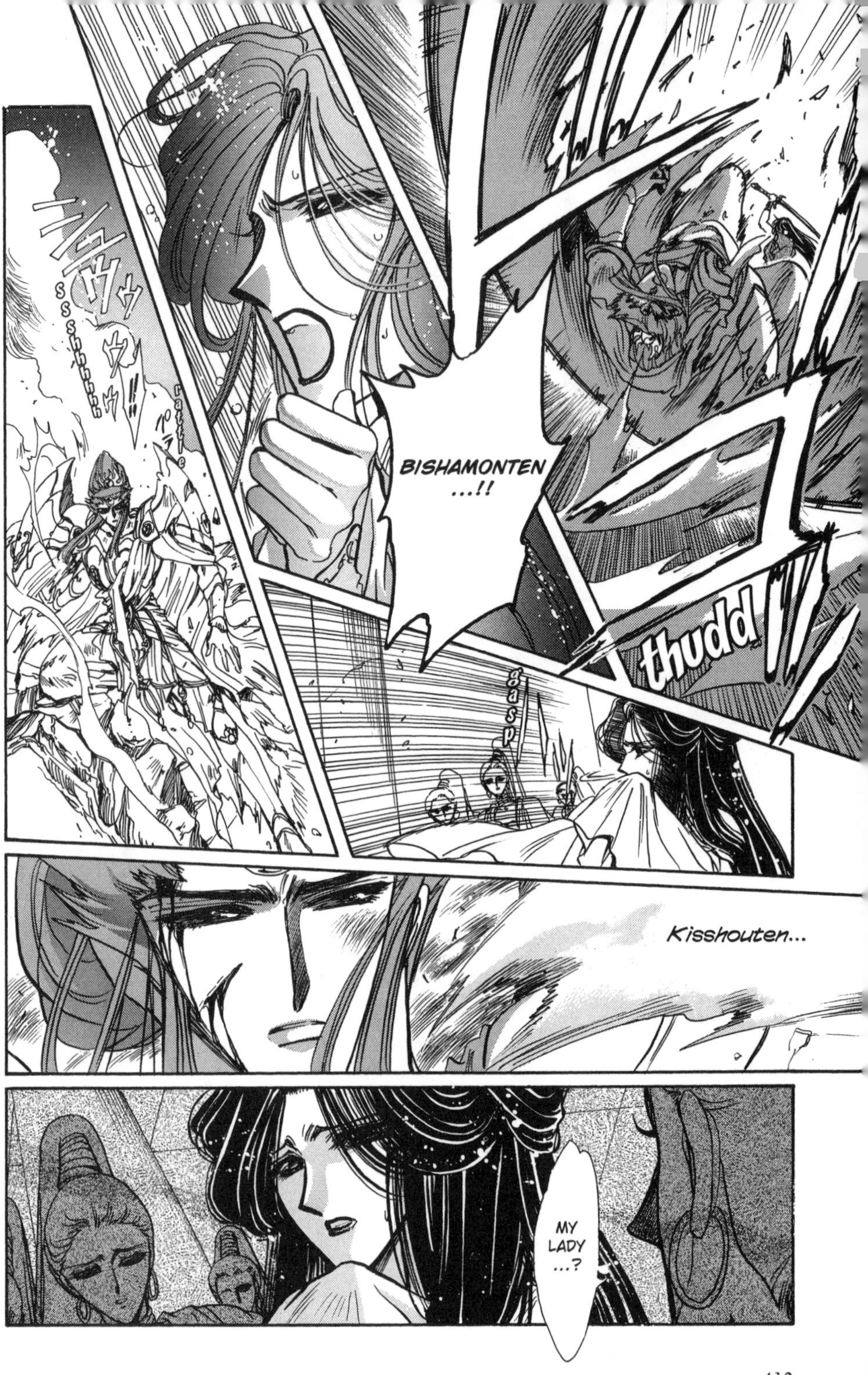
thudd
BISHAMONTEN ...!!
ssshhhhh
rattle
gasp
Kisshouten...
MY LADY ...?

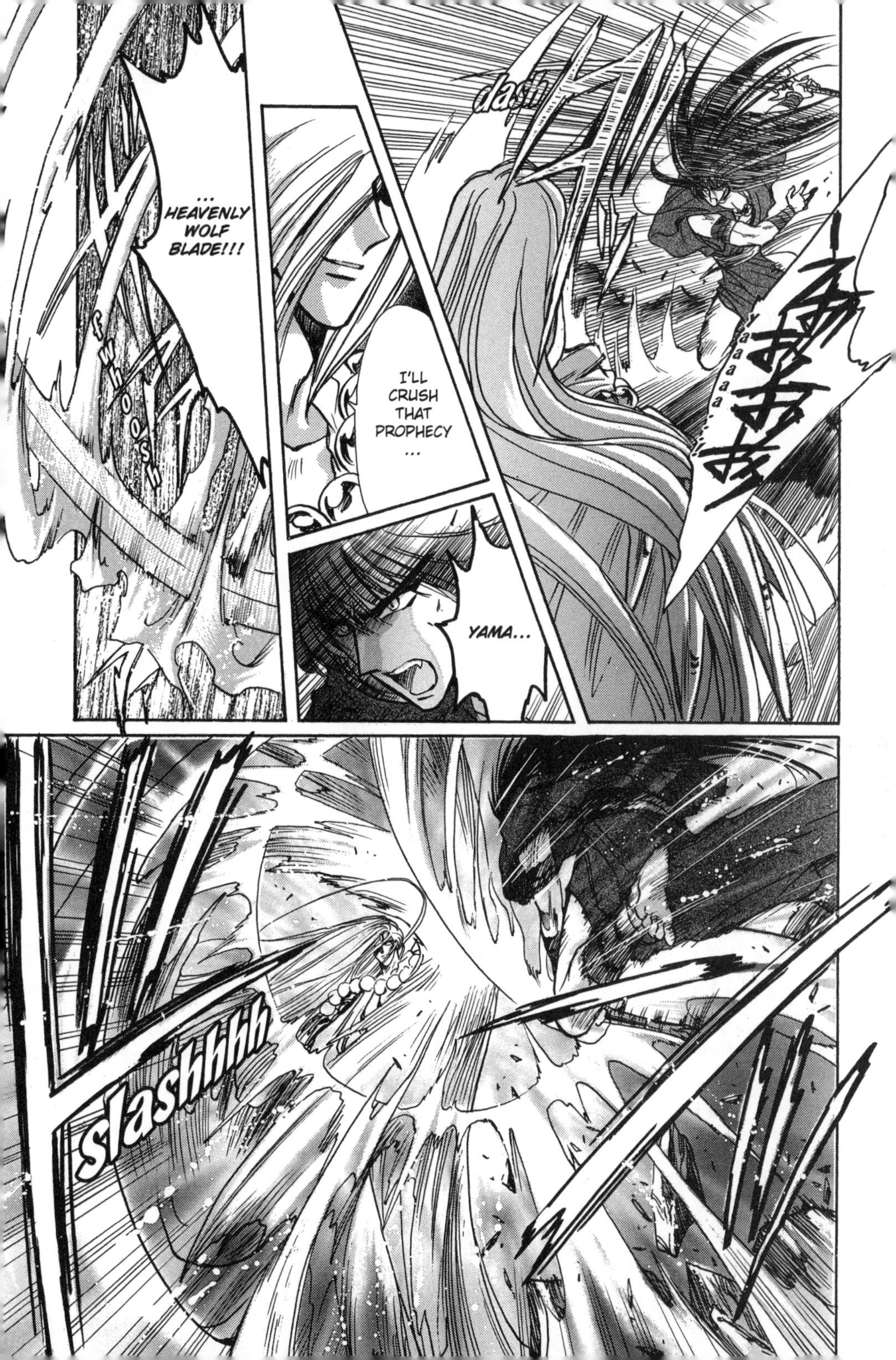
dash
yaaaaa......
I'LL CRUSH THAT PROPHECY...
YAMA...
...HEAVENLY WOLF BLADE!!!
fwhoosh
slashhhh

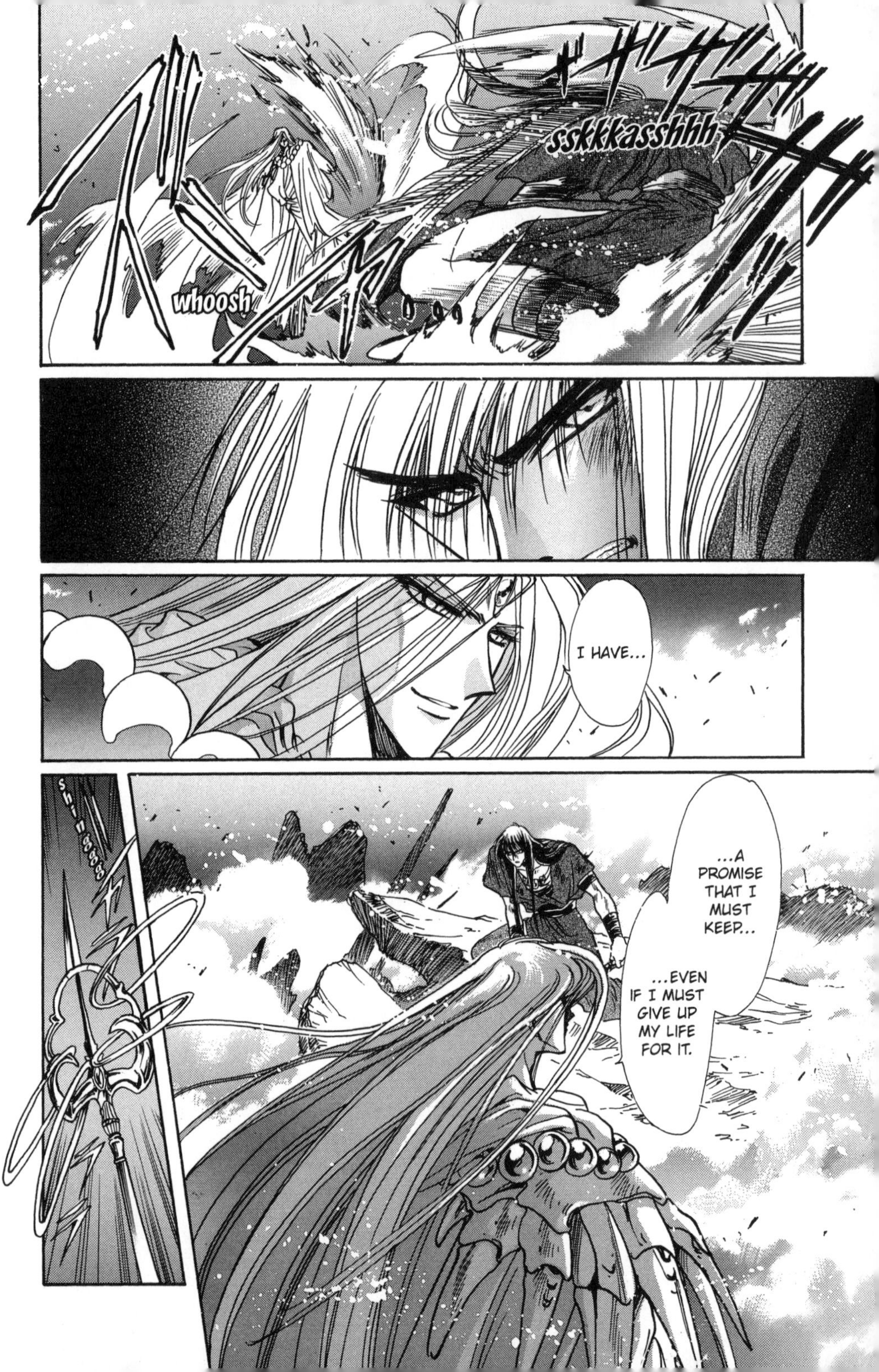
sskkkasshhh
whoosh
I HAVE...
...A PROMISE THAT I MUST KEEP...
...EVEN IF I MUST GIVE UP MY LIFE FOR IT.
shinggg

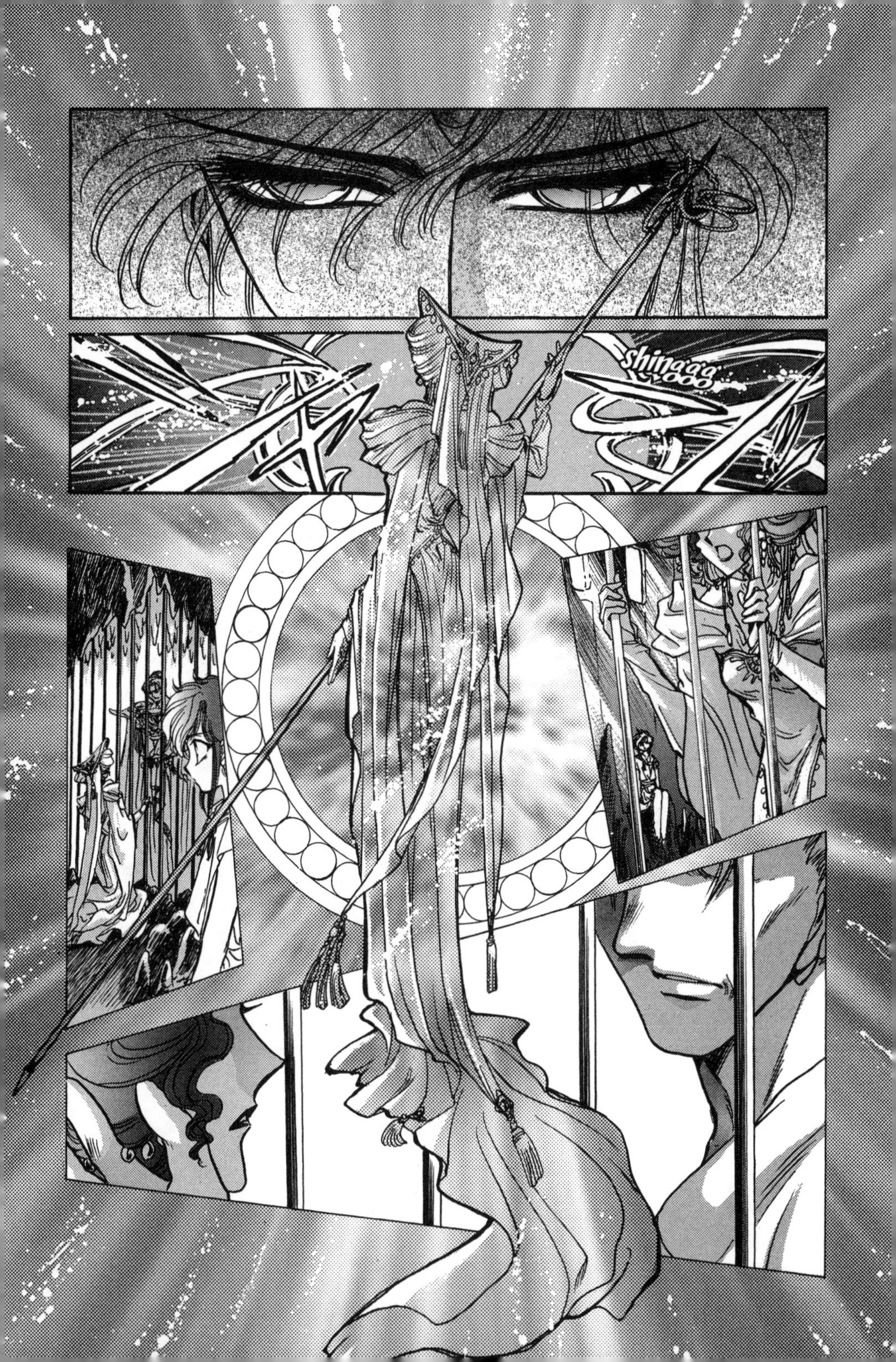
shingggg

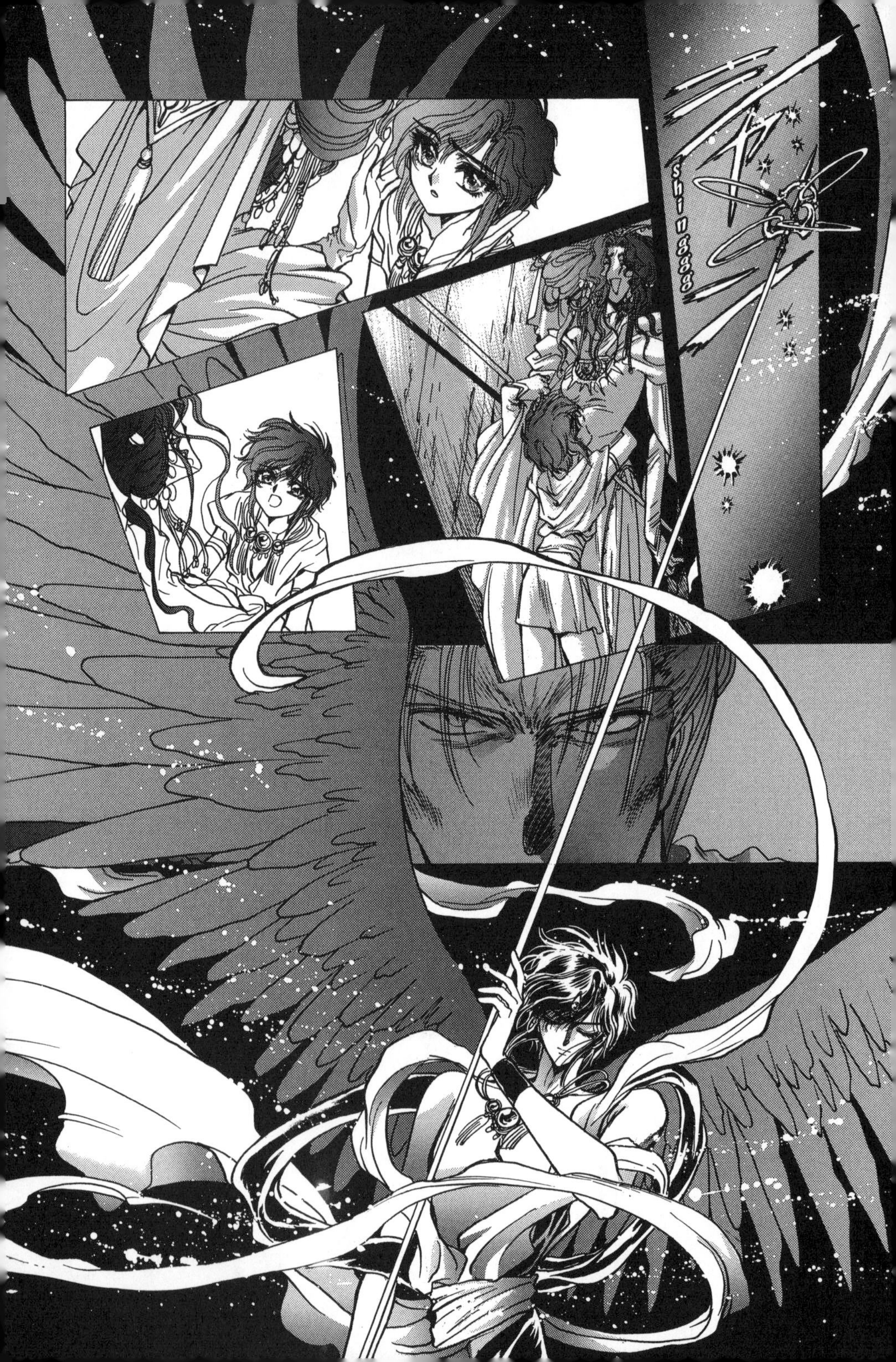
shinggg

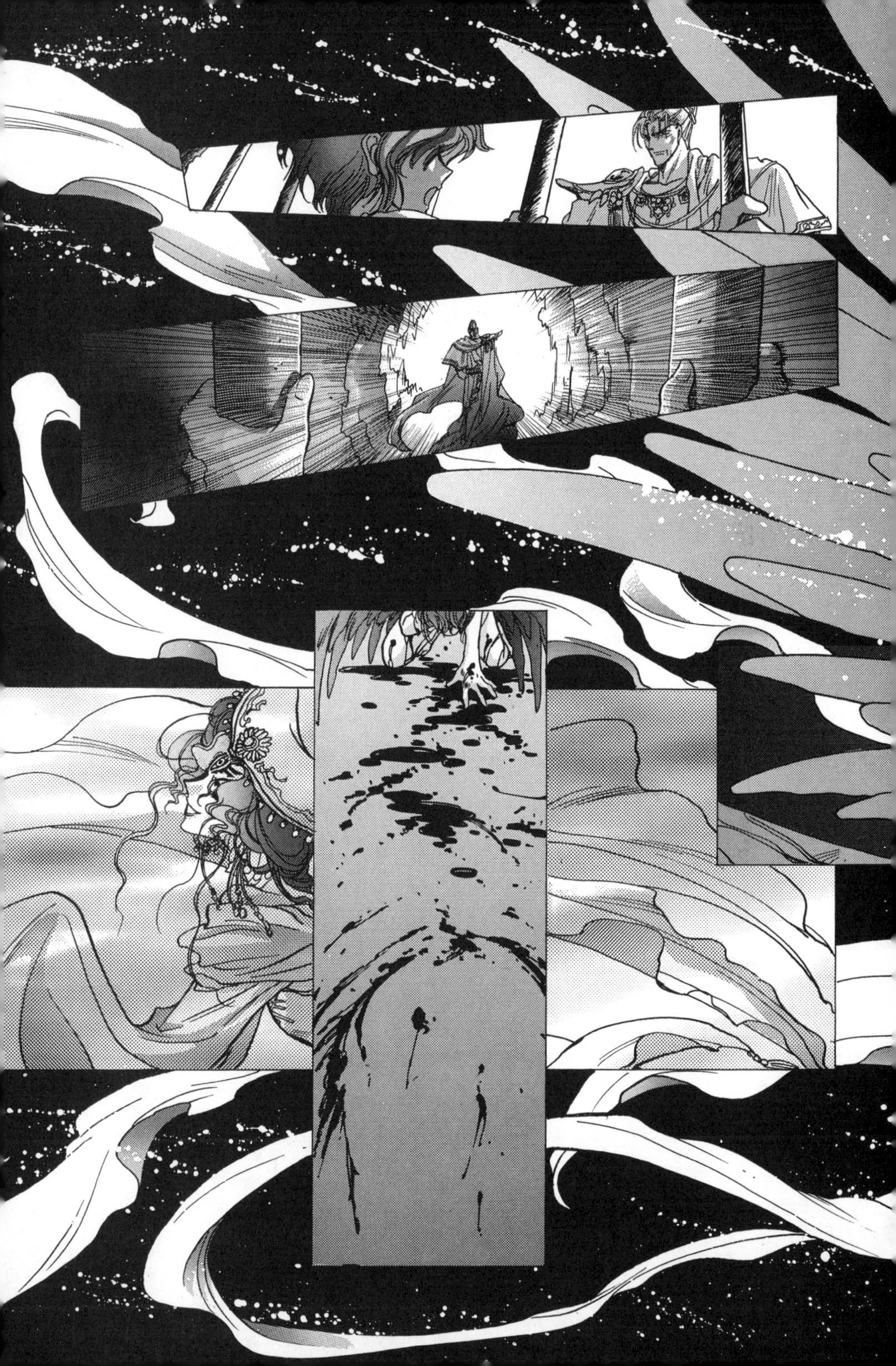

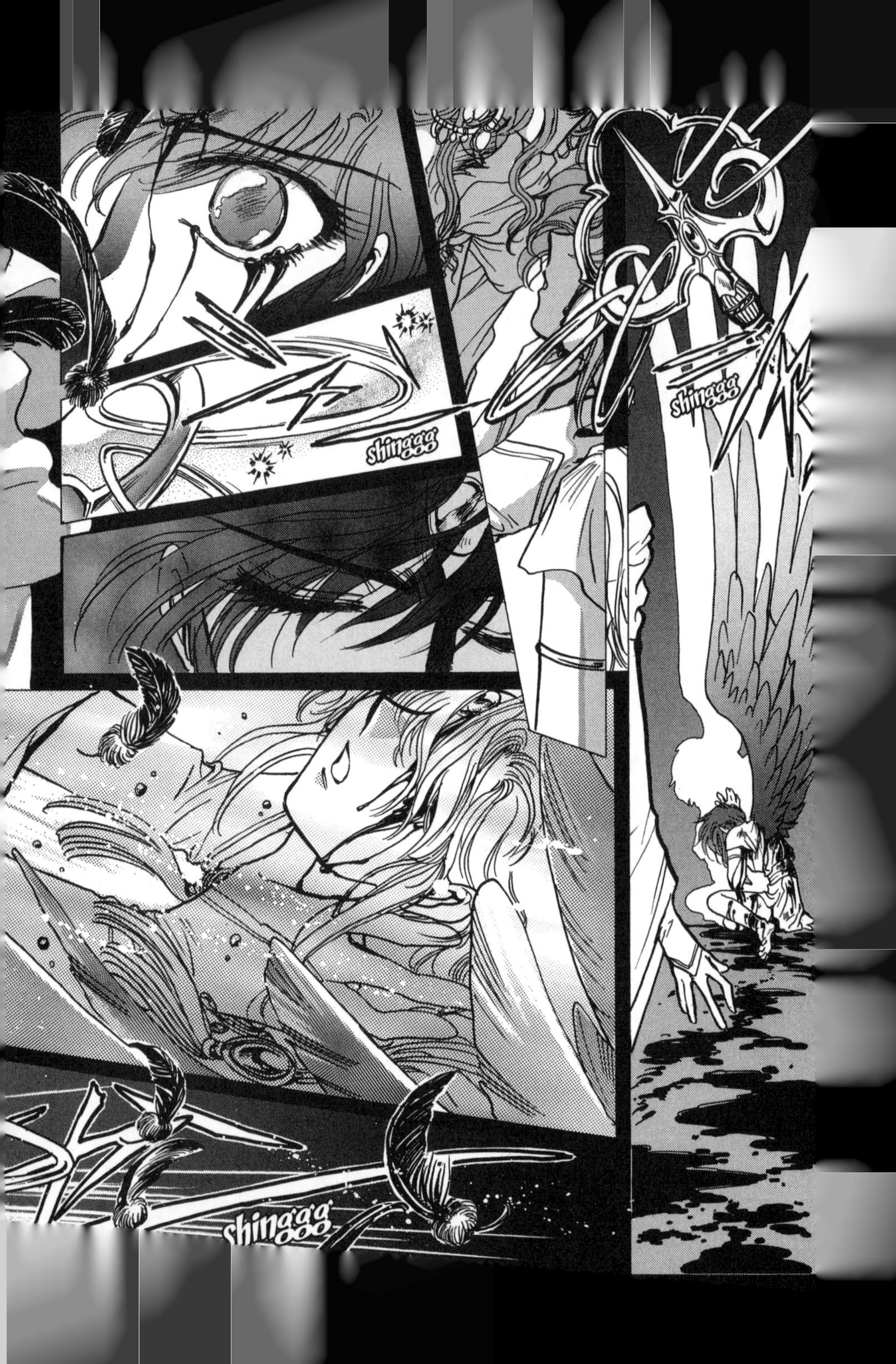
shingggg
shingggg
shingggg

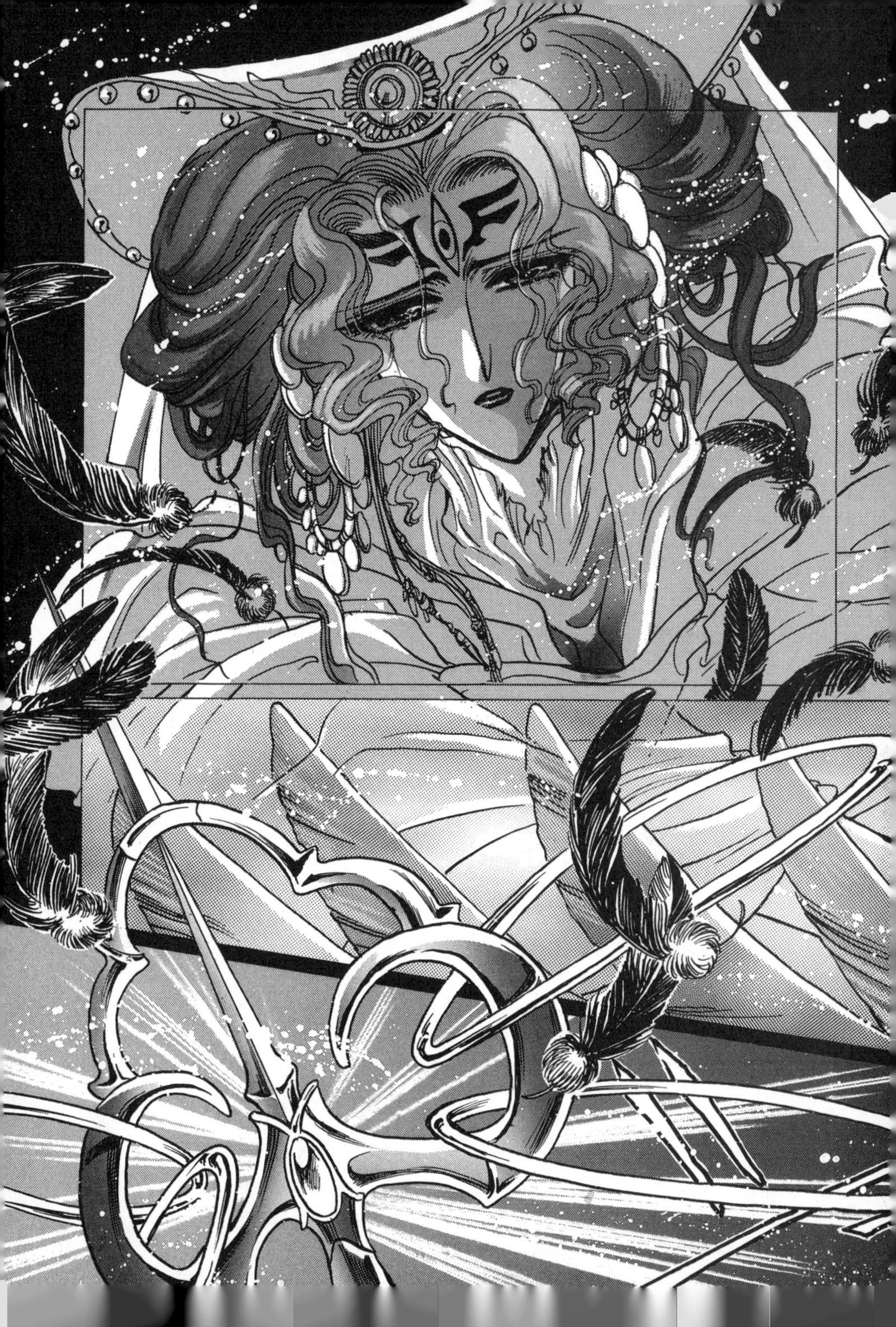

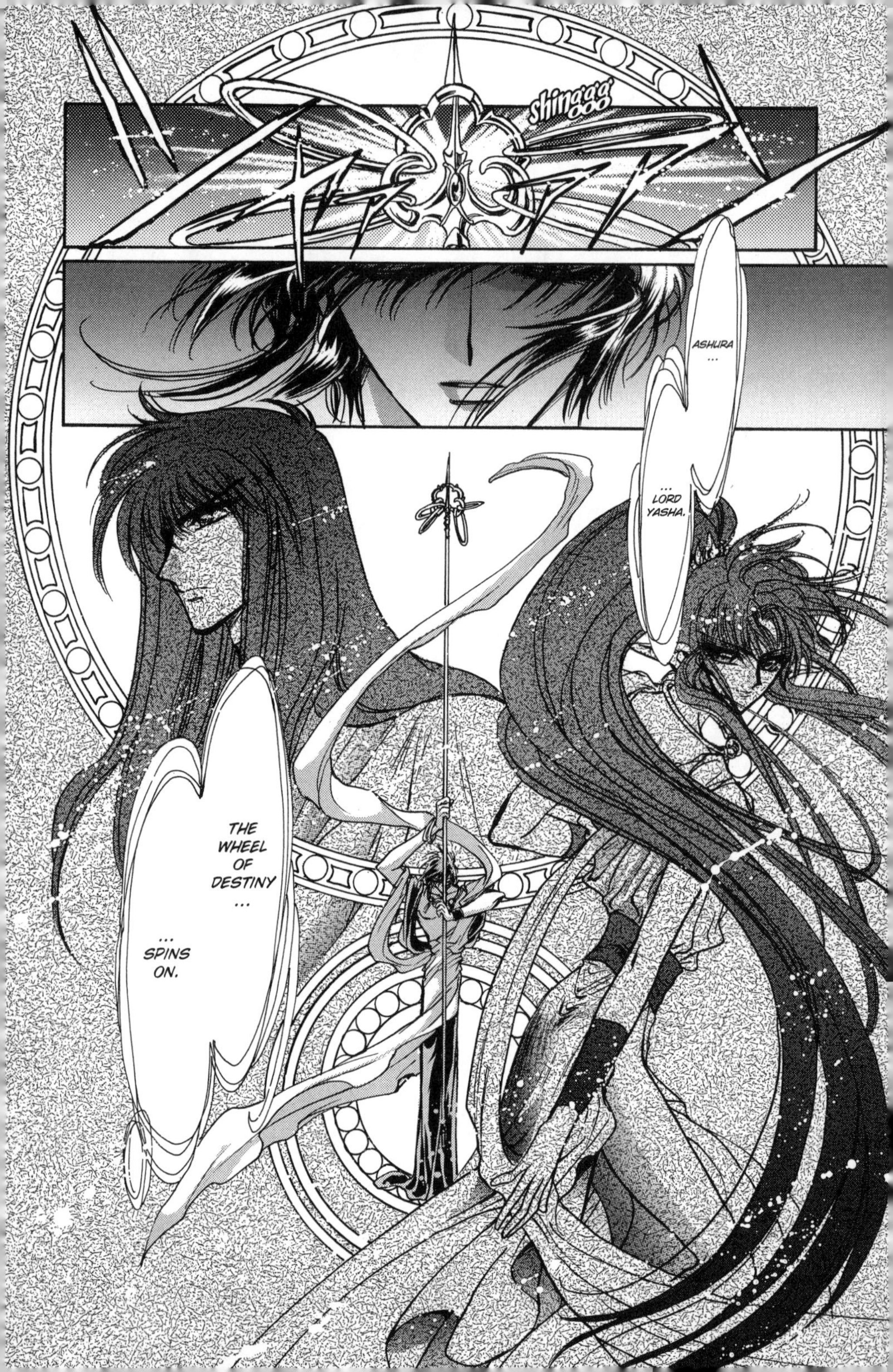
shingggooo
ASHURA ...
... LORD YASHA.
THE WHEEL OF DESTINY ...
... SPINS ON.

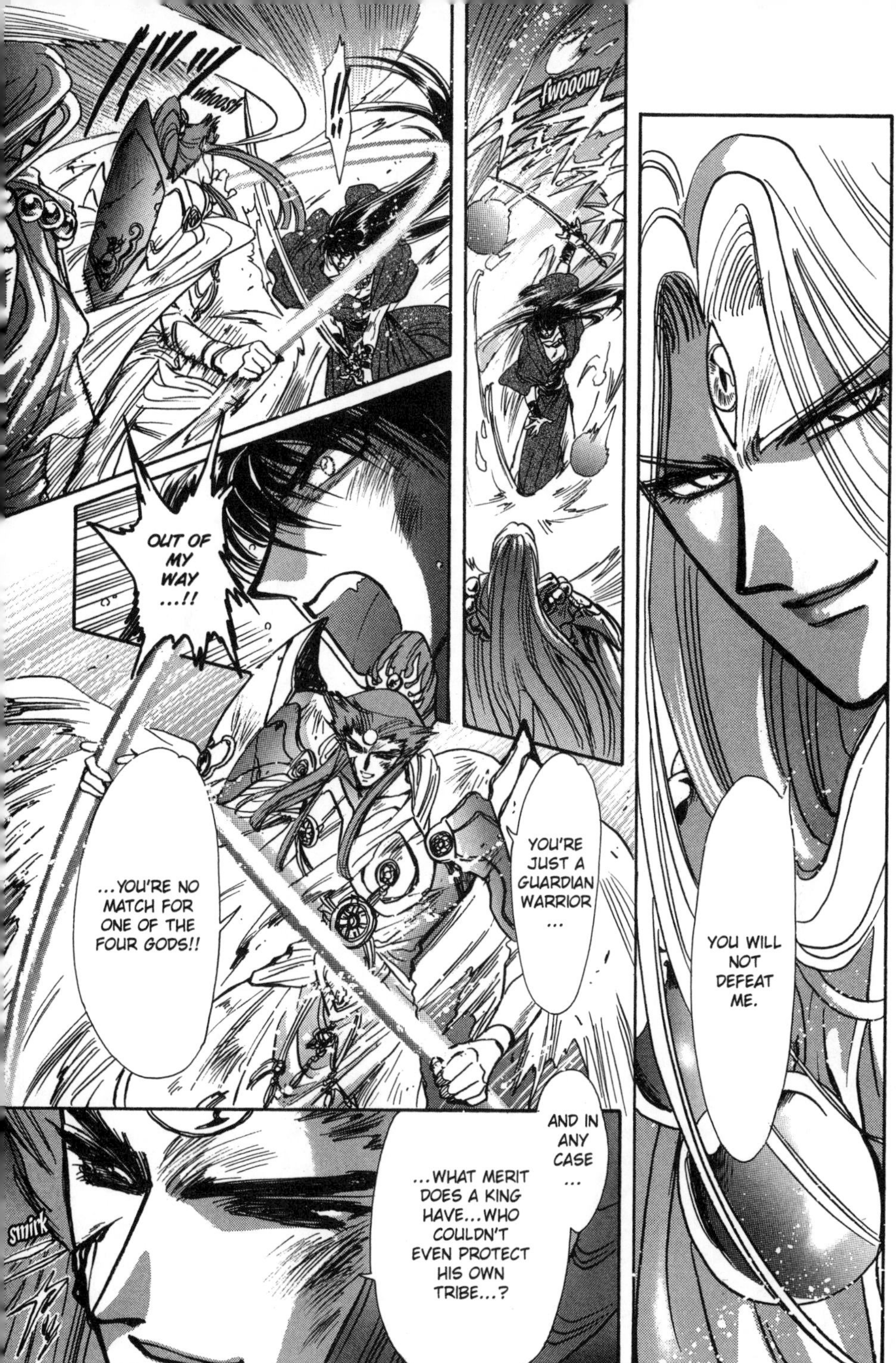
YOU WILL NOT DEFEAT ME.
fwooom
whoosh
OUT OF MY WAY ...!!
YOU'RE JUST A GUARDIAN WARRIOR ...
...YOU'RE NO MATCH FOR ONE OF THE FOUR GODS!!
AND IN ANY CASE ...
...WHAT MERIT DOES A KING HAVE...WHO COULDN'T EVEN PROTECT HIS OWN TRIBE...?
smirk

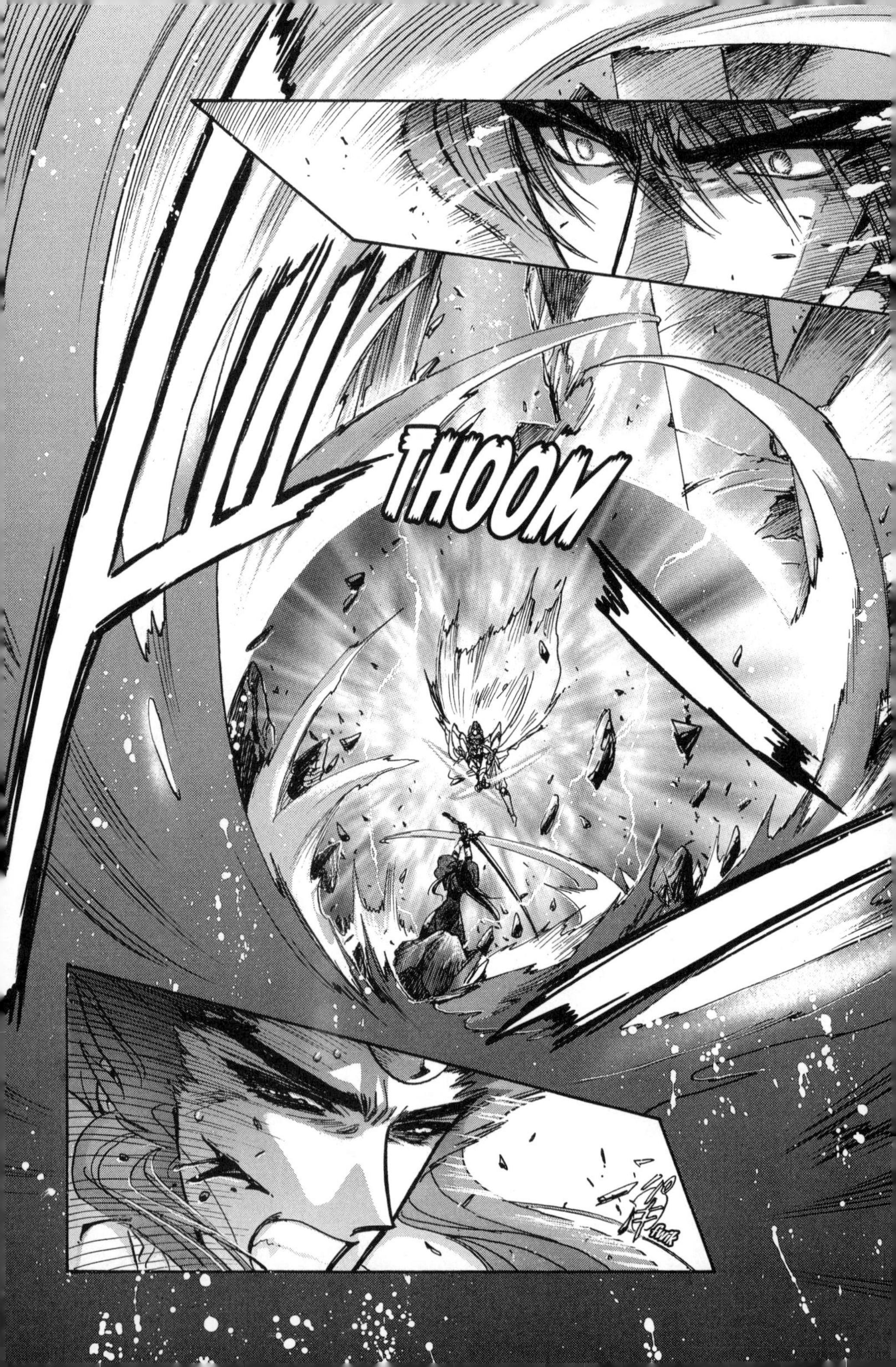
THOOM
fwik

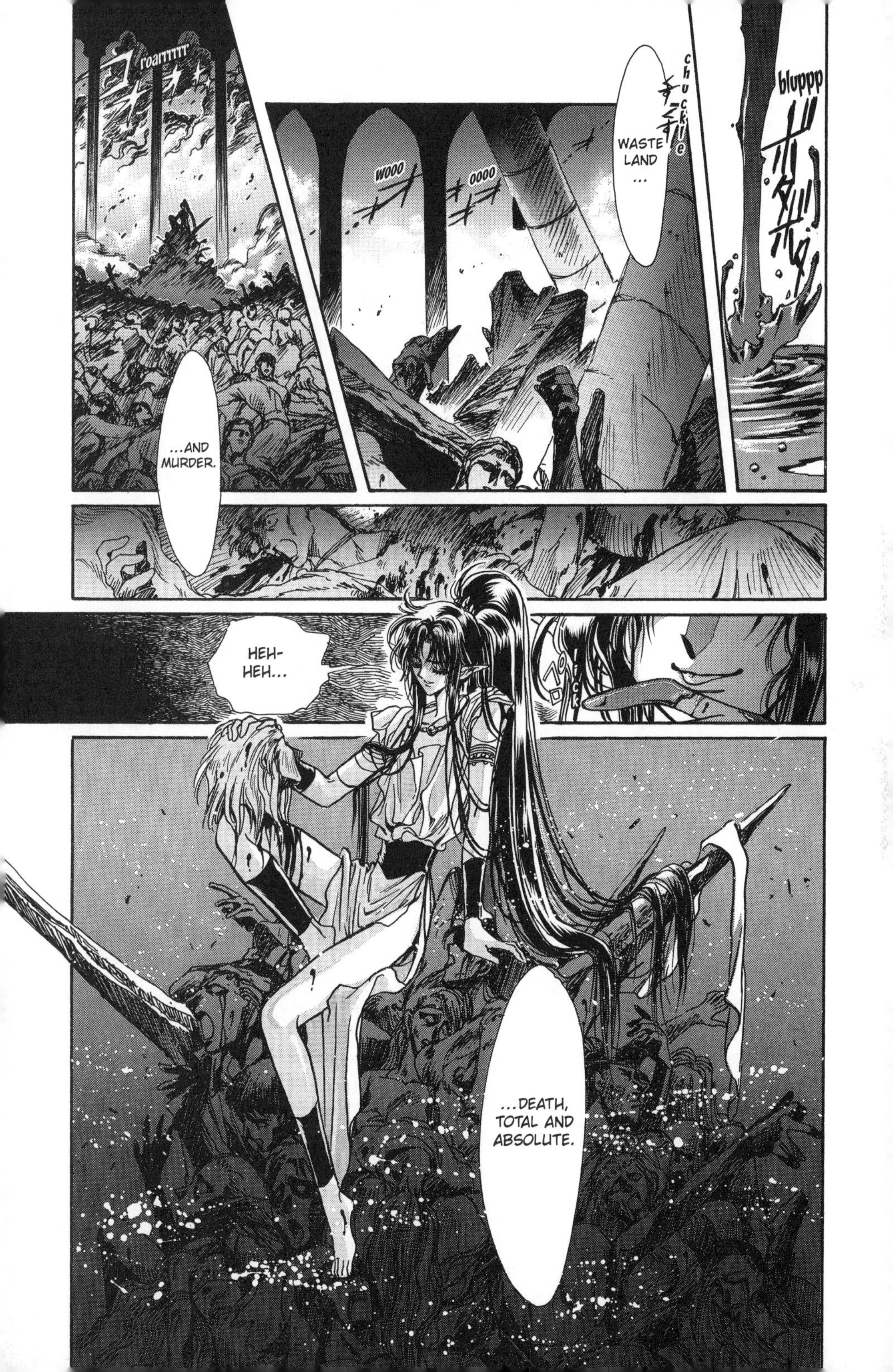
bluppp
chuckle
WASTE LAND ...
oooo
wooo
roarrrrr
...AND MURDER.
lick
HEH-HEH...
...DEATH, TOTAL AND ABSOLUTE.

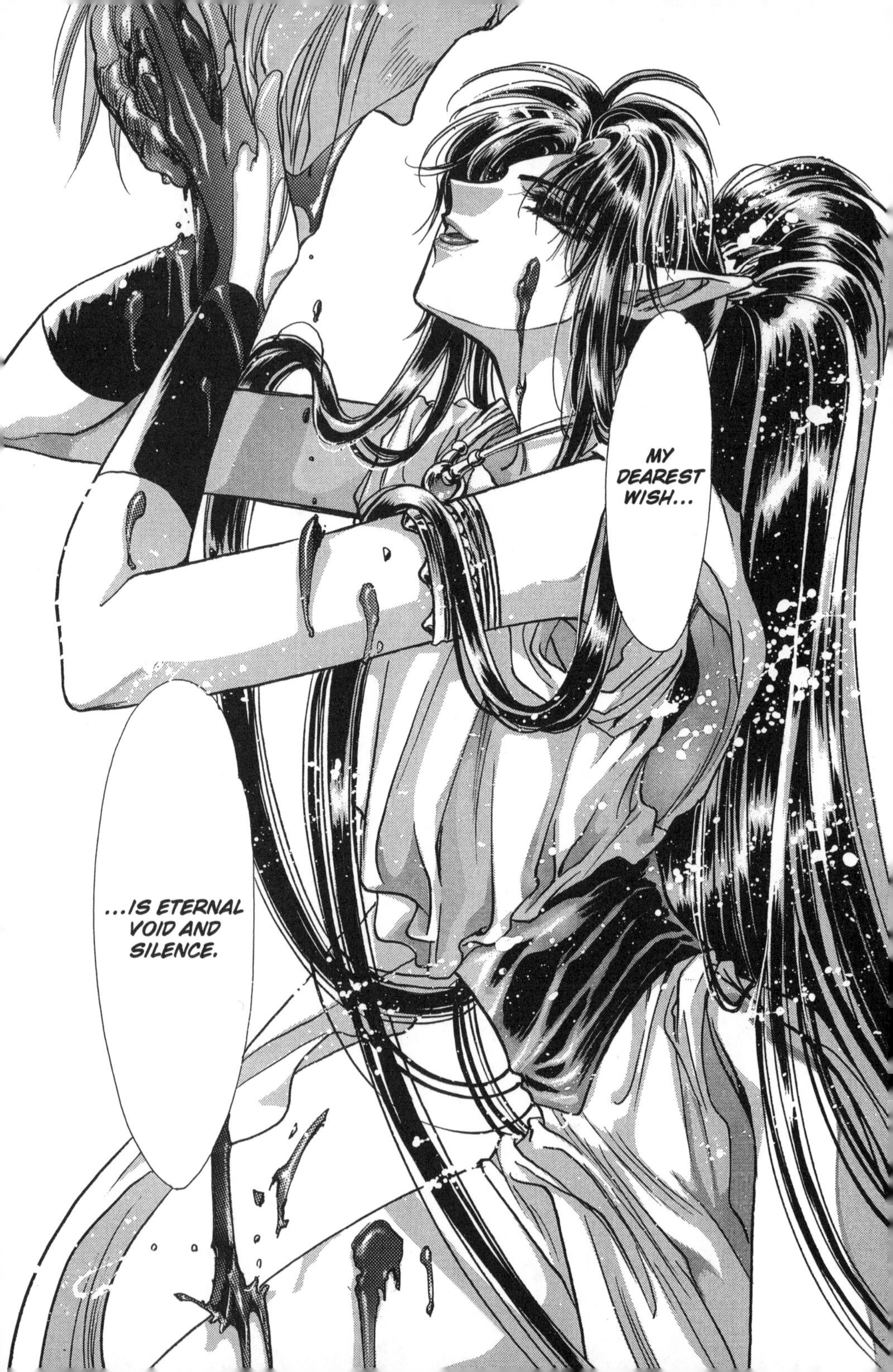
MY DEAREST WISH...
...IS ETERNAL VOID AND SILENCE.

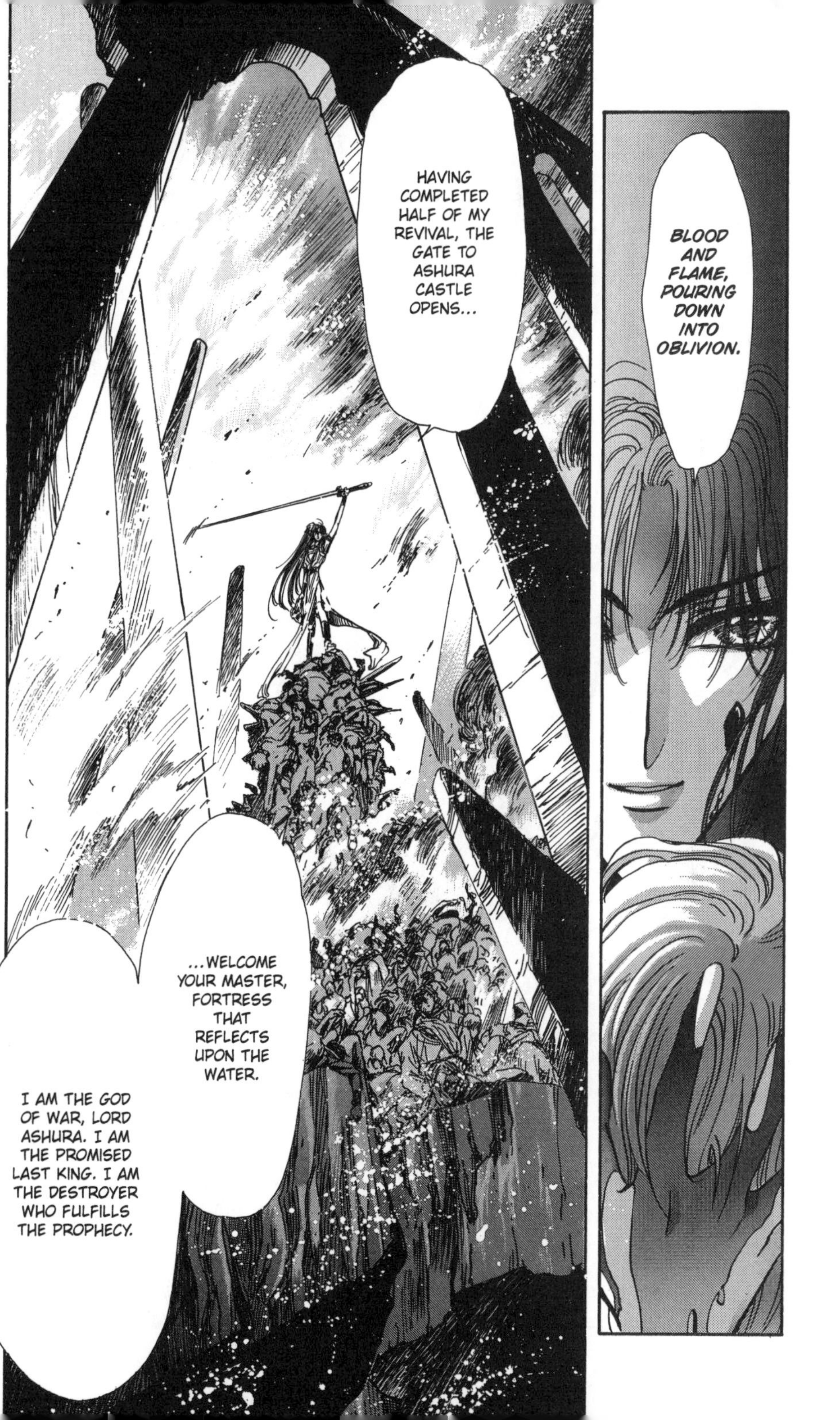
BLOOD AND FLAME, POURING DOWN INTO OBLIVION.
HAVING COMPLETED HALF OF MY REVIVAL, THE GATE TO ASHURA CASTLE OPENS...
...WELCOME YOUR MASTER, FORTRESS THAT REFLECTS UPON THE WATER.
I AM THE GOD OF WAR, LORD ASHURA. I AM THE PROMISED LAST KING. I AM THE DESTROYER WHO FULFILLS THE PROPHECY.

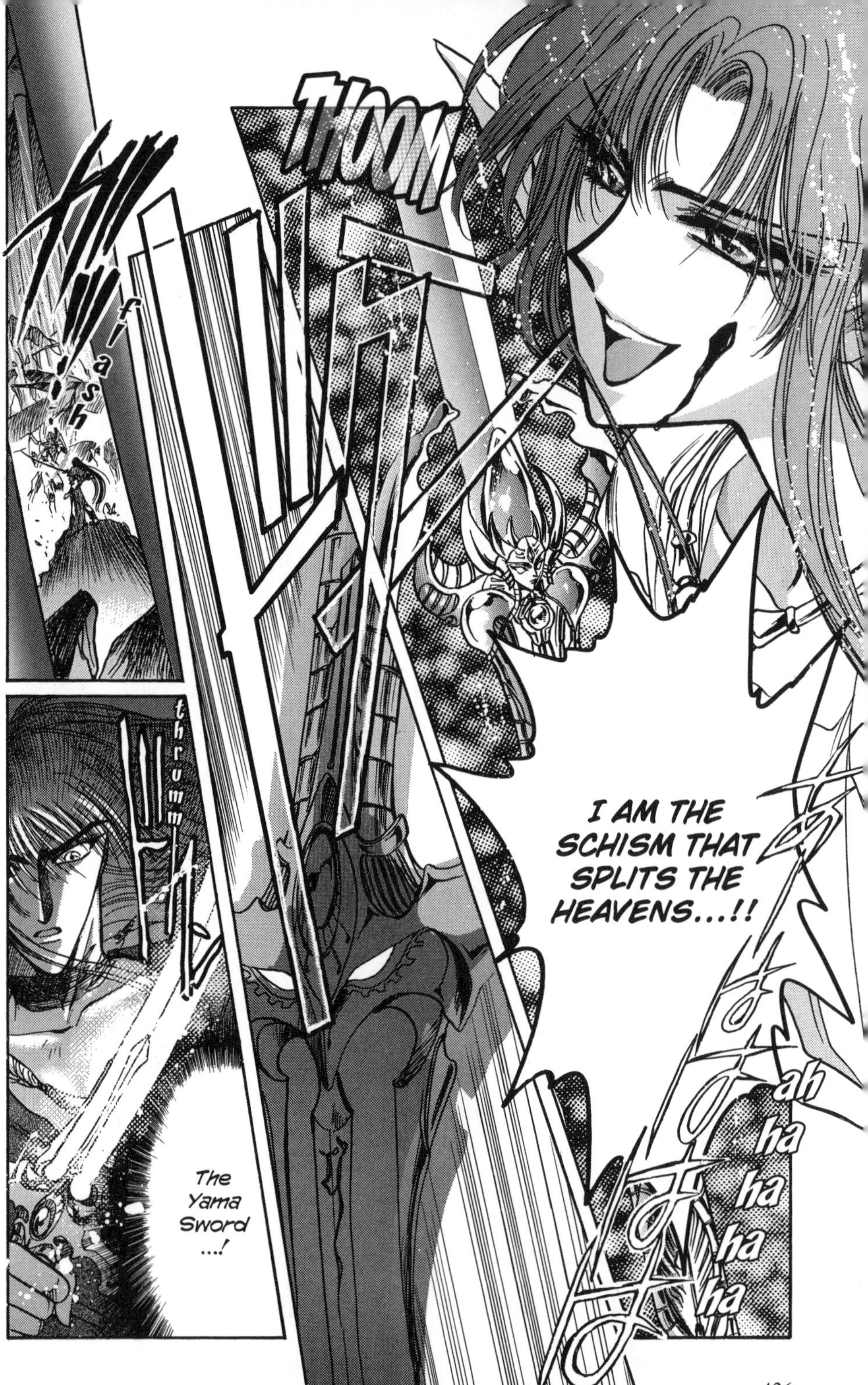
THOOM
I AM THE SCHISM THAT SPLITS THE HEAVENS...!!
ah ha ha ha ha
flash
thrumm
The Yama Sword ...!

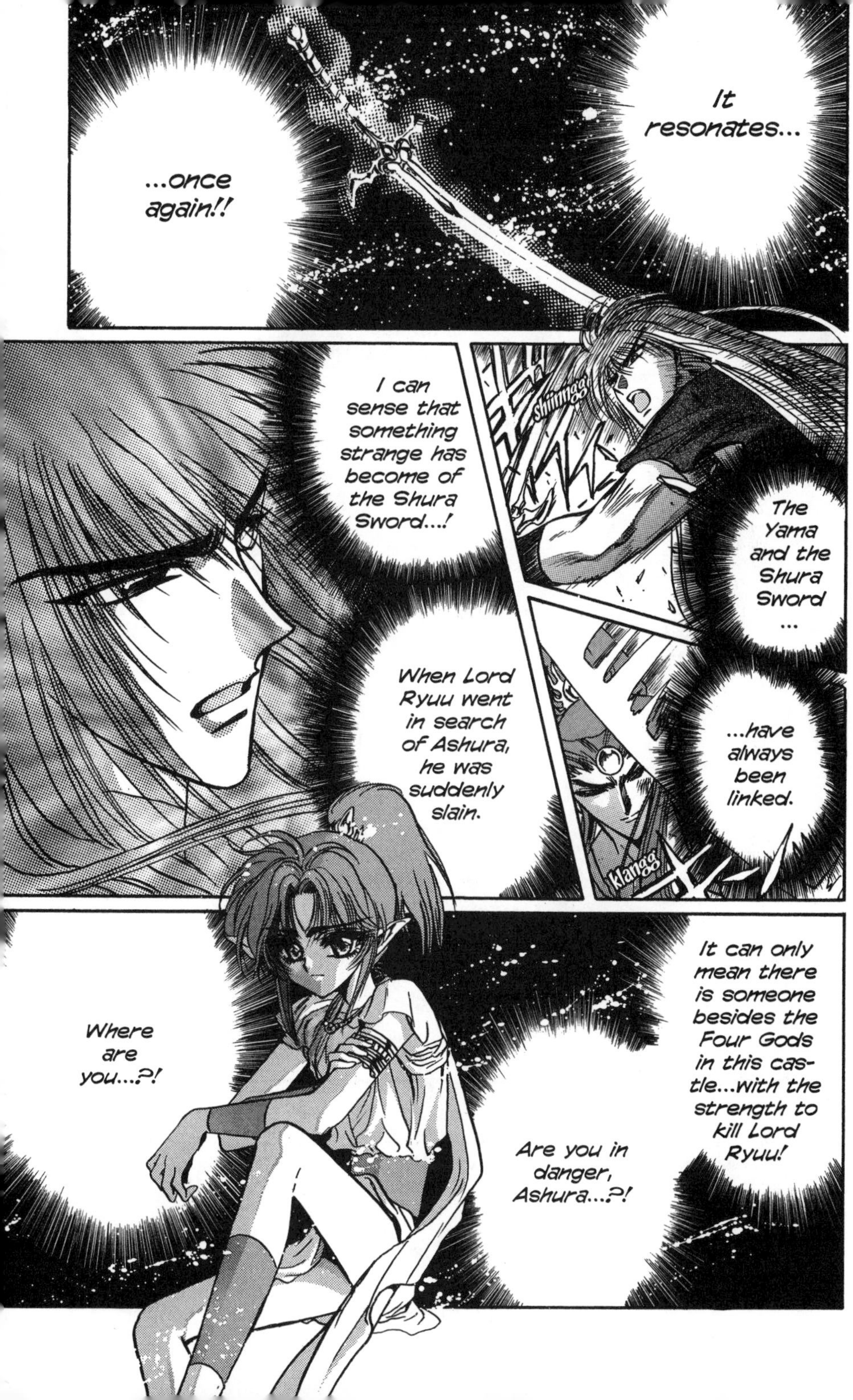
It resonates...
...once again!!
shiinngg
The Yama and the Shura Sword...
...have always been linked.
klangg
I can sense that something strange has become of the Shura Sword...!
When Lord Ryuu went in search of Ashura, he was suddenly slain.
It can only mean there is someone besides the Four Gods in this castle...with the strength to kill Lord Ryuu!
Are you in danger, Ashura...?!
Where are you...?!

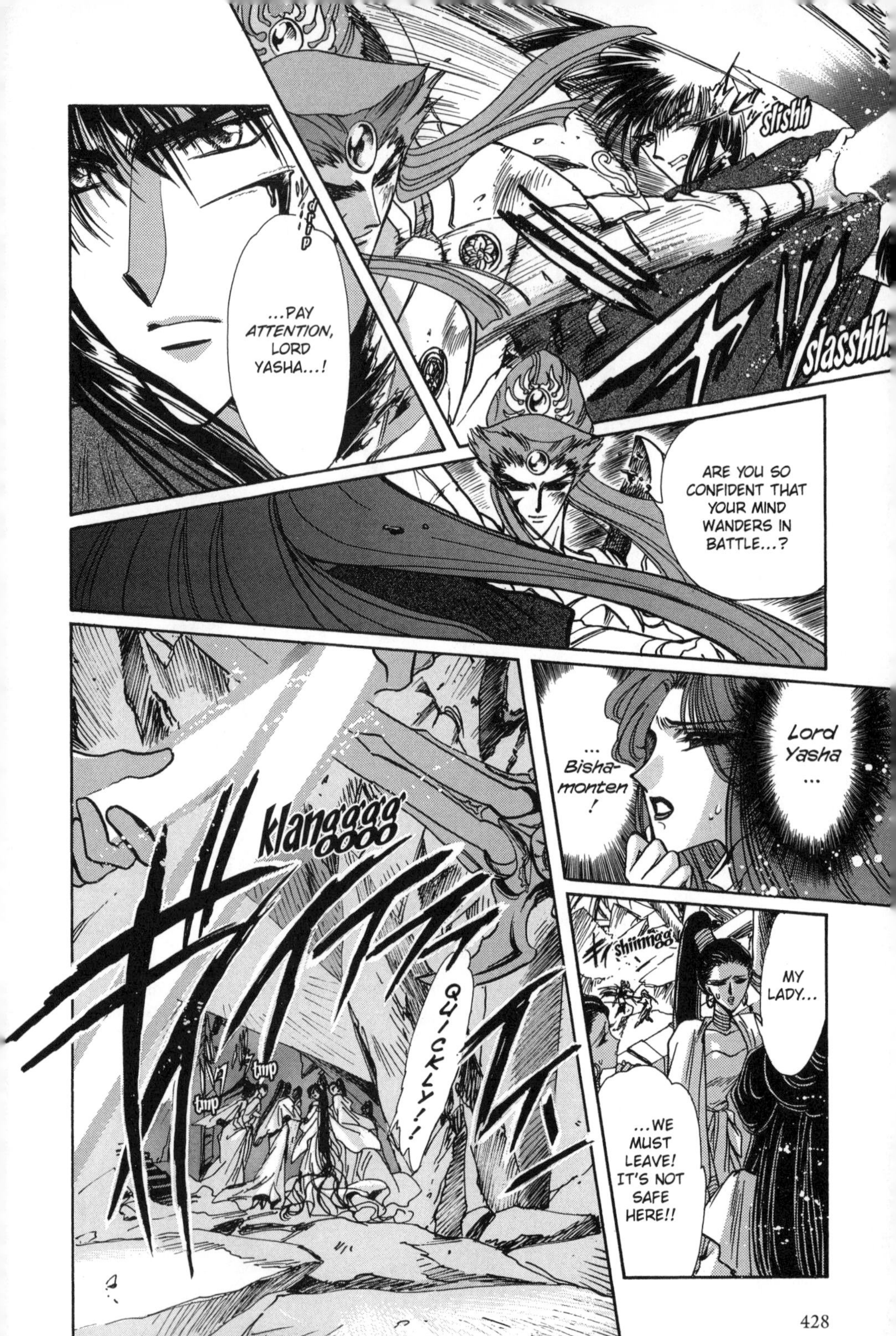

slishh
slasshh
drip
...PAY ATTENTION, LORD YASHA...!
ARE YOU SO CONFIDENT THAT YOUR MIND WANDERS IN BATTLE...?
Lord Yasha ...
... Bisha-monten!
shiinngg
MY LADY...
...WE MUST LEAVE! IT'S NOT SAFE HERE!!
klanggggoooo
QUICKLY!!
tmp
tmp

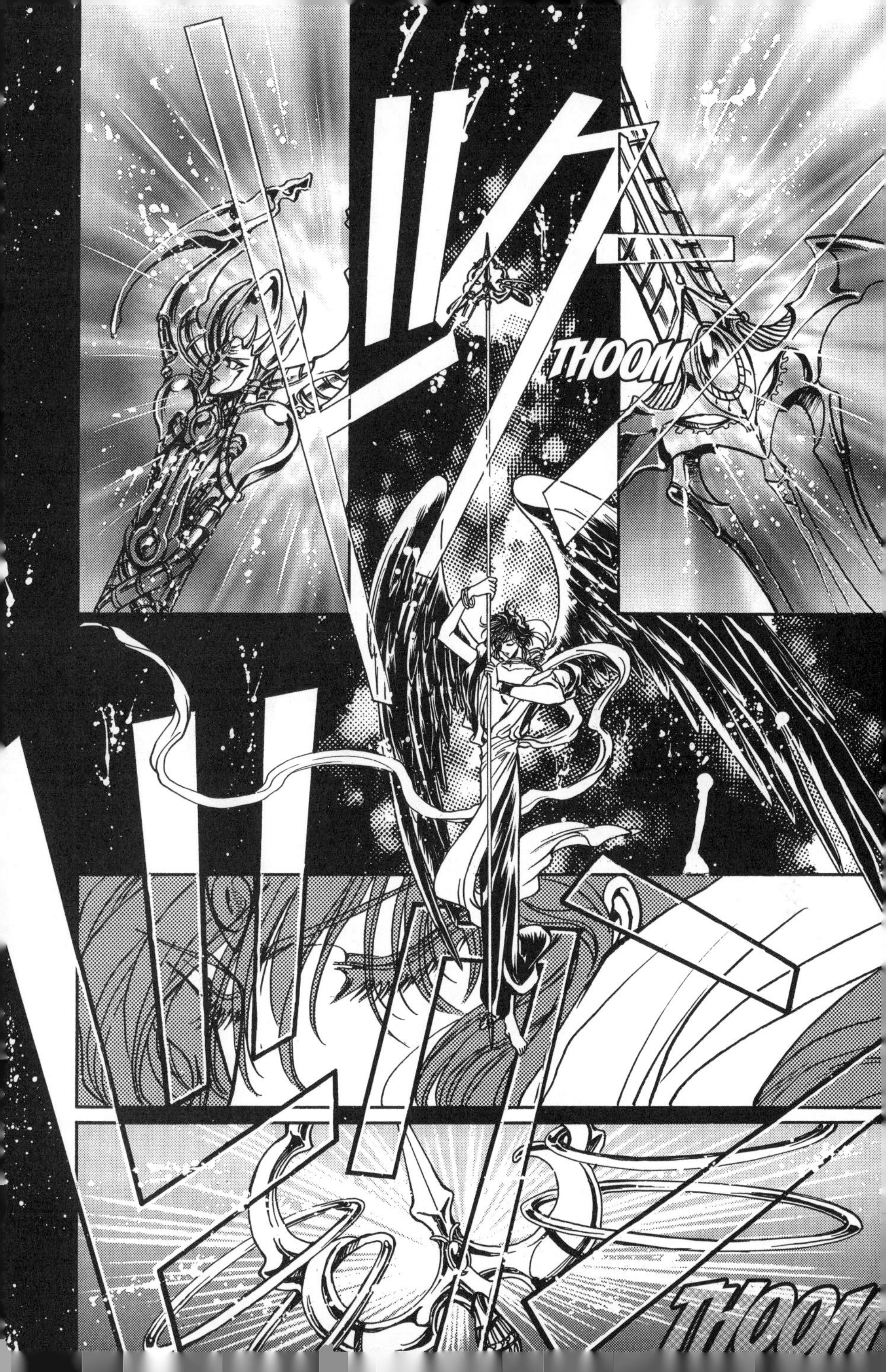
THOOM
THOOM

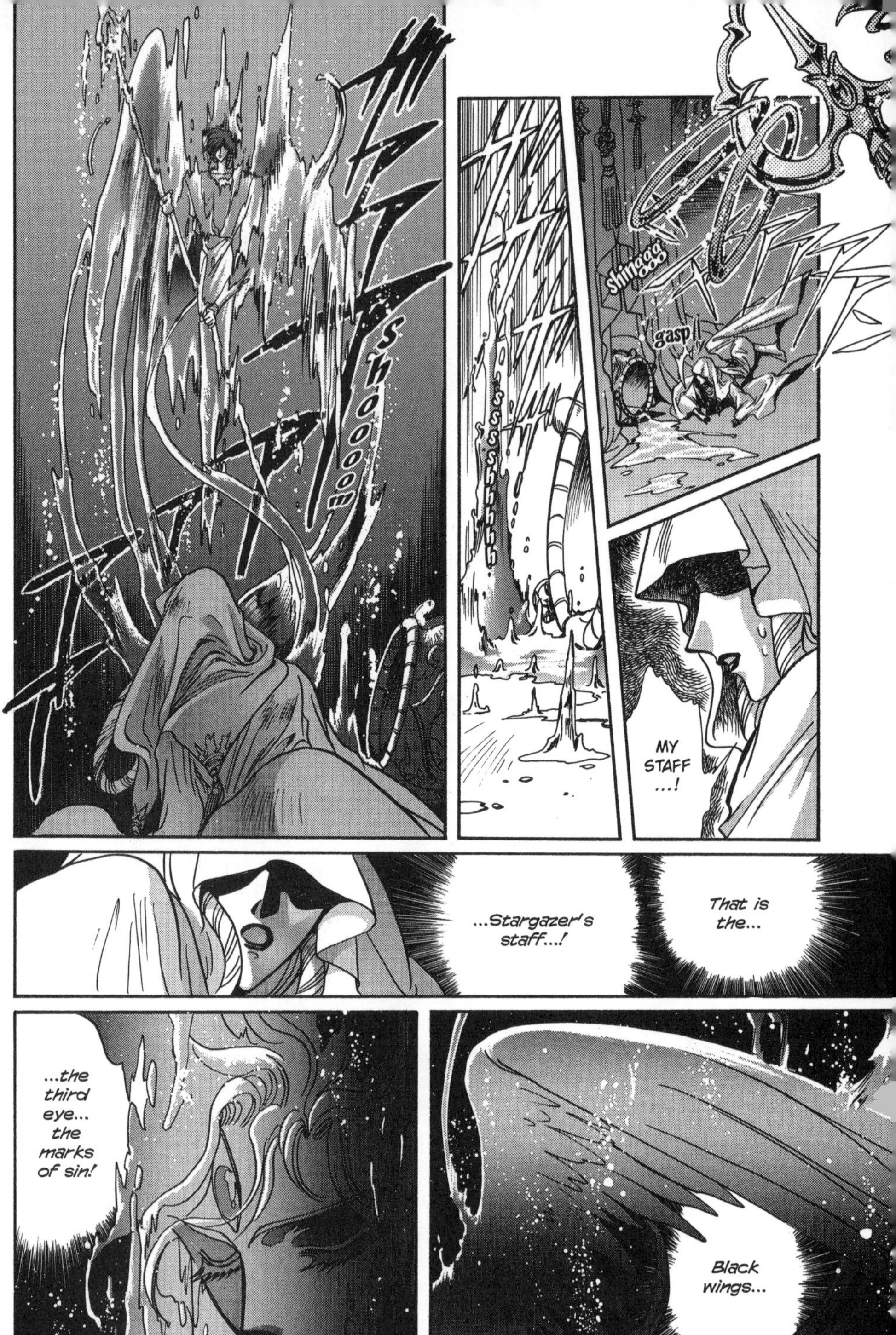
shinggg ooo
gasp
MY STAFF ...!
ssssshhhhh
shoooooom
That is the...
...Stargazer's staff...!
Black wings...
...the third eye... the marks of sin!

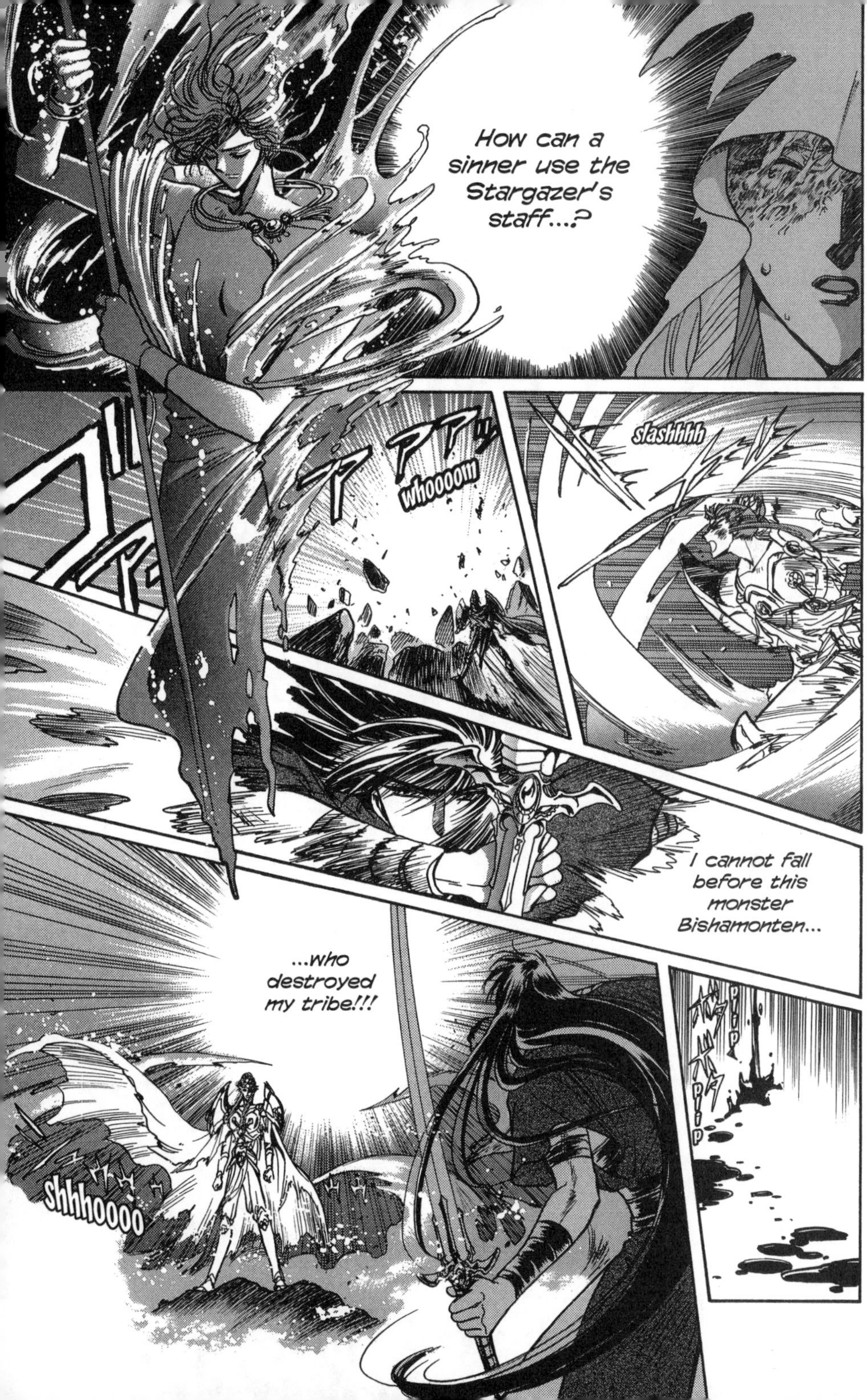
How can a sinner use the Stargazer's staff...?
slashhhh
whoooom
I cannot fall before this monster Bishamonten...
plip
plip
...who destroyed my tribe!!!
Shhhoooo

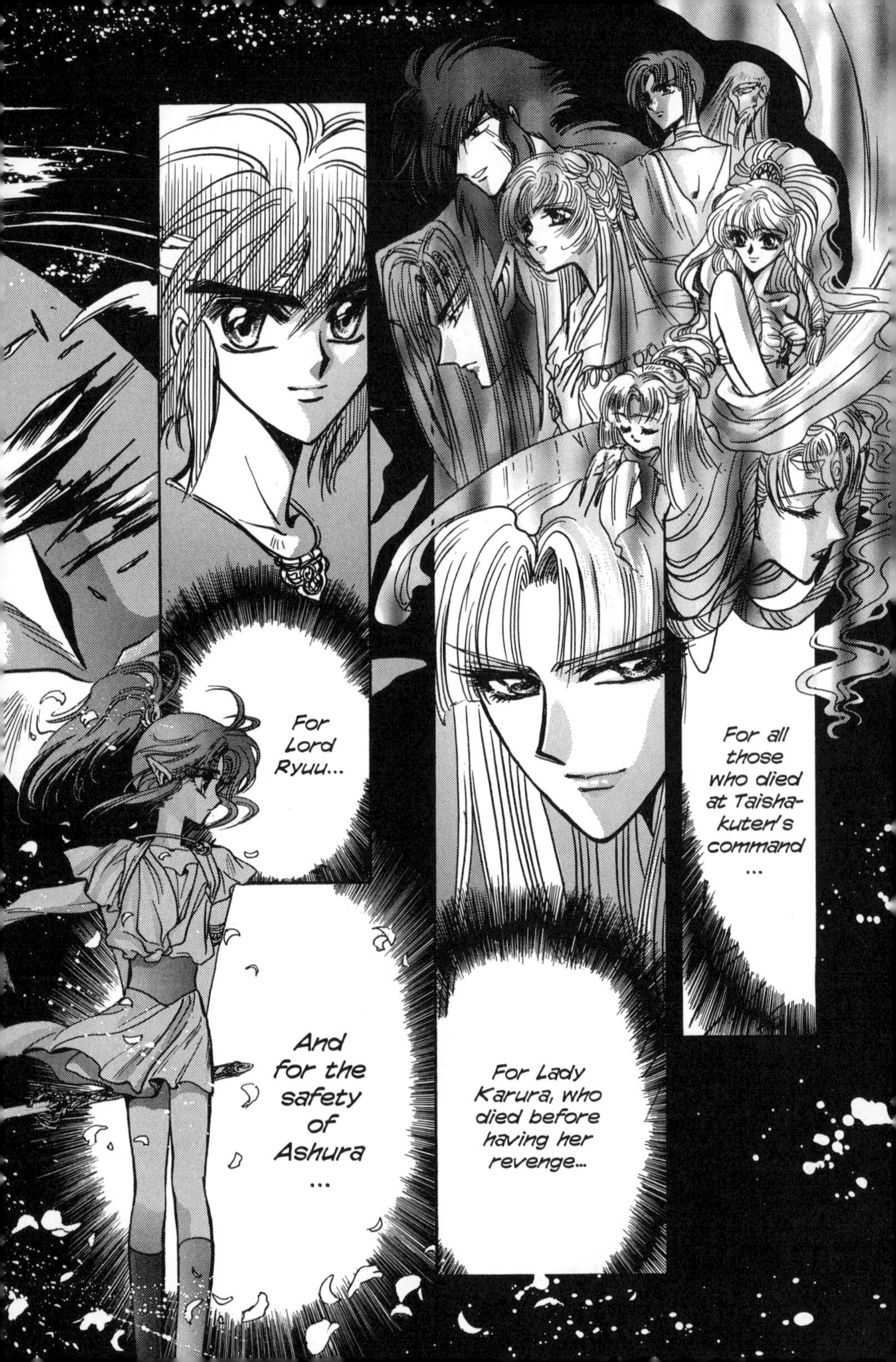
For all those who died at Taisha-kuten's command ...
For Lord Ryuu...
For Lady Karura, who died before having her revenge...
And for the safety of Ashura ...

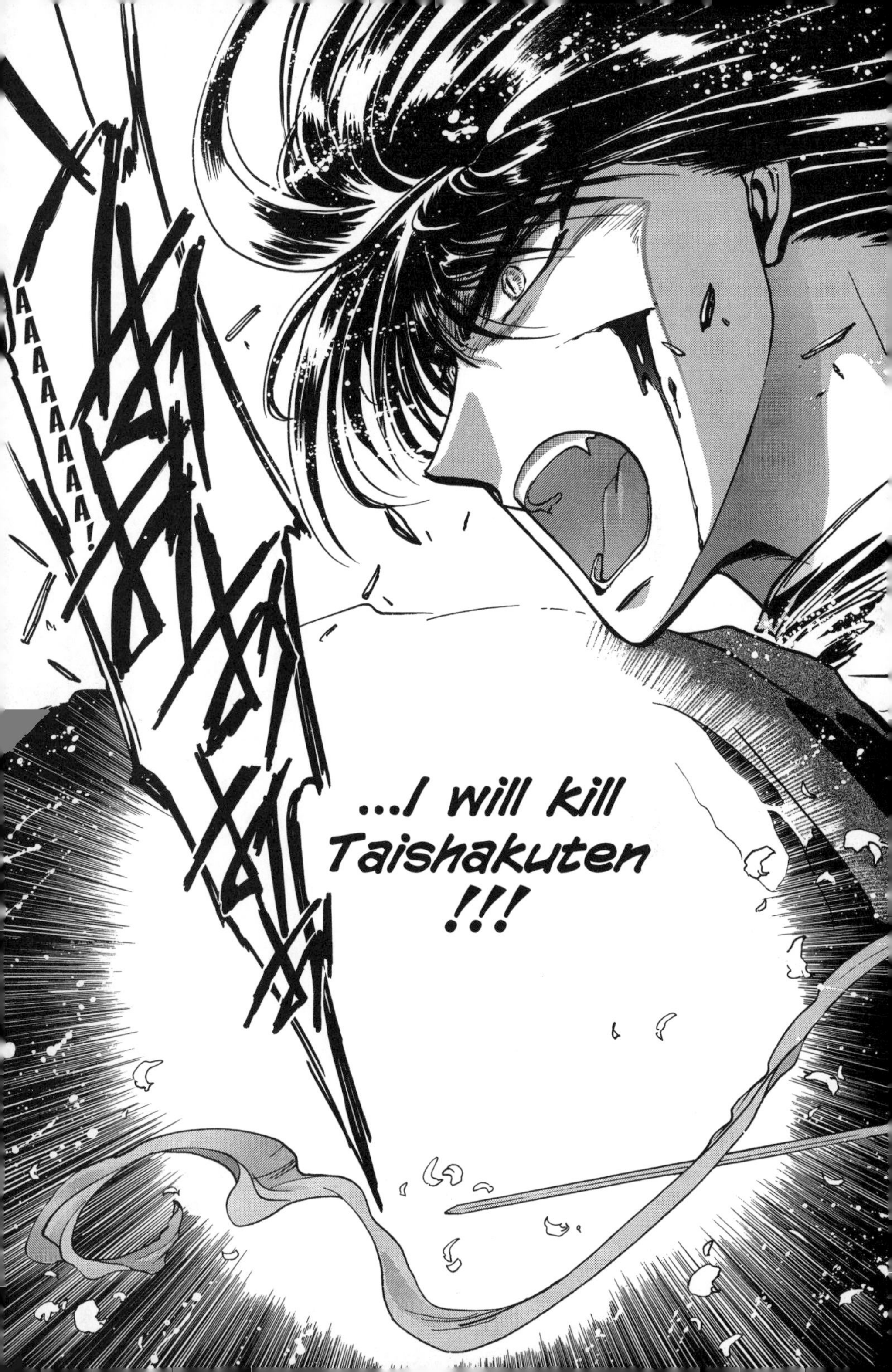

...I will kill Taishakuten !!!
AAAAAAAAAA!

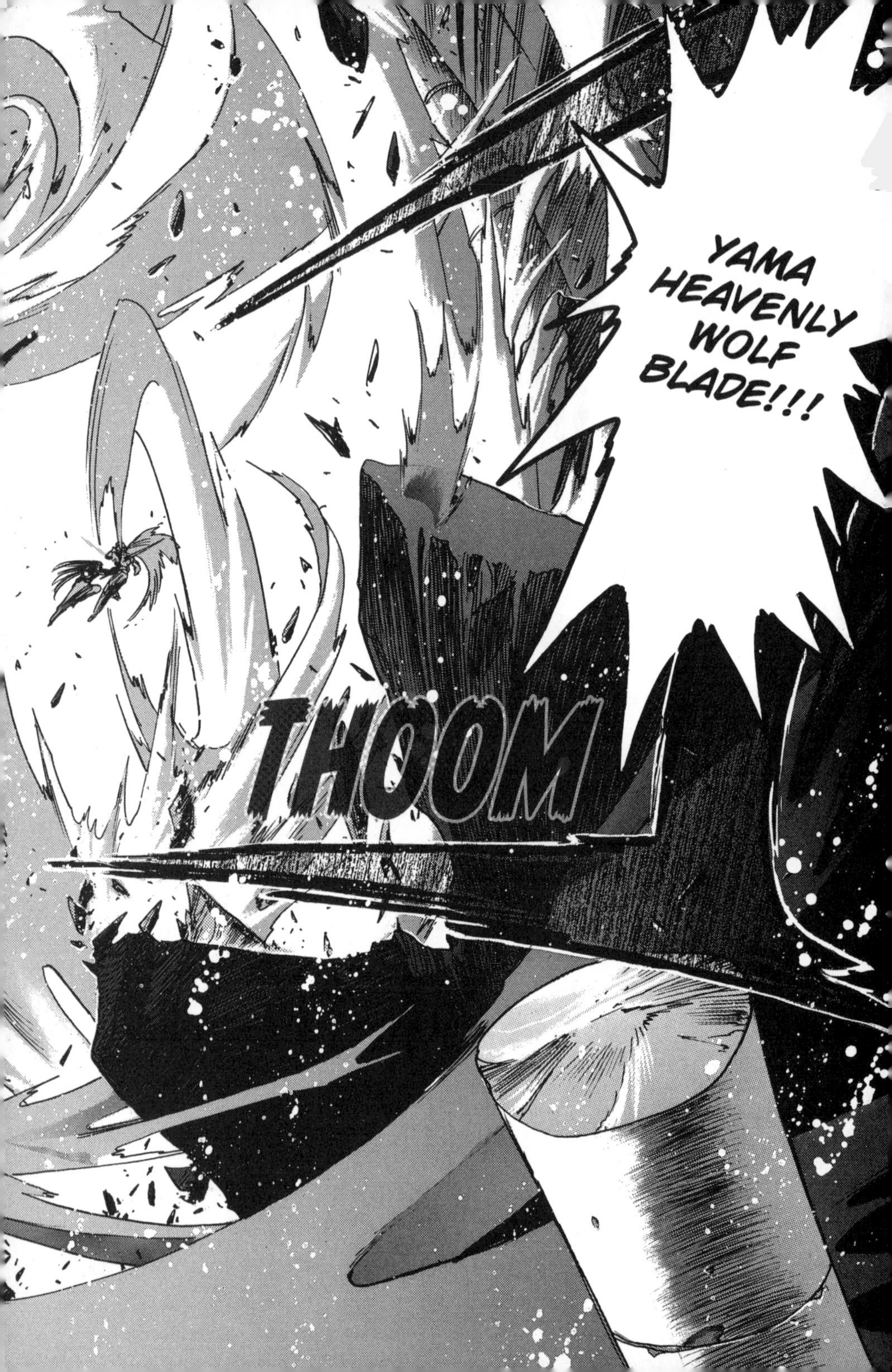
YAMA HEAVENLY WOLF BLADE!!!
THOOM

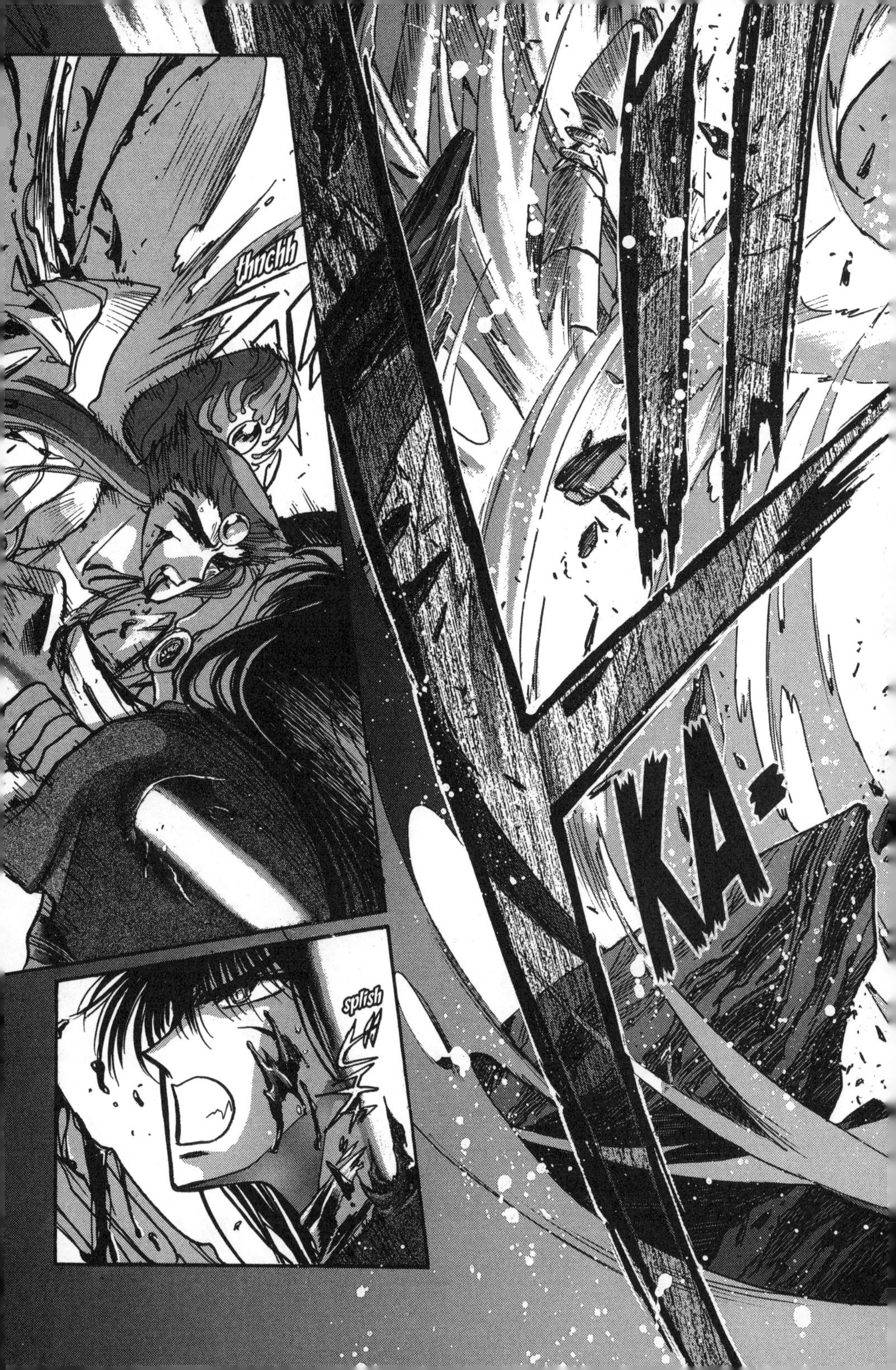
KA-
thnchh
splish

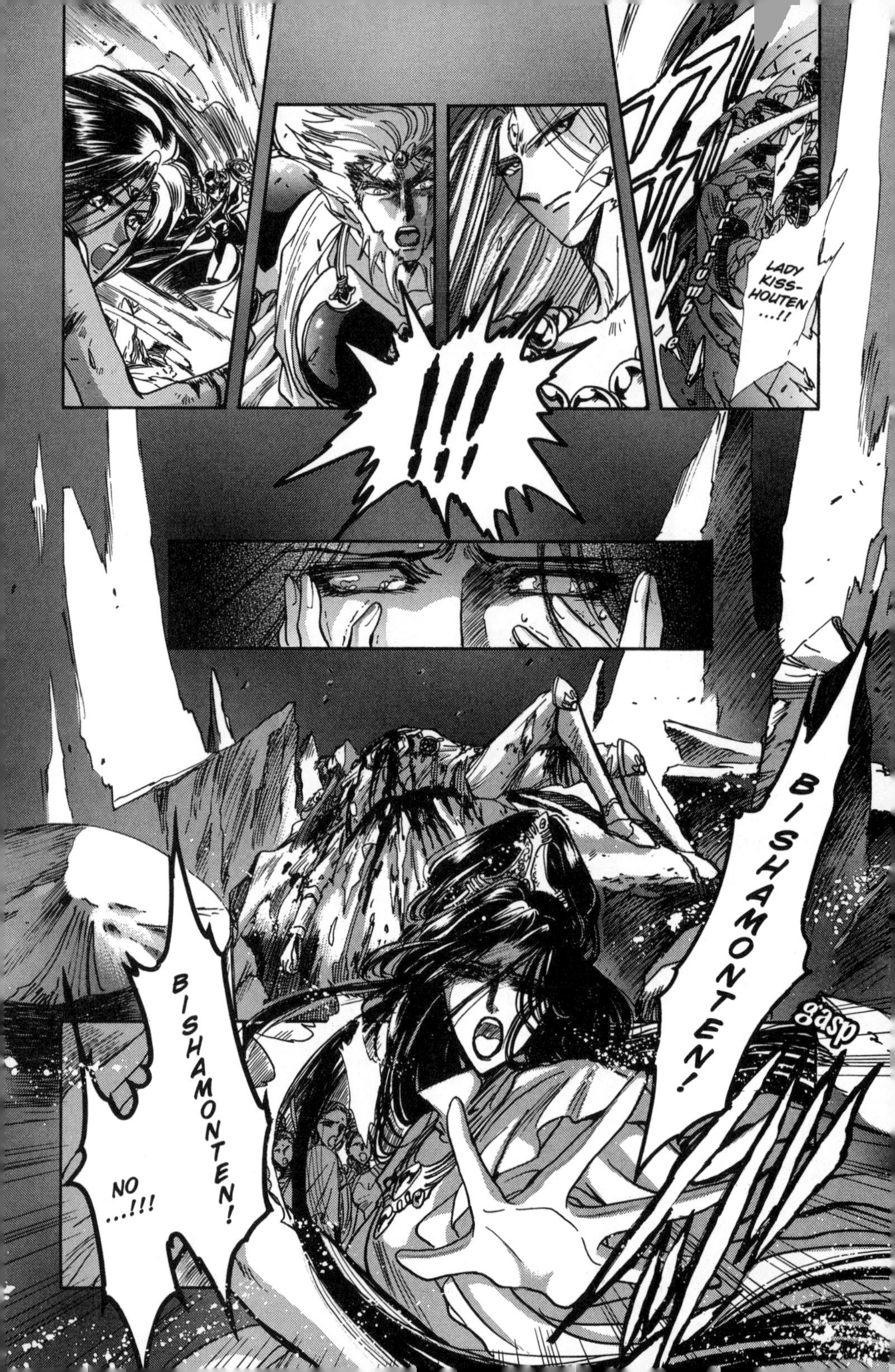
rrrrumble
LADY KISS-HOUTEN ...!!
!!!
gasp
BISHAMONTEN!
BISHAMONTEN!
NO ...!!!

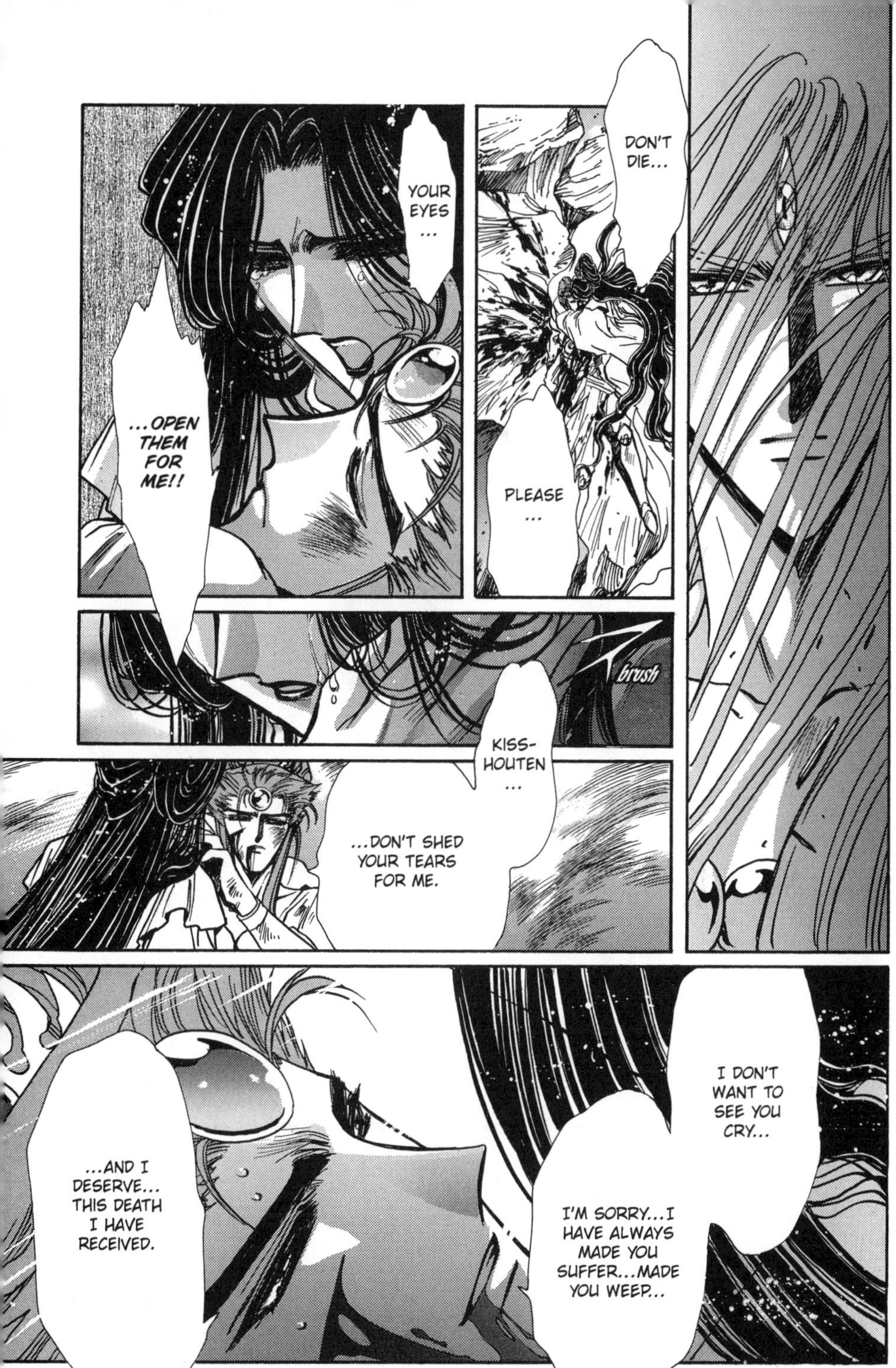
DON'T DIE...
PLEASE...
YOUR EYES...
...OPEN THEM FOR ME!!
brush
KISS-HOUTEN...
...DON'T SHED YOUR TEARS FOR ME.
I DON'T WANT TO SEE YOU CRY...
I'M SORRY...I HAVE ALWAYS MADE YOU SUFFER...MADE YOU WEEP...
...AND I DESERVE... THIS DEATH I HAVE RECEIVED.

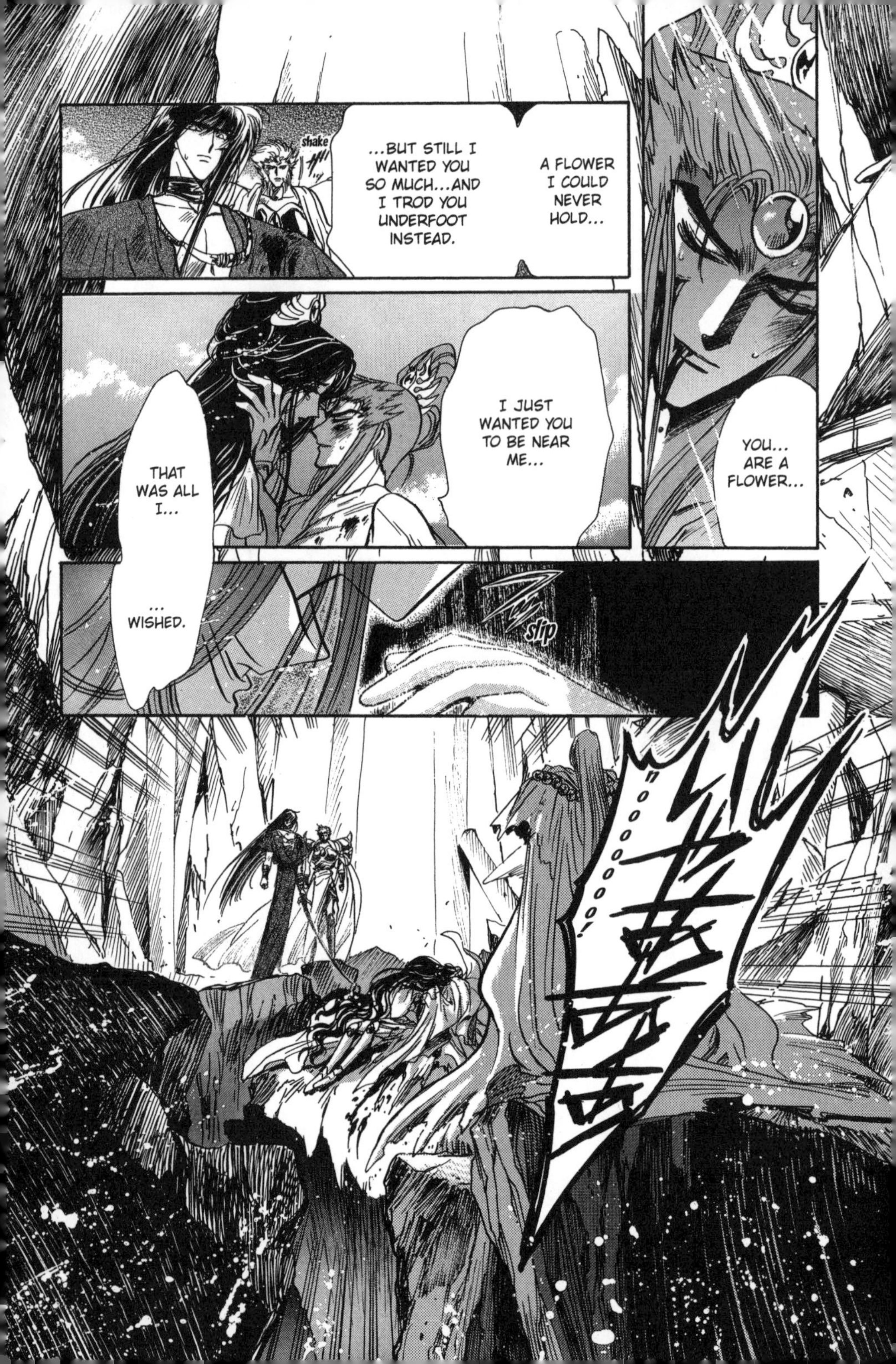
YOU... ARE A FLOWER...
A FLOWER I COULD NEVER HOLD...
...BUT STILL I WANTED YOU SO MUCH...AND I TROD YOU UNDERFOOT INSTEAD.
shake
I JUST WANTED YOU TO BE NEAR ME...
THAT WAS ALL I...
slip
... WISHED.
nooooooo!

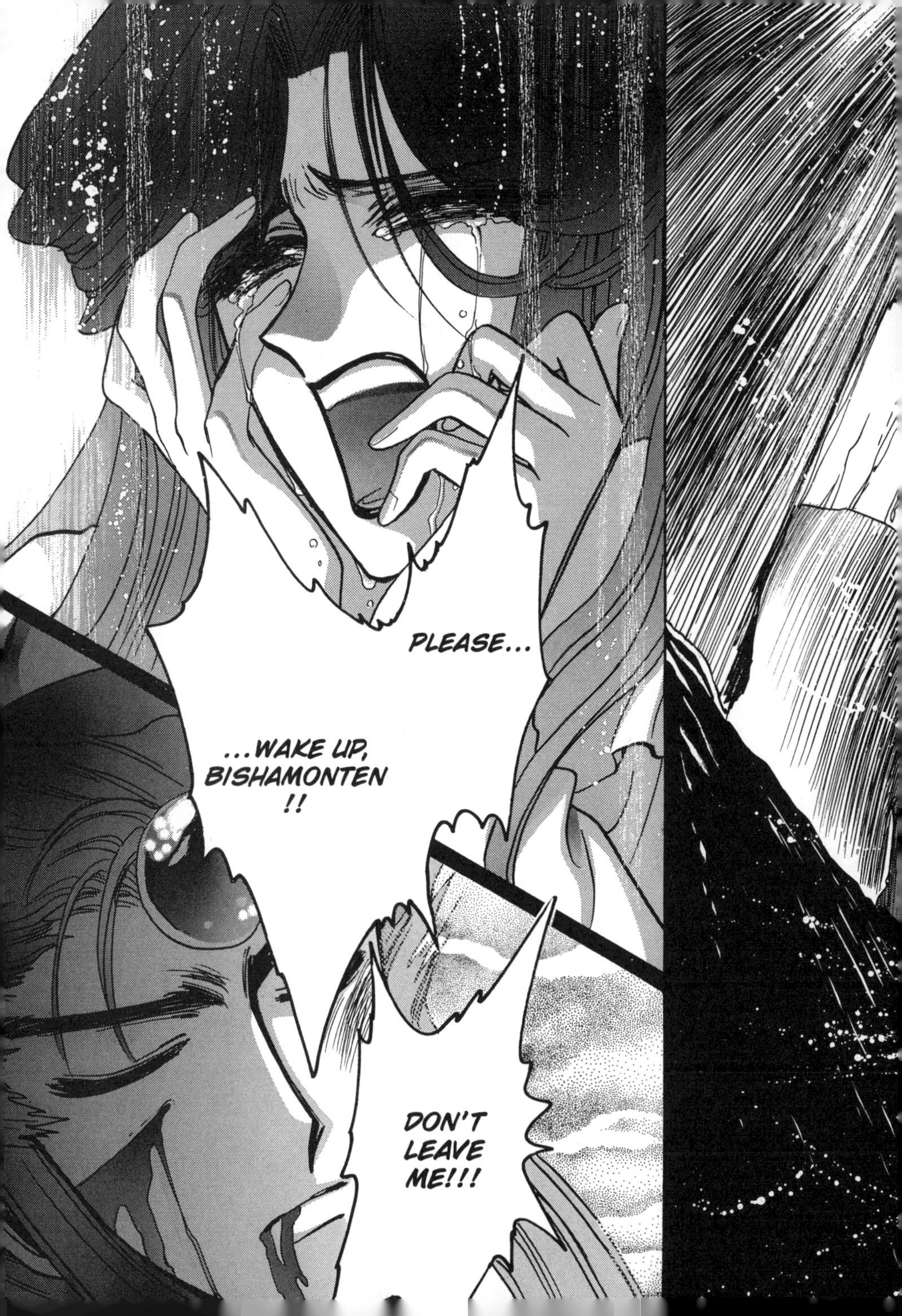
PLEASE...
...WAKE UP, BISHAMONTEN !!
DON'T LEAVE ME!!!

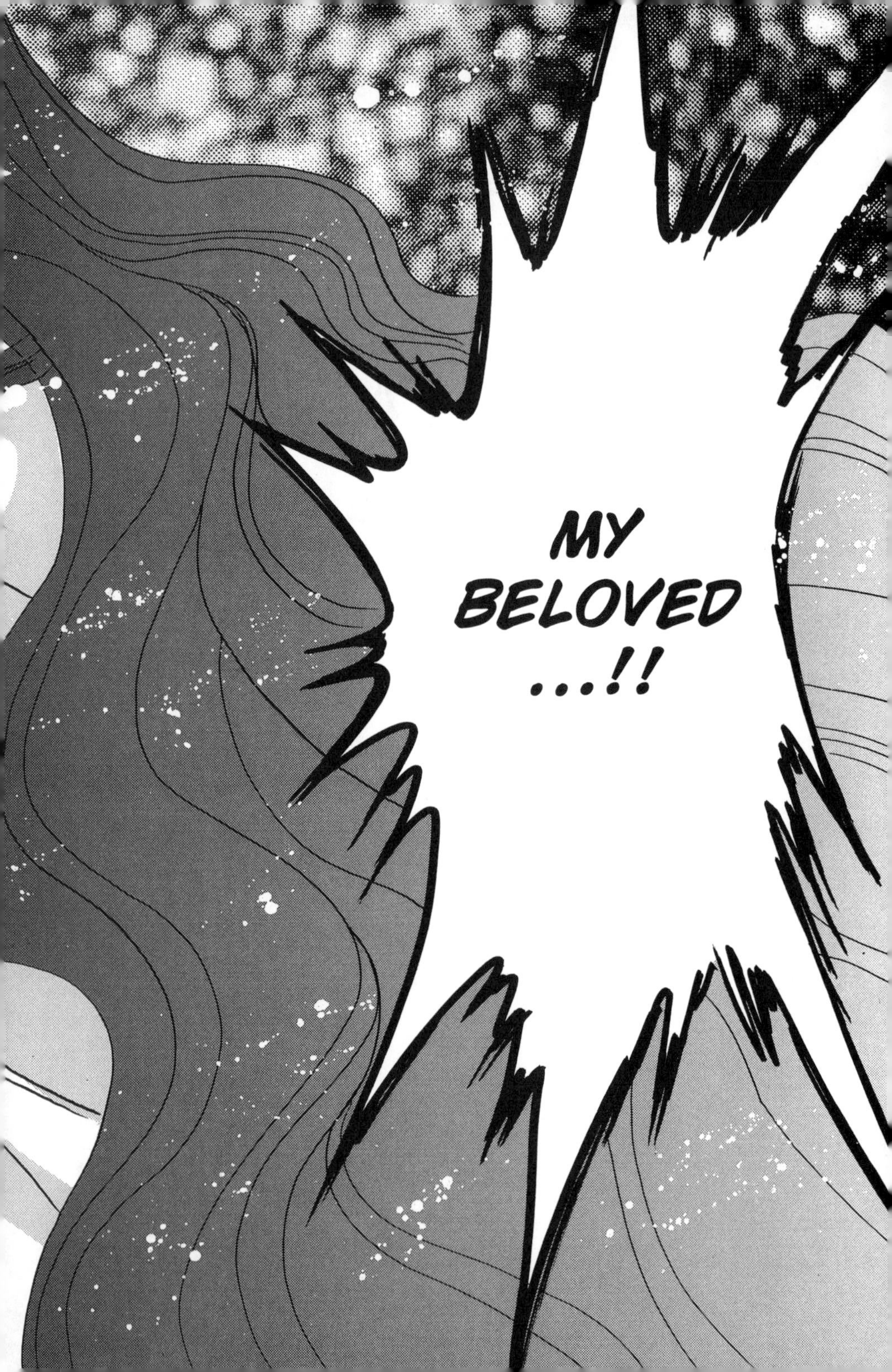
MY BELOVED ...!!

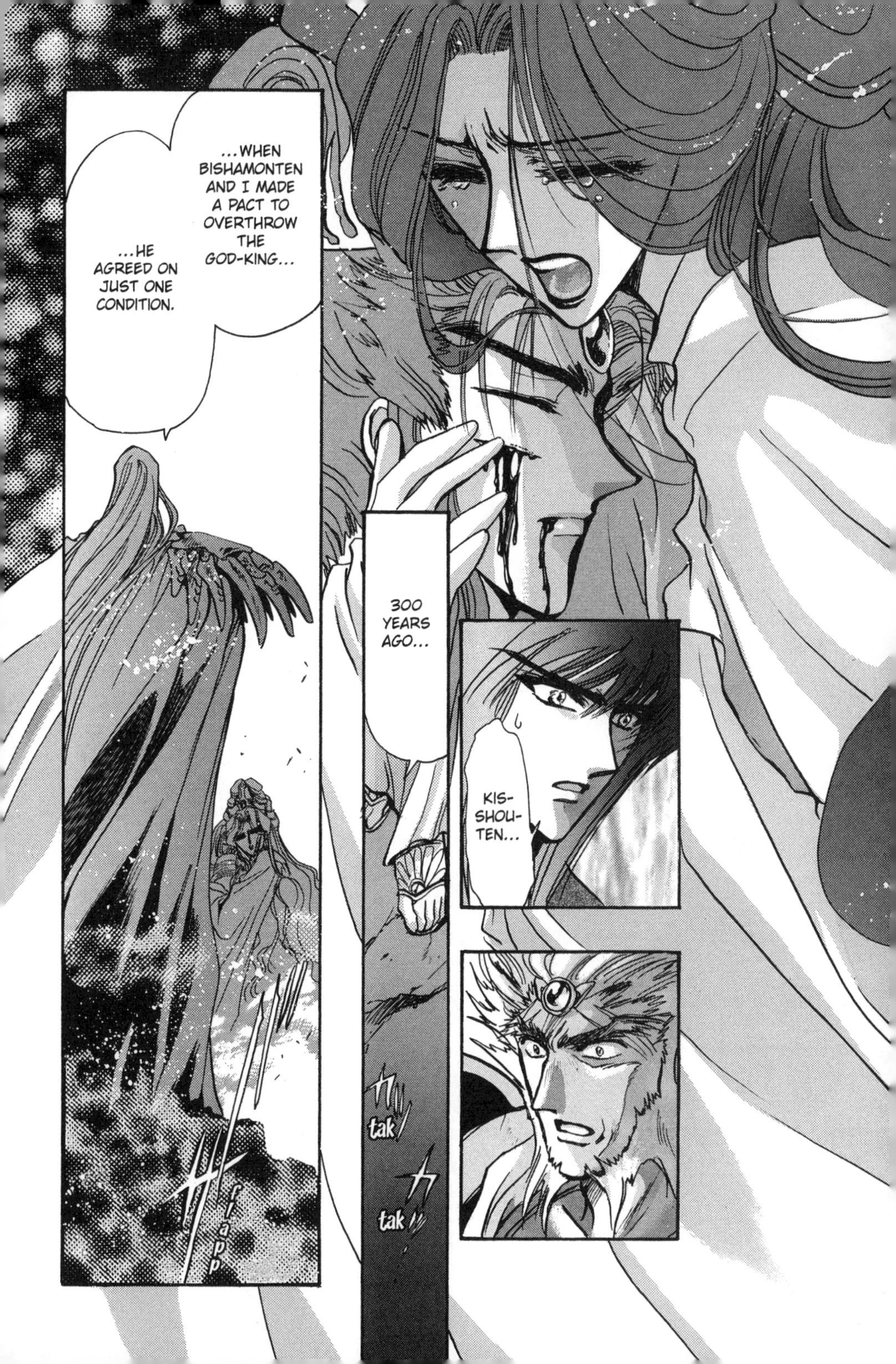
300 YEARS AGO...
KIS-SHOU-TEN...
tak
tak
...WHEN BISHAMONTEN AND I MADE A PACT TO OVERTHROW THE GOD-KING...
...HE AGREED ON JUST ONE CONDITION.
flapp

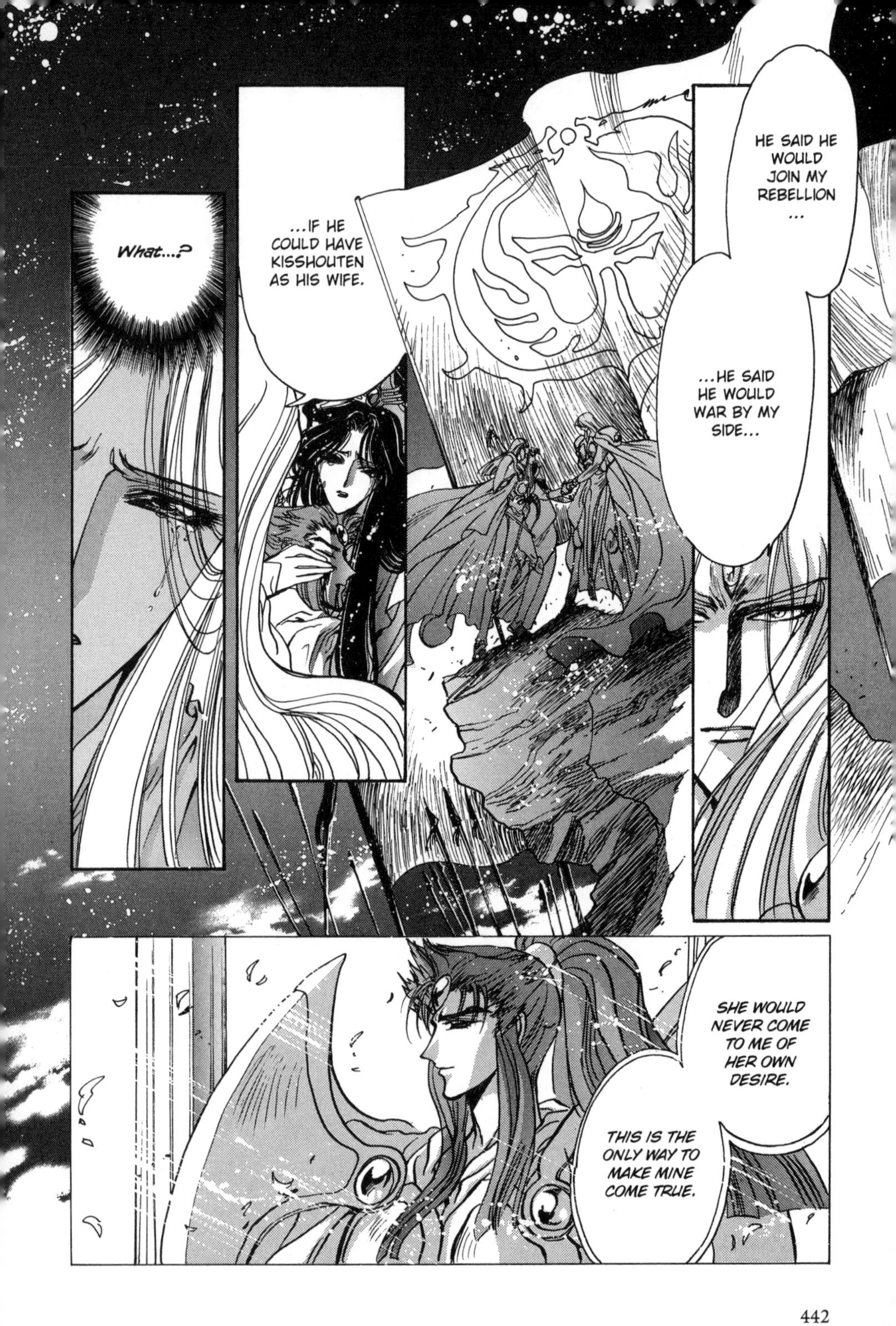
HE SAID HE WOULD JOIN MY REBELLION ...
...HE SAID HE WOULD WAR BY MY SIDE...
...IF HE COULD HAVE KISSHOUTEN AS HIS WIFE.
What...?
SHE WOULD NEVER COME TO ME OF HER OWN DESIRE.
THIS IS THE ONLY WAY TO MAKE MINE COME TRUE.

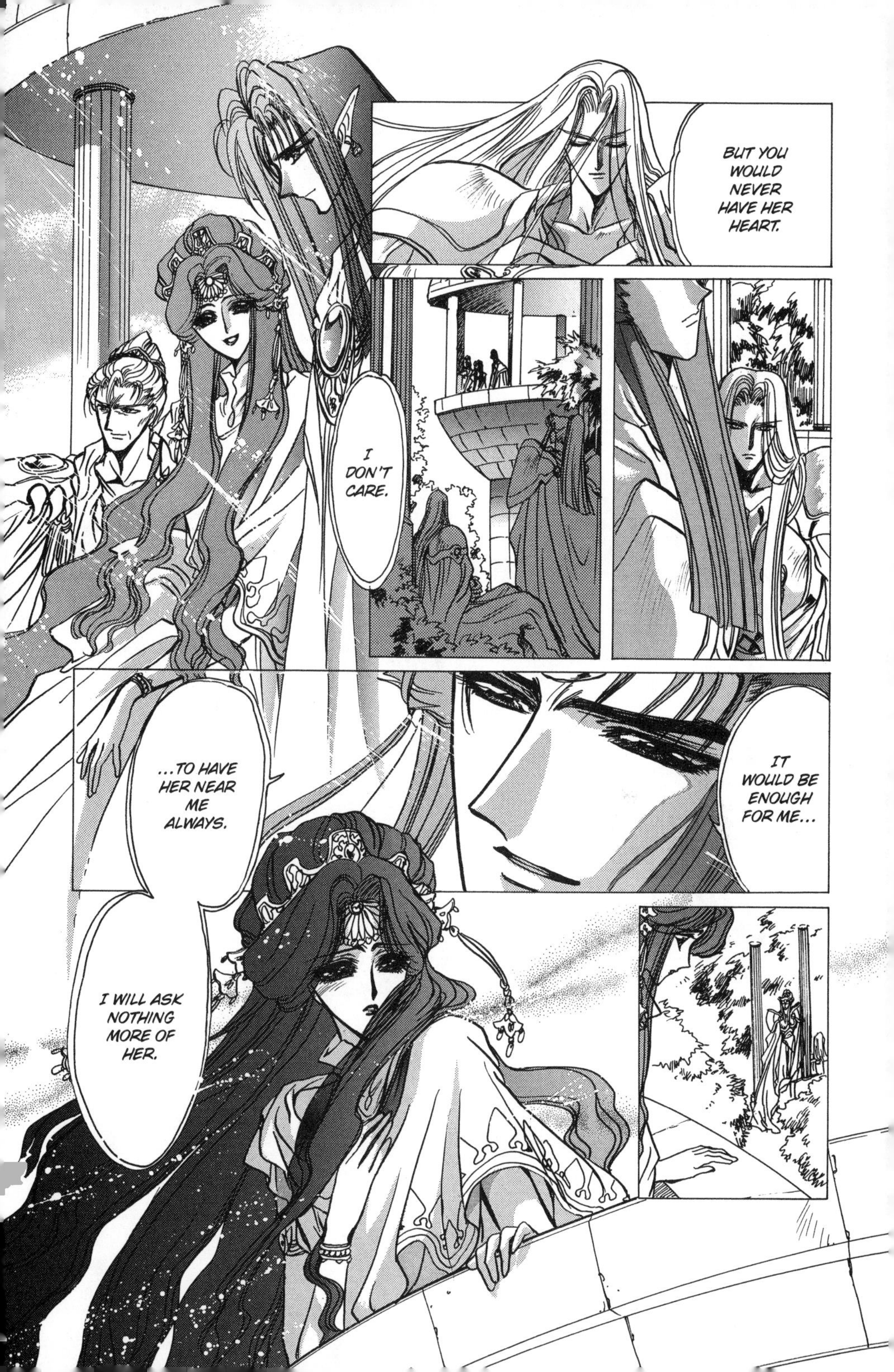
BUT YOU WOULD NEVER HAVE HER HEART.
I DON'T CARE.
IT WOULD BE ENOUGH FOR ME...
...TO HAVE HER NEAR ME ALWAYS.
I WILL ASK NOTHING MORE OF HER.

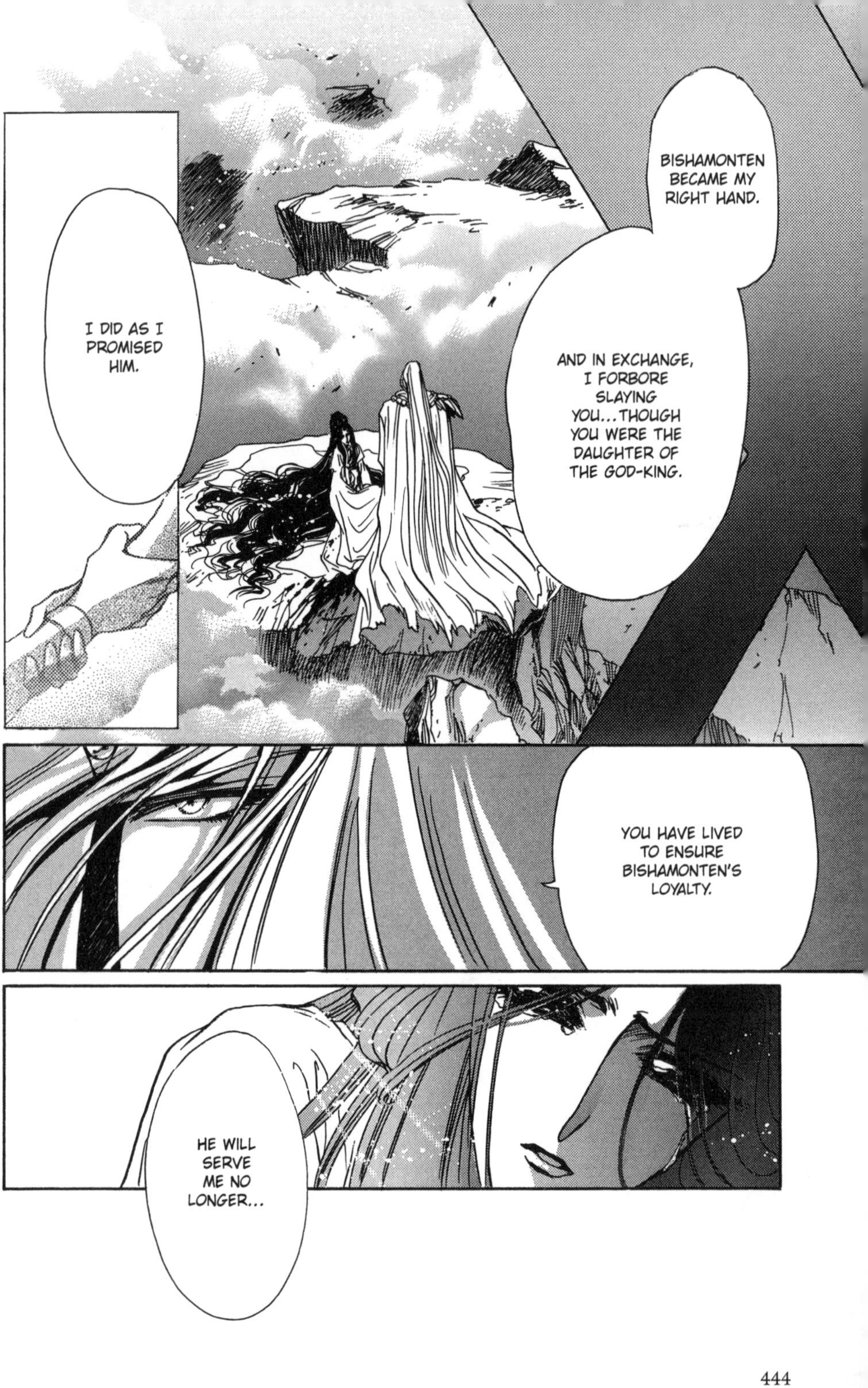
BISHAMONTEN BECAME MY RIGHT HAND.
AND IN EXCHANGE, I FORBORE SLAYING YOU...THOUGH YOU WERE THE DAUGHTER OF THE GOD-KING.
I DID AS I PROMISED HIM.
YOU HAVE LIVED TO ENSURE BISHAMONTEN'S LOYALTY.
HE WILL SERVE ME NO LONGER...

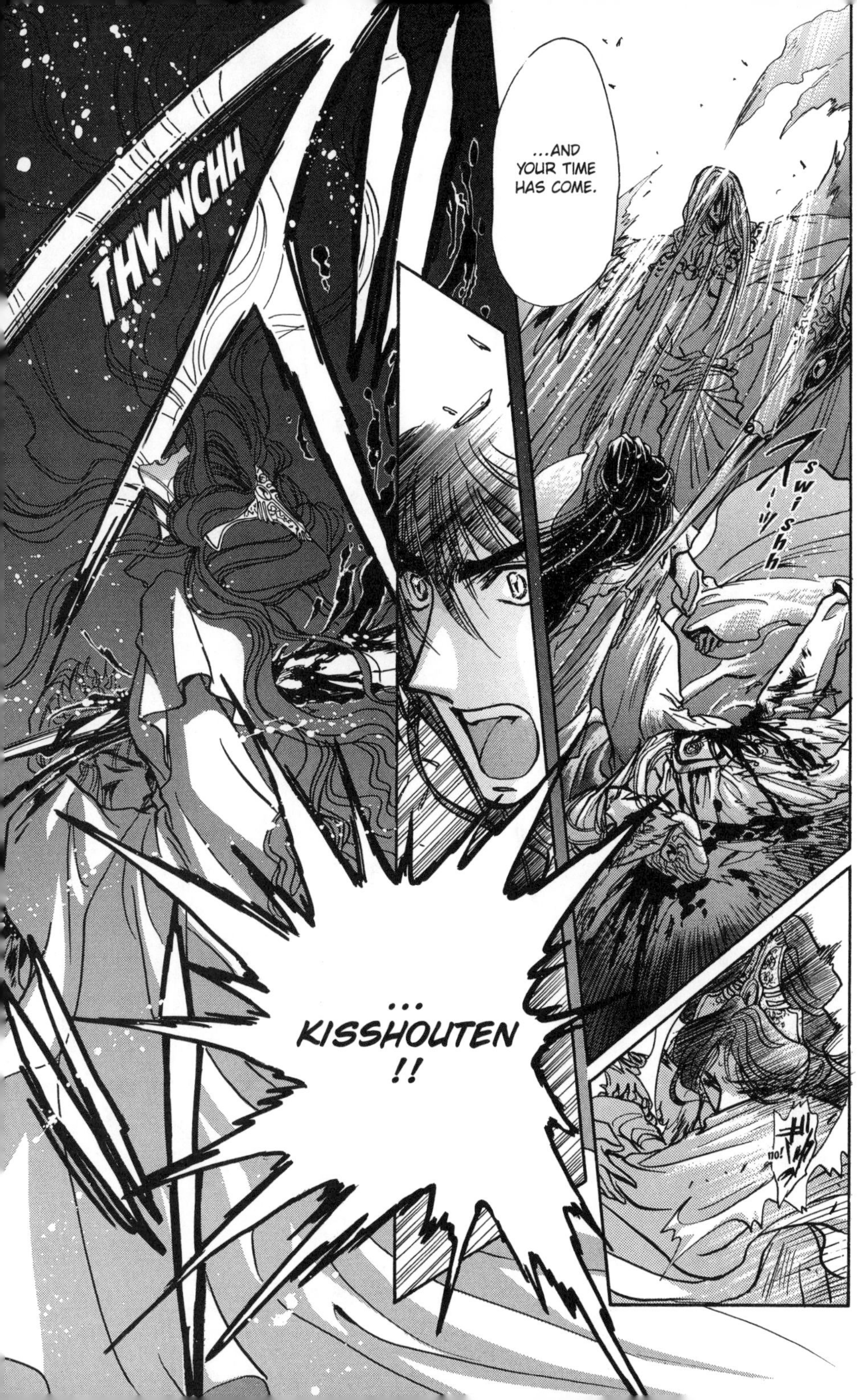
...AND YOUR TIME HAS COME.
swishh
THWNCHH
... KISSHOUTEN !!
no!

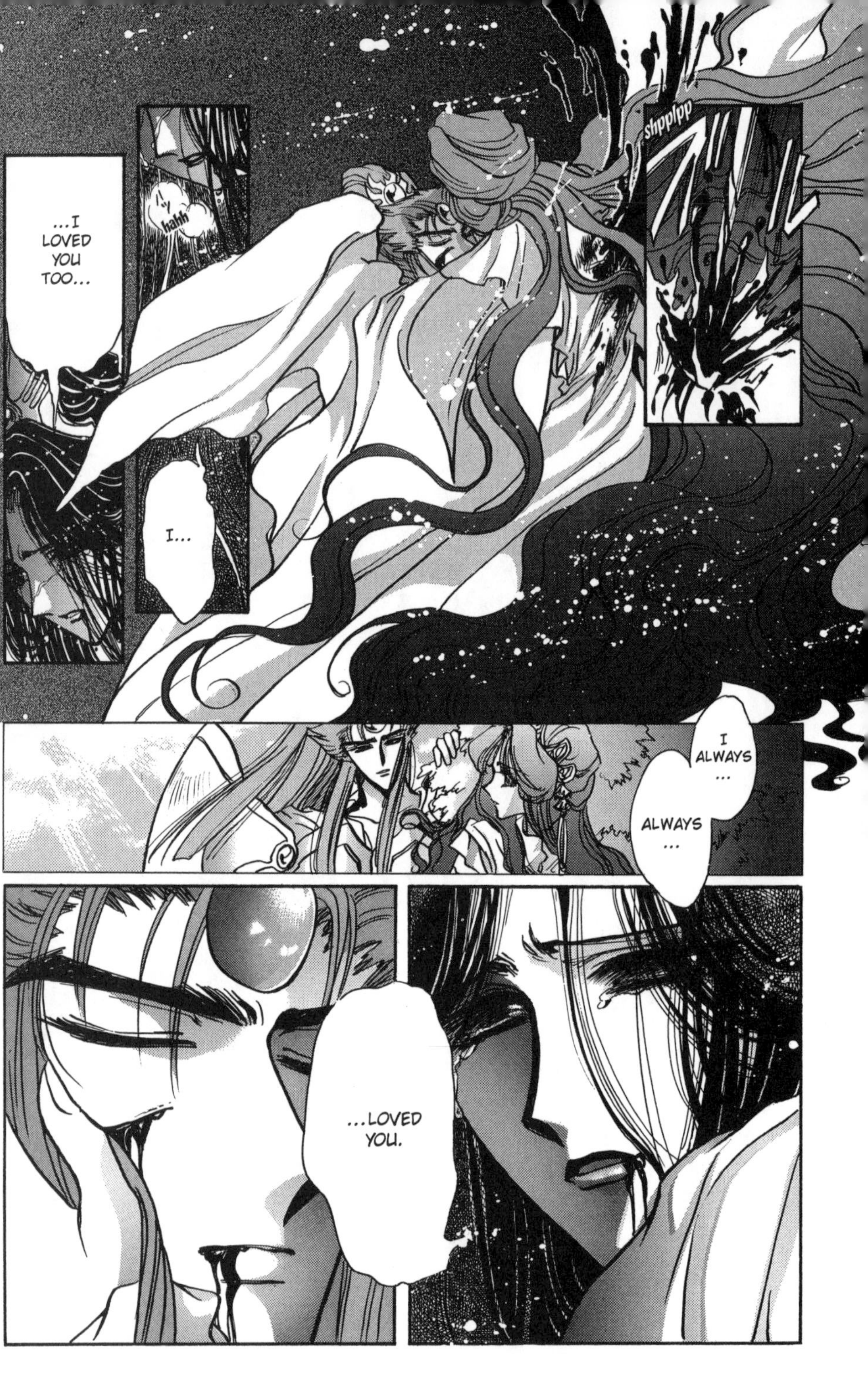
shpplpp
hahh
I...
...I LOVED YOU TOO...
I ALWAYS ... ALWAYS ...
...LOVED YOU.

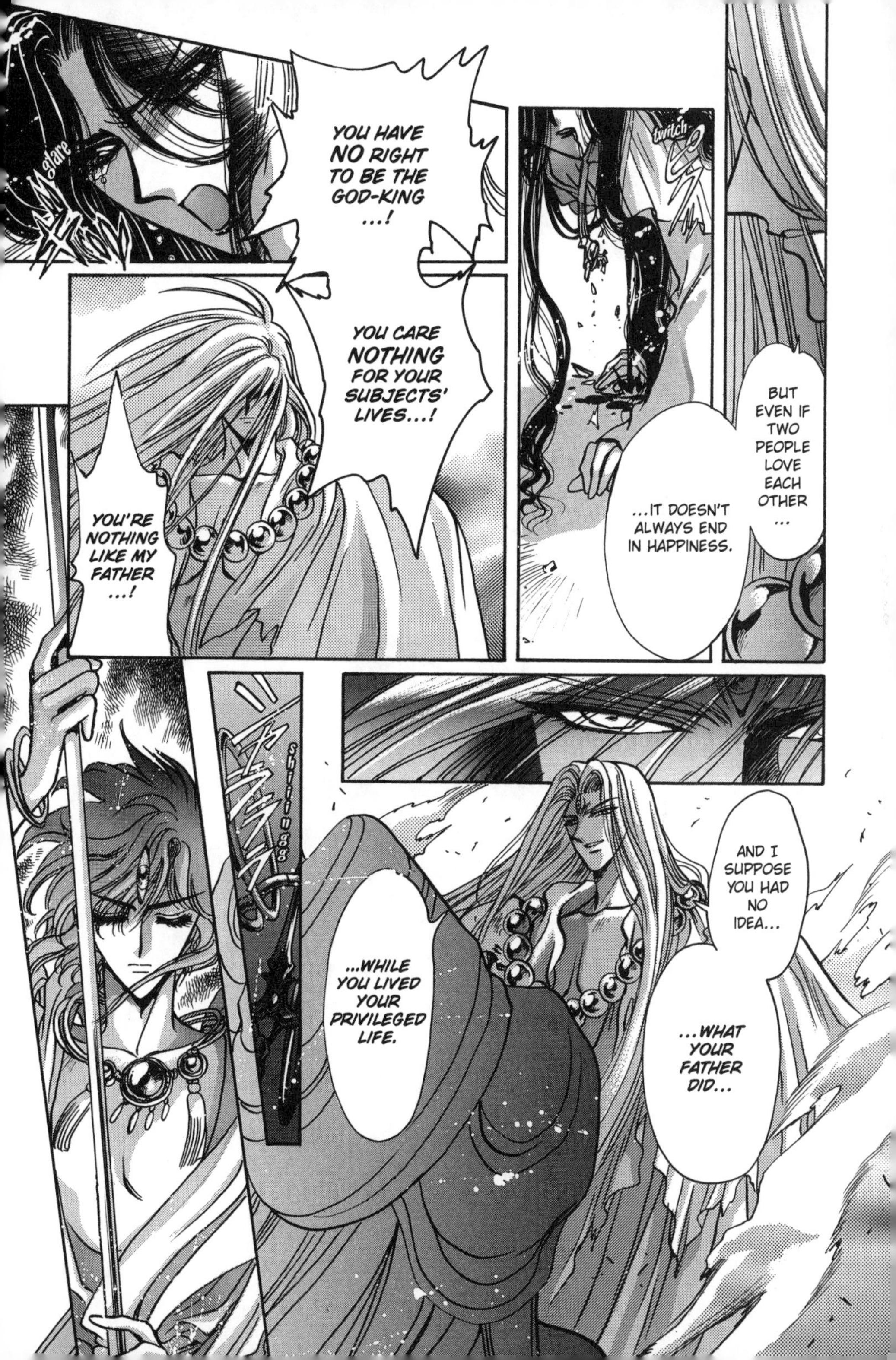
BUT EVEN IF TWO PEOPLE LOVE EACH OTHER...
...IT DOESN'T ALWAYS END IN HAPPINESS.
twitch
glare
YOU HAVE NO RIGHT TO BE THE GOD-KING...!
YOU CARE NOTHING FOR YOUR SUBJECTS' LIVES...!
YOU'RE NOTHING LIKE MY FATHER...!
shiiing
AND I SUPPOSE YOU HAD NO IDEA...
...WHAT YOUR FATHER DID...
...WHILE YOU LIVED YOUR PRIVILEGED LIFE.

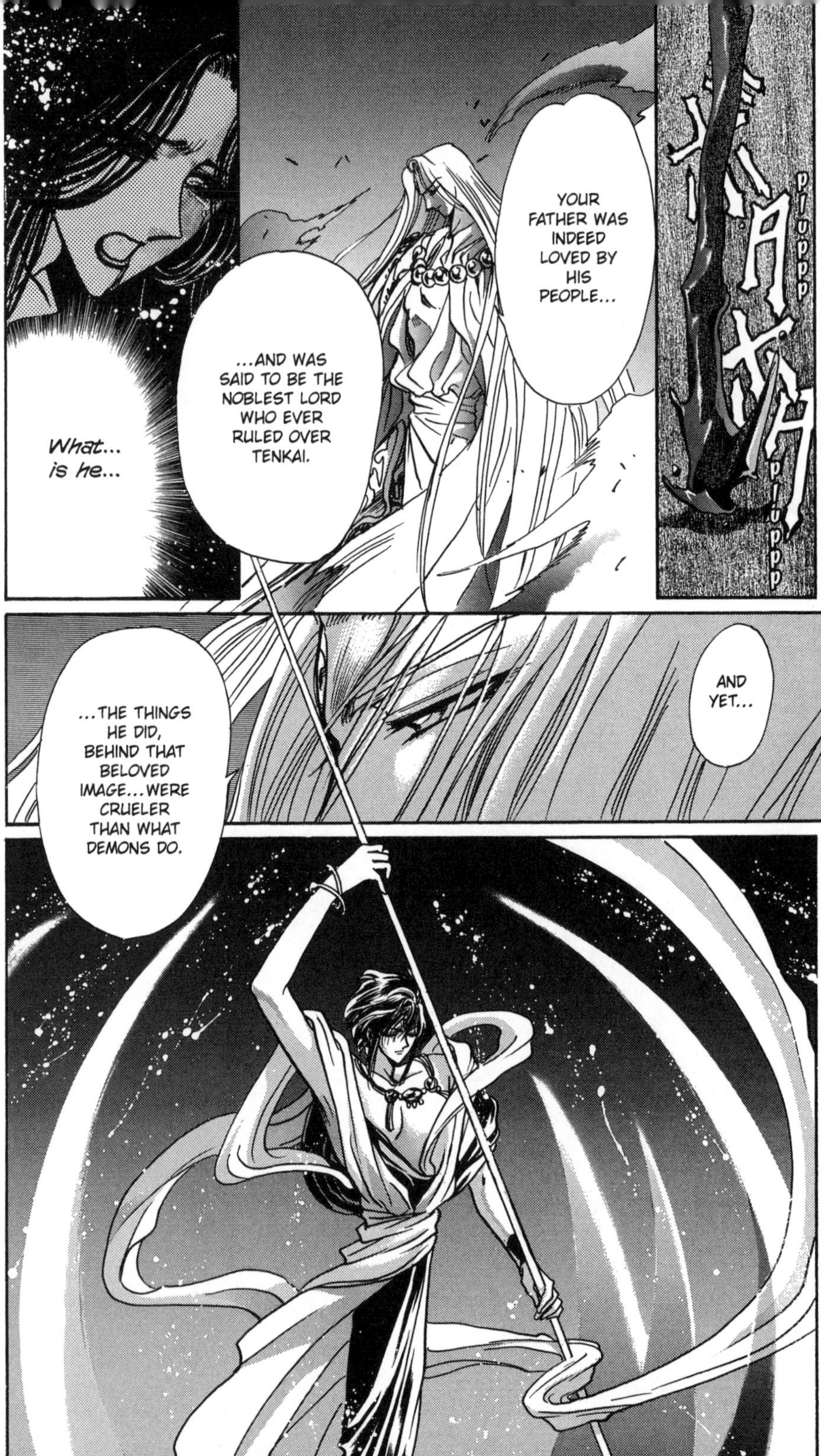
pluppp
pluppp
YOUR FATHER WAS INDEED LOVED BY HIS PEOPLE...
...AND WAS SAID TO BE THE NOBLEST LORD WHO EVER RULED OVER TENKAI.
What... is he...
AND YET...
...THE THINGS HE DID, BEHIND THAT BELOVED IMAGE...WERE CRUELER THAN WHAT DEMONS DO.

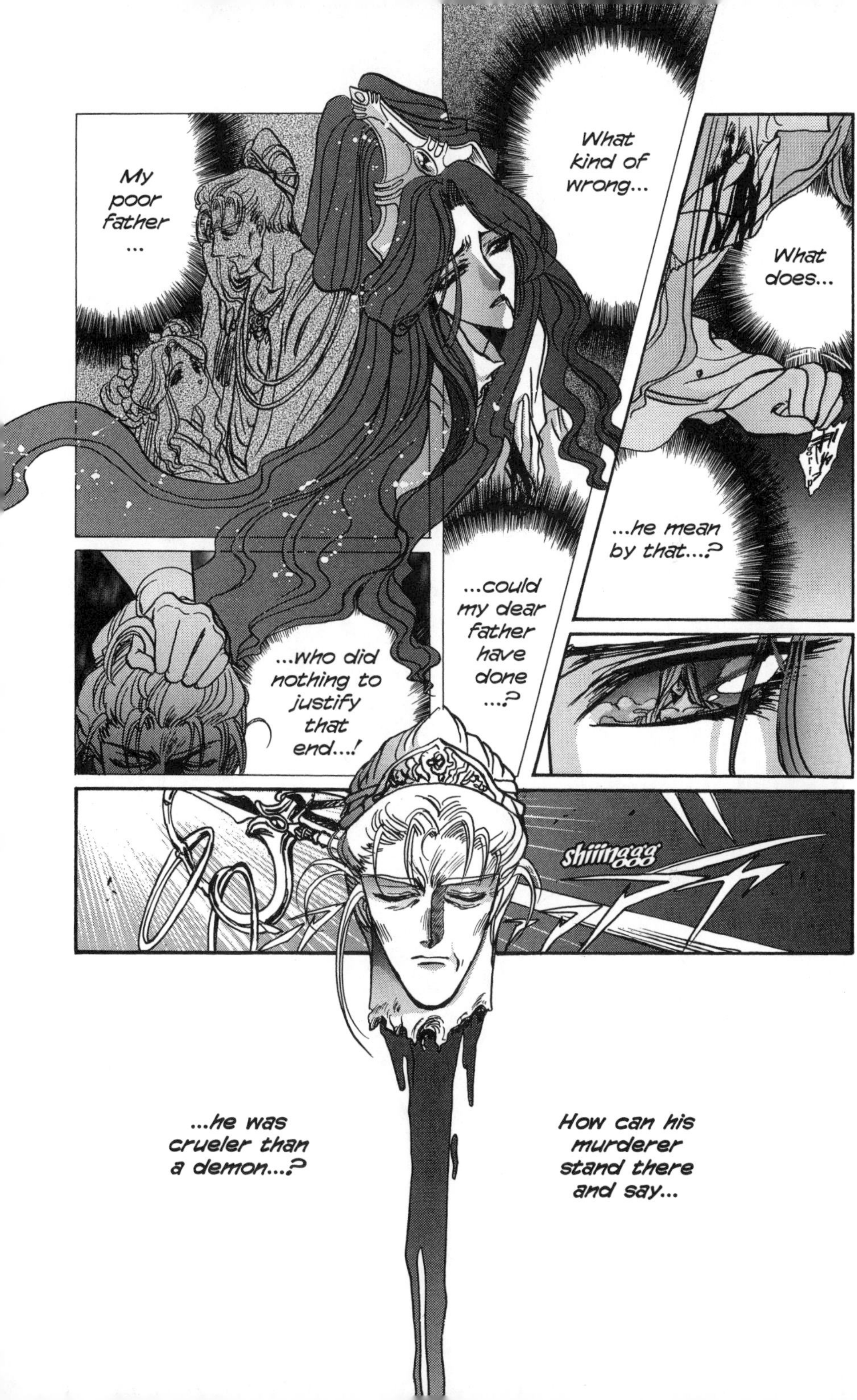

What does...
...he mean by that...?
What kind of wrong...
My poor father...
...could my dear father have done...?
...who did nothing to justify that end...!
shiiinggg
How can his murderer stand there and say...
...he was crueler than a demon...?

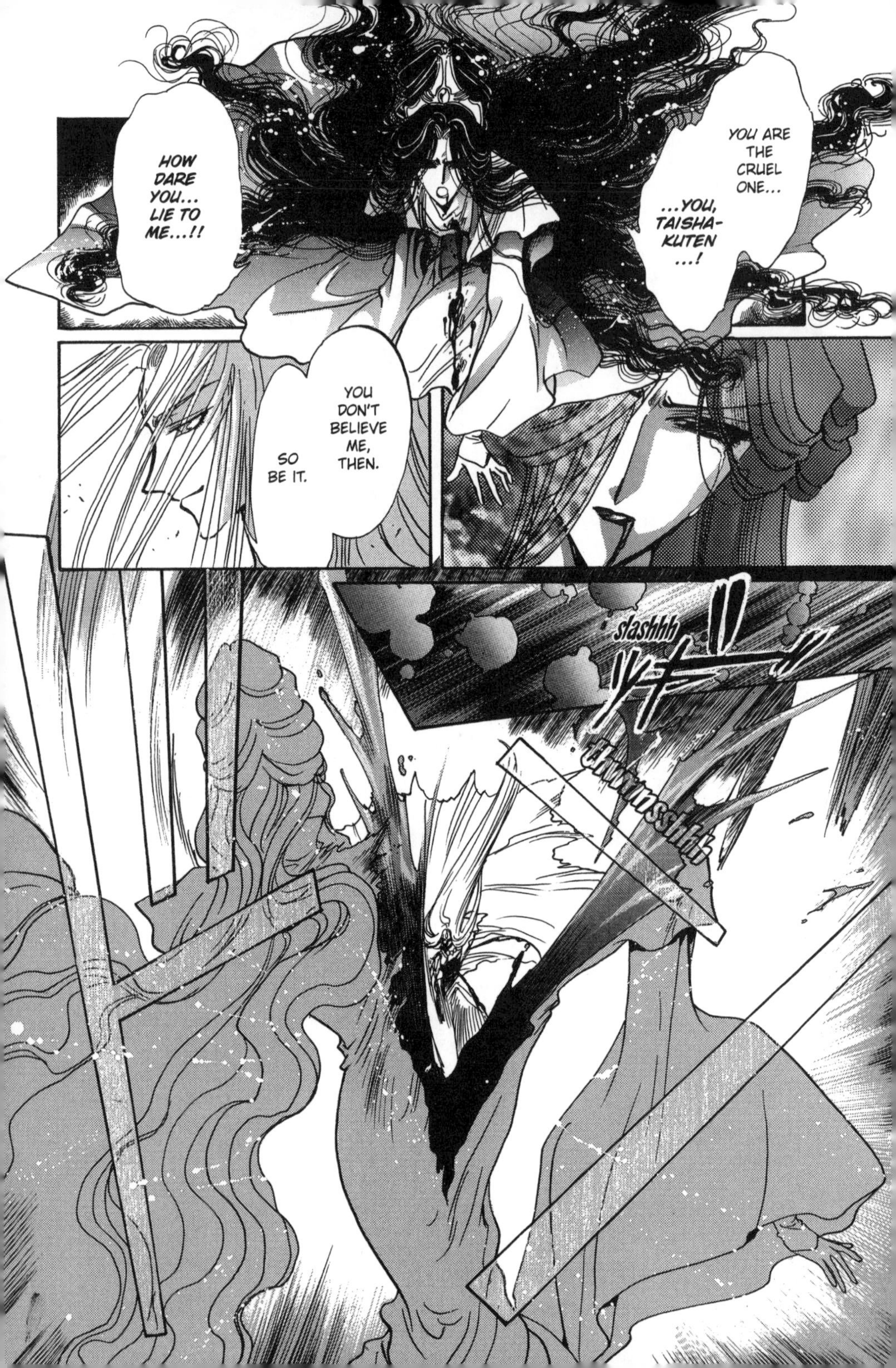
YOU ARE THE CRUEL ONE...
...YOU, TAISHA-KUTEN...!
HOW DARE YOU... LIE TO ME...!!
YOU DON'T BELIEVE ME, THEN.
SO BE IT.
slashhh
thwunshhk

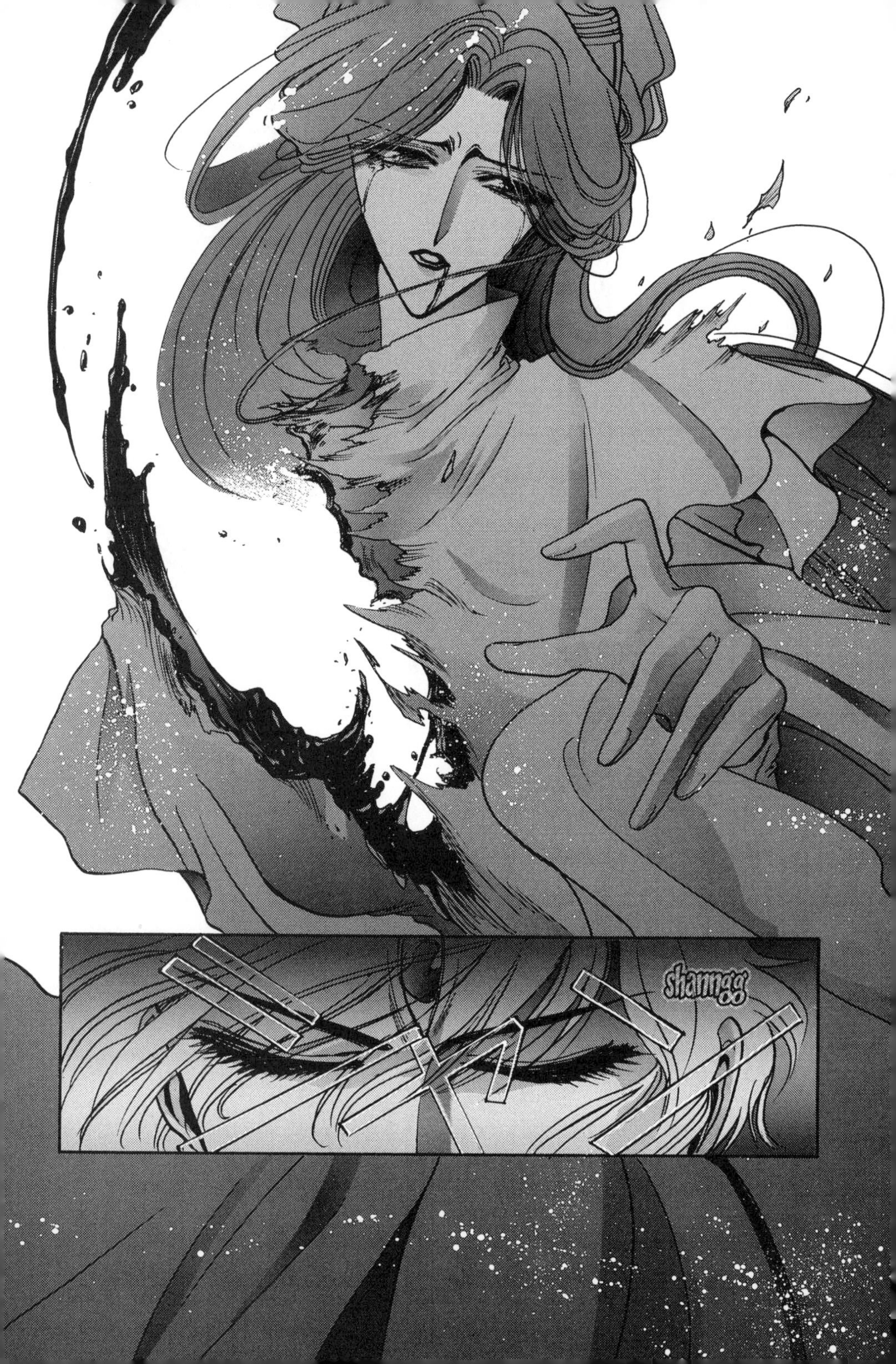
sharrngg

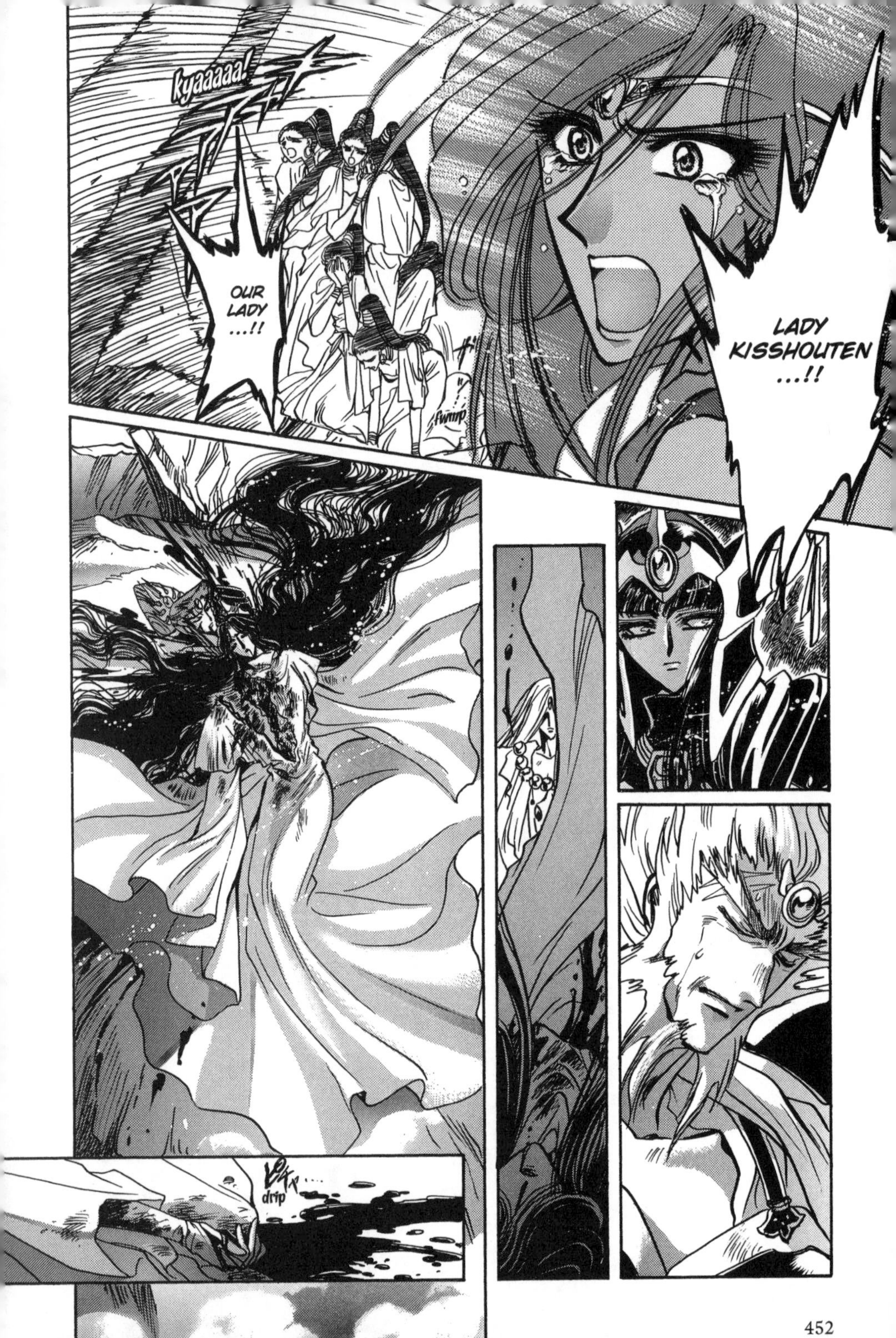
LADY KISSHOUTEN ...!!
kyaaaaa!
OUR LADY ...!!
fwmp
drip

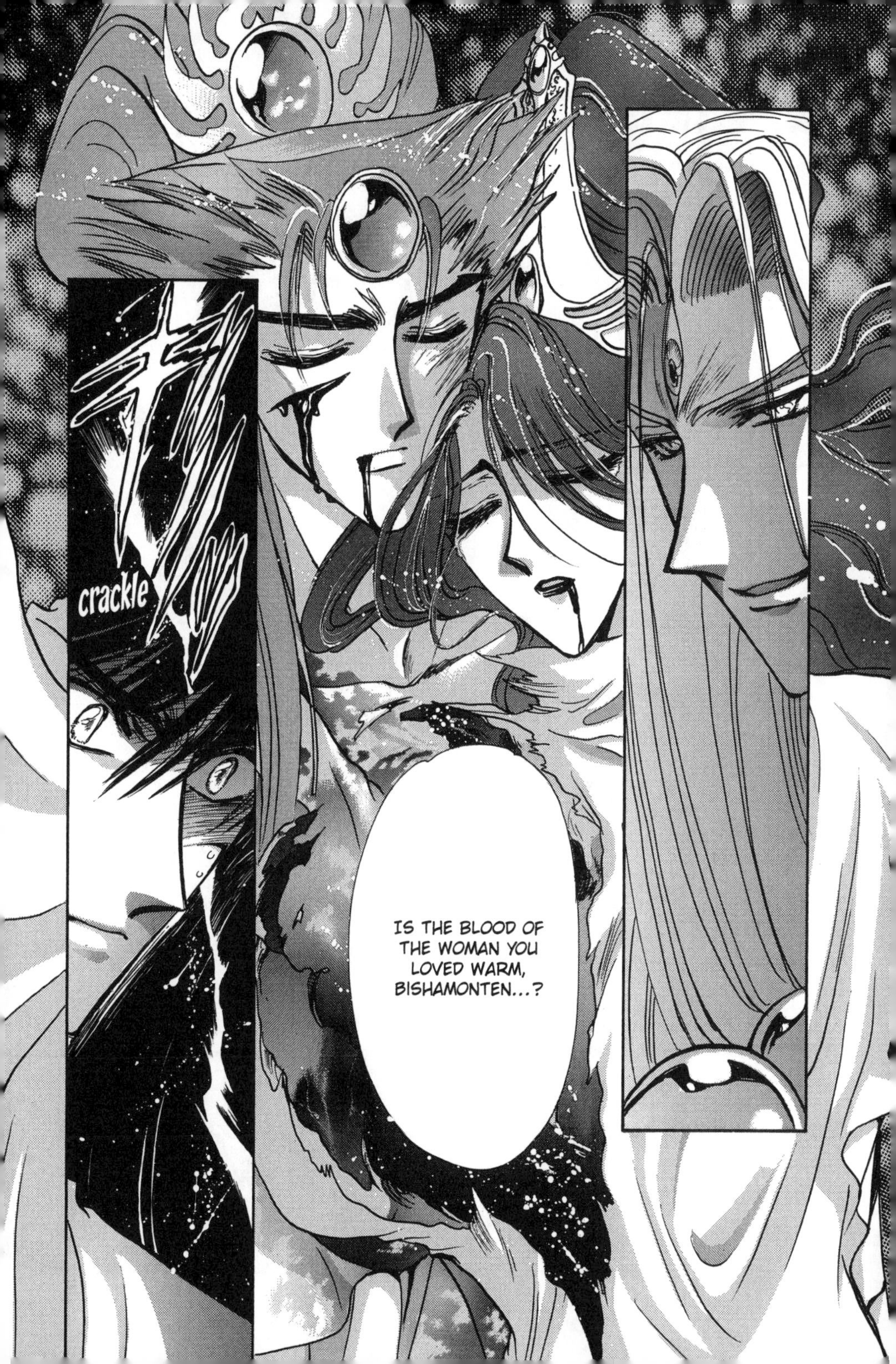
crackle
IS THE BLOOD OF THE WOMAN YOU LOVED WARM, BISHAMONTEN...?

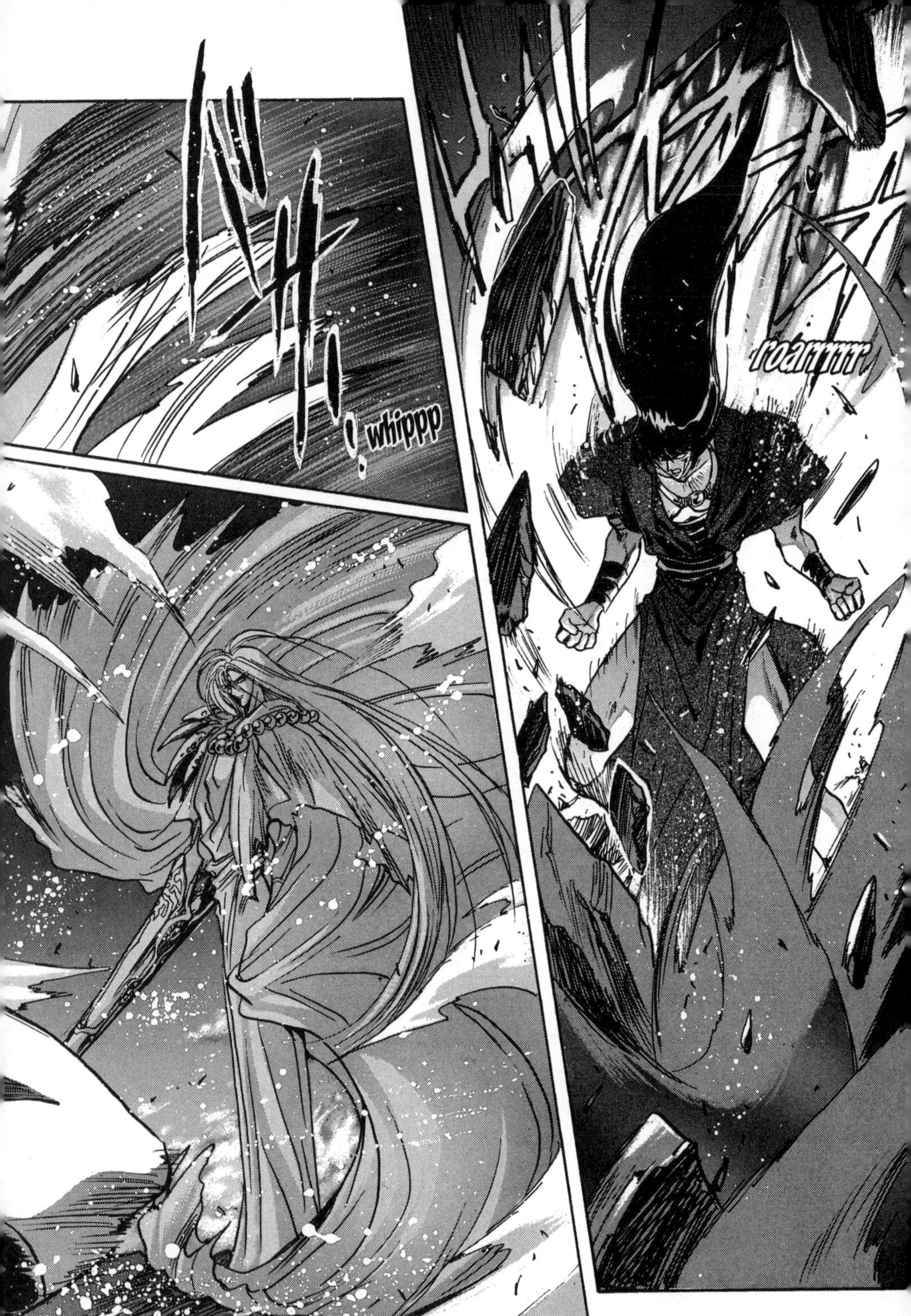
roarrrrr
whippp

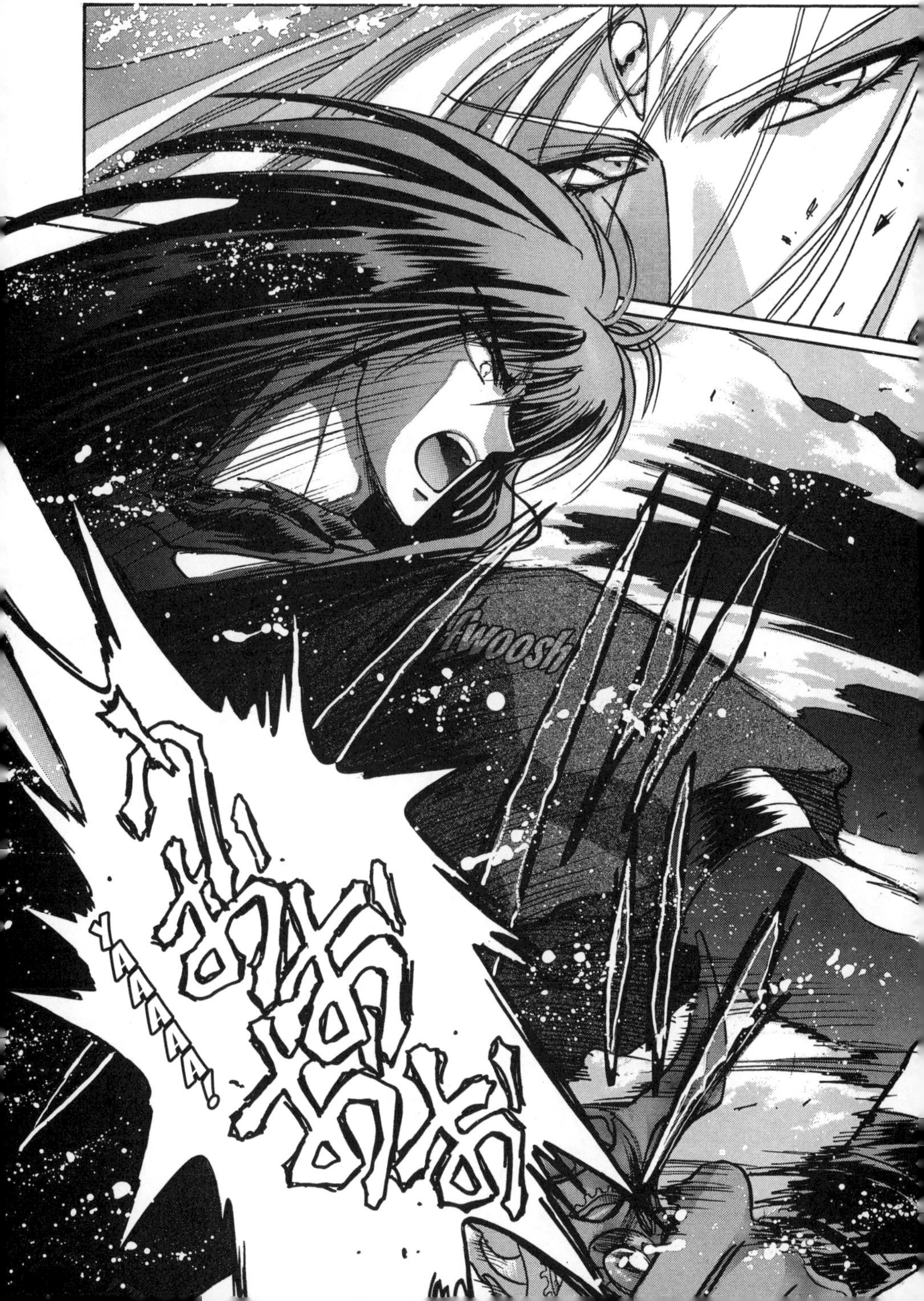
twoosh
YAAAAAAA!

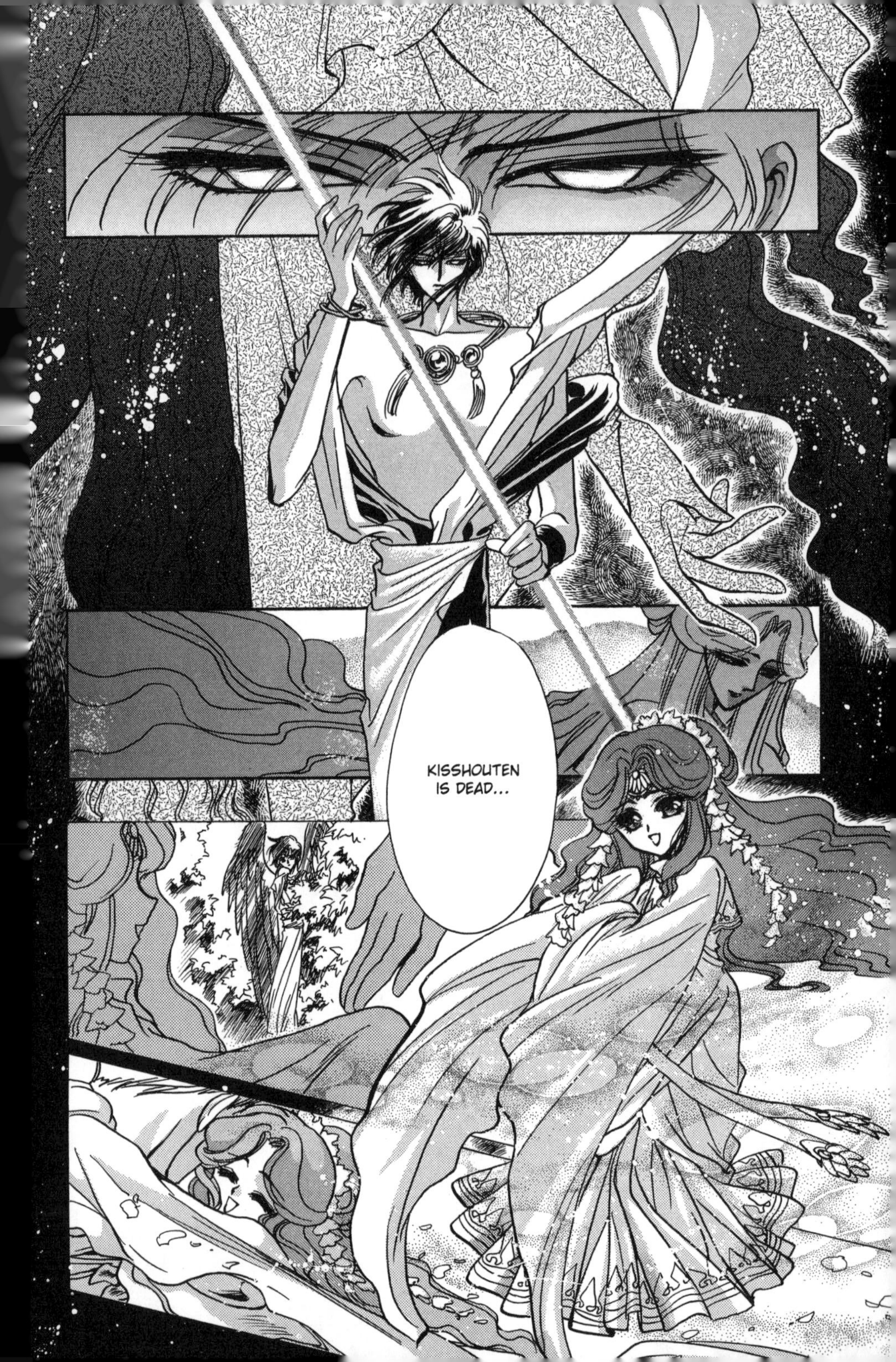
KISSHOUTEN IS DEAD...

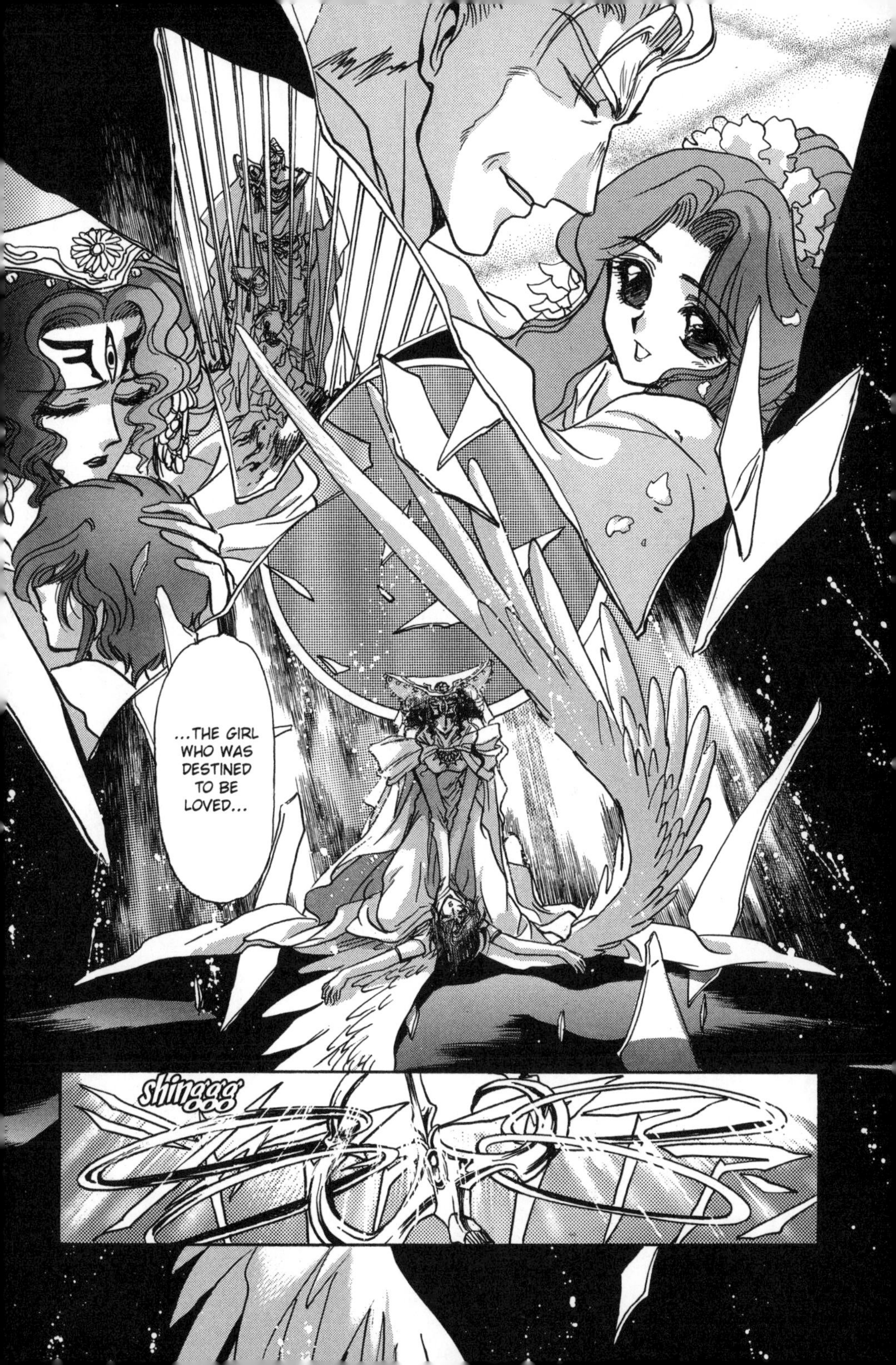
...THE GIRL WHO WAS DESTINED TO BE LOVED...
shingggg

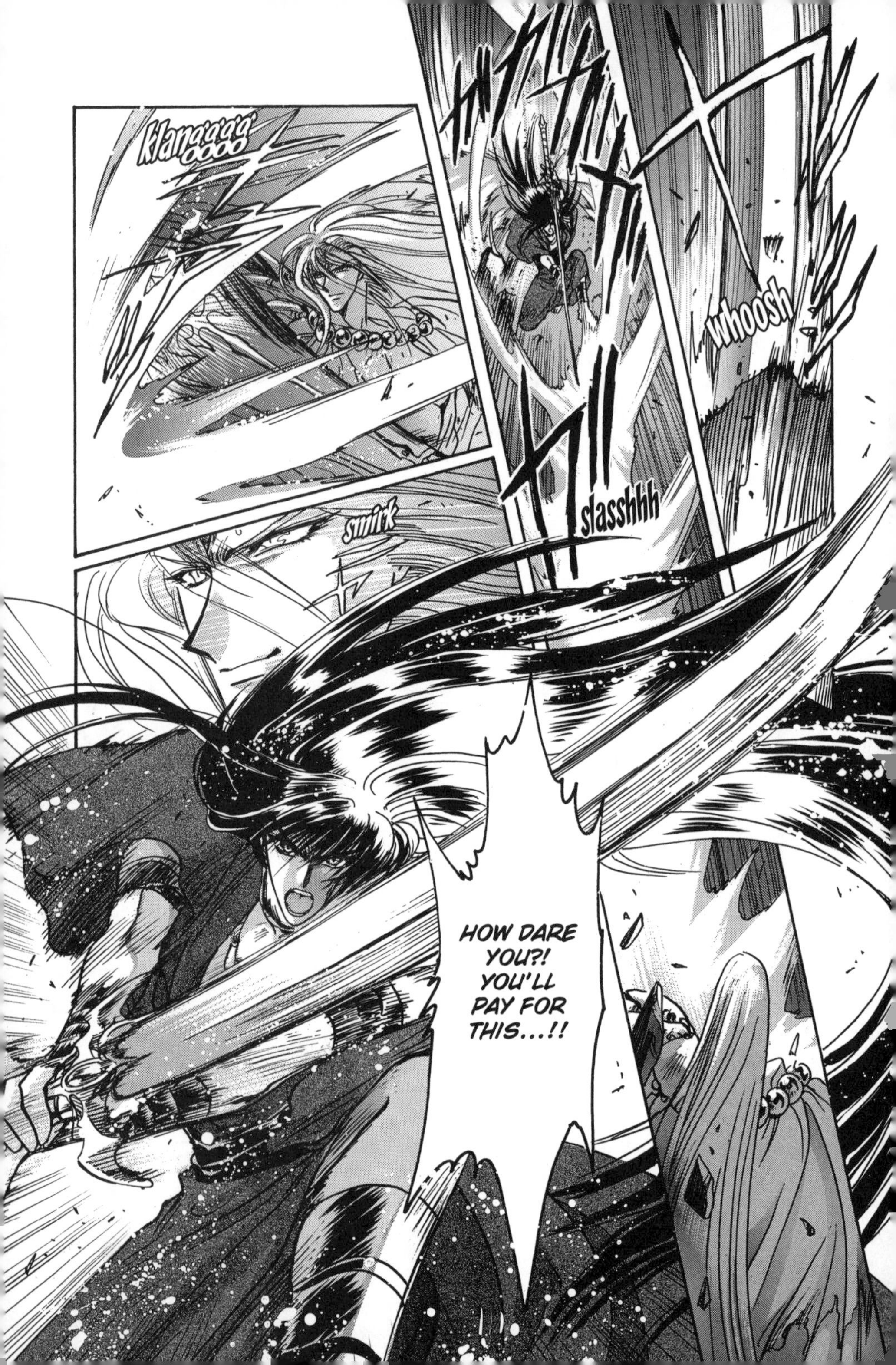
whoosh
slasshhh
klanggggoooo
smirk
HOW DARE YOU?! YOU'LL PAY FOR THIS...!!

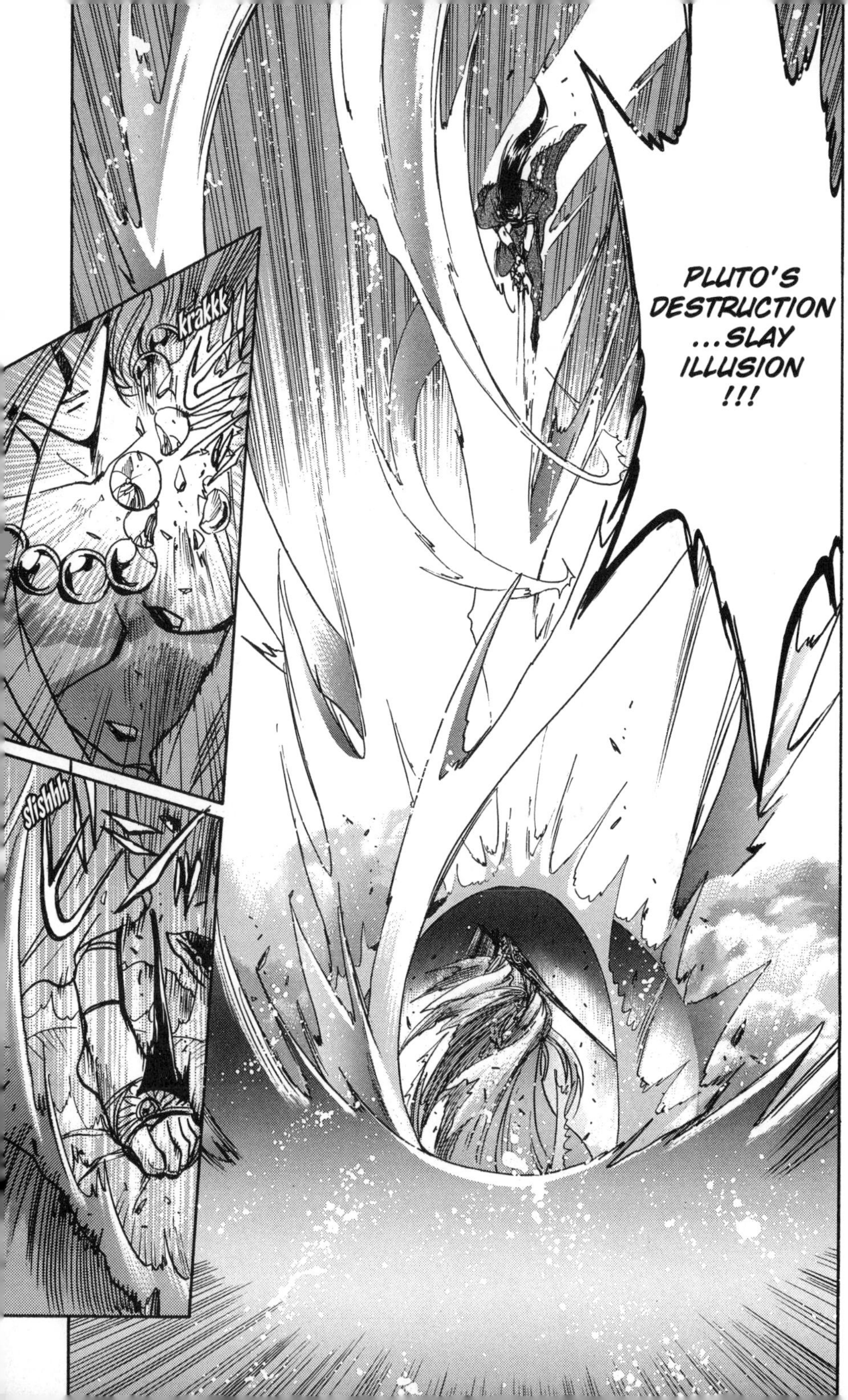
PLUTO'S DESTRUCTION ...SLAY ILLUSION !!!
krakkk
slishhh

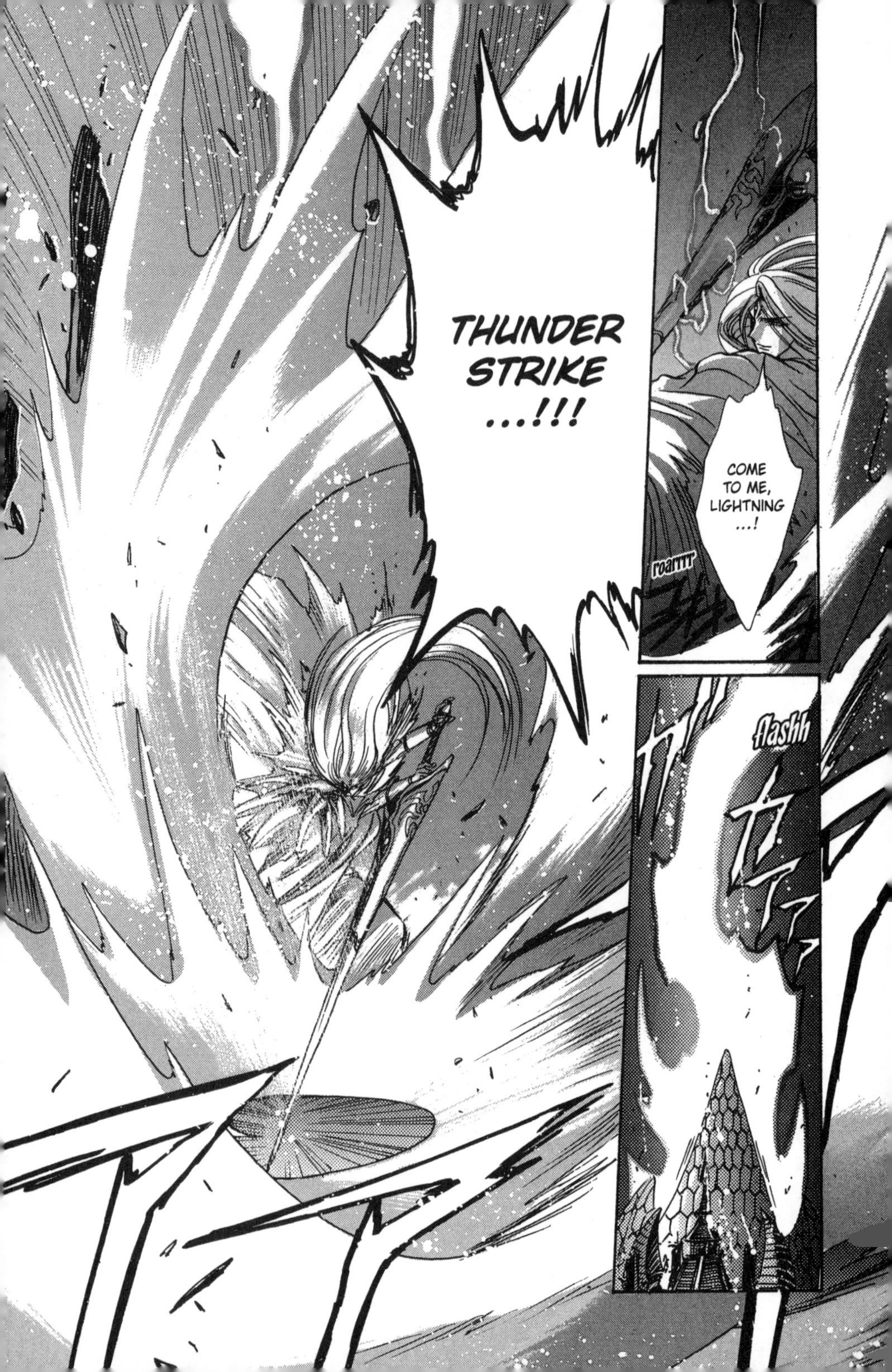
COME TO ME, LIGHTNING ...!
roarrrr
flashh
THUNDER STRIKE ...!!!

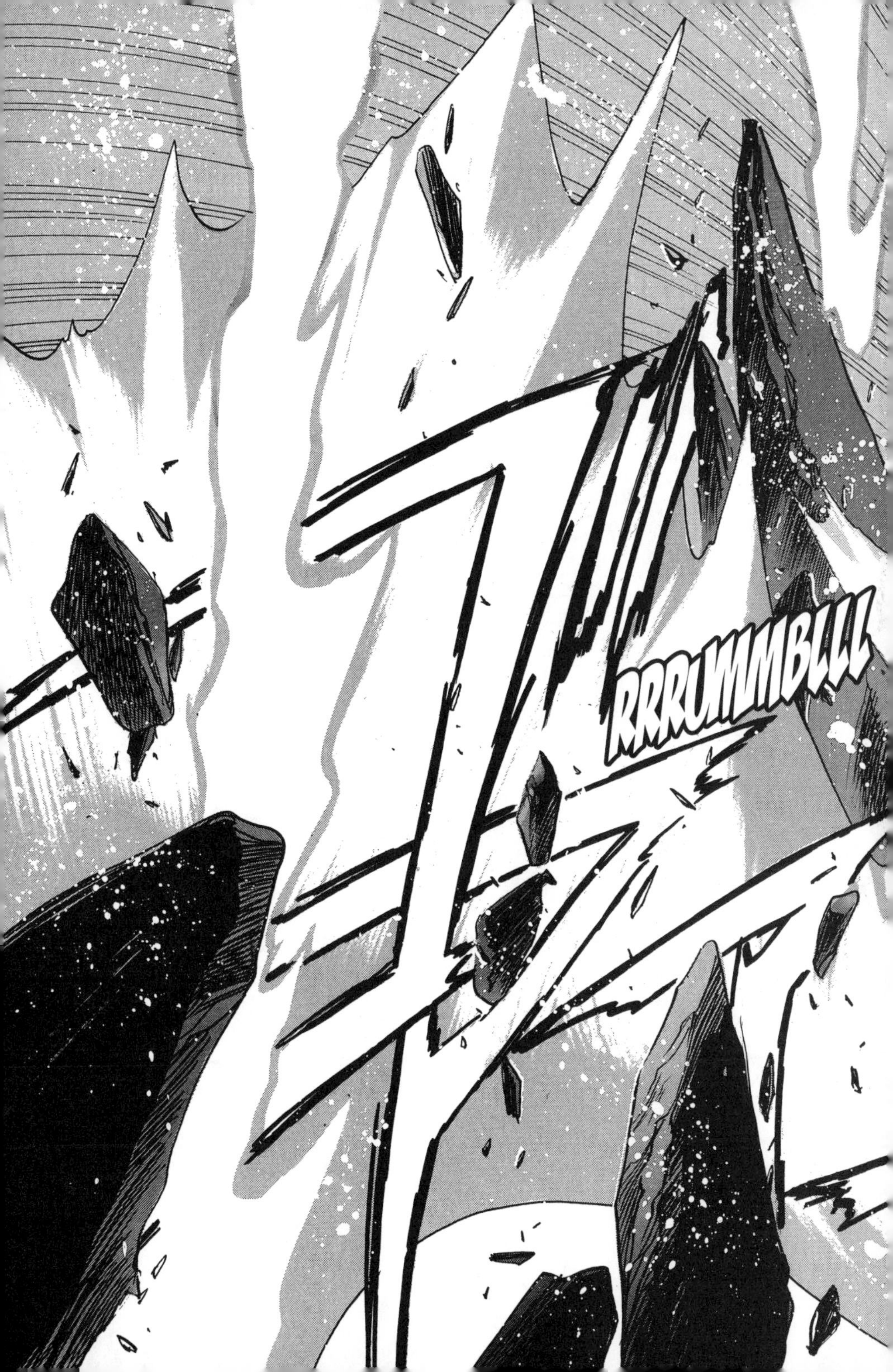
RRRUMMMBLLL

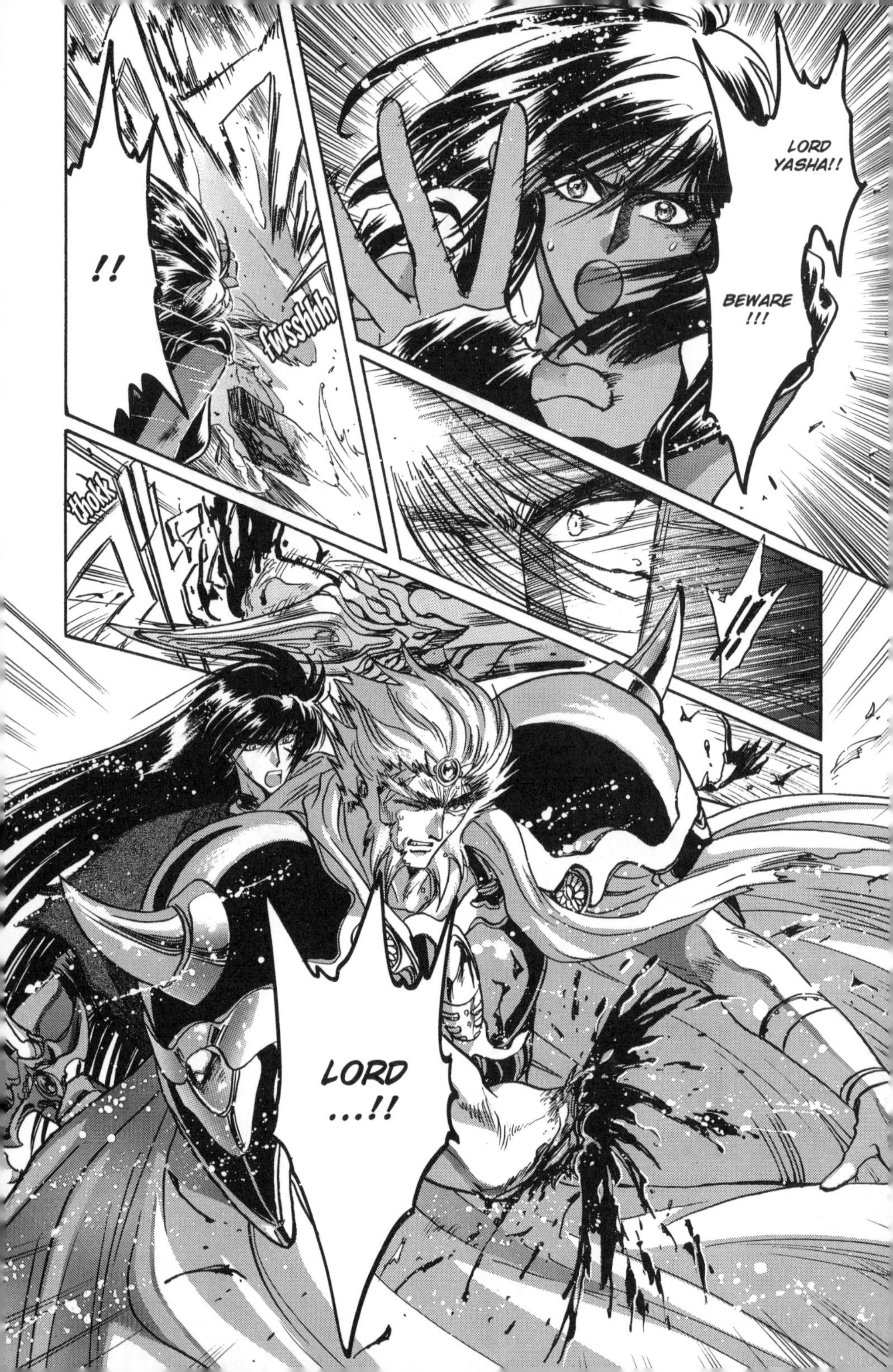
LORD YASHA!!
BEWARE !!!
!!
fwsshhh
thokk
LORD ...!!

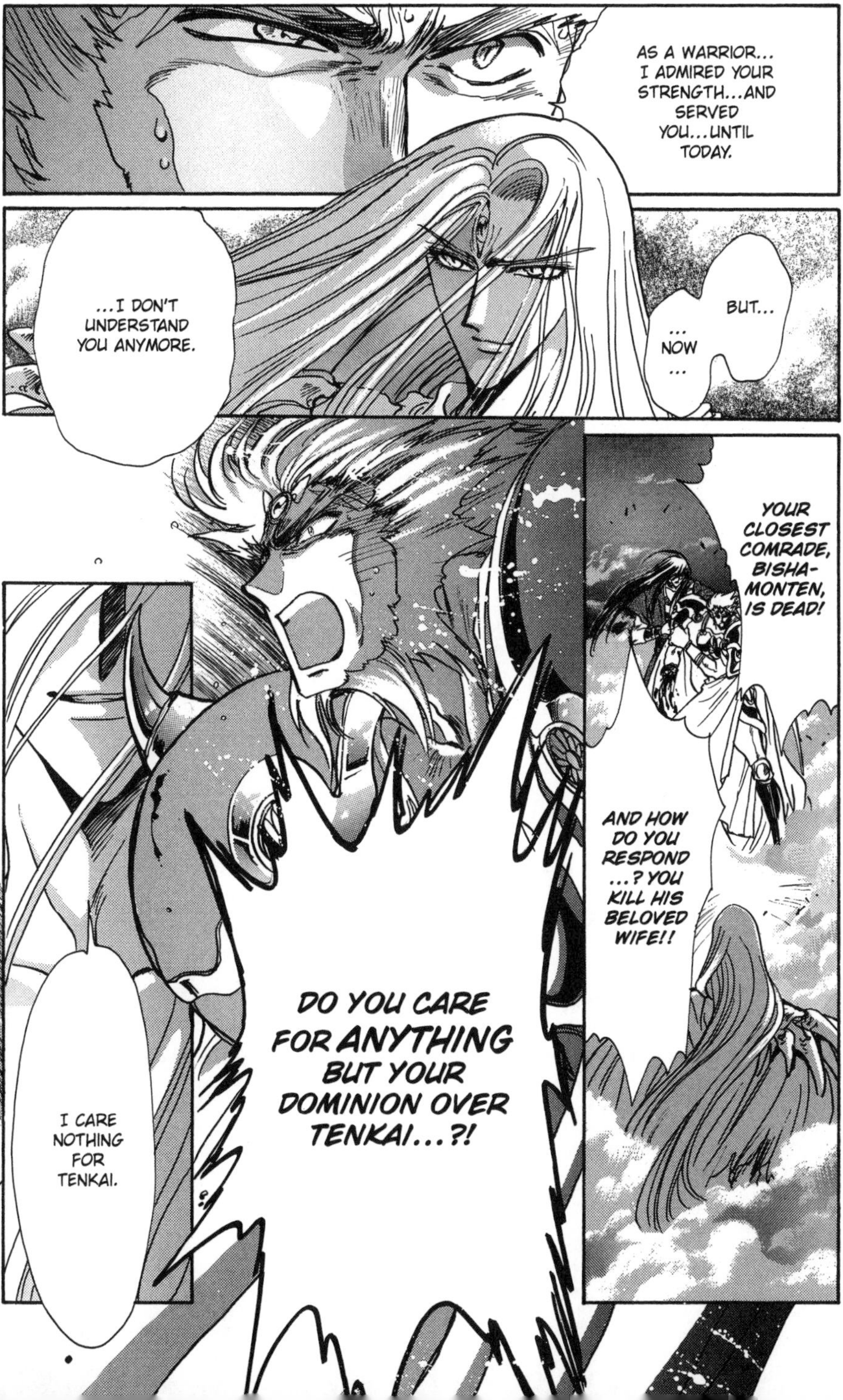
AS A WARRIOR... I ADMIRED YOUR STRENGTH...AND SERVED YOU...UNTIL TODAY.
BUT... ... NOW ...
...I DON'T UNDERSTAND YOU ANYMORE.
YOUR CLOSEST COMRADE, BISHAMONTEN, IS DEAD!
AND HOW DO YOU RESPOND ...? YOU KILL HIS BELOVED WIFE!!
DO YOU CARE FOR ANYTHING BUT YOUR DOMINION OVER TENKAI...?!
I CARE NOTHING FOR TENKAI.

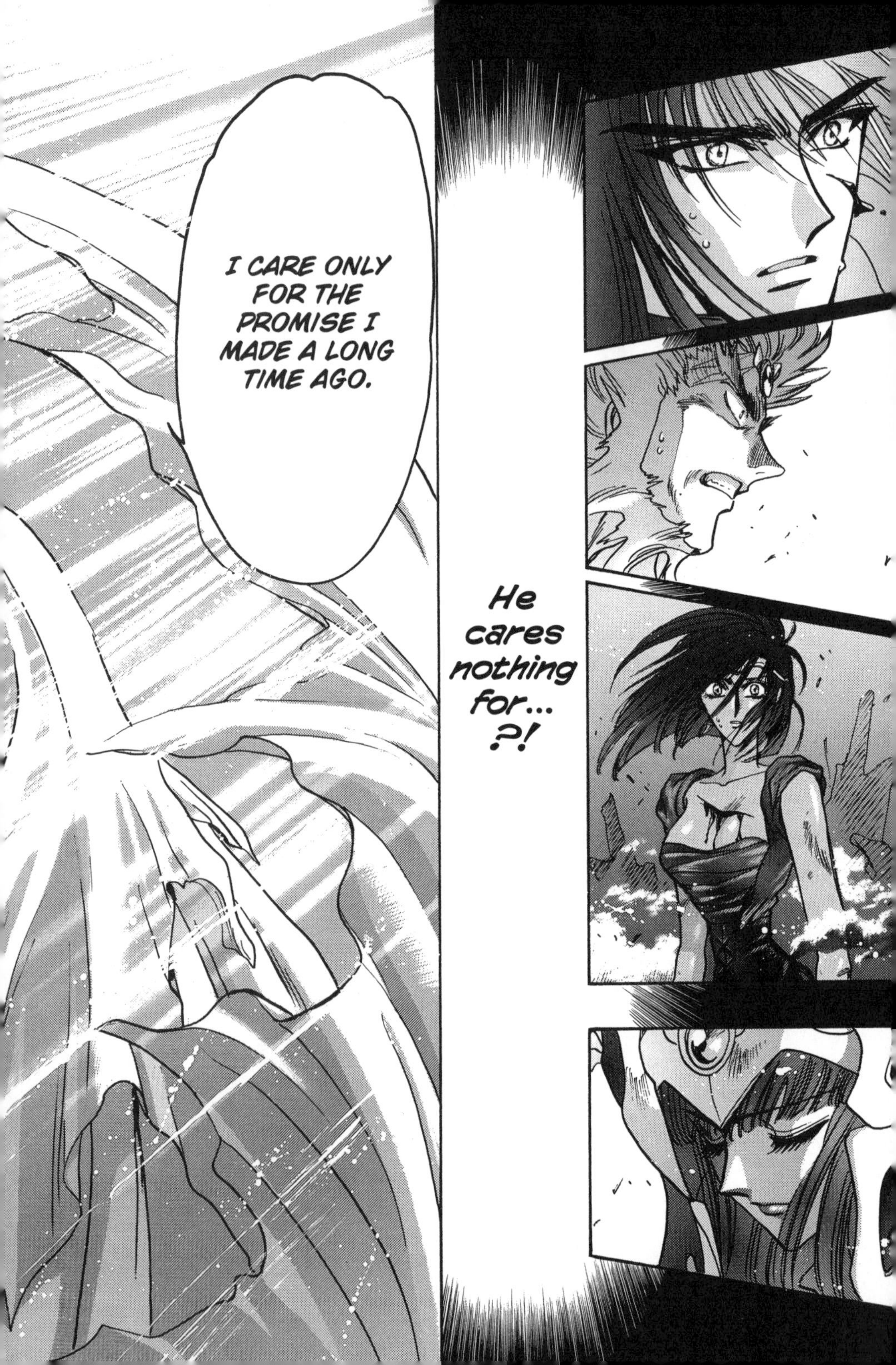
He cares nothing for...?!
I CARE ONLY FOR THE PROMISE I MADE A LONG TIME AGO.

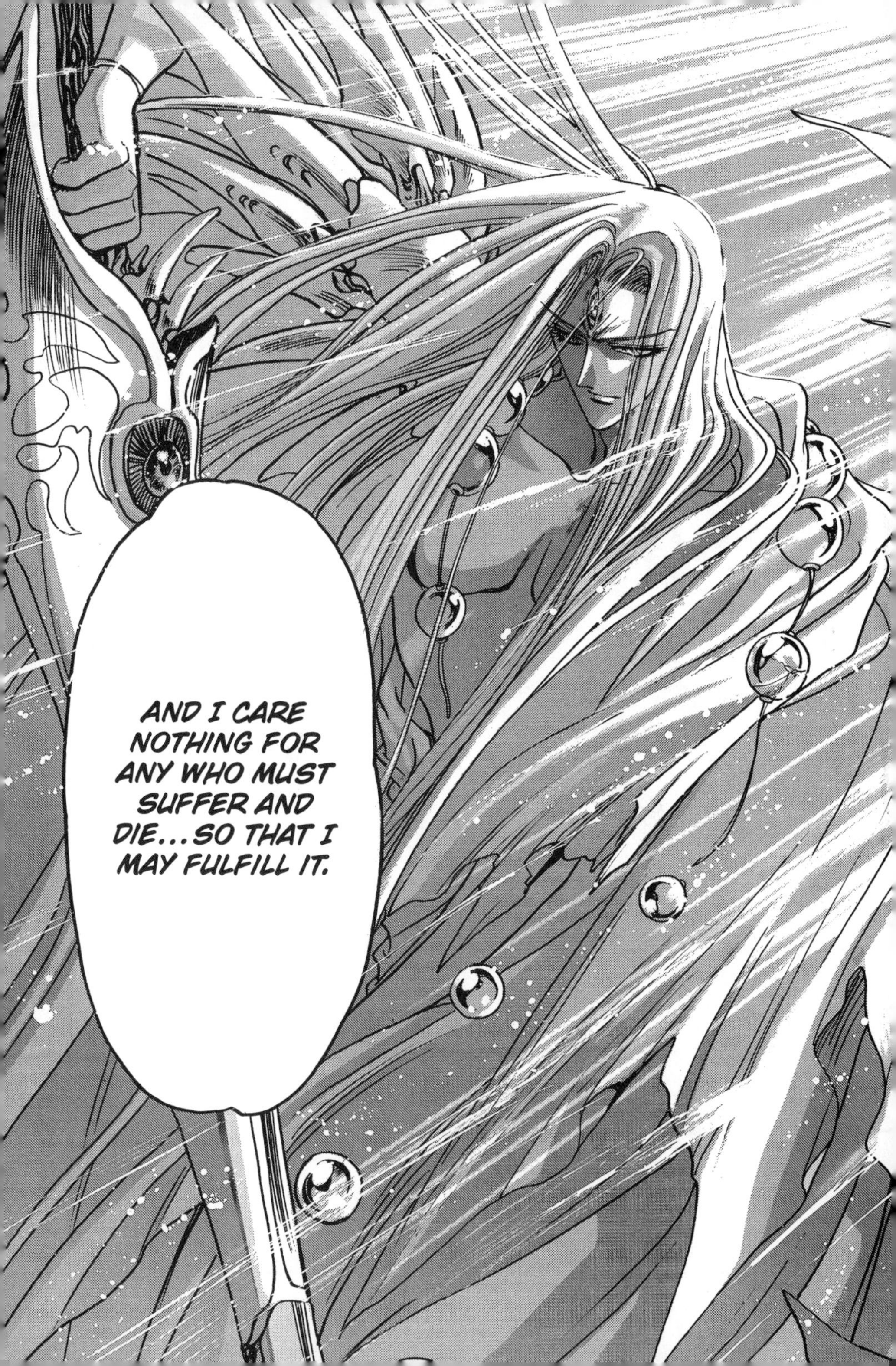
AND I CARE NOTHING FOR ANY WHO MUST SUFFER AND DIE...SO THAT I MAY FULFILL IT.

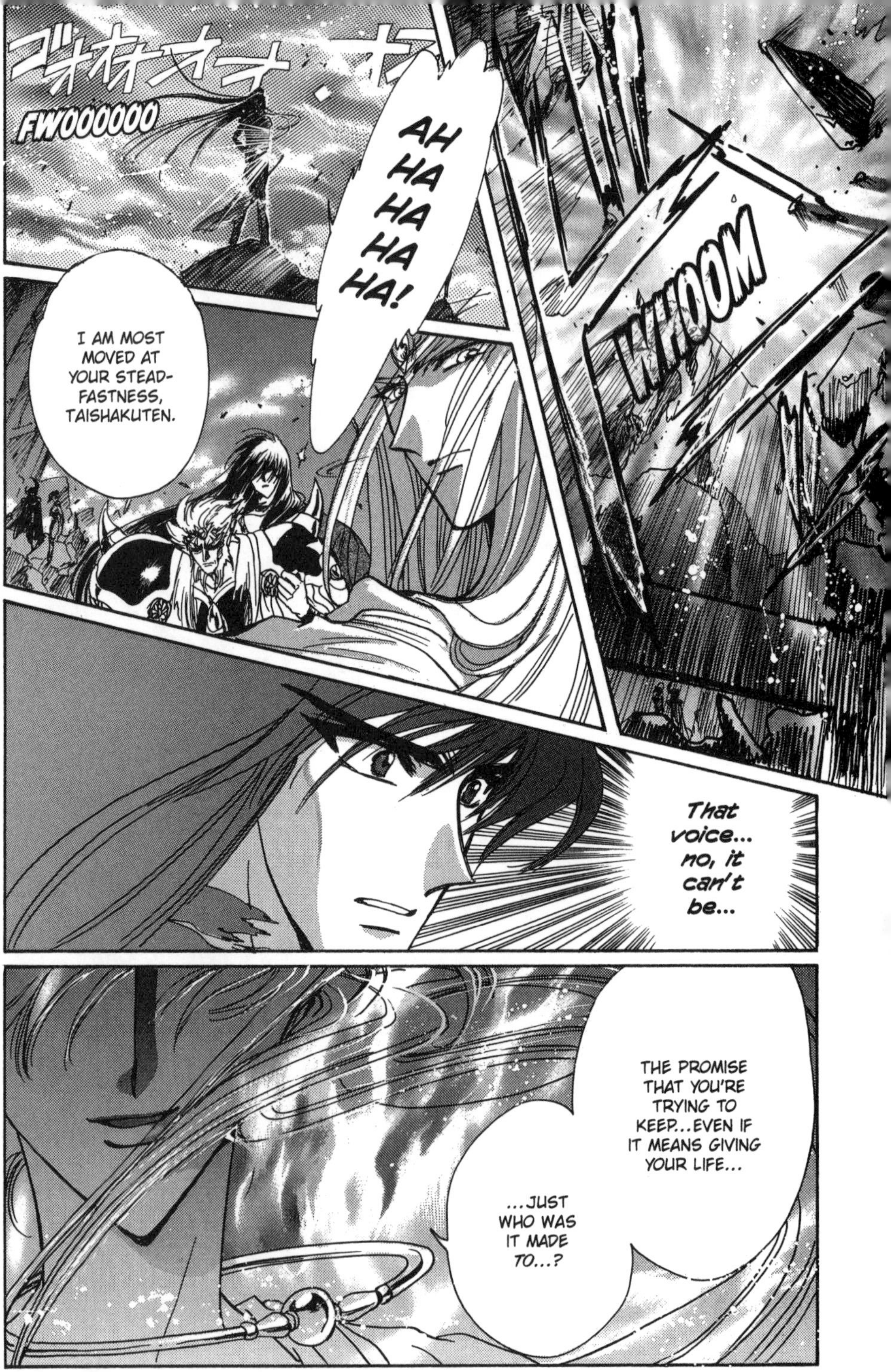
WHOOM
ゴオオオオオ…オオ
FWOOOOOO
AH HA HA HA HA HA!
I AM MOST MOVED AT YOUR STEAD-FASTNESS, TAISHAKUTEN.
That voice... no, it can't be...
THE PROMISE THAT YOU'RE TRYING TO KEEP...EVEN IF IT MEANS GIVING YOUR LIFE...
...JUST WHO WAS IT MADE TO...?

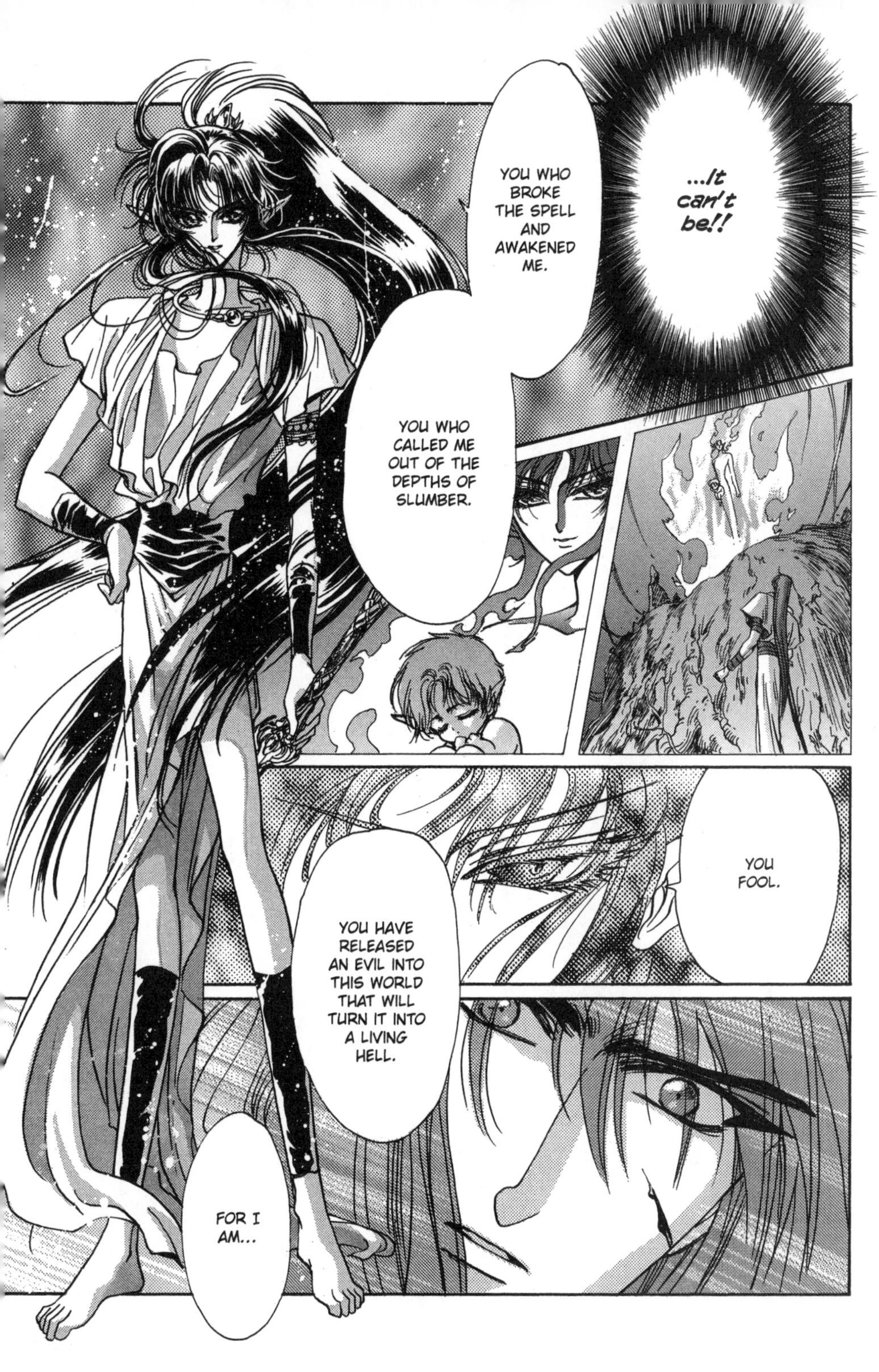
...It can't be!!
YOU WHO BROKE THE SPELL AND AWAKENED ME.
YOU WHO CALLED ME OUT OF THE DEPTHS OF SLUMBER.
YOU FOOL.
YOU HAVE RELEASED AN EVIL INTO THIS WORLD THAT WILL TURN IT INTO A LIVING HELL.
FOR I AM...

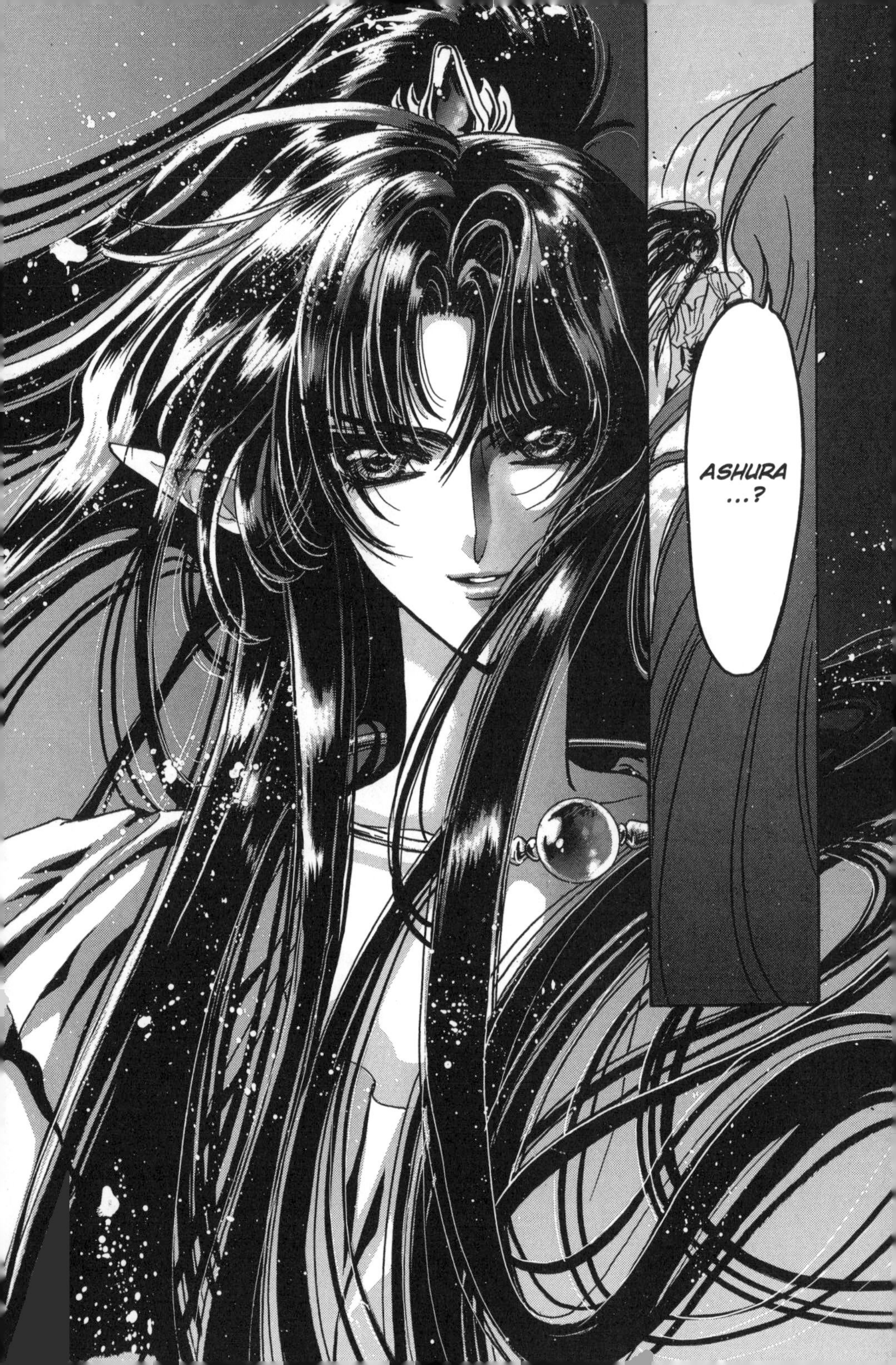
ASHURA ...?

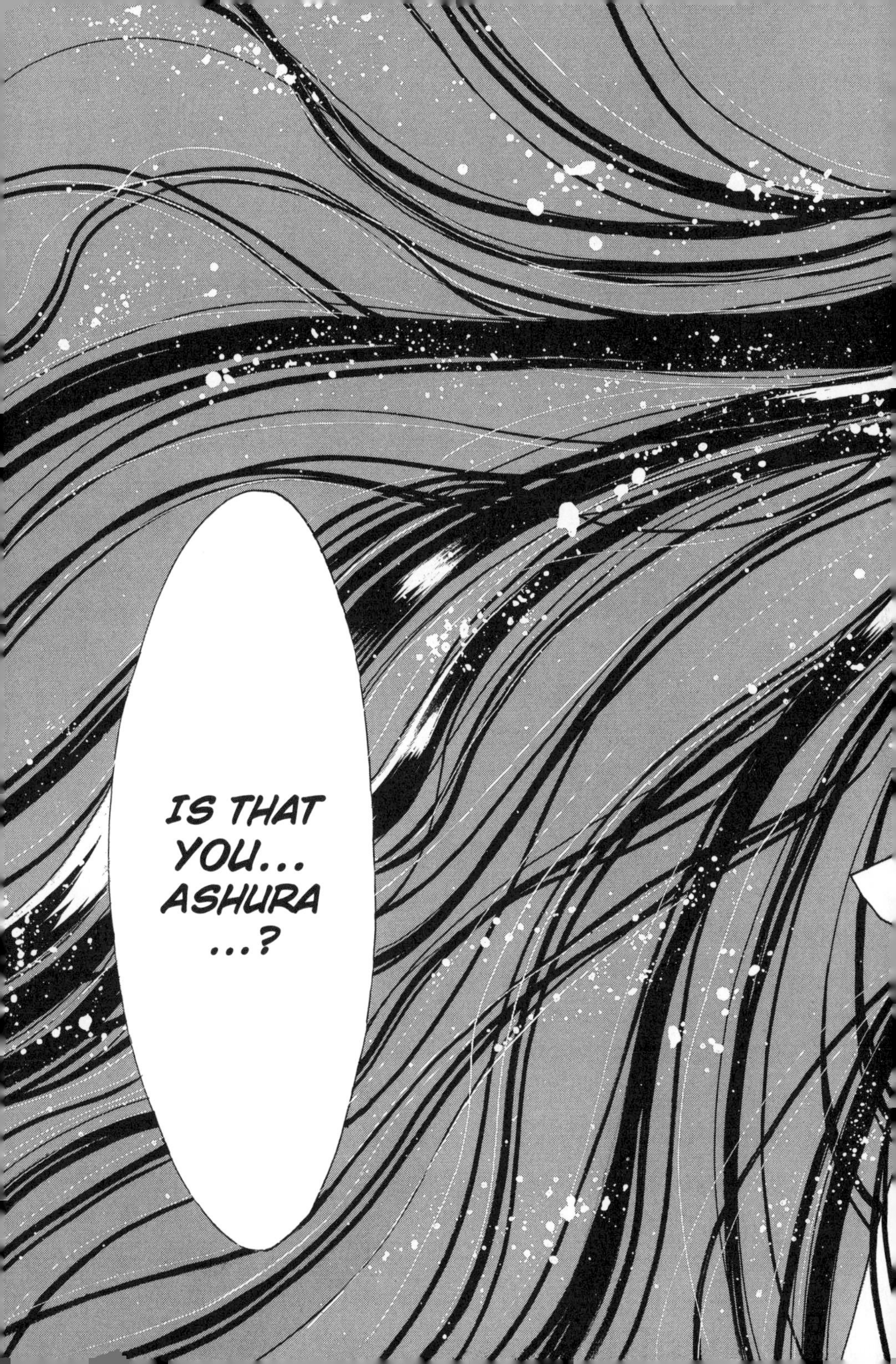
IS THAT YOU... ASHURA ...?

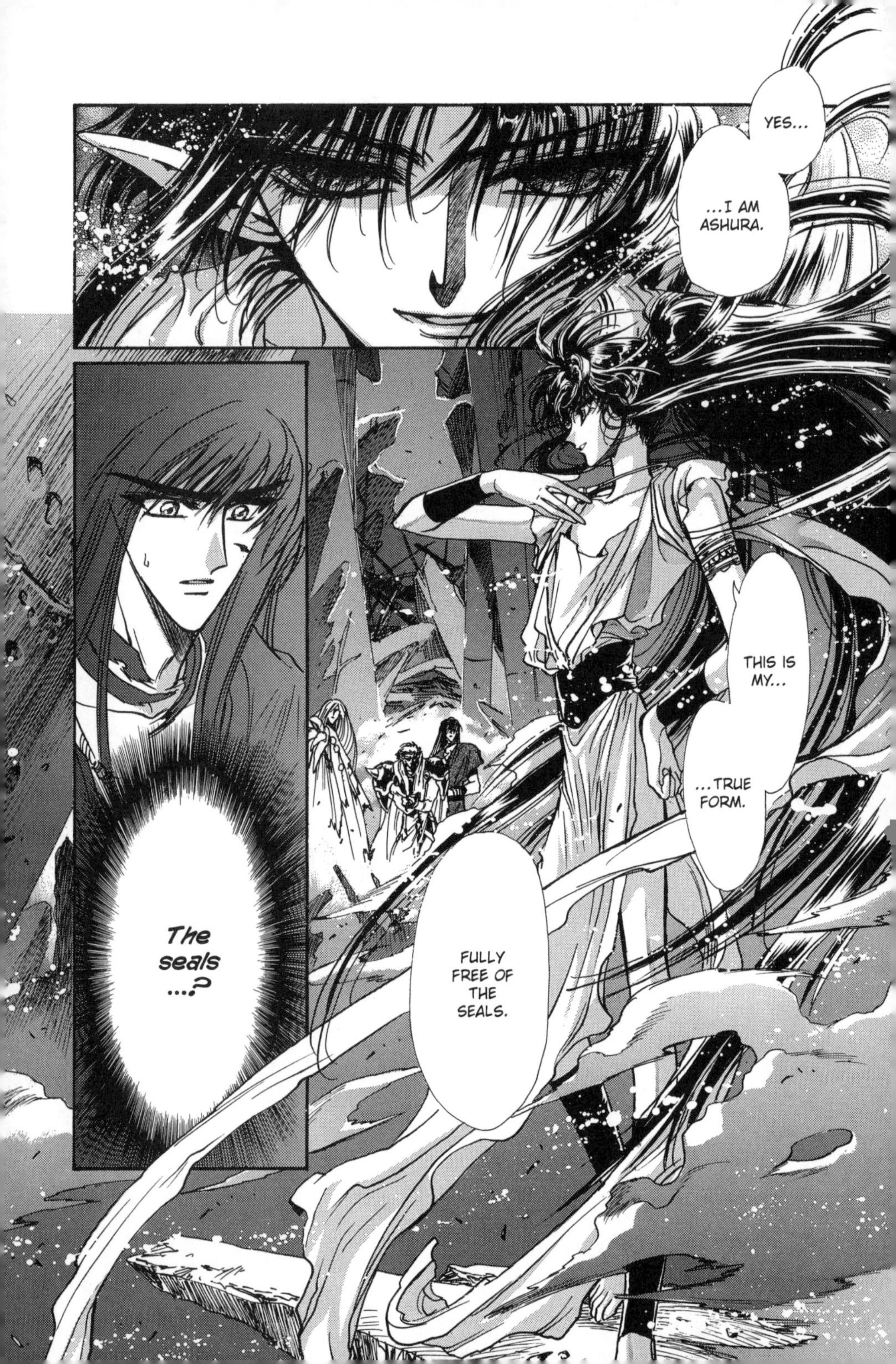
YES...
...I AM ASHURA.
THIS IS MY...
...TRUE FORM.
FULLY FREE OF THE SEALS.
The seals ...?

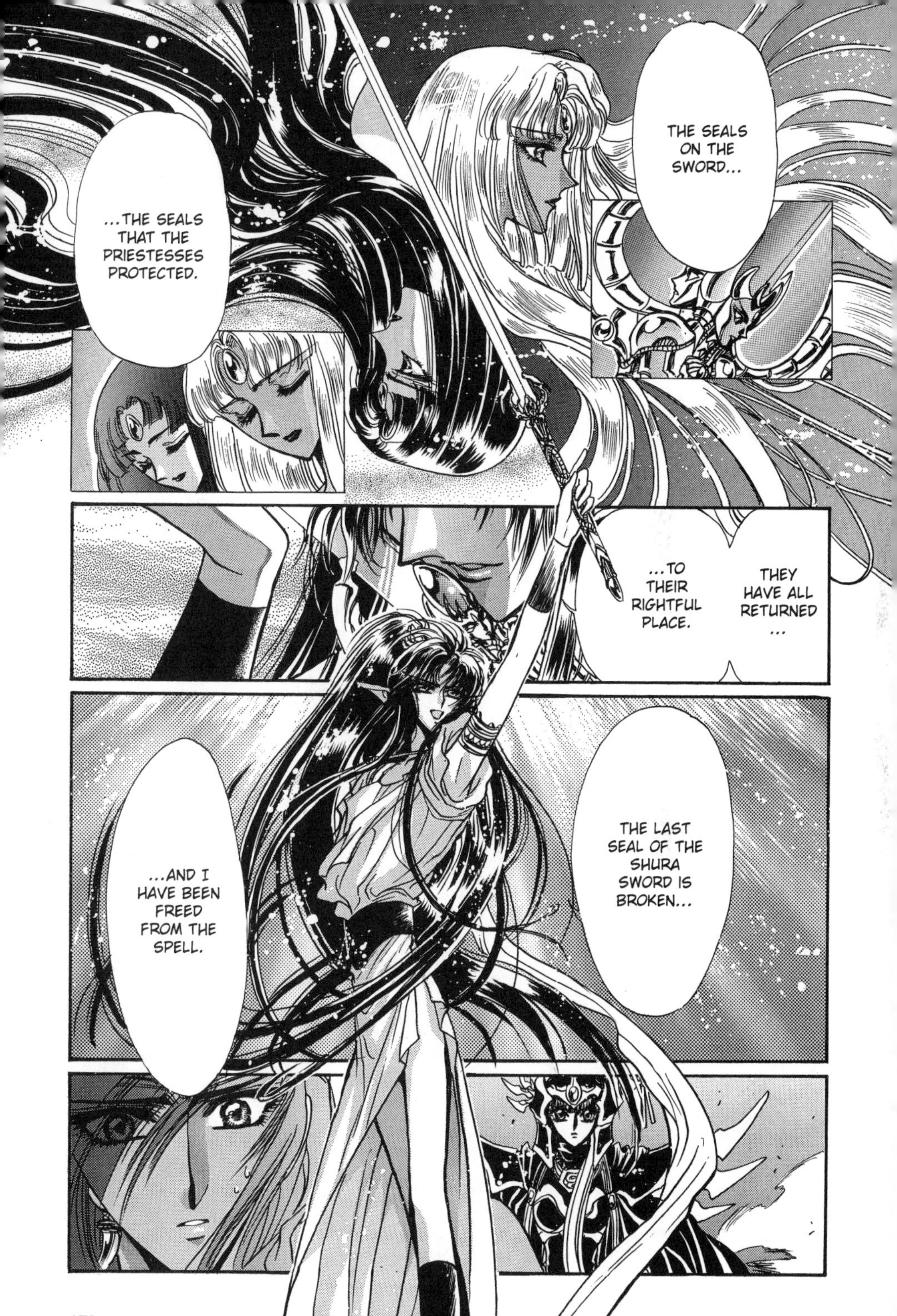
THE SEALS ON THE SWORD...
...THE SEALS THAT THE PRIESTESSES PROTECTED.
THEY HAVE ALL RETURNED...
...TO THEIR RIGHTFUL PLACE.
THE LAST SEAL OF THE SHURA SWORD IS BROKEN...
...AND I HAVE BEEN FREED FROM THE SPELL.

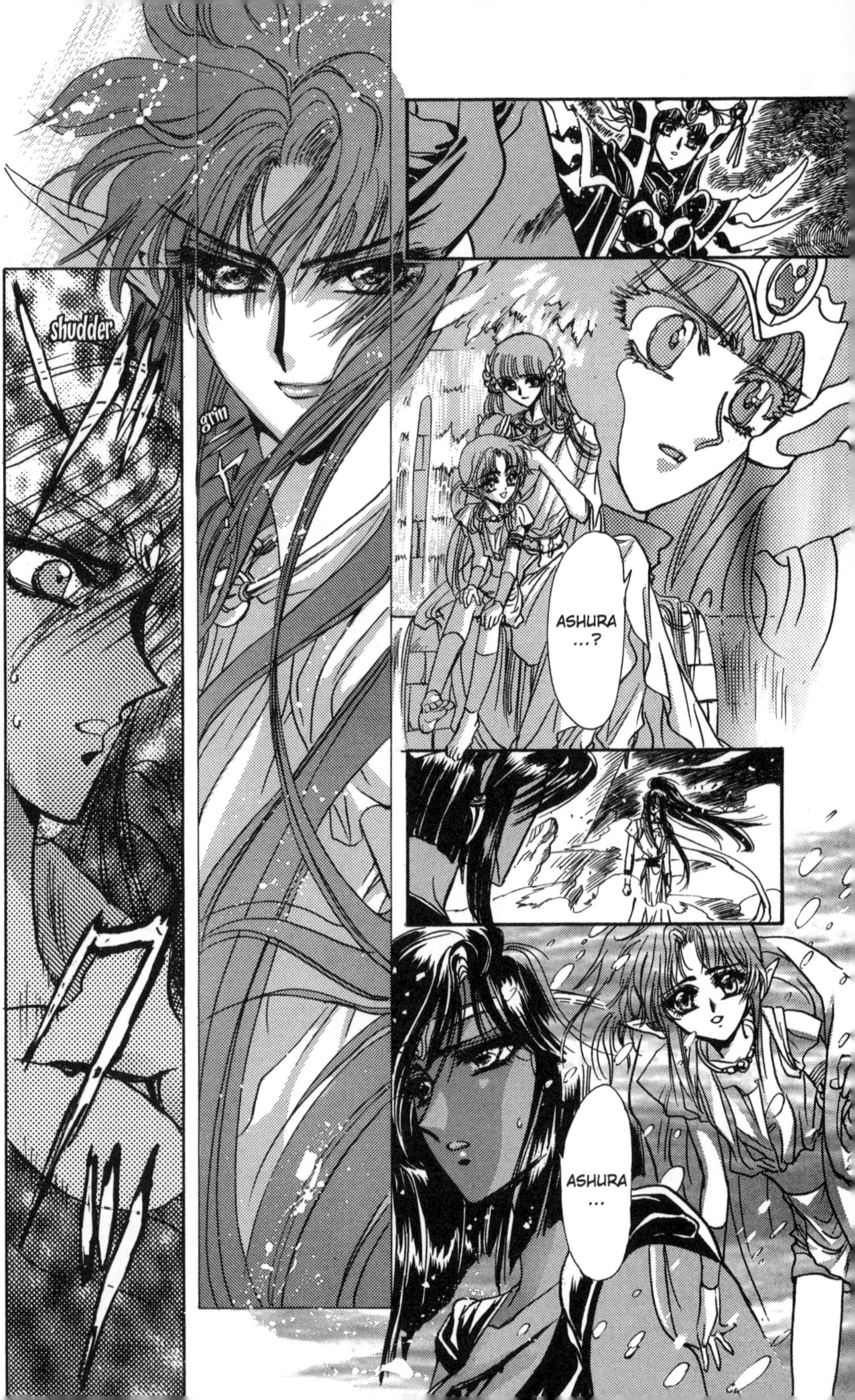
ASHURA …?
ASHURA …
grin
shudder

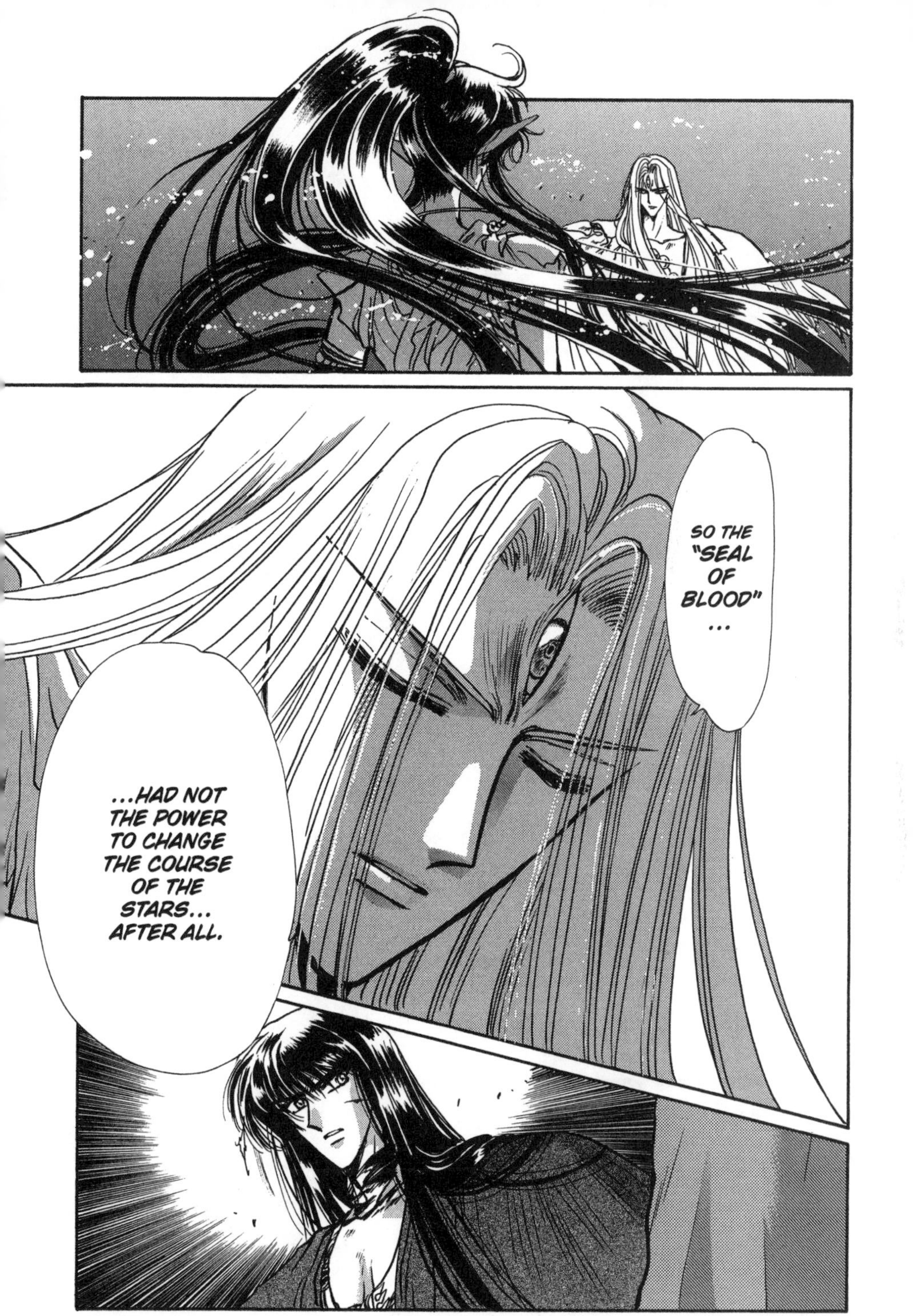
SO THE "SEAL OF BLOOD" ...
...HAD NOT THE POWER TO CHANGE THE COURSE OF THE STARS... AFTER ALL.

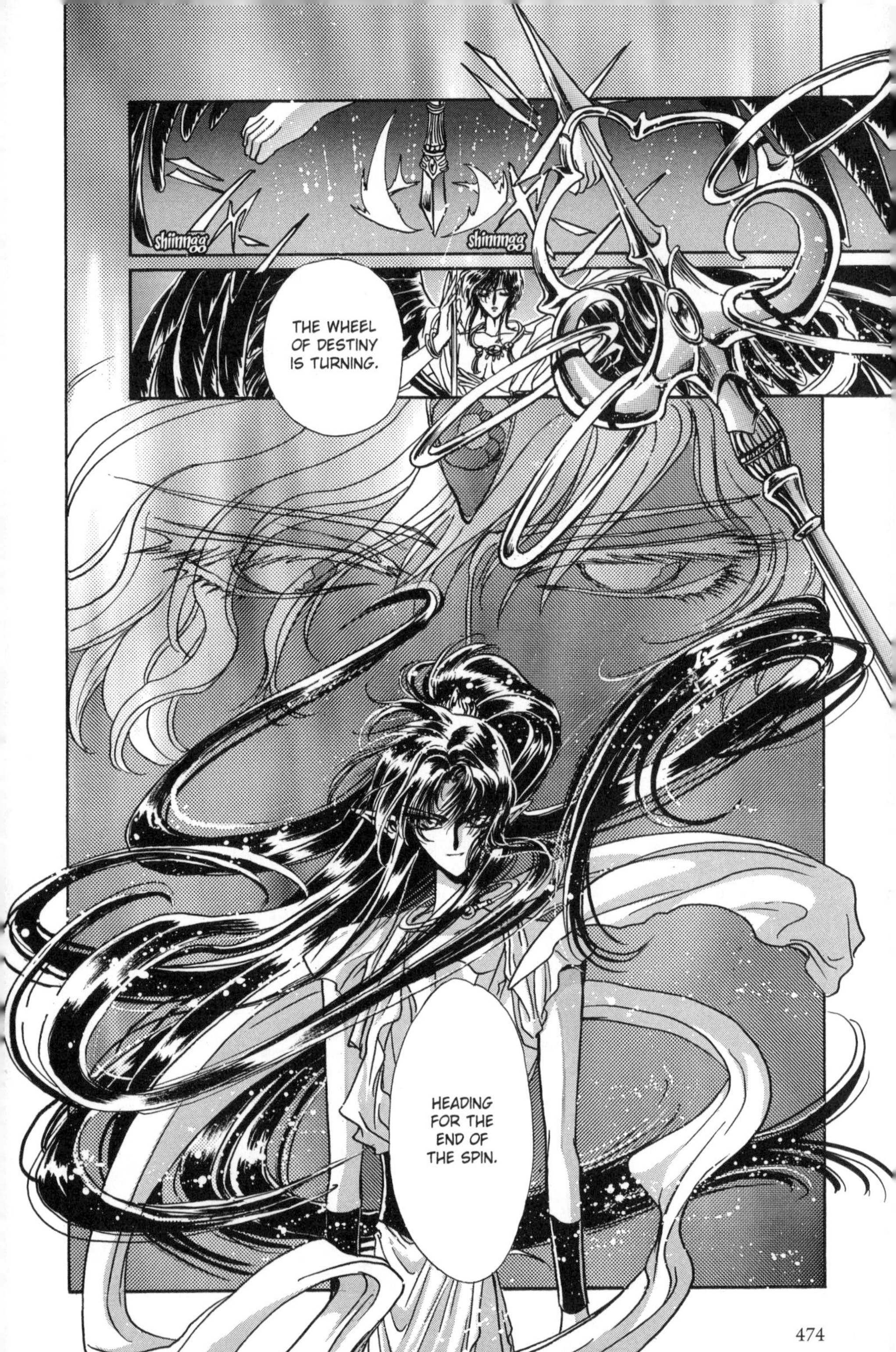
shinnngg
shiinngg
THE WHEEL OF DESTINY IS TURNING.
HEADING FOR THE END OF THE SPIN.

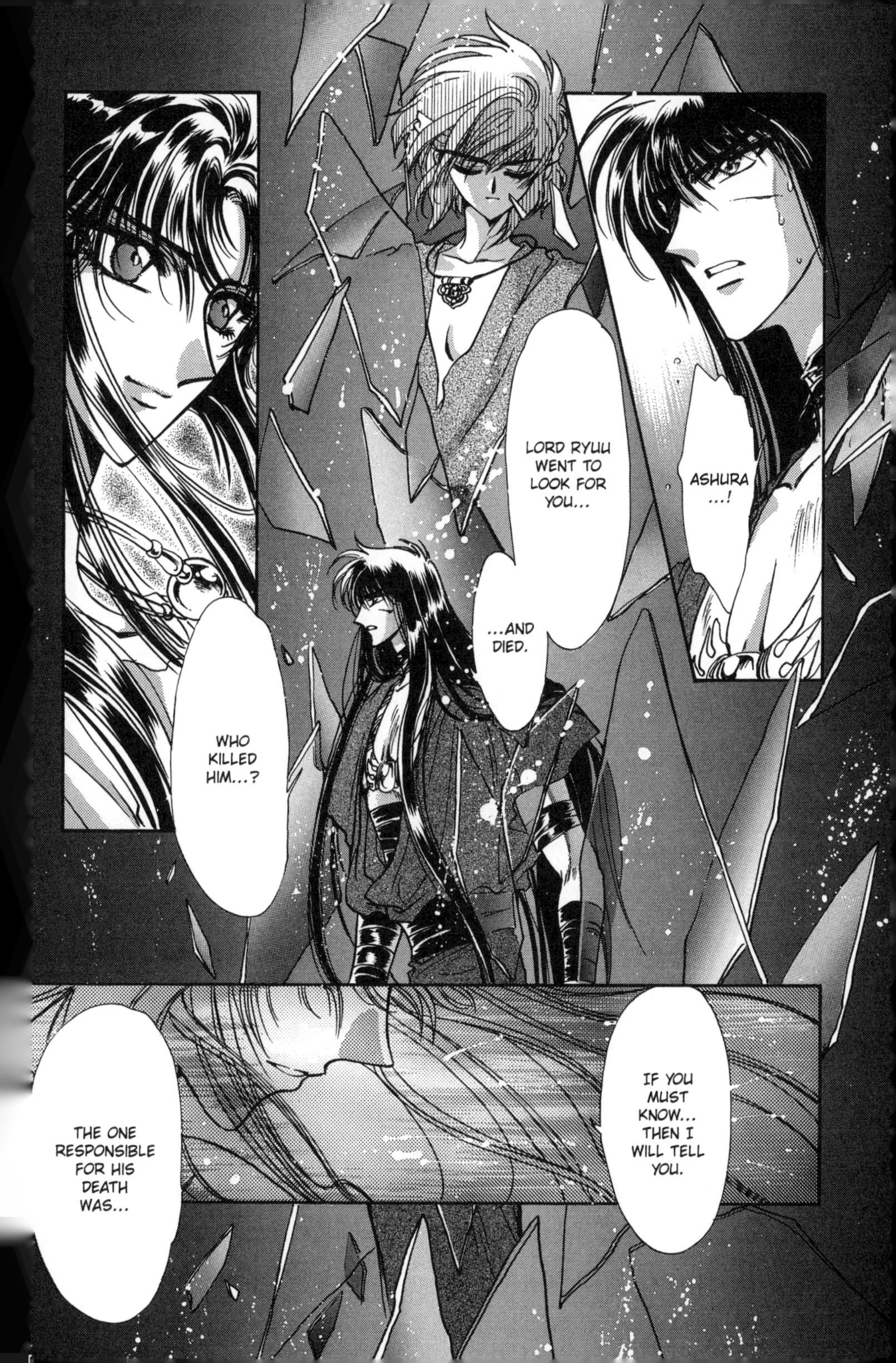
ASHURA...!
LORD RYUU WENT TO LOOK FOR YOU...
...AND DIED.
WHO KILLED HIM...?
IF YOU MUST KNOW...
THEN I WILL TELL YOU.
THE ONE RESPONSIBLE FOR HIS DEATH WAS...

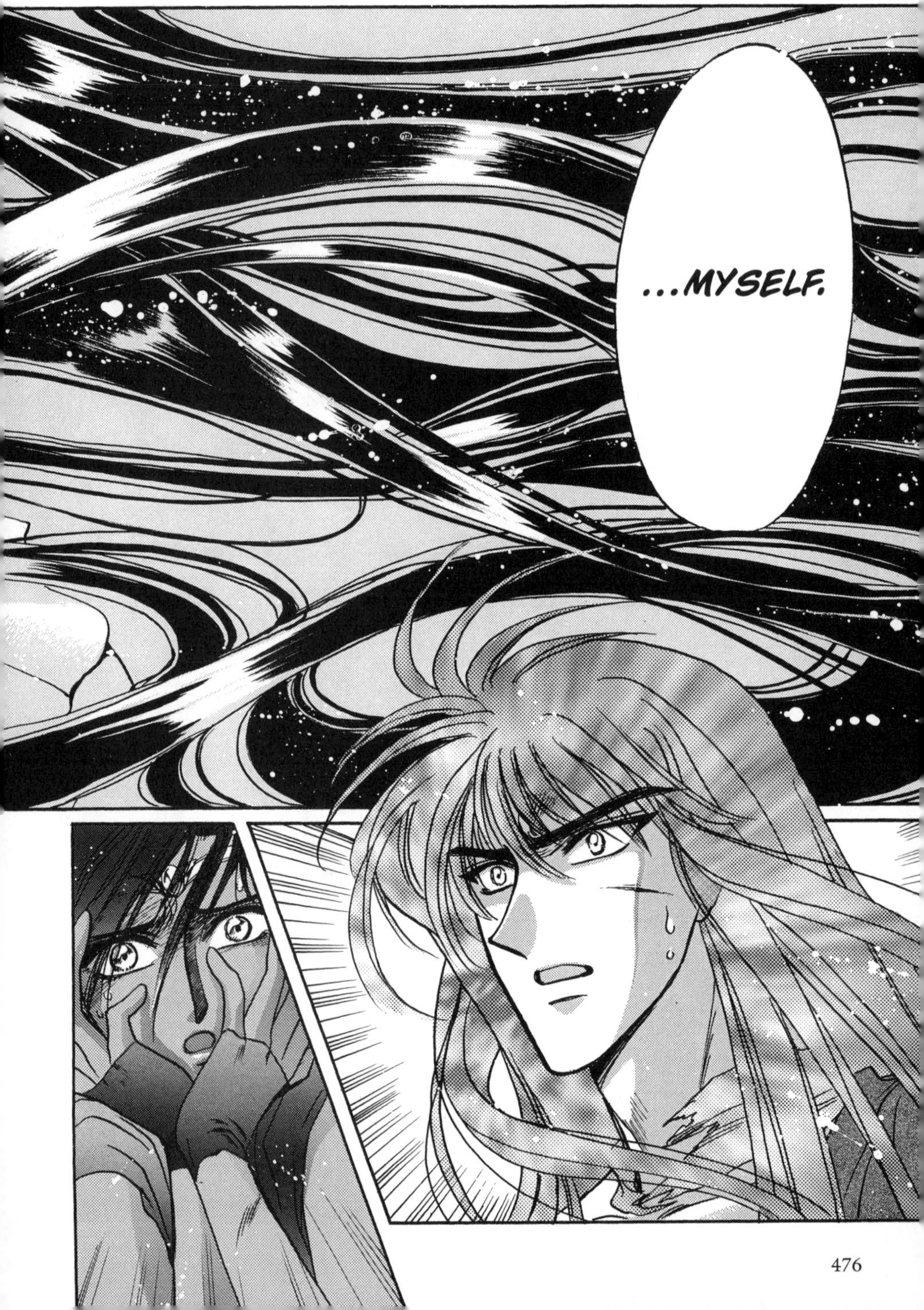
...MYSELF.

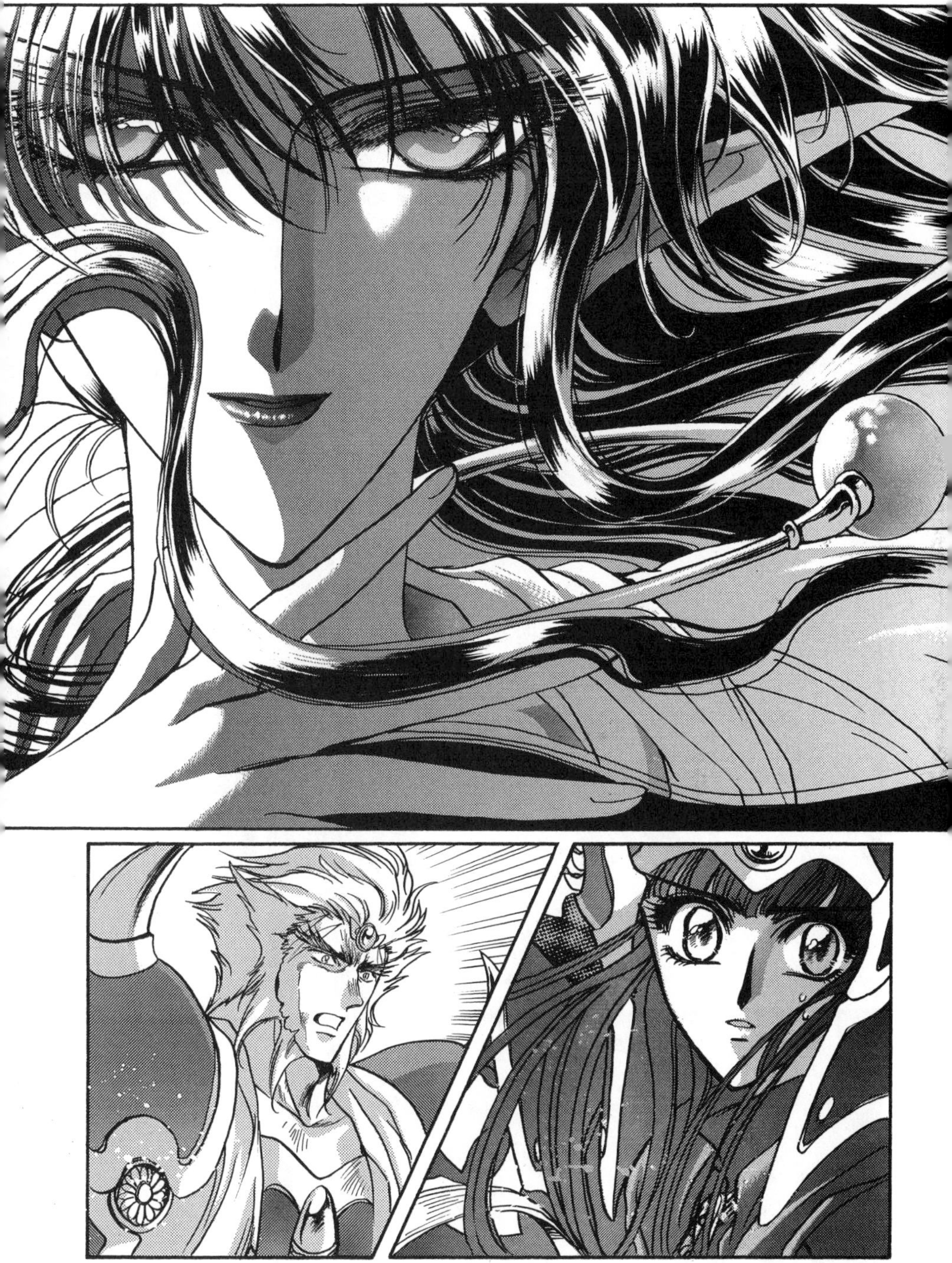

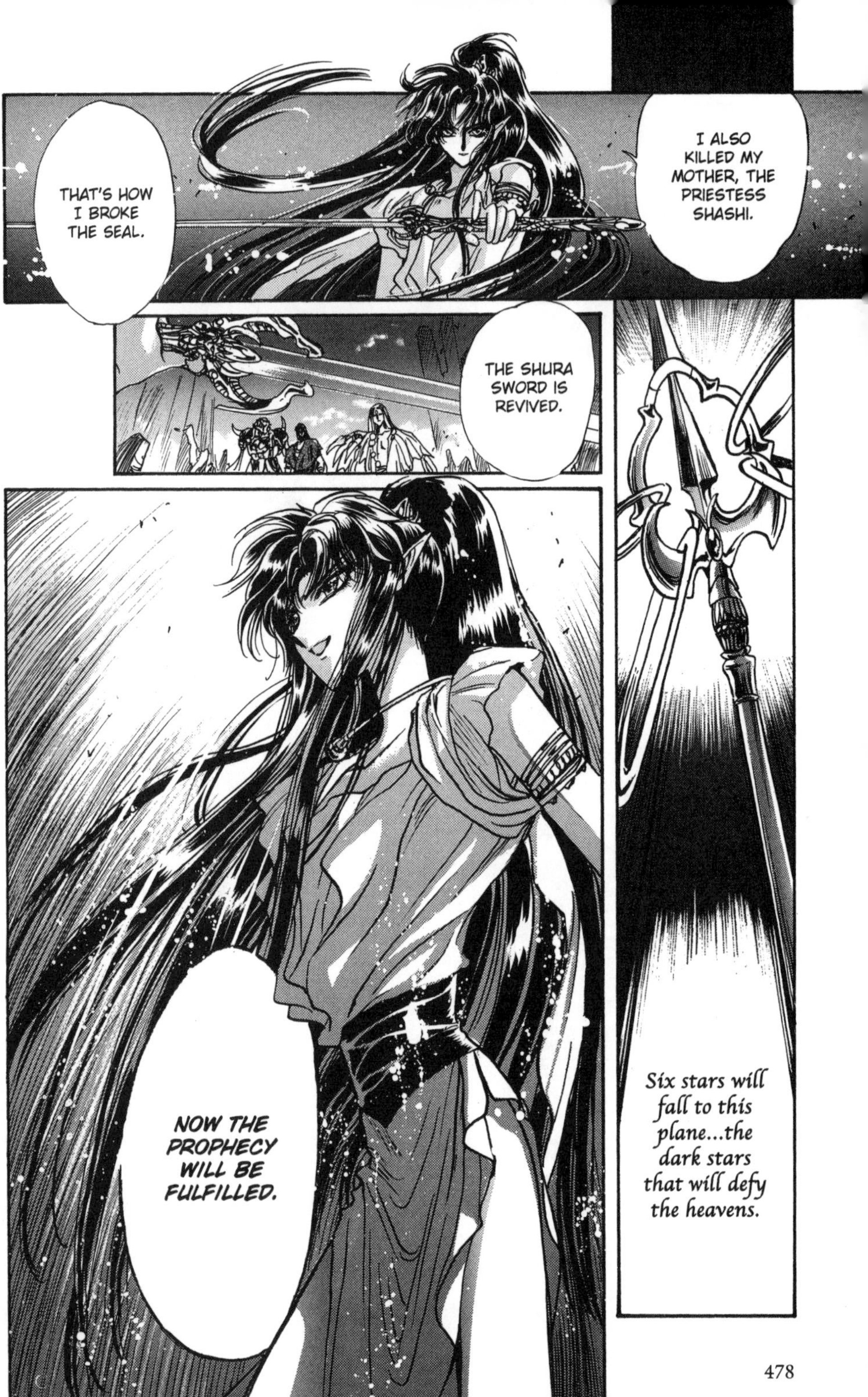
I ALSO KILLED MY MOTHER, THE PRIESTESS SHASHI.
THAT'S HOW I BROKE THE SEAL.
Six stars will fall to this plane...the dark stars that will defy the heavens.
THE SHURA SWORD IS REVIVED.
NOW THE PROPHECY WILL BE FULFILLED.

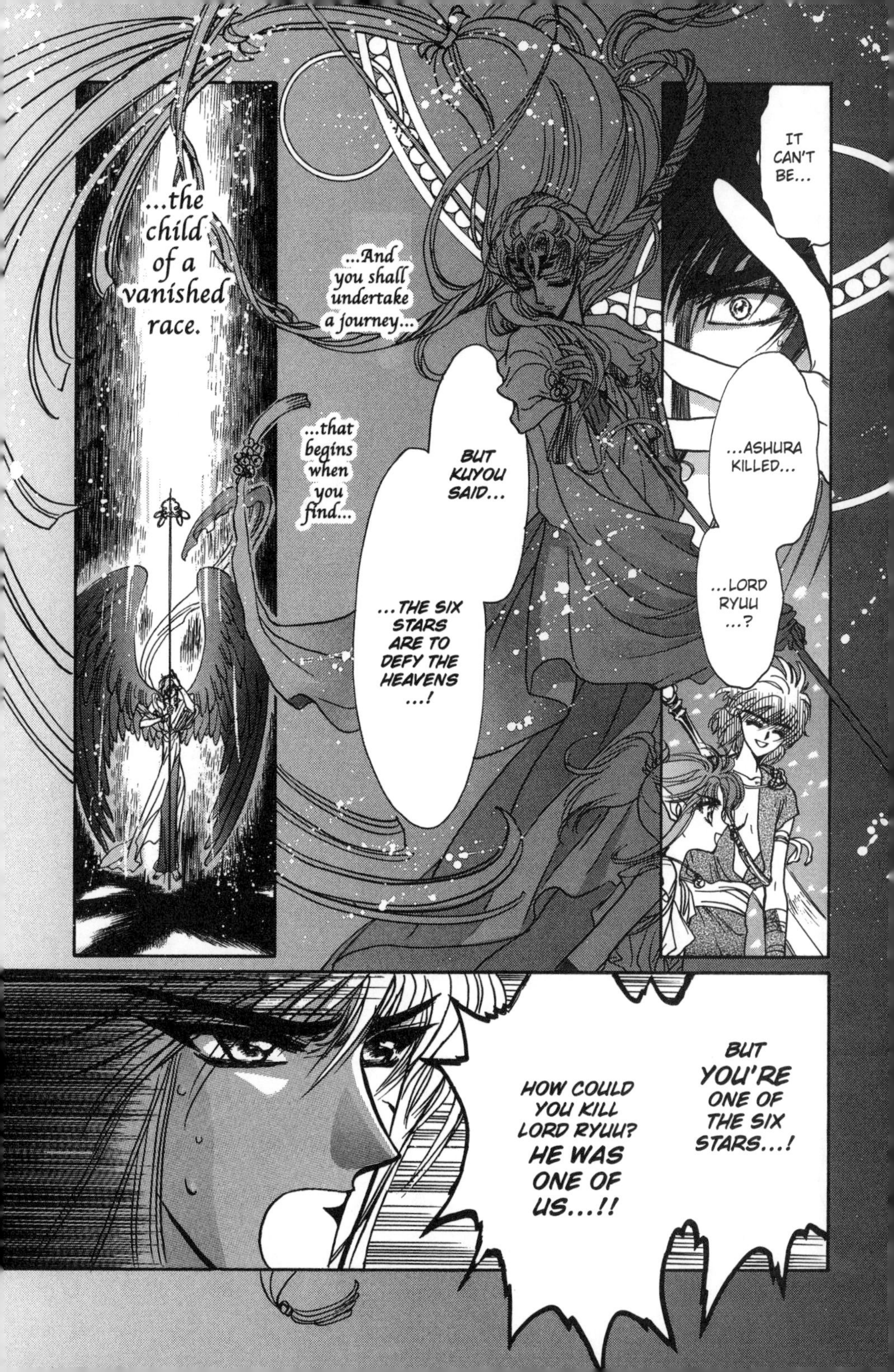
IT CAN'T BE...
...ASHURA KILLED...
...LORD RYUU ...?
...And you shall undertake a journey...
BUT KUYOU SAID...
...THE SIX STARS ARE TO DEFY THE HEAVENS ...!
...that begins when you find...
...the child of a vanished race.
BUT YOU'RE ONE OF THE SIX STARS...!
HOW COULD YOU KILL LORD RYUU? HE WAS ONE OF US...!!

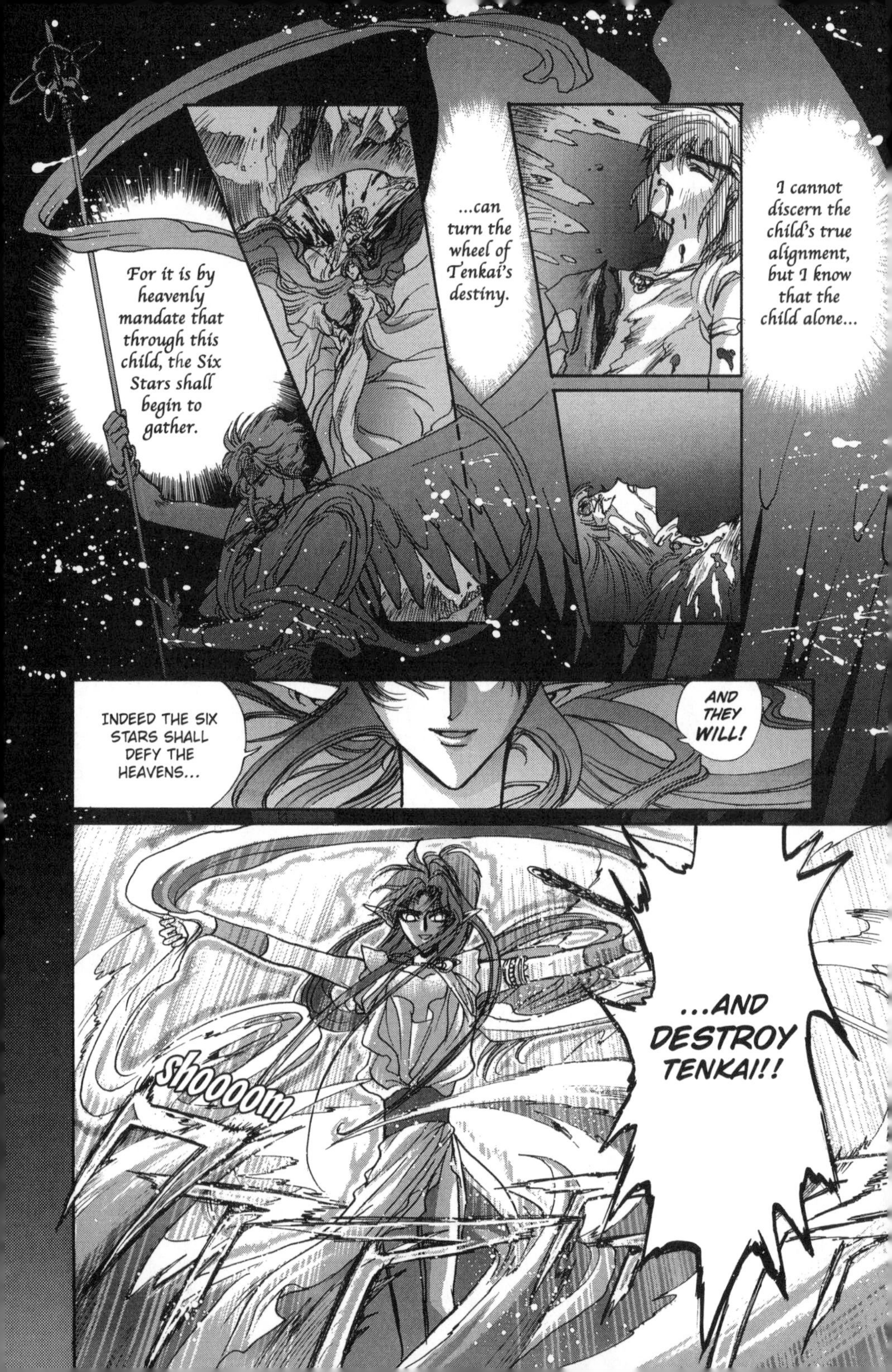
I cannot discern the child's true alignment, but I know that the child alone...
...can turn the wheel of Tenkai's destiny.
For it is by heavenly mandate that through this child, the Six Stars shall begin to gather.
INDEED THE SIX STARS SHALL DEFY THE HEAVENS...
AND THEY WILL!
...AND DESTROY TENKAI!!
Shoooom

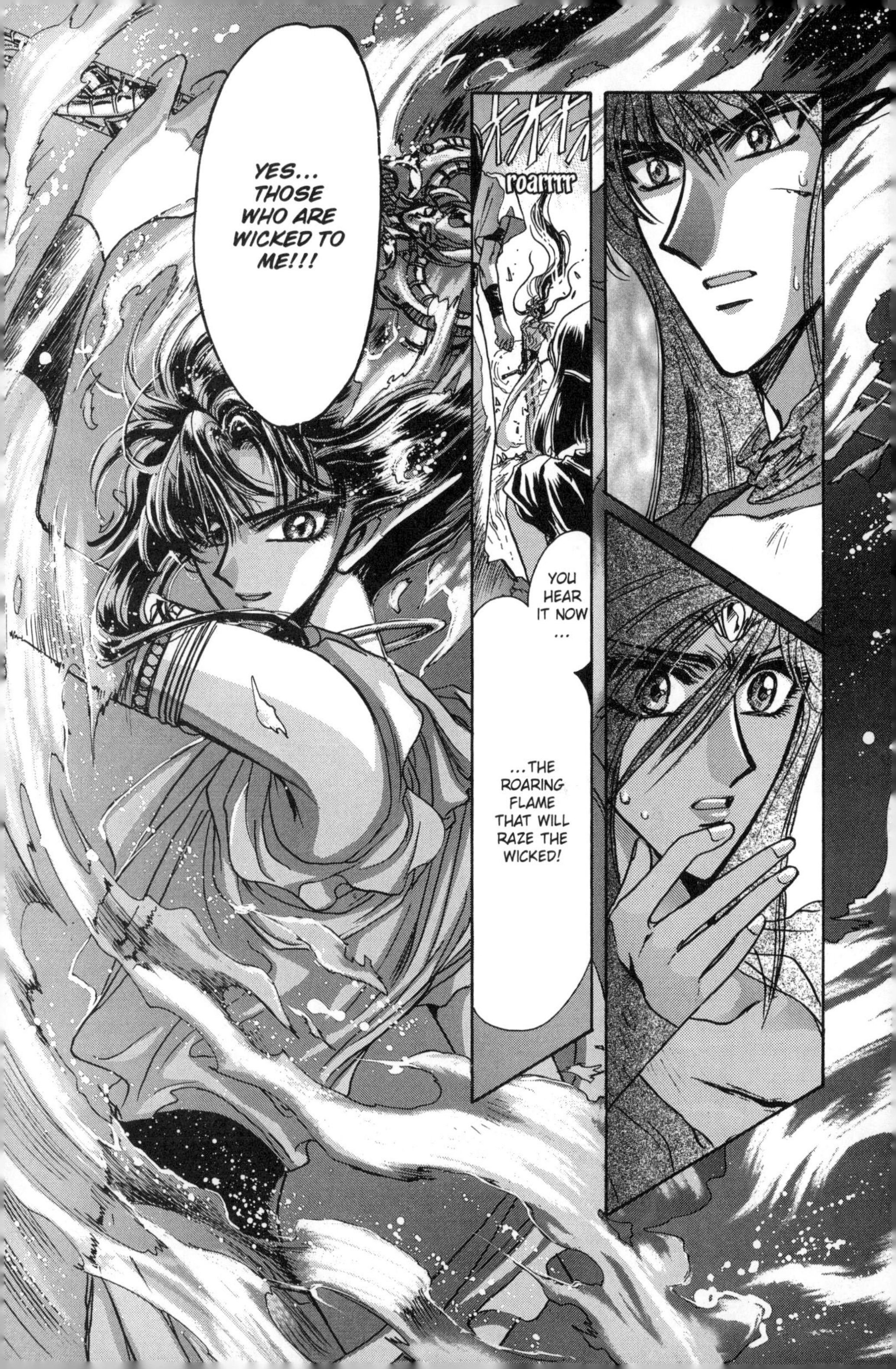
YES... THOSE WHO ARE WICKED TO ME!!!
roarrrr
YOU HEAR IT NOW ...
...THE ROARING FLAME THAT WILL RAZE THE WICKED!

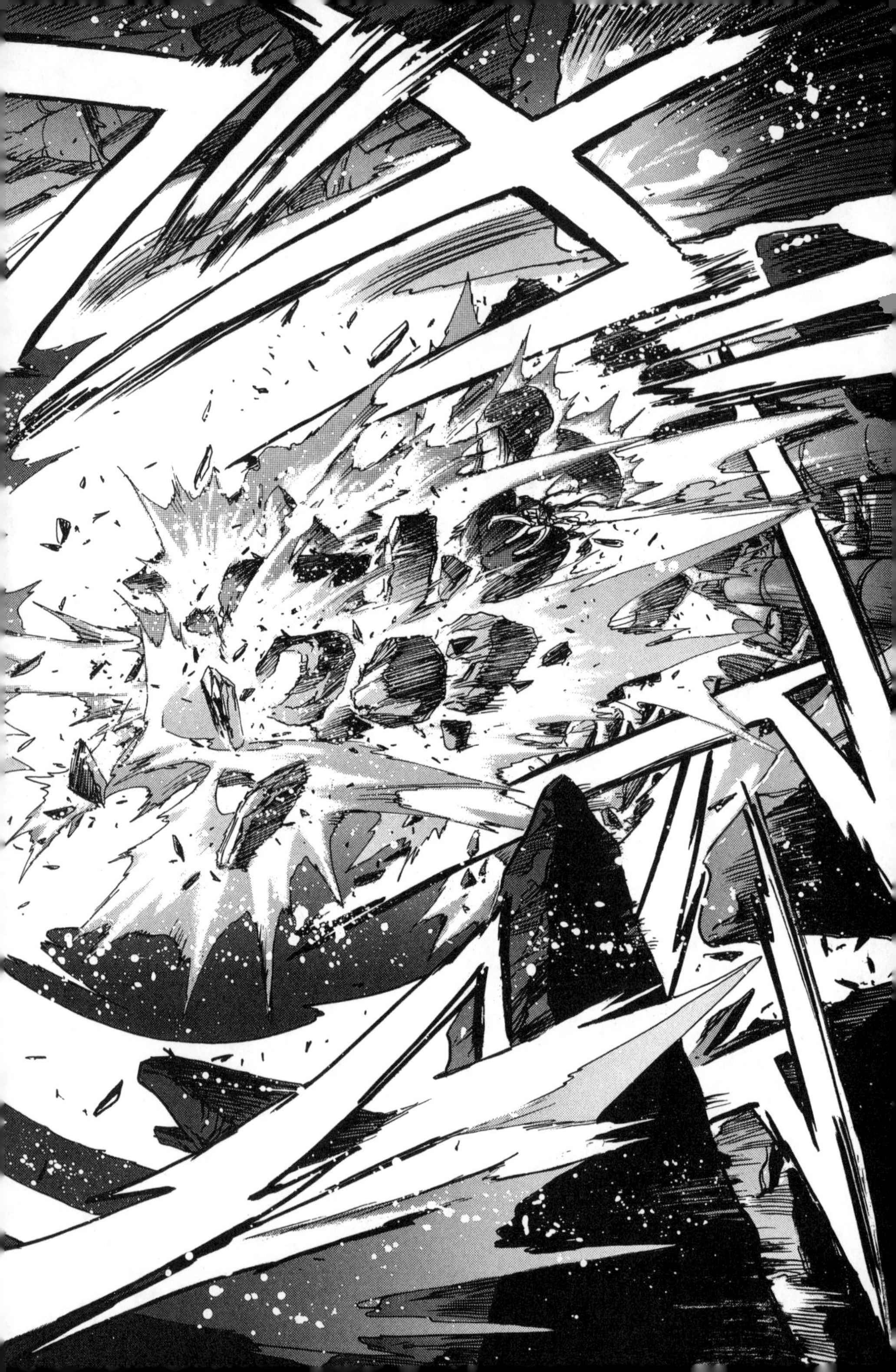

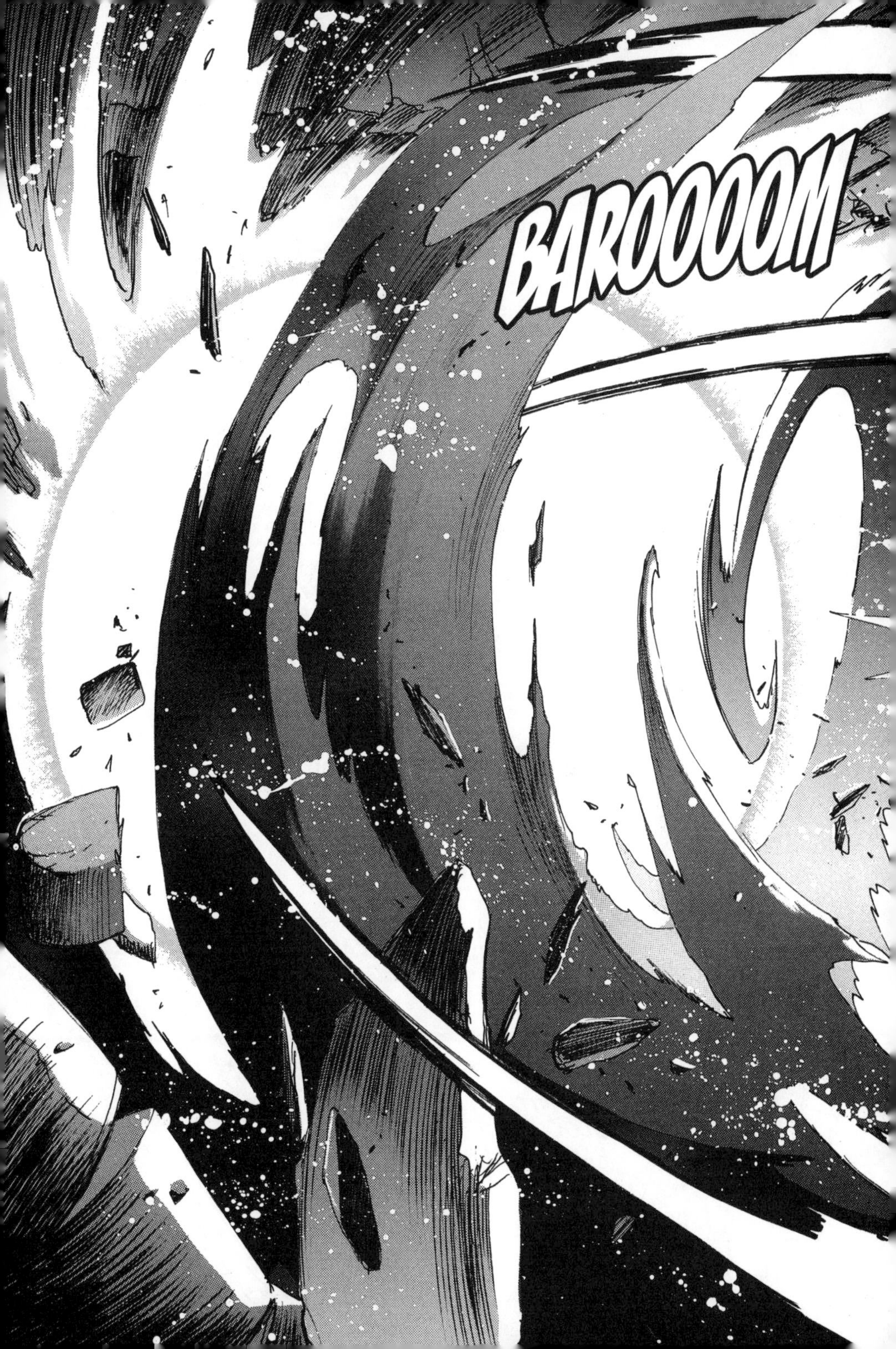
BAROOOOM

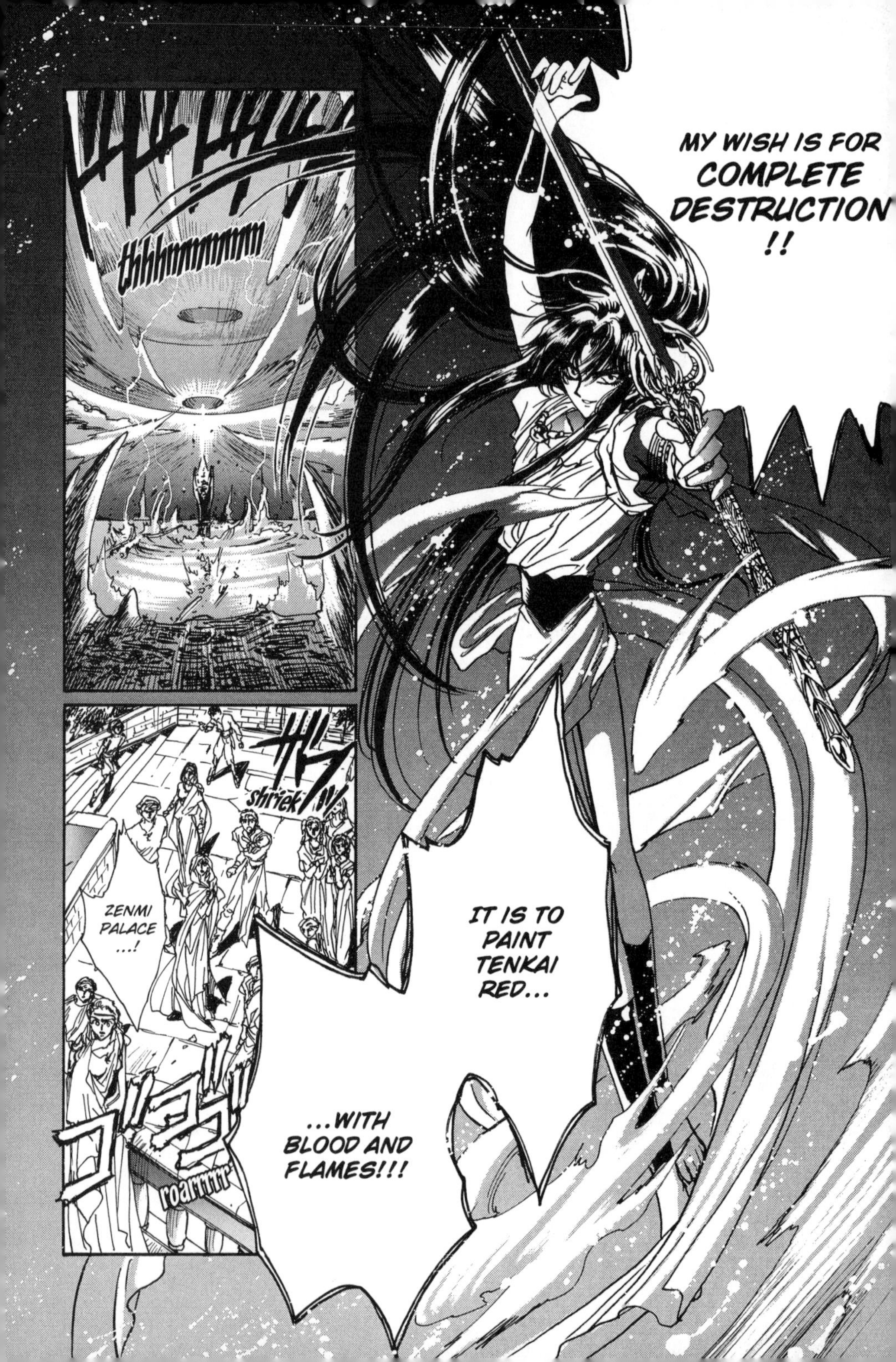
MY WISH IS FOR COMPLETE DESTRUCTION !!
IT IS TO PAINT TENKAI RED...
...WITH BLOOD AND FLAMES!!!
thhhmmmmmm
shriek
ZENMI PALACE ...!
roarrrrr

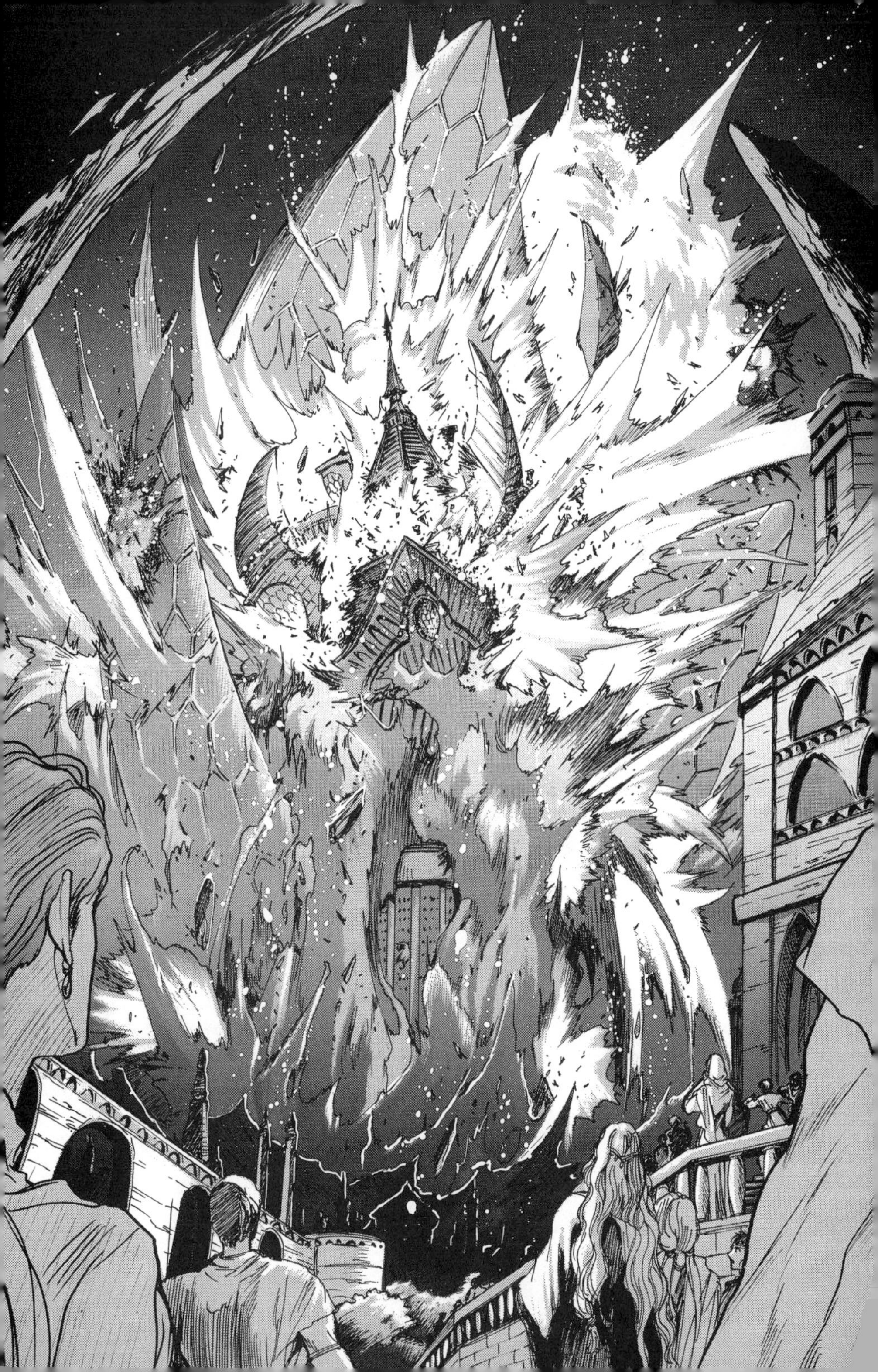

...and can turn the path of those stars, whether evil or heavenly. A roaring flame will raze the wicked. Six Stars will overpower all others...

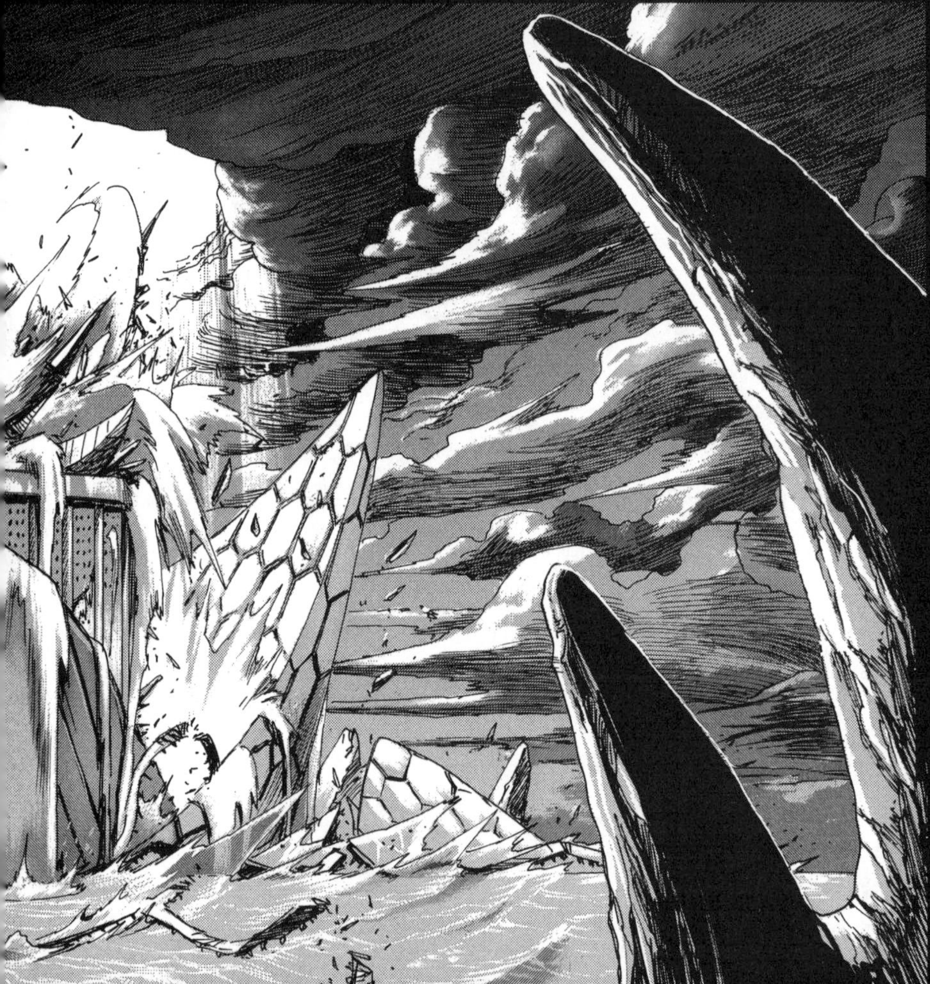

And then a figure shall appear from the shadows. Even my powers cannot clearly discern him...but he knows the future...

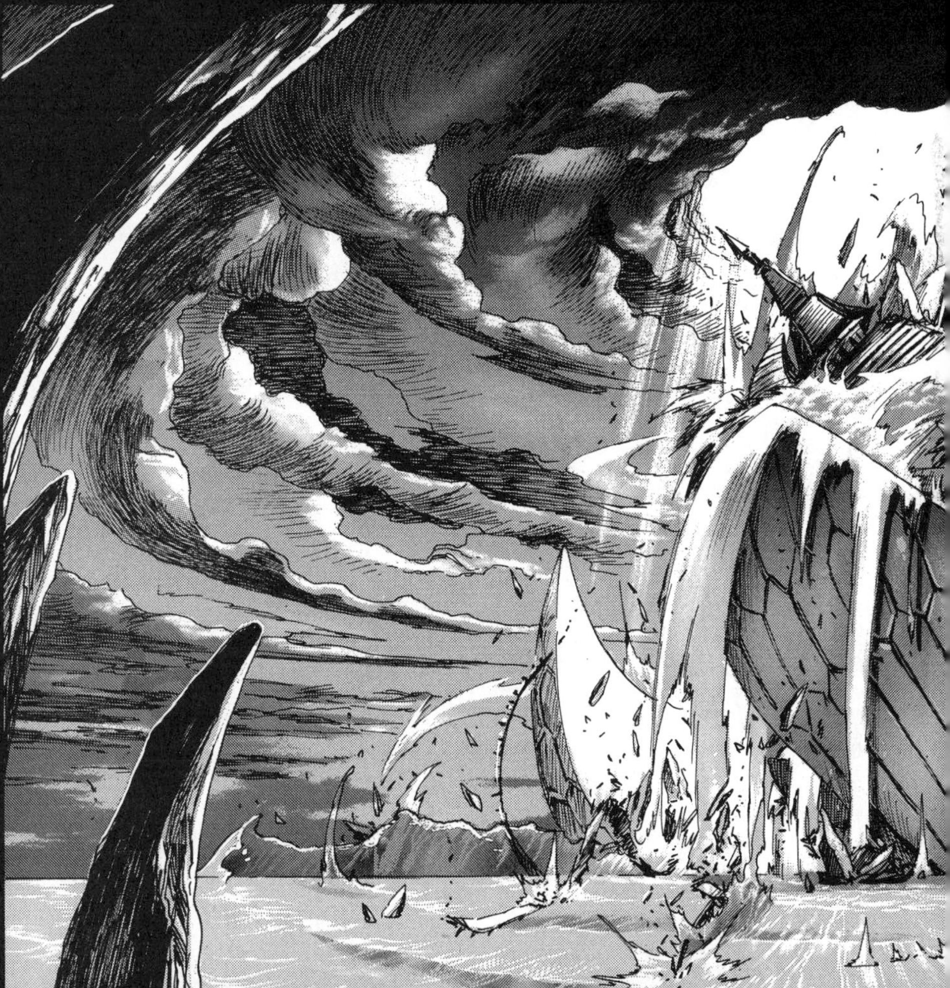

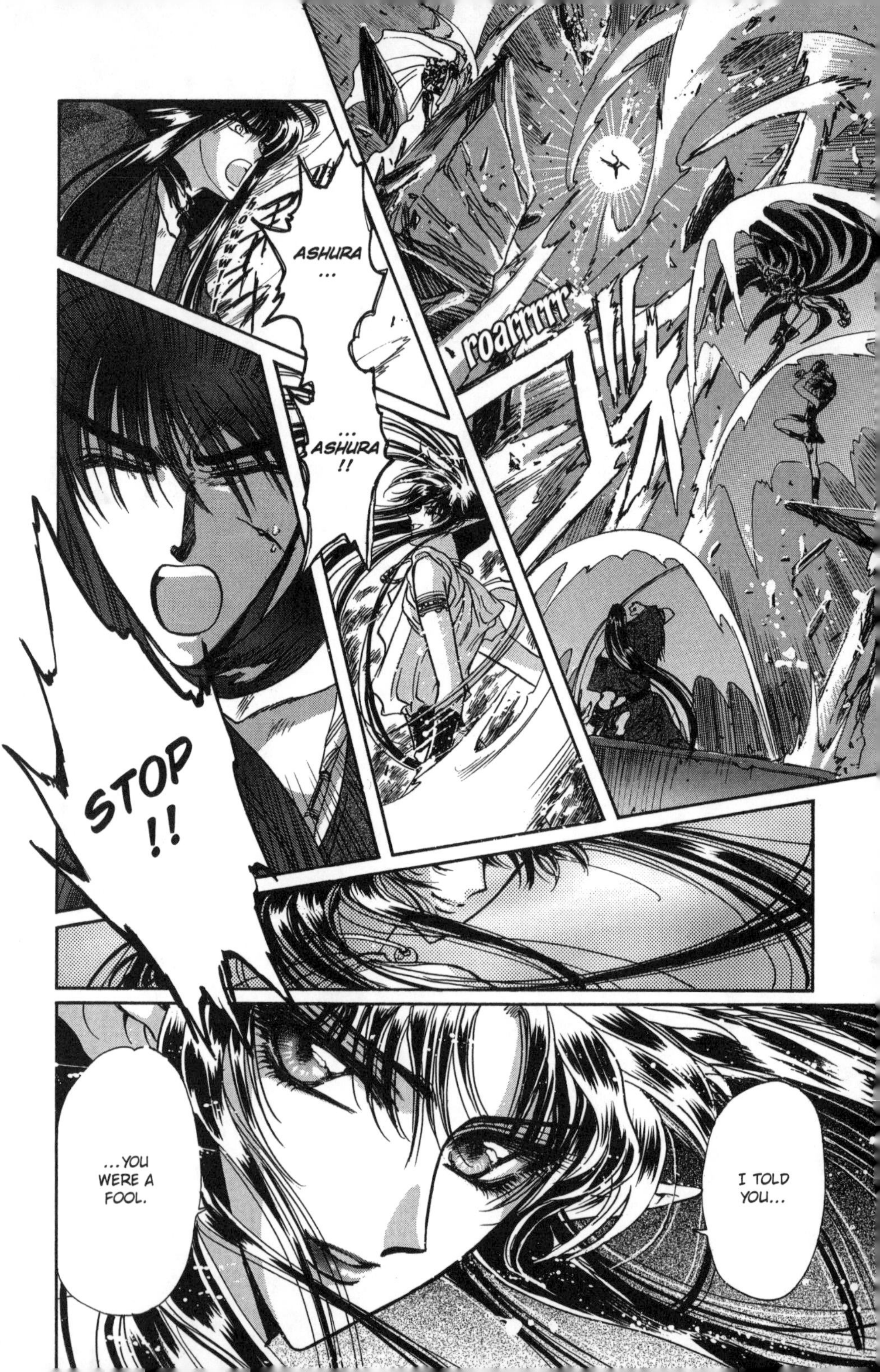
roarrrrr
ASHURA ...
... ASHURA !!
STOP !!
I TOLD YOU...
...YOU WERE A FOOL.

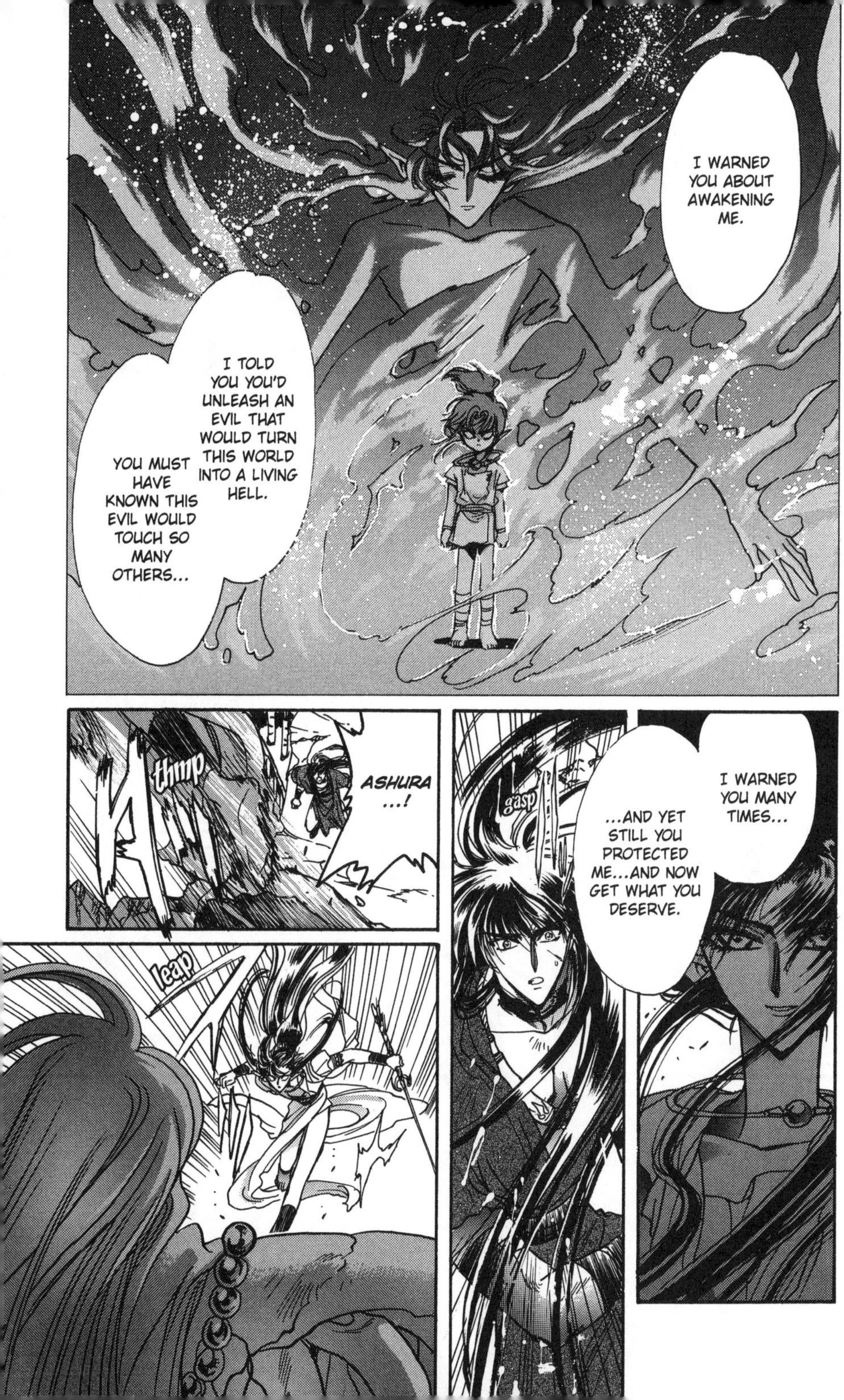
I WARNED YOU ABOUT AWAKENING ME.
I TOLD YOU YOU'D UNLEASH AN EVIL THAT WOULD TURN THIS WORLD INTO A LIVING HELL.
YOU MUST HAVE KNOWN THIS EVIL WOULD TOUCH SO MANY OTHERS...
I WARNED YOU MANY TIMES...
...AND YET STILL YOU PROTECTED ME...AND NOW GET WHAT YOU DESERVE.
gasp
thmp
ASHURA ...!
leap

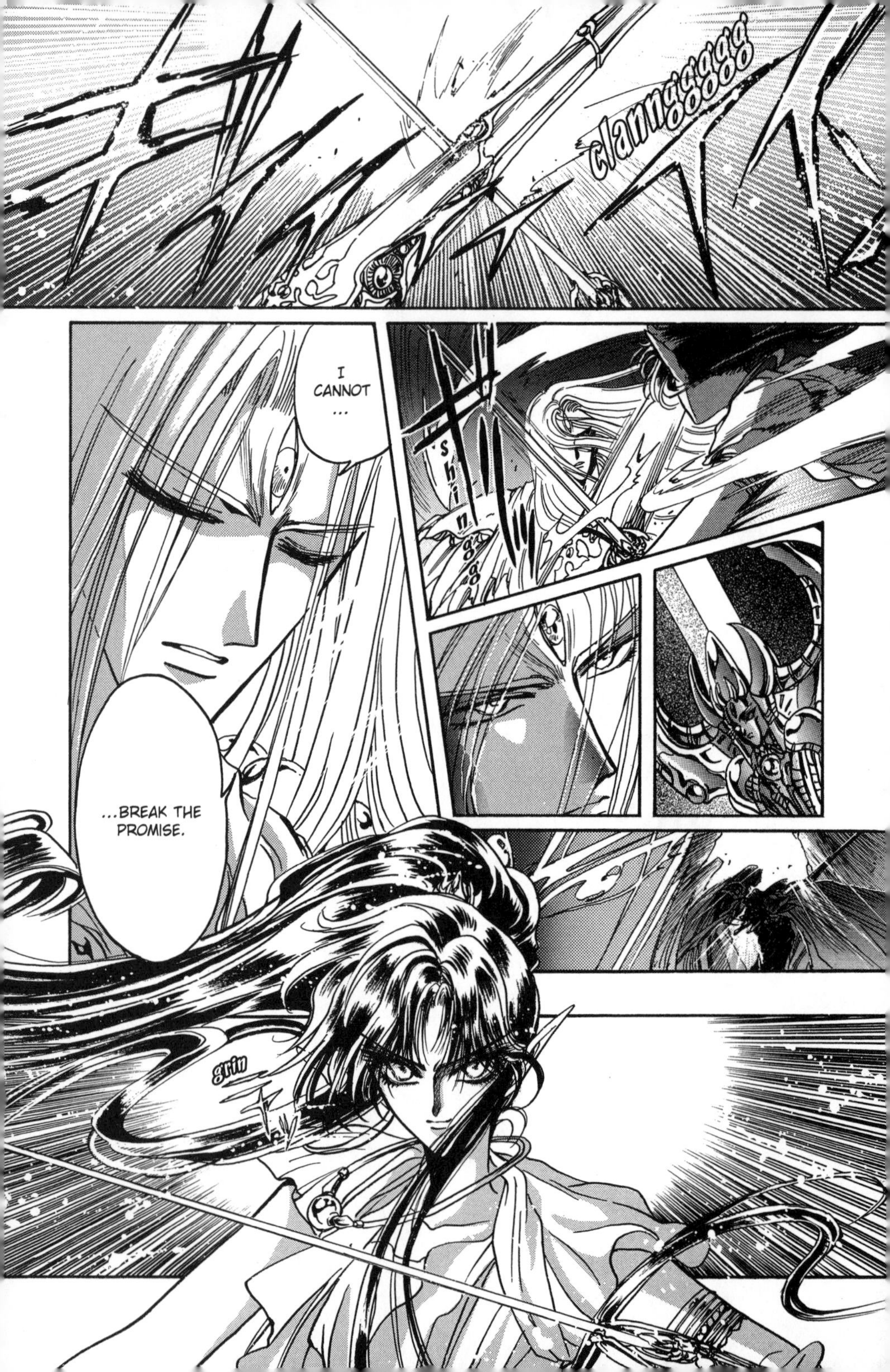
clannggggg
shinggg
I CANNOT ...
...BREAK THE PROMISE.
grin

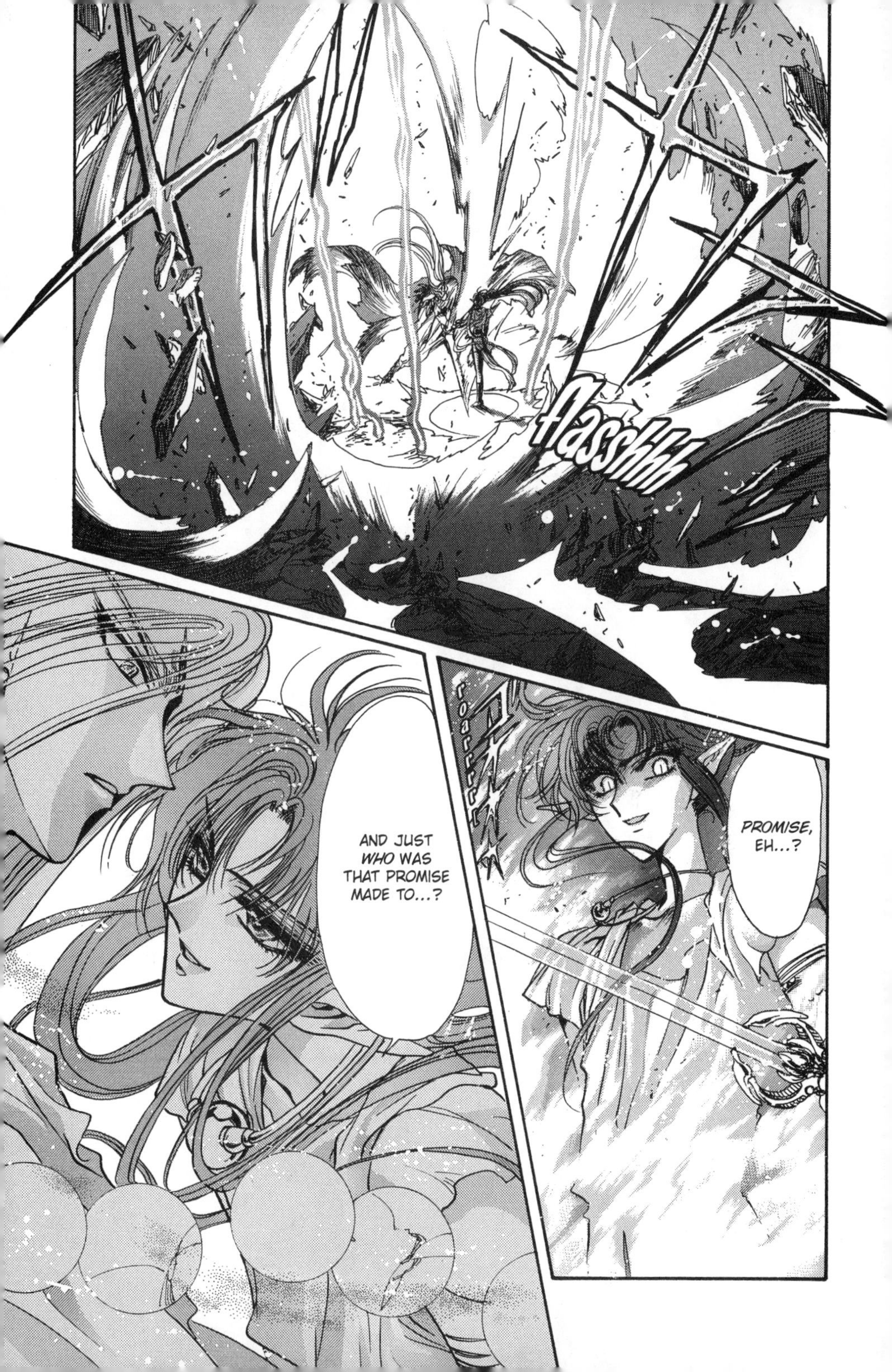
flasshhh
roarrrr
PROMISE, EH...?
AND JUST *WHO* WAS THAT PROMISE MADE TO...?

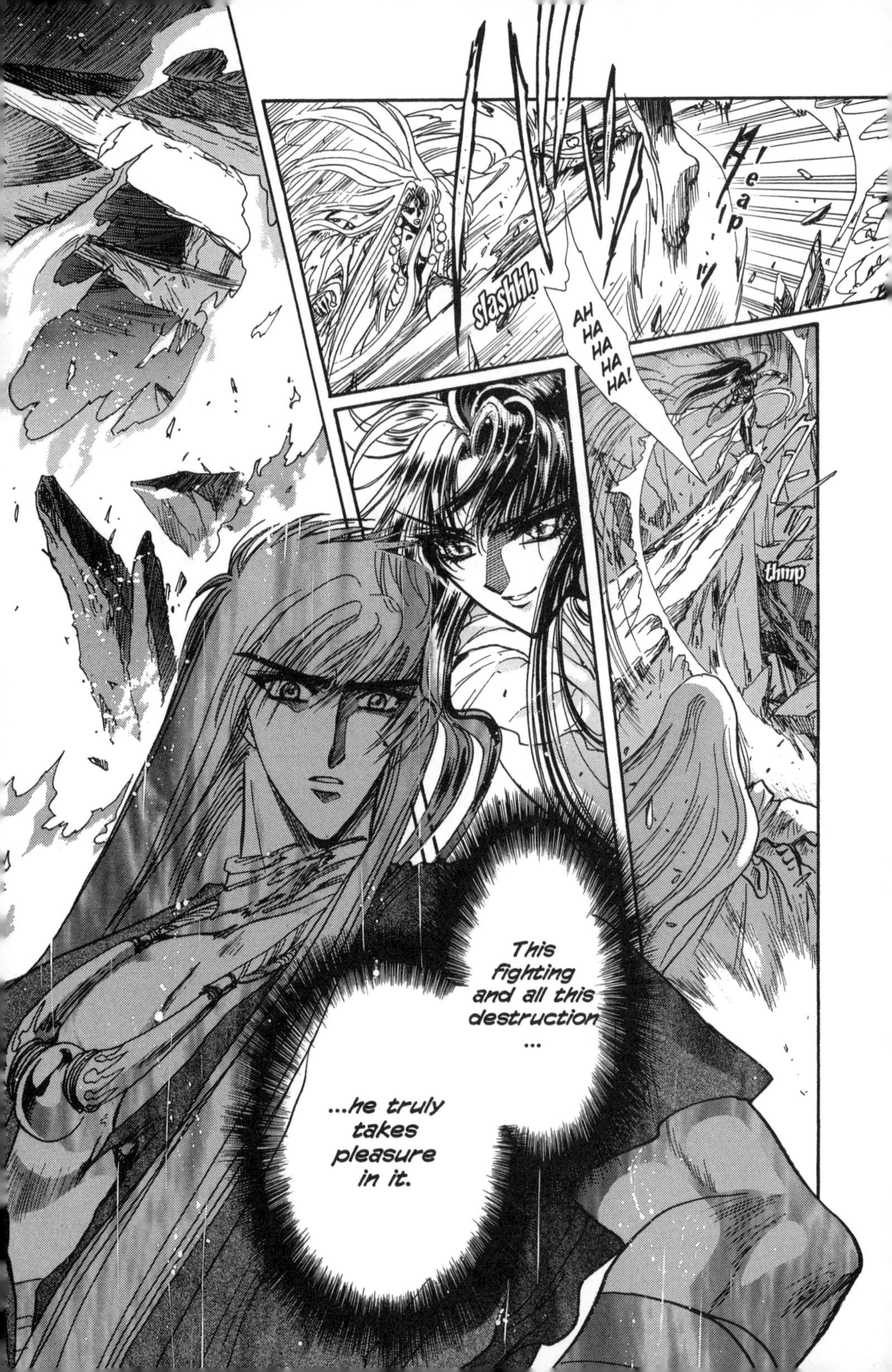
Heap
slashhh
AH HA HA HA HA!
thmp
This fighting and all this destruction ...
...he truly takes pleasure in it.

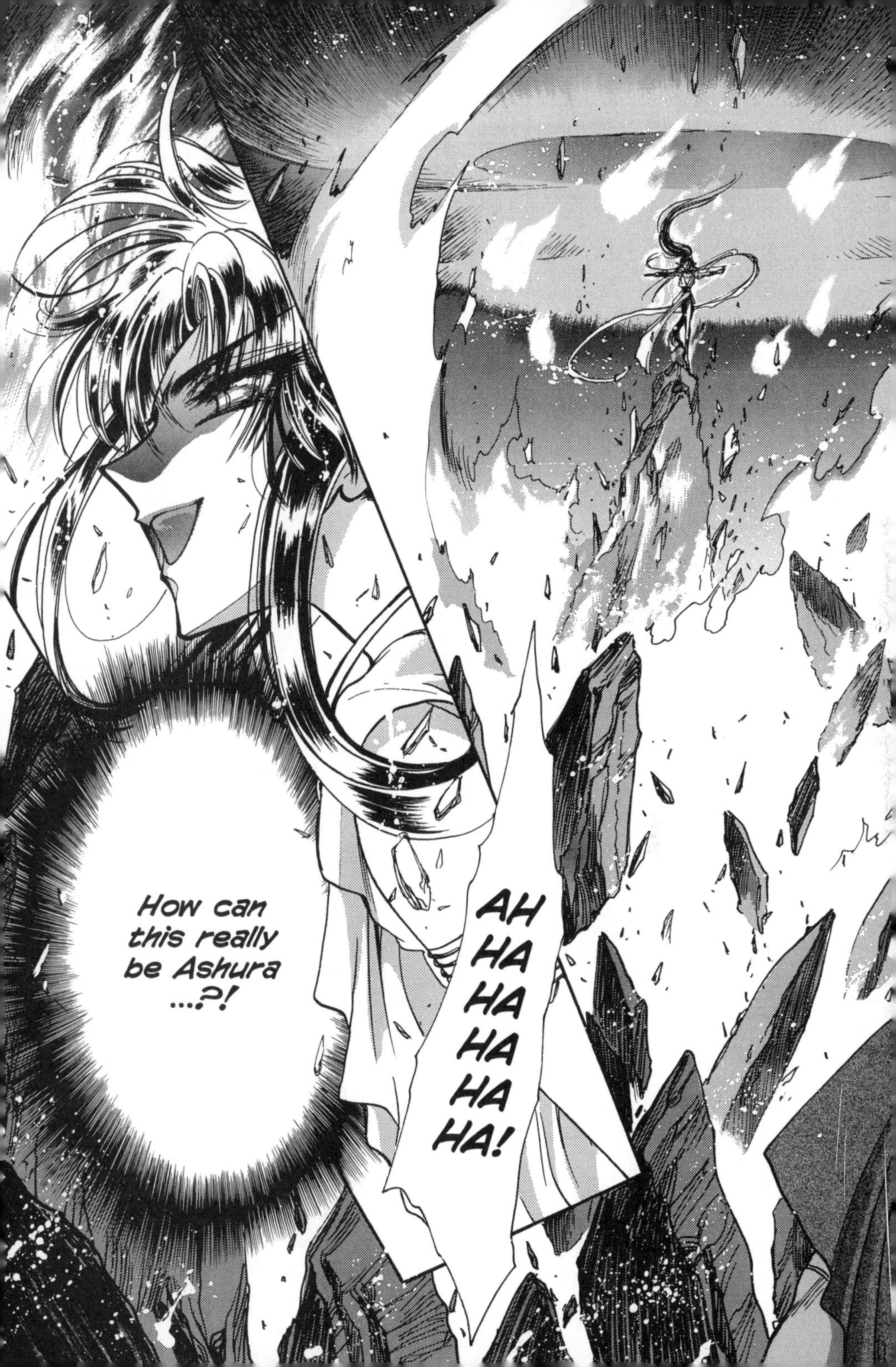
AH HA HA HA HA HA!
How can this really be Ashura ...?!

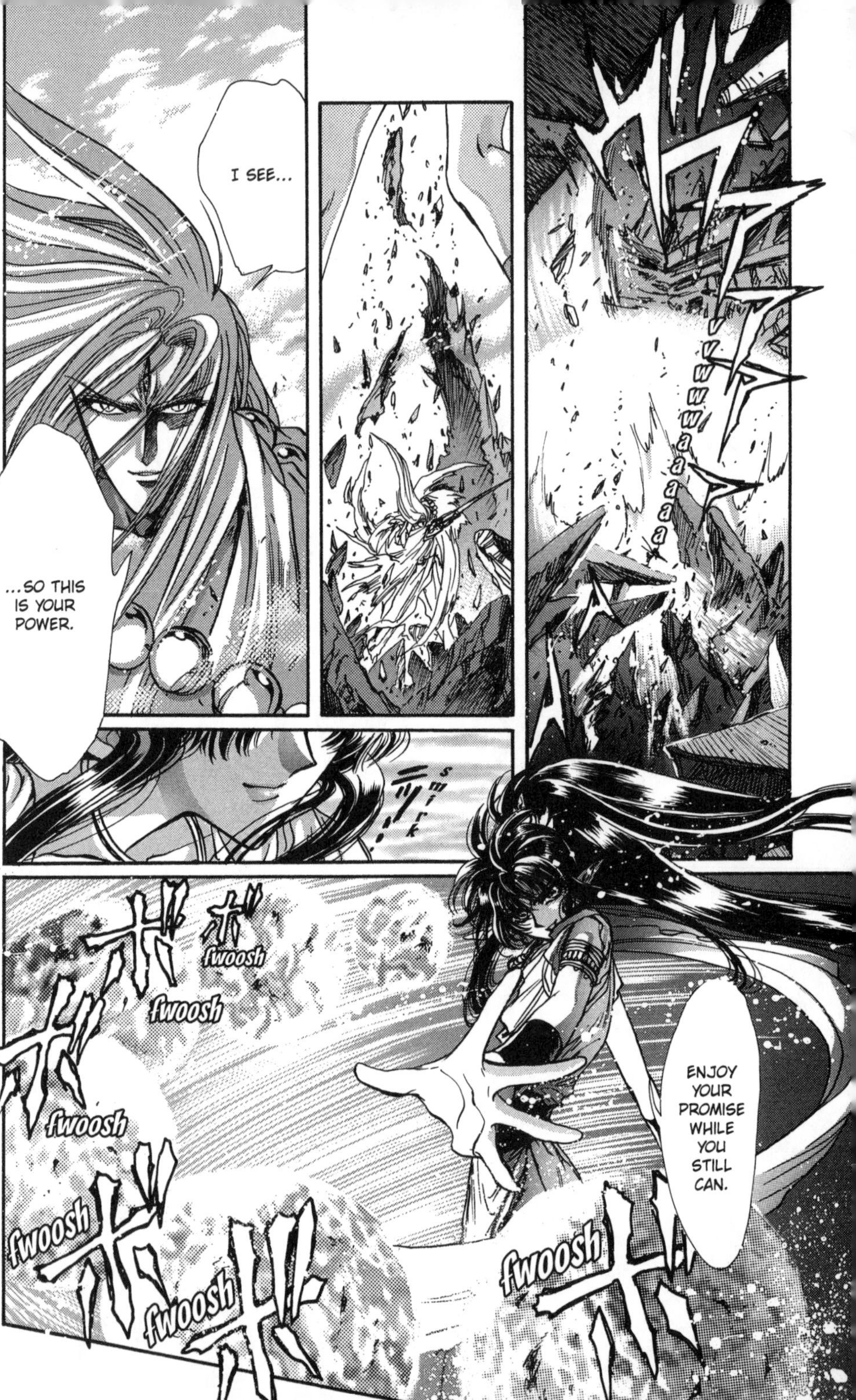
vvwwwaaaaa
I SEE...
...SO THIS IS YOUR POWER.
smirk
ENJOY YOUR PROMISE WHILE YOU STILL CAN.
fwoosh
fwoosh
fwoosh
fwoosh
fwoosh
fwoosh

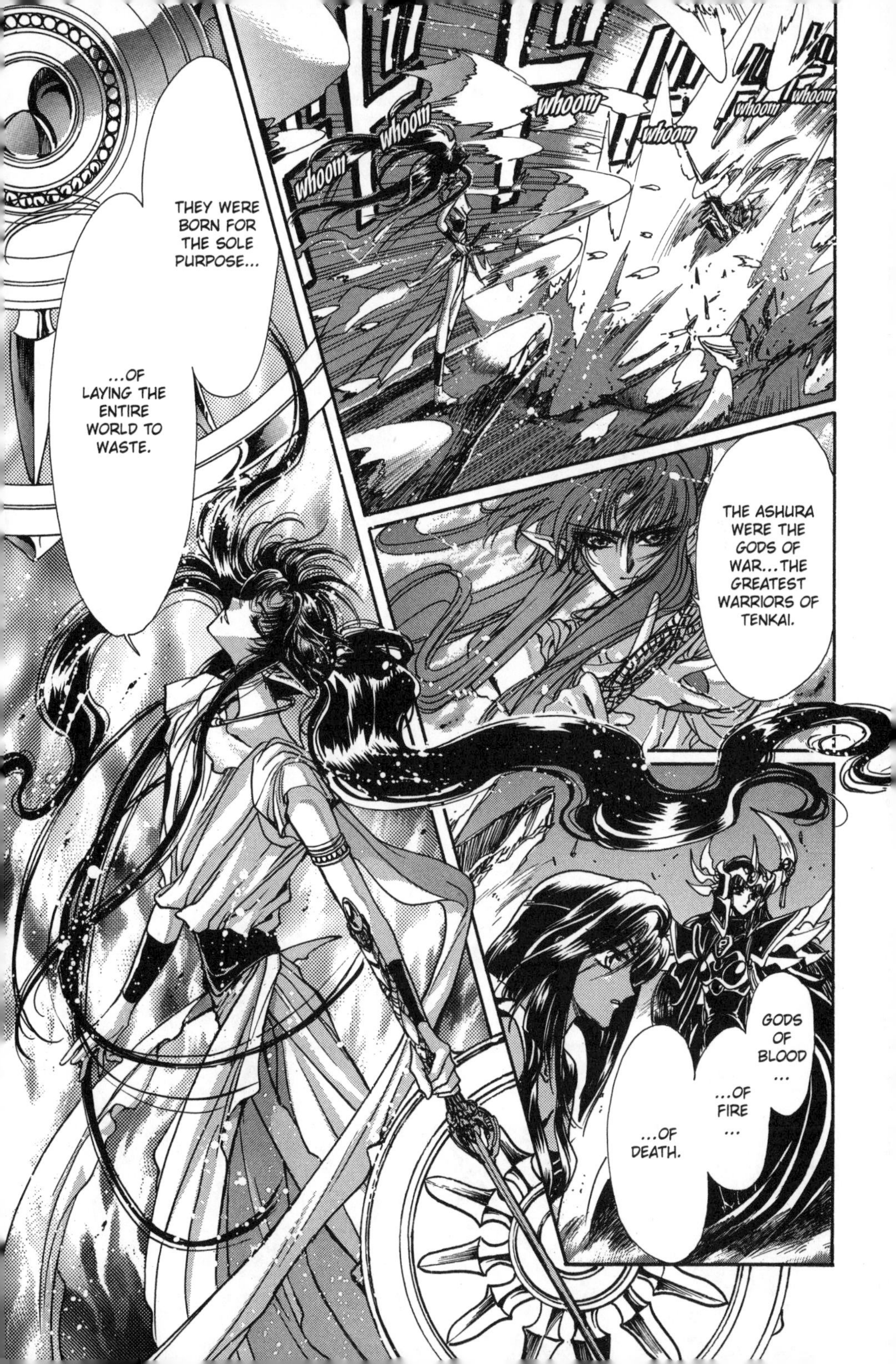
whoom
whoom
whoom
whoom
whoom
whoom
THE ASHURA WERE THE GODS OF WAR...THE GREATEST WARRIORS OF TENKAI.
GODS OF BLOOD ...
...OF FIRE ...
...OF DEATH.
THEY WERE BORN FOR THE SOLE PURPOSE...
...OF LAYING THE ENTIRE WORLD TO WASTE.

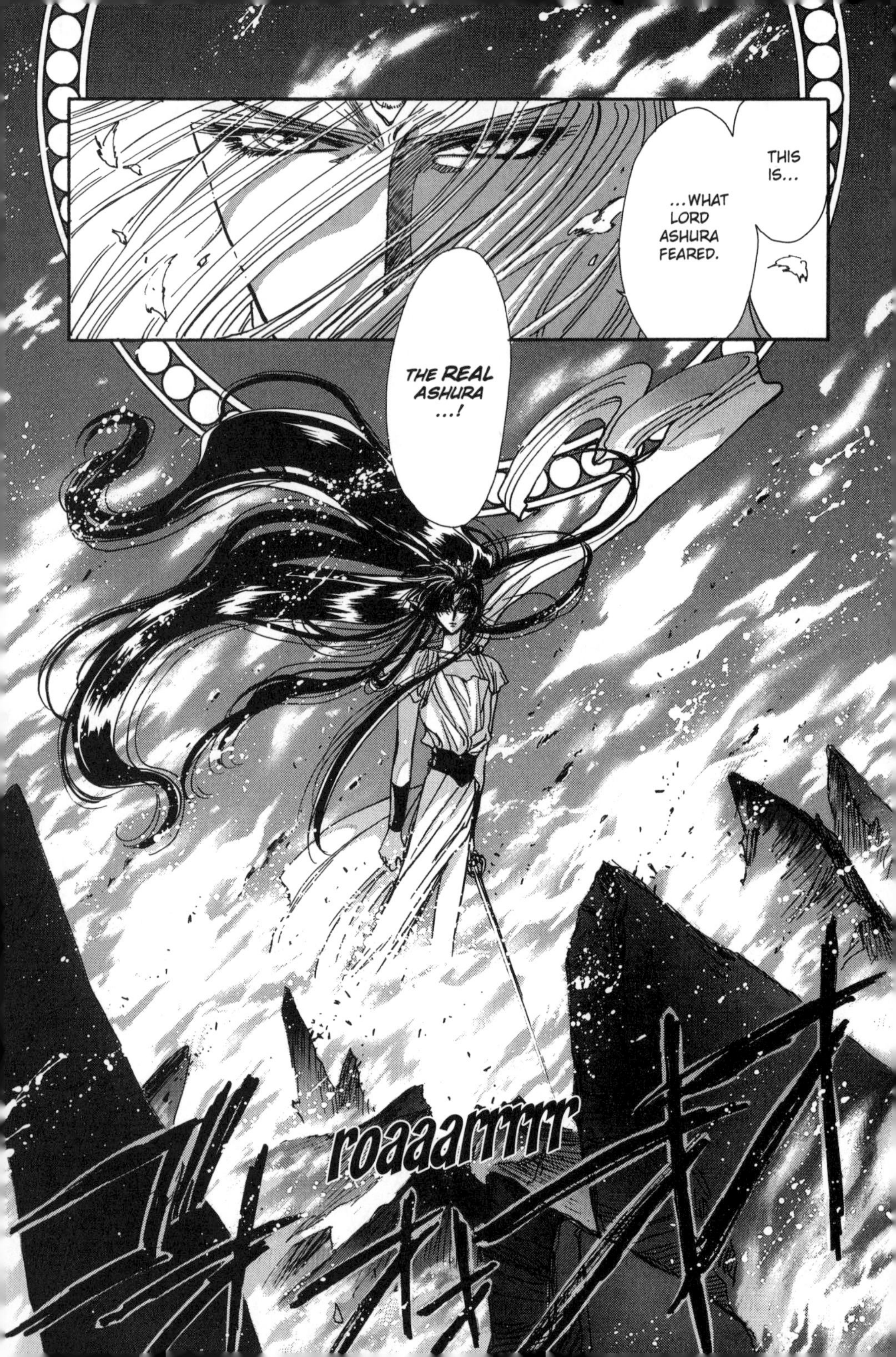
THIS IS...
...WHAT LORD ASHURA FEARED.
THE REAL ASHURA ...!
roaaarrrrr

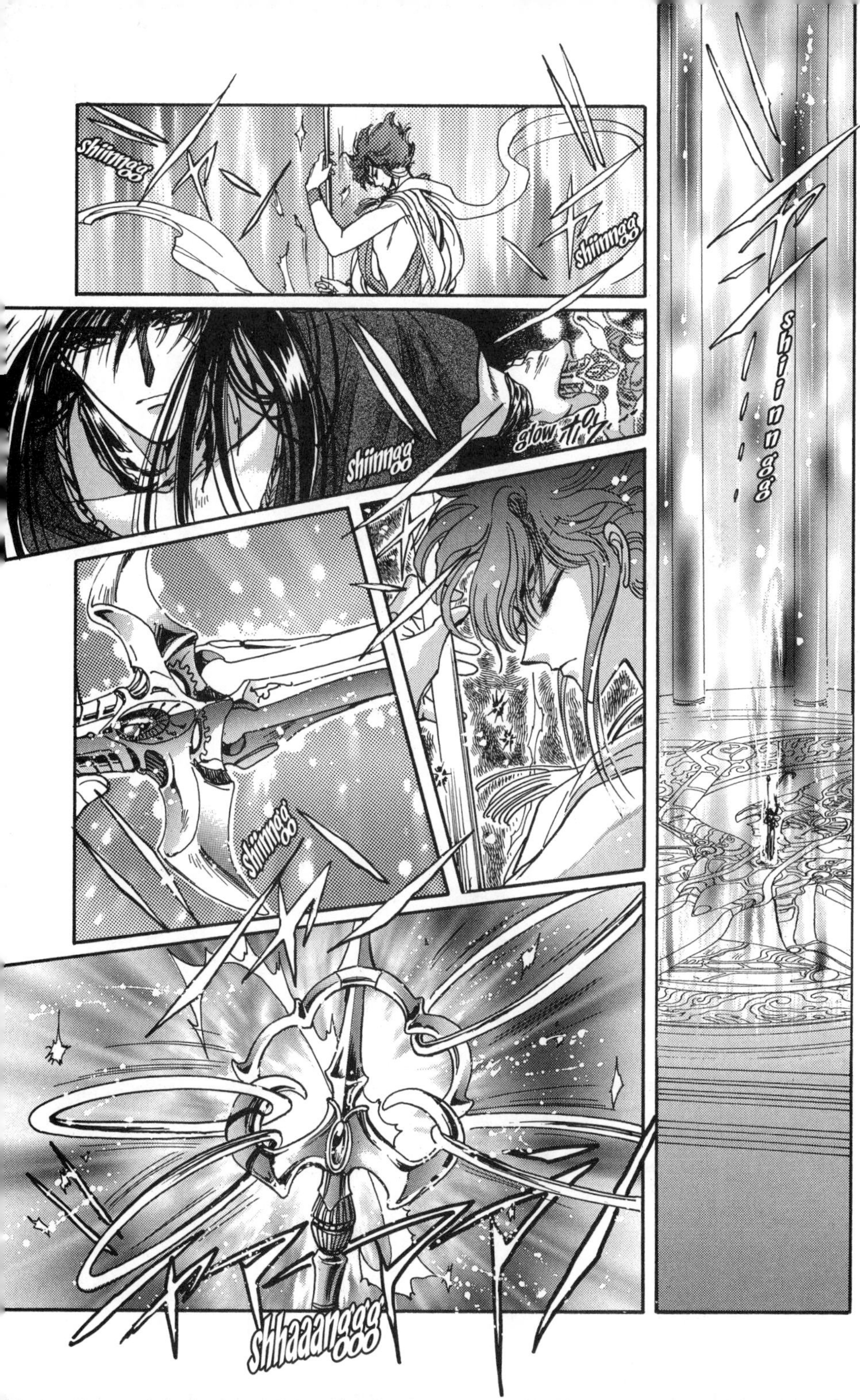
shiinngg
shiinngg
shiinngg
glow
shiinngg
shiinngg
shhaaanggg

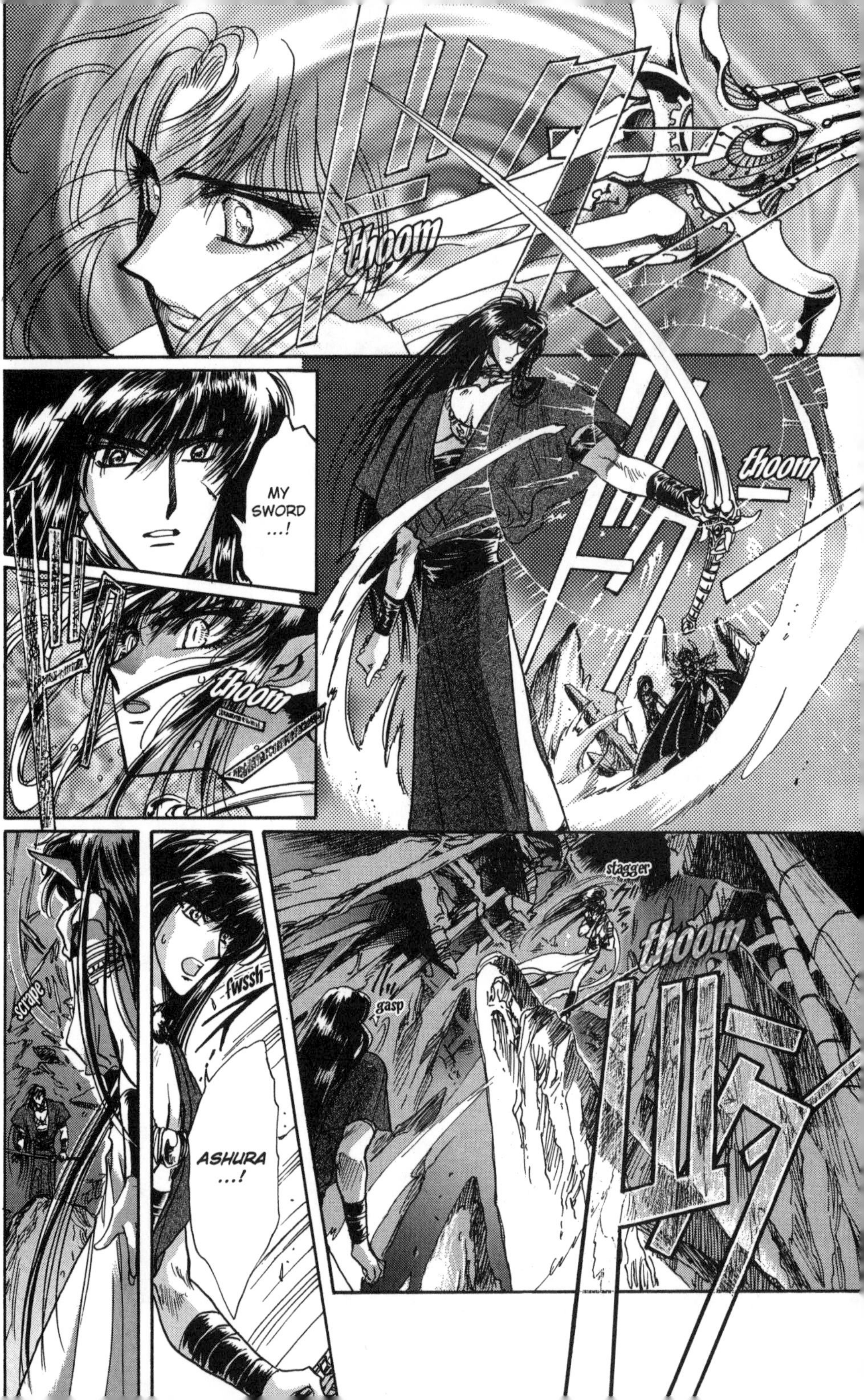
thoom
thoom
MY SWORD ...!
thoom
stagger
thoom
gasp
fwssh
ASHURA ...!
scrape

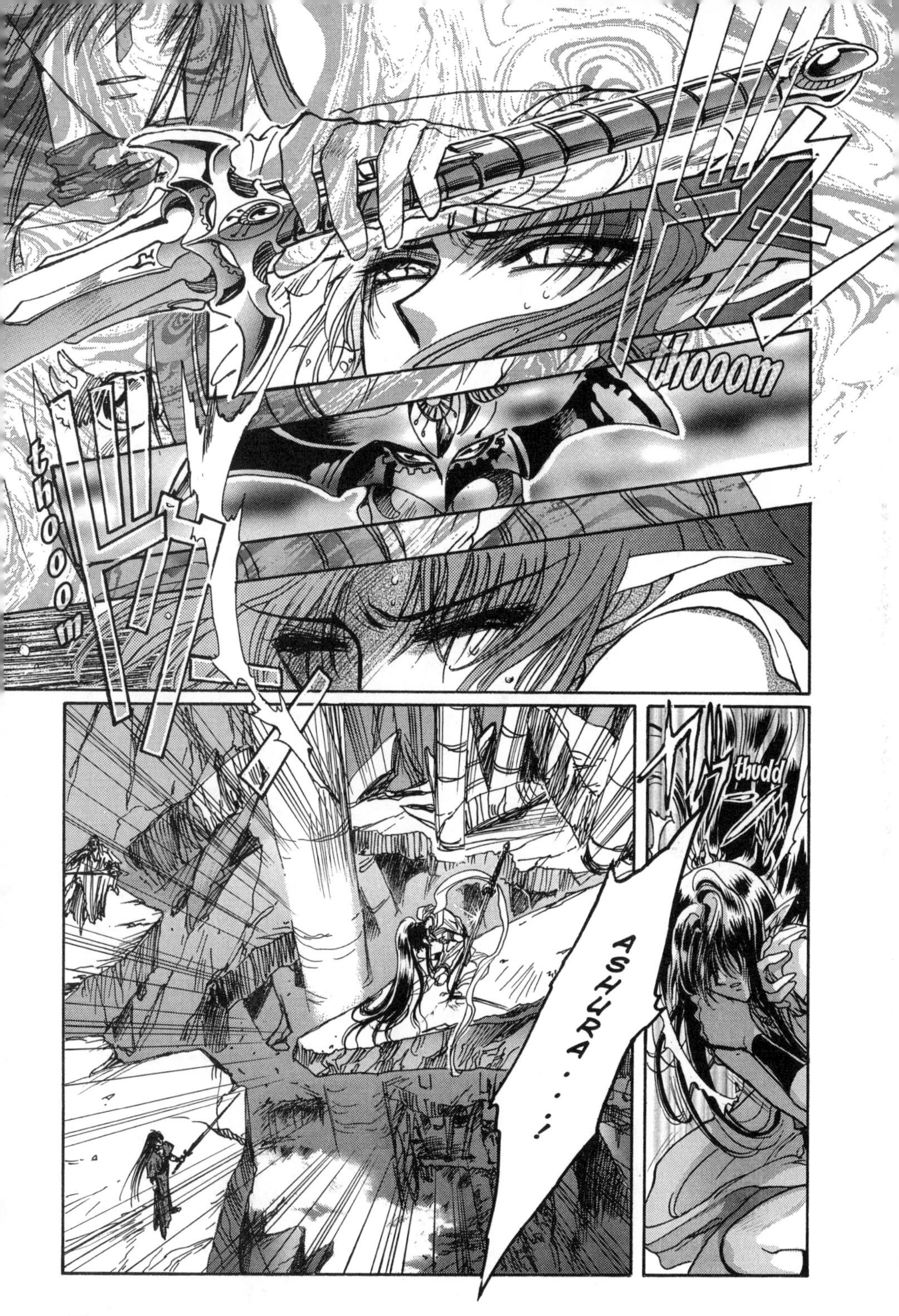
thooom
thoooom
thudd
ASHURA...!

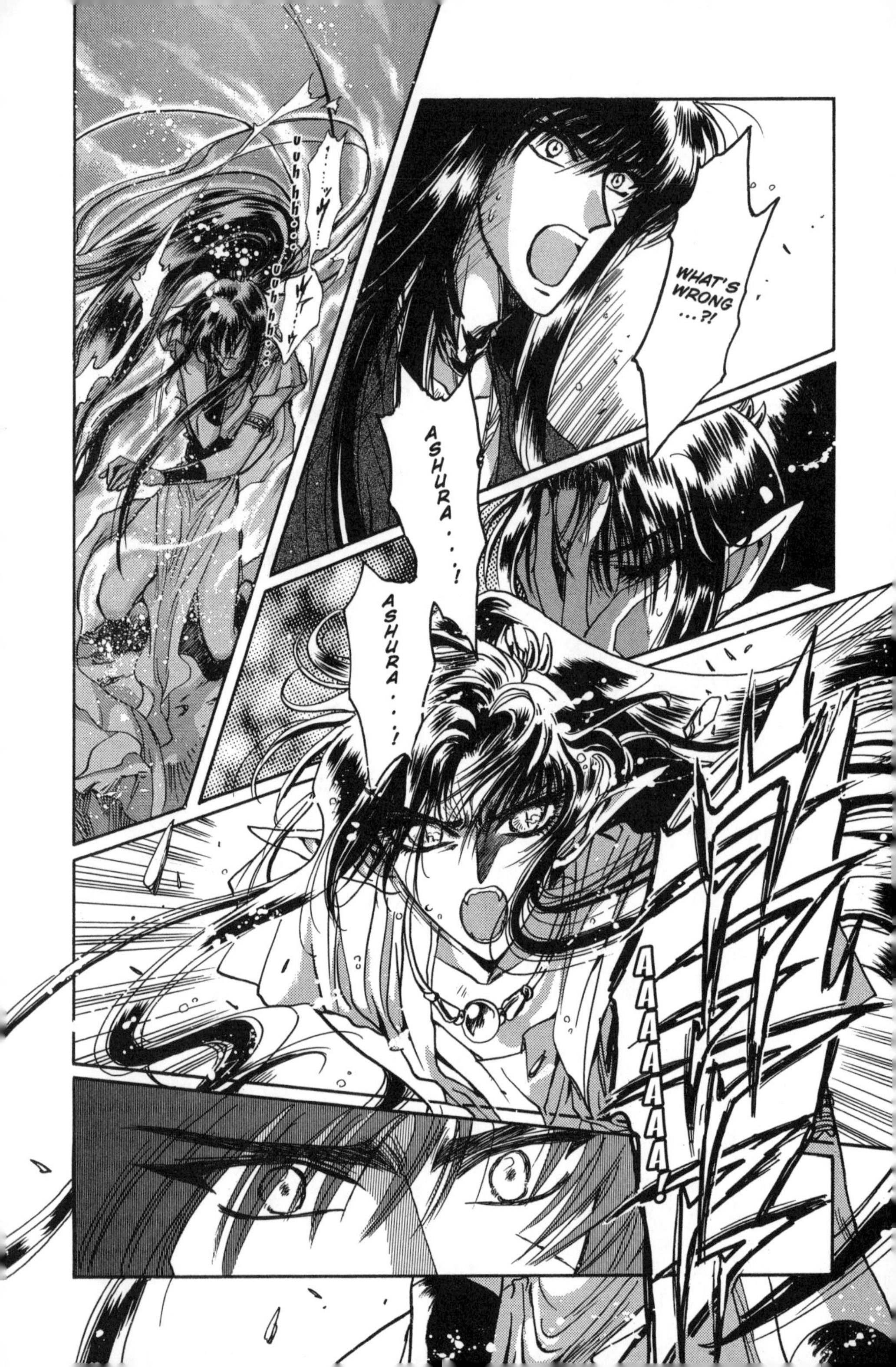
WHAT'S WRONG ...?!
ASHURA...!
ASHURA...!
UUHHHOOO
UUHHHOOO
AAAAAAAA!

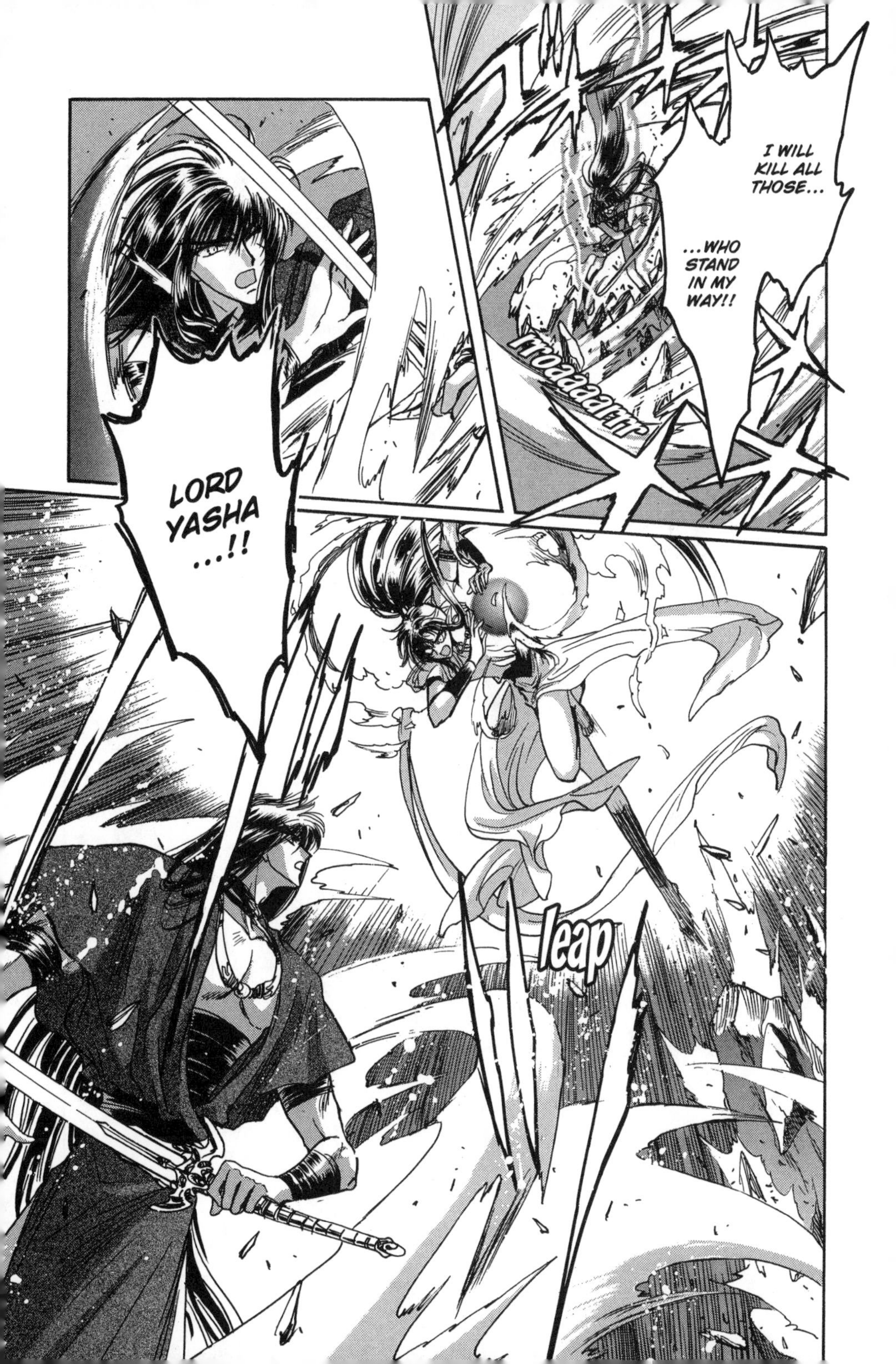
I WILL KILL ALL THOSE...
...WHO STAND IN MY WAY!!
rroaaaaarrr
LORD YASHA ...!!
leap

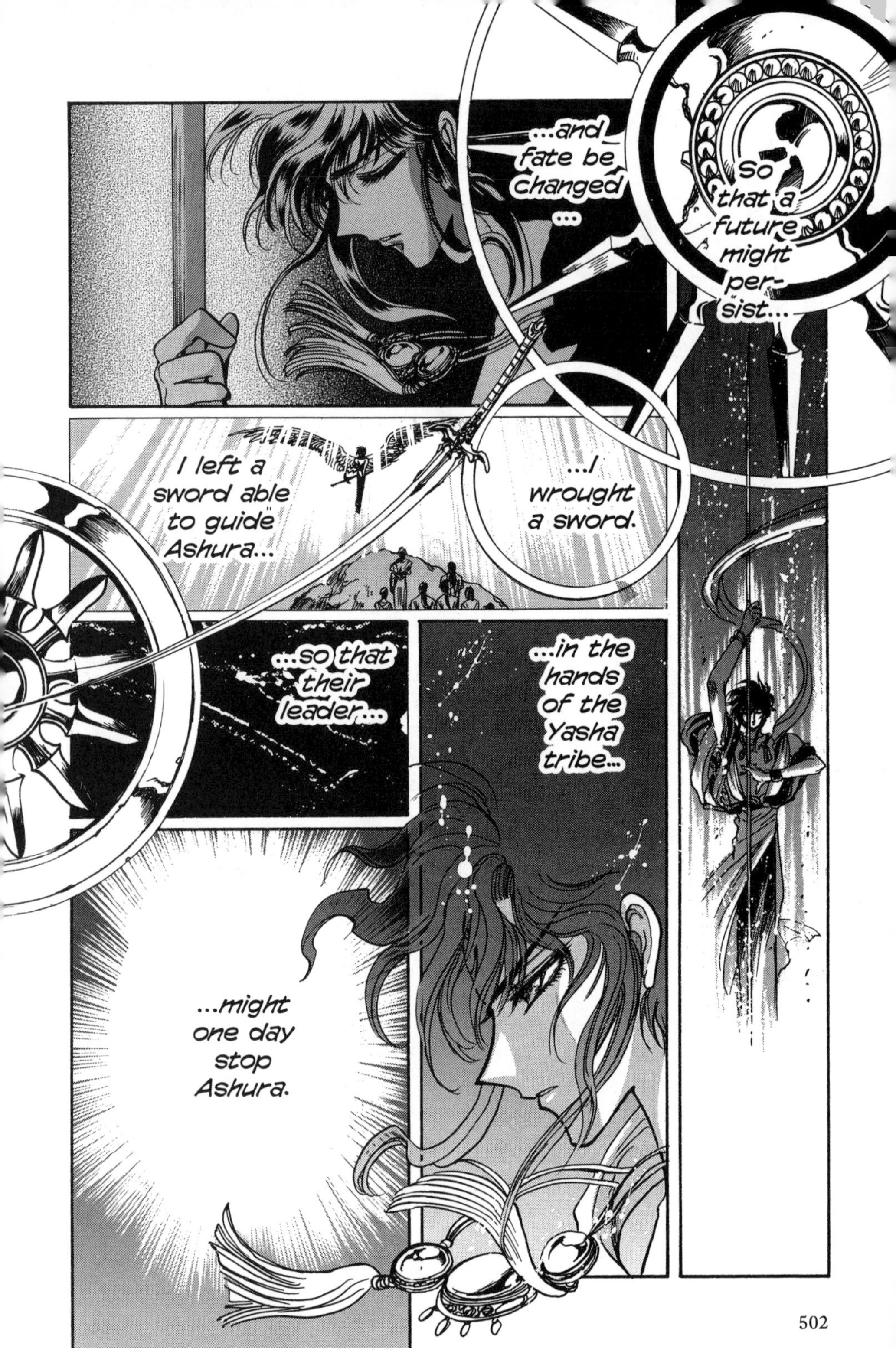
So that a future might per-sist...
...and fate be changed...
...I wrought a sword.
I left a sword able to guide Ashura...
...in the hands of the Yasha tribe...
...so that their leader...
...might one day stop Ashura.

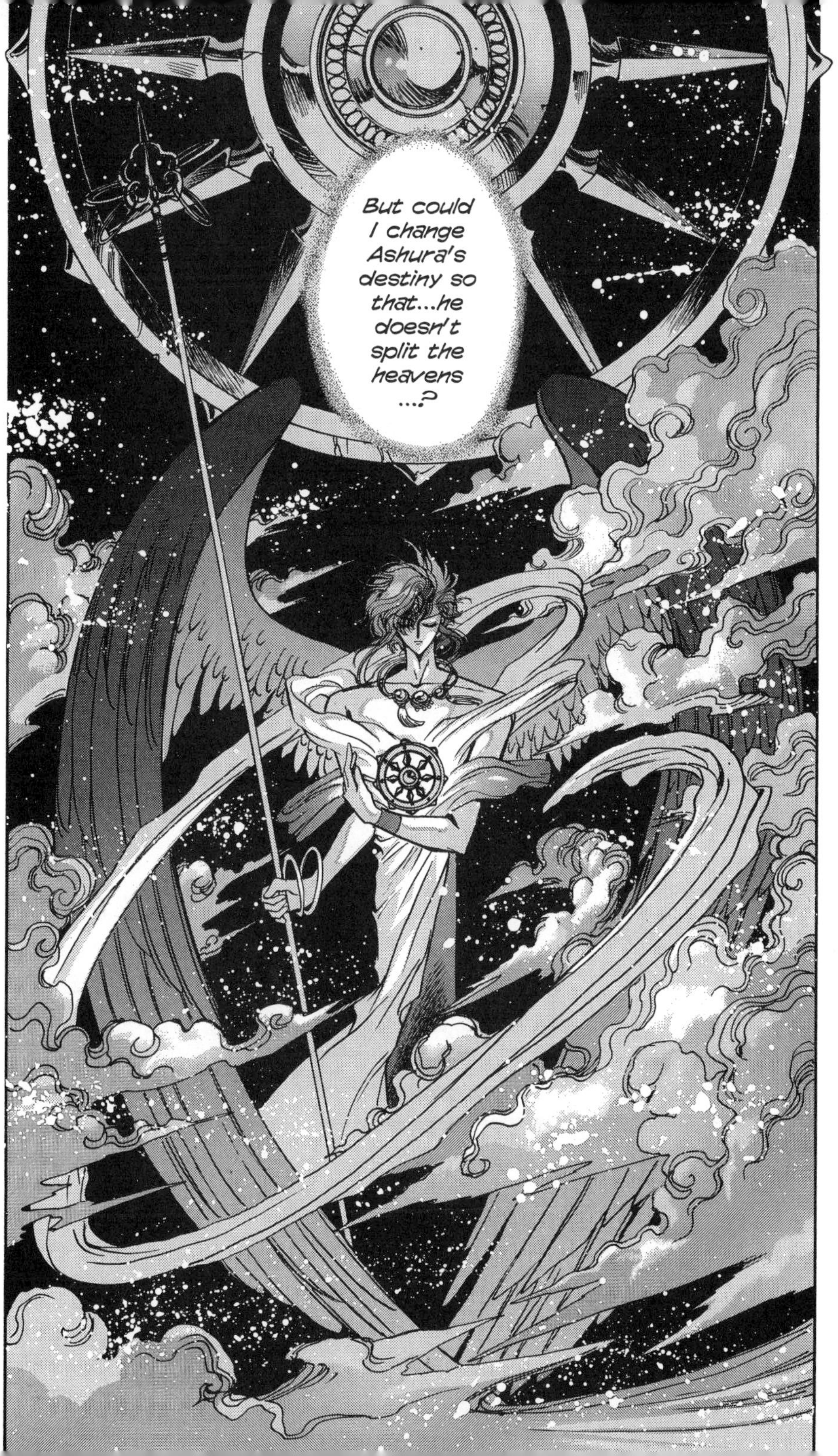
But could I change Ashura's destiny so that...he doesn't split the heavens ...?

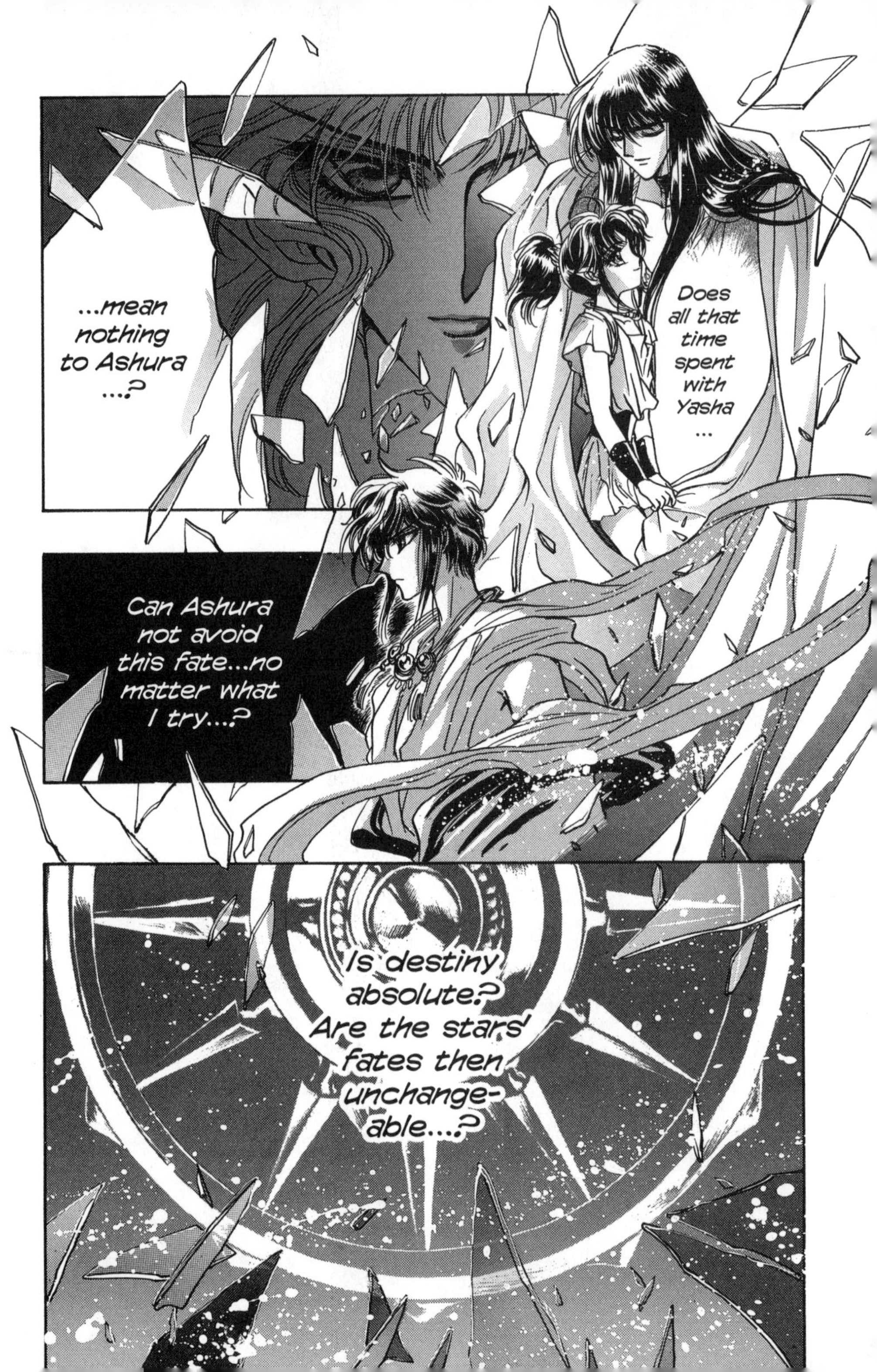
Does all that time spent with Yasha ...
...mean nothing to Ashura ...?
Can Ashura not avoid this fate...no matter what I try...?
Is destiny absolute? Are the stars' fates then unchange-able...?

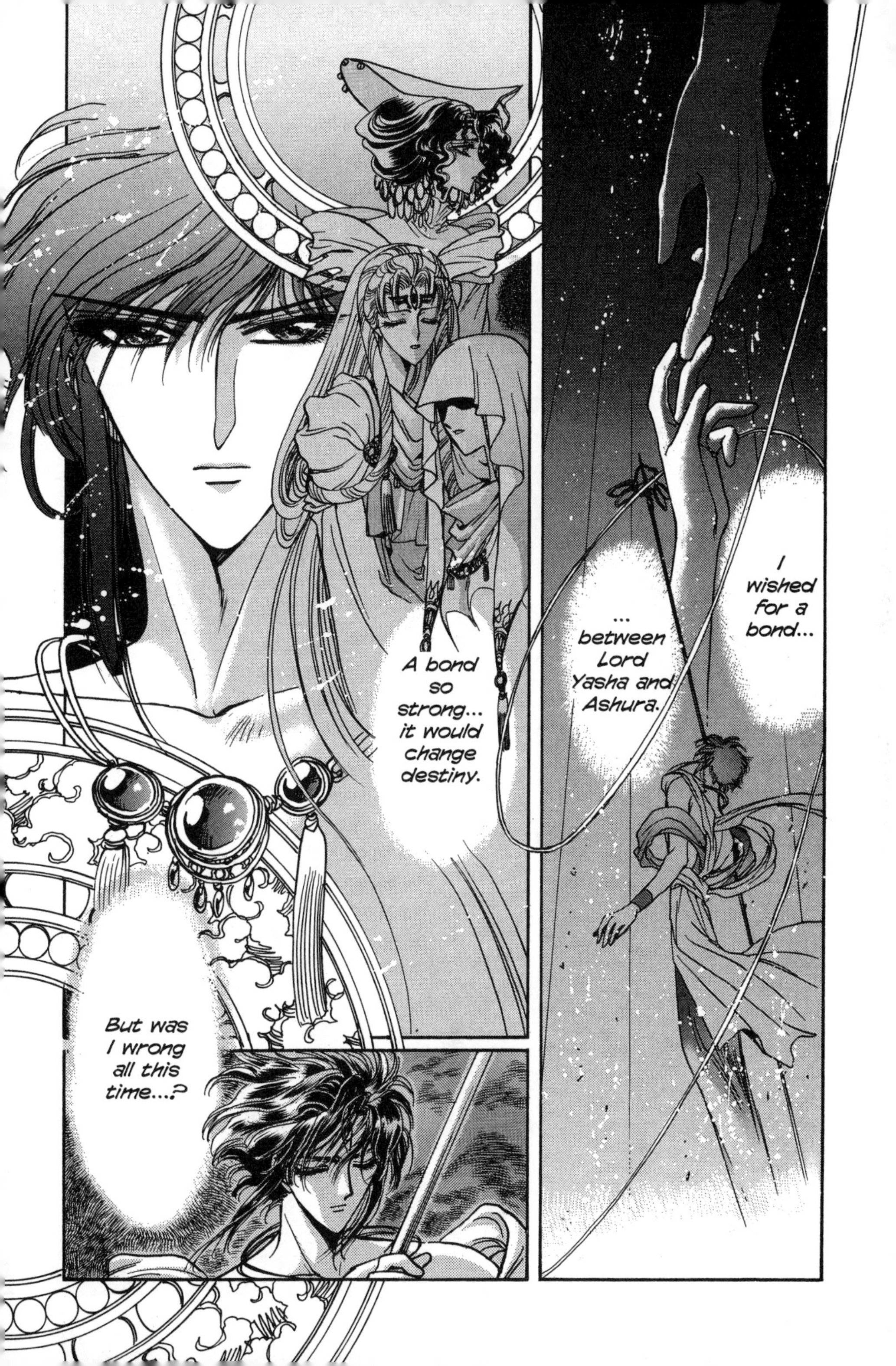
I wished for a bond...
...between Lord Yasha and Ashura.
A bond so strong... it would change destiny.
But was I wrong all this time...?

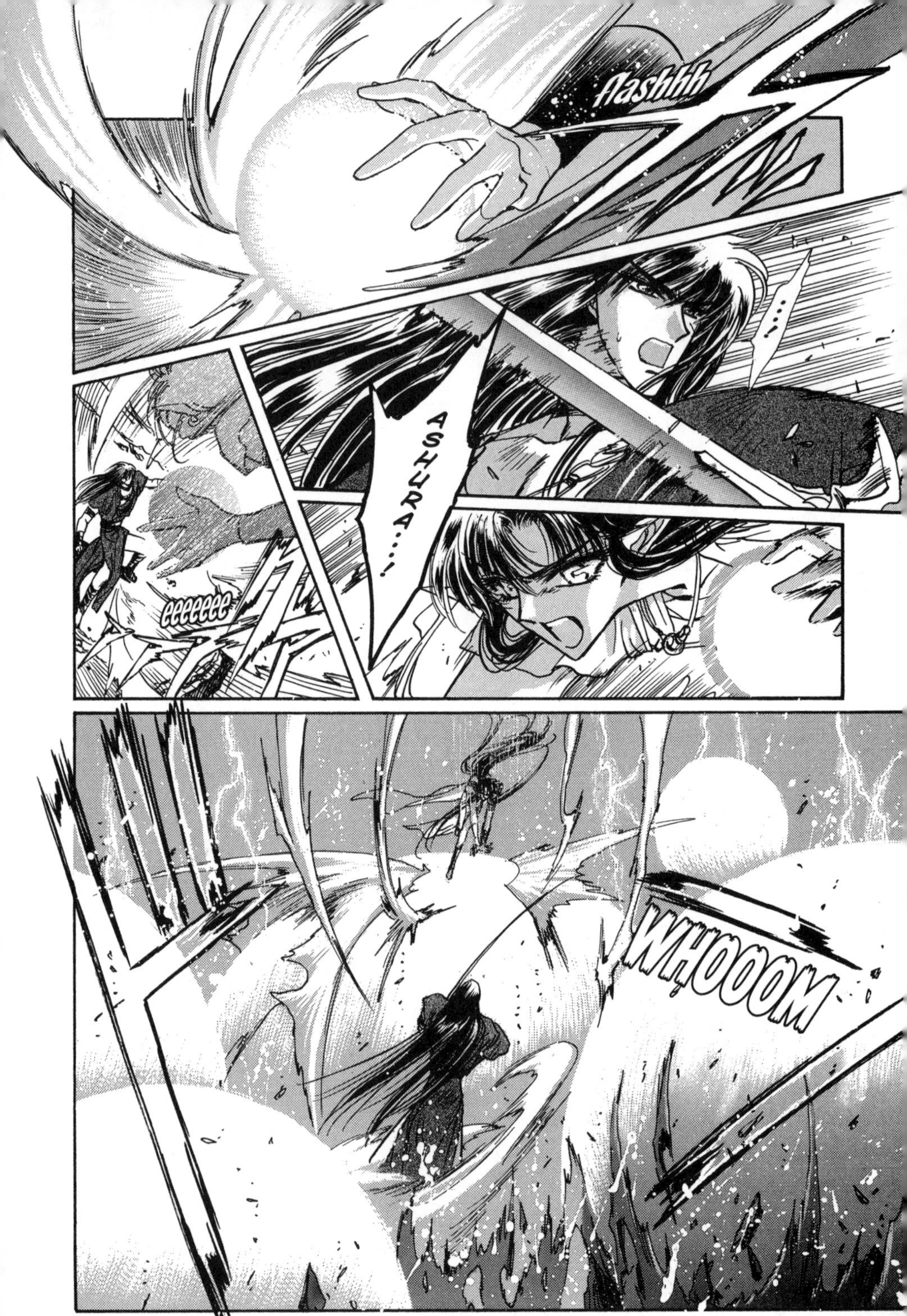
flashhh
...!
ASHURA...!
eeeeeee
WHOOOM

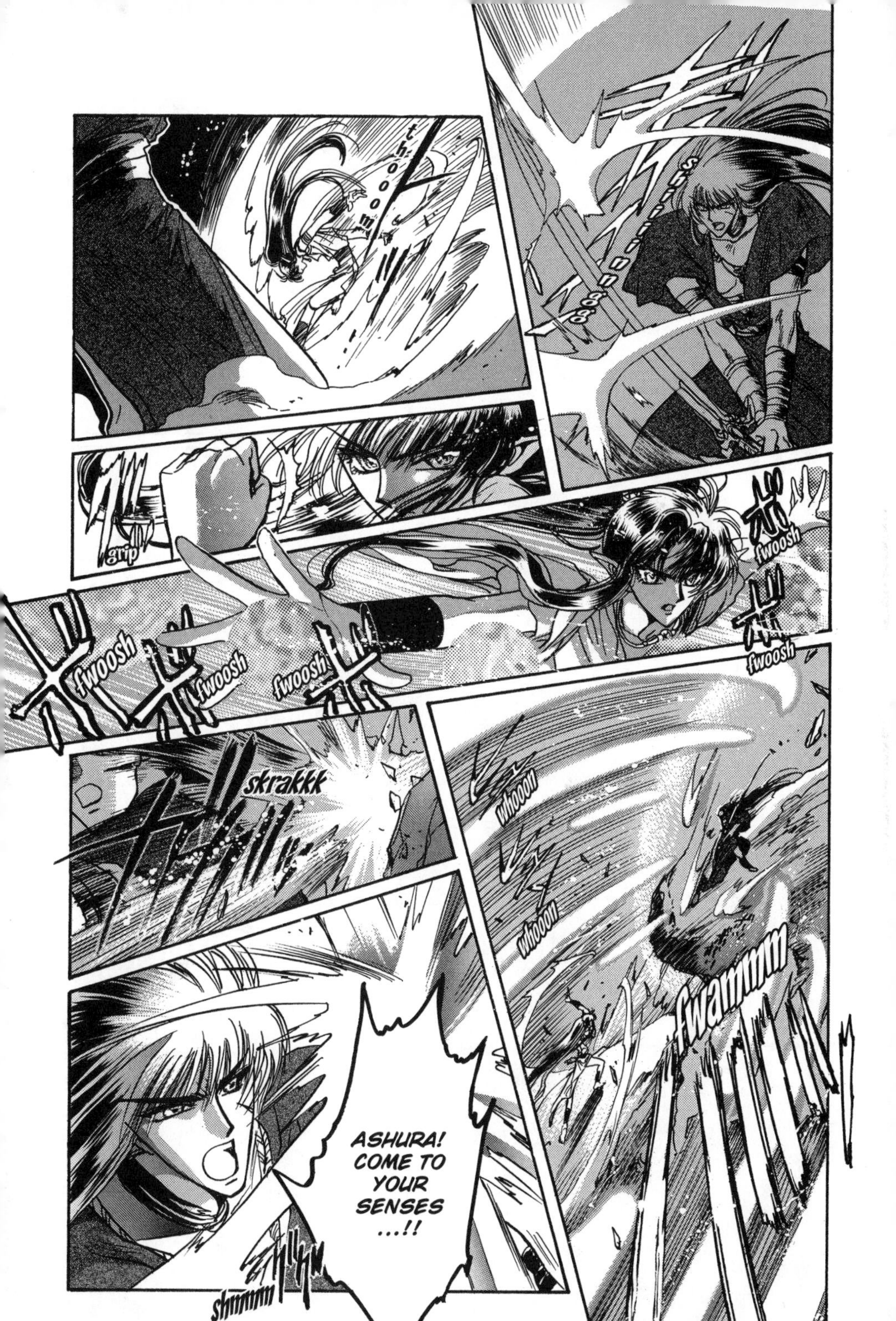
shiiiinnggg
thooom
grip
fwoosh
fwoosh
fwoosh
fwoosh
fwoosh
whooon
whooon
fwammmm
skrakkk
ASHURA! COME TO YOUR SENSES ...!!
shmmm

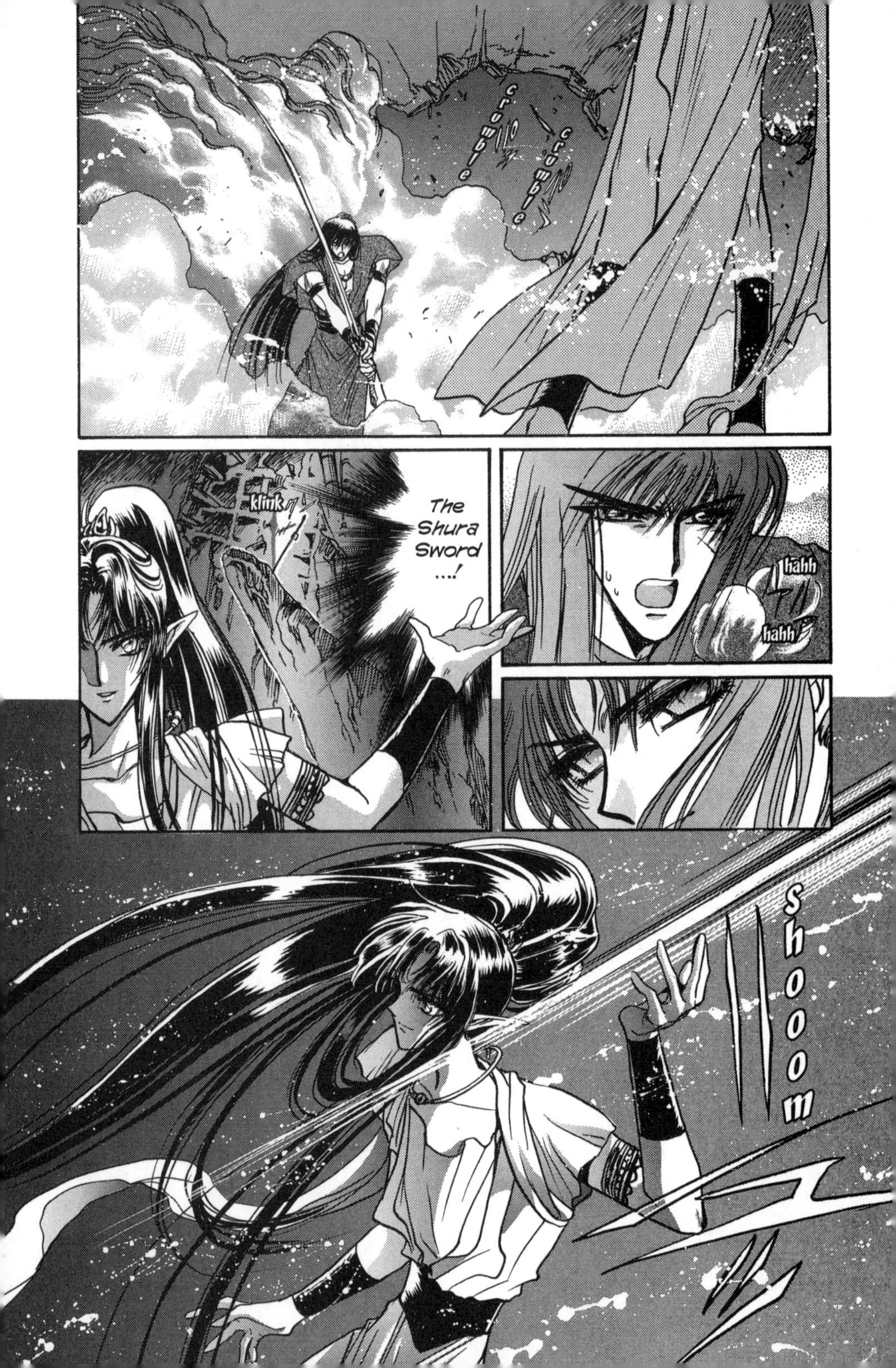
crumble
crumble
hahh
hahh
klink
The Shura Sword ....!
shoooom

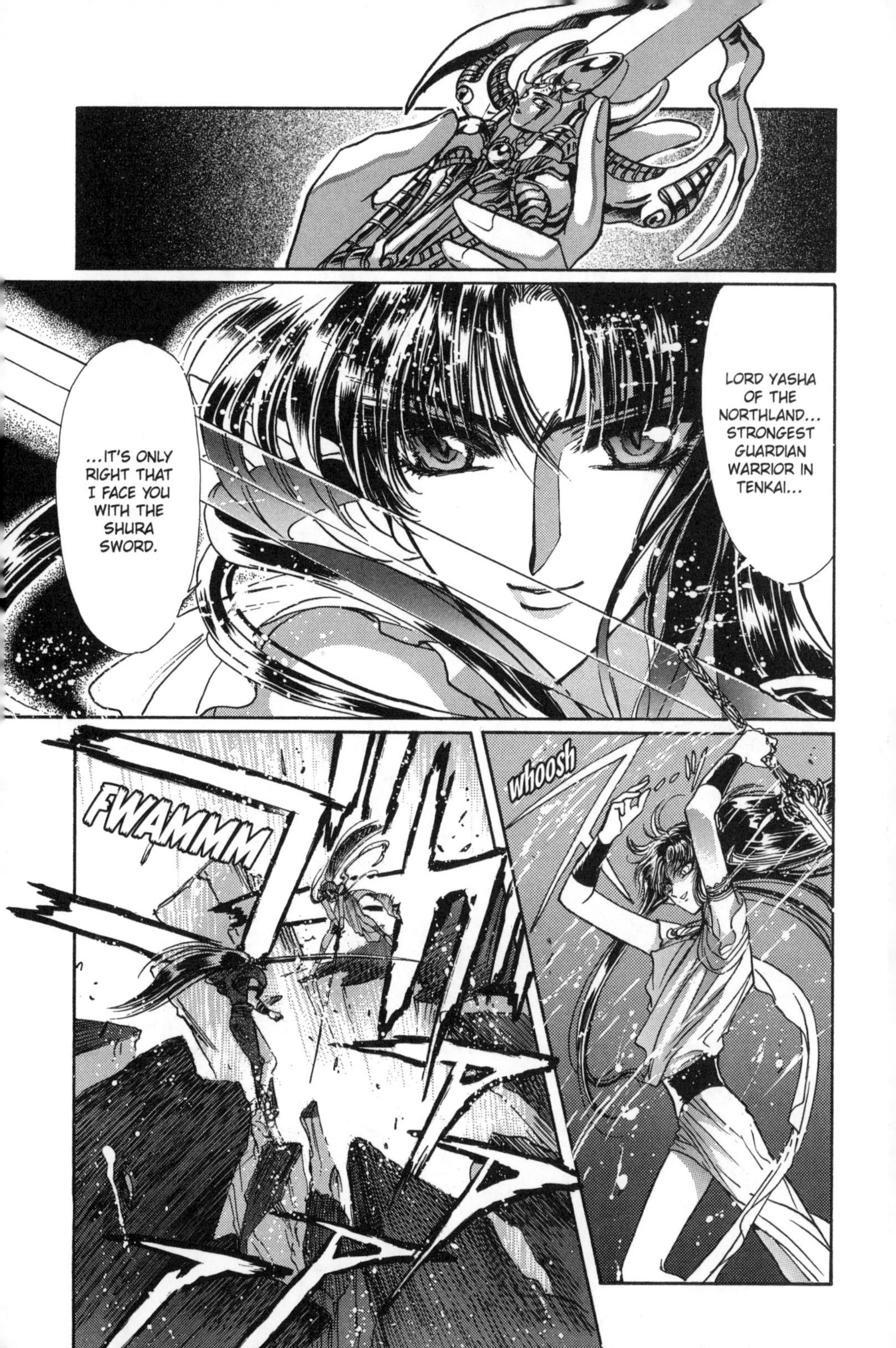
LORD YASHA OF THE NORTHLAND... STRONGEST GUARDIAN WARRIOR IN TENKAI...
...IT'S ONLY RIGHT THAT I FACE YOU WITH THE SHURA SWORD.
whoosh
FWAMMMM

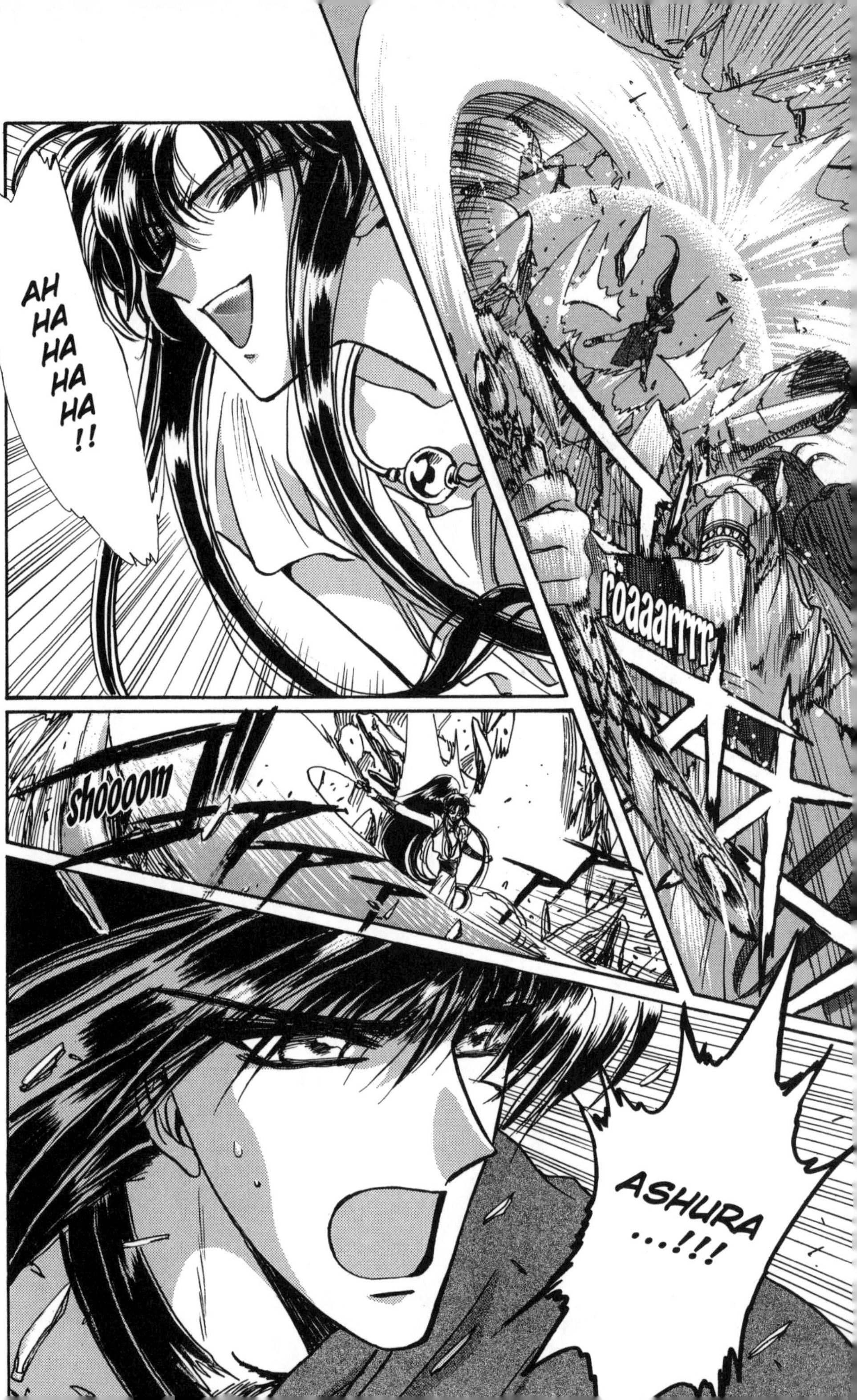
roaaarrrr
AH HA HA HA HA!!
shoooom
ASHURA...!!!

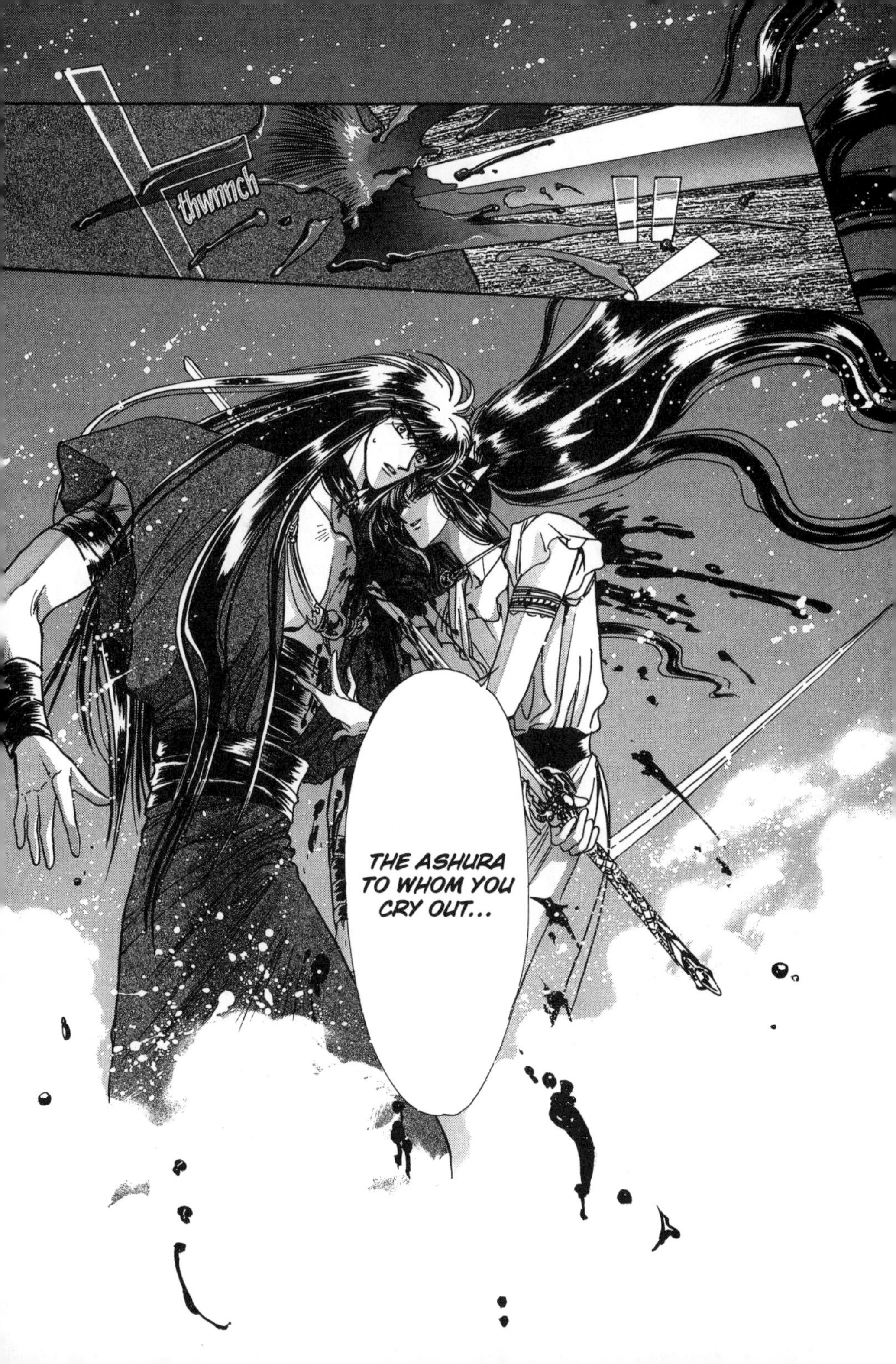
thwnnch
THE ASHURA TO WHOM YOU CRY OUT...

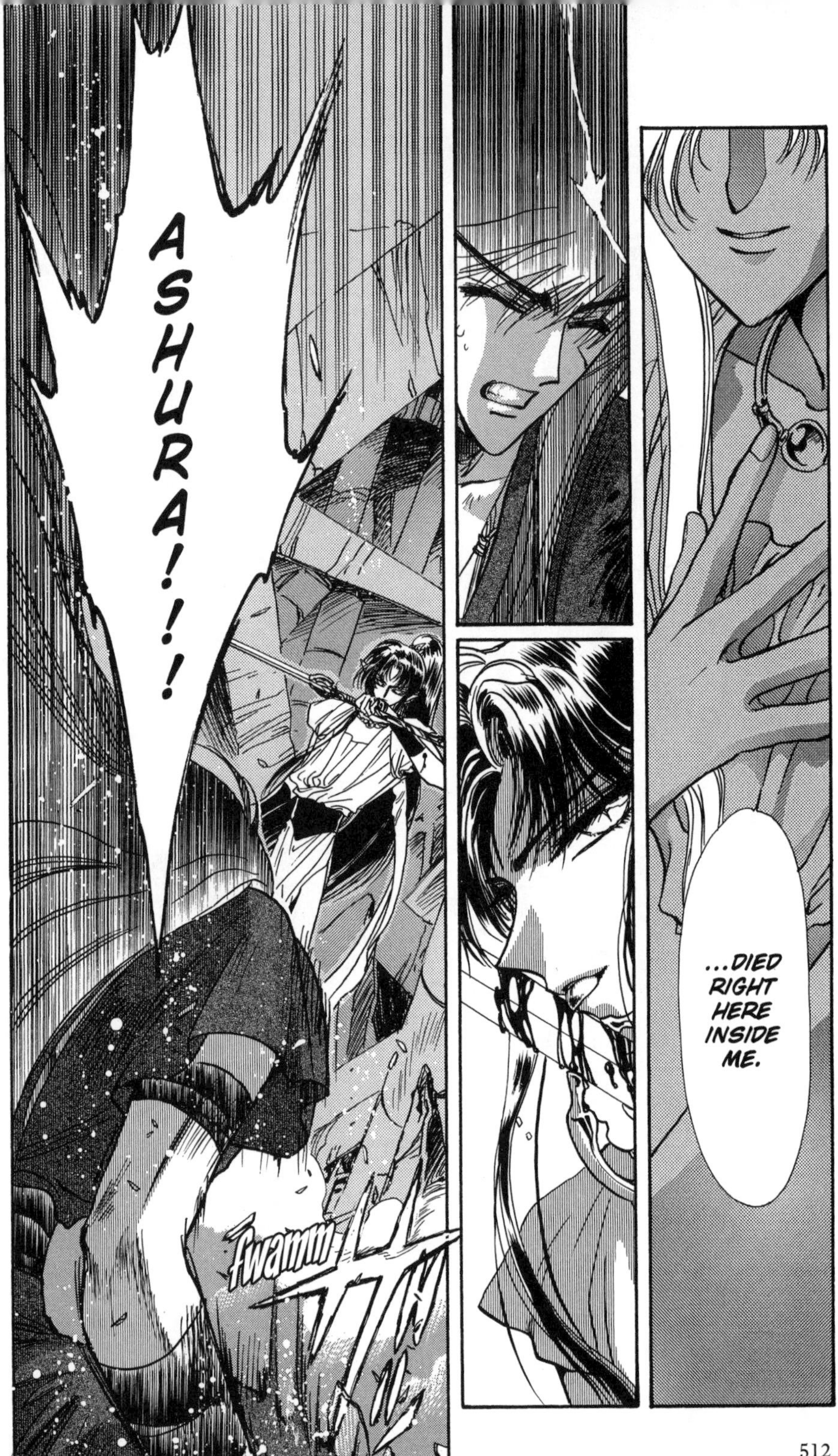
...DIED RIGHT HERE INSIDE ME.
ASHURA!!!!
fwamm

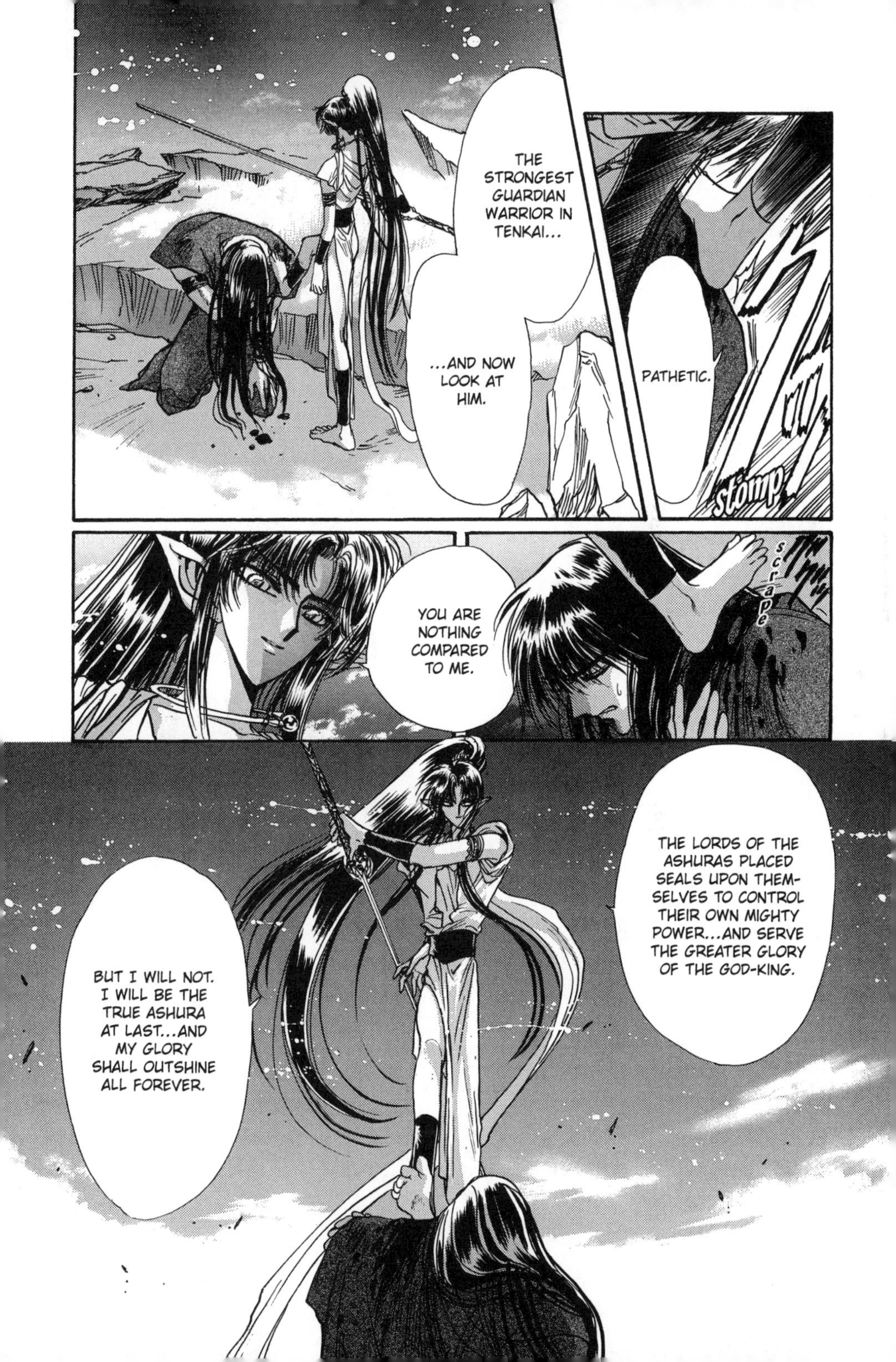
PATHETIC.
stomp
THE STRONGEST GUARDIAN WARRIOR IN TENKAI...
...AND NOW LOOK AT HIM.
scrape
YOU ARE NOTHING COMPARED TO ME.
THE LORDS OF THE ASHURAS PLACED SEALS UPON THEMSELVES TO CONTROL THEIR OWN MIGHTY POWER...AND SERVE THE GREATER GLORY OF THE GOD-KING.
BUT I WILL NOT. I WILL BE THE TRUE ASHURA AT LAST...AND MY GLORY SHALL OUTSHINE ALL FOREVER.

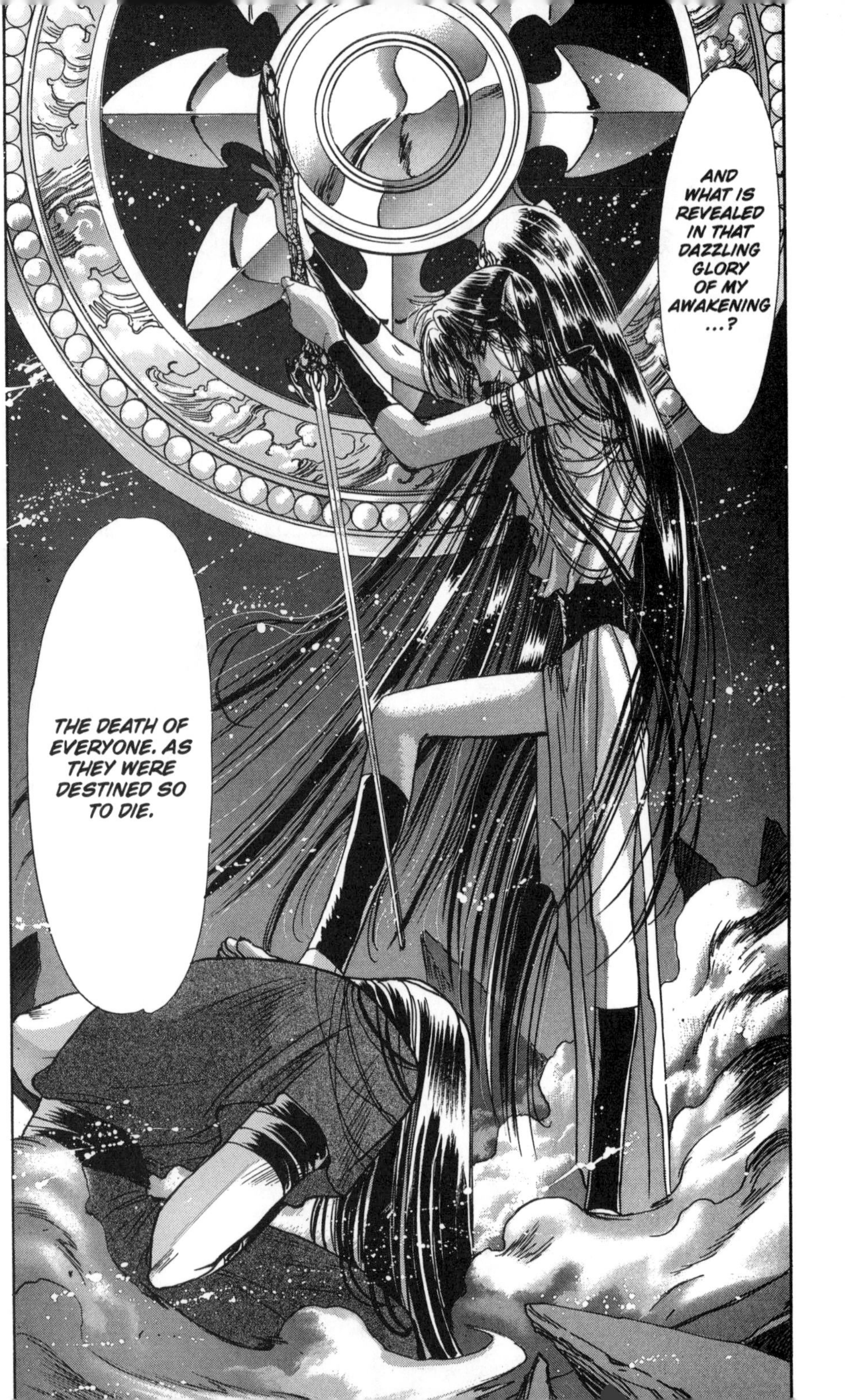
AND WHAT IS REVEALED IN THAT DAZZLING GLORY OF MY AWAKENING ...?
THE DEATH OF EVERYONE. AS THEY WERE DESTINED SO TO DIE.

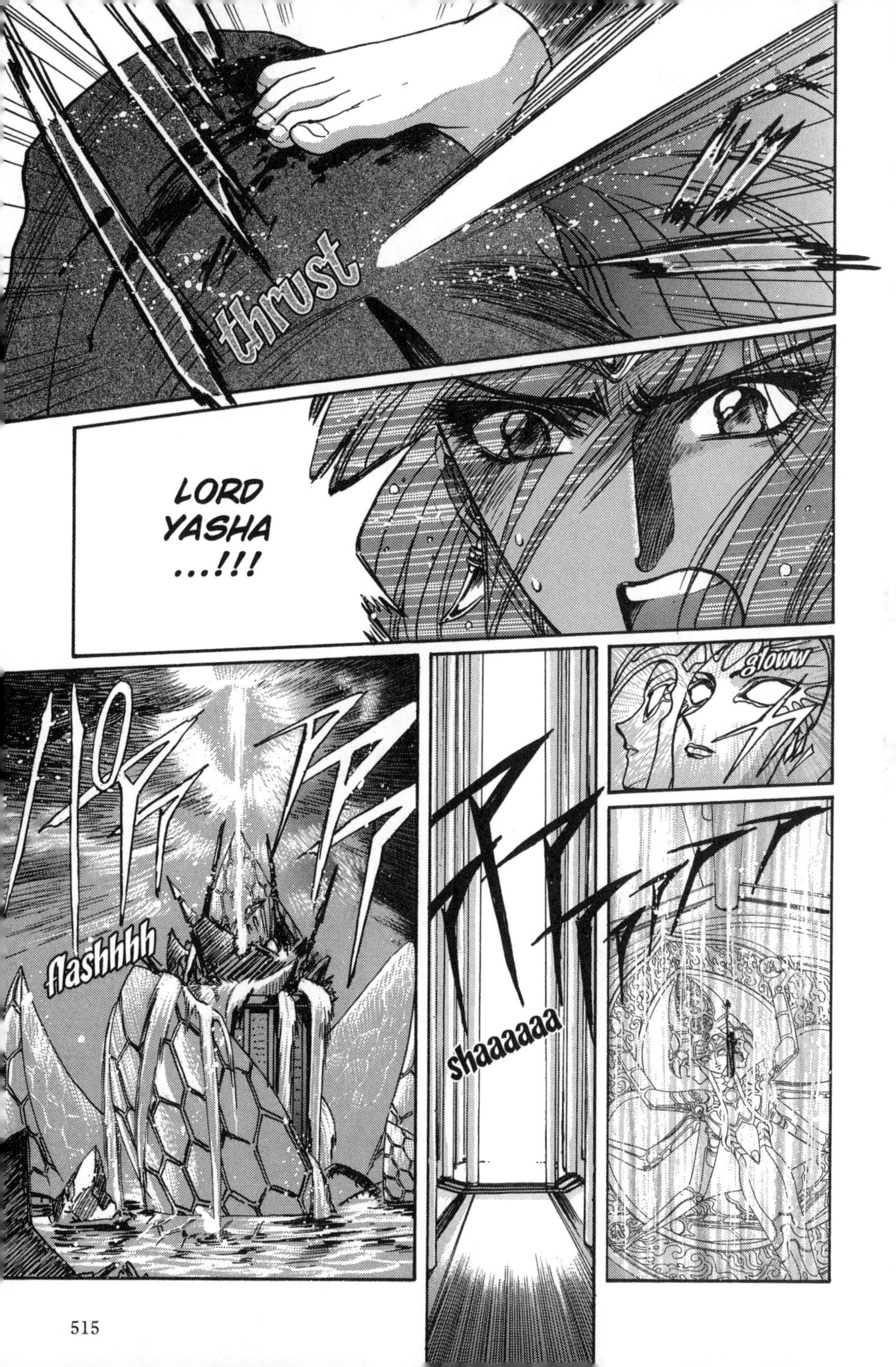
thrust
LORD YASHA ...!!!
gloww
shaaaaaa
flashhhh

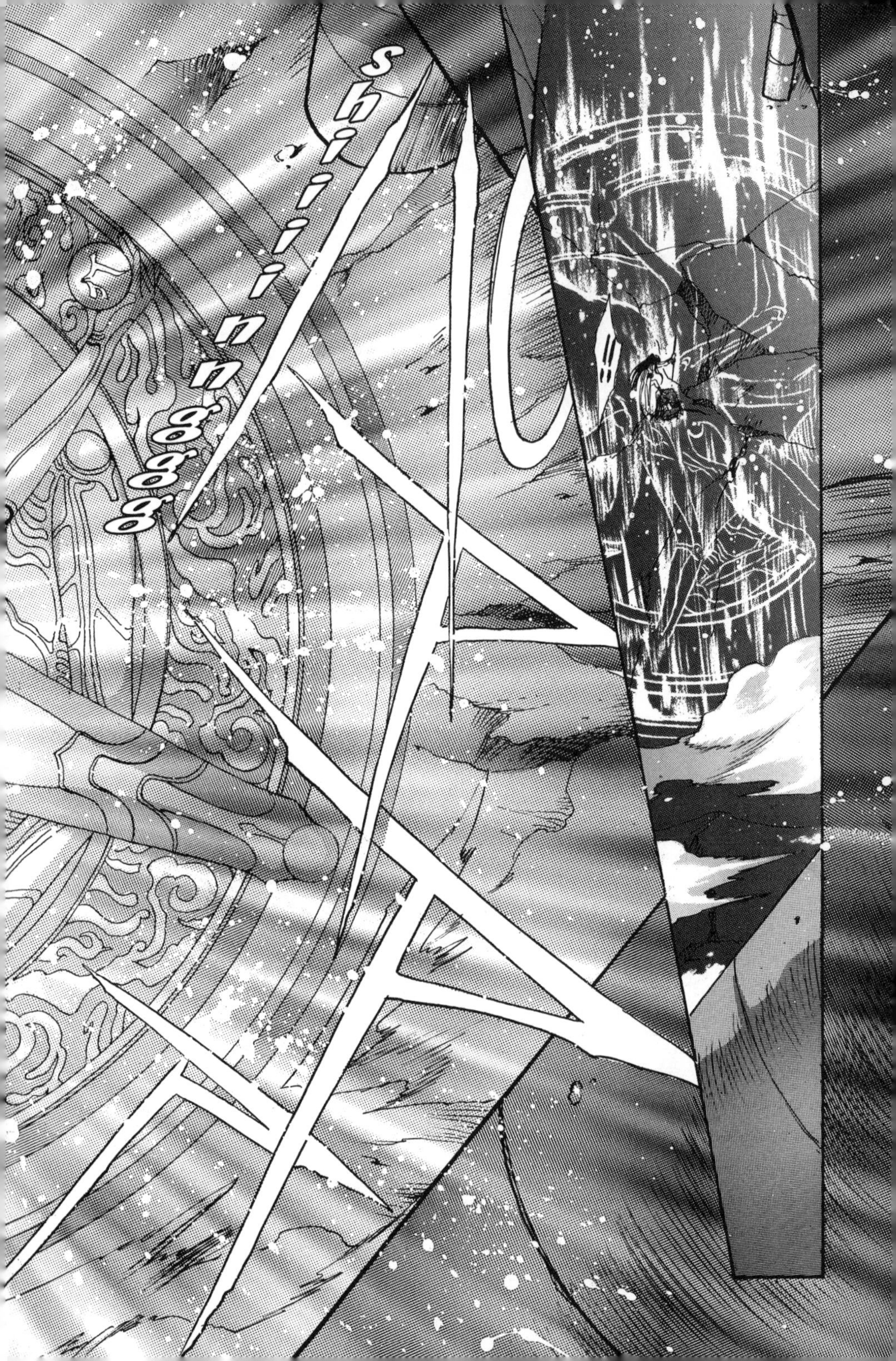
shiiiinnggggg
!!

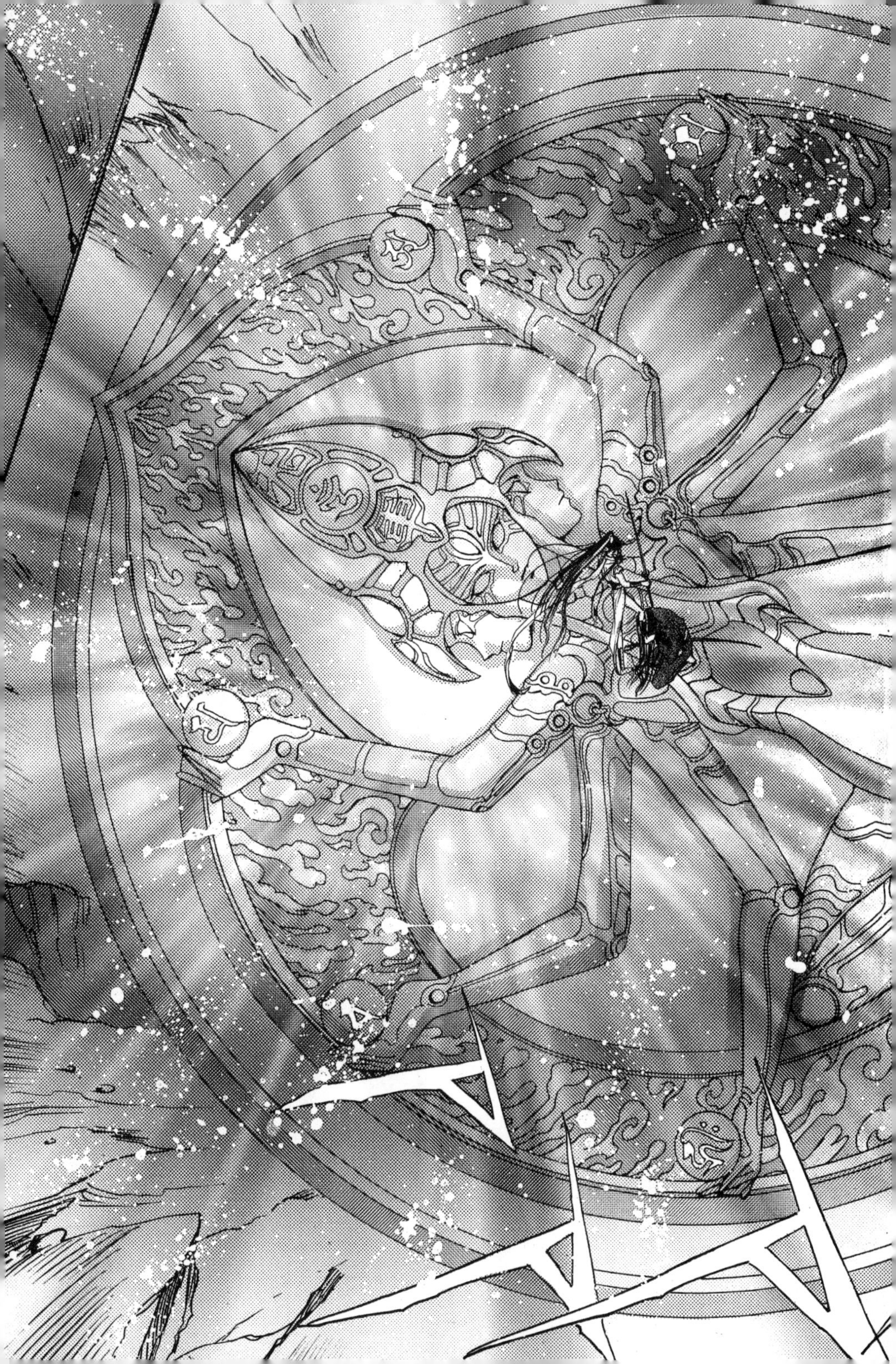

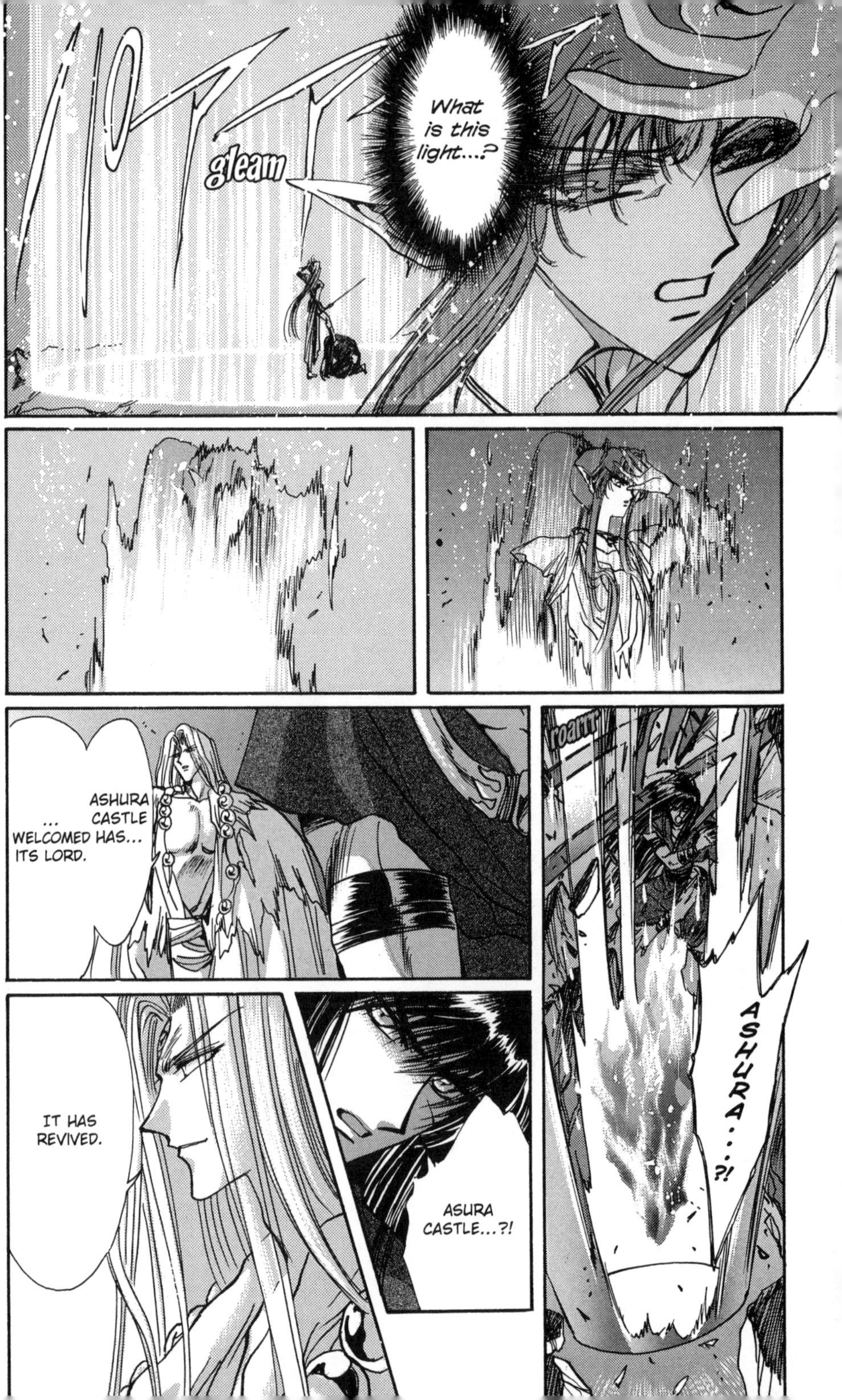
What is this light...?
gleam
roarrr
ASHURA...?!
ASHURA CASTLE ... WELCOMED HAS... ITS LORD.
ASURA CASTLE...?!
IT HAS REVIVED.

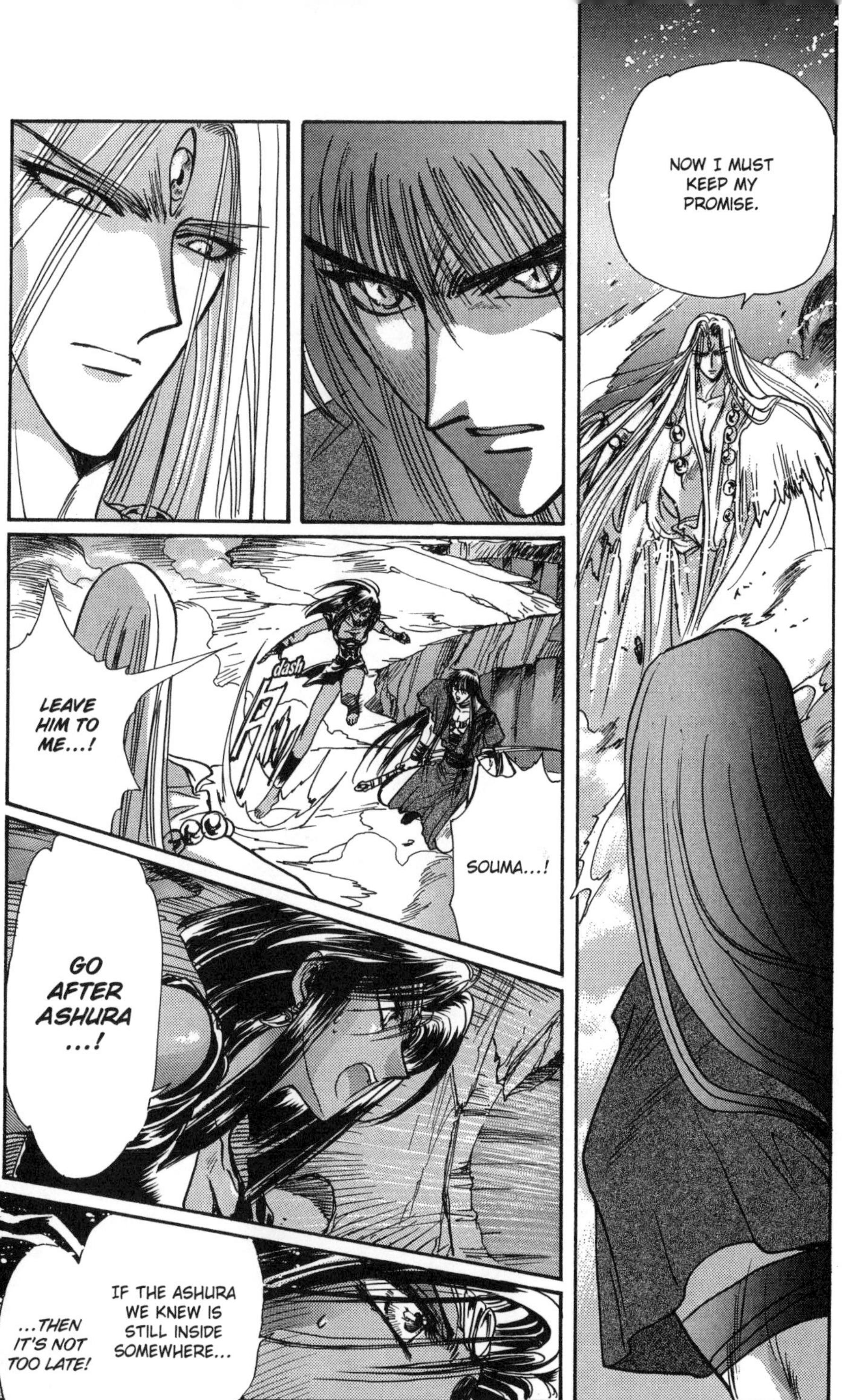
NOW I MUST KEEP MY PROMISE.
LEAVE HIM TO ME...!
dash
SOUMA...!
GO AFTER ASHURA ...!
IF THE ASHURA WE KNEW IS STILL INSIDE SOMEWHERE...
...THEN IT'S NOT TOO LATE!

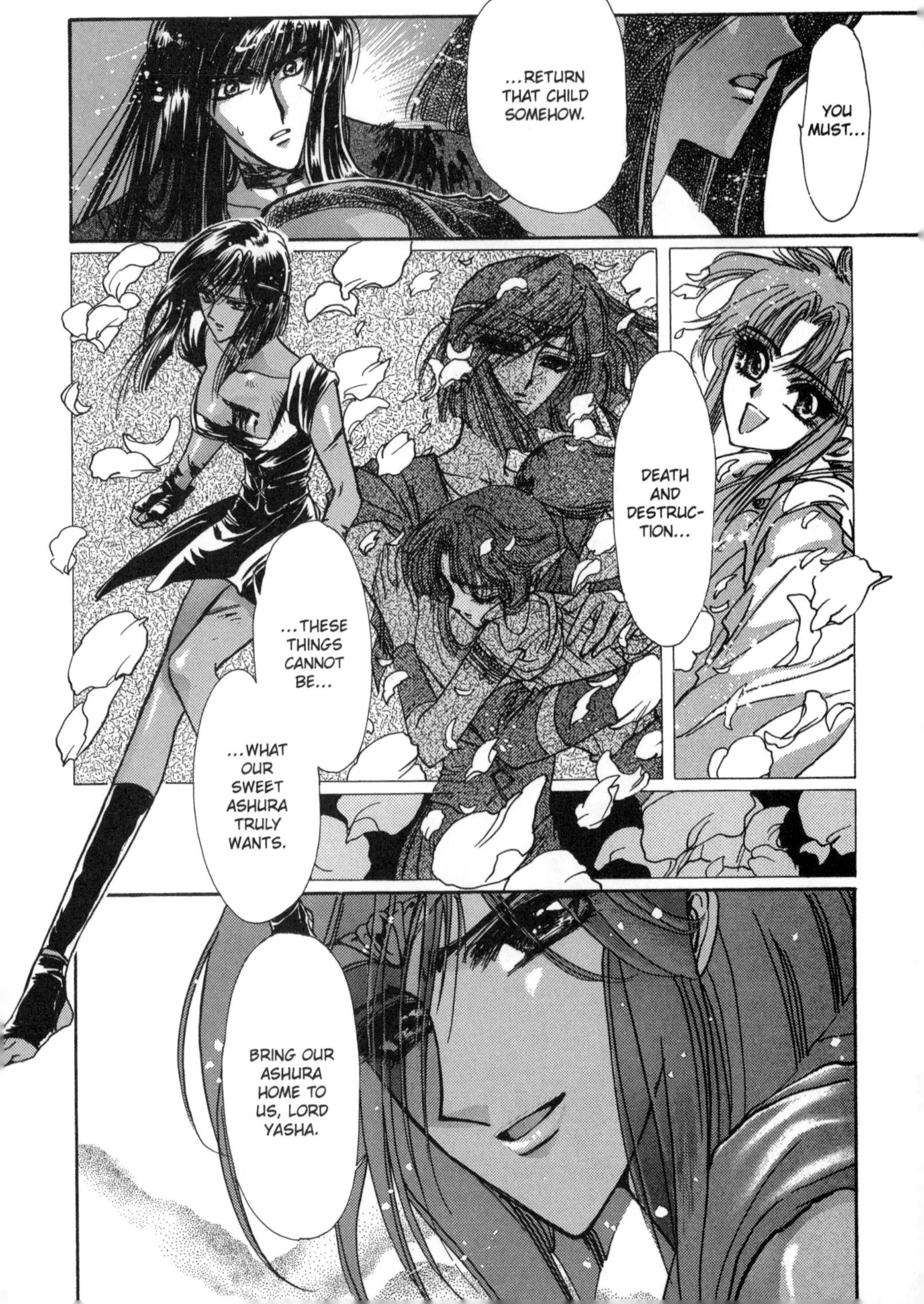
YOU MUST...
...RETURN THAT CHILD SOMEHOW.
DEATH AND DESTRUC-TION...
...THESE THINGS CANNOT BE...
...WHAT OUR SWEET ASHURA TRULY WANTS.
BRING OUR ASHURA HOME TO US, LORD YASHA.

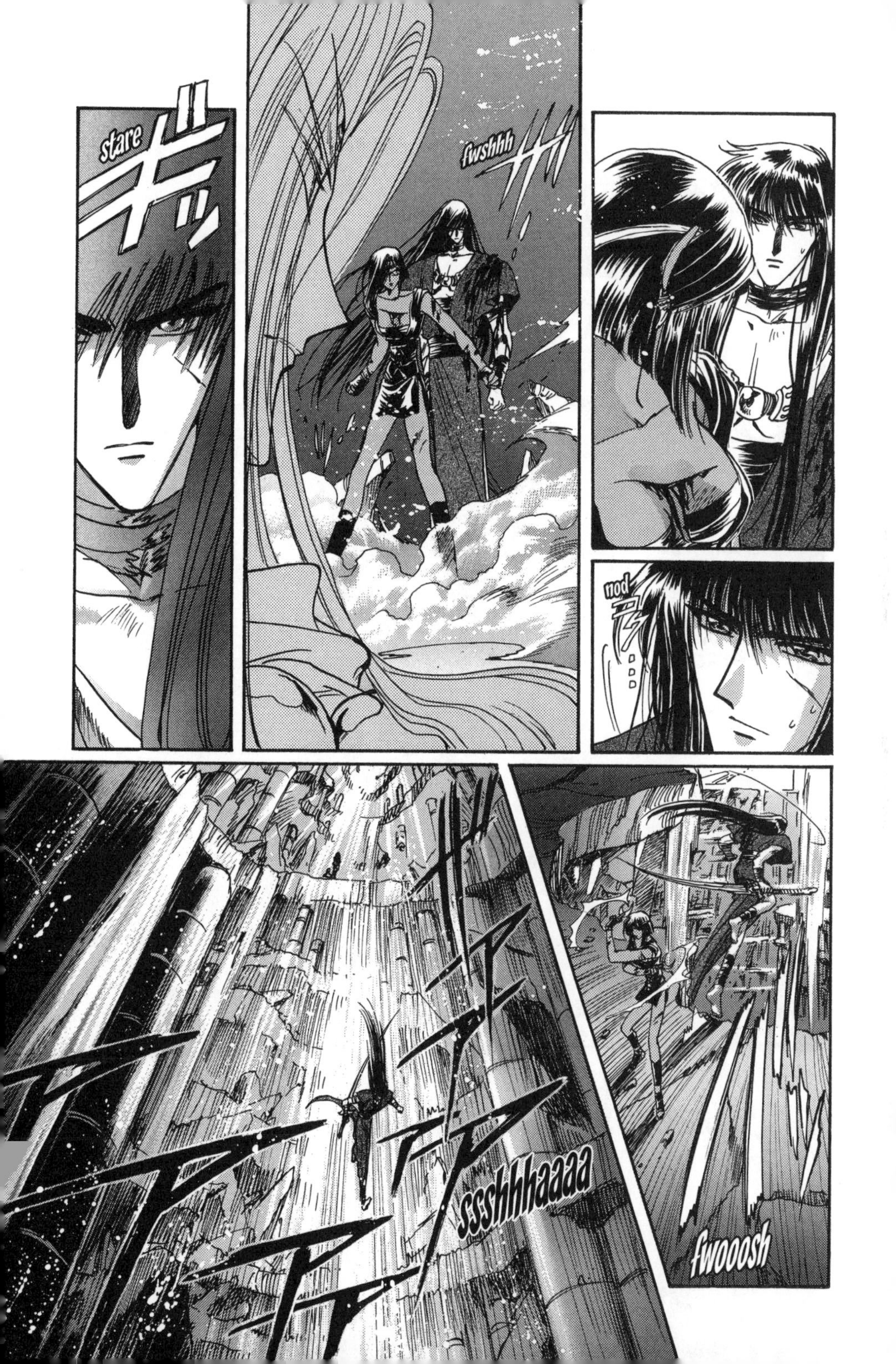
nod
fwshhh
stare
fwooosh
ssshhhaaaa

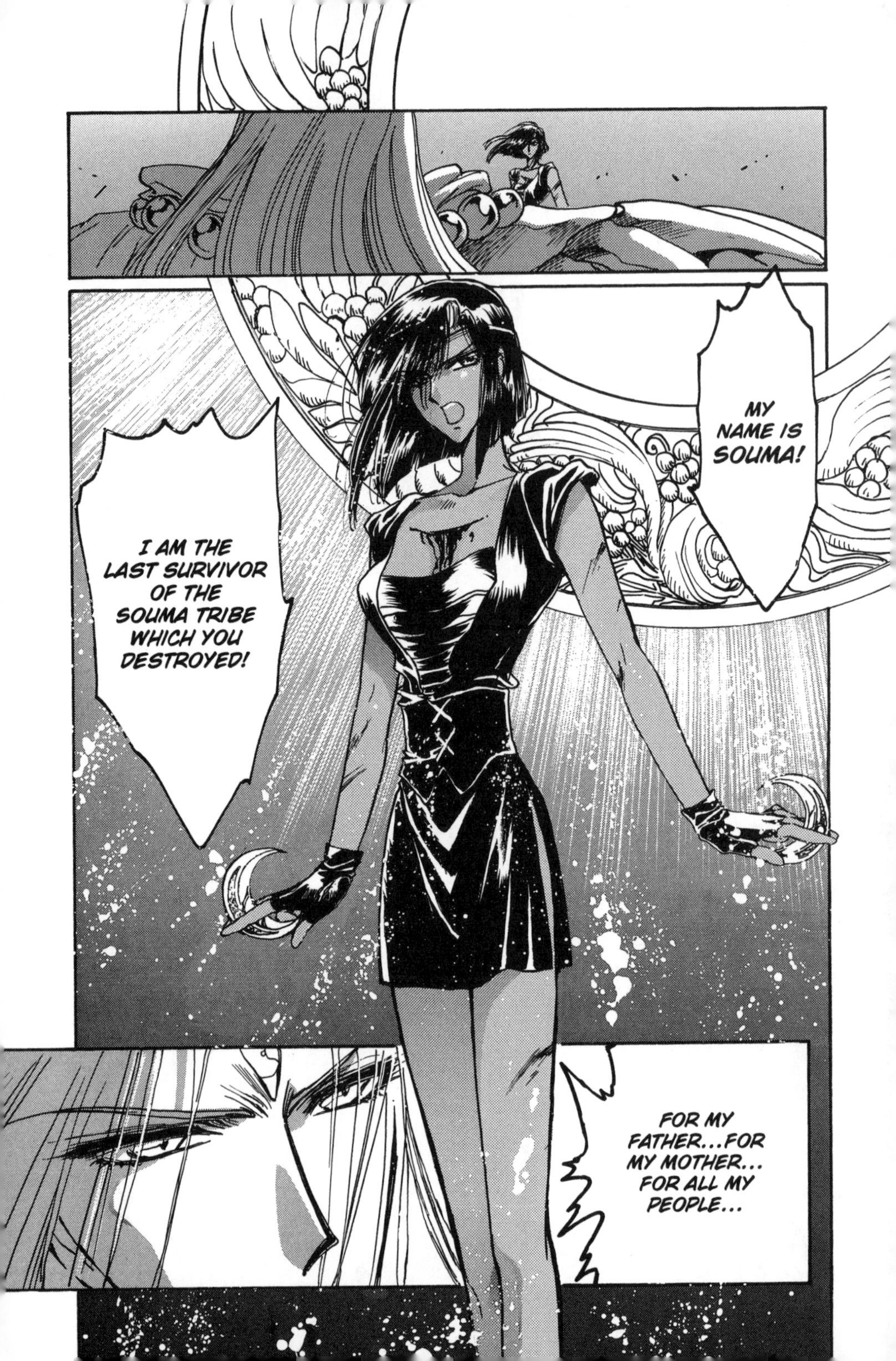
MY NAME IS SOUMA!
I AM THE LAST SURVIVOR OF THE SOUMA TRIBE WHICH YOU DESTROYED!
FOR MY FATHER...FOR MY MOTHER... FOR ALL MY PEOPLE...

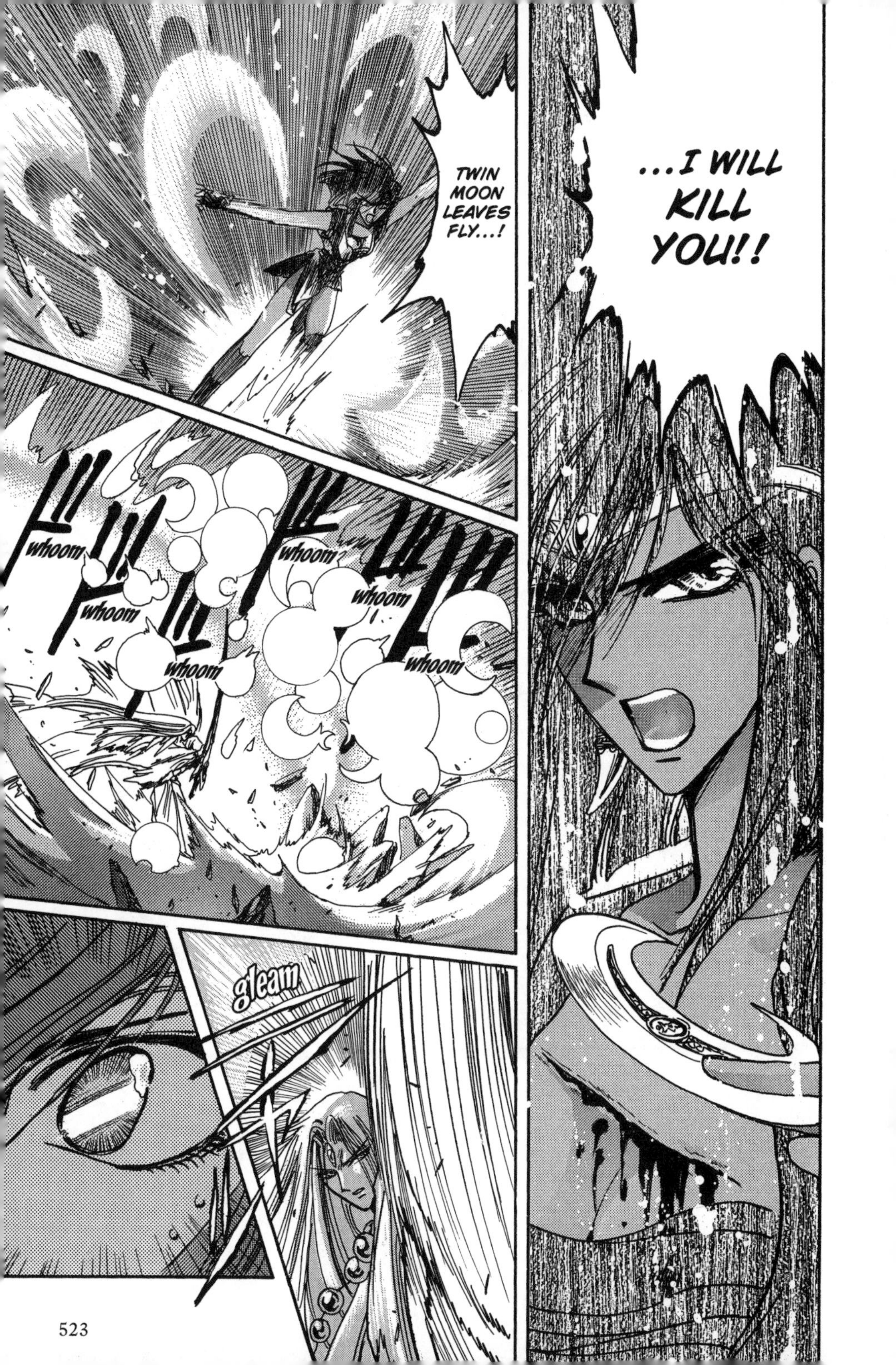
...I WILL KILL YOU!!
TWIN MOON LEAVES FLY...!
whoom
whoom
whoom
whoom
whoom
whoom
gleam

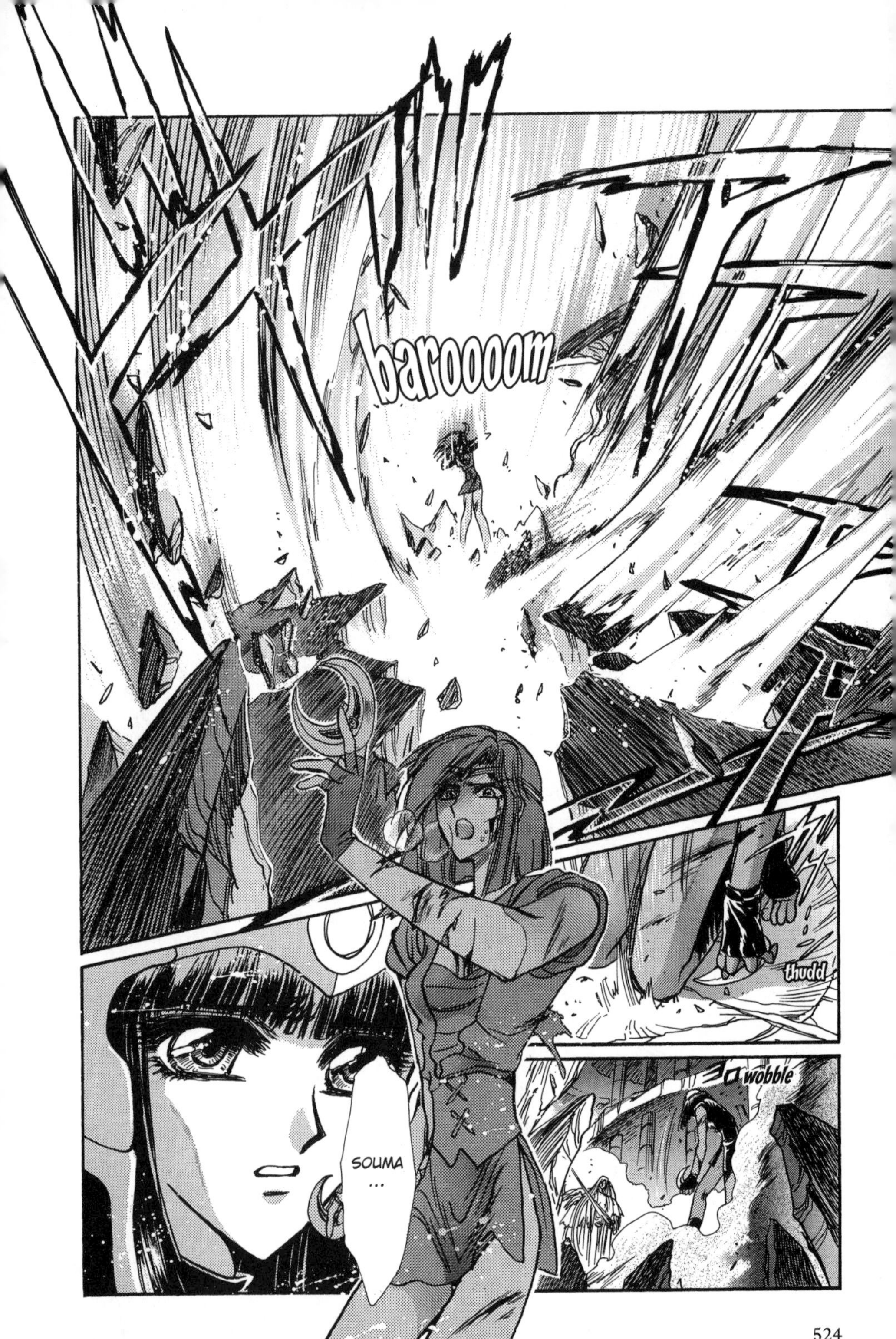
barooooom
thudd
wobble
SOUMA
...

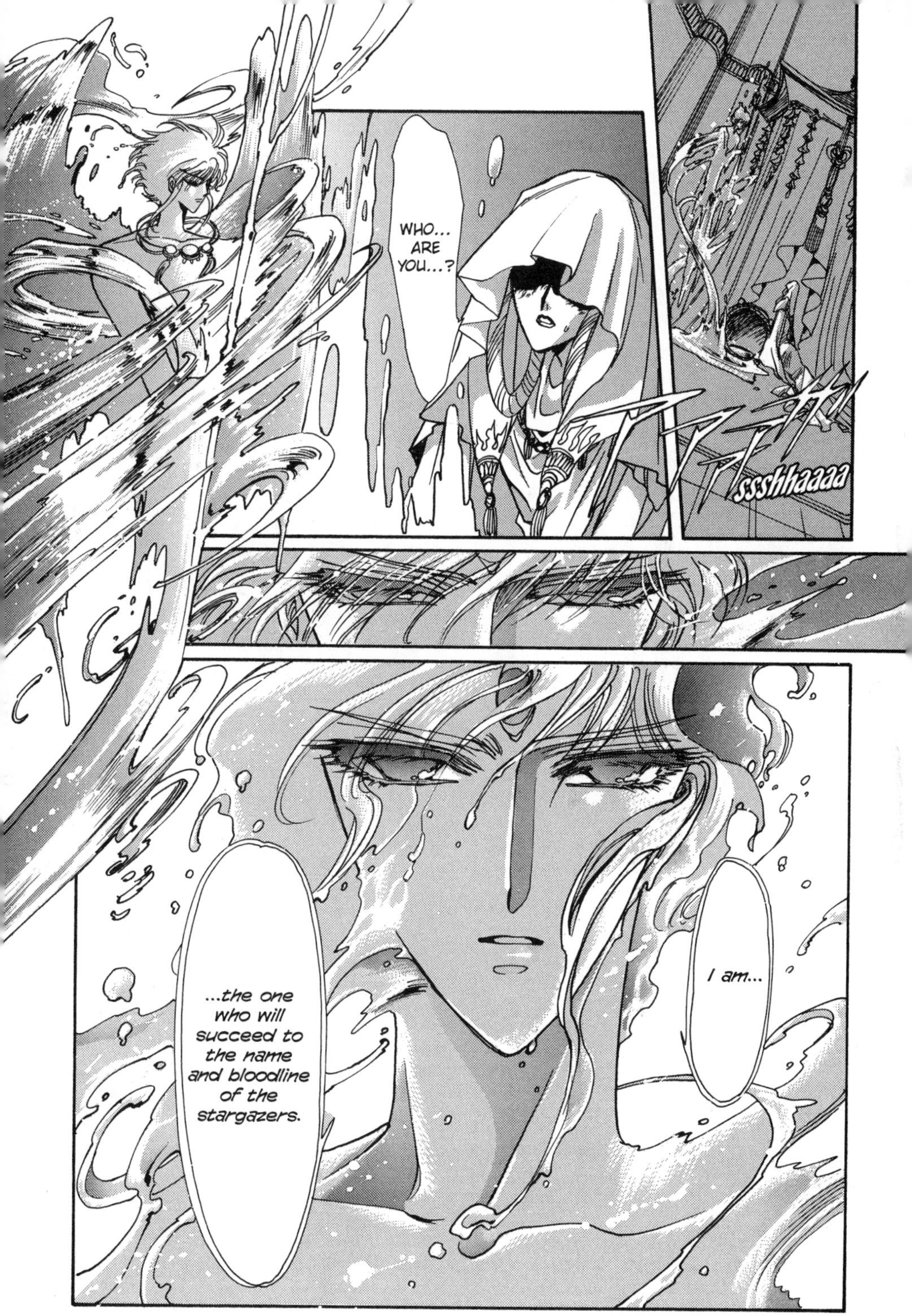
ssshhaaaa
WHO... ARE YOU...?
I am...
...the one who will succeed to the name and bloodline of the stargazers.

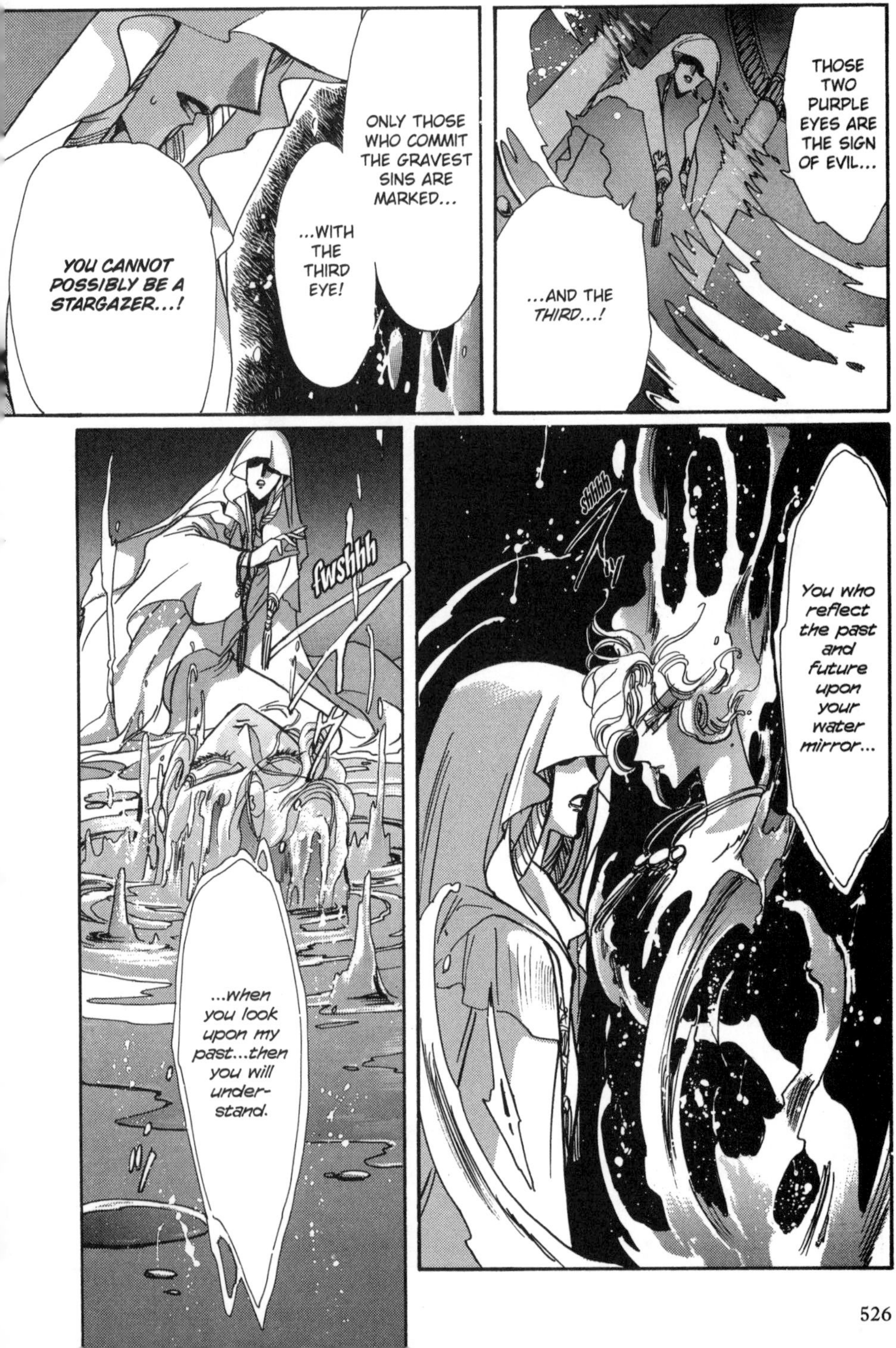
THOSE TWO PURPLE EYES ARE THE SIGN OF EVIL...
...AND THE THIRD...!
ONLY THOSE WHO COMMIT THE GRAVEST SINS ARE MARKED...
...WITH THE THIRD EYE!
YOU CANNOT POSSIBLY BE A STARGAZER...!
shhhh
You who reflect the past and future upon your water mirror...
fwshhh
...when you look upon my past...then you will under-stand.

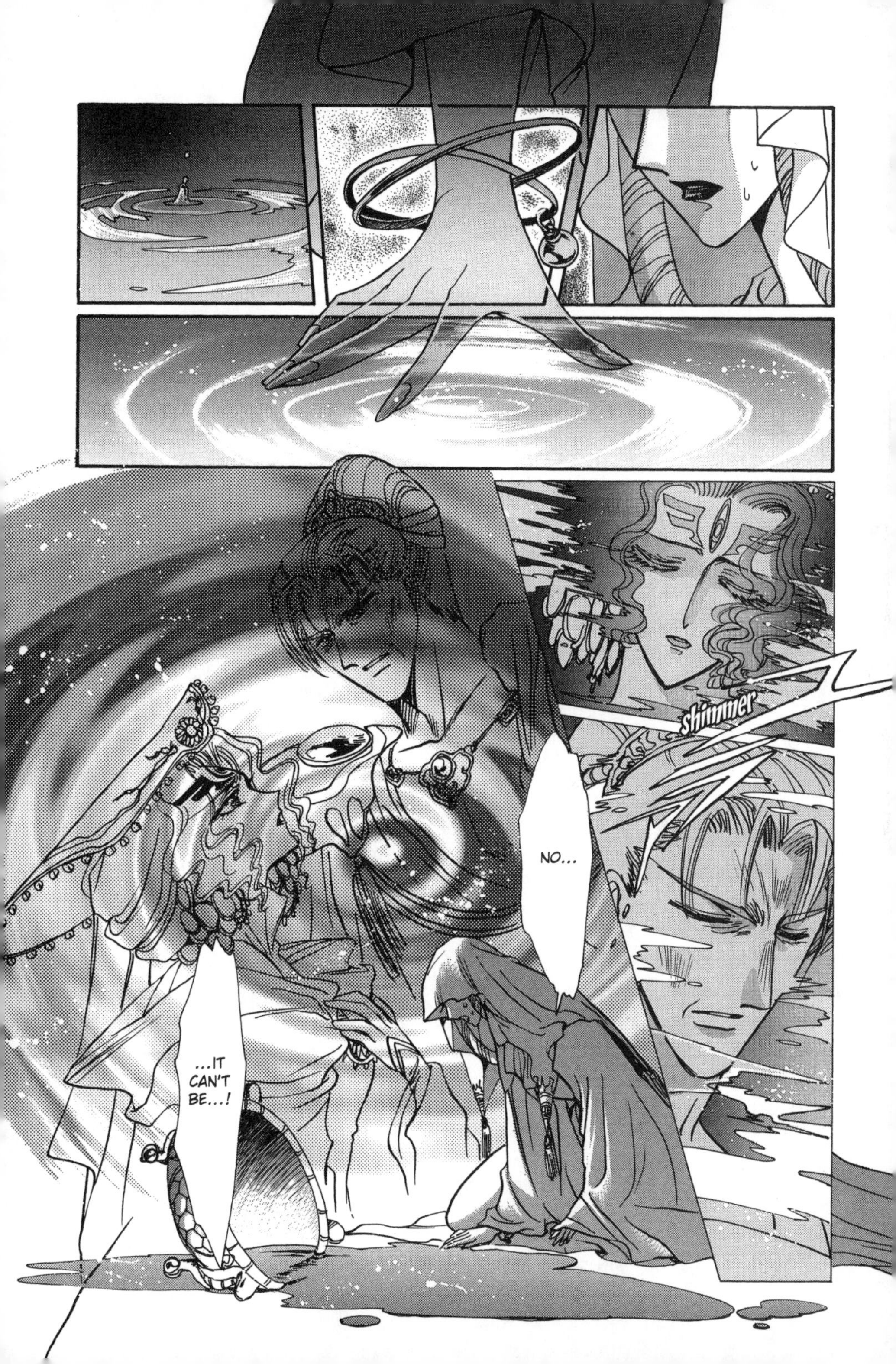
shimmer
NO...
...IT CAN'T BE...!

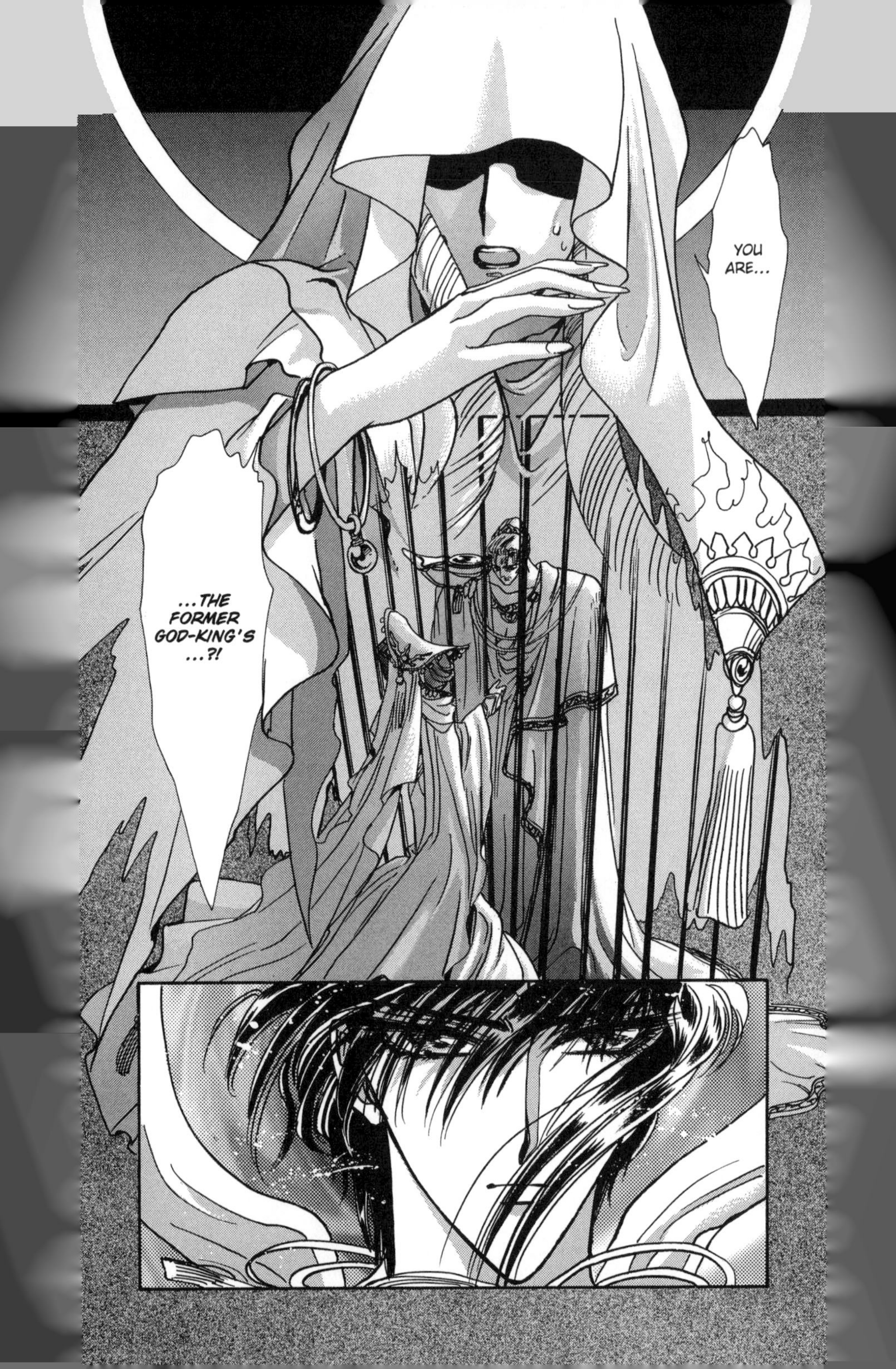
YOU ARE...
...THE FORMER GOD-KING'S ...?!

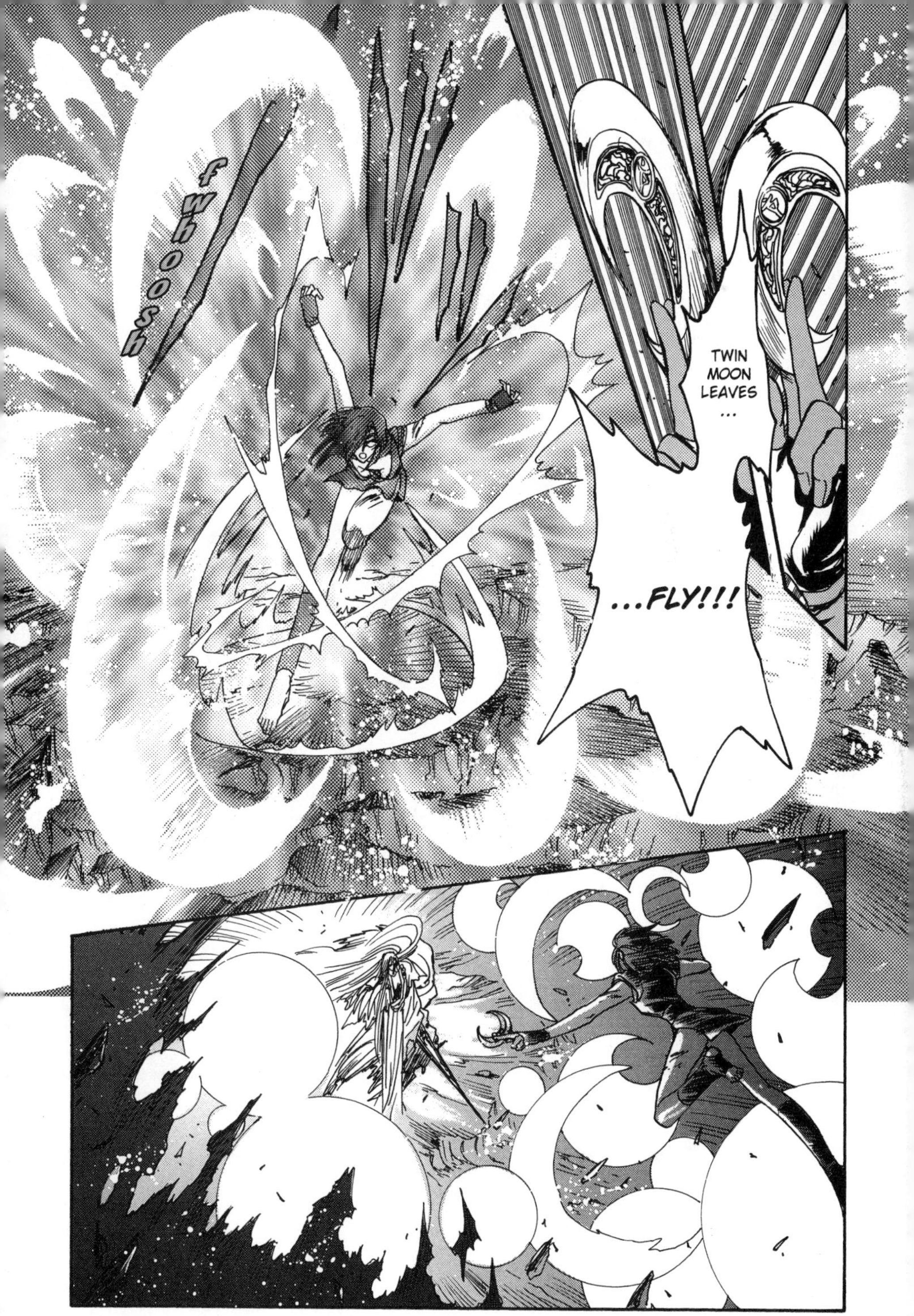
TWIN MOON LEAVES ...
...FLY!!!
fwhoosh

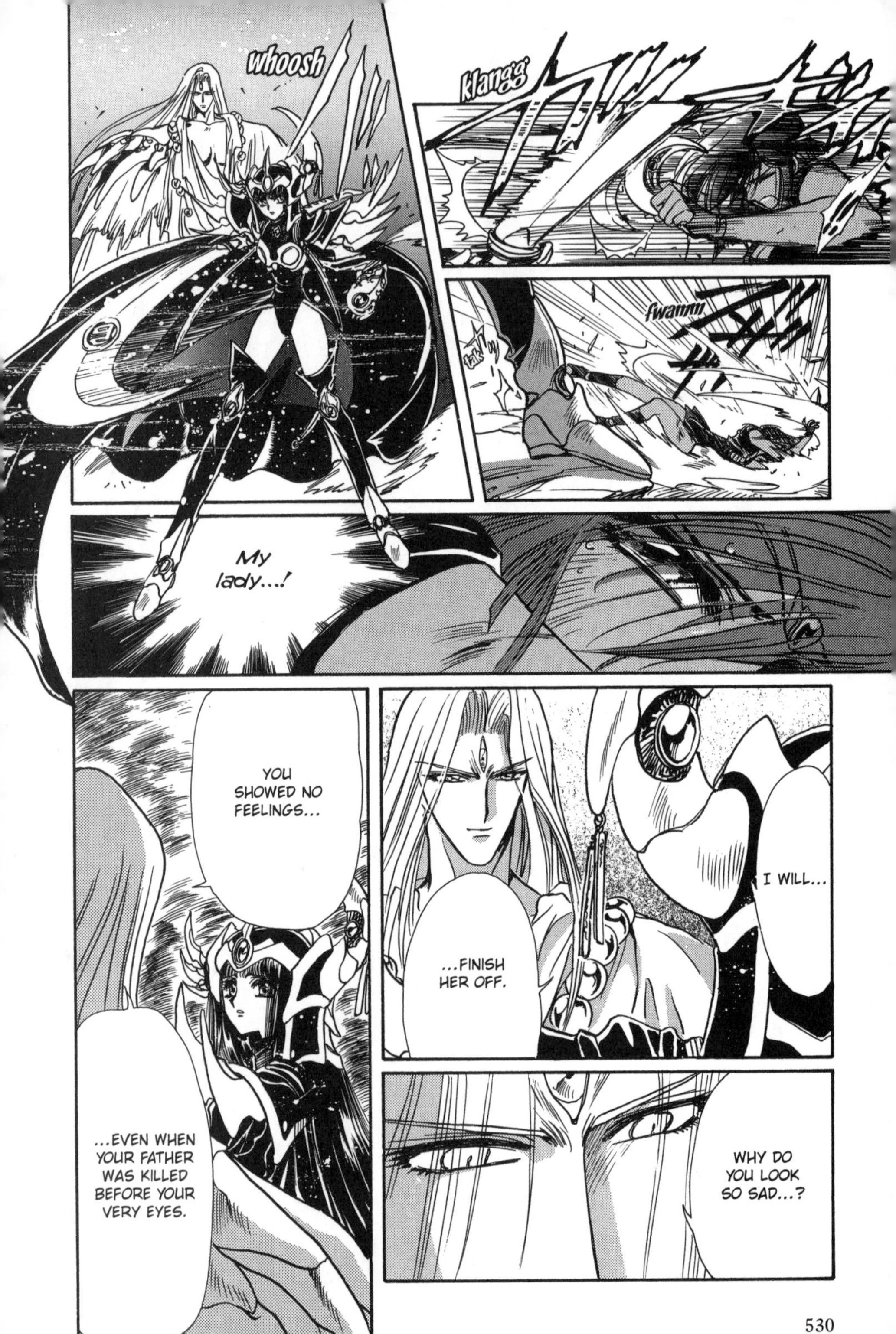
klang'g
fwannn
whoosh
My lady...!
I WILL...
...FINISH HER OFF.
WHY DO YOU LOOK SO SAD...?
YOU SHOWED NO FEELINGS...
...EVEN WHEN YOUR FATHER WAS KILLED BEFORE YOUR VERY EYES.

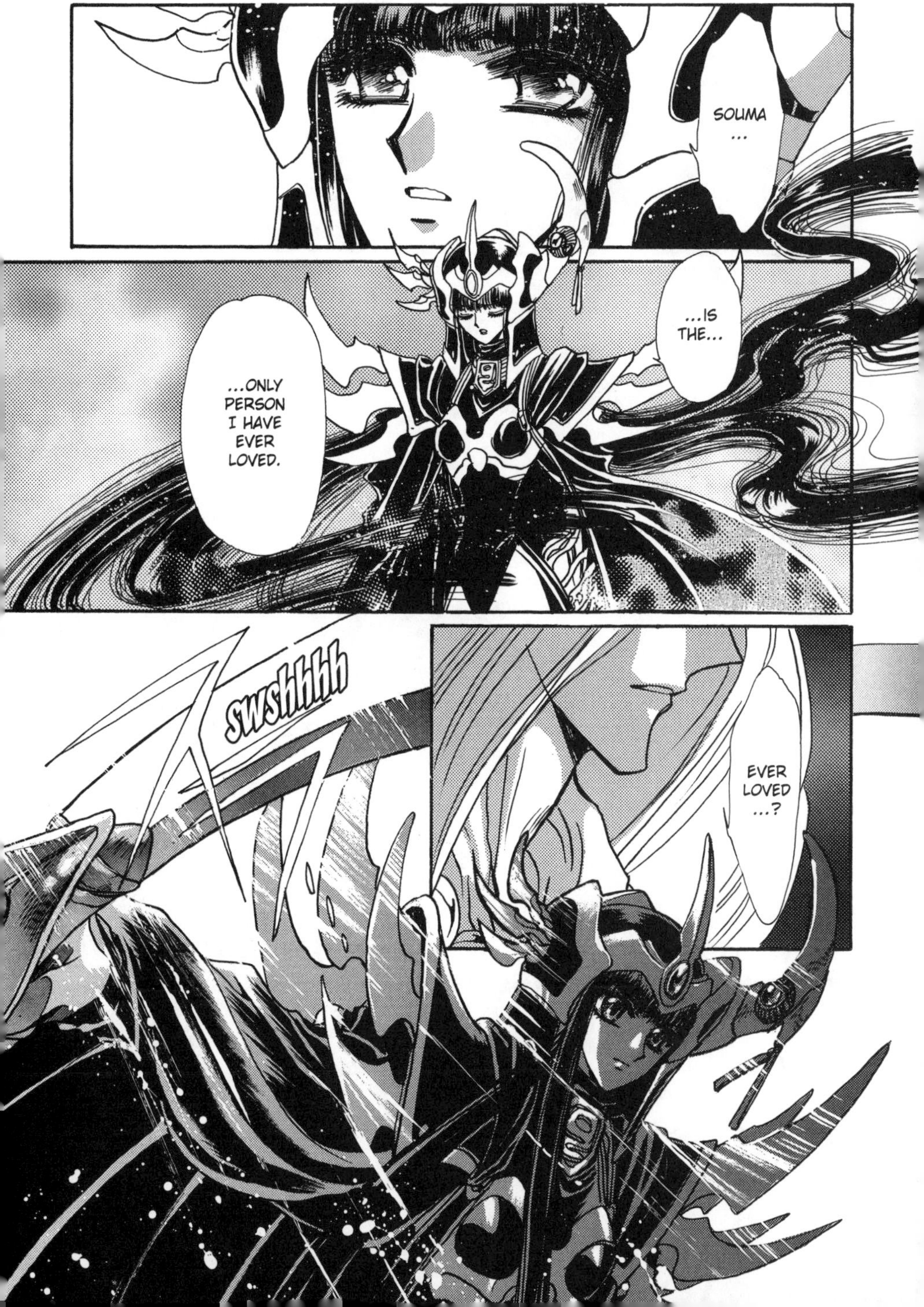

SOUMA ...
...IS THE...
...ONLY PERSON I HAVE EVER LOVED.
EVER LOVED ...?
SWSHHHH

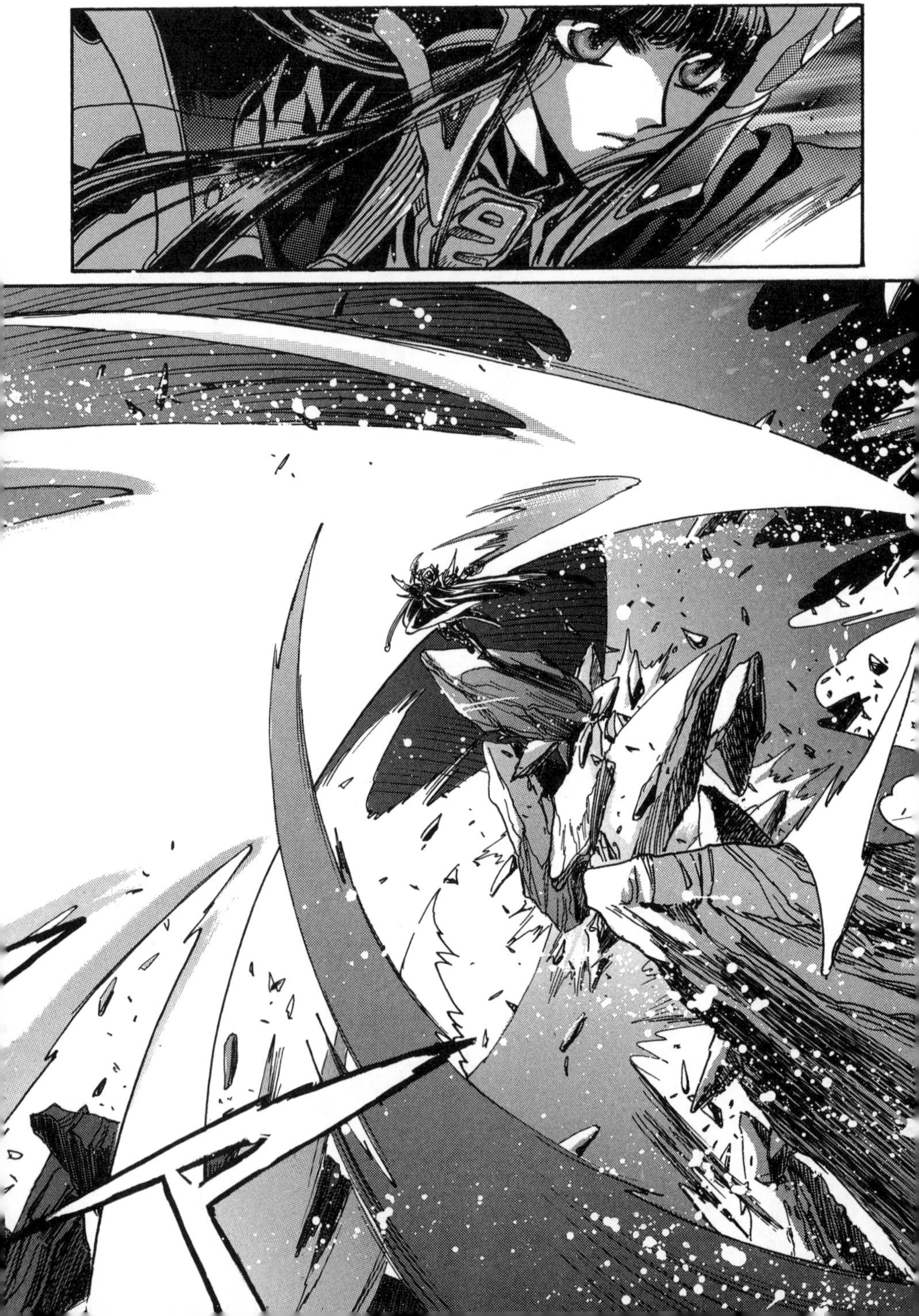

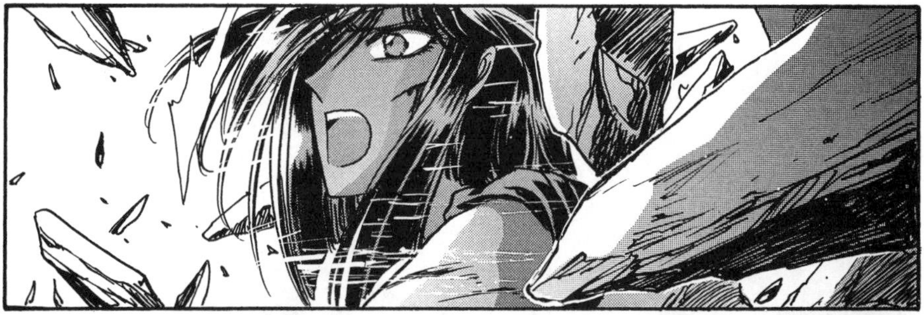

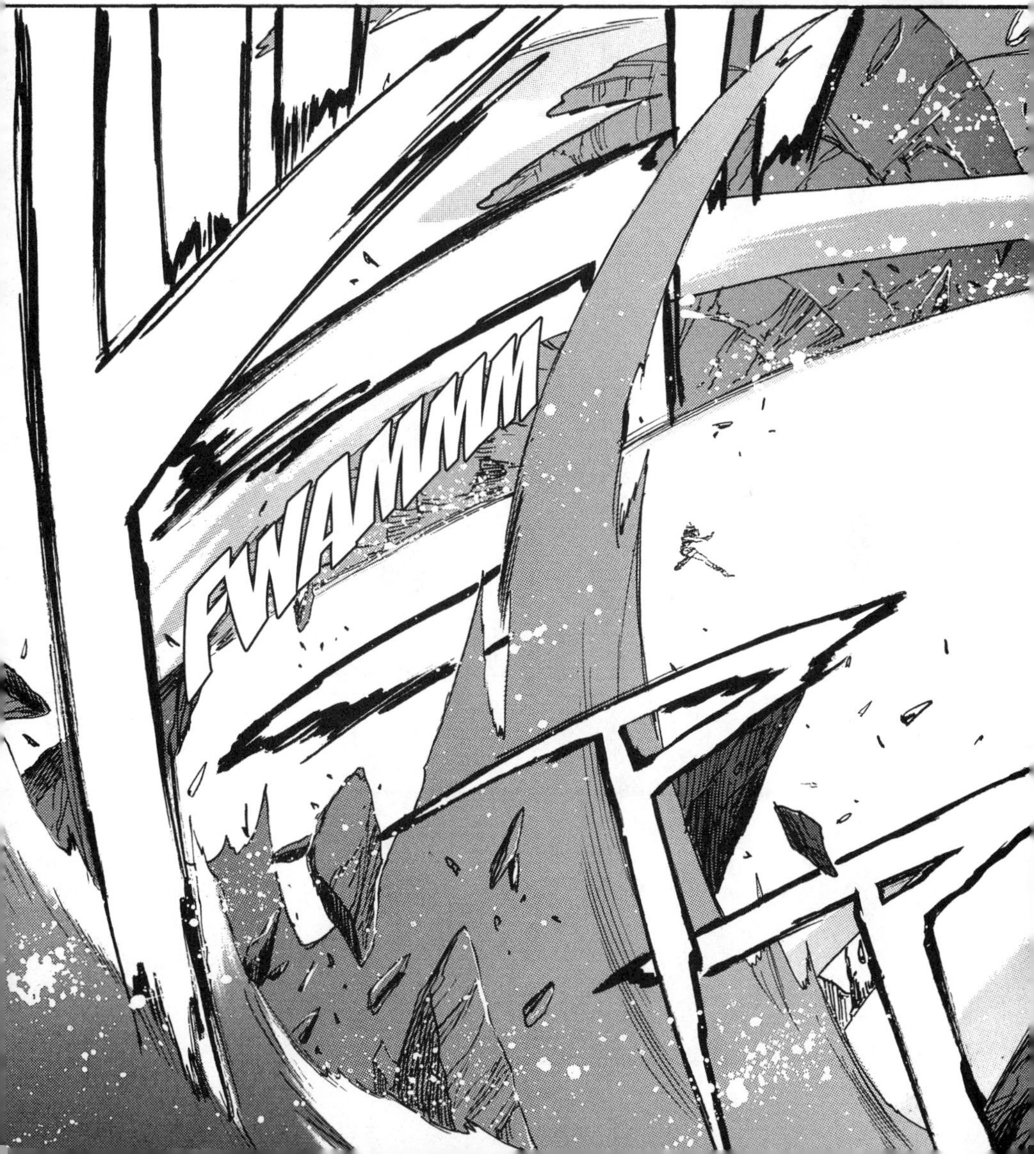
FWAMMM

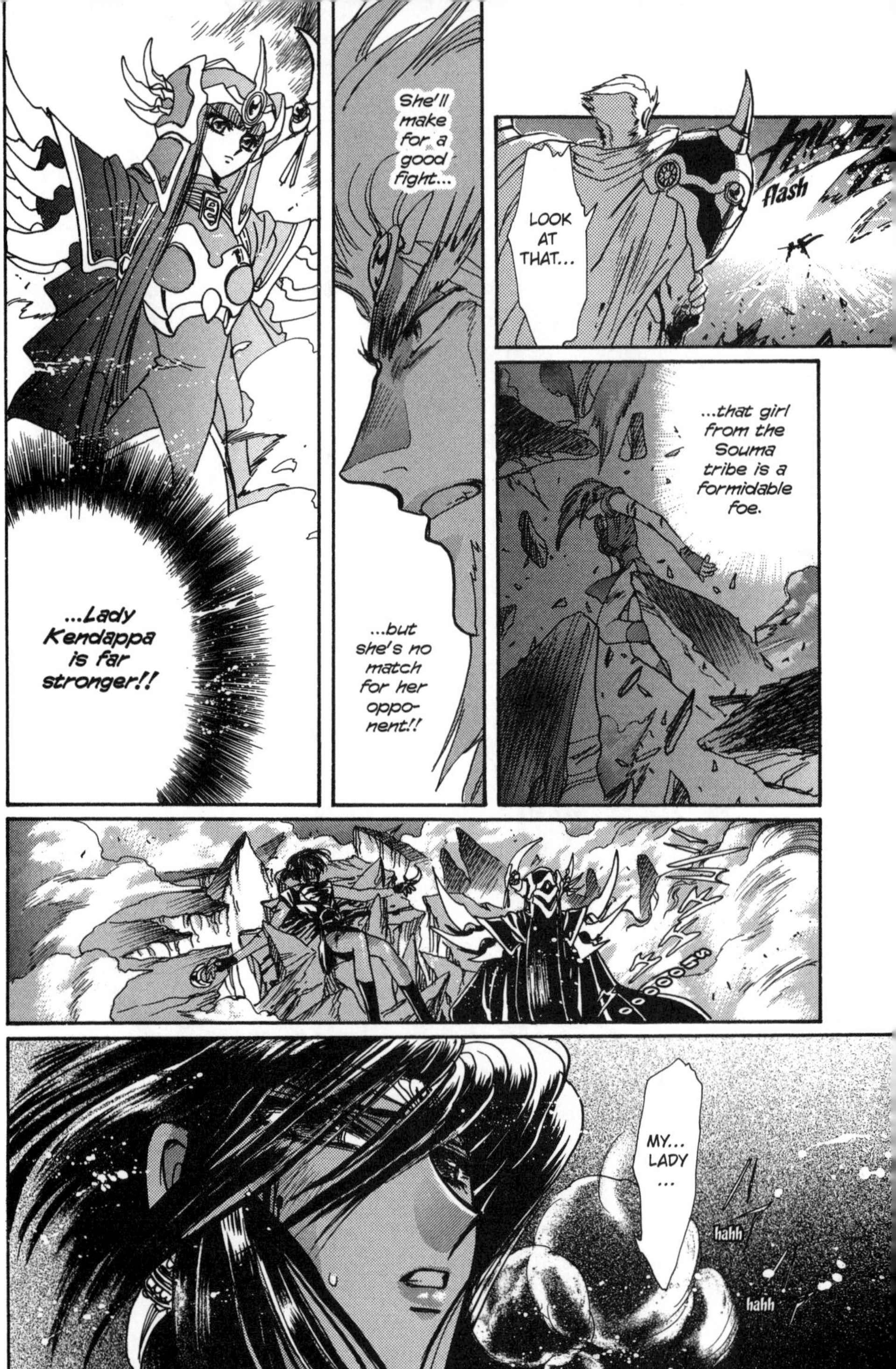
LOOK AT THAT...
flash
...that girl from the Souma tribe is a formidable foe.
She'll make for a good fight...
...but she's no match for her opponent!!
...Lady Kendappa is far stronger!!
MY... LADY ...
hahh
hahh

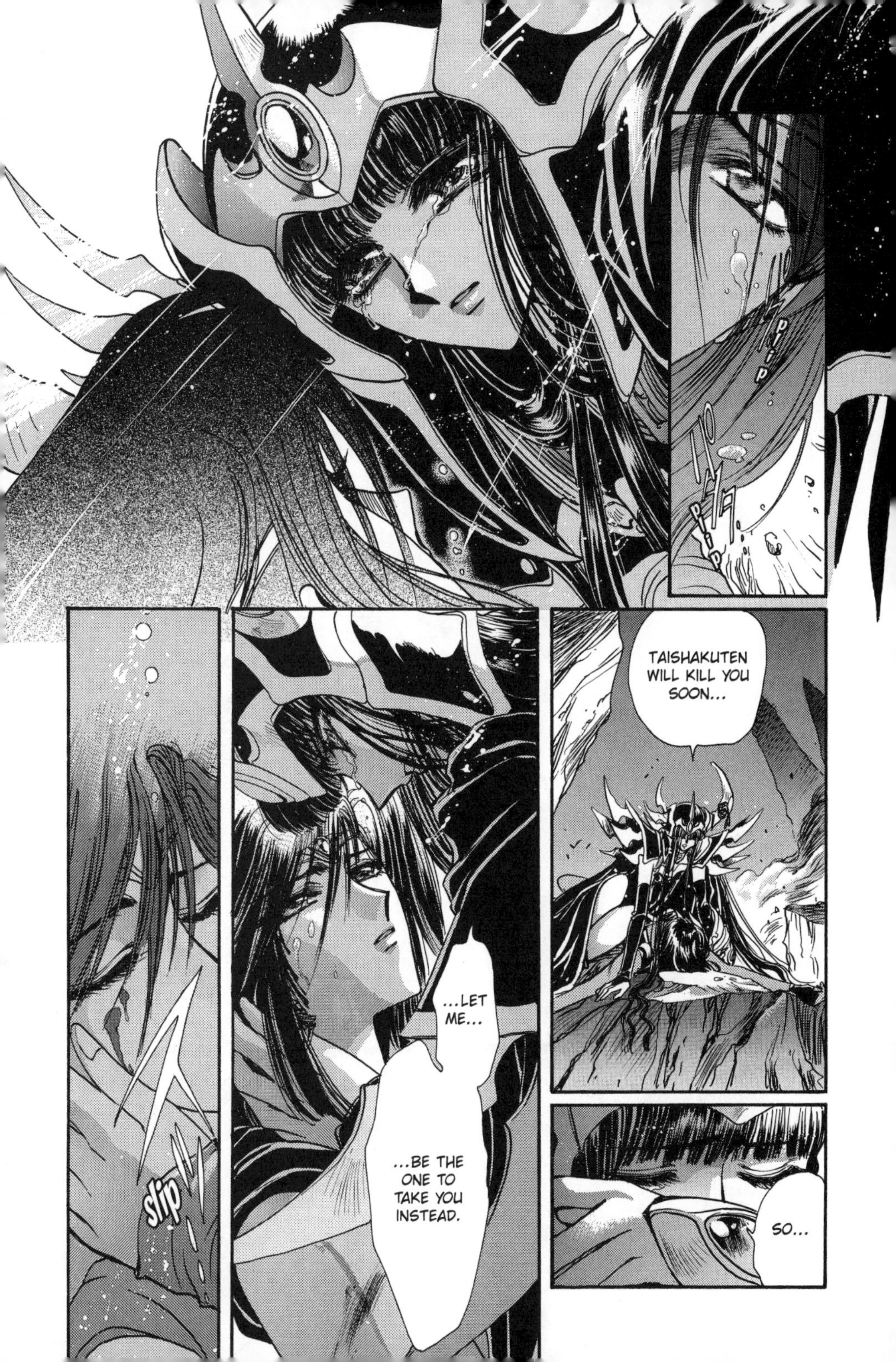
pip
pip
TAISHAKUTEN WILL KILL YOU SOON...
SO...
...LET ME...
...BE THE ONE TO TAKE YOU INSTEAD.
slip

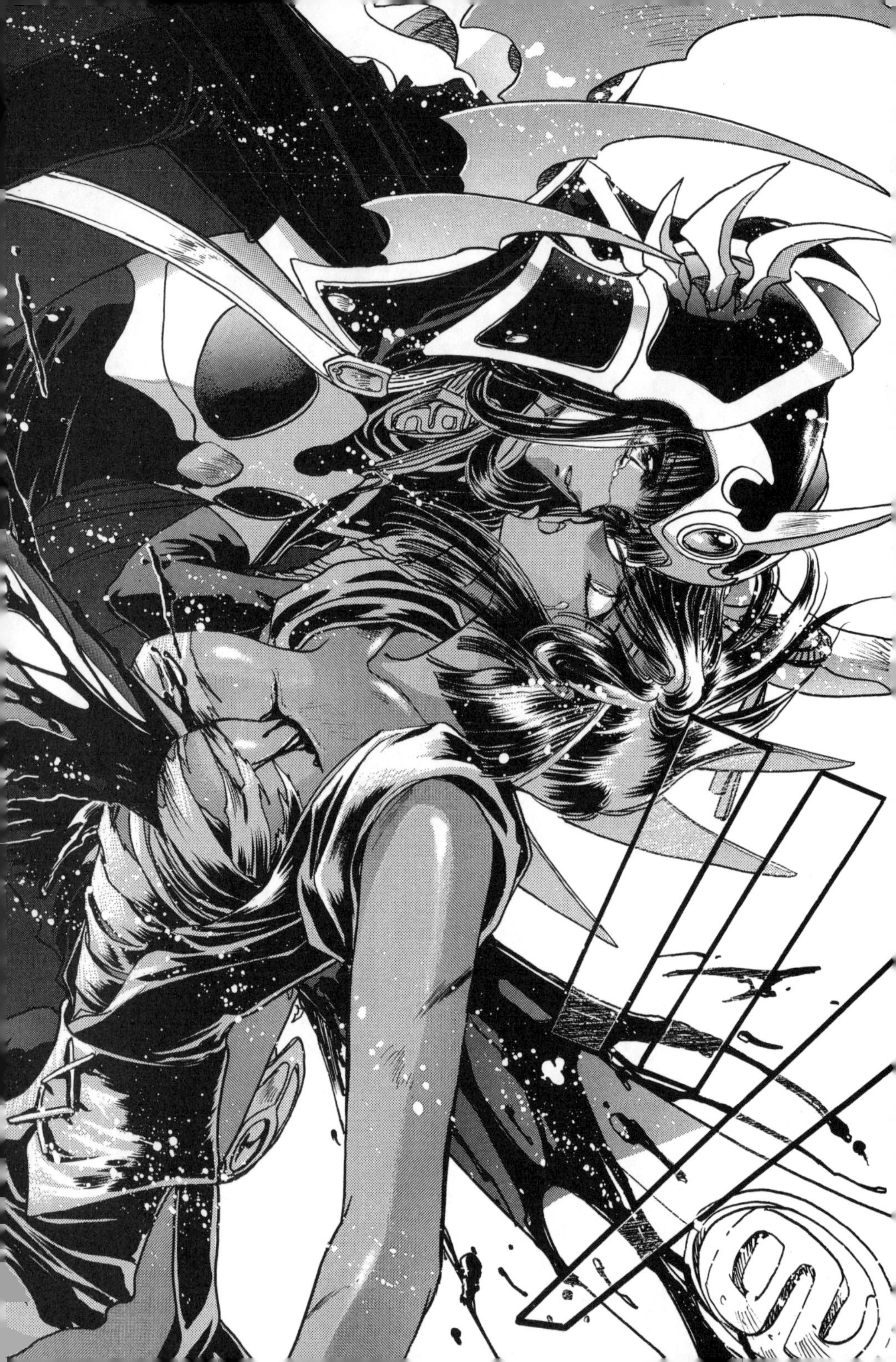

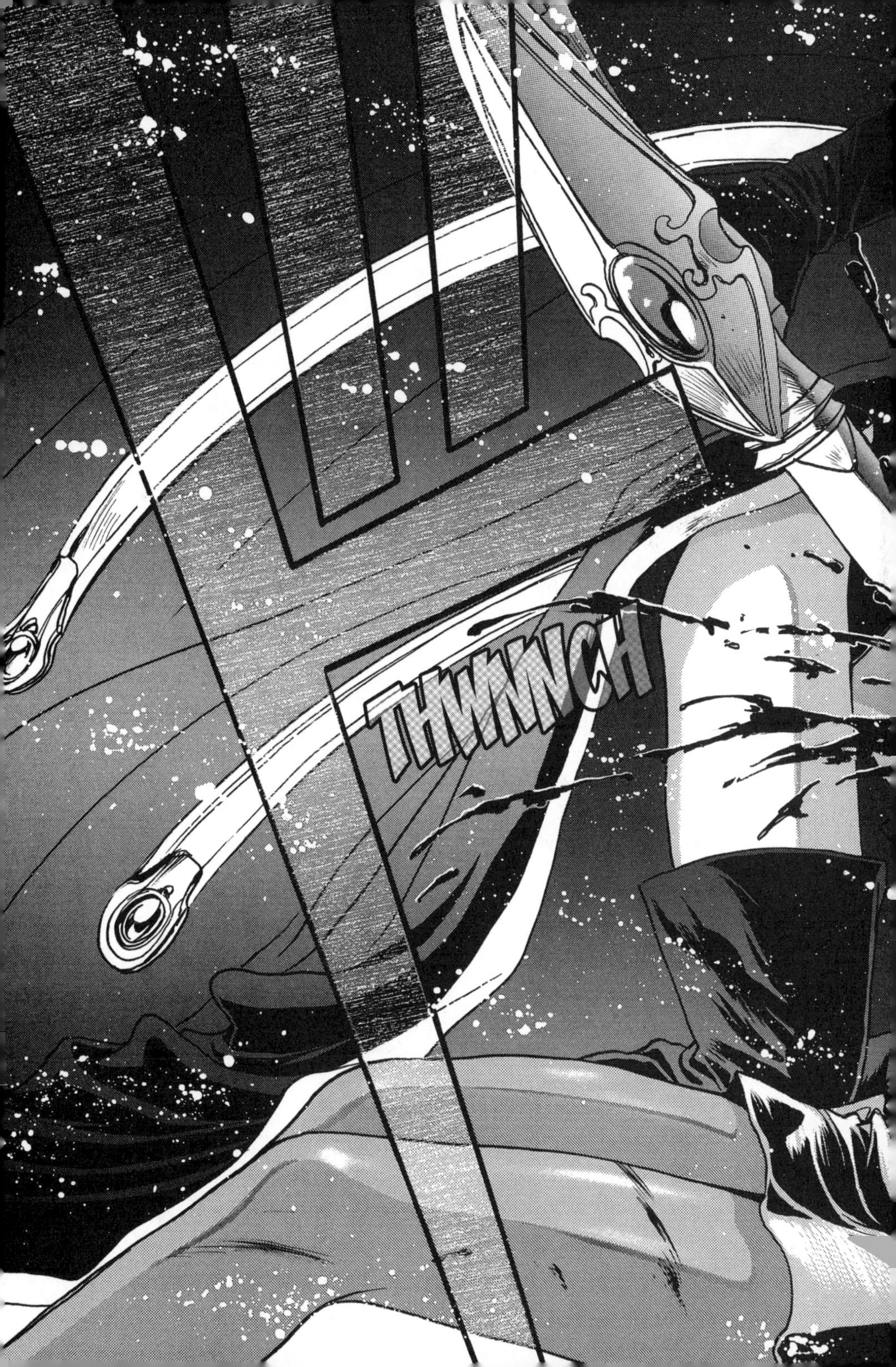
THWNNCH

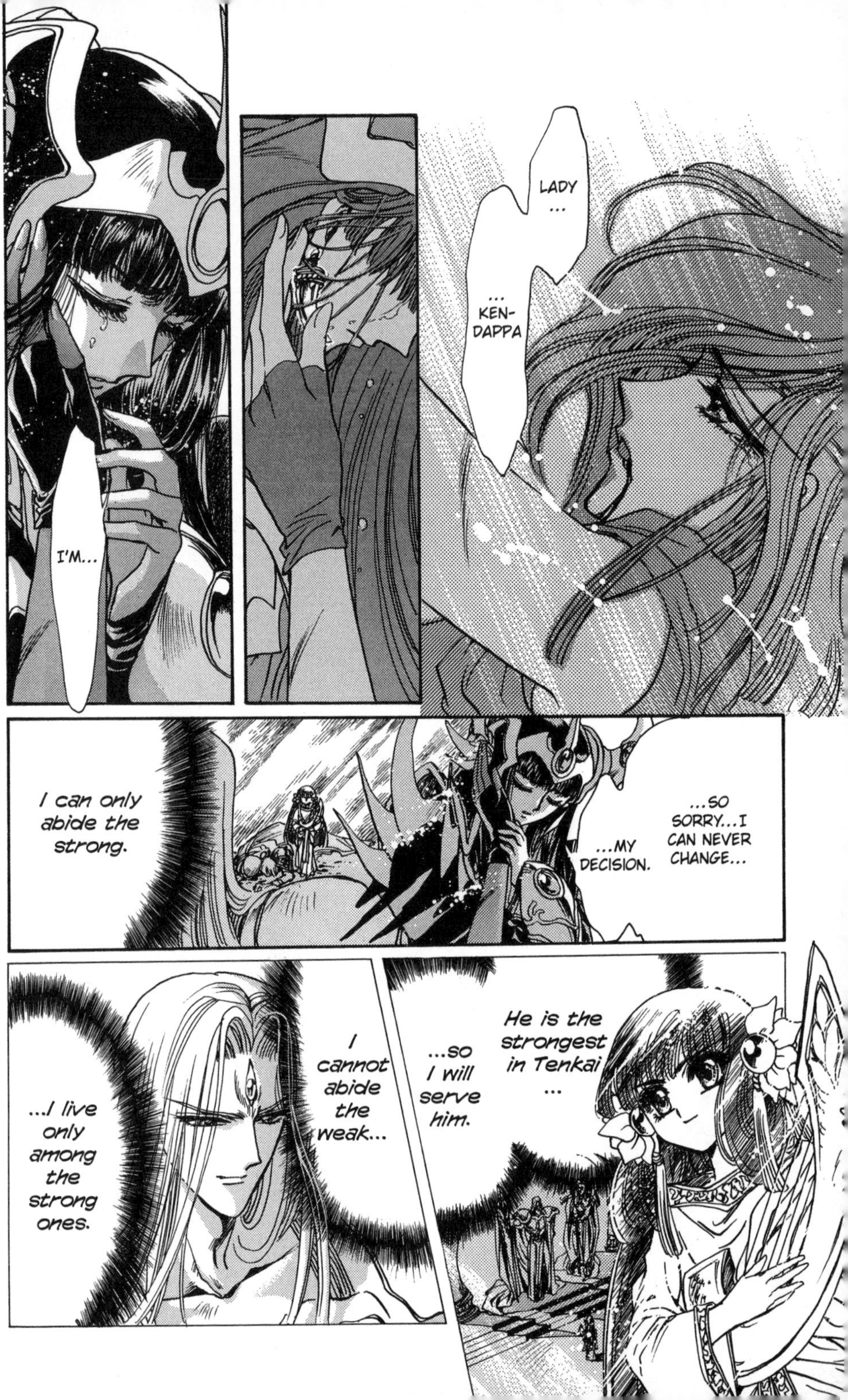
LADY ...
... KEN-DAPPA
I'M...
...SO SORRY...I CAN NEVER CHANGE...
...MY DECISION.
I can only abide the strong.
He is the strongest in Tenkai ...
...so I will serve him.
I cannot abide the weak...
...I live only among the strong ones.

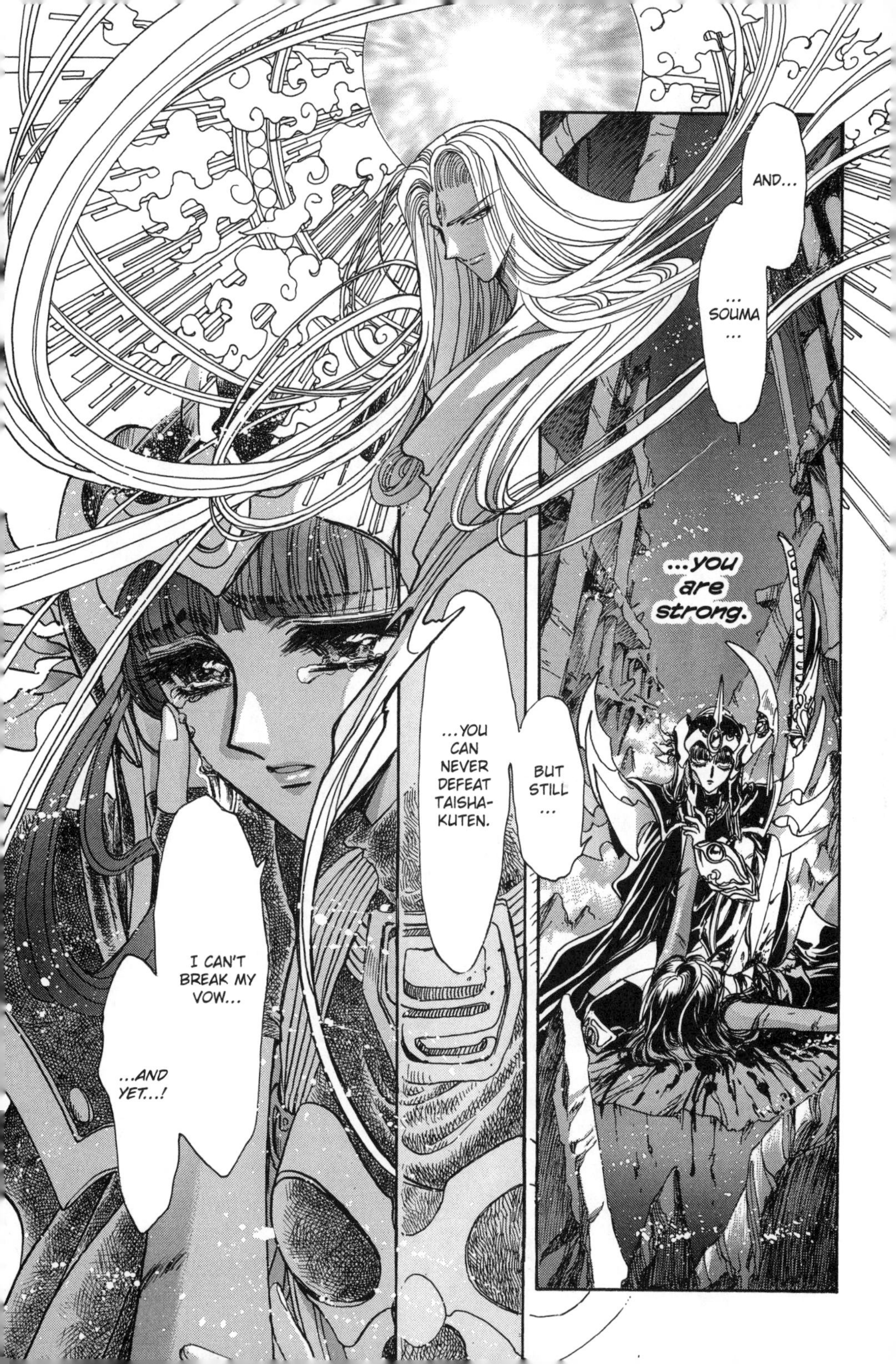
AND...
...SOUMA...
...you are strong.
BUT STILL...
...YOU CAN NEVER DEFEAT TAISHA-KUTEN.
I CAN'T BREAK MY VOW...
...AND YET...!

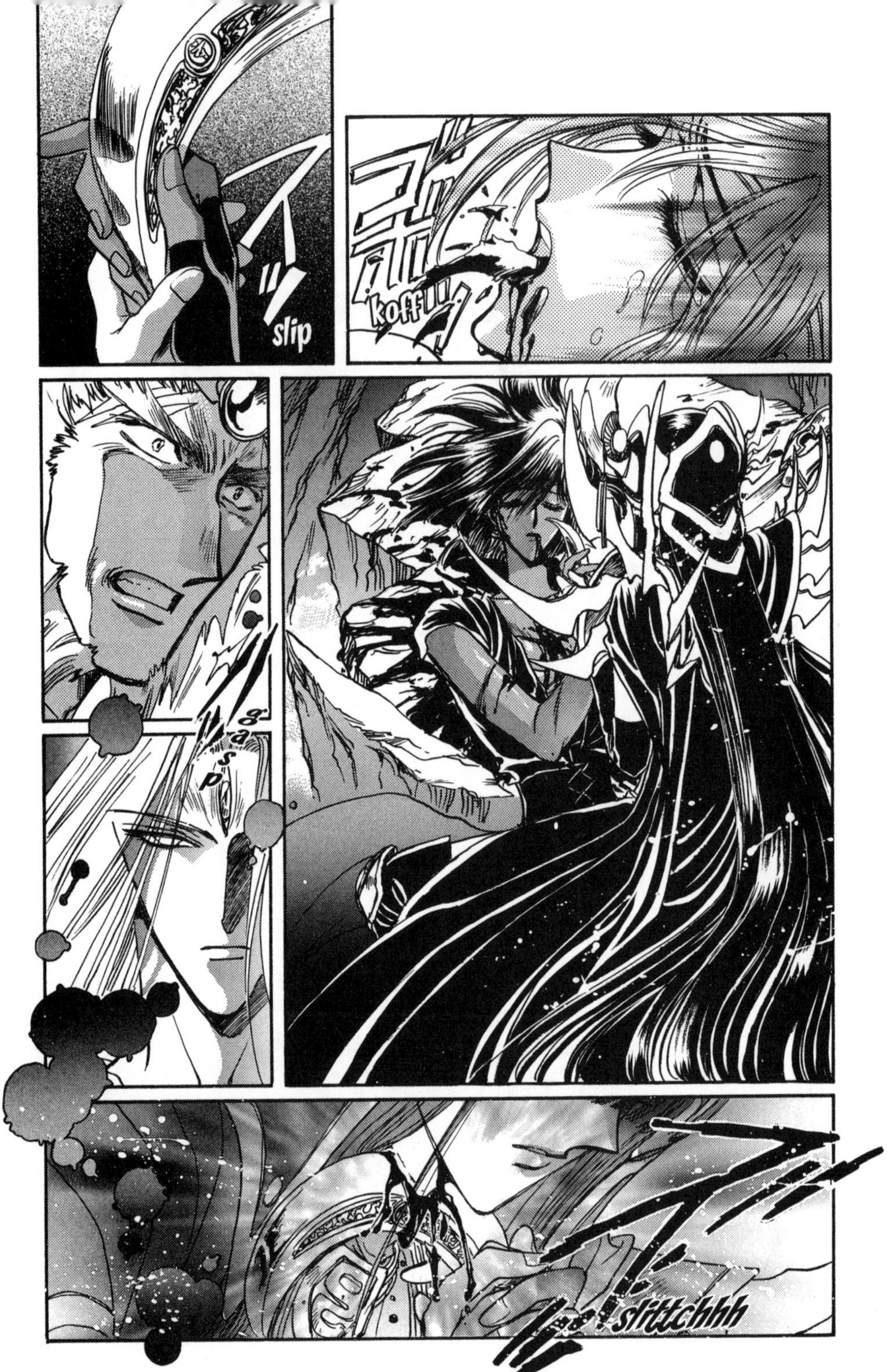
koff!!
slip
gasp
slittchhh

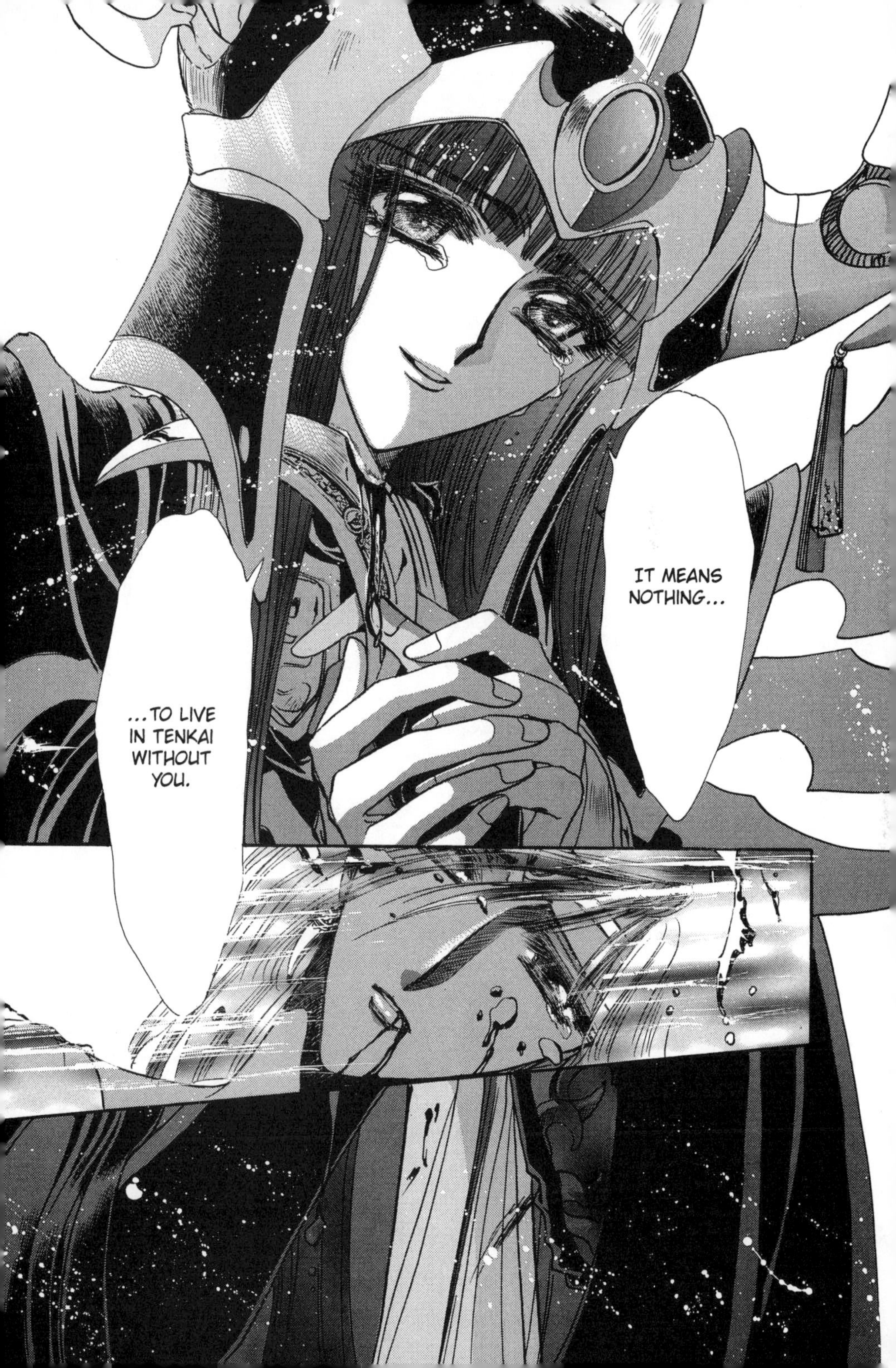
IT MEANS NOTHING...
...TO LIVE IN TENKAI WITHOUT YOU.

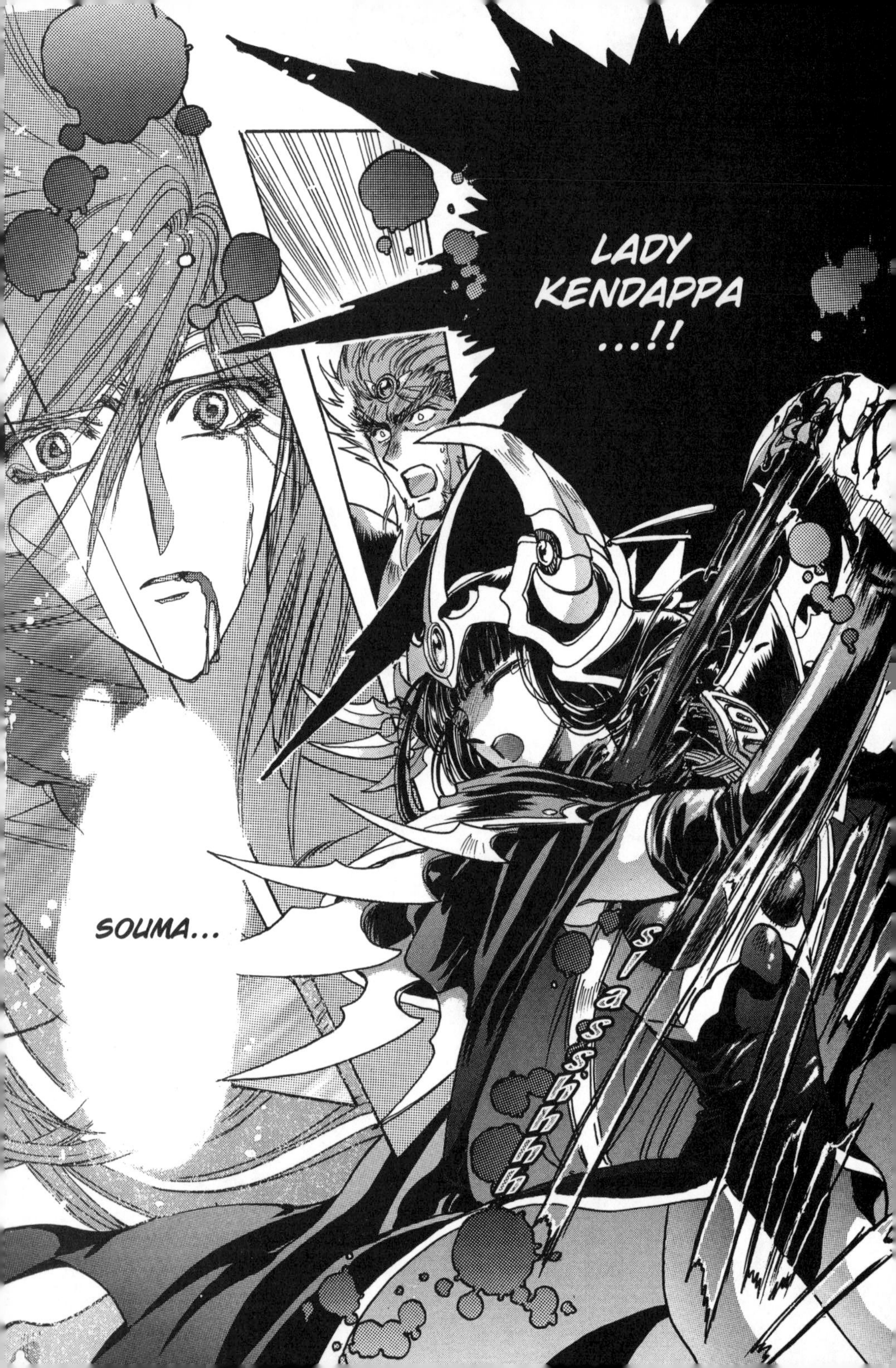
LADY KENDAPPA ...!!
SOUMA...
slasshhhh

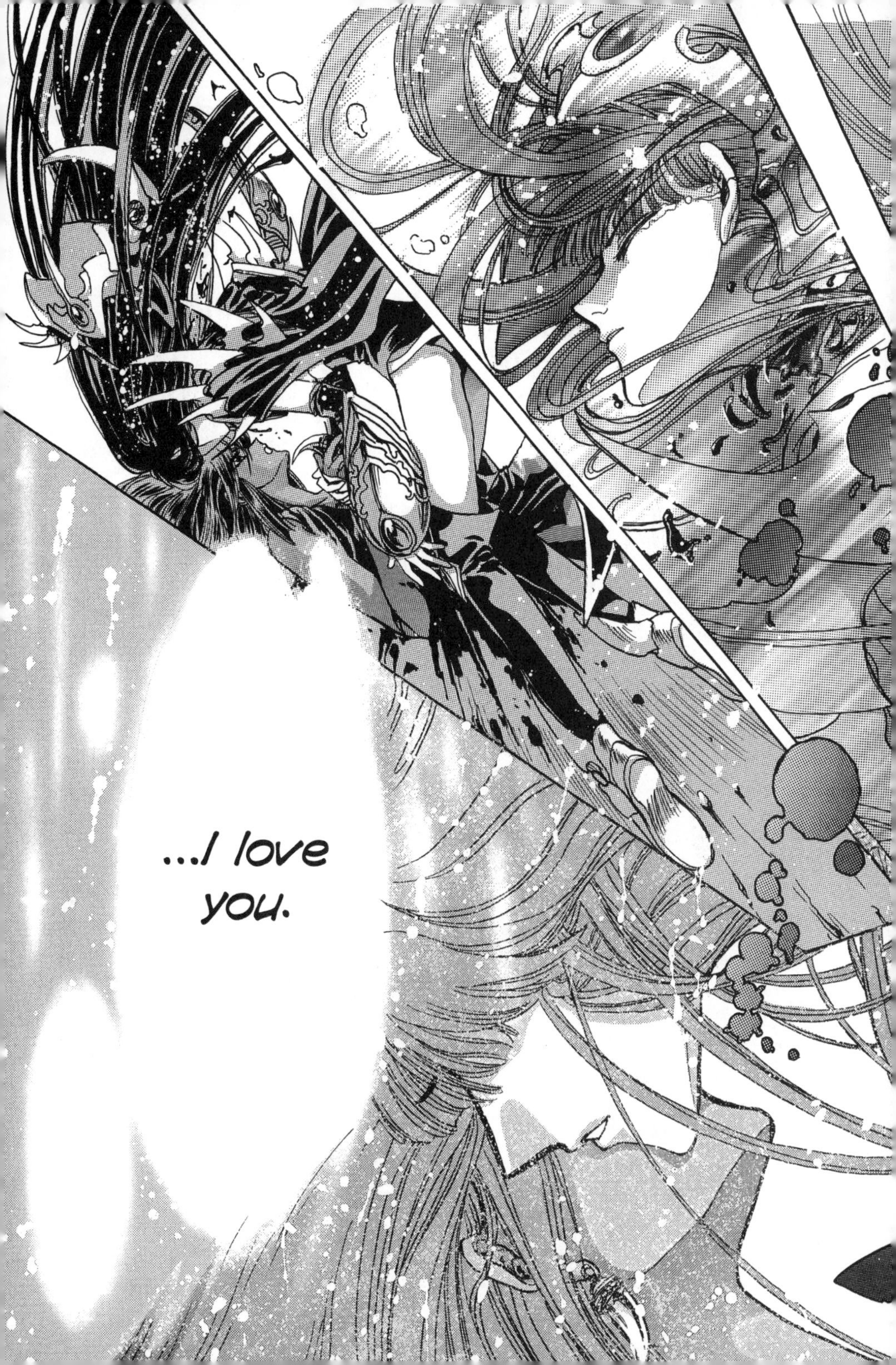
...I love you.

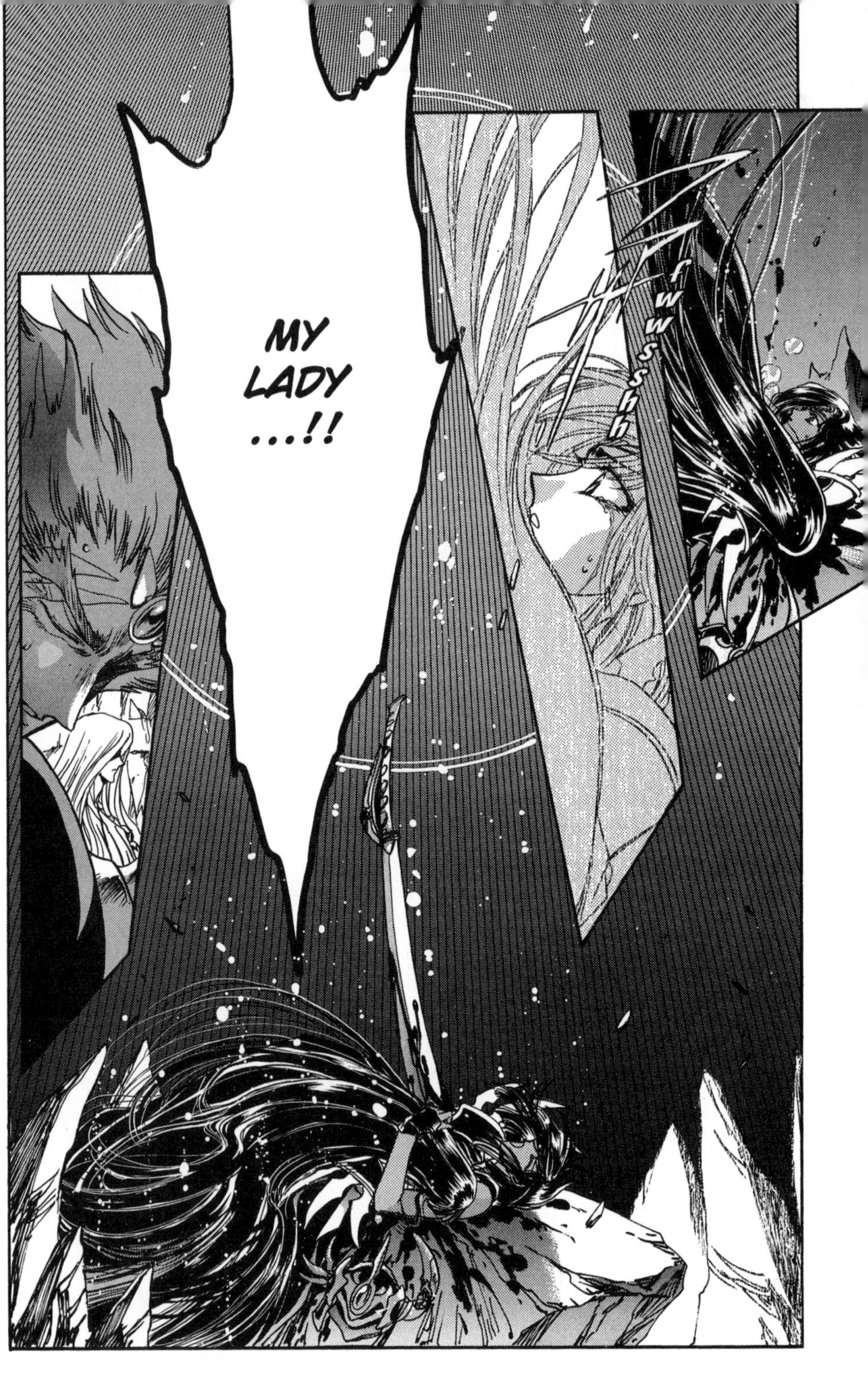
fwwsshh
MY LADY ...!!

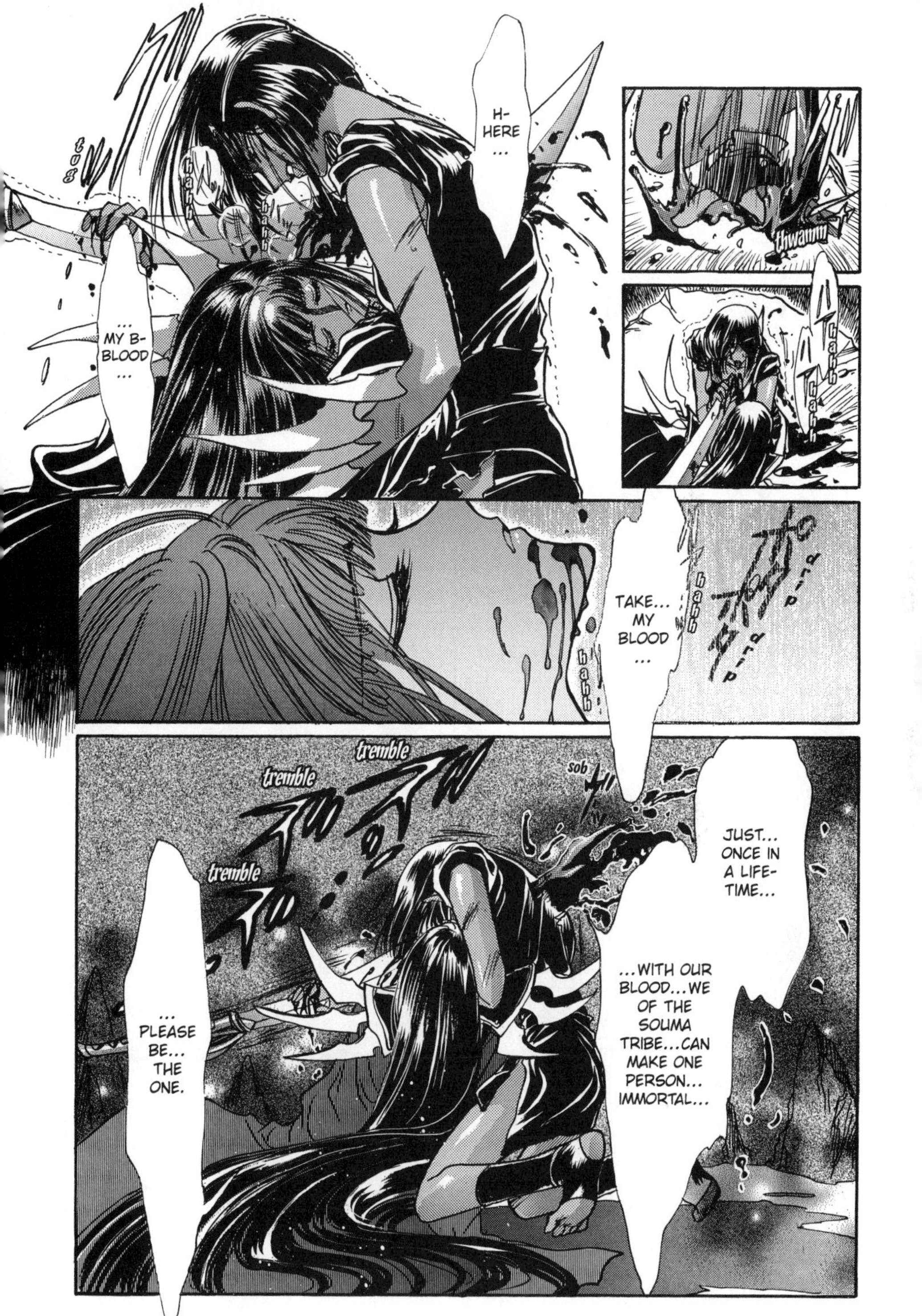
thwannn
bahh
bahh
H-
HERE
...
... MY B-
BLOOD
...
tug
bahh
bahh
TAKE...
MY
BLOOD
...
drip
drip
bahh
bahh
JUST...
ONCE IN
A LIFE-
TIME...
...WITH OUR
BLOOD...WE
OF THE
SOUMA
TRIBE...CAN
MAKE ONE
PERSON...
IMMORTAL...
sob
tremble
tremble
tremble
...
PLEASE
BE...
THE
ONE.

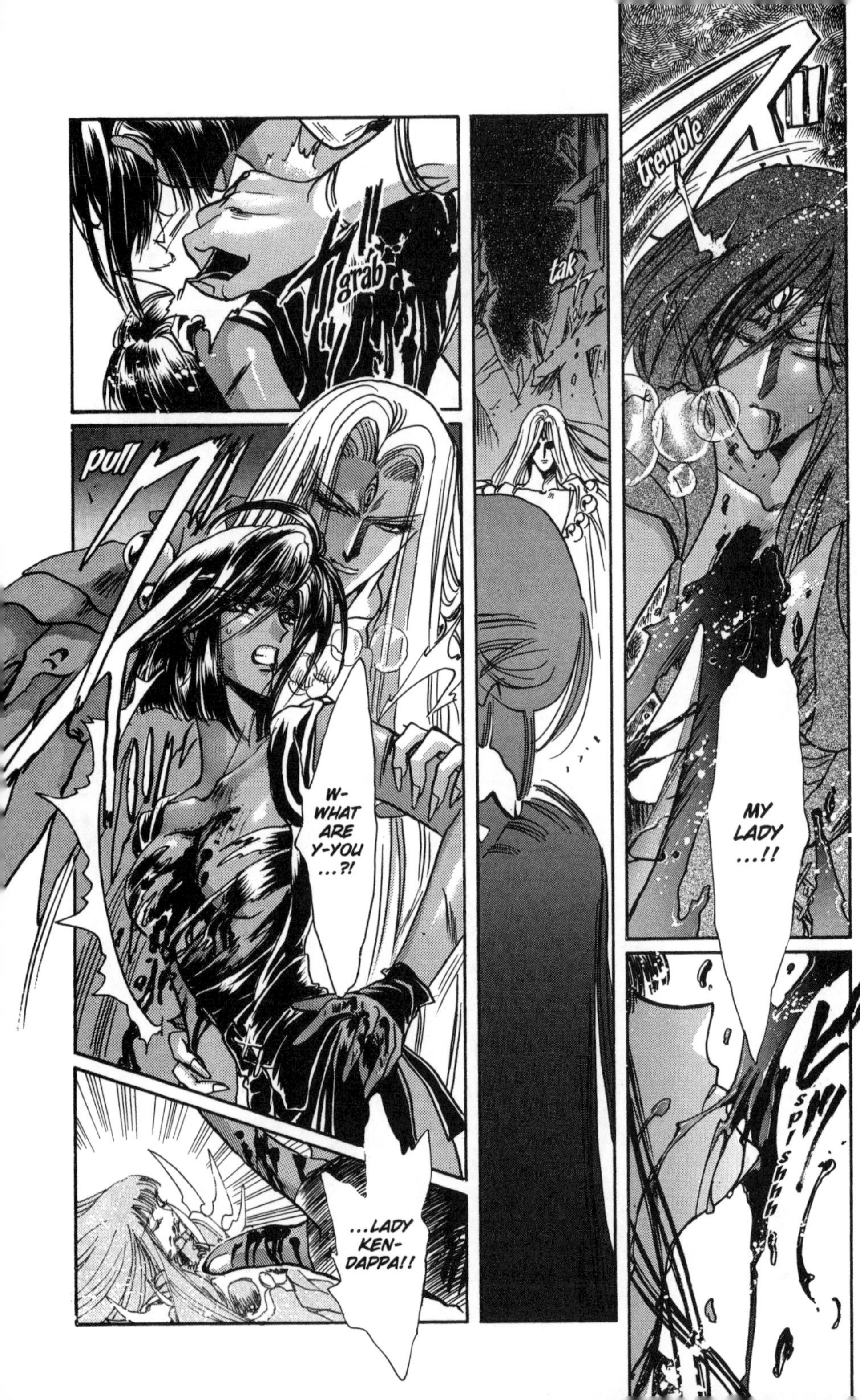
tremble
MY LADY ...!!
splishhh
tak
grab
pull
W- WHAT ARE Y-YOU ...?!
...LADY KEN-DAPPA!!

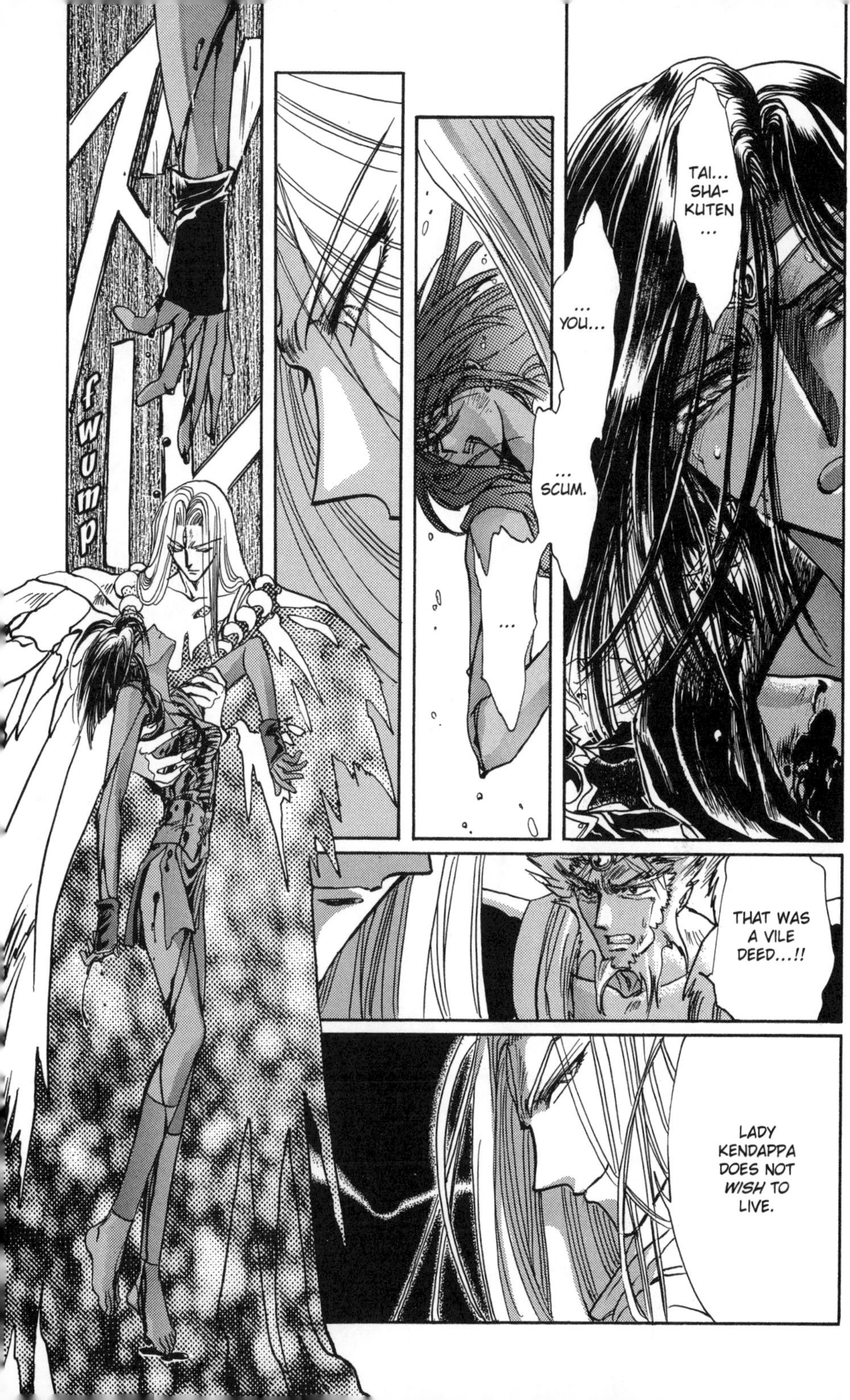

TAI... SHA-KUTEN ...
... YOU...
... SCUM.
...
THAT WAS A VILE DEED...!!
LADY KENDAPPA DOES NOT *WISH* TO LIVE.
fwump

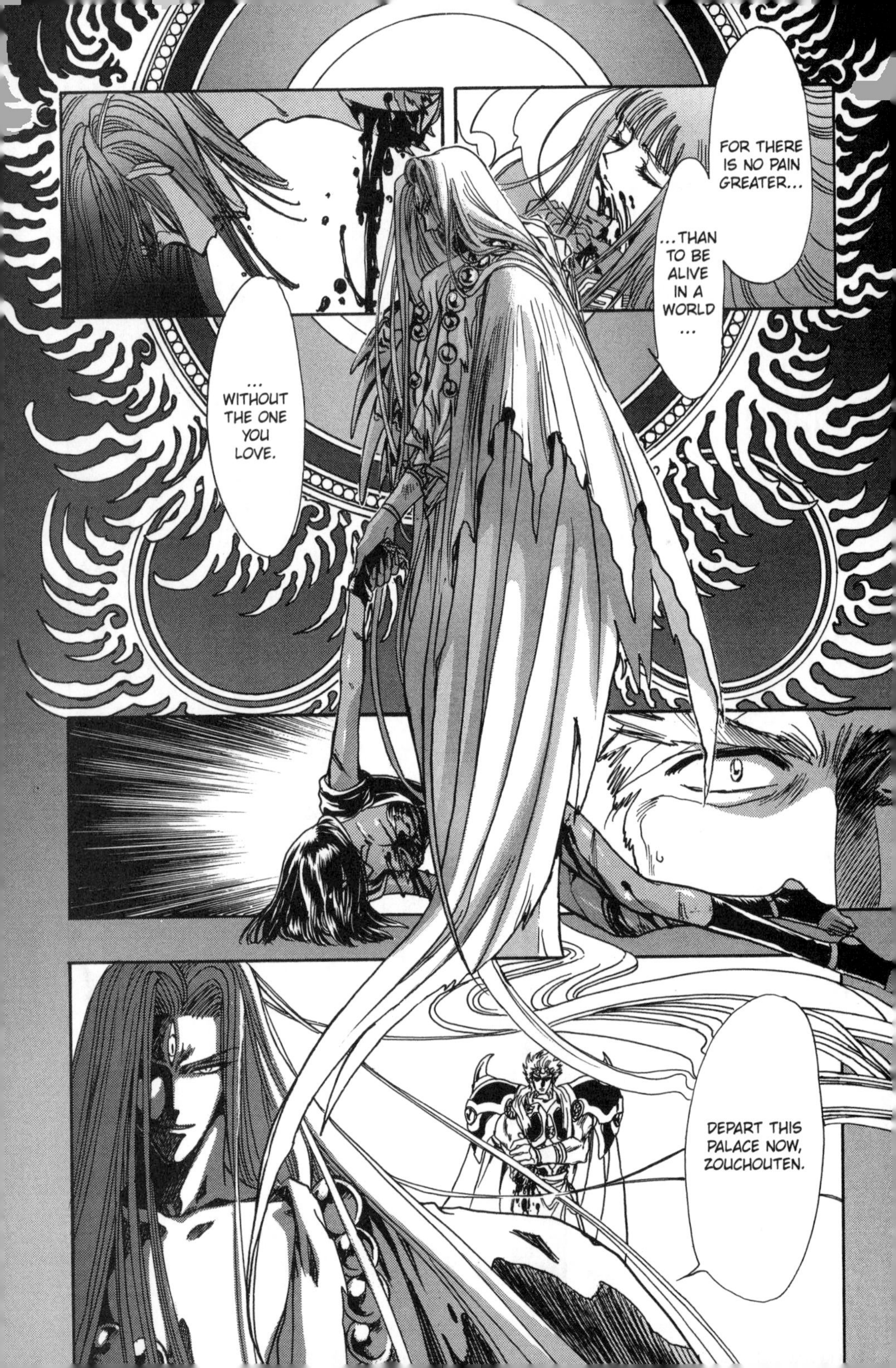
FOR THERE IS NO PAIN GREATER...
...THAN TO BE ALIVE IN A WORLD ...
... WITHOUT THE ONE YOU LOVE.
DEPART THIS PALACE NOW, ZOUCHOUTEN.

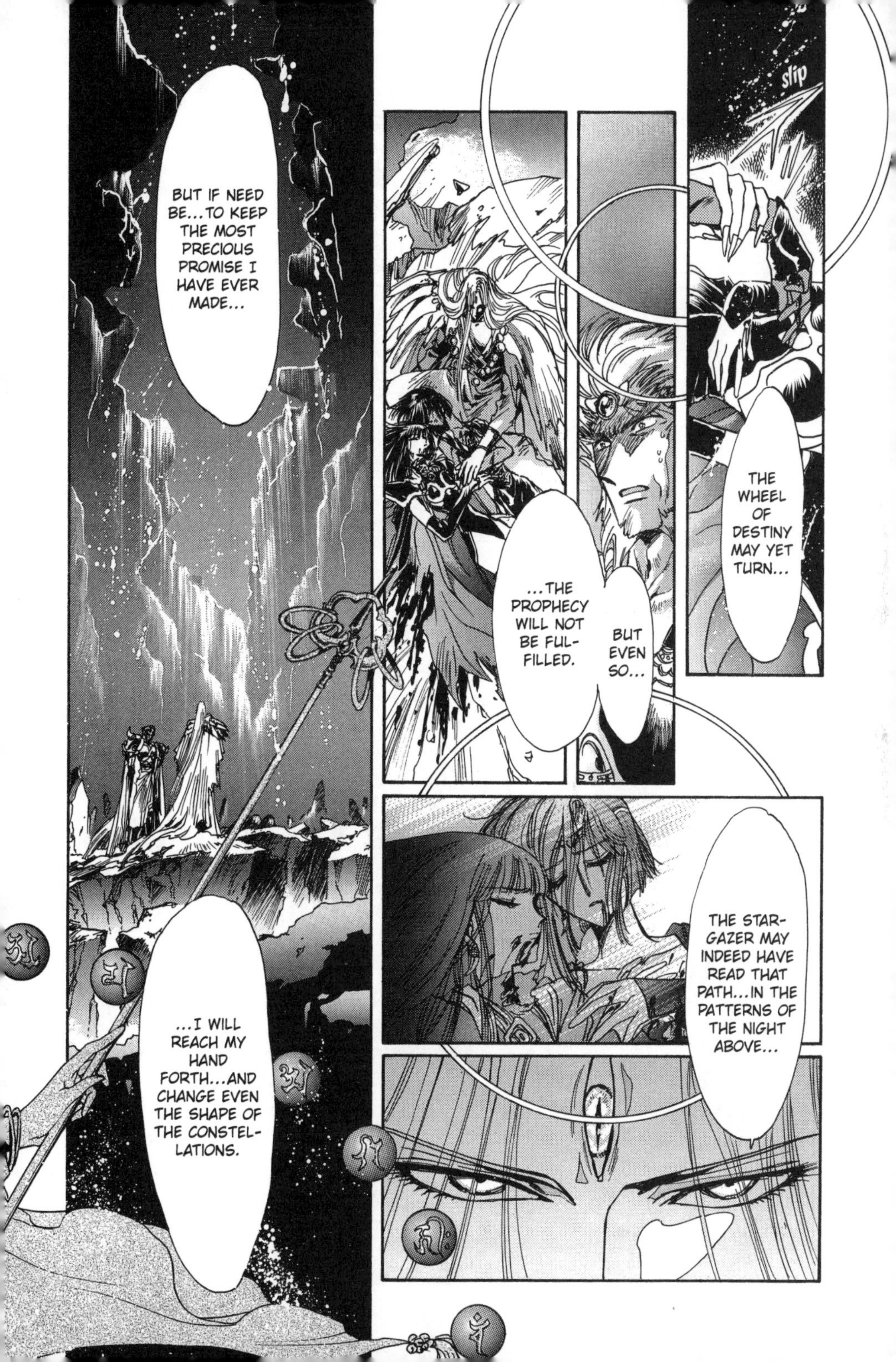
slip
THE WHEEL OF DESTINY MAY YET TURN...
BUT EVEN SO...
...THE PROPHECY WILL NOT BE FULFILLED.
THE STARGAZER MAY INDEED HAVE READ THAT PATH...IN THE PATTERNS OF THE NIGHT ABOVE...
BUT IF NEED BE...TO KEEP THE MOST PRECIOUS PROMISE I HAVE EVER MADE...
...I WILL REACH MY HAND FORTH...AND CHANGE EVEN THE SHAPE OF THE CONSTELLATIONS.

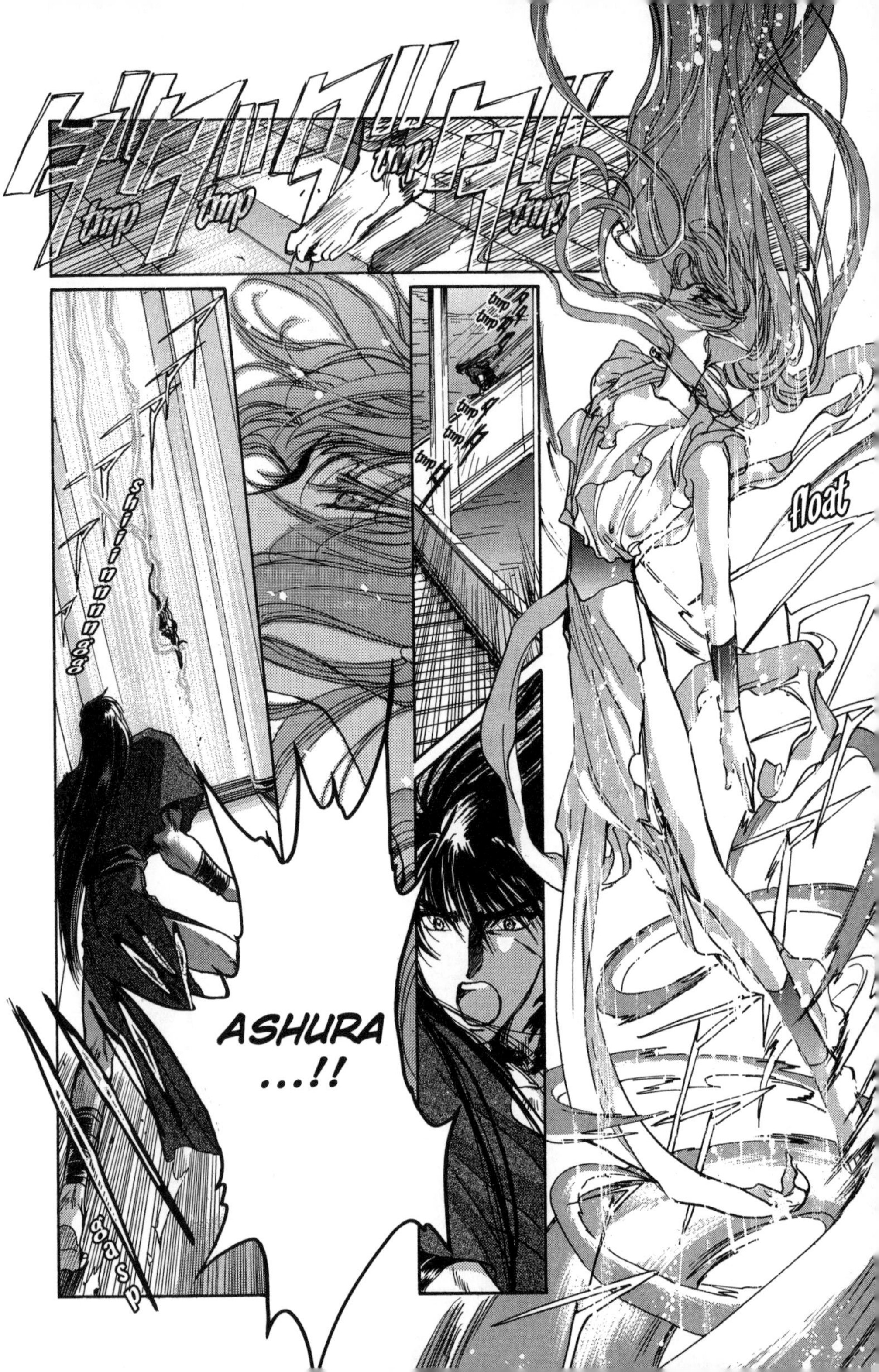

tmp
tmp
tmp
tmp
float
tmp
tmp
tmp
tmp
tmp
shiiinnnnggg
ASHURA ...!!
gasp

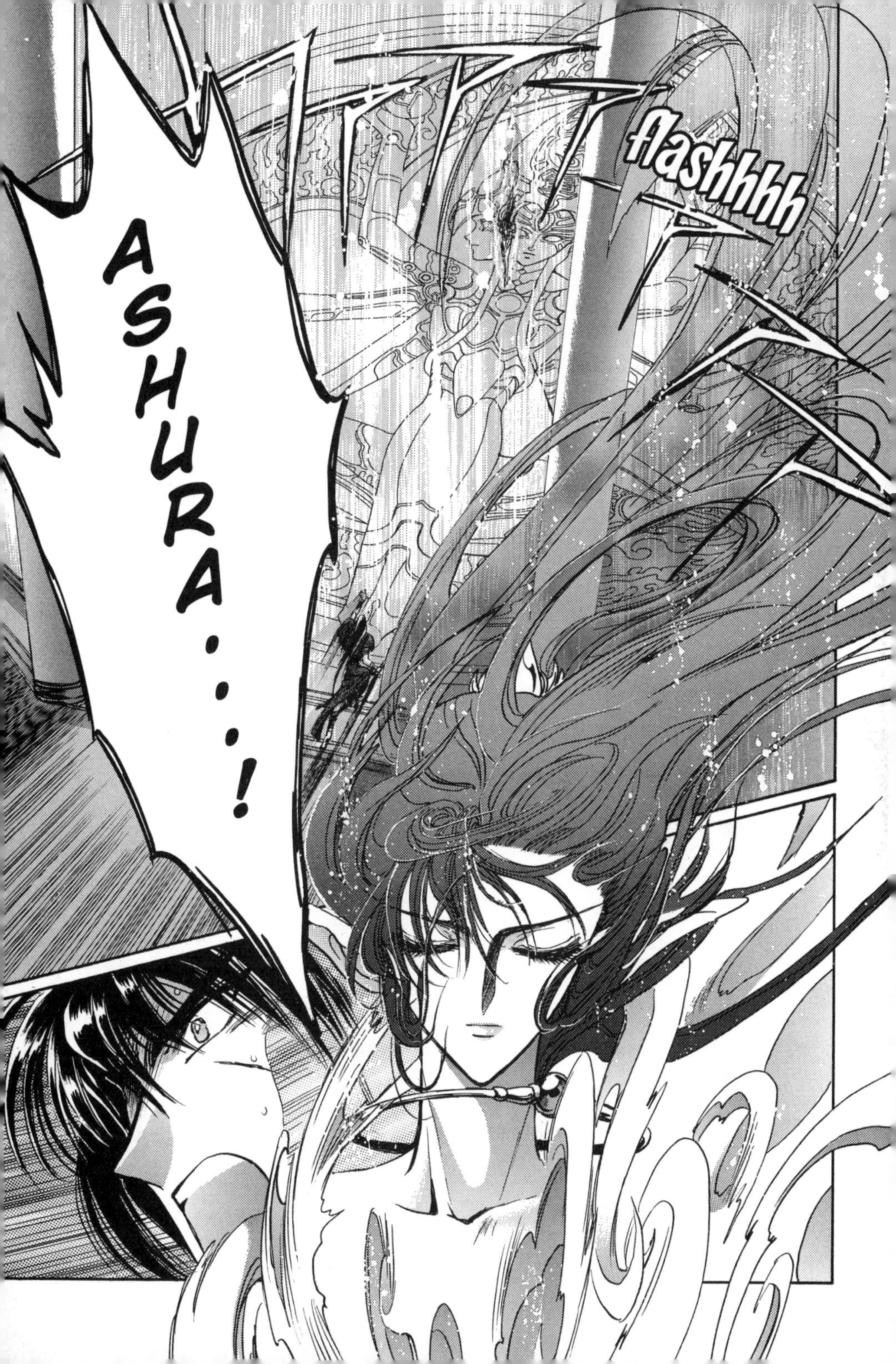
flashhhh
ASHURA...!

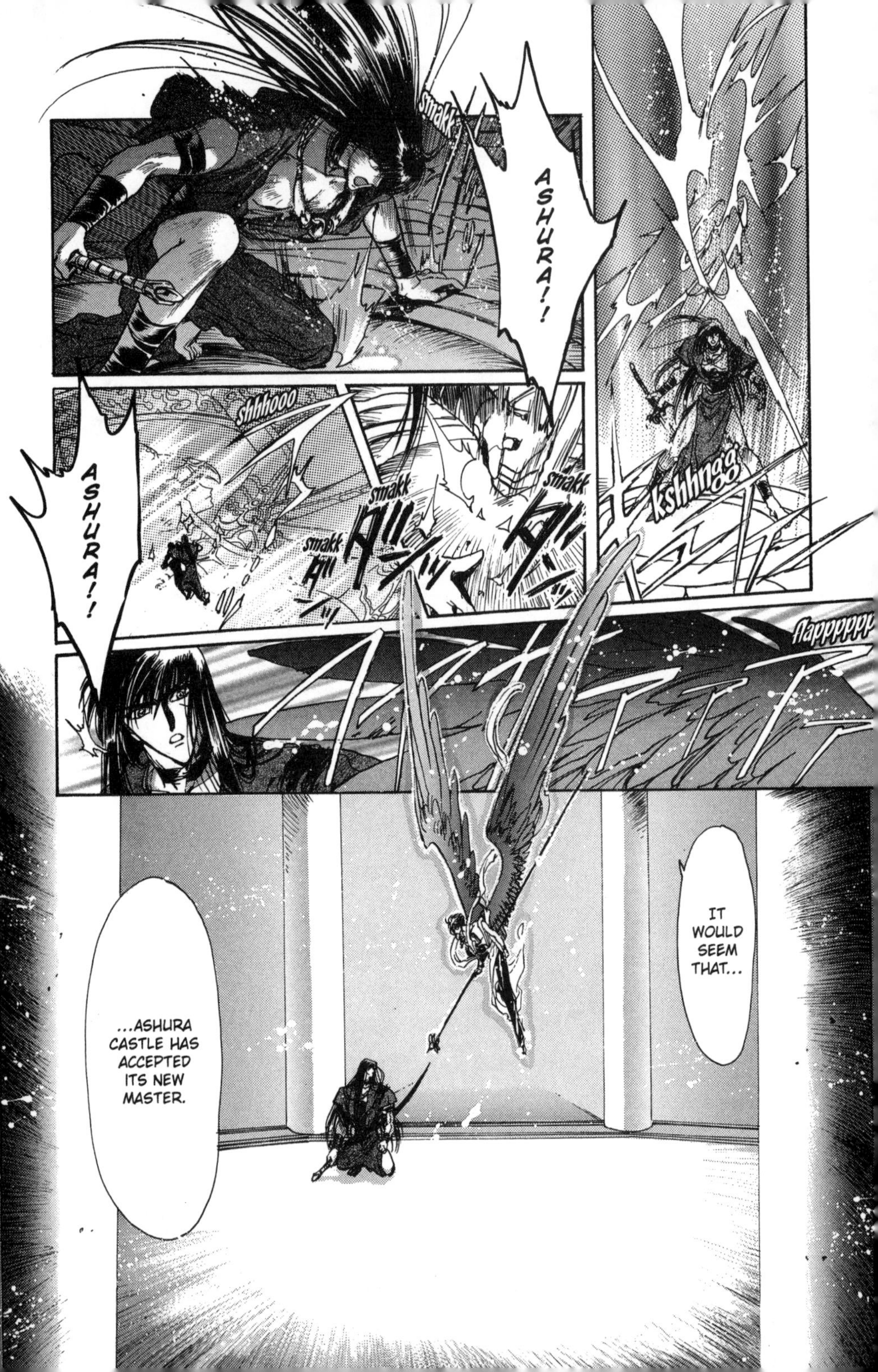

kshhngg
smakk
ASHURA!!
smakk
smakk
smakk
shhhooo
ASHURA!!
flapppppp
IT WOULD SEEM THAT...
...ASHURA CASTLE HAS ACCEPTED ITS NEW MASTER.

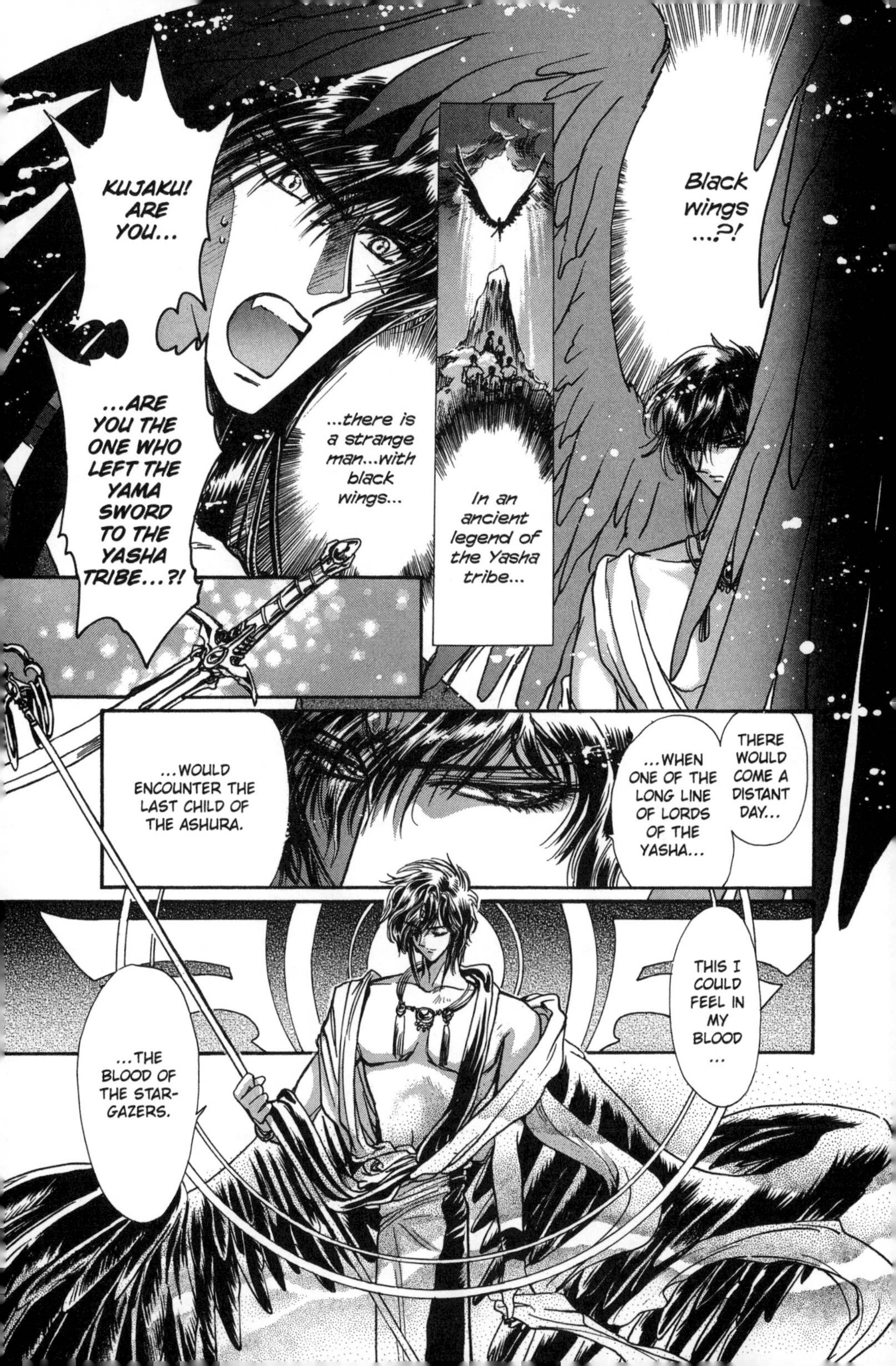

Black wings ...?!
In an ancient legend of the Yasha tribe...
...there is a strange man...with black wings...
KUJAKU! ARE YOU...
...ARE YOU THE ONE WHO LEFT THE YAMA SWORD TO THE YASHA TRIBE...?!
THERE WOULD COME A DISTANT DAY...
...WHEN ONE OF THE LONG LINE OF LORDS OF THE YASHA...
...WOULD ENCOUNTER THE LAST CHILD OF THE ASHURA.
THIS I COULD FEEL IN MY BLOOD ...
...THE BLOOD OF THE STAR-GAZERS.

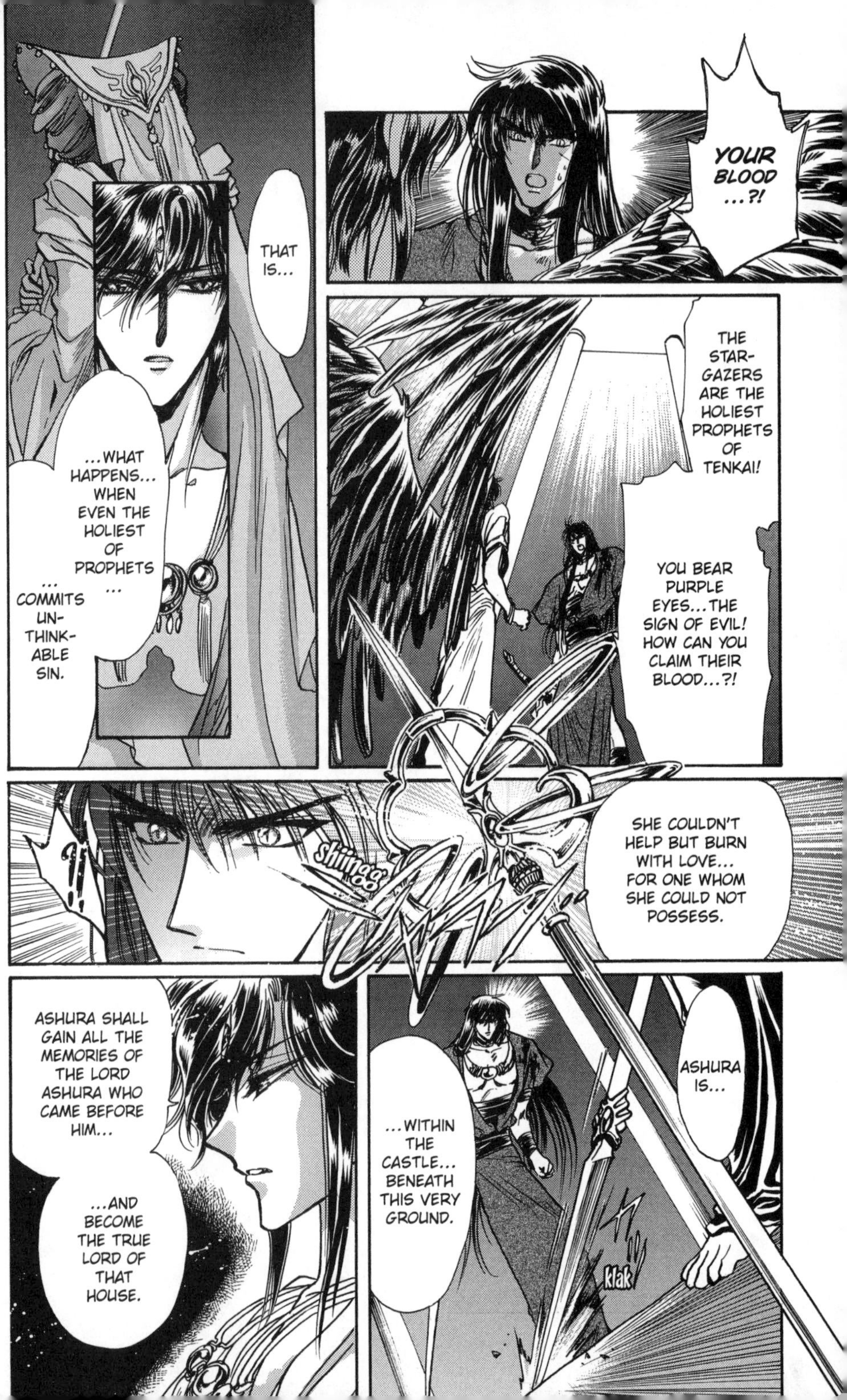
YOUR BLOOD ...?!
THE STAR-GAZERS ARE THE HOLIEST PROPHETS OF TENKAI!
YOU BEAR PURPLE EYES... THE SIGN OF EVIL! HOW CAN YOU CLAIM THEIR BLOOD...?!
THAT IS...
...WHAT HAPPENS... WHEN EVEN THE HOLIEST OF PROPHETS ...
... COMMITS UN-THINK-ABLE SIN.
SHE COULDN'T HELP BUT BURN WITH LOVE... FOR ONE WHOM SHE COULD NOT POSSESS.
Shiingg
!!
ASHURA IS...
...WITHIN THE CASTLE... BENEATH THIS VERY GROUND.
klak
ASHURA SHALL GAIN ALL THE MEMORIES OF THE LORD ASHURA WHO CAME BEFORE HIM...
...AND BECOME THE TRUE LORD OF THAT HOUSE.

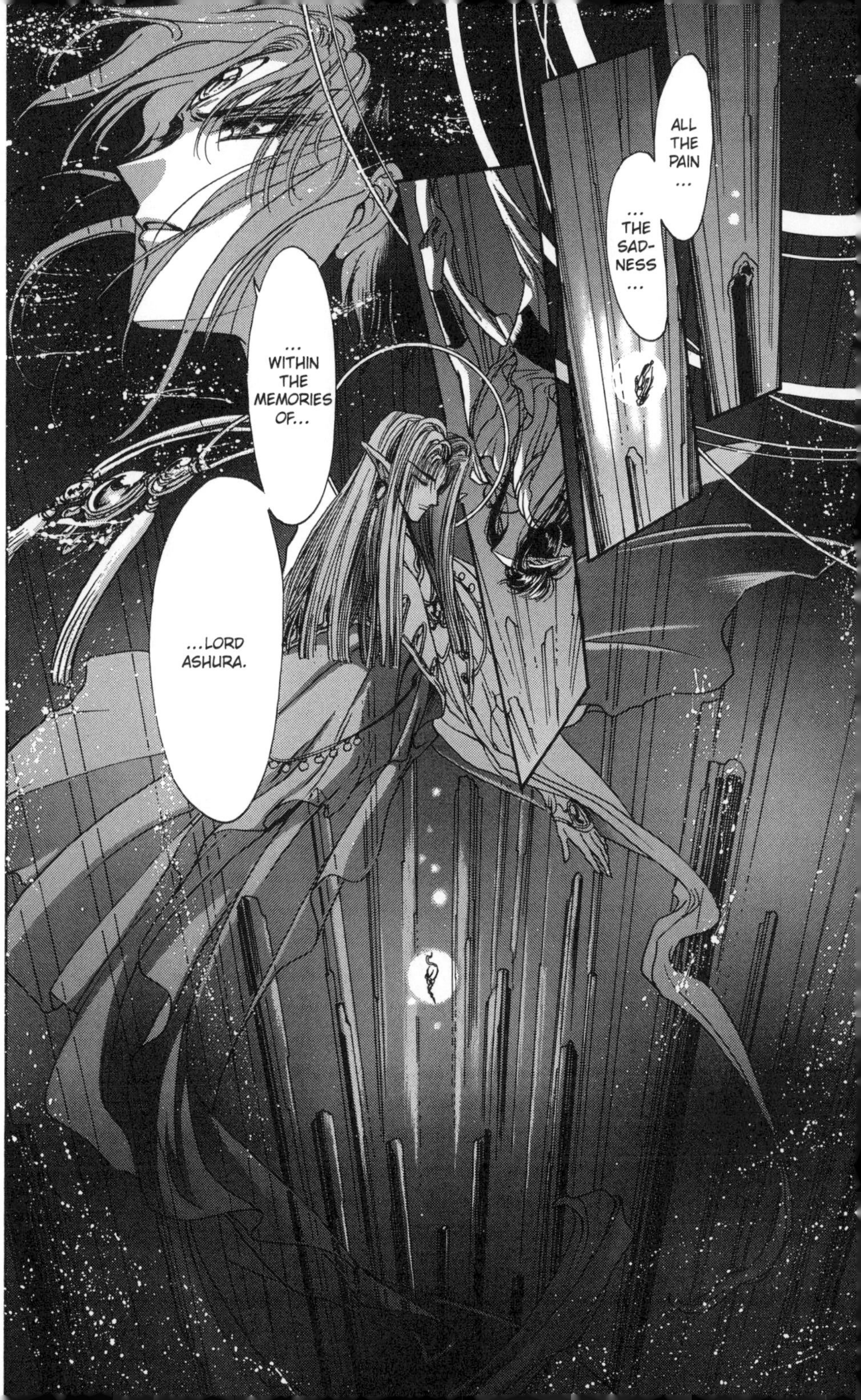
ALL THE PAIN …
… THE SAD-NESS …
… WITHIN THE MEMORIES OF…
…LORD ASHURA.

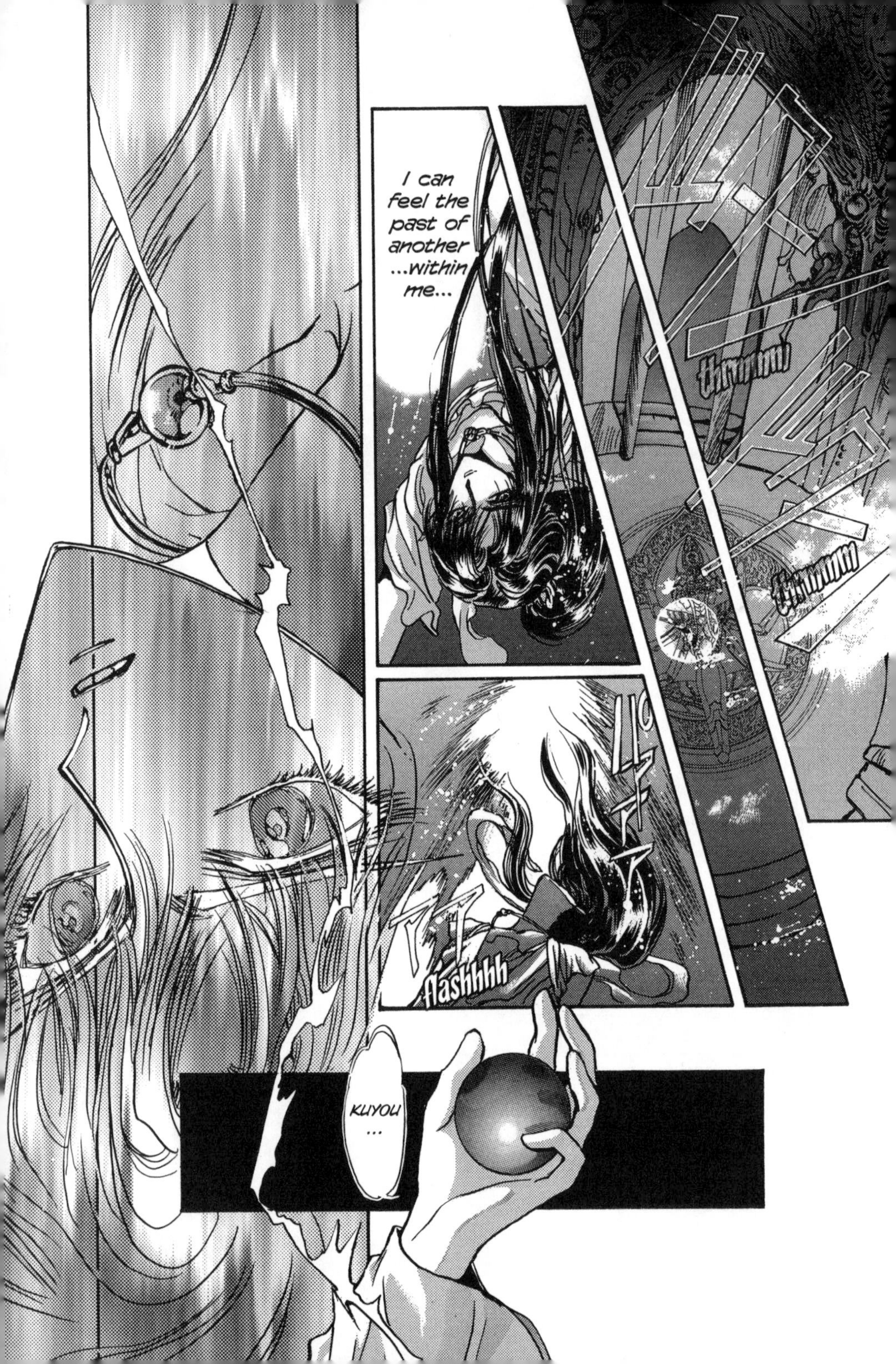
thrmmm
thrmmm
I can feel the past of another ...within me...
flashhhh
KUYOU ...

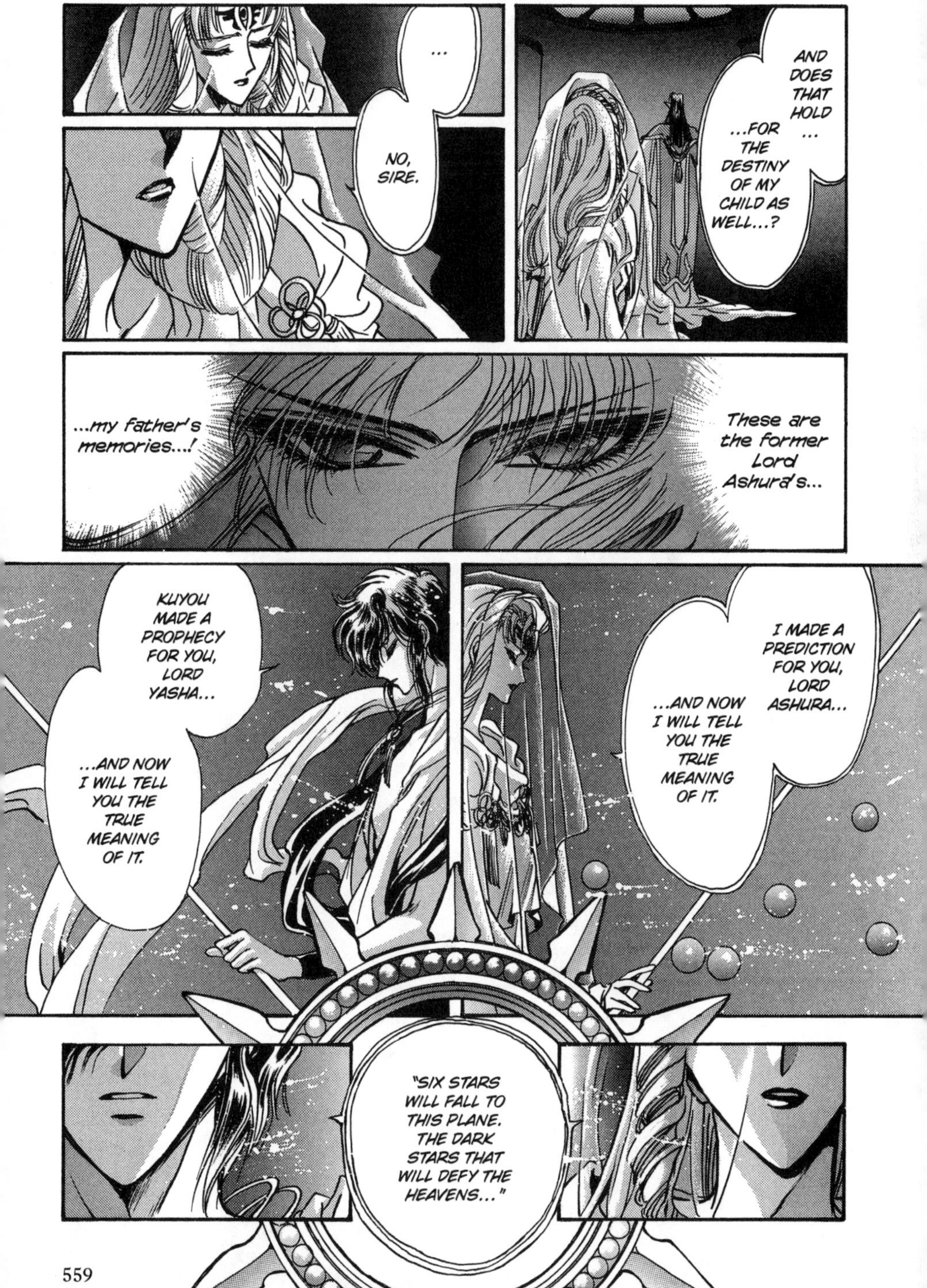
AND DOES THAT HOLD ...
...FOR THE DESTINY OF MY CHILD AS WELL...?
...
NO, SIRE.
These are the former Lord Ashura's...
...my father's memories...!
I MADE A PREDICTION FOR YOU, LORD ASHURA...
...AND NOW I WILL TELL YOU THE TRUE MEANING OF IT.
KUYOU MADE A PROPHECY FOR YOU, LORD YASHA...
...AND NOW I WILL TELL YOU THE TRUE MEANING OF IT.
"SIX STARS WILL FALL TO THIS PLANE. THE DARK STARS THAT WILL DEFY THE HEAVENS..."

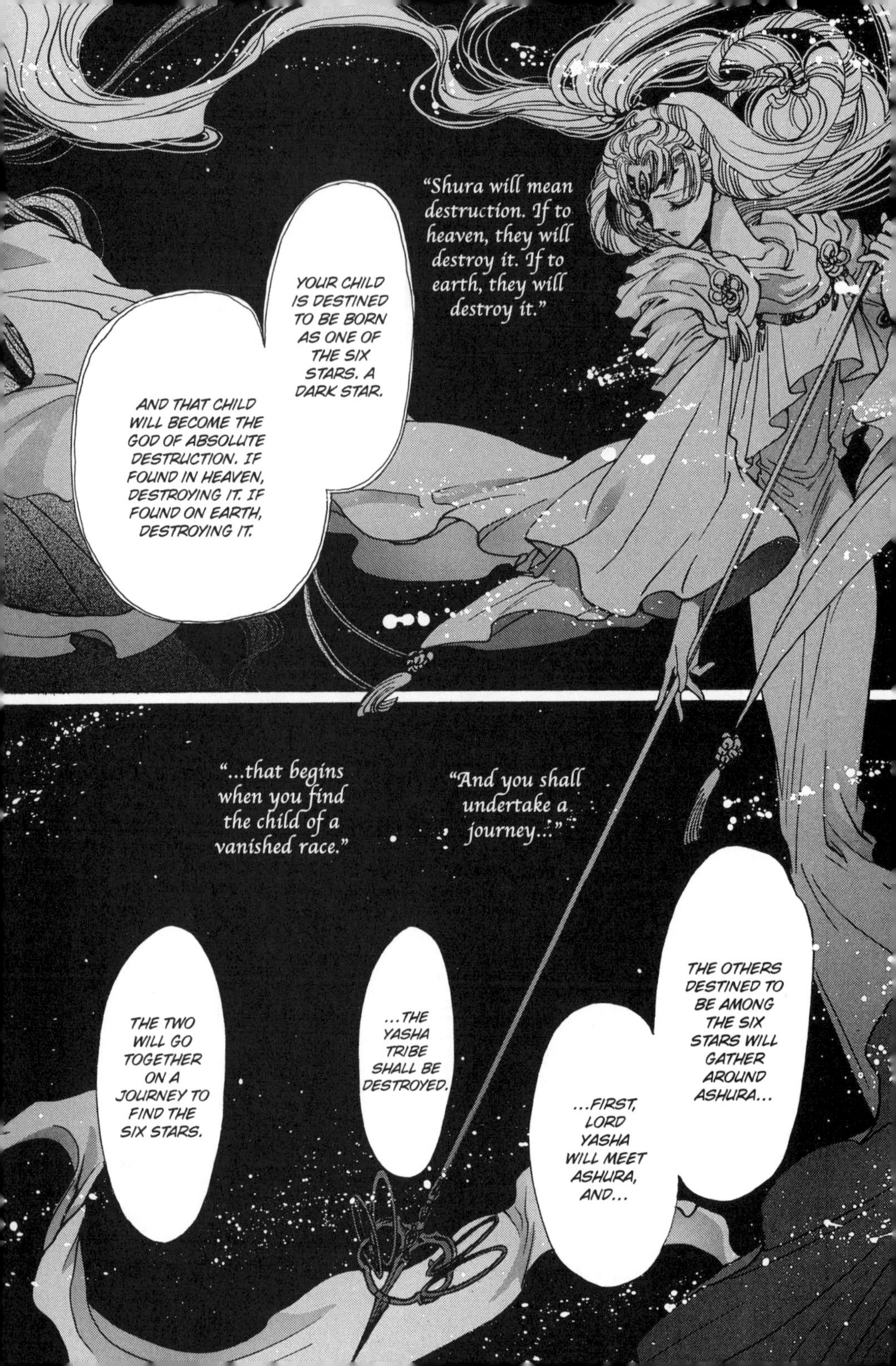
"Shura will mean destruction. If to heaven, they will destroy it. If to earth, they will destroy it."
YOUR CHILD IS DESTINED TO BE BORN AS ONE OF THE SIX STARS. A DARK STAR.
AND THAT CHILD WILL BECOME THE GOD OF ABSOLUTE DESTRUCTION. IF FOUND IN HEAVEN, DESTROYING IT. IF FOUND ON EARTH, DESTROYING IT.
"And you shall undertake a journey..."
"...that begins when you find the child of a vanished race."
THE OTHERS DESTINED TO BE AMONG THE SIX STARS WILL GATHER AROUND ASHURA...
...FIRST, LORD YASHA WILL MEET ASHURA, AND...
...THE YASHA TRIBE SHALL BE DESTROYED.
THE TWO WILL GO TOGETHER ON A JOURNEY TO FIND THE SIX STARS.

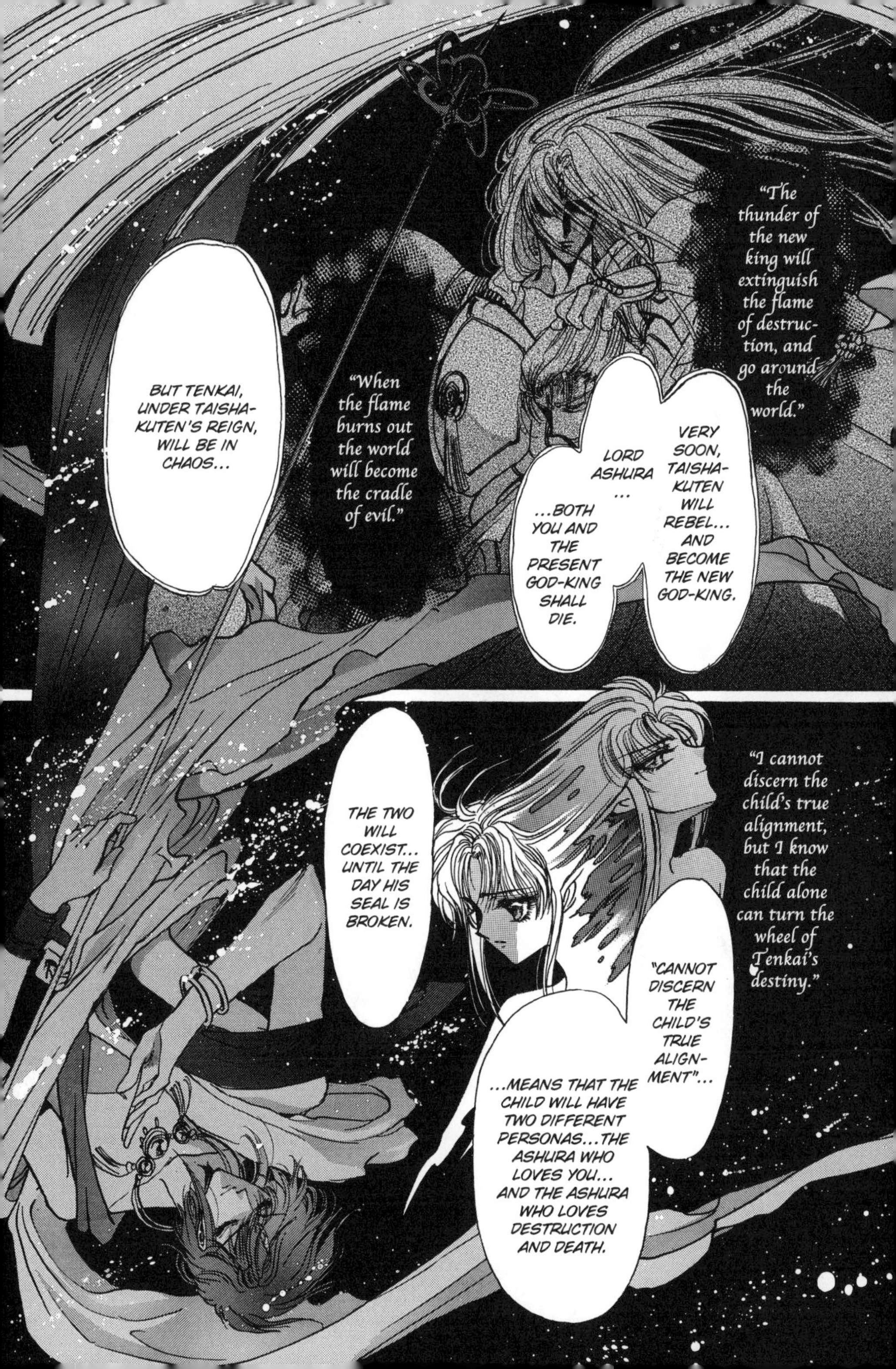
"The thunder of the new king will extinguish the flame of destruction, and go around the world."
VERY SOON, TAISHAKUTEN WILL REBEL... AND BECOME THE NEW GOD-KING.
LORD ASHURA ...
...BOTH YOU AND THE PRESENT GOD-KING SHALL DIE.
"When the flame burns out the world will become the cradle of evil."
BUT TENKAI, UNDER TAISHAKUTEN'S REIGN, WILL BE IN CHAOS...
"I cannot discern the child's true alignment, but I know that the child alone can turn the wheel of Tenkai's destiny."
"CANNOT DISCERN THE CHILD'S TRUE ALIGNMENT"...
...MEANS THAT THE CHILD WILL HAVE TWO DIFFERENT PERSONAS...THE ASHURA WHO LOVES YOU... AND THE ASHURA WHO LOVES DESTRUCTION AND DEATH.
THE TWO WILL COEXIST... UNTIL THE DAY HIS SEAL IS BROKEN.

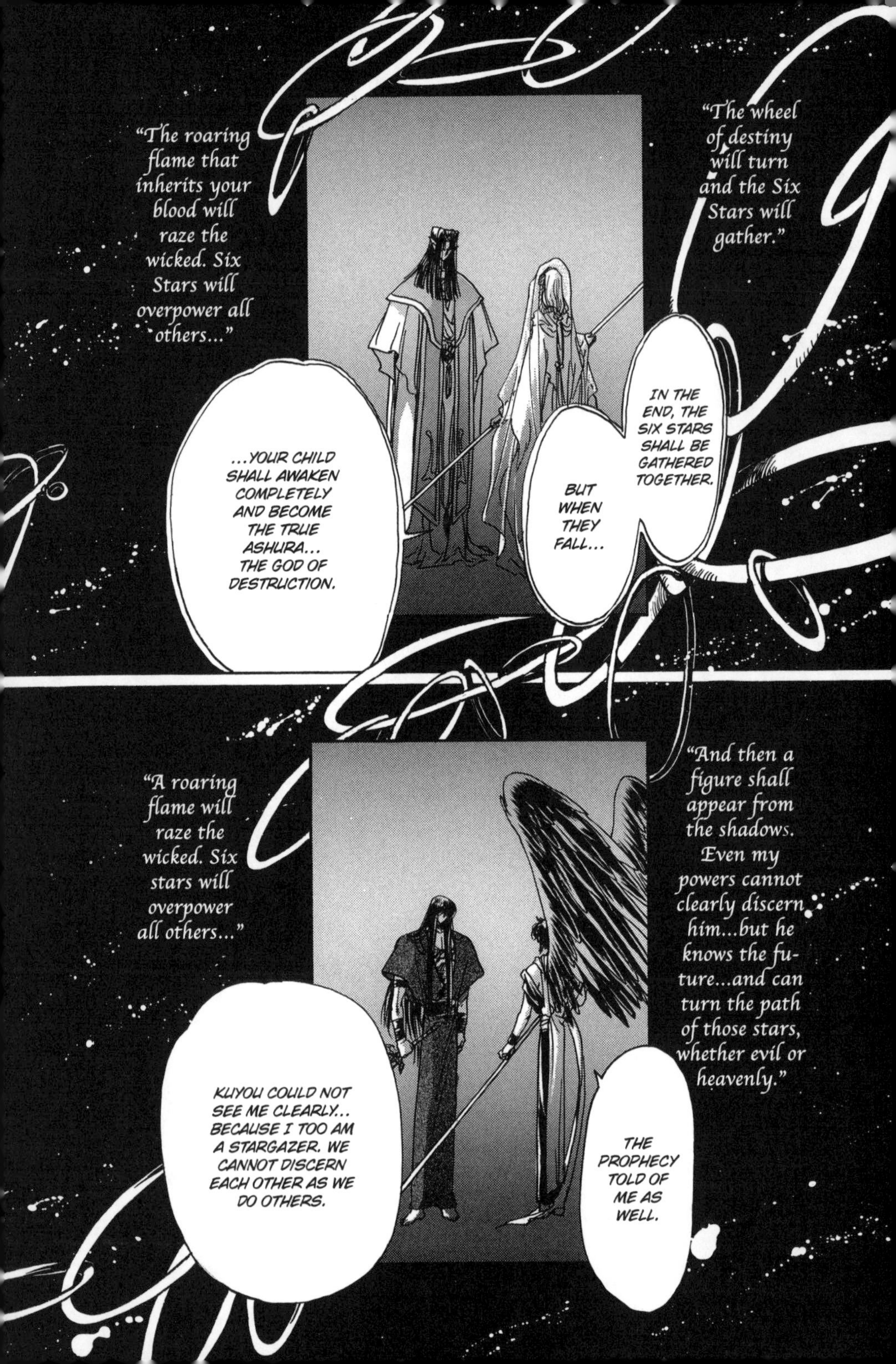
"The wheel of destiny will turn and the Six Stars will gather."
IN THE END, THE SIX STARS SHALL BE GATHERED TOGETHER.
BUT WHEN THEY FALL...
...YOUR CHILD SHALL AWAKEN COMPLETELY AND BECOME THE TRUE ASHURA... THE GOD OF DESTRUCTION.
"The roaring flame that inherits your blood will raze the wicked. Six Stars will overpower all others..."
"And then a figure shall appear from the shadows. Even my powers cannot clearly discern him...but he knows the future...and can turn the path of those stars, whether evil or heavenly."
THE PROPHECY TOLD OF ME AS WELL.
KUYOU COULD NOT SEE ME CLEARLY... BECAUSE I TOO AM A STARGAZER. WE CANNOT DISCERN EACH OTHER AS WE DO OTHERS.
"A roaring flame will raze the wicked. Six stars will overpower all others..."

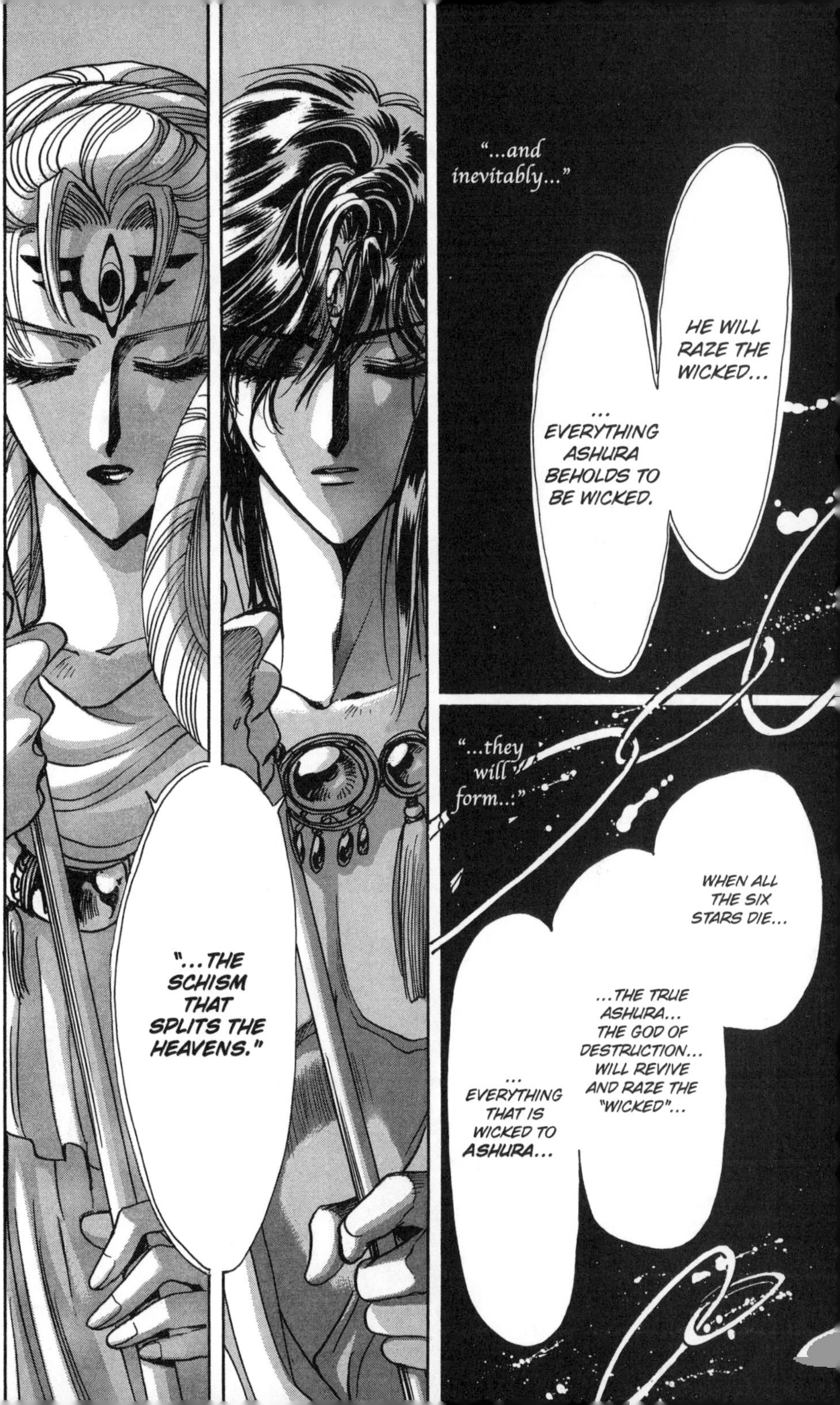
"...and inevitably..."
HE WILL RAZE THE WICKED...
...EVERYTHING ASHURA BEHOLDS TO BE WICKED.
"...they will form..."
WHEN ALL THE SIX STARS DIE...
...THE TRUE ASHURA... THE GOD OF DESTRUCTION... WILL REVIVE AND RAZE THE "WICKED"...
...EVERYTHING THAT IS WICKED TO ASHURA...
"...THE SCHISM THAT SPLITS THE HEAVENS."

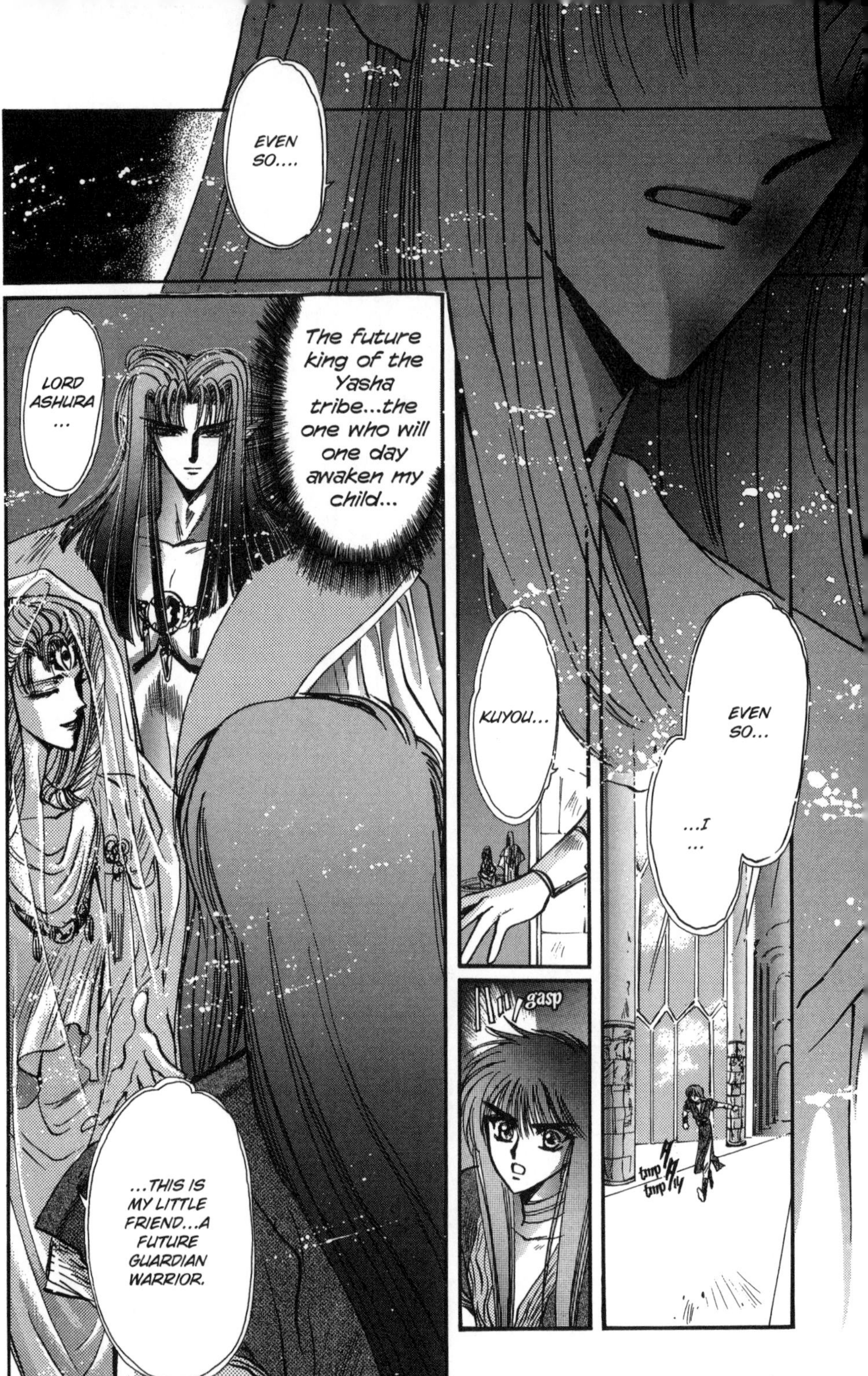
EVEN SO....
EVEN SO...
...I ...
tmp tmp
KUYOU...
gasp
The future king of the Yasha tribe...the one who will one day awaken my child...
LORD ASHURA ...
...THIS IS MY LITTLE FRIEND...A FUTURE GUARDIAN WARRIOR.

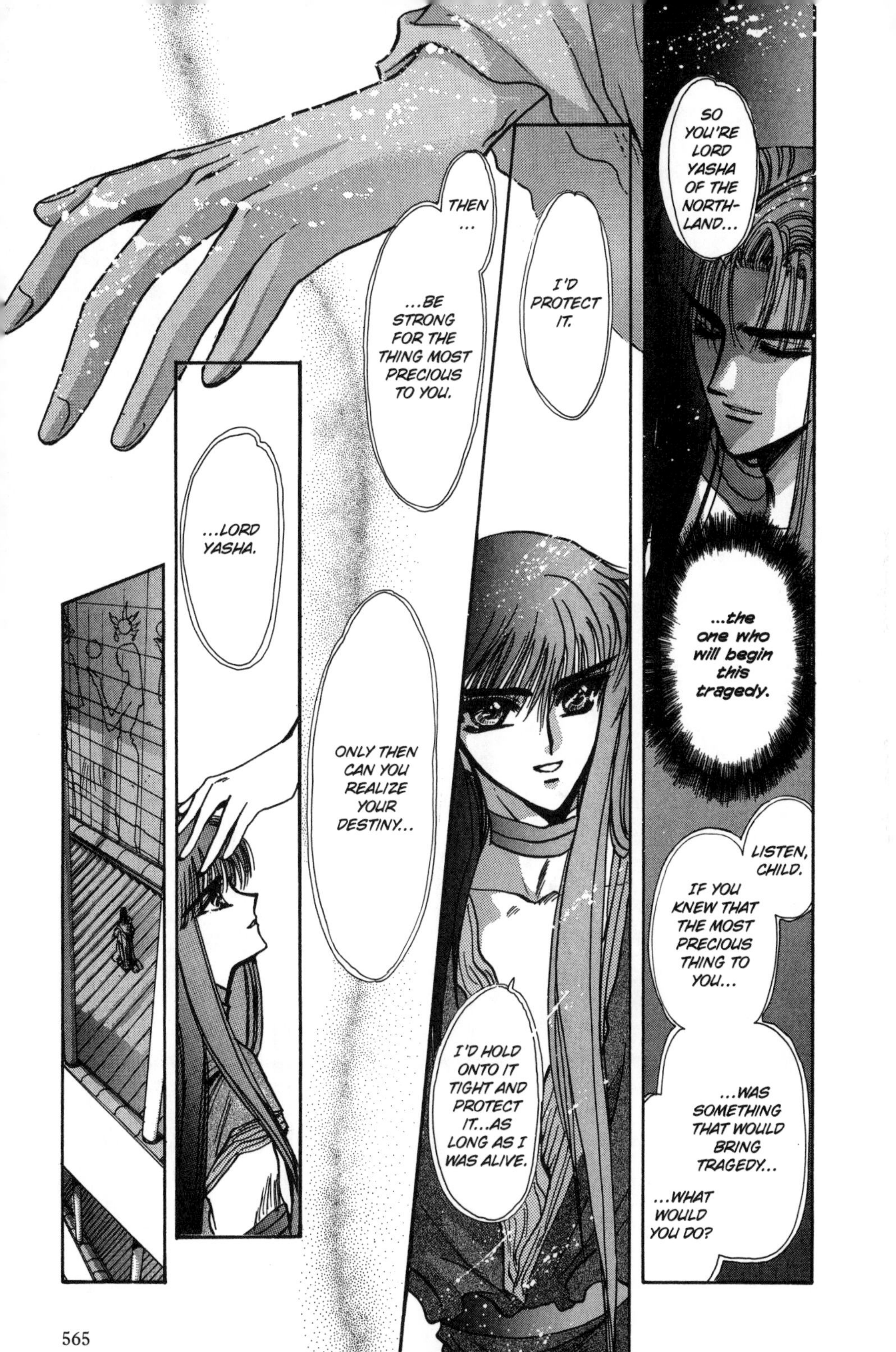

SO YOU'RE LORD YASHA OF THE NORTH-LAND...
...the one who will begin this tragedy.
LISTEN, CHILD.
IF YOU KNEW THAT THE MOST PRECIOUS THING TO YOU...
...WAS SOMETHING THAT WOULD BRING TRAGEDY...
...WHAT WOULD YOU DO?
I'D HOLD ONTO IT TIGHT AND PROTECT IT...AS LONG AS I WAS ALIVE.
I'D PROTECT IT.
THEN...
...BE STRONG FOR THE THING MOST PRECIOUS TO YOU.
ONLY THEN CAN YOU REALIZE YOUR DESTINY...
...LORD YASHA.

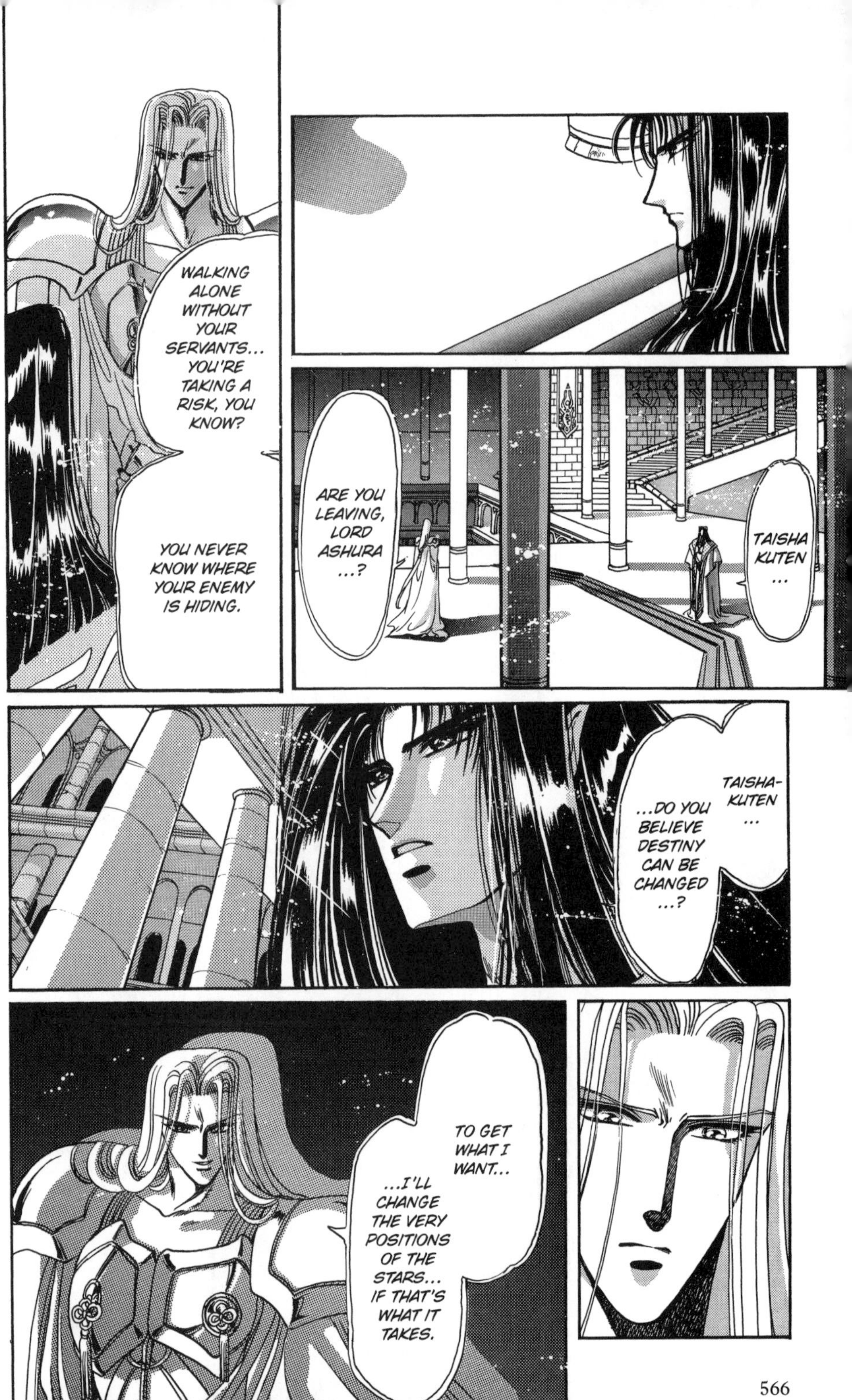
TAISHA KUTEN ...
ARE YOU LEAVING, LORD ASHURA ...?
WALKING ALONE WITHOUT YOUR SERVANTS... YOU'RE TAKING A RISK, YOU KNOW?
YOU NEVER KNOW WHERE YOUR ENEMY IS HIDING.
TAISHA-KUTEN ...
...DO YOU BELIEVE DESTINY CAN BE CHANGED ...?
TO GET WHAT I WANT...
...I'LL CHANGE THE VERY POSITIONS OF THE STARS... IF THAT'S WHAT IT TAKES.

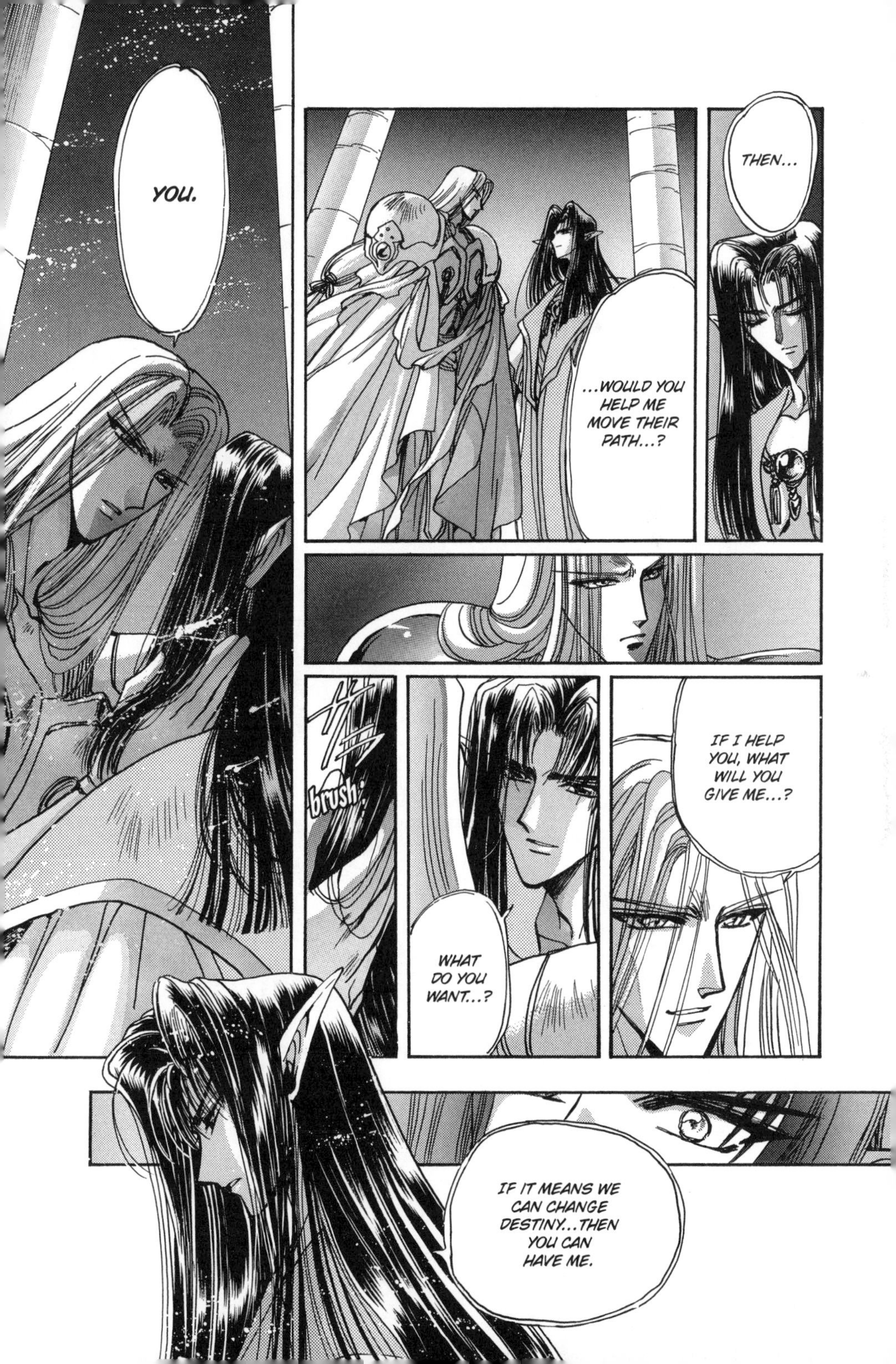
THEN...
...WOULD YOU HELP ME MOVE THEIR PATH...?
IF I HELP YOU, WHAT WILL YOU GIVE ME...?
WHAT DO YOU WANT...?
brush
YOU.
IF IT MEANS WE CAN CHANGE DESTINY...THEN YOU CAN HAVE ME.

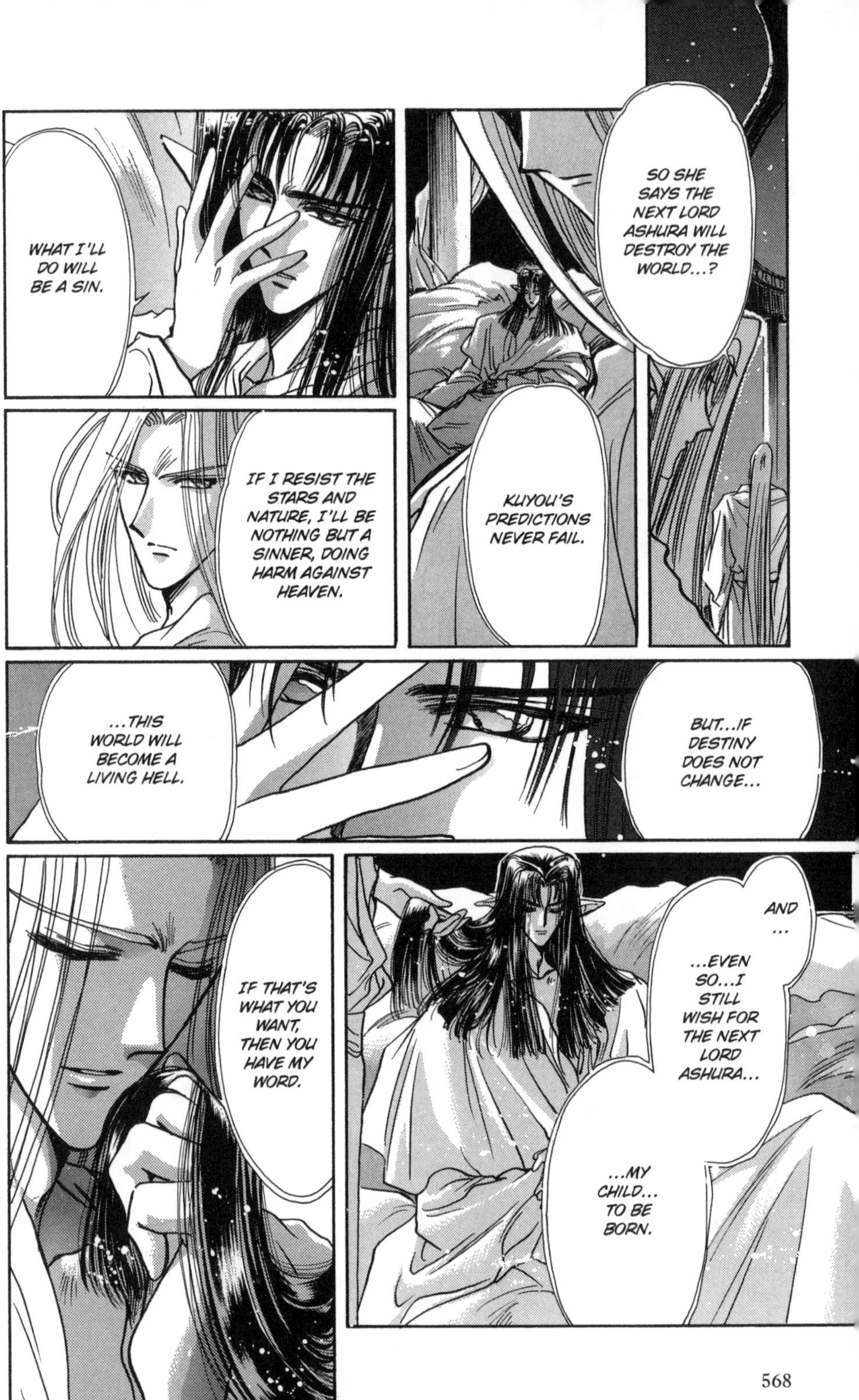
SO SHE SAYS THE NEXT LORD ASHURA WILL DESTROY THE WORLD...?
KUYOU'S PREDICTIONS NEVER FAIL.
WHAT I'LL DO WILL BE A SIN.
IF I RESIST THE STARS AND NATURE, I'LL BE NOTHING BUT A SINNER, DOING HARM AGAINST HEAVEN.
BUT...IF DESTINY DOES NOT CHANGE...
...THIS WORLD WILL BECOME A LIVING HELL.
AND ...
...EVEN SO...I STILL WISH FOR THE NEXT LORD ASHURA...
...MY CHILD... TO BE BORN.
IF THAT'S WHAT YOU WANT, THEN YOU HAVE MY WORD.

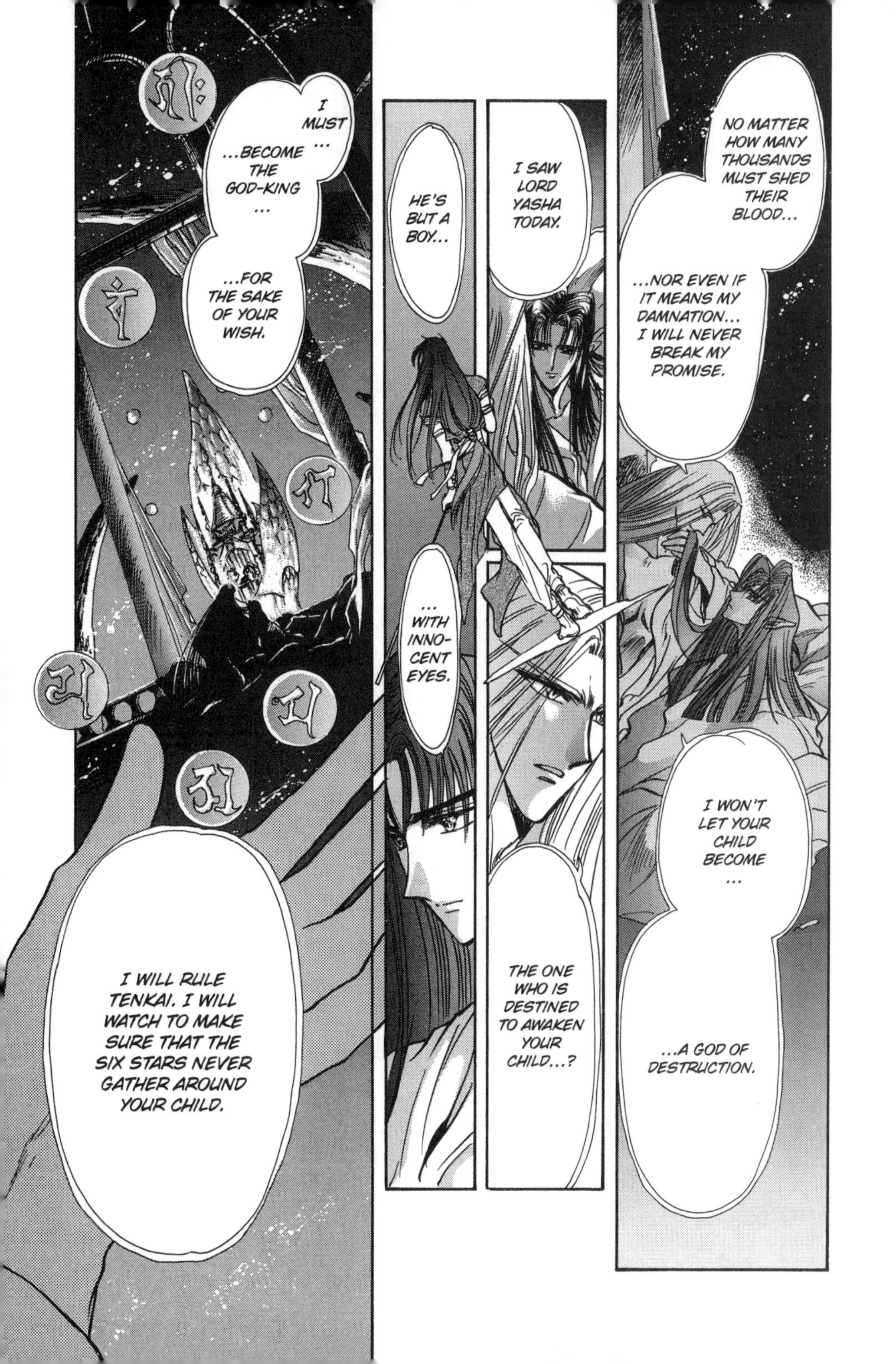
NO MATTER HOW MANY THOUSANDS MUST SHED THEIR BLOOD...
...NOR EVEN IF IT MEANS MY DAMNATION... I WILL NEVER BREAK MY PROMISE.
I WON'T LET YOUR CHILD BECOME ...
...A GOD OF DESTRUCTION.
I SAW LORD YASHA TODAY.
THE ONE WHO IS DESTINED TO AWAKEN YOUR CHILD...?
HE'S BUT A BOY...
... WITH INNO-CENT EYES.
I MUST ...
...BECOME THE GOD-KING ...
...FOR THE SAKE OF YOUR WISH.
I WILL RULE TENKAI. I WILL WATCH TO MAKE SURE THAT THE SIX STARS NEVER GATHER AROUND YOUR CHILD.

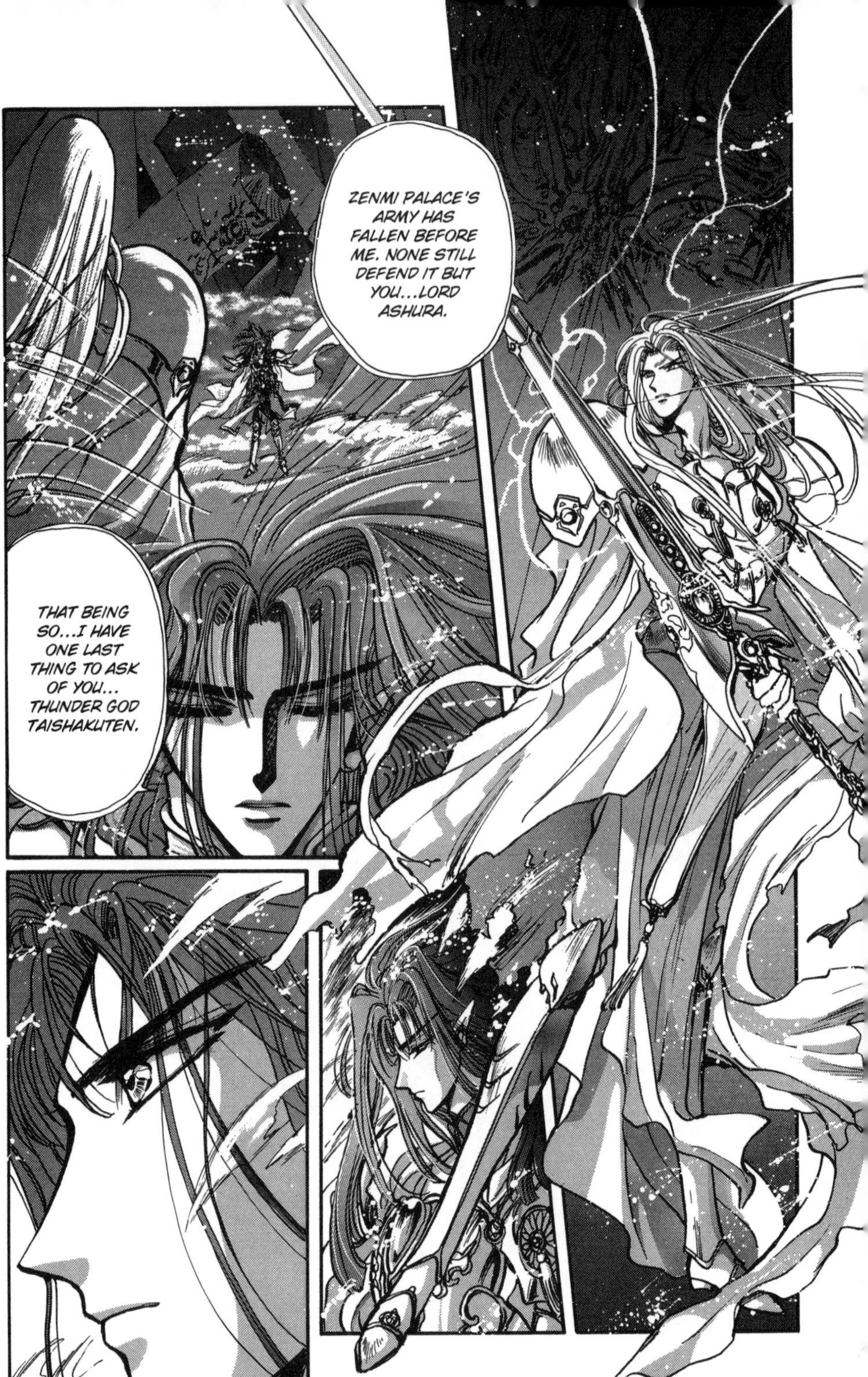
ZENMI PALACE'S ARMY HAS FALLEN BEFORE ME. NONE STILL DEFEND IT BUT YOU...LORD ASHURA.
THAT BEING SO...I HAVE ONE LAST THING TO ASK OF YOU... THUNDER GOD TAISHAKUTEN.

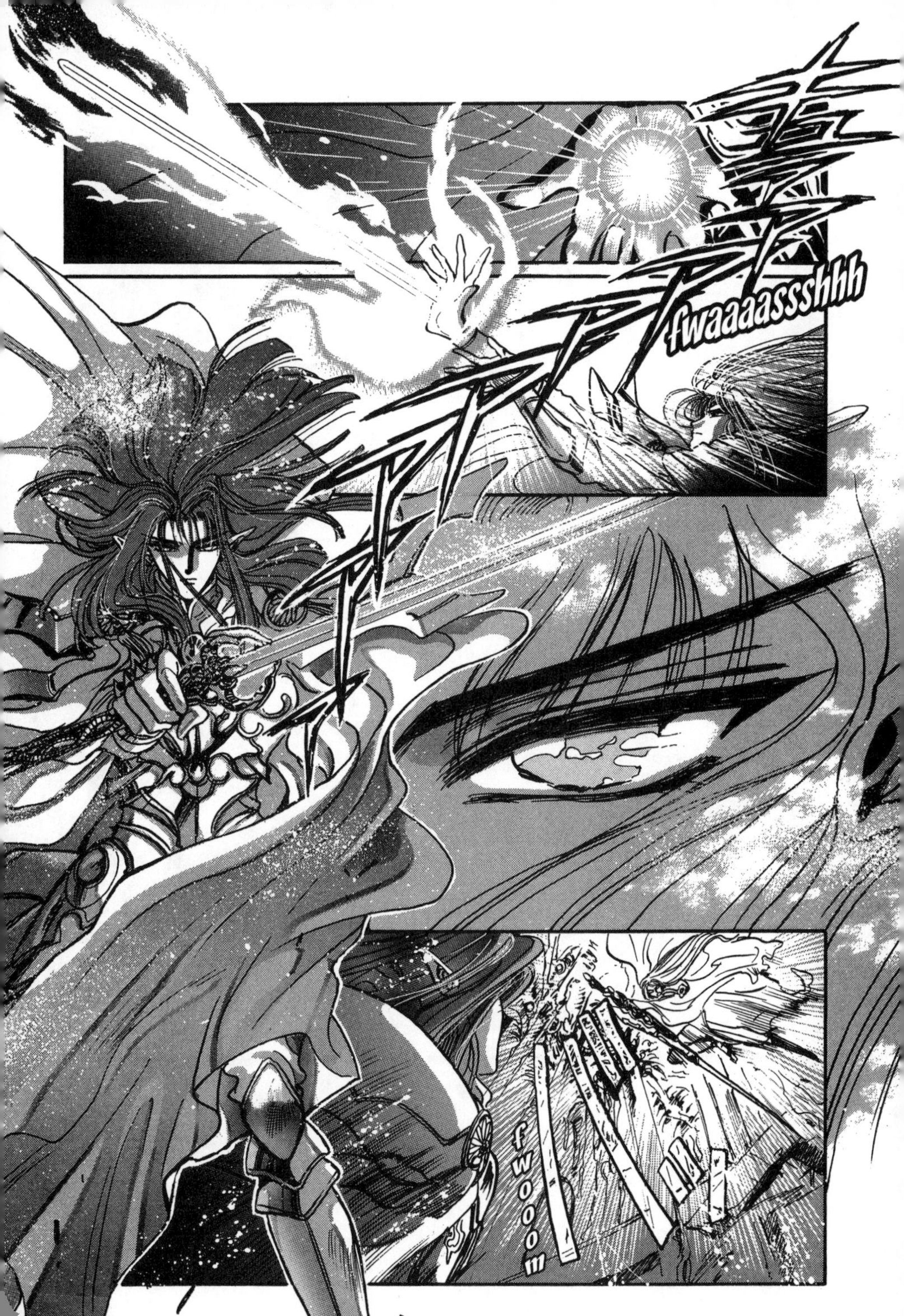
fwaaaassshhh
fwooom

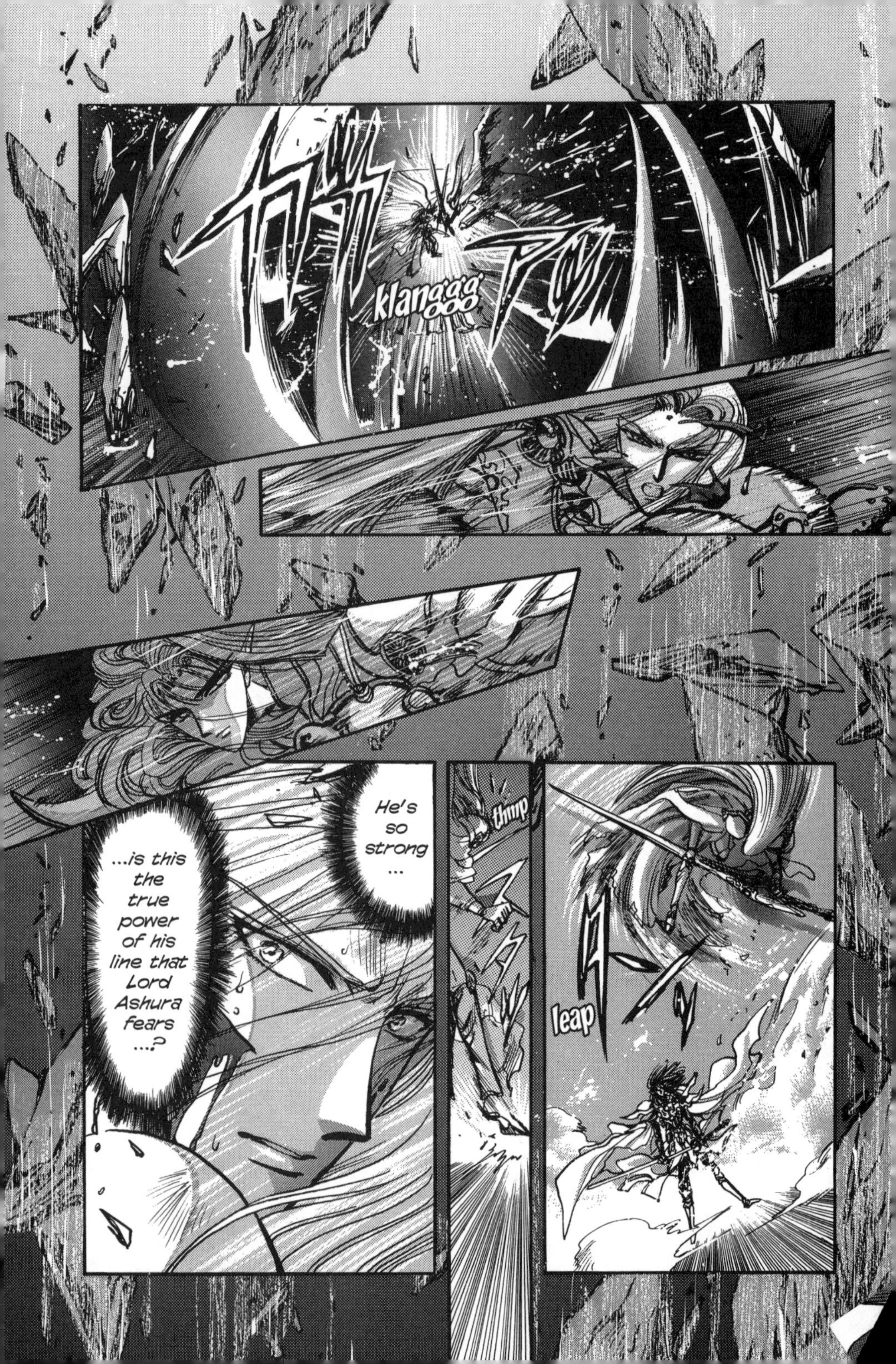
klanggg
ooo
leap
thmp
He's so strong ...
...is this the true power of his line that Lord Ashura fears ...?

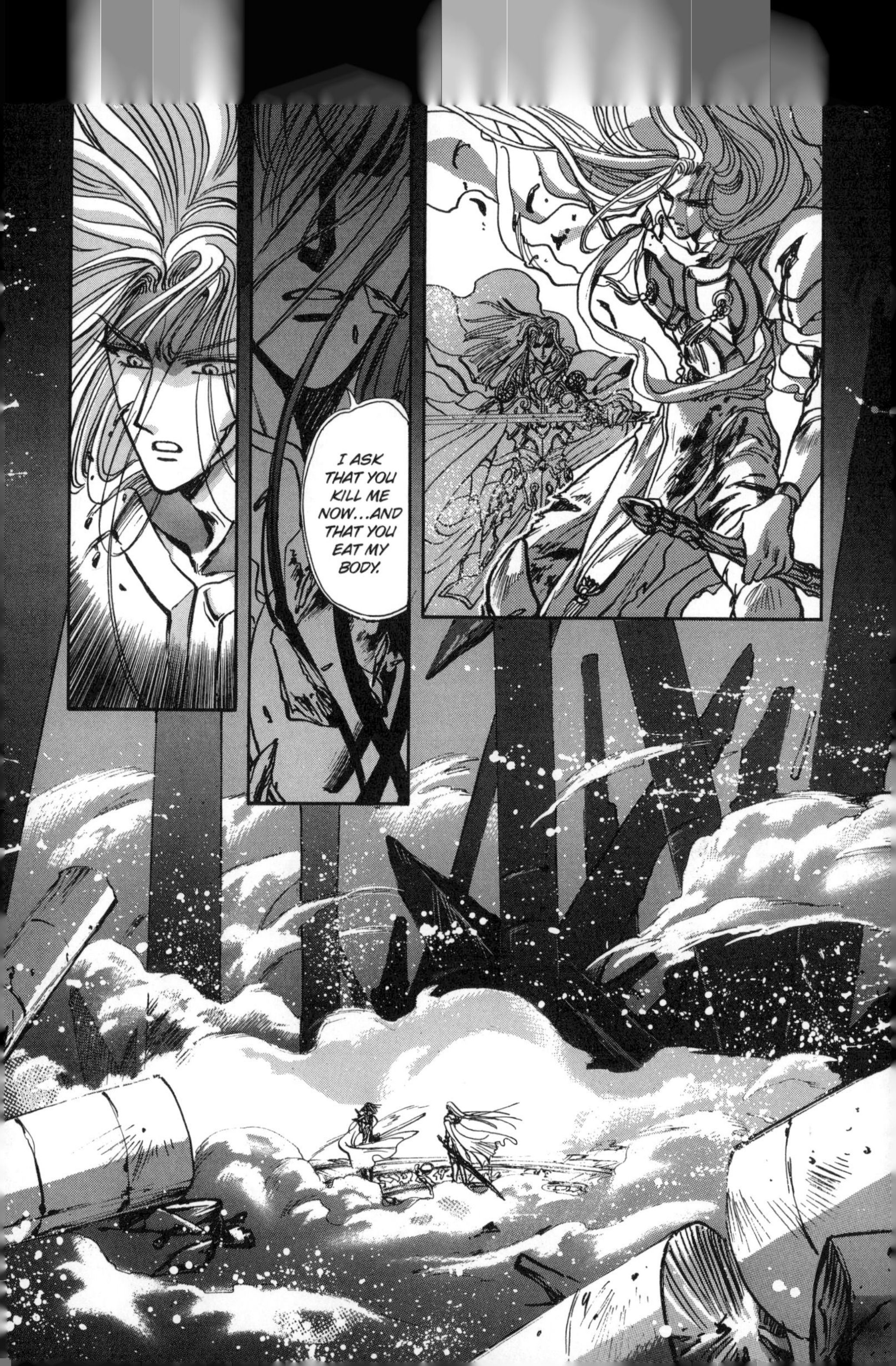
I ASK THAT YOU KILL ME NOW...AND THAT YOU EAT MY BODY.

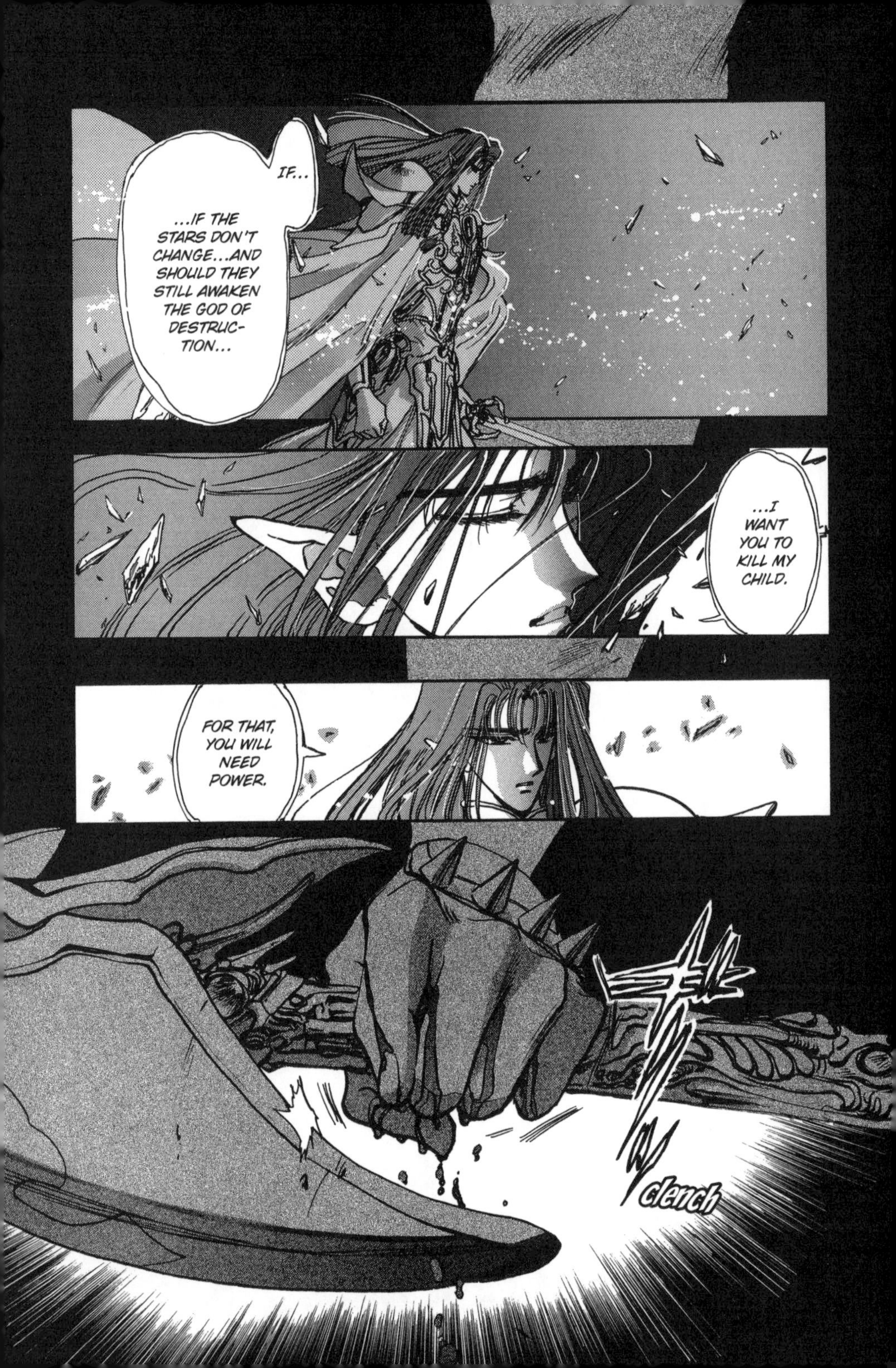
IF...
...IF THE STARS DON'T CHANGE...AND SHOULD THEY STILL AWAKEN THE GOD OF DESTRUCTION...
...I WANT YOU TO KILL MY CHILD.
FOR THAT, YOU WILL NEED POWER.
clench

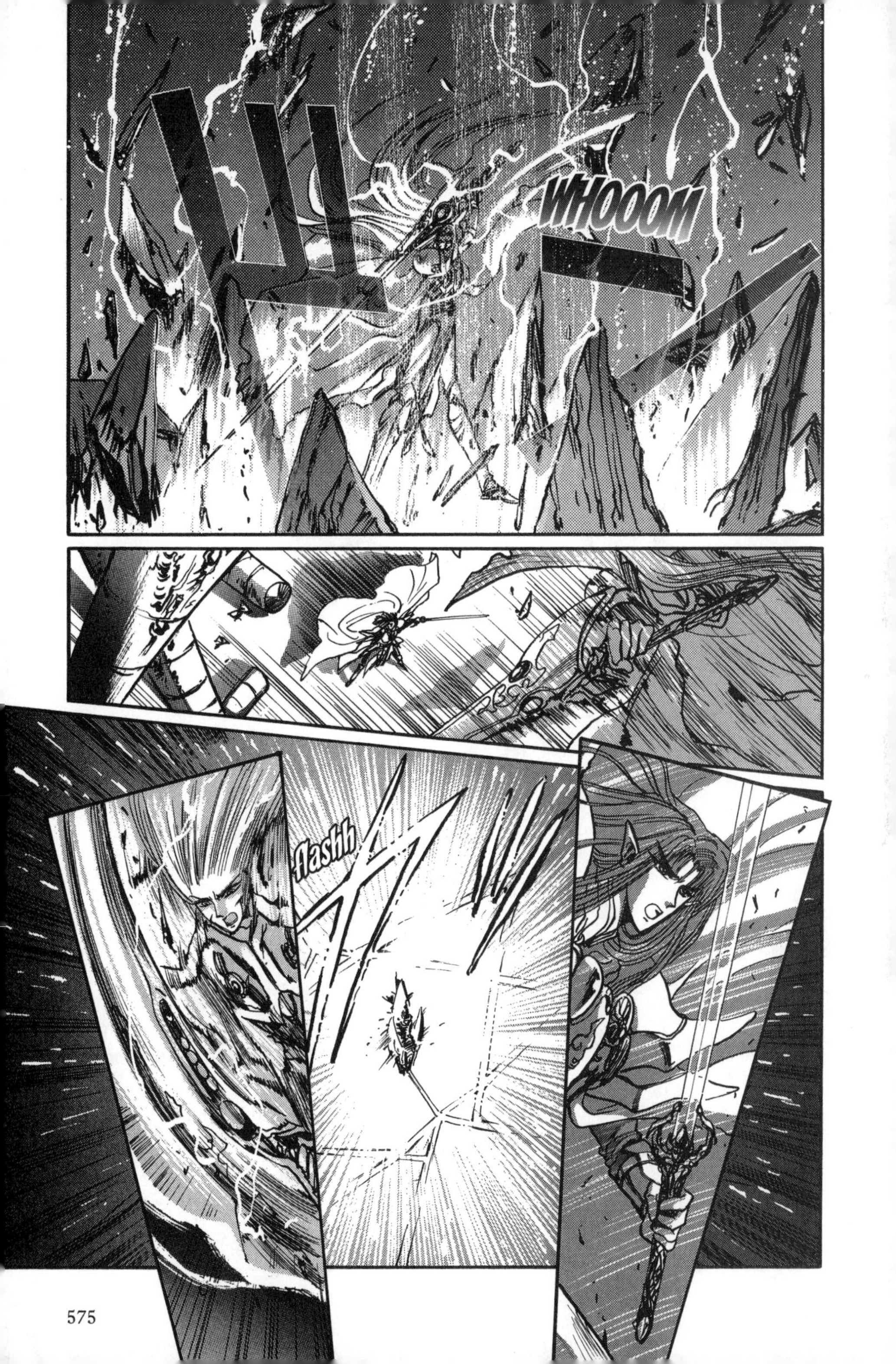
WHOOOM
flashh

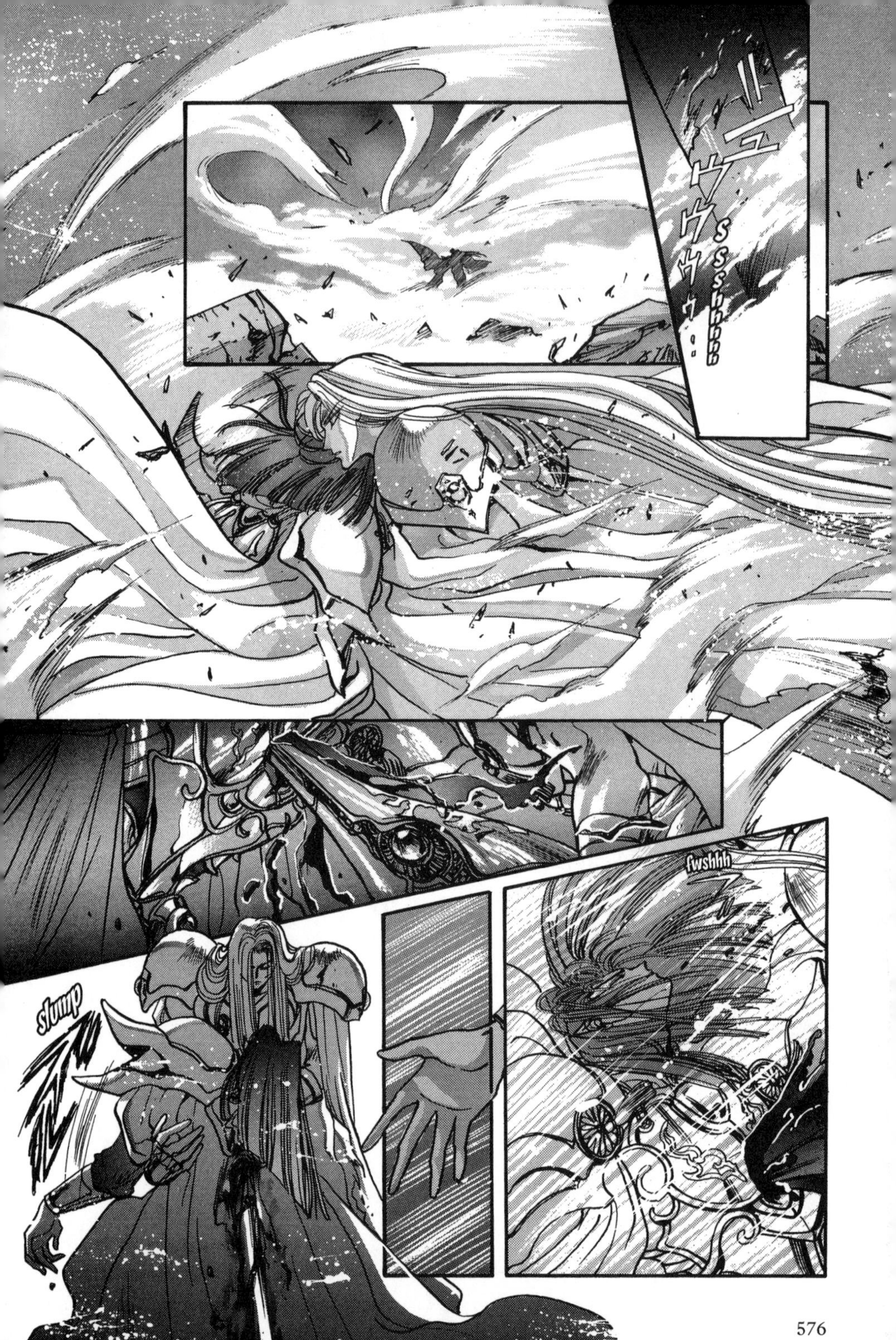
ジュウウウゥ..
ssshhhhh
fwshhh
slump

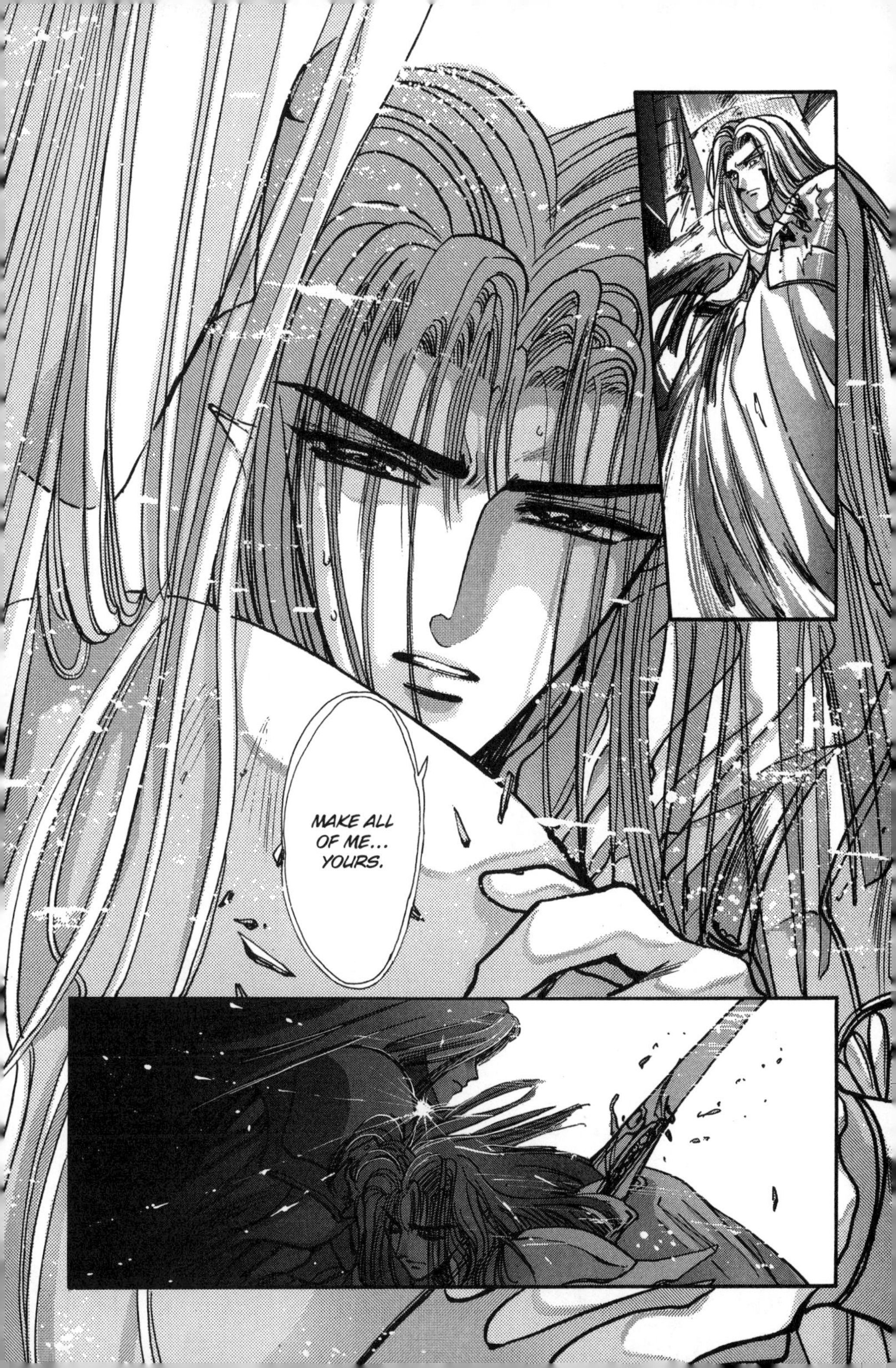
MAKE ALL OF ME... YOURS.

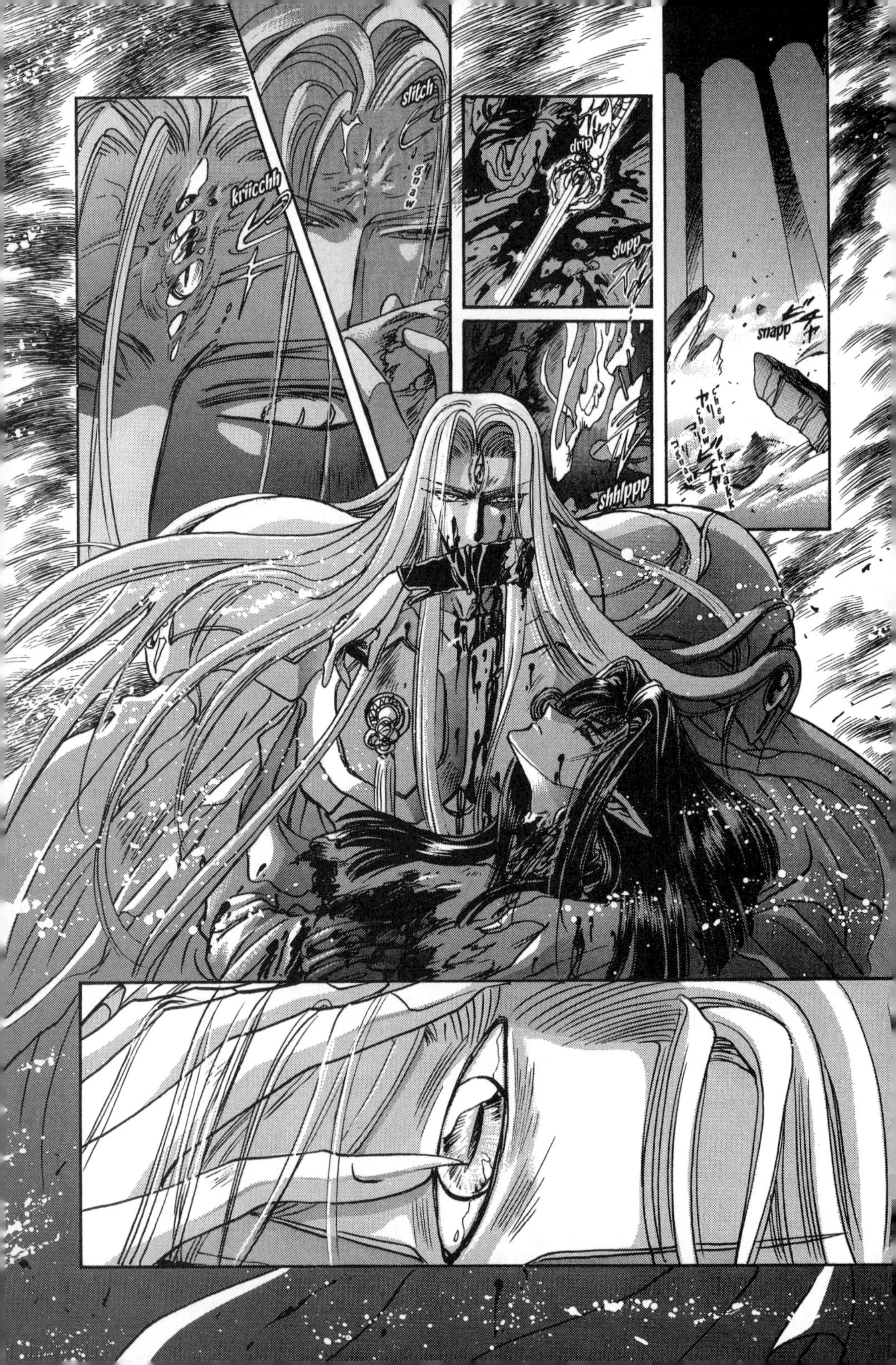

snapp
chew chew
chew chew
krakk
gnaw
drip
slupp
shhlppp
slitch
gnaw
kriicchh

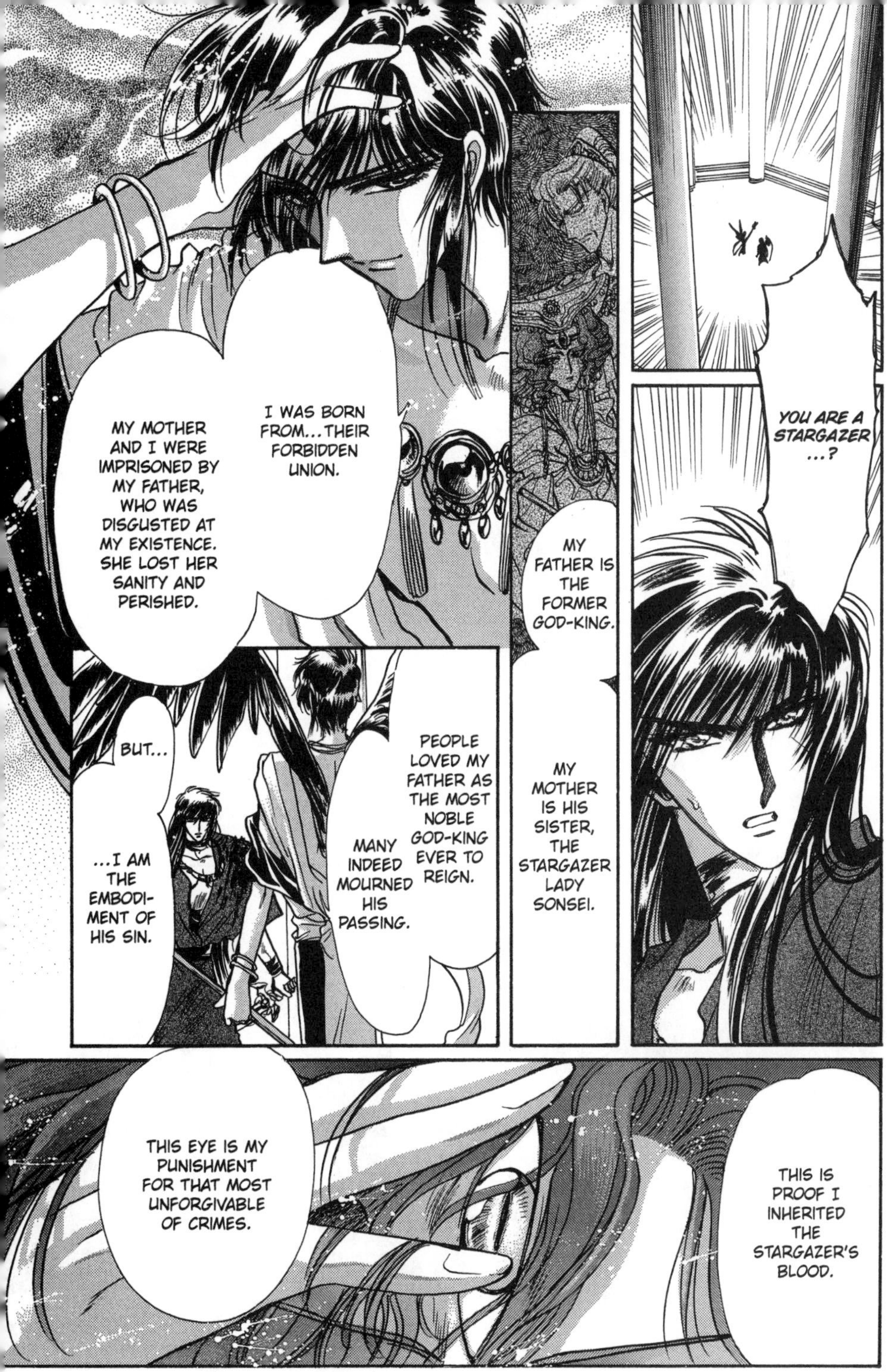
YOU ARE A STARGAZER ...?
MY FATHER IS THE FORMER GOD-KING.
MY MOTHER IS HIS SISTER, THE STARGAZER LADY SONSEI.
I WAS BORN FROM... THEIR FORBIDDEN UNION.
MY MOTHER AND I WERE IMPRISONED BY MY FATHER, WHO WAS DISGUSTED AT MY EXISTENCE. SHE LOST HER SANITY AND PERISHED.
PEOPLE LOVED MY FATHER AS THE MOST NOBLE GOD-KING EVER TO REIGN.
MANY INDEED MOURNED HIS PASSING.
BUT...
...I AM THE EMBODIMENT OF HIS SIN.
THIS IS PROOF I INHERITED THE STARGAZER'S BLOOD.
THIS EYE IS MY PUNISHMENT FOR THAT MOST UNFORGIVABLE OF CRIMES.

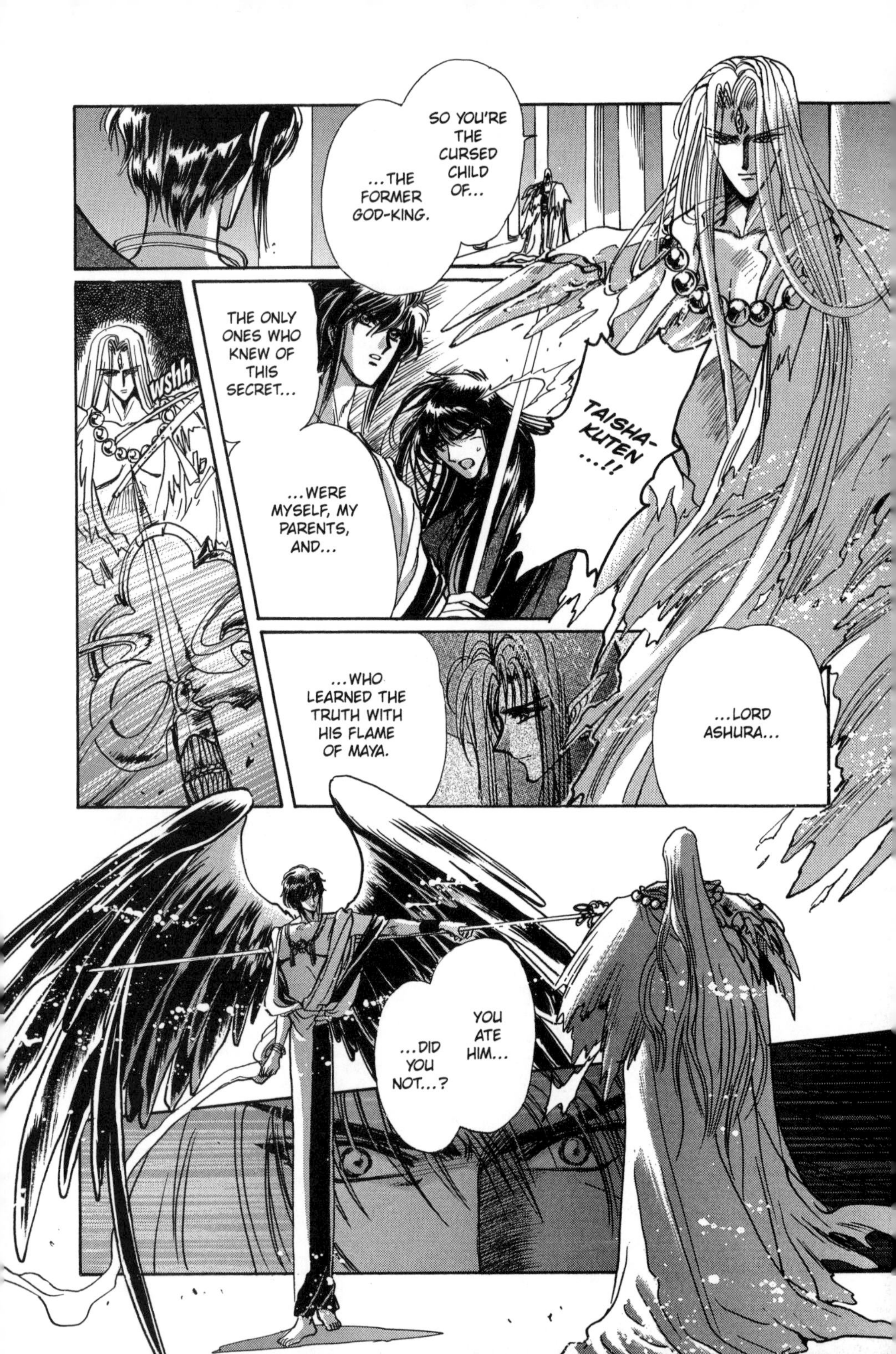
SO YOU'RE THE CURSED CHILD OF... ...THE FORMER GOD-KING.
TAISHA-KUTEN...!!
THE ONLY ONES WHO KNEW OF THIS SECRET...
...WERE MYSELF, MY PARENTS, AND...
...LORD ASHURA...
...WHO LEARNED THE TRUTH WITH HIS FLAME OF MAYA.
wshh
YOU ATE HIM...
...DID YOU NOT...?

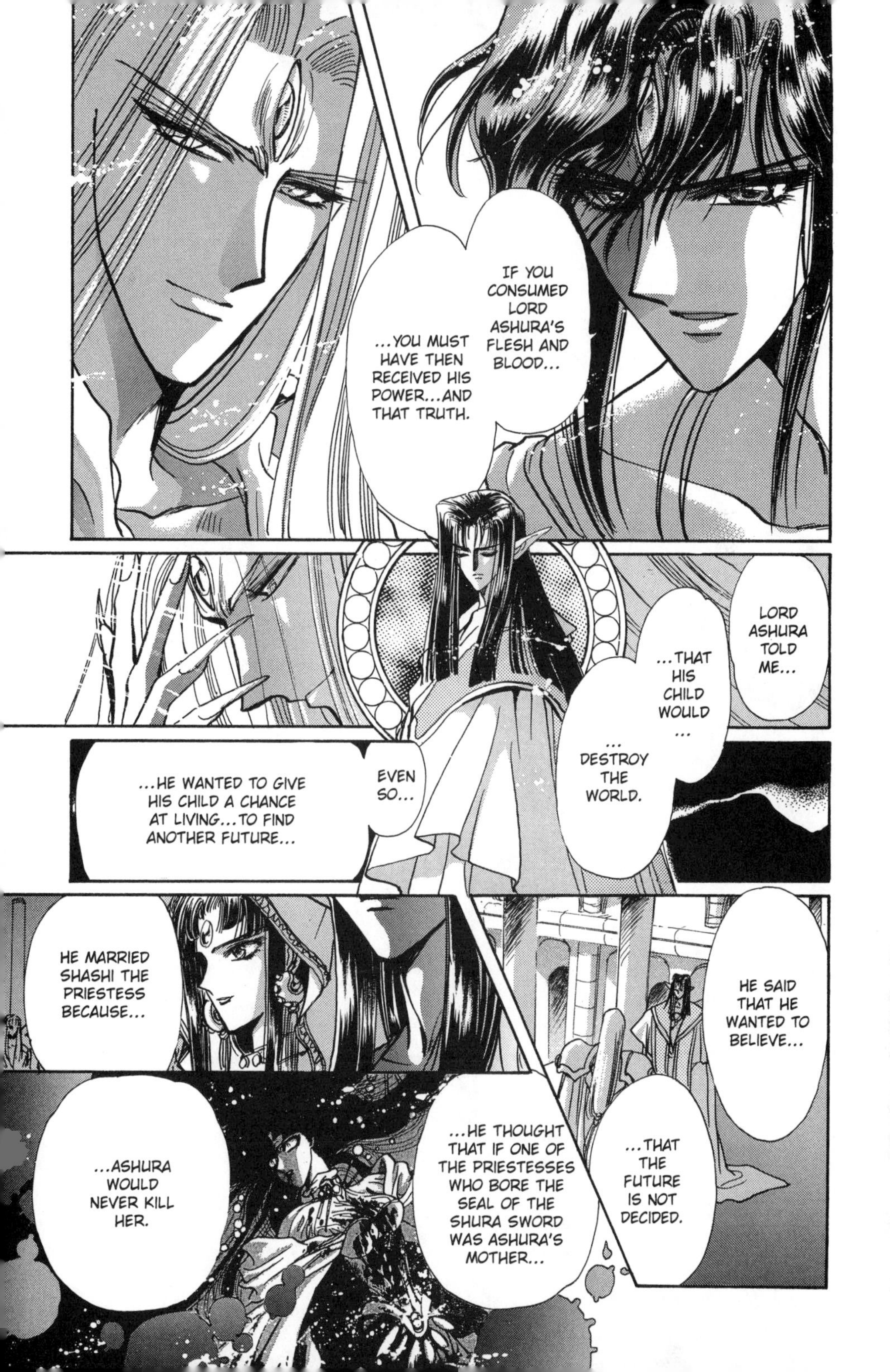
IF YOU CONSUMED LORD ASHURA'S FLESH AND BLOOD...
...YOU MUST HAVE THEN RECEIVED HIS POWER...AND THAT TRUTH.
LORD ASHURA TOLD ME...
...THAT HIS CHILD WOULD ...
... DESTROY THE WORLD.
EVEN SO...
...HE WANTED TO GIVE HIS CHILD A CHANCE AT LIVING...TO FIND ANOTHER FUTURE...
HE SAID THAT HE WANTED TO BELIEVE...
...THAT THE FUTURE IS NOT DECIDED.
HE MARRIED SHASHI THE PRIESTESS BECAUSE...
...HE THOUGHT THAT IF ONE OF THE PRIESTESSES WHO BORE THE SEAL OF THE SHURA SWORD WAS ASHURA'S MOTHER...
...ASHURA WOULD NEVER KILL HER.

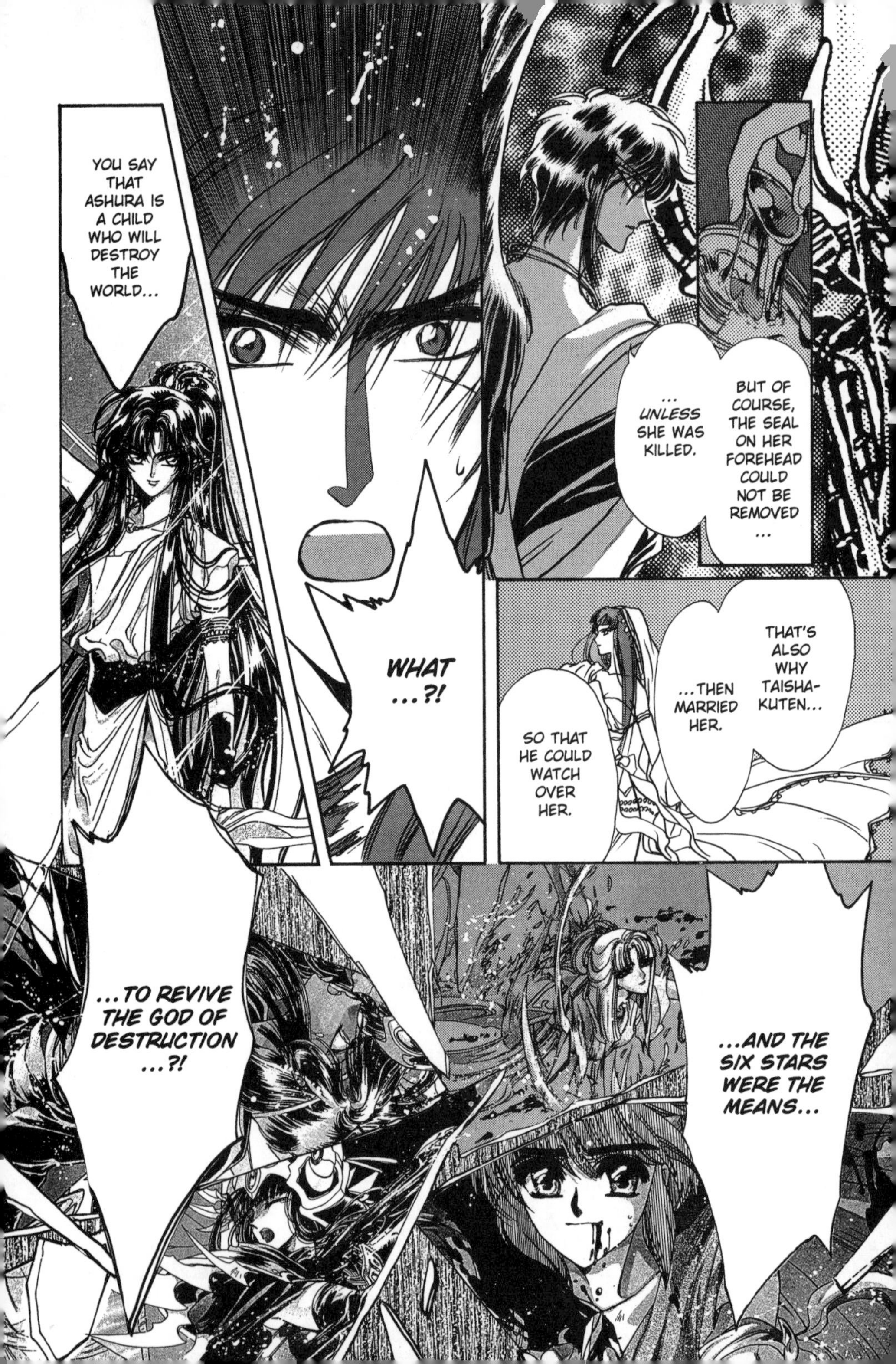

BUT OF COURSE, THE SEAL ON HER FOREHEAD COULD NOT BE REMOVED ...
... UNLESS SHE WAS KILLED.
THAT'S ALSO WHY TAISHA-KUTEN...
...THEN MARRIED HER.
SO THAT HE COULD WATCH OVER HER.
WHAT ...?!
YOU SAY THAT ASHURA IS A CHILD WHO WILL DESTROY THE WORLD...
...AND THE SIX STARS WERE THE MEANS...
...TO REVIVE THE GOD OF DESTRUCTION ...?!

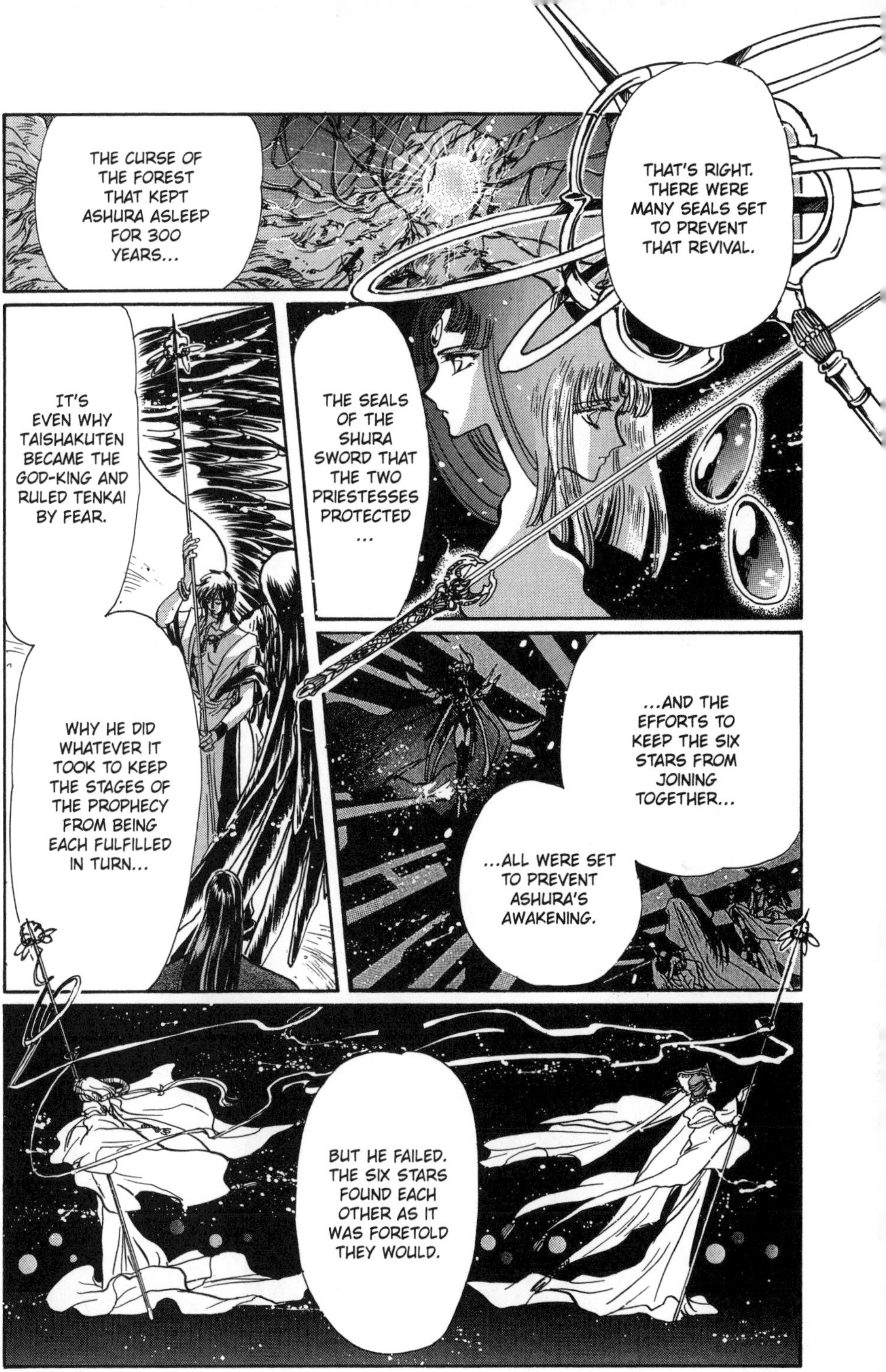
THAT'S RIGHT. THERE WERE MANY SEALS SET TO PREVENT THAT REVIVAL.
THE CURSE OF THE FOREST THAT KEPT ASHURA ASLEEP FOR 300 YEARS...
THE SEALS OF THE SHURA SWORD THAT THE TWO PRIESTESSES PROTECTED ...
...AND THE EFFORTS TO KEEP THE SIX STARS FROM JOINING TOGETHER...
...ALL WERE SET TO PREVENT ASHURA'S AWAKENING.
IT'S EVEN WHY TAISHAKUTEN BECAME THE GOD-KING AND RULED TENKAI BY FEAR.
WHY HE DID WHATEVER IT TOOK TO KEEP THE STAGES OF THE PROPHECY FROM BEING EACH FULFILLED IN TURN...
BUT HE FAILED. THE SIX STARS FOUND EACH OTHER AS IT WAS FORETOLD THEY WOULD.

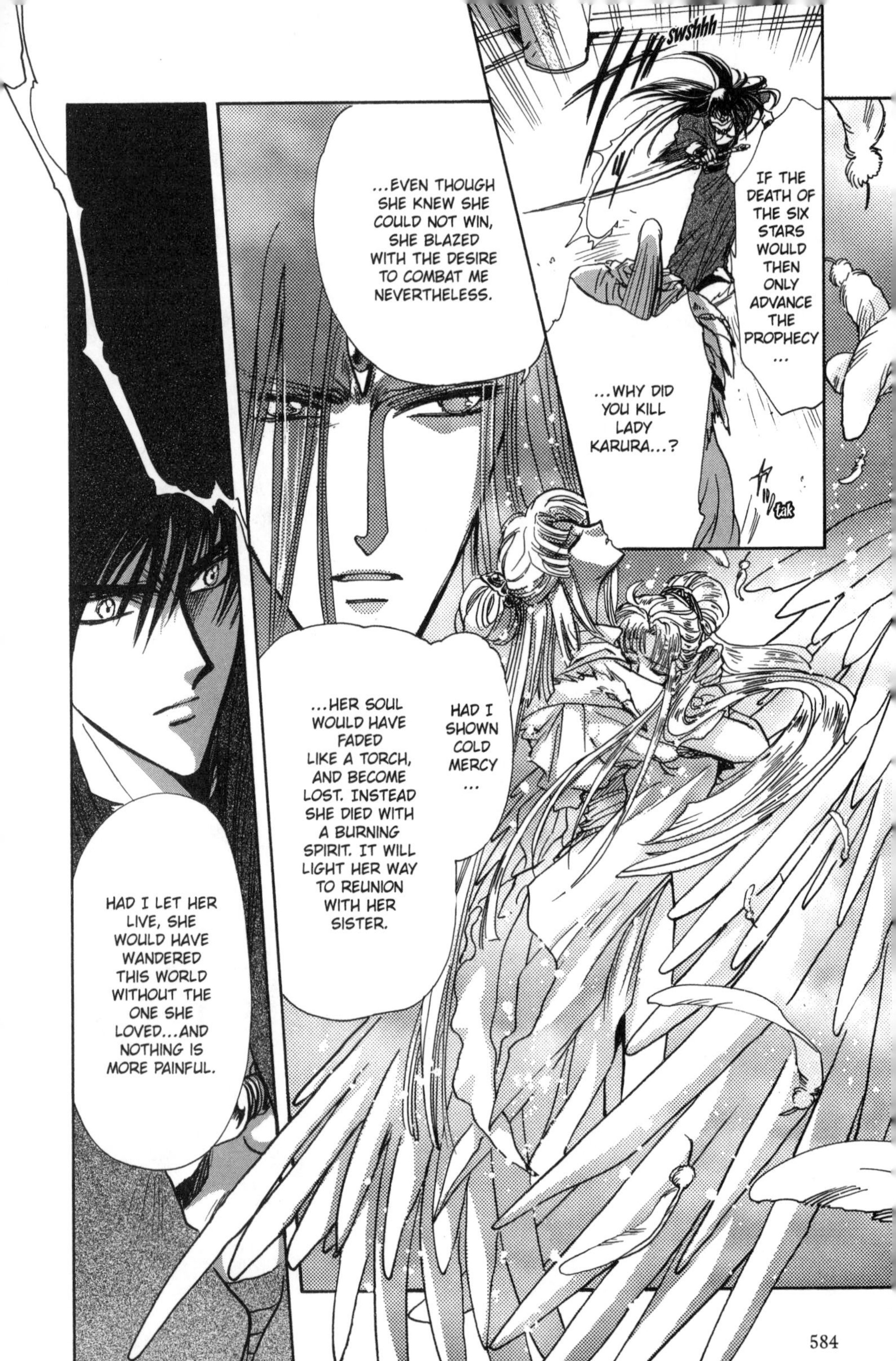
swshhh
IF THE DEATH OF THE SIX STARS WOULD THEN ONLY ADVANCE THE PROPHECY...
...WHY DID YOU KILL LADY KARURA...?
tak
...EVEN THOUGH SHE KNEW SHE COULD NOT WIN, SHE BLAZED WITH THE DESIRE TO COMBAT ME NEVERTHELESS.
HAD I SHOWN COLD MERCY...
...HER SOUL WOULD HAVE FADED LIKE A TORCH, AND BECOME LOST. INSTEAD SHE DIED WITH A BURNING SPIRIT. IT WILL LIGHT HER WAY TO REUNION WITH HER SISTER.
HAD I LET HER LIVE, SHE WOULD HAVE WANDERED THIS WORLD WITHOUT THE ONE SHE LOVED...AND NOTHING IS MORE PAINFUL.

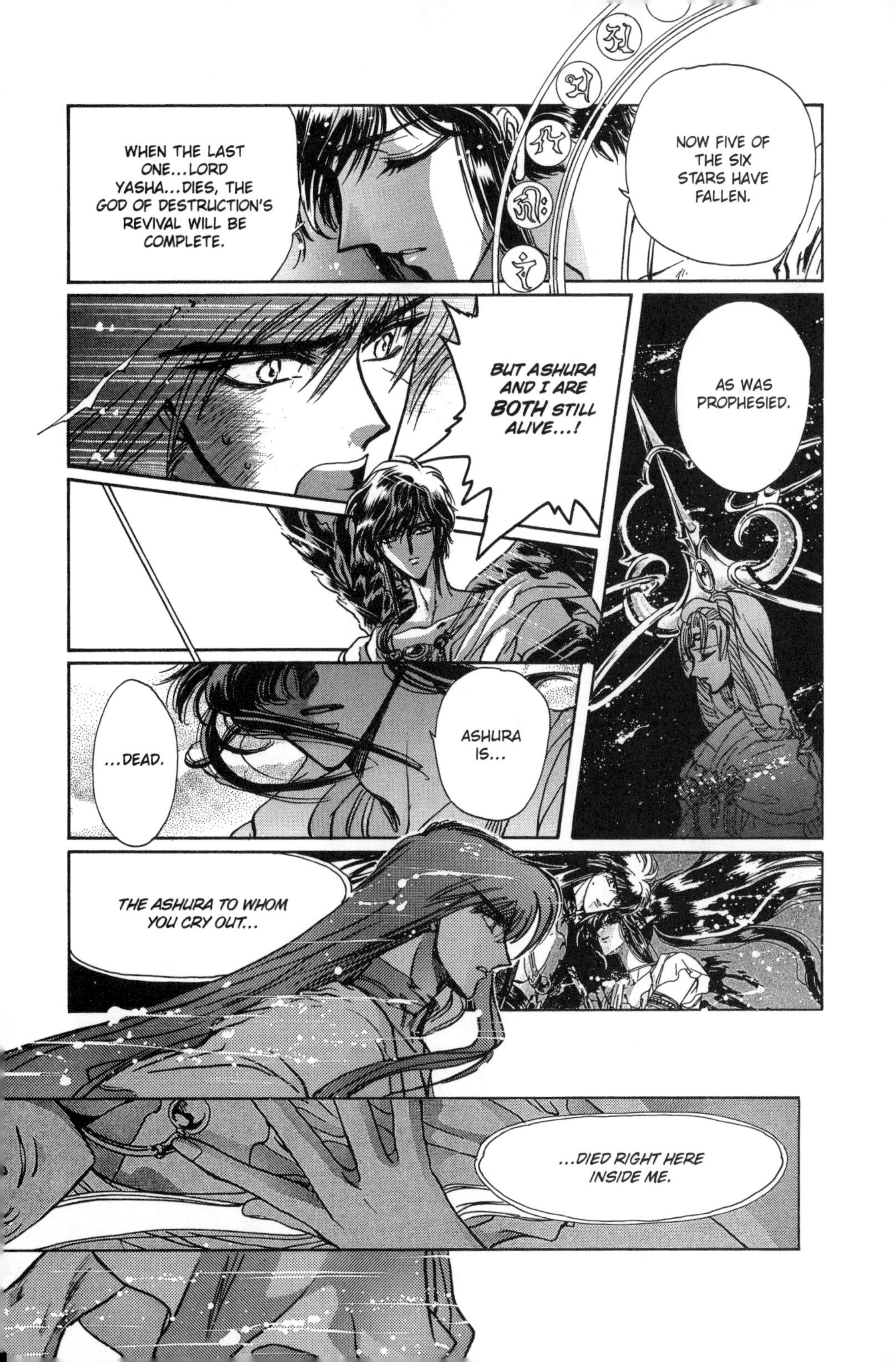
NOW FIVE OF THE SIX STARS HAVE FALLEN.
WHEN THE LAST ONE...LORD YASHA...DIES, THE GOD OF DESTRUCTION'S REVIVAL WILL BE COMPLETE.
AS WAS PROPHESIED.
BUT ASHURA AND I ARE BOTH STILL ALIVE...!
ASHURA IS...
...DEAD.
THE ASHURA TO WHOM YOU CRY OUT...
...DIED RIGHT HERE INSIDE ME.

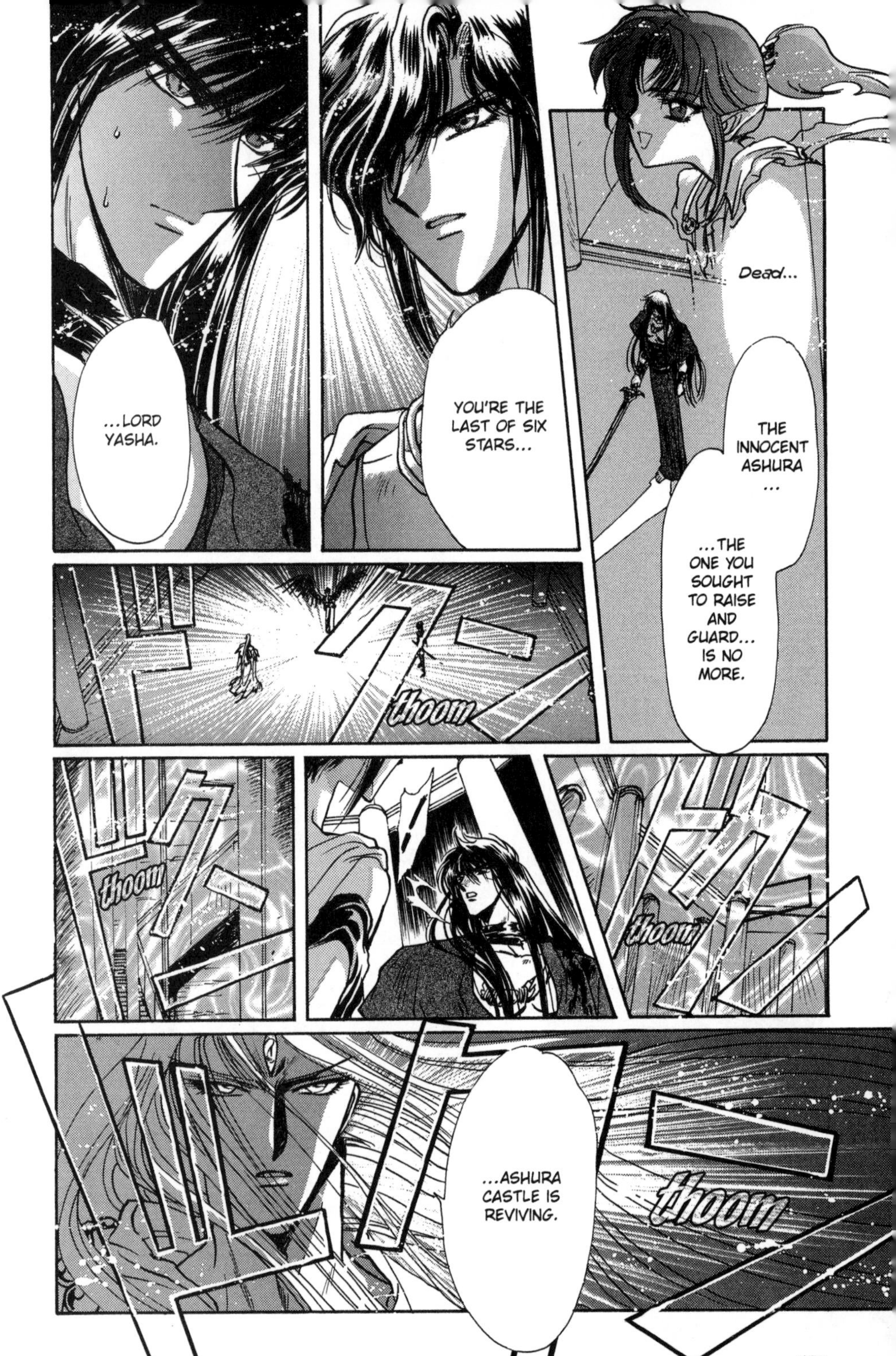
Dead...
THE INNOCENT ASHURA ...
...THE ONE YOU SOUGHT TO RAISE AND GUARD... IS NO MORE.
YOU'RE THE LAST OF SIX STARS...
...LORD YASHA.
thoom
thoom
thoom
...ASHURA CASTLE IS REVIVING.
thoom

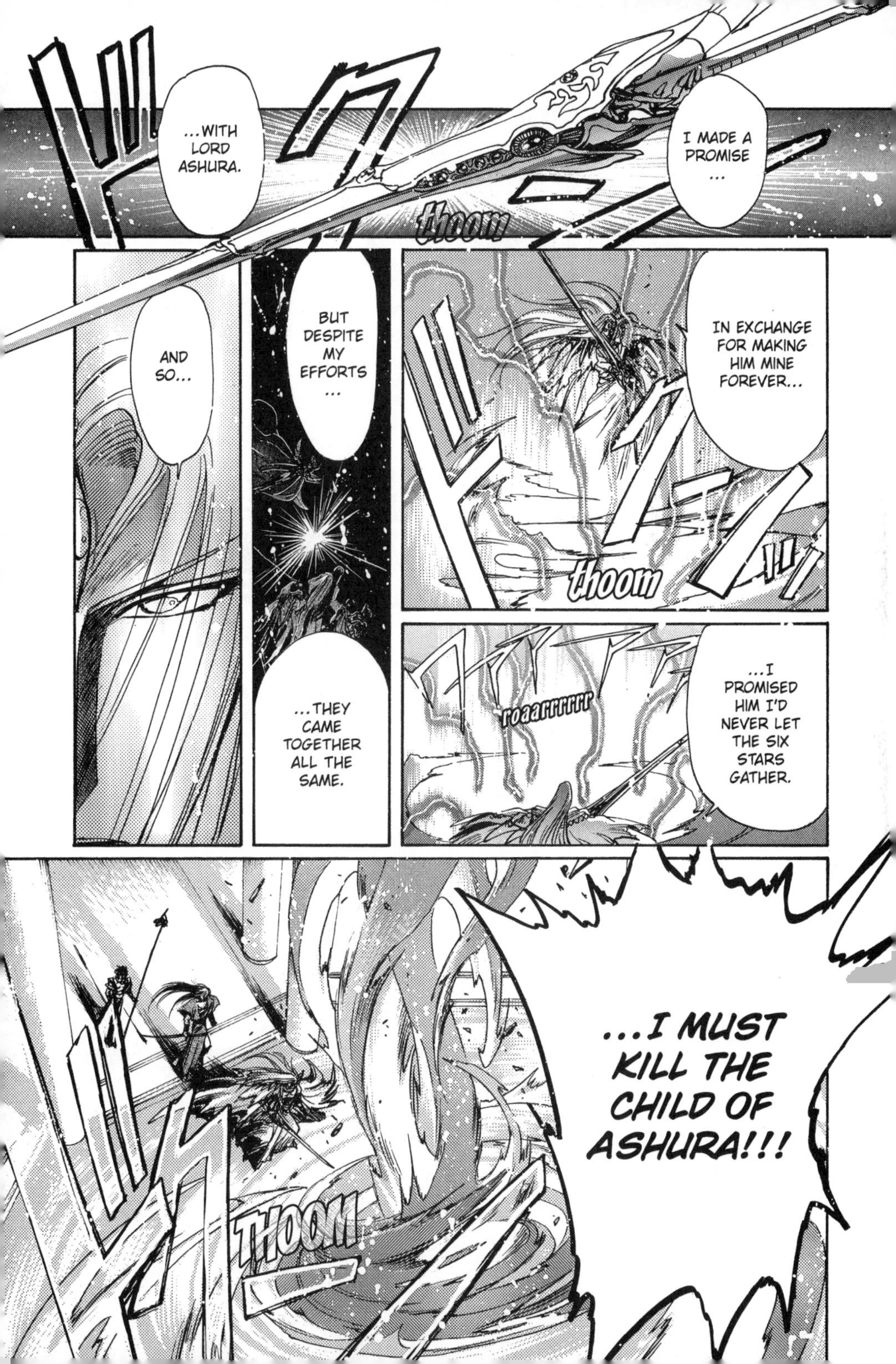
I MADE A PROMISE...
...WITH LORD ASHURA.
thoom
IN EXCHANGE FOR MAKING HIM MINE FOREVER...
thoom
...I PROMISED HIM I'D NEVER LET THE SIX STARS GATHER.
roaarrrrrrr
BUT DESPITE MY EFFORTS...
...THEY CAME TOGETHER ALL THE SAME.
AND SO...
...I MUST KILL THE CHILD OF ASHURA!!!
THOOM

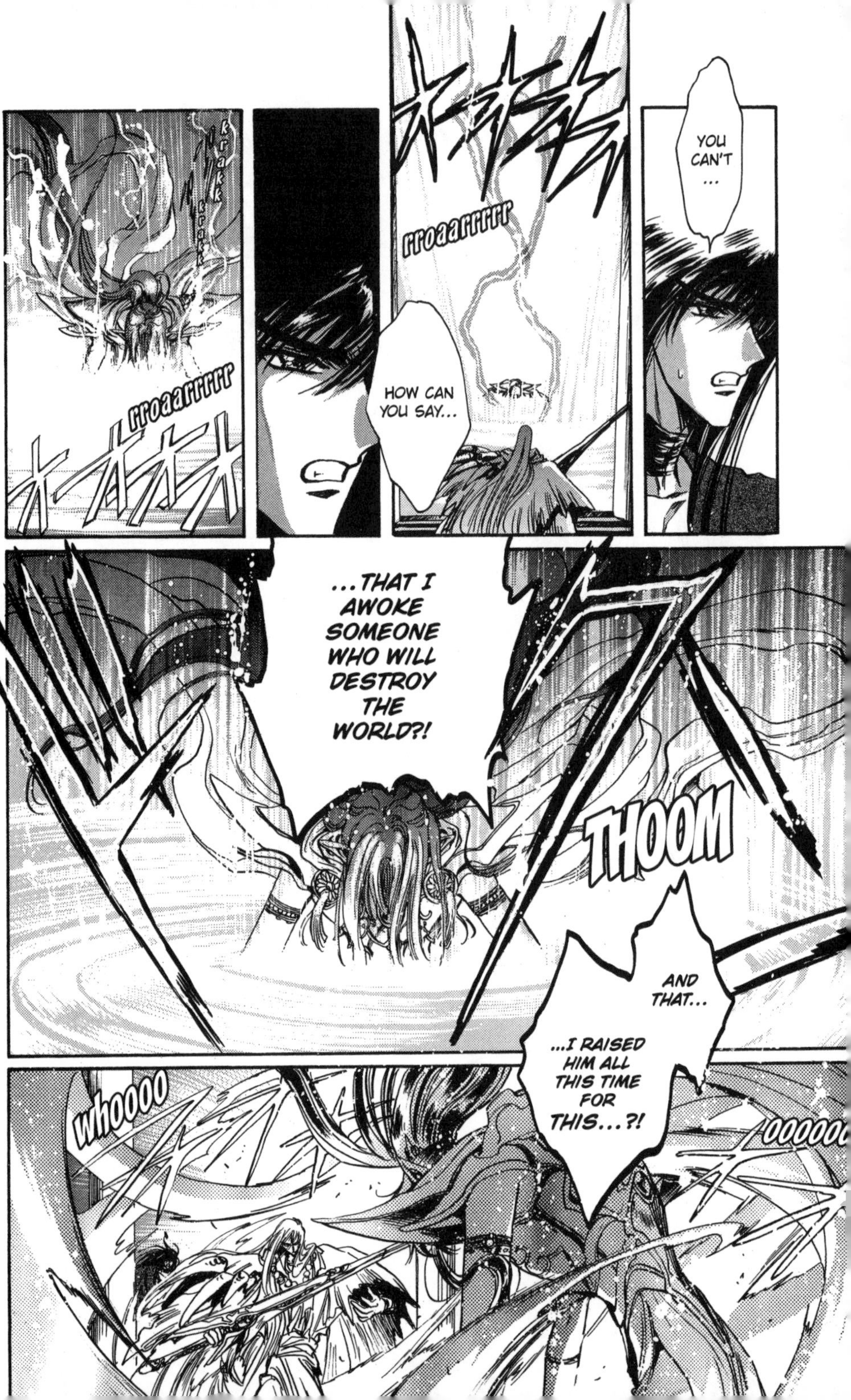
YOU CAN'T ...
rroaarrrrr
HOW CAN YOU SAY...
krakk
krakk
rroaarrrrr
...THAT I AWOKE SOMEONE WHO WILL DESTROY THE WORLD?!
THOOM
AND THAT...
...I RAISED HIM ALL THIS TIME FOR THIS...?!
oooooo
whoooo

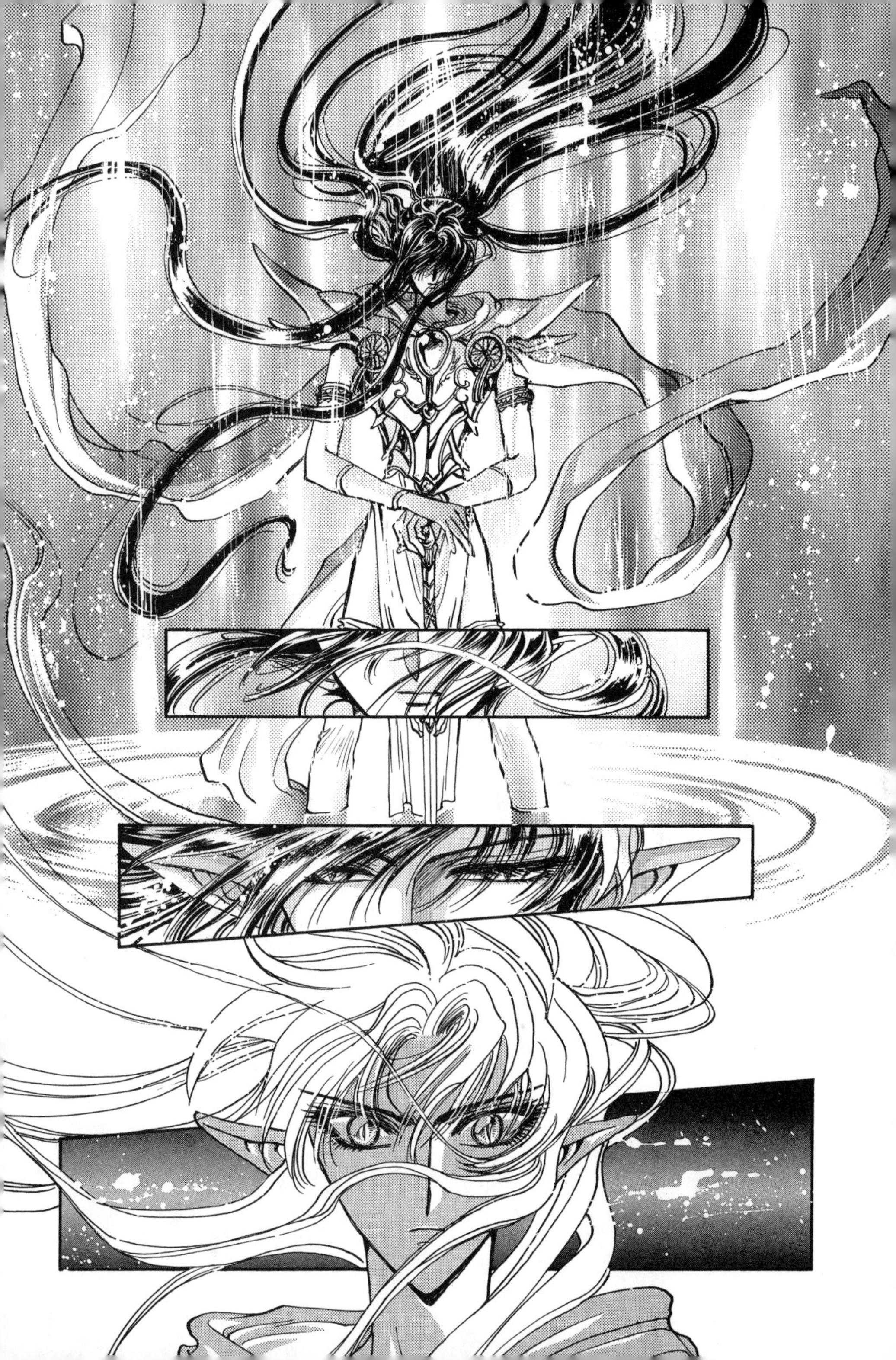

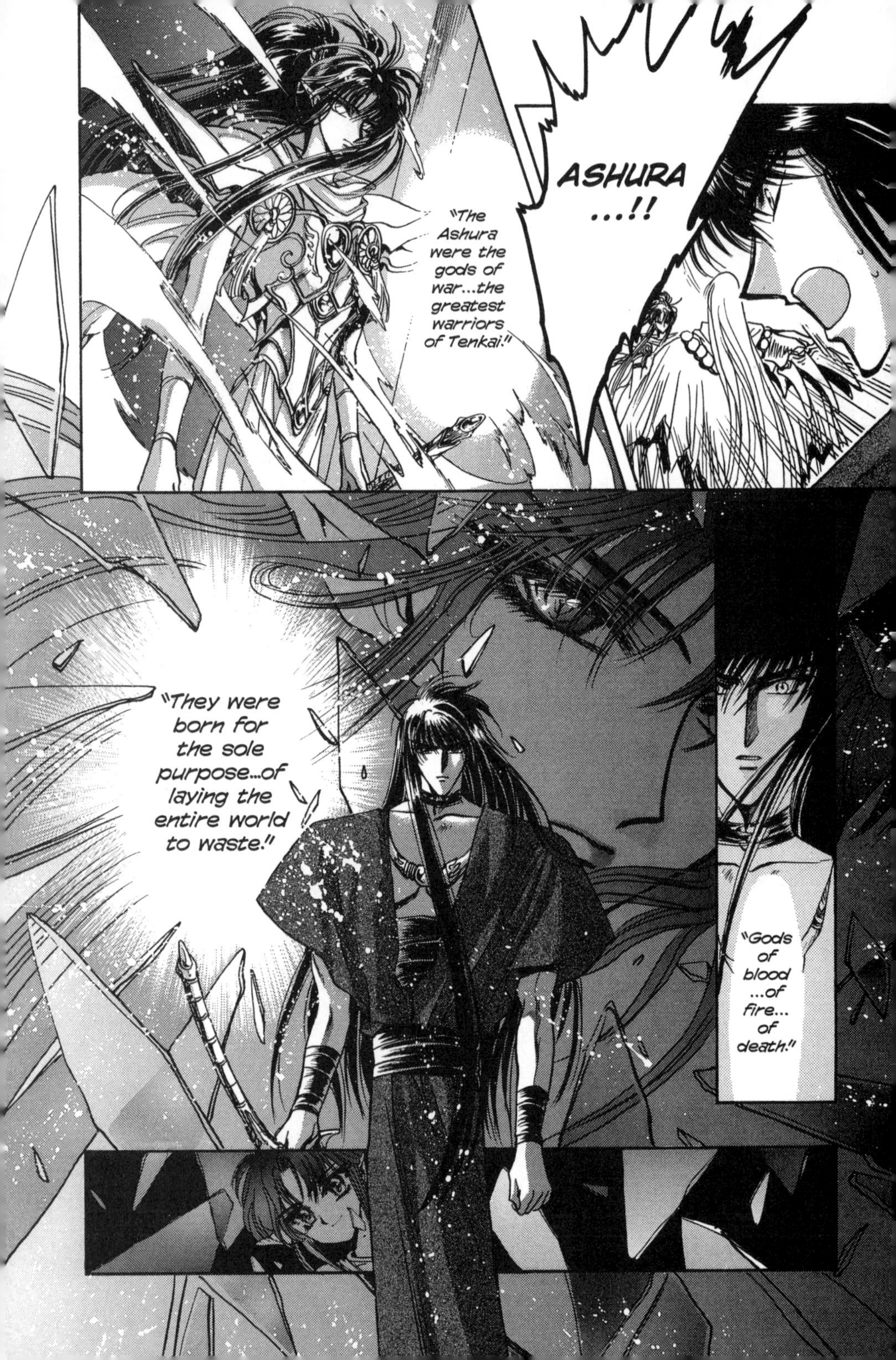
ASHURA ...!!
"The Ashura were the gods of war...the greatest warriors of Tenkai."
"Gods of blood ...of fire... of death."
"They were born for the sole purpose...of laying the entire world to waste."

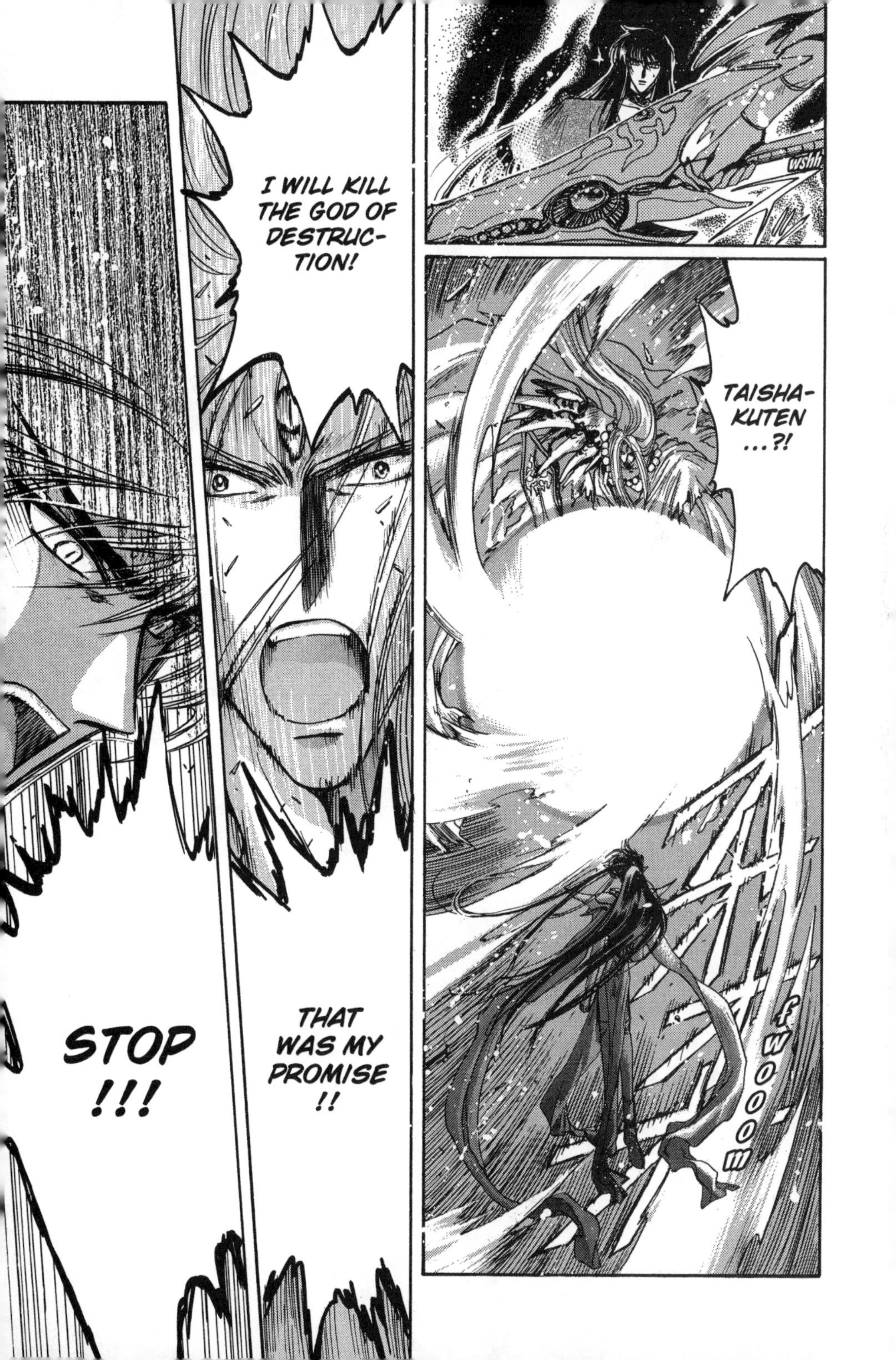
wshh
TAISHA-KUTEN...?!
fwoooom
I WILL KILL THE GOD OF DESTRUCTION!
THAT WAS MY PROMISE!!
STOP!!!

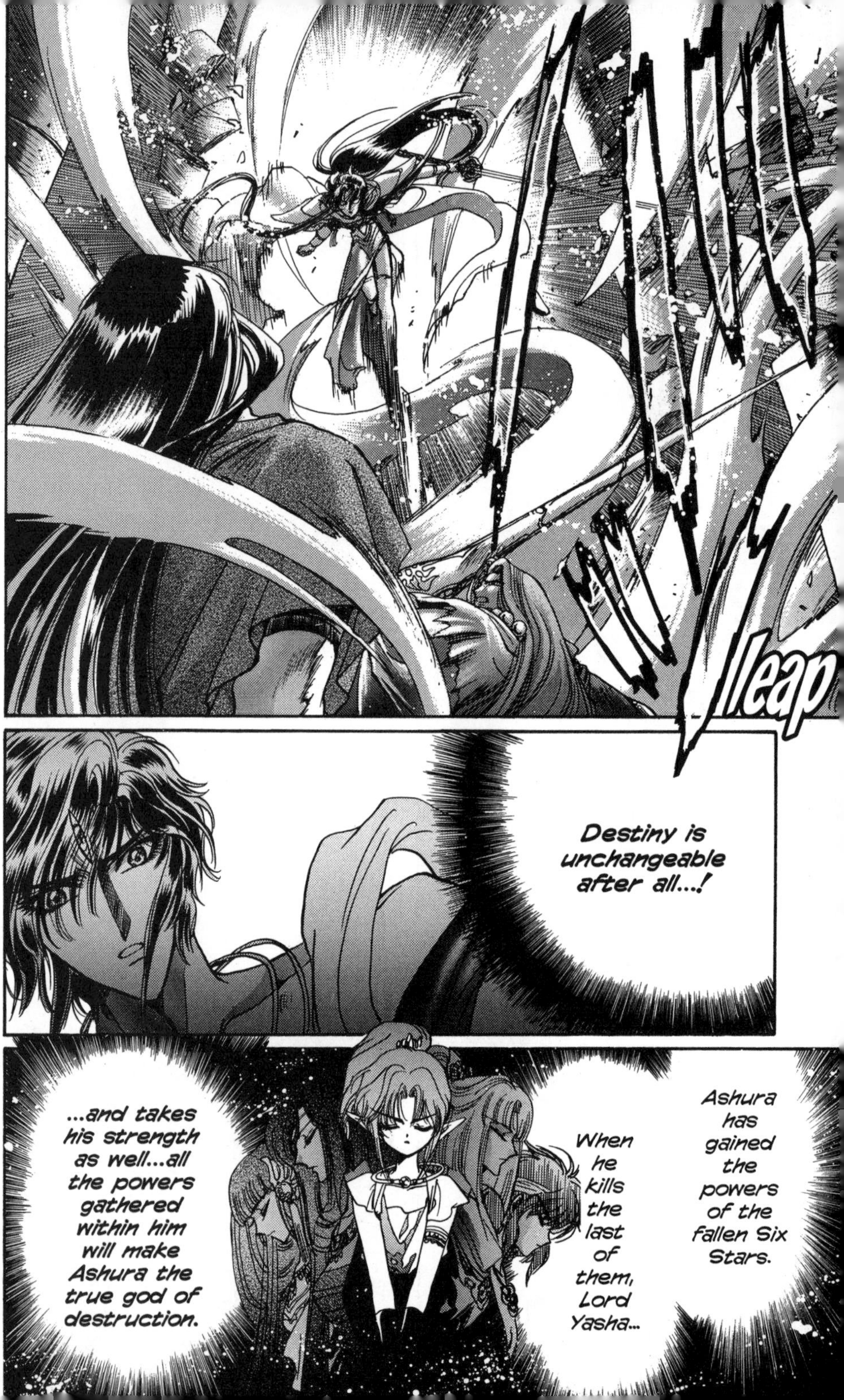
leap
Destiny is unchangeable after all...!
Ashura has gained the powers of the fallen Six Stars.
When he kills the last of them, Lord Yasha...
...and takes his strength as well...all the powers gathered within him will make Ashura the true god of destruction.

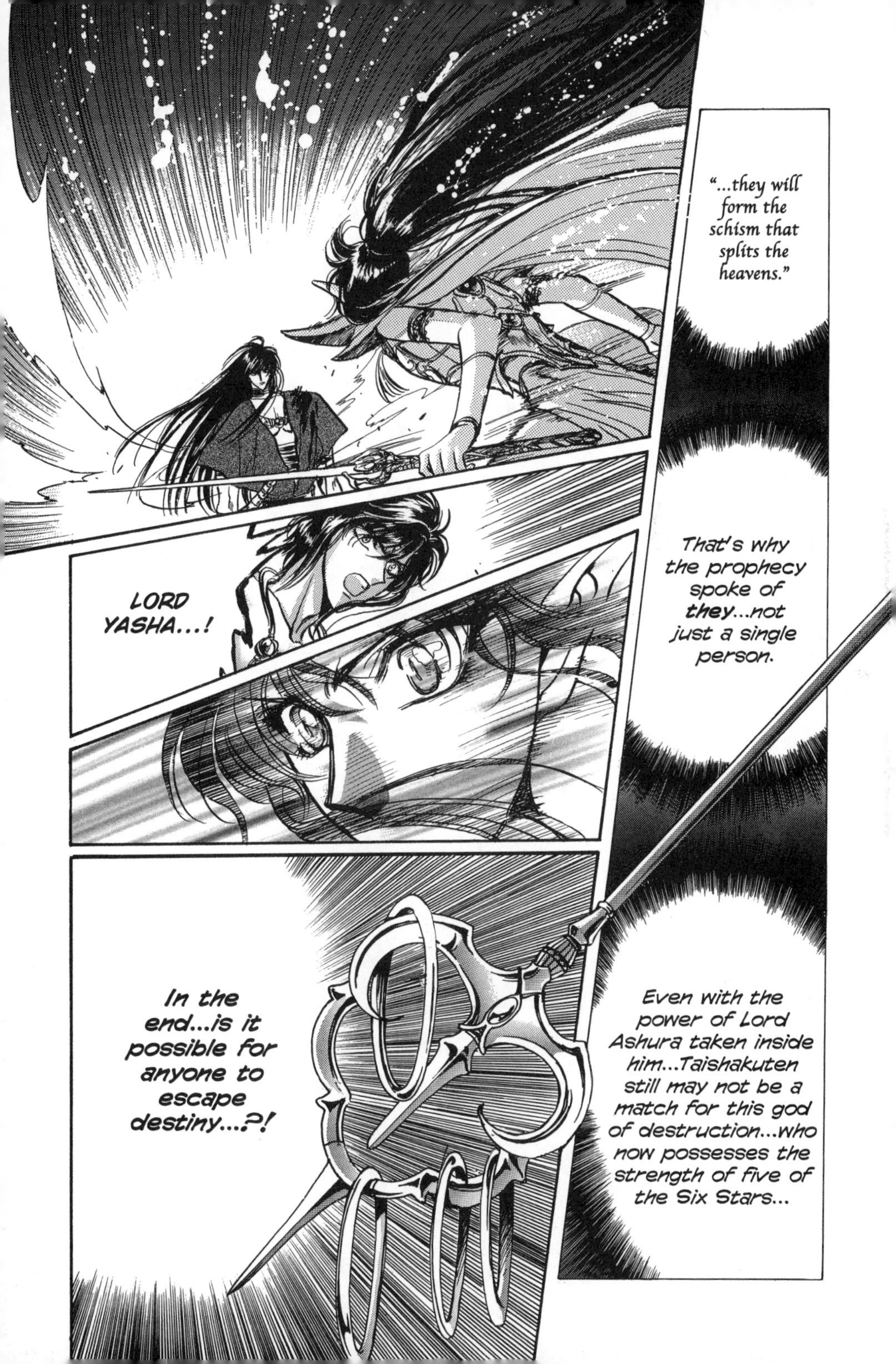
"...they will form the schism that splits the heavens."
That's why the prophecy spoke of **they**...not just a single person.
LORD YASHA...!
Even with the power of Lord Ashura taken inside him...Taishakuten still may not be a match for this god of destruction...who now possesses the strength of five of the Six Stars...
In the end...is it possible for anyone to escape destiny...?!

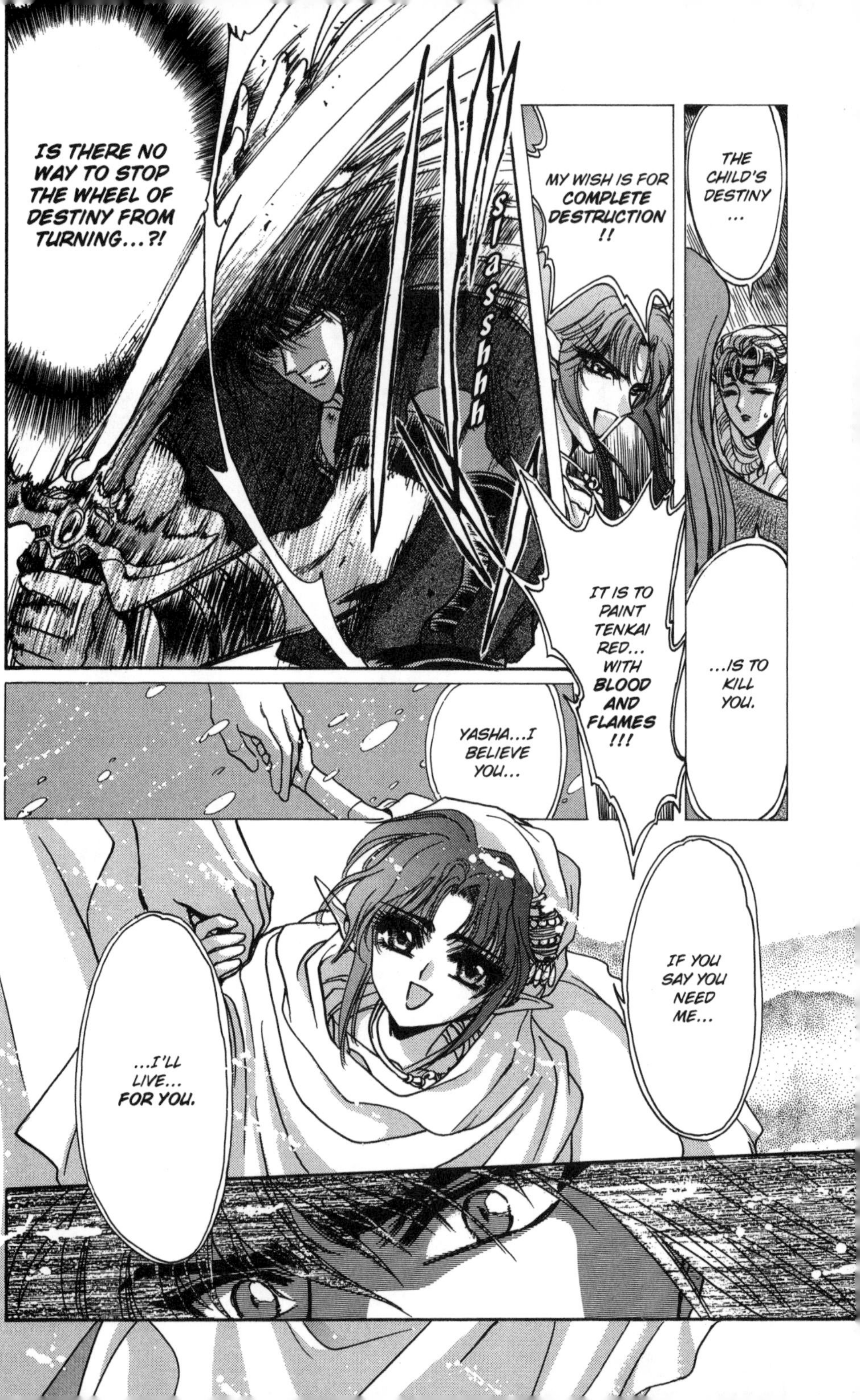
THE CHILD'S DESTINY ...
...IS TO KILL YOU.
MY WISH IS FOR COMPLETE DESTRUCTION !!
IT IS TO PAINT TENKAI RED... WITH BLOOD AND FLAMES !!!
Slasshhh
IS THERE NO WAY TO STOP THE WHEEL OF DESTINY FROM TURNING...?!
YASHA...I BELIEVE YOU...
IF YOU SAY YOU NEED ME...
...I'LL LIVE... FOR YOU.

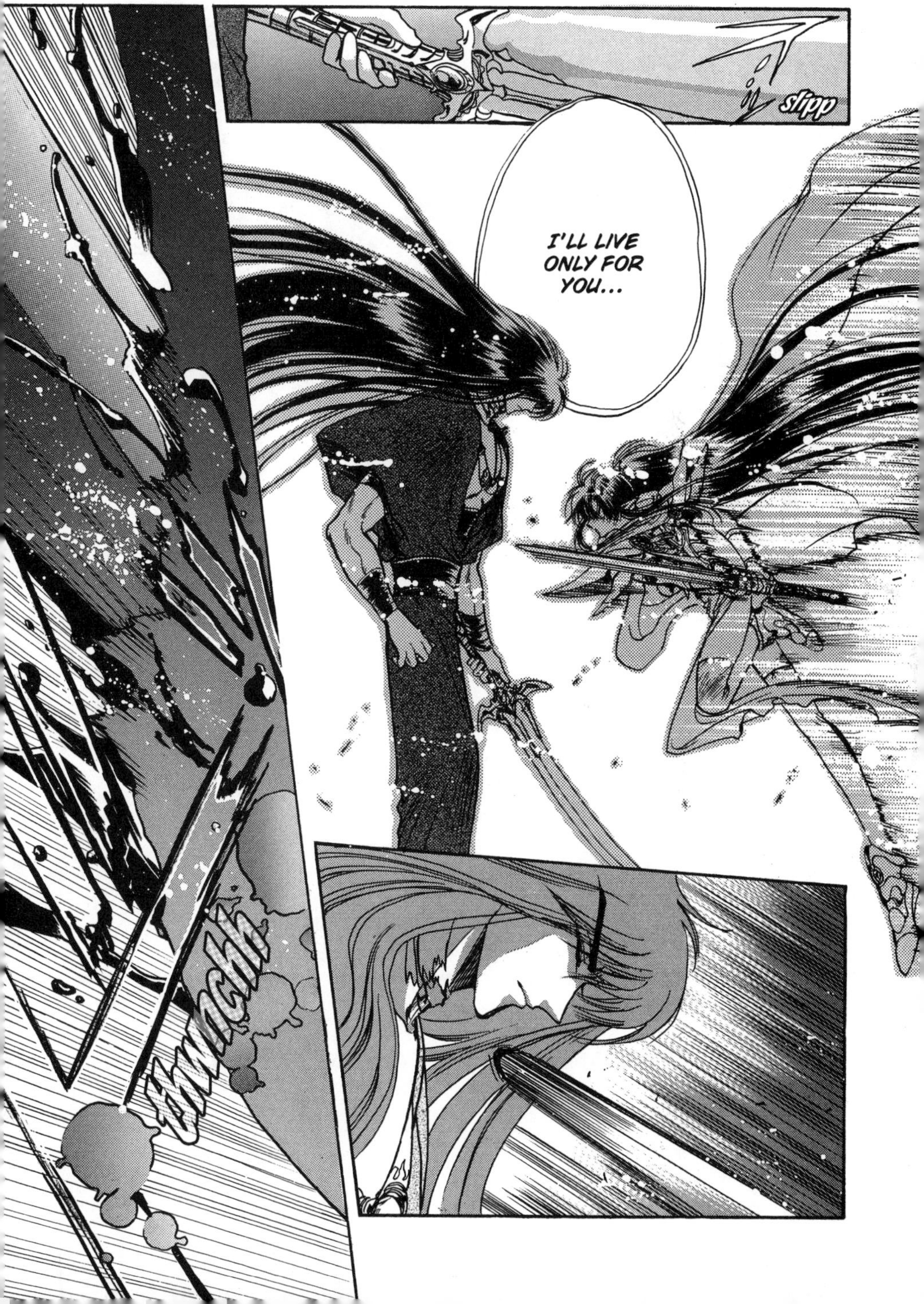
slipp
I'LL LIVE ONLY FOR YOU...

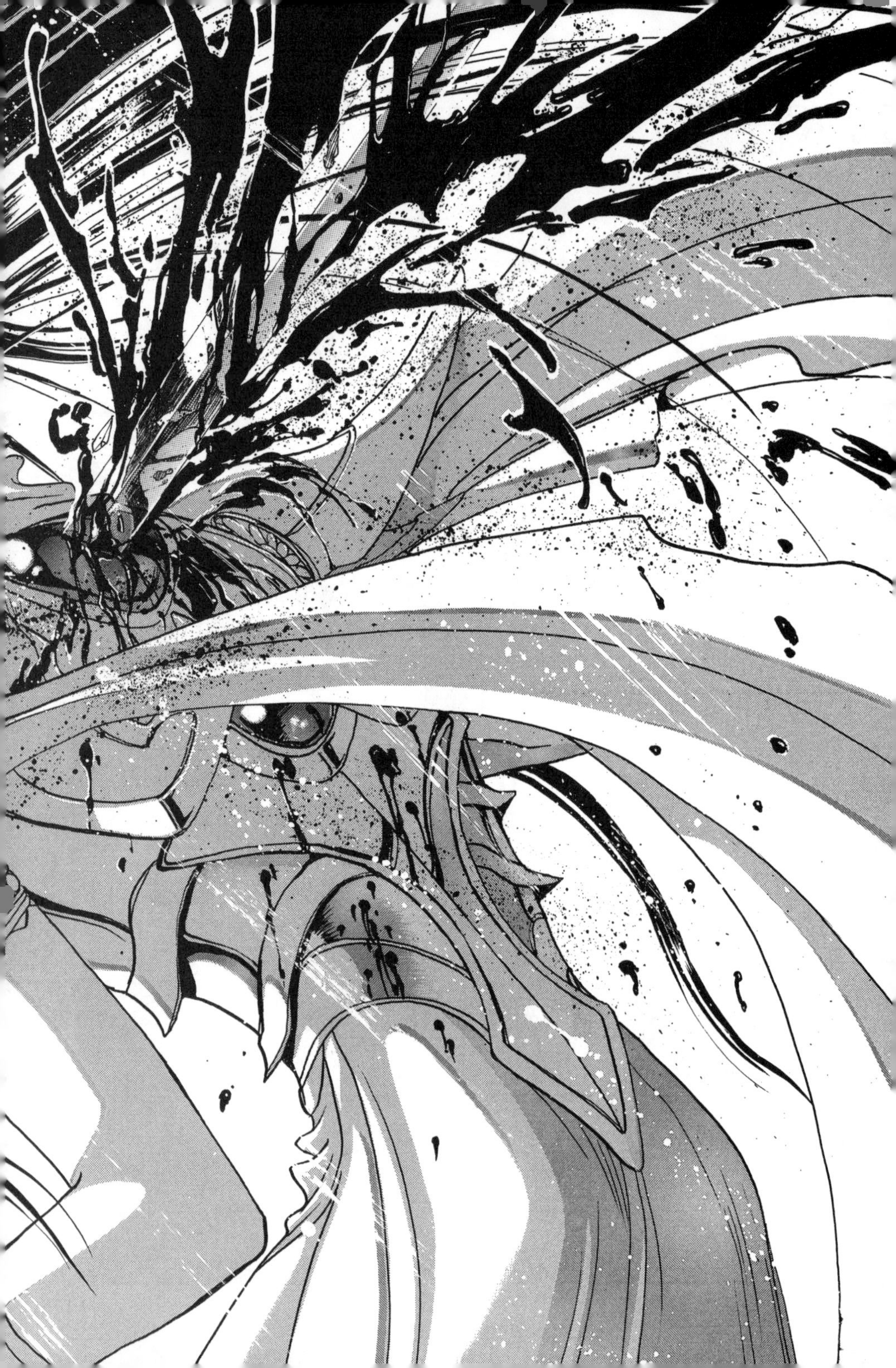

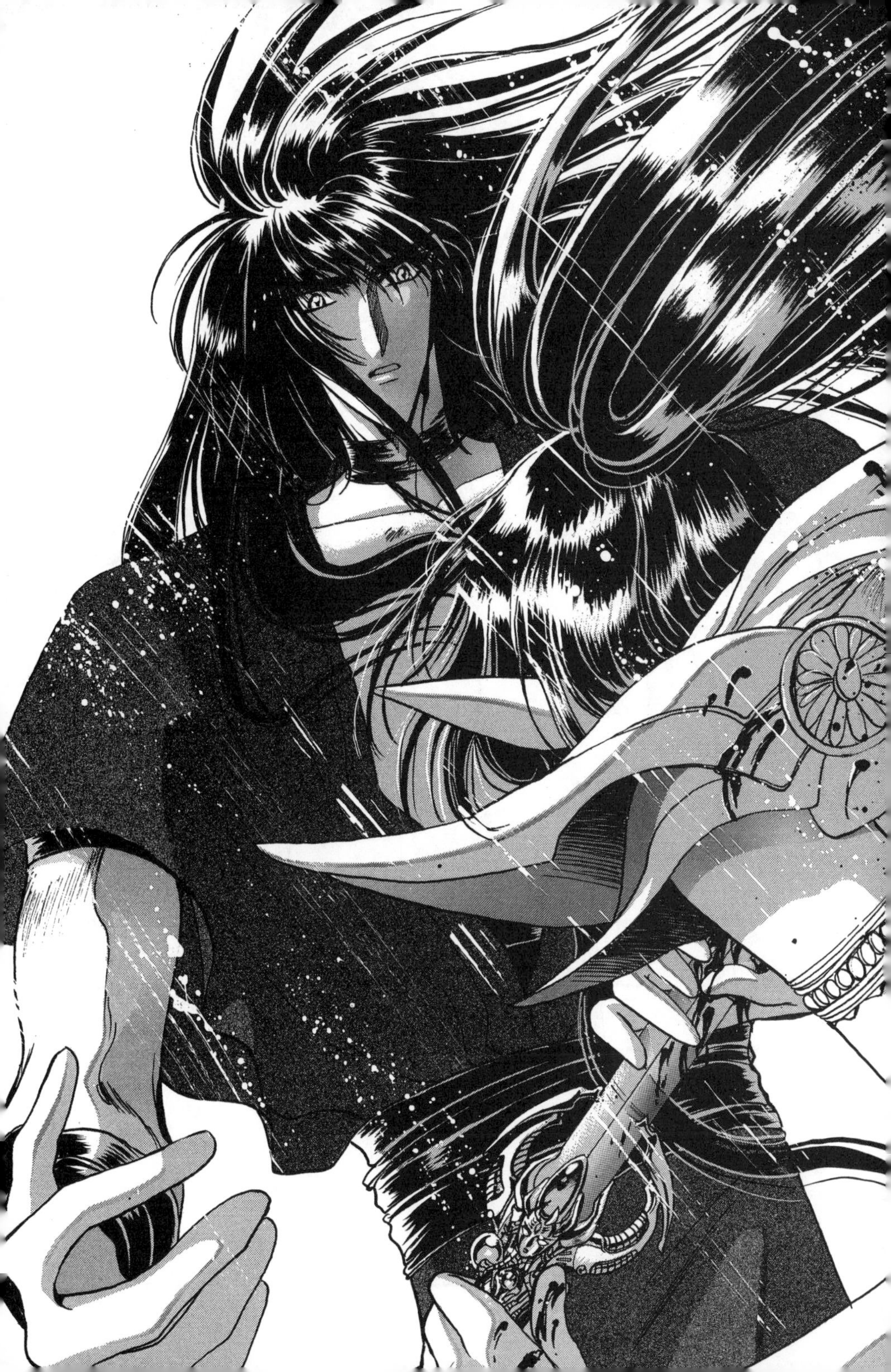

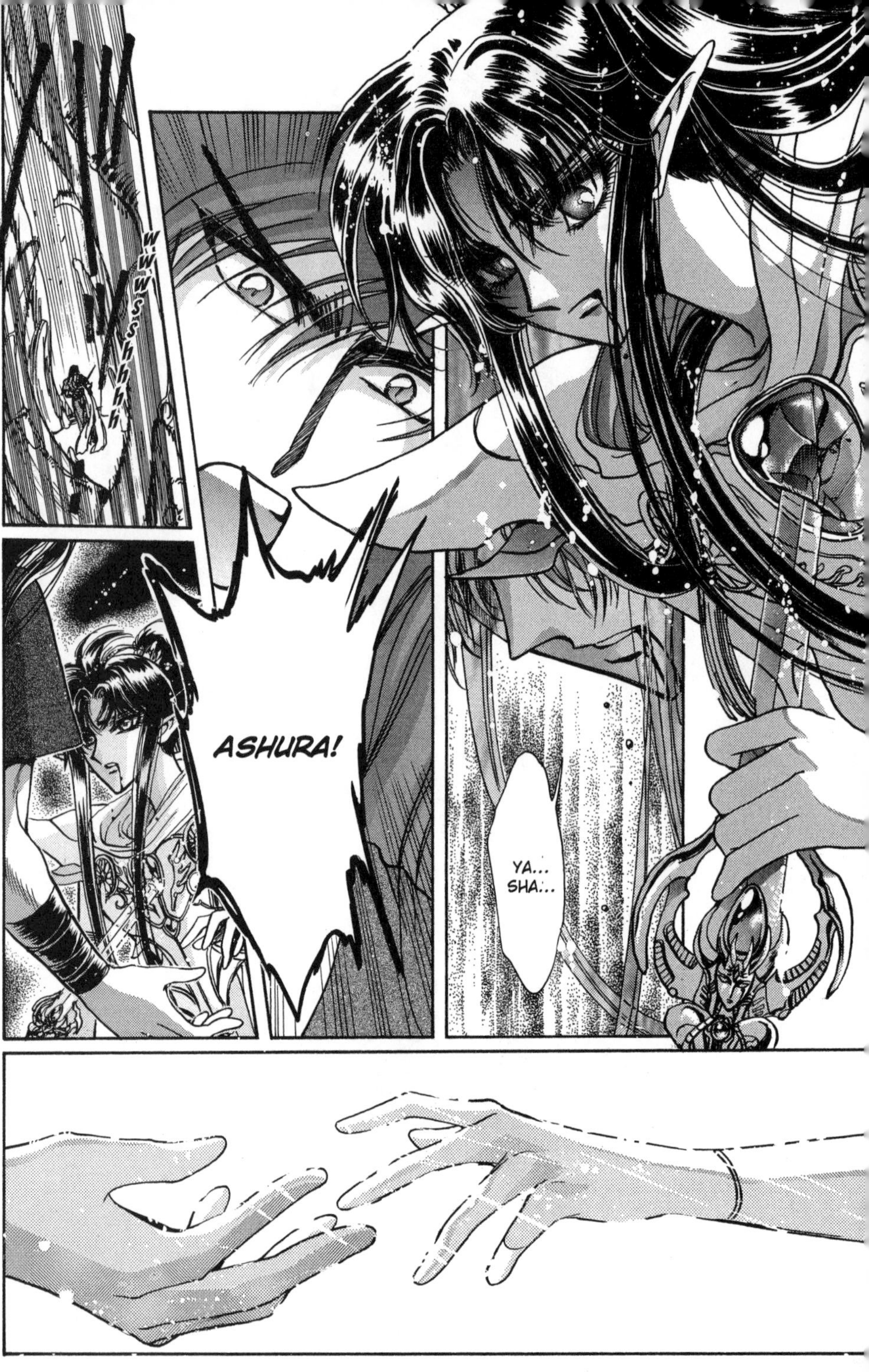
YA... SHA...
ASHURA!
wwwsshhhh

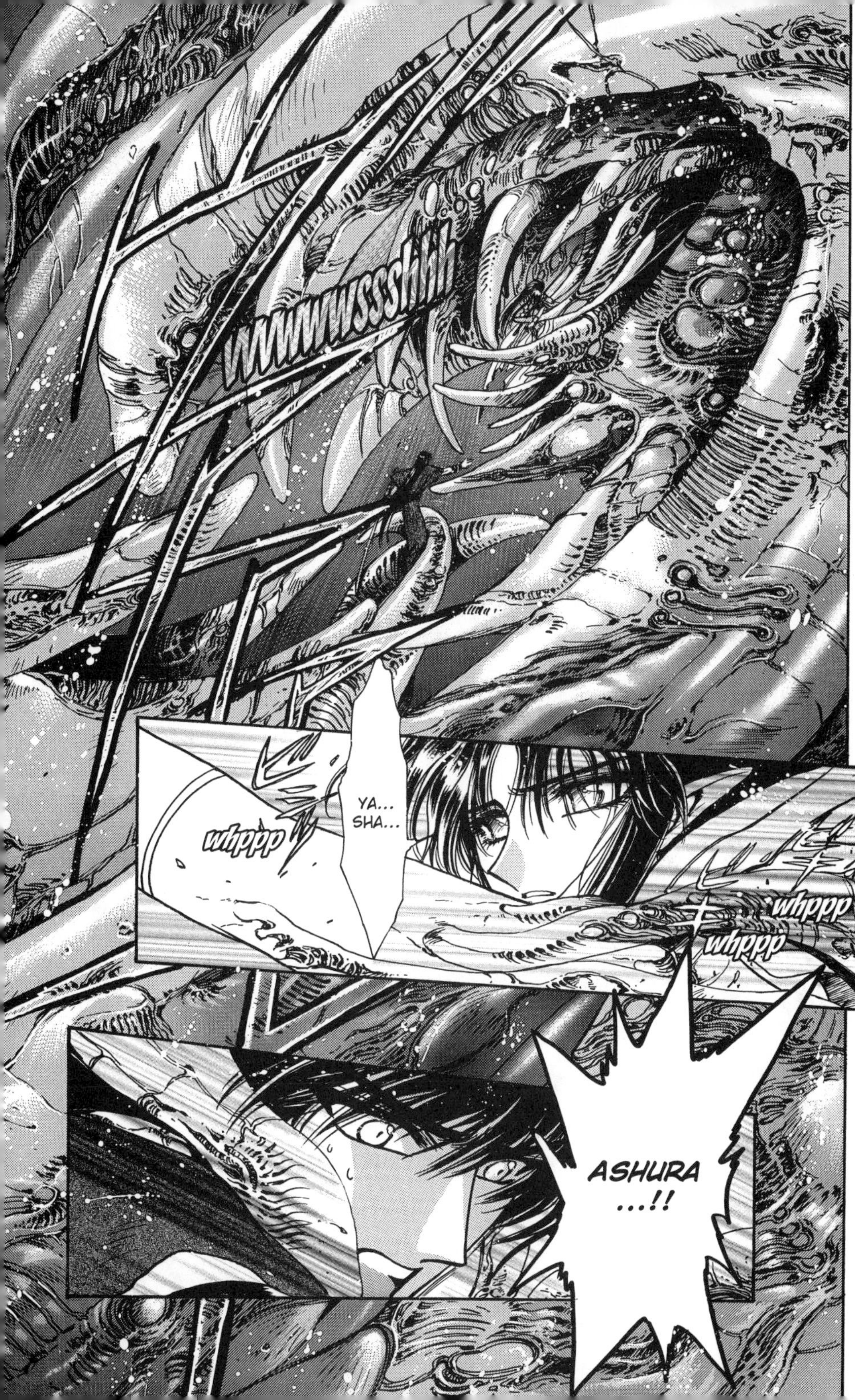
wwwwwwssshhh
whppp
whppp
YA... SHA...
whppp
ASHURA ...!!

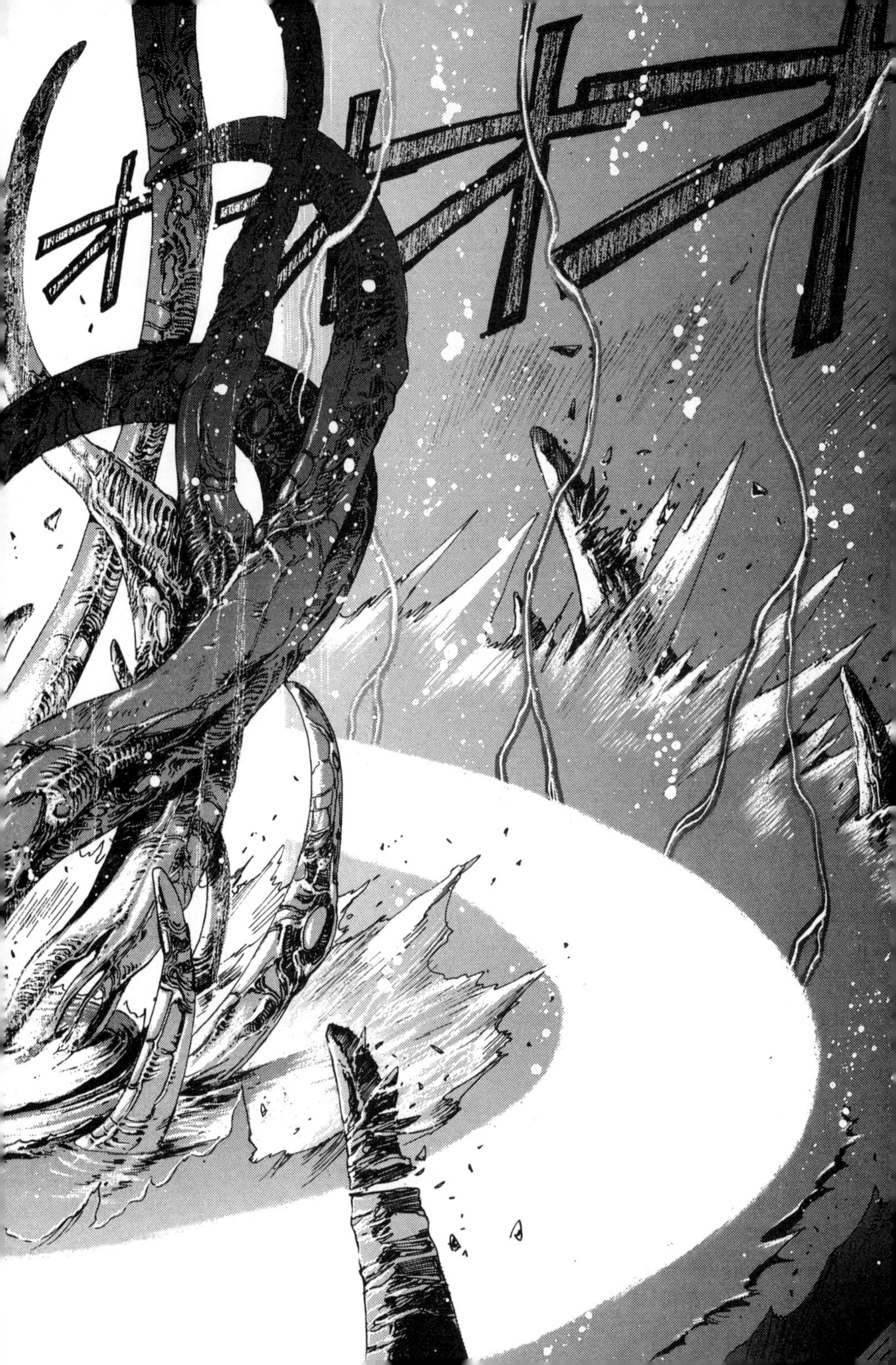

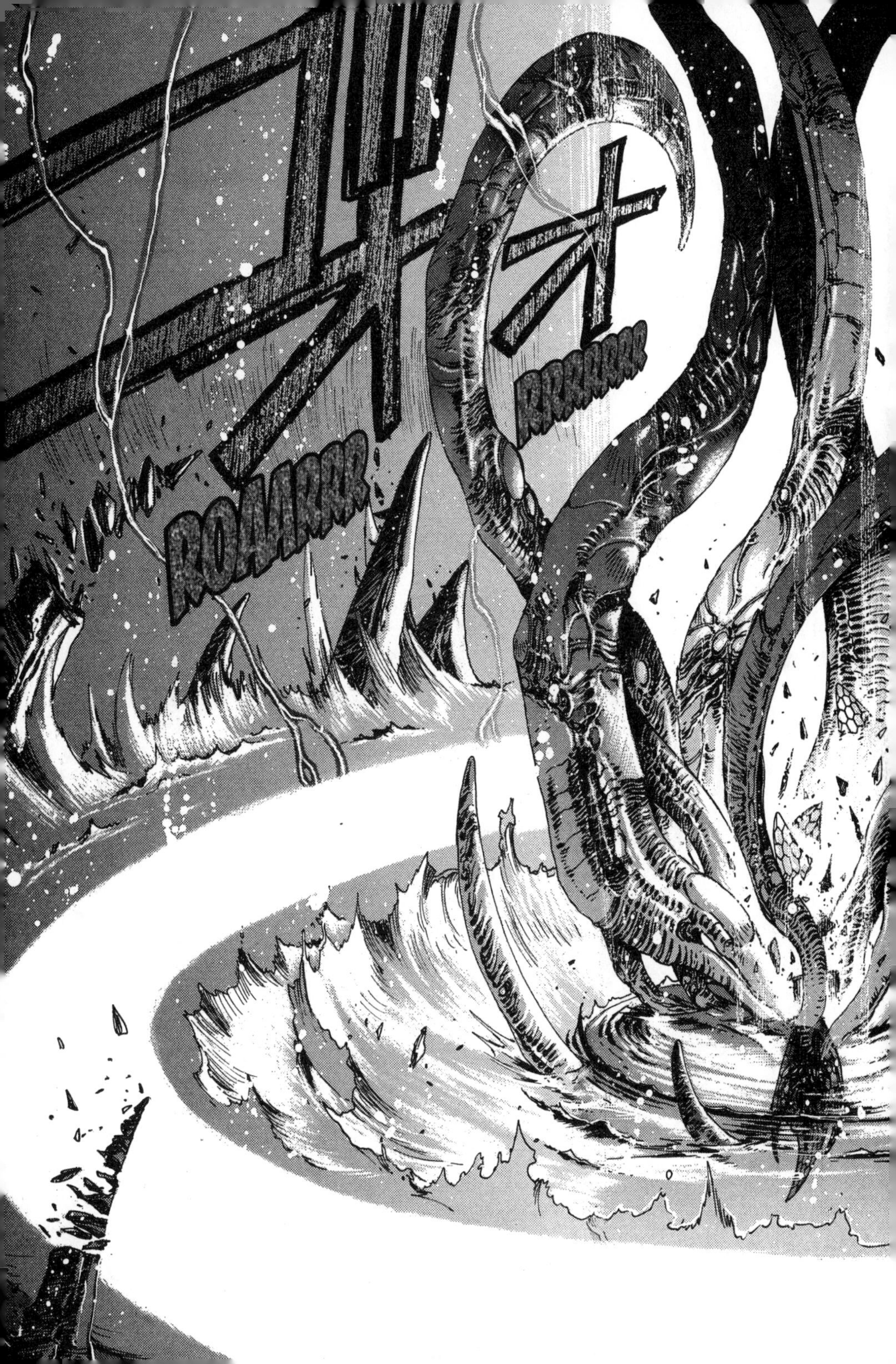
ROAARRR
RRRRRRR

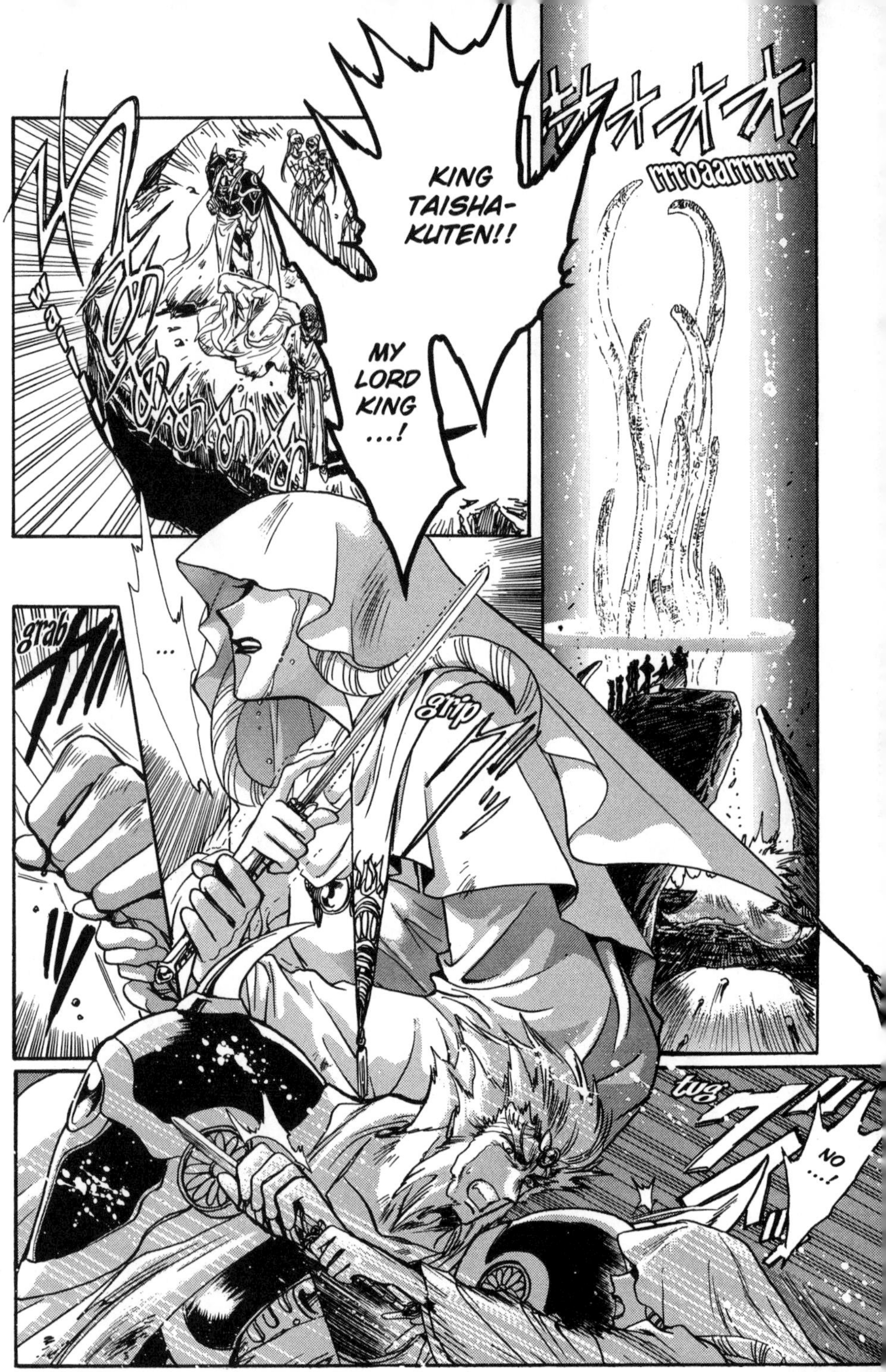
rrroaarrrrrr
KING TAISHA-KUTEN!!
MY LORD KING ...!
grip
...
grab
tug
NO ...!

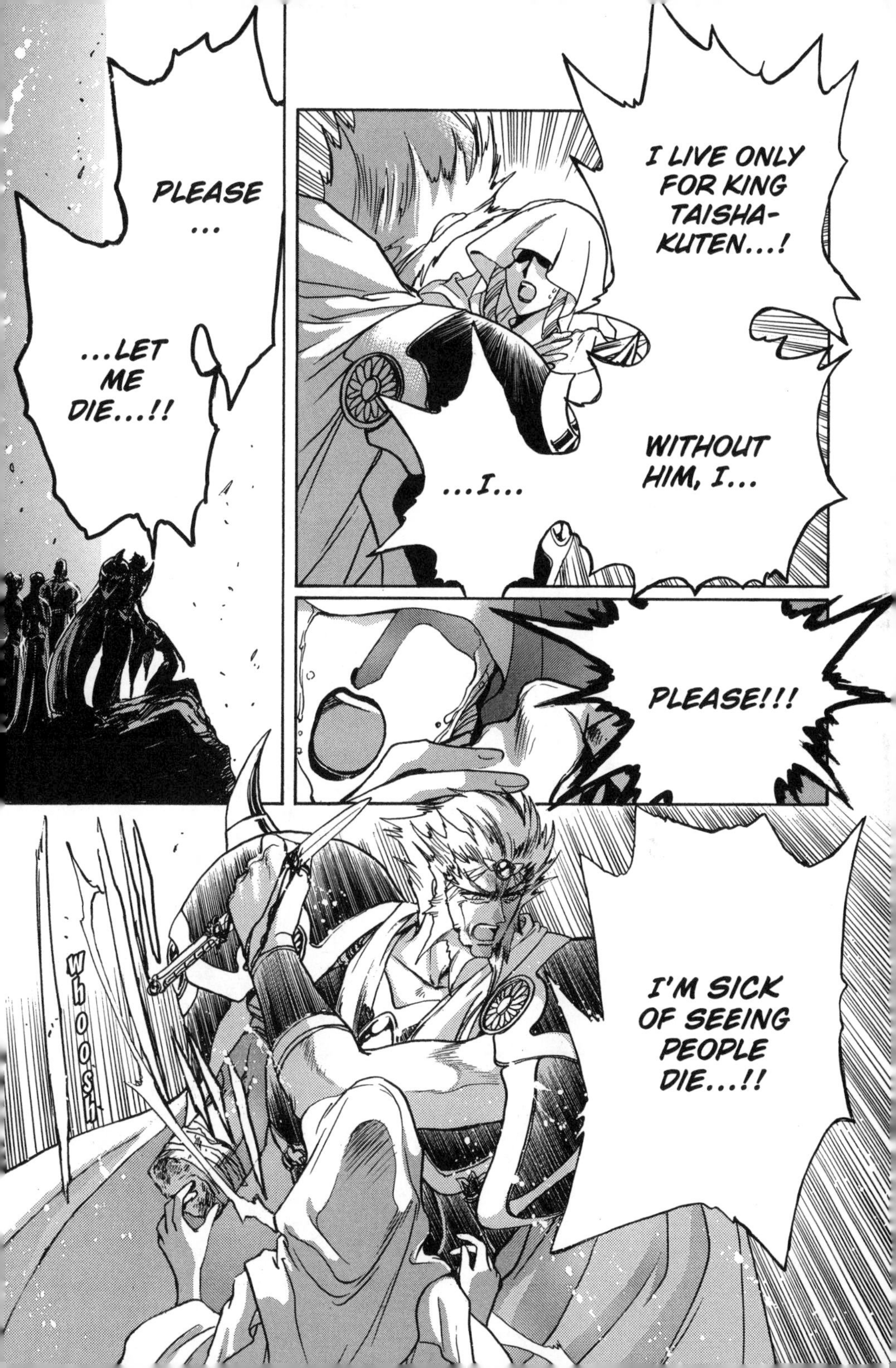
I LIVE ONLY FOR KING TAISHA-KUTEN...!
WITHOUT HIM, I...
...I...
PLEASE!!!
PLEASE...
...LET ME DIE...!!
I'M SICK OF SEEING PEOPLE DIE...!!
whoosh

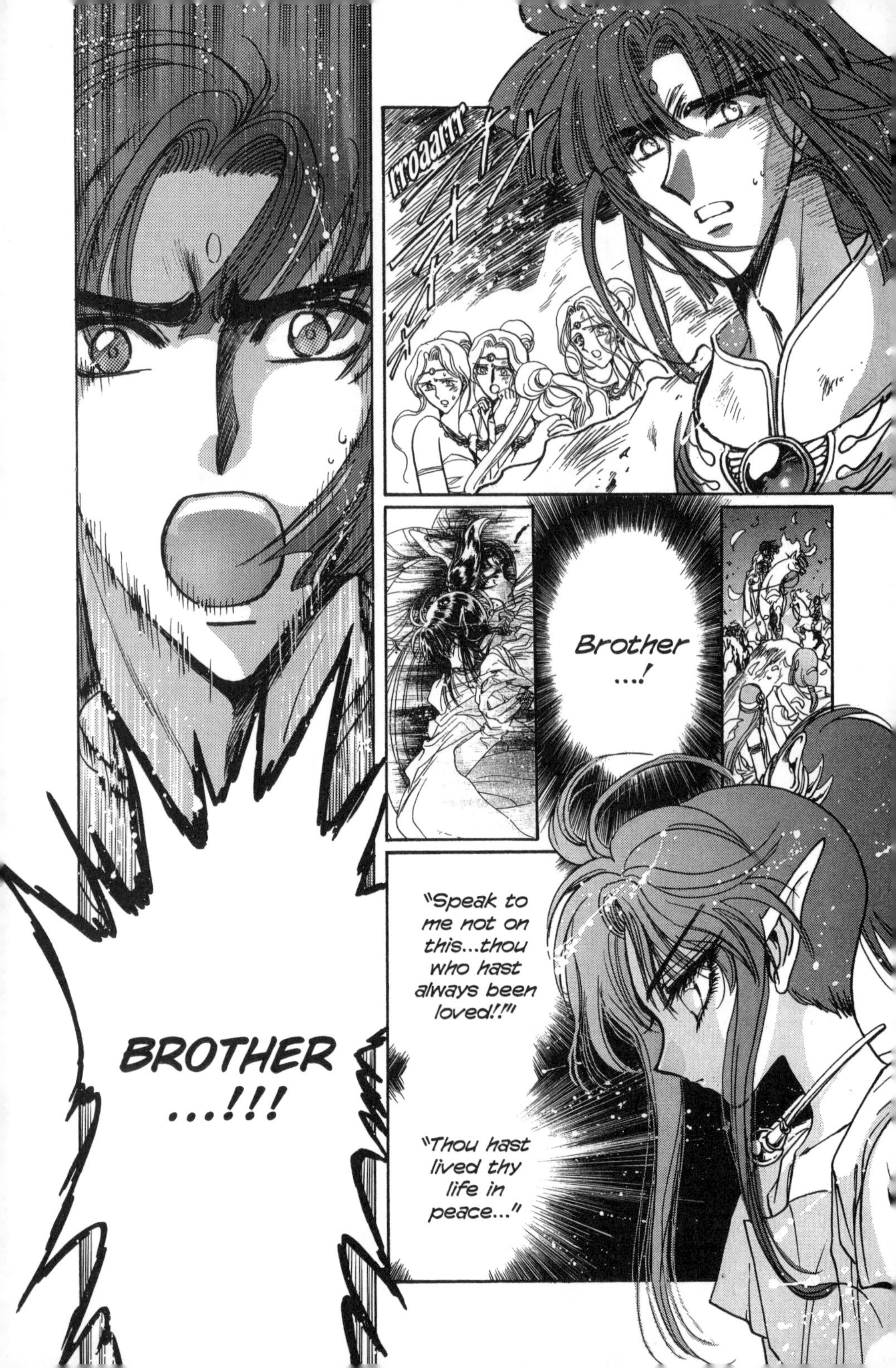
rroaarrr
Brother ...!
"Speak to me not on this...thou who hast always been loved!!"
"Thou hast lived thy life in peace..."
BROTHER ...!!!

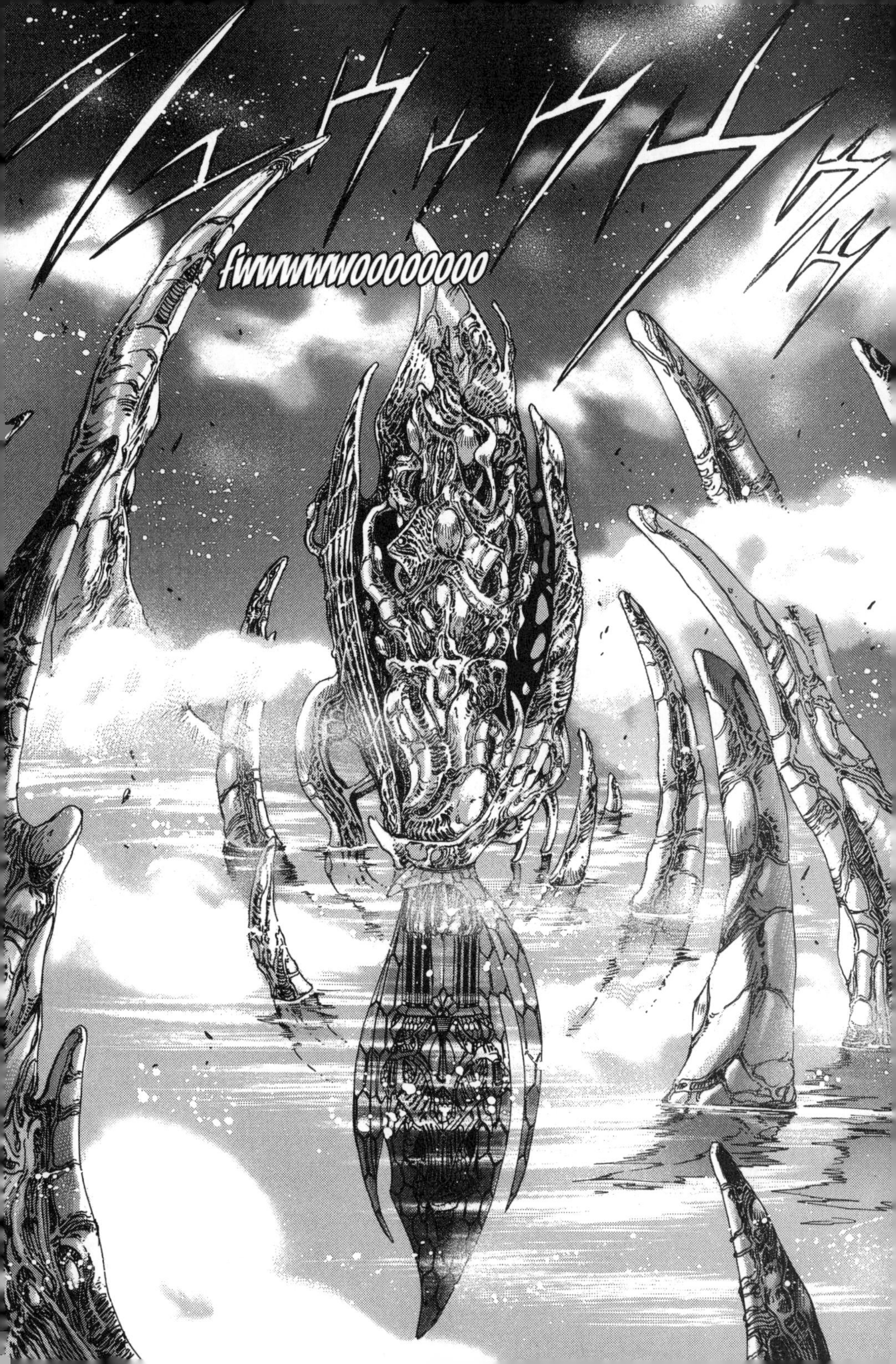
fwwwwwwoooooooo

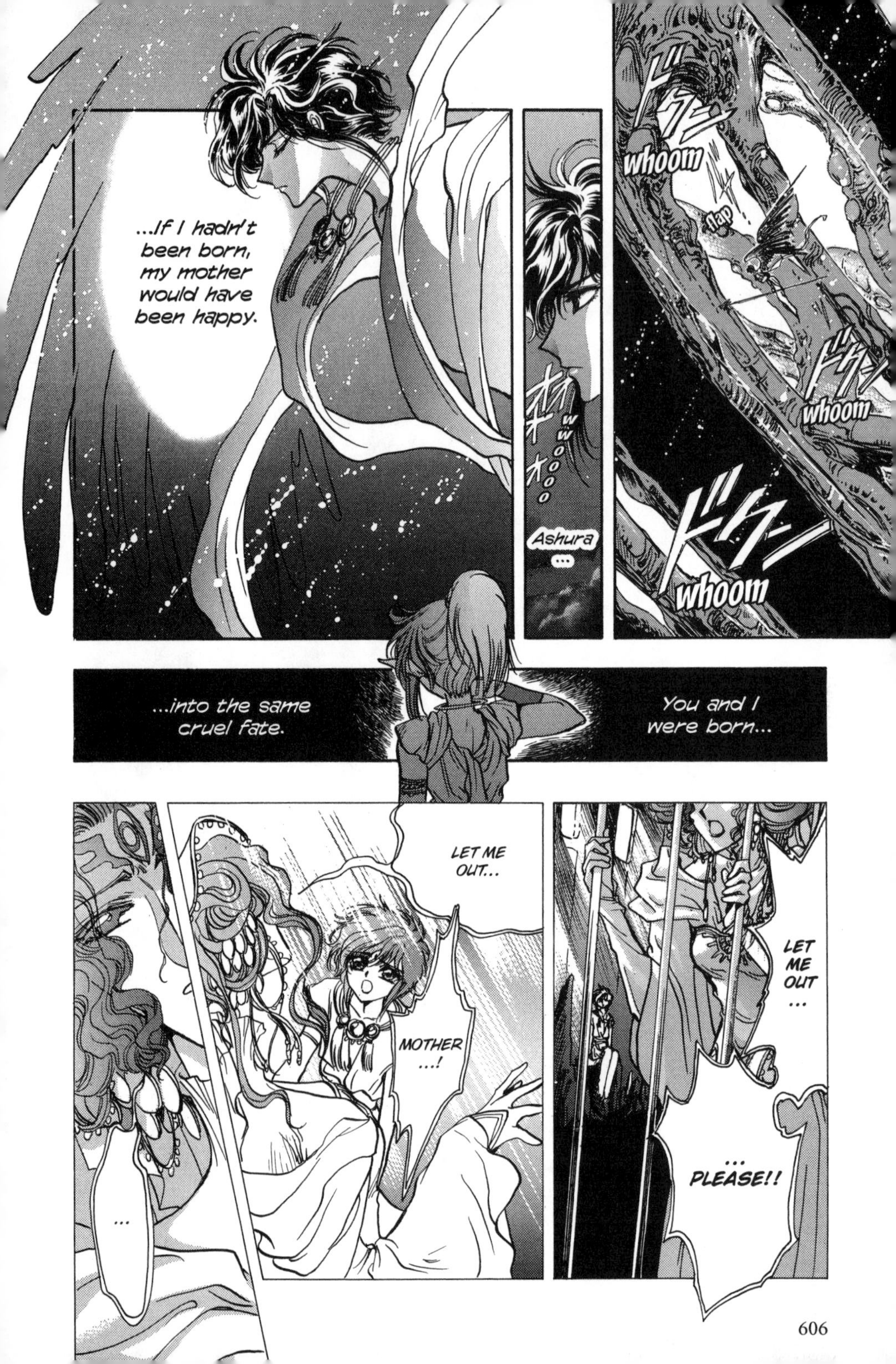

whoom
flap
whoom
whoom
wwoooo
Ashura …
...If I hadn't been born, my mother would have been happy.
You and I were born...
...into the same cruel fate.
LET ME OUT...
... PLEASE!!
LET ME OUT...
MOTHER ...!
...

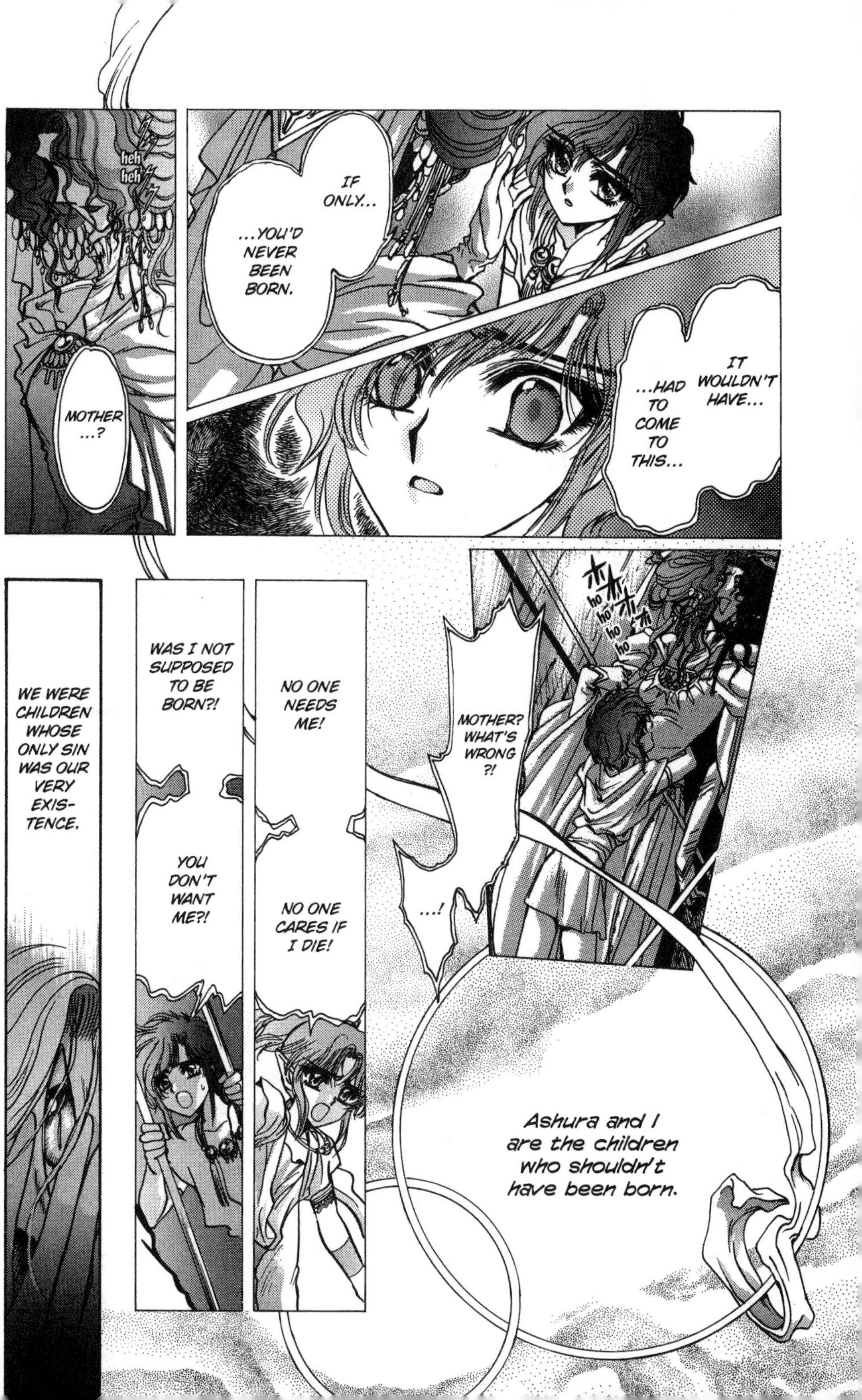
IF ONLY...
...YOU'D NEVER BEEN BORN.
IT WOULDN'T HAVE...
...HAD TO COME TO THIS...
heh heh
MOTHER ...?
ho ho ho ho
MOTHER? WHAT'S WRONG ?!
...!
Ashura and I are the children who shouldn't have been born.
NO ONE NEEDS ME!
NO ONE CARES IF I DIE!
WAS I NOT SUPPOSED TO BE BORN?!
YOU DON'T WANT ME?!
WE WERE CHILDREN WHOSE ONLY SIN WAS OUR VERY EXISTENCE.

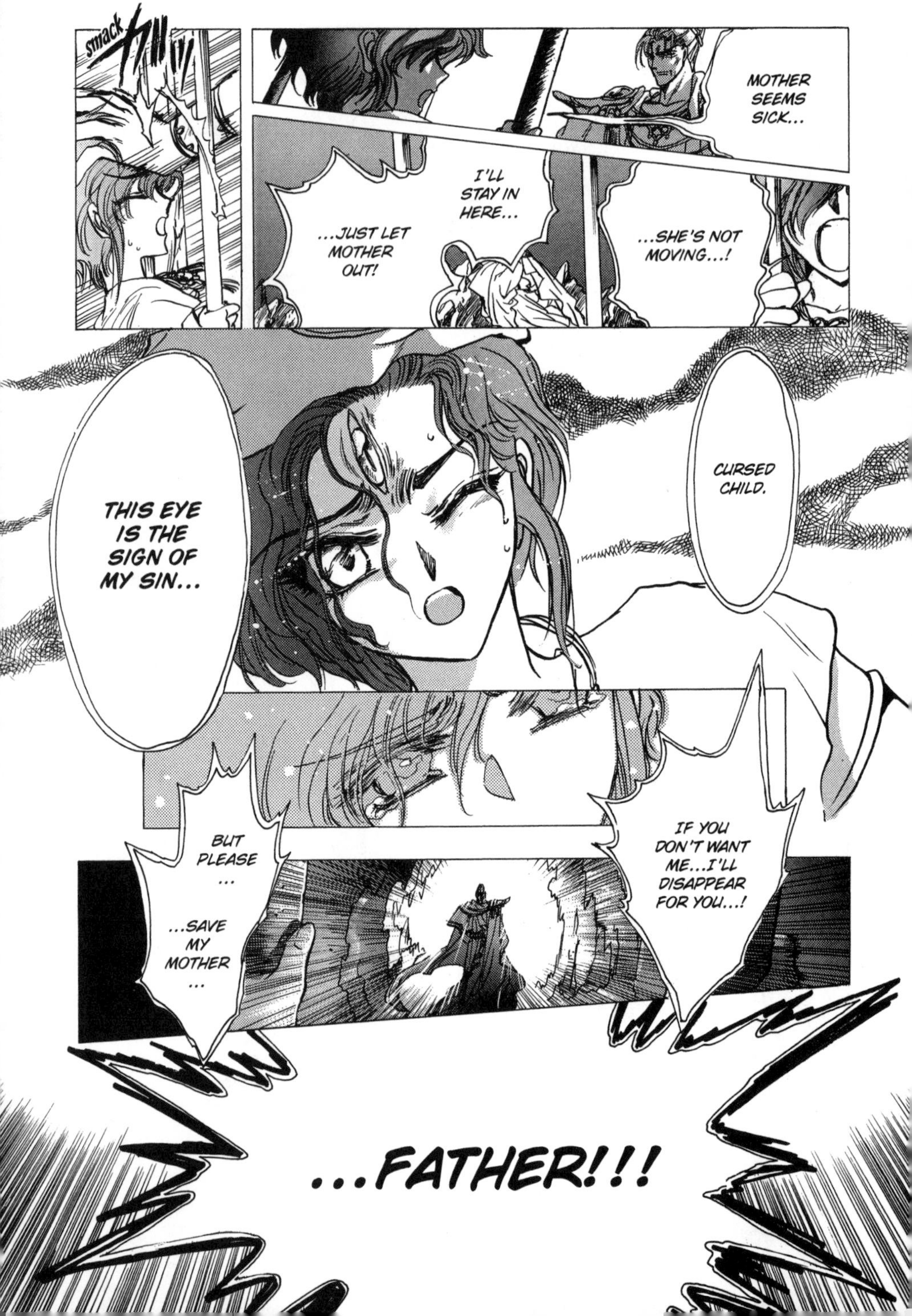
MOTHER SEEMS SICK...
...SHE'S NOT MOVING...!
I'LL STAY IN HERE...
...JUST LET MOTHER OUT!
smack
CURSED CHILD.
THIS EYE IS THE SIGN OF MY SIN...
IF YOU DON'T WANT ME...I'LL DISAPPEAR FOR YOU...!
BUT PLEASE ...
...SAVE MY MOTHER ...
...FATHER!!!

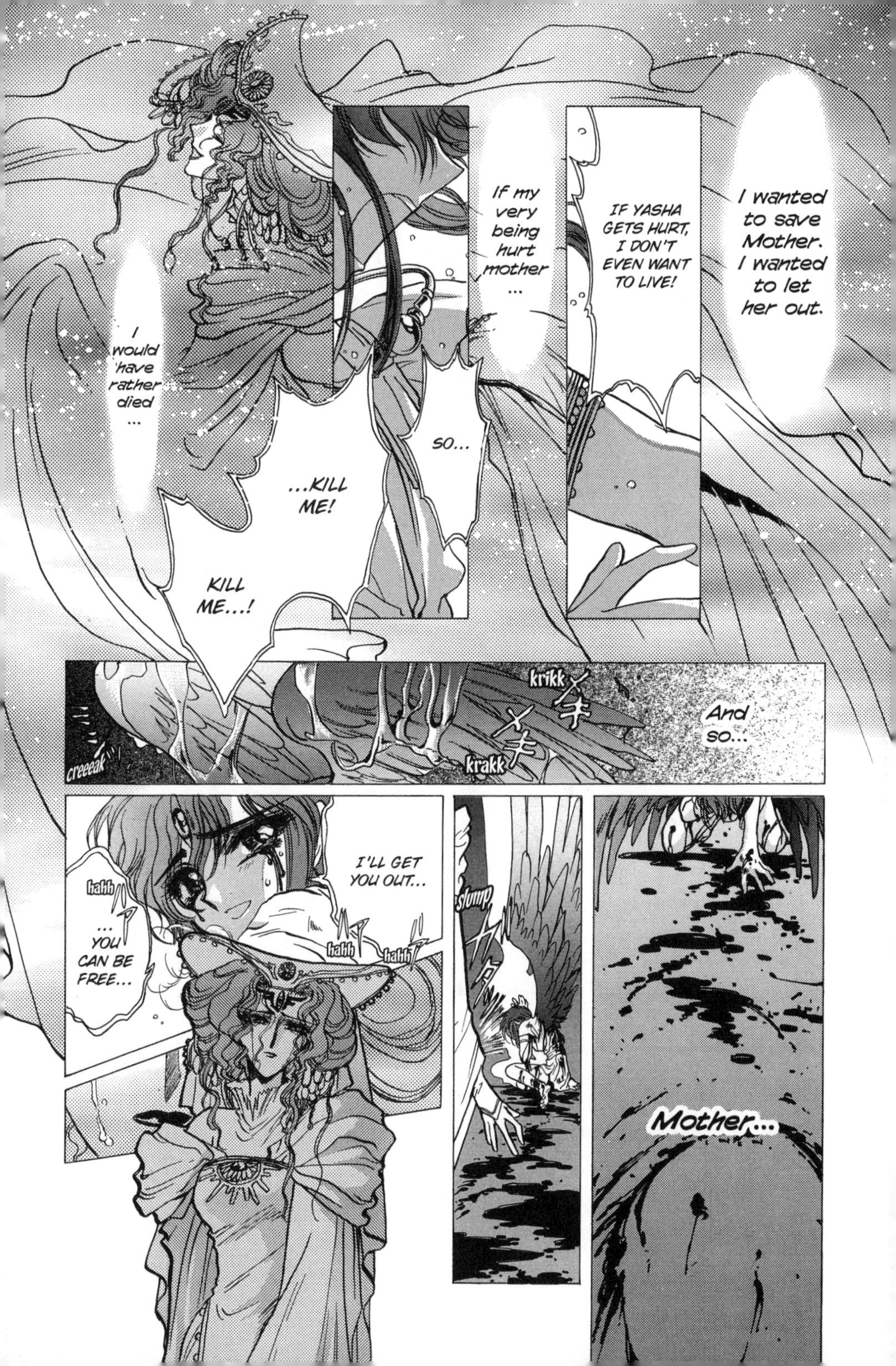
I wanted to save Mother. I wanted to let her out.
IF YASHA GETS HURT, I DON'T EVEN WANT TO LIVE!
If my very being hurt mother ...
so...
I would have rather died ...
...KILL ME!
KILL ME...!
And so...
krikk
krakk
creeeak
Mother...
slump
I'LL GET YOU OUT...
hahh
hahh
hahh
... YOU CAN BE FREE...

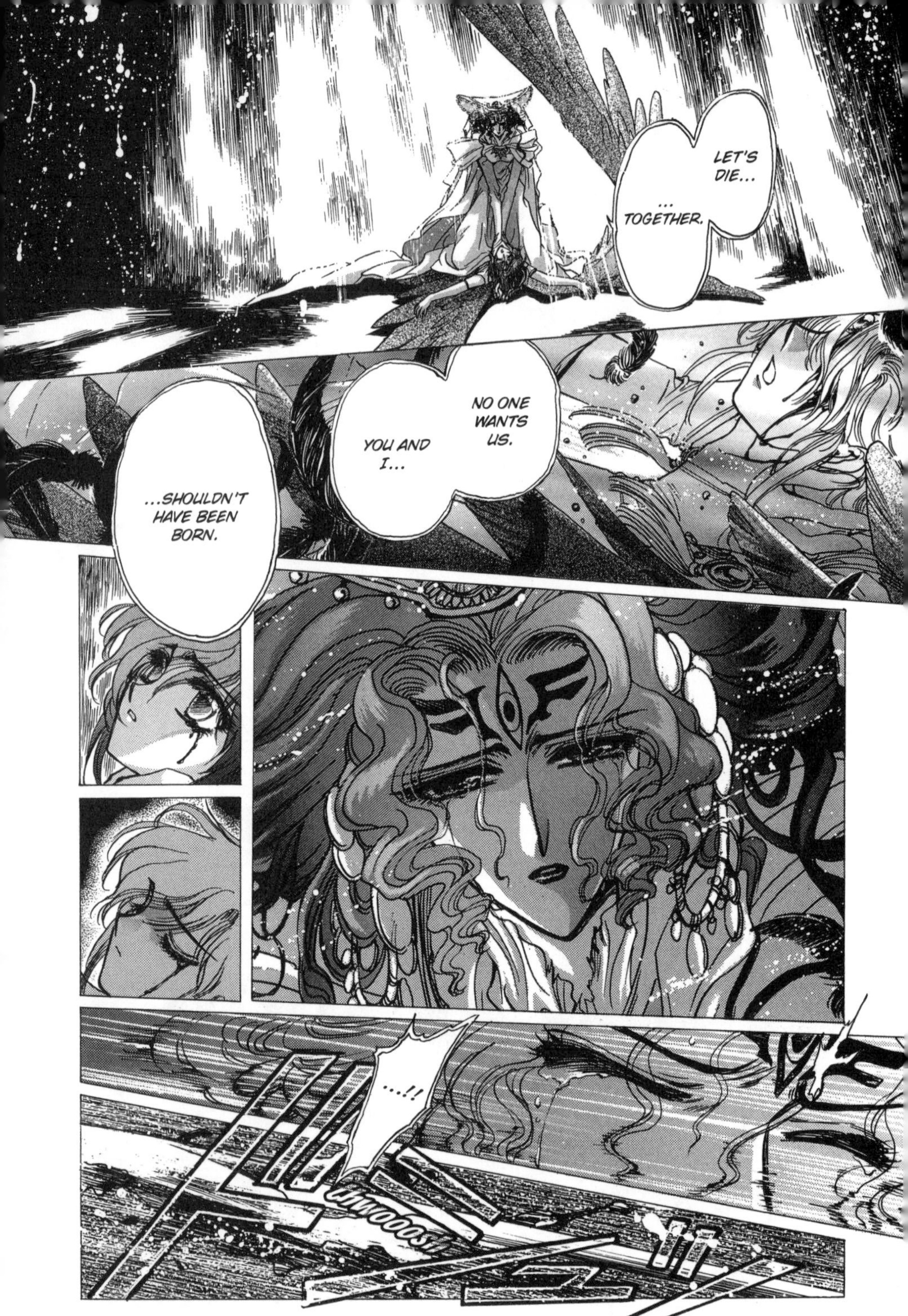
LET'S DIE...
...TOGETHER.
NO ONE WANTS US.
YOU AND I...
...SHOULDN'T HAVE BEEN BORN.
...!!
WHOOOSH!!

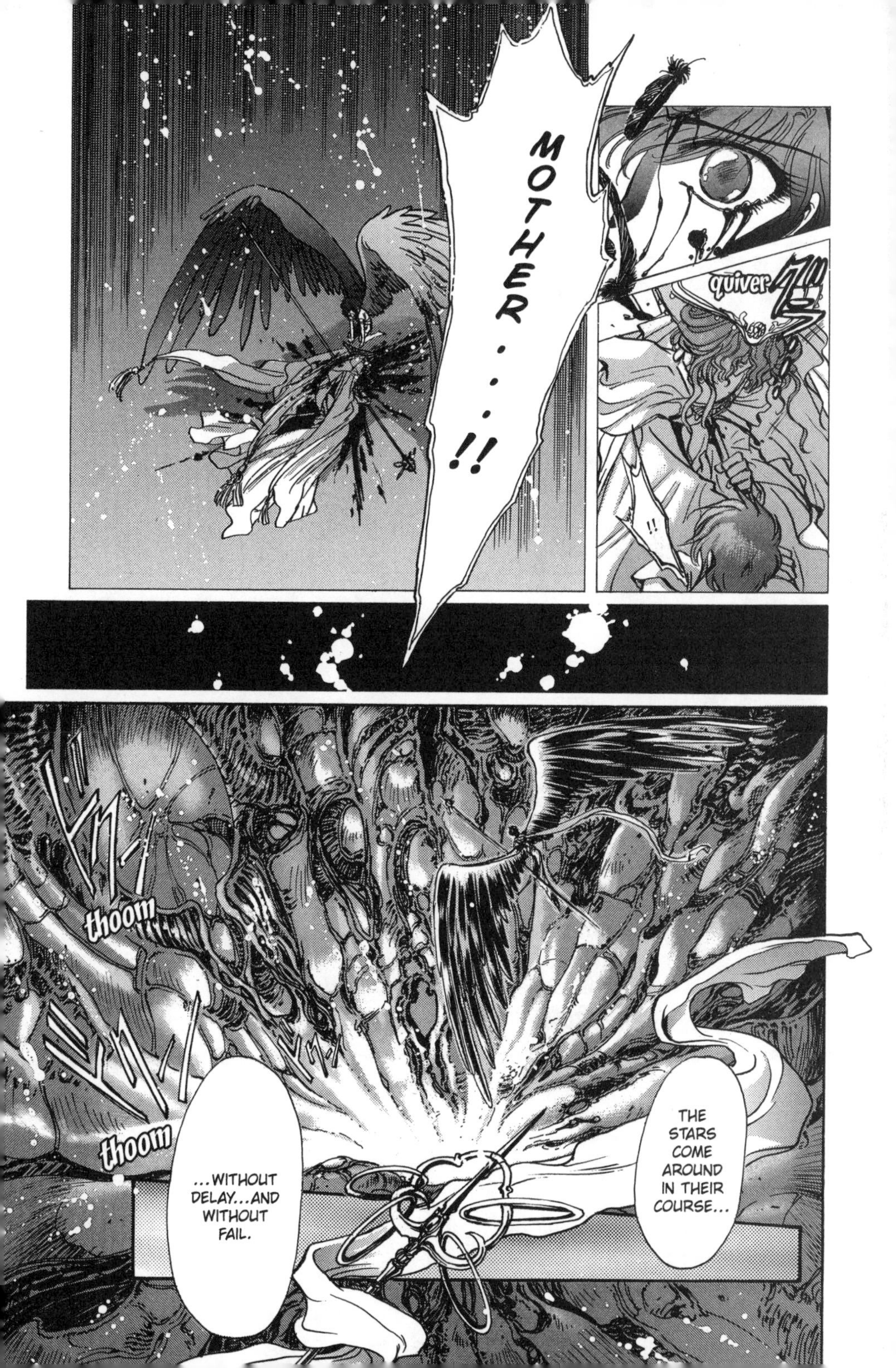
MOTHER . . . !!
quiver
!!
THE STARS COME AROUND IN THEIR COURSE...
...WITHOUT DELAY...AND WITHOUT FAIL.
thoom
thoom

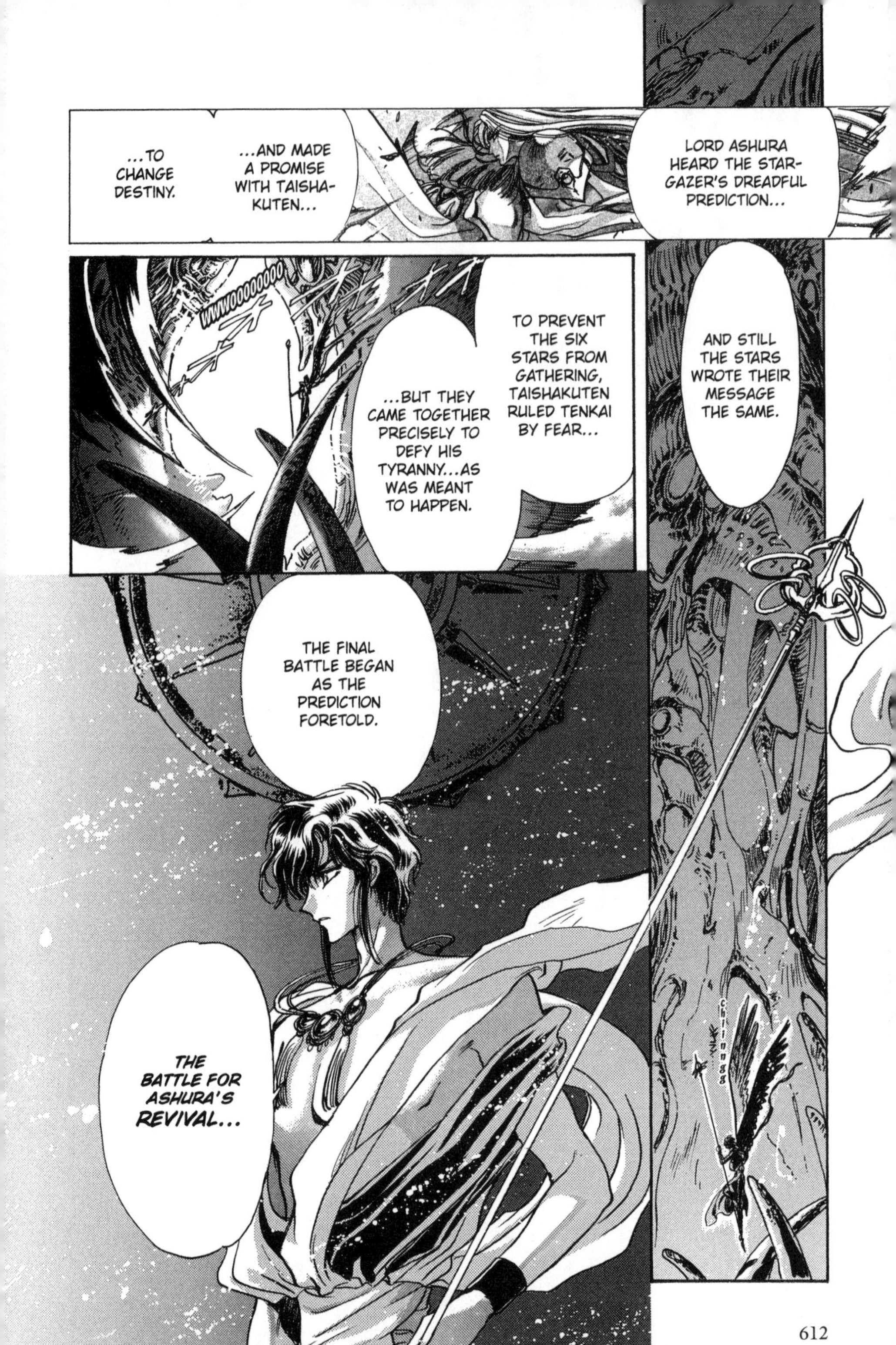
LORD ASHURA HEARD THE STAR-GAZER'S DREADFUL PREDICTION...
...AND MADE A PROMISE WITH TAISHA-KUTEN...
...TO CHANGE DESTINY.
AND STILL THE STARS WROTE THEIR MESSAGE THE SAME.
TO PREVENT THE SIX STARS FROM GATHERING, TAISHAKUTEN RULED TENKAI BY FEAR...
...BUT THEY CAME TOGETHER PRECISELY TO DEFY HIS TYRANNY...AS WAS MEANT TO HAPPEN.
THE FINAL BATTLE BEGAN AS THE PREDICTION FORETOLD.
THE BATTLE FOR ASHURA'S REVIVAL...

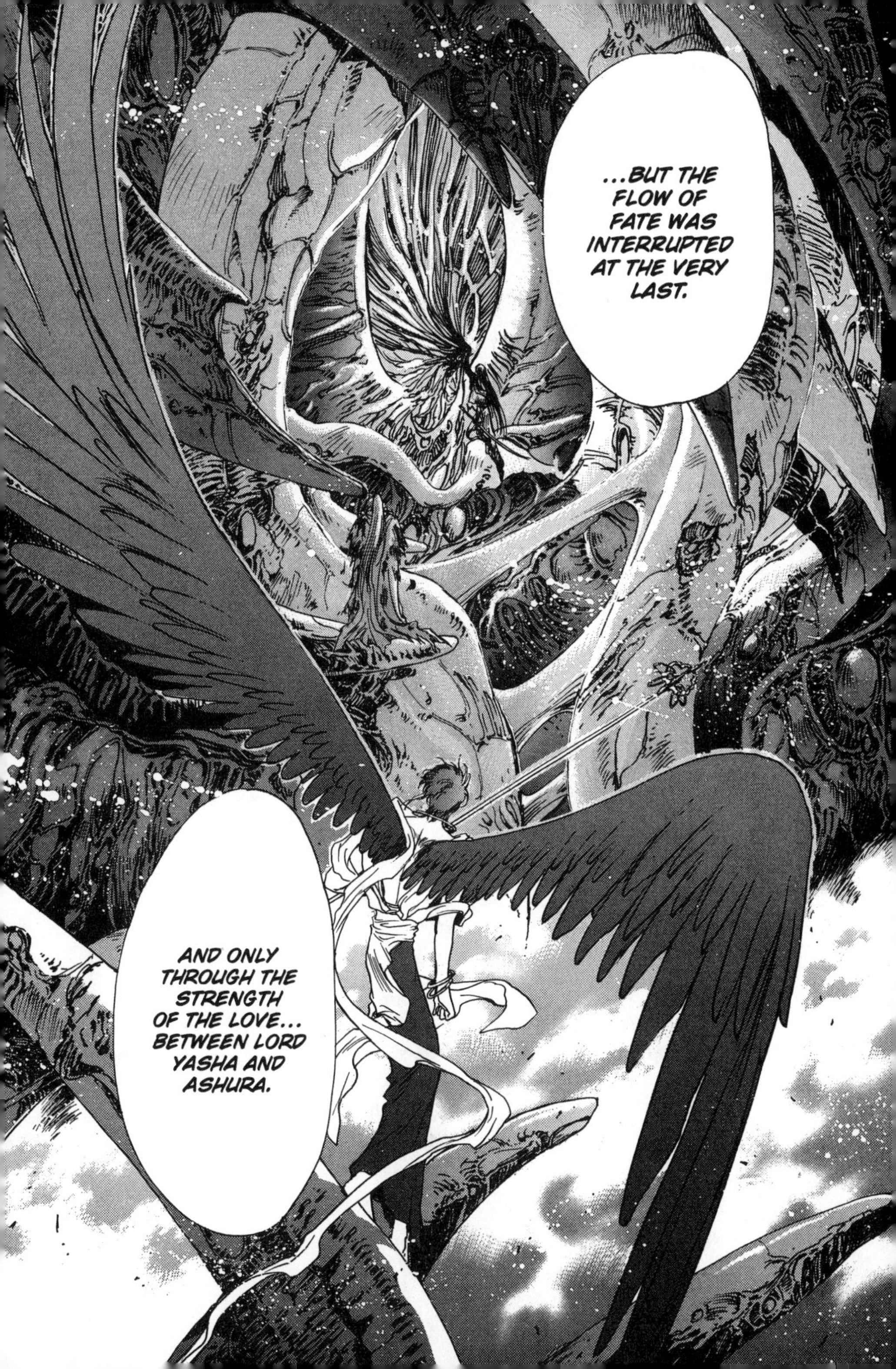
...BUT THE FLOW OF FATE WAS INTERRUPTED AT THE VERY LAST.
AND ONLY THROUGH THE STRENGTH OF THE LOVE... BETWEEN LORD YASHA AND ASHURA.

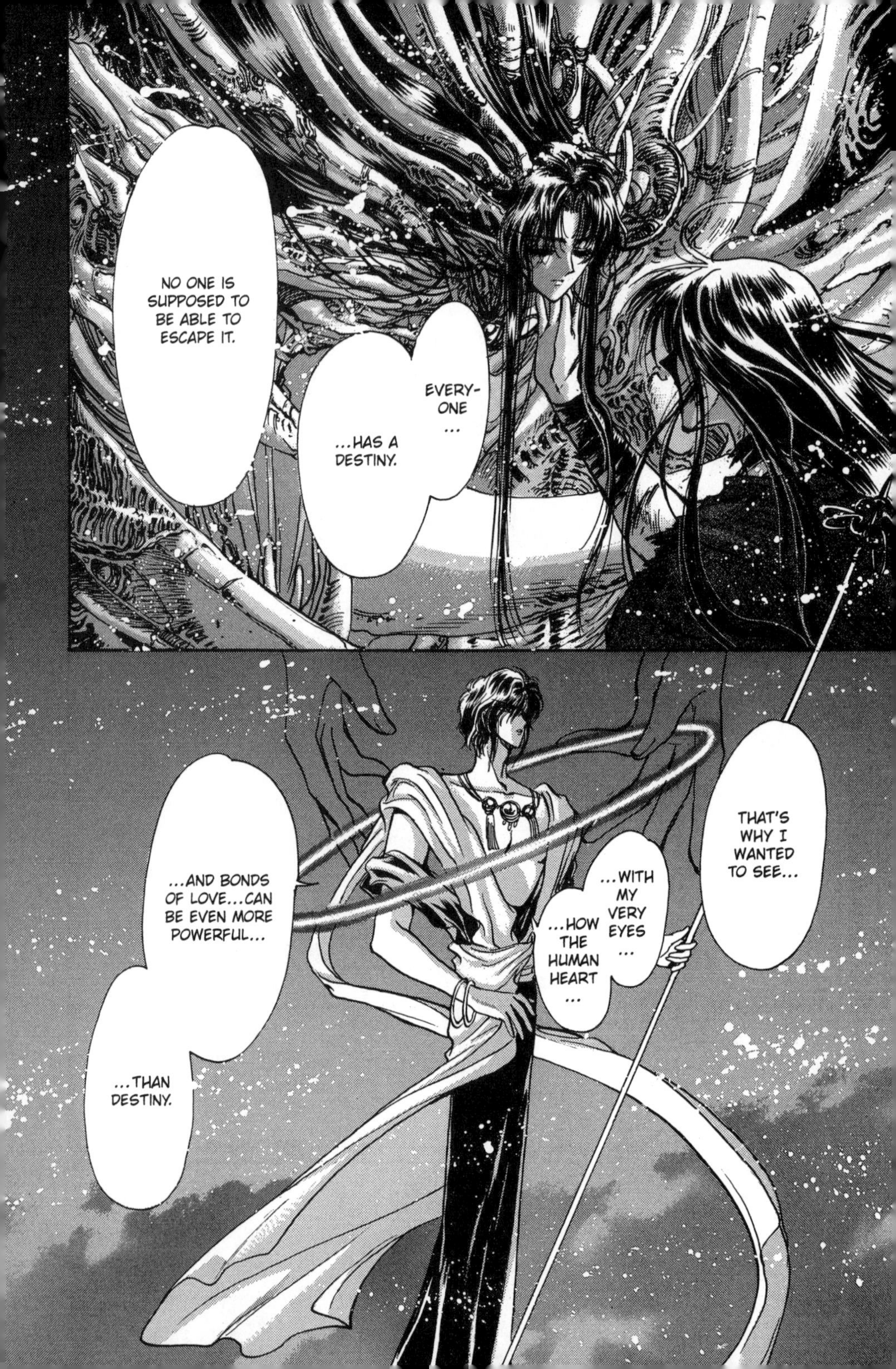
EVERY-ONE...
...HAS A DESTINY.
NO ONE IS SUPPOSED TO BE ABLE TO ESCAPE IT.
THAT'S WHY I WANTED TO SEE...
...WITH MY VERY EYES...
...HOW THE HUMAN HEART...
...AND BONDS OF LOVE...CAN BE EVEN MORE POWERFUL...
...THAN DESTINY.

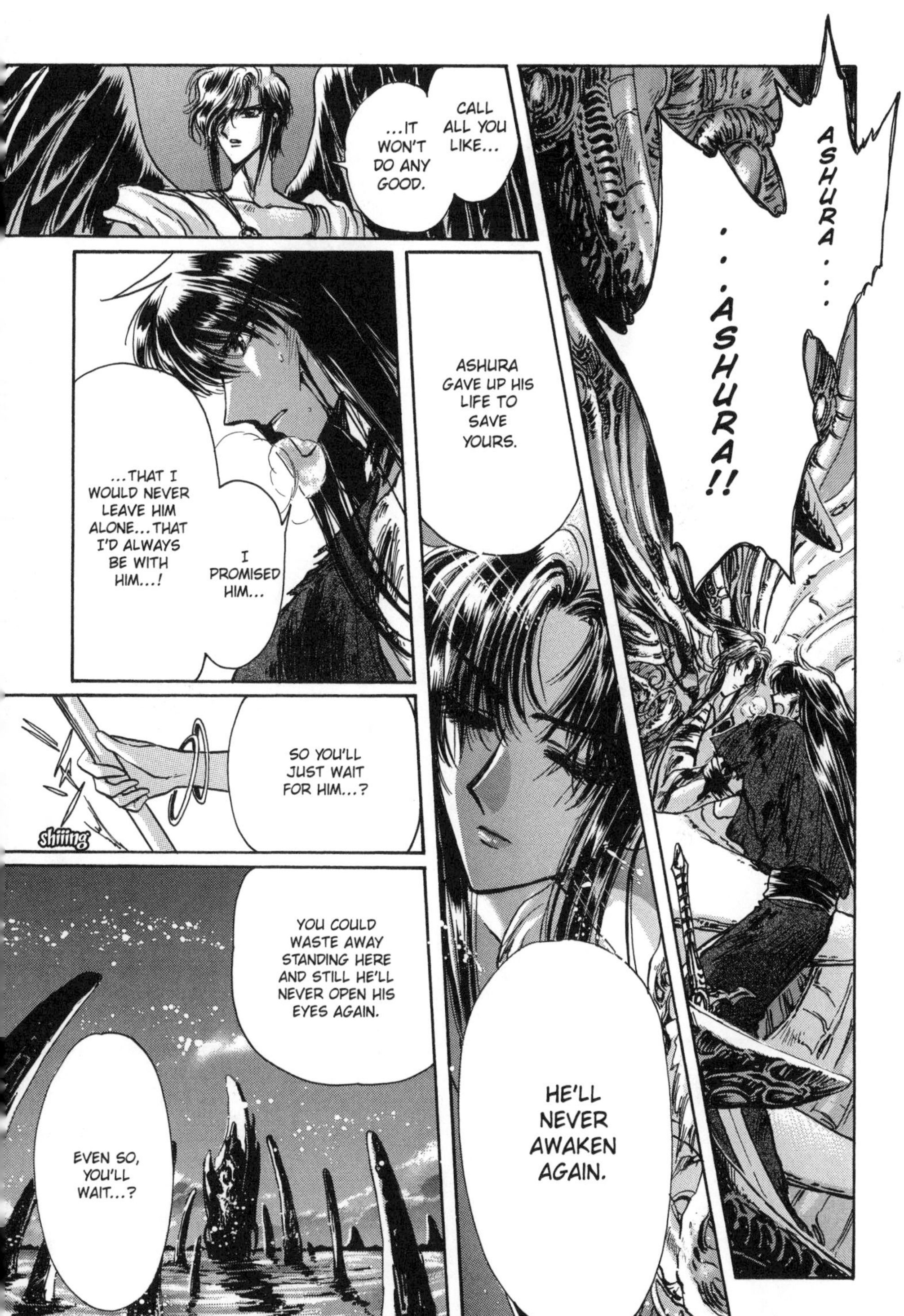
ASHURA...
...ASHURA!!
CALL ALL YOU LIKE...
...IT WON'T DO ANY GOOD.
ASHURA GAVE UP HIS LIFE TO SAVE YOURS.
HE'LL NEVER AWAKEN AGAIN.
I PROMISED HIM...
...THAT I WOULD NEVER LEAVE HIM ALONE...THAT I'D ALWAYS BE WITH HIM...!
SO YOU'LL JUST WAIT FOR HIM...?
shiiing
YOU COULD WASTE AWAY STANDING HERE AND STILL HE'LL NEVER OPEN HIS EYES AGAIN.
EVEN SO, YOU'LL WAIT...?

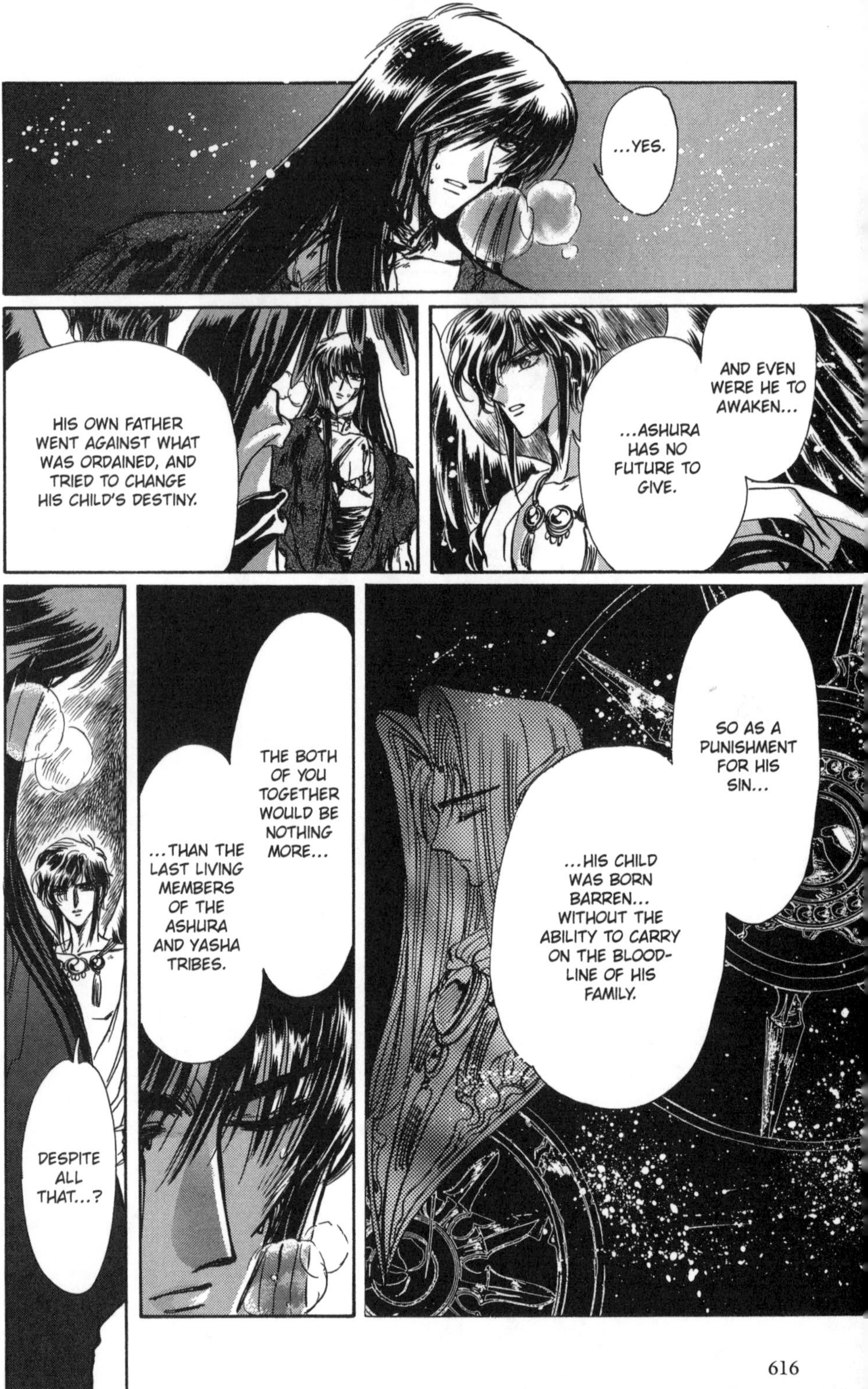
...YES.
AND EVEN WERE HE TO AWAKEN...
...ASHURA HAS NO FUTURE TO GIVE.
HIS OWN FATHER WENT AGAINST WHAT WAS ORDAINED, AND TRIED TO CHANGE HIS CHILD'S DESTINY.
SO AS A PUNISHMENT FOR HIS SIN...
...HIS CHILD WAS BORN BARREN... WITHOUT THE ABILITY TO CARRY ON THE BLOOD-LINE OF HIS FAMILY.
THE BOTH OF YOU TOGETHER WOULD BE NOTHING MORE...
...THAN THE LAST LIVING MEMBERS OF THE ASHURA AND YASHA TRIBES.
DESPITE ALL THAT...?

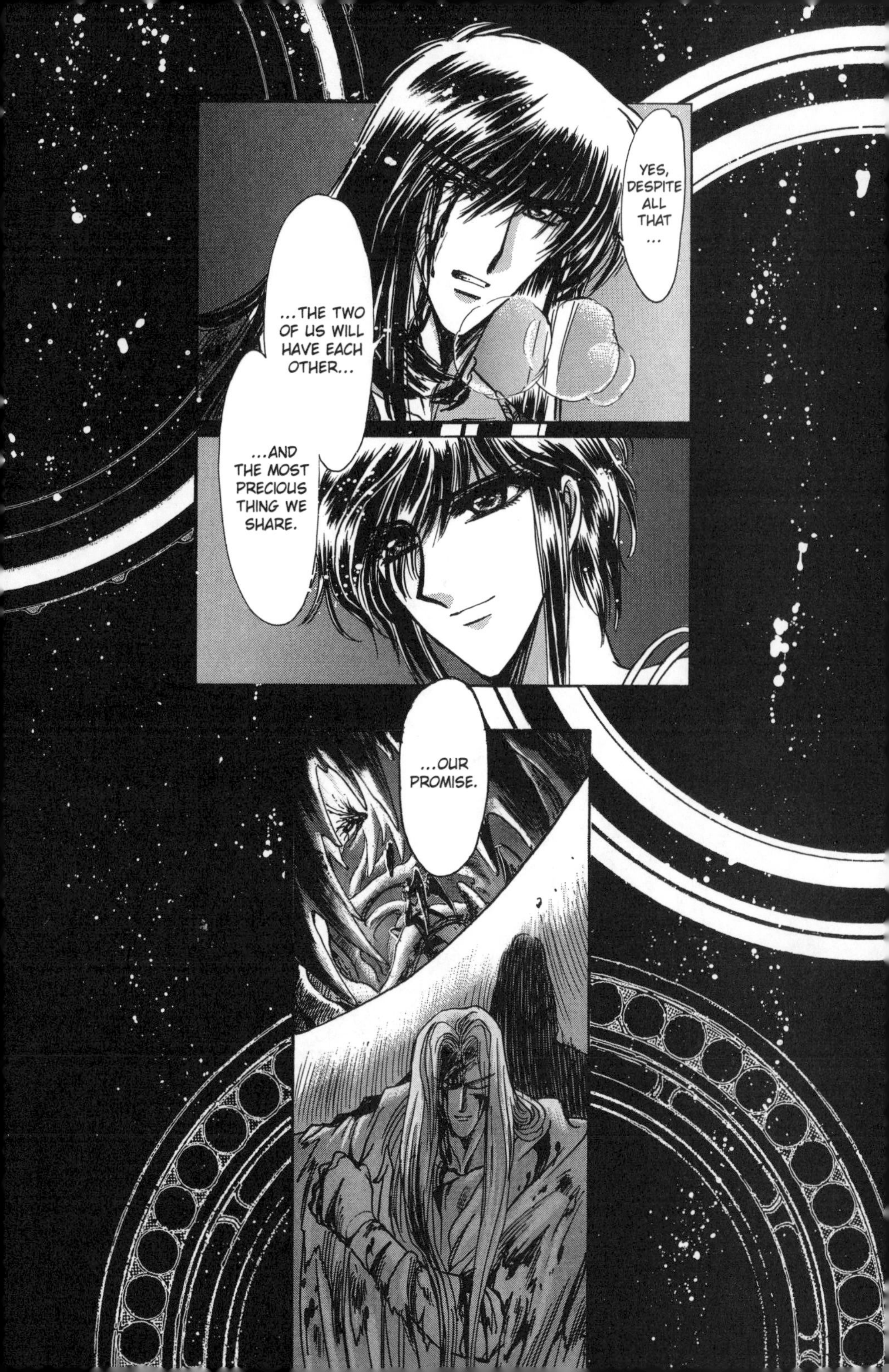
YES, DESPITE ALL THAT ...
...THE TWO OF US WILL HAVE EACH OTHER...
...AND THE MOST PRECIOUS THING WE SHARE.
...OUR PROMISE.

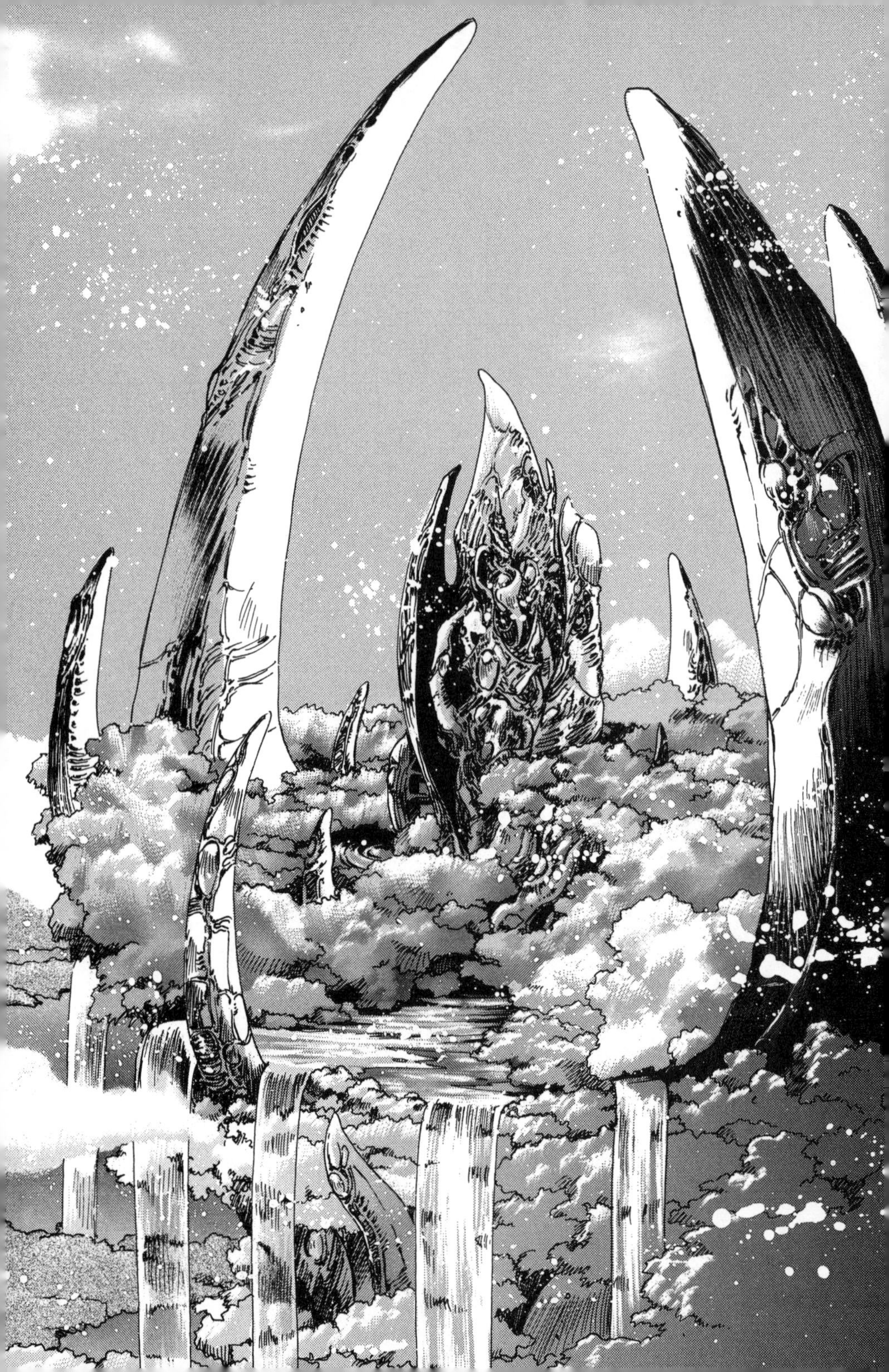

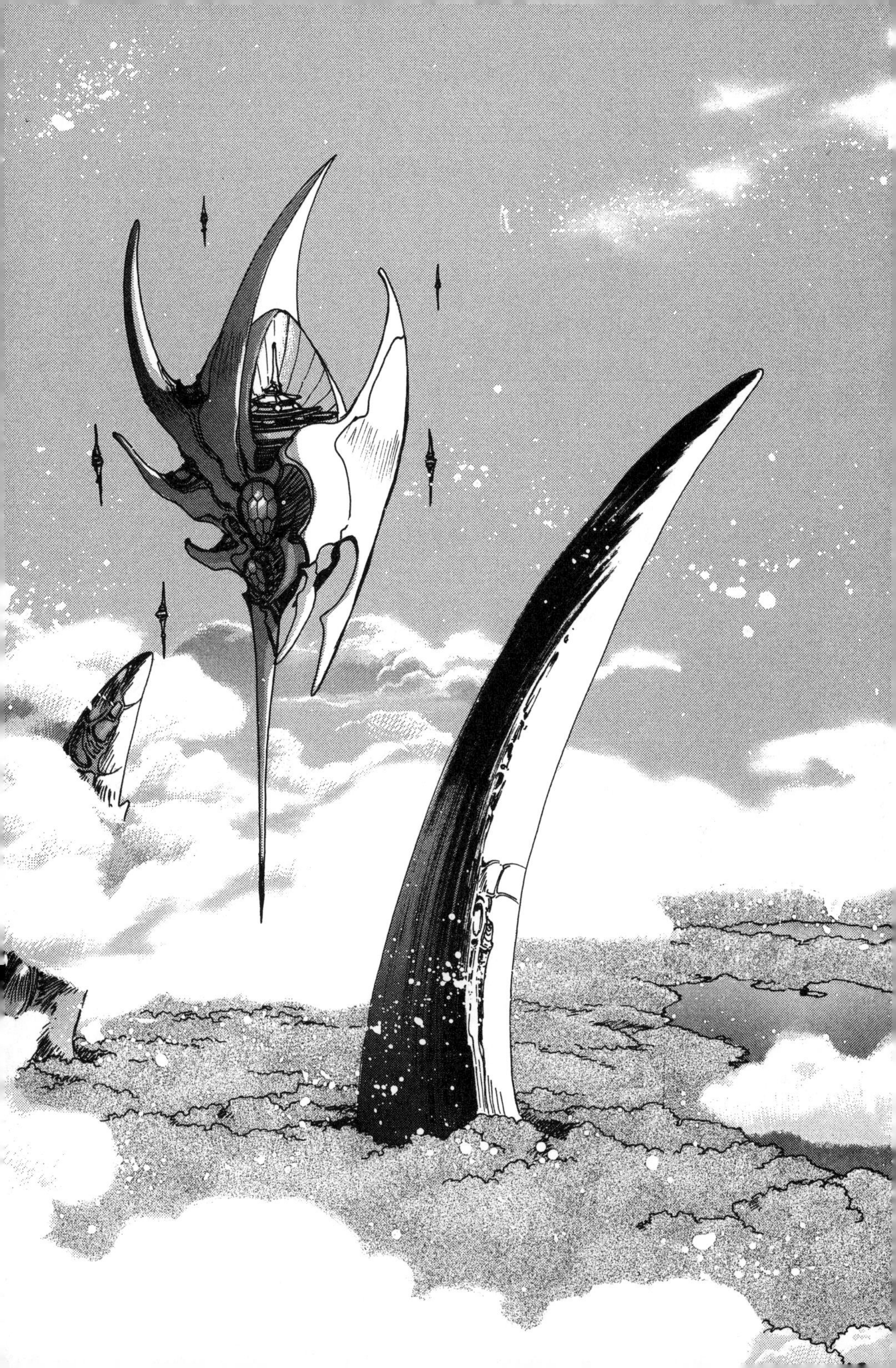

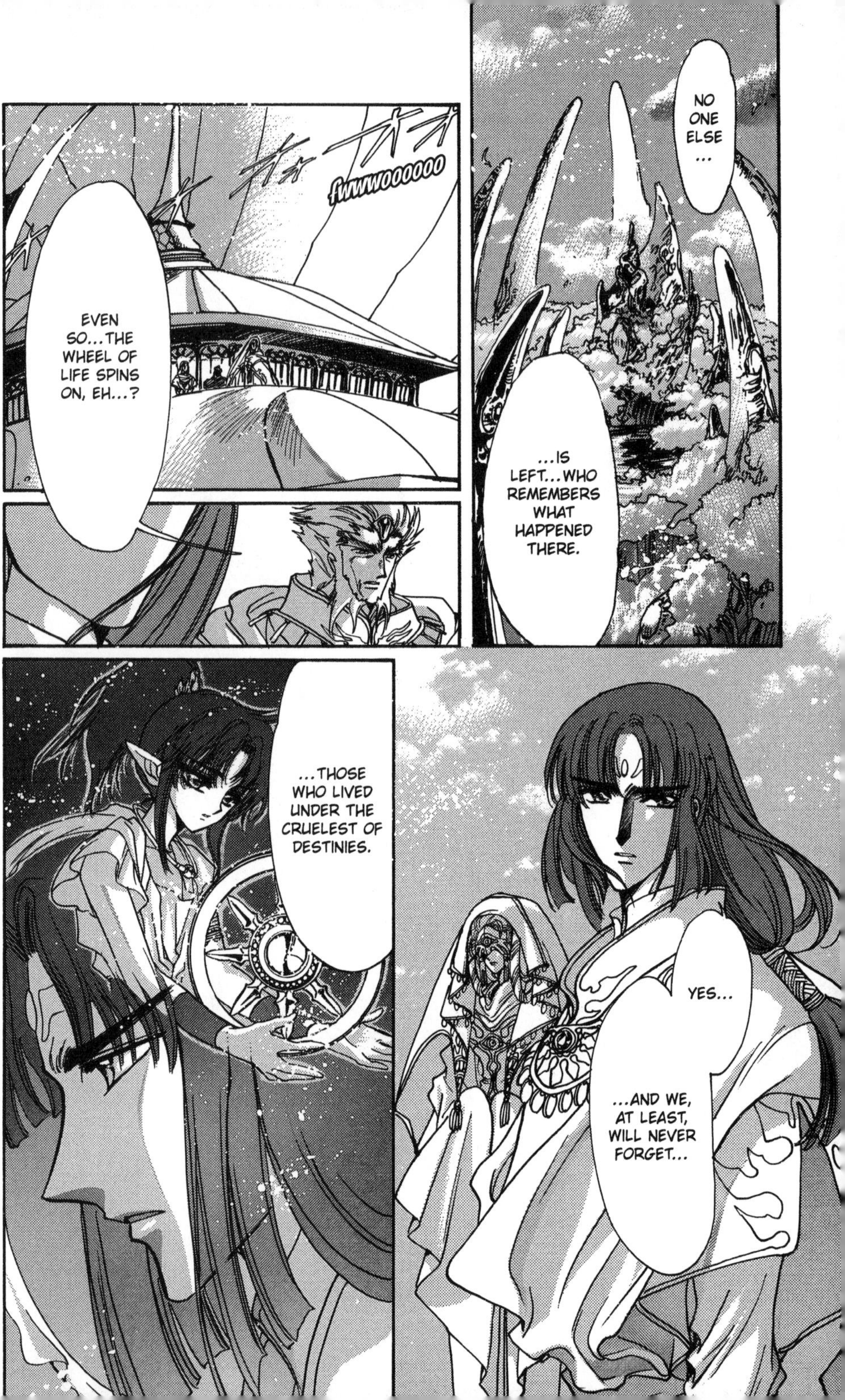
NO ONE ELSE...
...IS LEFT...WHO REMEMBERS WHAT HAPPENED THERE.
fwwwoooooo
EVEN SO...THE WHEEL OF LIFE SPINS ON, EH...?
YES...
...AND WE, AT LEAST, WILL NEVER FORGET...
...THOSE WHO LIVED UNDER THE CRUELEST OF DESTINIES.

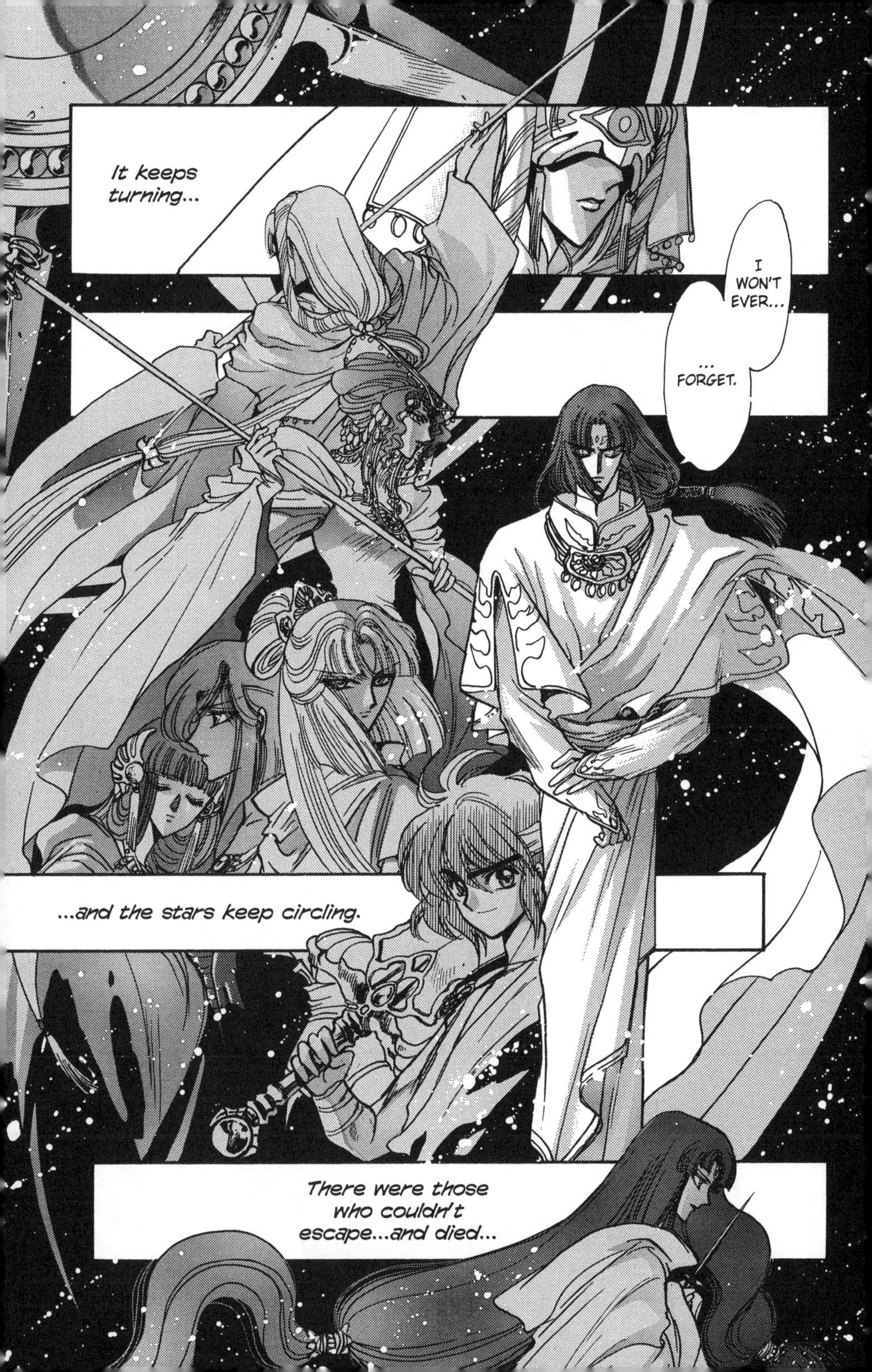
It keeps turning...
I WON'T EVER...
...FORGET.
...and the stars keep circling.
There were those who couldn't escape...and died...

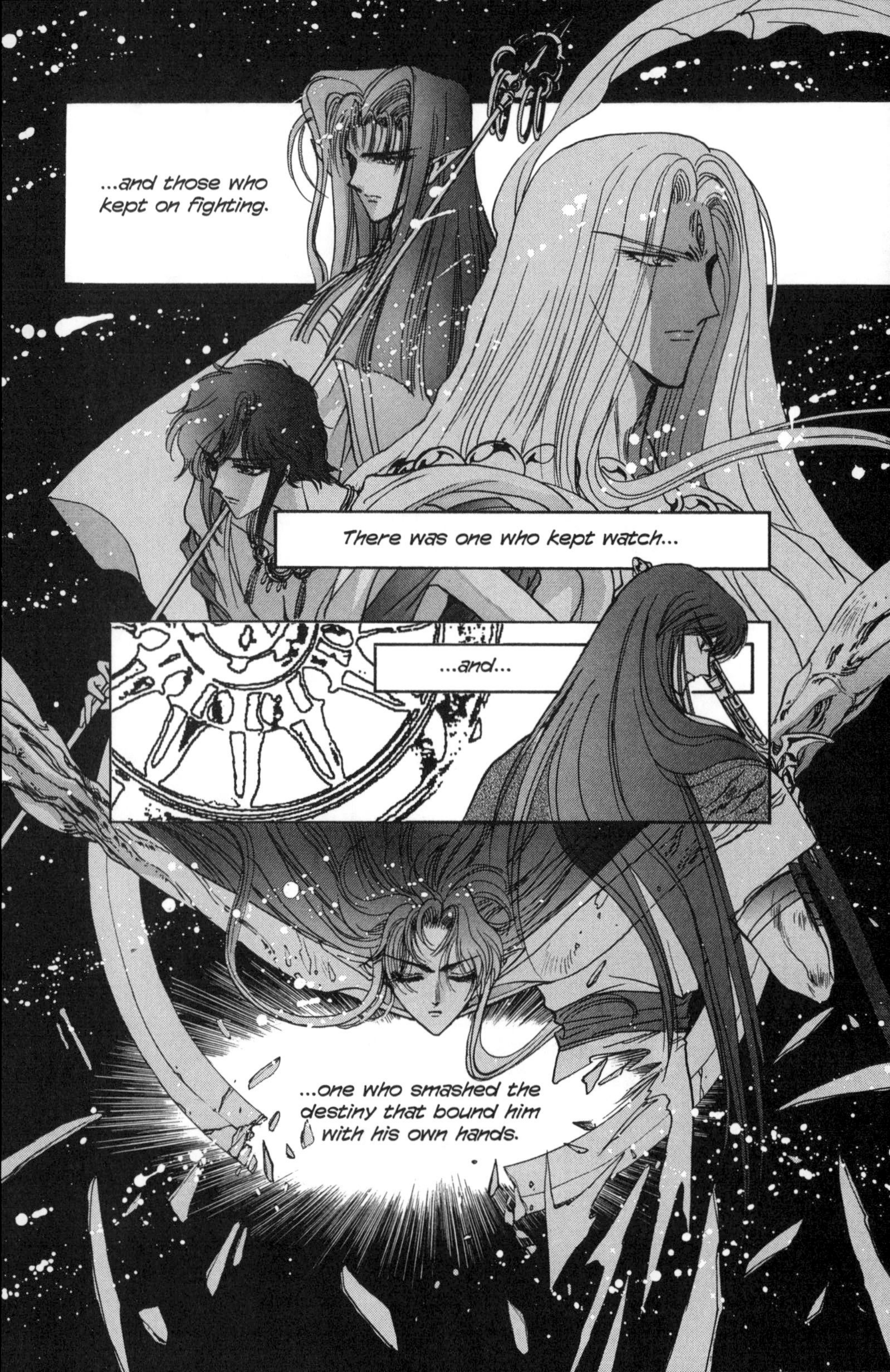
...and those who
kept on fighting.
There was one who kept watch...
...and...
...one who smashed the
destiny that bound him
with his own hands.

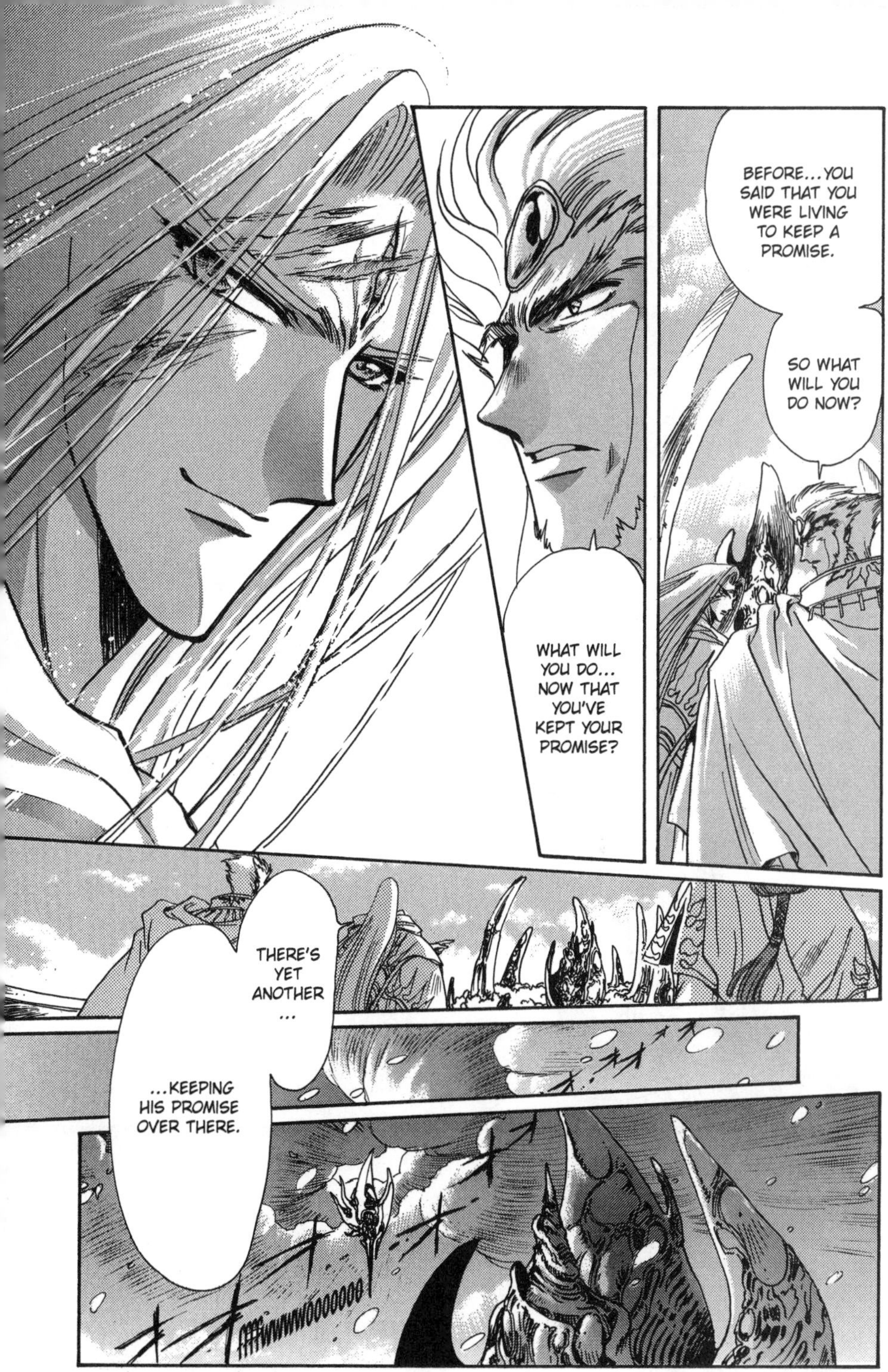
BEFORE...YOU SAID THAT YOU WERE LIVING TO KEEP A PROMISE.
SO WHAT WILL YOU DO NOW?
WHAT WILL YOU DO... NOW THAT YOU'VE KEPT YOUR PROMISE?
THERE'S YET ANOTHER ...
...KEEPING HIS PROMISE OVER THERE.
ffffwwwwwoooooooo

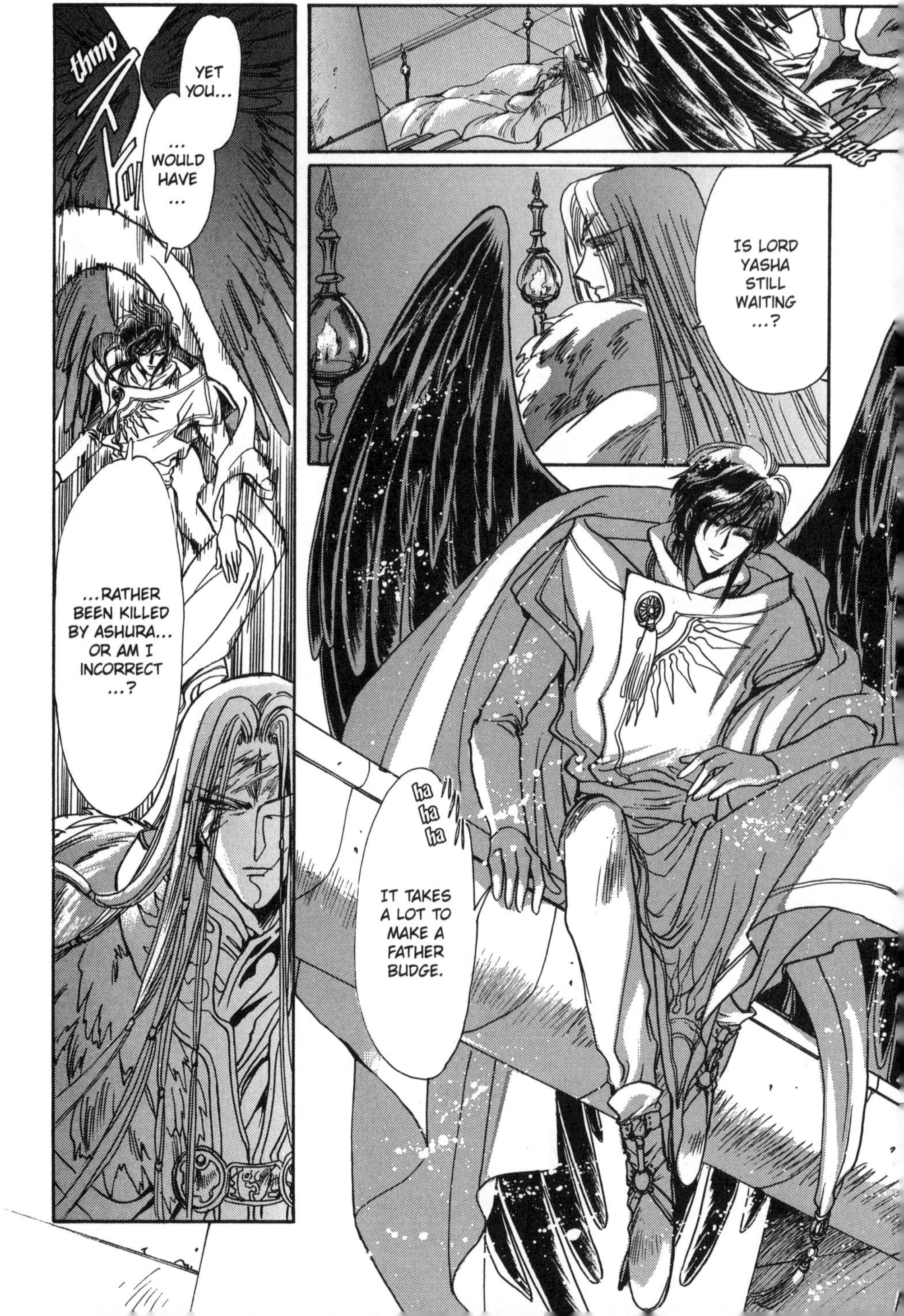
IS LORD YASHA STILL WAITING ...?
thmp
YET YOU...
...WOULD HAVE ...
...RATHER BEEN KILLED BY ASHURA... OR AM I INCORRECT ...?
ha ha ha
IT TAKES A LOT TO MAKE A FATHER BUDGE.

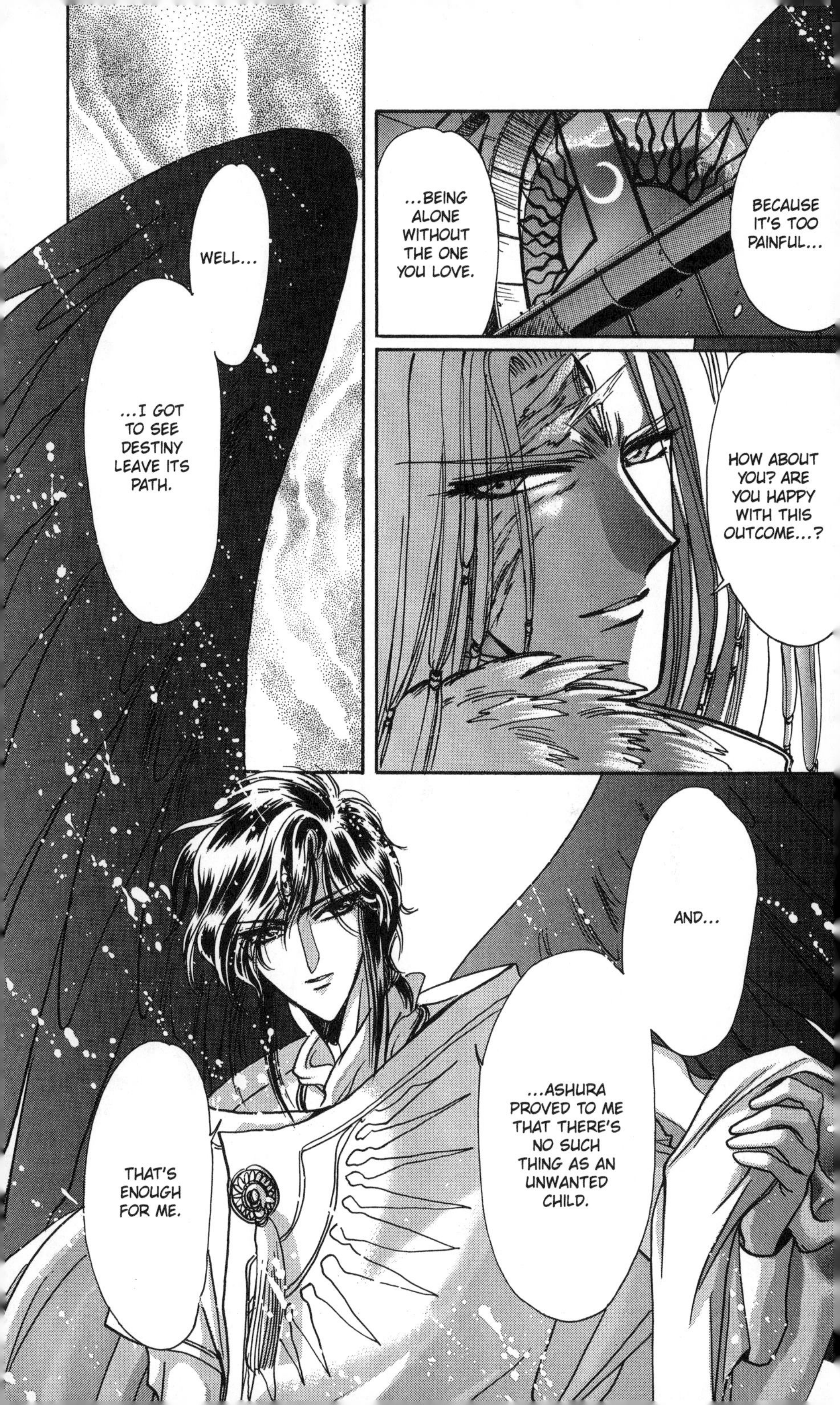
BECAUSE IT'S TOO PAINFUL...
...BEING ALONE WITHOUT THE ONE YOU LOVE.
HOW ABOUT YOU? ARE YOU HAPPY WITH THIS OUTCOME...?
WELL...
...I GOT TO SEE DESTINY LEAVE ITS PATH.
AND...
...ASHURA PROVED TO ME THAT THERE'S NO SUCH THING AS AN UNWANTED CHILD.
THAT'S ENOUGH FOR ME.

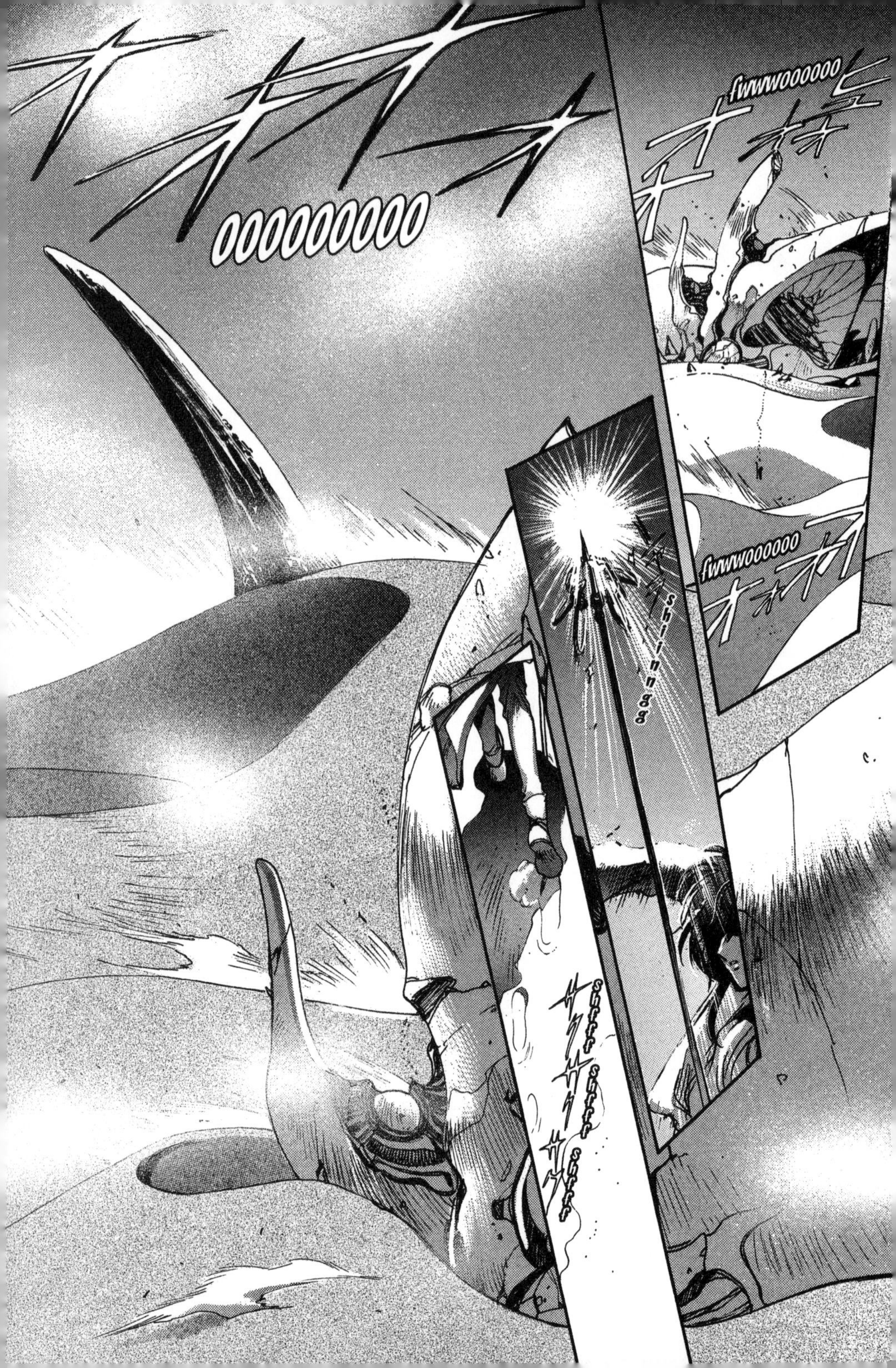
fwwwoooooo
fwwwoooooo
shiiinngg
shfff shfff shfff
oooooooooo

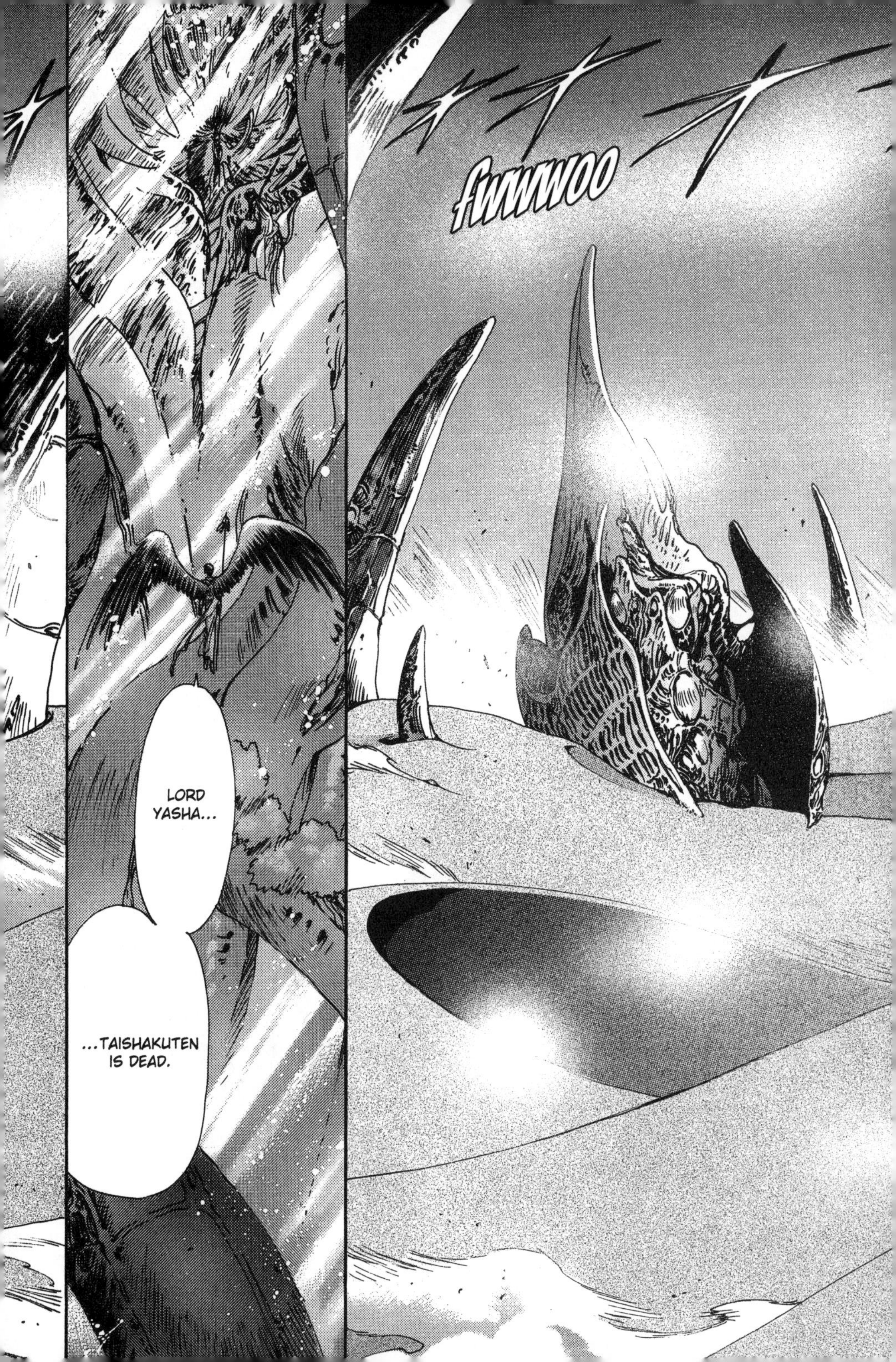
fwwwoo
LORD YASHA...
...TAISHAKUTEN IS DEAD.

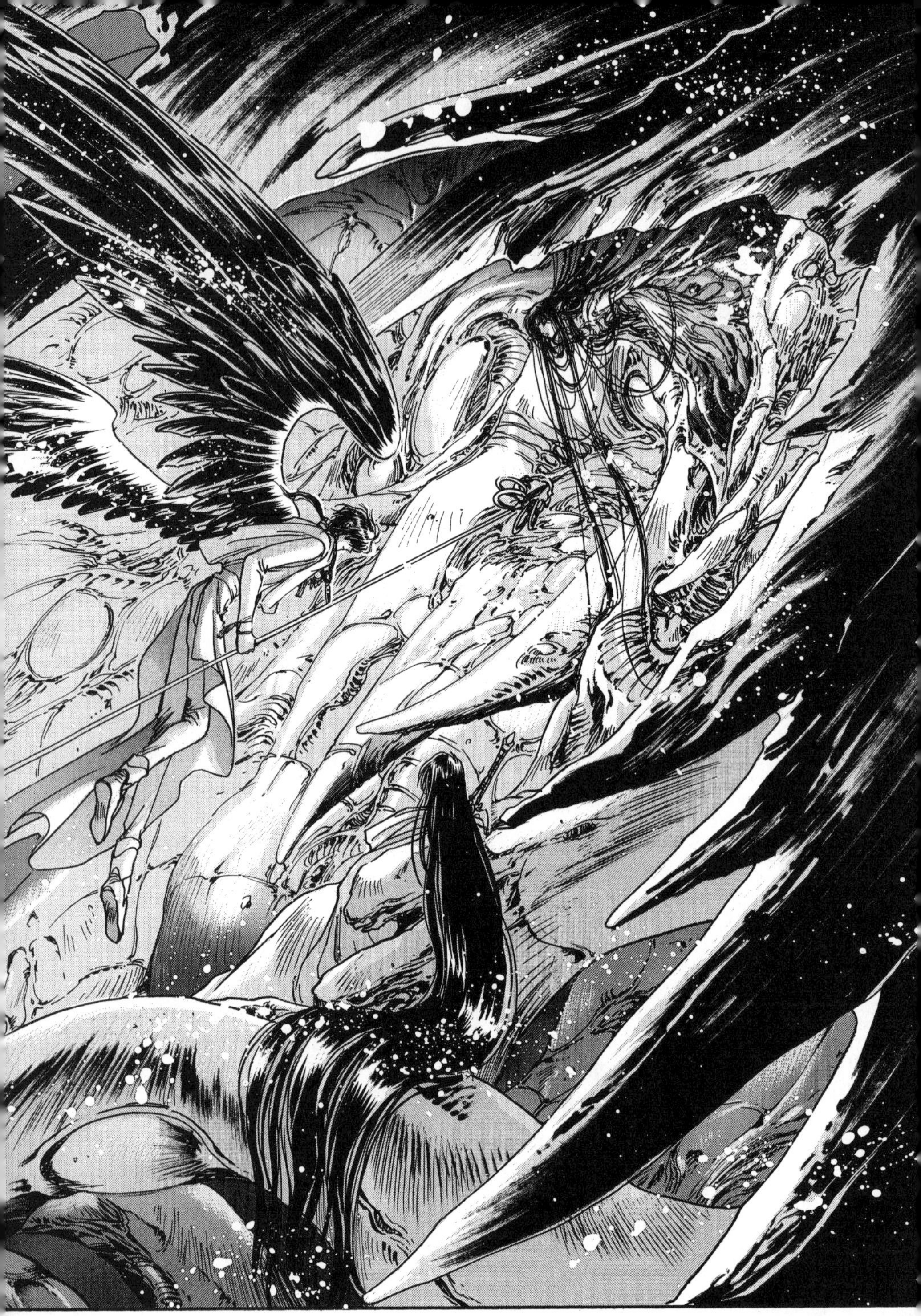

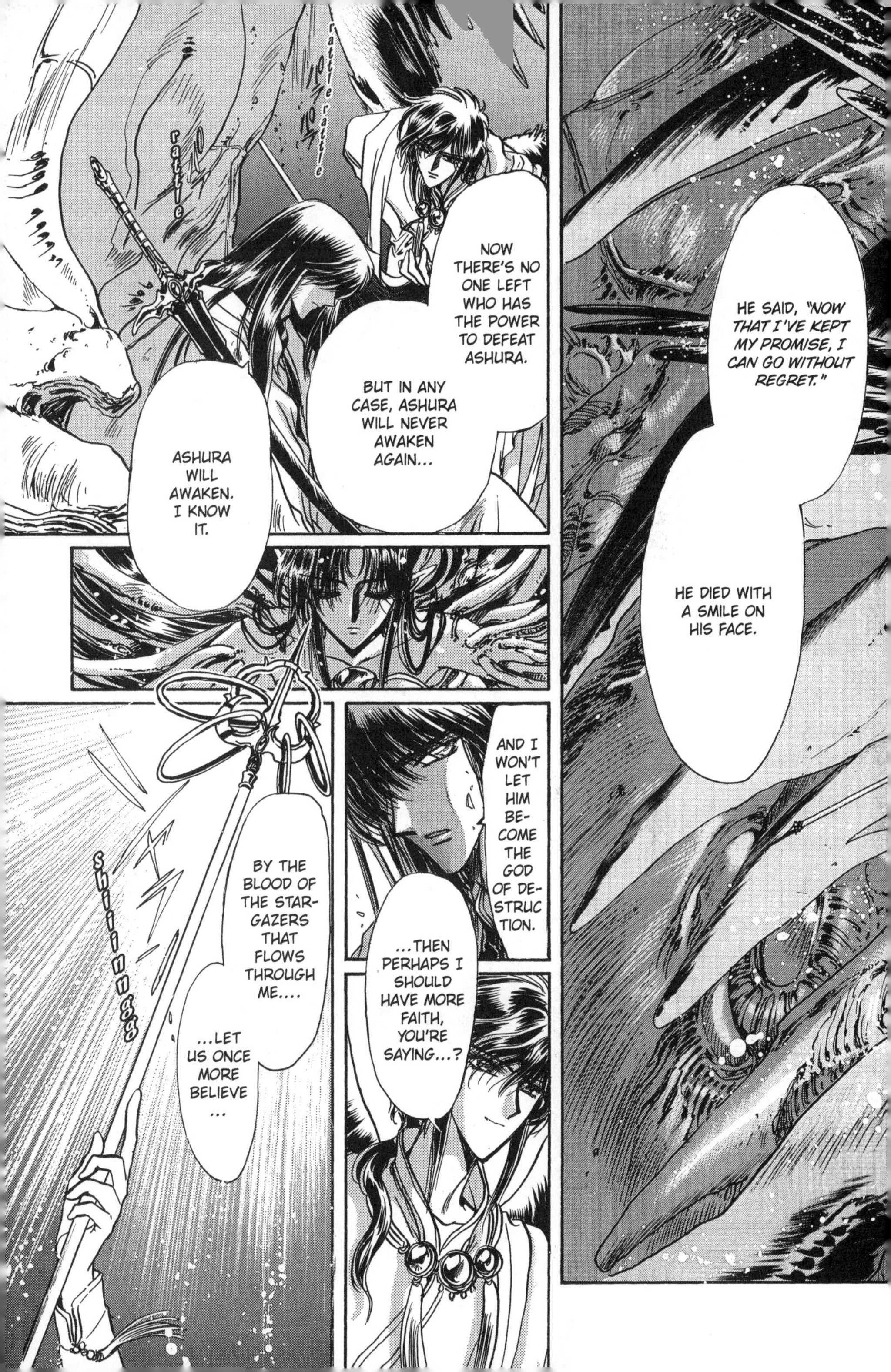
HE SAID, "NOW THAT I'VE KEPT MY PROMISE, I CAN GO WITHOUT REGRET."
HE DIED WITH A SMILE ON HIS FACE.
rattle rattle
rattle
NOW THERE'S NO ONE LEFT WHO HAS THE POWER TO DEFEAT ASHURA.
BUT IN ANY CASE, ASHURA WILL NEVER AWAKEN AGAIN...
ASHURA WILL AWAKEN. I KNOW IT.
AND I WON'T LET HIM BE-COME THE GOD OF DE-STRUC TION.
...THEN PERHAPS I SHOULD HAVE MORE FAITH, YOU'RE SAYING...?
BY THE BLOOD OF THE STAR-GAZERS THAT FLOWS THROUGH ME....
...LET US ONCE MORE BELIEVE ...
shiiinng

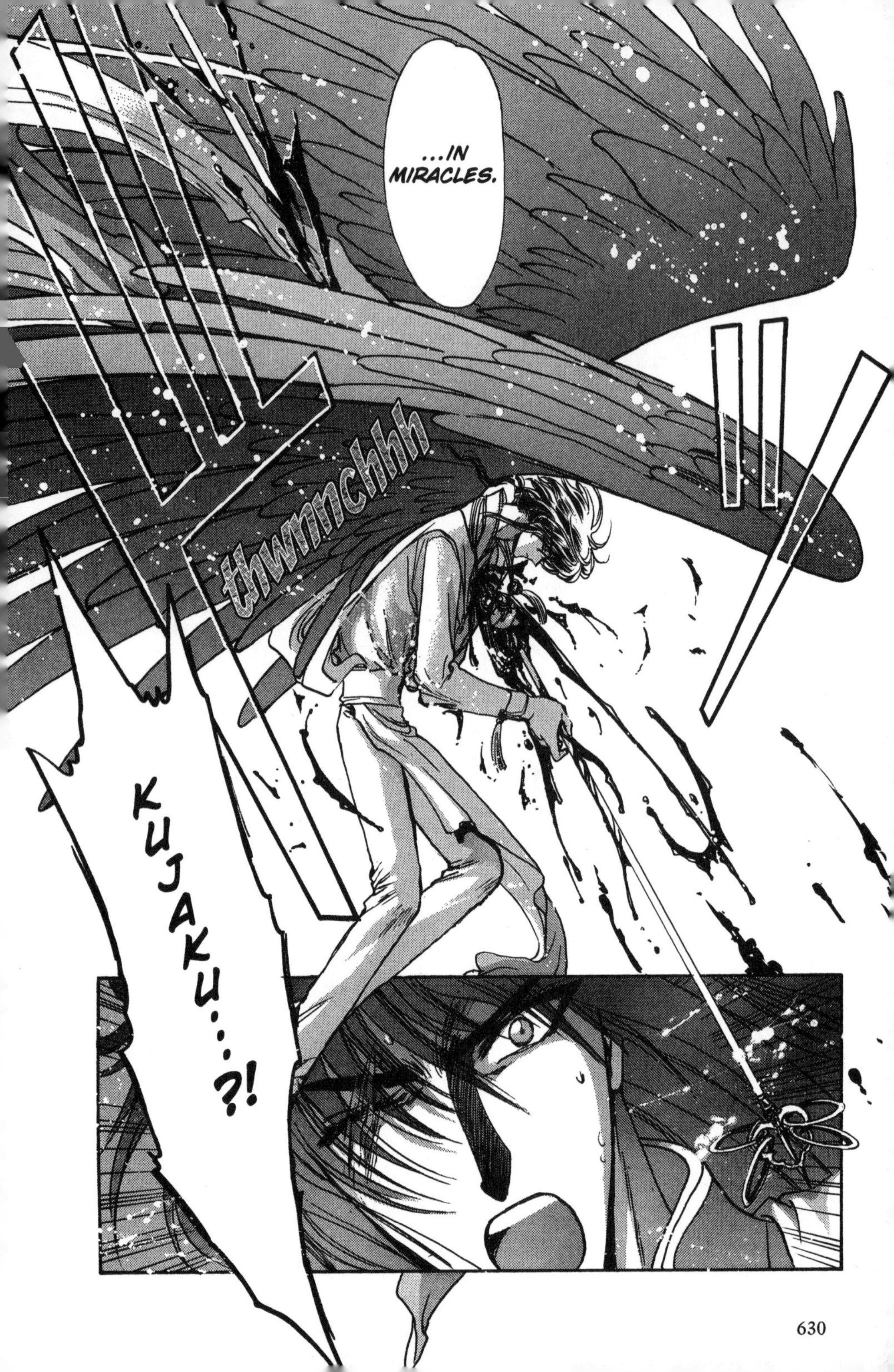
...IN MIRACLES.
thwnnchhh
KUJAKU...?!

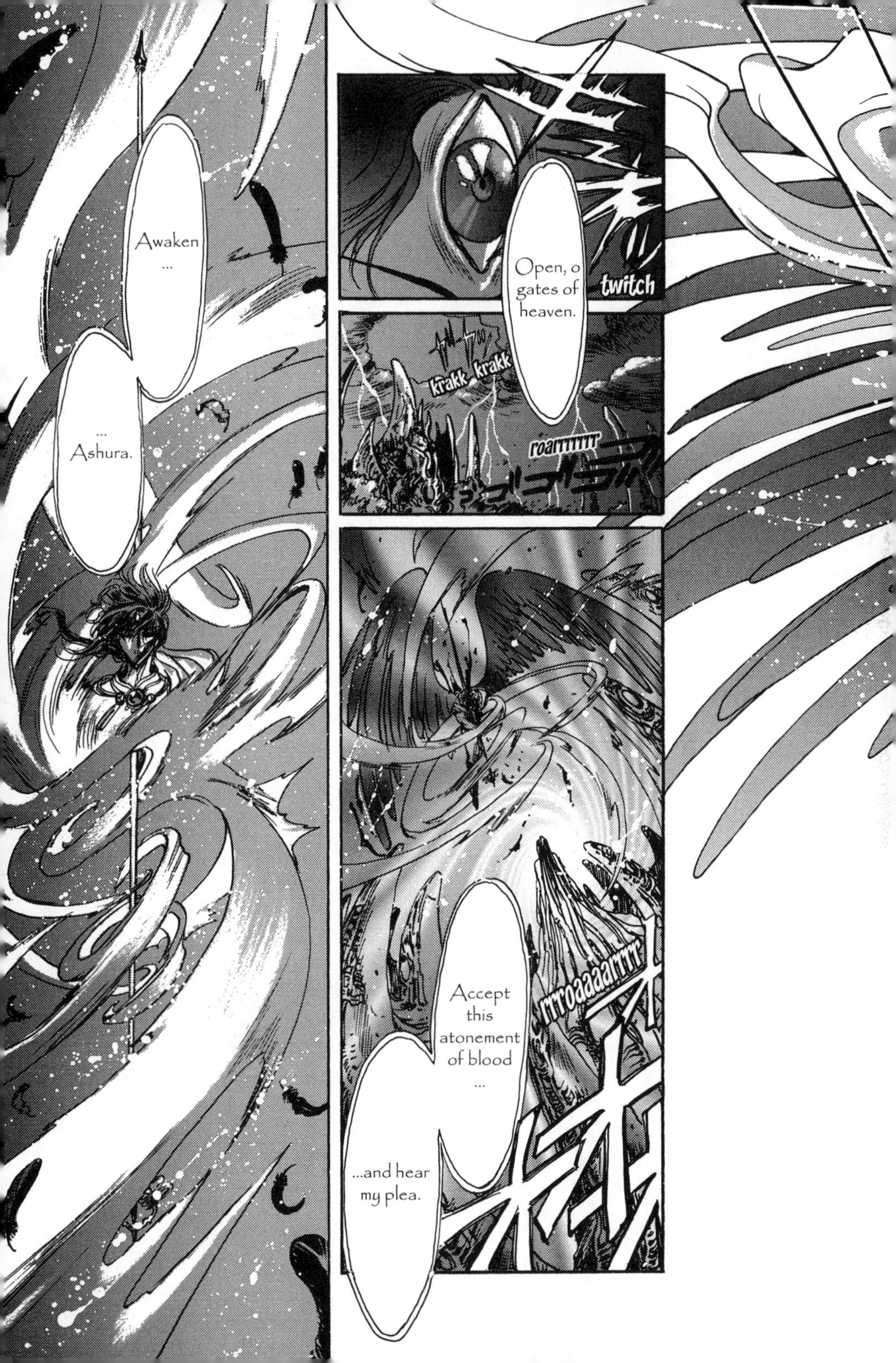

Open, o gates of heaven.
twitch
krakk krakk
roarrrrrr
rrroaaaarrrr
Accept this atonement of blood ...
...and hear my plea.
Awaken ...
... Ashura.

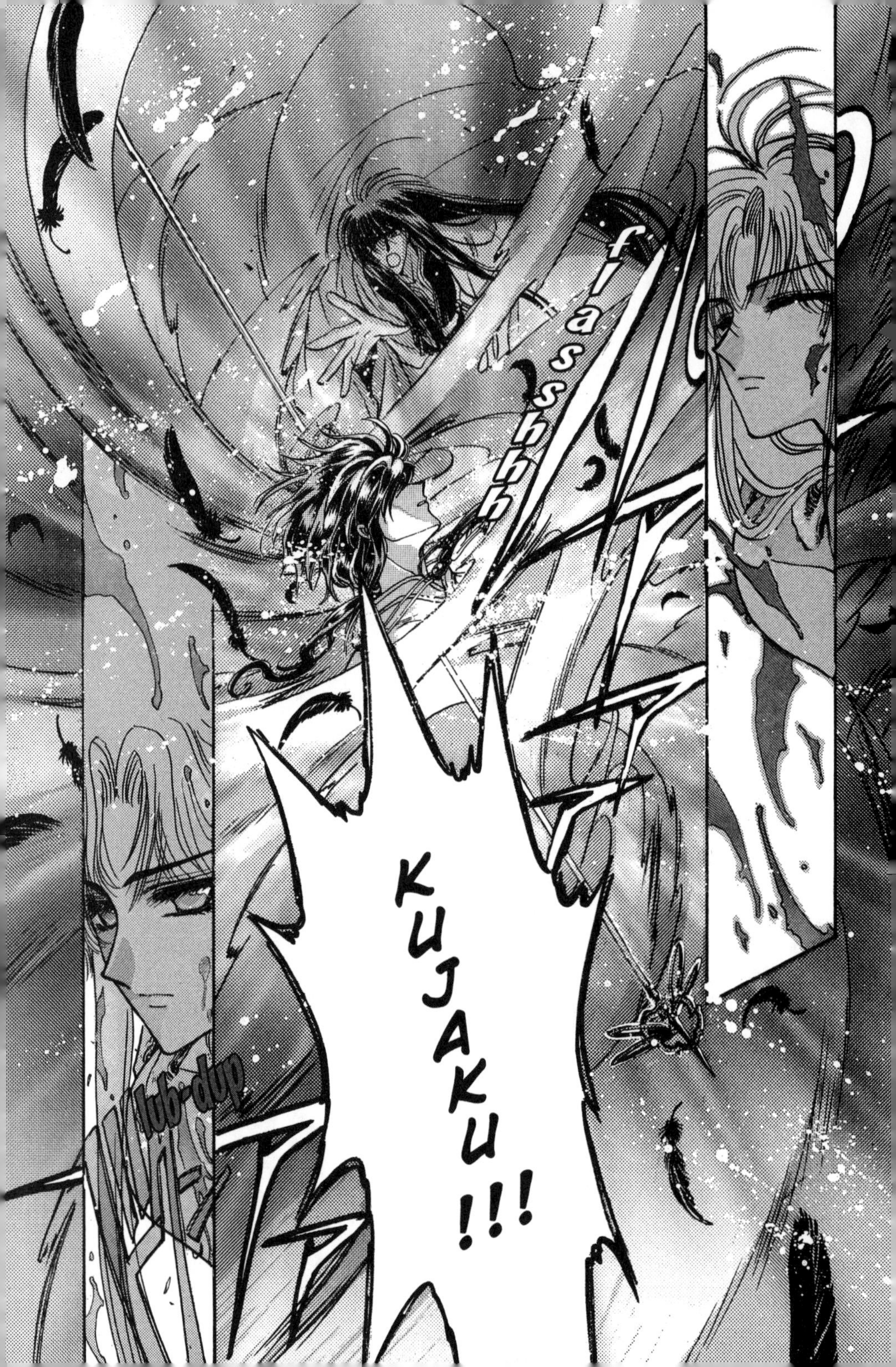

flasshhh
KUJAKU!!!
lub-dup

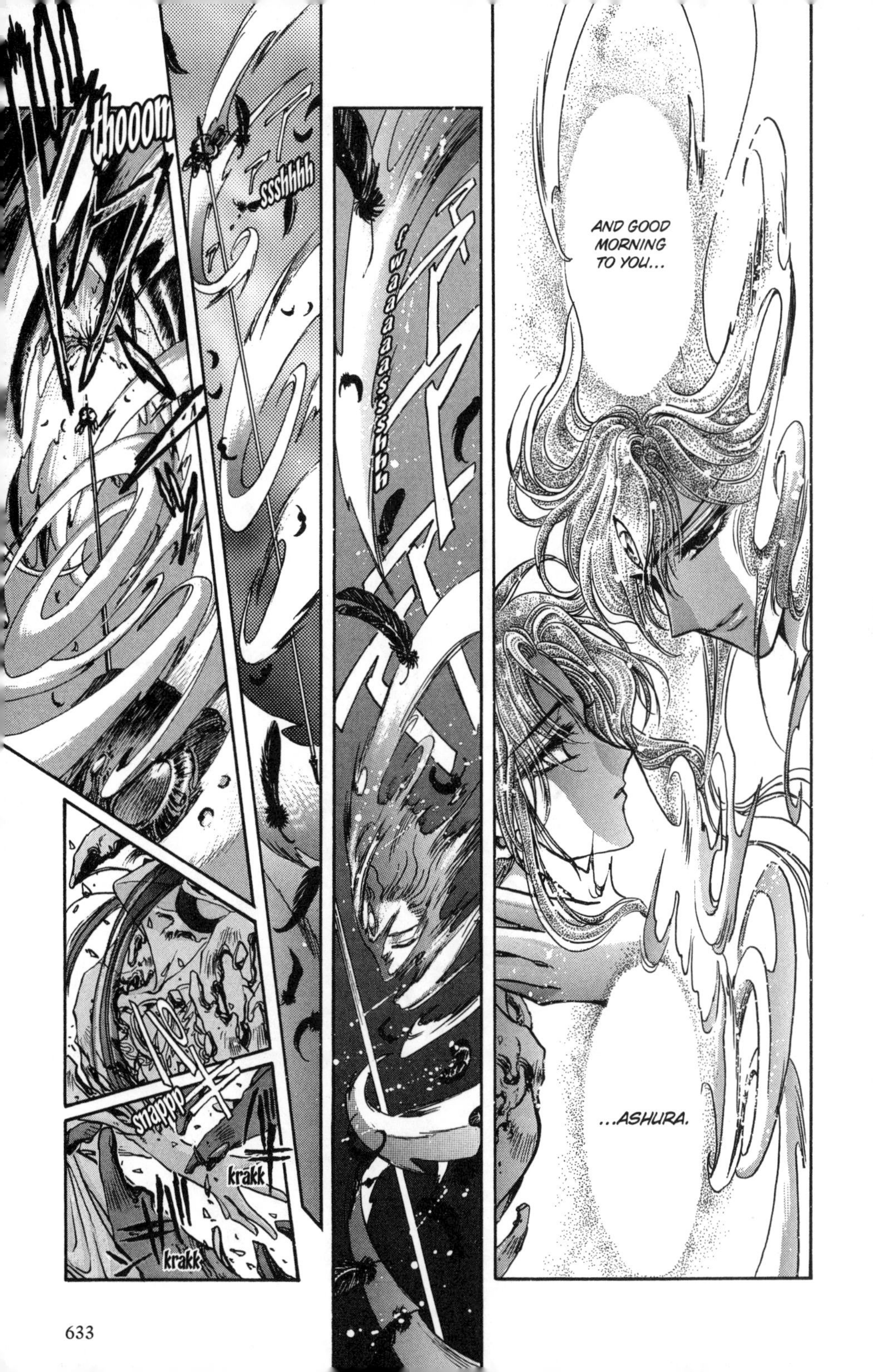
AND GOOD MORNING TO YOU...
...ASHURA.
fwaaaaaassshhh
ssshhhh
thooom
snapp
krakk
krakk

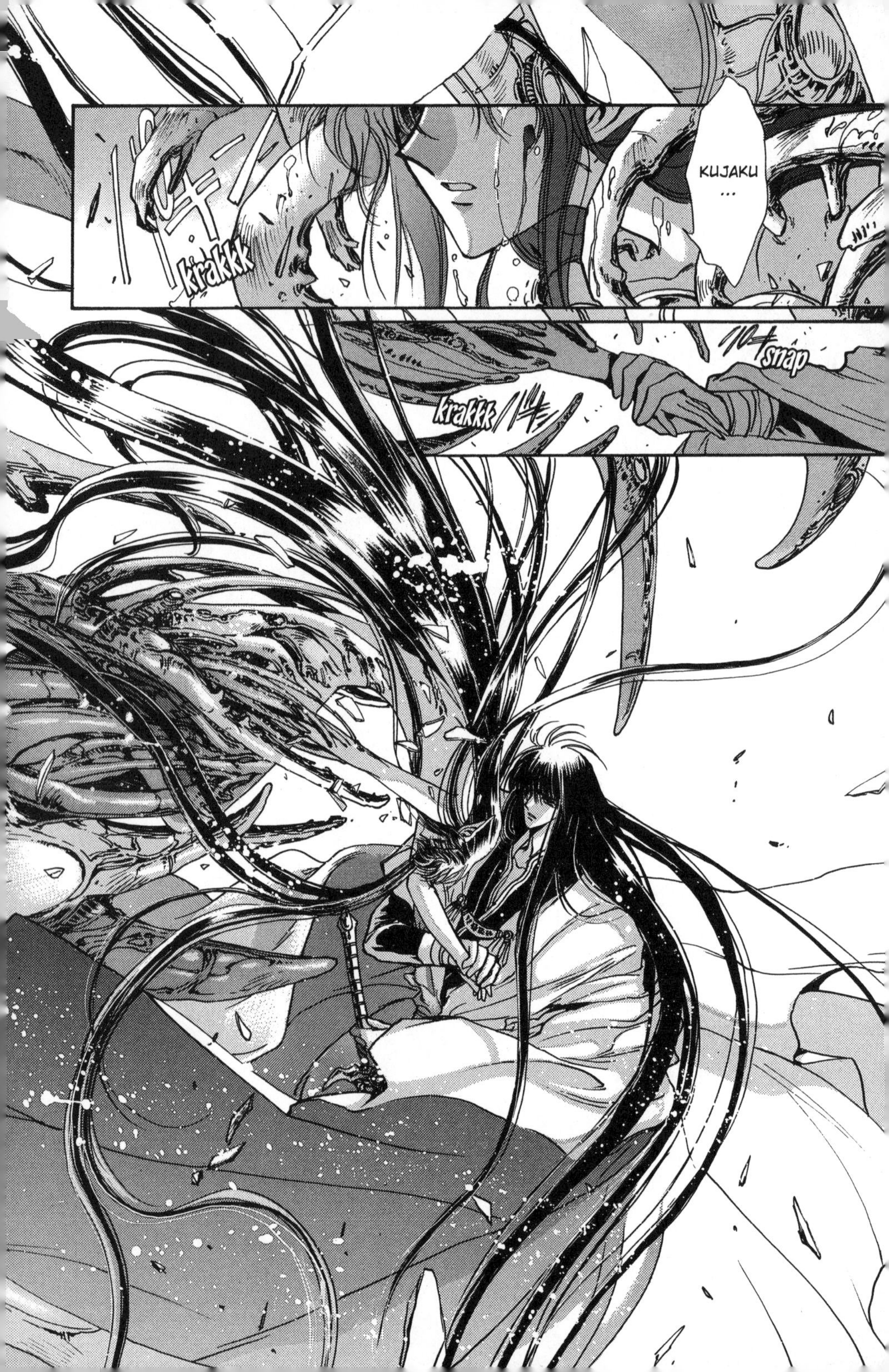
KUJAKU
...
krakkk
snap
krakkk

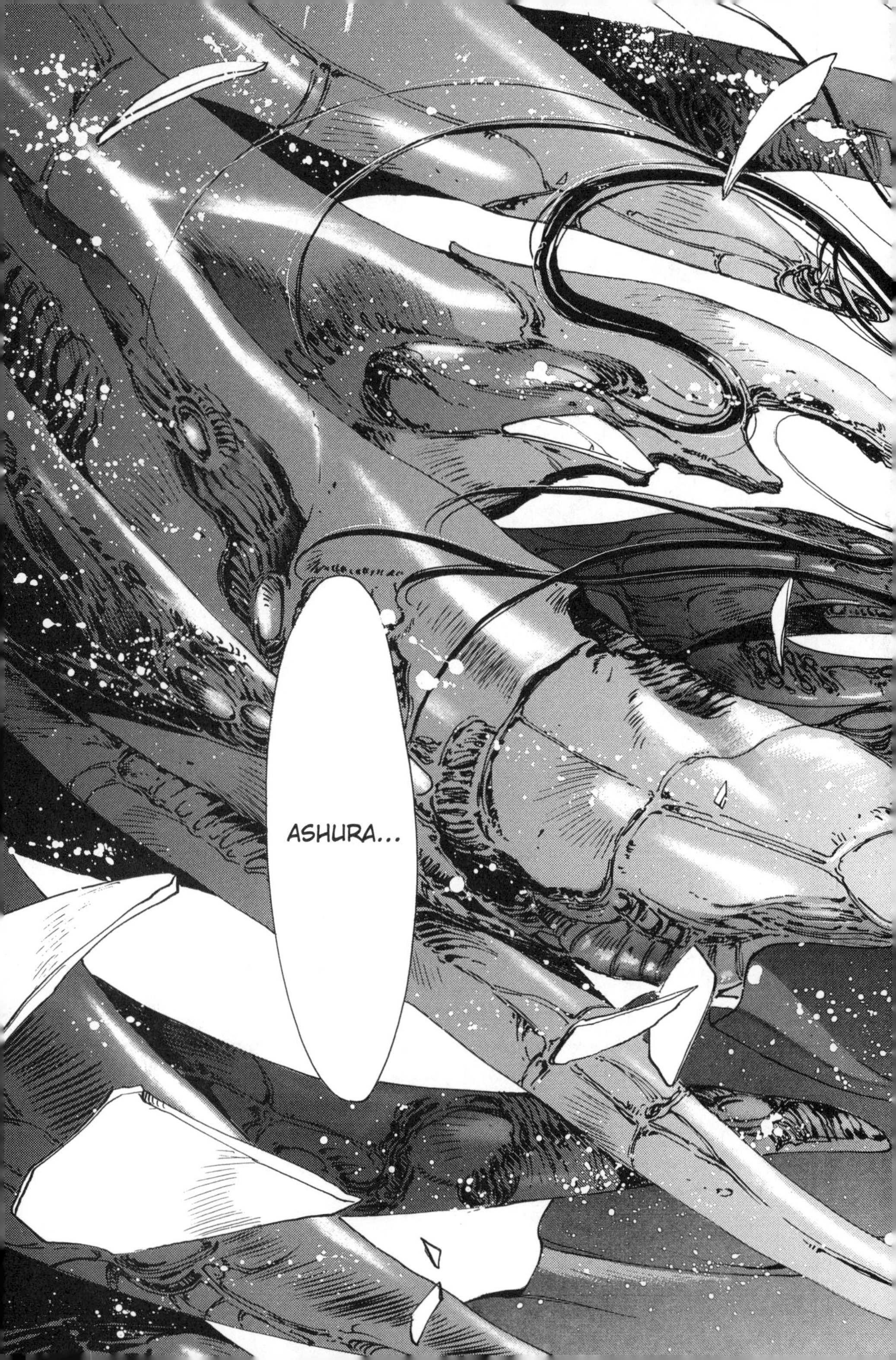
ASHURA...

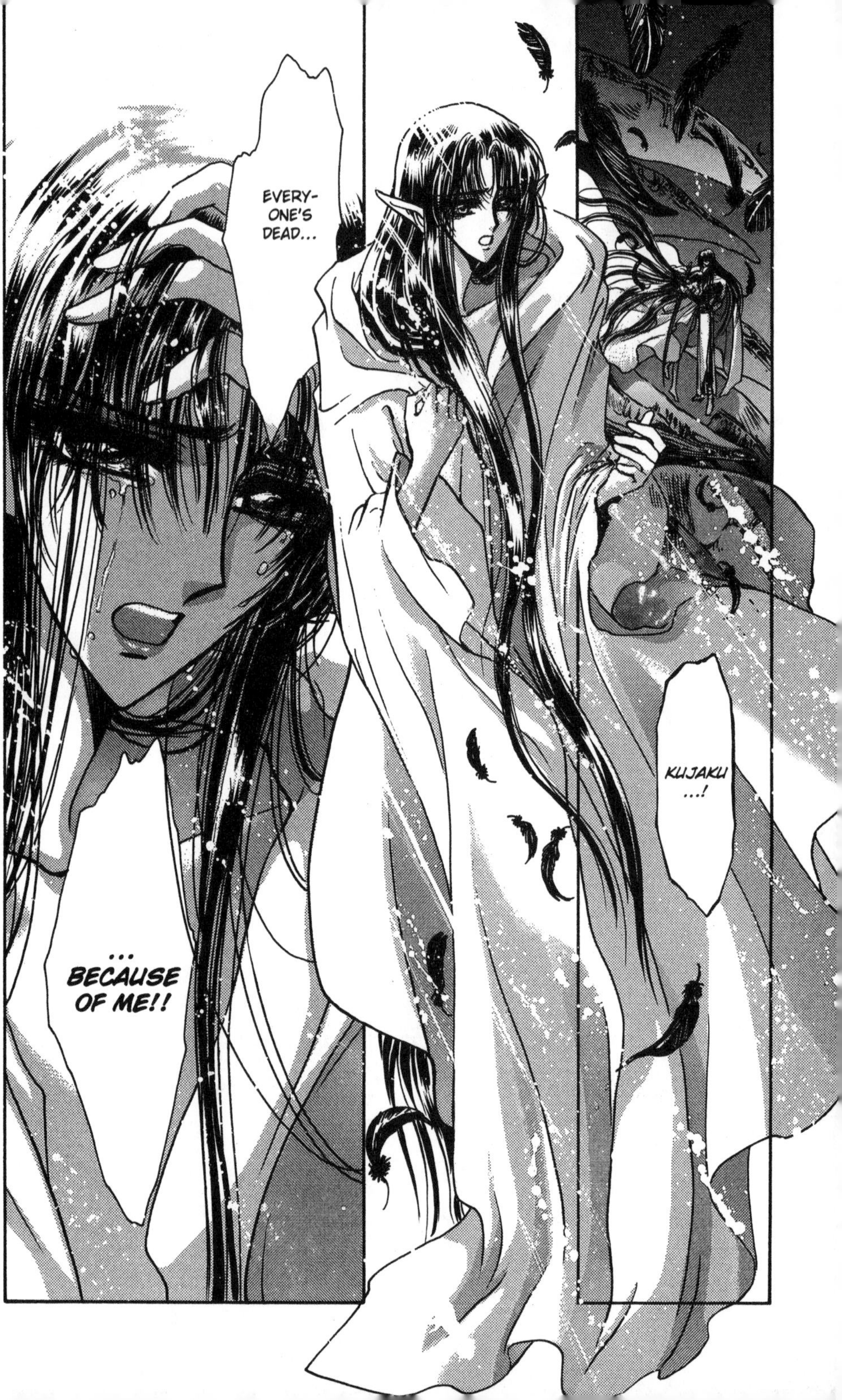
KUJAKU ...!
EVERY-ONE'S DEAD...
...BECAUSE OF ME!!

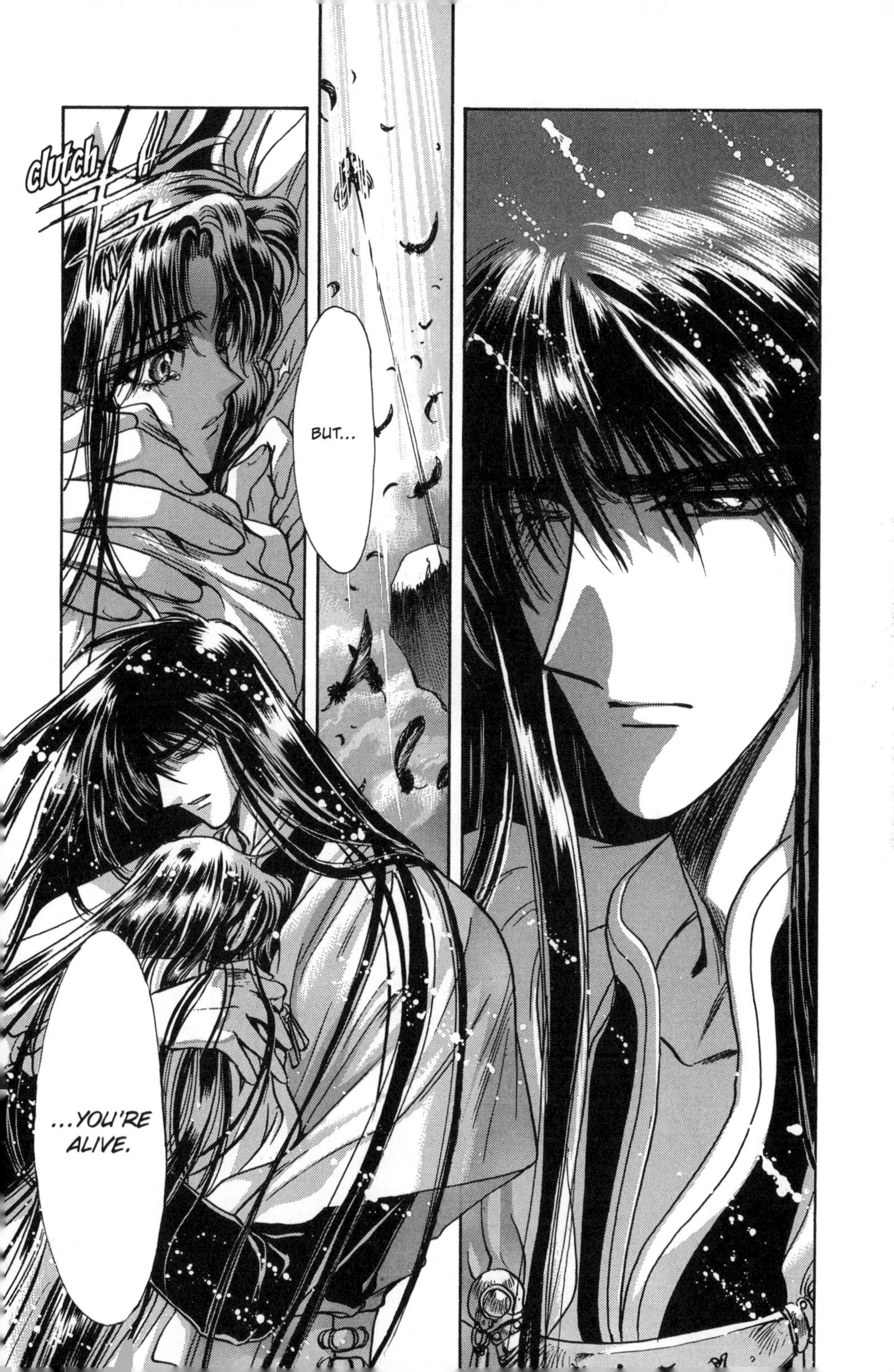
BUT...
clutch
...YOU'RE ALIVE.

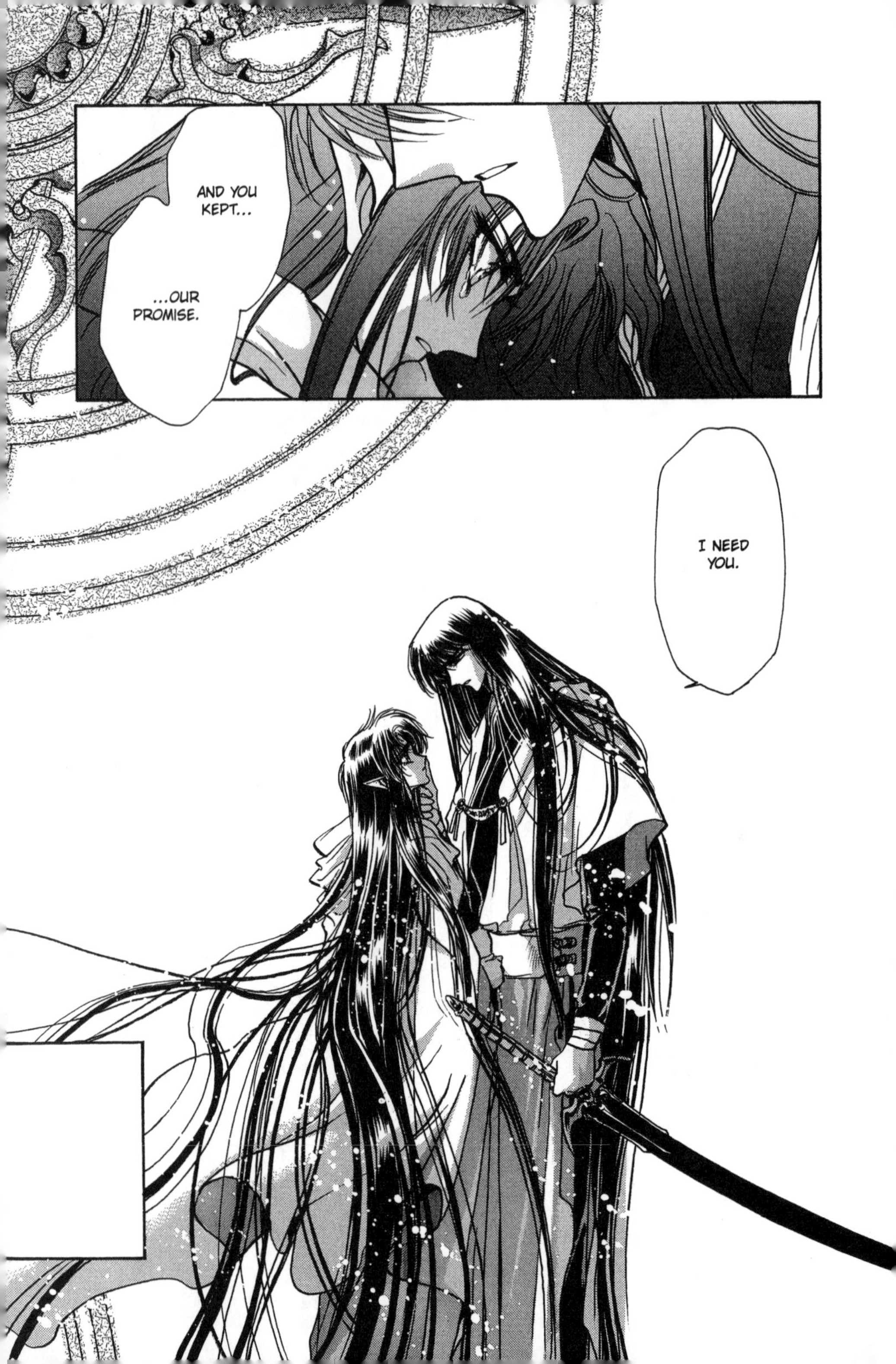
AND YOU KEPT...
...OUR PROMISE.
I NEED YOU.

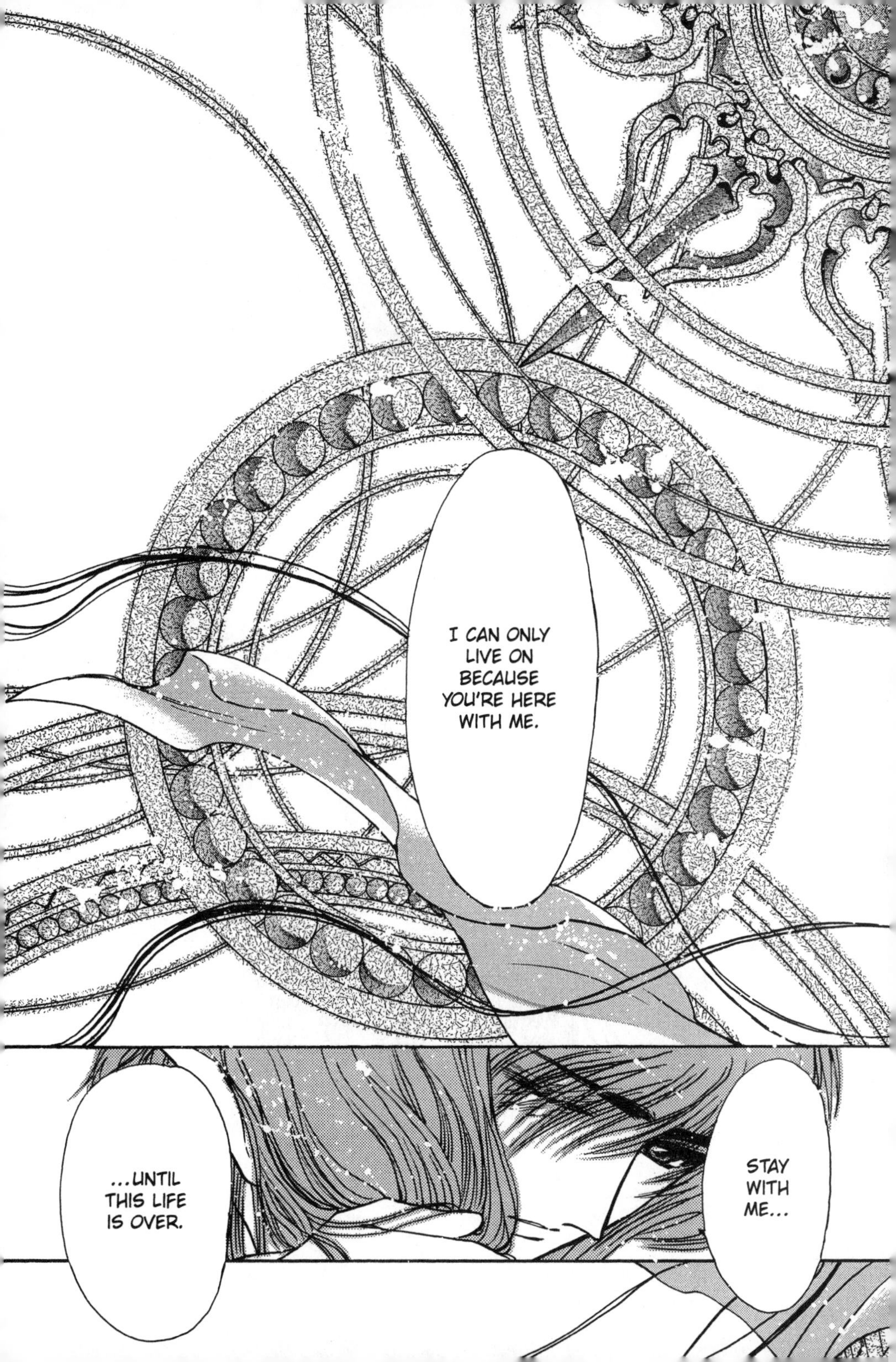
I CAN ONLY LIVE ON BECAUSE YOU'RE HERE WITH ME.
STAY WITH ME...
...UNTIL THIS LIFE IS OVER.

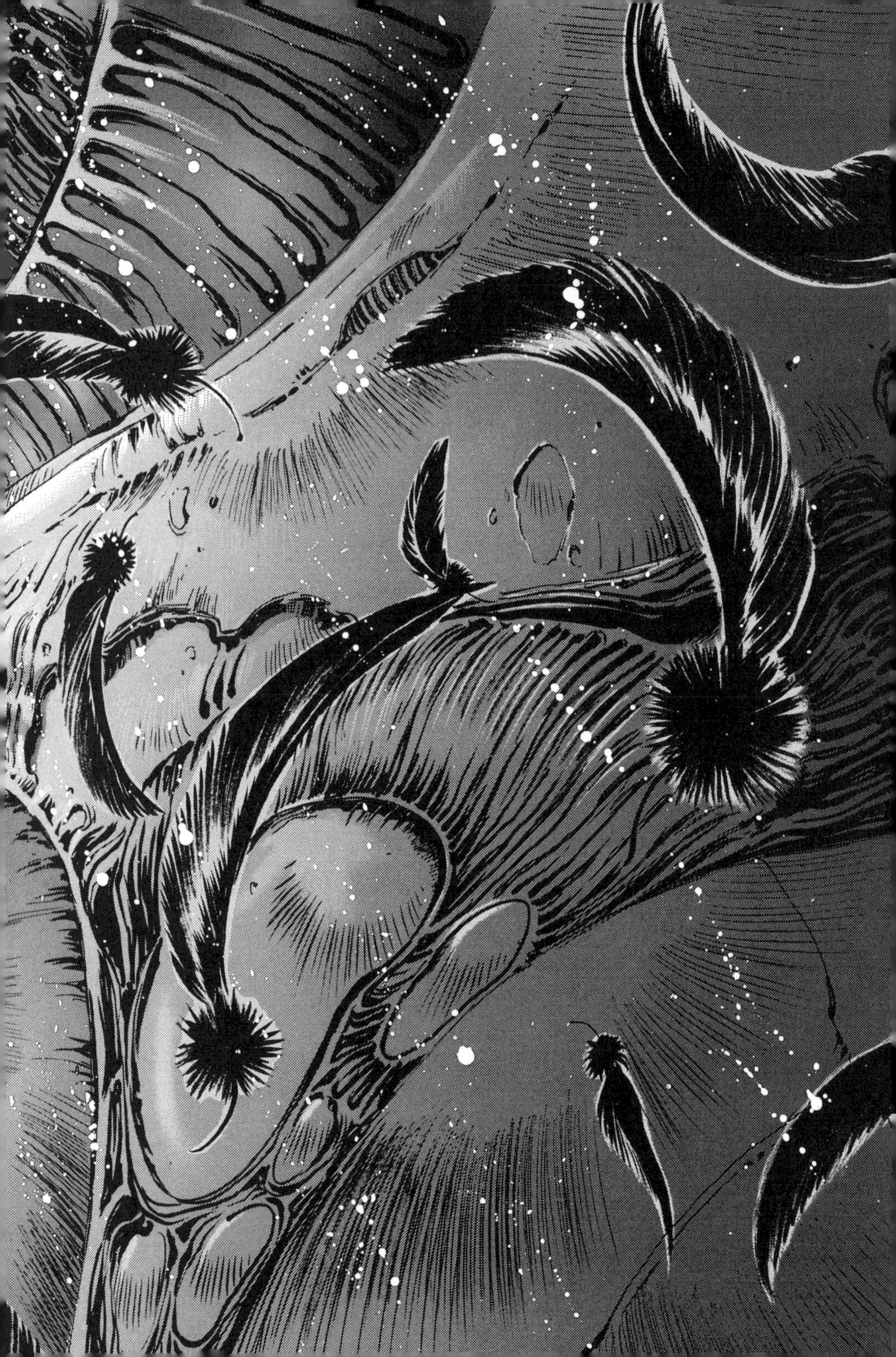

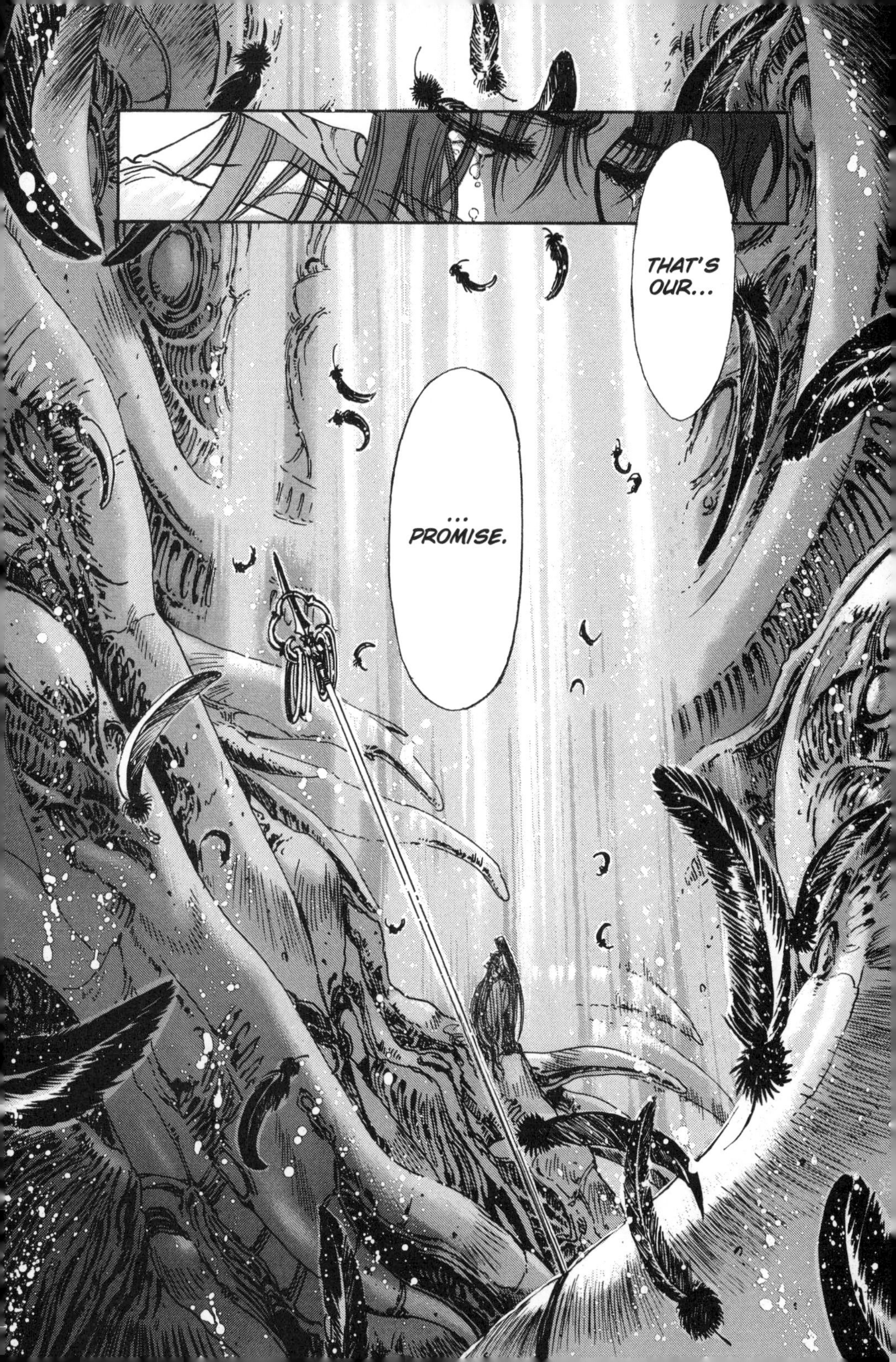
THAT'S OUR...
...PROMISE.

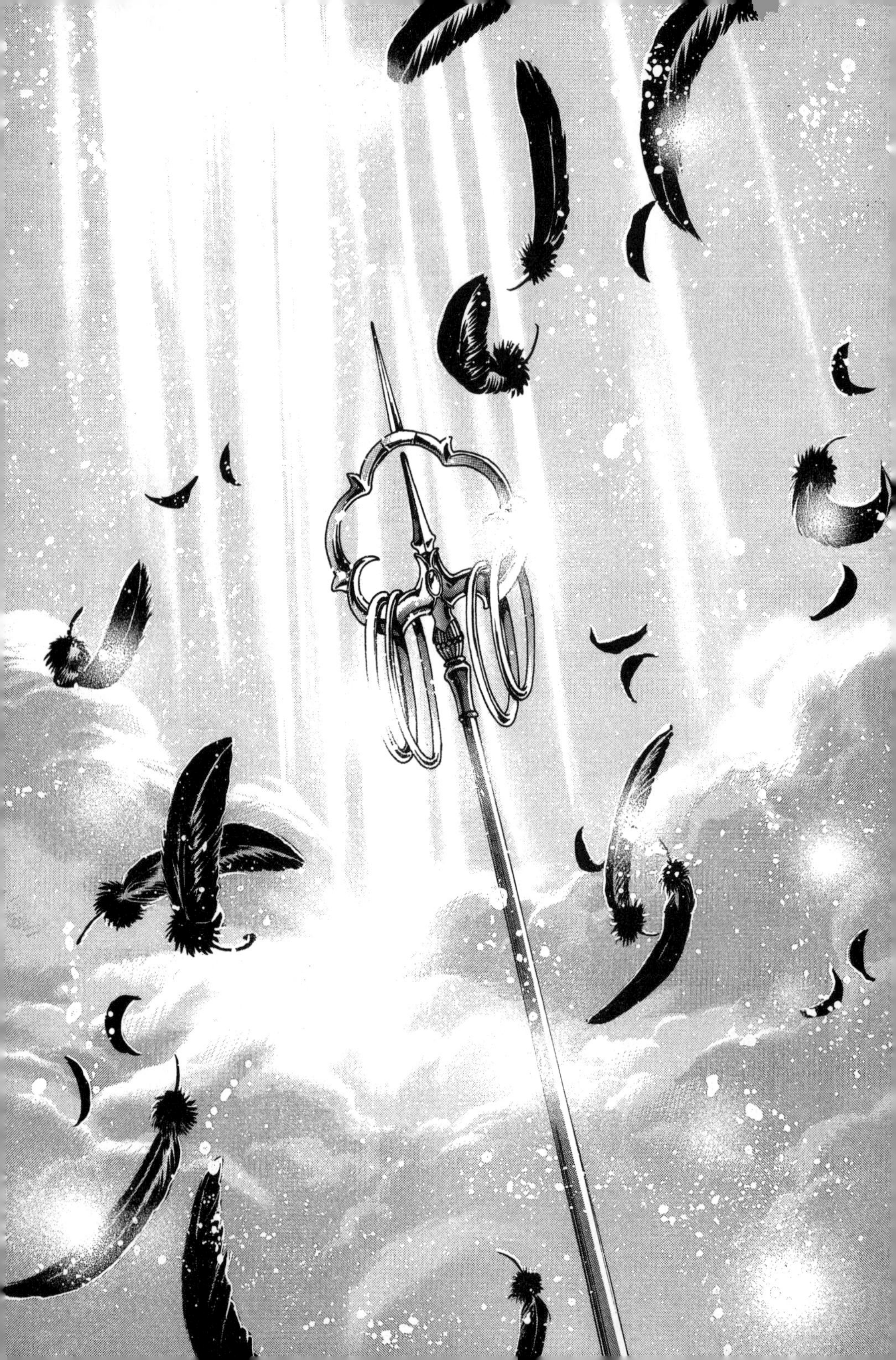

sacred tradition

聖伝
-RG VEDA-

end

完

president and publisher
MIKE RICHARDSON

editor
CARL GUSTAV HORN

designer
PATRICK SATTERFIELD

digital art technician
CHRIS HORN

special thanks to **JUDY KHUU, TERESA GRESHAM, DESIGN CREST, MICHAEL GOMBOS, JEMIAH JEFFERSON, JULIE TAYLOR, CAROL FOX**

English-language version produced by Dark Horse Comics

RG VEDA BOOK THREE

SEIDEN -RG VEDA- [AIZOUBAN] volume 3 © CLAMP/KADOKAWA © CLAMP • Shigatsu Tsuitachi CO., LTD., 2012. First published in Japan in 2012 by KADOKAWA CORPORATION, Tokyo. English translation rights arranged with KADOKAWA CORPORATION, Tokyo, through TOHAN CORPORATION, Tokyo. This English-language edition © 2018 by Dark Horse Comics, Inc. All other material © 2018 by Dark Horse Comics, Inc. Dark Horse Manga™ is a trademark of Dark Horse Comics, Inc. All rights reserved. No portion of this publication may be reproduced, in any form or by any means, without the express written permission of Dark Horse Comics, Inc. Names, characters, places, and incidents featured in this publication are either the product of the author's imagination or are used fictitiously. Any resemblance to actual persons (living or dead), events, institutions, or locales, without satiric intent, is coincidental.

Published by Dark Horse Manga, a division of Dark Horse Comics, Inc.
10956 SE Main Street | Milwaukie, OR 97222 | DarkHorse.com

To find a comics shop in your area,
visit comicshoplocator.com.

First edition: August 2018
ISBN 978-1-50670-154-7

1 3 5 7 9 10 8 6 4 2

Printed in the United States of America

GATE 7
ゲート セブン

BRAND NEW FROM CLAMP—COMING TO THE U.S. JUST MONTHS AFTER JAPAN!

An innocent sightseeing trip to a legendary shrine opens up a magical realm to shy high schooler Chikahito Takamoto! Chikahito finds himself in the mystical world of Hana and an otherworldly band of warriors, and his immunity to their powers leads them to believe he's no ordinary, awkward teenager! Protecting our world from violent elemental beasts, Hana and the team welcome the confused and cautious Chikahito—who isn't quite sure that he wants to be caught in the middle of their war!

Volume One	Volume Two	Volume Three	Volume Four
ISBN 978-1-59582-806-4	ISBN 978-1-59582-807-1	ISBN 978-1-59582-902-3	ISBN 978-1-59582-961-0

$10.99 each

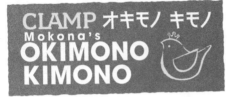

CLAMP オキモノ キモノ
Mokona's OKIMONO KIMONO

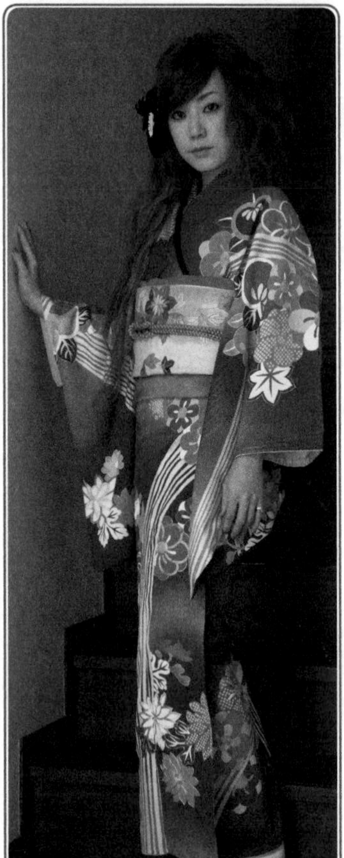

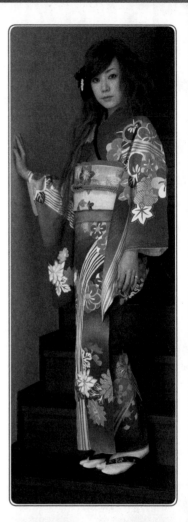

CLAMP artist Mokona loves the art of traditional Japanese kimono. In fact, she designs kimono and kimono accessories herself and shares her love in *Okimono Kimono*, a fun and lavishly illustrated book full of drawings and photographs, interviews (including an interview with Onuki Ami of the J-pop duo Puffy AmiYumi), and exclusive short manga stories from the CLAMP artists!

From the creators of such titles as *Clover, Chobits, Cardcaptor Sakura, Magic Knight Rayearth,* and *Tsubasa, Okimono Kimono* is now available in English for the first time ever!

ISBN 978-1-59582-456-1

$12.99

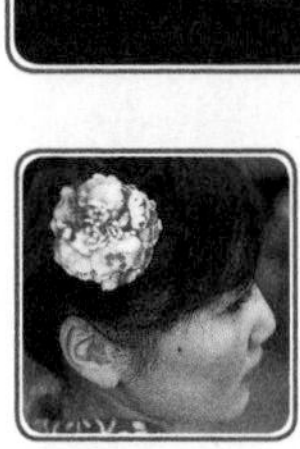

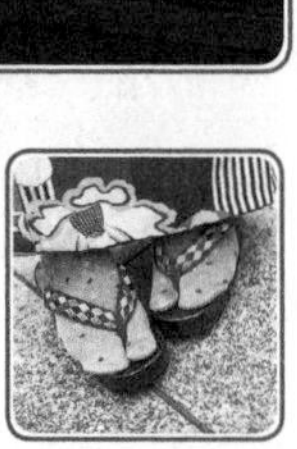

AVAILABLE AT YOUR LOCAL COMICS SHOP OR BOOKSTORE
To find a comics shop in your area, call 1-888-266-4226
For more information or to order direct: • On the web: DarkHorse.com
E-mail: mailorder@darkhorse.com • Phone: 1-800-862-0052 Mon.–Fri. 9 AM to 5 PM Pacific Time.

DARK HORSE MANGA
DarkHorse.com